www.wadsworth.com

wadsworth.com is the World Wide Web site for Wadsworth and is your direct source to dozens of online resources.

At wadsworth.com you can find out about supplements, demonstration software, and student resources. You can also send email to many of our authors and preview new publications and exciting new technologies.

wadsworth.com
Changing the way the world learns®

Fourth Edition

Social and Personality Development

Fourth Edition

Social and Personality Development

David R. Shaffer
University of Georgia

Wadsworth
Thomson Learning™

Australia • Canada • Denmark • Japan • Mexico • New Zealand • Philippines
Puerto Rico • Singapore • South Africa • Spain • United Kingdom • United States

Psychology Editor: Stacey Purviance
Editorial Assistant: Amy Wood
Marketing Manager: Lauren Harp
Marketing Assistant: Jenna Burrill
Project Editor: Tanya Nigh
Print Buyer: Karen Hunt
Permissions Editor: Bob Kauser
Production Service: Ruth Cottrell
Text Designer: Janet Bollow

Photo Researcher: Bobbie Broyer
Copy Editor: Patterson Lamb
Illustrators: Judith L. Mcdonald, Lori Heckelman, ColorType
Compositor: ColorType
Cover Designer: Janet Bollow
Cover Image: © Ed Horowitz, Tony Stone Images
Cover Printer: Phoenix Color
Printer/Binder: RR Donnelley, Crawfordsville

**Library of Congress
Cataloging-in-Publication Data**

Shaffer, David R. (David Reed) , 1946–
   Social and personality development / David R.
     Shaffer. — 4th ed.
       p. cm.
   Includes bibliographical references and index.
   ISBN 0-534-36819-0
   1. Personality development.   2. Socilization.
     I. Title.   II. Title: Social and personality
     development.
  BF723.P4S48   1999
  155.4'18—DC21.   99–30186

Wadsworth/Thomson Learning
10 Davis Drive
Belmont, CA 94002-3098
USA
www.wadsworth.com

International Headquarters
Thomson Learning
290 Harbor Drive, 2nd Floor
Stamford, CT 06902-7477
USA

UK/Europe/Middle East
Thomson Learning
Berkshire House
168-173 High Holborn
London WC1V 7AA
United Kingdom

Asia
Thomson Learning
60 Albert Street #15-01
Albert Complex
Singapore 189969

Canada
Nelson/Thomson Learning
1120 Birchmount Road
Scarborough, Ontario M1K 5G4
Canada

This book is printed on acid-free recycled paper.

I dedicate this book to
the memory of my mother,

Gerrie Doris Shaffer
(1926–1998),

whose strong encouragement
and support of my endeavors
contributed mightily to the
successes I have had in life.

About the Author

David R. Shaffer is a professor of psychology, chair of the Social Psychology program, and past chair of the Life-Span Developmental Psychology program at the University of Georgia, where he has taught courses in human development to graduate and undergraduate students for the past 25 years. His many research articles have concerned such topics as altruism, attitudes and persuasion, moral development, sex roles and social behavior, self-disclosure, and social psychology and the law. He has also served as associate editor for the Journal of Personality and Social Psychology, Personality and Social Bulletin, and Journal of Personality. In 1990 Dr. Shaffer received the Josiah Meigs award for Excellence in Instruction, the University of Georgia's highest instructional honor.

Brief Contents

Chapter 1   Introduction   1

Chapter 2   Classical Theories of Social and
             Personality Development   36

Chapter 3   Recent Perspectives on Social and
             Personality Development   67

Chapter 4   Early Social and Emotional Development I: Emotional Growth
             and the Establishment of Intimate Relationships   104

Chapter 5   Early Social and Emotional Development II:
             Individual Differences and Their Implications
             for Future Development   135

Chapter 6   Development of the Self and Social Cognition   163

Chapter 7   Achievement   199

Chapter 8   Sex Differences, Gender-Role Development, and Sexuality   230

Chapter 9   Aggression and Antisocial Conduct   271

Chapter 10   Altruism and Moral Development   305

Chapter 11   The Family   355

Chapter 12   Extrafamilial Influences I: Television,
             Computers, and Schooling   400

Chapter 13   Extrafamilial Influences II: Peers As Socialization Agents   435

Chapter 14   Epilogue   472

             References   492

             Glossary   483

             Name Index   533

             Subject Index   551

Contents

Preface

Introduction 1
The Universal Parenting Machine–A Thought Experiment   3
Social-Personality Development in Historical Perspective   6
   Childhood in Premodern Times   6
   Children as Subjects: The Baby Biographies   7
   Emergence of a Psychology of Childhood   8
   The Role of Theory in the Scientific Enterprise   8
Questions and Controversies About Human Development   10
Early Philosophical Perspectives on Human Nature   11
   Nature Versus Nurture   11
   Activity Versus Passivity   12
   Continuity Versus Discontinuity   12
   Is Development Universal or Particularistic?   13
Research Methods   15
   The Scientific Method   15
   Gathering Data: Basic Fact-Finding Strategies   15
Detecting Relationships: Correlational and Experimental Designs   21
   The Correlational Design   21
   The Experimental Design   23
   The Natural (or Quasi-) Experiment   25
Designs for Studying Development   26
   The Cross-Sectional Design   26
   The Longitudinal Design   28
   The Sequential Design   29
Cross-Cultural Comparisons   30
Postscript: On Becoming a Wise Consumer of Developmental Research   32
Summary   33

Chapter 1

Box 1.1
Cultural Influences: On the
"Invention" of Adolescence   9

Box 1.2
Developmental Issues:
How Do You Stand on Major
Developmental Issues?   14

Box 1.3
Focus on Research: Assessing
Causal Relationships in the
Real World: The Field
Experiment   25

Box 1.4
Cultural Influences: A Cross-
Cultural Comparison of Gender
Roles   32

Classical Theories of Social and Personality Development   36
The Psychoanalytic Viewpoint   37
   Freud's Psychosexual Theory   37
   Contributions and Criticisms of Freud's Theory   40
   Erikson's Theory of Psychosocial Development   40
   Contributions and Criticisms of Erikson's Theory   41
   Psychoanalytic Theory Today   43
The Behaviorist (or Social-Learning) Viewpoint   43
   Watson's Behaviorism   43
   Skinner's Operant-Learning Theory (Radical Behaviorism)   44

Chapter 2

Box 2.1
Focus on Research: An
Example of No-Trial
(Observational) Learning
Without Reinforcement   46

Bandura's Cognitive Social-Learning Theory   44
Social Learning as Reciprocal Determinism   48
Contributions and Criticism of the Social Learning Perspective   49
Piaget's Cognitive-Developmental Viewpoint   50
Piaget's View of Intelligence and Intellectual Growth   51
Four Stages of Cognitive Development   52
Contributions and Criticisms of Piaget's Theory   63
Summary   65

**Recent Perspectives on Social
and Personality Development   67**

Ethology: A Modern Evolutionary Perspective   68
Assumptions of Classical Ethology   69
Ethology and Human Development   69
Contributions and Criticisms of Evolutionary Viewpoints   71
Behavioral Genetics: Biological Bases for Individual Differences   73
Methods of Estimating Hereditary Influences   74
Estimating the Contributions of Genes and Environment   75
Hereditary Contributions to Personality and Mental Health   78
Heredity and Environment as Developmental Co-Conspirators   82
Contributions and Criticisms of the Behavioral Genetics Approach   84
Ecological Systems Theory: A Modern Environmentalist Perspective   86
Bronfenbrenner's Contexts for Development   88
Contributions and Criticisms of Ecological Systems Theory   90
Modern Cognitive Perspectives   91
Vygotsky's Sociocultural Theory   91
Contributions and Criticisms of the Sociocultural Perspective   93
The Social Information-Processing (or Atributional) Viewpoint   94
Contributions and Criticisms of the Social Information-Processing Viewpoint   97
Theories and World Views   98
Summary   102

**Early Social and Emotional Development I: Emotional Growth
and the Establishment of Intimate Relationships   104**

An Overview of Emotional Development   105
Displaying Emotions: The Development and Regulation of Emotional
Expressions   105
Recognizing and Interpreting Emotions   110
Emotions and Early Social Development   112
Temperament and Development   112
Hereditary and Environmental Influences on Temperament   113
Stability of Temperament   114
Early Temperamental Profiles and Later Development   115
What Are Emotional Attachments?   116
Early Emotional Bonding   118
Establishment of Interactional Synchrony   119
How Do Infants Become Attached?   121
The Growth of Primary Attachments   121
Theories of Attachment   122
Two Attachment-Related Fears of Infancy   126
Stranger Anxiety   127
Separation Anxiety   127

Box 2.2
Current Controversies: Can
Newborns Imitate?   55

Box 2.3
Focus on Research: Children's
Responses to a Hypothetical
Proposition   61

Chapter 3

Box 3.1
Focus on Research: Is Altruism
a Part of Human Nature?   72

Box 3.2
Current Controversies: Some
Common Misconceptions about
Hereditary Estimates   78

Box 3.3
Current Controversies: Need
Parenting Be "Good" or Simply
"Good Enough"?   86

Chapter 4

Box 4.1
Cultural Influences: Is
Shyness a Social
Disadvantage? It Depends
on One's Culture   117

Box 4.2
Applying Developmental
Research: Combating Stranger
Anxiety: Some Helpful Hints
for Doctors and Child-Care
Professionals   128

Box 4.3
Applying Developmental
Research: On Easing the Pain
of Separation   132

Why Do Infants Fear Strangers and Separations?   127
Reactions to the Loss of an Attachment Object   131
Summary   133

Early Social and Emotional Development II: Individual Differences and Their Implications for Future Development   135

Individual Differences in Attachment Quality   136
  Assessing Attachment Security   136
  Cultural Variations in Attachment   139
Factors That Influence Attachment Security   139
  Quality of Caregiving   140
  Infant Characteristics   142
Fathers as Attachment Objects   145
  Fathers as Caregivers   145
  Fathers' Influence on Early Intellectual Development   146
  Fathers as Contributors to Early Social and Emotional Development   146
Attachment and Later Development   147
  Long-Term Correlates of Secure and Insecure Attachments   147
  Why Might Attachment Quality Forecast Later Outcomes?   148
  Is Attachment History Destiny?   150
The Unattached Infant   151
  Effects of Social Isolation in Dogs   151
  Harlow's Studies of Socially Deprived Monkeys   152
  Social Deprivation in Humans   153
Maternal Employment, Day Care, and Early Emotional Development   157
  Benefits of High-Quality Alternative Care   158
The Importance of High-Quality Parenting   159
  How Might We Assist Working Parents?   159
Summary   161

Box 5.1
Current Controversies: Alternative Methods of Assessing Attachment Quality   138

Box 5.2
Focus on Research: On the Intricate Interplay between Caregiving and Temperament in Shaping Infant Attachments   144

Box 5.3
Developmental Issues: Emotional Deprivation and the Failure to Thrive   156

Development of the Self and Social Cognition   163

Chapter 6

Development of the Self-Concept   165
  The Emerging Self: Differentiation, Discrimination, and Self-Recognition   165
  Who Am I?: Responses of Preschool Children   168
  Children's Theory of Mind and Emergence of the Private Self   169
  Conceptions of Self in Middle Childhood and Adolescence   171
Self-Esteem: The Evaluative Component of Self   172
  Origins and Development of Self-Esteem   173
  Social Contributors to Self-Esteem   177
The Development of Self-Control   178
  Emergence of Self-Control in Early Childhood   179
  Delay of Gratification in Childhood and Adolescence   181
Who Am I to Be?: Forging an Identity   183
  Developmental Trends in Identity Formation   184
  How Painful Is Identity Formation?   185
  Personal and Social Influences on Identity Formation   186
The Other Side of Social Cognition: Knowing About Others   188
  Age Trends in Person Perception   189
  Theories of Social-Cognitive Development   191
Summary   196

Box 6.1
Cultural Influences: Cultural Influences on the Self-Concept   174

Box 6.2
Developmental Issues: Adolescent Suicide: The Tragic Destruction of Self   178

Box 6.3
Cultural Influences: Identity Formation Among Minority Adolescents   186

Box 6.4
Developmental Issues: Racial Categorization and Racism in Young Children   190

Achievement   199

The Concept of Achievement Motivation   200
  The Motivational View of Achievement   201
  A Behavioral View of Achievement   201
Early Reactions to One's Accomplishments: From Mastery to Self-Evaluation   202
Theories of Achievement Motivation and Achievement Behavior   203
  Need Achievement Theories   204
  Weiner's Attribution Theory   207
  Dweck's Learned Helplessness Theory   211
  Reflections on Theories of Achievement   213
Cultural and Subcultural Influences on Achievement   215
  Individualistic Versus Collectivistic Perspectives on Achievement   215
  Ethnic Variations in Achievement   216
  Social Class Differences in Achievement   218
Home and Family Influences on Achievement   222
  Quality of Attachments on Achievement   222
  The Home Environment   222
  Child-Rearing and Achievement   224
  Configural Influences: Birth Order, Family Size, and Children's Achievement
    Behavior   225
On Sex Differences in Achievement and a Look Ahead   227
Summary   228

Sex Differences, Gender-Role Development, and Sexuality   230

Categorizing Males and Females: Gender-Role Standards   232
Some Facts and Fictions About Sex Differences   234
  Actual Psychological Differences between the Sexes   234
  Cultural Myths   236
  Do Cultural Myths Contribute to Sex Differences in Ability (and Vocational
    Opportunity)?   238
Developmental Trends in Gender Typing   239
  Development of the Gender Concept   240
  Development of Gender-Role Stereotypes   240
  Development of Gender-Typed Behavior   242
  Subcultural Variations in Gender Typing   244
Theories of Gender Typing and Gender-Role Development   245
  Money and Ehrhardt's Biosocial Theory   246
  Evidence for Social-Labeling Influences   249
  Freud's Psychoanalytic Theory   252
  Social Learning Theory   253
  Kohlberg's Cognitive-Developmental Theory   255
  Gender Schema Theory   256
  An Integrative Theory   257
Psychological Androgyny: A Prescription for the Future?   259
  Do Androgynous People Really Exist?   259
  Are There Advantages to Being Androgynous?   260
  Applications: On Changing Gender-Role Attitudes and Behavior   260
Sexuality and Sexual Behavior   263
  Cultural Influences on Sexuality   263
  Adolescent Sexual Attitudes and Behaviors   263
  Personal and Social Consequences of Adolescent Sexual Activity   266
Summary   269

Chapter 7

Box 7.1
Applying Developmental
Research: On Restructuring
Achievement Goals to Minimize
(or Prevent) Learned
Helplessness   214

Box 7.2
Focus on Research: A Threat in
the Air: How Social Stereotypes
Can Influence Academic
Performance   219

Box 7.3
Applying Developmental
Research: Recipes for
Effective Compensatory
Interventions   220

Chapter 8

Box 8.1
Developmental Issues: What
Traits Characterize Males and
Females?   233

Box 8.2
Focus on Research: Do
Gender Stereotypes Color
Children's Interpretations
of Counterstereotypic
Information?   237

Box 8.3
Current Controversies: Is
Biology Destiny?   250

Box 8.4
Applying Developmental
Research: Combating Gender
Stereotypes with Cognitive
Interventions   262

Box 8.5
Current Controversies: On
Sexual Orientation and the
Origins of Homosexuality   264

Aggression and Antisocial Conduct   271

What Is Aggression?   272
  Aggression as an Instinct   272
  Behavioral Definitions of Aggression   273
  Aggression as a Social Judgment   274
Theories of Aggression   274
  Instinct Theories   274
  Learning Theories   277
  Dodge's Social Information-Processing Theory   281
Developmental Trends in Aggression   284
  Early Conflict and the Origins of Aggression   284
  Age-Related Changes in the Nature of Aggression   284
  Is Aggression a Stable Attribute?   288
Sex Differences in Aggression   289
  The Biological Viewpoint   289
  The Social-Learning Viewpoint   290
  The Interactive Viewpoint   291
Cultural and Subcultural Influences on Aggression   291
Family Influences on Aggression   294
  Parental Child-Rearing Practices and Children's Aggression   294
  Family Climate and Children's Aggression   296
Methods of Controlling Aggression and Antisocial Conduct   300
  Catharsis: A Dubious Strategy   300
  Creating "Nonaggressive" Environments   301
  Eliminating the Payoffs for Aggression   301
  Social-Cognitive Interventions   302
Summary   303

Chapter 9

Box 9.1
Focus on Research: Adult Reactions to Roughhousing: Boys Will Be Boys, but Girls Are Aggressors   275

Box 9.2
Focus on Research: How Girls Are More Aggressive Than Boys   292

Box 9.3
Applying Developmental Research: Helping Children (and Parents) Who Are "Out of Control"   298

Altruism and Moral Development   305

What Are Altruism and Prosocial Behavior?   306
The Motivational (or Intentional) Definition of Altruism   307
A Behavioral Definition of Altruism   307
Theories of Altruism and Prosocial Development   308
  Biological Theories: Are We Programmed for Prosocial Conduct?   308
  Psychoanalytic Theory: Let Your Conscience (Superego) Be Your Guide   309
  Social-Learning Theory: What's in It for Me?   309
  Cognitive Theories of Altruism: Maturity Is the Medium   311
Developmental Trends in Altruism   313
  Origins of Prosocial Behavior   313
  Age-Related Changes in Altruism   314
Cognitive and Affective Contributors to Altruism   315
  Role-Taking and Altruism   316
  Prosocial Moral Reasoning   316
  Empathy: An Important Affective Contributor to Altruism   317
  Viewing Oneself as Altruistic   319
Cultural and Social Influences on Altruism   320
  Cultural Influences   320
  Reinforcing Altruism   321
  Modeling Influences: Practicing and Preaching Altruism   322
  Who Raises Altruistic Children?   324
What Is Morality?   326
  How Developmentalists Look at Morality   326

Chapter 10

Box 10.1
Cultural Influences: Cultural Differences in Thinking About Prosocial Conduct   322

Psychoanalytic Explanations of Moral Development   327
  Freud's Theory of Oedipal Morality   327
  Evaluating Freud's Theory and Newer Psychoanalytic Ideas About Morality   328
Cognitive-Developmental Theory: The Child as a Moral Philosopher   328
  Piaget's Theory of Moral Development   329
  An Evaluation of Piaget's Theory   331
  Kohlberg's Theory of Moral Development   333
  Support for Kohlberg's Theory   336
  Criticisms of Kohlberg's Approach   339
Morality as a Product of Social Learning (and Social Information Processing)   344
  How Consistent Are Moral Conduct and Moral Character?   344
  Learning to Resist Temptation   345
Who Raises Children Who Are Morally Mature?   348
Summary   352

The Family   355

Functions of the Family   356
The Family as a Social System   358
  Direct and Indirect Influences   359
  Families Are Developing Systems   360
  Families Are Embedded Systems   361
  A Changing Family System in a Changing World   361
Parental Socialization During Childhood and Adolescence   363
  Two Major Dimensions of Parenting   363
  Four Patterns of Parenting   364
  Social Class and Ethnic Variations in Child-Rearing   367
  The Quest for Autonomy: Renegotiating the Parent/Child Relationship During
    Adolescence   371
The Influence of Siblings and Sibling Relationships   373
  Changes in the Family System When a New Baby Arrives   373
  Sibling Relationships over the Course of Childhood   375
  Positive Contributions of Sibling Relationships   377
  Characteristics of Only Children   378
Diversity in Family Life   379
  Adoptive Families   379
  Gay and Lesbian Families   380
  The Impacts of Family Conflict and Divorce   380
  Remarriage and Blended Families   385
  Maternal Employment Revisited   387
When Parenting Breaks Down: The Problem of Child Abuse   390
  Who Are the Abusers?   391
  Who Is Abused?   391
  Social-Situational Triggers: The Ecology of Child Abuse   392
  Consequences of Abuse and Neglect   393
  How Can We Solve the Problem?   394
Reflections on the Family   397
Summary   398

Extrafamilial Influences I: Television, Computers, and Schooling   400

The Early Window: Effects of Television on Children and Adolescents   401
  Television and Children's Lifestyles   401

Box 10.2
Cultural Influences: Cultural Differences in Moral Reasoning   340

Box 10.3
Focus on Research: Temperament, Discipline, and Moral Internalization   351

Chapter 11

Box 11.1
Developmental Issues: Family Instability, Homelessness, and Child Development   370

Box 11.2
Developmental Issues: Does Part-Time Employment Foster a Healthy Sense of Autonomy (and Positive Developmental Outcomes)?   374

Box 11.3
Applying Developmental Research: Smoothing the Rocky Road to Recovery from a Divorce   384

Box 11.4
Developmental Issues: Childhood Sexual Abuse   394

Chapter 12

Development of Television Literacy   402
Effects of Televised Violence   403
Other Potentially Undesirable Effects of Television   408
Television As an Educational Tool   410
Should Television Be Used to Socialize Children?   412
Child Development in the Computer Age   413
Computers in the Classroom   413
Concerns About Computers   415
The School as a Socialization Agent   416
Does Schooling Promote Cognitive Development?   416
Determinants of Effective (and Ineffective) Schooling   417
The Teacher's Influence   422
Do Our Schools Meet the Needs of All Our Children?   427
How Well-Educated Are Our Children? Cross-Cultural Comparisons   431
Summary   433

Extrafamilial Influences II: Peers As Socialization Agents   435

Who Is a Peer and What Functions Do Peers Serve?   437
The Significance of Peer Interaction   437
Frequency of Peer Contacts   438
Peers as Promoters of Positive Developmental Outcomes   439
The Development of Peer Sociability   440
Peer Sociability in Infancy and Toddlerhood   441
Sociability During the Preschool Period   442
Peer Sociability in Middle Childhood and Adolescence   444
Personal and Social Influences on Sociability   448
Peer Acceptance and Popularity   452
Measuring Children's Popularity with Peers   453
Why Are Children Accepted, Neglected, or Rejected By Peers?   454
On Improving the Social Skills of Rejected Children   459
Children and Their Friends   461
On the Development of Friendship   461
Social Interactions Among Friends and Acquaintances   462
Are There Distinct Advantages to Having Friends?   463
How Do Peers Exert Their Influence?   466
Peer Reinforcement and Modeling Influences   466
Peers as Critics and Agents of Persuasion   466
The Normative Function of Peer Groups   467
Peer Versus Adult Influences and the Question of Cross-Pressures   468
Summary   470

Epilogue   472

Major Themes in Human Social and Personality Development   473
Human Development Is an Holistic Enterprise   473
We Are Active Contributors to Our Own Development   473
There Is Both Continuity and Discontinuity in Development   474
There Is Much Plasticity in Human Development   475
The Nature-Nurture Distinction Is a False Dichotomy   475
Both Normative and Idiosyncratic Developments Are Important   476
We Develop in a Cultural and Historical Context   477

Box 12.1
Focus on Research: Do "The Mighty Morphin Power Rangers" Promote Children's Aggression?   406

Box 12.2
Current Controversies: Should Preschoolers Attend School?   418

Box 12.3
Developmental Issues: On the Difficult Transition to Secondary Schools   424

Chapter 13

Box 13.1
Focus on Research: Robber's Cave: An Experimental Analysis of Group Formation and Intergroup Conflict   446

Box 13.2
Cultural Influences: A Cross-Cultural Examination of Parenting and Children's Social Skills   452

Box 13.3
Developmental Issues: A Longitudinal Analysis of the Benefits of Chumships   465

Chapter 14

Development Is Best Viewed from Multiple Perspectives   477

Patterns of Parenting (and Adult Guidance) Clearly Matter   478

Many Social Forces Conspire to Shape Development   480

We've Come a Long Way, Baby . . . but Have So Far to Go   481

References   492

Glossary   483

Name Index   533

Subject Index   551

In the preface of the first edition, I expressed an opinion that the study of social and personality development had come of age and the hope that my book reflected that fact. Clearly, the former premise turned out to be correct—so correct, in fact, that the information explosion that has occurred over the past 21 years has rendered earlier editions of this volume hopelessly obsolete.

My purpose in revising *Social and Personality Development* has been to produce a current and comprehensive overview of the discipline that reflects the best theories, research, and practical wisdom that developmentalists have to offer. Throughout my many years of teaching, I have tried to select rigorous, research-based textbooks that are also interesting, accurate, up to date, and written in concise, precise language that my students can easily understand. I believe that a good text should talk with, rather than at, its readers, anticipating their interests, questions, and concerns and treating them as active participants in the learning process. A good "developmental" text should also stress the processes that underlie developmental change, so that students come away from the course with a firm understanding of the causes and complexities of whatever aspect(s) of development the test strives to present. Last, a good text is a relevant text—one that shows how the theory and research that students are asked to digest can be applied to a number of real-life settings. The present volume represents my attempt to accomplish all these objectives.

Philosophy

Certain philosophical views are inherent in any systematic treatment of a discipline as broad as social and personality development. My philosophy can be summarized as follows:

■ *I emphasize theory and believe in theoretical eclecticism.* And my reasons for doing so are straightforward: The study of social and personality development is now a well-established scientific discipline—one that has advanced because of the efforts of a large number of researchers who have taught us so much about developing children by formulating theory and systematically evaluating their theoretical hypotheses. This area of study has a very rich theoretical tradition, and all the theories we will review have contributed in important ways to our understanding of social and personality development. Consequently, this book will not attempt to convince its readers that any one theoretical viewpoint is "best." The psychoanalytic, behavioristic, cognitive-developmental, social information-processing, ethological, ecological, sociocultural, and behavioral genetic viewpoints (as well as several less encompassing theories that address selected aspects of development) are all treated with respect.

■ *The best information about human development comes from systematic research.* To teach this course effectively, I believe that one must convince students of the value of theory and systematic research. Although there are many ways to achieve these objectives, I have chosen to contrast modern developmental psychology with its "prescientific" origins, and then, to discuss and illustrate the many methodological approaches that researchers use to test their theories and answer important questions about developing children and adolescents. I've taken care to explain why there is no one "best method" for studying social and personality development, and I've repeatedly stressed that our most reliable knowledge is based on outcomes that can be replicated using a variety of methods.

■ *I favor a strong "process" orientation.* A major complaint with many developmental texts is that they describe human development without adequately explaining why it occurs. In recent years, investigators have increasingly become concerned about identifying and understanding developmental processes—the biological and environmental factors that cause us to change—and this book clearly reflects this emphasis. My own "process orientation" is based on the belief that students are more likely to remember what develops and when if they know and understand the reasons these developments take place.

■ *I favor a strong "contextual" orientation.* One of the more important lessons that developmentalists have learned is that children and adolescents live in historical eras and sociocultural contexts that affect every aspect of their development. I have chosen to highlight these contextual influences in three major ways. First, *cross-cultural comparisons* are discussed throughout the text. Not only do students enjoy learning about the development of people in other cultures and ethnically diverse subcultures, but cross-cultural research also helps them to see how human beings can be so much alike and at the same time, so different from one another. In addition, the impacts of such immediate contextual influences as our families, neighborhoods, schools, and peer groups are considered (1) throughout the first 10 chapters as we discuss important aspects of social and personality development, and (2) again in Chapters 11–13, as important topics in their own right.

■ *Human development is a holistic process.* Although individual researchers may concentrate on particular topics such as physical development, cognitive development, emotional development, or the development of moral reasoning, development is not piecemeal but *holistic:* Human beings are at once physical, cognitive, social, and emotional creatures, and each of these components of "self" depends, in part, on the changes that are taking place in other areas of development. Clearly, this is a "specialty" book that focuses primarily on the social and emotional aspects of development. However, I have striven to paint a holistic portrait of the developing person by stressing the fundamental interplay between biological, cognitive, social, and ecological influences in my coverage of each facet of social and personality development that we will discuss.

■ *A developmental text should be a resource book for students—one that reflects current knowledge.* I have chosen to cite more than 600 very recent studies and reviews (published since the third edition) to ensure that my coverage, as well as any outside readings that students may undertake, will represent our current understanding of a topic or topics. However, I have avoided the tendency, common in textbooks, to ignore older research simply because it is older. In fact, many of the "classics" of social and personality development are prominently displayed throughout the text to illustrate important breakthroughs and to show how our knowledge about developing persons gradually builds on these earlier findings and insights.

Content

Though not formally divided into parts, the book can be viewed in that way. The first three chapters (which could be construed as Part One) present an orientation to the discipline and the tools of the trade, including a thorough discussion and illustration of research methodologies (Chapter 1), and substantive reviews of both classical (Chapter 2) and contemporary (Chapter 3) theories of social and personality development. An important feature of this coverage is its analyses of the contributions and limitations of each research method and each of the major theoretical traditions.

Chapters 4–10 (which could be labeled Part Two) focus on the "products," or outcomes, of social and personality development, including early social and emotional development (Chapter 4) and its implications for later development (Chapter 5); development of the self (Chapter 6); achievement (Chapter 7); gender typing and gender-role development (Chapter 8); aggression and antisocial conduct (Chapter 9); and altruism and moral development (Chapter 10).

The third section (or Part Three) of the text explores the settings and contexts in which people develop and could be labeled the "ecology" of development. Here the focus is on the family as an agent of socialization (Chapter 11) and on four important extrafamilial influences: television, computers, schools (Chapter 12), and children's peer groups (Chapter 13).

Finally, a brief Epilogue (Chapter 14) has been added to remind readers of the bigger picture—that is, the central themes and processes that underlie human social and personality development. My hope is that students will retain this knowledge and put it to good use in guiding their own transactions with developing persons, even if they should forget the many, many studies that they have read about and by which these important guiding principles have come to light.

New to This Edition

The fourth edition contains many important changes in the treatment of theoretical, empirical, and practical issues, reinforcing themes that are at the forefront of research today. At the most general level, these changes include (1) increased attention throughout to cultural/subcultural/historical influences, with emphasis on the impacts of economic disadvantage on child development; (2) an even stronger focus on the intricate interplays among biological and environmental forces in shaping development; (3) stronger and more frequent illustrations that developmental outcomes depend very crucially on the "goodness of fit" between persons and their socializing environments; (4) greater emphasis on the importance of good peer relations and high-quality friendships (and on the interplays between families and peers as socializing agents); and (5) expanded coverage of adolescent development. The empirical literature has been updated extensively, with the result that a majority of the references were published in the 1990s, and most of these recent citations have appeared since mid-1993, when the previous edition of this text went into production.

In a word, each chapter has been thoroughly revised and updated to add the new topics that reflect current trends in our discipline. To make way for the additions, I have condensed or otherwise reorganized other topics or, in some cases, have eliminated coverage that the newer evidence has rendered obsolete. Here is a small sampling of these changes:

- Incorporation of ethnography and updated examples of many other research strategies (Chapter 1).
- Reorganization of the theories chapters to present classical theories of social and personality development (Chapter 2), followed by more contemporary viewpoints (Chapter 3).
- Expanded coverage of Vygotsky's sociocultural theory, Bronfenbrenner's ecological systems theory, and social information-processing theory (Chapter 3).
- Greater attention to temperament as a foundation for child and adolescent development (Chapter 4).
- Expanded coverage of cultural variations in emotional development (Chapter 4).
- New research to (1) illustrate that parenting attributes other than sensitivity contribute to attachment security and (2) clarify the interaction between parenting and child temperament in fostering secure and insecure attachments (Chapter 5).
- Updated coverage of the maternal employment/day care controversy, which highlights important conclusions drawn by the NICHD Early Child Care Research Network reports (Chapter 5).
- A new section on children's theory of mind as a contributor to the developing self-concept, including research illustrating family and cultural contributions to one's theory of mind (Chapter 6).
- New research on the early origins of self-esteem in young children and on factors that contribute most heavily to adolescent self-esteem (Chapter 6).
- Coverage of the origins and development of racial prejudice and on strategies for preventing or reducing it (Chapter 6).
- Updated and expanded coverage of ethnic identity formation (Chapter 6).
- Inclusion of Steele's exciting work on stereotype threat as a contributor to ethnic differences in academic achievement (Chapter 7).
- A new section on effective compensatory education programs to combat academic underachievement among economically disadvantaged children (Chapter 7).
- New evidence on the long-term impacts of gender reassignment (Chapter 8).
- Addition of Halpern's psychobiosocial viewpoint on sex differences and gender-role development (Chapter 8).
- Expanded coverage of cognitive and social interventions to reduce gender stereotyping, including those appropriate for elementary school instructors (Chapter 8).
- New findings on adolescent sexuality and effective interventions for reducing teenage pregnancies (Chapter 8).
- New findings on sex differences in aggression (Chapter 9).
- New research distinguishing proactive from reactive aggression and their linkage to bullying and victimization (Chapter 9).
- New evidence for the intergenerational transmission of aggression and antisocial conduct (Chapter 9).
- Dramatic illustrations that culture influences the ways in which children think about prosocial behaviors and reason about moral issues (Chapter 10).
- Inclusion of Kochanska's exciting research on the early origins of conscience and the "goodness-of-fit" between temperament and moral socialization (Chapter 10).
- New research on the impacts of family instability and homelessness on developing children (Chapter 11).
- A new section on ethnic variations in child rearing (Chapter 11).
- A *new* look at the impacts of part-time employment on adolescent development (Chapter 11).
- Expanded coverage on diversity in family life, including new sections on adoptive families and gay/lesbian families (Chapter 11).
- Inclusion of coverage on the correlates, contributors to, and long-term implications of childhood sexual abuse (Chapter 11).

- New information on the prevalence of TV violence and on strategies for reducing its potentially harmful effects (Chapter 12).
- Expanded coverage of the positive effects and of concerns about children's computer use (Chapter 12).
- Dramatic new data on the benefits of participating in after-school extracurricular activities (Chapter 12).
- Research showing that the effectiveness of schooling depends very crucially on its "goodness of fit" with students' cultural traditions and developmental needs (Chapter 12).
- Expanded coverage of the interface between the parenting children receive and their social skills/peer relations (Chapter 13).
- *Prospective* evidence that having high-quality friendships contributes, over and above establishing favorable peer relations, to positive developmental outcomes (Chapter 13).
- A new Epilogue chapter that succinctly reviews the important themes and processes that underlie social and personality development (Chapter 14).

Writing Style

My goal has been to write a book that treats its readers as active participants in an ongoing discussion. I have tried to be relatively informal and down to earth in my writing style and to rely heavily on questions, thought problems, and a number of other exercises to stimulate student interest and involvement. Many of the chapters were pretested on my own students, who provided many useful ideas for clarification and suggested several of the analogies and occasional anecdotes that I've used when introducing and explaining complex ideas. So, with the valuable assistance of my student-critics, I have attempted to prepare a volume that is substantive and challenging but that reads more like a story than an encyclopedia.

Special Features

The pedagogical features of the text have been expanded considerably in this fourth edition. Among the more important features that are included to encourage student interest and involvement and to make the material easier to learn are the following:

- *New design.* An attractive new design gives the book a more "open" look, which increases the effectiveness of photographs, drawings, and other illustrations.
- *Outlines and chapter summaries.* An outline and brief introductory section at the beginning of each chapter provide the reader with a preview of what will be covered. Each chapter concludes with a summary of its coverage, organized according to the chapter's major subdivisions and highlighting key terms, that allows one to quickly review the chapter's major themes.
- *Subheadings.* Subheadings are employed very frequently to keep the material well-organized and to divide the coverage into manageable bites.
- *Glossaries.* A running glossary provides on-the-spot definitions of more than 400 boldfaced key terms as they appear in the text. A complete glossary of key terms for the entire text appears at the end of the book.
- *Boxes.* Each chapter contains three to five boxes that call attention to important issues, ideas, or applications. The aim of the boxes is to permit a closer and more personal examination of selected topics while stimulating the reader to think about the questions, controversies, and practices under scrutiny. The majority of these

boxes are new to this edition, and most of the holdovers have been substantially updated, as dictated by new findings that have emerged. The boxes fall into five categories: *Cultural Influences,* which examine the impacts of cultures, subcultures, or other social contexts on selected aspects of child/adolescent development ("Culture Differences in Moral Reasoning"); *Focus on Research,* which discuss a study of series of related studies that have been highly influential in illuminating the cause(s) of development or individual differences in development ("How Girls Are More Aggressive Than Boys"); *Current Controversies,* which address hotly debated issues today ("Must Parenting Be 'Good' or Simply Good Enough"); *Developmental Issues,* which examine a variety of developmentally significant topics or processes ("A Longitudinal Analysis of the Benefits of Chumships"); and *Applying Developmental Research,* which focus on applying what we know to optimize developmental outcomes ("Helping Children [and Parents] Who Are 'Out of Control'"). All these boxes are carefully woven into the chapter narrative and were selected to reinforce central themes in the text.

■ *Illustrations.* Photographs, figures, and tables appear frequently throughout the text. Although these features are designed, in part, to provide visual relief and to maintain student interest, they are not merely decorations. All visual aids, including the occasional cartoons, were selected to illustrate important principles and outcomes and thereby further the educational goals of the text.

■ *Testing file* (for the instructor). An extensive testing file is available to all instructors who adopt *Social and Personality Development.* The text file for each chapter consists of 70 to 115 multiple-choice items, five to ten discussion questions, and page references for the answer to each question. Discussion questions in this file may serve instructors in another way by serving as springboards for class discussions.

■ *Visit the Wadsworth Psychology Study Center on the World Wide Web.* More information on developmental issues and a host of links to related websites are available when you visit the Wadsworth Psychology Study Center at the following address: **http://psychology.wadsworth.com**

Acknowledgments

As is always the case with projects as large as this one, there are many individuals whose assistance was invaluable in the planning and production of this volume. I'll begin by expressing my gratitude to the following expert reviewers for their many, many constructive and insightful comments on and suggestions for the Fourth Edition: Michelle R. Dunlap, Connecticut College; Jane A. Goldman, University of Connecticut; Craig H. Hart, Brigham Young University; Lauri A. Jensen-Campbell, Florida Atlantic University; Michelle L. Kelley, Old Dominion University; Kathleen A. Lawler, University of Tennessee-Knoxville; Sarah C. Magelsdorf, University of Illinois; Diane Mello-Goldner, Pine Manor College; and Joseph Pleck, University of Illinois.

Special thanks go to Pam Riddle, who somehow was able to decipher the many, many handwritten insertions that often ran up and down the page margins and produce an error-free final manuscript. I also benefited immensely from Pam's editorial skills at various points throughout the project and am extremely grateful for her tireless efforts on my behalf.

Once again, the staff at Wadsworth has displayed its professionalism and skill in the production of *Social and Personality Development,* fourth edition. I am most grateful to Patterson Lamb, the manuscript editor, for a skillful job of editing; to Bob Kauser and Roberta Broyer for securing the necessary permissions; to Janet Bollow for lending her talent and creativity to the design of the book; to Roberta Broyer for securing photos that help the text content to "come alive"; to Kathy Garcia who did the initial indexing; and to Ruth Cottrell, of Ruth Cottrell Books, who coordinated the efforts of all these important contributors and carried out the production of the book with skill and efficiency.

Finally, Stacey Purviance, my editor, came on board about a third of the way through the project. As an experienced author who was behind schedule owing to two recent deaths in my family, I quipped to Stacey in our first conversation that she need not be concerned about the fate of the volume for "I am rolling now. Just stay out of my way and I'll tell you what to do and when to do it." Fortunately, she knew I was kidding and is still talking to me. I say "fortunately" because Ms. Purviance has very skillfully guided this headstrong author through another challenging production process and is responsible for many of the improvements in this latest edition of the book.

David R. Shaffer

Fourth Edition

Social and Personality Development

Chapter One

Introduction

**The Universal Parenting Machine—
A Thought Experiment**

**Social-Personality Development
in Historical Perspective**
Childhood in Premodern Times
Children as Subjects: The Baby Biographies
Emergence of a Psychology of Childhood
The Role of Theory in the Scientific Enterprise

**Questions and Controversies
About Human Development**
Early Philosophical Perspectives on Human Nature
Nature Versus Nurture
Activity Versus Passivity
Continuity Versus Discontinuity
Is Development Universal or Particularistic?

Research Methods
The Scientific Method
Gathering Data: Basic Fact-Finding Strategies

**Detecting Relationships: Correlational
and Experimental Designs**
The Correlational Design
The Experimental Design
The Natural (or Quasi-) Experiment

Designs for Studying Development
The Cross-Sectional Design
The Longitudinal Design
The Sequential Design

Cross-Cultural Comparisons

**Postscript: On Becoming a Wise
Consumer of Developmental Research**

Summary

*T*o this day I can recall how I made the decision to major in psychology. I was a first-quarter junior who had dabbled in premed, chemistry, zoology, and oceanography without firmly committing myself to any of these fields. Perhaps the single most important event that prompted me to walk over to the psychology table on that fateful fall registration day had actually occurred 18 months earlier. It was the birth of my niece.

This little girl fascinated me. I found it quite remarkable that by the age of 18 months she was already quite proficient at communicating with others. I was also puzzled to discover that, although she and I were pals when she was 5 months old, she seemed to fear me nine months later when I returned home for the summer. This toddler knew the names of a number of objects, animals, and people (mostly TV personalities), and she had already become very fond of certain individuals, particularly her mother and her grandmother. To my way of thinking she was well on her way to "becoming human," and the process intrigued me.

After studying developing children for more than 25 years, I am more convinced than ever that the process of "becoming human," as I had called it, is remarkable in several respects. Consider the starting point. Newborns, or *neonates,* are often perceived as cute, cuddly, and lovable by their parents, but they are essentially unknowing, dependent, and occasionally demanding little creatures. Newborns have no prejudices or preconceptions; they speak no language; they obey no man-made laws; and they sometimes behave as if they were living for their next feeding. It is not hard to understand how John Locke (1690/1913) could describe the neonate as a *tabula rasa* (blank slate) who is receptive to any and all kinds of experience.

Irvin Child (1954, p. 655) has noted that despite the enormous number of behavioral options available to the child, he is "led to develop actual behavior which is confined within a much narrower range—the range of what is customary and acceptable according to the standards of his group." Indeed, English children will learn to speak English whereas French children learn French. Jewish children will often develop an aversion to pork, Hindus will not eat the flesh of the sacred cow, and Christians learn that it is perfectly acceptable to consume either of these foods. American children are taught they will someday play an active role in electing their leaders; Jordanian and Saudi Arabian children learn that their rulers assume that role as a birthright. Children who grow up in certain areas of the United States are likely to prefer square dancing and country music; those who live in other areas will prefer hip-hop and rap music. Some children are permitted to question their parents' pronouncements whereas others are taught to obey the commands of their elders without comment. In short, children develop in a manner and direction prescribed by their societies, communities, and families.

What I had originally described as becoming human is more commonly labeled **socialization**—the process through which the child acquires the beliefs, behaviors, and values deemed significant and appropriate by other members of society. The socialization of each succeeding generation serves society in at least three ways. First, it is a means of regulating behavior. I suspect that the penalties for rape, robbery, and murder are not the most important inhibitors of these heinous acts. Any one of us could probably walk outside, snatch someone's purse, and stand a reasonably good chance of making a few dollars without getting caught. Then why don't we mug little old ladies or commit several other low-risk but socially inappropriate behaviors? Probably it's because the control of antisocial acts is largely a personal matter that stems from the standards of morality—right and wrong—that we have acquired from our interactions with parents, teachers, peers, and many other agents of socialization. Second, the socialization process helps to promote the personal growth of the individual. As children interact with and become like other members of their culture, they acquire the knowledge, skills, motives, and aspirations that will enable them to func-

socialization: the process by which individuals acquire the beliefs, values, and behaviors considered desirable or appropriate by their culture or subculture.

tion effectively within their communities. Finally, socialization perpetuates the social order. Socialized children become socialized adults who will impart what they have learned to their own children.

On the first day of class one year, I asked my students to write, in 50 words or less, the main reason they elected to take a course in social and personality development. One perceptive sophomore wrote, "I want to know why all of us turn out so much alike and, at the same time, so *different* from one another." Clearly, humans are alike in certain respects because as members of the same species, we share a common evolutionary heritage that tends to channel development along a similar path. What's more, those of us living within any given culture or subculture are also encouraged to adopt similar norms and values. Yet, it is also true that no two individuals are exactly alike and that each of us has a unique personality. Why is this? One important reason is that no two of us, with the exception of identical twins, inherit precisely the same set of genes. A second and equally important contributor to our "uniqueness" is that every individual—even identical twins raised in the same home—has somewhat different (and often dramatically different) experiences growing up. So social and personality development represents far more than the unfolding of a genetic program or the impact of cultures on individuals. As we will see, it is more accurately characterized as a long and involved interplay among a variety of social, cultural, and biological influences that conspire to make us humans similar in certain ways but very different from one another in many other respects.

The Universal Parenting Machine—A Thought Experiment

Jones, Hendrick, and Epstein (1979) have described an interesting thought experiment that touches on the major issues that we will discuss throughout this book. They title their hypothetical experiment the "Universal Parenting Machine" and describe the project as follows:

> Suppose that six infants are placed immediately after birth into a "universal parenting machine" (the UPM). To enliven the scenario, we may suppose that three infants are male and three female. The UPM is . . . an enclosed building with advanced machinery and technology capable of taking care of all the infants' physical needs from immediately after birth to maturity. The most critical feature of the UPM is that it is constructed so that the infants will have no human contact other than with each other during their first 18 years of life. In fact, they will not even know that other human beings exist. (p. 52)

Now imagine that the creation of a UPM is within the range of our technical capabilities. Let's also assume that the UPM can be set up in such a way as to create a modern-day "Garden of Eden," complete with trees, flowers, the sounds of birds chirping, and a transparent domed room so that our experimental children are exposed to the sights and sounds of the weather and the movements of the sun, the moon, and the stars. In other words, try to imagine that we have simulated a very pleasant acre of the real world that lacks at least one potentially important feature: we have omitted all other people and, indeed, the concept of a culture. Were we to expose six infants to this environment, there are many questions we might wish to ask about their development. Here are a few:

- Perhaps the most basic question is this: Would these children interact with one another and become sociable creatures? If they did, several other questions might be asked.
- Would the children love one another, depend on one another, or develop stable friendships?

- Would the children ever develop a spoken language or some other efficient method of communicating complex ideas?
- Would this environment provide the kinds of stimulation that children need to develop intellectually so that they might have complex ideas to express?
- Would these children develop gender roles and/or become sexual beings at maturity?
- Would the children develop a sense of pride in their accomplishments (assuming, of course, that they were able to accomplish anything meaningful on their own)?
- Would the children's interactions be benevolent (guided by a spirit of togetherness, cooperation, and altruism) or belligerent (antagonistic and aggressive)?
- Would these children ever develop standards of good and evil or right and wrong to govern their day-to-day interactions?

How would the experiment turn out? That's hard to say, for this kind of project has not been conducted and, if current ethical guidelines prevail, never will be. But this is a thought experiment, and there is nothing to prevent us from speculating about possible outcomes, with the help of what we know about social and personality development.

Recall that the product of socialization is a person who has acquired the beliefs, attitudes, and behaviors that are thought to be appropriate for members of his or her culture. How does the child become socialized? One point of view is that children are shaped by their culture. Were we to adopt this viewpoint quite literally, we might predict that our six experimental children would become little vegetables or semihumans in the absence of a prevailing social structure. The opposite side of the coin is that culture is shaped by people. Thus, it is conceivable that our six children would show enough initiative to interact, to develop strong affectional ties, and to create their own little culture, complete with a set of rules or customs to govern their interactions. Although this suggestion may seem improbable, there is at least one case in which a small group of Jewish war orphans did indeed form their own "society" in the absence of adult supervision while in a German prison camp during the Second World War (Freud & Dann, 1951). We will take a closer look at this intriguing "peer-only" culture in Chapter 13.

Of course, we can't be absolutely certain that infants raised by the UPM would create the same kind of social order the young war orphans did. Furthermore, the war orphans were integrated into adult society at a very early age, so that they provide few clues about the kinds of people that our experimental children might eventually become. So where do we turn to develop some predictions about the outcome of our experiment? One possibility is to examine the existing theories of social and personality development to see what hints they provide.

There are now several such theories to examine, each of which makes assumptions about children and the ways they develop. In the following sections of this chapter, we will compare and contrast the different assumptions that theorists make about human nature and the character of human development. Our theoretical overview will then carry over into Chapters 2 and 3, where we will take an in-depth look at both classical and contemporary theories of social and personality development.

Once we have had an opportunity to examine the major theories, our focus will shift to a most important aspect of social development: the child's earliest interpersonal relationships. You may have noticed that young infants are drawn to their mothers and often voice their displeasure if separated from this intimate companion. How does this attachment originate? How does it affect the infant's reactions to strangers? Why and under what circumstances will an infant become distressed when separated from its mother or from another close companion? These issues are explored in some detail in Chapter 4. Chapter 5 addresses another important question: What happens to children who do not become securely attached to an adult or do not develop a positive sense of social responsiveness during the first two to three years of life? The answers to all these questions—particularly the last—would almost certainly provide some basis for speculation about the development of children raised by a universal parenting machine.

People clearly differ in their willingness to engage others in social interaction and to seek their attention or approval. Some individuals can be described as loners whereas others are outgoing and gregarious. These two types differ in what is called *sociability,* or the value they place on the presence, attention, and approval of other people. Competence is another way in which people clearly differ. Some people take great pride in their accomplishments and seem highly motivated to achieve. Others do not appear to be terribly concerned about what they have accomplished or what they are likely to accomplish in the future. Would our six experimental children come to value the presence, attention, or approval of one another? Would they develop a motive to achieve? Perhaps a review of the factors that influence children's sociability, achievement motivation, and achievement behavior will help us decide. These topics are discussed in Chapters 6 and 7, which explore the development of the self and the growth of one's propensities for achievement.

Recall that the children selected for our experiment were balanced with respect to biological sex (three males and three females). Would they eventually differentiate themselves on the basis of gender? Would they develop a sense of masculinity and femininity and pursue different activities? Would they become sexual beings at maturity? There are reasons for predicting that the answers to all these questions would be yes, for gender is, after all, a biological attribute. But we should keep in mind that gender roles and standards of sexual conduct are almost certainly affected by social values and customs. Thus, the gender typing and the sexual behavior of our six experimental children might well depend on the kind of social order they created, as well as on their biological heritage. The determinants of gender typing and gender-role behaviors are explored in detail in Chapter 8.

Earlier, we asked whether interactions among our six experimental children would turn out to be benevolent or belligerent. Children raised in a typical home setting display both kinds of behavior, but we should keep in mind that the socializing experiences provided by a UPM could hardly be described as typical. Nevertheless, it might be possible to make some educated guesses about the positive or negative character of these children's interactions if we had some information about the development of aggression and altruism in children reared under more normal circumstances. The factors that affect children's aggression and antisocial conduct are discussed in Chapter 9. The development of altruism and prosocial behavior (generosity, helpfulness, and cooperation) is covered in Chapter 10.

Of course, a major reason that human beings are able to live together in ordered societies is that they have devised laws and moral norms that distinguish right from wrong and govern their day-to-day interactions. How do children acquire a knowledge of these moral principles? What roles do parents, teachers, peers, and other agents of socialization play in a child's moral development? The answers to these questions may well provide some hints about the likelihood that children raised by a universal parenting machine would develop their own moral norms. Moral development is the primary focus of Chapter 10.

As our experimental children are to be raised by a machine, they will not be exposed to a nuclear family as we know it, consisting of a mother, a father, and any number of brothers and sisters. How would the lack of family ties and familial influence affect their development? Perhaps we can gain some insight on this issue after focusing on the family as an agent of socialization in Chapter 11.

Although families have an enormous impact on their young throughout childhood and adolescence, it is only a matter of time before other societal agents begin to exert their influence. For example, infants and toddlers are frequently exposed to alternative caregivers and a host of new playmates when their working parents place them in some kind of day care. Even those toddlers who remain at home will soon begin to learn more about the outside world once they develop an interest in television and computer technology. And by age 6 to 7, virtually all youngsters in Western societies are venturing outside the home to school, a setting that requires them to adjust to the demands of a new authority figure—the classroom teacher—and to interact effectively with other little people who are similar to themselves. Does exposure to television, computers, and formal schooling contribute in any meaningful ways to the shaping of one's character? Do playmates and the peer group have a significant impact on a child's or an adolescent's social and personality development? The answers to these questions are of obvious importance to the development of our six experimental children, who are to be raised with no exposure to the electronic media and no companions other than peers. Thus, our overview of social and personality development will conclude with in-depth discussions of the major "extra-familial" agents of socialization—television, computers, and schools (Chapter 12) and children's peer groups (Chapter 13).

In sum, we cannot specify *exactly* how children raised by a universal parenting machine would turn out. After all, we have no empirical precedents from which to work. Although we will not dwell further on our hypothetical children in the text, you may want to keep them in mind and to make some educated guesses about their future as we examine the major theories of social and personality development and review a portion of the data on developing children and adolescents that has been collected over the past 80 years. We will begin our discussion by briefly considering how scientists became interested in the socialization process and why they have settled on theoretically inspired empirical research as the preferred method of acquiring knowledge about human development.

Social-Personality Development in Historical Perspective

CHILDHOOD IN PREMODERN TIMES

Childhood and adolescence were not always regarded as the special and sensitive periods we know them to be today. In the early days of recorded history, children had few if any rights, and their lives were not always valued by the elders. For example, archaeological research has shown that as far back as 7000 B.C., children were killed as religious sacrifices and sometimes embedded in the walls of buildings to "strengthen" these structures (Bjorklund & Bjorklund, 1992). Until the fourth century A.D., Roman parents were legally entitled to kill their deformed, illegitimate, or otherwise unwanted infants; and even after this active infanticide was outlawed, unwanted babies were often left to die in the wilderness or sold as servants upon reaching childhood (deMause, 1974).

Historian Philippe Aries (1962) has analyzed documents and paintings from medieval Europe and concluded that European societies had little or no concept of childhood as we know it before 1600. Medieval children were closely cared for until they could feed, dress, and bathe themselves, but they were not often coddled by their elders (Aries, 1962; deMause, 1974). At about age 6, children were dressed in downsized ver-

PHOTO 1.1 Medieval children were often dressed and sometimes treated like miniature adults.

sions of adult clothing and were depicted in artwork as working alongside adults (usually close relations) in shops or fields or as drinking and carousing with adults at parties and orgies. And except for exempting infants from criminal culpability, medieval law generally made no distinctions between childhood and adult offenses (Borstelmann, 1983; Kean, 1937).

During the 17th and 18th centuries, attitudes about children and child rearing began to change. Religious leaders of that era stressed that children were fragile creatures of God who should be shielded from the wild and wanton behavior of adults and, at the same time, diverted from their own stubborn and devilish ways. One method of accomplishing these objectives was to send young people to school. Although the primary purpose of schooling was to civilize children—to provide them with a proper moral and religious education—society recognized that important subsidiary skills such as reading and writing should be taught to transform the innocents into "servants and workers" who would become "a good labor force" (Aries, 1962, p. 10). Children were still considered family possessions, but parents were now discouraged from abusing their sons and daughters and were urged to treat them with more warmth and affection (Aries, 1962; Despert, 1965).

CHILDREN AS SUBJECTS: THE BABY BIOGRAPHIES

The first glimmering of a systematic study of children can be traced to the late 19th century. This was a period in which investigators from a variety of academic backgrounds began to observe the development of their own children and to publish these data in works known as **baby biographies.**

Perhaps the most influential of the baby biographers was Charles Darwin, who made daily records of the early development of his son (Darwin, 1877; see also Charlesworth, 1992). Darwin's curiosity about child development stemmed from his earlier theory of evolution. Quite simply, he believed that young, untrained infants shared many characteristics with their nonhuman ancestors and he advanced the (now discredited) *law of recapitulation*—the notion that an individual who develops from a single cell at conception into a marvelously complex, thinking human being as a young adult will retrace the entire evolutionary history of the species, thereby illustrating the "descent of man." So Darwin and many of his contemporaries viewed the baby biography as a means of answering questions about our evolutionary past.

Unfortunately, baby biographies left much to be desired as works of science. Observations for many of the biographies were made at irregular intervals, and different

baby biography: a detailed record of an infant's growth and development over a period of time.

biographers emphasized very different aspects of their children's behavior. Consequently, the data provided by various biographers were often not comparable. In addition, the persons making observations in these biographical studies were generally proud parents who were likely to record incidents selectively—noting pleasant or positive events while downplaying unpleasant or negative episodes. Finally, almost every baby biography was based on observations of a single child; and it is difficult to know whether conclusions based on a single case would hold for other children.

Despite these shortcomings, baby biographies were a step in the right direction. For eminent scientists such as Charles Darwin to be writing about developing children implied that human development was a topic worthy of scientific scrutiny.

PHOTO 1.2 American psychologist G. Stanley Hall (1844–1924) is recognized as one of the founders of developmental psychology.

EMERGENCE OF A PSYCHOLOGY OF CHILDHOOD

Introductory textbooks in virtually all academic areas typically credit someone as the "founder" of the discipline. In developmental psychology, there are several influential pioneers who might merit consideration for this honor. Still, the person most often cited as the founder of developmental psychology is G. Stanley Hall.

Well aware of the shortcomings of baby biographies based on single children, Hall set out in the late 19th century to collect more objective data on larger samples. Specifically, he was interested in the character of children's thinking, and he developed a familiar research tool—the *questionnaire*—to "discover the contents of children's minds" (Hall, 1891). What he found was that children's understanding of worldly events increases rapidly over the course of childhood and that the "logic" of young children is not very logical at all. Hall later wrote an influential book titled *Adolescence* (1904), the first work to recognize adolescence as a unique phase of the life span (see Box 1.1). Here, then, were the first large-scale scientific investigations of developing youth, and it is on this basis that G. Stanley Hall merits consideration as the founder of developmental psychology (White, 1992).

At about the time Hall was using questionnaires to study children's thinking, a young European neurologist was trying a different method of probing the mind and revealing its contents. The neurologist's approach was very fruitful, providing information that led him to propose a theory that revolutionized thinking about children and childhood. The neurologist was Sigmund Freud. His ideas came to be known as *psychoanalytic theory.*

In many areas of science, new theories are often revisions or modifications of old theories. But in Freud's day, there were few "old" theories of human behavior to modify. Freud was truly a pioneer, formulating his psychoanalytic theory from the thousands of notes and observations he made while treating patients for various kinds of emotional disturbances.

Freud's highly creative and unorthodox theorizing attracted a lot of attention. Shortly after the publication of his earliest theoretical monographs, the *International Journal of Psychoanalysis* was founded, and other researchers began to report their tests of Freud's thinking. By the mid-1930s much of Freud's work had been translated into other languages, and the impact of psychoanalytic theory was felt around the world. Over the years, Freud's theory proved to be quite *heuristic*—meaning that it continued to generate new research and to prompt other researchers to extend Freud's thinking. Clearly, the field of child development was alive and well by the time Freud died, in 1939.

THE ROLE OF THEORY IN THE SCIENTIFIC ENTERPRISE

Freud's work and other scientists' reactions to it aptly illustrate the role theories play in the modern, scientific study of human development. Although the word *theory*

Box 1.1   *Cultural Influences*

On the "Invention" of Adolescence

Although modern-day concepts of childhood date to the 1700s, formal recognition of *adolescence* as a distinct phase of life came even later—during the early years of this century (Hall, 1904). Ironically, the spread of industry in Western societies is probably the event most responsible for the "invention" of adolescence. As immigrants poured into industrialized nations and took jobs that had formerly been filled by children and teenagers, young people became economic liabilities rather than assets or, as one person put it, "economically worthless but emotionally priceless" (Zelizer, cited in Remley, 1988). Moreover, the increasingly complex technology of industrial operations placed a premium on obtaining an educated labor force. So the late 19th century was a period when laws were passed to restrict child labor and make schooling compulsory (Kett, 1977). Suddenly teens were spending much of their time surrounded by age-mates and separated from adults. And as they hung out with friends and developed their own colorful "peer cultures," teenagers came to be viewed as a distinct class of individuals—those who had clearly emerged from the innocence of childhood but who were not yet ready to assume adult responsibilities (Hall, 1904).

After World War II, the adolescent experience broadened as increasing numbers of high school graduates postponed marriages and careers to pursue college (and postgraduate) educations. Today, it is not at all unusual for young people to delay their entry into the workaday adult world until their mid to late 20s (Hartung & Sweeney, 1991; Vobejda, 1991). And we might add that society condones this "extended adolescence" by requiring workers to obtain increasingly specialized training to pursue their chosen careers (Elder, Liker, & Cross, 1984).

Interestingly, many of the world's cultures have no concept of adolescence as a distinct phase of life. The St. Lawrence Eskimos, for example, simply distinguish boys from men (or girls from women), following the tradition of many preliterate societies that passage to adulthood occurs at puberty (Keith, 1985). And yet, other cultures' depictions of the life span are much more intricate than our own. The Arasha of East Africa, for example, have at least *six* meaningful age strata for males: youths, junior warriors, senior warriors, junior elders, senior elders, and retired elders.

In some cultures, passage to adulthood occurs at puberty, and adolescents are expected to assume adult responsibilities.

The fact that age does not have the same meaning in all eras or cultures reflects a basic truth that we have already touched on and will emphasize repeatedly throughout this book: The course of human development in one historical or cultural context is apt to differ, and to differ substantially, from that observed in other eras and cultural settings. Aside from our biological link to the human race, we are largely products of the times and places in which we live!

may seem imposing, theories are something everyone has. If I were to ask you why males and females appear so different as adults when they seem so very similar as infants, you would undoubtedly have something to say on the issue. In answering, you would be stating or at least reflecting your own underlying theory of sex differences. So a **theory** is really nothing more than a set of concepts and propositions that allow the theorist to describe and explain some aspect of experience. In the field of psychology, theories help us to describe various patterns of behavior and to explain why those behaviors occur.

A *scientific* theory is a public pronouncement that indicates what a scientist believes to be true about his or her specific area of investigation (Green, 1987). And the beauty of scientific theo-

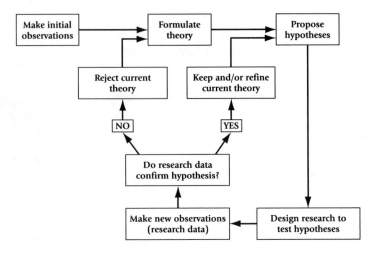

FIGURE 1.1 The role of theory in scientific investigation.

ries is that they allow us to organize our thinking about a broad range of observations and events. Imagine what life might be like for a researcher who plugs away at collecting data and recording fact after fact without organizing this information around a set of concepts and propositions. Probably, this person would eventually be swamped by a large number of seemingly unconnected facts, thus qualifying as a trivia expert who lacks a "big picture." So theories are of critical importance to the developmental sciences (or any other scientific discipline), for each of them provides us with a "lens" though which we might interpret any number of specific observations about developing individuals.

What are the characteristics of a good theory? Ideally, it should be concise, or **parsimonious,** and yet be able to explain a broad range of phenomena. A theory with few principles that accounts for a large number of empirical observations is much more useful than a second theory that requires many more concepts and propositions to explain the same number (or a lesser number) of observations. In addition, good theories are **falsifiable**—that is, capable of making explicit predictions about future events so that the theory can be supported or disconfirmed. And as implied by the falsifiability criterion, good theories have **heuristic value**—meaning that they build on existing knowledge by continuing to generate testable **hypotheses** that, if confirmed by future research, will lead to a much richer understanding of the phenomena under investigation (see Figure 1.1).

Today there are several "good" theories that have contributed to our understanding of social and personality development, and in Chapters 2 and 3 we will examine critically some of the more influential of these viewpoints. As we will see in our later review, each theory makes somewhat different assumptions about human nature as well as about the course and causes of development. So before we discuss the major theories of social and personality development, it may be helpful to consider some of the more basic issues on which they differ.

Questions and Controversies About Human Development

Developmental theorists have different points of view on at least five basic issues:

1. Are children inherently good or inherently bad?
2. Is nature (biological forces) or nurture (environmental forces) the primary influence on human development?

theory: a set of concepts and propositions designed to organize, describe, and explain an existing set of observations.

parsimony: a criterion for evaluating the scientific merit of theories; a parsimonious theory is one that uses relatively few explanatory principles to explain a broad set of observations.

falsifiability: a criterion for evaluating the scientific merit of theories; a theory is falsifiable when it is capable of generating predictions that could be disconfirmed.

heuristic value: a criterion for evaluating the scientific merit of theories. A heuristic theory is one that continues to stimulate new research and new discoveries.

hypothesis: a theoretical prediction about some aspect of experience.

3. Are children actively involved in the developmental process, or are they passive recipients of social and biological influences?
4. Is development continuous or discontinuous?
5. Are the most noteworthy aspects of development "universals" that all humans display or the "particularistic" or ideographic developments that characterize each individual?

Early Philosophical Perspectives on Human Nature

What kind of animal are we? After debating this issue for centuries, social philosophers have produced viewpoints ranging from Thomas Hobbes's (1651/1904) doctrine of **original sin**, which held that children are inherently selfish egoists who must be controlled by society, to Jean Jacques Rousseau's (1762/1955) doctrine of **innate purity**—the notion that children are born with an intuitive sense of right and wrong that is often misdirected by society. These two viewpoints clearly differ in their implications for child rearing. Proponents of original sin argued that parents must actively restrain their egoistic offspring whereas the innate purists viewed children as "noble savages" who should be given the freedom to follow their inherently positive inclinations.

Another view on children and child rearing was offered by John Locke (1690/1913), who believed that the mind of an infant is a **tabula rasa,** or "blank slate," that is written on by experience. In other words, children were portrayed as neither inherently good nor inherently bad, and how they will turn out should depend entirely on how they are raised. Like Hobbes, Locke argued in favor of disciplined child rearing to ensure that children develop good habits and acquire few if any unacceptable impulses.

As it turns out, each of these three philosophical perspectives on human nature remains with us today in one or more contemporary theories of social and personality development. Although one may search in vain for explicit statements about human nature, the theorist will typically emphasize the positive or the negative aspects of children's character or perhaps will note that positivity or negativity of character depends on the child's experiences. These assumptions about human nature are important, for they influence the content of each developmental theory—particularly what the theory has to say about child rearing.

NATURE VERSUS NURTURE

One of the oldest controversies among developmental theorists is the **nature versus nurture issue:** Are human beings a product of their heredity and other biological predispositions, or are they shaped by the environment in which they are raised? Here are two opposing viewpoints:

> Heredity and not environment is the chief maker of man. . . . Nearly all of the misery and nearly all of the happiness in the world are due not to environment. . . . The differences among men are due to differences in the germ cells with which they were born. (Wiggam, 1923, p. 42)
>
> Give me a dozen healthy infants, well formed, and my own specified world to bring them up in and I'll guarantee to take any one at random and train him to become any type of specialist I might select—doctor, lawyer, artist, merchant, chief, and yes, even beggar man and thief, regardless of his talents, penchants, tendencies, abilities, vocations, and race of his ancestors. There is no such thing as an inheritance of capacity, talent, temperament, mental constitution, and behavioral characteristics. (Watson, 1925, p. 82)

original sin: the idea that infants are born with an intuitive sense of right and wrong that is often misdirected by the demands and restrictions of society.

innate purity: the idea that infants are born with an intuitive sense of right and wrong that is often misdirected by societal demands and restrictions.

tabula rasa: the idea that the mind of an infant is a "blank slate" and that all knowledge, abilities, behaviors, and motives are acquired through experience.

nature versus nurture issue: debate within developmental psychology over the relative importance of biological predispositions (nature) and environmental influences (nurture) as determinants of human development.

Of course, there is a middle ground, one that is endorsed by most contemporary developmentalists who believe that the relative contributions of nature and nurture depend on the particular aspect of development in question. However, today's developmentalists generally agree that all complex human attributes such as intelligence, temperament, and personality are the end products of a long and involved interplay between biological predispositions and environmental forces (see, for example, Plomin et al., 1997). Their advice to us, then, is to think less about *nature* versus *nurture* and more about how these two sets of influences combine or *interact* to produce developmental change.

ACTIVITY VERSUS PASSIVITY

Another topic of theoretical debate is the **activity/passivity issue.** Are children curious, active creatures who largely determine how agents of society treat them? Or are they passive souls on whom society fixes its stamp? Consider the implications of these opposing viewpoints. If we could show that children are extremely malleable—literally at the mercy of those who raise them—then perhaps individuals who turned out to be less than productive would be justified in suing their overseers for malfeasance. Indeed, one young man in the United States recently used this logic to bring a malfeasance suit against his parents. Perhaps you can anticipate the defense the parents' lawyer would offer. Counsel would surely argue that the parents tried many strategies in an attempt to raise their child right but that he responded favorably to none of them. The implication is that this young man played an active role in determining how his parents treated him and therefore bears a large share of the responsibility for creating the climate in which he was raised.

As we will see in the next two chapters, there is an intermediate stance on this activity/passivity issue, one that leans more in the direction of an active child than a passive one. This middle ground is the view that human development is best described as a continuous *reciprocal interaction* between children and their environments (*reciprocal determinism*): the environment clearly affects the child, but the child's mannerisms and behaviors will also affect the environment. The implication is that children are *actively involved* in creating the very environments that will influence their growth and development.

CONTINUITY VERSUS DISCONTINUITY

Now think for a moment about the concept of developmental change. Do you think that the changes we experience occur very gradually? Or would you say that these changes are rather abrupt?

On one side of the **continuity/discontinuity issue** are continuity theorists, who view human development as an additive process that occurs in small steps, without sudden changes. They might represent the course of development change with a smooth growth curve like the one in Figure 1.2A. By contrast, discontinuity theorists describe the road to maturity as a series of abrupt changes, each of which elevates the child to a new and presumably more advanced level of functioning. These levels, or "stages," are represented by the plateaus of the discontinuous growth curve in Figure 1.2B.

A second aspect of the continuity/discontinuity issue centers on whether developmental changes are quantitative or qualitative in nature. Quantitative changes are changes in *degree*. For example, children grow taller; they run a little faster with each passing year; and they acquire more and more knowledge about the world around them. By contrast, qualitative changes are changes in *kind*—changes that make the individual fundamentally different in some way from the way he or she was before.

activity/passivity issue: debate among developmental theorists about whether children are active contributors to their own development or passive recipients of environmental influence.

continuity/discontinuity issue: debate among theorists about whether developmental changes are best characterized as gradual and quantitative or abrupt and qualitative.

The transformation of a tadpole into a frog is a qualitative change. Similarly, we might regard the infant who lacks language as qualitatively different from a preschooler who speaks well, or the adolescent who is sexually mature as fundamentally different from a classmate who is yet to reach puberty. Continuity theorists generally think that developmental changes are both gradual and quantitative in nature, whereas discontinuity theorists tend to view such changes as more abrupt and qualitative. Indeed, discontinuity theorists are the ones who argue that we progress through **developmental stages**. Presumably, each of these stages represents a distinct phase within a larger sequence of development—a period of the life cycle characterized by a particular set of abilities, motives, behaviors, or emotions that occur together and form a coherent pattern. Furthermore,

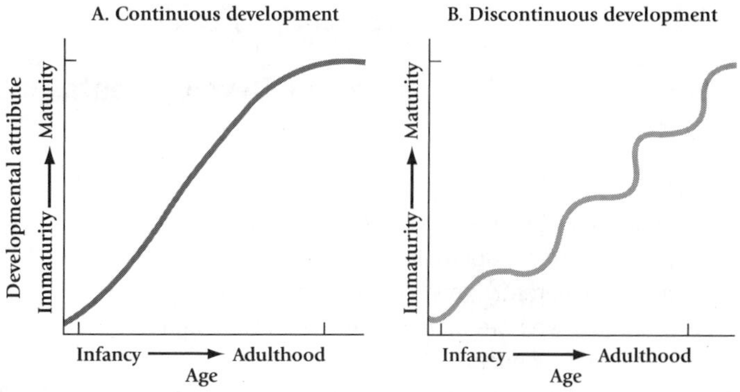

FIGURE 1.2 The course of development as described by continuity and discontinuity (stage) theorists. (Adapted from D. R. Shaffer, "Social Psychology from a Social-Developmental Perspective." In C. Hendrick [Ed.], *Perspectives on Social Psychology.* Copyright © 1977 by Lawrence Erlbaum Associates. Used by permission.)

each of these stages is qualitatively different from the stage that proceeds or follows it. By contrast, continuity theorists view development as an additive process that occurs continuously and is not at all stagelike.

Finally, there is a third aspect of the continuity/discontinuity debate: Are there close connections between early developments and later ones, or do changes that occur early in life have little bearing on future outcomes? Continuity in this sense implies a sense of *connectiveness* between earlier and later developments. Those who argue against the concept of developmental stages might see such connectiveness in the *stability* of attributes over time, as might be indicated, for example, if aggressive toddlers routinely become aggressive adolescents or if particularly curious preschoolers are the ones most often recognized, as adults, for creative accomplishments. Even a theorist who proposes that we pass through qualitatively distinct stages might still see some connectiveness (or continuity) to development if the abilities that characterize each successive stage are thought to evolve from those of the previous stage.

Interestingly, societies often take different positions on the continuity/discontinuity issue. Some Pacific and Far Eastern cultures, for example, have words for infant qualities that are never used to describe older children, and adult terms such as *intelligent* or *angry* that are never used to characterize infants (Kagan, 1991). People in these cultures view personality development as discontinuous, and infants are regarded as so fundamentally different from adults that they cannot be judged on the same personality dimensions. By contrast, North Americans and Northern Europeans are more inclined to assume that personality development is a continuous process and to search for the seeds of adult personality in babies' temperaments.

In sum, the debate about developmental continuities and discontinuities is very complex. There is the issue of whether developmental change is gradual or abrupt, the issue of whether it is quantitative or qualitative, and the issue of whether it is or is not reliably connected to earlier developments.

IS DEVELOPMENT UNIVERSAL OR PARTICULARISTIC?

Finally, theorists often disagree about whether the most noteworthy aspects of development are **universal** (that is, normative outcomes that everyone is said to display) or **particularistic** (trends or outcomes that vary from person to person). Stage theorists typically believe that their developmental sequences apply to all normal people in all cultures and are therefore universal. For example, all normal humans begin to

developmental stage: a distinct phase within a larger sequence of development; a period characterized by a particular set of abilities, motives, behaviors, or emotions that occur together and form a coherent pattern.

universal development: normative developments that all individuals display.

particularistic development: developmental outcomes that vary from person to person.

Box 1.2   *Developmental Issues*

How Do You Stand on Major Developmental Issues?

1. Children are
   a. creatures whose basically negative or selfish impulses must be controlled.
   b. neither inherently good nor inherently bad.
   c. creatures who are born with many positive and few negative tendencies.
2. Biological influences (heredity, maturational forces) and environmental influences (culture, parenting styles, learning experiences) are thought to contribute to development. Overall,
   a. biological factors contribute more than environmental factors.
   b. biological and environmental factors are equally important.
   c. environmental factors contribute more than biological factors.
3. People are basically
   a. active beings who play a major role in determining their own abilities and traits.
   b. passive beings whose characteristics are molded either by social influences (parents and other significant people, outside events) or by biological factors beyond their control.

4. Developmental proceeds
   a. through stages, so that the individual changes rather abruptly into a quite different kind of person from the one he or she was in an earlier stage.
   b. continuously—in small increments without abrupt changes or distinct stages.
5. Traits such as aggressiveness or dependency
   a. emerge in childhood and remain largely stable over the years.
   b. first appear in childhood but often disappear or give way to quite different traits at some later time.
6. When we compare the development of different individuals, we see
   a. mainly similarities; children and adults develop along universal paths and experience similar changes at similar ages.
   b. mainly differences; different people often undergo different sequences of change and have widely different timetables of development.

		Question			
1	2	3	4	5	6

Your pattern
of answers: _____ _____ _____ _____ _____ _____

---

use language at 11 to 14 months of age, experience cognitive changes that prepare them for school at 5 to 7 years of age, reach sexual maturity during the preteen or teenage period, and show some signs of aging (for example, wrinkles, a decline in certain sensory abilities) by midlife. From this perspective, then, the most important aspects of development are the universal patterns that all humans display.

However, other theorists believe that a singular focus on developmental universals is woefully incomplete. Why? Because it ignores all the factors that conspire to make each of us unique. Paths of development followed in one culture may be very different from those followed in another culture. And within any culture, developmental outcomes may vary across different subcultural or ethnic groups, from family to family, and from individual to individual. So the message of these "particularistic" theorists is that human development can (and does) proceed in many directions and is much less universal than stage theorists would have us believe.

These, then, are the major developmental controversies that different theories resolve in different ways. Perhaps you may wish to clarify your own stand on the issues by completing the brief questionnaire in Box 1.2. At the end of Chapter 3, Table 3-3 (on page 100) indicates how the major developmental theorists might answer these questions so that you can compare their assumptions about human development with your own.

In the next section of the chapter, we will focus on the "tools of the trade"—that is, the research methods and designs that developmentalists use to test their theories and gain a better understanding of the social development of children and adolescents.

Research Methods

When detectives are assigned cases to solve, they will first gather the facts, formulate hunches, and then sift through the clues or collect additional information until one of their hunches proves correct. Unraveling the mysteries of social and personality development is in many ways a similar endeavor. Investigators must carefully observe their subjects, study the information they have collected, and then use it to draw conclusions about the ways people develop.

Our focus in this section is on the methods that researchers use to gather information about developing children and adolescents. Our first task is to understand why developmentalists consider it absolutely essential to gather all these facts. We will then discuss the advantages and disadvantages of several basic fact-finding strategies and see how these techniques might be used to detect developmental change.

THE SCIENTIFIC METHOD

The study of social and personality development is appropriately labeled a scientific enterprise because modern developmentalists have adopted a value system called the **scientific method** that guides their attempts at understanding. The scientific method is really more of an attitude or a value than a method; the attitude dictates that, above all, investigators must be *objective* and must allow their observations (or data) to decide the merits of their thinking.

In earlier eras, when social philosophers such as Hobbes, Locke, and Rousseau were presenting their views on children and childrearing, people were apt to interpret these pronouncements as fact. It was as if the public assumed that great minds always had great insights. Very few individuals questioned the word of well-known scholars because the scientific method was not yet an important criterion for evaluating wisdom or knowledge.

The intent here is not to criticize the early social philosophers. In fact, today's developmentalists (and children) are indebted to these men for helping to modify the ways in which society thought about, treated, and often exploited its young. However, so-called great minds may produce miserable ideas on occasion, and if such poorly conceived notions have implications for the ways human beings are to be treated, it behooves us to discover these erroneous assumptions before they harm anyone. The scientific method, then, is a value that helps to protect the scientific community and society at large against flawed reasoning. The protection comes from the practice of evaluating the merits of various theoretical pronouncements against the objective record rather than simply relying on the academic, political, or social credibility of the theorist. Of course, this means that the theorist whose ideas are being evaluated must be equally objective and, thus, willing to discard pet notions when there is evidence that they have outlived their usefulness.

GATHERING DATA: BASIC FACT-FINDING STRATEGIES

No matter what aspect of social development we hope to study—be it the emotional reactions of newborn infants, the growth of friendships among children, or the origins of drug use among adolescents—we must find ways to measure what interests us. Today researchers are fortunate to have many tried-and-true procedures that they can use to measure behavior and to test their hypotheses about human development. But regardless of the technique one employs, scientifically useful measures must always display two important qualities: **reliability** and **validity.**

A measure is *reliable* if it yields consistent information over time and across observers. Suppose you go into a classroom and record the number of times each child

scientific method: an attitude or value about the pursuit of knowledge that dictates that investigators must be objective and must allow their data to decide the merits of their theorizing.

reliability: the extent to which a measuring instrument yields consistent results, both over time and across observers.

validity: the extent to which a measuring instrument accurately reflects what the researchers intended to measure.

behaves in an aggressive manner toward others, but your research assistant, using the same scheme to observe the same children, does not agree with your measurements. Or you measure each child's aggressiveness one week but come up with very different aggressiveness scores while applying the same measure to the same children a week later. Clearly, your observational measure of aggression is unreliable because it yields highly inconsistent information. To be reliable and thus useful for scientific purposes, your measure would have to produce comparable estimates of children's aggression from independent observers (*interrater reliability*) and would yield similar scores for individual children from one testing to another shortly thereafter (*temporal stability*).

A measure is *valid* if it measures what it is supposed to measure. Perhaps you can see how an instrument must be reliable and measure consistently before it can possibly be valid. Yet reliability, by itself, does not guarantee validity. For example, a reliable observational scheme that is intended to measure children's aggression may provide grossly overinflated estimates of aggressive behavior if the investigator simply classifies all acts of physical force as examples of aggression. What the researcher has failed to recognize is that many such high-intensity antics may simply represent enjoyable forms of rough-and-tumble play that children display without any harmful or aggressive intent. Clearly, researchers must demonstrate that they are measuring the attribute they say they are measuring before we can have much faith in the data they collect or the conclusions they reach.

With the importance of establishing the reliability and validity of measures in mind, let us consider some of the different ways in which aspects of social and personality development might be measured.

Self-Report Methodologies   Three common procedures that developmentalists use to gather information and test hypotheses are interviews, questionnaires (including psychological tests), and the clinical method. Although these approaches are similar in that each asks subjects to answer questions posed by the investigator, they differ in the extent in which the investigator treats individual participants alike.

Interviews and Questionnaires   Researchers who opt for the interview or the questionnaire techniques will ask the child (or the child's parents) a series of questions pertaining to such aspects of development as the child's feelings, beliefs, and characteristic patterns of behavior. Collecting data with a questionnaire (and most psychological tests) simply involves putting questions on paper and asking participants to respond to them in writing, whereas interviews require participants to respond orally to the investigator's queries. If the procedure is a **structured interview** or **structured questionnaire,** all who participate in the study are asked the same questions in the same order. The purpose of this standardized or structured format is to treat all respondents alike so that the responses of different participants can be compared.

One interesting use of the interview technique is a project in which kindergarten, second-grade, and fourth-grade children responded to 24 questions designed to assess their knowledge of social stereotypes about males and females (Williams, Bennett, & Best, 1975). Each question came in response to a different short story in which the central character was described by stereotypically masculine adjectives (for example, *aggressive, forceful, tough*) or stereotypically feminine adjectives (for example, *emotional, excitable*). The child's task was to indicate whether the character in each story was male or female. Williams and his associates found that even kindergartners could usually tell whether the stories referred to boys or girls. In other words, these 5-year-olds were quite knowledgeable about gender stereotypes, although children's thinking became much more stereotyped between kindergarten and the second grade. One implication of these results is that stereotyping of the sexes must begin very early if kindergartners are already thinking along stereotyped lines.

structured interview or **structured questionnaire:**   a technique in which all participants are asked the same questions in precisely the same order so that the responses of different participants can be compared.

Interviews and questionnaires have some very real shortcomings. First, neither approach can be used with very young children who cannot read or comprehend speech very well. Second, investigators must hope that the answers they receive are honest and accurate and are not merely attempts by respondents to present themselves in a favorable manner. Might many children, for example, be reluctant to admit that they have snitched money from mother's purse or played "doctor" with the child next door? Clearly, inaccurate or untruthful responses will lead to erroneous conclusions. Finally, investigators must be careful to ensure that participants of different ages interpret questions in the same way; otherwise, the age trends observed in the study may reflect differences in children's ability to comprehend and communicate rather than real underlying changes in children's feelings, thoughts, or behaviors.

Despite these potential shortcomings, structured interviews and questionnaires can be excellent methods of obtaining large amounts of useful information in a short period of time. Both approaches are particularly useful when the interviewer *challenges* participants to display what they know about an issue, for the socially desirable response to such a challenge is likely to be a truthful or accurate answer. In the gender stereotyping study, for example, the young participants probably considered each question a personal challenge or a puzzle to be solved and were thus motivated to answer accurately and to display exactly what they knew about males and females. Under the circumstances, then, the structured interview was an excellent method of assessing children's perceptions of the sexes.

The Clinical Method   The **clinical method** is a very close relative of the interview technique. The investigator is usually interested in testing a hypothesis by presenting the research participant with a task or problem of some sort and then inviting a response. When the participant has responded, the investigator will typically ask a second question or introduce a new problem in the hope of clarifying the participant's original answer. This questioning then continues until the investigator has the information needed to evaluate her hypothesis. Although participants are often asked the same questions in the initial stages of the research, their answers to each question determine what the investigator asks next. And since participants' answers often differ, it is possible that no two participants will ever receive exactly the same line of questioning. Thus, the clinical method considers each subject to be unique.

Jean Piaget, a famous Swiss psychologist, relied extensively on the clinical method to study children's moral reasoning and general intellectual development. The data from Piaget's research are largely protocol records of his interactions with individual children. Here is a small sample from Piaget's (1932/1965, p. 140) work on the development of moral reasoning—a sample showing that this young child thinks about lying very differently from the way adults do.

Piaget: Do you know what a lie is?
Clai: It's when you say what isn't true.
Piaget: Is 2 + 2 = 5 a lie?
Clai: Yes, it's a lie.
Piaget: Why?
Clai: Because it isn't right.
Piaget: Did the boy who said 2 + 2 = 5 know it wasn't right or did he make a mistake?
Clai: He made a mistake.
Piaget: Then if he made a mistake, did he tell a lie or not?
Clai: Yes, he told a lie.

Like structured interviews, clinical methods are often useful for gathering large amounts of information in relatively brief periods. Proponents of this approach also

clinical method: a type of interview in which a participant's response to each successive question (or problem) determines what the investigator will ask next.

cite its flexibility as an advantage: By asking follow-up questions that are tailored to the participant's original answers (as Piaget did in the above example), a researcher can often obtain a rich understanding of the meaning of those answers. However, the flexibility of the clinical method is also a potential shortcoming. It may be difficult, if not impossible, to compare directly the answers of participants who are asked different questions. Furthermore, this nonstandardized treatment of participants raises the possibility that the examiner's preexisting theoretical biases may affect the particular follow-up questions asked and the interpretations provided. Because conclusions drawn from the clinical method depend, in part, on the investigator's *subjective* interpretations, it is always desirable to verify these insights using other research techniques.

Observational Methodologies   Often researchers prefer to observe people's behavior directly rather than asking them questions about it. One method that many developmentalists favor is **naturalistic observation**—observing people in their common, everyday (that is, natural) surroundings. To observe children, this would usually mean going into homes, schools, or public parks and playgrounds and carefully recording what happens. Rarely will the investigator try to record every event that occurs; he or she will usually be testing a specific hypothesis about one type of behavior, such as cooperation or aggression, and will focus exclusively on acts of this kind. One strength of naturalistic observation is the ease at which it can be applied to infants and toddlers, who often cannot be studied though methods that demand verbal skills. But perhaps the greatest advantage of the observational technique is that it is the only method that can tell us how people actually behave in everyday life (Willems & Alexander, 1982).

However, naturalistic observation also has its limitations. First, some behaviors occur so infrequently (for example, heroic rescues) or are so socially undesirable (for example, overt sex play; thievery) that they are unlikely to be witnessed by a strange observer in the natural environment. Second, many events are usually happening at the same time in the natural setting, and any (or some combination) of them may be affecting people's behavior. Consequently, pinpointing the causes of participants' actions or of any developmental trends in behavior can be quite difficult. Finally, the mere presence of an observer can sometimes make people behave differently from the way they otherwise would. Children may "ham it up" when they have an audience whereas parents may be on their best behavior, showing a strong reluctance, for example, to spank a misbehaving child. For these reasons, researchers will often attempt to minimize **observer influence** by (1) videotaping their participants from a concealed location or (2) by spending time in the setting before collecting their "real" data so that the individuals they are observing will grow accustomed to their presence and behave more naturally.

Several years ago, Mary Haskett and Janet Kistner (1991) conducted an excellent piece of naturalistic observation to compare the social behaviors of nonabused preschoolers with those of daycare classmates identified by child protection agencies as having been physically abused by their parents. The investigators first defined examples of the behaviors they wished to record—both *desirable* behaviors such as friendly social greetings and cooperative play, and *undesirable* behaviors such as aggression and negative verbalizations. They then monitored 14 abused and 14 nonabused preschool children as they mingled with peers in a play area of a

naturalistic observation: a method in which the scientist tests hypotheses by observing people as they engage in everyday activities in their natural habitats (for example, at home, at school, or on the playground).

PHOTO 1.3   Children's tendency to perform for an observer is one of the problems researchers must overcome when using the method of naturalistic observation.

day-care facility. Each child was observed during three 10-minute play sessions on three different days. To minimize their influence on the play activities, observers stood outside the play area while making their observations.

The results were disturbing. As shown in Figure 1.3, abused children initiated fewer social interactions than their nonabused classmates and were somewhat socially withdrawn. And when they did interact with playmates, the abused youngsters displayed many more aggressive acts and other negative behaviors than did their nonabused companions. Indeed, nonabused children would often blatantly ignore the positive social initiations of an abused child, as if they did not want to get involved with him or her.

In sum, Haskett and Kistner's observational study shows that abused children are unattractive playmates who are likely to be disliked and even rejected by peers. But as is almost always the case in naturalistic observational research, pinpointing the exact cause of these findings is difficult. Did the negative behaviors of abused children cause their peers to reject them? Or did peer rejection cause the abused children to display negative behaviors? Either possibility can account for Haskett and Kistner's results.

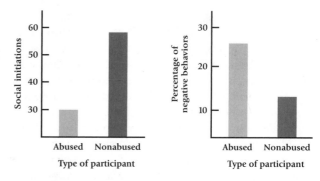

FIGURE 1.3 Social initiations and negative behaviors of abused and nonabused preschool children. Compared to their nonabused companion, abused youngsters initiate far fewer social interactions with peers and behave much more negatively toward them.

How might observational researchers study unusual or undesirable behaviors that they are unlikely to observe in the natural environment? By conducting **structured observations** in the laboratory. In a structured observational study, each participant is exposed to a setting that might cue the behavior in question and is then surreptitiously observed (by a hidden camera or through a one-way mirror) to discover whether he or she performs the behavior. For example, Leon Kuczynski (1983) got children to promise to help him with a boring task and then left them alone to work at it in a room where attractive toys were present. This procedure enabled Kuczynski to determine whether youngsters would break a promise to work (an undesirable act that many children displayed) when they thought there was no one present to observe their transgression.

Aside from being a most feasible way of studying behaviors that occur infrequently or are not openly displayed in the natural environment, structured observations also ensure that every participant in the sample is exposed to the *same* eliciting stimuli and has an *equal opportunity* to perform the target behavior—circumstances that are not always true in the natural setting. Of course, the major disadvantage of structured observations is that participants may not always respond to a contrived laboratory setting as they would in everyday life.

Case Studies Any or all of the data collection methods we have discussed—structured interviews, questionnaires, clinical methods, and behavioral observations—can be used to compile a detailed portrait of a single individual's development through the **case study** method. In preparing an individualized record, or "case," the investigator will typically seek many kinds of information about the participant, such as his or her family background, socioeconomic status, health records, academic or work history, and performance on psychological tests. Much of the information included in any case history comes from interviews with and observations of the individual, although the questions asked and observations made are typically not standardized and may vary considerably from case to case.

The baby biographies of the 19th and early 20th centuries are examples of case studies, and Sigmund Freud prepared many fascinating case studies of his clinical patients.

observer influence: tendency of participants to react to an observer's presence by behaving in unusual ways.

structured observation: an observational method in which the investigator cues the behavior of interest and observes participants' responses in a laboratory.

case study: a research method in which the investigator gathers extensive information about the life of an individual and then tests developmental hypotheses by analyzing the events of the person's life history.

In analyzing his cases, Freud noticed that different patients often described very similar events and experiences that had been noteworthy to them as they were growing up. He inferred from the observations that there must be important milestones in human development that all people share. As he continued to observe his patients and to listen to accounts of their lives, Freud concluded that each milestone in the life history of a patient was meaningfully related to earlier events. He then inferred that he had the data—the pieces of the puzzle—to construct a comprehensive explanation of human development, the account we know today as *psychoanalytic theory.*

Although Freud and many other developmentalists have used case studies to great advantage, there are major drawbacks to this approach. For example, it is often difficult to compare directly cases who have been asked different questions, have taken different tests, and have been observed under different circumstances. Case studies may also lack *generalizability;* that is, conclusions drawn from the experiences of the small number of individuals studied may simply not apply to most people. In fact, one recurring criticism of Freud's psychoanalytic theory is that it was formulated from the life histories of *emotionally disturbed patients* who are hardly typical of the general population. For these reasons, any conclusions drawn from case studies should always be verified through the use of other research techniques.

Ethnography Ethnography—a form of participant observation often used in the field of anthropology—is becoming increasingly popular among researchers who hope to understand the impact of culture on developing children and adolescents. To collect their data, ethnographers often live within the cultural or subcultural community they are studying for periods of months, or even years. The data they collect is typically diverse and extensive, consisting largely of naturalistic observations, notes made from conversations with members of the culture, and the researcher's initial interpretations of these events. These data are eventually used to compile a detailed portrait of the cultural community and to draw conclusions about how the community's unique values and traditions influence one or more aspects of the development of its children and adolescents.

Clearly detailed ethnographic portraits of a culture or subculture that arise from close and enduring contact with members of the community can lead to a richer understanding of that community's traditions and values than is possible through a small number of visits, in which outsiders make limited observations and conduct a few interviews (LeVine et al., 1994). In fact, these extensive cultural or subcultural descriptions are particularly useful to investigators hoping to understand cultural conflicts and other developmental challenges faced by minority children and adolescents in diverse multicultural societies (Segal, 1991; see also Patel, Power, & Bhavnagri, 1996). But despite these clear strengths, ethnography is a highly subjective method—one in which researchers' own cultural values and theoretical biases can cause them to misinterpret what they have experienced. In addition, ethnographic conclusions pertain only to the culture or subculture studied and cannot be assumed to generalize to other contexts or social groups.

Table 1-1 provides a brief review of the data-gathering schemes that we have examined thus

ethnography: method in which the researcher seeks to understand the unique values, traditions, and social processes of a culture or subculture by living with its members and making extensive observations and notes.

PHOTO 1.4 Ethnographic researchers attempt to understand cultural influences by living within the community and participating in all aspects of community life.

TABLE 1-1 Strengths and limitations of common research methods

METHOD	STRENGTHS	LIMITATIONS
SELF-REPORTS		
Interviews and questionnaires	Offer a relatively quick way to gather much information; standardized format allows the investigator to make direct comparisons between data provided by different participants.	Data collected may be inaccurate, may be less than completely honest, or may reflect variations in respondents' verbal skills and ability to understand the questions.
Clinical methods	Provide a flexible methodology that treats participants as unique individuals; freedom to probe can be an aid in ensuring that the participant understands the meaning of the questions one asks.	Conclusions drawn may be unreliable in that participants are not all treated alike; flexible probes depend, in part, on the investigator's subjective interpretations of the participant's responses; can be used only with highly verbal participants.
SYSTEMATIC OBSERVATION		
Naturalistic observation	Allows study of behavior as it actually occurs in the natural environment.	Observed behaviors may be influenced by observer's presence; unusual or undesirable behaviors are unlikely to be observed during the periods when observations are made.
Structured observation	Offers a standardized environment that provides every child an opportunity to perform target behavior. Excellent way to observe infrequent or socially undesirable acts.	Contrived observations may not always capture the ways children behave in the natural environment.
Case studies	Offer a very broad method that considers many sources of data when drawing inferences and conclusions about individual participants.	Kind of data collected often differs from case to case and may be inaccurate or less than honest; conclusions drawn from individual cases are subjective and may not apply to other people.
Ethnography	Provides a richer description of cultural beliefs, values, and traditions than is possible in brief observational or interview studies.	Conclusions may be biased by the investigator's values and theoretical viewpoints; results cannot be generalized beyond the groups and settings that were studied.

far. In the sections that follow, we will consider how investigators might design their research to test hypotheses and detect developmental continuities and changes.

Detecting Relationships:
Correlational and Experimental Designs

Once researchers have decided what they want to study, they must then formulate a research plan, or design, that permits them to identify associations among events and behaviors and to specify the causes of these relationships. Here we consider two general research designs that investigators might employ: correlational and experimental.

THE CORRELATION DESIGN

In a **correlational design,** the investigator gathers information to determine whether two or more variables of interest are meaningfully related. If the researcher is testing a specific hypothesis (rather than conducting preliminary exploratory research), he or she will be checking to see whether these variables are related as the hypothesis specifies they should be. No attempts are made to structure or to manipulate the participants' environment in any way. Instead, correlational researchers take people as they find them—already "manipulated" by natural life experiences—and try to determine

correlational design: a type of research design that indicates the strength of associations among variables; though correlated variables are systematically related, these relationships are not necessarily causal.

whether variations in people's life experiences are associated with differences in their behaviors or patterns of development.

To illustrate the correlational approach to hypothesis testing, let's work with a simple theory specifying that youngsters learn a lot from watching television and are apt to imitate the actions of the characters they observe. One hypothesis we might derive from this theory is that the more often children observe TV characters who display violent and aggressive acts, the more inclined they will be to behave aggressively toward their own playmates. After selecting a sample of children to study, our next step in testing our hypothesis is to measure the two variables that we think are related. To assess children's exposure to aggressive themes on television, we might use the interview or naturalistic observational methods to determine what each child watches, and then count the number of violent and aggressive acts that occur in this programming. To measure the frequency of the children's own aggressive behavior toward peers, we could observe our sample on a playground and record how often each child behaves in a hostile, aggressive manner toward playmates. After gathering the data, we evaluate our hypothesis.

The presence (or absence) of a relationship between variables can be determined by subjecting the data to a statistical procedure that yields a **correlation coefficient.** A correlation coefficient (symbolized by an r) provides a numerical estimate of the strength and the direction of the association between two variables. It can range in value from +1.00 to –1.00. The absolute value of r (disregarding its sign) tells us the *strength* of the relationship. Thus, correlation coefficients of –.70 and +.70 are of equal strength, and both are stronger than a moderate correlation of .50. An r of .00 indicates that the two variables are unrelated.

The sign of the correlation coefficient indicates the *direction* of the relationship. If the sign is positive, this means that as one variable increases, the other variable also increases. For example, height and weight are positively correlated: as children grow taller, they (usually) get heavier (Tanner, 1990). Negative correlations, however, indicate inverse relationships; as one variable increases, the other *decreases.* Among grade-school students, for example, aggression and popularity are negatively correlated: children who behave more aggressively tend to be less popular with their peers (Crick, 1996).

Now let's return to our hypothesized positive relationship between viewing televised violence and children's aggressive behavior. A number of investigators have conducted correlational studies similar to the one we have designed, and the results (reviewed in Liebert & Sprafkin, 1988) suggest a moderate positive correlation (between +.30 and +.50) between the two variables of interest: children who watch a lot of violent television programming are more likely to behave aggressively toward playmates than do other youngsters who watch little violent programming (see Figure 1.4 for a visual display).

Do these correlational studies establish that exposure to violent TV programming *causes* children to behave more aggressively? *No, they do not!* Though we have detected a relationship between exposure to televised violence and children's aggressive behavior, the causal direction of the relationship is not at all clear. An equally plausible alternative explanation is that relatively aggressive children are the more inclined to prefer violent programming. Another possibility is that the association between TV viewing and ag-

correlation coefficient: a numerical index, ranging from –1.00 to +1.00, of the strength and direction of the relationship between two variables.

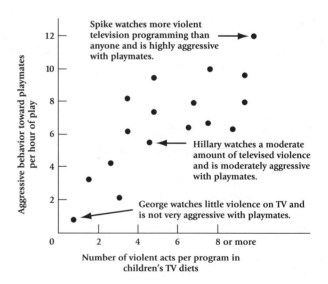

FIGURE 1.4 Plot of a hypothetical positive correlation between the amount of violence children see on television and the number of aggressive responses they display. Each dot represents a specific child who views a particular level of televised violence (shown on the horizontal axis) and commits a particular number of aggressive acts (shown on the vertical axis). Although the correlation is less than perfect, we see that the more acts of violence a child watches on TV, the more inclined he or she is to behave aggressively toward peers.

gressive behavior is actually caused by a third variable we have not measured. Perhaps parents who fight a lot at home (an unmeasured variable) cause their children to become more aggressive *and* to favor violent TV programming. If this were true, the latter two variables might be correlated, even though their relationship to each other would not be one of cause and effect.

In sum, the correlational design is a versatile approach that can detect systematic relationships between any two or more variables that we might be interested in and that can be measured. However, its major limitation is that *it cannot unambiguously indicate that one thing causes another.* How, then, might a researcher establish the underlying causes of various behaviors or other aspects of human development? By conducting experiments.

THE EXPERIMENTAL DESIGN

In contrast to correlational studies, **experimental designs** permit a precise assessment of the cause-and-effect relationship that may exist between two variables. Let's return to the issue of whether viewing violent television programming *causes* children to become more aggressive. In conducting a laboratory experiment to test this (or any) hypothesis, we would bring participants to the lab, expose them to different treatments, and record as data their responses to these treatments.

The different treatments to which we expose our participants represent the **independent variable** of our experiment. To test the hypothesis that we have proposed, our independent variable (or treatments) would be the type of television program our participants observe. Half the children might view a program in which one or more characters behave in a violent or otherwise aggressive manner toward others, whereas the other half would watch a program that contains little if any violence.

Children's reactions to the television shows would become the data, or **dependent variable,** in our experiment. Because our hypothesis centers on children's aggression, we would want to measure (as our dependent variable) how aggressively children behave after watching each type of television show. A dependent variable is called "dependent" because its value presumably "depends" on the independent variable. In the present case, we are hypothesizing that future aggression (our dependent variable) will be greater for children who watch violent programs (one level of the independent variable) than for children who watch nonviolent programs (the second level of the independent variable). If we are careful experimenters and exercise precise control over *all* other factors that may affect children's aggression, then the pattern of results that we have anticipated would allow us to draw a strong conclusion: watching violent television programs *causes* children to behave more aggressively.

Many years ago, an experiment similar to the one we have proposed was actually conducted (Liebert & Baron, 1972). Half of the 5- to 9-year-olds in this study watched a violent 3½ minute clip from *The Untouchables*—one that contained two fistfights, two shootings, and a stabbing. The remaining children watched 3½ minutes of a nonviolent but exciting track meet. So, the independent variable was the type of program the children had watched. Then each child was taken into another room and seated before a box that had wires leading into the adjoining room. On the box was a green button labeled HELP, a red button labeled HURT, and a white light between the buttons. The experimenter told him or her that a second child in the adjoining room would soon be playing a handle-turning game that would illuminate the white light. The participant was told that, by pushing the buttons when the light was lit, he or she could either *help* the other child by making the handle easy to turn, or *hurt* the child by making the handle become very hot. When it was clear that the participant understood the instructions, the experimenter left the room, and the light came on 20 times over the next several minutes. So each participant had 20 opportunities

experimental design: a research design in which the investigator introduces some change in the participant's environment and then measures the effect of that change on the participant's behavior.

independent variable: the aspect of the environment that an experimenter modifies or manipulates to measure its impact on behavior.

dependent variable: the aspect of behavior that is measured in an experiment and assumed to be under the control of the independent variable.

to help or hurt another child. The total amount of time each participant spent pushing the HURT button served as a measure of his or her aggression—the dependent variable in this study.

The results were clear: despite the availability of an alternative helping response, *both boys and girls were much more likely to press the HURT button* (that is, *behave aggressively*) *if they had watched the violent television program*. It appears that a mere 3½-minute exposure to televised violence can cause children to behave more aggressively toward a peer, even though the aggressive acts they witnessed on television bore no resemblance to those they committed themselves.

When students discuss this experiment in class, someone invariably challenges this interpretation of the results. For example, one student proposed an alternative interpretation that "maybe kids who saw the violent film were naturally more sadistic than those who saw the track meet." In other words, he was suggesting that a confounding variable—children's *preexisting* levels of sadism—had determined their willingness to hurt a peer and that the independent variable (type of television programming) had had no effect at all! Could he have been correct? How do we know that children in the two experimental conditions didn't differ in some important way that may have affected their willingness to hurt a peer?

This question brings us to the crucial issue of **experimental control.** To conclude that the independent variable is causally related to the dependent variable, the experimenter must ensure that all other factors that could affect the dependent variable are *controlled*—that is, equivalent in each experimental condition. One way to equalize these extraneous factors is to do what Liebert and Baron (1972) did: randomly assign children to their experimental treatments. The concept of *randomization,* or **random assignment**, means that each research participant has an equal probability of being exposed to each experimental treatment or condition. Assignment of individual participants to a particular treatment is accomplished by an unbiased procedure such as the flip of a coin. If the assignment is truly random, there is only a very slim chance that participants in the two (or more) experimental conditions will differ on *any* characteristic that might affect their performance on the dependent variable: all these "confounding" characteristics or **confounding variables** will have been randomly distributed within each condition and equalized across the different conditions. Since Liebert and Baron randomly assigned children to experimental conditions, they could be reasonably certain that the group of children who watched the violent TV program were not naturally more sadistic than children who watched the nonviolent program. So it was reasonable for them to conclude that the former group of children were the more aggressive group *because* they had watched a TV program in which violence and aggression was a central theme.

A Possible Limitation of Laboratory Experiments   Clearly, the greatest strength of the experimental method is its ability to establish conclusively that one thing causes another. Yet critics of laboratory experimentation have argued that the tightly controlled laboratory environment is often contrived and artificial and that children are likely to behave very differently in these surroundings from the way they would in a natural setting. Urie Bronfenbrenner (1977) has charged that a heavy reliance on laboratory experiments has made developmental psychology "the science of the strange behavior of children in strange situations with strange adults" (p. 19). Similarly, Robert McCall (1977) notes that experiments tell us what *can* cause a developmental change, but do not necessarily identify the factors that *actually do* cause such changes in natural settings. Consequently, it is quite possible that conclusions drawn from laboratory experiments will not always apply to the real world. In Box 1.3 we will consider a step that experimentalists can take to counter this criticism and assess the **ecological validity** of their laboratory findings.

experimental control: steps taken by an experimenter to ensure that all extraneous factors that could influence the dependent variable are roughly equivalent in each experimental condition; these precautions must be taken before an experimenter can be reasonably certain that observed changes in the dependent variable were caused by the manipulation of the independent variable.

random assignment: a control technique in which participants are assigned to experimental conditions through an unbiased procedure so that the members of the groups are not systematically different from one another.

confounding variable: some factor other than the independent variable which, if not controlled by the experimenter, could explain any differences across treatment conditions in participants' performance on the dependent variable.

ecological validity: state of affairs in which the findings of one's research are an accurate representation of processes that occur in the natural environment.

Box 1.3   *Focus on Research*

Assessing Causal Relationships in the Real World: The Field Experiment

How can we be more certain that a conclusion drawn from a laboratory experiment also applies in the real world? One way is to seek converging evidence for that conclusion by conducting a similar experiment *in a natural setting*—that is, a **field experiment.** This approach combines all the advantages of naturalistic observation with the more rigorous control that experimentation allows. In addition, subjects are typically not apprehensive about participating in a "strange" experiment because all the activities they undertake are everyday activities. Indeed, they may not even be aware that they are being observed or participating in an experiment.

Let's consider a field experiment (Leyens et al., 1975) that sought to test the hypothesis that heavy exposure to media violence can cause viewers to become more aggressive. The subjects were Belgian delinquents who lived together in cottages at a minimum-security institution for adolescent boys. Before the experiment began, the experimenters observed each boy in their research sample to measure his characteristic level of aggression. These initial assessments served as a *baseline* against which future increases in aggression could be measured. The baseline observations suggested that the institution's four cottages could be divided into two subgroups consisting of two cottages populated by relatively aggressive inmates and two cottages populated by less aggressive peers. Then the experiment began. For a period of one week, *violent* movies (such as *Bonnie and Clyde* and *The Dirty Dozen*) were shown each evening to one of the two cottages in each subgroup, and *neutral* films (such as *Daddy's Fiancée* and *La Belle Américaine*) were shown to the other cottages. Instances of physical and verbal aggression among residents of each cottage were recorded twice daily (at lunchtime and in the evenings after the movie) during the movie week and once daily (at lunchtime) during a posttreatment week.

The most striking result of this field experiment was the significant increase in *physical* aggression that occurred in the evenings among residents of both cottages assigned to the violent-film condition. Since the violent

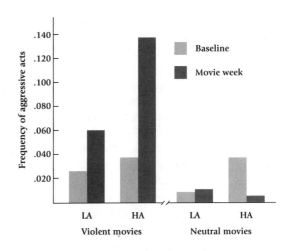

Mean physical aggression scores in the evening for highly aggressive (HA) and less aggressive (LA) boys under baseline conditions and after watching violent or neutral movies. Adapted from Leyens, Parke, Camino, & Berkowitz, 1975.

movies contained a large number of physically aggressive incidents, it appears that they evoked similar responses from the boys who watched them. But as shown in the figure, violent movies prompted larger increases in aggression among boys who were already relatively high in aggression. Furthermore, exposure to the violent movies caused the highly aggressive boys to become more *verbally aggressive* as well—an effect that these boys continued to display through the movie week *and* the posttreatment week.

Clearly, the results of the Belgian field experiment are consistent with Liebert and Baron's (1972) laboratory study in suggesting that exposure to media violence does indeed instigate aggressive behavior. Yet it also qualifies the laboratory findings by implying that the instigating effects of media violence *in the natural environment* are likely to be stronger and more enduring for the more-aggressive members of the audience (and see Friedrich & Stein, 1973 for similar results with nursery school children).

THE NATURAL (OR QUASI-) EXPERIMENT

There are many issues to which the experimental method cannot be applied or should not be used for ethical reasons. Suppose, for example, that we wish to study the effects of early social deprivation on infants' social and emotional development. Obviously, we

> **field experiment:** an experiment that takes place in a naturalistic setting such as the home, the school, or a playground.

cannot ask one group of parents to lock their infants in an attic for two years so that we can collect the data we need. Submitting children to any experimental treatment that may adversely affect their physical or psychological well-being is simply unethical.

However, we might be able to accomplish our research objectives through a **natural (or quasi-) experiment**—a study in which we observe the consequences of a natural event to which participants have been exposed. So if we were able to locate a group of children who were raised in impoverished institutions with very little contact with caregivers over the first two years, we could compare their social and emotional development with that of children raised at home with their families. This comparison would provide some valuable information about the likely impact of early social deprivation on children's social and emotional development. (Indeed, precisely this kind of natural experiment is described in detail in Chapter 5). The "independent variable" in a natural experiment is the "event" that participants experience (in our example, the social deprivation experienced by institutionalized infants). The "dependent variable" is whatever outcome measure one chooses to study (in our example, social and emotional development).

Note, however, that researchers conducting natural experiments do not control the independent variable, nor do they randomly assign participants to experimental conditions; they merely observe and record the apparent outcomes of a natural happening or event. So in the absence of tight experimental control, it is often hard to determine precisely what factor is responsible for any group differences that are found. Suppose, for example, that our socially deprived institutionalized children showed a poorer pattern of emotional outcomes than did children raised at home. Is the *social deprivation* experienced by institutionalized children the factor that accounts for this difference? Or did the institutionalized children differ in other ways from family-reared children (for example, were more sickly as infants, were more poorly nourished) that might explain their poorer outcomes? Without randomly assigning participants to treatments and controlling other factors that may vary across treatments (for example, nutrition received), we simply cannot be *certain* that *social deprivation* is the factor responsible for the poor emotional outcomes that institutionalized children display.

Despite its inability to make precise statements about cause and effect, the natural experiment is useful nonetheless. Why? Because it can tell us whether a natural event could *possibly* have influenced those who experienced it and, thus, can provide some meaningful clues about cause and effect.

Table 1-2 summarizes the strengths and limitations of each of the general research designs we have discussed. Now let's consider designs that focus more specifically on detecting developmental continuities and changes.

Designs for Studying Development

Social developmentalists are not interested merely in examining children's behavior at one particular point in time; instead, they hope to determine how children's feelings, thoughts, abilities, and behaviors *develop* or *change* over time. How might we design research to chart these developmental trends? Let's briefly consider three approaches: the cross-sectional design, the longitudinal design, and the sequential design.

THE CROSS-SECTIONAL DESIGN

In a **cross-sectional design**, groups of children who *differ in age* are studied at *the same point in time*. For example, a researcher interested in determining whether children become more generous as they mature might place 6-, 8-, and 10-year-olds in

natural (or quasi-) experiment: a study in which the investigator measures the impact of some naturally occurring event that is assumed to affect people's lives.

cross-sectional design: a research design in which subjects from different age groups are studied at the same point in time.

TABLE 1-2 Strengths and limitations of general research designs

DESIGN	PROCEDURE	STRENGTHS	LIMITATIONS
Correlational	Gathers information about two or more variables without researcher intervention.	Estimates the strength and direction of relationships among variables in the natural environment.	Does not permit determination-and-effect relationships among variables.
Laboratory experiment	Manipulates some aspect of participants' environment (independent variable) and measures its impact on participants' behavior (dependent variable).	Permits determination of cause-and-effect relationships among variables.	Data obtained in artificial environment may lack generalizability to the real world.
Field experiment	Manipulates independent variable and measures its impact on the dependent variable in a natural setting.	Permits determination of cause-and-effect relationships and generalization of findings to the real world.	Experimental treatments may be less potent and harder to control when presented in the natural environment.
Natural (Quasi-experiment)	Gathers information about the behavior of people who experience a real-world (natural) manipulation of their environment.	Permits a study of the impact of natural events that would be difficult or impossible to simulate in an experiment; provides strong clues about cause-and-effect relationships.	Lack of precise control over the natural events or the participants exposed to them prevents the investigator from establishing definitive casual relationships.

a situation where they are afforded an opportunity to share a valuable commodity (say, candy or money) with needy youngsters who are less fortunate than themselves. By comparing the responses of children in the different age groups, investigators can often identify age-related changes in generosity (see Chapter 10 for a review of this topic) or in whatever aspect of development they have chosen to study.

An important advantage of the cross-sectional method is that the investigator can collect data from subjects of different ages over a short time. For example, an investigator would not have to wait four years for her 6-year-olds to become 10-year-olds to determine whether children's generosity increases over this age range. She can merely sample children of different ages and test all samples at approximately the same time.

Notice, however, that in cross-sectional research, participants at each age level are *different* people who come from different cohorts. A *cohort* is a group of people of the same age who are exposed to similar cultural environments or historical events as they are growing up. The fact that different cohorts are always involved in cross-sectional comparisons means that any age-related effects that are found in the study may not always be due to age or development but, rather, to some other feature that distinguishes individuals in different cohorts. For example, early cross-sectional research had consistently indicated that young adults score higher on intelligence tests than do middle-age adults, who, in turn, score higher than the elderly. But does intelligence decline with age, as these findings would seem to indicate? Not necessarily! More recent research (Schaie, 1986, 1990) reveals that individuals' intelligence test scores remain reasonably stable over the years and that the earlier studies were really measuring something quite different: cohort differences in education. The older adults in earlier cross-sectional studies had had less schooling, which could explain why they scored lower on intelligence tests than the middle-age or young adult samples. Their test scores had not declined but, rather, had always been lower than those of the younger adults with whom they were compared. So the earlier cross-sectional research had discovered a **cohort effect** rather than true developmental change.

cohort effect: age-related difference among cohorts that is attributable to cultural/historical differences in cohorts' growing-up experiences rather than to true developmental change.

This example points directly to a second problem with the cross-sectional method: It tells us nothing about the development of *individuals* because each person is observed *at only one point in time*. So cross-sectional comparisons cannot provide answers to questions such as "When will *my* child become more generous?" or "Will aggressive 2-year-olds become aggressive 5-year-olds?" To address issues like these, an investigator will often rely on a second kind of developmental comparison, the longitudinal design.

THE LONGITUDINAL DESIGN

In a **longitudinal design,** the same participants are observed repeatedly over time. For example, a researcher interested in determining whether generosity increases over middle childhood might provide 6-year-olds an opportunity to behave in a charitable fashion toward needy youngsters and then follow up with similar assessments of the generosity of *these same children* at ages 8 and 10.

The period spanned by a longitudinal study may be very long or reasonably short. The investigators may be looking at one particular aspect of development, such as generosity, or at many. By repeatedly testing the same participants, investigators can assess the *stability* of various attributes and the patterns of developmental *change* for each person in the sample. In addition, they can identify *general* developmental trends by looking for commonalities in development that most or all individuals share. Finally, tracking several children over time will help investigators understand the bases for *individual differences* in development, particularly if they are able to establish that different kinds of earlier experiences lead to very different outcomes.

Several very noteworthy longitudinal projects have followed children for decades and have assessed many aspects of development (see, for example, Kagan & Moss, 1962; Newman et al., 1997). However, most longitudinal studies are much more modest in direction and scope. For example, Carolee Howes and Catherine Matheson (1992) conducted a study in which the pretend play activities of a group of 1- to 2-year-olds were repeatedly observed at six-month intervals over the next three years. Using a classification scheme that assessed the cognitive complexity of play, Howes and Matheson sought to determine (1) whether play did reliably become more complex with age, (2) whether children reliably differed in the complexity of their play, and (3) whether the complexity of a child's play reliably forecast his or her social competencies with peers. Not surprisingly, all children displayed increases in the complexity of their play over the three-year period, although there were reliable individual differences in play complexity at each observation point. In addition, there was a clear relationship between the complexity of a child's play and social competence with peers: children who engaged in more complex forms of play at any given age were the ones who were rated as most outgoing and least aggressive at the next observation period six months later. So this longitudinal study shows that complexity of pretend play not only increases with age but is also a reliable predictor of children's future social competencies with peers.

Although we have focused on the important advantages of the longitudinal comparison, this procedure does have several drawbacks. For example, longitudinal research can be very costly and time-consuming, particularly if the project spans a period of several years. Moreover, the focus of theory and research in social and personality development is constantly changing, so that longitudinal questions that seem very exciting at the beginning of a long-term project may seem rather trivial by the time the study ends. **Selective attrition** may also become a problem: Children may move away, get sick, become bored with repeated testing, or have parents who, for one reason or another, will not allow them to continue in the study. The result is a smaller and potentially **nonrepresentative sample** that not only provides less infor-

longitudinal design: a research design in which one group of subjects is studied repeatedly over a period of months or years.

selective attrition: nonrandom loss of participants during a study which results in a nonrepresentative sample.

nonrepresentative sample: a subgroup that differs in important ways from the larger group (or population) to which it belongs.

PHOTOS 1.5 Leisure activities of the 1930s (left) and the 1990s (right). As these photos illustrate, the kinds of experiences that children growing up in the 1930s had were very different from those of today's youth. Many believe that cross-generational changes in the environment may limit the results of a longitudinal study to the youngsters who were growing up while the research was in progress.

mation about the developmental issues in question but also may limit the conclusions of the study to those healthy children who do not move away and who remain cooperative over the long run.

Another shortcoming of these very long-term longitudinal studies that students often see right away is the **cross-generational problem.** Children in longitudinal research are typically drawn from one cohort; as a result, they will experience cultural, family, and school environments somewhat different from those children in other cohorts. Consider, for example, how the times have changed since the 1930s and 1940s, when children in some of the early long-term longitudinal studies were growing up. In this age of dual-career families, more youngsters are attending day-care centers and nursery schools than ever before. Modern families are smaller than those of years past, meaning that children now have fewer brothers and sisters. Families also move more frequently than they did in the 1930s and 1940s, so that many children from the modern era are exposed to a wider variety of people and places than was typical in years gone by. And no matter where they may be living, today's youngsters grow up in front of television sets and computers, influences that were nonexistent during the 1930s and 1940s. So children of earlier eras lived in a very different world, and we cannot be certain that these youngsters developed in precisely the same way as today's children. Stated another way, cross-generational changes in the environment may limit the conclusions of a longitudinal project to those participants who were growing up while the study was in progress.

We have seen that the cross-sectional and the longitudinal designs each have distinct advantages and disadvantages. Might it be possible to combine the best features of both approaches? A third kind of developmental comparison—the **sequential design**—tries to do just that.

THE SEQUENTIAL DESIGN

Sequential designs combine the best features of cross-sectional and longitudinal studies by selecting participants of different ages and following each of these cohorts over time. To illustrate, imagine that we wished to study the development of moral reasoning in children between the ages of 6 and 12. We might begin in the year 2000

cross-generational problem: the fact that long-term changes in the environment may limit conclusions of a longitudinal project to that generation of children who were growing up while the study was in progress.

sequential design: a research design in which subjects from different age groups are studied repeatedly over a period of months or years.

by testing the logical reasoning of a sample of 6-year-olds (the 1994 birth cohort) and a sample of 8-year-olds (the 1992 birth cohort). We could then retest the reasoning abilities of both those groups in 2002 and 2004. Notice that the design calls for us to follow the 1994 cohort from age 6 through age 10 and the 1992 cohort from age 8 through age 12. A graphic representation of this research plan appears in Figure 1.5.

This sequential design has three major strengths. First, it allows us to determine whether cohort effects are influencing our results by comparing the moral reasoning of same-age children who were born in different years. As shown in Figure 1.5, cohort effects are assessed by comparing the moral judgments of the two samples at age 8 and age 10. If the samples do not differ, we can assume that cohort effects are not operating. The figure also illustrates a second major advantage of our sequential design: It allows us to make both longitudinal and cross-sectional comparisons in the same study. If the age trends in reasoning are similar in both the longitudinal

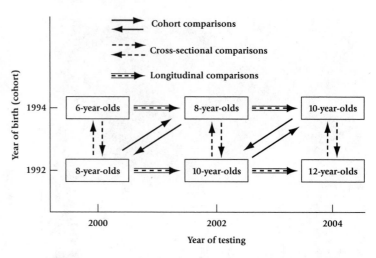

FIGURE 1.5 Example of a sequential design. Two samples of children, one born in 1992 and one born in 1994, are observed longitudinally over a 4-year period. The design permits the investigator to assess cohort effects by comparing children of the same age who were born in different years. In the absence of cohort effects, the longitudinal and cross-sectional comparisons in this design permit the researcher to make strong statements about the strength and direction of any developmental changes.

and the cross-sectional comparisons, we can be quite confident that they represent true developmental changes in moral reasoning abilities. Finally, sequential designs are often more efficient than standard longitudinal designs. In our example, we could trace the development of moral reasoning over a 6-year age range, even though our study would take but four years to conduct. A standard longitudinal comparison that initially sampled 6-year-old participants would take six years to provide similar information. Clearly, this combination of the cross-sectional and longitudinal designs is a versatile alternative to either of these approaches.

To help you review and compare the three major developmental designs, Table 1-3 provides a brief description of each, along with its major strengths and weaknesses.

Cross-Cultural Comparisons

Developmentalists are often hesitant to publish a new finding or conclusion until they have studied enough people to determine that their "discovery" is reliable. However, their conclusions are frequently based on participants living at one point in time within one particular culture or subculture, and it is difficult to know whether these conclusions will apply to future generations or even to children currently growing up in other societies or subcultures (Lerner, 1991). Today, the generalizability of findings across samples and settings has become an important issue, for many theorists have implied that there are "universals" in human development—events and outcomes that all children share as they progress from infancy to adulthood.

Cross-cultural studies are those in which participants from different cultural, sub-cultural, racial, or ethnic backgrounds are observed, tested, and compared on one or more aspects of development. Studies of this kind serve many purposes. For example, they allow the investigator to determine whether conclusions drawn about the development of children from one social context (such as middle-class, White youngsters in the United States) also characterize children growing up in other societies or even those from different ethnic or socioeconomic backgrounds within the same so-

TABLE 1-3   Strengths and limitations of three developmental designs

DESIGN	PROCEDURE	STRENGTHS	LIMITATIONS
Cross-sectional	Observes people of different ages (or cohorts) at one point in time.	Demonstrates age differences; hints at developmental trends; is relatively inexpensive; takes little time to conduct.	Age trends may reflect extraneous differences between cohorts rather than true developmental change; provides no data on the development of individuals because each participant is observed at only one point in time.
Longitudinal	Observes people of one cohort repeatedly over time.	Provides data on the development of individuals; can reveal links between early experiences and later outcomes; indicates how individuals are alike and how they are different in the ways they change over time.	Relatively time-consuming and expensive; selective attrition may yield nonrepresentative sample that limits the generalizability of one's conclusions; cross-generational changes may limit one's conclusions to the cohort that was studied.
Sequential	Combines the cross-sectional and the longitudinal approaches by observing different cohorts repeatedly over time.	Discriminates true developmental trends from cohort effects; indicates whether developmental changes experienced by one cohort are similar to those experienced by other cohorts; often less costly and time-consuming than the longitudinal approach.	More costly and time-consuming than cross-sectional research; despite being the strongest design, may still leave questions about whether a developmental change is generalizable beyond the cohorts studied.

ciety (for example, American children of Latino ancestry or those from economically disadvantaged homes). So the **cross-cultural comparison** guards against the over-generalization of research findings and, indeed, is the only way to determine whether there are truly "universals" in human development.

However, many investigators who favor the cross-cultural approach are looking for *differences* rather than similarities. They recognize that human beings develop in societies and subcultures that have very different ideas about issues such as the proper times and procedures for disciplining children, the activities that are most appropriate for boys and for girls, the time at which childhood ends and adulthood begins, the treatment of the aged, and countless other aspects of life. They have also learned that people from various cultures differ in the ways they perceive the world, express their emotions, think, and solve problems. So apart from its focus on universals in development, the cross-cultural approach also illustrates that human development is heavily influenced by the cultural context in which it occurs (see Box 1.4 for a dramatic illustration of cultural diversity in gender roles).

Isn't it remarkable how many methods and designs developmentalists have at their disposal? This diversity of available procedures is a definite strength because findings gained through one procedure can then be confirmed (or perhaps disconfirmed) through other procedures. Indeed, providing *converging evidence* serves a most important function by demonstrating that the discovery one has made is truly a "discovery" and not merely an artifact of the method or the design used to collect the original data. So there is no "best method" for studying children and adolescents; each of the approaches we have considered has contributed substantially to our understanding of social and personality development.

cross-cultural comparison: a study that compares the behavior and/or development of people from different cultural or sub-cultural backgrounds.

Box 1.4   Cultural Influences

A Cross-Cultural Comparison of Gender Roles

One of the greatest values of cross-cultural comparisons is that they can tell us whether a developmental phenomenon is or is not universal. Consider the roles that males and females play in our society. In our culture, the masculine role has traditionally required traits such as independence, assertiveness, and dominance. By contrast, females are expected to be more nurturant and sensitive to other people. Are these masculine and feminine roles universal? Could biological differences between the sexes lead to inevitable sex differences in behavior?

Some years ago, anthropologist Margaret Mead (1935) compared the gender roles adopted by people in three tribal societies on the island of New Guinea, and her observations are certainly thought provoking. In the Arapesh tribe, both men and women were taught to play what we would regard as a feminine role: they were co-operative, nonaggressive, and sensitive to the needs of others. By contrast, both men and women of the Mundugumor tribe were brought up to be hostile, aggressive, and emotionally unresponsive to other people— a masculine pattern of behavior by Western standards. Finally, the Tchambuli displayed a pattern of gender-role development opposite to the Western pattern: males were passive, emotionally dependent, and socially sensitive, whereas females were dominant, independent, and assertive!

Mead's cross-cultural comparison suggests that cultural dictates may have far more to do with the characteristic behavior patterns of men and women than biological differences do. So we very much need cross-cultural comparisons such as Mead's. Without them, we might easily make the mistake of assuming that whatever holds true

The roles assumed by men and women may vary dramatically from culture to culture.

in our society holds true everywhere; with their help, we can begin to understand the contributions of biology and environment to human development.

Postscript: On Becoming a Wise Consumer of Developmental Research

At this point, you may be wondering "Why do I need to know so much about the methods developmentalists use to conduct research?" This is a reasonable question given that the vast majority who take this course will pursue other careers and will never conduct a scientific study of developing children or adolescents.

My answer is straightforward: Although survey courses such as this one are designed to provide a solid overview of theory and research in the discipline to which they pertain, they should also strive to help you evaluate the relevant information you may encounter in the years ahead. And you will encounter such information. Even if you don't read academic journals in your role as a teacher, school administrator, nurse, probation officer, social worker, or other professional who works with developing persons, then certainly you will be exposed to such information through the popular media—television, newspapers, magazines, and the like. How can you know whether that seemingly dramatic and important new finding you've just read or heard about can be taken seriously?

This is an important issue, for new information about social and personality development is often chronicled in the popular media several months or even years before the data on which the media reports are based finally make their appearance in professional journals (if they ever do). What's more, less than 30% of the papers developmentalists submit are judged sufficiently worthy to be published by reputable journals in our discipline. So many media reports of "dramatic" new findings are based on research that other scientists don't view as very dramatic, or even worth publishing.

Even if a media report is based on a published article, coverage of the research and its conclusions is often misleading. For example, one bold network story reported on a published article saying that there was clear evidence that "alcoholism is inherited." As we will see in Chapter 3, this is a far more dramatic conclusion than the authors actually drew. Another metropolitan newspaper report summarized an article from the prestigious journal *Developmental Psychology* with the headline "Day Care Harmful for Children." What was never made clear in the newspaper article was the researcher's (Howes, 1990) conclusion that *very low quality* day care may be harmful to the social and intellectual development of *some* preschool children, but that most youngsters receiving good day care suffer no adverse effects. (The issue of day care and its impact on developing children is explored in depth in Chapter 5.)

I do not mean to imply that you can never trust what you read; rather, I'd caution you to be skeptical and to evaluate media (and journal) reports, using the methodological information presented in this chapter. You might start by asking "How were the data gathered and how was the study designed? Were appropriate conclusions drawn given the limitations of the method of data collection and the design (correlational vs. experimental; cross-sectional vs. longitudinal) that the investigators used? Were proper control groups used? Have the results of the study been reviewed by other experts in the field and published in a reputable academic journal?" And please don't assume that published articles are beyond criticism. Many theses and dissertations in the developmental sciences are based on problems and shortcomings that students have identified in previously published research. So take the time to read and evaluate published reports that seem especially relevant to your profession or to your role as a parent. Not only will you have a better understanding of the research and its conclusions, but any lingering questions and doubts you may have can often be addressed through a letter, a phone call, or an e-mail message to the author of the article.

In sum, you must become a knowledgeable consumer to get the most from what the field of social and personality development has to offer. Our discussion of research methodology was undertaken with these objectives in mind, and a solid understanding of these methodological lessons should help you to evaluate properly the research you will encounter, not only throughout this text but from many, many other sources in the years to come.

Summary

- **Socialization** is the process through which children acquire the beliefs, behaviors, and values deemed significant and appropriate by members of society. Social and personality development is the product of a long and involved interplay among social, cultural, and biological influences that make humans similar in certain ways and very different from one another in many respects.

THE UNIVERSAL PARENTING MACHINE—A THOUGHT EXPERIMENT

■ The universal parenting machine, a hypothetical thought experiment in which children are raised with peers and without parents or a prevailing culture, provides an interesting context for thinking about the processes and products of normal social and personality development.

SOCIAL-PERSONALITY DEVELOPMENT IN HISTORICAL PERSPECTIVE

■ In medieval times, children were afforded few of the rights and protections of today's youth. During the 17th and 18th centuries came a more humane outlook on children, and shortly thereafter, some parents began to record the development of their infant sons and daughters in **baby biographies**. The scientific study of development did not emerge until nearly 1900 as G. Stanley Hall, in the United States, and Sigmund Freud, in Europe, began to collect data and formulate **theories** about human development. Soon, other researchers were deriving **hypotheses** and conducting research to evaluate and extend early theories.

■ A theory is a set of concepts and propositions that describe and explain observations one has made. Theories are particularly useful when they are **parsimonious, falsifiable,** and **heuristic**.

QUESTIONS AND CONTROVERSIES ABOUT HUMAN DEVELOPMENT

■ Theories of human development differ with respect to their stands on five basic issues: (1) Whether human beings are inherently good or bad (as illustrated by the doctrines of **original sin, innate purity,** and **tabula rasa**); (2) the **nature/nurture issue;** (3) the **activity/passivity issue;** (4) the **continuity-discontinuity issue;** and (5) the issue of whether the most important aspects of development are **universal** or **particularistic**.

RESEARCH METHODS

■ Today's developmentalists, guided by the **scientific method,** allow objective data to determine the adequacy of their thinking. Acceptable research methods are those that possess both **reliability** and **validity**. A method is reliable if it produces consistent, replicable results; it is valid if it accurately reflects what it was intended to measure.

■ The most common methods of data collection in the field of social and personality development are self-reports, observational methodologies, case studies, and ethnography. Self-reports include standardized procedures, such as **structured interviews** or **structured questionnaires,** that allow direct comparisons among research participants, and flexible approaches like the **clinical method,** which yields an individualized portrait of each participant's feelings, thoughts, and behaviors.

■ **Naturalistic observations** are obtained in the natural environments of children or adolescents, whereas **structured observations** take place in laboratories where the investigator cues the behavior of interest.

■ **Case studies** allow investigators to obtain an in-depth understanding of individual children or adolescents by collecting data based on interviews, observations, and test scores of the individual in question, as well as information about that person from such knowledgeable sources as teachers and parents.

■ **Ethnography,** used originally by anthropologists, is a descriptive procedure in which the researcher becomes a participant observer within a cultural or subcultural context. He or she will carefully observe the community members, make notes from conversations, and compile such information into a detailed portrait of the group's values and traditions and their impacts on developing children and adolescents.

DETECTING RELATIONSHIPS: CORRELATIONAL AND EXPERIMENTAL DESIGNS

■ Two general research designs permit researchers to identify relationships among variables that interest them. **Correlational designs** examine relationships as they naturally occur, without any intervention. The **correlation coefficient** is used to estimate the strength and magnitude of the association between variables. However, correlational studies cannot specify whether correlated variables are causally related.

■ The **experimental design** does point to cause-and-effect relationships. The experimenter manipulates one (or more) **independent variables,** exercises **experimental control** over all other **confounding variables** (often by **random assignment** of participants to treatments), and observes the effect(s) of the manipulation(s) on the **dependent variable**. Experiments may be performed in the laboratory, or alternatively, in the natural environment (that is, a **field experiment**), thereby increasing the **ecological validity** of the results. The impact of events that researchers cannot manipulate or control can be studied in **natural (quasi-) experiments**. However, lack of control over natural events prevents the quasi-experimenter from drawing definitive conclusions about cause and effect.

DESIGNS FOR STUDYING DEVELOPMENT

- Cross-sectional, longitudinal, and sequential designs are employed to detect developmental change. The **cross-sectional design**, which compares different age groups at a single point in time, is easy to conduct; but it cannot tell us how individuals develop, and its results may be misleading if the age trends one observes are actually due to **cohort effects** rather than true developmental change.

- The **longitudinal design** detects developmental change by repeatedly examining the same participants as they grow older. Though it identifies developmental continuities and changes and individual differences in development, the longitudinal design is subject to such problems as **selective attrition,** which results in **nonrepresentative samples.** Moreover, the **cross-generational** problem of long-term longitudinal studies implies that results may be limited to the particular cohort studied.

- The **sequential design,** a combination of the cross-sectional and longitudinal designs, offers researchers the advantages of both approaches and allows them to discriminate true developmental trends from troublesome cohort effects.

CROSS-CULTURAL COMPARISONS

- **Cross-cultural studies,** in which participants from different cultures or subcultures are compared on one or more aspects of development, are becoming increasingly important. Only by comparing people from many cultures can we identify "universal" patterns of development and, at the same time, demonstrate that other aspects of development are heavily influenced by the social context in which they occur.

Classical Theories of Social and Personality Development

The Psychoanalytic Viewpoint

Freud's Psychosexual Theory

Contributions and Criticisms of Freud's Theory

Erikson's Theory of Psychosocial Development

Contributions and Criticisms of Erikson's Theory

Psychoanalytic Theory Today

The Behaviorist (or Social-Learning) Viewpoint

Watson's Behaviorism

Skinner's Operant-Learning Theory (Radical Behaviorism)

Bandura's Cognitive Social-Learning Theory

Social Learning as Reciprocal Determinism

Contributions and Criticisms of the Social Learning Perspective

Piaget's Cognitive-Developmental Viewpoint

Piaget's View of Intelligence and Intellectual Growth

Four Stages of Cognitive Development

Contributions and Criticisms of Piaget's Theory

Summary

In our introductory chapter, we talked only briefly about theories, portraying them as sets of concepts and propositions that describe and explain certain aspects of our experience. We also noted that everyone is a "theorist," for each of us has definite points of view reflecting what we believe to be true about many issues, observations, and events. How important are theories to today's developmentalists? They are so important that many contemporary researchers cannot conceive of how knowledge might be advanced without them. In fact, when developmentalists describe themselves to other developmentalists, they are most likely to mention (1) their primary area of interest (for example, emotional development in infancy) and (2) the theoretical perspectives that guide their research. So a developmentalist's professional identity may depend, in part, on the theories he or she favors.

Our focus in this chapter is on some of the earliest and most highly influential ideas about human social and personality development—theories that guided the majority of research conducted before 1975. We begin by briefly considering Freud's *psychoanalytic* theory, an approach that depicts human beings as servants to inborn *biological* instincts that mature gradually over the course of childhood and play a major role in determining who we are and what we are likely to become. After reviewing Freud's theory and comparing it to a rival psychoanalytic viewpoint, we consider a very different perspective—*behaviorism* and *social-learning theory*—that downplays biological contributions to human development and portrays the child as a *tabula rasa* who is heavily influenced by his or her socializing *environment*. Finally, we conclude this chapter by examining the *cognitive-developmental* viewpoint of Jean Piaget. This is an *interactionist* theory contending that biological forces (maturation) in concert with environmental experiences promote intellectual growth, which, in turn, has major implications for all aspects of social and personality development.

Of course, each of the three theoretical perspectives that we examine in this chapter has its strengths and its weaknesses, and new theories of social-personality development—models that question and build on earlier insights—are constantly emerging. In Chapter 3, we will consider some of these newer ideas, focusing on models that emphasize biological contributions (for example, behavioral genetics and ethology), environmental forces (ecological systems theory), and cognitive underpinnings (sociocultural theory; social information-processing theory) of social and personality development.

Let's now begin our survey of the "classic" theories with Freud's psychoanalytic approach.

The Psychoanalytic Viewpoint

With the possible exception of evolutionist Charles Darwin, it is difficult to think of a theorist who has had a greater impact on Western thought than Sigmund Freud, the Viennese physician who lived from 1856 to 1939. This revolutionary thinker challenged prevailing notions about human nature by proposing that we are driven by motives and conflicts *of which we are largely unaware* and that our personalities are shaped by early life experiences. In this section of the chapter, we first consider Freud's fascinating **psychosexual theory** of human development and then compare Freud's theory with that of his best known follower, Erik Erikson.

FREUD'S PSYCHOSEXUAL THEORY

Freud's view of human nature is essentially a restatement of Thomas Hobbes's *doctrine of original sin*. Central to his psychoanalytic theory is the notion that human beings

That's only true in theory, not in practice.

—Anonymous

There is nothing as practical as a good theory.

—Kurt Lewin

psychosexual theory: Freud's theory which states that maturation of the sex instinct underlies stages of personality development, and that how parents manage children's instinctual impulses will determine the traits children come to display.

are driven by powerful biological urges that must be satisfied. What kinds of urges? Undesirable ones! Freud (1940/1964) viewed the newborn as a "seething cauldron"—an inherently selfish creature who is relentlessly driven by two kinds of **instincts** that he called **Eros** and **Thanatos.** *Eros,* or the life instinct, was said to promote survival by directing such life-sustaining activities as breathing, eating, sex, and the fulfillment of all other bodily needs. By contrast, *Thanatos*—the death instinct—was viewed as a destructive force present in human beings and expressed through such behaviors as arson, fistfights, sadistic aggression, murder, and even masochism (harm directed against the self).

Recall that Freud was a practicing neurologist who formulated his theory of human development from his analyses of the life histories of his emotionally disturbed patients. As he worked with his patients, seeking to relieve their nervous symptoms and anxieties, he came to rely heavily on such methods as hypnosis, *free association* (a quick spelling out of one's thoughts) and dream analysis because they gave some indication of **unconscious motives** that patients had **repressed** (that is, forced out of conscious awareness). By analyzing these motives and the events that had caused them to be suppressed, Freud concluded that human development is a conflictual process: as biological creatures, we have basic sexual and aggressive *instincts* that *must* be served; yet society dictates that many of these needs are undesirable and *must* be restrained. According to Freud, the ways in which parents have managed these sexual and aggressive urges in the first few years of life play a major role in shaping their child's conduct and character.

Three Components of Personality   Freud's psychosexual theory specifies that three components of personality—the id, ego, and superego—develop and gradually become integrated in a series of five psychosexual stages. The **id** is all that is present at birth. Its sole function is to satisfy inborn biological instincts, and it will try to do so immediately. If you think about it, young infants do seem to be "all id." When hungry or wet, they simply fuss and cry until their needs are met, and they are not known for their patience.

The **ego** is the conscious, rational component of the personality that reflects the child's emerging abilities to perceive, learn, remember, and reason. Its function is to find realistic means of gratifying the instincts, as when a hungry toddler, remembering how she gets food, seeks out mom and says "cookie." As their egos mature, children become better at controlling their irrational ids and finding realistic ways to gratify needs on their own.

However, realistic solutions to needs are not always acceptable, as a hungry 3-year-old who is caught snitching cookies between meals may soon discover. The final component of personality, or **superego,** is the seat of the conscience. It develops between the ages of 3 and 6 as children *internalize* (take on as their own) the moral values and standards of their parents (Freud, 1933). Once the superego emerges, children do not need an adult to tell them they have been good or bad; they are now aware of their own transgressions and will feel guilty or ashamed of their unethical conduct. So the superego is truly an internal censor. It insists that the ego find socially acceptable outlets for the id's undesirable impulses.

Obviously, these three components of personality do not see eye-to-eye and conflict is inevitable (Freud, 1940/1964). In the mature, healthy personality a dynamic balance operates: the id communicates basic needs, the ego restrains the impulsive id long enough to find realistic methods of satisfying these needs, and the superego decides whether the ego's problem-solving strategies are morally acceptable. The ego is clearly "in the middle"; it must serve two harsh masters by striking a balance between the opposing demands of the id and the superego, all the while accommodating to the realities of the external environment.

PHOTO 2.1   The psychoanalytic theory of Sigmund Freud (1856–1939) changed our thinking about developing children.

instinct: an inborn biological force that motivates a particular response or class of responses.

Eros: Freud's name for instincts such as respiration, hunger, and sex that help the individual (and the species) to survive.

Thanatos: Freud's name for inborn, self-destructive instincts that were said to characterize all human beings.

unconscious motives: Freud's term for feelings, experiences, and conflicts that influence a person's thinking and behavior, but lie outside the person's awareness.

repression: a type of motivated forgetting in which anxiety-provoking thoughts and conflicts are forced out of conscious awareness.

id: psychoanalytic term for the inborn component of the personality that is driven by the instincts.

ego: psychoanalytic term for the rational component of the personality.

superego: psychoanalytic term for the component of the personality that consists of one's internalized moral standards.

Stages of Psychological Development Freud thought that sex was the most important of the instincts because he discovered that the mental disturbances of his patients often revolved around childhood sexual conflicts they had repressed. But are *young children* really sexual beings? Yes, said Freud (1940/1964), whose view of sex was very broad, encompassing such activities as thumb-sucking and urinating that we might not consider at all erotic. Freud believed that as the sex instinct matured, its focus would shift from one part of the body to another, and that each shift brought on a new stage of psychosexual development. Table 2-1 briefly describes each of Freud's five stages of psychosexual development.

Clearly, the most controversial aspect of Freud's theory was his description of the **phallic stage**—a period when 3- to 6-year-olds were said to develop a hostile rivalry with their same-sex parent that stemmed from their own *incestuous* desire for the opposite-sex parent. This state of affairs (no pun intended) was called the **Oedipus complex** for boys and the **Electra complex** for girls. Freud believed that anxieties stemming from such rivalrous conflicts would build until children felt compelled to renounce their incestuous desires and to identify with their same-sex parental rival. As we will see in Chapters 8 and 10, this **identification** process was said to be the primary mechanism by which children acquire "masculine" or "feminine" identities and a strong internalized conscience, or superego.

Freud believed that parents must walk a fine line with their child at each psychosexual stage. Permitting either too much or too little gratification of sexual needs was thought to cause the child to become obsessed with whatever activity was strongly encouraged or discouraged. He might then **fixate** on that activity (that is, display arrested development) and retain some aspect of it throughout life. For example, an infant who was strongly punished for and thus conflicted about sucking her thumb

TABLE 2-1 Freud's stages of psychosexual development

PSYCHOSEXUAL STAGE	AGE	DESCRIPTION
Oral	Birth– 1 year	The sex instinct centers on the mouth, as infants derive pleasure from such oral activities as sucking, chewing, and biting. Feeding activities are particularly important. For example, an infant weaned too early or too abruptly may later crave close contact and become overdependent on a spouse.
Anal	1–3 years	Voluntary urination and defecation become the primary methods of gratifying the sex instinct. Toilet training produces major conflicts between children and parents. The emotional climate parents create can have lasting effects. For example, children punished for toileting "accidents" may become inhibited, messy, or wasteful.
Phallic	3–6 years	Pleasure is now derived from stimulating the genitals. Children develop an incestuous desire for the opposite-sex parent (called the *Oedipus complex* for boys and *Electra complex* for girls). Anxiety stemming from this conflict causes children to internalize the sex-role characteristics and moral standards of their same-sex parental rival.
Latency	6–11 years	Traumas of the phallic stage cause sexual conflicts to be repressed and sexual urges to be rechanneled into school work and vigorous play. The ego and superego continue to develop as the child gains more problem-solving abilities at school and internalizes societal values.
Genital	age 12 onward	Puberty triggers a reawakening of sexual urges. Adolescents must now learn how to express these urges in socially acceptable ways. If development has been healthy, the mature sex instinct is satisfied by marriage and child rearing.

phallic stage: Freud's third stage of psychosexual development (from 3- to 6 years of age), in which children gratify the sex instinct by fondling their genitals and developing an incestuous desire for the parent of the other sex.

Oedipus complex: Freud's term for the conflict that 3- to 6-year-olds boys experience when they develop an incestuous desire for their mothers and, at the same time, a jealous and hostile rivalry with their fathers.

Electra complex: female version of Oedipus complex, in which a 3- to 6-year-old girl was believed to envy her father for possessing a penis and to seek him as a sex object in the hope of sharing the organ that she lacks.

identification: Freud's term for the child's tendency to emulate another person, usually the same-sex parent.

fixation: arrested development at a particular psychosexual stage, often occurs as a means of coping with existing conflicts and preventing movement to the next stage, where stress may be even greater.

might express this oral fixation through such substitute activities as chain smoking or oral sex as an adult. Note the implication here: Freud is saying that early childhood experiences and conflicts may haunt us for years and influence our adult interests, activities, and personalities.

CONTRIBUTIONS AND CRITICISMS OF FREUD'S THEORY

How plausible do you think Freud's ideas are? Do you think that we are all relentlessly driven by sexual and aggressive instincts? Or might the sexual conflicts that Freud thought so important merely have been reflections of the sexually repressive Victorian era in which he and his patients lived?

Few developmentalists today are strong proponents of Freud's theory. There is not much evidence that any of the oral, anal, and genital conflicts that Freud thought so important reliably predict one's later personality (see, for example, Bem, 1989; Crews, 1996). One reason may be that Freud's account of human development was based on the recollections of a relatively small number of emotionally disturbed adults whose experiences may not apply to most people.

Yet, we should not reject all Freud's ideas simply because some of them may seem a bit outlandish. Perhaps Freud's greatest contribution was his concept of *unconscious motivation*. When psychology came into being in the mid-19th century, investigators were concerned with understanding isolated aspects of *conscious* experience, such as sensory processes and perceptual illusions. It was Freud who first noted that these scientists were studying the tip of an iceberg when he proclaimed that the vast majority of psychic experience lay below the level of conscious awareness. Freud also deserves considerable credit for focusing attention on the importance of early experience for later development. Debates continue about exactly how critical early experiences are, but few developmentalists today doubt that some early experiences *can* have lasting effects. Finally, we might thank Freud for studying the emotional side of human development—the loves, fears, anxieties, and other powerful emotions that play important roles in our lives. Unfortunately, these aspects of life have often been overlooked by developmentalists who have tended to concentrate on observable behaviors or on rational thought processes.

In sum, Freud was truly a great pioneer who dared to navigate murky, uncharted waters that his predecessors had not even thought to explore. In the process, he changed our views of humankind.

ERIKSON'S THEORY OF PSYCHOSOCIAL DEVELOPMENT

As Freud became widely read, he attracted many followers. However, Freud's pupils did not always agree with the master, and eventually they began to modify some of his ideas and become important theorists in their own right. Among the best known of these *neo-Freudian* scholars was Erik Erikson.

Comparing Erikson with Freud   Although Erikson (1963, 1982) accepted many of Freud's ideas, he differed from Freud in two important respects. First, Erikson (1963) stressed that children are *active,* curious explorers who seek to adapt to their environments, rather than passive slaves to biological urges who are molded by their parents. Erikson has been labeled an "ego" psychologist because he believed that at each stage of life, people must cope with social *realities* (in ego function) in order to adapt successfully and show a normal pattern of development. So in Erikson's theory, the ego is far more than a simple arbiter of the opposing demands of the id and superego.

A second critical difference between Erikson and Freud is that Erikson places much less emphasis on sexual urges and far more emphasis on cultural influences than Freud did. Clearly, Erikson's thinking was shaped by his own varied experiences. He was born in Denmark, raised in Germany, and spent much of his adolescence wandering throughout Europe. After receiving his professional training, Erikson came to the United States, where he studied college students, combat soldiers, civil rights workers in the South, and American Indians. Having observed many similarities and differences in development across these diverse social groups, it is hardly surprising that Erikson would emphasize *social* and *cultural* aspects of development in his own **psychosocial theory.**

PHOTO 2.2 Erik Erikson (1902–1994) emphasized the sociocultural determinants of personality in his theory of psychosocial development.

Eight Life Crises Erikson believed that human beings face eight major crises, or conflicts, during the course of their lives. Each conflict has its own time for emerging, as dictated by both biological maturation and the social demands that developing people experience at particular points in life. And each must be resolved successfully to prepare the individual for a satisfactory resolution of the next life crisis. Table 2-2 briefly describes each of Erikson's eight crises (or psychosocial stages) and lists the Freudian psychosexual stage to which it corresponds. Notice that Erikson's developmental stages do not end at adolescence or young adulthood as Freud's do. Erikson believed that the problems of adolescents and young adults are very different from those faced by parents who are raising children or by the aged who might be grappling with the specter of retirement, a sense of uselessness, and impending death. Most contemporary developmentalists would definitely agree.

An analysis of the first psychosocial stage—**trust versus mistrust**—should help to illustrate Erikson's thinking. Recall that Freud emphasized the infant's oral activities during the first year of life, and he believed that a mother's feeding practices could have a lasting impact on her child's personality. Erikson agreed. However, he argued that what is most important to an infant's later development is not merely the caregiver's feeding practices but rather her *overall responsiveness* to all the infant's needs. To develop a basic sense of *trust,* infants must be able to count on their primary caregivers to provide food, to relieve discomfort, to come when beckoned, to smile when smiled upon, and to display warmth and affection. But should close companions often neglect, reject, or respond inconsistently to an infant, that child will learn a very simple lesson: other people are not to be trusted. Indeed, we will see in Chapters 5 and 13 that infants who establish untrusting, insecure relationships with their caregivers often make few, if any, close supportive friendships and tend to have conflictual, nonharmonious interactions with their peers.

CONTRIBUTIONS AND CRITICISM OF ERIKSON'S THEORY

Many people prefer Erikson's theory to Freud's because they simply refuse to believe that human beings are dominated by sexual instincts. An analyst like Erikson, who stresses our *rational, adaptive* nature, is much easier to accept. In addition, Erikson emphasizes many of the social conflicts and personal dilemmas that people may remember, are currently experiencing, can easily anticipate, or can see affecting people they know.

Erikson does seem to have captured many of the central issues in life in his eight psychosocial stages. In fact, we will see just how stimulating his ideas have been as we discuss such topics as the emotional development of infants (Chapters 4 and 5), the growth of self-concept in childhood and the identity crisis facing adolescents (Chapter 6), and the influence of friends and playmates on social and personality development (Chapter 13) (see also Sigelman, 1999, for a discussion of Erikson's contributions to the field of adult development). On the other hand, Erikson's theory can be criticized for being vague about the *causes* of development. What kinds of experiences must children have to develop autonomy as a toddler, initiative as a preschool

psychosocial theory: Erikson's revision of Freud's theory which emphasizes sociocultural (rather than sexual) determinants of development and posits a series of eight psychosocial conflicts that people must resolve successfully to display healthy psychological adjustment.

trust versus mistrust: the first of Erikson's eight psychosocial stages, in which infants must learn to trust their closest companions or else run the risk of mistrusting other people later in life.

TABLE 2-2 Erikson's and Freud's stages of development

APPROXIMATE AGE	ERIKSON'S STAGE OR PSYCHOSOCIAL CRISIS	ERIKSON'S VIEWPOINT: SIGNIFICANT EVENTS AND SOCIAL INFLUENCES	CORRESPONDING FREUDIAN STAGE
Birth to 1 year	Basic trust versus mistrust	Infants must learn to trust others to care for their basic needs. If caregivers are rejecting or inconsistent in their care, the infant may view the world as a dangerous place filled with untrustworthy or unreliable people. The mother or primary caregiver is the key social agent.	Oral
1 to 3 years	Autonomy versus shame and doubt	Children must learn to be "autonomous"—to feed and dress themselves, to look after their own hygiene, and so on. Failure to achieve this independence may force the child to doubt his or her own abilities and feel shameful. Parents are the key social agents.	Anal
3 to 6 years	Initiative versus guilt	Children attempt to act grown up and will try to accept responsibilities that are beyond their capacity to handle. They sometimes undertake goals or activities that conflict with those of parents and other family members, and these conflicts may make them feel guilty. Successful resolution of this crisis requires a balance: The child must retain a sense of initiative and yet learn not to impinge on the rights, privileges, or goals of others. The family is the key social agent.	Phallic
6 to 12 years	Industry versus inferiority	Children must master important social and academic skills. This is a period when the child compares himself or herself with peers. If sufficiently industrious, children will acquire the social and academic skills to feel self-assured. Failure to acquire these important attributes leads to feelings of inferiority. Significant social agents are teachers and peers.	Latency
12 to 20 years	Identity versus role confusion	This is the crossroad between childhood and maturity. The adolescent grapples with the question "Who am I?" Adolescents must establish basic social and occupational identities, or they will remain confused about the roles they should play as adults. The key social agent is the society of peers.	Early genital (adolescence)
20 to 40 years (young adulthood)	Intimacy versus isolation	The primary task at this stage is to form strong friendships and to achieve a sense of love and companionship (or a shared identity) with another person. Feelings of loneliness or isolation are likely to result from an inability to form friendships or an intimate relationship. Key social agents are lovers, spouses, and close friends (of both sexes).	Genital
40 to 65 years (middle adulthood)	Generativity versus stagnation	At this stage, adults face the tasks of becoming productive in their work and raising their families or otherwise looking after the needs of young people. These standards of "generativity" are defined by one's culture. Those who are unable or unwilling to assume these responsibilities will become stagnant and/or self-centered. Significant social agents are the spouse, children, and cultural norms.	Genital
Old age	Ego integrity versus despair	The older adult will look back at life, viewing it as either a meaningful, productive, and happy experience or a major disappointment full of unfulfilled promises and unrealized goals. One's life experiences, particularly social experiences, will determine the outcome of this final life crisis.	Genital

child, or a stable identity during adolescence? Why, exactly, is a sense of trust so important for the development of autonomy, initiative, or industry? Unfortunately, Erikson is not very explicit about these important issues. So, Erikson's theory is really a *descriptive* overview of human social and emotional development that does not adequately *explain* how or why this development takes place.

Freud and Erikson are only two of many psychoanalysts who have had (or are having) a strong influence on the field of social and personality development (Tyson & Tyson, 1990). Karen Horney (1967), for example, has challenged Freud's ideas about sex differences in development and is now widely credited as a founder of the discipline we know today as the psychology of women. Alfred Adler (1929/1964), a contemporary of Freud, was among the first to suggest that *siblings* (and sibling rivalries) are critically important influences on social and personality development—a proposition that we will explore in detail in Chapter 11. And American psychoanalyst Harry Stack Sullivan (1953) wrote extensively about how *chumships* (close friendships) during preadolescence set the stage for the development of intimate love relationships later in life (see Chapter 13 for a discussion of this and other contributions that friends make to social and personality development). Although their theories clearly differ in focus, all these neo-Freudians place much more emphasis than Freud did on *social* contributions to personality development—and much less emphasis on the role of sexual instincts.

Despite the many important contributions that psychoanalytic theorists have made, only a small minority of contemporary developmentalists adhere strongly to this perspective. One reason that many researchers have abandoned the psychoanalytic approach (particularly Freud's theory) is because its propositions are difficult to verify or disconfirm. Suppose, for example, that we wanted to test the basic Freudian proposition that the healthy personality is one in which psychic energy is evenly distributed among the id, ego, and superego. How could we do it? There are objective tests that we could use to select "mentally healthy" subjects, but we have no instrument that measures psychic energy or the relative strengths of the id, ego, and superego. The point is that many psychoanalytic assertions are untestable by any method other than the interview or a clinical approach, and unfortunately, these techniques are time-consuming, expensive, and among the least objective of all methods used to study developing persons.

Of course, the main reason that so many developmentalists have abandoned the psychoanalytic perspective is that other theories seem more compelling. One perspective favored by many was the *behaviorist,* or *social-learning* approach, to which we now turn.

behaviorism: a school of thinking in psychology that holds that conclusions about human development should be based on controlled observations of overt behavior rather than speculation about unconscious motives or other unobservable phenomena; the philosophical underpinning for social-learning theories.

The Behaviorist (or Social-Learning) Viewpoint

In Chapter 1, we encountered a developmentalist who claimed that he could take a dozen healthy infants and train them to be whatever he chose—doctor, lawyer, beggar, and so on—regardless of their backgrounds or ancestry. What a bold statement! It implies that nurture is everything and that nature, or hereditary endowment, counts for nothing. The statement was made by John B. Watson, a strong proponent of the importance of learning in human development and the father of a school of psychology that came to be known as **behaviorism** (Horowitz, 1992).

WATSON'S BEHAVIORISM

A basic premise of Watson's (1913) behaviorism is that conclusions about human development should be based on observations of overt behavior rather than on speculations about unconscious motives or cognitive processes that are unobservable. Furthermore, Watson believed that well-*learned* associations between external stimuli

PHOTO 2.3 John B. Watson (1878–1958) was the father of behaviorism and the first social-learning theorist.

and observable responses (called **habits**) are the building blocks of human development. Like John Locke, Watson viewed the infant as a *tabula rasa* to be written on by experience. Children have no inborn tendencies; Watson was a *social-learning* theorist who believed that how children turn out will depend entirely on their rearing environments and the ways their parents and other significant people in their lives treat them. According to the behaviorist perspective, it is a mistake to assume that children progress through a series of distinct stages, dictated by biological maturation, as Freud (and others) had argued. Instead, behaviorists viewed development as a continuous process of behavioral change that is shaped by the person's unique environment and may differ dramatically from person to person.

To prove just how malleable children are, Watson set out to demonstrate that infantile fears and other emotional reactions are acquired rather than inborn. In one demonstration, for example, Watson and Rosalie Raynor (1920) presented a gentle white rat to a 9-month-old named Albert. Albert's initial reactions were positive ones; he crawled toward the rat and played with it as he had previously with a dog and a rabbit. Then, two months later, came an attempt to instill a fear response. Every time Albert reached for the white rat, Watson, standing behind him, would bang a steel rod with a hammer. Did little Albert eventually associate the white rat with the loud noise and come to fear his furry playmate? Indeed he did, thus illustrating that fears are easily learned.

Watson's belief that children are shaped by their social environments carried a stern message for parents—that it was they who were largely responsible for what their child would become. Watson (1928) cautioned parents that they should begin to train their child at birth and to cut back on the coddling if they hoped to instill good habits. Treat them, he said,

> as though they were young adults. . . . Let your behavior always be objective and kindly firm. Never hug and kiss them, never let them sit on your lap. . . . Shake hands with them in the morning. Give them a pat on the head if they have made an extraordinally good job of a difficult task. . . . In a week's time, you will find how easy it is to be perfectly objective . . . [yet] kindly. You will be utterly ashamed at the mawkish, sentimental way you have been handling [your child]. (pp. 81–82)

Since Watson's day, several theories have been proposed to explain how we learn from our social experiences and form the habits that Watson viewed as "bricks in the edifice of human development." Perhaps the one theorist who did more than anyone to advance the behaviorist approach was B. F. Skinner.

SKINNER'S OPERANT-LEARNING THEORY (RADICAL BEHAVIORISM)

Through his research with animals, Skinner (1953) came to understand a very important form of learning that he believed to be the basis for most of the habits that organisms form. Quite simply, Skinner proposed that both animals and humans will repeat acts that lead to favorable outcomes and will suppress those that produce unfavorable outcomes. So a rat that presses a bar and receives a tasty food pellet is apt to perform that response again. In the language of Skinner's theory, the freely emitted bar-pressing response is called an *operant*, and the food pellet that strengthens this response (by making it more probable in the future) is called a **reinforcer**. Similarly, a girl may form a long-term habit of showing compassion toward distressed playmates if her parents consistently reinforce her kindly behavior with praise, or a teenage boy may become more studious should such conduct earn him higher grades. **Punishers**, on the other hand, are consequences that suppress a response and decrease the likelihood that it will occur in the future. If the rat who had been reinforced for bar pressing were suddenly given a painful shock each time it pressed the

habits: well-learned associations between stimuli and responses that represent the stable aspects of one's personality.

reinforcer: any consequence of an act that increases the probability that the act will recur.

punisher: any consequence of an act that suppresses that act and/or decreases the probability that it will recur.

bar, the "bar pressing" habit would begin to disappear. Similarly, a teenage girl who is grounded every time she stays out beyond her curfew should become more concerned about being home on time.

Like Watson, then, Skinner believed that the habits that each of us develop result from our unique **operant learning** experiences. One boy's aggressive behavior may be reinforced over time because his playmates "give in to" (reinforce) his forceful tactics. Another boy may become relatively nonaggressive because his peers actively suppress (punish) aggressive conduct by fighting back. The two may develop in entirely different directions based on their different histories of reinforcement and punishment. According to Skinner, there is no need to speak of an "aggressive stage" in child development or of an "aggressive instinct" within human beings. Instead, he claims that the majority of habits children acquire—the very responses that make up a "personality" and make us unique—are freely emitted operants that have been shaped by their consequences. So Skinner's *operant learning theory* claims that the directions in which we develop depend very critically on *external* stimuli (reinforcers and punishers) rather than on internal forces such as instincts, drives, or biological maturation.

Today's developmentalists have come to realize that human behavior can take many forms and that habits can emerge and disappear over a lifetime, depending on whether they have positive or negative consequences (Gewirtz & Pelaez-Nogueras, 1992). Yet many believe that Skinner placed far too much emphasis on operant behaviors shaped by *external* stimuli (reinforcers and punishers) while ignoring important *cognitive* contributors to social learning. One such critic is Albert Bandura, who has proposed a *social-cognitive* theory of human development that is widely respected today.

BANDURA'S COGNITIVE SOCIAL-LEARNING THEORY

Are we on firm ground in trying to explain human social learning on the basis of research with animals? Bandura (1977, 1986, 1992) doesn't think so. He agrees with Skinner that operant conditioning is an important type of learning, particularly for animals. However, Bandura stresses that humans are *cognitive* beings—active information processors—who, unlike animals, are likely to think about the relationships between their behavior and its consequences and are often more affected by what they *believe* will happen than by the events they actually experience. Consider your own plight as a student. Your education is costly and time-consuming and may impose many demands that you find less than satisfying. Yet, you tolerate the costs and unpleasantries because you can probably *anticipate* greater rewards once you obtain your degree. Your behavior is not shaped by its immediate consequences; if it were, few students would ever make it through the trials and turmoils of college. Instead, you persist as a student because you have *thought about* the long-term benefits of obtaining an education and have decided that they outweigh the short-term costs you must endure.

Nowhere is Bandura's cognitive emphasis clearer than in his decision to highlight **observational learning** as a central developmental process. Observational learning is simply learning that results from observing the behavior of other people (called models). A 2-year-old may learn how to approach and pet the family dog by simply noting how his older sister does it. An 8-year-old may acquire a very negative attitude toward a minority group (as well as learn derogatory labels for these people) after hearing her parents talk about this group in a disparaging way. Observational learning simply could not occur unless cognitive processes were at work. We must *attend* carefully to the model's behavior, actively digest, or *encode,* what we observe, and then *store* this information in memory (as an image or a verbal label) if we are to imitate what we have observed at a later time. Indeed, as we will see in Box 2.1 children need not even be reinforced in order to learn this way.

PHOTO 2.4 B. F. Skinner (1904–1990) proposed a social-learning theory that emphasized the role of external stimuli in controlling human behavior.

operant learning: a form of learning in which voluntary acts (or operants) become either more or less probable, depending on the consequences they produce.

observational learning: learning that results from observing the behavior of others.

PHOTO 2.5 Albert Bandura (1925–   ) has emphasized the cognitive aspects of learning in his social-learning theory.

Box 2.1   *Focus on Research*

An Example of No-Trial (Observational) Learning Without Reinforcement

In 1965, Bandura made what was then considered a radical statement: Children can learn by merely observing the behavior of a social model, *even without first performing the responses themselves or receiving any reinforcement for performing them.* Clearly, this "no-trial" learning is inconsistent with Skinner's theory, which claims that one must perform a response and then be reinforced to have learned that response.

Bandura (1965) conducted a now-classic experiment to prove his point. Nursery school children each watched a short film in which an adult model directed an unusual sequence of aggressive responses toward an inflatable Bobo doll, hitting the doll with a mallet while shouting "sockeroo," throwing rubber balls while shouting "bang, bang," and so on. There were three experimental conditions:

1. Children in the *model-rewarded* condition saw a second adult give the aggressive model candy and soda for a "championship performance."
2. Children in the *model-punished* condition saw a second adult scold and spank the model for beating up Bobo.
3. Children in the *no-consequence* condition simply saw the model behave aggressively.

When the film ended, each child was left alone in a playroom that contained a Bobo doll and the props that the model had used to work Bobo over. Hidden observers then recorded all instances in which the child imitated one or more of the model's unusual aggressive acts. These observations revealed how willing children were to *perform* the responses they had witnessed. The results of this "performance" test appear on the left-hand side of the figure. Notice that children in the model-rewarded and no-consequences conditions imitated more of the model's aggressive acts than those who had seen the model punished for aggressive behavior. Clearly, this looks very much like the kind of no-trial observational learning that Bandura had proposed.

But an important question remained. Had children in the first two conditions actually learned more from observing the model than those who had seen the model punished? To find out, Bandura devised a test to see just how much they had learned. Each child was now offered

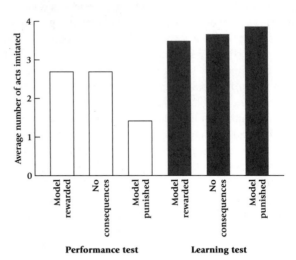

Average number of aggressive responses imitated during the performance test and the learning test for children who had seen a model rewarded, punished, or receiving no consequences for her actions. (Adapted from "Influence of Models' Reinforcement Contingencies on the Acquisition of Imitative Responses," by A. Bandura, 1965, *Journal of Personality and Social Psychology, 1,* 589–595. Copyright 1965 by the American Psychological Association. Adapted by permission.)

trinkets and fruit juice for reproducing all the model's behaviors he or she could recall. As we see in the right-hand side of the figure, this "learning test" revealed that children in each of the three conditions had learned about the same amount by observing the model. Apparently, children in the model-punished condition had imitated fewer of the model's responses on the initial performance test because they felt that they too might be punished for striking Bobo. But when offered a reward, they showed that they had learned much more than their initial performances had implied.

In sum, it is important to distinguish what children *learn* by observation from their willingness to *perform* these responses. Clearly, reinforcement is not necessary for observational learning—that is, for the formation of images or verbal descriptions that would enable the observer to imitate the model's acts. However, the reinforcing or punishing consequences the model has received may well affect the observer's tendency to *perform* what he or she has already learned by observation.

Why does Bandura stress observational learning in his social-learning theory? Because this active, cognitive form of learning permits young children to quickly acquire literally thousands of new responses in a variety of settings where their "models" are simply pursuing their own interests and are not trying to teach them anything. In fact, many of the behaviors that children attend to, remember, and may imitate are actions that models display but would like to discourage—practices such as swearing, smoking, or eating between meals. So Bandura claims that children are continually learning both desirable and undesirable responses by "keeping their eyes (and ears) open," and he is not at all surprised that human development proceeds so very rapidly along so many different paths.

Developmental Trends in Imitation and Observational Learning Bandura's theory of observational learning assumes that an observer can construct images or other **symbolic representations** of a model's behavior and then use these mediators to reproduce what he or she has witnessed. When do these capabilities first appear? When do children begin to take advantage of their emerging powers of observation to acquire important new skills? And how does the character of observational learning change over time? Although Bandura had little to say about these important issues, other researchers have addressed them and have provided some answers.

Origins of Imitation and Observational Learning Although newborns are able to imitate a limited number of motor responses, such as sticking out their tongue (Kaitz et al., 1988), moving their head as an adult model does (Meltzoff & Moore, 1989), and possibly even mimicking facial expressions of happiness and sadness (Field, Woodson, Greenberg, & Cohen, 1982; and see Box 2.2 on page 55), these early imitative capabilities soon disappear and may be nothing more than involuntary reflexes (Abravanel & Sigafoos, 1984; Vinter, 1986). Voluntary imitation of novel responses first appears and becomes more reliable between 8 and 12 months of age (Piaget, 1951). Initially the model must be present and must continue to perform a response before the child is able to imitate. But by age 9 months, some infants can imitate very simple acts with a toy up to 24 hours after they first witness them (Meltzoff, 1988c). This **deferred imitation**—the ability to reproduce the actions of a model at some point in the future—develops rapidly during the second year. By age 14 months, nearly half the infants in one study imitated the simple actions of a *televised* model after a 24-hour delay (Meltzoff, 1988a), and nearly all the 14-month-olds in a second experiment were able to imitate at least three (of six) novel behaviors displayed by a live model *after a delay of one week* (Meltzoff, 1988b).

Clearly, deferred imitation is an important developmental milestone—one indicating that children are now capable of constructing symbolic representations of their experiences and then retrieving this information from memory to guide their reproduction of past events. So 14- to 24-month-old infants should now be prepared to *learn* a great deal by observing the behavior of their companions. But do they take advantage of their newly acquired imitative capabilities?

Yes, indeed! Leon Kuczynski and his associates (1987) asked mothers to record the immediate and the delayed reactions of their 12- to 20-month-old infants and their 25- to

symbolic representations: the images and verbal labels that observers generate in order to retain the important aspects of a model's behavior.

deferred imitation: reproduction of a modeled activity that has been witnessed at some point in the past.

PHOTO 2.6 By age 2, toddlers are already acquiring important personal and social skills by imitating the adaptive acts of older social models.

33-month-old toddlers to the behavior of parental and peer models. The results were quite interesting. All the children imitated their models a fair percentage of the time, but there were clear age differences in the content of these imitations. The 12- to 20-month-olds tended to imitate affective displays, such as laughing and cheering, and other high-intensity antics like jumping, shaking the head to and fro, and pounding on the table. In other words, their imitations were largely playful in character. By contrast, the 25- to 33-month-olds more often imitated *instrumental* behaviors, such as household tasks and self-care routines. What's more, their imitations had more of a self-instructional quality to them, as if the older toddlers were now making an active attempt (1) to acquire skills their models had displayed or (2) to understand the events they had witnessed. When imitating disciplinary encounters, for example, the 12- to 20-month-olds simply repeated verbal prohibitions and physical actions such as hand slapping, usually directing these responses to themselves. However, the older toddlers tended to reenact the entire scenario, including the social influence strategies the disciplinarian had used, and they usually directed these responses to another person, an animal, or a doll. So it seems that between the ages of 2 and 3, observational *learning* is becoming an important means by which children acquire basic personal and social competencies and gain a richer understanding of the rules and regulations they are expected to follow (see also Rogoff, 1997).

A Later Development in Observational Learning: Use of Verbal Mediators   Although preschool children are rapidly acquiring language and becoming more accomplished as conversationalists, they are less likely than older children to rely on verbal labels to help them retain modeled sequences. In a study by Coates and Hartup (1969), 4- to 5-year-olds and 7- to 8-year-olds watched a short film in which an adult model displayed a number of unusual responses, such as shooting at a tower of blocks with a pop gun and throwing a beanbag between his legs. Some of the children from each age group were told to describe the model's actions as they observed them (*induced-verbalization condition*); others simply watched the model without having received any instructions (*passive-observation condition*). As shown in Figure 2.1, 4- to 5-year-olds who described what they were observing were later able to reproduce much more of the model's behavior than their age-mates in the passive-observation condition. By contrast, 7- to 8-year-olds reproduced the same number of the model's responses regardless of whether they had been told to describe what the model was doing. This latter finding suggests that 7- to 8-year-olds will use verbal labels to describe what they have seen, *even if they are not told to.* One important implication of this study is that preschool children may generally learn *less* from social models because they, unlike older children, do not spontaneously produce the verbal mediators that would help them retain what they have observed.

SOCIAL LEARNING AS RECIPROCAL DETERMINISM

Early versions of learning theory were largely tributes to Watson's doctrine of **environmental determinism:** young, unknowing children were viewed as passive recipients of environmental influence—they would become whatever parents, teachers, and other agents of society groomed them to be. Bandura (1986, 1989) takes strong exception to this point of view, stressing that children and adolescents are active, thinking beings who contribute in many ways to their own development. Observational learning, for example, requires the observer to *actively* attend to, encode, and retain the behaviors displayed by social

environmental determinism: the notion that children are passive creatures who are molded by their environments.

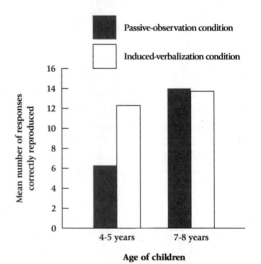

FIGURE 2.1 Children's ability to reproduce the behavior of a social model as a function of age and verbalization instructions. (Adapted from "Age and Verbalization in Observational Learning," by B. Coates and W. W. Hartup, 1969, *Developmental Psychology, 1,* 556–562. Copyright © 1969 by the American Psychological Association. Adapted by permission of the authors.)

models. And children are often free to choose the models to whom they will attend; so they have some say about *what* they will learn from others.

Bandura (1986) has proposed the concept of **reciprocal determinism** to describe his view that human development reflects an interaction between the person (P), the person's behavior (B), and the environment (E) (see Figure 2.2). Unlike the early behaviorists, who maintained that the environment (E) shaped the child and his (her) behavior, Bandura and others (most notably Richard Bell, 1979) propose that the links between the person, behaviors, and environments are bidirectional, so that children, for example, might influence their environments by virtue of their own conduct. Consider an example.

Suppose a 4-year-old discovers that he can gain control over desirable toys by assaulting his playmates. In this case, control over a desired toy is a satisfying outcome that reinforces the child's aggressive behavior. But note that the reinforcer here is produced by the child himself—through his aggressive actions. Not only has bullying behavior been reinforced (by obtaining the toy), *but the character of the play environment has changed.* Our bully becomes more inclined to victimize his playmates in the future, whereas those playmates who are victimized may become even more inclined to "give in" to the bully (see Figure 2.3).

In sum, cognitive-social–learning theorists describe development as a continuous *reciprocal interaction* between children and their environments. The situation or "environment" that a child experiences will surely affect her, but her behavior is thought to affect the environment as well. The implication is that children are actively involved in shaping the very environments that will influence their growth and development.

CONTRIBUTIONS AND CRITICISMS OF THE SOCIAL-LEARNING PERSPECTIVE

Perhaps the major contribution of the social-learning viewpoint is the wealth of information it has provided about developing children and adolescents. Social-learning theories are very precise and testable (Horowitz, 1992). And by conducting tightly controlled experiments to determine how their participants react to various environmental influences, social-learning theorists have begun to understand how and why developing persons might form emotional attachments, adopt gender roles, make friends, learn to abide by moral rules, and change in countless other ways over the course of childhood and adolescence. As we will see throughout the text, the social-learning perspective has contributed substantially to our knowledge of many aspects of social and personality development (Grusec, 1992).

The social-learning theorist's emphasis on overt behavior and its immediate causes has also produced a number of important clinical insights and practical applications.

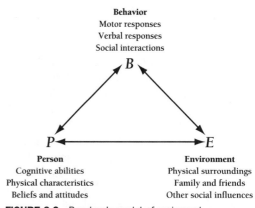

FIGURE 2.2 Bandura's model of reciprocal determinism. (Adapted from A. Bandura, 1978, "The Self System in Reciprocal Determinism." *American Psychologist, 33*, 344–358. Copyright © 1978 by the American Psychological Association.)

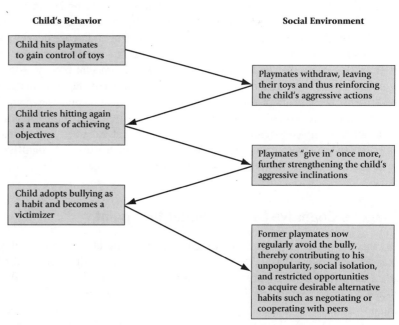

FIGURE 2.3 Reciprocal determinism: A hypothetical example showing how a child both influences and is influenced by the social environment.

reciprocal determinism: the notion that the flow of influence between children and their environments is a two-way street; the environment may affect the child, but the child's behavior will also influence the environment.

For example, many problem behaviors can now be quickly eliminated by behavioral modification techniques in which the therapist (1) identifies the reinforcers that sustain undesirable habits and eliminates them, while (2) modeling or reinforcing alternative behaviors that are more socially desirable. Thus, distressing antics such as bullying or name-calling can often be eliminated in a matter of days or weeks, rather than the months (or years) that a psychoanalyst might take, probing the child's unconscious, searching for a conflict that may underlie these hostilities.

Despite its strengths, many view the social-learning approach as an oversimplified account of social and personality development. Consider its explanation of individual differences. Presumably, individuals follow different developmental paths because no two persons grow up in exactly the same environment. Yet, critics are quick to note that each person comes into the world with something else that is an equally plausible explanation for his or her "individuality"—a unique genetic inheritance. So social-learning theorists may have badly oversimplified the issue of individual differences in development by downplaying the contribution of important biological influences.

Yet another group of critics, whose viewpoint we will examine in Chapter 3, can argue with the behaviorists that development depends very heavily on the contexts in which it occurs. However, these *ecological systems theorists* argue that the "environment" that so powerfully influences development is really a series of social systems (for example, families, communities, and cultures) that interact with each other (and with the individual) in complex ways that are impossible to simulate in a laboratory. Their point is that only by studying the children and adolescents in their *natural settings* are we likely to understand how environments truly influence development.

One final criticism. Despite the popularity of recent cognitively oriented learning theories that stress the child's active role in the developmental process, some critics maintain that *no* learning theorist pays enough attention to *cognitive* influences on development. Proponents of this third or cognitive-developmental viewpoint believe that the child's mental abilities undergo a series of qualitative changes (or stages) that behaviorists completely ignore. Further, they argue that a child's impressions of and reactions to the environment depend largely on his or her level of **cognitive development.** Let's now turn to this viewpoint and see what it has to offer.

Piaget's Cognitive-Developmental Viewpoint

No theorist has contributed more to our understanding of children's thinking than Jean Piaget (1896–1980), a Swiss scholar who began to study intellectual development during the 1920s. Piaget was truly a remarkable individual. At age 10, he published his first scientific article about the behavior of a rare albino sparrow. His early interest in the ways that animals adapt to their environments eventually led him to pursue a Ph.D. in zoology, which he completed in 1918. Piaget's secondary interest was *epistemology* (the branch of philosophy concerned with the origins of knowledge), and he hoped to be able to integrate his two interests. Thinking that psychology was the answer, Piaget journeyed to Paris, where he accepted a position at the Alfred Binet laboratories, working on the first standardized intelligence test. His experiences in this position would have a profound influence on his career.

In the testing approach to the study of mental ability, an estimate is made of the person's intelligence based on the number and kinds of questions that he or she answers correctly. However, Piaget soon found that he was more interested in children's *incorrect* answers than their correct ones. He first noticed that children of about the same age were producing the same kinds of wrong answers. But why? As he proceeded to question children about their misconceptions, using the clinical method he

cognitive development: age-related changes that occur in mental activities such as attending, perceiving, learning, thinking, and remembering.

had learned earlier while working in a psychiatric clinic, he began to realize that young children are not simply less intelligent than older children; their thought processes are completely different. Piaget then set up his own laboratory and spent 60 years charting the course of intellectual growth and attempting to determine how children progress from one mode (or stage) of thinking to another.

PIAGET'S VIEW OF INTELLIGENCE AND INTELLECTUAL GROWTH

Influenced by his background in biology, Piaget (1950) defined intelligence as a basic life process that helps an organism to adapt to its environment. By adapting, Piaget means that the organism is able to cope with the demands of its immediate situation. For example, the hungry infant who grasps a bottle and brings it to her mouth is behaving adaptively, as is the adolescent who successfully interprets a road map while traveling or changes a tire should the need arise. As children mature, they acquire ever more complex "cognitive structures" that aid them in adapting to their environments.

PHOTO 2.7 The cognitive-developmental theory of Swiss scholar Jean Piaget (1896–1980) has several important implications for our understanding of social and personality development.

Cognitive (Intellectual) Schemes   A cognitive structure—or what Piaget called a **scheme**—is an organized pattern of thought or action that is used to cope with or explain some aspect of experience. For example, many 3-year-olds will insist that the sun is alive because it comes up in the morning and goes down at night. These children are operating on the basis of a simple cognitive scheme—the idea that things that move are alive. The earliest **schemes,** formed in infancy, are simple motor habits such as reaching, grasping, and lifting, that prove to be adaptive indeed. For example, a curious infant who combines the responses of extending an arm (reaching) and grasping with the hand is suddenly capable of satisfying her curiosity by exploring almost any interesting object that is no more than an arm's length away. Simple as these **behavioral schemes** may be, they permit infants to operate toys, to turn dials, to open cabinets, and to otherwise master their environments. Late in infancy, children are able to represent experiences mentally, forming such **symbolic schemes** as visual images. Shortly after entering grade school, children's schemes become **operational,** taking the form of internal mental activities or "actions of the head" (for example, cognitive addition or subtraction) that allow them to manipulate information mentally and think logically about the issues and problems they encounter in everyday life. At any age, children rely on their current cognitive structures to understand the world around them. As a result, younger and older children, who construct very different kinds of schemes, will often interpret and respond to the same objects and events in very different ways.

Constructing Schemes: Piaget's Intellectual Functions   How do children develop more complex schemes and grow intellectually? Piaget claimed that infants have no inborn knowledge or ideas about reality as some philosophers have claimed. Nor are children simply handed information or taught how to think by adults. Instead, Piaget viewed children as **constructivists** who actively create new understandings of the world based on their own experiences. How? By being the curious and active explorers that they are. Children watch what goes on around them; they experiment with objects they encounter; they make connections or associations between events; and they are puzzled when their current understanding (or schemes) fail to explain what they have experienced.

According to Piaget, children are able to construct new schemes because they have inherited two *intellectual functions,* which he calls *organization* and *adaptation. Organization* is the process by which children combine existing schemes into new and more complex intellectual structures. For example, a toddler may initially believe that

scheme: an organized pattern of thought or action that a child constructs to make sense of some aspect of his or her experience; Piaget sometimes uses the term cognitive structures as a synonym for schemes.

behavioral schemes: organized patterns of behavior that are used to represent and respond to objects and experiences.

symbolic schemes: internal mental symbols (such as images or verbal codes) that one uses to represent aspects of experience.

operational schemes: Piaget's term for schemes that utilize cognitive operations, or mental "actions of the head," that enable one to transform objects of thought and to reason logically.

constructivist: one who gains knowledge by acting or otherwise operating on objects or events to discover their properties.

organization: an inborn tendency to combine and integrate available schemes into coherent systems or bodies of knowledge.

anything that flies is a "birdie." As he gradually discovers that many things that are not birds can also fly, he may organize this knowledge into new and more complex hierarchical structures such as this one:

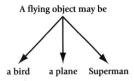

A flying object may be

a bird · a plane · Superman

According to Piaget, organization is inborn and automatic: children are constantly organizing their available schemes into higher-order systems or structures.

The goal of organization is to further the process of adaptation. As its name implies, **adaptation** is the process of adjusting to the demands of the environment. According to Piaget, adaptation occurs through two complementary activities: assimilation and accommodation.

To illustrate the adaptive function, let's return to the 3-year-old who believes that the sun is alive. Surely this idea is not something the child learned from an adult; it was apparently constructed by the child on the basis of her own worldly experiences. After all, many things that move *are* alive. So long as the child clings to this understanding, she may regard any new moving object as alive; that is, new experiences will be interpreted in terms of her current cognitive structures, a process Piaget called **assimilation.** Eventually, however, this child will encounter moving objects that almost certainly couldn't be alive, such as a paper airplane that was nothing more than a sheet of newsprint before dad built it, or a wind-up toy that invariably stops moving unless she winds it again. Now here are contradictions (or what Piaget termed **disequilibriums**) between the child's understanding and the facts to be understood. It becomes clear to the child that her "objects-that-move-are-alive" scheme needs to be revised. So she will be prompted by these disconfirming experiences to **accommodate**—that is, to alter her existing schemes so that they provide a better explanation of the events she has witnessed (perhaps by concluding that only things that move under their own power are alive).

So it goes through life; Piaget believes that we are continually relying on the complementary processes of assimilation and accommodation to adapt to our environments. Initially, we attempt to understand new experiences or to solve problems using our current cognitive structures (assimilation). But we often find our existing schemes to be inadequate for these tasks, which then prompts us to revise them (through accommodation) and to integrate them with other relevant schemes (organization) to provide a better "fit" with reality (Piaget, 1952). Biological maturation also plays an important role: As the brain and nervous system mature, children become capable of increasingly complex cognitive activities that help them to construct better understandings of what they have experienced (Piaget, 1970). Eventually, curious, active children, who are always forming new schemes and reorganizing this knowledge, will have progressed far enough to be thinking about old issues in entirely new ways; that is, they pass from one stage of cognitive development to the next higher stage.

FOUR STAGES OF COGNITIVE DEVELOPMENT

Piaget proposed four major periods (or stages) of cognitive development: the *sensorimotor* stage (birth to age 2), the *preoperational* stage (ages 2 to 7), the *concrete-operational* stage (ages 7 to 11 or 12), and the *formal-operational* stage (ages 11–12 and beyond). These stages form what Piaget called an **invariant developmental se-**

adaptation: inborn tendency to adjust to the demands of the environment.

assimilation: Piaget's term for the process by which children interpret new experiences by incorporating them into their existing schemes.

disequilibriums: imbalances or contradictions between one's thought processes and environmental events. By contrast, *equilibrium* refers to a balanced, harmonious relationship between one's cognitive structures and the environment.

accommodation: Piaget's term for the process by which children modify their existing schemes in order to incorporate or adapt to new experiences.

AN INFANT ACCOMMODATING HIS MOUTH TO THE SHAPE OF AN OBJECT

quence—that is, all children progress through the stages in exactly the order in which they are listed. There is no skipping of stages because each successive stage builds on the previous stage and represents a more complex way of thinking.

The Sensorimotor Stage (Birth to Approximately Two Years) The **sensorimotor stage** spans the first two years, or the period that developmentalists refer to as infancy. The dominant cognitive structures are behavioral schemes, which evolve as infants begin to coordinate their *sensory* input and *motor* responses in order to "act on" and get to "know" the environment.

During the first two years of life, infants evolve from reflexive creatures with very limited knowledge into planful problem solvers who have already learned a great deal about themselves, their close companions, and the objects and events in their everyday worlds. So dramatic are the infant's cognitive advances that Piaget divides the sensorimotor period into six substages (see Table 2-3 on p. 57), which describe the child's gradual transition from a reflexive to a reflective organism. Our review concentrates on those aspects of sensorimotor development that have influenced current thinking about children's social and personality development.

Growth of Intentional or Goal-Directed Behavior Over the first eight months, infants begin to act on objects and to discover that they can make interesting things happen. However, these discoveries emerge very gradually. Piaget believes that **neonates** are born with only a few basic reflexes (for example, sucking, grasping) that assist them in satisfying biological needs such as hunger. During the first month, their activities are pretty much confined to exercising their innate reflexes, assimilating new objects into these reflexive schemes (for example, sucking on objects other than nipples), and accommodating their reflexes to these novel objects.

The first coordinated habits emerge at 1 to 4 months of age as infants discover by chance that various responses they can produce (for example, sucking their thumbs, making sounds by cooing) are satisfying and thus worthy of repetition. These responses, called **primary circular reactions,** are centered on the infant's own body. They are called "primary" because they are the first habits to appear and "circular" because the pleasure they bring stimulates their repetition.

Between 4 and 8 months of age, infants discover (again by chance) that they can make interesting things happen to *external* objects (such as making a rubber duck quack by squeezing it). These responses, called **secondary circular reactions,** also tend to be repeated for the pleasure they bring. Of what possible significance are these simple habits for social and personality development? According to Piaget, infants are discovering the limits and capabilities of their own bodies during the first four months and then recognizing that external objects are separate from their "physical selves" by the middle of the first year. Thus, making a distinction between "self" and "nonself" is viewed as the first step in the development of a personal identity, or self-concept.

Between 8 and 12 months of age, infants are suddenly able to coordinate two or more actions to achieve simple objectives. For example, were you to place a toy that the child wanted under a cushion, the child might lift the cushion with one hand while using the other to grab the toy. In this case, the act of lifting the cushion is not pleasurable in itself; nor is it done by chance. Rather, it represents part of a larger *intentional* scheme in which two initially unrelated responses—lifting and grasping— are coordinated as a means to an end. Piaget believed that these simple means-ends activities represent the earliest form of true problem solving.

At 12 to 18 months of age, infants begin to experiment with objects and will try to invent totally new methods of solving problems or reproducing interesting results. For example, a child who originally squeezed a rubber duck to make it quack may now

invariant developmental sequence: a series of developments that occur in one particular order because each development in the sequence is a prerequisite for the next.

sensorimotor stage: Piaget's first stage of cognitive development, from birth to 2 years, when infants are relying on behavioral schemes to adapt to the environment.

neonate: a newborn infant from birth to approximately one month of age.

primary circular reaction: a pleasurable response, centered on the infant's own body, that is discovered by chance and performed over and over.

secondary circular reaction: a pleasurable response, centered on an object external to the self, that is discovered by chance and performed over and over.

decide to drop it, step on it, or crush it with a pillow to see whether these actions will have the same or different effects on the toy. These trial-and-error exploratory schemes, called **tertiary circular reactions**, signal the emergence of true curiosity.

A dramatic development takes place between 18 and 24 months of age: children begin to internalize their behavioral schemes to construct mental symbols, or images. Suddenly, 18- to 24-month-olds are capable of solving problems mentally, without resorting to trial-and-error experimentation. This ability, called **inner experimentation**, is illustrated in Piaget's interaction with his son, Laurent:

> Laurent is seated before a table and I place a bread crust in front of him, out of reach. Also, to the right of the child I place a stick, about 25cm. long. At first, Laurent tries to grasp the bread . . . and then he gives up. . . . Laurent again looks at the bread, and without moving, looks very briefly at the stick, then suddenly grasps it and directs it to the bread . . . [he then] draws the bread to him. (Piaget, 1952, p. 335)

Clearly, Laurent had an important insight: the stick can be used as an extension of his arm to obtain a distant object. Trial-and-error experimentation is not apparent in this case, for Laurent's "problem solving" occurred at an internal, symbolic level.

Development of Imitation Imitation intrigued Piaget because he viewed it as a highly adaptive activity—a means by which infants might actively participate in social exchanges and add many new skills to their behavioral repertoires. However, his own observations suggested that infants are incapable of imitating *novel* responses displayed by a model until 8 to 12 months of age (the same age at which they show clear evidence of intentionality in their own behavior). Furthermore, the imitative schemes of an 8-month-old are rather imprecise. Were you to bend and straighten your finger, the infant might mimic you by opening and closing her entire hand (Piaget, 1951). Voluntary imitation becomes much more precise between 12 and 18 months, and as we noted earlier, a major accomplishment of the second year is refinement of *deferred imitation*—the ability to reproduce actions modeled earlier in time. Clearly, this capacity for deferred imitation implies that infants are capable of generating the kinds of *symbolic* representations of their experiences that promote observational learning.

What are we to make of recent claims that *neonates* are capable of imitating simple facial gestures and motor responses? In Box 2.2, we explore this phenomenon that Piaget overlooked and discuss its possible adaptive significance.

Development of Object Permanence One of the more notable achievements of the sensorimotor period is the development of **object permanence**—the idea that objects continue to exist when they are no longer visible or detectable through the other senses. If you were to remove your watch and cover it with a coffee mug, you would be well aware that the watch continues to exist. Objects have a permanence for us; out of sight is not necessarily out of mind.

According to Piaget, babies are not initially aware of this basic fact of life. Throughout the first four months, infants will not search for attractive objects that vanish; were they interested in a watch that was then covered by a mug, they would soon lose interest, almost as if they believed that the watch had lost its identity by being transformed into a mug (Bower, 1982). At age 4 to 8 months, infants will retrieve attractive objects that are partly concealed or hidden under a transparent cover; but their continuing failure to search for objects that are completely concealed suggests that, from their perspective, disappearing objects may no longer exist.[1]

tertiary circular reaction: an exploratory scheme in which infants devise new methods of acting on objects to reproduce interesting results.

inner experimentation: the ability to solve simple problems on a mental, or symbolic, level without having to rely on trial-and-error experimentation.

object permanence: the realization that objects continue to exist when they are no longer visible or detectable through the other senses.

---

[1]However, Piaget's conclusion has been hotly debated. Many investigators now believe that even very young infants *know* that objects continue to exist; they simply *forget* where the objects are if those objects remain hidden for more than a second or two (cf. Bjorklund, 2000, for a review).

Box 2.2   *Current Controversies*

Can Newborns Imitate?

Researchers once believed that infants were unable to imitate the actions of another person until the latter half of the first year (Piaget, 1951). But beginning in the late 1970s, a number of studies reported that babies younger than 7 days old were apparently able to imitate a number of adult facial gestures, including sticking out their tongues, opening and closing their mouths, protruding their lower lips (as if they were sad), and even posing displays of happiness (Field et al., 1982; Meltzoff & Moore, 1977; Reissland, 1988; see the figure below).

Some critics have dismissed these expressive responses as an artifact. Perhaps infants pucker, open their mouths, or stick out their tongues because face-to-face interaction with the adult has excited them (Olson & Sherman, 1983). Or perhaps they are trying to *explore* with their mouths those sights they find particularly interesting (Jones, 1996). Others have wondered whether the adult model might not be subconsciously mimicking the facial expressions of the infants. And these early "matching" displays become much harder to elicit over the first 3 to 4 months of life (Abravanel & Sigafoos, 1984). Some have interpreted this to mean that the neonate's limited capacity for mimicking is an *involuntary reflexive*

scheme that disappears with age (as many other reflexes do), only to be replaced later by voluntary imitation (Kaitz et al., 1988; Vinter, 1986).

However, Andrew Meltzoff (1990; Meltzoff & Moore, 1992) argues quite strongly that babies' early matching displays are *voluntary imitative responses.* He thinks this because babies only a few days old will often match an adult's facial expression *after a short delay,* even though the model is no longer posing that expression. According to Meltzoff, these imitative responses are possible because babies match facial movements they "see" in the model's face to movements they can "feel" in their own faces.

Regardless of whether one chooses to call babies' early capacity for mimicry a form of imitation, exploration, or a reflex, it almost certainly warms the hearts of many caregivers and helps to ensure that they and their baby get off to a good start. Indeed, we will see in Chapter 4 that very young infants have a number of other inborn characteristics that elicit the kinds of affectionate social contacts from caregivers that promote healthy social and emotional development. So it is quite conceivable that the newborn's ability to match facial displays serves this same important function and is highly adaptive indeed!

Sample photographs from videotaped recordings of 2- and 3-week-old infants imitating tongue protrusion, mouth opening, and lip protrusion.

According to Piaget, the first signs of an emerging object concept appear at 8 to 12 months of age. However, object permanence is far from complete, as we see in Piaget's demonstration with 10-month-old Jacqueline:

> Jacqueline is seated on a mattress without anything to disturb or distract her. . . . I take her [toy] parrot from her hands and hide it twice in succession under the mattress, on her left [point A]. Both times Jacqueline looks for the object immediately and grabs it. Then I take it from her hands and move it very slowly before her eyes to the corresponding place on her right, under the mattress [point B]. Jacqueline watches this movement . . . but at the moment when the parrot disappears [at point B], she turns to her left and looks where it was before [at point A]. (1954, p. 51)

Jacqueline's response is typical of children at this age. When searching for a disappearing object, the 8- to 12-month-old will often look in the place where it was previously *found* rather than the place where it was last seen. In other words, the child acts as if her *behavior* determined where the object was to appear, and consequently she does not treat the object as if it existed independent of her own activity.

Between 12 and 18 months of age, the object concept improves. Infants will now track the visible movements of objects and search for them where they were last seen. Yet, the object concept is not complete, for the child cannot make the mental inferences necessary to represent and understand *invisible* displacements. Thus, if you conceal an attractive toy in your hand, place your hand behind a barrier and deposit the toy there, remove and open your empty hand, and ask the child to find the toy, 12- to 18-month-olds will search where the toy was last seen—in your hand—rather than looking behind the barrier.

By 18 to 24 months of age, children are capable of mentally representing invisible displacements and using these mental inferences to guide their search for objects that disappear. The object concept is now complete.

Of what social significance is the object concept? In Chapter 4, we will see that it may play a very important role in the development of an infant's first true emotional attachments. Cognitive theorists (for example, Schaffer, 1977, 1990) have proposed that infants cannot form close emotional ties to regular companions unless these individuals have a "permanence" about them. After all, it would seem rather difficult to establish a meaningful and lasting relationship with a person who "ceases to exist" whenever he or she passes from view.

In sum, the child's intellectual achievements during the sensorimotor period are truly remarkable. In two short years, infants have evolved from reflexive and largely immobile creatures into planful thinkers who can move about on their own, solve some problems in their heads, form simple concepts, and even communicate many of their thoughts to their companions. Table 2-3 presents a brief summary of the major intellectual accomplishments of the first two years.

The Preoperational Stage (Approximately Two to Seven Years)   During the **preoperational stage**, children become increasingly proficient at constructing and using mental symbols (words and images) to think about the objects, situations, and events they encounter. But despite these advances in symbolic reasoning, Piaget's descriptions of preoperational intelligence focus mainly on the limitations or deficiencies in children's thinking. Indeed, he calls this period "preoperational" because he believes that preschool children have not yet acquired the **cognitive operations**—such internal mental activities such as cognitive addition or subtraction—that would enable them to think logically. As we review this intellectual stage, we once again focus on characteristics of preoperational thought that have implications for social and personality development.

Symbolism and Pretend Play   The early preoperational period (ages 2 to 3) is marked by a dramatic increase in children's use of the **symbolic function**: the ability to make one thing—a word or an object—stand for, or represent, something else. Consider, for example, that because 2- to 3-year-olds can use words and images to represent their experiences, they are now quite capable of reconstructing past events and thinking about or even comparing objects that are no longer present.

A second hallmark of the early preoperational period—one made possible by the growth of symbolism—is a dramatic increase in both the frequency and complexity of *pretend play*: toddlers often pretend to be people they are not (mommies, super heroes) and they may assume these roles with props (such as a shoe box or a stick) that symbolize role-relevant objects (a baby's crib or a ray gun). Although parents are oc-

preoperational stage: Piaget's second stage of cognitive development, lasting from about age 2 to age 7, when children are thinking at a symbolic level but are not yet using cognitive operations.

cognitive operation: an internal mental activity that one performs on objects of thought.

symbolic function: the ability to use symbols (for example, images and words) to represent objects and experiences.

TABLE 2-3 Summary of the substages and intellectual accomplishments of the sensorimotor period

PIAGETIAN SUBSTAGE	METHODS OF SOLVING PROBLEMS OR PRODUCING INTERESTING OUTCOMES	IMITATION SKILLS	OBJECT CONCEPT
1. Reflex activity (0–1 month)	Exercising and accommodating inborn reflexes	Some imitation of facial expressions and gross motor responses[1]	Tracks moving object but ignores its disappearance
2. Primary circular reactions (1–4 months)	Repeating interesting acts that are centered on one's own body	Repetition of own behavior that is mimicked by a companion	Looks intently at the spot where an object disappeared[2]
3. Secondary circular reactions (4–8 months)	Repeating interesting acts that are directed toward external objects	Same as in substage 2	Searches for partly concealed object
4. Coordination of secondary schemes (8–12 months)	Combining actions to solve simple problems (first evidence of intentionality)	Ability to eventually imitate novel responses after gradually accommodating a crude first attempt at imitation	Searches for and finds concealed object that has not been visibly displaced—first glimmering of notion of object permanence
5. Tertiary circular reactions (12–18 months)	Experimenting to find new ways to solve problems or reproduce interesting outcomes	Systematic imitation of novel responses; deferred imitation of simple motor acts	Searches for and finds object that has been visibly displaced
6. Invention of new means through mental combinations (18–24 months)	Solving problems at an internal symbolic level—first evidence of child's using insight	Deferred imitation of complex behavioral sequences	Searches for and finds objects that have been hidden through invisible displacements—object concept is complete

[1]Imitation of facial expressions is apparently an inborn ability that may bear little relation to the voluntary imitation that appears later in the first year.

[2]Many researchers now believe that the object concept may be present very early and that Piaget's research badly underestimates what young infants may know about objects (see Bjorklund, 2000; Shaffer, 1999).

SOURCES: Adapted from T. M. Field, R. Woodson, R. Greenberg, & D. Cohen, 1982, "Discrimination and Imitation of Facial Expressions by Neonates." *Science, 218,* 179–181; also A. N. Meltzoff & M. K. Moore, 1977, "Imitation of Facial and Manual Gestures by Human Neonates." *Science, 198,* 75–78.

casionally concerned when their preschoolers immerse themselves in a world of make-believe, Piaget viewed pretend play as serious business—an activity that promotes the child's social, emotional, and intellectual development. And there is ample support for Piaget's argument. For example, preschool children who "pretend" a lot are judged to be more creative, more socially mature, and (if their play often includes peers), more popular than age-mates who pretend less often (Connolly & Doyle, 1984; Howes & Matheson, 1992). Finally, play may foster healthy emotional development by allowing children to express feelings that bother them or to resolve emotional conflicts (Fein, 1986). If Jennie, for example, has been scolded at lunch for failing to eat her peas, she may gain control of the situation at play as she scolds her doll for picky eating or persuades the doll to "eat healthy" and consume the peas. Playful resolution of such emotional conflicts may even be an important contributor to children's understanding of authority and to the rationales that underlie the rules they must follow (Piaget & Inhelder, 1969).

Let it never be said, then, that play is useless. Although children play because it is fun, not because it sharpens their skills, players indirectly contribute to their own social, emotional, and intellectual development, enjoying themselves all the while. In this sense, play is truly the child's work—and is serious business indeed!

Deficiencies in Preoperational Reasoning Despite the adaptive characteristics of children's symbolism and pretend play, much of what Piaget had to say about preoperational thought dwelled on its limitations. The most striking deficiency that he saw was the child's **egocentrism**—a tendency to view the world from one's own perspec-

tive and to have difficulty recognizing another person's divergent point of view. Piaget demonstrated this by first familiarizing children with an asymmetrical mountain scene (see Figure 2.4) and then asking them what an observer would see as he gazed at the scene from a vantage point other than their own. Often 3- to 4-year-olds said that the other person would see exactly what they see, which Piaget interpreted as the child's failure to consider the other's divergent perspective.

If young children often have trouble with *perceptual perspective-taking,* or inferring what others can see and hear, imagine the difficulties they must face with *conceptual perspective taking*—that is, correctly inferring what another person may be feeling, thinking, or intending. Indeed, we will see that preschoolers do often rely on their own perspectives and thus fail to make accurate judgments about other people's motives, intentions, and desires; also, they often assume that if they know something, others will too (Hala & Chandler, 1996; Ruffman et al., 1993). Furthermore, the egocentrism that younger children display may help to explain why they may sometimes appear rather cruel, selfish, inconsiderate, or unwilling to help one another. If these "insensitive" youngsters do not realize how their own actions make others feel, they may not readily experience the remorse and sympathy that might inhibit antisocial behavior or elicit acts of kindness. This hypothesized link between children's cognitive abilities (namely their empathic capabilities and role-taking skills) and their social conduct will be explored in detail when we consider the topics of aggression, altruism, and moral development in Chapters 9 and 10.

Between the ages of 4 and 7, egocentrism declines somewhat and children are becoming much more proficient at classifying objects on the basis of shared perceptual features such as size, shape, and color. In fact, Piaget characterized the thinking of the 4- to 6-year-old as **intuitive** because her understanding of objects and events tends to "center" on their single, most salient *perceptual* feature—the way things appear to be—rather than or logical on rational thought processes.

The deficiencies of intuitive reasoning are quite clear if we examine the results of Piaget's famous *conservation* studies (Flavell, 1963). One of these experiments begins with the child adjusting the volumes of liquid in two identical containers until each is said to have "the same amount to drink." Next the child sees the experimenter pour the liquid from one of these tall, thin containers into a short, broad container. He is then asked whether the remaining tall, thin container and the shorter, broader container have the same amount of liquid (see Figure 2.5 for an illustration of the procedure). Children younger than 6 or 7 will usually say that the tall, thin receptacle contains more liquid than the short, broad one. The child's thinking about liquids is apparently **centered** on one perceptual feature—the relative heights of the columns (tall column = more liquid). In Piaget's terminology, preoperational children are incapable of **conservation:** They do not yet realize that certain properties of a substance (such as its volume or mass) remain unchanged when its appearance is altered in some superficial way.

Why do preoperational children fail to conserve? Simply because their thinking is not yet *operational.* According to Piaget, either of two cognitive operations is necessary for conservation. The first is **reversibility**—the ability to mentally undo, or reverse, an action. At the intuitive level, the child is incapable of mentally reversing the flow of action and therefore does not realize that the liquid in the short, broad container would attain its former height if it were poured back into the tall, thin container. Second, the child must be able to overcome his or her "centered" thinking in

FIGURE 2.4 Piaget's three-mountain problem. Young preoperational children are egocentric. They cannot easily assume another person's perspective and will often say that another child viewing the mountain from a different vantage point will see exactly what they see from their own location.

egocentrism: the tendency to view the world from one's own perspective while failing to recognize that others may have different points of view.

intuitive thought: Piaget's term for reasoning that is dominated by appearances (or perceptual characteristics of objects and events) rather than by rational thought processes.

centered thinking (centration): the tendency to focus on only one aspect of a problem when two or more aspects are relevant.

conservation: the recognition that the properties of an object or substance do not change when its appearance is altered in some superficial way.

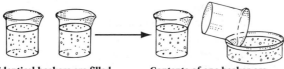

| Liquids: | Two identical beakers are filled to the same level, and the child agrees that they have the same amount to drink. | Contents of one beaker are poured into a different-shaped beaker so that the two columns of water are of unequal height. | Conserving child recognizes that each beaker has the same amount to drink (on the average, conservation of liquids is attained at age 6–7 years). |

| Mass (continuous substance): | Two identical balls of playdough are presented. The child agrees that they have equal amounts of dough. | One ball is rolled into the shape of a sausage. | Conserving child recognizes that each object contains the same amount of dough (average age, 6–7). |

FIGURE 2.5 Two of Piaget's famous conservation problems.

order to recognize that immediate appearances can be deceiving. Piaget suggests that children begin to "decenter" as they acquire a cognitive operation called **compensation**—the ability to focus on several aspects of a problem at the same time. Children at the intuitive stage are unable to attend simultaneously to both height and width when trying to solve the liquid conservation problem. Consequently, they fail to recognize that an increase in the width of the column of liquid compensates for a decrease in its height to preserve its absolute amount.

Let's consider one implication of the young child's intuitive reasoning for social and personality development. Three- to 5-year-olds clearly understand that they are boys or girls and that everyone can be classified according to gender. But the thinking of these young children about gender and its implications is quite egocentric and is dominated by appearances. Thus, a 4-year-old boy might well say he could become a mommy if he really wanted to or might conclude that a woman who cuts her hair short, wears men's clothing, and goes to work as a construction worker is now a man (McConaghy, 1979; Slaby & Frey, 1975). Impressions such as these suggest that preschool children have not yet conserved the concept of gender. In Chapter 8, we will see that the conservation of gender is an important contributor to gender-role development that is not attained until age 5 to 7—precisely the age at which children begin to conserve "nonsocial" attributes such as liquids and mass.

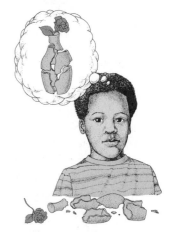

Reversibility is an important cognitive operation that develops during middle childhood.

The Concrete-Operational Stage (Approximately 7 to 11 Years) According to Piaget, children at the **concrete-operational stage** are rapidly acquiring cognitive operations and applying these important new skills when thinking about objects and events that they've seen, heard, or otherwise experienced. Recall from our earlier discussion that a cognitive operation is an internal mental activity that enables the child to modify and reorganize her images and symbols to reach a logical conclusion (Flavell, Miller, & Miller, 1993). For example, the operation of *reversibility* allows a child to mentally reverse the flow of action and thereby recognize that a column of water that has assumed a new appearance would once again look the same if she were to pour it back into its original container. Armed with this cognitive operation, then, the concrete operator now *knows* that the two different containers have the same amount of liquid; he uses *logic,* not misleading appearances, to reach his conclusion. So, the ability to operate on one's objects of thought takes the 7- to 11-year-old far beyond the static and centered thinking of the preoperational stage.

The Growth of Relational Logic One of the hallmarks of preoperational thinking— an ability that permits us to (among other things) sharpen our self-concepts by

reversibility: the ability to reverse, or negate, an action by mentally performing the opposite action.

compensation: the ability to consider more than one aspect of a problem at a time (also called decentration).

concrete-operational stage: Piaget's third stage of cognitive development, lasting from about age 7 to age 11, when children are acquiring cognitive operations and thinking more logically about tangible objects and experiences.

comparing our skills and attributes with those of other people—is a better understanding of relations and relational logic. Can you remember an occasion when your gym teacher said "Line up by height from tallest to shortest"? Carrying out such a request is really quite easy for concrete operators who are now capable of **seriation**—the ability to mentally arrange items along a quantifiable dimension such as height and weight. By contrast, preoperational youngsters perform miserably on mental seriation tasks and would struggle to comply with the gym teacher's request.

Closely related to seriation is the concept of **transitivity**: the ability to accurately infer the relations among elements in a serial order. If, for example, Jane is taller than Susan, who is taller than Jo, then Jane has to be taller than Jo. Elementary as this inference may seem to us, Piaget claimed that children show little awareness of the transitivity principle before the stage of concrete operations.

Interestingly, however, the transitive inferences of concrete operators are generally limited to *real objects* that are *physically present*; 7- to 11-year-olds cannot yet apply this relational logic to abstract signifiers such as the x's, y's, and z's that we use in algebra. Indeed, Piaget names this period *concrete* operations because his research implied that 7- to 11-year-olds are not yet able to apply their operational schemes to think *logically* about abstract ideas or about any hypothetical proposition that violates their conceptions of reality. Let's see why he came to this conclusion.

The Formal-Operational Stage (Age 11–12 and Beyond) By age 11 or 12, many children are entering the last of Piaget's intellectual stages: **formal operations.** Recall that concrete operations are mental actions performed on material aspects of experience and that concrete operators can think quite logically about tangible objects and events. By contrast, formal operations are mental actions performed on *ideas* and *propositions.* No longer is thinking tied to the factual or observable, for formal operators can reason quite logically about hypothetical processes and events that may have no basis in reality.

Reactions to Hypothetical Propositions One way to determine whether a preadolescent has crossed over into the stage of formal operations is to present a thought problem that violates her views about the real world. The concrete operator, whose thinking is tied to objective reality, will often balk at hypothetical propositions. In fact, she may even reply that it is impossible to think logically about objects that don't exist or events that could never happen. By contrast, formal operators enjoy thinking about hypotheticals and are likely to generate some very unusual and creative responses. In Box 2.3 we see the differences between concrete-operational and formal-operational thinking as children consider a hypothetical proposition that was presented in the form of an art assignment.

Hypothetico-Deductive Reasoning: The Systematic Search for Answers and Solutions The formal operator's approach to problem solving becomes increasingly systematic and abstract—much like the **hypothetico-deductive reasoning** of a scientist. We can easily compare the reasoning of formal operators with that of their youngest counterparts by examining their responses to Piaget's famous *pendulum problem* (Inhelder & Piaget, 1958). Given strings of different lengths, objects of different weights to attach to one end of the strings, and a hook on which to hang the other end, the subject's task is to discover which factor influences how fast the pendulum oscillates (that is, swings back and forth during a given time period). Is it the length of the string? The heaviness of the weight? The force with which the weight is pushed? The height from which the weight is released? Or might two or more of these variables be important?

The key to solving this problem is to first identify the four factors that might control the pendulum's oscillation and then systematically test all of these "hypotheses,"

seriation: a cognitive operation that allows one to order a set of stimuli along a quantifiable dimension such as height or weight.

transitivity: the ability to infer relations among elements in a serial order (for example, if A > B and B > C, then A > than C).

formal-operational stage: Piaget's fourth and final stage of cognitive development, from age 11 to 12 and beyond, when the individual begins to think more rationally and systematically about abstract concepts and hypothetical events.

hypothetico-deductive reasoning: a style of problem solving in which all possible solutions to a problem are generated and then systematically evaluated to determine the correct answer(s).

Box 2.3   *Focus on Research*

Children's Responses to a Hypothetical Proposition

Piaget (1970) has argued that the thinking of concrete operators is reality bound. Presumably most 9-year-olds would have a difficult time thinking about objects that don't exist or events that could never happen. By contrast, children entering the stage of formal operations were said to be quite capable of considering hypothetical propositions and carrying them to a logical conclusion. Indeed, Piaget suspected that many formal operators would even enjoy this type of cognitive challenge.

Several years ago a group of concrete operators (9-year-old fourth-graders) and a group of children who were at or rapidly approaching formal operations (11- to 12-year-old sixth-graders) completed the following assignment:

> Suppose that you were given a third eye and that you could choose to place this eye anywhere on your body. Draw me a picture to show where you would place your "extra" eye, and then tell me why you would put it there.

All the 9-year-olds placed the third eye *on the forehead between their two natural eyes*. It seems as if these children called on their concrete experiences to complete their assignment: eyes are found somewhere around the middle of the face in all people. One 9-year-old boy remarked that the third eye should go between the other two because "that's where a cyclops has his eye." The rationales for this eye placement were rather unimaginative. Consider the following examples:

> *Jim* (age 9½): I would like an eye beside my two other eyes so that if one eye went out, I could still see with two.

> *Vickie* (age 9): I want an extra eye so I can see you three times.

> *Tanya* (age 9½): I want a third eye so I could see better.

By contrast, the older, formal-operational children gave a wide variety of responses that were not at all dependent on what they had seen previously. Furthermore, these children thought out the advantages of this hypothetical situation and provided rather imaginative rationales for placing the "extra" eye in unique locations. Here are some sample responses:

> *Ken* (age 11½): (*Draws the extra eye on top of a tuft of hair.*) I could revolve the eye to look in all directions.

> *John* (age 11½): (*Draws his extra eye in the palm of his left hand.*) I could see around corners and see what kind of cookie I'll get out of the cookie jar.

> *Tony* (age 11): (*Draws a close-up of a third eye in his mouth.*) I want a third eye in my mouth because I want to see what I am eating.

When asked their opinions of the "three eye" assignment, many of the younger children considered it rather silly and uninteresting. One 9-year-old remarked "This is stupid. Nobody has three eyes." However, the 11–12-year-olds enjoyed the task and continued to pester their teacher for "fun" art assignments "like the eye problem" for the remainder of the school year (Shaffer, 1973).

So the results of this demonstration are generally consistent with Piaget's theory. Older children who are at or rapidly approaching the stage of formal operations are more likely than younger, concrete operators to generate logical and creative responses to a hypothetical proposition and to enjoy this type of reasoning.

Tanya's, Ken's, and John's responses to the "third eye" problem.

varying one factor at a time while holding all the other factors constant. Formal operators, who rely on this systematic approach to hypothesis generation and testing, eventually discover that the oscillation of the pendulum depends on only one factor: the length of the string. By contrast, 9- to 10-year-old concrete operators are not able to generate and systematically test the full range of possibilities that would permit them to draw a logical conclusion. They often test one variable (say, string length) without holding another (weight) constant; and should they find that a short string with a heavy weight oscillates faster than a longer one with a lighter weight, they are apt to conclude erroneously that both string length and weight control the pendulum's oscillation.

In sum, formational-operational reasoning is rational, systematic, and abstract; the formal operator can think logically about *ideas* and *possibilities* as well as tangible objects and events.

Personal and Social Consequences of Formal Thought   Formal-operational thinking is a powerful tool that may change the adolescent in many ways—some good and some not so good. First the good news: As we will see in Chapter 6, formal operations may pave the way for thinking about what is possible in one's life, forming a stable identity, and achieving a much richer understanding of other people's psychological perspectives and the underlying causes of their behavior. The formal operator is also better equipped to make difficult personal decisions that involve weighing alternative courses of action and their probable consequences for the decision maker as well as other people (see Chapter 10, for example, on the development of moral reasoning). So advances in cognitive growth do help to lay the groundwork for changes in other aspects of social and personality development.

Now the bad news: Formal operations may also be related to some of the more painful aspects of the adolescent experience. Unlike younger children, who tend to accept the world as it is and to heed the dictates of authority figures, formal operators, who can imagine hypothetical alternatives to present realities, may begin to question everything—from their parents' authority to restrict their choice of friends to the need for spending billions on space exploration and cruise missiles when so many people are hungry and homeless. Indeed, the more logical inconsistencies and other flaws that adolescents detect in the real world, the more inclined they are to become frustrated with or even rebelliously angry toward the agents (for example, parents, the government) they hold responsible for these imperfect states of affairs. Piaget (1970) viewed this idealistic fascination with the way things "ought to be" as a perfectly normal outgrowth of the adolescent's newly acquired abstract reasoning abilities, and he proclaimed formal operations the primary cause of the "generation gap."

According to Piaget, adolescents can be so focused on themselves and their thinking that they actually appear more egocentric than they were during the grade-school years. David Elkind (1967, 1981) has identified two kinds of "egocentrism" that adolescents often display. The **imaginary audience** phenomenon refers to the adolescent's feeling that she is constantly "on stage" and that everyone around her is just as concerned with and as critical of her actions or appearance as she is. Thus a teenage girl who has spent hours making up her face to hide a few pimples may be convinced that her date is repulsed by them whenever he looks away—when, in truth, the equally self-conscious boy may be turning away because he's convinced that her looks of concern imply that his mouthwash has failed him.

The second form of adolescent egocentrism is what Elkind calls the **personal fable**—a belief in the *uniqueness* of oneself and one's thinking. For example, a teenager who has just been dumped by his first love may feel that no one in human history has ever experienced anything quite like *his* crushing agony. The personal fable may also help to explain many of the risks that adolescents take. After all, *they*

imaginary audience: allegedly a form of adolescent egocentrism that involves confusing one's own thoughts with those of a hypothesized audience and concluding that others share your preoccupations.

personal fable: allegedly a form of adolescent egocentrism in which the individual thinks that he and his thoughts and feelings are special or unique.

PHOTO **2.8** An adolescent may feel that others are as preoccupied with her appearance or her conduct as she is—allegedly a form of egocentrism known as the imaginary audience phenomenon.

are unique and are unlikely to be harmed by snorting cocaine or having unsafe sex: The negative consequences are much more likely to happen to others, not to me.

Elkind believed that both forms of adolescent egocentrism would increase as youngsters are first acquiring formal operations and would gradually decline over time as idealism wanes. However, the data are not always consistent with his point of view. Apparently, teenagers perceive just as many personal dangers in risky acts such as drug use, driving while intoxicated, and having unsafe sex as middle-age adults do, thus questioning the idea that adolescents feel especially unique or invulnerable (Beyth-Marom et al., 1993). Indeed, much of adolescent risk taking apparently reflects a desire to have exciting experiences rather than any feelings of invulnerability (Arnett & Balle-Jensen, 1993). And although the imaginary audience phenomenon is stronger among 13- to 15-year-olds than among older adolescents, it is often the 13- to 15-year-olds still functioning at the *concrete-operational* level who show more of this self-consciousness (Gray & Hudson, 1984; O'Conner & Nikolic, 1990)—just the reverse of what Elkind would expect. Consequently, some developmentalists now believe that the apparent self-preoccupation that adolescents display may be linked less closely to formal-operational thinking than to the development of advanced social perspective-taking skills (discussed in Chapter 6) that allow teenagers to contemplate how *other people* might perceive them or react to their behavior (Lapsley et al., 1986; Vartanian & Powlishta, 1996). Viewed in this way, adolescent egocentrism is not very "egocentric" after all.

CONTRIBUTIONS AND CRITICISMS OF PIAGET'S THEORY

Like Freud and Watson, Piaget was an innovative renegade. He was unpopular with psychometricians because he claimed that their intelligence tests measure only what children know and tell us nothing about the most important aspect of intellect—how children think. In addition, Piaget dared to study an unobservable, mentalistic concept, "cognition," that had fallen from favor among psychologists from the behaviorist tradition (Beilin, 1992).

By the 1960s, the times had clearly changed. Not only had Piaget's early theorizing and research legitimized the study of children's thinking, but his early work linking moral development to cognitive development (see Chapter 10 for an extended discussion) has contributed immensely to a whole new area of developmental research—the study of **social cognition.** Recent social-cognitive theorists such as Lawrence Kohlberg and Robert Selman have found that the same mind that gradually constructs increasingly sophisticated understandings of the physical world also comes, with age, to form more complex ideas about sex differences, moral values, the significance of human emotions, the meaning and obligations of friendship, and countless other aspects of social life. The development of social cognition is a primary focus of Chapter 6, and the links between one's social-cognitive abilities and various aspects of social and personality development are discussed throughout the text.

Piaget's theory has also had a strong impact on education. For example, popular *discovery-based* educational programs are grounded on the premise that young children do not think like adults and will learn best by having "hands-on" educational experiences with familiar aspects of their environment. So a preschool teacher in a Piagetian classroom might introduce the difficult concept of number by presenting her pupils with different quantities of objects to stack, color, or arrange. Presumably, new concepts like number are best transmitted by methods in which curious, active children can apply their existing schemes and make the critical "discoveries" for themselves.

Although Piaget is clearly a giant among behavioral scientists whose work has left deep and lasting imprints on our thinking about human development (Fischer & Bidell, 1998; Flavell, 1996), many of his ideas have now been challenged. For

social cognition: the thinking that people display about the thoughts, feelings, motives, and behaviors of themselves and other people.

example, we now know that Piaget's reliance on clinical interviews often *underestimated* children's mental competencies and social understandings, either because children were incapable of articulating what they actually knew or were unmotivated to do their best on the kinds of problems Piaget presented for them (Bjorklund, 2000). Other critics have noted that performances on Piagetian problems can often be improved dramatically through training programs—a finding that would seem to challenge Piaget's assumption that individualized discovery learning, rather than direct instruction, is necessarily the best way to promote intellectual growth.

Piaget's notion that cognitive growth proceeds through a universal and invariant sequence of stages has also been challenged, both in theory and in research (Bjorklund, 2000). In his own *sociocultural theory,* Russian developmentalist Lev Vygotsky (1978) focused on how *culture*—the beliefs, values, traditions, and skills of a social group—is transmitted from generation to generation. Vygotsky challenged the belief that children were independent explorers who make critical discoveries on their own. Instead, he saw their cognitive growth as a *socially mediated activity*—one in which children gradually acquire new ways of thinking and behaving through cooperative dialogues with more knowledgeable members of society. Vygotsky also rejected the notion that all children progress through the same stages of cognitive growth. Why? Because the new skills that children master through their interactions with more competent associates are often specific to their culture rather than being universal cognitive structures. So from Vygotsky's perspective (which we will explore more carefully in Chapter 3), Piaget largely ignores important social and cultural influences on human development.

Is cognitive development at all stagelike? In Piaget's theory, each new stage of cognitive development is portrayed as a coherent mode of thinking that is applied across a wide range of problems. Yet there is often little consistency in an individual's performance across different tasks that presumably measure the abilities defining a given stage. For example, it may be months (or even more than a year) before a 6-year-old concrete operator who can seriate is able to pass other concrete-operational problems such as conservation of liquids. These inconsistencies have led many developmentalists to conclude that cognitive growth is much less "stagelike" than Piaget had assumed (Fischer & Bidell, 1998; Flavell et al., 1993).

Finally, even those contemporary theorists who think that cognitive growth *is* stagelike are nonetheless bothered by Piaget's account of how children move from one stage of intellect to the next. Recall what Piaget says: Biological maturation, in conjunction with the constant interplay among the intellectual functions of assimilation, accommodation, and organization, permit children to construct increasingly complex schemes. Eventually they will view their experiences in completely new ways as they move to the next higher intellectual stage. Clearly, this rather vague explanation of cognitive growth raises more questions than it answers. What maturational changes are necessary before children can progress from sensorimotor to preoperational intellect or from concrete operations to formal operations? What kinds of experiences must a child have before he will construct mental symbols, use cognitive operations, or begin to operate on ideas and think about hypotheticals? Piaget is simply not very explicit about these or any other mechanisms that might enable a child to move to a higher stage of reasoning. As a result, a growing number of researchers now look on his theory as an elaborate *description* of cognitive development that has limited explanatory power (Bruner, 1997; Kuhn, 1992).

Despite these criticisms, almost no one today would challenge Piaget's notion that social and personality development depends, in part, on cognitive development. And the reason is simple: Social-developmentalists of the past half century have found—over and over again—that many important social and emotional developments occur at roughly the same time that children reach noteworthy Piagetian cognitive milestones. So even though Piaget's theory has its shortcomings, it nonetheless provides a valuable framework for understanding changes that occur in many aspects of development. It is truly a "classic" in the field of developmental psychology.

Summary

- This chapter examines three "classic" perspectives on social and personality development: the *psychoanalytic* viewpoint, *behaviorism* (or the *social-learning* viewpoint), and Piaget's *cognitive-developmental* viewpoint.

THE PSYCHOANALYTIC VIEWPOINT

- The psychoanalytic perspective originated with Sigmund Freud whose **psychosexual theory** claimed that humans are driven by inborn sexual and aggressive **instincts** (**Eros** and **Thanatos**) that must be controlled. Much of human behavior was said to reflect **unconscious motives** that people have **repressed.** Freud proposed five stages of psychosexual development—oral, anal, phallic, latency, and genital—in which three components of personality, the **id, ego,** and **superego,** emerge and become closely integrated.

- Freud's description of the **phallic stage,** and the **Oedipus** and **Electra complexes** that 3- to 6-year-olds were said to experience, has been highly controversial. According to Freud, parents must handle these sexual conflicts carefully to prevent their children from **fixating** on immature activities and showing arrested development.

- Eric Erikson's **psychosocial theory** revises and extends Freud's theory by concentrating less on the sex instinct and more on important sociocultural determinants of human development. According to Erikson, people progress through a series of eight psychosocial conflicts beginning with "**trust versus mistrust**" in infancy and concluding with "integrity versus despair" in old age. Each conflict must be resolved in favor of the positive trait (trust, for example) if development is to be healthy.

THE BEHAVIORIST (OR SOCIAL-LEARNING) VIEWPOINT

- The learning viewpoint, or **behaviorism,** originated with John B. Watson, who argued that infants are *tabulae rasae* who develop **habits** as a result of their social experiences. Development was viewed as a continuous process that could proceed in many different directions, depending on the kinds of environments to which a person is exposed. B. F. Skinner, who extended Watson's theory, claimed that development reflects the **operant** conditioning of children who are *passively* shaped by the **reinforcers** and **pun-**ishments that accompany their behaviors. By contrast, Albert Bandura's cognitive social-learning theory viewed children as *active* information processors who quickly develop many new habits through **observational learning.** Bandura rejects Watson's **environmental determinism,** proposing instead that children have a hand in creating the environments that influence their development (**reciprocal determinism**).

PIAGET'S COGNITIVE DEVELOPMENTAL VIEWPOINT

- Jean Piaget's theory of intellectual development has many important implications for social and personality development. According to Piaget, intellectual activity is a basic life function that helps the child to adapt to the environment. He describes children as active, inventive explorers (that is, **constructivists**) who are constantly constructing **schemes** to represent what they know and modifying these cognitive structures throughout the processes of **organization** and **adaptation.** Organization is the process by which children rearrange their existing knowledge into higher-order schemes. Adaptation is the process of adjusting successfully to the environment, and it occurs through two complementary activities: **assimilation** and **accommodation.**

- Piaget believed that intellectual growth proceeds through an **invariant sequence** of stages that can be summarized as follows:
  - Sensorimotor stage (0–2 years). Over the first two years, infants come to "know" and understand objects and events by acting on them. The **behavioral (or sensorimotor) schemes** that a child creates to adapt to his surroundings are eventually internalized to form mental symbols (or **symbolic schemes**) that enable the child to understand **object permanence,** to display **deferred imitation,** and to solve simple problems on a mental level without resorting to trial and error.
  - Preoperational stage (roughly 2–7 years). Symbolic reasoning becomes increasingly apparent during the **preoperational stage** as children begin to use words and images in inventive ways in their play activities. Although 2- to 7-year-olds are becoming more and more

knowledgeable about the world in which they live, their thinking is quite deficient by adult standards. Piaget describes preschool children as highly **egocentric:** They view events from their own perspective and have difficulty assuming another person's point of view. And their thinking is characterized by **centration:** When they encounter something new, they tend to focus on only one aspect of it—its most obvious or perceptually salient feature. Consequently, these **intuitive thinkers** often fail to solve such problems as **conservation** tasks that require them to evaluate several pieces of information simultaneously.

■ Concrete operations (roughly 7–11 years). During the period of **concrete operations,** children can think logically and systematically about concrete objects, events, and experiences. They can now perform arithmetical operations in their heads and mentally **reverse** the outcomes of physical actions and behavioral sequences. The acquisition of these and other **cognitive operations** permits the child to conserve, **seriate,** and make **transitive inferences.** However, concrete operators still cannot think logically about hypothetical propositions that violate their conceptions of reality.

■ Formal operations (age 11 or 12 and beyond). **Formal-operational thinking** is rational, abstract, and much like the **hypothetico-deductive reasoning** of a scientist. At this stage, adolescents can "think about thinking" and operate on ideas as well as tangible objects and events. These newly emerging cognitive powers may help to explain why adolescents are so idealistic and display such thinking as the **imaginary audience** and the **personal fable.**

■ Although Piaget has accurately described the general *sequences* of intellectual development, he often underestimates and occasionally overestimates the child's cognitive capabilities. Some investigators have challenged Piaget's assumption that development occurs in stages, while others have criticized his theory for largely ignoring social and cultural influences or failing to specify how children progress from one stage of intellect to the next. But despite its shortcomings, Piaget's theory has contributed enormously to our understanding of cognitive development, has been applied extensively in the field of education, has helped spawn the field of **social cognition,** and has provided important insights about many other aspects of social and personality development.

Chapter Three

Recent Perspectives on Social and Personality Development

Ethology: A Modern Evolutionary Perspective

Assumptions of Classical Ethology

Ethology and Human Development

Contributions and Criticisms of Evolutionary Viewpoints

Behavioral Genetics: Biological Bases for Individual Differences

Methods of Estimating Hereditary Influences

Estimating the Contributions of Genes and Environment

Hereditary Contributions to Personality and Mental Health

Heredity and Environment as Developmental Co-Conspirators

Contributions and Criticisms of the Behavioral Genetics Approach

Ecological Systems Theory: A Modern Environmentalist Perspective

Bronfenbrenner's Contexts for Development

Contributions and Criticisms of Ecological Systems Theory

Modern Cognitive Perspectives

Vygotsky's Sociocultural Theory

Contributions and Criticisms of the Sociocultural Perspective

The Social Information-Processing (or Attributional) Viewpoint

Contributions and Criticisms of the Social Information-Processing Viewpoint

Theories and Worldviews

Summary

J magine that we have been transported back to 1974 and are in the second week of a new semester, taking the first course in social and personality development that our college has ever offered. Having already reviewed the psychoanalytic and behavioristic perspectives on developing children, our professor introduced what she calls the "new look" at child development—Piaget's cognitive-developmental theory. Indeed, Piaget's theory does appear to be a fresh insight. After all, children are portrayed not as passive agents shaped by biological instincts or environmental influences but as *active* beings who play a prominent role in their own development. Furthermore, Piaget emphasizes neither nature nor nurture, choosing instead to characterize development as an intricate interplay between biological maturation and the experiences that curious, active children have and create for themselves.

Piaget's theory clearly qualified as the "new look" at social-personality development in the early 1970s. However, several new theories have emerged over the past 25 years—models that challenged, built on, and extended earlier viewpoints. Some of these recent theories emphasize biological forces, whereas others concentrate more on either environmental influences or on cognitive contributors to social and personality development. But as we will see in reviewing these theories, they all acknowledge the two points that Piaget sought to emphasize: (1) Developing persons are *active* rather than passive beings, and (2) development results from a variety of complex transactions between the forces of nature and nurture.

In the first two sections of the chapter, we become acquainted with two modern "biological" theories. The first of them—*ethology*—has strong evolutionary overtones. It focuses heavily on inherited attributes that characterize all members of the species and conspire to make us *alike* (that is, contribute to normative developmental outcomes). By contrast, the second, or *behavioral genetics*, viewpoint is concerned mainly with determining how the unique combination of genes that each person inherits might be implicated in making individuals *different* from one another.

Ethology: A Modern Evolutionary Perspective

Biological theories of human development have a long and illustrious history. Freud's psychoanalytic theory obviously had strong biological overtones. Not only were inborn instincts the motivational components of Freud's theory, but *maturation* of the sex instinct was said to determine the course (or at least the stages) of social and personality development.

Interestingly, behaviorist John B. Watson may have taken his extreme environmental stance partly in response to Freud and to other prominent biological theorists of his day, most notably Arnold Gesell (1880–1961), who argued that human development is largely a matter of biological maturation. Gesell's (1933) view was that children, much like plants, simply "bloomed," following a pattern and timetable laid out in their genes; how parents raised their young was thought to be of little importance.

Although today's developmentalists have largely rejected Gesell's radical claims, the notion that biological influences play a significant role in human development is alive and well in **ethology**—the scientific study of the evolutionary basis of behavior and the contributions of such evolved responses to the survival and development of a species (Archer, 1992b). The origins of this discipline can be traced to Charles Darwin; however, modern ethology arose from the work of Konrad Lorenz and Niko Tinbergen, two European zoologists whose animal research highlighted some important links between evolutionary processes and adaptive behaviors (Dewsbury, 1992). Here we briefly examine the central assumptions of classical ethology and their implications for human development.

ethology: the study of the bio-evolutionary bases of behavior and development.

ASSUMPTIONS OF CLASSICAL ETHOLOGY

According to Lorenz (1937, 1981) and Tinbergen (1973), members of all animal species are born with a number of "biologically programmed" behaviors that are (1) products of evolution and (2) adaptive in that they contribute to survival. Many species of birds, for example, come biologically prepared to engage in such instinctual behaviors as following their mothers (a response called *imprinting,* which helps to protect the young from predators and to ensure that they find food), building nests, and singing songs. These biologically programmed characteristics are thought to have evolved as a result of the Darwinian process of **natural selection;** that is, over the course of evolution, birds with genes responsible for these "adaptive" behaviors were more likely to survive and to pass their genes on to future generations than were birds lacking these adaptive characteristics. Over many, many generations, then, the genes underlying the most adaptive behaviors would become more widespread in the species, characterizing nearly all individuals.

So ethologists focus on inborn or instinctual responses (1) that members of a species share and (2) that seem to steer individuals along similar developmental paths. Where might one search for these adaptive behaviors and study their developmental implications? Ethologists have always preferred to study their subjects in the natural environment. They believe that the inborn attributes that shape human (or animal) development are most easily identified and understood if observed in the natural settings where they evolved and have proven to be adaptive (Hinde, 1989).

ETHOLOGY AND HUMAN DEVELOPMENT

Instinctual responses that promote survival are relatively easy to spot in animals. But do humans really display such behaviors? And if they do, how might these preprogrammed responses influence their development?

Human ethologists such as John Bowlby (1969, 1973) not only believe that children display a wide variety of preprogrammed behaviors, but they also claim that each of these responses promotes a particular kind of experience that will help the individual to survive and develop normally. For example, the cry of a human infant is thought to be a biologically programmed "distress signal" that brings caregivers running. Infants are said to be biologically programmed to convey their distress with loud, lusty cries, and ethologists also believe that caregivers are biologically predisposed to respond to such signals. So the adaptive significance of an infant's crying is to ensure (1) that the infant's basic needs (for example, for food, liquid, safety) will be met and (2) that the infant will have sufficient contact with other human beings to form primary social and emotional attachments (Bowlby, 1973).

Although ethologists are especially critical of learning theorists for largely ignoring the biological basis of human development, they are well aware that development could not progress very far without learning. For example, the cry of an infant may be an innate signal that promotes the human contact from which emotional attachments emerge. However, these emotional attachments do not simply "happen" automatically. The infant must first *learn* to discriminate familiar faces from those of strangers before he will show any evidence of being emotionally attached to a regular companion. Presumably, the adaptive significance of this discriminatory learning goes back to that period in evolutionary history when humans traveled in nomadic tribes and lived outdoors. In those days, it was crucial that an infant become attached to familiar companions and fearful of strangers, for failure to cry in response to a strange face might make the infant an easy target for a predatory animal.

Now consider the opposite side of the coin. Some caregivers who suffer from various life stresses of their own (for example, prolonged illnesses, depression, an unhappy

natural selection: an evolutionary process, proposed by Charles Darwin, stating that individuals with characteristics that promote adaptation to the environment will survive, reproduce, and pass these adaptive characteristics to offspring; those lacking these adaptive characteristics will eventually die out.

marriage, or even a habitually cranky baby) may be routinely inattentive or neglectful, so that the infant's cries rarely promote any contact with them. Such an infant is not likely to form strong emotional attachments to her caregivers and could remain rather shy and emotionally unresponsive to other people for years to come (Ainsworth, 1979, 1989). What this infant has *learned* from her early experiences is that her closest companions are undependable and are not to be trusted. Consequently, she may become ambivalent or wary around her caregivers and may later assume that other regular associates, such as teachers and peers, are equally untrustworthy individuals who should be avoided whenever possible.

How important are an individual's early learning experiences? Like Freud, the ethologists believe they are *very* important. In fact, they have argued that there may be "critical periods" for the development of many attributes and behaviors. A *critical period* is a short part of the life cycle during which the developing organism is uniquely sensitive or responsive to specific environmental influences; outside this period, the same environmental events or influences are thought to have no lasting effects. Although this concept of critical period does seem to explain certain aspects of animal development, such as imprinting in young fowl, many human ethologists think that the term *sensitive period* is a more accurate portrayal of human development. A **sensitive period** refers to a time that is optimal for the emergence of particular competencies or behaviors and in which the individual is particularly sensitive to environmental influences. The time frames of sensitive periods are less rigid, or well-defined, than those of critical periods. And development can occur outside a sensitive period, but it is much more difficult to foster then.

PHOTO **3.1** The cry is a distress signal that attracts the attention of caregivers.

To illustrate, some ethologists believe that the first three years of life are a sensitive period for the development of social and emotional responsiveness in human beings (Bowlby, 1973). Presumably, we are most susceptible to forming close emotional ties during the first three years, and should we have little or no opportunity to do so during this period, we would find it difficult to make close friends or to enter into intimate emotional relationships with other people later in life. Clearly, this is a most interesting and provocative claim about the emotional lives of human beings—one that we will examine carefully when we consider the long-term effects of early social and emotional development in Chapter 5.

In sum, ethologists clearly acknowledge that we are heavily influenced by our experiences. Yet they are quick to remind us that we are inherently biological creatures whose inborn characteristics affect the kinds of learning experiences we are likely to have.

Ethology Versus Modern Evolutionary Theory Like ethologists, proponents of a movement known as *modern evolutionary theory* are also interested in specifying how natural selection might predispose us to develop adaptive traits, motives, and behaviors. However, evolutionary theorists make assumptions about the workings of evolution that are different from those of ethologists. Recall the ethological notion that preselected adaptive behaviors are those that ensure survival of the *individual*. Evolu-

sensitive period: period of time that is optimal for the development of particular capacities, or behaviors, and in which the individual is particularly sensitive to environmental influences that would foster these attributes.

tionary theorists disagree, arguing instead that preselected, adaptive motives and behaviors are those that ensure the survival and spread of the *individual's genes*. This may seem like a subtle distinction, but it is an important one. Consider the personal sacrifice made by a father who perished after saving his children from a house fire. This is hard for an ethologist to explain, for the father's selflessness does not promote his survival. Evolutionary theorists, however, view the father's motives and behavior as highly adaptive because his children carry his genes and have many more reproductive years ahead of them than he does. Thus, from the modern evolutionary perspective, the father has ensured the survival and spread of *his genes* (or literally, of those who carry his genes), even if he should perish from his actions.

Let's briefly consider how the evolutionary history of our species might have led to sex differences in one socially significant attribute—human mating preferences (Buss, 1995). The average male produces billions of sperm in his lifetime, making sperm plentiful compared to ova. Thus, if males are interested in spreading and preserving their genes, it stands to reason from an evolutionary perspective that they might best serve this unconscious biological motive by seeking to fertilize many females. Moreover, males ought to seek *youthful, attractive* partners because these attributes imply fertility, sexual interest, and hence, reproductive success. Females should be just as interested as males are in preserving their genes for posterity. But because a woman can produce fewer offspring than a man and her investment in her offspring is great (having to bear, nurse, and raise them), she should be inclined to seek a mate who has the tangible resources (wealth, power) and psychological attributes (kindness, a capacity for love) that will aid her in protecting and nurturing her children.

Interestingly, men's and women's mating preferences do tend to confirm these predictions, with men the world over being more inclined than women to seek mates who are younger and attractive, and women being more inclined to seek an older and kindly mate with ample resources who is emotionally attracted to her (see Buss, 1995; Myers, 1999). So modern evolutionary theorists contend that the largely unconscious purpose of protecting and maximizing the number of genes we leave to posterity can explain sex differences in mating preferences. (Of course, other interpretations are possible. As an exercise, you might see whether you can explain the findings cited here using one or more of the other theories covered in this or the previous chapter).

CONTRIBUTIONS AND CRITICISMS OF EVOLUTIONARY VIEWPOINTS

If this text had been written in 1974, it would not have included any evolutionary perspectives. Although ethology came into its own during the 1960s, the early ethologists studied animal behavior; only within the past 15 to 20 years have proponents of ethology or modern evolutionary theory made a serious attempt to specify evolutionary contributions to human development, and many of their hypotheses could still be considered speculative (Lerner & von Eye, 1992). Nevertheless, proponents of evolutionary perspectives have already contributed importantly to our discipline by reminding us that every child is a biological creature who comes equipped with a number of adaptive, genetically programmed characteristics—attributes that will influence other people's reactions to the child and thus the course that development is likely to take. In addition, the ethologists have made a major methodological contribution by showing us the value of (1) studying human development in normal, everyday settings and (2) comparing human development with that of other species.

One very intriguing ethological notion that we will discuss in detail in Chapter 4 is that infants are inherently sociable creatures who are quite capable of promoting and sustaining social interactions from the day they are born. This viewpoint contrasts

Box 3.1   *Focus on Research*

Is Altruism a Part of Human Nature?

Darwin's notion of "survival of the fittest" seems to argue against altruism as an inborn motive. Many have interpreted Darwin's idea to mean that powerful, self-serving individuals who place their own needs ahead of others' are the ones who are most likely to survive. If this were so, evolution would favor the development of selfish, egoistic motives—not altruism—as basic components of human nature.

Martin Hoffman (1981) has challenged this point of view, listing several reasons that the concept of "survival of the fittest" actually implies altruism. His arguments hinge on the assumption that human beings are more likely to receive protection from natural enemies and to satisfy all their basic needs if they have genes that predispose them to be socially outgoing and to live together in cooperative social groups. If this assumption is correct, cooperative, altruistic individuals would be the ones who are most likely to survive long enough to pass along their "altruistic genes" to their offspring; individualists who "go it alone" would probably succumb to famine, predators, or some other natural disaster that they could not cope with by themselves. So, over thousands of generations, natural selection would favor the development of such innate social motives as altruism. Presumably, the tremendous survival value of being "social" makes altruism, cooperation, and other social motives much more plausible as components of human nature than competition, selfishness, and the like.

It is obviously absurd to argue that infants routinely help other people. However, Hoffman believes that even newborn babies are capable of recognizing and experiencing the emotions of others. This ability, known as **empathy,** is thought to be an important contributor to altruism, for a person must recognize that others are distressed in some way before he or she is likely to help. So Hoffman is suggesting that at least one precursor of altruism—empathy—is present at birth.

Hoffman's claim is based on an experiment (Sagi & Hoffman, 1976) in which infants less than 36 hours old listened to (1) another infant's cries, (2) an equally loud computer simulation of a crying infant, or (3) no sounds at all (silence). The infants who heard a real infant crying soon began to cry themselves, to display physical signs of agitation such as kicking, and to grimace. Infants exposed to the simulated cry or to silence cried much less and seemed not to be very discomforted. (A second study by Martin & Clark, 1982, has confirmed these observations).

Hoffman argues that there is something quite distinctive about the human cry. His contention is that infants listen to and experience the distress of (that is, empathize with) another crying infant and become distressed themselves. Of course, this finding does not conclusively demonstrate that humans are altruistic by nature. But it does imply that the capacity for empathy may be present at birth and thus serve as a biological foundation for the eventual development of altruistic behavior.

---

sharply with that of behaviorists, who portray the newborn as a *tabula rasa,* or with Piaget's "asocial" infant, who is said to enter the world equipped with only a few basic reflexes. Ethologists also believe that we humans have evolved in ways that predispose us to develop and display prosocial motives such as *altruism* that contribute to the common good and permit us to live and work together in harmony. Box 3.1 describes some observations suggesting that there may be a biological basis for certain aspects of altruism.

By way of criticism, evolutionary approaches are like psychoanalytic theory in being very hard to test. How does one demonstrate that various motives, mannerisms, and behaviors are inborn, are adaptive, or are products of evolutionary history? Such claims are difficult to confirm. Harvard paleontologist Steven Jay Gould (1978) has criticized all evolutionary theorists for constructing "just-so stories" to explain how various forms of social behavior have been naturally selected because of their adaptive value. A just-so story is an explanation that sounds plausible and, in fact, may be true but is not supported by any *conclusive* evidence. (Indeed, the explanation given in Box 3.1 for the evolution of altruism in group contexts could be con-

empathy: the ability to experience the same emotions that someone else is experiencing.

sidered a just-so story.) This is a strong critique, for theories that easily lend themselves to just-so stories lack one important characteristic of a *useful* scientific model: They are nearly impossible to falsify. Evolutionary theories have also been criticized as being *retrospective* or "post hoc" explanations of development. One can easily apply evolutionary concepts to explain what has already happened, but can the theories *predict* what is likely to happen in the future? Many developmentalists believe that they cannot.

Finally, proponents of other viewpoints (mostly notably, social-learning theory) have argued that even if the bases for certain motives or behaviors are biologically programmed, these innate responses will soon become so modified by learning that it may not be helpful to spend much time wondering about their prior evolutionary significance. Even some strong, genetically influenced attributes can easily be modified by experience. Consider, for example, that young mallard ducklings clearly prefer their mothers' vocal calls to those of other birds (for example, chickens)—a behavior that ethologists say is innate and adaptive, as well as being a product of mallard evolution. Yet Gilbert Gottlieb (1991) has shown that duckling embryos that were exposed to chicken calls before hatching came to prefer the call of a chicken to that of a mallard mother! In this case, the ducklings' prenatal *experiences* overrode a genetic predisposition. Of course, human beings have a much greater capacity for learning than ducklings do, thus leading many critics to argue that cultural learning experiences quickly overshadow innate evolutionary mechanisms in shaping human conduct and character. Albert Bandura (1973), for example, makes the following observation when comparing the aggressive behavior of humans and animals:

> [Unlike animals], man does not rely heavily on auditory, postural, or olfactory signals for conveying aggressive intent or appeasement. He has [developed] a much more intricate system of communication—namely language—for controlling aggression. National leaders can . . . better safeguard against catastrophic violence by verbal communiques than by snapping their teeth or erecting their hair, especially in view of the prevalence of baldness among the higher echelons. (p. 16)

Despite these criticisms, evolutionary viewpoints are most valuable additions to the developmental sciences. Not only have they provided a healthy balance to the heavily environmental emphasis of learning theories, but they have also convinced more developmentalists to look for the causes of development in the *natural environment* where it actually occurs.

Now let's turn to a second modern biological perspective that is becoming increasingly influential: the *behavioral genetics* approach.

Behavioral Genetics: Biological Bases for Individual Differences

In recent years, investigators from a number of academic disciplines have asked the question, "Are there specific abilities, traits, and patterns of behavior that depend very heavily on the *particular combination* of genes that an individual inherits, and if so, are these attributes likely to be modified by one's experiences?" Those who focus on these issues in their research are known as *behavioral geneticists.*

Before we take a closer look at the field of **behavioral genetics,** let's dispel a common myth. Although behavioral geneticists view development as the process through which one's **genotype** (the set of genes one inherits) comes to be expressed as a **phenotype** (one's observable characteristics and behaviors), they are *not* strict hereditarians. Instead, they claim that most behavioral attributes are the end product of a long and involved interplay between hereditary predispositions and environmental influences.

behavioral genetics: the scientific study of how genotype interacts with environment to determine behavioral attributes such as intelligence, personality, and mental health.

genotype: the genetic endowment that an individual inherits.

phenotype: the ways in which a person's genotype is expressed in observable or measurable characteristics.

Consider an example. A child who inherits genes for tall stature will almost certainly grow taller than one who inherits genes for short stature if these children are raised in the same environment. But if the first child receives very poor nutrition early in life and the second is well nourished, they may be about the same height as adults. Thus, the behavioral geneticist is well aware that even attributes such as physical stature that seem to have a very strong hereditary component are often modified in important ways by environmental influences.

How, then, do behavioral geneticists differ from ethologists and modern evolutionary theorists, who are also interested in the biological bases of development? The answer is relatively simple. As we noted earlier, proponents of evolutionary viewpoints study inherited attributes that characterize *all* members of a species and conspire to make them *alike* (that is, attributes that contribute to *common* developmental outcomes). By contrast, behavioral geneticists focus on the biological bases for *variation* among members of a species. They are concerned with determining how the unique combination of genes that each of us inherits might be implicated in making us *different* from one another. Let's now consider the methods they use to approach this task.

METHODS OF ESTIMATING HEREDITARY INFLUENCES

Behavioral geneticists rely on two major strategies to assess hereditary contributions to behavior: *selective breeding* and *family studies*. Each of these approaches attempts to specify the **heritability** of various attributes—that is, the amount of variation in a trait or a class of behavior that is attributable to hereditary factors.

Selective Breeding   Some investigators have looked for hereditary contributions to various behavioral attributes by deliberately manipulating animal genotypes in an attempt to "breed" for these attributes. A classic example of such a **selective breeding experiment** is R. C. Tryon's (1940) attempt to show that maze-learning ability is a heritable attribute in rats. Tryon first tested a large number of rats for the ability to run a complex maze. Rats that made few errors were labeled "maze-bright"; those that made many errors were termed "maze-dull." Then, across several generations, Tryon mated bright rats with other bright rats and dull rats with dull rats. He also controlled the environments to which the rats were exposed to rule out their contribution to differences in maze-learning performance. As we see in Figure 3.1, differences across generations in the maze-learning performances of the maze-bright and maze-dull groups became progressively greater. Clearly, Tryon showed that maze-learning ability in rats is influenced by their genetic makeup. Other investigators have used this same selective breeding technique to show that genes contribute to such attributes as activity level, emotionality, aggressiveness, and sex drive in rats, mice, and chickens (Plomin et al., 1997).

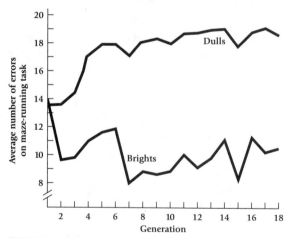

FIGURE 3.1   Maze-running performance by inbred maze-bright and maze-dull rats over 18 generations. (From Plomin et al., 1997.)

Family Studies   Because people don't take kindly to the idea of being selectively bred by experimenters, human behavioral genetics relies on an alternative methodology known as the family study. In a typical family study, people who live in the same household are compared to see how similar they are on one or more attributes. If the attribute in question is heritable, then the similarity between any two pairs of individuals who live in the same environment should increase as a function of their **kinship**—that is, the extent to which they have the same genes.

heritability: the amount of variability in a trait that is attributable to hereditary factors.

selective breeding experiment: a method of studying genetic influences by determining whether traits can be bred in animals through selective mating.

kinship: the extent to which two individuals have genes in common.

twin design: study in which sets of twins that differ in zygosity (kinship) are compared to determine the heritability of an attribute.

adoption design: study in which adoptees are compared with their biological relatives and their adoptive relatives to estimate the heritability of an attribute.

concordance rate: the percentage of cases in which a particular attribute is present for one member of a twin pair if it is present for the other.

Two kinds of family (or kinship) studies are common today. The first is the **twin design,** or **twin study,** which asks the question, "Are pairs of identical twins reared together more similar to each other on various attributes than pairs of fraternal twins reared together?" If genes affect the attribute(s) in question, then identical twins should be more similar, for they have 100% of their genes in common (kinship = 1.00), whereas fraternal twins share only 50% (kinship = .50).

The second common family study, or **adoption design,** focuses on adoptees who are genetically unrelated to other members of their adoptive families. A researcher searching for hereditary influences would ask, "Are adopted children similar to their biological parents, whose *genes* they share (Kinship = .50), or are they similar to their adoptive parents, whose *environment* they share?" If adoptees resemble their biological parents in temperament or personality, even though these parents did not raise them, then genes must be influential in determining such attributes.

Family studies can also help us to estimate the extent to which various abilities and behaviors are influenced by the environment. To illustrate, consider a case in which two genetically unrelated adopted children are raised in the same home. Their degree of kinship with each other and with their adoptive parents is .00. Consequently, there is no reason to suspect that these children will resemble each other or their adoptive parents unless their common environment plays some part in determining their standing on the attribute in question. Another way the effects of environment can be inferred is to compare identical twins raised in the same environment with identical twins raised in different environments. The kinship of all pairs of identical twins, reared together or apart, is 1.00. So, if identical twins reared together are more alike on an attribute than identical twins reared apart, we can infer that the environment plays a role in determining that attribute.

ESTIMATING THE CONTRIBUTIONS OF GENES AND ENVIRONMENT

Behavioral geneticists rely on some reasonably simple mathematical calculations to determine (1) whether a trait is genetically influenced and (2) the degree to which heredity *and* environment account for individual differences in that trait. When studying traits that a person either does or does not display (for example, a drug habit or clinical depression), researchers calculate and compare **concordance rates**—the percentages of pairs of people (for example, identical twins, fraternal twins, parents and their adoptive children) in which *both* members of the pair display the trait if one member does. Suppose you are interested in determining whether homosexuality in men is genetically influenced. You might locate gay men who have twins, either identical or fraternal, and then track down their twin siblings to determine whether they too are gay. As shown in Figure 3.2, the concordance rate for identical twins in one such study was much higher (29 of the 56 co-twins of gay men were also gay) than the concordance rate for fraternal twins (12 of the 54 co-twins were also gay). This suggests that genotype does contribute to a man's sexual orientation. But because identical twins are not perfectly concordant for sexual orientation, we can also conclude that their *experiences* (that is, environmental influences) must also influence their sexual orientations, despite their identical genes.

For continuous traits that can assume many values (for example, aggressiveness, intelligence), behavioral geneticists estimate hereditary contributions by calculating *correlation coefficients* rather than concordance rates. In a study of IQ scores, for example,

PHOTO 3.2 Because identical twins have identical genotypes, they are a rich source of information about possible hereditary contributions to personality and social behavior.

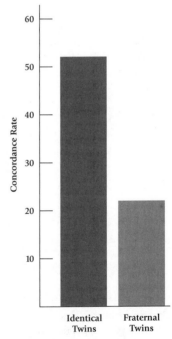

FIGURE 3.2 Concordance rates for homosexuality in 110 male twin pairs. From the higher concordance for identical twin pairs, we can infer that genes influence one's sexual orientation. Yet, the fact that only half the identical twin pairs share the same sexual orientation despite their identical genes also implies that environment contributes to one's sexual orientation as well. (Adapted from Bailey & Pillard, 1991.)

a correlation coefficient indicates whether the IQ scores of twins are systematically related to the IQ scores of their co-twins. Larger correlations indicate closer resemblances in IQ, thus implying that if one twin is bright, the other is bright too, and if one twin is dull, the other is probably dull as well.

As we noted earlier, behavioral genetics studies always tell us about *both* genetic and environmental influences on development. This point is easily illustrated by considering a review of family studies of intellectual performance (IQ) based on 112,942 pairs of children, adolescents, or adults, the results of which appear in Table 3-1. Here we will focus on the twin correlations (identical and fraternal) to show how behavioral geneticists can estimate the contributions of three factors to individual differences in intellectual performance (IQ).

Gene Influences   Genetic influences on IQ are clearly evident in Table 3-1. The correlations become higher when pairs of people are more closely related genetically and are highest when the pairs are identical twins. But just how strong is the hereditary influence?

Behavioral geneticists use statistical techniques to estimate the amount of variation in a trait that is attributable to hereditary factors. This index, called a **heritability coefficient**, is calculated as follows from twin data.

$$H = (r \text{ identical twins} - r \text{ fraternal twins}) \times 2$$

Translated, the equation reads: Heritability of an attribute equals the correlation between identical twins minus the correlation between fraternal twins, all multiplied by a factor of 2 (Plomin, 1990).

Now we can estimate the contribution that genes make to individual differences in intellectual performance. If we focus on sets of twins raised together from Table 3-1, our estimate becomes

$$H = (.86 - .60) \times 2 = .52$$

The resulting heritability estimate for IQ is .52; on a scale ranging from 0 (not at all heritable) to 1.00 (totally heritable), this figure is moderate at best. We might conclude that within the population from which we drew our twins reared together, IQ is influenced to a moderate extent by hereditary factors. However, it appears

---

TABLE 3-1   Average correlation coefficients for intelligence-test scores from family studies involving persons at four levels of kinship

GENETIC RELATIONSHIP (KINSHIP)	REARED TOGETHER (IN SAME HOME)	REARED APART (IN DIFFERENT HOMES)
Unrelated siblings (kinship = .00)	+.34	−.01[a]
Adoptive parent/adoptive offspring (kinship = .00)	+.19	—
Half-siblings (kinshiip = .25)	+.31	—
Biological parent/child (kinship = .50)	+.42	+.22
Siblings (kinship = .50)	+.47	+.24
Twins		
Fraternal (kinship = .50)	+.60	+.52
Identical (kinship = 1.00)	+.86	+.72

[a]This is the correlation obtained from random pairings of unrelated people living apart.
SOURCE: From Bouchard & McGue, 1981.

heritability coefficient: a numerical estimate, ranging from .00 to +1.00, of the amount of variation in an attribute that is due to hereditary factors.

that much of the variability among people on this trait is attributable to non-hereditary factors—that is, to environmental influences and to errors we may have made in measuring the trait (no measure is perfect). Interestingly, the data in Table 3-1 also allow us to estimate the contributions of *two* sources of environmental influence.

Nonshared Environmental Influences (NSE)   Experiences that are unique to the individual—*not* shared by other members of the family—are called **nonshared environmental influences.** These nonshared experiences are thought to make family members *different* from each other (Rowe & Plomin, 1981; Rowe, 1994). Where is evidence of nonshared environmental influence in Table 3-1? Notice that identical twins raised together are not perfectly similar in IQ, even though they share 100% of their genes and the same family environment: A correlation of +.86, though substantial, is less than a perfect correlation of +1.00. Because identical twins share the same genes and family environment, any *differences* between twins raised together must necessarily be due to differences in their *experiences.* Perhaps they were treated differently by friends, or perhaps one twin favors puzzles and other intellectual games more than the other twin does. Because the only factor that can make identical twins raised together any *different* from each other are experiences they do *not* share, we can estimate the influence of nonshared environmental influences by the following formula (Rowe & Plomin, 1981):

$$NSF = 1 - r \text{ (identical twins reared together)}$$

So, the contribution of nonshared environmental influences to individual differences in IQ performance (that is, $1 - .86 = .14$) is small but detectable nevertheless. As we will see, nonshared environmental influences make a greater contribution to other attributes, most notably personality traits.

Shared Environmental Influences (SE)   Experiences that individuals living in the same home environment share and that conspire to make them *similar* to each other are called **shared environmental influences.** As you can see in Table 3-1, both identical and fraternal twins (and, indeed, biological siblings and pairs of unrelated individuals) show a greater intellectual resemblance if they live together than if they live apart. One reason that growing up in the same home may increase children's degree of intellectual similarity is that parents model similar interests for *all* their children and tend to rely on similar strategies to foster their intellectual growth (Hoffman, 1991; Lewin et al., 1993).

How do we estimate the contribution of shared environmental influence (SE) to a trait? One rough estimate can be made as follows:

$$SE = 1 - (H + NSE)$$

Translated, the equation reads: Shared environmental influences on a trait equal 1 (the total variation for that trait) minus the variation attributable to genes (H) *and* nonshared environmental influences (NSE). Previously, we found that the heritability of IQ in our twins-reared-together sample was .52, and the contribution of nonshared environment was .14. So, the contribution of shared environmental influences to individual differences in IQ (that is, $SE = 1 - [.52 + .14] = .34$) is moderate and meaningful.

One final note: While heritability coefficients are useful for estimating whether genes make any meaningful contribution to various human attributes, these statistics are poorly understood and often misinterpreted. In Box 3.2, we take a closer look at what heritability estimates *can* and *cannot* tell us.

nonshared environmental influence (NSE):   an environmental influence that people living together do not share and should make these individuals different from one another.

shared environmental influence (SE):   an environmental influence that people living together share and should make these individuals similar to one another.

Box 3.2   *Current Controversies*

Some Common Misconceptions about Heritability Estimates

Heritability coefficients are controversial statistics that are poorly understood and frequently misapplied. One of the biggest misconceptions that people hold is the notion that heritability coefficients can tell us whether we have inherited a trait. *This idea is simply incorrect.* When we talk about the heritability of an attribute, we are referring to the extent to which *differences* among individuals on that attribute are related to differences in the genes they have inherited (Plomin, 1994). To illustrate that *heritable* means something other than *inherited,* consider that everyone inherits two eyes. Agreed? Yet the heritability of eyes is .00, simply because everyone has two and there are no individual differences in "eyeness" (except for those attributable to environmental events such as accidents).

In interpreting heritability coefficients, it is important to recognize that these estimates apply only to populations and *never to individuals.* So if you studied the heights of many pairs of 5-year-old twins and estimated the heritability of height to be .70, you could infer that a major reason that 5-year-olds *differ* in height is that they have different genes. But since heritability estimates say nothing about individuals, it is clearly inappropriate to conclude from an *H* of .70 that 70% of Freddie Jones's height is inherited, while the remaining 30% reflects the contribution of environment.

Let's also note that heritability estimates refer only to the particular trait in question as displayed by members of a *particular population* under *particular environmental circumstances.* Indeed, heritability coefficients may differ substantially for different populations raised in different environments. Suppose, for example, we located a large number of identical and fraternal twin infants, each of whom was raised in an impoverished orphanage in which his or her crib was lined with sheets that prevented much visual or social contact with other infants or with adult caregivers. Previous research (that we will examine in Chapter 5) suggests that if we measured how sociable these infants are, we would find that they vary somewhat in sociability but that virtually all of them would be much less sociable than babies raised at home—a finding we could reasonably attribute to their socially impoverished early environment. But because these twins experienced *the same depriving environment,* the only reason they might show any *differences* in sociability is due to differences in their genetic predispositions. The heritability coefficient for sociability would actually approach 1.0 in this sample—a far cry from the *H*s of .25 to .40 found in studies of other infants raised at home with parents (Plomin, 1994).

Finally, people have often assumed that genetically influenced traits cannot be modified by environmental influences. *This, too, is a false assumption!* In Chapter 5, for example, we will see that the depressed sociability of institutionalized infants can be improved substantially by placing them with responsive, socially stimulating adoptive families. To assume that *heritable* means *unchangeable* (as some critics of social programs for the socially and intellectually disadvantaged have done) is to commit a potentially grievous error based on a common misconception about the meaning of heritability coefficients.

In sum, the term *heritable* is not a synonym for *inherited,* and heritability estimates, which may vary widely across populations and environments, can tell us nothing about the development of individuals. And though heritability estimates are useful for helping us to determine whether there is any hereditary basis for the *differences* people display on any attribute we might care to study, they say nothing about children's capacity for change and should not be used to make public policy decisions that could constrain children's development or adversely affect their welfare.

HEREDITARY CONTRIBUTIONS TO PERSONALITY AND MENTAL HEALTH

Although psychologists have typically assumed that the relatively stable habits and traits that make up our personalities are shaped by our environments, family studies and other longitudinal projects reveal that many core dimensions of personality are genetically influenced (Loehlin, 1992; Plomin, 1994). For example, **introversion-extroversion**—the extent to which a person is shy, retiring, and uncomfortable

introversion/extroversion: the opposite poles of a personality dimension: Introverts are shy, anxious around others, and tend to withdraw from social situations; extroverts are highly sociable and enjoy being with others.

around others versus outgoing and socially oriented—shows about the same moderate level of heritability as IQ does (Martin & Jardine, 1986).

Another important attribute that may be genetically influenced is **empathic concern.** A person high in empathy recognizes the needs of others and is concerned about their welfare. In Box 3.1 we saw that newborn infants will react to the distress of another infant by becoming distressed themselves—a finding that implies that the capacity for empathy may be innate. But are there any biological bases for *individual differences* in empathic concern?

Indeed there are. As early as 14 to 20 months of age, identical twin infants are already more similar in their levels of concern for distressed companions than fraternal twin infants are (Zahn-Waxler, Robinson, & Emde, 1992). And by middle age, identical twins who have lived apart for many years since leaving home still resemble each other on measures of empathic concern ($r = + .41$), whereas fraternal twins do not ($r = + .05$), thus suggesting that this attribute is a reasonably heritable trait (Matthews et al., 1981). In fact, the authors of this adult twin study noted that "if empathic concern . . . leads to altruistic motivation, [our] study provides evidence for a genetic basis for individual differences in altruism" (p. 246).

How Much Genetic Influence?   To what extent are our personalities influenced by the genes we have inherited? We get some idea by looking at personality resemblances among family members, as shown in Table 3-2. Note that identical twins are more similar to each other on this composite measure of personality than are fraternal twins. Were we to use the twin data to estimate the genetic contribution to personality, we might conclude that many personality traits are moderately heritable (that is, $H = + .40$ in this sample). Of course, one implication of a moderate heritability coefficient is that personality is strongly influenced by environmental factors.

Which Aspects of Environment Influence Personality?   Developmentalists have traditionally assumed that the home environment that individuals *share* is especially important in shaping their personalities. Now examine Table 3-2 again and see whether you can find some problems with this logic. Notice, for example, that genetically unrelated individuals who live in the same home barely resemble each other on the composite personality measure ($r = .07$). Therefore, aspects of the home environment that all family members *share* must not contribute much to the development of personality.

How, then, does environment affect personality? According to behavioral geneticists David Rowe and Robert Plomin (1981; Rowe, 1994), the aspects of environment

TABLE 3-2   Personality resemblances among family members at three levels of kinship

	KINSHIP			
	1.00 (IDENTICAL TWINS)	.50 (FRATERNAL TWINS)	.50 (NONTWIN SIBLINGS)	.00 (UNRELATED CHILDREN RAISED IN THE SAME HOUSEHOLD)
Personality attributes (average correlations across several personality traits)	.50	.30	.20	.07

SOURCES: J. C. Loehlin, "Fitting Heredity-Environment Models Jointly to Twin and Adoption Data from the California Psychological Inventory." *Behavior Genetics,* 1985, *15,* 199–221. Also J. C. Loehlin & R. C. Nichols, *Heredity, Environment, and Personality.* Copyright © 1976 by the University of Texas Press.

empathic concern: a measure of the extent to which an individual recognizes the needs of others and is concerned about their welfare.

that contribute most heavily to personality are *nonshared environmental influences*—influences that make individuals *different* from each other. And there are many sources of nonshared experience in a typical home. Parents, for example, often treat sons differently from daughters, or first-born children differently from later-borns. To the extent that siblings are not treated alike by parents, they will experience different environments, which will increase the likelihood that their personalities will differ in important ways. Interactions among siblings provide another source of nonshared environmental influence. For example, an older sibling who habitually dominates a younger one may become generally assertive and dominant as a result of these home experiences. But for the younger child, this home environment is a dominating environment that may foster the development of such personality traits as passivity, tolerance, and cooperation.

Measuring the Effects of Nonshared Environments　How could we ever measure the impact of something as broad as nonshared environments? One strategy used by Denise Daniels and her associates (Daniels, 1986; Daniels & Plomin, 1985a) is simply to ask pairs of adolescent siblings whether they were treated differently by parents and teachers or experienced other important differences in their lives—for example, differences in their popularity with peers. Daniels finds that siblings do report such differences, and more important, the greater the *differences* in parental treatment and other experiences that siblings report, the more dissimilar siblings are in their personalities. Although correlational studies of this sort do not conclusively establish that differences in experiences *cause* differences in personality, they suggest that some of the most important environmental influences on development may be nonshared experiences unique to each member of the family (Dunn & Plomin, 1990).

Now an important question: Do siblings have different experiences because they have different genes? Stated another way, isn't it possible that a child's genetically influenced attributes might affect how other people respond to her, so that a physically attractive youngster, for example, is apt to be treated very differently by parents and peers than a less attractive sibling would be? Although genes do contribute to some extent to the different experiences that siblings have (Baker & Daniels, 1990; Pike et al., 1996; Plomin et al., 1994), there is ample reason to believe that our highly individualized, unique environments are not entirely due to our having inherited different genes. How do we know this?

The most important clue comes from studies of identical twins. Since identical twins are perfectly matched from a genetic standpoint, any *differences* between them must necessarily reflect the contribution of environmental influences that they do *not* share. Clearly, these nonshared environmental influences cannot be attributed to the twins' different genes, because identical twins have identical genotypes! This is why the formula for estimating the contribution of nonshared environmental influences (that is, $1 - r$ [identical twins raised together]) makes sense, because the estimate it provides is based on environmental influences that are *not* in any way influenced by genes.

With these facts in mind, let's return to Table 3-2. Here we see that the average correlation for identical twins across many personality traits is only + .50, which implies that identical twins are alike in some respects and different in others. Applying the formula for estimating NSE ($1 - .50 = .50$) tells us that nonshared environmental influences are very important contributors to personality—at least as important as genes are.

In sum, the family environment does contribute importantly to personality, but not simply because it has a standard effect on all family members that makes them alike. True, there are some important areas of socialization for which parents do treat all their children alike and foster similarities among them (Hoffman, 1991). For example, parents often model and encourage the same moral, religious, and political interests and values in all their children. For these and many other psychological characteristics, *shared environmental influences* are often as important or even more important than genes are in creating likenesses between brothers and sisters (Hoffman, 1991, 1994; Plomin, 1990). But when it comes to the shaping of many other basic personality traits, it is the *nonshared* experiences people have—in concert with genetic influences—that contribute most to their phenotypes (Plomin, et al., 1997; McGue, Sharma, & Benson, 1996; Pike et al., 1996).

Hereditary Contributions to Behavior Disorders and Mental Illnesses   Is there a hereditary basis for mental illness? Might some people be genetically predisposed to commit deviant or antisocial acts? Although these ideas seemed absurd 30 years ago, it now appears that the answer to both questions is a qualified yes.

Consider the evidence for **schizophrenia**—a serious mental illness characterized by severe disturbances in logical thinking, emotional expression, and social behavior, which typically emerges in late adolescence or early adulthood. A survey of several twin studies of schizophrenia suggests an average concordance rate of .46 for identical twins but only .14 for fraternal twins (Gottesman & Shields, 1982). In addition, children who have a biological parent who is schizophrenic are at increased risk of becoming schizophrenic themselves, even if they are adopted and raised by another family early in life (Loehlin, 1992). These are strong indications that schizophrenia is genetically influenced. In fact, investigators have recently found *genetic markers* for schizophrenia (that is, parts of genes that are suspected to be linked to the illness) on two of the 23 pairs of human chromosomes (DeAngelis, 1997a).

In recent years, it has also become quite clear that heredity contributes to abnormal behaviors and conditions such as alcoholism, criminality and delinquency, depression, hyperactivity, *manic-depressive* psychosis, and a number of *neurotic disorders* (Baker et al., 1989; Plomin et al., 1997; Rowe, 1994). Now, you may have or have had close relatives who were diagnosed as alcoholic, neurotic, manic-depressive, or schizophrenic. Rest assured that does *not* mean that you or your children will develop these problems. Only 5% to 10% of children who have one schizophrenic parent ever develop any symptoms that might be labeled "schizophrenic" (DeAngelis, 1997a). Even if you are an identical twin whose co-twin has a serious psychiatric disorder, the odds are between 1 in 2 (for schizophrenia) and 1 in 20 (for most other disorders) that you would ever experience anything that even approaches the problem that affects your twin.

Since identical twins are often *discordant* (that is, not alike) with respect to mental illness and behavioral disorders, environment must be a very important contributor to these conditions. In other words, people do not inherit behavioral disorders; instead, they inherit *predispositions* to develop certain illnesses or deviant patterns of behavior. And even when a child's family history suggests that such a genetic predisposition may exist, usually one or more very stressful experiences (for example, rejection by parents, a failure or series of failures at school, or dissolution of the family due to divorce) is required to trigger a disorder (Plomin & Rende, 1991; Rutter, 1979). Clearly, these findings provide some basis for optimism, for it may be possible someday to prevent the onset of most genetically influenced disorders should we (1) learn more about the environmental triggers that precipitate these disturbances while (2) striving to develop interventions or therapeutic techniques that will help high-risk individuals maintain their emotional stability in the face of environmental stress.

schizophrenia: a serious form of mental illness characterized by disturbances in logical thinking, emotional expression, and interpersonal behavior.

HEREDITY AND ENVIRONMENT
AS DEVELOPMENTAL CO-CONSPIRATORS

After reviewing a portion of the literature and seeing how behavioral geneticists estimate the contribution of heredity to various attributes, we should be able to see that both heredity and environment contribute in important ways to our cognitive performances, personalities, and mental health. But how? Our discussion thus far might lead us to think that heredity and environment are *independent* sources of influence, much as they were portrayed 35 years ago when developmentalists were embroiled in the great nature/nurture debate. Today, behavioral geneticists believe that our genes may actually influence the kinds of environments we are likely to experience (Plomin et al., 1997; Scarr & McCartney, 1983). How? In at least three ways.

Passive Genotype/Environmental Correlations   According to Sandra Scarr and Kathleen McCartney (1983), the home environment parents provide for their children is influenced, in part, by the parents' own genotypes. And since parents also provide their children with genes, the rearing environments to which children are exposed are correlated with (and are likely to suit) their own genotypes.

The following example illustrates a developmental implication of these **passive genotype/environment correlations.** Parents who are genetically predisposed to be athletic may create a very athletic home environment by encouraging their children to play vigorously and to take an interest in sports. Besides being exposed to an athletic environment, the children may have inherited their parents' athletic genes, which might make them particularly responsive to that environment. So children of athletic parents may come to enjoy athletic pursuits for *both* hereditary and environmental reasons, and the influences of heredity and environment are tightly intertwined.

Evocative Genotype/Environment Correlations   Earlier, we noted that the environmental influences that contribute most heavily to many aspects of personality are "nonshared" experiences that make individuals *different* from one another. Might the differences in environments that children experience be partly because they have inherited different genes and may elicit different reactions from their companions?

Scarr and McCartney (1983) think so. Their notion of **evocative genotype-environment correlations** assumes that a child's genetically influenced attributes will affect the behavior of others toward him or her. For example, smiley, active babies may receive more attention and social stimulation than moody and passive ones. Teachers may respond more favorably to physically attractive students than to their less attractive classmates. Clearly, these *reactions* of other people to the child (and the child's genetically influenced attributes) are environmental influences that play an important role in shaping that child's personality. So once again, we see an intermingling of hereditary and environmental influences: Heredity affects the character of the social environment in which the personality develops.

Active Genotype/Environment Correlations   Finally, Scarr and McCartney propose that the environments children prefer and seek out will be those most compatible with their genetic predispositions. For example, a child genetically predisposed to be extroverted is likely to invite friends to the house, to be an avid party goer, and to generally prefer activities that are socially stimulating. By contrast, a child genetically predisposed to be shy and introverted may actively avoid large social gatherings and choose instead to pursue activities such as coin collecting that can be done alone. So one implication of these **active genotype/environment correlations** is that people with different genotypes will *select* different "environmental niches" for themselves—niches that may then have a powerful effect on their future social, emotional, and intellectual development.

passive genotype/environment correlations: the notion that the rearing environments that biological parents provide are influenced by the parents' own genes, and hence are correlated with the child's own genotype.

evocative genotype/environment correlations: the notion that our heritable attributes affect others' behavior toward us and thus influence the social environment in which development takes place.

active genotype/environment correlations: the notion that our genotypes affect the types of environments that we prefer and seek out.

How Do Genotype/Environment Correlations Influence Development?   According to Scarr and McCartney (1983), the relative importance of active, passive, and evocative gene influences changes over the course of development. During the first few years, infants, toddlers, and preschool children are not free to roam the neighborhood, choosing friends and building environmental niches. Most of their time is spent at home in an environment that parents structure for them, so that passive genotype/environment interactions are particularly important early in life. But once children reach school age and venture away from home on a daily basis, they suddenly become much freer to pick their own interests, activities, friends, and hangouts. Thus, active, niche-building interactions should exert more and more influence on development as the child matures (see Figure 3.3). Finally, evocative genotype-environment interactions are always important; that is, a person's genetically influenced attributes and patterns of behavior may influence the ways other people react to him or her throughout life.

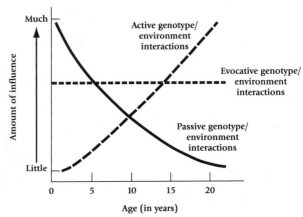

FIGURE 3.3   Relative influence of passive, evocative, and active (niche-picking) genotype/environment interactions as a function of age.

If Scarr and McCartney's theory has any merit, then virtually all siblings other than identical twins should become much less similar over time as they emerge from the relatively similar rearing environments parents impose during the early years and begin actively to select different environmental niches for themselves. Indeed, there is ample support for this idea. Pairs of genetically unrelated adoptees who live in the same home do show some definite similarities in conduct and in intellectual performance during early and middle childhood (Scarr & Weinberg, 1978). As these adoptees share no genes with each other or with their adoptive parents, their resemblances must be due to their common rearing environments. Yet by late adolescence, genetically unrelated siblings no longer resemble each other in intelligence or personality, presumably because they have selected very different environmental niches which, in turn, have steered them along differing developmental paths (Scarr & McCartney, 1983; Scarr et al., 1981). Even fraternal twins, who have 50% of their genes in common, are much less alike as adolescents and adults than they were as children (McCartney, Harris, & Bernieri, 1990). Apparently the genes that fraternal twins do *not* share cause these individuals to select somewhat different environmental niches which, in turn, will contribute to their declining resemblance over time. By contrast, pairs of identical twins continue to display some very noteworthy similarities throughout life. Not only do identical twins elicit similar reactions from other people, but their identical genotypes also predispose them to prefer and to select very *similar* environments (that is, friends, interests, and activities), which in turn exert comparable influences on these twin pairs and virtually guarantee that they will continue to resemble one another over time. Even identical twins raised *apart* should be similar in some respects if their identical genes cause them to seek out and to prefer similar activities and experiences. Let's take a closer look.

Separated Identical Twins   Thomas Bouchard and his associates (Bouchard et al., 1990; Farber, 1981) have studied more than 30 pairs of *separated identical twins* who were raised in different home environments. One such pair was Oscar Stohr and Jack Yufe. Oscar was raised as a Catholic by his mother in Nazi-dominated Europe. He became involved in the Hitler Youth Movement during World War II and is now employed as a factory supervisor in Germany. Jack, a store owner, was raised as a Jew and came to loathe Nazis while growing up in a Caribbean country halfway around the world. Today, Jack is a political liberal whereas Oscar is very conservative.

Like every pair of separated identical twins that Bouchard has studied, Oscar and Jack are different in some very noteworthy respects. One twin is usually more self-assured, outgoing, or aggressive than the other, or perhaps has a different religious or political philosophy (as Jack and Oscar do). Yet perhaps the more remarkable finding is that all these twin pairs show a number of striking similarities as well. As young men, for example, Oscar and Jack both excelled at sports and had difficulty with math. They have similar mannerisms, and both tend to be absent-minded. And then there are the little things, such as their common tastes for spicy foods and sweet liqueurs, their habit of storing rubber bands on their wrists, and their preference for flushing the toilet *before* and after using it.

PHOTO **3.3**   Jack Yufe (left) and Oscar Stohr (right).

How can separated identical twins be so different and at the same time so similar to each other? The concept of *active gene influences* helps to explain the uncanny resemblances. When we learn that twins grow in different environments, we tend to think of these settings as more dissimilar than they really are. In fact, identical twins raised apart are members of the same life cohort who are likely to be exposed to many of the same kinds of objects, activities, educational experiences, and historical events as they are growing up. So, if identical twins are genetically predisposed to select comparable aspects of the environment for special attention, and if their "different" environments provide them with reasonably similar sets of experiences from which to build their environmental niches, then these individuals should resemble each other in many of their habits, mannerisms, abilities, and interests.

Why, then, do separated identical twins often differ? According to Scarr and McCartney (1983), twins could be expected to differ on any attribute for which their rearing environments are so dissimilar as to prevent them from ever establishing comparable niches. Oscar Stohr and Jack Yufe are a prime example. They are alike in many ways because their separate rearing environments permitted them access to many of the same kinds of experiences (for example, sports, math classes, spicy foods, rubber bands), thereby enabling those genetically identical individuals to develop several similar habits, mannerisms, and interests. However, it was almost inevitable that they would differ in their political ideologies because their sociopolitical environments (Nazi-dominated Europe vs. the laid-back Caribbean) were so *dissimilar* as to prevent them from ever building the kinds of "niches" that would make them staunch political allies.

CONTRIBUTIONS AND CRITICISMS OF THE BEHAVIORAL GENETICS APPROACH

Behavioral genetics is a relatively new discipline that is having a strong influence on the way scientists look at human development. We now know, for example, that many attributes previously thought to be shaped by environment are influenced, in part, by genes. As Scarr and McCartney put it, we are products of "cooperative efforts of the nature/nurture team, directed by the genetic quarterback" (1983, p. 433). In effect, genes may exert many of their influences on human development by affecting the experiences we have, which in turn influence our behavior. And one very important implication of their viewpoint is that many of the "environmental" influences on development that have previously been identified may reflect, in part, the workings of heredity (Plomin, 1990; Plomin et al., 1997).

Of course, not all developmentalists would agree that genetic endowment is the "quarterback" of the "nature/nurture team" (Gottlieb, 1996; Wachs, 1992; and see the debate about parenting in Box 3.3). Students often object to Scarr and McCartney's theory because they sometimes read it to mean that genes *determine* environments. But this is not what the theory implies. What Scarr and McCartney are saying is this:

1. People with different genotypes are likely to evoke different responses from others and to select different environmental niches for themselves.
2. Yet, the responses they evoke and the niches they select depend to no small extent on the particular individuals, settings, and circumstances they encounter. Although a child must be genetically predisposed to be outgoing and extroverted, for example, it would be difficult to act on this predisposition if she lived in the wilds of Alaska with a reclusive father. In fact, this youngster could well become rather shy and reserved when raised in such an asocial environment.

In sum, genotypes and environments *interact* to produce developmental change and variations in developmental outcomes. True, genes exert some influence on those aspects of the environment that we are likely to experience. But the particular environments available to us limit the possible phenotypes that are likely to emerge from a particular genotype (Gottlieb, 1991, 1996). Perhaps Donald Hebb (1980) was not too far off when he said that behavior is determined 100% by heredity and 100% by the environment, for it seems that these two sets of influences are intertwined in a very complex way.

Interesting as these new ideas may be, critics argue that the behavioral genetics approach is merely a descriptive overview of how development might proceed rather than a well-articulated *explanation* of development. One reason for this sentiment is that we know so little about how genes exert their effects. Genes are encoded to manufacture proteins and enzymes, not to produce such attributes as intelligence or sociability. Though we now suspect that genes affect behavior *indirectly* by influencing the experiences we evoke from others or create for ourselves, we still know very little about how or why genes might impel us to prefer particular kinds of stimulation or to find certain activities especially satisfying (Plomin & Rutter, 1998). In addition, behavioral geneticists apply the term *environment* in a very global way, making few if any attempts to measure environmental influences directly or to specify *how* environments act on individuals to influence their behavior. Perhaps you can see the problem: The critics contend that one has not *explained* development by merely postulating that *unspecified* environmental forces influenced in *unknown* ways by our genes *somehow* shape our abilities, conduct, and character (Bronfenbrenner & Ceci, 1994; Gottlieb, 1996).

How exactly do environments impinge on children and adolescents to influence their abilities, conduct, and character? What environmental influences, at what ages, are particularly important? These are questions we will seek to answer throughout the remainder of this text. Recall that we briefly examined one *environmentalist* perspective—the social-learning approach in Chapter 2—that relies on laboratory experimentation to describe how children and adolescents learn from their experiences. Now let's consider a very different environmentalist viewpoint—one that criticizes the heavy experimental emphasis of social-learning theory and insists that only by studying people in their *natural settings* are we likely to understand how environments truly influence development.

Box 3.3   Current Controversies

Need Parenting Be "Good" or Simply "Good Enough"?

True or False?   Within typical families, parenting practices have a major influence on children's development.

In Chapter 2, we saw that John Watson (1928) advised parents to take their role very seriously, for he believed that parents had the power to shape their children's destiny. Sandra Scarr (1992) disagrees, arguing that parents do not have the power to mold children in any way they see fit. Yet, in some ways, Scarr's viewpoint is every bit as controversial as Watson's. She believes that human beings have evolved in ways that make them responsive to a wide range of environments and that

1. Within the broad range of home environments that are typical of the human species, children display normal, adaptive patterns of development.
2. Particular child-rearing practices do not influence developmental outcomes to any great extent.
3. Only those home environments that fall far outside the normal range (for example, those in which parents are violent, abusive, or neglectful) are likely to seriously constrain development and produce maladaptive outcomes.

Of course, Scarr assumes that different children respond in somewhat different ways to the typical (or "average expectable") home environment due, in large part, to the fact that they have different genes. However, Scarr also believes that a child's or an adolescent's development is so heavily influenced by the reactions he or she evokes from people other than parents and by the environmental niches he or she constructs that parental child-rearing practices have little effect on development—provided that these practices are "good enough" (that is, within the range of what might be considered normal for human beings). So, in contrast to Watson, who advocated super parenting, Scarr states that parents need only provide an "average expectable environment" to foster healthy development and fulfill their own role as effective guardians. She states:

> Children's outcomes do not depend on whether parents take (them) to a ball game or a museum so much as they depend on genetic transmission, on plentiful opportunities, and on having a *good enough* environment that supports children's development to become themselves. (Scarr, 1992, p. 15, emphasis added)

What do you think about Scarr's propositions? Many developmentalists were quick to criticize them. Diana Baumrind (1993), for example, points out that different child-rearing practices that fall well within what Scarr considers the range of "good enough" parenting produce *very large differences* in children's and adolescents' develop-

Ecological Systems Theory: A Modern Environmentalist Perspective

Imagine a discussion in which leading "environmentalists" are brought together and asked a very straightforward question: "What is this entity you people call *environment*?" We have just criticized behavioral geneticists for being vague on this issue, and interestingly enough, social-learning theorists aren't much better. Behaviorists John B. Watson and B. F. Skinner depicted "environment" as any and all external forces that shape the individual's development. Although current social-learning theorists such as Bandura (1986, 1989) have backed away from this extremely mechanistic view by acknowledging that environments both influence and *are influenced by* developing individuals, they continue to provide only vague descriptions of the environmental contexts in which development takes place.

By contrast, Urie Bronfenbrenner's (1979, 1989, 1993) **ecological systems theory** is an exciting new look at human development that provides the most detailed

PHOTO 3.4   In his ecological systems theory, Urie Bronfenbrenner (1917–   ) describes how multiple levels of the surrounding environment influence child and adolescent development.

mental outcomes. In her own research, Baumrind consistently finds that "highly demanding—highly responsive" parents have children and adolescents who perform better academically and who show better social adjustment than do parents who are only moderately demanding or responsive but well within the "normal range" on these parenting dimensions. Baumrind also argues that just because children are active agents who, in part, shape their own environments in no way implies that parents are powerless to influence those environments in ways that might promote (or inhibit) adaptive outcomes. Finally, Baumrind worries that telling parents they need only be "good enough" may cause them to become less invested in promoting children's competencies and quicker to absolve themselves of responsibility should their children founder. This would be unfortunate, in her view, because research consistently indicates that parents who feel personally responsible for fostering adaptive development typically have competent, well-adjusted sons and daughters, whereas those who are less personally involved tend to have offspring whose outcomes are less adaptive. For all these reasons, Baumrind concludes that Scarr's "good enough" parenting is simply *not* good enough.

Other critics (for example, Jackson, 1993) are concerned about the possible implications of Scarr's views for public policy were they to be accepted by those in power. Specifically, if we endorse Scarr's ideas that the "average expectable environment" is all children need to approximate their genetically influenced developmental potentials, then there would be little reason to intervene in an attempt to optimize the development of economically disadvantaged children from homes that fall within the normal range of family environments. Yet Jackson (1993) notes that many such interventions designed to promote the cognitive and emotional development of African-American (and other) populations have had impressive results. If we assumed that these interventions are unnecessary, as Scarr's theory implies to Jackson, then we would hardly be serving the best interests of perhaps 25% to 30% of America's children (not to mention the majority of children in many other countries around the world; see Baumrind, 1993).

Clearly, this debate about the influence of parenting practices illustrates the very different perspectives on development taken by behavioral geneticists (Scarr) and environmentalists (Baumrind, Jackson). At this point, the debate is far from resolved, although we will see throughout the text that parenting does seem to have a meaningful effect on the developmental outcomes of children and adolescents and that many developmentalists would advise parents to strive to be much better than "good enough."

analyses of environmental influences that has appeared to date. And since it also concedes that a person's biologically influenced characteristics interact with environmental forces to shape development, this perspective could be described more accurately as a *bioecological* theory (Bronfenbrenner, 1995).

Bronfenbrenner (1979) begins by assuming that *natural* environments are the major source of influence on developing persons—and one that is often overlooked (or simply ignored) by researchers who choose to study development in the highly artificial context of the laboratory. He then proceeds to define "environment" (or the natural ecology) as "a set of nested structures, each inside the next, like a set of Russian dolls" (p. 22). In other words, the developing person is said to be at the center of and embedded in several environmental systems, ranging from immediate settings such as the family to more remote contexts such as the broader culture (see Figure 3.4). Each of these systems is thought to interact with the others and with the individual to influence development in important ways. Let's take a closer look.

ecological systems theory:
Bronfenbrenner's model emphasizing that the developing person is embedded in a series of environmental systems that interact with one another and with the person to influence development.

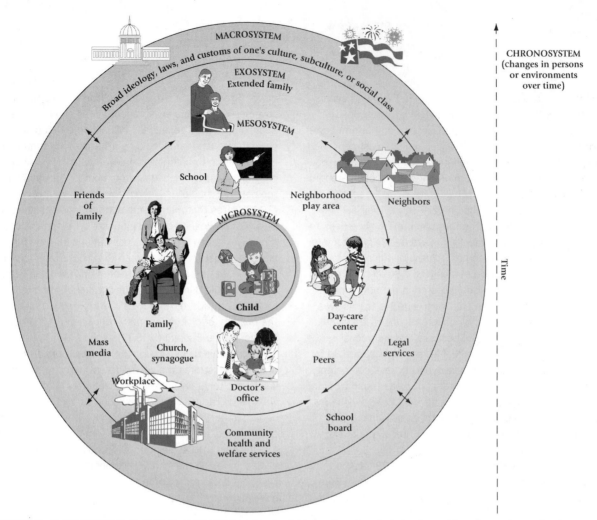

FIGURE 3.4 Bronfenbrenner's ecological model of the environment as a series of nested structures. The microsystem refers to relations between the child and the immediate environment, the mesosystem to connections among the child's immediate settings, the exosystem to social settings that affect but do not contain the child, and the macrosystem to the overarching ideology of the culture. (Based on Bronfenbrenner, 1979.)

BRONFENBRENNER'S CONTEXTS FOR DEVELOPMENT

The Microsystem Bronfenbrenner's innermost environmental layer, or **microsystem,** refers to the activities and interactions that occur in the person's immediate surroundings. For most young infants, the microsystem may be limited to the family. Yet, the natural environment eventually becomes much more complex as children are exposed to such other microsystems as day care, preschool classes, youth groups, and peers in neighborhood play areas. Not only are children influenced by the people in their microsystems, but their own biologically and socially influenced characteristics—their habits, temperaments, physical characteristics, and capabilities—influence the behavior of companions as well. For example, an extremely irritable or temperamentally difficult infant can alienate her parents or even create friction between them that may be sufficient to impair their marital relationship (Belsky, Rosenberger, & Crnic, 1995). And interactions between any two individuals in a microsystem are likely to be influenced by third parties. Fathers, for example, clearly influence mother-infant interactions: Happily married mothers who have close supportive re-

microsystem: the immediate settings (including role relationships and activities) that the person actually encounters; the innermost of Bronfenbrenner's environmental layers, or contexts.

lationships with their spouses tend to interact much more patiently and sensitively with their infants than mothers who experience marital tension, have little support from their spouses, and feel that they are raising their children on their own (Cox et al., 1989, 1992). Microsystems are truly dynamic contexts for development in which each person influences and is influenced by all other persons in the system.

The Mesosystem The second of Bronfenbrenner's environmental layers, or **mesosystem,** refers to the connections or interrelationships among such microsystems as homes, schools, and peer groups. Bronfenbrenner believes that development is likely to be optimized by strong, supportive links between microsystems. For example, youngsters who have established secure and harmonious relationships with parents are especially inclined to be accepted by peers and to enjoy close, supportive friendships during childhood and adolescence (Gavin & Furman, 1996; Kerns, Klepec, & Cole, 1996; Shulman, Elicker, & Sroufe 1994). A child's ability to master lessons at school depends not only on the quality of instruction his teachers provide but also on the extent to which parents value these scholastic activities and consult or cooperate with teachers (Luster & McAdoo, 1996; Stevenson, Chen, & Lee, 1993). On the other hand, nonsupportive links between microsystems can spell trouble. For example, when peer groups devalue academics, they often undermine an adolescent's scholastic performance, despite the best efforts of parents and teachers to encourage academic achievement (Steinberg, Dornbusch, & Brown, 1992).

The Exosystem Bronfenbrenner's third environmental layer, or **exosystem,** consists of contexts that children and adolescents are not a part of but which may nevertheless influence their development. For example, the parents' work environment is an exosystem influence, and children's emotional relationships at home can be influenced considerably by whether their parents enjoy their work (Greenberger, O'Neil, & Nagel, 1994). Similarly, children's experiences in school may also be affected by their exosystem—by a social integration plan adopted by the school board, or by a plant closing in their community that results in a decline in the school's revenue.

The Macrosystem Bronfenbrenner also stresses that development occurs in a **macrosystem**—that is, a cultural, or subcultural, or social class context in which microsystems, mesosystems, and exosystems are embedded. The macrosystem is really a broad, overarching ideology that dictates (among other things) how children should be treated, what they should be taught, and the goals for which they should strive. Of course, these values differ from culture to culture (and across subcultures and social classes) and can greatly influence the kinds of experiences children have in their homes, neighborhoods, schools, and all other contexts that affect them, directly or indirectly. To cite one example, the incidence of child abuse in families (a microsystem experience) is much lower in those cultures (or macrosystems) that discourage physical punishment of children and advocate nonviolent ways of resolving interpersonal conflict (Belsky, 1993; Levinson, 1989).

Finally, Bronfenbrenner's model includes a temporal dimension, or **chronosystem,** which emphasizes that changes *in the child* or in any of the ecological contexts of development can affect the direction development is likely to take. Cognitive and biological changes that occur at puberty, for example, seem to contribute to increased conflict between young adolescents and their parents (Paikoff & Brooks-Gunn, 1991; Steinberg, 1996). And the impacts of environmental changes will also depend upon another chronological variable—the age of the child. For example, even though a divorce hits hard at youngsters of all ages, adolescents are less likely than younger children to experience the strong blow of feeling that *they* were the cause of the break-up (Hetherington & Clingempeel, 1992).

mesosystem: the interconnections among an individual's immediate settings, or microsystems. The second of Bronfenbrenner's environmental layers, or contexts.

exosystem: social systems that children and adolescents do not directly experience but that may nonetheless influence their development; the third of Bronfenbrenner's environmental layers, or contexts.

macrosystem: the larger cultural or subcultural context in which development occurs; Bronfenbrenner's outermost environmental layer, or context.

chronosystem: in ecological systems theory, changes in the individual or the environment that occur over time and influence the direction development takes.

CONTRIBUTIONS AND CRITICISMS OF ECOLOGICAL SYSTEMS THEORY

Though we have touched briefly on the ecological perspective here and will explore its propositions through the text, perhaps you can already see that it provides a much richer description of environment (and environmental influences) than anything offered by learning theorists. Each of us functions in particular microsystems that are linked by a mesosystem and embedded in the larger contexts of an exosystem and a macrosystem. It makes little sense to ecological theorists to try to study environmental influences in contrived laboratory contexts. They argue that only by observing transactions between developing persons and their constantly changing *natural* settings will we ever understand how individuals influence and are influenced by their environments.

Bronfenbrenner's detailed analyses of environmental influences has suggested many ways in which the development of children and adolescents might be optimized. To illustrate, imagine a working mother who is having a tough time establishing a pleasant relationship with her temperamentally difficult infant. At the level of the microsystem, a successful intervention might assist the father to become a more sensitive companion—one who assumes some of the drudgery of child care and who encourages the mother to be more responsive to and patient with their baby (Howes & Markman, 1989). At the level of the exosystem, mothers (and fathers) can often be helped to improve their relationships with their children if their community has parenting classes available in the adult education curriculum or, alternatively, if parenting groups exist in which parents with problems can express their concerns, enlist others' emotional support, and learn from each other how to elicit more favorable reactions from their children (Lyons-Ruth et al., 1990). And at the level of the macrosystem, a social policy guaranteeing parents the right to take paid or unpaid leave from their jobs to attend to family matters might be an especially important intervention indeed—one that not only allows distressed parents more time to resolve difficulties that arise with their children (Clark et al., 1997) but also conveys an attitude that society views the resolution of family problems as important to children's (and ultimately to society's) well-being (Bronfenbrenner & Neville, 1995).

Yet, despite its strengths, ecological systems theory falls far short of being a complete account of human development. Though Bronfenbrenner characterizes the theory as a bioecological model, it really has very little to say about specific biological contributors to development. And even though developmentalists are indebted to the ecological systems perspective for describing the complexities of the natural environments that influence and are influenced by developing persons, we must still understand how children and adolescents *process* environmental *information* and *learn* from their experiences before we can fully comprehend how environments influence human development. So the ecological systems approach is an important addition to the field—but one that is best described as a complement to rather than a replacement for other developmental theories.

PHOTO 3.5 Parenting classes are an "exosystem" influence that can help parents establish more harmonious relationships with their children.

Modern Cognitive Perspectives

In this section of the chapter, we complete our review of recent perspectives on human development by examining two influential cognitive approaches: Vygotsky's *sociocultural theory* and the *social information-processing* approach.

VYGOTSKY'S SOCIOCULTURAL THEORY

Earlier in Chapter 2, we reviewed the cognitive-developmental theory of Jean Piaget—a viewpoint specifying that children progress through a universal and invariant sequence of cognitive stages that have many implications for their social and personality development. To view Piaget's work from a new vantage point, let's consider a perspective on cognitive development and its implications that has been arousing a great deal of interest lately: the **sociocultural theory** of Russian developmentalist Lev Vygotsky (1934/1962, 1930–1935/1978; see Rogoff, 1990, 1998; Wertsch & Tulviste, 1992). Vygotsky was an active scholar in the 1920s and 1930s when Piaget was formulating his theory, and his ideas qualify as "recent" only in the sense that they are now being translated from Russian and have begun to influence Western thinking in important ways. Vygotsky died of tuberculosis at age 38, before his own theory was fully developed. Nevertheless, he left us with important food for thought by insisting that (1) human development occurs in a particular sociocultural context that influences the form that it takes, and (2) many of a child's most noteworthy personal characteristics and cognitive skills evolve from *social interactions* with parents, teachers, and other more competent associates.

PHOTO 3.6 The sociocultural theory of Lev Vygotsky (1896–1934) views human development as a socially mediated process that may vary from culture to culture.

The Role of Culture in Intellectual Development Vygotsky (1930–1935/1978) claimed that infants are born with a few *elementary mental functions*—attention, sensation, perception, and memory—that are eventually transformed by the culture into new and more sophisticated mental processes that he called *higher mental functions*. Take memory, for example. Young children's early memorial capabilities are limited by biological constraints to the images and impressions they can produce. However, each culture provides its children **tools of intellectual adaptation** that permit them to use their basic mental functions more adaptively. Thus, children in Western societies may learn to remember more efficiently by taking notes on what to remember, whereas their age-mates in preliterate societies may have learned other memory strategies, such as representing each object they must remember by tying a knot in a string or by tying a string around their fingers to remind them to perform a chore. Such *socially transmitted* memory strategies and other cultural tools teach children how to use their minds: in short, *how* to think. And since each culture also transmits specific beliefs and values, it teaches children *what* to think as well.

In sum, Vygotsky claimed that human cognition, even when carried out in isolation, is inherently *sociocultural* because it is affected by the beliefs, values, and tools of intellectual adaptation passed to individuals by their culture. And since these values and intellectual tools may vary dramatically from culture to culture, Vygotsky believed that neither the course nor the content of intellectual growth was as "universal" as Piaget had assumed.

The Social Origins of Early Competencies Vygotsky agreed with Piaget that young children are curious explorers who are actively involved in learning and discovering new principles. However, he placed much less emphasis than Piaget did on *self-initiated discovery*, choosing instead to stress the importance of *social* contributions to personal growth.

sociocultural theory: Vygotsky's perspective on development, in which children acquire their culture's values, beliefs, and problem-solving strategies through collaborative dialogues with more knowledgeable members of society.

tools of intellectual adaptation: Vygotsky's term for methods of thinking and problem-solving strategies that children internalize from their interactions with more competent members of society.

According to Vygotsky, many of the truly important "discoveries" that children make occur within the context of cooperative, or collaborative, *dialogues* between a skillful tutor, who may model the activity and transmit verbal instructions, and a novice pupil, who first seeks to understand the tutor's instruction and eventually internalizes this information, using it to regulate his or her own performance.

Vygotsky claims that **collaborative (or guided) learning** occurs most readily within the child's **zone of proximal development**—a term he uses to describe the difference between what a learner can accomplish independently and what he or she can accomplish with the guidance and encouragement of a more skilled partner. To illustrate collaborative learning as Vygotsky sees it, let's imagine that a 4-year-old boy is eager to learn to hit a whiffle ball with his plastic bat; try as he might, however, he cannot make contact when Dad pitches to him. His father, noticing that the boy always takes his eye off the ball and holds his arms too close to his body, quickly concludes that his son is not about to become the next Mark McGwire without assistance. How might this father help his son to become a better hitter?

One feature of social collaboration that fosters cognitive growth and the acquisition of other skills is **scaffolding**—willingness of the more expert participants to tailor the support they provide to the novice learner's current abilities so he can profit from this assistance and increase his understanding of the problem. So our father, observing that his son can't hit what he doesn't track, might first build a tee, allowing the whiffle ball to remain *stationary*. He then might place the boy before the tee and give relevant verbal instructions ("bring your arms out," "keep your head up," and "WATCH THE BALL") before encouraging his son to knock the ball into the next county.

Vygotsky assumes that the child's role in collaborative learning is to take the language of the verbal instructions and to use it to guide his own activities. Thus, our 4-year-old's **private speech** might include such statements as "arms out" or "watch the ball" as he takes his first several dozen swings at it. As the boy learns these initial lessons, the father will provide new and more complex instructions (such as "turn your hips as you swing") to further his son's skills, whereas the boy will verbalize these new directives (out loud or to himself) as he continues to refine his techniques. After several such dialogues (or exchanges of information), the boy should have internalized the instructions and gained a pretty fair verbal representation of the component skills involved in batting and may now be ready to put this "private speech" to good use in guiding his attempts to hit a *moving* ball.

Note that collaborative learning is a form of *social learning*—but one very different from the kinds of learning emphasized by social-learning theorists. It does not depend on the shaping of new responses through administration of tangible reinforcers, nor does it rest solely on lessons learned by observation (although the tutor's demonstrations of the new skill or activity may often help to clarify his verbal instructions). Instead, guided learning is really more of an "apprenticeship" in thinking and doing—one in which novice children learn any number of culturally relevant skills and activities through their day-to-day, "hands-on" participation in such activities as preparing food, tracking prey, harvesting crops, solving puzzles, or hitting a baseball, with the guidance of their parents, teachers, older siblings, or their more skillful and accomplished peers (Rogoff, 1998). So collaborative (or guided) learning, which can occur only through *social* transactions between tutor and tutee, appears to be a

PHOTO 3.7 According to Vygotsky, new skills are often easier to acquire if children receive guidance and encouragement from a more competent associate.

---

collaborative (guided) learning: process of learning or acquiring new skills that occurs as novices participate in activities under the guidance of a more skillful tutor.

zone of proximal development: Vygotsky's term for the range of tasks that are too complex to be mastered alone but can be accomplished with guidance and encouragement from a more skillful partner.

scaffolding: process by which an expert, when instructing a novice, responds contingently to the novice's behavior in a learning situation, so that the novice gradually increases his or her understanding of a problem.

private speech: Vygotsky's term for the subset of a child's verbal utterances that serve a self-communicative function and guide the child's activities.

very meaningful socialization process—and one that social-learning theorists seem to have overlooked.

CONTRIBUTIONS AND CRITICISMS OF THE SOCIOCULTURAL PERSPECTIVE

Vygotsky's sociocultural theory offers a new lens through which to view human development by stressing the importance of specific social processes other theorists have not emphasized. According to Vygotsky, children's minds, skills, and personalities develop as they (1) take part in cooperative dialogues with skilled partners on tasks that are within their zone of proximal development and (2) incorporate what skillful tutors say to them into what they say to themselves. As social speech is translated into private speech and ultimately, into covert, **inner speech,** the culture's preferred methods of thinking and problem solving—or tools of intellectual adaptation—work their way from the language of competent tutors into the child's own thinking.

Unlike Piaget, who stressed *universal* sequences of cognitive growth that were said to promote *universal* stages of social-personality development, Vygotsky leads us to expect wide variations across cultures in the course of development—variations that reflect differences in children's cultural learning experiences. For example, children in Western cultures often learn to work *independently* on puzzles and other intellectual challenges that adults provide: experiences that prepare them for the *individual mastery* of academic assignments in highly structured Western classrooms. By contrast, children in some Australian and African bushman hunter societies are encouraged to *collaborate* early and to acquire elaborate spatial reasoning skills that prepare them to successfully track and corner the prey on which their livelihoods absolutely depend. Neither orientation to problems or set of cognitive capacities is necessarily any better or more advanced than the other; instead, they represent alternative forms of development that have evolved because they enable children to adapt successfully to values and traditions of their own cultures (Rogoff, 1998; Vygotsky, 1978).

Vygotsky's emphasis on collaborative learning has caused many (particularly developmentalists interested in education) to look anew at the roles that peers may play as agents of socialization. Indeed, research in educational settings reveals that children are often quicker to master important lessons when they collaborate with fellow students as opposed to working alone (Azmitia, 1992; Johnson & Johnson, 1989), and the youngsters who gain the most from these collaborations are usually the less competent collaborators who clearly profit from the guidance provided by their more skillful peers (Azmitia, 1988; Tudge, 1992). Not only are such collaborative learning projects of some academic benefit to participants, but as we will see in Chapter 12, they may also help to foster racial harmony and to improve the social standing and self-esteem of children with learning disabilities and other special needs.

There are, of course, criticisms. Many of Vygotsky's writings are only now being translated from Russian to other languages (Wertsch & Tulviste, 1992), and his theory has not received the intense scrutiny that Piaget's theory has. Nevertheless, at least some of his ideas have already been challenged. Barbara Rogoff (1990, 1998), for example, argues that guided participations that rely heavily on the kinds of verbal instruction that Vygotsky emphasized may be less adaptive in some cultures or less useful for some forms of learning than for others. A young child learning to stalk prey in Australia's outback or to plant, care for, and harvest rice in Southeast Asia may profit more from observation and practice than from verbal instruction and encouragement (see also Rogoff et al., 1993). Other investigators are finding that

inner speech: internalized private speech; covert verbal thought.

collaborative problem solving among peers does not always benefit the collaborators and may actually *undermine* task performance if the more competent collaborator is not very confident about what he knows or fails to adapt his instruction to a partner's level of understanding (Levin & Druyan, 1993; Tudge, 1992). But despite whatever criticism his theory should generate in the years ahead, Vygotsky has provided a valuable service by reminding us that both cognitive growth and social development are (1) much less "universal" than some theorists contend and (2) are best understood when studied in the cultural and social contexts in which they occur.

THE SOCIAL INFORMATION-PROCESSING (OR ATTRIBUTIONAL) VIEWPOINT

Our final "grand theory" pertaining to social and personality development stems from the efforts of cognitive theorists, social psychologists, and social-developmentalists who were concerned with explaining (1) how people process information and interpret their experiences and/or (2) how these interpretations influence their social behavior and personality development. Today, many developmentalists call this viewpoint the **social information-processing (or attributional) perspective.**

Premises of Social Information-Processing Theory Social information-processing theorists depict human beings as active processors of social information who are constantly generating explanations, or **causal attributions,** for their own and other people's behavior. These "attribution" theorists propose that children's impressions of themselves, other people, and their social experiences will change, becoming much deeper and more abstract, as they become better at inferring the reasons that people behave as they do. Unlike Piaget, however, many social information-processing theorists view the course of both cognitive growth and social information processing as a *continuous, incremental* process that is not at all stagelike.

Theorizing about attributional processes can be traced to Fritz Heider (1958), a social psychologist who believed that all human beings are characterized by two strong motives: (1) the need to form a coherent understanding of the world and (2) the need to exert some control over the environment and, thus, become the "captain of one's own ship." To satisfy these motives, a person must be able to predict how people are likely to behave in a variety of situations and to understand why they behave in these ways.

According to Heider, a person who is seeking to explain some noteworthy behavior will tend to attribute it either to *internal* causes (for example, some characteristic or disposition of the actor) or to *external* causes (for example, something about the situation that elicited the actor's behavior or is otherwise responsible for it). This is an important distinction, for the kinds of causal attributions we make about our own or other people's behavior can influence our reactions to that behavior. Consider the following example.

Suppose a 10-year-old boy is walking across the playground when he is suddenly smacked in the back of the head by a Frisbee. He turns around and sees a single classmate, who is laughing at this turn of events. What kind of attribution does the child make about his classmate's behavior? It is likely that the boy will interpret the laughter as a sign that the classmate *intended* to hit him, and he will probably attribute the classmate's behavior to some internal (or dispositional) cause, such as the classmate's aggressiveness. Consequently, the boy is likely to be angry and may respond with some form of rejection or counteraggression. Had the classmate expressed concern

social information-processing (or attributional) theory: social-cognitive theory stating that the explanations we construct for social experiences largely determine how we react to those experiences.

causal attributions: conclusions drawn about the underlying causes of our own or another person's behavior.

about having hit the boy with the Frisbee, and had there been another classmate present to whom the Frisbee was apparently being thrown, it is more likely that the boy would view the harm done to him as *unintentional* and perhaps attribute it to some external (or situational) cause, such as the wind deflecting the Frisbee's path. Given this kind of attribution, the child is not as likely to be angry, and his behavior might be very different from what it would be if he had held the classmate personally responsible for the harm he had experienced.

In sum, social information-processing theorists contend that the implications of our experiences for our social conduct and personality development depend not so much on what these experiences are as on the attributions we make about them. Stated another way, we are largely products of our *interpretations* of our social experiences (that is, social information-processing) rather than the objective character of those experiences. Of course, one implication of this viewpoint is that the same experience can have very different effects on individuals who make different attributions about it.

Heider and other early attribution theorists (for example, Kelley, 1973) were social psychologists who studied the causal attributions of adults and were not interested in developmental issues. Yet once the principles underlying adult attributions had been established, an obvious next step was to study children's interpretations of social behavior, seeking to determine how their causal attributions differ from those of adults and why they change over time. To provide a flavor of this research, let's briefly consider how children come to view people as possessing stable dispositions, or *traits*—a milestone that critically influences the kinds of impressions they form of themselves and their companions.

Inferring Dispositional Attributes   If asked to characterize yourself or another person you know well, you are likely to mention several psychological qualities that you or your companion display—perhaps traits such as friendliness, integrity, and intelligence. Interestingly, children younger than 8 or 9 years old rarely make traitlike attributions about themselves or anyone else. Early thinking about this issue (Secord & Peevers, 1974) presumed that to describe oneself or another person in traitlike terms, a child must (1) know that individuals can be the *cause* of various behaviors, (2) recognize that such actions are often guided by *intentions,* and (3) realize that particular individuals are likely to behave in *consistent* and *predictable* ways over time and across situations.

Even very young children understand that people are *causal* agents who often perform acts fully *intending* to produce a given effect. By age 2, toddlers frequently display their awareness of causality and intentionality in their own language (for example, "I left it [TV] on *cause* I want to watch it") and are much more likely to recall causal event sequences than noncausal ones two weeks after observing them (Bauer & Mandler, 1989; Miller & Aloise, 1989). And 3-year-olds recognize that actors clearly *intend* to succeed when striving to achieve a goal and that failures are unintentional (Shultz & Wells, 1985; Stipek, Recchia, & McClintic, 1992). In fact, the attributional error most often made by preschool children is to assume that *most effects that other people produce are intentional;* consequently, children younger than 6 or 7 may often fail to distinguish deliberate acts from either accidents or from other behaviors that produce consequences the actor could not have foreseen (Nelson-LeGall, 1985; Shultz & Wells, 1985).

Yet, the knowledge that an actor has caused a foreseeable and intended outcome is not, in itself, an indication that the actor possess a stable trait. Attribution theorists argue that to view someone as exhibiting a trait, the perceiver must first (1) judge the actor's behavior to be *internally* caused, rather than attribute it to situational constraints, and then (2) infer that this internal cause is reasonably *stable over time and across situations.*

Understanding Traitlike Attributions If preschool children often make *dispositional* attributions, deciding that an actor's behavior reflects her personal *motives* or *intentions* (internal causes), then why do they not use psychological constructs, or traits, to describe themselves or their companions? A study by Steven Rholes and Diane Ruble (1984) suggests one answer.

In Rholes and Ruble's study, 5- to 10-year-olds first heard stories in which an actor's behavior varied in its consistency. Some actors produced outcomes that were highly *consistent* over time whereas other actors produced *inconsistent* outcomes. Earlier research (Kelley, 1973) had shown that adults often rely on a **consistency schema,** generally making traitlike attributions about actors who behave consistently over time and across situations. Here is a sample of a "high consistency" story that might lead perceivers to attribute the actor's behavior to a trait he displays, namely *high ability:*

> Yesterday Sam threw the basketball through the hoop almost every time he tried. In the past, Sam has almost always thrown the ball through the hoop when he tried.

After hearing such consistent (or inconsistent) stories, the 5- to 10-year-olds in Rholes and Ruble's study were asked to make either dispositional or situational attributions for the actor's behavior and to answer a series of questions to determine whether they viewed an actor's dispositions as *stable* causes of his or her outcomes. In the basketball story, for example, children might be asked, "How many times do you think Sam could throw the ball through the hoop in the future?" (stability over time)

PHOTO 3.8 Although this 5-year-old knows that his brother is good at fixing bikes (a dispositional attribution), he is unlikely to describe him in trait-like terms because he may not realize that his brother probably has the mechanical skill to perform many kinds of repairs.

consistency schema: attributional heuristic implying that actions that a person consistently performs are likely to be internally caused (reflecting a dispositional characteristic).

or "How many other kinds of throwing games would Sam do well?" (stability over situations).

Rholes and Ruble found that even 5- and 6-year-olds made dispositional attributions about the actor's *current behavior* if the action was high in consistency, but when it came to the *prediction* questions, children younger than 9 did not seem to recognize that dispositions are stable across situations. Thus, 5- to 8-year-olds who viewed Sam as being good at basketball today did not realize that Sam probably has the perceptual-motor skills to do well at other, similar games, today or in the future.

In sum, children younger than 8 or 9 may fail to describe themselves and others in "traitlike" terms not because they fail to make dispositional attributions (as attribution theorists had originally thought) but because they are often uncertain about the *stability* of these dispositions. Stated another way, traitlike terms may not be very meaningful for younger children. Should they hear a teacher describe a classmate as "smart" because he made the highest grade on a recent test, they are likely to treat this term more as a description of how well the classmate did this time than as an indication of his enduring intellectual abilities (Rholes, Jones, & Wade, 1988; Rholes & Ruble, 1984). By contrast, traitlike terms are much more meaningful to a 9-year-old, who can use a label like "smart" as a brief and convenient way of expressing her knowledge that the person who is smart in one situation is likely to display the same inclination (and be smart) in other similar situations. Of course, understanding the implications of traits is an important advance in person perception because it enables us to predict more confidently how associates who display the traits we attribute to them are likely to behave in a variety of social settings.

CONTRIBUTIONS AND CRITICISMS OF THE SOCIAL INFORMATION-PROCESSING VIEWPOINT

Clearly, we have touched only briefly here on the social information-processing perspective. Yet, we will see over and over again that its proponents have contributed importantly to our understanding of such central social-developmental issues as the development of our self-concepts and self-esteem (Chapter 6), the growth of achievement orientations (Chapter 7), gender-role socialization (Chapter 8), and the bases for individual differences in aggressive behavior, (Chapter 9), moral conduct (Chapter 10), and peer acceptance/popularity (Chapter 13), to name a few. Indeed, the central proposition of social information-processing theory—that developing persons are active information seekers who are often influenced more by their *interpretations* of social experiences than by the objective character of these experiences—has proved to be a crucial theoretical insight.

By way of criticism, social information-processing theorists can be rather vague about the factors responsible for developmental changes in the attributions children make. For example, why do children younger than 8 or 9 not understand that dispositional characteristics can be stable over time and across situations, thereby implying the existence of psychological *traits*? Social information-processing theorists answer by arguing that younger children simply have not had enough *experience* at appraising the causes of their own and other people's behavior, and at comparing actors' behaviors over time and across situations, to have developed the concept of consistent and enduring psychological traits (Rholes & Ruble, 1984). Although we will see in Chapter 6 that social experience does contribute to the development of traitlike attributions, this "social-experience" hypothesis still leaves many questions unanswered. For example, what kinds of social experiences with what kinds of people are most likely to foster the growth of trait-like attributions? The social information-processing perspective is largely silent on this and other potentially important contributors to children's social-cognitive development.

What's more, many alternative explanations for the emergence of traitlike attributions are possible and highly plausible. We will see in Chapter 6, for example, that theorists influenced by Piaget would argue that young children make few traitlike attributions because of their *cognitive immaturity;* that is, they are highly egocentric, lack role-taking skills, and display centered thinking, focusing on the way things appear to be at present—all of which may prevent them from detecting regularities or invariances in conduct over time (and across situations) that might lead to stable traitlike attributions. Other researchers (for example, Eder, 1989) have shown that even 3- to 5-year-old preschool children are aware of regularities in the conduct of well-known playmates but apparently do not yet know what words to use to describe the rudimentary "traits" they have detected. So although social information-processing theory is a valuable addition to the field of social and personality development, it rarely provides a complete account of the phenomena to which it applies and is best viewed as a complement to rather than a replacement for the other theoretical viewpoints we have considered.

Theories and Worldviews

Now that we have completed our survey of the major theories of human development, how might we compare them? One way is to group the theories into even grander categories, for each is grounded in a broader set of philosophical assumptions, or *worldview.* By examining the fundamental assumptions that underlie different theories, we can perhaps appreciate just how deeply some of their disagreements run.

Early developmental theories adopted either of two broad worldviews (Overton, 1984). The first, or **mechanistic model,** likens human beings to machines by viewing them (1) as a collection of parts (behaviors) that can be decomposed, much as machines can be taken apart piece by piece, (2) as *passive,* changing mostly in response to outside influences (much as machines depend on external energy sources to operate), and (3) as changing gradually or *continuously* as their parts (specific behavior patterns) are added or subtracted. By contrast, the **organismic model** compares humans to plants and other living organisms by viewing them (1) as whole beings who cannot be understood as a simple collection of parts, (2) as *active* in the developmental process, changing under the guidance of internal forces (such as instincts or maturation), and (3) as evolving through distinct (discontinuous) *stages* as they mature.

Which theorists have adopted which model? Clearly, early learning theorists such as Watson and Skinner favored the mechanistic worldview, for they saw human beings as passively shaped by environmental events and they analyzed human behavior response by response. Bandura's social learning theory is primarily mechanistic; yet it does reflect the important organismic assumption that human beings are active creatures who both influence and are influenced by their environments. By contrast, psychoanalytic theorists such as Freud and Erikson and cognitive-developmentalists from the Piagetian tradition all base their theories primarily on the organismic model: Given some nourishment from their surroundings, human beings will progress through discontinuous steps or stages as directed by forces lying within themselves—much as seeds evolve into blooming plants.

mechanistic model: view of children as passive entities whose developmental paths are primarily determined by external (environmental) influences.

organismic model: view of children as active entities whose developmental paths are primarily determined by forces from within themselves.

Another broad worldview, the **contextual model,** has recently evolved and become the perspective that many developmentalists favor (Lerner, 1996). The contextual model views development as the product of a dynamic interplay between person and environment. People are assumed to be active in the developmental process (as in the organismic model) *and* the environment is active as well (as in the mechanistic model). Development may have both universal aspects *and* aspects peculiar to certain cultures, times, or individuals. The potential exists for both continuous and discontinuous change, and development may proceed along many different paths depending on the intricate interplay between internal forces (nature) and external influences (environment).

Although none of the theories we've reviewed provides a pure example of the contextual worldview, several come reasonably close: Information-processing theorists describe children and adolescents as active processors of environmental input whose processing capabilities are influenced by maturation *and* by the kinds of social and cultural experiences they encounter. (Note that Vygotsky's sociocultural theory makes similar assumptions.) Although they view development as basically continuous rather than stagelike, many information-processing theorists concede that changes within particular developmental domains may be uneven and that qualitative leaps in one's intellectual performances or social information-processing capabilities are not unknown.

Ethologists and behavioral geneticists also seem to favor a contextual worldview. They clearly make the "organismic" assumptions that humans are active beings who are born genetically equipped to display certain attributes, many of which promote adaptive developmental outcomes. However, they know full well that biological predispositions, by themselves, do not guarantee healthy development and that a child's outcomes may depend very critically on the environment she experiences. In addition, ethologists claim that we are *continuously* developing adaptive behaviors over the course of our lives (a mechanistic premise), although they stress that change can be abrupt, or *discontinuous,* as when a new, adaptive response unfolds during its sensitive period for development (an organismic premise).

Finally, Bronfenbrenner's ecological systems theory makes the "mechanistic" assumption that we humans are heavily influenced by many environmental contexts, ranging from our home settings to the wider society in which we live. Yet Bronfenbrenner is keenly aware that children and adolescents are active biological beings who change as they mature, and whose behaviors and biologically influenced attributes influence the very environments that are influencing their development. So development is viewed as the product of a truly dynamic interplay between an active person and an ever-changing "active" environment, and it is on this basis that the ecological systems approach qualifies as a contextual theory.

Table 3-3 summarizes the philosophical assumptions and "worldviews" underlying each of the broad theoretical perspectives we have reviewed. As you compare the viewpoints you expressed in Box 1.2 (on page 14) with those of the theorists, see if you can clearly determine your own worldview on human nature and the character of human development.

Although we have loosely classified the major theories as biological, environmental, or cognitive viewpoints, it should be clear by now that each of these models (with the possible exceptions of the radical behaviorism of Watson and Skinner) acknowledges the contributions of forces other than those it emphasizes. In other words, all modern-day theorists are well aware that biological factors, cognitive growth, and environmental influences are intertwined in complex ways and that changes in one aspect of development may have important implications for other developmental domains. Consider the following example.

contextual model: view of children as active entities whose developmental paths represent a continuous, dynamic interplay between internal forces (nature) and external influences (nurture).

TABLE 3-3   A Summary of the philosophies underlying eight major developmental perspectives

THEORY	ACTIVE VERSUS PASSIVE PERSON	CONTINUOUS VERSUS DISCONTINUOUS DEVELOPMENT	NATURE VERSUS NURTURE	WORLDVIEW
Psychoanalytic perspective	*Active:* Children are driven by inborn instincts that are channeled (with the assistance of others) into socially desirable outlets.	*Discontinuous:* Emphasizes stages of psychosexual development (Freud) or psychosocial development (Erikson).	*Both nature and nurture:* Biological forces (instincts; maturation) precipitate psychosexual stages and psychosocial crises; parental child-rearing practices influence the outcomes of these stages.	Organismic
Learning perspective	*Passive:* Children are molded by their environments (although Bandura claims that developing persons also influence these environments).	*Continuous:* Emphasizes the gradual addition of learned responses (habits) that make up one's personality.	*Nurture most important:* Environmental input rather than biological influences determines the course of development.	Mechanistic
Piaget's cognitive developmental theory	*Active:* Children actively construct more sophisticated understandings of the self, others, and the environment to which they adapt.	*Discontinuous:* Emphasizes an invariant sequence of qualitatively distinct cognitive stages.	*Both nature and nurture:* Children have an inborn need to adapt to the environment; they are nurtured by a stimulating environment that provides many adaptive challenges.	Organismic
Ethological perspective	*Active:* Humans are born with biologically determined behaviors that promote adaptive developmental outcomes.	*Both:* Emphasizes that adaptive behaviors are added continuously, but that some adaptive capabilities emerge abruptly (or fail to emerge) during sensitive periods of their development.	*Nature:* Biologically programmed adaptive behaviors are stressed, although an appropriate environment (which is influenced by the biological predispositions of companions) is necessary for successful adaptation.	Contextual
Behavioral genetics	*Active:* By virtue of genetically influenced characteristics we elicit responses from others and we select environmental niches for ourselves.	*Continuous:* Genotype/environment interactions occur continuously, influencing the form that development takes.	*Both nature and nurture:* Emphasis is on nature, however, genes are said to exert a heavy influence on the environments in which development takes place.	Contextual

What determines a person's popularity with peers? If you were to say that social skills are important, you would be right. Social skills such as warmth, friendliness, and a willingness to cooperate—all of which are heavily influenced by rearing environments—are characteristics that popular children typically display. And yet, we will see in Chapter 13 that such genetically influenced attributes as facial attractiveness and the age at which a child reaches puberty can have a very real effect on social life. For example, boys who reach puberty early enjoy better relations with their peers than boys who reach puberty later. Also note that bright children who do well in school tend to be more popular with their peers than children of average intelligence or below who perform somewhat less admirably in the classroom.

In sum, one's popularity depends not only on social skills but also on cognitive prowess and physical characteristics. As this example illustrates, development is not piecemeal but **holistic**: Human beings are biological, cognitive, and social creatures, and each of these components of "self" depends, in part, on changes that are taking place in other areas of development. This holistic perspective is perhaps the domi-

holistic perspective: a unified view of the developmental process that emphasizes the interrelationships among the physical/biological, mental, social, and emotional aspects of human development.

TABLE 3-3 *(continued)*

THEORY	ACTIVE VERSUS PASSIVE PERSON	CONTINUOUS VERSUS DISCONTINUOUS DEVELOPMENT	NATURE VERSUS NURTURE	WORLDVIEW
Ecological systems perspective	*Both:* Humans actively influence the environmental contexts that influence their development.	*Both:* Emphasizes that transactions between ever-changing individuals and ever-changing environments lead to quantitative developmental changes. However, discontinuous personal or environmental events (for example, reaching puberty; parents' divorce) can produce abrupt qualitative changes.	*Nurture:* Impacts of environmental contexts on development are most clearly emphasized, although children's biologically influenced attributes can affect their environments.	Contextual
Modern cognitive viewpoints Vygotsky Social information-processing theory	*Active:* Children actively possess environmental information to answer questions, interpret the causes of their own and others' behavior, and acquire culturally valued attributes and modes of thinking.	*Continuous:* Emphasize gradual acquisition of social information-processing skills and of other culturally valued attributes.	*Emphasis on nurture:* Capabilities that develop are heavily influenced by one's social and cultural experiences. However, some information-processing theorists clearly acknowledge that biological maturation permits older children and adolescents to process information faster.	Contextual
My viewpoint (Review Box 1.2)	_____ _____ _____ _____ _____	_____ _____ _____ _____ _____	_____ _____ _____ _____ _____	_____ _____ _____ _____ _____

nant theme of human development today—and the theme around which the remainder of this book is organized.

In case you are wondering, no one expects you to choose one of the major theories as a favorite and to reject the others. The fact that each theory emphasizes different aspects of development, combined with the realization that human development is truly a *holistic* enterprise, have led many developmentalists to become theoretical **eclectics:** individuals who recognize that none of the grand theories can explain all aspects of social and personality development and that each has contributed to what we know about developing children and adolescents. The plan for the remainder of this book is to take an *eclectic approach,* borrowing from many theories to integrate their contributions into a unified, holistic portrait of the developing person. Indeed, the benefits of this approach will become quite clear in our next chapter, where we will see that psychoanalysts, ethologists, social-learning theorists, and cognitive-developmentalists have all helped us to understand how and why infants establish (or, in some cases, fail to establish) secure emotional ties with their closest companions.

eclectics: those who borrow from many theories in their attempts to predict and explain human development.

Summary

- This chapter examines several recent perspectives on social and personality development—theories that have challenged, built on, and extended the three classical viewpoints we reviewed in Chapter 2.

ETHOLOGY: A MODERN EVOLUTIONARY PERSPECTIVE

- The evolutionary viewpoint, as expressed in **ethology**, is that humans are born with a number of adaptive attributes that have evolved through **natural selection** and channel development in ways that promote survival. Ethologists recognize that humans are influenced by their experiences and even claim that certain adaptive characteristics are most likely to develop during **sensitive periods,** provided that the environment fosters this development. However, they remind us that humans are biological beings whose biologically influenced attributes affect the kind of learning experiences they are likely to have.

BEHAVIORAL GENETICS: BIOLOGICAL BASES FOR INDIVIDUAL DIFFERENCES

- *Behavioral genetics* is the study of how **genotypes** and environment contribute to individual variations in **phenotypes.** Although animals can be studied in *selective breeding* experiments, human behavioral geneticists must conduct family studies (often **twin designs** or **adoption designs**), estimating the **heritability** of various attributes from similarities and differences among family members who differ in **kinship.** Hereditary contributions to various attributes are estimated by evaluating **concordance rates** and **heritability coefficients.** Behavioral geneticists can also determine the amount of variability in a trait that is attributable to **nonshared environmental influences** and **shared environmental influences.**

- Family studies reveal that the genes people inherit influence their intellectual performances, such core dimensions of personality as **introversion-extroversion** and **empathic concern,** and even their predispositions to display such abnormalities as **schizophrenia,** neurotic disorders, alcoholism, and criminality. However, none of these complex attributes is genetically "determined"; all are heavily influenced by environment.

- Behavioral geneticists have sought to explain how heredity and environment combine to produce developmental change. One recent model proposes three avenues by which genes influence the environments we are likely to experience: through **passive genotype/environment correlations,** through **evocative genotype/environment correlations,** and through **active (or niche-building) genotype/environment correlations.** However, the behavioral genetics approach has been criticized as an incomplete theory of development that describes, but fails to *explain,* how either genes or environment influence our abilities, conduct, and character.

ECOLOGICAL SYSTEMS THEORY: A MODERN ENVIRONMENTALIST PERSPECTIVE

- Urie Bronfenbrenner's **ecological systems theory** views development as the product of transactions between an ever-changing person and an ever-changing environment. Bronfenbrenner proposes that the natural environment in which development occurs actually consists of several interacting contexts or systems—**microsystem, mesosystem, exosystem,** and **macrosystem**—each of which is also influenced by the **chronosystem**—that is, by changes that occur over time in the individual or in other environmental contexts. This detailed analysis of person-environment interactions has suggested many new interventions to optimize development.

MODERN COGNITIVE PERSPECTIVES

- Vygotsky's **sociocultural theory** proposes that children's minds, skills, and personalities develop as they acquire the **tools of intellectual adaption** that pertain to their culture. Children acquire cultural beliefs, values, and problem-solving strategies in the context of *collaborative dialogues* with more skillful partners as they gradually internalize their tutors' instructions to master tasks within their **zone of proximal development. Collaborative learning** is most effective when more skillful associates properly **scaffold** their instruction, thereby allowing the child to profit from it and begin to function more independently.

- Social information-processing theorists propose that children's reactions to their social experiences depend largely on the **causal attributions** they make about their own and other people's behavior. This crucial insight has been supported consistently by research and has contributed importantly to our understanding of many social-developmental issues. However, social information-processing theory rarely provides a complete account of the phenomena to which it applies and is best viewed as an important complement to, rather than a replacement for, other theoretical viewpoints.

THEORIES AND WORLDVIEWS

■ Theories can be grouped into families based on the "worldviews" that underlie them. As developmentalists have come to appreciate the incredible complexity and **holistic character** of human development, more of them are favoring a **contextual model** over the **mechanistic model** that guides learning theories or the **organismic** model that underlies stage theories. Indeed, most contemporary developmentalists are theoretically **eclectic**, recognizing that no single theory offers a totally adequate account of human development and that each contributes importantly to our understanding of developing persons.

Chapter Four

Early Social and Emotional Development I:

EMOTIONAL GROWTH AND THE ESTABLISHMENT OF INTIMATE RELATIONSHIPS

An Overview of Emotional Development

Displaying Emotions: The Development and Regulation of Emotional Expressions

Recognizing and Interpreting Emotions

Emotions and Early Social Development

Temperament and Development

Hereditary and Environmental Influences on Temperament

Stability of Temperament

Early Temperamental Profiles and Later Development

What Are Emotional Attachments?

Early Emotional Bonding

Establishment of Interactional Synchrony

How Do Infants Become Attached?

The Growth of Primary Attachments

Theories of Attachment

Two Attachment-Related Fears of Infancy

Stranger Anxiety

Separation Anxiety

Why Do Infants Fear Strangers and Separations?

Reactions to the Loss of an Attachment Object

Summary

$\mathcal{T}$wo 18-month-olds, Caryn and Cherry, are each holding their mother's hand, patiently awaiting the entrance of a department store Santa. Upon appearing and seeing these toddlers, Santa quickly approaches them, bends over and belts out a deep HO! HO! HO!, and inquires rather intrusively "Have you been good little girls this year?" Cherry, obviously startled and fearful, whimpers and nearly falls over backward as she turns away to clutch at her mother. Caryn, too, is cautious, but she's highly curious as well. She looks intently at Santa, then at her mother, who says "Tell Santa yes I've been good and that I'd like a doll for Christmas this year." Caryn then turns and approaches Santa, allowing him to pick her up and place her on his lap.

Clearly, these toddlers had very different emotional reactions on meeting this loud, bearded stranger in a bright red suit. Cherry, noticeably upset, sought comfort from her mother, whereas Caryn, more intrigued than scared, first looked at her mother for clarification and guidance before exploring the situation for herself. Why might these two children have reacted so differently to the same novel experience?

In this and the following chapter, we address such issues by turning to the literature on children's emotions and the development of emotional ties to caregivers and other close companions. We begin by charting age-related changes in children's displays and interpretations of emotions and by considering the roles that emotions play in early social and personality development. We then look at individual differences in emotional reactivity, or *temperament,* and see that the early temperamental attributes that so often explain why young children react differently to both novel and everyday events are now considered by many developmentalists to be important building blocks of our adult personalities. We then turn to the topic of emotional *attachments* and explore the processes by which infants and their closest companions establish these intimate affectional ties. Next we consider two common fears that attached infants often display and see why these wary reactions often emerge during the latter half of the first year. And in Chapter 5 we will continue our discussion of early social and emotional development by reviewing a rapidly expanding base of evidence suggesting that the kind of emotional attachments infants are able to establish (or the lack thereof) can have important implications for their later social, emotional, and intellectual development.

An Overview of Emotional Development

Do babies have feelings? Do they experience and display specific emotions such as happiness, sadness, fear, and anger the way older children and adults do? Most parents think so. In one study, more than half the mothers of 1-month-olds claimed that their babies displayed at least five distinct emotional expressions: interest, surprise, joy, anger, and fear (Johnson et al., 1982). Although one might argue that this is simply a case of proud mothers reading much too much into the behavior of their babies, there is now reliable evidence that even very young infants are emotional creatures.

DISPLAYING EMOTIONS: THE DEVELOPMENT AND REGULATION OF EMOTIONAL EXPRESSIONS

Carroll Izard and his colleagues at the University of Delaware have studied infants' emotional expressions by videotaping babies' responses to such events as grasping an ice cube, having a toy taken away, or seeing their mothers return after a separation (Izard, 1982, 1993). Izard's procedure is to ask raters, who are *unaware* of the events that an infant has experienced, to tell him what emotion the infant is experiencing from the facial expression the infant displays. These studies reveal that different adult raters observing the same expressions reliably see the same emotion in a baby's face

Interest: brows raised; mouth may be rounded; lips may be pursed.

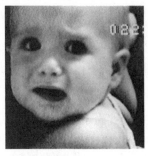

Fear: mouth retracted; brows level and drawn up and in; eyelids lifted.

Disgust: tongue protruding; upper lip raised; nose wrinkled.

Joy: bright eyes; cheeks lifted; mouth forms a smile.

Sadness: corners of mouth turned down; inner portion of brows raised.

Anger: mouth squared at corners; brows drawn together and pointing down; eyes fixed straight ahead.

FIGURE 4.1 Young infants display a variety of emotional expressions.

(see Figure 4.1.) What's more, infants respond in predictable ways to particular kinds of experiences. For example, soft sounds and novel visual displays are likely to elicit smiles and looks of interest, whereas inoculations and other painful stimuli will elicit distress from a younger infant and anger from an older one (Izard, Hembree, & Huebner, 1987). Babies also express emotions vocally. For example, 2-month-olds often coo when contented and may also display "blurts" of excitation when they are happy or interested in something—signals that parents interpret as positive emotions and will attempt to prolong by talking to or playing with their babies (Keller & Scholmerich, 1987).

Interestingly, adults can usually tell what *positive* emotion a baby is experiencing (for example, interest versus joy) from facial expressions, but specific negative emotions (fear versus anger, for example) are much more difficult to pinpoint on the basis of facial cues alone (Izard et al., 1995; Matias & Cohn, 1993). Nevertheless, most researchers agree that babies communicate a variety of feelings through their facial and vocal expressions, and that each expression becomes a more recognizable sign of a particular emotion with age (Camras et al., 1992; Izard et al., 1995).

Sequencing of Discrete Emotions Various emotions appear at different times over the first two years. At birth, babies show interest, distress, disgust, and contentment (as indicated by a rudimentary smile). Other **primary (or basic) emotions** that emerge between 2.5 months and 7 months of age are anger, sadness, joy, surprise, and fear (Izard et al., 1995). These so-called primary emotions seem to be biologically programmed, for they emerge in all normal infants at roughly the same ages and are dis-

primary (or basic) emotions:
the set of emotions present at birth or emerging early in the first year that some theorists believe to be biologically programmed.

played and interpreted similarly in all cultures (Camras et al., 1992; Izard, 1982, 1993; Malatesta et al., 1989). Yet some learning (or cognitive development) may be necessary before babies will express any emotion not present at birth. Indeed, one of the strongest elicitors of surprise and joy among 2- to 8-month-olds is their discovery that they can exert some control over objects and events. And disconfirmation of these *learned* expectancies (as when someone or something prevents them from exerting control) is likely to *anger* many 2- to 4-month-olds and may *sadden* the 4- to 6-month-olds as well (Lewis, Alessandri, & Sullivan, 1990; Sullivan, Lewis, & Alessandri, 1992).

Later in the second year, infants begin to display such **secondary (or complex) emotions** as embarrassment, shame, guilt, envy, and pride. These feelings are sometimes called *self-conscious emotions* because each involves some damage to or enhancement of our sense of self. Michael Lewis and his associates (1989) believe that embarrassment, the simplest self-conscious emotion, will not emerge until the child can recognize herself in a mirror or a photograph (a self-referential milestone we will discuss in detail in Chapter 6), whereas *self-evaluative* emotions such as shame, guilt, and pride may require both self-recognition *and* an understanding of rules and standards for evaluating one's conduct.

Most of the available evidence is consistent with Lewis's theory. For example, the only toddlers who became noticeably embarrassed by lavish praise or by requests to "show off" for strangers were those who displayed self-recognition (Lewis et al., 1989). By about age 3, when children are better able to evaluate their performances as good or bad, they begin to show clear signs of *pride* (smiling, applauding, or shouting "I did it") when they succeed at a difficult task, as well as *shame* (a downward gaze with a slumped posture, often accompanied by statements such as "I'm no good at this") should they fail at an easy task (Lewis, Alessandri, & Sullivan, 1992; Stipek, Recchia, & McClintic, 1992).

Of course, parents can clearly influence a child's experience and expression of self-evaluative emotions. In one recent study (Alessandri & Lewis, 1996), mothers' reactions were observed as their 4- to 5-year-olds succeeded or failed at a variety of puzzles. As expected, children generally showed some signs of pride over their successes and shame over their failures. Yet the amounts of pride and shame they displayed largely depended on their mothers' reactions to these outcomes. Mothers who accentuated the negative by being especially critical of failures tended to have children who displayed high levels of shame after a failure and little pride after successes. By contrast, mothers who were more inclined to react positively to successes had children who displayed more pride in their accomplishments and less shame on those occasions when they failed to achieve their objectives.

Interestingly, toddlers and young preschool children are likely to display self-evaluative emotions only when an adult is present to observe their conduct (Harter & Whitesell, 1989; Stipek et al., 1992). It seems that young children's self-evaluative emotions may stem largely from the reactions they anticipate receiving from adult evaluators. In fact, children may be well into the elementary school period before they fully internalize many rules or evaluative standards and come to feel especially prideful, shameful, or guilty about their conduct in the absence of external surveillance (Bussey, 1992; Harter & Whitesell, 1989).

Socialization of Emotions and Emotional Self-Regulation Each society has a set of **emotional display rules** that specify the circumstances under which various emotions should or should not be expressed (Gross & Ballif, 1991; Harris, 1989). Children in the United States, for example, learn that they are supposed to express happiness or gratitude when they receive a gift from grandma and, by all means, to suppress any disappointment they may feel should the gift turn out to be underwear.

secondary (or complex) emotions: self-conscious or self-evaluative emotions that emerge in the second year and depend, in part, on cognitive development.

emotional display rules: culturally defined rules specifying which emotions should or should not be expressed under which circumstances.

These emotional "codes of conduct" are rules that children must acquire and use to get along with other people and to maintain their approval. When does this learning begin?

Earlier than you might imagine! Consider that when mothers play with 7-month-old infants, they restrict themselves mainly to displays of joy, interest, and surprise, thus serving as models of positive emotions for their babies (Malatesta & Haviland, 1982). Mothers also respond selectively to their infants' emotions; over the first several months, they become increasingly attentive to babies' expressions of interest or surprise and less responsive to the infant's negative emotions (Malatesta et al., 1986). Through basic learning processes, then, babies are being trained to display more pleasant faces and fewer unpleasant ones—and they do just that over time.

However, the emotions that are considered socially acceptable may be quite different in different cultures. American parents love to stimulate their babies until they reach peaks of delight. By contrast, Gusii mothers in Kenya hardly ever take part in face-to-face play with their babies, seeking instead to keep young infants as calm and contented as possible (LeVine et al., 1994). American babies learn that intense emotion is okay as long as it is positive, whereas Gusii babies learn to restrain both positive and negative emotions.

Regulating Emotions   To comply with these lessons, babies must learn **emotional self-regulation.** That is, they must devise strategies for regulating and controlling their emotions. This is a difficult task for very young infants, who do manage to reduce at least some of their negative arousal by turning their bodies away from unpleasant stimuli or by sucking vigorously on objects (Mangelsdorf, Shapiro, & Marzolf, 1995). Nevertheless, young infants must often depend on caregivers to soothe them when they are experiencing strong emotional distress (Cole, Michel, & Teti, 1994). There is one interesting sex difference in early emotional regulation that is as yet not well explained. Six-month-old boys have more difficulties than 6-month-old girls do at regulating negative affect and are more inclined than 6-month-old girls are to emit negative emotions in an attempt to receive regulatory support from their mothers (Weinberg et al., 1999).

By the end of the first year, infants develop other strategies for reducing negative arousal such as rocking themselves, chewing on objects, and moving away from people or events that upset them (Kopp, 1989; Mangelsdorf et al., 1995). And by age 18 to 24 months, toddlers are now more likely to try to control the actions of people or objects (for example, mechanical toys) that upset them (Mangelsdorf et al., 1995), and they are beginning to cope with frustrations of having to wait for snacks or gifts by talking to companions, playing with toys, or otherwise distracting themselves from the source of their disappointments (Grolnick, Bridges, & Connell, 1996). In fact, toddlers this young have even been observed to knit their brows or to compress their lips as they actively attempt to suppress their anger or sadness (Malatesta et al., 1989). However, even 18-month-old toddlers have a very difficult time regulating any *fear* they may have experienced (Buss & Goldsmith, 1998); instead, fearful toddlers often develop styles of emotional expression that are successful at attracting attention and soothing from caregivers (Bridges & Grolnick, 1995).

As young preschool children become more talkative and begin to discuss their feelings, parents and other close companions will often help them to deal constructively with negative emotions by distracting them from the most distressing aspects of unpleasant situations (for example, telling a child who is about to receive an inoculation to look at a brightly colored poster on the wall) or by otherwise helping them to understand frightening, frustrating, or disappointing experiences (Thompson, 1994, 1998). These supportive interventions are a form of guided instruction of the kind that Vygotsky wrote about—experiences that should help preschoolers to

emotional self-regulation: strategies for managing emotions or adjusting emotional arousal to a comfortable level of intensity.

devise effective strategies for regulating their own emotions. Indeed, 2- to 6-year-olds do become better and better at coping with unpleasant emotional arousal by directing their attention away from frightening events ("I scared of the shark. Close my eyes"), by thinking pleasant thoughts to overcome unpleasant ones ("Mommy left me; but when she comes back, we are going to the movies"), and by reinterpreting the cause of their distress in a more satisfying way ("He [story character] didn't *really* die . . . it's just pretend") (Thompson, 1994). Unfortunately, youngsters who express a good deal of negative emotionality and do not learn how to regulate it are likely to alienate both adults and peers when they "act out" their anger or frustrations (Eisenberg et al., 1995, 1997).

Interestingly, adaptive regulation of emotions may sometimes involve *maintaining* or *intensifying* one's feelings rather than suppressing them. For example, children may learn that *conveying* their anger helps them to stand up to a bully (Thompson, 1994). And as we will see in Chapter 10, parents often call attention to (and thereby seek to maintain) the uneasiness young children experience after causing another person distress or breaking a rule. They hope to persuade youngsters to *reinterpret* these feelings in ways that cause them (1) to *sympathize* with victims of distress and to act on this concern or (2) to feel *guilty* about their transgressions and become less inclined to repeat them (Dunn, Brown, & Maguire, 1995; Kochanska, 1991). Another form of emotional arousal that we may seek to maintain or enhance is pride in our accomplishments—an important contributor to a healthy sense of achievement and to the development of a positive academic self-concept (see Chapter 7 for further discussion of this point). So, effective regulation of emotions involves an ability to suppress, maintain, or even intensify our emotional arousal in order to remain productively engaged with the challenges we face or the people we encounter (Buss & Goldsmith, 1998; Thompson, 1994).

Acquiring Emotional Display Rules   An ability to regulate emotions is only the first skill children must acquire to comply with a culture's emotional display rules. Indeed, these prescriptions often dictate that we not only suppress whatever "unacceptable" emotions we are actually experiencing, but that we also *replace* them (outwardly, at least) with whatever feeling the display rule calls for in that situation (for example, acting happy rather than sad upon receiving a disappointing gift).

By about age 3, children are beginning to show some limited ability to hide their true feelings. Michael Lewis and his associates (Lewis, Stanger, & Sullivan, 1989), for example, found that 3-year-olds who had lied about peeking at a forbidden toy showed subtle signs of anguish (detectable on film played in slow motion); however, they were able to mask their feelings well enough to make it impossible for uninformed adult judges to discriminate them from other children who truthfully reported that they hadn't peeked. With each passing year, preschool children become a little better at posing outward expressions that differ from their inner feelings (Peskin, 1992; Ruffman et al., 1993). Still, preschoolers are not especially skilled at disguising their true emotions; they typically wear their feelings on their face and express them freely.

Throughout the grade-school years, children become increasingly aware of socially sanctioned display rules, learning more and more about which emotions to express (and which to suppress) in particular social situations (Jones, Abbey, & Cumberland, 1998; Zeman & Shipman, 1997). Perhaps because parents place stronger pressures on girls to "act nice" in social situations, girls are both more motivated and more skilled at complying with display rules than boys are (Davis, 1995). Furthermore, mothers who emphasize positive emotions and who deemphasize negative feelings in their parent-child interactions tend to have children who are better able to mask disappointment and other negative emotions (Garner & Power, 1996; Jones et al., 1998).

Yet even simple display rules take some time to master fully. As we see in Figure 4.2, many 7- to 9-year-olds (especially boys) are still unable to act thrilled and to mask all their disappointment on receiving a lousy gift. And even many 12- to 13-year-olds will fail to suppress all their anger when a respected adult exercises authority and thwarts their plans (Underwood, Coie, & Herbsman, 1992).

Compliance with culturally specified rules for displaying emotions occurs early and is especially strong in communal societies like Japan that stress social harmony and place the needs of the larger social group over those of the individual (Matsumoto, 1990). Clearly, this socialization of emotions works for the good of society. Even in an individualistic culture like the United States, children's increasing compliance with emotional display rules is largely motivated by a desire to maintain social harmony and to avoid disapproval (Saarni, 1990; Zeman & Garber, 1996), and children who have mastered these emotional codes of conduct are viewed as more likable and more socially competent by their teachers and peers (Jones et al., 1998).

RECOGNIZING AND INTERPRETING EMOTIONS

When do infants first notice and respond to the emotional expressions of other people? Surprising as it may seem, they are prepared to react to certain vocal signals at birth or shortly thereafter. In Box 3.1, for example, we learned that newborns who hear another infant cry will soon begin to cry themselves, thus showing their responsiveness to the distress of another baby. Over the first year, parents the world over speak to infants in high-pitched tones that are acoustic concomitants of positive emotions such as happiness (Fernald & Mazzie, 1991; Grieser & Kuhl, 1988), and even 2-day-old infants pay more attention to this highly intonated speech than to the "flatter" speech that adults use when communicating with each other (Cooper & Aslin, 1990; Kaplan et al., 1996).

Currently there is some debate about when babies begin to recognize and interpret the facial expressions of emotion that others display. Although 3-month-olds prefer to look at photos of happy faces rather than at photos of neutral, sad, or angry ones (Kuchuk, Vibbert, & Bornstein, 1986; La Barbera et al., 1976), their looking preferences may simply reflect their powers of visual discrimination and not necessarily imply that infants this young interpret various expressions as "happy," "angry," or "sad" (Ludemann, 1991; Nelson, 1987). Yet, there is some evidence to suggest that young infants do attend carefully and *react appropriately* to more natural displays of emotion. For example, 3-month-olds will not only discriminate their mother's happy, sad, or angry expressions when these facial configurations are accompanied by a happy, sad, or angry tone of voice, but they also become rather gleeful in response to a happy expression and distressed by their mother's anger or sadness (Haviland & Lelwica, 1987; Tronick, 1989).

Social Referencing Infants' ability to interpret emotional expressions becomes rather obvious between 8 and 10 months of age—the point at which they begin to monitor their parents' emotional reactions to uncertain situations and to use this information to regulate their own behavior (Feinman, 1992). This **social referencing** becomes more common with age (Walden & Baxter, 1989) and soon extends to people other than parents. By the end of the first year, for example, infants will typically approach and play with unfamiliar toys if a nearby stranger is smiling, but they are apt to avoid these objects if the stranger displays a fearful expression (Klinnert et al., 1986). An adult's *vocal*

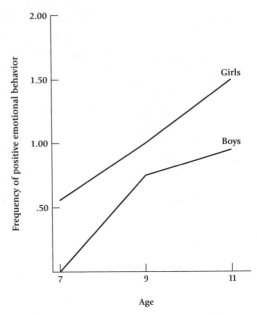

FIGURE 4.2 With age, children are more able to display positive emotional reactions after receiving a disappointing gift. (Based on C. Saarni, 1984.)

social referencing: the use of others' emotional expressions to infer the meaning of otherwise ambiguous situations.

expressions of emotion seem to convey as much or more information for a 12-month-old infant than her facial expressions do (Mumme, Fernald, & Herrera, 1996), and some investigators have wondered whether these emotional signals might not best be interpreted as commands (for example, "don't touch") rather than as active information seeking on the infant's part (Baldwin & Moses, 1996). But during the second year, toddlers will often look to their companions *after* they have appraised a new object or situation, thereby suggesting that they are now using another person's emotional reactions as *information* to assess the accuracy of their own judgments (Hornik & Gunnar, 1988).

PHOTO 4.1 Family conversations about emotional experiences help young children to better understand their own and other people's feelings.

Conversations About Emotions   Once toddlers begin to talk about emotions at 18 to 24 months of age, family conversations that center on emotional experiences can help them achieve a much richer understanding of their own and others' feelings. In fact, Judy Dunn and her associates (1991; Herrera & Dunn, 1997) found that the more often 3-year-olds had discussed emotional experiences with other family members, the better they were at interpreting others' emotions and at settling disputes with friends three years later in grade school (see also Denham, Zoller, & Couchoud, 1994; Oppenheim et al., 1997). Of course, the ability to identify how others are feeling and to understand why they feel that way is a central aspect of social cognition—and one that may have important social consequences. We will see in Chapter 10, for example, that understanding the *causes* of others' emotions is an important contributor to **empathy**, which often motivates children to comfort or otherwise assist distressed companions. In fact, these "prosocial" inclinations may largely explain why children who score high on tests of emotional understanding tend to be rated high in social competence by teachers and enjoy especially good relations with their peers (Cassidy et al., 1992; Garner, Jones, & Miner, 1994; Oppenheim et al., 1997).

Later Milestones in Emotional Understanding   The ability to recognize and interpret the emotional displays of others improves steadily throughout childhood. By age 4 to 5, children can correctly infer whether a person is happy, angry, or sad from his or her expressive body movements (Boone & Cunningham, 1998). What's more, they can offer explanations for why playmates are happy, angry, or sad, although they tend to focus more on *external* events as causes of emotions than on internal needs, desires, moods, or motives (Fabes et al., 1991). As grade-school children gradually begin to rely more on both internal and situational information to interpret emotions, they achieve several important breakthroughs in emotional understanding. For example, they eventually recognize at about age 8 that many situations (for example, the approach of a big dog) will elicit different emotional reactions (for example, fear versus joy) from different individuals (Gnepp & Klayman, 1992). Furthermore, 6- to 9-year-olds are also beginning to understand that a person can experience more than

empathy: the ability to experience the emotions others display.

one emotion (for example, excitement and wariness) at the same time (Arsenio & Kramer, 1992; Brown & Dunn, 1996), and they are displaying some ability to integrate contrasting facial, behavioral, and situational cues to infer what those emotions might be (Hoffner & Badzinski, 1989; see also Friend & Davis, 1993).

Notice that these advances in emotional understanding emerge at about the same age that children can integrate more than one piece of information (for example, height and width of a column of liquid) in Piagetian conservation tasks, and they may depend, in part, on the same underlying cognitive developments. However, social experiences are also important. Jane Brown and Judy Dunn (1996), for example, found that 6-year-olds who show an early understanding of conflicting emotions have often discussed the causes of emotions with their parents earlier in childhood. Apparently, these discussions prepared them to analyze mixed feelings that might have arisen from squabbles with siblings and peers.

EMOTIONS AND EARLY SOCIAL DEVELOPMENT

What role do emotions play in early social development? Clearly, a baby's displays of emotion serve a *communicative* function that is likely to affect the behavior of caregivers. For example, cries of distress summon close companions. Early suggestions of a smile or expressions of interest may convince caregivers that their baby is willing and even eager to strike up a social relationship with them. Later expressions of fear or sadness may indicate that the infant is insecure or feeling blue and needs some attention or comforting. Anger may imply that the infant wishes her companions to cease whatever they are doing that is upsetting her, whereas joy serves as a prompt for caregivers to prolong an ongoing interaction or perhaps signals the baby's willingness to accept new challenges. So, infant emotions are adaptive in that they promote social contact and help caregivers adjust their behavior to the infant's needs and goals. Stated another way, the emotional expressions of infancy help infants and their close companions "get to know each other" (Tronick, 1989).

At the same time, the infant's emerging ability to recognize and interpret others' emotions is an important achievement that enables him to infer how he should be feeling or behaving in a variety of situations (see Table 4-1). The beauty of this "social referencing" is that children can quickly acquire *knowledge* in this way. For example, a sibling's joyful reaction to the family dog should indicate that this "ball of fur" is a friend rather than an unspeakable monster. A mother's pained expression and accompanying vocal concern might immediately suggest that the knife in one's hand is an implement to be avoided. And given the frequency with which expressive caregivers direct an infant's attention to important aspects of the environment or display their feelings about an infant's appraisal of objects and events, very likely the information contained in their emotional displays will contribute in a major way to the child's understanding of the world in which he lives (Rosen, Adamson, & Bakeman, 1992).

Temperament and Development

As parents well know, every baby has a distinct personality. In trying to describe infant personality, researchers have focused on aspects of **temperament**—an individual's tendency to respond in predictable ways to environmental events that many believe to be the emotional and behavioral building blocks of the adult personality (Caspi & Silva, 1995; Goldsmith et al., 1987). Although different researchers do not always define or measure temperament in precisely the same ways, most would agree

temperament: a person's characteristic modes of emotional and behavioral responding to environmental events, including such attributes as activity level, irritability, fearfulness, and sociability.

TABLE 4-1 An overview of emotional development

AGE	EMOTIONAL EXPRESSIONS/REGULATIONS	EMOTIONAL UNDERSTANDINGS
Birth to 6 months	■ All primary emotions appear ■ Displays of positive emotion are encouraged and become more commonplace ■ Attempts to regulate negative emotions by sucking or turning away are observed	■ Child can discriminate such facial expressions as happiness, anger, and sadness
7 to 12 months	■ Primary emotions such as anger, fear, and sadness become more apparent ■ Emotional self-regulation improves as infants rock themselves, chew on objects, or move away from distressing stimuli	■ Recognition of others' primary emotions improves ■ Social referencing appears
1 to 3 years	■ Secondary (self-conscious) emotions appear ■ Emotional self-regulation improves as toddlers distract themselves from or attempt to control stimuli that upset them	■ Toddlers begin to talk about and play-act emotions ■ Empathic responding appears
3 to 6 years	■ Cognitive strategies for regulating emotions appear and are refined ■ Some masking of emotions and compliance with simple display rules appear	■ Child uses expressive body movements to recognize emotions ■ Understanding of the external causes and consequences of emotions improves ■ Empathic responding becomes more common
6 to 12 years	■ Compliance with display rules improves ■ Self-conscious emotions become more closely tied to internalized standards of "right" or "competent" behavior ■ Self-regulation strategies (including those allowing one to intensify emotions when appropriate) become more varied and more complex	■ Children integrate internal and external cues to understand others' emotions ■ Empathic responding becomes stronger ■ Child becomes aware that people may differ in their emotional reactions to the same event ■ Understands that others may experience mixed emotions

that the following five attributes are important components of temperament (Buss & Plomin, 1984; Goldsmith et al., 1987; Rothbart, 1981):

1. *Activity level*—typical pace or vigor of one's activities
2. *Irritability/negative emotionality*—how easily or intensely upset one becomes over negative events
3. *Soothability*—ease with which one calms after becoming upset
4. *Fearfulness*—one's wariness of intense or highly unusual stimulation
5. *Sociability*—one's receptiveness to social stimulation

HEREDITARY AND ENVIRONMENTAL INFLUENCES ON TEMPERAMENT

To many, the very term *temperament* implies a biological foundation for individual differences in behavior—a foundation that is genetically influenced and stable over time (Buss & Plomin, 1984; DiLalla, Kagan, & Reznick, 1994). Behavioral geneticists have looked for hereditary influences by comparing the temperamental similarities of pairs of identical and pairs of fraternal twins. By the middle of the first year, identical twins are already more similar than fraternal twins are on most temperamental attributes, including activity level, demands for attention, irritability, and sociability (Braungart et al., 1992; Emde et al., 1992; see Figure 4.3). Although the heritability coefficients for most temperamental attributes are moderate at best throughout infancy and the preschool period (Goldsmith, Buss, & Lemery, 1997), many important components of temperament seem to be genetically influenced.

Environmental Influences Of course, because most temperamental attributes are only moderately heritable, we know that environment is also implicated in shaping children's temperaments. Which aspects of environment are most important? The home environment that siblings share clearly influences one temperamental attribute—the tendency to smile and display positive affect (Goldsmith et al., 1997). Yet shared environment plays little part in shaping other temperamental attributes, for genetically unrelated adoptees and nontwin siblings who live together often barely resemble each other in activity level, fearfulness, and the other aspects of temperament (Plomin et al., 1997; Schmitz et al., 1996). Thus, behavioral geneticists now believe that the strongest environmental contributors to temperament are *nonshared environmental influences*—those aspects of environment that siblings do not share and that conspire to make them temperamentally *dissimilar.* Nonshared environmental influences on temperament are likely if parents notice early behavioral differences among their children and adjust their parenting to them. For example, if a mother observes that her infant son Jimmy is much less outgoing with strangers than her 3-year-old Jennifer was at Jimmy's age, she may allow Jimmy more freedom to avoid social contacts and to pursue solitary activities, thereby encouraging him to become much more reclusive and socially inhibited than his sister is (Park et al., 1997).

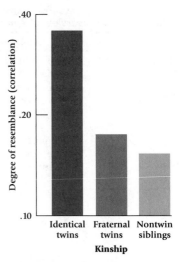

FIGURE 4.3 Average correlations in infant temperament among identical twins, fraternal twins, and nontwin siblings born at different times. (Sources: Braungart et al., 1992; Emde et al., 1992.)

STABILITY OF TEMPERAMENT

How stable is early temperament over time? Is the "fearful" 8-month-old who is highly upset by a strange face likely to remain wary of strangers at 24 months and to shun new playmates as a 4-year-old? Longitudinal research indicates that several components of temperament—namely, activity level, irritability, sociability, and shyness—are moderately stable through infancy, childhood, and sometimes even into the early adult years (Caspi & Silva, 1995; Lemery et al., 1999; Pedlow et al., 1993; Ruff et al., 1990). In fact, one longitudinal study in New Zealand found that several components of temperament measured when participants were 3 years old were not only moderately stable between ages 3 and 18 but also predicted individual differences in participants' antisocial tendencies and the quality of their personal and family relationships at ages 18 to 21 (Caspi & Silva, 1995; Henry et al., 1996; Newman et al., 1997). Findings such as these illustrate why many developmentalists consider temperament to be the cornerstone of the adult personality. However, not all individuals are so temperamentally stable.

Consider what Jerome Kagan and his associates found while conducting longitudinal studies of a temperamental attribute they call **behavioral inhibition**: the tendency to withdraw from unfamiliar people or situations (Kagan, 1992; Snidman et al., 1995). At age 4 months, inhibited infants are already fussing and showing heightened motor activity to such novel objects as a brightly colored mobile, and they often display intense physiological arousal (for example, high heart rates) to situations that barely faze uninhibited infants. When tested at age 21 months, toddlers classified as inhibited were rather shy and sometimes even fearful when they encountered unfamiliar people, toys, or settings, whereas most uninhibited children responded quite adaptively to these events. And when retested at 4, 5.5, and 7.5 years of age, inhibited youngsters were still less sociable with strange adults and peers and more cautious than uninhibited children were about engaging in activities that involved an element of risk (for example, walking a balance beam).

behavioral inhibition: a temperamental attribute reflecting one's tendency to withdraw from unfamiliar people or situations.

So behavioral inhibition is a moderately stable attribute that may have deep biological roots. Indeed, researchers have been finding that infants easily upset by novelty show greater electrical activity in the right cerebral hemisphere of the brain (the center for negative emotions) than in the left hemisphere, whereas infants who are less reactive show either the opposite pattern or no hemispheric differences in electrical activity (Calkins, Fox, & Marshall, 1996; Fox, Bell, & Jones, 1992). In addition, family studies clearly indicate that behavioral inhibition is a genetically influenced attribute (DiLalla et al., 1994; Robinson et al., 1992). Nevertheless, both Kagan and his associates and a research team in Sweden (Kerr et al., 1994) found that only those children at the extremes of the continuum—the most highly inhibited and most highly uninhibited youngsters—displayed such long-term stability, with most other children showing considerable fluctuation in their levels of inhibition over time. What these latter observations imply is that genetically influenced aspects of temperament are often modified by environmental influences (see also Rothbart & Bates, 1998). Interestingly, a similar conclusion emerges from Alexander Thomas and Stella Chess's classic longitudinal research on the stability of temperamental profiles from infancy to adulthood.

EARLY TEMPERAMENTAL PROFILES AND LATER DEVELOPMENT

In their earliest reports, Thomas and Chess (1977; Thomas, Chess, & Birch, 1970) noted that certain aspects of infant temperament tend to cluster in predictable ways, forming broader temperamental profiles. In fact, the majority of the 141 infants in their *New York Longitudinal Study* could be placed into one of three temperamental profiles:

1. **Easy temperament** (40% of the sample): Easygoing children are even-tempered, are typically in a positive mood, and are quite open and adaptable to new experiences. Their habits are regular and predictable.
2. **Difficult temperament** (10% of the sample): Difficult children are active, irritable, and irregular in their habits. They often react very vigorously to changes in routine and are very slow to adapt to new persons or situations.
3. **Slow-to-warm-up temperament** (15% of the sample): These children are quite inactive, somewhat moody, can be slow to adapt to new persons and situations. But unlike the difficult child, they typically respond to novelty in mildly rather than intensely negative ways. For example, they may resist cuddling by looking away rather than by kicking or screaming.

The remaining children fit none of these profiles, showing their own unique patterns of temperamental attributes.

Temperamental Profiles and Children's Adjustment   Apparently, these broader temperamental patterns may persist over time and influence a child's adjustment to a variety of settings later in life. For example, temperamentally "difficult" children are more likely than other children to have problems adjusting to school activities, and they are often irritable and aggressive in their interactions with siblings and peers (Lytton, 1990; Thomas, Chess, & Korn, 1982). By contrast, about half of all children who are "slow to warm up" show a different kind of adjustment problem, as their hesitancy to embrace new activities and challenges may cause them to be ignored or neglected by peers (Chess & Thomas, 1984).

Child Rearing and Temperament   Do those observations imply that early temperamental profiles are difficult to alter and will largely determine our personalities and social adjustment? No, they do not! Thomas and Chess (1986; Chess & Thomas, 1984) find that early temperamental characteristics *sometimes do* and *sometimes do not* carry over into later life (see also Cohen et al., 1998). In other words, temperament

easy temperament: temperamental profile in which the child quickly establishes regular routines, is generally good-natured, and adapts easily to novelty.

difficult temperament: temperamental profile in which the child is irregular in daily routines and adapts slowly to new experiences, often responding negatively and intensely.

slow-to-warm-up temperament: temperamental profile in which the child is inactive and moody and displays mild passive resistance to new routines and experiences.

can change, and one factor that often determines whether it does change is the "**goodness of fit**" between the child's temperamental style and patterns of child rearing used by parents. Let's first consider a "good fit" between temperament and child rearing. Difficult infants who fuss a lot and have trouble adapting to new routines often become less cranky and more adaptable over the long run if parents remain calm, exercise restraint, and allow these children to respond to novelty at a more leisurely pace. Indeed, many difficult infants who experience such patient and sensitive caregiving are no longer classifiable as temperamentally difficult later in childhood or adolescence (Chess & Thomas, 1984). Yet it is not always easy for a parent to be patient and

PHOTO **4.2** Difficult infants are likely to retain their difficult temperaments if parents are impatient and forceful with them.

sensitive with a highly active, moody child who resists their bids for attention; in fact, many parents become irritable, impatient, demanding, and punitive with difficult children (van den Boom, 1995). Unfortunately, these attitudes and behaviors constitute a "poor fit" with a difficult child, who is apt to become all the more fussy and resistant in response to the parent's forceful and punitive tactics. And Chess and Thomas (1984) found that, true to form, difficult infants were especially likely to remain difficult and to display behavior problems later in life if their parents had been impatient, demanding, and forceful with them.

Finally, there is a great deal of variation across cultures in what qualifies as a "desirable" temperament and in the developmental outcomes that are associated with particular temperamental attributes. Box 4.1 briefly examines some cross-cultural differences in the developmental implications of childhood and adolescent shyness.

What Are Emotional Attachments?

Although babies can communicate many of their feelings right from the start, their social lives will change rather dramatically as they become emotionally attached to their caregivers. What is an emotional **attachment**? John Bowlby (1969) uses the term to describe the strong affectional ties that we feel for the special people in our lives. According to Bowlby (1969), people who are securely attached will take pleasure in their interactions and will feel comforted by their partner's presence in times of stress or uncertainty. So 10-month-old Michael may reflect the attachment relationship he shares with his mother by reserving his biggest grins for her and by crying out to her or crawling in her direction whenever he is upset, discomforted, or afraid.

Bowlby (1969) also stressed that parent/infant attachments are *reciprocal relationships;* infants become attached to parents, and parents become attached to infants. Parents clearly have an edge on infants when it comes to forming these intimate affectional ties, although people sometimes find it hard to understand how a parent might become emotionally involved with a neonate. Many years ago, a classmate of mine, listening to our professor describing just how drawn he was to his newborn son, remarked:

> Why do you feel that way? Newborn infants drool, spit up, fuss, cry, dirty their diapers on a regular basis, and often require lots of attention at all hours of the day and night. Since babies are associated with so many unpleasant consequences, wouldn't learning theory predict that their parents should learn to dislike them?

"goodness-of-fit" model: Thomas and Chess's notion that development is likely to be optimized when parents' child-rearing practices are sensitively adapted to the child's temperamental characteristics.

attachment: a close emotional relationship between two persons, characterized by mutual affection and a desire to maintain proximity.

Box 4.1   *Cultural Influences*

Is Shyness a Social Disadvantage? It Depends on One's Culture

In the United States, children who are shy and reserved are at a social disadvantage. They run the risk of being neglected or even rejected by peers—an outcome that can lead to low self-esteem, depression, and a number of other adjustment problems that we will discuss in detail in Chapter 13. Furthermore, even if shy adolescents or young adults are otherwise well adjusted, they often fail to act boldly or assertively enough to take advantage of many opportunities, and they typically lag far behind non-shy peers in getting married, having children, and firmly establishing themselves in a career (Caspi et al., 1988).

By contrast, many Asian cultures value what Americans would call a shy and somewhat inhibited demeanor. In China, for example, children who are shy and reserved are perceived as socially mature by their teachers (Chen, Rubin, & Li, 1995), and they are much more likely than active, assertive, children to be popular with their peers—precisely the opposite pattern to what we see in the United States and Canada (Chen, Rubin, & Sun, 1992). And the boisterous classroom behaviors that most Western children display on occasion (and that American teachers view as normal) are likely to be branded *conduct disorders* by teachers in Thailand, who expect their pupils to be reserved, respectful, and obedient (Weisz et al., 1995).

There are even differences among Western cultures in outcomes associated with shyness. Swedes, for example, view shyness somewhat more positively than Americans do and prefer shy, reserved behaviors to bold assertive or attention-seeking antics. Consequently, shyness is not really a disadvantage for Swedish men. Like shy American men, shy Swedish men married and had children later than their non-shy counterparts; however shyness did not constrain their careers the way it does for American men (Kerr, Lambert, & Bem, 1996). What about Swedish women? Shyness posed no problems for them in establishing intimate relationships, for shy Swedish girls married and had children at roughly the same age as their non-shy peers. But unlike shy American women, who were generally well educated and who married successful men, shy Swedish women completed *fewer* years of education than their non-shy counterparts and married men who made less money, thus suggesting that shyness may place them at some risk of economic disadvantage. Why did shy Swedish girls receive less education than their non-shy peers? Margaret Kerr and her associates (1996) speculate that Swedish teachers are more likely to encourage shy students to continue their educations if the students are males. So, lacking the initiative to approach teachers and seek their guidance, shy Swedish girls end up having fewer educational opportunities than their non-shy female peers or shy boys do.

We see, then, that outcomes associated with shyness can vary dramatically across cultures (and even within a culture, depending on one's gender). Clearly, some temperamental qualities provide "better fits" with a culture's specific values and traditions than others do. And because cultural traditions vary so widely, we can safely conclude that there is no one temperamental profile that is "most adaptive" in all cultures.

Since that day in the late 1960s, social-developmentalists have begun to understand how parents might be drawn to a newborn infant. Even before their baby is born, many parents display their readiness to become attached by talking blissfully about the baby, formulating grand plans for him or her, and expressing delight in such milestones as feeling their fetus kick or hearing his heart beat with the aid of a stethoscope (Grossman, Eicher, Winickoff, & Associates, 1980). Furthermore, Marshall Klaus and John Kennell (1976, 1982) have proposed that the first few hours after birth can be a special time for a mother to thoroughly enjoy her baby, provided she is given the opportunity. Let's take a closer look at Klaus and Kennell's ideas.

According to Klaus and Kennell (1976), one reason that so many mothers can overlook or discount the negative aspects of child care is that they have often begun to forge strong emotional ties to their infant *before* they experience many of the unpleasantries of parenthood. Specifically, Klaus and Kennell believe that the first few hours after birth are a *sensitive period* for the **emotional bonding** of a mother to her infant—a time when the mother is especially ready to respond to and develop a strong sense of affection for her baby. To test his hypothesis, Klaus and Kennell (1976) studied 28 economically disadvantaged mothers who had just delivered full-term healthy infants. During their three-day stay in the hospital, half the mothers followed the traditional routine: They saw their babies briefly after delivery, visited with them 6 to 12 hours later, and then had half-hour feeding sessions with their infants every four hours thereafter. Mothers assigned to a second, or "extended contact" group were permitted five "extra" hours a day to cuddle their babies, including an hour of skin-to-skin contact that took place within three hours of birth.

When observed one month later, mothers who had had extended contact with their newborns stood nearer and soothed their infants more during a routine physical examination, and they held their babies closer while feeding than did mothers who had followed the normal hospital routine. A year later, extended contact mothers were still more soothing, cuddling, and nurturing than mothers in the "normal routine" condition. As for the year-old infants, those who had had extended early contact with their mothers outperformed those who had not on tests of physical and mental development. Thus, it seemed to Klaus and Kennell that mothers had formed closer and more enduring emotional ties with their babies if they had had early contact with them in the first hours after giving birth.

Why Might Early Contact Matter?   Why might mothers build these emotional bridges to their infants just after giving birth? Kennell, Voos, and Klaus (1979) suggested that hormones present at the time of delivery may help to focus the mother's attention on her baby and make her more susceptible to forming a strong emotional bond. If these hormones should dissipate before a mother has any extended contact with her infant, she will presumably become less responsive to her baby, much as animals do if separated from their offspring in the first few hours after giving birth.

Although this "hormonal mediation" hypothesis may sound quite plausible, there are observations it can't easily explain. Consider, for example, that fathers who are present at birth (or soon thereafter) often become just as fascinated with a neonate as mothers do, wishing to touch, hold, or caress the baby (Chandler & Field, 1997; Greenberg & Morris, 1974). Clearly, a father's early **engrossment** with his infant is an emotional reaction very similar to that experienced by mothers and is obviously *not* due to the action of pregnancy hormones.

If the hormonal mediation hypothesis does not explain the early affection that parents display toward their newborn infants, what does? One idea offered by ethologists is that caregivers are biologically predisposed to react favorably and with affection to a neonate's pleasing social overtures (Bowlby, 1969). Another possibility stems from social-psychological research on the interpretation and misattribution of emotions. Perhaps the intense emotional arousal (fear or apprehension) that parents experience during childbirth is *reinterpreted* in a positive light when they are handed an infant who gazes attentively at them, grasps their fingers, and seems to snuggle in response to their caresses. If parents should then attribute these positive feelings to *the baby and its behavior,* it is easy to see how they might feel rather affectionate toward their neonate and become emotionally involved with him or her. However, parents who have little or no early contact with their newborn are unable to attribute

emotional bonding: term used to describe the strong affectional ties that parents may feel toward a neonate; some theorists believe that the strongest bonding occurs shortly after birth, during a sensitive period.

engrossment: paternal analogue of maternal emotional bonding; term used to describe fathers' fascination with their neonates, including their desire to touch, hold, caress, and talk to the newborn baby.

their existing emotional arousal to a beautiful, responsive baby. In fact, they often end up labeling their emotions as exhaustion or a sense of relief that the ordeal of pregnancy and childbirth is finally over (Grossman, Eichler, Winickoff, & Associates, 1980). Perhaps you can see that these latter attributions are unlikely to make parents feel especially drawn toward a newborn child when they finally do have contact with him or her.

Is Early Contact Necessary for Optimal Development? Klaus and Kennell's sensitive-period hypothesis implies that new parents show a basic "readiness" to become emotionally involved with their infant during the first few hours after the baby is born. As we have seen, there is clear evidence to support this proposition. However, Klaus and Kennell also implied that parents who have had little or no contact with their neonates during the sensitive period may never become as attached to these infants as they might had they had skin-to-skin contact with them during the first few hours. This second theoretical proposition is much more controversial.

Susan Goldberg (1983) has carefully reviewed the emotional bonding literature and concluded that, contrary to Klaus and Kennell's claim, "early contact" effects are neither large nor long-lasting. In one well-controlled study in which mothers and neonates were carefully observed for a nine-day period, the advantages of early contact steadily declined over time. By the ninth day after birth, early-contact mothers were no more affectionate or responsive toward their infants than mothers who had had no skin-to-skin contact with their babies for several hours after delivery. Indeed, the delayed-contact mothers showed a dramatic increase in responsiveness over the nine-day observation period—suggesting that the hours immediately after birth are not nearly so critical as Klaus and Kennell assumed (Goldberg, 1983; see also Myers, 1987). Michael Rutter (1981) adds that most adoptive parents are quite satisfied with and will develop close emotional ties to their adoptees, even though they have rarely had any contact with them during the neonatal period (see also Levy-Shiff, Goldshmidt, & Har-Even, 1991). In fact, the likelihood that a mother and her infant will become securely attached is just as high in adoptive families as in nonadoptive ones (Singer, et al., 1985).

In sum, research on early emotional bonding suggests that parents can become highly involved with their infants during the first few hours after birth, and the advantages of such early contact appear to be greatest for younger, economically disadvantaged mothers who know very little about babies or infant care (Eyer, 1992). As a result, many hospitals have altered their routines to permit and encourage these kinds of experiences. Yet, it is important to note that this early contact is neither crucial nor sufficient for the development of strong parent/infant attachments. Stable attachments between infants and caregivers are not formed in a matter of minutes, hours, or days. They build rather slowly from social interactions that take place over *many weeks and months*. So there is absolutely no reason for parents who have not had early skin-to-skin contact with their infant to assume that they will have problems establishing a warm and loving relationship with their child.

ESTABLISHMENT OF INTERACTIONAL SYNCHRONY

One important contributor to the growth of attachments is the **synchronized routines** that caregivers and infants often establish over the first few months of a baby's life (Stern, 1977; Tronick, 1989). These coordinated interactions, which have been likened to "dances," are most likely to develop if the caregiver attends carefully to her baby's state, provides playful stimulation when the baby is alert and attentive, and avoids pushing things when an overexcited or tired infant is fussy and sending the message "Cool it! I just need a break from all this excitement." Edward Tronick (1989,

synchronized routines: generally harmonious interactions between two persons in which participants adjust their behavior in response to the partner's actions.

p. 112) described one very synchronous interaction that unfolded as a mother played peek-a-boo with her infant:

> The infant abruptly turns away from his mother as the game reaches its "peek" of intensity and begins to suck on his thumb and stare into space with a dull facial expression. The mother stops playing and sits back watching. . . . After a few seconds the infant turns back to her with an inviting expression. The mother moves closer, smiles, and says in a high-pitched, exaggerated voice, "Oh, now you're back!" He smiles in response and vocalizes. As they finish crowing together, the infant reinserts his thumb and looks away. The mother again waits. [Soon] the infant turns . . . to her and they greet each other with big smiles.

Notice that much information is exchanged in this simple but synchronous exchange. By turning away and sucking, the excited infant is saying "Hey, I need to slow down and regulate my emotional state." His mother tells him she understands by patiently awaiting his return. As he returns, mom tells him she's glad he's back, and he acknowledges that signal with a smile and an excitable blurt. And when the baby becomes overstimulated a minute or two later, his mother waits for him to calm once again, and he communicates his thanks by smiling wide for her when he turns back the second time. Clearly, this is a dyad that not only interacts smoothly but quickly repairs any interactive errors.

How important are synchronous exchanges to the establishment of affectional ties? We can get some idea by contrasting synchronous interactions with conflictual, nonsynchronous ones. Suppose the mother in the example had been less patient when her infant turned away, choosing instead to click her tongue to attract his attention and to follow up by sticking her face in the baby's line of vision. According to Tronick (1989), what might well happen is that the baby would grimace, turn further away, and perhaps even push at his mother's face. The mother's intrusive actions have communicated something like "Cut the coy stuff and come play with me," whereas the infant's negative response implies "No, you cool it and give me some space." Here, then, is an exchange in which messages go unheeded and interactive errors persist— one that is undoubtedly much less pleasant for both the mother and her baby than the highly affectionate, synchronous interplay described earlier.

In sum, infants play an important role in winning others' affection by virtue of their responsiveness to social overtures and their emerging ability to synchronize their behaviors with those of sensitive companions. Daniel Stern (1977) believes that synchronized interactions between infants and their caregivers may occur several times a day and are particularly important contributors to emotional attachments. As an infant continues to interact with a particular caregiver, he will learn what this person is like and how he can regulate her attention. Of course, the caregiver should become better at interpreting the baby's signals and will learn how to adjust her behavior to successfully capture and maintain his

PHOTO 4.3 Early synchrony of affect and behavior is one of the best predictors of strong, mutually satisfying attachments between infants and their caregivers.

attention. As the caregiver and the infant practice their routines and become better "dance partners," their relationship should become more satisfying for both parties and eventually blossom into a strong reciprocal attachment (Isabella, 1993; Isabella & Belsky, 1991).

How Do Infants Become Attached?

Although many parents do find themselves emotionally drawn to their infant very soon after their baby is born, an infant requires some time before she is developmentally ready to form a genuine attachment to another human being. Many theories have been proposed to explain how and why infants become emotionally involved with the people around them. But before we consider these theories, we should briefly discuss the phases that babies go through in becoming attached to a close companion.

THE GROWTH OF PRIMARY ATTACHMENTS

Many years ago, Rudolph Schaffer and Peggy Emerson (1964) studied the development of emotional attachments by following a group of Scottish infants from early infancy to 18 months of age. Once a month, mothers were interviewed to determine (1) how the infant responded when separated from close companions in seven situations (for example, being left in a crib; being left in the presence of strangers) and (2) the persons to whom the infant's separation responses were directed. A child was judged to be attached to someone if separation from that person reliably elicited a protest.

Schaffer and Emerson found that infants pass through the following phases as they develop close ties with their caregivers:

1. The **asocial phase** (0–6 weeks). The very young infant is somewhat "asocial" in that many kinds of social or nonsocial stimuli will produce a favorable reaction, and few produce any kind of protest. By the end of this period, infants are beginning to show a preference for such social stimuli as a smiling face.

2. The **phase of indiscriminate attachments** (6 weeks to 6–7 months). Now infants clearly enjoy human company but tend to be somewhat indiscriminate: They smile more at people than at such other lifelike objects as talking puppets (Ellsworth, Muir, & Hains, 1993) and are likely to fuss whenever any adult puts them down. Although 3- to 6-month-olds reserve their biggest grins for familiar companions (Watson et al., 1979) and are more quickly soothed by a regular caregiver, they seem to enjoy the attention they receive from just about anyone (including strangers).

3. The **specific attachments phase** (about age 7–9 months). Between 7 and 9 months of age, infants begin to protest only when separated from one particular individual, usually the mother. Now able to crawl, infants may try to follow along behind mother to stay close and will often greet her warmly when she returns. They also become somewhat wary of strangers. According to Schaffer and Emerson, these babies have established their first genuine attachments.

The formation of a strong attachment to a caregiver has another important consequence: it promotes the development of exploratory behavior. Mary Ainsworth (1979) emphasizes that an attachment figure serves as a **secure base** for exploration; a point of safety from which an infant can feel free to venture away. Thus Juan, a securely attached infant visiting a neighbor's home with his mother, may be quite comfortable exploring the far corners of the living room so long as he can

asocial phase (of attachment): approximately the first six weeks of life, in which infants respond in an equally favorable way to increasing social and nonsocial stimuli.

phase of indiscriminate attachments: period between 6 weeks and 6 to 7 months of age in which infants prefer social to nonsocial stimulation and are likely to protest whenever any adult puts them down or leaves them alone.

phase of specific attachment: period between 7 and 9 months of age when infants are attached to one close companion (usually the mother).

secure base: use of a caregiver as a base from which to explore the environment and to which to return for emotional support.

check back occasionally to see that Mom is still seated on the sofa. But should she disappear into the bathroom, Juan may become wary and reluctant to explore. Paradoxical as it may seem, then, infants apparently need to rely on another person in order to feel confident about acting independently.

4. The **phase of multiple attachments.** Within weeks after forming their initial attachments, about half the infants in Schaffer and Emerson's study were becoming attached to other people (fathers, siblings, grandparents, or perhaps even a regular baby-sitter). By 18 months of age, very few infants were attached to only one person, and some were attached to five or more.

Schaffer and Emerson originally believed that infants who are multiply attached have a "hierarchy" of attachment objects and that the individual at the top of the list is their most preferred companion. However, later research indicates that each of the infant's attachment objects may serve different functions, so that the person an infant prefers most may depend on the situation. For example, most infants prefer the mother's company if they are upset or frightened. However, fathers seem to be preferred as playmates, possibly because much of the time they spend with their infants is "play time" (Bretherton, 1985; Lamb, 1981). Schaffer (1977) later concluded that "being attached to several people does not necessarily imply a shallower feeling toward each one, for an infant's capacity for attachment is not like a cake that has to be [divided]. Love, even in babies, has no limits" (p. 100).

THEORIES OF ATTACHMENT

If you have ever had a kitten or a puppy, you may have noticed that pets often seem especially responsive and affectionate to the person who feeds them. Might the same be true of human infants? Developmentalists have long debated this very point, as we will see in examining four influential theories of attachment: psychoanalytic theory, learning theory, cognitive-developmental theory, and ethological theory.

Psychoanalytic Theory: I Love You Because You Feed Me According to Freud, young infants are "oral" creatures who derive satisfaction from sucking and mouthing objects and should be attracted to any person who provides oral pleasure. Since it is usually mothers who "pleasure" oral infants by feeding them, it seemed logical to Freud that the mother would become the baby's primary object of security and affection, particularly if she was relaxed and generous in her feeding practices.

Erik Erikson also believed that a mother's feeding practices will influence the strength or security of her infant's attachments. However, he claimed that a mother's *overall responsiveness* to her child's needs is more important than feeding itself. According to Erikson, a caregiver who consistently responds to all an infant's needs will foster a sense of trust in other people, whereas unresponsive or inconsistent caregiving breeds mistrust. He adds that children who have learned not to trust caregivers during infancy may come to avoid close mutual-trust relationships throughout life.

Before we examine the research on feeding practices and attachments, we need to consider another viewpoint that assumes that feeding is important—learning theory.

Learning Theory: Rewardingness Leads to Love For quite different reasons, some learning theorists have also assumed that infants will become attached to persons who feed them and gratify their needs. Feeding was thought to be particularly important for two reasons (Sears, 1963). First, it should elicit positive responses from a contented infant (smiles, coos) that are likely to increase a caregiver's affection for the baby. Second, feeding is often an occasion when mothers can provide an infant with

phase of multiple attachments: period when infants are forming attachments to companions other than their primary attachment object.

many comforts—food, warmth, tender touches, soft, reassuring vocalizations, changes in scenery, and even a dry diaper (if necessary)—*all in one sitting*. Over time, an infant should come to associate his mother with pleasant or pleasurable sensations, so that the mother herself becomes a valuable commodity. Once the mother (or any other caregiver) has attained this status as a **secondary reinforcer**, the infant is attached; he or she will now do whatever is necessary (smile, cry, coo, babble, or follow) to attract the caregiver's attention or to remain near this valuable and rewarding individual.

Just how important *is* feeding? In 1959, Harry Harlow and Robert Zimmerman reported the results of a study designed to compare the importance of feeding and tactile stimulation for the development of attachments in infant monkeys. The monkeys were separated from their mothers in the first day of life and reared for the next 165 days by two surrogate mothers. As you can see in Photo 4.4, each surrogate mother had a face and well-proportioned body constructed of wire. However, the body of one surrogate (the "cloth mother") was wrapped in foam rubber and covered with terry cloth. Half the infants were always fed by this warm, comfortable cloth mother, the remaining half by the rather uncomfortable "wire mother."

The research question was simple: Would these infants become attached to the "mother" who fed them, or would they instead prefer the soft, cuddly terry cloth mother? It was no contest! Even if fed by the wire mother, infants clearly preferred the cloth mother, spending more than 15 hours a day clutching this surrogate, compared with only an hour or so (mostly at mealtimes) with the wire mother (see Figure 4.4). Furthermore, all infants ran directly to the cloth mother when they were frightened by such novel stimuli as marching toy bears or wooden spiders that were placed in their cages. Apparently the cloth mothers provided the reassurance the infants were seeking, for Harlow and Zimmerman noted that

> In spite of their abject terror, the infant monkeys, after reaching the cloth mother and rubbing their bodies about hers, rapidly come to lose their fear of the frightening stimuli. Indeed, within a minute or two most of the babies were visually exploring the thing which so shortly before had seemed an object of evil. The bravest of the babies would actually leave the mother and approach the fearful monsters, under, of course, the protective gaze of their mothers. (1959, p. 423)

Clearly Harlow and Zimmerman's classic study implies that *contact comfort* is a more powerful contributor to attachment in monkeys than feeding or the reduction of hunger.

Apparently, feeding is not any more important to human infants than to baby monkeys. When Schaffer and Emerson (1964) asked mothers the feeding schedules (regular interval versus demand feeding) they had used and the age at which they had weaned their infants, they found that the generosity of a mother's feeding practices simply did not predict the quality of her infant's attachment to her. In fact, for 39% of these infants, the person who usually fed, bathed, and changed a baby was not even the child's primary attachment object!

Current Viewpoints Although it is now quite clear that feeding is *not* the primary contributor to attachments in either monkeys or humans, modern learning theorists

PHOTO 4.4 The wire and cloth surrogate mothers used in Harlow's research. Infant monkeys remain with the cloth mother even though they must stretch to the wire mother to feed. This was one observation that led Harlow to conclude that feeding is not the most important contributor to primary social attachments.

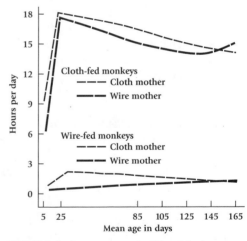

FIGURE 4.4 Average amount of time infant monkeys spent in contact with their cloth and wire mother surrogates. The monkeys spent much more of their time clinging to the cloth mother, regardless of which mother had fed them. (From Harlow & Zimmerman, 1959.)

secondary reinforcer: an initially neutral stimulus that acquires reinforcement value by virtue of its repeated association with other reinforcing stimuli.

continue to argue that *reinforcement* is the mechanism responsible for social attachments (Gewirtz & Petrovich, 1982). Their revised viewpoint, which is similar to that of Erik Erikson, is that infants will be attracted to any individual who is quick to respond to all their needs and who provides them with a variety of pleasant or rewarding experiences. Indeed, Schaffer and Emerson (1964) found that the two aspects of a mother's behavior that predicted the character of her infant's attachment to her were her *responsiveness* to the infant's behavior and the *total amount of stimulation* she provided. Mothers who responded reliably and appropriately to their infants' bids for attention and who often played with their babies had infants who were closely attached to them.

Cognitive-Developmental Theory: To Love You, I Must Know You Will Be There

Cognitive-developmental theory has little to say about which adults are most likely to appeal to infants, but it does remind us of the holistic character of development by suggesting that the ability to form attachments depends, in part, on the infant's level of intellectual development. Before an attachment can occur, the infant must be able to discriminate familiar companions from strangers. He must also recognize that familiar companions have a "permanence" about them (object permanence), for it would be difficult indeed to form a stable relationship with a person who ceases to exist whenever she passes from view (Schaffer, 1971). So perhaps it is no accident that attachments first emerge at age 7 to 9 months—precisely the time infants are entering Piaget's *fourth sensorimotor substage,* the point at which they first begin to search for and find objects that they've seen someone hide from them.

Barry Lester and his associates (1974) evaluated this hypothesis by giving 9-month-old infants a test of object permanence before exposing them to brief separations from their mothers, their fathers, and a stranger. They found that 9-month-olds who scored high (substage 4 or above) in object permanence protested only when separated from their mothers, whereas age-mates who scored lower (substage 3 or below) showed little evidence of *any* separation protest. So it seemed that only the cognitively advanced 9-month-olds had formed a primary attachment (to their mothers)—implying that the timing of this important emotional milestone does depend, in part, on the infant's level of object permanence.

Ethological Theory: Perhaps I Was Born to Love

Ethologists have proposed a most interesting and influential explanation for emotional attachments that has strong evolutionary overtones. A major assumption of the ethological approach is that all species, including human beings, are born with a number of innate behavioral tendencies that have in some way contributed to the survival of the species over the course of evolution. Indeed, John Bowlby (1969, 1980), who was originally a psychoanalyst, came to believe that many of these built-in behaviors are specifically designed to promote attachments between infants and their caregivers. Even the attachment relationship itself is said to have adaptive significance, serving to protect the young from predators and other natural calamities and to ensure that their needs are met. Of course, ethologists would argue that the long-range purpose of the primary attachment is to permit members of each successive generation to live long enough to reproduce, thereby enabling the species to survive.

Origins of the Ethological Viewpoint The ethological theory of attachment was prompted by research with animals. In 1937, Konrad Lorenz reported that very young goslings would follow almost any moving object—their mothers, a duck, or even a human being—a behavior he labeled **imprinting.** Lorenz also noted that (1) imprinting is automatic—young fowl do not have to be taught to follow; (2) imprinting occurs only within a narrowly delimited *critical period* after the bird has

imprinting: an innate or instinctual form of learning in which the young of certain species will follow and become attached to moving objects (usually their mothers).

hatched; and (3) imprinting is irreversible—once the bird begins to follow a particular object, it will remain attached to it.

Lorenz then concluded that imprinting was an adaptive response. Young birds should generally survive if they follow their mothers so that they are led to food and afforded protection. Those that wander away may starve or be eaten by predators and thus fail to pass their genes to future generations. So over the course of many, many generations, the imprinting response eventually became an inborn, **preadapted characteristic** that attaches a young fowl to its mother, thereby increasing its chances of survival.

Attachment in Humans   Although human infants do not imprint on their mothers in the same way that young fowl do, they have inherited a number of attributes that help them to maintain contact with others and to elicit caregiving. Lorenz (1943), for example, suggested that a baby's *kewpie doll* appearance (that is, large forehead, chubby cheeks, and soft, rounded features; see Figure 4.5) makes the infant appear cute or lovable to caregivers. Thomas Alley (1981) agrees. Alley found that adults judged line drawings of infant faces (and profiles) to be "adorable"—much cuter than those of 2-, 3-, and 4-year-old children. So babyish facial features may well help to elicit the kinds of positive attention from others that will promote social attachments, and the more attractive the baby, the more favorably mothers and other companions respond to him or her (Barden et al., 1989; Langlois et al., 1995). Nevertheless, babies need not be adorable to foster close attachments, for a clear majority of relatively unattractive infants end up securely attached to their caregivers (Speltz et al., 1997).

Not only do most infants have "cute" faces, but many of their inborn, reflexive responses may have an endearing quality about them (Bowlby, 1969). For example, an infant's sucking and grasping reflexes may lead parents to believe that their baby enjoys being close to them. Smiling, which is initially a reflexive response to almost any pleasing stimulus, is a particularly potent signal to caregivers, as are cooing, excitable blurting, and spontaneous babbling (Keller & Scholmerich, 1987). In fact, an adult's typical response to a baby's smiles and positive vocalizations is to smile at (or vocalize to) the infant (Gewirtz & Petrovich, 1982; Keller & Scholmerich, 1987), and parents often interpret their baby's grins, laughs, and babbles as an indication that the child is contented and that they are effective caregivers. So a smiling or babbling infant can reinforce caregiving activities and thereby increase the likelihood that parents or other nearby companions will want to attend to this happy little person in the future.

Finally, Bowlby insists that under normal circumstances, adults are just as biologically predisposed to respond favorably to a baby's signals as the baby is to emit them. It is difficult, he claims, for parents to ignore an urgent cry or to fail to warm up to a baby's big grin. In sum, human infants and their caregivers are said to have evolved in ways that predispose them to respond favorably to each other and to form close attachments, thus enabling infants (and ultimately, the species) to survive.

Does this mean that attachments are automatic? No indeed! Bowlby claims that secure attachments develop gradually as parents become more proficient at reading and reacting appropriately to the baby's signals and the baby is *learning* what his parents are like and how he might regulate their behavior. Yet, the process can easily go awry as illustrated by the finding that an infant's preprogrammed signals will eventually wane if they fail to produce favorable reactions from an unresponsive companion, such as a depressed mother or an unhappily married father (Ainsworth et al., 1978). So while Bowlby believes that human beings are biologically *prepared* to form close attachments, he also stresses that secure emotional

preadapted characteristics: an innate attribute that is a product of evolution and serves some function that increases the chances of survival for the individual and the species.

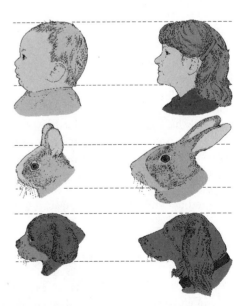

FIGURE 4.5 Infants of many species display the "kewpie-doll" effect that makes them appear lovable and elicits caregivers' attention. (Adapted from Lorenz, 1943.)

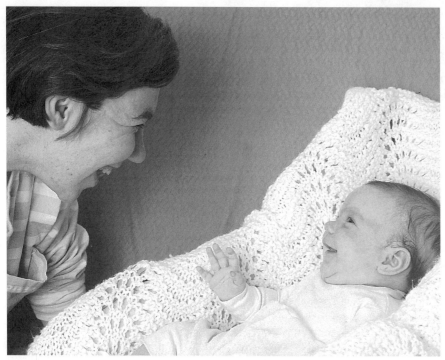

PHOTO 4.5 Few signals attract as much attention as a baby's social smile.

bonds will not develop unless each participant has *learned* how to respond appropriately to the behavior of the other.

Comparing the Four Theoretical Approaches Although the four theories we have reviewed differ in many respects, each has something to offer. Clearly, feeding practices are not as important to human attachments as psychoanalysts had originally thought; but it was Freud who stressed that we will need to know more about mother/infant interactions if we hope to understand how babies form attachments. Erik Erikson and the learning theorists pursued Freud's early leads and concluded that caregivers do play an important role in an infant's emotional development. Presumably infants are likely to view a responsive companion who provides many comforts as a trustworthy and rewarding individual who is worthy of affection. Ethologists can agree with this point of view, but they add that infants are *active participants* in the attachment process who emit preprogrammed responses that enable them to promote the very interactions from which attachments are likely to develop. Finally, cognitive theorists have contributed by showing that the timing of emotional attachments is related to the infant's level of cognitive development. It makes little sense to tag one of these theories as "correct" and to ignore the others, for each theory has helped us to understand how infants become attached to their most intimate companions.

Two Attachment-Related Fears of Infancy

At about the same time infants are establishing close affectional ties to a caregiver, they often begin to display negative emotional reactions that may puzzle or perhaps even annoy their companions. In this section we look briefly at two of the common fears of infancy: *stranger anxiety* and *separation anxiety*.

STRANGER ANXIETY

Nine-month-old Billy is sitting on the floor in the den when his mother leads a strange person into the room. The stranger suddenly walks closer, bends over, and says "Hi, Billy! How are you?" If Billy is like many 9-month-olds, he may stare at the stranger for a moment and then turn away, whimper, and crawl toward his mother.

This wary reaction to a stranger, or **stranger anxiety,** stands in marked contrast to the smiling, babbling, and other positive greetings that infants often display when approached by a familiar companion. Most infants react positively to strangers until they form their first attachment, and they become apprehensive shortly thereafter (Schaffer & Emerson, 1964). Wary reactions to strangers—which are often mixed with signs of interest—peak at 8 to 10 months of age, and gradually decline in intensity over the second year (Sroufe, 1977). However, even an 8- to 10-month-old is not afraid of every strange face she sees and may occasionally react rather positively to strangers. In Box 4.2, we consider the circumstances under which stranger anxiety is most likely to occur and see how medical personnel and other child-care professionals might use this knowledge to head off outbreaks of fear and trembling in their offices.

SEPARATION ANXIETY

Many infants who have formed primary attachments also begin to display obvious signs of discomfort when separated from their mothers or other attachment objects. Ten-month-old Tony, for example, is likely to cry as he sees his mother put on a coat and pick up her purse as she prepares to go shopping, whereas 15-month-old Doris might even follow her mother to the door while whining and pleading not to be left at home. These reactions reflect the children's **separation anxiety.** Separation anxiety normally appears at 6 to 8 months of age (at about the time infants are forming emotional attachments, peaks at 14 to 18 months, and gradually becomes less frequent and less intense throughout infancy and the preschool period (Kagan, Kearsley, & Zelazo, 1978; Weinraub & Lewis, 1977). However, grade-school children and even adolescents may still show signs of anxiety and depression when separated for long periods from their loved ones (Thurber, 1995).

Children raised in some cultural settings protest separations from their mothers at an earlier age than North American or European infants. For example, Mary Ainsworth (1967) found that Ugandan infants begin to fear such separations as early as 5 to 6 months of age. Why? One reason may be that Ugandan babies have much closer contact with their mothers than is typical in Western cultures. These infants sleep with their mothers, nurse for at least two years, and go wherever their mothers go, riding on the mother's hips or across her back in a cotton sling. So Ugandan infants may be quick to protest separations from their mothers because these separations are very unusual events.

WHY DO INFANTS FEAR STRANGERS AND SEPARATIONS?

Why do infants who are just beginning to experience the pleasures of love suddenly become wary of strangers and anxious when separated from their objects of affection? Let's consider three very different points of view.

The "Conditioned Anxiety" (or Fear of Separation) Hypothesis Psychoanalysts and some social learning theorists have proposed that infants may learn to fear separations from their caregivers if prior discomforts (for example, hunger, wet diapers, and pain)

stranger anxiety: a wary or fretful reaction that infants and toddlers often display when approached by an unfamiliar person.

separation anxiety: a wary or fretful reaction that infants and toddlers often display when separated from the person(s) to whom they are attached.

Box 4.2   *Applying Developmental Research*

Combating Stranger Anxiety: Some Helpful Hints for Doctors and Child-Care Professionals

It is not at all unusual for toddlers visiting the doctor's office to break into tears and to cling tenaciously to their parents. Some youngsters who remember previous visits may be suffering from "shot anxiety" rather than stranger anxiety, but many are simply reacting fearfully to the approach of an intrusive physician who may poke, prod, and handle them in ways that are atypical and upsetting. Fortunately, there are steps that caregivers and medical personnel (or any other stranger) can take to make such encounters less terrifying for an infant or toddler. What can we suggest?

1. *Keep familiar companions available.* Infants react much more negatively to strangers when they are separated from their mothers or other close companions. Indeed, most 6- to 12-month-olds are not particularly wary of an approaching stranger if they are sitting on their mother's laps; however, they will frequently whimper and cry at the stranger's approach if seated only a few feet from their mothers (Morgan & Ricciuti, 1969; and see Bohlin & Hagekull, 1993). Clearly, doctors and nurses can expect a more constructive response from their youngest patients if they can avoid separating them from their caregivers.
2. *Arrange for companions to respond positively to the stranger.* Stranger anxiety is less likely to occur if the caregiver issues a warm greeting to the stranger or uses a positive tone of voice when talking to the infant about the stranger (Feinman, 1992). These actions permit the child to engage in *social referencing* and to conclude that maybe the stranger really isn't all that scary if mom and dad seem to like him. It might not hurt, then, for medical personnel to strike up a pleasant conversation with the caregiver before directing their attention to the child.
3. *Make the setting more "familiar."* Stranger anxiety occurs less frequently in familiar settings than in unfamiliar ones. For example, few 10-month-olds are especially wary of strangers at home, but most react negatively to strange companions when tested in an unfamiliar laboratory (Sroufe, Waters, & Matas, 1974). Although it may be unrealistic to advise modern physicians to make home visits, they could make at least one of their examination rooms more homelike for young children, perhaps by placing an attractive mobile in one corner and posters of cartoon characters on the wall, or by having a stuffed toy or two available for the child to play with. The infant's familiarity with a strange setting also makes a difference: Whereas the vast majority (90%) of 10-month-olds become upset if a stranger approaches them within a minute after being placed in an unfamiliar room, only about half will react negatively to the stranger when they have had 10 minutes to grow accustomed to this setting (Sroufe et al., 1974). Perhaps trips to the doctor would become more tolerable for an infant or toddler

have been especially frequent or intense during periods when caregivers were not present to relieve them. In other words, infants may associate discomfort with the caregiver's absence and then express their "conditioned anxiety" by protesting whenever the caregiver is about to depart. Stranger anxiety is presumably a simple extension of separation anxiety: The child protests the approach of intrusive strangers because she fears becoming separated from or losing the person(s) to whom she is attached.

Although this **"conditioned anxiety" hypothesis** is appealing for its simplicity, there are problems with it. For example, it cannot easily explain why infants are less likely to protest separations from a loved one at home (where they have previously suffered many discomforts) than in a laboratory where they have never been before (Rinkoff & Corter, 1980). Nor does it adequately explain the *early* separation protests seen among Ugandan infants who have rarely been separated from their mothers and therefore have had little or no opportunity to associate pain and discomfort with the mother's absence. Let's now consider a second point of view that does explain these findings.

"conditioned anxiety" hypothesis: notion that infants fear separations from caregivers (and strangers who might cause such separations) because prior discomforts have been especially intense when caregivers were not present to relieve them.

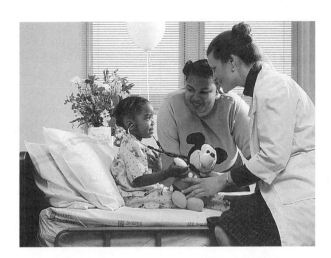

Most toddlers respond favorably to a friendly stranger—even a doctor—who offers a toy.

familiar activity (Bretherton, Stolberg, & Kreye, 1981; Sroufe, 1977). It also helps if the stranger, like any sensitive caregiver, takes his or her cues from the infant (Mangelsdorf, 1992). Babies prefer strangers they can control! Intrusive strangers who approach quickly and force themselves on the child (for example, by trying to pick infants up before they have time to adjust) probably get the response they deserve.

5. *Try looking a little less strange to the child.* Stranger anxiety depends, in part, on the stranger's physical appearance. Jerome Kagan (1972) has argued that infants form mental representations, or *schemas,* for the faces that they encounter in daily life and are most likely to be afraid of people whose appearance is not easily assimilated into these existing schemas. So a doctor in a sterile white lab coat with a strange stethoscope around her neck (or a nurse with a pointed hat that may give her a "witchlike" look) can make infants and toddlers rather wary indeed! Pediatric professionals may not be able to alter various physical features (for example, a huge nose or a facial scar) that might make children wary; but they can and often do shed their strange instruments and white uniforms in favor of more "normal" attire that will help their youngest patients to recognize them as members of the human race. Baby-sitters with spiked hair or nose rings might also heed this advice if establishing rapport with their young companions is a priority.

if medical personnel gave the child a few minutes to familiarize himself with the examination room before making their entrance.

4. *Be a sensitive, unobtrusive stranger.* Not surprisingly, an infant's response to a stranger depends on the stranger's behavior (Sroufe, 1977). The meeting is likely to go best if the stranger initially keeps his or her distance and then approaches slowly while smiling, talking, and offering a familiar toy or suggesting a

The Ethological Viewpoint Ethologist John Bowlby (1973) claims that many situations infants face qualify as *natural clues to danger*—situations that have been so frequently associated with danger throughout human evolutionary history that a fear or avoidance response has become "biologically programmed." Among the situations that infants may be programmed to fear are strange faces (which, in earlier eras, may have belonged to predatory animals), strange settings, and the "strange circumstance" of being separated from familiar companions.

Critics scoffed at this explanation when it was first proposed. After all, couldn't one reasonably argue that many stimuli, including the child's eventual attachment objects, should be sufficiently unfamiliar to elicit a protest almost from birth if Bowlby's notion of programmed fears were correct? Yet it is important to understand that Bowlby was *not* suggesting that a fear of the unfamiliar is present *at birth.* Quite the contrary; he argued that a neonate's cognitive and perceptual capabilities are very immature and that it will take some time for the child to learn what is "familiar" and to discriminate these persons, objects, and events from those that are unfamiliar. But once such discriminations are possible, the infant's preprogrammed "fear of the unfamiliar" should be readily apparent.

The ethological viewpoint easily explains many observations that the "conditioned anxiety" hypothesis cannot. For example, Bowlby would expect infants to show stronger separation protests in an unfamiliar laboratory than at home because the "strangeness" of the laboratory setting magnifies the apprehension they will ordinarily experience when separated from a caregiver. Furthermore, ethologists would argue that Ainsworth's (1967) Ugandan infants were quick to protest separations from their mothers because these separations occur so very infrequently that they qualify as very strange and fear-provoking events.

Ethological theory also explains why stranger and separation anxieties decline during the second year. Once infants begin to walk and can use their attachment objects as *secure bases* for exploration, they actively initiate separations and will eventually discover that many novel stimuli (including friendly strangers) can be interesting and enjoyable in their own right.

In sum, ethologists view the anxieties of infancy as biologically influenced and highly adaptive concerns that help to protect the young of a species from harm by ensuring that they will remain near their caregivers. Yet the caregivers who serve this protective function are also instrumental in alleviating these programmed fears. By serving as a secure base for exploratory activities, a caregiver encourages her infant to become more familiar with the broader environment. As a result, the child should eventually become more tolerant of separations and much less wary of stimuli (strangers and unfamiliar settings) that have previously been a source of concern (Ainsworth, 1979; Posada et al., 1995).

The Cognitive-Developmental Viewpoint   Cognitive theorists view both stranger anxiety and separation anxiety as natural outgrowths of the infant's perceptual and cognitive development. Jerome Kagan (1972, 1976) suggests that 6- to 10-month-olds have finally developed stable schemes for (1) the faces of familiar companions and (2) these companions' probable whereabouts at home (if they are not present). Suddenly a strange face that is discrepant with the infants' schemes for caregivers now upsets children because they can't *explain* who this is or what has become of familiar caregivers. Kagan also proposes that 7- to 10-month-olds will not protest most separations at home because they have a pretty good idea where a caregiver has gone should he leave them in the living room and proceed to a familiar locale, such as the kitchen. But should a caregiver violate this "familiar faces in familiar places" scheme by lifting his briefcase and walking out the front door, an infant cannot easily account for his whereabouts and will probably cry.

Indeed, toddlers observed at home are more likely to protest when mothers depart through an unfamiliar doorway (such as the entry to the cellar) than through a familiar one (Littenberg, Tulkin, & Kagan, 1971). Even more revealing are the results of an interesting laboratory study (Corter, Zucker, & Galligan, 1980) in which 9-month-old infants first accompanied their mothers to a strange room (Room A) and shortly thereafter watched their mothers exit into a second room (Room B). Though few infants protested immediately, they soon crawled into the adjoining room in search of their mothers. In cognitive terms, it is reasonable to assume that the infants had formed a scheme for the mother's whereabouts once they had found her in Room B. At this point, the infants and their mothers reentered Room A and spent a short time together before the mother departed once again. But on this second trial, she went into another room (Room C), thus violating the infant's scheme for her probable whereabouts. This time, the majority of the infants fussed or cried! And where did these distressed youngsters go to search for their mothers? Generally, they crawled to the doorway that matched their schemes (Room B) rather than to the portal through which they had most recently watched the mother depart (Room C). Here, then, is clear support for Kagan's theory: Infants are most likely to protest separations from a caregiver when they are uncertain of her whereabouts.

Notice that Corter's 9-month-olds were looking for Mom *where they had previously found her* rather than where she was last seen. This is precisely the type of error made by Piaget's 8- to 12-month-old infants as they first began to search for disappearing objects in object permanence tests. Must infants have reached this "searching" phase (that is, the fourth sensorimotor substage that Piaget believed to be the beginning of true *object permanence*) before they will begin forming hypotheses about the probable location of an absent caregiver? Probably so. If an infant did not recognize that a departing caregiver continued to exist somewhere out of view, he or she would not try to determine her location and might not even protest her absence. As it turns out, we have already discussed a study that supports this line of reasoning. Recall that Barry Lester and his associates (1974) found that infants who had not yet reached the point at which they search for disappearing objects generally failed to protest when separated from their mothers.

Summing Up   Clearly, stranger anxiety and separation anxiety are complex emotional responses that may stem, in part, from (1) a child's general *apprehension of the unfamiliar* (the ethological viewpoint); (2) her inability to explain who a stranger may be, what he may want, or what has become of familiar companions (the cognitive-developmental viewpoint); and (3) perhaps even a *fear of losing a companion* who provides so much warmth and security (the "conditioned anxiety" interpretation). So there is no one correct explanation for these interesting fears of infancy: Each of the theories helped us to understand why infants may be wary of strangers and upset when separated from loved ones. In Box 4.3, we see how parents and substitute caregivers might use this knowledge to make necessary separations easier for infants and toddlers to bear.

Reactions to the Loss of an Attachment Object

To this point, the research we have reviewed has focused on children's rather immediate responses to *short-term* separations from attachment objects. How do young children react to prolonged or permanent separations from their loved ones? Do they eventually stop protesting or perhaps even forget these special companions? Seeking to answer these questions, John Bowlby (1960) studied the behavior of children aged 15 to 30 months who were hospitalized for chronic illnesses and thus separated from their mothers for a long period. According to Bowlby, most of these children progressed through three behavioral phases during their separations:

1. In an initial *protest phase,* children tried to regain their mothers by crying, demanding her return, and resisting the attention of substitute caregivers. This phase lasted from a few hours to more than a week.
2. In a second *phase of despair,* children seemed to lose hope of ever being reunited with their mothers. They often became apathetic and unresponsive to toys and other people and seemed to be in a deep state of mourning.
3. Finally, many children progressed to what Bowlby called the *detachment phase.* They appeared to have "recovered" in that they showed renewed interest in toys and substitute caregivers; but their relationships with their mothers had changed. When the mother visited, her child was often cool and indifferent, showing little if any protest when she left once again. It almost seemed as if the children were in the process of undoing their attachments to their mothers.

Box 4.3   *Applying Developmental Research*

On Easing the Pain of Separation

At some point, most parents find it necessary to leave their infants and toddlers in an unfamiliar setting (such as a nursery or a day-care center) or in the company of a stranger (for example, a baby-sitter) for hours at a time. How can they make these necessary separations easier for their child to bear? Here are three simple recommendations:

1. *Provide an explanation for the separation.* Cognitive-developmental theorists tell us that separations are most upsetting when infants and toddlers cannot explain where caregivers have gone or when they will return. Thus, an explanation for the separation may help immensely. Indeed, toddlers who are left in unfamiliar settings cry less and play much more constructively if their mothers have taken a moment to explain that they are leaving and will soon return (Weinraub & Lewis, 1977). Brief explanations work better than lengthy ones (Adams & Passman, 1981), and one need not prepare a toddler days in advance for an upcoming separation. In fact, 2-year-olds who are prepared in advance often worry in advance; moreover, they protest more and play less constructively once the separation actually occurs than do age-mates who have received little advance preparation (Adams & Passman, 1980).

2. *Provide some reminder of home.* Ethologists tell us that separations involving a *strange* caregiver in a *strange* setting are likely to be particularly upsetting. Not surprisingly, then, separations can be made less painful for older infants and toddlers if they have some reminder of home with them, such as a favorite stuffed animal or a security blanket (Passman & Weisberg, 1975). Indeed, giving the toddler a sharply focused photograph of his mother (or having one available for the substitute caregiver to show the child) may also help him to respond more constructively to a necessary separation (Passman & Longeway, 1982).

3. *Choose a sensitive substitute caregiver.* Finally, all developmentalists advise parents to select a substitute caregiver who enjoys children and is sensitive to their concerns. Although infants 8 months of age and older are likely to become visibly upset when first left with an unfamiliar sitter, their adjustment to this arrangement clearly depends on the sitter's behavior (Gunnar

Necessary separations are easier to bear when toddlers have their favorite toys with them and their sitters act more like playmates than like caretakers.

et al., 1992). If the sitter assumes a "caretaker" role by first settling the child in and then pursuing her own interests, most infants and toddlers will continue to display signs of distress. But if the sitter acts as a "playmate" by providing toys and attracting the child's interest, most infants and toddlers will quickly stop protesting and join in the fun (Gunnar et al., 1992). Clearly, a sitter who enjoys interacting with young children is a far better choice than one who sees her function as quickly attending to the child's most basic needs before heading to the telephone or refrigerator.

Bowlby's observations were later replicated by Heinicke and Westheimer (1965) who studied the behavior of 2- to 3-year-old children left by their parents in a residential nursery for periods ranging from two weeks to three months.

Bowlby noted that a fourth separation phase, *permanent withdrawal from human relationships,* may occur if the child's separation from the mother is extremely prolonged or if the child loses a series of temporary attachment objects, such as nurses or baby-sitters, while separated from the mother. In either case, the child often becomes uninterested in contacting others. He or she is still able to communicate with other people on their initiative but becomes more egocentric as attention shifts from human beings to fuzzy toys or other inanimate objects.

Michael Rutter (1981) has carefully reviewed these and other pertinent data and concluded that children's reactions to long-term separations are nowhere near as uniform as Bowlby suggests (see also Schaffer, 1990). According to Rutter, the majority of children who are securely attached to their caregivers may protest and show some "despair" over a long-term separation, but they are unlikely to "detach" themselves either from their close companions (that is, parents) or from human beings in general. Yet, Rutter acknowledges that infants and toddlers who have *shaky, insecure* relationships with companions at home may well put some psychological distance between themselves and these persons, almost as if they were becoming detached. And should the child's attachments be extremely insecure, he or she may occasionally withdraw from human contact, sinking into a state of "affectionless psychopathology" in which it becomes exceedingly difficult to be emotionally involved with anyone (see also DeAngelis, 1997).

Clearly Rutter is proposing that there are perhaps several kinds of attachments that children may form with caregivers and that different kinds of attachments may have different implications for the child's future social and emotional well-being. In Chapter 5, we will see that he is right on both counts. And would you care to hazard a guess about whether an insecure attachment with a close companion is better than no attachment at all? This is another issue we will consider in the next chapter as we review what is known about the social, emotional, and intellectual development of children who are denied opportunities to form emotional attachments during the early years of their lives.

Summary

AN OVERVIEW OF EMOTIONAL DEVELOPMENT

- Human infants are clearly emotional beings. At birth, babies reliably display interest, distress, disgust, and contentment (as indicated by their facial expressions), with the remaining **primary emotions** (that is, anger, sadness, surprise, and fear) normally appearing by the middle of the first year. Such **secondary emotions** as embarrassment, pride, guilt, and shame emerge in the second (or third) year, after children reach such cognitive milestones as self-recognition and have acquired standards for evaluating their conduct.

- The socialization of emotions and **emotional self-regulation** begin very early, as parents model positive emotions for their infants, attend carefully to and try to prolong their infants' pleasant feelings, and become less responsive to infants' negative emotional displays. By the end of the first year, infants develop simple strategies for regulating aversive arousal; soon thereafter they will be making active attempts to suppress their sadness or anger. However, the ability to regulate and control emotions develops very slowly, and children may be well into the grade-school years before they become proficient at complying with culturally defined **emotional display rules.**

- The infant's ability to recognize and interpret others' emotions improves dramatically over the first year. By 8 to 10 months of age, infants are capable of **social referencing,** and their ability to identify and interpret others' emotions continues to improve throughout childhood, aided in part by cognitive development and by family conversations centering on the causes of one's own and others' emotions.

- Emotions play at least two important roles in an infant's life. The child's emotional displays promote social contact with caregivers and help caregivers adjust their behaviors to her needs and goals. The infant's ability to recognize and interpret others' emotions serves an important *knowledge* function by helping the child to infer how he should feel, think, or behave in uncertain situations.

TEMPERAMENT AND DEVELOPMENT

- Many components of **temperament,** a person's tendency to respond in predictable ways to environmental events, are genetically influenced. Environment also contributes heavily to temperament, with nonshared environmental influences having the larger impact.

- Such components of temperament as activity level, irritability, sociability, and **behavioral inhibition** are moderately stable over time and forecast later variations in adult personality. Stability is greatest for individuals at the extremes of a temperamental dimension.

- Temperamental attributes often cluster in predictable patterns such as the **easy, difficult,** and **slow-to-warm-up profiles.** Although children with difficult and slow-to-warm-up temperaments are at greater risk of experiencing adjustment problems, whether they actually develop these problems depends on the **goodness of fit** between the parenting they receive and their own temperamental attributes.

WHAT ARE EMOTIONAL ATTACHMENTS?

- Infants normally form affectional ties to their close companions during the first year of life. These **attachments** are reciprocal relationships, for an infant's **attachment objects** (parents and other intimate companions) will normally become attached to him or her. Parents' initial **emotional bonding/engrossment** with their infant builds in strength as they gear their behavior to the infant's social signals and establish **synchronized routines.** These exquisite interactions are pleasing for both parents and infants and are thought to contribute to strong reciprocal attachments.

HOW DO INFANTS BECOME ATTACHED?

- Infants pass through an **asocial phase** and a **phase of indiscriminate attachment** before forming their first true attachments at 7 to 9 months of age during the **phase of specific attachments.** Attached infants become more curious, using their attachment object as a **secure base** for exploration. They eventually enter the **phase of multiple attachments,** forming affectional ties to more than one person.

THEORIES OF ATTACHMENT

- Early *psychoanalytic* and *learning* theories were largely discredited by the finding that feeding plays much less a role in human attachments than these models expected. The *cognitive-developmental* notion that attachments depend, in part, on cognitive development has received some support. *Ethological* theory, which specifies that humans have **preadapted characteristics** that predispose them to form attachments, has become especially influential in recent years. Yet, all these theories have contributed to our understanding of infant attachments.

TWO ATTACHMENT-RELATED FEARS OF INFANCY

- At about the time infants are becoming attached to a close companion, they often begin to display **stranger anxiety** and **separation anxiety.** These two fears, which stem from infants' wariness of strange situations and their inability to explain who strangers are and the whereabouts of absent companions, usually decline dramatically in the second year as toddlers mature intellectually and venture away from their secure bases to explore.

REACTIONS TO THE LOSS OF AN ATTACHMENT OBJECT

- Prolonged or permanent separations from a loved one are very stressful for young children, and a child's ability to cope with such loss will depend on the quality of his or her emotional relationship with the departed person. Children who have stable, secure ties with caregivers often protest and may show some short-term depression, or despair, over the loss of an attachment object. However, those who are insecure in their emotional relationships may become "detached" from close companions and, in extreme cases, may withdraw from human contact and experience difficulties becoming involved with anyone.

Chapter Five

Early Social and Emotional Development II:

INDIVIDUAL DIFFERENCES AND THEIR IMPLICATIONS FOR FUTURE DEVELOPMENT

**Individual Differences
in Attachment Quality**

Assessing Attachment Security

Cultural Variations in Attachment

**Factors That Influence
Attachment Security**

Quality of Caregiving

Infant Characteristics

Fathers as Attachment Objects

Fathers as Caregivers

Fathers' Influence on Early Intellectual Development

Fathers as Contributors to Early Social
and Emotional Development

Attachment and Later Development

Long-term Correlates of Secure
and Insecure Attachments

Why Might Attachment Quality
Forecast Later Outcomes?

Is Attachment History Destiny?

The Unattached Infant

Effects of Social Isolation in Dogs

Harlow's Studies of Socially Deprived Monkeys

Social Deprivation in Humans

**Maternal Employment, Day Care,
and Early Emotional Development**

Benefits of High-Quality Alternative Care

The Importance of High-Quality Parenting

How Might We Assist Working Parents?

Summary

M y sister once asked whether it was normal for a 10-month-old to be a "mama's boy." She then proceeded to tell me that her son Jacob often cried when she left him alone and would try to crawl to wherever she had gone. Actually, she was overstating the case. Jacob would cry occasionally when his mother disappeared from view at grandma's house or left him alone for more than five to ten minutes at home. But in most cases Jacob reacted rather normally to a separation from his mother: He watched intently as she left and then usually continued whatever he was doing. My sister and I talked for a while about the nature of relationships between mothers and infants, and we eventually decided that Jacob's attachment to her was one indication that he was well on his way to becoming a socially responsive little boy.

Had he been there, Sigmund Freud would surely have agreed. Freud (1905/1930) repeatedly argued that the emotional events and experiences of infancy can have any number of long-term effects on developing children. In fact, he stressed that the formation of a stable mother/infant emotional bond is absolutely necessary for normal social and personality development, a sentiment shared by ethologist John Bowlby and the best-known psychoanalytic theorist of recent times, Erik Erikson. Erikson's view was that secure emotional attachments to caregivers provide the infant with a basic sense of trust that will permit him or her to form close affectional ties to other people later in life. Learning theorists such as Harry Harlow (who studied monkeys) and Robert Sears (who studied humans) believed that close contact with a mother figure allows the infant to acquire a repertoire of social skills that will enable him or her to interact effectively and appropriately with other members of the species. In sum, almost everyone agrees that the emotional events of infancy are very influential in shaping one's future development.

There are at least two ways to evaluate this **"early experience" hypothesis.** First, we could try to determine whether infants who do not become securely attached to their parents turn out any different from those who do. Second, we could look at what happens to infants who have had little or no contact with a mother figure during the first two years and do not become attached to anyone. In the pages that follow, we will consider the findings and implications of both these lines of inquiry.

Individual Differences in Attachment Quality

The attachment relationships that virtually all home-reared infants establish with their caregivers clearly differ in quality. Some infants are quite comfortable and relaxed around caregivers whereas others seem highly anxious or uncertain about what to expect next. Why are some infants secure and others insecure in their attachment relationships? And does the security of a child's early attachments have any impact on later development? To answer these questions, researchers first had to find ways of measuring attachment quality.

ASSESSING ATTACHMENT SECURITY

The most widely used technique for measuring the quality of attachments that 1- to 2-year-olds have established with their mothers or other caregivers is Mary Ainsworth's Strange Situation procedure (Ainsworth et al., 1978). The **Strange Situation** consists of a series of eight episodes (summarized in Table 5-1) that attempt to simulate (1) naturalistic caregiver/infant interactions in the presence of toys (to see whether the infant uses the caregiver as a *secure base* from which to explore); (2) brief separations from the caregiver and encounters with strangers (which will often stress

"early experience" hypothesis: the notion that the social and emotional events of infancy are very influential in determining the course of one's future development.

Strange Situation: a series of eight separation and reunion episodes to which infants are exposed in order to determine the quality of their attachments.

TABLE 5-1 The eight episodes of the strange situation

EPISODE	EVENTS	POTENTIAL ATTACHMENT BEHAVIORS NOTED
1.	Experimenter introduces parent and baby to playroom and leaves.	
2.	Parent sits while baby plays.	Parent as a secure base
3.	Stranger enters, sits, and talks to parent.	Stranger anxiety
4.	Parent leaves, stranger offers comfort if the baby is upset.	Separation anxiety
5.	Parent returns, greets baby, and offers comfort if baby is upset. Stranger leaves.	Reunion behaviors
6.	Parent leaves room.	Separation anxiety
7.	Stranger enters and offers comfort.	Ability to be soothed by stranger
8.	Parent returns, greets baby, offers comfort if necessary, and tries to interest baby in toys.	Reunion behaviors

Note: All episodes except the first last 3 minutes, although separation episodes may be abbreviated and reunion episodes extended for babies who become extremely upset.

the infant); and (3) reunion episodes (to determine whether a stressed infant derives any comfort and reassurance from the caregiver and can once again become involved with toys). By recording and analyzing an infant's responses to these episodes—that is, exploratory activities, reactions to strangers and to separations, and, in particular, behaviors when reunited with the close companion—an observer can usually characterize the child's attachment to the caregiver in one of four ways:

1. **Secure attachment.** About 65% of 1-year-old North American infants fall into this category. The securely attached infant actively explores while alone with the mother and may be visibly upset by separations. The infant *often greets the mother warmly when she returns and, if highly distressed, will often seek physical contact with her,* which helps to alleviate that distress. The child may be outgoing with strangers while the mother is present.
2. **Resistant attachment.** About 10% of 1-year-olds show this type of "insecure" attachment. These infants try to stay close to their mother but explore very little while she is present. They become very distressed as the mother departs. But when she returns, the infants are ambivalent: they will *remain near her,* although they seem angry at her for having left them and are likely to *resist physical contact initiated by the mother.* Resistant infants are quite wary of strangers, even when their mothers are present.
3. **Avoidant attachment.** These infants (about 20% of 1-year-olds) also display an "insecure" attachment. They often show little distress when separated from the mother and will generally *turn away from and may continue to ignore the mother even when she tries to gain their attention.* Avoidant infants are often rather sociable with strangers but may occasionally avoid or ignore them in much the same way that they avoid or ignore their mothers.
4. **Disorganized/disoriented attachment.** This recently discovered attachment pattern characterizes the 5% to 10% of American infants who are most stressed by the Strange Situation and who may be the most insecure (Hertsgaard et al., 1995). It appears to be a curious combination of the resistant and the avoidant patterns that reflects confusion about whether to approach or avoid the caregiver (Main & Solomon, 1990). When reunited with their mothers, these infants may act dazed and freeze; or they may move closer but then abruptly move away as the mother draws near; or they may show both patterns in different reunion episodes.

secure attachment: an infant/caregiver bond in which the child welcomes contact with a close companion and uses this person as a secure base from which to explore the environment.

resistant attachment: an insecure infant/caregiver bond, characterized by strong separation protest and a tendency of the child to remain near but resist contact initiated by the caregiver, particularly after a separation.

avoidant attachment: an insecure infant/caregiver bond, characterized by little separation protest and a tendency of the child to avoid or ignore the caregiver.

disorganized/disoriented attachment: an insecure infant/caregiver bond, characterized by the infant's dazed appearance on reunion or a tendency to first seek and then abruptly avoid the caregiver.

Box 5.1   Current Controversies

Alternative Methods of Assessing Attachment Quality

Soon after its appearance, the Strange Situation was criticized as an unnecessarily cumbersome and potentially invalid assessment of infants' attachment relationships. Urie Bronfenbrenner (1979), for example, has argued that the very "strangeness" of the Strange Situation (rapid exposure to strange environments, abrupt separations, and unfamiliar, semi-intrusive adults) may prompt exaggerated emotional reactions that are not very representative of an infant's day-to-day behavior at home or the true character of his or her relationships with caregivers. Furthermore, the Strange Situation is not very useful for characterizing the attachments of children much older than 2, who are becoming quite accustomed to (and less stressed by) brief separations from loved ones and encounters with strangers. Finally, the Strange Situation is a "costly" procedure in that investigators seeking to classify the quality of attachments that children have established must first receive extensive training to do so at satisfactory levels of reliability.

Recently, an alternative assessment of attachment quality—the **Attachment Q-set (AQS)**—has become quite popular. Appropriate for use with 1- to 5-year-olds, the Attachment Q-set requires an observer—usually a parent or trained observer—to sort a set of 90 descriptors of attachment-related behaviors (for example, "Child looks to mother for reassurance when wary"; "Child greets mother with a big smile"; "Child easily grows fond of [friendly strangers]" into three categories: "most characteristic . . . ," "neither characteristic nor uncharacteristic . . . ," or "most uncharacteristic . . ." of this child. The resulting patterning of items represents how *secure* the child is with his or her caregiver *at home* (Waters et al., 1995). Trained observers' Q-set data can also be scored to indicate the particular type of attachment an infant or toddler has established, and these assessments are usually concordant with Strange Situation attachment classifications (Pederson & Moran, 1996; Vaughn & Waters, 1990). Clearly, the ability to assess both the type of attachment and the overall attachment security that in-

fants, toddlers, and older preschool children display *in their natural environments* makes AQS a versatile alternative to the Strange Situation.

Other, newer methods of assessing the quality of older participants' attachments and/or their mental representations of attachment relationships include (1) Main and Cassidy's (1988) analogue of the Strange Situation, which focuses on the ways preschool and young grade-school children respond to unusual and potentially frightening separations from loved ones; and (2) the Adult Attachment Interview (George, Kaplan, & Main, 1985) in which adults are questioned extensively about their recollections of and feelings about early childhood relationships and, on the basis of their responses, are classified as having secure, resistant, or avoidant mental representations of attachment relationships (Main & Goldwyn, 1994). Finally, social psychologists (for example, Bartholomew & Horowitz, 1991; Hazan & Shaver, 1987) have constructed simple paper-and-pencil self-report measures, with items modeled after Ainsworth's and Main's verbal descriptions of secure, resistant, avoidant, and disorganized/disoriented attachments, to assess adults' mental models of intimate relationships and predispositions to form similar attachments with romantic partners or spouses.

In sum, there are now many alternatives to Ainsworth's Strange Situation—measures that permit researchers to assess the kinds of attachments that infants, children, adolescents, and adults have established with loved ones. Of course, the development of these new measures permit us to seek answers for some intriguing questions. For example, is the quality of an infant's primary attachments stable over time? Do these attachments forecast the kinds of attachments she will establish with other people (such as romantic partners or her own children) in the years ahead? Later in the chapter we address these very issues and discuss several other ways that an early history of secure or insecure attachments might influence a child's development.

A clear majority of infants in any research sample can be classified into one of the four attachment categories that Ainsworth and her associates have described. Nevertheless, the Strange Situation procedure has been criticized, and newer attachment measures are now favored by many researchers. In Box 5.1, we briefly consider some alternatives to the Strange Situation, including self-report measures that are suitable for adolescents and adults.

Attachment Q-set: alternative method of assessing attachment security that is based on observations of the child's attachment-related behaviors at home: can be used with infants, toddlers, and preschool children.

CULTURAL VARIATIONS IN ATTACHMENT

Both Bowlby (1973) and Ainsworth (1979) claimed that infants and toddlers around the world respond similarly to separations from loved ones, and they concluded that a desire to maintain proximity to primary caregivers is a *universal* human phenomenon. Yet cross-cultural comparisons reveal that the percentages of infants who fall into the secure and the various insecure attachment classifications may vary substantially from culture to culture (van IJzendoorn & Kroonenberg, 1988). Does this mean that the Strange Situation is an invalid measure of attachment security for children in other cultures? Might the meaning or the significance of close infant/caregiver attachments vary across cultures as LeVine (1989; LeVine et al., 1994) has argued? Or do cultural differences in the distributions of attachment classifications reflect cultural variations in child-rearing and the meaning of various attachment behaviors?

Attachment theorists (for example, Bretherton, 1995) cite several findings as support for the latter viewpoint. Parents in northern Germany, for example, encourage their infants to be independent and discourage close, clingy contact, perhaps explaining why more German than North American babies display reunion behaviors characteristic of the *avoidant* attachment pattern (Grossmann et al., 1985). Furthermore, intense separation and stranger anxieties, which characterize the *resistant* attachment pattern, are much more common in cultures such as Japan, where caregivers do not encourage early separation and rarely leave infants with substitute caregivers, and Israel, among communally reared kibbutz children who sleep in infant houses without their parents being accessible to them at night (Sagi et al., 1994). So the different distributions of attachment classifications across cultures is at least partially attributable to cultural variations in child-rearing practices.

PHOTO 5.1 Although child-rearing practices vary dramatically across cultures, secure attachments are more common than insecure attachments around the world.

Do cultural differences in attachment classifications imply that secure infant/caregiver attachments are less valued or are viewed as less adaptive in some cultures than in others? Probably not. In fact, parents around the world generally prefer their young children to feel secure in their relationships with them (Posada et al., 1995), and more infants around the world do fall into the secure attachment category than into any of the insecure categories (van IJzendoorn & Kroonenberg, 1988). So, far from undermining the validity or universality of the attachment construct, cultural variations in attachment have actually fostered our understanding of early emotional development by helping to illustrate how various patterns of caregiving may contribute to the formation of different kinds of attachment relationships (Bretherton, 1995). Now let's pursue this lead and see how infants might become securely or insecurely attached to a close companion.

Factors That Influence Attachment Security

Among the many factors that seem to influence the kinds of attachments that infants establish are the quality of caregiving they receive, the character or emotional climate of their homes, and their own health conditions and temperaments.

QUALITY OF CAREGIVING

Mary Ainsworth (1979) believes that the quality of an infant's attachment to his mother (or any other close companion) depends largely on the kind of attention he has received. According to this **caregiving hypothesis,** mothers of *securely attached* infants are thought to be sensitive, responsive caregivers from the very beginning. And apparently they are. One recent review of 66 studies found that mothers who display the characteristics described in Table 5-2 tend to have infants who form secure attachments with them (De Wolff & van IJzendoorn, 1997). So if a caregiver has a positive attitude toward her baby, is usually sensitive to his needs, has established interactional synchrony with him, and provides ample stimulation and emotional support, the infant will often derive comfort and pleasure from their interactions and is likely to become securely attached.

Babies who show a *resistant* rather than a secure pattern of attachment sometimes have irritable and unresponsive temperaments (Cassidy & Berlin, 1994; Waters et al., 1980); but more often they have parents who are *inconsistent* in their caregiving—reacting enthusiastically or indifferently depending on their moods and being unresponsive a good deal of the time (Ainsworth, 1979; Isabella, 1993; Isabella & Belsky, 1991). The infant copes with this inconsistent caregiving by trying desperately—through clinging, crying, and other attachment behaviors—to obtain emotional support and comfort and then becomes *angry* or *resentful* when these efforts often fail.

There are at least two patterns of caregiving that place infants at risk of developing *avoidant* attachments. Ainsworth and others (for example, Isabella, 1993) find that some mothers of avoidant infants are often impatient with their babies and unresponsive to their signals, are likely to express negative feelings about their infants, and seem to derive little pleasure from close contact with them. Ainsworth (1979) believes that these mothers are rigid, self-centered people who are likely to *reject* their babies. In other cases, however, avoidant babies have overzealous parents who chatter endlessly and provide high levels of stimulation even when their babies do not want it (Belsky et al., 1984; Isabella & Belsky, 1991). Infants may be responding quite adaptively by learning to avoid adults who seem to dislike their company or who bombard them with stimulation they cannot handle. Whereas resistant infants make vigorous attempts to gain emotional support, avoidant infants seem to have learned to do without it (Isabella, 1993).

Finally, Mary Main believes that infants who develop *disorganized/disoriented* attachments are often drawn to but are also *fearful* of caregivers because of past episodes in which they were neglected or physically abused (Main & Solomon, 1990). Indeed, the infant's approach/avoidance (or totally dazed demeanor) at reunion is quite understandable if she has experienced cycles of acceptance and abuse (or neglect) and doesn't know whether to approach the caregiver for comfort or to retreat from her to

---

TABLE 5-2 Aspects of caregiving that promote secure mother-infant attachments

CHARACTERISTIC	DESCRIPTION
Sensitivity	Responding promptly and appropriately to the infant's signals
Positive attitude	Expressing positive affect and affection for the infant
Synchrony	Structuring smooth, reciprocal interactions with the infant
Mutuality	Structuring interactions in which mother and infant attend to the same thing
Support	Attending closely to and providing emotional support for the infant's activities
Stimulation	Frequently directing actions toward the infant

NOTE: These six aspects of caregiving are moderately correlated with each other
SOURCE: De Wolff and van IJzendoorn, 1997.

caregiving hypothesis:
Ainsworth's notion that the type of attachment an infant develops with a particular caregiver depends primarily on the kind of caregiving he has received from that person.

safety. Available research supports Main's theorizing: Although disorganized/disoriented attachments are occasionally observed in any research sample, they seem to be especially common among groups of abused infants (Carlson, 1998; Carlson et al., 1989). And this same curious mixture of approach and avoidance, coupled with sadness upon reunion, also characterizes many infants of severely depressed mothers, who may be inclined on occasion to mistreat or neglect their babies (Lyons-Ruth et al., 1990; Murray et al., 1996; Teti et al., 1995).

Who Is at Risk of Becoming an Insensitive Caregiver?   Several personal characteristics place parents at risk of displaying the insensitive patterns of parenting that contribute to insecure attachments. For example, insecure attachments of one kind or the other are the *rule* rather than the exception when a child's primary caregiver has been diagnosed as clinically depressed (Radke-Yarrow et al., 1985; Teti et al., 1995). Depressed parents often ignore babies' social signals and generally fail to establish satisfying and synchronous relationships with them. And infants often become angry at these caregivers' lack of responsiveness and may soon begin to match their depressive symptoms, even when interacting with other *nondepressed* adults (Campbell, Cohn, & Meyers, 1995; Field et al., 1988; Pickens & Field, 1993).

Another group of parents who are often insensitive caregivers are those who themselves felt unloved, neglected, or abused as children. These formerly mistreated caregivers often start out with the best intentions, vowing never to do to their children what was done to them—but they often expect their infants to be "perfect" and to love them right away. So when their babies are irritable, fussy, or inattentive (as all infants will be at times), these emotionally insecure adults are likely to feel as if they are being rejected once again (Steele & Pollack, 1974). They may then back off or withdraw their own affection (Biringen, 1990; Crowell & Feldman, 1991), sometimes to the point of neglecting or even abusing their babies.

Finally, adults whose pregnancies were unplanned and their babies unwanted can be particularly insensitive caregivers whose children fare rather poorly in all aspects of development. In one longitudinal study in Czechoslovakia (Matejcek, Dytrych, & Schuller, 1979), mothers who had been denied permission to abort an unwanted pregnancy were judged to be less closely attached to their children than a group of same-aged mothers of similar marital and socioeconomic status who had not requested an abortion. Although both the "wanted" and the "unwanted" children were physically healthy at birth, over the next nine years the unwanted children were more frequently hospitalized, made lower grades in school, had less stable family lives and poorer relations with peers, and were generally more irritable and antisocial than the children whose parents had wanted them. Follow-up observations in young adulthood tell much the same story: compared to their "wanted" peers, the formerly "unwanted" children were now much less satisfied with their marriages, their jobs, their friendships, and their general mental health, having more often sought treatment for a variety of psychological disorders (David, 1992, 1994). Clearly, parents are unlikely to be very sensitive or to foster the development of children they do not care to raise.

Ecological Constraints on Caregiving Sensitivity   Of course, parent-child interactions always take place in a broader ecological context that may influence how caregivers respond to their children. Insensitive parenting, for example, is much more likely among caregivers who are experiencing health-related, legal, or financial problems, and it is hardly surprising that the incidence of insecure attachments is highest among poverty-stricken families that receive inadequate health care (Murray et al., 1996; NICHD Early Child Care Research Network, 1997).

The quality of a caregiver's relationship with his or her spouse can also have a dramatic effect on parent/infant interactions. Consider that parents who were unhappily married prior to the birth of their child (1) are less sensitive caregivers after the baby is born, (2) express less favorable attitudes about their infants and the parenting role, and (3) establish less secure ties with their infants and toddlers, compared to other parents from similar socioeconomic backgrounds whose marriages are close and confiding (Cox et al., 1989; Howes & Markman, 1989). Happily married couples, on the other hand, usually support each other's parenting efforts, and this positive social support for parenting is especially important if the baby has already shown a tendency to be irritable and unresponsive. In fact, Jay Belsky (1981) found that newborns who are "at risk" for later emotional difficulties (as indicated by their sluggish reactions to social stimulation and the ease with which they become irritated) are likely to have nonsynchronous interactions with their parents *only when the parents are unhappily married.* So it seems that a stormy marriage is a major environmental hazard that can hinder or even prevent the establishment of secure emotional ties between parents and their infants.

What Can Be Done to Assist Insensitive Caregivers? Fortunately, there are ways of assisting at-risk parents to become more sensitive and responsive caregivers. In one intervention, depressed poverty-stricken mothers were visited regularly by a professional, who first established a friendly, supportive relationship and then taught them how to elicit more favorable responses from their babies and encouraged their participation in weekly parenting groups. Toddlers whose mothers received this support later scored higher on intelligence tests and were much more likely to be securely attached than those of other depressed mothers who had not participated in an intervention (Lyons-Ruth et al., 1990).

In another intervention in Holland, economically disadvantaged mothers whose babies were *extremely irritable* received a three-month intervention designed to improve their sensitivity and responsiveness to their infants' difficult temperaments. Not only did these mothers become more sensitive caregivers, but their infants were more likely than those of comparable mothers who received no intervention to be securely attached at age 12 months and to remain more secure with their mothers at 3.5 years of age (van den Boom, 1995).

So the intervention studies clearly indicate that caregiving sensitivity can be fostered and that it promotes secure attachments.

INFANT CHARACTERISTICS

Thus far, we have talked as if parents are responsible for the kind of attachments that infants establish. But since it takes two people to form an attachment *relationship,* we might suspect that babies can also influence the quality of parent/infant emotional ties. For example, the sluggish and often irritable demeanor that characterizes many low birth weight babies (and those born seriously ill or addicted to drugs) is a behavioral profile that can alienate caregivers and contribute to insensitive parenting and insecure attachments (Field, 1987; Lester et al., 1991). Indeed, low birth weight babies are at higher risk than full-term healthy ones of establishing insecure primary attachments (Mangelsdorf et al., 1996), although most of these at-risk infants who receive sensitive parenting end up quite secure with their caregivers (Goldberg et al., 1986; Pederson & Moran, 1995).

Do the large temperamental variations that infants display influence attachment classifications? Jerome Kagan (1984, 1989) certainly thinks so. He argues that the Strange Situation really measures individual differences in infants' temperaments rather than the quality of their attachments. This idea grew from his observation that the percentages of 1-year-olds who have established *secure, resistant,* and *avoidant* attachments corresponds closely to the percentages of babies who fall into Thomas and

TABLE 5-3 Comparison of the percentages of young infants who can be classified as temperamentally "easy," "difficult," and "slow-to-warm-up" with the percentages of 1-year-olds who have established secure, resistant, and avoidant attachments with their mothers

TEMPERAMENTAL PROFILE	PERCENTAGE OF "CLASSIFIABLE" INFANTS	ATTACHMENT CLASSIFICATION	PERCENTAGE OF 1-YEAR-OLDS
Easy	60	Secure	65
Difficult	15	Resistant	10
Slow-to-warm-up	23	Avoidant	20

SOURCES: Ainsworth, Blehar, Waters, & Wall, 1978; Thomas & Chess, 1977.

Chess's *easy, difficult,* and *slow-to-warm-up* temperamental profiles (see Table 5-3). And the linkages even make some sense. Kagan suggests that a temperamentally "difficult" infant who actively resists changes in routine and is upset by novelty may become so distressed by the Strange Situation that he is unable to respond constructively to his mother's comforting and is thus classified as *resistant.* By contrast, a friendly, easygoing child is apt to be classified as *securely attached,* whereas one who is shy or "slow to warm up" may appear distant or detached in the Strange Situation and will probably be classified as *avoidant.* So Kagan's **temperament hypothesis** implies that infants, not caregivers, are the primary architects of their attachment classifications. Presumably, the attachment behaviors that a child displays reflect his or her own temperament.

Does Temperament Explain Attachment Security? Although such components of temperament as irritability and negative emotionality do predict certain attachment behaviors (for example, intensity of separation protests) and can certainly contribute to the quality of an infant's attachments (Goldsmith & Alansky, 1987; Seifer et al., 1996; Vaughn et al., 1992), most experts view Kagan's temperament hypothesis as far too extreme. Consider, for example, that many infants are securely attached to one close companion and insecurely attached to another—a pattern that we would not expect to see if attachment classifications were merely reflections of the child's relatively stable temperamental characteristics (Goossens & van IJzendoorn, 1990; Sroufe, 1985). In addition, we have already seen that when mothers of temperamentally difficult Dutch infants were trained to be more patient, sensitive, and responsive, the vast majority of their babies established secure rather than insecure attachments—a finding indicating that sensitive caregiving is *causally* related to attachment quality (van den Boom, 1995). Finally, one review of 34 studies revealed that maternal characteristics that often predict insensitive parenting—factors such as illness, depression, and other life stresses—were associated with a sharp increase in insecure attachments (see Figure 5.1). However, child problems such as prematurity, illness, and other psychological disorders had virtually no impact on attachment quality (van IJzendoorn et al., 1992).

Although the findings cited above make it seem as if caregivers, not infants, are the primary architects of the quality of infant attachments, there is another "middle-of-the-road" position that suggests that both the caregiving hypothesis and the temperament hypothesis are partially correct. This integrative theory contends that quality of caregiving largely determines whether infants establish secure *versus* insecure attachments with their parents; however, the *type* of insecurity young children display, should caregiving be less than positive and sensitive, may largely depend on their own temperamental qualities (Kochanska, 1998).

There is now ample evidence that quality of caregiving is the more important factor in determining whether emerging attachments are secure or insecure. Consider that a clear majority of temperamentally difficult babies will establish *secure* attachments to

temperament hypothesis: Kagan's view that the Strange-Situation measures individual differences in infants' temperaments rather than the quality of their attachments.

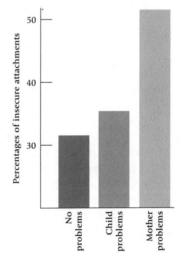

FIGURE 5.1 Comparing the impact of maternal and child problem behaviors on the incidence of insecure attachments. Maternal problems were associated with a sharp increase in insecure attachments, whereas child problems were not.

Box 5.2   Focus on Research

On the Intricate Interplay between Caregiving and Temperament in Shaping Infant Attachments

Recently, Grazyna Kochanska (1998) sought to test an integrative theory of infant/caregiver attachments—one specifying that (1) quality of caregiving is most important in determining whether an infant's emerging attachments or secure or insecure, but (2) infant temperament is the better predictor of the *type* of insecurity infants display, should their attachments be insecure. Kochanska began by measuring qualify of caregiving mothers provided (that is, maternal responsiveness to her infant; the synchrony of positive emotions between mother and infant) when their babies were 8-10 and 13-15 months old. She also assessed the aspect of infant temperament known as fearfulness. *Fearlful* children are prone to showing strong distress in new and uncertain situations and are similar to those children that Kagan calls behaviorally *inhibited*. *Fearless* children, by contrast, are largely unperturbed by strange settings, people, or separations, and are similar to children whom Kagan refers to as behaviorally *uninhibited*. Finally, Kochanska used the Strange Situation to assess the quality of infants' attachments to their mothers at age 13-15 months. Thus, she had data allowing her to determine whether caregiving or temperament contributed more strongly to the security and specific type of attachments that infants display.

The study produced two particularly interesting sets of results. First, as anticipated by the integrative theory, quality of caregiving (but not infant temperament) clearly predicted whether infants established secure or insecure attachments with their mothers, with positive, responsive parenting being associated with secure attachments. And yet, quality of caregiving did *not* predict the specific *type* of insecurity that infants with insecure attachments displayed.

What, then, predicted type of insecurity? Infant fearfulness did! As anticipated by the integrative theory and a knowledge of the fearful-fearless dimension, temperamentally fearful children who had insecure attachments were prone to display *resistant* attachments, whereas the insecure infants who were temperamentally fearless were more likely to display *avoidant* attachments.

Clearly, these findings imply that the quality of attachment relationships that infants develop represent the end result of an intricate interplay between the caregiving they receive and their own individual temperaments. In other words, strong versions of both the caregiving hypothesis and the temperament hypothesis are overstatements, and only by adopting an *eclectic* approach that recognizes the merits of both positions do we achieve a richer understanding of the variations in attachment quality that infants display.

caregivers who display lots of patience and positive affect and adapt their caregiving to their baby's temperamental characteristics (Mangelsdorf et al., 1990; van den Boom, 1995; van IJzendoorn et al., 1992). By contrast, even many babies who are good natured may end up establishing insecure relationships with mothers who are experiencing serious psychological difficulties that prevent them from being sensitive, responsive companions (van IJzendoorn et al., 1992). And yet, the research presented in Box 5.2 clearly illustrates that the *specific type of insecurity* that infants display, should they receive rather insensitive parenting, is largely a function of their own temperaments.

Taken together, the findings we have reviewed are quite consistent with Thomas and Chess's (1977) *goodness-of-fit model* introduced in Chapter 4. Secure attachments evolve from relationships in which there is a "good fit" between the caregiving a baby receives and his or her own temperament, whereas different kinds of insecure attachments are likely to develop when highly stressed or otherwise inflexible caregivers fail to accommodate their infants' particular temperamental qualities (van den Boom, 1995). Indeed, one reason "caregiver sensitivity" predicts attachment security is that the very notion of *sensitive* care implies an ability to tailor one's routines to whatever temperamental qualities a baby might display (Sroufe, 1985; van den Boom, 1997).

To this point we have focused only on the quality of the infant's attachment to her mother. Do you think that the kind of attachment an infant has with her mother will have any effect on the infant's relationship with her father? We explore this issue in the next section as we look at some of the ways fathers contribute to their infants' social and emotional development.

Fathers as Attachment Objects

In 1975, Michael Lamb described fathers as the "forgotten contributors to child development." And he was right. Until the mid-1970s, fathers were treated as biological necessities who played only a minor role in the social and emotional development of their infants and toddlers. One reason for overlooking or discounting the father's early contributions may have been that fathers spend less time interacting with babies than mothers do (Belsky, Gilstrap, & Rovine, 1984; Parke, 1995). Nevertheless, fathers appear to be just as "engrossed" with their *newborn* infants as mothers are (Nichols, 1993), and they become increasingly involved with their babies over the first year of life (Belsky et al., 1984), spending an average of nearly an hour a day interacting with their 9-month-olds (Ninio & Rinott, 1988). Fathers are most highly involved with their infants and hold more favorable attitudes about them when they are happily married (Belsky, 1996; Cox et al., 1989, 1992) and when their wives encourage them to become an important part of their babies' lives (Palkovitz, 1984).

FATHERS AS CAREGIVERS

Most infants in two-parent homes form secure attachments to their fathers during the latter half of the first year (Lamb, 1981, 1997), particularly if the father has a positive attitude about parenting, is extraverted and agreeable, spends a lot of time with them, and is a sensitive caregiver (Cox et al., 1992; van IJzendoorn & De Wolff, 1997). And how do fathers compare to mothers as companions? Research conducted in Australia, Israel, India, Italy, Japan, and the United States reveals that mothers and fathers in all these societies tend to play somewhat different roles in a baby's life. Mothers are more likely than fathers to hold their infants, to soothe and talk to them, to play traditional games, such as peekaboo, and to care for their physical needs; fathers are more likely than mothers to provide playful physical stimulation and to initiate unusual or unpredictable games that infants often enjoy. Although most infants prefer their mothers' company when upset or afraid, fathers are often preferred as playmates (Lamb & Oppenheim, 1989; Roopnarine et al., 1990).

However, the playmate role is but one of many that modern fathers fulfill, particularly if their wives are working and they must necessarily assume at least some of the caregiving burden (Cox et al., 1992; Pleck, 1997). And what kinds of caregivers do Dads make? Many of them are (or soon become) rather skillful at virtually all phases of routine care (including diapering, bathing, and soothing a distressed infant). Moreover, once fathers become objects of affection they begin to serve as a *secure base* from which their babies will venture to explore the environment (Hwang, 1986; Lamb, 1997). So fathers are rather versatile companions who can assume any and all functions normally served by the other parent (of course, the same is true of mothers).

Although research on fatherhood is still a relatively new endeavor, social-developmentalists have already learned that the father is a very important contributor to his infant's social, emotional, and intellectual development. Let's take a closer look at some of these findings.

PHOTO 5.2 The "playmate" role is only one of many that fathers assume.

FATHERS' INFLUENCE ON EARLY INTELLECTUAL DEVELOPMENT

In some of the earliest research on fathering, Alison Clarke-Stewart (1978, 1980) found that infants whose fathers were highly involved with them scored higher on infant intelligence tests than those whose fathers were less involved. Easterbrooks and Goldberg (1984) have corroborated these findings with a sample of young toddlers. Children whose fathers were highly involved with them and sensitive to their needs expressed more positive affect while working at a cognitive challenge (a jigsaw puzzle) and persisted longer at the task than those whose fathers were less sensitive and involved. Indeed, fathers continue to influence the intellectual and academic performance of their children throughout middle childhood (Pleck, 1997), *even when they no longer reside at home*. Rebekah Coley (1998), for example, found that third-graders and fourth-graders in single-parent, mother-headed households performed much better academically if they had maintained a warm relationship with an absent father who encouraged them to do well and who monitored their progress to ensure that they did. Interestingly, contact with an absent father was every bit as (or even more) important for girls and for black children (who are more likely than whites to live in a single-parent home) than for boys and for whites (see also Florsheim, Tolan, & Gorman-Smith, 1998). Although much remains to be determined about exactly how fathers foster intellectual and academic achievement, fathers quite clearly can play a most important role in these crucial areas of development.

FATHERS AS CONTRIBUTORS TO EARLY SOCIAL AND EMOTIONAL DEVELOPMENT

Although many infants form the same kind of attachment with their fathers that they have established with their mothers (Fox, Kimmerly, & Schafer, 1991; Rosen & Rothbaum, 1993), it is not at all unusual for a child to be securely attached to one parent and insecure with the other (Cox et al., 1992; van IJzendoorn & De Wolff, 1997). For example, when Mary Main and Donna Weston (1981) used the Strange Situation to measure the quality of 44 toddlers' attachments to their mothers and their fathers, they found that 12 toddlers were securely attached to both parents, 11 were secure with the mother but insecure with the father, 10 were insecure with the mother but secure with the father, and 11 were insecurely attached to both parents.

What does the father add to a child's social and emotional development? One way to find out is to compare the social behavior of children who are securely attached to their fathers to those whose relationships with their fathers are insecure. Main and Weston did just that by exposing their four groups of toddlers to a friendly stranger in a clown outfit who spent several minutes trying to play with the child and then turned around and cried when a person at the door told the clown he would have to leave. As the clown went through his routine, the toddlers were each observed and rated for (1) the extent to which they were willing to establish a positive relationship with the clown (low ratings indicated that the infant was wary or distressed) and (2) signs of emotional conflict (that is, indications of psychological disturbance such as curling up in the fetal position on the floor or vocalizing in a "social" manner to a wall). Figure 5.2 shows the results of this stranger test. Note that toddlers who were securely attached to both parents were the most socially responsive group. Equally important is the finding that toddlers who were securely attached to *at least one parent* were more friendly toward the clown and less emotionally conflicted than those who had insecure relationships with both parents. So this study illustrates the important role that fathers can play in early social and emotional development. Not only are children more socially responsive when they are securely attached to both the mother and the father, but a secure attachment with the father may buffer the potentially negative effects of an insecure mother-infant attachment (see also Biller, 1993).

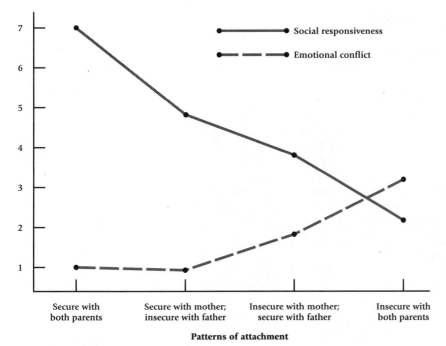

FIGURE 5.2 Average levels of social responsiveness and emotional conflict shown by toddlers who were either securely or insecurely attached to their mothers and fathers. (Adapted from Main & Weston, 1981.)

Attachment and Later Development

Both psychoanalytic theorists (Erikson, 1963; Freud, 1905/1930) and ethologists (Bowlby, 1969) believe that the feelings of warmth, trust, and security that infants gain from secure attachments will set the stage for healthy psychological development later in life. Of course, one implication of this viewpoint is that insecure attachments may forecast less than optimal developmental outcomes in the years ahead.

LONG-TERM CORRELATES OF SECURE AND INSECURE ATTACHMENTS

Although the existing data are somewhat limited in that they focus almost exclusively on infants' attachments to their mothers, it seems that infants who have established secure primary attachments are likely to display more favorable developmental outcomes. For example, babies who were securely attached at age 12 to 18 months are better problem solvers as 2-year-olds (Frankel & Bates, 1990), are more complex and creative in their symbolic play (Pipp, Easterbrooks, & Harmon, 1992), and are more attractive to toddlers as playmates (Fagot, 1997; Jacobson & Wille, 1986) than children who were insecurely attached. In fact, infants whose primary attachments are disorganized/disoriented are at risk of becoming hostile and aggressive preschool and grade-school children whom peers are likely to reject (Lyons-Ruth, Alpern, & Repacholi, 1993; Lyons-Ruth, Easterbrooks, & Cibelli, 1997).

Many other studies of securely and insecurely attached children paint a similar picture. Everett Waters and his associates (1979), for example, first measured the quality of children's attachments at 15 months of age and then observed these children in a nursery school setting at 3.5 years of age. Children who had been securely attached to their mothers at age 15 months were now social leaders in the nursery school: They often initiated play activities, were generally sensitive to the needs and feelings of other children, and were very popular with their peers. Observers described these children as curious, self-directed, and eager to learn. By contrast, children who had been insecurely attached at age 15 months were somewhat socially and emotionally withdrawn, hesitant to engage other children in play activities, and were described by observers as less curious, less interested in learning, and much less forceful in pursuing their goals (see also Bost et al., 1998). A follow-up in a camp setting when these children were 11 to 12 years old revealed that those who had been securely attached as infants and toddlers displayed better social skills and were more likely to have close friends than age-mates whose primary attachments had been insecure (Elicker, Egeland, & Sroufe, 1992; Shulman, Elicker, & Sroufe, 1994). And recent studies with other samples consistently reveal that youngsters whose early attachment relationships were insecure are somewhat more likely than those who were securely attached to experience poor peer relations and to display deviant behaviors (for example, disobedience at school) and other psychopathological systems later in adolescence (see, for example, Allen et al., 1998; Carlson, 1998).

So it seems that the quality of their early attachments can influence children for many years to come. And one reason is that attachments are often stable over time: Most children (84% in one American sample and 82% in a German sample) experience the same kind of attachment relationships with their parents during the grade-school years that they did in infancy (Main & Cassidy, 1988; Wartner et al., 1994). In fact, young adults who characterize their early parental attachments as secure, resistant, or avoidant on the *Adult Attachment Interview* or other self-report measures tend to establish the same kinds of attachment relationships with their current romantic partners (Berscheid & Reis, 1998; Hazan & Shaver, 1987).

WHY MIGHT ATTACHMENT QUALITY FORECAST LATER OUTCOMES?

Why is the quality of one's early attachments so often stable over time? And how might attachments shape one's behavior and influence the character of future interpersonal relationships?

Erikson's Viewpoint Clearly, both the short-term and long-term correlates of secure and insecure attachments are consistent with Erik Erikson's ideas about the importance of developing an early sense of *trust* in other people. Perhaps securely attached infants who have learned to trust an easily accessible and responsive caregiver become curious problem solvers later in life because they feel comfortable at venturing *away* from an attentive parent to explore and, as a result, they learn how to answer questions and how to solve problems *on their own*. In addition, securely attached infants may become quite sociable and rather popular with their peers because they have already established pleasant relationships with responsive caregivers and have learned from these experiences that human beings are likely to react positively to their social overtures. By contrast, an anxious, insecure infant who has not learned to trust her caregivers may be reluctant either to (1) explore the environment and gain the initiative that would help her to answer questions or (2) completely trust other people with whom she may have dealings, including teachers, peers, and future romantic partners.

The Ethological Viewpoint: Attachments as "Working Models" of Self and Others Ethologists can agree in principle with Erikson's analyses but have chosen to explain any enduring effects of early attachment histories in a different way. John Bowlby (1980, 1988) and Inge Bretherton (1985, 1990) believe that as infants continue to interact with primary caregivers, they will develop **internal working models**—that

Internal working models: cognitive representations of self, others, and relationships that infants construct from their interactions with caregivers.

is, cognitive representations of *themselves* and *other people*—that they use to interpret events and to form expectations about the character of human relationships. Sensitive, responsive caregiving should lead the child to conclude that people are dependable (positive working model of others), whereas insensitive, neglectful, or abusive caregiving may lead to insecurity and a lack of trust (negative working model of others). Although this sounds very similar to Erik Erikson's earlier ideas about the importance of trust, ethologists proceed one step further, arguing that an infant will also develop a working model of the self based largely on her ability to elicit attention and comfort *when she needs it*. So an infant whose caregivers respond quickly and appropriately to her bids for attention is apt to believe that "I'm lovable" (positive working model of self), whereas one whose signals are ignored or misinterpreted may conclude that "I'm unworthy or loathful" (negative working model of self). Presumably, these two models will combine to influence the quality of the child's primary attachments and the expectations she has about future relationships. What kinds of expectations might she form?

A recent version of this "working models" theory appears in Figure 5.3 As shown, infants who construct positive working models of themselves and their caregivers are the ones who should (1) form secure primary attachments, (2) have the *self*-confidence to approach and to master new challenges, and (3) be inclined to establish secure, mutual-trust relationships with friends and spouses later in life. By contrast, a positive model of self coupled with a negative model of others (as might result when infants can successfully attract the attention of an insensitive, overintrusive caregiver) is thought to predispose the infant to form *avoidant* attachments and to "dismiss" the importance of close emotional bonds. A negative model of self and a positive model of others (as might result when infants sometimes can but often cannot attract the attention and care they need) should be associated with *resistant* attachments and a "preoccupation" with establishing secure emotional ties. Finally, a negative working model of both the self and others is thought to underlie *disorganized/disoriented* attachments and an emerging "fear" of being hurt (either physically or emotionally) in intimate relationships (Bartholomew & Horowitz, 1991).

Recently, Jay Belsky, Becky Spritz, and Keith Crnic (1996) demonstrated for the first time that children who had secure and insecure attachments as infants have different styles of processing information that suggest they have formed very different internal working models of self and other. These researchers treated 3-year-olds to a series of puppet shows dramatizing positive events such as getting a birthday present and negative ones such as spilling juice. They expected children who had been securely attached as infants to expect positive experiences in life and to attend to them and remember them especially well; they expected children with histories of insecure attachment to expect and find that life is less pleasant. The securely and insecurely attached children in the study did not differ in their attention to positive and negative events, but as Figure 5.4 shows, securely attached children excelled at remembering positive events, whereas insecurely attached children excelled at remembering negative events. This was true even when group differences in temperament were controlled. The implication? Bowlby was on the right track in theorizing that differences in the internal working models that securely and insecurely attached individuals form may be significant for later development.

Indeed, other early returns with preschool and grade-school children tend to support Bowlby's thinking. Consider that 3½- to 6-year-olds with secure and resistant attachment histories—the very children who presumably have formed a *positive*

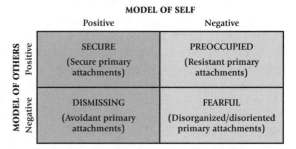

	MODEL OF SELF	
	Positive	Negative
MODEL OF OTHERS Positive	SECURE (Secure primary attachments)	PREOCCUPIED (Resistant primary attachments)
MODEL OF OTHERS Negative	DISMISSING (Avoidant primary attachments)	FEARFUL (Disorganized/disoriented primary attachments)

FIGURE 5.3 Four perspectives on close emotional relationships that evolve from the positive or negative "working models" of self and others that people construct from their experiences with intimate companions. (Adapted from Bartholomew & Horowitz, 1991.)

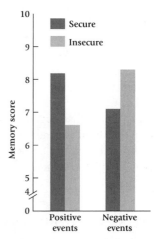

FIGURE 5.4 Due to differences in their internal working models, securely attached children are biased to remember positive experiences and insecurely attached children to remember negative experiences. (Based on means in Table 1, p. 113, in J. Belsky, B. Spritz, & K. Crnic, "Infant Attachment Security and Affective-Cognitive Information Processing at Age 3." *Psychological Science, 7,* 1996, 11–114.)

working model of others—already perceive peers in more positive ways than do age-mates with avoidant attachments. Furthermore, children with more positive cognitive representations of peers have established more reciprocated friendships than those whose peer representations are less positive (Cassidy et al., 1996). Other research with grade-school students indicates that children with negative *self*-representations do make lower grades later in adolescence than those with positive working models of self (Jacobsen & Hofmann, 1997). So the available evidence is quite consistent with the notion that working models established early in life may persist for long periods, influencing our reactions to cognitive challenges and the character of our future interpersonal relationships.

Parents' Working Models and Attachment Interestingly, parents also have positive or negative working models of themselves and others based on their own life experiences. Several methods now exist to measure adults' working models, based on either a detailed analysis of their memories of childhood attachment experiences as indicated in the *Adult Attachment Interview* or by their current views of themselves, other people, and the character of interpersonal relationships as reported on paper-and-pencil measures (Bartholomew & Horowitz, 1991; Main & Goldwyn, 1994). Using these instruments, adults can be reliably cast into the classifications described earlier in Figure 5.3. Do their own working models influence the kinds of attachments their babies form?

Indeed they do. Peter Fonagy and his associates (1991), for example, found that English mothers' working models of attachment relationships measured *before their babies were born* accurately predicted about 75% of the time whether their infants would establish secure or insecure attachments with them. Similar results have now been reported in studies conducted in Canada, Germany, the Netherlands, and the United States (Benoit & Parker, 1994; Das Eiden, Teti, & Corns, 1995; Steele, Steele, & Fonagy, 1996; van IJzendoorn, 1995), with an exact matching of working models occurring in 60% to 70% of the mother-infant dyads. Interestingly, mothers' working models of attachment relationships and the sensitivity of caregiving mothers provide contribute *independently* to the types of attachment infants form (Pederson et al., 1998), and at least one study found that mothers' working models were actually better predictors of infants' attachment classifications than maternal sensitivity was (Ward & Carlson, 1995).

So it seems that cognitive representations of intimate relationships are often transmitted from generation to generation. Indeed, Bowlby (1988) proposed that once formed early in life, working models may stabilize, becoming an aspect of personality that continues to influence the character of one's close emotional ties throughout life.

IS ATTACHMENT HISTORY DESTINY?

Although it appears that early working models can be long lasting and that there are some clear advantages to having formed secure emotional attachments early in life, the future is not always so bleak for infants who are insecurely attached. As we learned earlier in this chapter, a secure relationship with another person such as the father (or perhaps a grandparent or a day-care provider) can help to offset whatever undesirable consequences might otherwise result from an insecure attachment with the mother (Clarke-Stewart, 1989).

Let's also note that secure attachments sometimes become insecure should a mother return to work, place her infant in day care, or experience such life stresses as marital problems, a major illness, or financial woes that drastically alter the ways that she and her infant respond to each other (Thompson, Lamb, & Estes, 1982). One reason

Bowlby (and later Bretherton) used the term *working* models was to underscore that a child's cognitive representations of self, others, and close emotional relationships are dynamic and can change (for better or for worse) if later experiences with caregivers, close friends, romantic partners, or spouses imply that a revision is necessary.

In sum, secure attachment histories are no guarantee of positive adjustment later in life; nor are insecure early attachments a certain indicator of poor life outcomes (Fagot & Kavanagh, 1990). Yet, we should not underestimate the adaptive significance of secure early attachments, for children who have functioned adequately as infants but very poorly (due to one or more major life stresses) during the preschool period are more likely to recover and to display good social skills and self-confidence during the grade-school years if their early attachment histories were secure rather than insecure (Sroufe, Egeland, & Kreutzer, 1990).

The Unattached Infant

Some infants have very limited contacts with adults during the first year or two of life and do not appear to become attached to anyone. Occasionally these socially deprived youngsters are reared at home by very abusive or neglectful caregivers, but most of them are found in understaffed institutions where they may see a caregiver only when it is time to be fed, changed, or bathed. Will these infants suffer as a result of their early experiences? Must infants form attachments to develop normally as Freud and Bowlby have argued?

We begin by looking at the immediate and long-range effects of social deprivation on puppies and infant monkeys—species that ordinarily form attachments and, in the case of rhesus monkeys, will develop complex social networks. As we will see, this tightly controlled experimental research has helped us to interpret quasi-experimental studies in which socially deprived children are found to differ from those raised at home with their parents.

EFFECTS OF SOCIAL ISOLATION IN DOGS

Thompson and Melzack (1956) describe an interesting series of experiments designed to measure the effects of social isolation on the development of Scottish-terrier puppies. Each puppy assigned to the experimental group was separated from its mother immediately after weaning and housed in a cage with opaque sides. These pups were then isolated from other puppies and humans for several months. By contrast, puppies assigned to the control group were reared (1) with other dogs in the laboratory or (2) in a home setting with human caretakers.

After seven to ten months, both groups were tested for their fear of strange stimuli, their relative dominance, and their social responsiveness. Thompson and Melzack found that the isolated puppies were much more agitated when exposed to novel stimuli, such as an umbrella opening, than the control puppies. They were also less dominant than control puppies when placed in a situation where they had to compete with the control puppies for a bone. The results of the social responsiveness test were particularly interesting. Social responsiveness was measured by releasing the puppy into a large pen that contained two other dogs confined to opposite corners of the pen by chicken-wire partitions. The isolates were observed to pay very little attention to other dogs, spending most of their time sniffing around and exploring the pen itself. Control pups, by contrast, spent a considerable amount of time barking at, wagging their tails at, and examining the other dogs. Follow-up observations revealed that the isolates' relative lack of social responsiveness persisted for several years.

Subsequent research has identified the period between 3 and 12 weeks of age as a *sensitive period* for the development of social responsiveness in dogs: Puppies that are socially isolated during this period typically remain quite unreceptive to the social overtures of other dogs or human beings (see Scott, 1962, 1968) and will often display such unusual behaviors as wedging their bodies into the corner of a novel testing room, as if they were trying to retreat from this strange new environment. They are rather atypical and asocial creatures indeed.

HARLOW'S STUDIES OF SOCIALLY DEPRIVED MONKEYS

Harry Harlow and his associates have studied the effects of early social deprivation on rhesus monkeys by isolating newborn infants in individualized stainless steel cubicles and then carefully monitoring their progress.[1]

What they found was remarkable. Even three months of social deprivation left infants in a state of emotional shock. When removed from isolation, these pitiful creatures gave the appearance of being terrified by clutching at themselves, crouching, or burying their heads in their arms as if trying to shut out this strange new world (see Photo 5.3). They also displayed such abnormal behaviors as self-biting, rocking, and pulling out tufts of their hair. However, the three-month isolates eventually recovered. Daily 30-minute play periods with a normal age-mate soon led to the development of competent social relationships that persisted into adolescence and adulthood.

PHOTO 5.3 Isolate monkeys often display unusual postures.

The prognosis was not nearly as optimistic for infant monkeys isolated six months or longer. The six-month isolates clearly avoided normal age-mates during free-play sessions, preferring instead to play by themselves with toys. What little social responsiveness they did show was directed toward other isolates, leading the Harlows to conclude that *misery prefers miserable company*. Normally reared infant monkeys usually go through a phase of aggressive play in the latter half of the first year. Yet, when the isolates were attacked by other infants, they accepted the abuse without offering much defense. Bad as this behavioral pattern may sound, the effects of 12 months of social isolation were even worse. The 12-month isolates were extremely withdrawn and apathetic, and they often had to be separated from their normal age-mates, who were likely to injure or even kill these passive creatures during periods of aggressive play (Harlow & Harlow, 1977).

Follow-up studies of monkeys isolated six months or longer have found that the isolates develop bizarre patterns of social and sexual behavior during adolescence and adulthood. Harlow describes the adult sexual behavior of these monkeys as follows:

> When the females were smaller than the [normally reared] males, the girls would back away and sit down facing the males [an inadequate attempt at sexual posturing], looking appealingly at their would-be consorts. Their hearts were in the right place but nothing else was. . . . [Isolate] males were equally unsatisfactory. They approached the females with a blind . . . misdirected enthusiasm. Frequently, they would grasp the females by the side of the body and thrust laterally, leaving them working at cross purposes with reality. (1962, p. 5)

---

[1]Harlow's original purpose in isolating rhesus infants was to protect them from a lethal virus in the monkey colony—one to which infant monkeys were particularly susceptible.

Can isolate monkeys recover? Harlow and his associates initially believed that the first six months of life was a *critical period* for the social development of rhesus monkeys: Presumably infants who were denied social stimulation and who remained unattached to another monkey for six months or longer would become forever incapable of establishing normal social and emotional relationships with other adult monkeys. However, a later experiment by Steven Suomi and Harry Harlow (1972) challenged this point of view by showing that the isolation syndrome can be reversed.

The "therapy" that proved so successful was to expose long-term isolates to daily play sessions with *younger,* 3-month-old monkeys. Why younger companions? Mainly because a 3-month-old infant has not yet become active and aggressive in its play; the initial response of these younger associates is to approach and cling tenaciously to their isolate partners rather than harassing them or working them over (as normally reared 6-month-old age-mates do). Suomi and Harlow believed that an emotionally disturbed isolate would not only tolerate a passive, nonaggressive infant but might eventually be "drawn out of his shell" if he ever began to respond to the younger monkey's playful antics. Progress did prove to be painfully slow, but by the end of 26 weeks of this **younger-peer therapy,** the isolates had recovered. Their social behaviors were normal and age appropriate and they bore no resemblance to the pitiful, socially inept crea-

PHOTO 5.4 Younger "therapist" monkey clinging to the back of her older isolate playmate.

tures described in earlier reports. Even profoundly disturbed 12-month isolates will eventually recover to become socially and sexually competent as adults if they are eased into a rehabilitative program with a younger therapist monkey (Novak, 1979).

Clearly, these dramatic recoveries contradict the critical period hypothesis—a viewpoint implying that the devastating social and emotional consequences of prolonged isolation were permanent and irreversible. Perhaps it is more accurate to say that the first six months of life is a "sensitive" period when normally reared monkeys are rapidly developing important social skills and becoming attached to their mothers. Although social deprivation interferes with these activities and produces a rather disturbed young monkey, recovery is possible if the patient is given the proper therapy.

SOCIAL DEPRIVATION IN HUMANS

In the 1940s, physicians and psychologists began to discover and study infants who were living under conditions of extreme social deprivation. For example, it was not uncommon for the impoverished institutions in which these infants lived to have but one caregiver for every 10 to 20 infants. Adult caregivers rarely interacted with the infants except to bathe and change them or to prop a bottle against their pillows at feeding time. Infants were often housed in separate cribs with sheets hung over the railings so that, in effect, they were isolated from the world around them. By today's standards, these babies were victims of extreme neglect (DeAngelis, 1997b).

Infants raised under these conditions appear quite normal for the first three to six months of life: They cry for attention, smile and babble at caregivers, and make the proper postural adjustments when they are about to be picked up. But in the second half of the first year, their behavior changes. Now they seldom cry, coo, or babble; they become rigid and fail to accommodate to the handling of caregivers; and they often appear rather depressed and uninterested in social contact (Goldfarb, 1943; Provence & Lipton, 1962; Ribble, 1943; Spitz, 1945). Here is a description of one such infant:

younger-peer therapy: a method of rehabilitating emotionally withdrawn individuals by regularly exposing them to younger but socially responsive companions.

PHOTO 5.5 Children raised in barren, understaffed institutions show many signs of developmental impairment.

Outstanding were his soberness, his forlorn appearance, and lack of animation. . . . He did not turn to adults to relieve his distress. . . . He made no demands. . . . As one made active and persistent efforts at a social exchange he became somewhat more responsive, animated and . . . active, but lapsed into his depressed . . . appearance when the adult became less active . . . if you crank his motor you can get him to go a little; but he can't start on his own. (Provence & Lipton, 1962, pp. 134–135)

What are these institutionalized infants like as schoolchildren and adolescents? The answer depends, in part, on how long they remain in the institution. William Goldfarb (1943, 1947) compared children who left an understaffed orphanage during the first year with similar children who spent their first three years at the orphanage before departing for foster homes. After interviewing, observing, and testing these children at ages 3½, 6½, 8½, and 12, Goldfarb found that youngsters who had spent three years in the institution lagged behind the early adoptees in virtually all aspects of development. They scored poorly on IQ tests, were socially immature, remarkably dependent on adults, had poor language skills, and were prone to behavior problems such as aggression and hyperactivity. By early adolescence, they were often loners who had a difficult time relating to peers or family members.

More recently, concerns have been expressed about serious maladjustment observed in some children from deprived institutions in Romania who were adopted into homes in the United States and Canada after the fall of the Romanian government in 1990 (Holden, 1996). Let's first note that infants adopted from modern orphanages in most countries today are usually no more or less likely than other infants to form secure attachments (Juffer & Rosenboom, 1997). However, the Romanian adoptees reportedly spent their infancies in orphanages with 20 to 30 children in a room and only one caregiver for every 10 to 20 children, most of the time rocking back and forth in their cribs with little human affection or bouts of play and virtually no synchronous routines with anyone (Fisher et al., 1997). Infants who spent eight months or more in such orphanages displayed eating problems as well as medical problems, and many were withdrawn and seemingly overwhelmed by later interactions with adoptive siblings and peers (Fisher et al., 1997). In one recent study, the majority of late-adopted

Romanian children were eventually able to establish attachment bonds with adoptive parents, although the incidence of insecure attachments was substantially higher in this sample than among age-mates raised with parents from birth (Chisholm, 1998). However, other investigators have found that a fair number of institutionalized Romanian adoptees display **reactive attachment disorder,** an inability to bond securely or otherwise, to adoptive or foster parents, even when these new caregivers have secure working models of attachment relationships (DeAngelis, 1997b). Indeed, the attachment difficulties that these children display may help to explain why they are often restless and troubled, and have few close friends later in childhood.

Finally, Box 5.3 reveals that institutionalized infants are not the only ones to suffer developmental impairments when seriously deprived of attention and affection.

Why Is Early Deprivation Harmful?   No one today questions that early social deprivation can have lasting effects, but there is some disagreement about why this is so. Proponents of the **maternal deprivation hypothesis** (Bowlby, 1969; Spitz, 1965) think that children in understaffed institutions and animals reared in isolation develop abnormally because they lack the warm, loving attention of a single mother-figure to whom they can become attached. But despite its popularity, there are many observations the maternal deprivation hypothesis cannot easily explain. Studies of adequately staffed institutions in Russia, China, and Israel, for example, reveal that infants who are cared for by dozens of responsive caregivers appear quite normal and are as well adjusted later in childhood as those who are reared at home (Bronfenbrenner, 1970a; Kessen, 1975; Oppenheim, Sagi, & Lamb, 1988). Similarly, Efe (Pygmy) infants in Zaire seem to thrive from birth on being cared for and even nursed by a variety of caregivers (Tronick, Morelli, & Ivey, 1992). So it seems that the impairments characterizing children in understaffed institutions probably reflect something other than their lack of an exclusive attachment to a singular mother figure.

Might socially deprived infants develop abnormally simply because they have little contact with anyone who responds to their social signals? Proponents of the **social stimulation hypothesis** think so, arguing that the normal development of Chinese, Russian, Israeli, and Efe infants raised by a multitude of caregivers implies that infants need *sustained* interactions with *responsive* companions—either one or several—to develop normally. Such stimulation may be particularly important because it often depends, in part, on the infant's own behavior: People often attend to the infant when he or she cries, smiles, babbles, burps, or gazes at them. This kind of association between one's own behavior and the behavior of caregivers may lead an infant to believe that she has some *control* over the social environment—an important contributor to a positive working model of self. And as she exerts this "control" and receives others' attention and affection, she should develop a positive working model of others and become more outgoing.

Now consider the plight of socially deprived infants who may emit many signals and rarely receive a response from their overburdened or inattentive caregivers. What are these children likely to learn from their early experiences? Probably that their attempts to attract the attention of others are useless (negative working model of self), for nothing they do seems to matter to anyone (negative working model of others). Consequently they may develop a sense of **learned helplessness** and simply stop trying to elicit responses from other people (Finkelstein & Ramey, 1977). Here, then, is a very plausible reason that socially deprived infants are often rather passive, withdrawn, and apathetic.

Can Children Recover from Early Deprivation Effects?   Earlier we noted that severely disturbed young monkeys can overcome the effects of prolonged social isolation if they receive the proper kinds of therapy. Is the same true of young human beings?

reactive attachment disorder: inability to form secure attachment bonds with other people; characterizes many victims of early social deprivation and/or abuse.

maternal deprivation hypothesis: the notion that socially deprived infants develop abnormally because they have failed to establish attachments to a primary caregiver.

social stimulation hypothesis: the notion that socially deprived infants develop abnormally because they have had little contact with companions who respond contingently to their social overtures.

learned helplessness: the failure to learn how to respond appropriately in a situation because of previous exposures to uncontrollable events in the same or similar situations.

Box 5.3 Developmental Issues

Emotional Deprivation and the Failure to Thrive

Otherwise healthy children who experience too much stress and too little affection are likely to lag far behind their age-mates in physical growth and motor development. This *failure-to-thrive* syndrome may characterize as many as 6% of preschool children in the United States and up to 5% of all patients admitted to pediatric hospitals (Lozoff, 1989).

Nonorganic failure to thrive is a growth disorder that appears early, usually by 18 months of age. Babies who display it stop growing and appear to be wasting away, in much the same way as do extremely malnourished infants in countries experiencing famine. These infants do not have an obvious illness, and no other biological cause for their condition is apparent. Affected babies often have trouble feeding and, in many cases, their growth retardation is undoubtedly attributable to poor nutrition (Brockington, 1996; Lozoff, 1989). Of course, a major question is why would an otherwise healthy baby have trouble feeding?

One clue comes from these babies' behaviors around caregivers. They are generally apathetic and withdrawn, often watch their caregivers closely, but are unlikely to smile or cuddle when they are picked up. Why? Because their caregivers are typically cool and aloof, impatient with them, and sometimes even physically abusive (Brockington, 1996). So even though caregivers offer enough food for these babies to thrive, their impatience and hostility causes babies to withdraw and to become aloof themselves to the point of feeding poorly and displaying few, if any, positive social responses.

Deprivation dwarfism is a second growth-related disorder that stems from emotional deprivation and a lack of affection. It appears later, usually between 2 and 5 years of age, and is characterized by small stature and dramatically reduced rates of growth, even though children who display this disorder do not look especially malnourished and usually receive adequate nutrition and physical care. What seems to be lacking in their lives is a positive involvement with another person, namely with their primary caregivers, who themselves are likely to be depressed by

an unhappy marriage, economic hardships, or some other personal problem (Brockington, 1996; Roithmaier et al., 1988). Apparently deprivation dwarfs grow very slowly because their emotional deprivation depresses the endocrine system and inhibits the production of the pituitary **growth hormone (GH),** a substance known to be essential for the normal growth and development of body cells (Tanner, 1990). Indeed, when these youngsters are removed from their homes and begin to receive attention and affection, secretion of GH quickly resumes, and they grow rapidly on the *same diet* on which they formerly failed to thrive (Brockington, 1996; Gardner, 1972).

The prognosis for children affected by nonorganic failure to thrive and deprivation dwarfism is very good if the caregiving problems responsible for these disorders are corrected by individual or family therapy, or if the affected child is placed with caring foster parents (Brockington, 1996). However, if nonorganic failure to thrive is not identified and corrected in the first two years, or if the emotional neglect that underlies deprivation dwarfism persists for several years, affected children may remain smaller than normal and display long-term emotional problems and intellectual deficiencies as well (Drotar, 1992; Lozoff, 1989).

In sum, failure to thrive provides yet another indication that children require love and responsive caregiving if they are to develop normally. Fortunately, there is hope for preventing these deprivation-related disorders if parents whose children are at risk can be identified early. And often they can be. Even before giving birth, women whose children may fail to thrive are more likely than other mothers to feel unloved by their parents, to reject their own mothers as a model, and to say their own childhoods were unhappy. Within days of giving birth, these mothers are already having more problems feeding and soothing their babies than other mothers are (Lozoff, 1989). Clearly, these families need help and would almost certainly benefit from early interventions that teach parents how to be more sensitive and responsive caregivers.

Fortunately, socially deprived children can overcome many of their initial handicaps if placed in homes where they receive lots of attention from affectionate and responsive caregivers (Clarke & Clarke, 1976; Rutter, 1981). Recovery seems to go especially well if children are deprived for less than two years, have not been physically abused, and are placed with *highly educated, relatively affluent* parents who have the personal, social, and financial resources to foster adaptive development (Chisholm, 1998; DeAngelis, 1997b; Hodges & Tizard, 1989). Audrey Clark and Jeannette Hanisee (1982), for example, studied a group of Asian orphans who had lived in institutions, foster homes, or hospitals before coming to the United States. Many were war orphans who had early histories of malnutrition or serious illness. But despite the severe environmental insults they had endured, these children made remarkable progress. After only two to three years in their highly stimulating, middle-class adoptive homes, the Asian adoptees scored significantly *above* average on both a standardized intelligence test and an assessment of social maturity.

In sum, infants who have experienced social and emotional deprivation over the first two years often show a strong capacity for recovery when they are placed in a stimulating home environment and receive individualized attention from responsive caregivers. However, the lingering deficiencies and reactive attachment disorders that many abuse victims and late adoptees display suggest that infancy and toddlerhood may be a *sensitive period* for the establishment of secure affectional ties and other capacities that these ties may foster. Can they make complete recoveries? Many researchers think so, although they remind us that especially severe or prolonged adversity may take longer to overcome and may require stronger interventions than merely placing these children in good homes. Fortunately, recently developed *attachment therapies,* specifically aimed at building emotional bridges to adoptive parents and at fostering more positive working models of others look quite promising. One recent study found that 85% of severely disturbed children who had undergone attachment therapy eventually established secure bonds to their caregivers (although the success rate with *teenage* victims of reactive attachment disorder was very poor) (DeAngelis, 1997b). So there is hope that new and improved interventions that begin as soon as children show signs of reactive attachment disorders will eventually enable victims of prolonged social adversity to leave their lingering deficiencies behind them.

Maternal Employment, Day Care, and Early Emotional Development

In recent years, an important question has arisen about the ways our infants, toddlers, and preschool children spend their time. Should they be cared for at home by a parent, or can they pursue their developmental agendas just as well in a day-care setting. Now that more than 60% of all mothers work outside the home at least part time, more and more young children are receiving alternative forms of care. In the United States today, about 40% of infants and toddlers are cared for regularly by their parents, whereas 21% receive day care from other relatives, 4% are cared for at home by a sitter, 14% receive care in day-care homes (typically run by a woman who takes a few children into her own home for payment), and 31% are enrolled in large day-care centers (Scarr, 1998).[2]

nonorganic failure to thrive: an infant growth disorder, caused by lack of attention and affection (and associated undernutrition) that causes growth to slow dramatically or stop.

deprivation dwarfism: a childhood growth disorder triggered by emotional deprivation and characterized by decreased production of growth hormone (GH), slow growth, and small stature.

growth hormone (GH): a pituitary hormone that stimulates the growth and development of body cells.

---

[2]These figures total more than 100% because 9% of American children have more than one regular care arrangement, such as morning enrollment in a day-care center and parental care at home during other hours (Hofferth, 1996).

TABLE 5-4   Characteristics of high-quality infant and toddler day care

Physical setting:	The indoor environment is clean, well lighted and ventilated; outdoor play areas are fenced, spacious, and free of hazards; they include age-appropriate implements (slides, swings, sandbox, etc.).
Child/caregiver ratio:	No more than three infants or four to six toddlers per adult caregiver.
Caregiver characteristics/ qualifications:	Caregivers should have some training in child development and first aid; they should be warm, emotionally expressive, and responsive to children's bids for attention. Ideally, staffing is consistent so that infants and toddlers can form relationships (even attachment relationships) with their caregivers.
Toys/activities:	Toys and activities are age appropriate; infants and toddlers are always supervised, even during free play indoors.
Family links:	Parents are always welcome and caregivers confer freely with them about their child's progress.
Licensing:	Day-care setting is licensed by the state and (ideally) accredited by the National Family Day Care Program or the National Academy of Early Childhood Programs.

Do infants who attend day-care homes or centers suffer in any way compared to those who stay at home with a parent? Research to date suggests that they usually do not (Clarke-Stewart, 1993; NICHD Early Child Care Research Network, 1997). In fact, high-quality day care promotes both the social responsiveness and the intellectual development of children from disadvantaged backgrounds, who are otherwise at risk of experiencing serious developmental delays (Campbell & Ramey, 1995; Ramey & Ramey, 1998). Furthermore, a large, well-controlled longitudinal study of 1,153 children in alternative care revealed that neither the age at which children enter day care nor the amount of care they receive was related to the security of their attachments to their mothers or their emotional well-being (NICHD Early Child Care Research Network, 1997).

However, this broad generalization does not tell the full story. Let's briefly consider two factors that are likely to influence how an infant or toddler adjusts to maternal employment and day care.

BENEFITS OF HIGH-QUALITY OF ALTERNATIVE CARE

Table 5-4 lists what experts believe to be the most important characteristics of high-quality day care for infants and toddlers (Howes, Phillips, & Whitebrook, 1992; Zigler & Gilman, 1993). Unfortunately, the quality of alternative care in the United States is very uneven compared to that widely available in many Western European countries. Large numbers of American infants and toddlers are cared for by sitters who have little knowledge of or training in child development, or in unlicensed day-care homes or centers that often fail to meet minimum health and safety standards (Scarr, 1998; Zigler & Gilman, 1993).

How important is high-quality care? Apparently there is far less risk that children will display insecure attachments (or any other adverse outcome) when children receive excellent day care—*even when that care begins very early.* Jerome Kagan and his associates (1978), for example, found that the vast majority of infants who entered a high-quality, university-sponsored day-care program at age 3½ to 5½ months not only developed secure attachments to their mothers but were just as socially, emotionally, and intellectually mature over the first two years of life as children from similar backgrounds who had been cared for at home. Studies conducted in Sweden (where day care is government subsidized, closely monitored, and typically of high quality) report similar positive outcomes (Broberg et al., 1997), and it seems that the earlier Swedish infants enter high quality day care, the better is their cognitive, social, and emotional development six to eight years later in elementary and junior high school (Andersson, 1989, 1992). Finally, Carollee Howes's (1990) longitudinal study of middle-class families in California indicates that early entry into day care is associated with poor social, emotional, and intellectual outcomes later in childhood only when the care children received was of low quality (see also Vandell, Henderson, & Wilson, 1988).

Unfortunately, children who receive the poorest and most unstable day care are often those whose parents are living complex, stressful lives of their own that may constrain their sensitivity as parents and their involvement in children's learning activities (Fuller, Holloway, & Liang, 1996; Howes, 1990). What this means is that a child's poor progress in day care may often stem as much from a disordered home life, in which parents are not very enthusiastic about parenting as from the less-than-optimal alternative care that he or she receives (NICHD Early Child Care Research Network, 1997; 1998a). Let's explore this idea further.

The Importance of High-Quality Parenting

According to Lois Hoffman (1989), a mother's attitudes about working and child care may be as important to her child's social and emotional well-being as her actual employment status. Mothers tend to be much happier and more sensitive as caregivers when their employment status matches their attitudes about working (Crockenberg & Litman, 1991; Hock & DeMeis, 1990; NICHD Early Child Care Research Network, 1998b). So, if a woman wants to work, it may make little sense to pressure her into staying home to care for her child when she might be depressed, hostile, or otherwise unresponsive in that role.

Even when children receive far less-than-optimal alternative care, their outcomes will depend greatly on the parenting they receive (NICHD Early Child Care Research Network, 1997, 1998b). Outcomes are likely to be better if a working mother has positive attitudes *both* about working and about being a mother (Belsky & Rovine, 1988; Crockenberg & Litman, 1991). And it also helps immensely if her spouse approves of her working and supports her in her parenting role (Spitze, 1988). Ultimately, parents' attitudes about parenting and the quality of care they provide at home has far more to do with an infant's or a toddler's development than the kind of alternative care he receives (Broberg et al., 1997; NICHD Early Child Care Research Network, 1997, 1998a).

Do such findings then imply that quality of alternative care doesn't really matter? *No, they do not.* As we have seen, high-quality alternative care can have social and intellectual benefits and it clearly buffers young children against risks of forming insecure attachments when the parenting they receive is not especially sensitive and responsive (Broberg et al., 1997; NICHD Early Child Care Research Network, 1997). Yet the weight of the evidence suggests that neither maternal employment nor a child's exposure to less than optimal day care are likely to impair early emotional development *as long as the child receives sensitive, responsive care from his or her parents when they are at home* (NICHD Early Child Care Research Network, 1997).

HOW MIGHT WE ASSIST WORKING PARENTS?

What, then, might be done to help working parents to establish and maintain more secure ties with their infants and toddlers and to otherwise optimize their development?

TABLE 5-5 Sample parental-leave policies in modern industrialized nations

Denmark:	Mothers receive 14 weeks' paid maternity leave after childbirth; at their option, either the mother or father may take an additional 10 weeks without pay.
Finland:	Leave for a mother or a father consists of 70 working days at full pay and an additional 188 working days at 70% pay. Unpaid leave may be extended for 3 years without jeopardizing the parent's employment.
France:	Working mothers receive 16 weeks of leave at 84% pay.
Israel:	Working mothers receive 12 weeks' paid leave and up to 40 weeks' unpaid leave.
Japan:	Working mothers receive 14 weeks' paid leave.
Poland:	Working mothers can take up to 6 months' leave with full pay and up to 2½ additional years with partial pay.
Sweden:	Working mothers receive 6 months' leave at 90% pay and an additional 6 months' unpaid leave. Mothers and fathers may share leave benefits if they wish.
United States:	Parents may take 12 weeks of unpaid leave in firms of 50 or more employees.

SOURCE: Adapted from Bjorklund & Bjorklund, 1992.

A national policy governing parental leave for child care is certainly one step in the right direction. Several years ago, the United States Congress passed the Family Leave and Medical Act of 1993—a law guaranteeing workers in firms with 50 or more employees the right to take 12 weeks of *unpaid* leave to spend time with their infant, without jeopardizing their jobs. Yet this guarantee (1) does not apply to the *majority* of American workers (who are employed by firms with fewer than 50 employees) and (2) seems almost miserly compared to the often-generous parental-leave policies that many other industrialized societies have enacted (see Table 5-5).

An early report on the impact of maternal leave reveals that longer leaves are more beneficial than shorter ones. Specifically, American mothers who took four-month leaves after giving birth displayed less negative affect when interacting with their babies than did mothers whose leaves lasted only two months (Clark et al., 1997). The benefits of longer leaves were most noticeable among mothers who reported depressive symptoms or who had babies with difficult temperaments: These mothers were much more *positively* involved with their infants and had more synchronous interactions with them if their leave had lasted a full four months. Longer leaves may allow depressed mothers to become more confident as caregivers, while allowing more time for those with difficult infants to establish a "good fit" between their parenting and the baby's temperamental attributes. Unfortunately, many mothers cannot afford to take four-month, *unpaid* leaves, thus prompting Clark et al. to recommend that the Family Leave and Medical Act of 1993 be revised to provide four to six months of leave with partial pay to employees in all firms, regardless of their size.

A workable national policy governing day care may be equally (or even more) important. At present, middle-class families are the ones caught most directly in a day-care squeeze. Upper-income families have the resources to purchase excellent day care; and the compensatory education (or other subsidized alternative care) that many lower-income children receive is typically of higher quality than the care middle-class parents can afford to purchase (Phillips et al., 1994; Scarr, 1998). Meanwhile, parents from all social backgrounds must often struggle to find and keep competent sitters or other high-quality day-care placements, which are in short supply—due, in part, to the continuing reluctance of the U.S. government to subsidize day care for all citizens and carefully monitor its quality, as many European countries have done. Increasingly, employers are realizing that it is in their best interest to help workers obtain quality day care. According to Sandra Scarr (1998), many corporations vie each year to be on the *Working Mother* magazine list of the top 100 most family-friendly companies, and some larger employers have established day-care centers at the work site. Edward Zigler (Zigler & Finn-Stevenson, 1996) has suggested that public schools, which are already established institutions in all communities, could be a relatively economical way to provide day care for preschool children, with costs funded by a mix of federal, state, and local tax dollars and parental fees. In fact, Zigler has prompted more than 400 school systems in the United States to incorporate child care into their educational programs. Yet, these efforts by corporations and the public schools are not widespread and appear unlikely to become public policy any time soon. Until more options are available, most working parents in the United States will continue to face the very real challenge of finding good alternative care at a cost they can afford.

Summary

- The **"early experience" hypothesis** contends that early emotional developments can have long-term implications for all other aspects of development. One way to evaluate this notion is to determine whether the security of attachments that infants establish influences their development in any meaningful ways.

INDIVIDUAL DIFFERENCES IN ATTACHMENT QUALITY

- Ainsworth's **strange situation** is most commonly used to assess the quality of attachments that 1- to 2-year-olds have formed, although the **Attachment Q-set** is a versatile alternative that is becoming quite popular. Four attachment classifications have been identified: **secure, resistant, avoidant, and disorganized/disoriented.**

- Although the distribution of various attachment classifications varies across cultures and often reflects cultural differences in child rearing, parents around the world prefer that their infants form secure attachments, and more infants around the world establish secure attachments than any other pattern.

FACTORS THAT INFLUENCE ATTACHMENT SECURITY

- Sensitive responsive caregiving is associated with the development of secure attachments, whereas inconsistent, neglectful, overintrusive, and abusive caregiving predict insecure attachments. Thus, there is ample support for the **caregiving hypothesis.** Fortunately, parents who are at risk of promoting insecure attachments can be trained to become more sensitive, responsive caregivers.

- Infant characteristics and temperamental attributes may also influence attachment quality by affecting the character of caregiver/infant interactions. However, the **temperament hypothesis**—that attachments are merely reflections of infant temperament—is clearly an overstatement.

- Today, some developmentalists favor an integrative, middle-of-the-road theory—one that holds caregiving as largely determining whether attachments are secure or not and child temperament as largely influencing the type of insecurity that might be displayed by a child who receives insensitive caregiving.

ATTACHMENT AND LATER DEVELOPMENT

- Secure attachment during infancy predicts intellectual curiosity and social competence later in childhood. One reason is that infants form **internal working models** of themselves and others that are often stable over time and influence their reactions to people and challenges for years to come. Parents' working models correspond closely with those of their children and are sometimes better predictors of attachment than parenting sensitivity is. However, children's working models can change, so that a secure attachment history is no guarantee of positive adjustment later in life; nor are insecure attachments a certain indication of poor life outcomes.

THE UNATTACHED INFANT

- Some infants have had very limited contacts with caregivers early in life and don't seem attached to anyone. Both monkeys and children who were socially deprived as infants are withdrawn and apathetic and (in the case of humans) may later display intellectual deficits, behavior problems, and **reactive attachment disorders.** Their problems appear to stem more from their lack of responsive social stimulation (**social stimulation hypothesis**) than from failure to receive care from a singular mother figure (**maternal deprivation hypothesis**), and they often display a strong capacity for recovery, overcoming many of their initial handicaps. However, such special interventions as **younger peer theory** (for monkeys) and *attachment therapy* (for humans) are needed for those whose early adversities were prolonged or severe.

MATERNAL EMPLOYMENT, DAY CARE, AND EARLY EMOTIONAL DEVELOPMENT

■ It was once feared that regular separations from working parents and placement into day care might prevent infants from establishing secure attachments or undermine the quality of attachments that were already secure. However, there is little evidence that either a mother's employment outside the home or alternative caregiving will have such effects, provided the day care is of good quality and that parents are sensitive and responsive caregivers when they are at home.

■ Stronger family-leave policies and national policies to make affordable, high-quality day care available to all parents are among the most important supports working parents need to optimize their children's social, emotional, and intellectual development.

Chapter Six

Development of the Self and Social Cognition

Development of the Self-Concept

The Emerging Self: Differentiation, Discrimination, and Self-Recognition

Who Am I? Responses of Preschool Children

Children's Theory of Mind and Emergence of the Private Self

Conceptions of Self in Middle Childhood and Adolescence

Self-Esteem: The Evaluative Component of Self

Origins and Development of Self-Esteem

Social Contributors to Self-Esteem

The Development of Self-Control

Emergence of Self-Control in Early Childhood

Delay of Gratification in Childhood and Adolescence

Who Am I to Be? Forging an Identity

Developmental Trends in Identity Formation

How Painful Is Identity Formation?

Personal and Social Influences on Identity Formation

The Other Side of Social Cognition: Knowing About Others

Age Trends in Person Perception

Theories of Social-Cognitive Development

Summary

*H*ow would you answer the "Who am I" question? If you are like most adults, you would probably respond by mentioning some of your noteworthy personal characteristics (honesty, friendliness), some roles you play in life (student, hospital volunteer), your religious or moral views, and perhaps your political leanings. In doing so, you would be describing that elusive concept that psychologists call the **self**.

Although no one else knows you as well as you do, it is a safe bet that much of what you know about yourself stems from your contacts and experiences with other people. When a college sophomore tells us that he is a friendly, outgoing person who is active in his fraternity, the Young Republicans, and the Campus Crusade for Christ, he is saying that his past experiences with others and the groups to which he belongs are important determinants of his personal identity. Many years ago, sociologists Charles Cooley (1902) and George Herbert Mead (1934) proposed that the self-concept evolves from social interactions and will undergo many changes over the course of a lifetime. Cooley used the term **looking-glass self** to emphasize that a person's understanding of self is a reflection of how other people react to him: the self-concept is the image cast by a social mirror.

Cooley and Mead believed that the self and social development are completely intertwined—that they emerge together and that neither can progress far without the other. Presumably, newborns experience people and events as simple "streams of impressions" and will have absolutely no concept of "self" until they realize that they exist independent of the objects and individuals that they encounter regularly. Once infants make this important distinction between self and nonself, they will establish interactive routines with close companions (that is, develop socially) and will learn that their behavior elicits predictable reactions from others. In other words, they are acquiring information about the "social self" based on the ways people respond to them. Mead (1934) concluded that

> the self has a character that is different from that of the physiological organism proper. The self is something which . . . is not initially there at birth but arises in the process of social development. That is, it develops in a given individual as a result of his relations to that process as a whole and to other individuals within the process.

Do babies really have no sense of self at birth? We explore this issue in the first section of the chapter, as we trace the growth of the self-concept from infancy through adolescence. We then consider how children and adolescents evaluate the self and construct a sense of *self-esteem*. Our focus next shifts to the development of one very important contributor to self-esteem, as we examine the growth of *self control*—an attribute that figures prominently in determining what we will be able to accomplish in life and how well we will be able to get along with other people. We then discuss a major developmental hurdle that adolescents face: the need to establish a firm, future-oriented self-portrait, or *identity*, with which to approach the responsibilities of young adulthood. Finally, we consider what developing children know about other people and interpersonal relationships and see that this aspect of **social cognition**, which parallels the development of the self-concept, nicely illustrates Cooley's and Mead's point that personal (self) and social aspects of development are intertwined in complex ways.

Of course, there are several other aspects of self-development that warrant more extended coverage as important topics in their own right. In Chapter 7, for example, we will see how curious infants and toddlers become fascinated by and begin to take pride in their ability to make things happen—a pride that may (or may not) blossom into a strong motive to achieve and a favorable academic self-concept. And we all develop conceptions of ourselves as males or females, as prosocial or antisocial beings, and as moral (or immoral) individuals. Research on these topics is now so extensive that each merits a chapter of its own (see Chapters 8–10).

Who Am I?

I'm a person who says what I think . . . not [one] who's going to say one thing and do the other. I'm really lucky. I've never [drunk or] done drugs, but I'm always high. I love life. I've got a lot of different business interests . . . a construction company, oil wells, land . . . I'm trying everything. I travel a lot . . . it's difficult to be traveling and in school at the same time. [People] perceive me as being unusual . . . very mysterious, and I hope they see me as being a competitor, because I do all my talking on the field.

Herschel Walker, former college student and Olympic bobsledder, Heisman Trophy winner, and all-pro running back for the Minnesota Vikings and the Dallas Cowboys (as quoted by Blount, 1986)

self: the combination of physical and psychological attributes that is unique to each individual.

looking-glass self: the idea that a child's self-concept is largely determined by the ways other people respond to him or her.

social cognition: thinking that people display about the thoughts, feelings, motives, and behaviors of themselves and other people.

For now, let's return to the starting point and see how children come to know this entity we call the *self*.

Development of the Self-Concept

When do infants first distinguish themselves from other people, objects, and environmental events? At what point do they become consciously aware of their uniqueness. What kinds of information do young children use to define the self? And how do their self-images and feelings of self-worth change over time? These are some of the issues we will explore as we trace the development of the **self-concept** from infancy through adolescence.

THE EMERGING SELF: DIFFERENTIATION, DISCRIMINATION, AND SELF-RECOGNITION

Like Mead, many developmentalists believe that infants are born without a sense of self. Psychoanalyst Margaret Mahler (Mahler, Pine, & Bergman, 1975) likens the newborn to a "chick in an egg" who has no reason to differentiate the self from the surrounding environment. After all, every need that the child has is soon satisfied by his or her ever-present companions, who are simply "there" and have no identities of their own.

By contrast, other developmentalists (see Brown, 1998; Butterworth, 1992) believe that even newborn infants have the *capacity* to distinguish the self from the surrounding environment. For example, newborns cry at hearing a recording of another baby's cries but *not* on hearing a recording of their *own* cries, thus implying that a differentiation of self and others is possible at birth (Butterworth, 1992). Furthermore, newborns anticipate the arrival of their own hands at their mouths, and as we noted in Box 2.2, seem capable of using **proprioceptive feedback** from their own facial expressions to mimic at least some of the facial expressions their caregivers display. These kinds of observations suggested to Andrew Meltzoff (1990a) that "the young infant possesses an embryonic 'body scheme.' . . . [Although] this body scheme develops [over time], some body scheme kernel is present as a 'psychological primitive' right from the earliest phases of infancy" (p. 160).

Of course, these observations are subject to alternative interpretations (many believe them to be mere reflexes), and it is by no means an easy task to clearly establish when infants first become self-aware. Yet, almost everyone agrees that the first glimmerings of this capacity can be seen in the first two or three months (Samuels, 1986; Stern, 1985). Recall Piaget's (and others') descriptions of cognitive development early in infancy. During the first two months, babies are exercising their reflexive schemes and repeating pleasurable acts centered in their own bodies (for example, sucking their thumbs and waving their arms). In other words, they are becoming acquainted with their own physical capabilities, and by 3 months of age, an infant who sees legs kicking on a TV monitor can already use proprioceptive and spatial cues about the directionality of those kicks to decide whether the legs he is observing are his own (Rochat & Morgan, 1995). We also learned in Chapter 4 that infants only 2 to 3 months old delight at producing interesting sights and sounds by kicking their legs or pulling their arms (which are attached by strings to mobiles or to audiovisual machinery (Lewis, Alessandri, & Sullivan, 1990; Rovee-Collier, 1995). Even an 8-week-old infant can recall how to produce these interesting events for two or three days; and if the strings are disconnected so she can no longer exert any control, she may pull or kick all the harder and become rather distressed (Lewis et al., 1990; Sullivan et al., 1992). Thus it seems that 2-month-old infants may have some limited

self-concept: one's perceptions of one's unique combination of attributes.

proprioceptive feedback: sensory information from the muscles, tendons, and joints that help one locate the position of one's body (or body parts) in space.

sense of **personal agency,** or understanding that *they* are responsible for at least some of the events that so fascinate them.

In sum, it is still an open question whether newborn infants can truly differentiate themselves from the surrounding environment. But even if they can't, it is likely that they learn the limits of their own bodies during the first month or two and differentiate this "physical self" from the external objects they can control shortly thereafter (Samuels, 1986). So if a 2- to 4-month-old could talk, he might answer the "Who am I" question by saying "I am a looker, a chewer, a reacher, and a grabber who acts on objects and makes things happen."

Self-Recognition   Once infants know that they *are* (that they exist independent of other people and other objects), they are in a position to find out *who* or *what* they are (Harter, 1983). When do infants perceive themselves as having unique physical characteristics? When do they construct firm self-images and view themselves as an object that has a sense of permanence over time?

One way to answer these questions is to expose infants to some visual representation of the self (that is, a videotape or mirror reflection) and see how they respond to these images. Research of this type reveals that infants only 5 months old seem to treat their own faces as familiar social stimuli. For example, Marie Legerstee and her associates (1998) found that 5-month-olds who viewed moving images of themselves and an age-mate (on videotape) could clearly discriminate their own image from that of the peer, as indicated by their preference to gaze at the peer's face (which was novel and interesting to them) rather than at their own (which was presumably familiar and, hence, less interesting). How might infants this young come to discriminate their own faces from those of other people? One explanation is that babies (in Western cultures, at least) often find themselves in front of mirrors, usually beside a caregiver who is playing a social game with them (Fogel, 1995; Stern, 1995). Such experiences may thus allow ample opportunity for infants to match their own movement-produced proprioceptive information with the actions of one of the figures in the mirror, thereby discriminating this "self" from an older social partner, whose movements do not correspond so closely with their own (Legerstee et al., 1998).

Yet, the remarkable feats that these young infants display may simply represent their powers of visual discrimination rather than any conscious awareness that the image in a mirror or on videotape is "me." How might we determine whether infants have truly constructed a firm *self*-image that is stable over time?

Michael Lewis and Jeanne Brooks-Gunn (1979) have studied the development of **self-recognition** by asking mothers to surreptitiously apply a spot of rouge to their infants' noses (under the pretext of wiping the infants' faces) and then place the infants before a mirror. If infants have a scheme for their own faces and recognize their mirror images as themselves, they should soon notice the new red spot and reach for or wipe their *own* noses. When infants 9 to 24 months old were given this **rouge test,** the younger ones showed no self-recognition: They seemed to treat the image in the mirror as if it were "some other kid." Signs of self-recognition were observed among some of the 15- to 17-month-olds, but only among the 18- to 24-month-olds did a majority of infants touch their own noses, apparently realizing that they had a strange mark on their faces. They knew exactly who that kid in the mirror was (see also Asendorph, Warkentin, & Baudonniere, 1996)!

Interestingly, infants from nomadic tribes, who have no experience with mirrors, begin to display self-recognition on the rouge test at the same age as city-reared infants (Priel & deSchonen, 1986). And many 18- to 24-month-olds can even recognize themselves in current photographs and will often use a personal pronoun ("me") or their own name to label their photographic image (Lewis & Brooks-Gunn, 1979). Yet, children this young are not yet fully aware that the self is an entity that

personal agency: the recognition that one can be the cause of an event or events.

self-recognition: the ability to recognize oneself in a mirror or a photograph, coupled with the conscious awareness that the mirror or photographic image is a representation of "me."

rouge test: test of self-recognition that involves marking a toddler's face and observing his or her reaction to the mark when placed before a mirror.

is stable over time. Not until age 3½ will they retrieve a brightly colored sticker placed surreptitiously on their heads if their first glimpse of it comes after a two- to three-minute delay on videotape or in a photograph (Povinelli, Landau, & Perilloux, 1996). Apparently 2- to 3-year-olds who display some self-recognition do not retrieve the sticker because they don't yet seem to realize that earlier events in which they have participated have happened to *them!* By contrast, 4- and 5-year-olds quickly retrieve the sticker after a *brief delay* but do not retrieve it if the videotape depicts events that happened a week earlier. These older preschoolers clearly recognize that the self is stable over time but that transient events are not. In other words, they know that the sticker they see a week later on film is *not* still on *their* heads because this event had happened to them a long time ago (Povinelli & Simon, 1998).

Contributors to Self-Recognition   Why do 18- to 24-month-olds suddenly begin to display clear evidence of self-recognition? Recall that this is precisely the age when toddlers are said to internalize their sensorimotor schemes to form mental images—at least one of which may be a now-clear image of their own facial features. Even children with severe mental retardation display self-recognition on the rouge test if they have attained a mental age of 18 to 20 months (Hill & Tomlin, 1981). And once 3½- to 4-year-olds finally begin to encode noteworthy experiences as autobiographical memories (Nelson, 1993), they now clearly realize that the self is a stable entity and that the earlier events that they can remember did indeed happen to *them* (Povinelli & Simon, 1998).

Although a certain level of cognitive development may be necessary for self-recognition, social experiences are probably of equal importance. Gordon Gallup (1979) found that adolescent chimpanzees can easily recognize themselves in a mirror (as shown by the rouge test) unless they have been reared in complete social isolation. In contrast to normal chimps, social isolates react to their mirror images as if they were looking at another animal! So the term *looking-glass self* may apply to chimpanzees as well as to humans: Reflections in a "social mirror" enable normal chimps to develop some self-awareness, whereas a chimpanzee that is denied these experiences will fail to acquire a clear self-image.

One social experience that contributes to self-awareness in humans is a secure attachment to a primary caregiver. Sandra Pipp and her associates (1992) administered a complex test of self-knowledge to 2- and 3-year-olds—a test assessing the child's awareness of his name and gender as well as tasks to assess self-recognition. As we see in Figure 6.1, securely attached 2-year-olds were outperforming their insecurely attached age-mates on the test, and differences in self-knowledge between secure and insecure 3-year-olds were even greater.

Social and Emotional Consequences of Self-Recognition   The growth of self-recognition and an emerging awareness of oneself as a participant in *social* interactions pave the way for many new social and emotional competencies. For example, we saw in Chapter 4 that the ability to experience *self-conscious* emotions such as embarrassment depends on self-recognition. Furthermore, toddlers who have reached this self-referential milestone soon become more outgoing and socially skilled. They now take great pleasure in imitating a playmate's activities (Asendorph & Baudonniere, 1993; Asendorph et al., 1996) and will occasionally even cooperate (as illustrated by one child's operating a handle so that another can retrieve toys from a container) to achieve shared goals (Brownell & Carriger, 1990).

Categorical Self   Once toddlers display clear evidence of self-recognition, they also become more sensitive to the ways in which people differ and begin to categorize themselves or these dimensions—a classification called the **categorical self** (Stipek,

PHOTO 6.1   Recognizing one's mirror image as "me" is a crucial milestone in the development of "self."

categorical self: a person's classification of the self along socially significant dimensions such as age and sex.

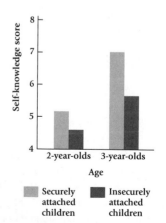

FIGURE 6.1   Average scores on a test of self-knowledge as a function of age and attachment quality. (Adapted from Pipp, Easterbrooks, & Harmon, 1992.)

Gralinski, & Kopp, 1990). Age, sex, and such evaluative dimensions as good–bad are the first social categories that toddlers incorporate into their self-concepts, as illustrated by such statements as "I *big boy*, not a *baby*" or "Jennie *good girl*."

Interestingly, young children are even becoming aware of racial and ethnic categories, although it may take a while before they can classify themselves correctly. Native American 3- to 5-year-olds, for example, can easily discriminate Indians from whites in photographs but are less often accurate in specifying which category they most resemble (Spencer & Markstrom-Adams, 1990). A similar "misidentification" phenomenon has been observed among African-American preschoolers, who show a clear pro-white bias and associate fewer positive attributes with the color black or with African-American people (Cross, 1985; Spencer, 1988). However, these "misidentifications" and pro-white biases do not necessarily mean that minority youngsters are unaware of their own ethnicity or are especially critical of themselves, for minority children typically display a strong pro-white sentiment *and* highly favorable self-concepts (see Spencer & Markstrom-Adams, 1990). Instead, the so-called "misidentifications" that minority preschoolers display may simply reflect the same early awareness of negative stereotypes about minorities that white children display (Bigler & Liben, 1993) and a desire to align themselves with what they believe to be the most socially desirable group (Spencer & Markstrom-Adams, 1990).

WHO AM I? RESPONSES OF PRESCHOOL CHILDREN

Until very recently, developmentalists believed that the self-concepts of preschool children were concrete, physicalistic, and nearly devoid of any *psychological* self-awareness. Why? Because when 3- to 5-year-olds are asked to describe themselves, they talk mostly about their physical attributes ("I have blue eyes"), their possessions ("I have a new bike"), or about *actions* of which they feel especially proud, such as hitting a baseball or walking to nursery school on their own. By contrast, psychological descriptors such as "I'm happy," "I'm good at sports," or "I like people" are rarely used by children this young (Damon & Hart, 1988; Keller, Ford, & Meachum, 1978).

These findings would hardly surprise Erik Erikson. In his theory of psychosocial development, Erikson (1963) proposes that 2- to 3-year-olds are struggling to become independent or autonomous, while 4- to 5-year-olds who have achieved a sense of autonomy are now acquiring new skills, achieving important objectives, and taking great pride in their accomplishments. According to Erikson, it is a healthy sign when preschool children define themselves in terms of their activities, for an activity-based self-concept reflects the sense of *initiative* they will need to cope with the many new lessons they must learn at school.

Evidence for an Early "Psychological" Self-Concept

However, not everyone agrees that preschoolers' self-concepts are limited to observable characteristics and devoid of any "psychological" self-awareness. Rebecca Eder (1989, 1990) finds that when 3½- to 5-year-old children are asked to respond to contrasting *forced choice* statements that require fewer verbal skills than open-ended "Who am I" questions, they can quickly characterize themselves on *psychological* dimensions such as sociability (by choosing, for example, between such statements as

PHOTO **6.2** Preschool children are already aware of their behavioral patterns and preferences and are using this information to form an early "psychological" portrait of the self.

"I like to play by myself" versus "I like to play with my friends"). Furthermore, they characterize themselves differently on different dimensions, and these self-characterizations are stable over time (Eder, 1990). Although preschool children may not be consciously aware of what it means to be "sociable" or "athletic" or to be an "achiever," Eder's research implies that they have rudimentary psychological conceptions of self long before they can express this knowledge in traitlike terminology (see also Flavell et al., 1993).

CHILDREN'S THEORY OF MIND AND EMERGENCE OF THE PRIVATE SELF

When adults think about the self, they know that it consists of a **public self** (or **me**) that others can see and a **private self** (or **I**) that has an inner, reflective (thinking) character not available to others. Are young children aware of both the public and private aspects of self? Such a distinction implies that they have a **theory of mind**—an understanding that people have mental states, such as desires, beliefs, and intentions, that are not always shared with or accessible to others, and that often guide their behavior.

Early Understandings of Mental States By 18 months of age, toddlers are demonstrating some awareness of their own and others' mental states. They will imitate the purposeful actions of human models but not those of a mechanical toy, thereby illustrating an early awareness that human behaviors reflect definite goals and intentions (Meltzoff, 1995). They can also reason accurately about other people's *desires*. So having seen an experimenter express disgust at the thought of eating crackers, they know that she would prefer raw vegetables to the crackers they prefer when offered a choice between these snacks (Repacholi & Gopnik, 1997).

By age 2 to 3, children often talk about such mental states as needs, feelings, and desires, and they are aware that (1) they may know something that others don't (O'Neill, 1996) and (2) that people cannot actually observe their thoughts (Flavell et al., 1993). But despite these early glimmerings of an emerging private self, 2- to 3-year-olds have a very primitive understanding of the connections between various mental states and behaviors. In fact, they might be labeled **desire theorists** because they think a person's actions generally reflect his *desires* and do not yet understand that what a person *believes* might also affect his behavior (Wellman & Woolley, 1990). But between ages 3 and 4, children develop a **belief-desire theory of mind** in which they recognize, as we adults do, that beliefs and desires are different mental states and that either or both can influence one's conduct (Wellman, 1990). So, a 4-year-old who has broken a vase while roughhousing may now try to overcome his mother's apparent *desire* to punish him by trying to make her *believe* that his breaking the vase was unintentional ("I didn't mean to Mama—it was an accident!").

Origins of a Belief-Desire Theory Very young children may view desire as the most important determinant of behavior because their own actions are so often triggered by desires and they may assume that other people's conduct reflects similar motives. In addition, 3-year-olds have a very curious view of beliefs, thinking that they are accurate reflections of reality that everyone shares. They don't seem to appreciate, as older children and adults do, that beliefs are merely *interpretations* of reality that may differ from person to person and may be *inaccurate*. Consider children's reactions to the following story—a **false-belief task** that assesses the understanding that people can hold incorrect beliefs and be influenced by them, wrong though they may be:

> Sam puts some chocolate in a blue cupboard and goes out to play. In his absence, his mother moves the chocolate to the green cupboard. When Sam returns, he wants his chocolate. Where does he look for it?

public self (or me): those aspects of self that others can see or infer.

private self (or I): those inner, or subjective, aspects of self that are known only to the individual and are not available for public scrutiny.

theory of mind: an understanding that people are cognitive beings with mental states that are not always accessible to others and that often guide their behavior.

desire theory: an early theory of mind in which a person's actions are thought to be a reflection of her desires rather than other mental states such as beliefs.

belief-desire theory: theory of mind that develops between ages 3 and 4; the child now realizes that both beliefs and desires may determine behavior and that people will often act on their beliefs, even if these are inaccurate.

false-belief task: method of assessing one's understanding that people can hold inaccurate beliefs that can influence their conduct, wrong as these beliefs may be.

Three-year-olds say "in the green cupboard." They know where the chocolate is, and because beliefs reflect reality for them, they assume that Sam will be driven by his *desire* for chocolate to look in the right place. By contrast, 4- to 5-year-olds display a *belief-desire theory of mind:* They now understand that beliefs are merely mental representations of reality that may be inaccurate and that someone else may not share; thus, they know that Sam will look for his chocolate in the blue cupboard where he *believes* it is (beliefs determine behavior, even if they are false) rather than in the green cupboard where they know it is (Wellman & Woolley, 1990).

Once children understand that people will act on the basis of false beliefs, they may use this knowledge to their own advantage by lying or attempting other deceptive ploys. For example, 4-year-olds (but not 3-year-olds) who are playing hide-the-object games will *spontaneously* generate false clues, trying to *mislead* their opponent about the object's true location (Sodian et al., 1991). Notice that these 4-year-olds are now making a clear distinction between public and private self, for they recognize that their deceptive *public* behavior may lead their opponent to adapt a belief that differs from their own *private* knowledge.

It's not that younger children haven't any capacity to recognize a false belief or its implications. For example, 3-year-olds can tell from thought-bubble deceptions or from knowledge that a story character is participating in pretense that the incorrect beliefs story characters have expressed really do contradict reality (Cassidy, 1998; Wellman, Hollander, & Schult, 1996). And if they have collaborated with an adult in formulating a deceptive strategy in a hide-the-object game, their performance improves dramatically on other false-belief tasks (Hala & Chandler, 1996). Nevertheless, between 3 and 4 is when children normally achieve a much richer understanding of mental life, distinguishing desires from beliefs and clearly discriminating the private-self-as-knower from the public self they present to others. How important are these developments? John Flavell and his colleagues (1993) answer by saying that if children had no theory of mind and no awareness that public appearances do not necessarily reflect private realities, they would be largely incapable of drawing meaningful *psychological* inferences about their own or others' behavior; in other words, the rich social-cognitive abilities that humans display would be impossible.

How Does a Theory of Mind Originate?   How do children manage to construct a theory of mind so early in life? One perspective is that human infants may be just as biologically prepared and as motivated to acquire information about mental states as they are to share meaning through language. Andrew Meltzoff (1995), for example, suggests that early *imitative* acts may reflect an infant's or toddler's attempts to share meaning by representing and understanding others' motives and intentions.

But even if humans are biologically predisposed to develop a theory of mind, there are many social experiences that foster its development. Pretend play, for example, is an activity that prompts children to think about mental states. As toddlers and preschool children conspire to make one object represent another or to enact pretend roles such as cops and robbers, they become increasingly aware of the creative potential of the human mind—an awareness that beliefs are merely mental constructions that can influence ongoing behavior, even if they misrepresent reality (as they do during many pretend play activities) (Hughes & Dunn, 1998, Taylor & Carlson, 1997; Youngblade & Dunn, 1995). Young children also have ample opportunity to learn how the mind works from family conversations centering on the discussion of motives and intentions, and other mental states (Sabbagh & Callanan, 1998), as well as on the resolution of conflicts among siblings and reasoning about moral issues (Dunn, 1994). In fact, researchers have been finding that preschoolers with siblings, especially those with older siblings, do better on false-belief tasks and are quicker to adopt a belief-desire theory of mind than only children are (see Ruffman et al., 1998, for a review). Having older siblings may provide children with more opportunities for complex pretend play, as well as more interactions involving deception and trickery—experiences that may clearly illustrate that beliefs need not reflect reality to influence one's own or another's behavior. However, preschoolers who perform especially well on false-belief tasks also interact with a larger number of adults—a finding that implies children are apprentices to a variety of tutors as they acquire a theory of mind (Lewis et al., 1996).

Cultural Influences   Do children in all cultures construct such a rich understanding of how the mind works during the preschool period? Apparently not. Even 8-year-olds among the Junin Quechua people of Peru have difficulties understanding that beliefs can be false (Vinden, 1996). Why? Probably because Junin Quechua speakers do not often talk about their own or others' mental states. Most of these people are subsistence farmers who work from dawn to dusk just to survive, and they do not need to reflect very often on what they or others may feel or believe in order to live productive lives. In fact, their language has few mental state words, and references to mental states are largely absent from their folktales. So the appearance of a belief-desire theory of mind by age 4 is not universal and is likely to be delayed in cultures that lack the social supports for its emergence.

CONCEPTIONS OF SELF IN MIDDLE CHILDHOOD AND ADOLESCENCE

Once children develop a theory of mind and clearly differentiate their public and private selves, their self-descriptions very gradually evolve from listings of their physical, behavioral, and other "external" attributes to sketches of their enduring inner qualities—that is, their traits, values, beliefs, and ideologies (Damon & Hart, 1988; Livesley & Bromley, 1973). This developmental shift toward a more abstract or "psychological" portrayal of self can be seen in the following three responses to the "Who am I" question (Montemayor & Eisen, 1977, pp. 317–318):

9-year-old: My name is Bruce C. I have brown eyes. I have brown hair. I love! sports. I have seven people in my family. I have great! eye sight. I have lots! of friends. I live at . . . I have an uncle who is almost 7 feet tall. My teacher is Mrs. V. I play hockey! I'm almost the smartest boy in the class. I love! food . . . I love! school.

11½-year-old: My name is A. I'm a human being . . . a girl . . . a truthful person. I'm not pretty. I do so-so in my studies. I'm a very good cellist. I'm a little tall for my age. I like several boys . . . I'm old fashioned. I am a very good swimmer . . . I try to be helpful . . . Mostly I'm good, but I lose my temper. I'm not well liked by some girls and boys. I don't know if boys like me . . .

17-year-old: I am a human being . . . a girl . . . an individual . . . I am a Pisces. I am a moody person . . . an indecisive person . . . an ambitious person. I am a big curious person . . . I am lonely. I am an American (God help me). I am a Democrat. I am a liberal person. I am a radical. I am conservative. I am a pseudoliberal. I am an Atheist. I am not a classifiable person (i.e., I don't want to be). (pp. 317–318)

In addition to using more psychological terms to describe the self than grade-school children do, adolescents are also becoming much more aware that they are not the same person in all situations—a fact that may puzzle or even annoy them. Susan Harter and Ann Monsour (1992) asked 13-, 15-, and 17-year-olds to describe themselves when they are with (1) parents, (2) friends, (3) romantic partners, and (4) teachers and classmates. Then each participant was asked to sort through the four self-descriptions, picking out any inconsistencies and indicating how confusing or upsetting they were. As we see in Figure 6.2, 13-year-olds reported few inconsistencies and were not bothered much by those they did detect. By contrast, 15-year-olds listed many oppositional attributes and were often confused about them. One 15-year-old talked about her tendency to be happy with friends but depressed at home. "I really think of myself as happy—and want to be that way because I think that's my true self, but I get depressed with my family and it bugs me." (Harter & Monsour, 1992, p. 253). These 15-year-olds seemed to feel that there were several different selves inside them and were concerned about finding the "real me."

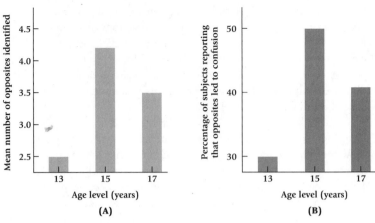

FIGURE 6.2 Average number of oppositional attributes reported by 13-, 15-, and 17-year-olds (panel A) and the percentages of 13-, 15-, and 17-year olds who said they were confused or "mixed up" by these inconsistencies in their self-portraits (panel B). (Adapted from Harter & Monsour, 1992.)

Interestingly, adolescents who are most upset over inconsistencies in their self-portrayals are those who put on false fronts, acting out of character in an attempt to improve their images or win the approval of parents or peers. Unfortunately, those who most often display these **false self behaviors** are the ones who feel least confident that they know who they truly are (Harter et al., 1996).

Inconsistent self-portrayals are somewhat less bothersome to older adolescents, who have often integrated them into a higher-order, more coherent view of themselves. A 17-year-old boy, for example, might conclude that it is perfectly understandable to be relaxed and confident in most situations but nervous on dates if one has not yet had much dating experience, or that "moodiness" can explain his being *cheerful* with friends on some occasions but *irritable* on others. Harter and Monsour believe that cognitive development—specifically the formal-operational ability to compare abstract traits like "cheerful" and "irritable" and to ultimately integrate them into more general concepts like "moodiness"—is behind this change in self-perceptions.

In sum, one's self-concept becomes more psychological, more abstract, and a more coherent, integrated self-portrait from childhood throughout adolescence. Truly, the adolescent becomes a sophisticated self-theorist who can reflect on and understand the workings of his or her personality.

One final point, but an important one: The overview of self-concept development presented here stems largely from research conducted in Western industrialized societies that value independence and view *personal* attributes as the hallmark of one's character. Yet, as we will see in Box 6.1 on pages 174–175, this Eurocentric perspective on the meaning of "self" may not completely capture the experiences of people from many *collectivist* societies around the world.

Self-Esteem: The Evaluative Component of Self

As children develop, they not only come to understand more and more about themselves and to construct more intricate self-portraits, but they also begin to *evaluate* the qualities that they perceive themselves as having. This evaluative aspect of self is called **self-esteem.** Children with high self-esteem are fundamentally satisfied with the type of person they are; they recognize their strong points, can acknowledge their weaknesses (often hoping to overcome them), and generally feel quite positive about

false self behavior: acting in ways that do not reflect one's true self or the "true me."

self-esteem: one's evaluation of one's worth as a person based on an assessment of the qualities that make up the self-concept.

the characteristics and competencies they display. By contrast, children with low self-esteem view the self in a less favorable light, often choosing to dwell on perceived inadequacies rather than on any strengths they may happen to have (Brown, 1998; Zupan, Hammen, & Jaenike, 1987).

ORIGINS AND DEVELOPMENT OF SELF-ESTEEM

Children's evaluations of themselves and their competencies is a most important aspect of self that can influence all other aspects of their conduct and their psychological well-being. How does self-esteem originate and when do children first establish a realistic sense of self-worth?

These questions are not easy to answer, but Bowlby's (1988) "working models" theory that we discussed in Chapter 5 provides some meaningful clues. The theory predicts that securely attached children, who presumably construct a *positive* working model of self, should soon begin to evaluate themselves more favorably than insecurely attached children, whose working models of self are not so positive. And apparently they do. In a recent study in Belgium, 4- to 5-year-olds were asked questions about their worthiness, which they answered through a hand puppet (for example, Do you [puppet] like to play with [this child]? Is [this child] a good [bad] boy/girl?). Children with secure ties to their mothers not only described themselves more favorably (through the puppet) than did children who were insecurely attached, but they were also rated as more competent and more socially skilled by their preschool teachers (Verschueren, Marcoen, & Schoefs, 1996). So it seems that by age 4 or 5 (and possibly sooner), children have already established an early and meaningful sense of self-esteem—one that is influenced by their attachment history and is a reasonably accurate reflection of how teachers evaluate their competencies.

Determinants of Global Self-Esteem When we adults think about self-esteem, a global appraisal of self comes to mind based on the strengths and weaknesses we display in several different life domains. The same is true for children, who first evaluate their competencies in many different areas and only later integrate these impressions into an overall self-evaluation (Harter, 1996; Marsh & Hattie, 1996).

Susan Harter (1982, 1990) has asked children of different ages to evaluate their competencies in such domains as *social acceptance, task/scholastic competence, physical/athletic competence,* and *behavioral conduct* by indicating the extent to which statements such as "Some kids are good at figuring out answers at school!" (scholastic competence) and "Some kids are always chosen for games" (athletic competence) are true of themselves. Figure 6.3 illustrates two sample questions from Harter's Self-Perception Profile for Children—items that tap children's perceptions of their *scholastic competence* (top) and *behavioral conduct* (bottom). As shown in the figure, each item

Type of item	Really true for me	Sort of true for me				Sort of true for me	Really true for me
Scholastic competence	1	2	Some kids have *trouble* figuring out the answers in school	BUT	Other kids almost *always* can figure out the answers	3	4
	Really true for me	Sort of true for me				Sort of true for me	Really true for me
Behavioral conduct	1	2	Some kids usually get in *trouble* because of things they do	BUT	Other kids usually *don't* do things that get them in trouble	3	4

FIGURE 6.3 Sample items from Harter's Self-Perception Profile for Children. (From Harter, 1988.)

Box 6.1 Cultural Influences

Cultural Influences on the Self-Concept

Indicate the extent to which you agree or disagree with each of the items below, on the following scale:

1	2	3	4	5	6	7
Strongly disagree						Strongly agree

_____ 1. I have respect for authority figures with whom I interact.

_____ 2. I am comfortable with being singled out for praise or rewards.

_____ 3. My happiness depends on the happiness of those around me.

_____ 4. Speaking up in class is not a problem for me.

_____ 5. I should take my parent's advice into consideration when making education/career plans.

_____ 6. My identity independent of others is very important to me.

SOURCE: Adapted from Singelis, 1994.

What is considered desirable in the way of a self-concept may vary dramatically across cultures. Western societies such as the United States, Canada, Australia, and the industrialized countries of Europe might be termed **individualistic societies:** They value competition and individual initiative and tend to emphasize ways in which people differ from each other. By contrast, many Asian cultures (for example, India, Japan, and China) could be considered **collectivist** or **communal** societies: People are more cooperative and interdependent rather than competitive and independent, and their identities are closely tied to the groups to which they belong (for example, families, religious organizations, and communities) rather than to their own accomplishments and personal characteristics (Triandis, 1995). In fact, people in East Asian cultures such as China, Korea, and Japan tend to value self-effacement and to view individuals who are preoccupied with personal concerns as somewhat abnormal and maladjusted (Marcus & Kitayama, 1994; Triandis, 1995).

Indeed, cross-cultural variations in the nature or content of people's self-concepts are quite clear in the responses of older American and Japanese adolescents to a "Who Am I" questionnaire (Cousins, 1989). The questionnaire required them to first rate themselves on *personal/individualistic* attributes (for example, "I am honest"; "I am smart") and *social/relational* attributes (for example, "I'm a student"; "I'm a son"). Then, participants were asked to place a check mark by the five responses they viewed as most self-descriptive and central to their self-concepts.

The results of this study were quite clear. As shown in the figure, the majority of American students' core self-descriptors (59%) were personal/individualistic attributes

is scored from 1 to 4, with higher scores indicating higher perceived competence for that item.

Between ages 4 and 7, children's self-evaluations center largely on two domains. They evaluate themselves in terms of how well others like them (social acceptance) and how good they think they are at accomplishing tasks (task/general competence). What's more, their self-evaluations are often overly positive and unrealistic, and they may partly reflect a *desire* to be liked or to be good at tasks more than any firm set of beliefs about the children's actual competencies (Harter & Pike, 1984).[1] But by about

---

[1]Not everyone, however, believes that the self-evaluations of 4- to 7-year-olds are limited to two domains and are totally unrealistic. Using a new method that is more engaging than questionnaires, Jeffrey Measelle and his associates (1998) found that 4½- to 7-year-olds interviewed by playful puppets provided reliable estimates of their standings on six dimensions: academic competence, achievement motivation, social competence, peer acceptance, depression-anxiety, and aggression-hostility. These self-appraisals were highly positive for the most part; but they were not totally unrealistic in that they were correlated with teachers' ratings of the children on five of the same six dimensions. Although this study is based on a new instrument and its results will need to be replicated before definitive conclusions can be drawn, it offers the intriguing suggestion that young children have a much broader picture of their academic, social, and emotional lives than previous researchers had thought.

individualistic society: society that values personalism and individual accomplishments, which often take precedence over group goals. These societies tend to emphasize ways in which individuals differ from each other.

collectivist (or communal) society: society that values cooperative interdependence, social harmony, and adherence to group norms. These societies generally hold that the group's well-being is more important than that of the individual.

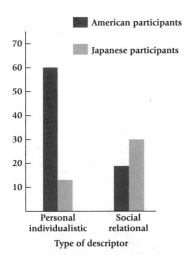

Average percentages of personal/individualistic and social/relational attributes listed as core dimensions of the self-concept by American and Japanese students who responded to a "Who Am I?" questionnaire. SOURCE: Adapted from Cousins, 1989.

whereas these same attributes made up only 19% of the core self-descriptors of the Japanese students. By contrast, Japanese students were much more inclined than American students were to list social/relational attributes as especially noteworthy components of their self-concepts. In terms of developmental trends, older

Japanese and Chinese adolescents are less inclined than preadolescents are to make distinctions among people on the basis of *individualistic* attributes, whereas American participants become more inclined to make such distinctions as they grow older (Crystal et al., 1998). Finally, research reveals that Asian-American adolescents, whose families often retain many collectivist values even after immigrating to the United States, tend to place more emphasis on their social identities and connections to other people than European-American adolescents do (see Brown, 1998).

Where do you stand on the individualist-collectivist continuum? If you are like most people from individualistic societies, you probably indicated greater agreement with items 2, 4, and 6 (which tap independence and individualistic concerns), whereas people from collectivist societies usually find it easier to agree with items 1, 3, and 5 (which tap interdependence or communal concerns).

Clearly, the traditional values and beliefs of one's culture can dramatically influence the kinds of self-concepts that emerge. And as we will see throughout the remainder of the text, the distinctions between individualistic and collectivist cultures and value systems are important ones that have implications for such aspects of self as the ways in which individuals look at and evaluate achievement behavior, aggression, altruism, and moral development, to name just a few.

age 8, children are not only evaluating their competencies in three domains—*physical competence, academic competence,* and *social acceptance*—but their appraisals now more accurately reflect other people's evaluations of them (Harter, 1982; Marsh, Craven, & Debus, 1998). For example, ratings of social self-esteem are now confirmed by peers who had been asked to rate their classmates' social competencies; and children with high athletic self-esteem are more frequently chosen for team sports and are rated higher in physical competence by gym teachers than classmates who feel physically inadequate. Taken together, these findings suggest that both self-knowledge and self-esteem may depend to a large extent on the way others perceive and react to our behavior (Harter, 1998). This is precisely the point that Charles Cooley (1902) was making when he coined the term *looking-glass self* to explain how we construct a self-image.

Yet, Harter (1986) also found that children differ in terms of the *importance* they assign to the various competency domains assessed by her scale. What's more, youngsters who rate themselves as very competent in the areas that *they* see as most important tend to be highest in overall self-worth. So it seems that older children's feelings of self-esteem depend both on how they think others evaluate them (that is, the social looking-glass) and on how they choose to evaluate themselves (Harter, 1990).

In early adolescence, one's perceptions of self-worth become increasingly differentiated and increasingly centered on interpersonal relationships. Susan Harter and her associates (1998), for example, use the term **relational self-worth** in describing their finding that adolescents often begin to perceive their self-worth somewhat differently in different relational contexts (for example, with parents, with teachers, with male classmates, and with female classmates). Clearly, all these domains of relational self-worth contribute to one's global self-esteem, although the same domain may be much more important for some teenagers than for others. Thus, one adolescent may enjoy high global self-esteem because he views himself as especially bright and as receiving ample support and admiration from his teachers, even though peers may consider him nerdy; another may enjoy equally high global self-esteem because she views her self-esteem with peers in a very favorable way, even though she feels much less efficacious in her relations with parents and teachers. Here, then, is another example of how self-appraisals depend not only on how others might evaluate us but also on *how we choose to evaluate ourselves* (that is, on the kinds of relationships and aspects of relational self-worth that we view as most central or important to our self-concepts).

Given the increasing importance of interpersonal relationships, it is hardly surprising that new relationship-oriented dimensions such as *romantic appeal* and *quality of close friendships* become very important contributors to an adolescent's global self-esteem (Masden et al., 1995; Richards et al., 1998), although they may influence the self-appraisals of boys and girls in somewhat different ways (Thorne & Michaelieu, 1996). Girls who enjoy very high self-esteem are often those who have had *supportive* relationships with friends, whereas boys are more likely to derive high self-esteem from their ability to successfully *influence* their friends. Low self-esteem in girls is most strongly associated with a failure to win friends' approval, whereas a major contributor to low self-esteem in adolescent boys is a lack of romantic competence, as reflected by their failure to win or maintain the affection of girls.

PHOTO 6.3 In adolescence, the quality of one's friendships becomes one of the strongest determinants of self-esteem.

Changes in Self-Esteem How stable are one's feelings of self-worth? Is a child who enjoys high self-esteem as an 8-year-old likely to feel especially good about himself as an adolescent? Or is it more reasonable to assume that the stresses and strains of adolescence cause most teenagers to doubt themselves and their competencies, thereby undermining their self-esteem?

Erik Erikson (1963) favored the latter point of view, arguing that young adolescents who experience the many physical, cognitive, and social changes associated with puberty often become confused and show at least some erosion of self-esteem as they leave childhood behind and begin to search for stable adult identity. Indeed, some young adolescents do experience a decline of self-esteem as they leave elementary school as the oldest and most revered students and enter junior high, where they are the youngest and least competent (Seidman et al., 1994; Simmons et al., 1987). This dip in self-esteem is likely to be greatest when multiple stressors pile up—for example, when adolescents are not only making the transition to junior high school but coping with pubertal changes, beginning to date, and perhaps dealing with family transitions, such as a divorce, all at the same time (Simmons et al., 1987). Furthermore, adolescents do experience more daily hassles and other negative events,

relational self-worth: feelings of self-worth within a particular relationship context (for example, with parents, with male classmates); may differ across relationship contexts.

both at home and at school, than younger children do, and these stresses largely account for the increased sulkiness and other negative emotions that seventh- to ninth-graders display (Larson & Ham, 1993; Seidman et al., 1994). So early adolescence can be a somewhat painful experience—one that can even drive some teenagers to consider taking their own lives (see Box 6.2 on pages 178–179).

But before we conclude that adolescence is hazardous to our sense of self-worth, let's note that most 11- to 14-year-olds show no appreciable decline in self-esteem (Nottelmann, 1987). In fact, teenagers generally display gradual though modest *increases* in self-esteem over the course of adolescence (Marsh, 1989; Mullis, Mullis, & Normandin, 1992; Savin-Williams & Demo, 1984). Perhaps owing to the lesser autonomy they are granted as part of female gender-role socialization, girls are less likely than boys to show such increases in self-esteem (Thorne & Michaelieu, 1996; Wichstrom, 1999); but most youths emerge from their teenage years with their self-worth intact, particularly if they enjoyed good self-esteem on entering adolescence (Block & Robins, 1993; Crain, 1996).

SOCIAL CONTRIBUTORS TO SELF-ESTEEM

Parenting Styles   Parents can play a crucial role in shaping a child's self-esteem. As we noted in Chapter 5, the sensitivity of parenting early in childhood clearly influences whether infants and toddlers construct positive or negative working models of self. Furthermore, grade-school children and adolescents with high self-esteem tend to have parents who are warm and supportive, who set clear standards for them to live up to, and who allow them a voice in making decisions that affect them personally (Coopersmith, 1967; Isberg et al., 1989; Lamborn et al., 1991). What's more, the link between high self-esteem and this nurturing/democratic parental style is much the same in Taiwan and Australia as it is in the United States and Canada (Scott, Scott, & McCabe, 1991). Although these child-rearing studies are correlational and we cannot be sure that warm, supportive parenting *causes* high self-esteem, it is easy to imagine such a causal process at work. Certainly, sending a message that "You're a good kid whom I trust to follow rules and make good decisions" is apt to promote higher self-esteem than more aloof or more controlling styles in which parents may be saying, in effect, "Your inadequacies turn me off."

Peer Influences   As early as age 5 or 6, children are beginning to recognize differences among themselves and their classmates as they use **social comparison** information to tell them whether they perform better or worse in various domains than their peers (Pomerantz et al., 1995). For example, they glance at each others' papers and say "How many did you miss?" or will make such statements as "I'm faster than you," after winning a footrace (Frey & Ruble, 1985). This kind of comparison increases and becomes more subtle with age (Pomerantz et al., 1995) and plays an important role in shaping children's self-esteem—particularly in Western cultures where competition and individual accomplishments are stressed. Interestingly, this preoccupation with evaluating oneself in comparison to peers is not nearly as strong among communally reared kibbutz children in Israel, perhaps because cooperation and teamwork are so strongly emphasized in the kibbutzim (Butler & Ruzany, 1993).

Peer influences on self-esteem become even more apparent during adolescence. Recall that some of the strongest contributions to adolescent self-appraisals are the quality of one's relationships with particularly close friends. In fact, when young adults reflect back on life experiences that were noteworthy to them and that may have influenced their self-esteem, they mention experiences with friends and romantic partners

social comparison: the process of defining and evaluating the self by comparing oneself to other people.

Box 6.2 *Developmental Issues*

Adolescent Suicide: The Tragic Destruction of Self

Surprising as it may seem to anyone who has never contemplated taking his own life, suicidal thoughts are shockingly common among adolescents and young adults (Committee on Adolescence, 1996). In one survey of adolescents, 56% reported at least one instance of suicidal thinking, and 5% had actually attempted suicide (Windle & Windle, 1997). Suicide rates among 15- to 24-year-olds have increased dramatically over the past 30 years, so much so that suicide is now the third leading cause of death for this age group, ranking behind only accidents and homicides (U.S. Bureau of the Census, 1996). Among some Native American groups, suicidal thoughts and behaviors are even more widespread (Garland & Zigler, 1993); in one sample of Zuni adolescents, for example, fully 30% had attempted suicide, most of them more than once (Howard-Pitney et al., 1992). Overall, females *attempt* suicide more often than males do; but males are more often successful in their attempts—by a ratio of about 3 to 1, a difference that holds up across most cultures studied (Girard, 1993). Males succeed more often simply because they shun slower-acting pills in favor of more abruptly lethal techniques such as nooses and guns.

Although teenagers *attempt* suicide more often than adults do, we see in the figure that adults are more likely to actually commit suicide. The suicide rate for women peaks in middle age, whereas it climbs for white males throughout adulthood. Because adolescents are far less successful than adults at killing themselves when they try, some researchers believe that their suicide attempts are often a desperate "cry for help." Unlike suicidal adults, who are often determined to end it all, many suicidal adolescents hope to *improve* their lives; they may see their suicide attempts as a way of forcing others to take their problems seriously, but by miscalculation or sudden impulse, they often die before they can be helped (Berman & Jobes, 1991; Rubenstein et al., 1989).

Unfortunately, there is no sure way to identify young people who will try to kill themselves. Suicidal adolescents come from all racial and ethnic groups, all social classes; and even popular adolescents of superior intelligence may take their own lives. Yet, there are some telltale warning signs. Suicidal adolescents are often severely depressed, abusing drugs, or displaying other forms of antisocial conduct (Committee on Adolescence, 1996; Vannatta, 1996). They often have experienced deteriorating relationships with parents, peers, or romantic partners, suffered academic failures, and lost all interest in hobbies or other enjoyable activities as they sink into a state of hopelessness

far more frequently than experiences with parents and family members (Thorne & Michaelieu, 1996).

Now that we have considered how developing children and adolescents acquire information about the self and evaluate this information to gain a sense of self-esteem, we turn to another crucial component of self: the development of *self-control*.

The Development of Self-Control

Developmentalists use the term **self-control** to refer to our ability to regulate our conduct and to *inhibit* actions (for example, rule violations) that we might otherwise be inclined to perform. Self-control is unquestionably an important attribute. If we had never learned to control our immediate impulses, we would constantly be at odds with other people for violating their rights, breaking rules, and failing to display the patience and self-sacrifice that would permit us to achieve important *long-range* objectives (for example, earning a diploma). Although many theorists have commented on the development of self-control (for example, Bandura, 1986; Freud, 1935/1960; Kopp, 1987; Mischel, 1986), all of them make two assumptions: (1) young children's

self-control: ability to regulate one's conduct and to inhibit actions that are unacceptable or that conflict with a goal.

and despair and feel incapable of coping with their problems (Berman & Jobes, 1991; Wagner, 1997).

Friends and associates can play an important role in preventing adolescent suicide by recognizing the warning signs and encouraging their deeply depressed or suddenly hostile young companions to talk about their problems—a step that adults often fail to take, thinking that the teenager's unruly or depressed demeanor reflects the typical "storm and stress" of adolescence. Should a troubled youngster divulge suicidal thoughts, companions might try to convince him or her that there are ways other than suicide to cope with distress. But perhaps the most important thing friends and associates can do is to tell what they have learned to other people who are in a better position to help, such as the adolescent's parents, a teacher, or a school counselor. Clearly, it is better to break a confidence than to let the person die.

As for parents, perhaps the best advice is to take *all* suicidal thinking seriously. And professional assistance is definitely called for after an unsuccessful suicide attempt, for adolescents who try once are at risk of succeeding in the future if they receive little help and continue to feel incapable of coping with their problems (Berman & Jobes, 1991).

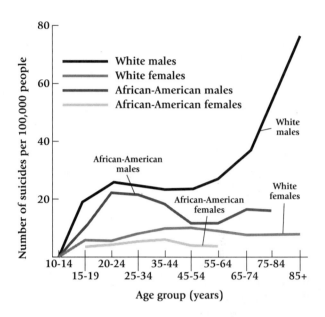

Number of suicides per 100,000 people by age and sex among whites and African Americans in the United States. Data about the oldest African Americans are not shown because too few cases were studied. Data from U.S. Bureau of the Census, *Statistical Abstract of the United States: 1996* (116th ed.). Washington, DC: U.S. Government Printing Office.

behavior is almost completely controlled by external agents (for example, parents); and (2) over time, control is gradually *internalized* as children adopt standards, or norms, that stress the value of self-control and acquire self-regulatory skills that permit them to adhere to these prescriptions.

EMERGENCE OF SELF-CONTROL IN EARLY CHILDHOOD

Emotional Self-Regulation as a Precursor to Early Self-Control When do children first display evidence of self-regulation and self-control? As we noted in Chapter 4 early signs of self-regulation are apparent during the first year as infants attempt to control their emotions. Yet, recall that caregivers must often assist young infants to regulate emotions by adjusting their own displays of positive affect to their baby's emotional state so as to alleviate distress and/or to maintain or intensify the baby's positive moods. This sensitive tailoring or synchronizing of caregiver affect to a baby's emotional displays is thought not only to promote affectionate caregiver–infant interactions and secure attachments but also to provide infants with strategies for regulating their own positive or negative emotions—an achievement that many believe to underlie children's eventual ability to obey restrictive and unpleasant rules, commands, and other requests (Emde et al., 1991; Kopp, 1987).

Ruth Feldman and her associates (1999) recently found that mothers who were quicker to help their 3-month-olds regulate emotions by adjusting their positive affect to the baby's demeanor did indeed seem to contribute positively to the emergence of self-control. That is, children of these affectively synchronous mothers were more likely to obey simply "do's" and "don't's" as 2-year-olds than were age-mates whose mothers had not been so quick to synchronize their moods with those of their babies. What's more, 9-month-old infants who have learned to *regulate* emotions so as to maintain synchronous interactions with their mothers were found to respond more favorably to simple commands at age 2 than did age-mates who had less synchronous interactions with their mothers at age 9 months. Finally, mother–infant synchrony of affect was an especially potent predictor of later self-control for youngsters with difficult temperaments—the very children who find it so hard to regulate negative affect and to alter ongoing behavior (Feldman et al., 1999). So it seems that emotional self-regulation, which develops in the context of synchronous face-to-face interactions among infants and caregivers, is indeed an important precursor of behavioral self-control.

Compliance, Self-Assertion, and Defiance By ages 18 to 24 months, most toddlers are showing clear evidence of **compliance.** They are now aware of caregiver expectations and can respond appropriately to many requests and commands (Crockenberg & Litman, 1990). They are also beginning to show clear signs of distress when they break things or otherwise do something that is prohibited, such as snitching a forbidden cookie (Cole, Barrett, & Zahn-Waxler, 1992; Kochanska, Casey, & Fukumoto, 1995). Yet their behavior is still largely *externally* controlled by the approval they anticipate for compliance and the disapproval they associate with noncompliance.

However, anyone who has ever spent much time with 2- to 3-year-olds knows that they can become extremely uncooperative and noncompliant on entering a phase that parents sometimes call the "terrible twos" (Bullock & Lutkenhaus, 1990; Erikson, 1963). According to Erikson, these toddlers are struggling with the psychosocial conflict of **autonomy versus shame and doubt:** They are resolved to display their independence and self-determination by doing things their own way, even if that means occasionally being noncompliant and risking others' disapproval.

An autonomy-seeking toddler who refuses to comply may do so through **self-assertion** (simply refusing a command or request) or **defiance** (saying "No!" and becoming angry or intensifying her ongoing behavior). Susan Crockenberg and Cindy Litman (1990) find that the strategies caregivers use to resolve autonomy conflicts with their self-assertive toddler play a major role in determining whether the child becomes negative and defiant toward authority figures or adopts a more cooperative and compliant posture that is likely to promote self-control. Specifically, mothers who reacted to their 2-year-olds' self-assertive refusals by intervening physically or threatening and criticizing were likely to elicit *defiance,* whereas those who took an initial "No" as an opportunity to remain firm in their demands while offering a rationale for complying were likely to elicit *compliance.* Grazyna Kochanska (1997b; Kochanska & Aksan, 1995) adds that a warm mother-child relationship in which a mother is responsive to her toddlers' needs and requests and sets reasonable expectations for mature conduct will promote **committed compliance**—an eagerness and readiness on the child's part to cooperate with the mother by internalizing her rules and obeying her commands. But if parents have often been insensitive to toddlers' needs and have shared few mutually enjoyable activities with them, their children are much more likely to display **situational compliance**—generally nonoppositional behavior that stems more from the parent's power to control the child's conduct than from the child's eagerness to cooperate and to embrace the parent's agenda. Clearly, 2- to 3-year-olds are quite capable of cooperation and are more likely to comply willingly

compliance: the act of obeying the requests or commands of others.

autonomy versus shame and doubt: the second of Erikson's psychosocial stages, in which toddlers either assert their wills and attend to their own basic needs or else become passive, dependent, and lacking in self-confidence.

self-assertion: noncompliant acts that are undertaken by children in the interest of doing things for themselves or otherwise establishing autonomy.

defiance: active resistance to others' requests or demands; noncompliant acts that are accompanied by anger and an intensification of ongoing behavior.

committed compliance: compliance based on an eagerness or readiness to cooperate with a responsive parent who has been willing to cooperate with the child.

situational compliance: compliance based primarily on the parent's power to control the child's conduct.

with a sensitive, caring parent who has demonstrated a willingness to cooperate with them. Sensitive, responsive parenting is particularly important for fostering the committed compliance and later self-control of temperamentally impulsive children, who are prone to tantrums when they don't get their own way (Kochanska, 1995).

As children acquire language, they begin to incorporate adult standards into their own speech, using those vocalizations to describe the implications of their actions and, eventually, to regulate and control their conduct. Even 2- to 2½-year-olds will occasionally say things like "No" or "Don't" when they are about to commit a prohibited act, such as jumping on the sofa (Kochanska, 1993). The self-instructional role that language may play in early self-control is also apparent in other contexts. In one study, Brian Vaughn and his associates (1984) presented 18- to 30-month-old toddlers with three challenges: (1) to refrain from touching a nearby toy telephone, (2) not to eat raisins hidden under a cup until told that they could, and (3) not to open a gift until the experimenter had finished her work. The child was then observed to see how long he or she could wait before succumbing to these powerful temptations. As shown in Figure 6.4 the ability to wait increased dramatically between 18 and 30 months of age. Furthermore, there were clear individual differences in the patience displayed by the 30-month-olds; those who were further along in their language development showed the most self-control. So it seems that the private speech that Vygotsky wrote about not only helps young children to master cognitive challenges but may also be involved in helping toddlers control their impulses.

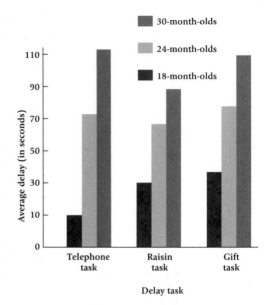

FIGURE 6.4 Average delay of gratification (in seconds) of 18-, 24-, and 30-month-olds exposed to three strong temptations. (Adapted from B. E. Vaughn, C. B. Kopp, & J. B. Krakow, "The Emergence and Consolidation of Self-Control from Eighteen to Thirty Months of Age: Normative Trends and Individual Differences." *Child Development*, 1984, 55, 990–1004. Copyright © 1984 by the Society for Research in Child Development.

DELAY OF GRATIFICATION IN CHILDHOOD AND ADOLESCENCE

One of the more fruitful approaches for studying the development of self-control has been the **delay of gratification** paradigm. In a typical delay of gratification study, participants are offered a choice between a small incentive available immediately and a larger (or more desirable) incentive for which they must wait. What these studies find is that (1) preschool children find it exceedingly difficult to be patient when the incentives they must resist are in plain sight, although (2) they do become better and better at delaying gratification over the grade-school years, eventually showing a strong preference to wait for larger delayed incentives by age 10 to 12 (Mischel, 1986). Why does this aspect of self-control improve so dramatically with age? Let's consider two possibilities.

Knowledge of Delay Strategies   In an early delay-of-gratification study, Walter Mischel and Ebbe Ebbesen (1970) found that 3- to 5-year-olds simply cannot keep their minds off tempting objects for long. The children in this study were told that if they waited 15 minutes, they would receive a very attractive snack; but if they couldn't wait that long, they could signal the experimenter by ringing a bell and would receive a less desirable snack. When both kinds of snacks were visible during the delay period, preschoolers waited an average of only a minute or two before losing their patience, signaling the experimenter, and receiving the less desirable treat. Only a handful of children were able to wait the entire 15-minute delay period to earn the more valuable incentive. How did they do it? By covering their eyes, singing songs, inventing games, or otherwise *distracting* themselves from the temptations they faced.

However, it should be emphasized that the vast majority of preschoolers do *not* know that distraction can help them to resist immediate temptations. They can be

delay of gratification: a form of self-control that involves the capacity to inhibit impulses to seek small rewards available immediately in the interest of obtaining larger, delayed incentives.

taught by adults to use distractive strategies (Mischel & Patterson, 1976)—even very complex ones that require them to mentally transform tempting objects (for example, marshmallows) into less tempting stimuli (for example, white, puffy clouds)—to help them maintain their resolve (Mischel & Baker, 1975). But they do not generate these distractive strategies on their own. In fact, if it is suggested to them that they might become more patient by choosing a self-instructional strategy, preschoolers are much more inclined to focus attention on the *desirable qualities* of the incentives they are trying to resist (Toner, 1981)—a very ineffective means of coping with the frustrations of a delay.

By ages 6 to 8, most children now realize that creating physical distractions (for example, by covering their eyes or the tempting objects) can help them to be more patient. And by ages 11 to 12 they know that *abstract ideation* (that is, cognitive distractions such as the marshmallows-are-clouds transformation or even such untrue self-instructions as "I hate marshmallows") can reduce their frustrations and make waiting easier (Mischel & Mischel, 1983). Abstract ideation probably takes so long to develop because it rests on hypothetical transformations of present realities—a formal-operational ability. Younger children can use abstract ideation if adults supply these distractors for them, but they will not generate them on their own.

So one reason that self-control improves over the grade-school years is that children are maturing intellectually and devising more *effective* strategies for regulating their thinking and conduct.

Self-Control as a Valued Attribute Another reason that older children and adolescents are better able to delay gratification, to comply with rules, or to otherwise control their impulses is that they are internalizing norms that stress the value of self-regulation and self-control. Evidence of this can be seen in the self-descriptions of preadolescents and adolescents. When asked what they like about themselves, adolescents will often mention conduct that reflects their self-discipline (for example, being persistent at pursuing their goals or being slow to lose their tempers), and teenagers are often quite concerned about breakdowns in self-control (for example, blowing up at someone over nothing or failing to complete their homework) (Rosenberg, 1979). So by early adolescence a capacity for self-control is viewed as a highly desirable and almost obligatory attribute—one that many teenagers hope to incorporate into their own self-concepts.

Could we foster children's self-control by working on their self-concepts—that is, by trying to convince them that they can be patient, persistent, honest, and even-tempered whenever they have shown some signs of displaying these attributes? Might children who are labeled "honest" or "patient" incorporate these attributions into their self-concepts and try to live up to this new self-image? Indeed they may. Nace Toner and his associates (1980) attempted to influence children's self-concepts by labeling youngsters "patient" individuals. Before beginning a typical delay-of-gratification experiment, the experimenter casually mentioned to half the 5½- to 9-year-old participants, "I hear that you are patient because you can wait for nice things when you can't get them right away." The remaining children heard a task-irrelevant attribution: "I hear that you have some very nice

PHOTO 6.4 Instructing children in how to be patient and bolstering their images of themselves as patient or self-disciplined individuals are important steps parents can take to foster self-control and delay of gratification.

friends." The results were clear: Even when no one was present to monitor their conduct, children who had been labeled "patient" were able to delay gratification far longer than those who had been labeled as having nice friends.

So in addition to suggesting effective self-instructional strategies for regulating conduct, it appears that adults can promote self-control by bolstering children's images of themselves as patient, honest, or otherwise self-disciplined individuals (see also Casey & Burton, 1982).

Early Self-Control as a Predictor of Later Life Outcomes   Developmentalists who study self-control cannot help but notice that some children are much more self-disciplined than others. Individual differences in compliance with rules and requests are already quite apparent by age 2; and relatively noncompliant toddlers whose mothers are either emotionally unresponsive or are critical and forceful with them (and who remain that way over time) are likely to become *defiant* and will often continue to display undercontrolled antisocial and disruptive behaviors from the preschool period throughout adolescence (Beckwith, Rodning, & Cohen, 1992; Henry et al., 1996; Shaw, Keenan, & Vondra, 1994). So there is reason to believe that a lack of self-discipline early in life can be a very maladaptive attribute.

Do children who display early evidence of self-control experience more *favorable* life outcomes? Indeed they may. Walter Mischel and his associates have conducted ten-year follow-up studies of individuals who had participated as preschoolers in Mischel's early delay-of-gratification experiments. In the follow-ups, parents completed questionnaires in which they described the competencies and shortcomings of their now-adolescent sons and daughters. These descriptions were highly informative. Apparently, self-control is a reasonably stable attribute, for adolescents who had been unable to delay gratification for long during the preschool years were the ones whom parents were now most likely to characterize as impatient and impulsive (Shoda, Mischel, & Peake, 1990). Adolescents who had been better at delaying gratification ten years earlier were generally described in more favorable terms (that is, more academically competent, more socially skilled, more confident and self-reliant, and better able to cope with stress) than their counterparts who had shown less self-control as preschoolers (Mischel, Shoda, & Peake, 1988; Shoda et al., 1990). And, consistent with the parents' reports of their teenagers' academic competencies, adolescents who had displayed the most self-control as preschoolers were the ones who made the highest scores on the Scholastic Assessment Test (SAT) (Shoda et al., 1990).

Perhaps we can now appreciate why developmentalists consider the establishment of self-regulatory skills and the emergence of self-control to be such important developmental hurdles. Not only is self-control a moderately stable characteristic, but it is reliably associated with the very attributes (cognitive competencies, social skills, self-confidence, self-reliance) that forecast high self-esteem in adolescence (Harter, 1990) and occupational success and good interpersonal relations in adulthood (Hunter & Hunter, 1984; Newman et al., 1997). So, one's capacity for self-control is a crucial component of this entity we call the "self"—a conclusion we will reach over and over again as we discuss such topics as achievement, aggression, altruism, moral development, and the establishment of favorable relations with people outside the family—namely, teachers and peers.

Who Am I to Be? Forging an Identity

According to Erik Erikson (1963), the major developmental hurdle that adolescents face is establishing an **identity**—a firm and coherent sense of who you are, where you are heading, and where you fit into society. Forging an identity involves grappling with

identity: a mature self-definition; a sense of who one is, where one is going in life, and how one fits into society.

many important choices: What kind of career do I want? What religious, moral, and political values should I adopt? Who am I as a man or a woman, and as a sexual being? Just where do I fit into society? All this is, of course, a lot for teenagers to have on their minds, and Erikson used the term **identity crisis** to capture the sense of confusion, and even anxiety, that adolescents may feel as they think about who they are today and try to decide "What kind of self can (or should) I become?"

.Can you recall a time during the teenage years when you were confused about who you were, what you should be, and what you were likely to become? Is it possible that you have not yet resolved these identity issues and are still seeking answers? If so, does that make you abnormal or maladjusted?

James Marcia (1980) has developed a structured interview that allows researchers to classify adolescents into one of four identity statuses—*Identity Diffusion, Foreclosure, Moratorium,* and *Identity Achievement*—based on whether they have explored various alternatives and made firm commitments to an occupation, a religious ideology, a sexual orientation, and a set of political values. These identity statuses are as follows:

1. **Identity diffusion:** Persons classified as "diffuse" have not yet thought about or resolved identity issues and have failed to chart future life directions. *Example:* "I haven't really thought much about religion, and I guess I don't know exactly what I believe."

2. **Foreclosure:** Persons classified as "foreclosed" are committed to an identity but have made this commitment without experiencing the "crisis" of deciding what really suits them best. *Example:* "My parents are Baptists and so I'm a Baptist; it's just the way I grew up."

3. **Moratorium:** Persons in this status are experiencing what Erikson called an identity crisis and are actively asking questions about life commitments and seeking answers. *Example:* "I'm evaluating my beliefs and hope that I will be able to describe what's right for me. I like many of the answers provided by my Catholic upbringing, but I'm skeptical about some teachings as well. I have been looking into Unitarianism to see whether it might help me answer my questions."

4. **Identity achievement:** Identity-achieved individuals have resolved identity issues by making *personal* commitments to particular goals, beliefs, and values. *Example:* "After a lot of soul-searching about my religion and other religions too, I finally know what I believe and what I don't."

DEVELOPMENTAL TRENDS IN IDENTITY FORMATION

Although Erikson assumed that the identity crisis occurs in early adolescence and is often resolved by ages 15 to 18, his age norms were overly optimistic. When Philip Meilman (1979) measured the identity statuses of males between the ages of 12 and 24, he observed a clear developmental progression. But as shown in Figure 6.5, the vast majority of 12- to 18-year-olds were identity diffuse or foreclosed, and not until age 21 or older had the majority of participants reached the moratorium status or achieved stable identities.

Is the identity formation process different for girls and women than it is for boys and men? In most respects, no (Archer, 1992; Kroger, 1996). Girls make progress toward achieving a clear sense of identity at about the same ages that boys do (Streitmatter, 1993). However, one intriguing sex difference has been observed: Although today's college women are just as concerned about establishing a career identity as men

identity crisis: Erikson's term for the uncertainty and discomfort that adolescents experience when they become confused about their present and future roles in life.

identity diffusion: identity status characterizing individuals who are not questioning who they are and have not yet committed themselves to an identity.

foreclosure: identity status characterizing individuals who have prematurely committed themselves to occupations or ideologies without really thinking about these commitments.

moratorium: identity status characterizing individuals who are currently experiencing an identity crisis and are actively exploring occupational and ideological positions in which to invest themselves.

identity achievement: identity status characterizing individuals who have carefully considered identity issues and have made firm commitments to an occupation and ideologies.

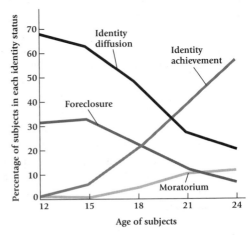

FIGURE 6.5 Percentages of subjects in each of Marcia's four identity statuses as a function of age. Note that resolution of the identity crisis occurs much later than Erikson assumed: only 4% of the 15-year-olds and 20% of the 18-year-olds had achieved a stable identity. (Adapted from Meilman, 1979.)

are, they attach greater importance to the aspects of identity that center on interpersonal relationships, gender roles, and sexuality (Archer, 1992; Kroger, 1996; Patterson, Sochting, & Marcia, 1992). They are also more concerned than men with the issue of how to balance career and family goals (Archer, 1992; Matula et al., 1992).

Judging from this research, identity formation takes quite a bit of time. Not until late adolescence—during the college years—do many young men and women move from the diffusion or foreclosure status into the moratorium status and then achieve a sense of identity (Waterman, 1982). But this is by no means the end of the identity formation process. Many adults are *still* struggling with identity issues or have reopened the question of who they are after thinking they had all the answers earlier in life (Waterman & Archer, 1990). A divorce, for example, may cause a homemaker to rethink what it means to be a woman and reraise questions about other aspects of her identity as well.

The process of achieving identity is also quite uneven (Archer, 1982; Kroger, 1996). For example, Sally Archer (1982) assessed the identity statuses of sixth- to twelfth-graders in four domains: occupational choice, gender-role attitudes, religious beliefs, and political ideologies. Only 5% of her adolescents were in the same identity status in all four areas, with 95% being in two or even three statuses across the four domains. So adolescents can achieve a strong sense of identity in one area and still be searching in others. Indeed, the process of identity formation may be particularly challenging for members of minority racial and ethnic groups in modern and diverse multicultural societies. As we see in Box 6.3, minority youth face the additional task of establishing a positive ethnic identity.

HOW PAINFUL IS IDENTITY FORMATION?

Perhaps it is unfortunate that Erikson used the term *crisis* to describe the adolescent's active search for an identity (or identities) because adolescents in the moratorium status do not appear all that "stressed out." In fact, James Marcia and his associates (1993) find that these active identity-seekers feel much better about themselves and their futures than do age-mates in the diffusion and foreclosure statuses. Yet, Erikson was right in characterizing identity achievement as a very healthy and adaptive development, for identity achievers do enjoy higher self-esteem and are less self-conscious or preoccupied with personal concerns than their counterparts in the other three identity statuses (Adams, Abraham, & Markstrom, 1987; O'Connor, 1995). Moreover, Erikson viewed the achievement of a stable identity as a prerequisite for establishing a truly intimate relationship (or *shared identity*) with another person during the psychological crisis of **intimacy versus isolation** that young adults face. And true to form, college students displaying mature identity statuses as freshman and sophomores had often established intimate relationships one year later, whereas those with diffuse identities had rarely established intimacy with anyone over the next 12 months (Fitch & Adams, 1983; see also Peterson et al., 1993). So the establishment of a stable personal identity is a significant milestone indeed—one that helps pave the way for positive psychological adjustment and the growth of deep and trusting emotional commitments that could conceivably last a lifetime.

What may be most painful or "crisislike" about identity seeking is a long-term failure to establish one. Erikson believed that individuals without a clear identity would eventually become depressed and lacking in self-confidence as they drift aimlessly, trapped in the "diffusion" status. Or alternatively, they might heartily embrace what Erikson called a *negative identity,* becoming a "black sheep," a "delinquent," or a "loser." Why? Because for these foundering souls, it is better to become everything that one is not supposed to be than to have no identity at all (Erikson, 1963). Indeed, many adolescents who are stuck in the diffusion status are highly apathetic and do express a

intimacy versus isolation: the sixth of Erikson's psychosocial conflicts, in which young adults must commit themselves to a shared identity with another person (that is, intimacy) or else remain aloof and unconnected to others.

Box 6.3   *Cultural Influences*

Identity Formation Among Minority Adolescents

In addition to the identity issues that confront all adolescents, members of ethnic minority groups must also establish an *ethnic identity*—a personal identification with an ethnic group and its values and traditions (Phinney, 1996). This is not always an easy task. As we saw earlier, some minority children may even identify at first with the culture's ethnic majority, apparently wanting to affiliate with the group that has the most status in society (Spencer & Markstrom-Adams, 1990). One Hispanic adolescent who had done this said, "I remember I would not say I was Hispanic. My friends . . . were White and Oriental and I tried so hard to fit in with them" (Phinney & Rosenthal, 1992, p. 158). It is not that young children have no knowledge of their subcultural traditions. Mexican-American preschoolers, for example, may learn such culturally relevant behaviors as giving a Chicano handshake; yet, not until about age 8 are they likely to fully understand which ethnic labels apply to them, what they mean, or that their ethnicity is a lifelong attribute (Bernal & Knight, 1997).

Forming a positive ethnic identity during adolescence seems to involve the same steps, or statuses, as forming a vocational or religious identity (Phinney, 1993). Young adolescents often say that they identify with their racial or ethnic group because their parents and other members of the group influenced them to do so (foreclosure status) or because that is what they are and they have not given the issue much thought (diffusion status) (Markstrom-Adams & Adams, 1995). But between ages 16 and 19, many minority youths move into the moratorium or achievement phases of ethnic identity. One

Forging a positive ethnic identity is an adaptive development for minority youths.

Mexican-American girl described her moratorium period this way: "I want to know what we do and how our culture is different from others. Going to festivals and cultural events helps me to learn more about my own culture and about myself" (Phinney, 1993, p. 70). Once ethnic identity is achieved, minority youth tend to enjoy higher self-esteem, better relations with parents and peers, and

sense of hopelessness about the future (Waterman & Archer, 1990). Others who enter high school with very low self-esteem often drift into delinquency and view their deviant self-image as having provided them with a boost in self-worth (Bynner, O'Malley, & Bachman, 1981; Wells, 1989). So it seems that a small minority of adolescents and young adults experience what might be termed an identity *crisis* after all.

PERSONAL AND SOCIAL INFLUENCES ON IDENTITY FORMATION

The adolescent's progress toward identity achievement is influenced by at least four factors: cognitive growth, parenting, schooling, and the broader social-cultural context.

Cognitive Influences   Cognitive development plays an important role in identity achievement. Adolescents who have achieved solid mastery of formal operational

more positive views of their own and other ethnicities than their counterparts who merely label themselves as a minority and are still ethnically diffuse or foreclosed (Phinney, 1996; Phinney, Ferguson, & Tate, 1997).

Interestingly, minority adolescents sometimes lag behind their majority-group peers at resolving other, more traditional identity issues. Why is this? Spencer and Markstrom-Adams (1990) suggest several possibilities. For one thing, minority adolescents may come to realize that prejudice and discrimination in society may limit their educational and vocational prospects, thus causing them to be less than optimistic about the future and hindering their establishment of an occupational identity (Ogbu, 1988). In addition, minority youths frequently encounter conflicts between the values of their subculture and those of the majority culture, and members of their subcultural communities (especially peers) often discourage identity explorations that clash with the social traditions of their own group. Virtually all North American minorities have a term for community members who are "too white" in orientation, be it the "apple" (red on the outside, white on the inside) for Native Americans, the Hispanic "coconut," the Asian "banana," or the African-American "Oreo." Clearly, minority adolescents must resolve these value conflicts and decide for themselves what *they* are inside.

Interestingly, biracial adolescents and minority adoptees in white adoptive homes sometimes face even greater conflicts. These youngsters may feel pressured to choose between minority and white peer groups, thereby encountering social barriers to achieving an identity as *both* African-American (for example) and white (DeBerry, Scarr, & Weinberg, 1996; Kerwin et al., 1993). About half the transracial adoptees in Scarr's classic Minnesota Transracial Adoption Study showed some signs of social maladjustment at age 17. Although African American in appearance, many of these adoptees regarded whites as their primary reference group. Thus, their maladjustment could reflect the fact that they were (1) not prepared to function effectively within the African-American community and (2) likely to face some prejudice and discrimination as a black trying to fit into a white ecological niche (DeBerry et al., 1996). Yet a stronger identification with *either* a white or an African-American reference group predicted better adjustment outcomes than did maintaining a more racially diffuse orientation. So here is another sign that establishing some kind of ethnic identity, or point of reference, is an adaptive developmental outcome for members of a minority group.

How can we help minority youths to forge positive ethnic identities? Their parents can play a major role by (1) teaching them about their group's cultural traditions and fostering ethnic pride, (2) preparing them to deal constructively with the prejudices and value conflicts they may encounter, and (3) simply being warm and supportive confidants (Bernal & Knight, 1997; Rosenthal & Feldman, 1992). Schools and communities can also help by promoting a greater understanding and appreciation of ethnic diversity and racism, starting early in the preschool years (Burnette, 1997) and continuing their efforts to ensure that educational and economic opportunities are extended to all (Spencer & Markstrom-Adams, 1990).

thought and who can reason logically about hypotheticals are now better able to imagine and contemplate future identities. Consequently, they are more likely to raise and resolve identity issues than are age-mates who are less intellectually mature (Boyes & Chandler, 1992; Waterman, 1992).

Parenting Influences The relationships that adolescents have with their parents can also affect their progress at forging an identity (Markstrom-Adams, 1992; Waterman, 1982). Adolescents in the diffusion status are more likely than those in other statuses to feel neglected or rejected by their parents and to be distant from them (Archer, 1994). Perhaps it is difficult to establish one's own identity without first having the opportunity to identify with respected parental figures and take on some of their desirable qualities. At the other extreme, adolescents in the identity foreclosure status are often extremely close to and sometimes fear rejection from relatively controlling parents (Kroger, 1995). Foreclosed adolescents may never question parental authority or feel any need to forge a separate identity.

By contrast, adolescents in the moratorium and identity achievement statuses appear to have a solid base of affection at home combined with considerable freedom to be individuals in their own right (Grotevant & Cooper, 1986). In family discussions, for example, these adolescents experience a sense of closeness and mutual respect while feeling free to disagree with their parents. So the same loving and democratic style of parenting that helps children gain a strong sense of self-esteem is also associated with healthy and adaptive identity outcomes in adolescence.

Scholastic Influences   Does attending college help one to forge an identity? The answer is yes—and no. Attending college does seem to push people toward setting career goals and making stable occupational commitments (Waterman, 1982); but college students are often far behind their working peers in terms of establishing firm political and religious identities (Munro & Adams, 1977). In fact, some collegians will regress from identity achievement to the moratorium or even the diffusion status in certain areas, most notably religion. But let's not be too critical of the college environment, for, like college students, many adults will later reopen the question of "who they are" if exposed to people or situations that challenge old viewpoints and offer new alternatives (Waterman & Archer, 1990).

Cultural-Historical Influences   Finally, identity formation is strongly influenced by the broader social and historical context in which it occurs—a point that Erikson himself emphasized. In fact, the very idea that adolescents should choose a personal identity after carefully exploring many options may well be peculiar to industrialized societies of the 20th century (Cote & Levine, 1988). As in past centuries, adolescents in many nonindustrialized societies today will simply adopt the adult roles they are expected to adopt, without any soul-searching or experimentation: Sons of farmers will become farmers; the children of fishermen will become (or perhaps marry) fishermen, and so on. For many of the world's adolescents, then, what Marcia calls identity foreclosure is probably the most adaptive route to adulthood. In addition, the specific life goals that adolescents pursue are necessarily constrained somewhat by whatever options are available and valued in their society at any given point in time.

In sum, Western societies permit and expect adolescents to raise serious questions about self and to answer them. And Erikson was right in claiming that the individual who achieves identity, regardless of the society in which he or she lives, is likely to be better off for it. Although Erikson recognized that identity issues can and do crop up later in life, even for those people who forge positive identities as adolescents, he quite rightly identified adolescence as the key time of life for defining who we are (and will likely become).

The Other Side of Social Cognition: Knowing About Others

Being appropriately "social" requires us to interact with other people, and these interactions are more likely to be harmonious if we know what our social partners are thinking or feeling and can predict how they are likely to behave (Heyman & Gelman, 1998). The development of children's knowledge about other people—their descriptions of others' characteristics and the inferences they make about others' thoughts and behaviors—constitutes perhaps the largest area of social-cognitive research. And there are so many questions to be answered. For example, what kinds of information do children use to form impressions of others? How do these impressions change over time? And what skills are children acquiring that might explain such changes in person perception? These are the issues we explore next.

AGE TRENDS IN PERSON PERCEPTION

Children younger than 7 or 8 are likely to characterize people they know in the same concrete, observable terms they use to describe the self (Livesley & Bromley, 1973; Peevers & Secord, 1973; see Box 6.4 on page 190). Five-year-old Jenny, for example, said: "My daddy is big. He has hairy legs and eats mustard. Yuck! My daddy likes dogs—do you?" Not much of a personality profile there! When young children do use a psychological term to describe others, it is typically a very general attribute such as "He's *nice*" or "She's *mean*" that they may use more as a description or evaluation of the other person's recent behavior than as an explanation of the person's enduring qualities (Rholes & Ruble, 1984; Ruble & Dweck, 1995).

It's not that preschoolers have no appreciation for the inner qualities that people display. As we noted earlier in the chapter, even 18-month-olds will imitate the purposeful acts of humans but not mechanical toys, thus reflecting an awareness that human behaviors are guided by intentions (Meltzoff, 1995). By age 3 to 5, children are aware of how their closest peer companions typically behave in a variety of different situations (Eder, 1989). And kindergartners already know that their classmates differ in academic competencies and social skills; furthermore, they reliably choose the "smart" ones as teammates for academic competitions and the "socially skilled" classmates as partners for play activities (Droege & Stipek, 1993).

Not only are 5- to 6-year-olds becoming more aware of *behavioral consistencies* that their companions display—recognizing, for example, that a boy who has done well in classroom exercises is likely to do well in the future—but they are also beginning to make other kinds of "traitlike" inferences based largely on their emerging understanding of such subjective mental states as desires and motives that might *explain* other people's conduct. For example, 5-year-olds who hear stories about a child who has often shared and a second child who rarely has can correctly infer that the first child will be *motivated* to share in the future and is "generous" (as opposed to selfish), whereas the second child will be *unmotivated* to share and is "selfish" (Yuill & Pearson, 1998). Thus, 5-year-olds (but not 4-year-olds) assume that individual differences in past behaviors imply different *motives* and different traits. And the links between thinking about motives and making accurate trait inferences is even clearer when the children in this study were asked to identify the emotions that children with contrasting traits might display to the same outcome. Five-year-olds (but not 4-year-olds) were quite capable of making appropriate emotional inferences, saying, for example, that the generous child would feel "happy" were she to share her birthday cake with other children, whereas a selfish child would feel "sad" were his stingy motive thwarted by being made to share (see also Heyman & Gelman, 1998, for similar results with 5- to 6-year-olds).

So by ages 5 to 6, children are quite capable of thinking about traits in *psychologically* meaningful ways. Why, then, do they not use many trait words to describe their companions? Possibly because they are still mainly using trait labels as adjectives to describe current behaviors (for example, "That joke of yours was *dumb*") and are not completely certain how to weave their "knowledge" of traits into their everyday speech.

Between ages 7 and 16, children come to rely less and less on concrete attributes and more on psychological descriptors to characterize their friends and acquaintances. These changes are nicely illustrated in a program of research by Carl Barenboim (1981) who asked 6- to 11-year-olds to describe three persons they know well. Rather than

Box 6.4   *Developmental Issues*

Racial Categorization and Racism in Young Children

Because toddlers and preschool children tend to define others in terms of their observable characteristics and to place people into categories, it may come as no surprise to learn that even 3- and 4-year-olds have formed racial categories and can apply labels such as *black* and *white* to different people or to photos of blacks and whites. Furthermore, studies conducted in Australia, Canada, and the United States reveal that by age 5, most white children have some knowledge of racial stereotypes (Bigler & Liben, 1993) and display at least some prejudicial attitudes toward blacks and Native Americans (Black-Gutman & Hickson, 1996; Doyle & Aboud, 1995).

Interestingly, parents often believe that their own children are largely oblivious to race and that racist attitudes and behaviors in other children arise when their bigoted parents pass their own intolerant views to them (Burnette, 1997). However, research suggests otherwise, for the racial attitudes of young children often bear little relationship to those of their parents or their friends (Aboud, 1988; Burnette, 1997). So the origins of racial prejudice may be more *cognitive* than social, reflecting the tendency of egocentric youngsters to rigidly categorize people by skin color (and other physical correlates of ethnicity) and to favor the group to which they belong.

As children enter concrete operations and become more flexible in their thinking, prejudicial attitudes often decline in strength. This increased tolerance of 8- to 9-year-olds reflects their more realistic evaluation of racial groups in which out-groups are viewed more favorably and their own group somewhat less favorably than was true during the preschool years (Doyle & Aboud, 1995). Nevertheless, social forces can obviously play a role in maintaining or even intensifying racial prejudice. Daisa Black-Gutman and Fay Hickson (1996) found that Euro-Australian children's prejudice toward black Aborigines declined between ages 5 and 9, and then intensified at age 10 to 12, returning to the high levels displayed by 5- to 6-year-olds! Since the 10- to 12-year-olds were no longer constrained by the egocentrism and rigid categorization schemes of a 5- or 6-year-old, their increased prejudice apparently reflected the influence of adult attitudes, namely, the deep-seated animosity that many Euro-Australians feel toward black Aborigines.

Developmentalists now believe that the best way to combat racism is for parents and teachers to talk

Mixed-ethnicity discussion groups can foster an appreciation of diverse subcultural traditions and combat the formation of prejudicial attitudes.

openly about race and ethnic diversity, beginning in the preschool period when prejudicial attitudes often take root (Burnette, 1997). One especially promising program in the public schools of western Massachusetts takes a three-pronged approach:

1. *Teacher training.* Teachers receive a four-month course that defines racism, explores how educators and children display it, and provides guidance for handling it at school.
2. *Youth groups.* Children of different races and ethnicities first meet for seven weeks with ethnic peers to discuss the values and traditions of their own subcultures. Then participants meet for seven more weeks in mixed-ethnicity groups to discuss their different perspectives and to devise strategies for getting along.
3. *Parent groups.* Once a month, parents of program participants attend classes to learn more about racism and how to comfortably discuss racial issues with their children.

This program is based on the proposition that the key to combating racism is to be honest about it with children rather than shunning the topic or trying to cover it up. As developmentalist Vonnie McLoyd (cited in Burnette, 1997, p. 33) has noted, "Racism is so deeply rooted that [overcoming it] is going to take hard work by open, honest, fair-minded people who are not easily discouraged."

simply listing the behaviors that close companions display, 6- to 8-year-olds often *compared* others on noteworthy behavioral dimensions, making such statements as "Billy *runs faster* than Jason" or "She *draws the best* pictures in our whole class." As shown in Figure 6.6, use of these **behavioral comparisons** increased between ages 6 and 8 and declined rapidly after age 9. One outgrowth of the behavioral comparison process is that children become increasingly aware of regularities in a companion's behavior and eventually begin to attribute them to stable **psychological constructs**, or traits, that the person is now presumed to have. So a 10-year-old who formerly described one of her acquaintances as drawing better than anyone else in her class may now convey the same impression by saying that the acquaintance is "very artistic." Notice in re-examining the figure that children's use of these psychological constructs increased rapidly between ages 8 and 11—the same period when behavioral comparisons became less common. Eventually, children begin to compare and contrast others on important psychological dimensions, making statements such as "Bill is more shy than Ted" or "Susie is the most artistic person in our class." Although few 11-year-olds generate these **psychological comparisons** when describing others (see Figure 6.6), the majority of 12- to 16-year-olds in Barenboim's second study were actively comparing their associates on noteworthy psychological dimensions.

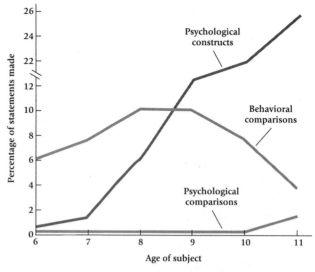

FIGURE 6.6 Percentages of descriptive statements classified as behavioral comparisons, psychological (traitlike) constructs, and psychological comparisons for children between the ages of 6 and 11. (From Barenboim, 1981.)

By age 14 to 16, adolescents are not only aware of the *dispositional* similarities and dissimilarities that characterize their acquaintances, but they are also beginning to recognize that any number of *situational* factors (for example, illness, family strife) can cause a person to act "out of character" (Damon & Hart, 1988). They now view people as unique individuals with distinctive combinations of personality traits and are able to analyze how a person's diverse and often inconsistent traits "fit together" and make sense, much as they do when constructing their own self-concepts. Todd, for example, may notice that Juanita brags about her abilities at times but seems very unsure of herself at other times, and he may integrate these seemingly discrepant impressions by concluding that Juanita is basically insecure and boasts to hide that insecurity.

So by mid- to late adolescence, young people are becoming sophisticated personality theorists and have become quite proficient at looking both "inside" and "outside" their regular companions to understand what really makes them tick.

Why do children's self-concepts and their impressions of others become increasingly abstract and coherent with age? In addressing these issues, we first examine two "cognitive" points of view before considering how social forces might contribute, both directly and indirectly, to the growth of social cognition.

THEORIES OF SOCIAL-COGNITIVE DEVELOPMENT

Cognitive Theories of Social Cognition   The two cognitive theories that are most often used to explain developmental trends in social cognition are Piaget's cognitive-developmental approach and Robert Selman's role-taking analysis.

Cognitive-Developmental Theory   According to cognitive-developmental theorists, the ways children think about the self and other people largely depend on their own levels of cognitive development. Recall that the thinking of 3- to 6-year-old "preoperational" children tends to center on the most salient *perceptual* aspects of stimuli

behavioral comparisons phase: the tendency to form impressions of others by comparing and contrasting their overt behaviors.

psychological constructs phase: tendency to base one's impressions of others on the stable traits these individuals are presumed to have.

psychological comparisons phase: tendency to form impressions of others by comparing and contrasting these individuals on abstract psychological dimensions.

and events. So it would hardly surprise a Piagetian to find that 3- to 6-year-olds describe their associates in very concrete, observable terms, mentioning their appearances and possessions, their likes and dislikes, and the actions they can perform.

The thinking of 7- to 10-year-olds will change in many ways as these youngsters enter Piaget's concrete-operational stage. Not only is egocentrism becoming less pronounced, but children are now *decentering* from perceptual illusions and beginning to recognize that certain properties of an object remain unchanged despite changes in the object's appearance (*conservation*). Clearly, these emerging abilities to look beyond immediate appearances and to infer underlying invariances might help to explain why 7- to 10-year-olds, who are actively comparing themselves with their peers, become more attuned to regularities in their own and others' conduct and use psychological constructs, or traits, to describe these patterns.

By ages 12 to 14, children are entering formal operations and are now able to think more logically and systematically about abstractions. Although the concept of a psychological trait is itself an abstraction, it is one based on regularities in concrete, observable behaviors, perhaps explaining why *concrete* operators can easily think in these terms. However, a trait *dimension* is even more of a mental inference or abstraction that has few if any concrete referents. Thus, the ability to think in dimensional terms and to reliably order people along these continua (as is necessary in making psychological comparisons) implies that a person is able to operate on abstract concepts—a formal-operational ability (O'Mahoney, 1989).

Although children do begin to make behavioral comparisons at ages 6-8 and psychological comparisons at ages 11 to 12—precisely the times that Piaget's theory implies they should—cognitive-developmental theory clearly underestimates the social-cognitive abilities of young children. We've seen, for example, that 4-year-olds with a belief-desire theory of mind are achieving a much richer understanding of the *subjective* nature of such mental states as desires and beliefs, and that by age 5—still the *preoperational* period in Piaget's theory—children can use their knowledge of mental states, along with their observations of behavioral regularities, to make at least some very accurate *trait* inferences (Yuill & Pearson, 1998). Clearly, general cognitive development contributes to the growth of social cognition as proponents of cognitive-developmental theory have claimed. Yet, Robert Selman (1980) believes there is one particular aspect of cognitive growth that underlies a mature understanding of the self and other people—the growth of **role-taking skills.**

Selman's Role-Taking Theory According to Selman (1980; Yeates & Selman, 1989), children will gain much richer understandings of themselves and other people as they acquire the ability to discriminate their own perspectives from those of their companions and to see the relationships between these potentially discrepant points of view. Simply stated, Selman believes that in order to "know" a person, one must be able to assume his perspective and understand his thoughts, feelings, motives, and intentions—in short, the *internal* factors that account for his behavior. If a child has not yet acquired these important role-taking skills, she may have little choice but to describe her acquaintances in terms of their external attributes—that is, their appearance, their activities, and the things they possess.

Selman has studied the development of role-taking skills by asking children to comment on a number of interpersonal dilemmas. Here is one example (from Selman, 1976, p. 302):

role taking: the ability to assume another person's perspective and understand his or her thoughts, feelings, and behaviors.

PHOTO 6.5 Robert Selman (1942–   ) has emphasized the relationship between the development of role-taking skills and the growth of interpersonal understanding.

Holly is an 8-year-old girl who likes to climb trees. She is the best tree climber in the neighborhood. One day while climbing down from a tall tree, she falls . . . but does not hurt herself. Her father sees her fall. He is upset and asks her to promise not to climb trees any more. Holly promises. Later that day, Holly and her friends meet Shawn. Shawn's kitten is caught in a tree and can't get down. Something has to be done right away or the kitten may fall. Holly is the only one who climbs trees well enough to reach the kitten and get it down but she remembers her promise to her father.

To assess how well a child understands the perspectives of Holly, her father, and Shawn, Selman asks: Does Holly know how Shawn feels about the kitten? How will Holly's father feel if he finds out she climbed the tree? What does Holly think her father will do if he finds out she climbed the tree? What would you do? Children's responses to such probes led Selman to conclude that role-taking skills develop in a stagelike manner, as shown in Table 6-1.

Notice in examining the table that children progress from largely egocentric beings, who seem unaware of any perspective other than their own (stage 0), to sophisticated social-cognitive theorists, who can keep several perspectives in mind and

TABLE 6-1 Selman's stages of social perspective taking

STAGE OF ROLE TAKING	TYPICAL RESPONSES TO THE "HOLLY" DILEMMA
0. Egocentric or undifferentiated perspective (roughly 3 to 6 years) Children are unaware of any perspective other than their own. They assume that whatever they feel is right for Holly to do will be agreed with by others.	Children often assume that Holly will save the kitten. When asked how Holly's father will react to her transgression, these children think he will be "happy because he likes kittens." In other words, these children like kittens themselves, and they assume that Holly and her father also like kittens.
1. Social-informational role taking (roughly 6 to 8 years) Children now recognize that people can have perspectives that differ from their own but believe that this happens *only* because these individuals have received different information.	When asked whether Holly's father will be angry because she climbed the tree, the child may say "If he didn't know why she climbed the tree, he would be angry. But if he knew why she did it, he would realize that she had a good reason."
2. Self-reflective role taking (roughly 8 to 10 years) Children now know that their own and others' points of view may conflict even if they have received the same information. They are now able to consider the other person's viewpoint. They also recognize that the other person can put himself in their shoes, so they are now able to anticipate the person's reactions to their behavior. However, the child cannot consider his own perspective and that of another person at the same time.	If asked whether Holly will climb the tree, the child might say "Yes. She knows that her father will understand why she did it." In so doing, the child is focusing on the father's consideration of Holly's perspective. But if asked whether the father would want Holly to climb the tree, the child usually says no, thereby indicating that he is now assuming the father's perspective and considering the father's concern for Holly's safety.
3. Mutual role taking (roughly 10 to 12 years) The child can now simultaneously consider her own and another person's points of view and recognize that the other person can do the same. The child can also assume the perspective of a disinterested third party and anticipate how each participant (self and other) will react to the viewpoint of his or her partner.	At this stage, a child might describe the outcome of the "Holly" dilemma by taking the perspective of a disinterested third party and indicating that she knows that both Holly and her father are thinking about what the other is thinking. For example, one child remarked: "Holly wanted to get the kitten because she likes kittens, but she knew that she wasn't supposed to climb trees. Holly's father knew that Holly had been told not to climb trees, but he couldn't have known about [the kitten]."
4. Societal role taking (roughly 12 to 15 and older) The adolescent now attempts to understand another person's perspective by comparing it with that of the social system in which he operates (that is, the view of the "generalized other"). In other words, the adolescent expects others to consider and typically assume perspectives on events that most people in their social group would take.	When asked if Holly should be punished for climbing the tree, the stage 4 adolescent is likely to say "No" and claim that the value of humane treatment of animals justifies Holly's act and that most fathers would recognize this point.

SOURCE: Adapted from Selman, 1976.

compare each with the viewpoint that "most people" would adopt (Stage 4). Apparently, these role-taking skills represent a true developmental sequence, for 40 of 41 boys who were repeatedly tested over a five-year period showed a steady forward progression from stage to stage, with no skipping of stages (Gurucharri & Selman, 1982). Perhaps the reason they develop in one particular order is that they are closely related to Piaget's invariant sequence of cognitive stages (Keating & Clark, 1980): Preoperational children are at Selman's first or second level of role taking (stage 0 or 1), whereas most concrete operators are at the third or fourth level (stage 2 or 3), and formal operators are about equally distributed between the fourth and fifth levels of role taking (stages 3 and 4).

Role Taking and Thinking About Relationships   As children acquire role-taking skills, their understanding of the meaning and character of human relationships begins to change. Consider what children of different ages say about the meaning of *friendship*. Preschoolers at Selman's egocentric (level 0) stage think that virtually any pleasant interactions between themselves and available playmates qualify those playmates as "friends." So 5-year-old Chang might describe Terry as a close friend simply because "he lives next door and plays games with me" (Damon, 1977).

Common activity continues to be the principal basis for friendship among 6- to 8-year-olds (Hartup, 1992). But because these youngsters have reached Selman's stage 1 and recognize that others may not always share their perspectives, they begin to view a friend as someone who *chooses* to "do nice things for me." Friendships are often one way at this stage, for the child feels no strong pressure to reciprocate these considerations. And should a friend fail to serve the child's interests (for example, by spurning an invitation to camp out in the back yard), she may quickly become a nonfriend.

Later, at Selman's stage 2, 8- to 10-year-olds show increasing concern for the needs of a friend and begin to see friendships as reciprocal relationships, based on *mutual trust,* in which two people exchange respect, kindness, and affection (Selman, 1980). No longer are common activities sufficient to brand someone a friend; as children appreciate how their own interests and perspectives and those of their peers can be similar or different, they insist that their friends be *psychologically* similar to themselves.

By early adolescence, many youngsters have reached Selman's stage 3 or 4. Although they still view friends as psychologically similar people who like, trust, and assist each other, they have expanded their notions of the obligations of friendship to emphasize the exchange of *intimate* thoughts and feelings (Berndt & Perry, 1990). They also expect their friends to stick up for them and be *loyal,* standing ready to provide close emotional support whenever they may need it (Berndt & Perry, 1990; Buhrmester, 1990).

So, with the growth of role-taking skills, children's conceptions of friendship gradually change from the one-sided, self-centered view of friends as "people who benefit me" to a harmonious, reciprocal perspective in which each party truly understands the other, enjoys providing him or her with emotional support and other niceties, and expects these same considerations in return. Perhaps because they rest on a firmer basis of intimacy and interpersonal understanding, the close friendships of older children and adolescents are viewed as more important and are more stable, or long-lasting, than those of younger children (Berndt, 1989; Berndt & Hoyle, 1985; Furman & Buhrmester, 1992).

Table 6-2 briefly summarizes the changes in thinking about the self and others that we have discussed—changes that are clearly influenced by cognitive development. Yet, as we will see in concluding the chapter, the growth of *social* cognition is also heavily influenced by *social* interactions and experiences that children and adolescents have had.

TABLE 6-2   Milestones in the development of self and social cognition

AGE (YEARS)	SELF-CONCEPT/SELF-ESTEEM	SELF-CONTROL	SOCIAL COGNITION
0–1	Can differentiate self from the external environment Sense of personal agency emerges Can discriminate own face from other faces	Suppresses negative emotions at times	Discriminates familiar from unfamiliar people Prefers familiar companions (attachment objects)
1–2	Self-recognition emerges Categorical self develops	Compliance emerges	Recognition that others act on intentions Categorization of others on socially significant dimensions
3–5	Self-concept emphasizes actions Evaluation of accomplishments emerges Undifferentiated self-esteem emerges Appearance of belief-desire theory of mind and private self	Compliance improves Can use adult-generated strategies to self-regulate and delay gratification	Impressions are based largely on others' actions and concrete attributes Knowledge of racial stereotypes and prejudicial attitudes emerge Friendships are based on shared activities
6–10	Self-concepts come to emphasize personality traits Self-esteem is based on one's academic, physical, and social competencies	Appearance of self-generated strategies for self-control Begins to value self-regulation/self-control	Impressions come to be based largely on the traits others display (psychological constructs) Prejudicial attitudes often decline in strength Friendships are based largely on psychological similarities and mutual trust
11 and beyond	Friendships, romantic appeal, and job competence become important to one's self-esteem Self-concepts now reflect one's values and ideologies, and become more integrated and abstract Identity is achieved	Generates abstract strategies to regulate conduct and defer gratification Internalizes norms that stress the value of self-control	Impressions are now based largely on others' dispositional similarities and dissimilarities (psychological comparisons) Prejudicial attitudes may decline or intensify, depending on social influences Friendships are based on loyalty and sharing of intimacies

Social Influences on Social-Cognitive Development   Many developmentalists have wondered whether the growth of children's self-awareness and their understanding of other people are as closely tied to cognitive development as cognitive theorists have assumed. Consider, for example, that even though children's role-taking abilities are related to their performances on Piagetian measures and IQ tests (Pellegrini, 1985), it is quite possible for a child to grow less egocentric and to mature intellectually without becoming an especially skillful role-taker (Shantz, 1983). So, there must be other, *noncognitive* factors that contribute to the growth of role-taking skills and that may even exert their own unique effects on children's social-cognitive development. Might social experiences play such a role? No less an authority than Jean Piaget thought so.

Social Experience as a Contributor to Role Taking   Many years ago, Piaget (1965) argued that playful interactions among grade-school children promote the development of role-taking skills and mature social judgments. In Piaget's view, children gradually become more aware of discrepancies between their own perspectives and those of playmates as they assume different roles while playing together. When conflicts arise in play, children must learn to coordinate their points of view with those of their companions (that is, compromise) for play to continue. So Piaget assumed that *equal-status contacts among peers* are a very important contributor to social perspective taking and the growth of interpersonal understanding.

Not only has research consistently supported Piaget's viewpoint, but it appears that some forms of peer contact may be better than others at fostering the growth of interpersonal understanding. Specifically, Janice Nelson and Francis Aboud (1985) propose that disagreements among *friends* are particularly important because children tend to be more open and honest with their friends than with mere acquaintances and are more motivated to resolve disputes with friends. As a result, disagreeing friends should be more likely than disagreeing acquaintances to provide each other with the information needed to understand and appreciate their conflicting points of view. Indeed, when 8- to 10-year-olds discuss an interpersonal issue on which they disagree, pairs of friends are much more critical of their partners than pairs of acquaintances are; but friends are also more likely to fully explain the rationales for their own points of view. Furthermore, disagreeing friends display increases in social understanding after these discussions are over, whereas disagreeing acquaintances do not (Nelson & Aboud, 1985). So it seems that equal-status contacts among friends may be especially important for the growth of role-taking skills and interpersonal understanding.

PHOTO **6.6** Equal-status contacts with peers are an important contributor to the development of role-taking skills and interpersonal understanding.

Social Experience as a Direct Contributor to Person Perception Social contacts with peers not only contribute *indirectly* to person perception by fostering the development of role-taking skills, but they are also a form of *direct experience* by which children can learn what others are like. In other words, the more experience a child has with peers, the more *motivated* she should be to try to understand them and the more *practiced* she should become at appraising the causes of their behavior (Higgins & Parsons, 1983).

Popularity is a convenient measure of social experience; that is, popular children interact more often with a wider variety of peers than do their less popular age-mates (LeMare & Rubin, 1987). So, if the amount of direct experience a child has with peers exerts its own unique influence on his or her social cognitive judgments, then popular children should outperform less popular age-mates on tests of social understanding, *even when their role-taking skills are comparable.* This is precisely what Jackie Gnepp (1989) found when she tested the ability of popular and less popular 8-year-olds to make appropriate traitlike inferences about an unfamiliar child from a small sample of the child's previous behaviors. So it seems that both social experience (as indexed by popularity) and cognitive competence (role-taking skills) each contribute in their own way to the development of children's understanding of other people. Apparently, Cooley (1902) and Mead (1934) were quite correct in suggesting that social cognition and social experience are completely intertwined—that they develop together, they are reciprocally related, and neither can progress very far without the other.

Summary

- The **self** is thought to arise from social interactions and largely to reflect other people's reactions to us (that is, a **looking-glass self**). The development of **social cognition** deals with how children's understandings of the self and other people change with age.

DEVELOPMENT OF THE SELF-CONCEPT

- Although there is some disagreement, most developmentalists believe that babies are born without a **self-concept** and will gradually differentiate themselves from the external environment over the first two to six months as they gain a sense of **personal agency** and learn (from their experiences before mirrors) to discriminate their faces from those of other people.

- By 18 to 24 months of age, toddlers begin to pass the **rouge test** and display true **self-recognition**—a milestone that depends on cognitive development and social experiences with companions. Soon thereafter, they form a **categorical self** as they classify themselves along socially significant dimensions such as age and sex.

- Although preschool children know how they typically behave in many situations and can classify themselves along psychological dimensions if asked to do so in ways that do not tax their verbal skills, the self-descriptions of 3- to 5-year-olds are typically very concrete, focusing mostly on their physical features, possessions, and the activities they can perform.

- Between the ages of 3 and 4, children's **theory of mind** progresses from a **desire theory** to a **belief-desire theory** that more closely resembles adults' conception of how the mind works. Once children achieve this milestone, which is fostered by pretend play and conversations about mental states with siblings and adults, they more clearly distinguish their **private self** from their **public self** and are better prepared to make meaningful psychological inferences about their own and others' behavior.

- By about age 8, children begin to describe themselves in terms of their inner and enduring psychological attributes. Adolescents have an even more integrated and abstract self-concept that includes not only their dispositional qualities (that is, traits, beliefs, attitudes, and values) but also a knowledge of how these characteristics might interact with each other and with situational influences to affect their behavior. However, frequent displays of **false self behaviors** can leave adolescents confused about who they really are.

SELF-ESTEEM: THE EVALUATIVE COMPONENT OF SELF

- **Self-esteem,** the judgments we make about our self-worth, begin to take shape early in life as infants form positive or negative working models of self from their interactions with caregivers. By age 8, children evaluate themselves in three domains: physical competence, academic competence, and social acceptance; in adolescence, feelings of **relational self-worth** and new dimensions such as job competence, romantic appeal, and quality of close friendships also become important contributors to global self-esteem. Except for a temporary decline associated with transition to junior high school, self-esteem is reasonably stable over time and often increases throughout adolescence, particularly for boys.

- Warm, responsive, democratic parenting fosters self-esteem, whereas aloof or controlling parenting styles seem to undermine it. Peers influence each others' self-esteem through **social comparison** during the grade-school years. For adolescents, some of the strongest determinants of self-worth are the quality of one's rela-

tionships with peers—particularly with close friends and prospective romantic partners.

DEVELOPMENT OF SELF-CONTROL

- The emergence of **self-control** is a major development. Although 2-year-olds are voluntarily complying with others' directives, their conduct is still largely externally controlled by the consequences they anticipate for **compliance** (or noncompliance). All toddlers are struggling with the psychological crisis of **autonomy versus shame and doubt** and can be **self-assertive** at times; but whether they display **defiance** largely depends on the parent-child relationship and on how parents respond to their bids for autonomy. Warm, responsive parenting is associated with **committed compliance** and internalization of parental rules, whereas control based on the parent's superior power leads to **situational compliance** and a hesitancy to fully embrace the parent's agenda. By the middle of the third year, children are displaying an increasing capacity to regulate and control their own thinking and behavior—aided, in part, by *private speech* as a regulatory mechanism.

- **Delay of gratification** is an important aspect of self-control—one that improves dramatically with age as children become more knowledgeable about effective delay strategies and internalize norms that stress the value of self-regulation and self-control. Preschoolers who have already developed a relatively strong capacity for delaying gratification tend to become self-disciplined adolescents whom parents describe as displaying attributes that contribute to high self-esteem and to favorable outcomes later in life.

WHO AM I TO BE? FORGING AN IDENTITY

- One of the more challenging tasks of adolescence is to resolve the **identity crisis** by forming a stable **identity** (or identities) with which to embrace the responsibilities of young adulthood. From the **diffusion** and **foreclosure** statuses, many college-age youths progress to the **moratorium** status (where they are experimenting to find an identity) and ultimately to **identity achievement**. Identity formation is an uneven process that often continues well into adulthood.

- The process of seeking an identity is a lot less crisislike than Erik Erikson assumed. Identity achievement and moratorium are psychologically healthy statuses. If there is a crisis surrounding the identity formation process, it is a long-term failure to form one, for adolescents stuck in the diffusion status often assume a *negative identity* and display poor psychological adjustment.

- Healthy identity outcomes are fostered by cognitive development; by warm, supportive parents who encourage individual self-expression; and by a culture that permits and expects adolescents to find their own niches. For minority youth, achieving a positive ethnic identity fosters healthy identity outcomes in other domains of life.

THE OTHER SIDE OF SOCIAL COGNITION: KNOWING ABOUT OTHERS

■ Although preschool children are not oblivious to other people's inner qualities and can make some accurate and appropriate traitlike inferences, children younger than 7 or 8 are more likely to describe friends and acquaintances in the same concrete observable terms they use to describe the self. As they compare themselves and others on noteworthy behavioral dimensions, they become more attuned to regularities in their own and others' conduct (**behavioral comparisons** phase), and begin to rely on stable psychological constructs, or traits, to describe these patterns (**psychological constructs** phase). Young adolescents' impressions of others become even more abstract as they begin to make **psychological comparisons** among their friends and acquaintances. And by ages 14 to 16, adolescents are becoming sophisticated "personality theorists" who know that any number of situational influences can cause a person to act "out of character."

■ The growth of children's social-cognitive abilities is related to cognitive development in general and to the emergence of **role-taking** skills in particular: To truly "know" a person, one must be able to assume her perspective and understand her thoughts, feelings, motives, and intentions. However, *social interactions*—particularly equal-status contacts with friends and peers—are important contributors to social-cognitive development. They contribute indirectly by fostering the growth of role-taking skills and in a more direct way by providing the experiences children need to learn what others are like.

Chapter Seven

Achievement

The Concept of Achievement Motivation

The Motivational View of Achievement

A Behavioral View of Achievement

Early Reactions to One's Accomplishments: From Mastery to Self-Evaluation

Theories of Achievement Motivation and Achievement Behavior

Need Achievement Theories

Weiner's Attribution Theory

Dweck's Learned Helplessness Theory

Reflections on Theories of Achievement

Cultural and Subcultural Influences on Achievement

Individualistic Versus Collectivistic Perspectives on Achievement

Ethnic Variations in Achievement

Social Class Differences in Achievement

Home and Family Influences on Achievement

Quality of Attachments and Achievement

The Home Environment

Child-Rearing and Achievement

Configural Influences: Birth Order, Family Size and Children's Achievement Behavior

On Sex Differences in Achievement and a Look Ahead

Summary

*O*ne basic aim of socialization is to urge children to pursue important goals and to take pride in their accomplishments. During my elementary and high school days, I had several heart-to-heart talks with my parents (of the kind you may remember) about the value of writing essays and memorizing the countless passages that were required of me in English and history classes. Both my parents took the position that I should strive to do my best, whatever the assignment, because successful completion of these scholastic activities would promote the self-confidence I would need to become a success in life. My parents' outlook was very typical of adults in many Western societies where children are often encouraged to be independent, and even competitive, and to do well in whatever activities they may undertake—in short, to become "achievers." As we will see, not all cultures believe that *competitive* successes and *individual* accomplishments are the best indicators of what it means to have "achieved." But even though the meaning of achievement varies somewhat from society to society, one survey of 30 cultures revealed that people all over the world value personal attributes such as self-reliance, responsibility, and a willingness to work hard to attain important objectives (Fyans et al., 1983).

Must these valued attributes be taught? Social-learning theorists thought so, although others disagree. Many years ago, psychoanalyst Robert White (1959) proposed that from infancy onward, human beings are intrinsically motivated to "master" their environments—to have an effect on or to cope successfully with a world of people and objects. We see this **mastery motive** in action as we watch infants struggle to turn knobs, open cabinets, and operate toys—and then notice their pleasure when they succeed (Mayes & Zigler, 1992).[1] Even infants and toddlers who are mentally retarded will actively seek out challenges just for the joy of mastering them (Hausen-Corn, 1995). Notice that White's viewpoint is very similar to that of Jean Piaget, who believed that children are intrinsically motivated to *adapt* to the environment by assimilating new experiences and then accommodating to these experiences.

If all infants are truly mastery-oriented and experience great joy in the effects they produce, why do school-age children vary so dramatically in their achievement strivings? Is there a "motive to achieve" that children must acquire? How do children's self-images and their expectations about succeeding or failing affect their aspirations and accomplishments? And what kinds of home and scholastic settings are likely to promote (or hinder) achievement behavior? These are some of the major issues we consider in the pages that follow.

The Concept of Achievement Motivation

One reason some children try harder than others to master their school assignments, music lessons, or the position they play on the neighborhood Tee-Ball team is that they differ in **achievement motivation**—their willingness to strive to succeed at challenging tasks and to meet high standards of accomplishment. Achievement motivation is reflected differently in different cultures. In Western industrialized societies, which tend to be *individualistic* cultures, achievement motivation is inferred from individual (and often competitive) accomplishments that can be compared against some standard of excellence. As we will see, most of the research on the growth of achievement motivation has been conducted in Western societies and reflects this largely Eurocentric view of achievement. By contrast, people from *collectivist* societies would argue that achievement motivation reflects a willingness to strive to succeed at

mastery motivation: an inborn motive to explore, understand, and control one's environment.

achievement motivation: a willingness to strive to succeed at challenging tasks and to meet high standards of accomplishment.

---

[1]White used the term *effectance motivation* to describe the infant's need for mastery, although most developmentalists today refer to it as mastery motivation.

objectives that promote *social harmony* or that *maximize the social welfare* of the groups to which they belong (see Triandis, 1995).

Yet, regardless of the culture in which one lives, the concept of "achievement" presumes some learning on the child's part. Not only must he or she acquire some idea of what constitutes acceptable or unacceptable performance in any given domain or context, but an achiever has also learned to use these standards to *evaluate* her accomplishments. Even though there is widespread agreement that one's propensity for achievement is largely an acquired attribute, however, different theorists look at this construct in very different ways.

THE MOTIVATIONAL VIEW OF ACHIEVEMENT

David McClelland and his associates (1953) speak of the child's **need for achievement (n Ach),** which they define as a "learned motive to compete and to strive for success whenever one's behavior can be evaluated against a standard of excellence" (p. 78). In other words, high "need-achievers" have learned to take *pride* in their ability to meet or exceed high standards, and it is this sense of *self*-fulfillment that motivates them to work hard, to be successful, and to try to outperform others when faced with new challenges.

McClelland measured achievement motivation by asking participants to examine a set of four pictures and then write a story about each as part of a test of "creative imagination." These four pictures show people working or studying, although each is sufficiently ambiguous to suggest any number of themes (see Photo 7.1). A person's need for achievement (*n* Ach) is determined by counting the achievement-related statements that he or she includes in the four stories (the assumption being that participants are projecting themselves and their motives into their themes). For example, a high need-achiever might respond to Photo 7.1 by saying that these men have been working for months on a new scientific breakthrough that will revolutionize the field of medicine, whereas a low need-achiever might say the workers are glad the day is over so that they can go home and relax.

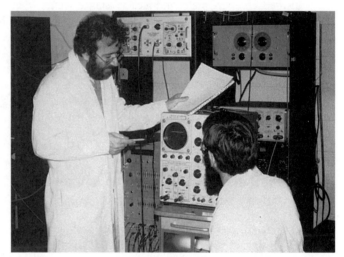

PHOTO 7.1 Scenes like this one were used by David McClelland and his associates to measure achievement motivation.

A BEHAVIORAL VIEW OF ACHIEVEMENT

In contrast to McClelland's viewpoint, Vaughn Crandall and his associates depict achievement as a behavioral rather than a motivational construct. According to Crandall, Katkovsky, and Preston (1960), "Achievement is any *behavior* directed toward the *attainment of approval or the avoidance of disapproval* for competence in performance in situations where standards of excellence are operable" (p. 789; italics added). Crandall and associates argue that there is no single, overriding motive to achieve that applies to all achievement tasks. Instead, they propose that children will show different strivings in different skill areas (for example, art, schoolwork, sports) depending on the extent to which they *value* doing well in each area and their *expectations* that they can succeed and be recognized for their accomplishments.

Notice that McClelland and Crandall clearly differ on the issue of what reinforces achievement behavior. McClelland and his associates have argued that the sense of *personal pride* stemming from one's high accomplishments is reinforcing (and will sustain achievement behavior in the future) because it satisfies an *intrinsic* need for

need for achievement (n Ach):
McClelland's depiction of achievement motivation as a learned motive to complete and to strive for success in situations in which one's performance can be evaluated against some standard of excellence.

competence or achievement. However, Crandall and his associates counterargue that one need not talk about internal needs that must be satisfied to explain why people strive to meet exacting standards. Instead, they propose that achievement behaviors are simply a class of instrumental responses designed to win the *approval* (or to avoid the disapproval) of significant others, such as parents, teachers, and peers.

Which of these viewpoints is correct? Perhaps both of them are. Susan Harter (1981) found that some children do view achievement tasks as a means of satisfying personal needs for competence or mastery (an **intrinsic orientation** very similar to McClelland's view of *n* Ach), whereas others strive to do well primarily to earn external incentives such as grades, prizes, or social approval (an **extrinsic orientation** that other theorists have called "social achievement"). Harter measured children's orientations to achievement with a 30-item questionnaire that asked whether the reasons they perform various activities are intrinsic justifications (I like challenging tasks; I like to solve problems myself) or extrinsic ones (I do things to get good grades, to win the teacher's approval, and so on). And her research revealed that children who are intrinsically oriented are more likely than those who are extrinsically oriented to prefer challenging problems over simpler ones and to view themselves as highly competent at schoolwork. Even when they must seek help to accomplish a task, intrinsically oriented children prefer indirect assistance (hints) that will allow *them* the personal satisfaction of deriving a solution, whereas extrinsically oriented children would just as soon be given the solution (Nelson-LeGall & Jones, 1990).

So by the early elementary school years, children in Western societies already differ in their orientations to achievement. Many theories have been proposed to explain how and why grade-school children (and, indeed, adolescents and adults) respond so differently to the challenges they face. But before we discuss these theoretical claims, let's first consider some of the milestones that toddlers and preschool children reach as they begin to evaluate their accomplishments.

Early Reactions to One's Accomplishments: From Mastery to Self-Evaluation

As we have noted, even infants can take pleasure in "mastering" a new toy or in producing other interesting outcomes. But when do they first acquire performance standards and begin to evaluate their outcomes as "successes" or "failures"? At what age do they understand the implications of winning or losing at a competitive activity with an age-mate? These are important questions in that Western definitions of achievement typically portray high achievers as those who reliably *evaluate* their accomplishments against standards of excellence and will try to *outperform* others when faced with new challenges.

Deborah Stipek and her associates (Stipek, Recchia, & McClintic, 1992) have conducted a series of studies with 1- to 5-year-olds to find out when children develop the capacity to evaluate their accomplishments against performance standards—a capacity central to achievement motivation. In Stipek's research, children were observed as they undertook activities that had clear-cut achievement goals (for example, hammering pegs into pegboards, working puzzles, knocking down plastic pins with a bowling ball). Tasks were structured so that children either could or could not master them so that reactions to success or failure could be observed. One of these studies even had 2- to 5-year-olds compete with a peer at a block-stacking task, and their reactions to winning or losing were noted. Based on this research, Stipek and her colleagues found that children progress through three phases in learning to evaluate their performances in achievement situations, phases we call *joy in mastery, approval seeking,* and *use of standards.*

intrinsic orientation: a desire to achieve in order to satisfy one's personal needs for competence or mastery.

extrinsic orientation: a desire to achieve in order to earn external incentives such as grades, prizes, or the approval of others.

Phase 1: Joy in mastery—Before the age of two, infants are visibly pleased to master challenges, displaying the mastery motivation White (1959) wrote about. However, they do not call other people's attention to their triumphs or otherwise seek recognition, and rather than being bothered by failures, they simply shift goals and attempt to master other toys. They are not yet evaluating their outcomes in relation to performance standards that define success and failure.

Phase 2: Approval-seeking—As they near age 2, toddlers begin to anticipate how others will evaluate their performances. They seek recognition when they master challenges and expect disapproval when they fail. For example, children as young as 2 who succeeded on a task often smiled, held their heads and chins up high, and made such statements as "I did it" as they called the experimenter's attention to their feats. Meanwhile, 2-year-olds who failed to master a challenge would often turn away from the experimenter as though they hoped to avoid criticism. It seems, then, that 2-year-olds are already appraising their outcomes as *mastery* successes or nonsuccesses and have already learned that they can expect approval after successes and disapproval after failures.

Phase 3: Use of standards—An important breakthrough occurred around age 3 as children began to react more independently to their successes and failures. They seemed to have adopted objective standards for appraising their performance and were not as dependent on others to tell them when they had done well or poorly. These Phase-3 children seemed capable of experiencing true *pride* (rather than mere pleasure) in their achievements and true *shame* (rather than mere disappointment) after failing to achieve an objective.

How do young children respond to competitive activities? Prior to age 33 months, competitors were neither happy about winning nor sad about losing. Instead, successfully completing (mastering) their individual tasks was what was most important to 24- to 32-month-olds. By contrast, 33- to 41-month-olds expressed much more positive affect on mastering a task if they finished first (and won a competition) than if they finished second. And by ages 42 to 60 months, losers tended to slow down or stop working when a winner had been declared; apparently they understood the competitive nature of the game and that there was little reason for them to rush to finish once an opponent had "won." Nevertheless, shameful responses were very infrequent among preschoolers who "lost" at a competitive activity. So, for 3½- to 5-year-olds, it appears that winning is divine but that losing is not typically interpreted as a clear failure.

In sum, infants are guided by a mastery motive and take pleasure in their everyday accomplishments; 2-year-olds begin to anticipate others' approval or disapproval of their performances; and children 3 and older evaluate their accomplishments against performance standards and are capable of experiencing pride or shame depending on how successfully they match those standards. Of course, Stipek's work looks at *normative* trends in young children's reactions to achievement outcomes and, as such, has little to say about the development of *individual differences* in achievement motivation. To address this issue, we now turn to the major theories of achievement—models that do seek to explain why individuals might adopt different achievement orientations and how this choice of an orientation might influence their future accomplishments.

Theories of Achievement Motivation and Achievement Behavior

The theories that have contributed most to our understanding of achievement motivation and achievement behavior are the McClelland/Atkinson need achievement models and more recent attributional (or social information-processing) approaches. In this section of the chapter, we compare and contrast these influential points of view.

NEED ACHIEVEMENT THEORIES

The first major theory of achievement was the "need achievement" approach, a motivational model that stemmed from the pioneering efforts of David McClelland and his associates at Wesleyan University and was later revised by John Atkinson of the University of Michigan.

McClelland's Theory of Achievement Motivation   In 1938, Henry Murray published *Explorations in Personality,* a text that had a profound influence on students of human behavior. Murray outlined a personality theory that included a taxonomy of human needs. He discussed 28 basic human needs—for example, the need for sex, the need for affiliation, the need for nurturance—including the need for achievement (*n* Ach), which he defined as "the desire of tendency to do things as rapidly and . . . as well as possible" (p. 164).

David McClelland and his associates at Wesleyan University read Murray's work and became interested in the development of achievement motivation. McClelland et al. (1953) viewed *n* Ach as a learned motive that, like all other complex social motives, is acquired on the basis of rewards and punishments that accompany certain kinds of behavior. If children are frequently reinforced for independence, competitiveness, and success and if they meet with disapproval when they fail, their achievement motivation should be rather strong. But a child can hardly be expected to develop a strong need for achievement if he or she is not often encouraged to be independent, competitive, and highly competent in day-to-day activities and endeavors. In sum, the strength of an individual's achievement motive was thought to depend on the quality of his or her "achievement" training. McClelland et al. believed that the quality of achievement training received by children varied as a function of their culture, their social class, and the attitudes of their parents about the value of independence and achievement.

The first task faced by the Wesleyan group was to develop a method of measuring achievement motivation. They needed an instrument that measured the strength of an individual's desire to compete and to excel in situations where standards of excellence are operable.

McClelland and his associates settled on the story-writing technique described earlier because they believed that a person's true underlying motives might well be reflected in his fantasy life—that is, dreams, wishes, idle thoughts, and daydreams. They soon discovered that people varied a great deal in the amount of achievement imagery they displayed when writing stories about ambiguous work or study scenes. The next step, then, was to validate this measure by showing that people who scored high in the need for achievement would actually turn out to be high achievers, whereas those who scored low would display more modest accomplishments.

The Relationship Between Achievement Motivation and Achievement Behavior   Is achievement motivation related in some meaningful way to achievement behavior? Early returns suggested that it was. Several studies conducted during the 1950s revealed that college students who score high in *n* Ach tend to have higher grade-point averages than those who score low and aspire to higher-status occupations as well (Bendig, 1958; McClelland et al., 1953; Minor & Neel, 1958). So it seemed that people who express a strong desire to achieve on the McClelland fantasy measure of *n* Ach often do achieve at higher levels than those who test low in achievement motivation.

The Achieving Society   What would happen if large numbers of high need-achievers were present in a culture at a given time? Would that culture take large strides forward, showing clear signs of technological or economic growth in the years ahead?

PHOTO 7.2   David McClelland (1917–1998) proposed a theory of achievement motivation that guided research on children's propensities for achievement throughout the 1950s and 1960s.

A direct test of this hypothesis appears in McClelland's (1961) book *The Achieving Society,* in which he assessed the mean *n* Ach of 23 countries in a most interesting fashion. He simply obtained readers used in the primary grades in each country and scored the stories in these books for achievement imagery in the same way he typically scored stories that children might produce themselves. Children's readers were selected for study because they represent the popular culture of the country and, as such, are probably a reasonably good indication of the amount of achievement training that grade-school children are receiving at any given time. Readers from the 1920s and the year 1950 were sampled. McClelland's goal was to see whether he could predict the subsequent economic growth of a country from the amount of achievement imagery present in its readers during the 1920s.

As anticipated, McClelland (1961) found a significant positive correlation ($r = +.53$) between the number of achievement themes in a country's readers during the 1920s and the country's increase in economic productivity for the period 1929 to 1950. Although this correlational relationship is consistent with his hypothesis, it does not necessarily mean that the *n* Ach of a society affects its subsequent economic growth. One rival hypothesis is that economic growth already under way during the 1920s was responsible for both a country's preoccupation with achievement during the 1920s *and* its later economic growth. But if prior economic growth had been the causal agent, then the country's economic growth between 1929 and 1950 should be highly correlated with the number of achievement themes in its readers in 1950. *No such relationship was observed.* Thus, McClelland's cross-cultural data suggest that achievement motivation precedes economic growth and that a nation's mean *n* Ach is a barometer of its future economic accomplishments.[2]

Problems with McClelland's Approach   Although McClelland's work seems to imply that achievement motivation is a reliable predictor of achievement behavior at both the individual and the group (or cultural) level, other investigators were having some difficulty replicating his findings. Virginia Crandall (1967), for example, found that children high in *n* Ach outperformed their low-need-achieving age-mates in fewer than half the studies she reviewed. Other studies (reviewed in Winter, 1996) reveal that McClelland's measure of *n* Ach is a better predictor of future success in entrepreneurial activities, such as establishing a business, than it is of success in the sciences or professions. Finally, John Atkinson (1964) noticed that people who actually do accomplish a lot (high achievers) often differed from people who accomplish much less (low achievers) in their *emotional reactions* to achievement contexts: high achievers welcomed new challenges, whereas low achievers seemed to dread them. Why does achievement motivation often fail to forecast achievement behavior? Could there be other, competing motives that make achievement contexts so threatening to some people that their performance is impeded? Atkinson thought so, as we will see in his revision of McClelland's theory.

Atkinson's Revision of Need Achievement Theory   In outlining his theory of achievement motivation, Atkinson (1964) proposed that

> in addition to a general disposition to achieve success [called the **motive to achieve success (M_s)**, or the achievement motive], there is also a general disposition to avoid failure [called **motive to avoid failure (M_{af})**]. Where the motive to achieve success might be characterized as a capacity for reacting with pride in accomplishment, the motive to avoid failure can be conceived as a capacity for reacting with shame and embarrassment

---

[2]This conclusion was strengthened by the results of a second study in which the *n* Ach scores for readers used in 39 countries in the year 1950 predicted the economic growth of those countries between 1952 and 1958 (McClelland, 1961).

when the outcome of performance is failure. When this disposition is aroused in a person, as it is aroused whenever it is clear . . . that his performance will be evaluated and failure is a distinct possibility, the result is anxiety and a tendency to withdraw from the situation. (p. 244)

So Atkinson claimed that a person's tendency to approach or avoid achievement activities depends on the relative strength of *two* competing motives. A person who willingly accepts new challenges and accomplishes a lot was presumed to have a motive to attain success that is considerably stronger than his or her motive to avoid failure (that is, $M_s > M_{af}$). By contrast, the low achiever who shies away from challenges and accomplishes little was thought to have a motive to avoid failure that is stronger than his or her motive to attain success (that is, $M_{af} > M_s$). In Atkinson's theory, then, the relationship between one's achievement motivation (M_s) and achievement behavior is clearly influenced by the strength of the motive to avoid failure (M_{af}).

Is It Worth Accomplishing? The Value of a Particular Goal Atkinson also believed that the *value* a person places on the success he might attain is an important determinant of achievement behavior. Virginia Crandall (1967) agreed. She noted that there are many, many areas in which children might achieve, including schoolwork, sports, hobbies, domestic skills, and making friends, to name a few. Presumably, a child's willingness to set high standards and to work to attain them may differ from area to area depending, in part, on the **achievement value** of accomplishing these objectives or winning recognition for her efforts.

Joel Raynor (1970) tested this hypothesis in an interesting study of introductory psychology students. Each student took McClelland's fantasy measure of *n* Ach (used to define M_s) and the Test Anxiety Questionnaire, an objective paper-and-pencil test that measures one's anxiety about being evaluated (used to define M_{af}). These students also made judgments about how relevant (hence, valuable) they thought their introductory psychology course would be to their future careers. Raynor's major prediction was that students high in achievement motivation (that is, those for whom $M_s > M_{af}$) would do much better in their intro psychology course if they considered the course relevant to their future (high value) as opposed to irrelevant (low value).

Table 7-1 shows the results. As predicted, students for whom $M_s > M_{af}$ (those in the top row) did make significantly *higher* grades if they considered introductory psychology relevant to their future careers. Apparently, achievement motivation is more likely to forecast noteworthy accomplishments when the goals one might attain are considered valuable or important. Notice also that participants for whom $M_{af} > M_s$ actually obtained *lower* grades if their psychology course was considered career relevant. So as Atkinson had suspected, a high fear of failure can actually undermine progress toward *valuable* goals.

We see, then, that one's performance in achievement contexts depends on far more than his or her absolute level of *n* Ach. To predict how a person is likely to fare when faced with a challenge, we also need to know something about (1) the person's fear of failure (M_{af}) and (2) the perceived *value* of success—a *cognitive* variable that differs across individuals and achievement domains and is a crucial determinant of achievement behavior.

Can I Achieve? The Role of Expectancies in Achievement Behavior Finally, Akinson (1964) proposed that a second *cognitive* variable—our expectations of succeeding or failing should we try to achieve an objective—is a critical determi-

motive to achieve success (M_s): Atkinson's term for the disposition describing one's tendency to approach challenging tasks and to take pride in mastering them; analogous to McClelland's need for achievement.

motive to avoid failure (M_{af}): Atkinson's term for the disposition describing one's tendency to shy away from challenging tasks so as to avoid the embarrassment of failing.

achievement value: perceived value of attaining a particular goal should one strive to achieve it.

TABLE 7-1 Mean grade-point averages in introductory psychology as a function of achievement-related motives and the relevance of the course to future careers

ACHIEVEMENT PROFILES	RELEVANCE OF COURSE TO ONE'S FUTURE	
	LOW	HIGH
$M_s > M_{af}$	2.93	3.37
$M_{af} > M_s$	3.00	2.59

NOTE: Mean grade-point averages are computed on a 4.00 scale where A = 4, B = 3, C = 2, D = 1, F = 0.

SOURCE: From Raynor, 1970. Reprinted by permission of the American Psychological Assn.

nant of achievement behavior. He claimed that people are more likely to work hard when they feel that they have a reasonable prospect of succeeding than when they see little chance of attaining a goal. How important are these **achievement expectancies?** Very important, and we can illustrate this point with the following example. Were we to review a massive literature, we would find that IQ is a moderate to strong correlate of academic achievement, with brighter children typically outperforming their average-IQ or low-IQ classmates (Neisser et al., 1996). Yet it is not uncommon for children with high IQs and low academic expectancies to earn *poorer* grades than their classmates with lower IQs but higher expectancies (Battle, 1966; Crandall, 1967; Phillips, 1984). In other words, expectations of success and failure are a powerful determinant of achievement behavior; children who expect to achieve usually do, whereas those who expect to fail may spend little time and effort pursuing goals they believe to be "out of reach" (Heckhausen & Dweck, 1999; Harter, 1988).

Summing Up   In sum, Atkinson's need achievement theory is a significant revision and extension of McClelland's earlier theory—a model which held that individual differences in achievement behavior are primarily attributable to the overall levels of achievement motivation (*n* Ach) that people display. Atkinson's theory is properly classified as a motivational model in that one's willingness to work hard to obtain various objectives is said to depend on the relative strength of two achievement-related motives: the motive to attain success (M_s) and the motive to avoid failure (M_{af}). But Atkinson also claims that two cognitive variables—*expectancies* of success (or failure) and the *value* of various objectives—are every bit as important as the motivational variables in determining our achievement strivings and our actual accomplishments.

Recently, attribution (or social information-processing) theorists have focused more extensively on cognitive determinants of achievement in general and on the origins of achievement expectancies in particular. Let's now turn to the attributional perspective to see what it can tell us about children's propensities for achievement.

WEINER'S ATTRIBUTION THEORY

Earlier in this chapter and throughout the text, we have noted that infants and toddlers are apt to view themselves as efficacious and to master many challenges when they have had ample opportunities to *control* their environments—that is, to regulate the behavior of responsive companions and to satisfy other objectives, such as successfully operating age-appropriate toys. Just how important is this sense of personal control to children's achievement expectancies and to the value they are likely to attach to their successes and failures?

Bernard Weiner (1974, 1986) has proposed an attributional theory of achievement which claims that a person's achievement behavior depends very critically on how he interprets prior successes and failures and on whether he thinks he can *control* these outcomes. Weiner believes that human beings are active information processors who will sift through the data available to them and formulate explanations, or **causal attributions,** for their achievement outcomes. What kinds of attributions will they make? Though they might not always use these precise labels, Weiner argues that people are likely to attribute their successes or failures to any of four causes: (1) their *ability* (or lack thereof), (2) the amount of *effort* expended, (3) the *difficulty* (or easiness) of the task, or (4) the influence of *luck* (either good or bad).

Notice that two of these causes, ability and effort, are *internal* causes, or qualities of the individual, whereas the other two, task difficulty and luck, are *external* or environmental factors. This grouping of causes along an "internal-external" dimension follows from Virginia Crandall's earlier research on a dimension or personality called **locus of control** (Crandall, 1967). Individuals with an *internal locus of control* assume

achievement expectancies: cognitive expectations of succeeding or failing at a particular achievement-related activity.

causal attributions: conclusions drawn made about the underlying causes of one's own or another person's behavior.

locus of control: personality dimension distinguishing people who assume that they are personally responsible for their life outcomes (internal locus) from those who believe that their outcomes depend more on circumstances beyond their control (external locus).

that they are personally responsible for what happens to them. If they received an A grade on an essay, they would probably attribute the mark to their superior writing ability or to their own hard work (internal causes). Individuals with an *external locus of control* believe that their outcomes depend more on luck, fate, or the actions of others than on their own abilities or efforts. They might say that an A grade was due to luck (the teacher happened to like this one), indiscriminate grading, or some other *external* cause. Crandall proposed that an internal locus of control is conducive to achievement: Children must necessarily believe that *they* can produce positive outcomes if they are to strive for success and become high achievers. Children with an external locus of control were not expected to strive for success or to become high achievers because they assume that their efforts do not necessarily determine their outcomes.

Children's locus of control is often measured by administering the Intellectual Achievement Responsibility Questionnaire, a 34-item scale that taps one's perceptions of responsibility for pleasant and unpleasant outcomes. Each item describes an achievement-related experience and asks the child to select either an internal or an external cause for that experience (see Figure 7.1 for sample items). The more "internal" responses the child selects, the higher will be his internality score. Children who choose few internal responses are classified as externalizers.

In their review of more than 100 studies, Maureen Findley and Harris Cooper (1983) found that internalizers do earn higher grades and will typically outperform externalizers on standardized tests of academic achievement. In fact, one rather extensive study of minority students in the United States revealed that children's beliefs in internal control were a better predictor of their academic achievements than were their *n* Ach scores, their parents' child-rearing practices, or the type of classroom and teaching styles to which these students had been exposed (Coleman et al., 1966). So Crandall was right in assuming that a willingness to take personal responsibility for one's successes is conducive to achievement behavior.

How, then, does Weiner's theory differ from Crandall's earlier ideas about locus of control? The answer is straightforward: Weiner claims that the four possible causes for achievement outcomes also differ along a *stability* dimension. Ability and task difficulty are relatively stable or unchangeable. If you have high verbal ability today, you'll have roughly the same high ability tomorrow; and if a particular kind of verbal problem is particularly difficult, similar problems are also likely to be difficult. By contrast, the amount of effort one expends on a task or the workings of luck are variable, or unstable, from situation to situation. So Weiner classifies the four possible causes for successes and failures along *both* a locus of causality and a stability dimension, as shown in Table 7-2.

1. *If a teacher passes you to the next grade, it would probably be*
   _____a. because she liked you or
   *_____b. because of the work that you did

2. *When you do well on a test at school, it is more likely to be*
   *_____a. because you studied for it
   _____b. because the test was especially easy

3. *When you read a story and can't remember much of it, it is usually*
   _____a. because the story wasn't well written or
   *_____b. because you weren't interested in the story

*Denotes the "internal" response for each sample item.

FIGURE 7.1 Sample items from the Intellectual Achievement Responsibility Questionnaire. (From V. C. Crandall, *Intellectual Achievement Responsibility Questionnaire.* Wright State University School of Medicine, Yellow Springs, Ohio.)

PHOTO 7.3 If youngsters believe they are personally responsible for their successes, they are more likely to become high achievers.

Contributions of "Stability" and "Locus of Control" Attributions to Future Achievement Behavior Why is it important to consider both *locus* of causality and *stability* to classify causal attributions? Simply because each of these judgments has different

TABLE 7-2   Weiner's classification of the causes of achievement outcomes (and examples of how you might explain a terrible test grade)

| | LOCUS OF CAUSALITY | |
	INTERNAL CAUSE	EXTERNAL CAUSE
Stable Cause	*Ability* "I'm hopeless in math."	*Task difficulty* "That test was incredibly hard and much too long."
Unstable Cause	*Effort* "I should have studied more instead of going out to the concert."	*Luck* "What luck! Every question seemed to be about the days of class I missed."

consequences. According to Weiner, the stability dimension determines achievement *expectancies:* Outcomes attributed to stable causes lead to stronger expectancies than those attributed to unstable causes. To illustrate, a *success* that you attribute to your high ability leads you to confidently predict similar successes in the future. Had you attributed that same success to an unstable cause that can vary from situation to situation (such as effort or luck), you should not be quite so confident of future successes. Conversely, *failures* attributed to stable causes that we can do little about (such as low ability or task difficulty) also lead to strong expectancies—this time to negative expectancies that lead us to anticipate similar failures in the future. By contrast, attributing a failure to an unstable cause (such as not trying very hard) allows for the possibility of improvement and hence, a less negative expectancy.

If the perceived stability of an achievement-related outcome determines achievement expectancies, what role does locus of causality (or control) play? According to Weiner, judgments about the internality or externality of an outcome determine its *value* to the perceiver. Presumably, successes are most valuable when attributed to *internal* causes such as hard work or high ability, and few of us would feel especially proud if we succeeded because of external causes such as blind luck or a ridiculously easy task. Yet, *failures* attributed to internal causes (especially to low ability) can be damaging to our self-esteem and may make us less inclined to strive for future success. Clearly, it seems fruitless to work hard to reverse a poor grade if we think we have little ability in the subject matter; in fact, the course may suddenly seem less valuable or important, and we might be inclined to drop it. But if we can attribute our poor mark to an *external* cause such as bad luck or an ambiguous exam, the failure should not make us feel especially critical of ourselves or necessarily undermine our feelings about the value of the course.

Perhaps you can see that it is adaptive to attribute our successes to high ability, for this internal and stable attribution causes us to *value* what we have accomplished and leads us to *expect* we can repeat our successes. By contrast, it is more adaptive to attribute *failures* to low effort (rather than low ability) because effort is unstable and we are more likely to believe that we can do better in the future if we just try harder.

In sum, Weiner's attribution model is like Atkinson's theory in stressing the importance of two cognitive variables: achievement expectancies and achievement value. But Weiner's approach assigns a primary role to the cognitive variables. Presumably, the perceived locus of causality for achievement outcomes affects our *valuation* of these successes and failures, whereas our attributions about the stability of these outcomes affect our *achievement expectancies.* Together, these two judgments (expectancy and value) determine our willingness (motivation) to undertake similar achievement-related activities in the future (see Figure 7.2 for a schematic overview of Weiner's theory).

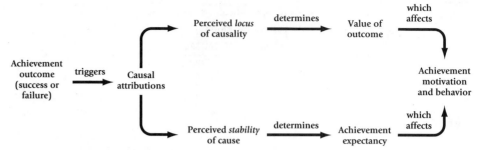

FIGURE 7.2 An overview of Weiner's attribution theory of achievement.

Age Differences in Achievement-Related Attributions If it seems to you as if Weiner's theory sounds a little too cognitive and too abstract to explain the achievement attributions that young children display, you would be right. Before age 7 or so, children tend to be unrealistic optimists who think they have the ability to succeed on almost any task, even those they have repeatedly failed to master in the past (Stipek & Mac Iver, 1989). Preschool and primary-grade teachers may contribute to this rosy optimism by setting mastery goals and by praising children more for their efforts than for the quality of their work, thus leading them to believe that they can accomplish much and "be smart" by working hard (Rosenholtz & Simpson, 1984; Stipek & Mac Iver, 1989). Indeed, 7-year-olds often equate effort expended with ability. They may say, for example, that John, who spent four hours at a task, is smarter than Jose, who accomplished the same result in only two hours; or they may claim that two children who expend the same amount of effort should achieve equal outcomes (see Nicholls & Miller, 1984; Nicholls, 1989). In fact, young children seem to adopt an **incremental view of ability:** They believe that ability is changeable, not stable, and that they can get smarter or become more capable through increased effort and lots of practice (Droege & Stipek, 1993; Dweck & Leggett, 1988).

Of course, we adults generally view effort and ability as *inversely related,* saying, for example, that John must have less ability than Jose if he had to expend twice as much effort to accomplish the same end. And judging from Weiner's (1982, 1986) findings, young adults see ability as more stable over time than young children do. So when do children begin to distinguish ability from effort? When do they move toward an **entity view of ability**—a perspective that ability is a fixed or stable trait that is not influenced much by effort or practice? It turns out that many 8- to 12-year-olds are beginning to distinguish effort from ability (Nicholls & Miller, 1984; Pomerantz & Ruble, 1997) due, in part, to cognitive development—particularly their concrete-operational ability to simultaneously classify objects, events, and outcomes on more than one dimension.

However, social experiences—especially the changing character of experiences at school—also contribute greatly to changes in children's thinking about ability and effort. Elementary schoolteachers gradually place more and more emphasis on *ability* appraisals; they assign grades that reflect the quality of work students perform rather than the amount of effort expended, and these performance evaluations are supplemented by such competitive activities as science fairs, spelling bees, and flash card contests, which also place a premium on the speed or *quality* rather than the quantity of students' work. Furthermore, older grade-school children are often placed into "ability groups" based on the teacher's appraisal of their competencies (Rosenholtz & Simpson, 1984; Stipek & Mac Iver, 1989). So all these practices, coupled with children's increased use of social comparison to appraise their outcomes (Pomerantz et al., 1995), help to explain why older grade-school students begin to distinguish effort

incremental view of ability: belief that one's ability can be improved through increased effort and practice.

entity view of ability: belief that one's ability is a highly stable trait that is not influenced much by effort or practice.

from ability and begin to make the kind of causal attributions for their successes and failures that Weiner's theory anticipates.

Interestingly, the late elementary school period (fourth to sixth grades) is also the time when many students begin to value academic achievement less and to develop rather negative academic self-concepts, a trend that becomes even stronger during the junior high school years (Butler, 1999; Eccles, Wigfield et al., 1993; Seidman et al., 1994). And as we are about to see, children's tendencies to distinguish ability and effort and to adopt an *entity view* of ability are major contributors to these trends.

DWECK'S LEARNED HELPLESSNESS THEORY

Carol Dweck and her colleagues (Dweck & Elliott, 1983; Dweck & Leggett, 1988) find that middle school children clearly differ in the attributions they offer for their achievement outcomes—particularly for their failures. Some children are **mastery-oriented**: They attribute their successes to their high ability but tend to externalize the blame for their failures ("That test was ambiguous and unfair") or attribute them to *unstable* causes that they can easily overcome ("I'll do better if I try harder"). These students are called "mastery oriented" because they persist in the face of failure, believing that their increased effort will ultimately allow them to succeed. Although they see their ability as a reasonably stable attribute that doesn't fluctuate radically from day to day (which allows them to feel confident about repeating their successes), they still think they can eventually improve their competencies (an *incremental* viewpoint) by trying harder after failures. So mastery-oriented youngsters are highly motivated to "master" new challenges, regardless of whether they have previously succeeded or failed at similar tasks (see Figure 7.3).

mastery orientation: a tendency to persist at challenging tasks because of a belief that one has high ability and/or that earlier failures can be overcome by trying harder.

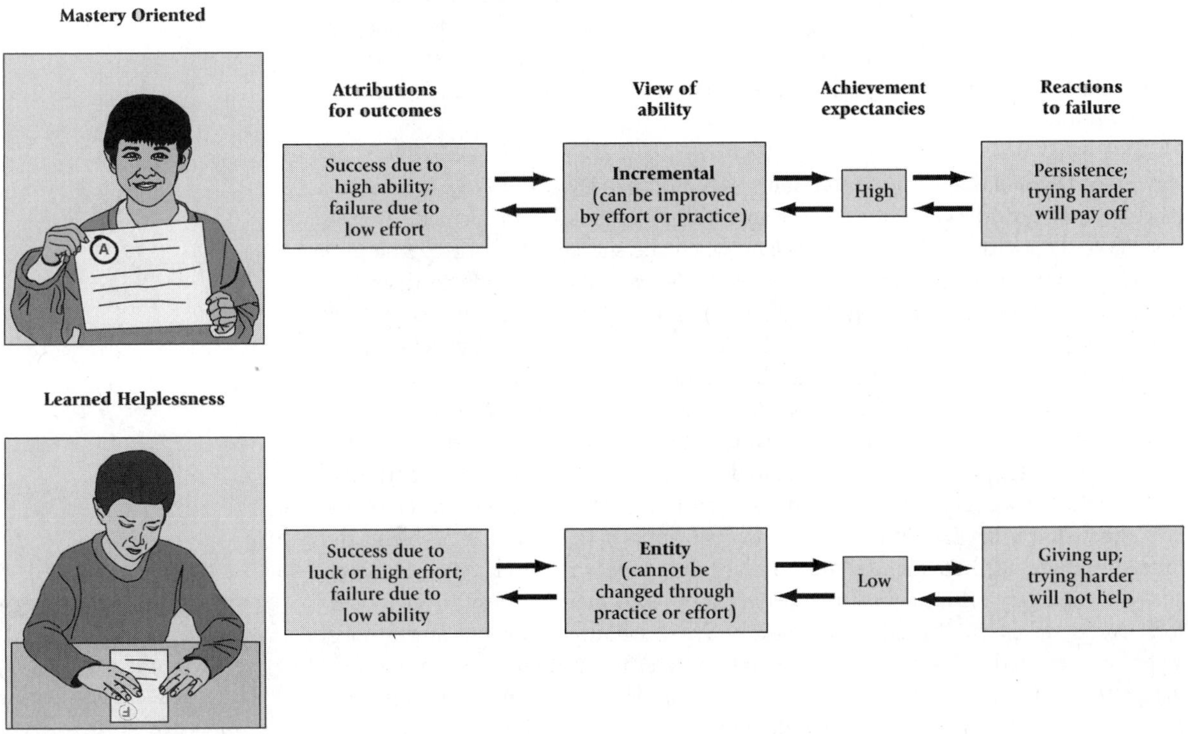

FIGURE 7.3 Characteristics of the mastery-oriented and learned-helplessness achievement orientations.

By contrast, other children often attribute their successes to the *unstable* factors of hard work or luck; they do not experience the pride and self-esteem that come from viewing themselves as highly competent. Yet, they often attribute their failures to a stable and internal cause—namely, their *lack of ability*—which leads them to form low expectations of future successes and to give up. It appeared to Dweck as if these youngsters were displaying a **learned helplessness orientation:** If failures are attributed to a *stable* cause—lack of ability—that the child thinks he can do little about (an *entity view* of ability), he becomes frustrated and sees little reason to try to improve. So he stops trying and acts helpless (see Figure 7.3).

Notice that children who give up after a failure may do so because they either believe (1) *they* personally have no *control* over their ability or (2) that ability is a fixed *capacity* that is unrelated to effort expenditure. To determine which of these impressions might contribute most to a helpless orientation, Eva Pomerantz and Diane Ruble (1997) first assessed the beliefs of second- through fifth-graders about the *controllability* of ability (for example, Can you change how smart you are?) and their impressions that ability is a *capacity* distinct from amount of effort one expends (for example, How come two kids get the same score if one tried hard and the other didn't?). These children then worked at some very difficult memory tasks, at which they initially failed, and their subsequent efforts to master these tasks were recorded. The results were clear. The perception that low ability was *uncontrollable* was the best predictor of giving up and not working hard in the face of failure. However, such performance deficits were greatest among children who also viewed ability as a personal *capacity,* quite apart from effort expenditure (see also Butler, 1999). According to Pomerantz & Ruble, "It may be that children who conceive of ability as [both] uncontrollable *and* as [a fixed] capacity feel that effort [after failing] is futile and . . . that exerting it only signals incompetence" (p. 1177).

It is also important to note that children who come to display helpless orientations are *not* merely the least competent members of a typical classroom. Instead, even highly talented students may adopt this unhealthy attributional style, which, once established, tends to persist over time and will eventually undermine their academic performances in subjects for which they feel helpless (Fincham, Hokoda & Sanders, 1989; Phillips, 1984).

How Does Learned Helplessness Develop?   According to Dweck (1978), parents and teachers may unwittingly foster the development of a helpless achievement orientation if they praise the child for *working hard* when she succeeds but criticize her *lack of ability* when she fails. Apparently even 4- to 6-year-olds can begin to develop a helpless orientation if their failures are often punished or otherwise criticized in ways that cause them to doubt their abilities (Burhans & Dweck, 1995; Heyman, Dweck, & Cain, 1992). By contrast, if parents and teachers praise the child's *abilities* when she succeeds but emphasize her *lack of effort* when she fails, the child may conclude that she is certainly smart enough and would do even better if she tried harder—the viewpoint adopted by mastery-oriented youngsters. In one clever experiment, Dweck and her associates (1978) demonstrated that fifth-graders who received the *helplessness-producing* pattern of evaluation while working at unfamiliar problems did indeed begin to attribute their failures to a lack of ability, whereas classmates who received the *mastery-oriented* evaluative pattern attributed their failures to a lack of effort, saying, in effect, "I need to try harder." These strikingly different attributional styles were created in less than one hour in this experiment, thus implying that similar patterns of evaluative feedback from parents or teachers, given consistently over a period of months or years, might well contribute to the development of the contrasting "helpless" and "mastery" orientations so often observed among grade-school (and older) students.

learned helplessness orientation: a tendency to give up or to stop trying after failing because these failures have been attributed to a lack of ability that one can do little about.

On Helping the Helpless to Achieve   Obviously, giving up as soon as one begins to founder is not the kind of achievement orientation that adults would hope to encourage. What can be done to help these "helpless" children to persist at tasks they have failed? According to Dweck, one effective therapy might be a form of **attribution retraining** in which children are persuaded to attribute their failures to unstable causes—namely insufficient effort—that they can do something about rather than continuing to view them as stemming from their lack of ability, which is not so easy to change.

Dweck (1975) tested her hypothesis by exposing children who had become "helpless" after failing a series of tough math problems to either of two "therapies." Over a period of 25 therapy sessions, half the children received a *success-only* therapy in which they worked problems they could solve and received tokens for their successes. The other half received *attribution retraining*—they experienced nearly as many successes over the 25 sessions as did the children in the other group but were also told after each of several prearranged failures that they had not worked fast enough and *should have tried harder.* Thus, an explicit attempt was made to convince these youngsters that failures can reflect a lack of effort rather than a lack of ability. Did this therapy work? Yes, indeed! At the end of the experiment, "helpless" children in the attribution-retraining condition now performed much better on the tough math problems they had initially failed; and when they did fail one, they usually attributed their outcome to a lack of effort and tried all the harder. By contrast, children in the success-only condition showed no such improvements, giving up once again after failing the original problems. So merely showing children who act helpless that they are capable of succeeding is not enough! To alleviate learned helplessness, one must teach children to respond more constructively to their *failures* by viewing these experiences as something they can overcome if they try harder.

Can we do better than this? Certainly we can by taking steps to *prevent* learned helplessness from developing. Parents and teachers can play a major part in these preventive efforts by simply praising the child's *abilities* when she succeeds and taking care not to undermine her self-worth by suggesting that failures reflect a lack of ability (Burhans & Dweck, 1995). In addition, the research presented in Box 7.1 implies that we might go a long way toward preventing learned helplessness with a little restructuring of classroom agendas.

REFLECTIONS ON THEORIES OF ACHIEVEMENT

Our review of four major achievement theories should make it obvious that children's propensities for achievement involve far more than an innate mastery motive or a global need for achievement. Clearly McClelland and his associates made an important contribution by showing that people reliably differ in their *motivation* to achieve and by suggesting how this motive might be nurtured, although their notion that achievement motivation was a global attribute that predicted one's reactions to all achievement tasks now seems badly overstated. Atkinson's revision of need achievement theory pointed to the existence of a competing "motive to avoid failure" that can make people shy away from challenging tasks to avoid the embarrassment of failing. Of course, Atkinson's model also broke important new ground by emphasizing that achievement-related cognitions—namely, one's *expectancies* of succeeding and the *value* of success—are important determinants of achievement behavior. Weiner's later attribution theory, which grew out of Crandall's earlier work on locus of control, has illustrated how our explanations, or *causal attributions,* for achievement outcomes contribute to our achievement expectancies and to the perceived value of our success and failure experiences. Finally, Dweck's learned helplessness theory takes us back to the starting point by demonstrating how

attribution retraining: therapeutic intervention in which helpless children are persuaded to attribute failures to their lack of effort rather than a lack of ability.

Box 7.1   *Applying Developmental Research*

On Restructuring Achievement Goals to Minimize (or Prevent) Learned Helplessness

Theory Regardless of whether they are pursuing academic or social objectives, children with different achievement orientations tend to pursue different kinds of goals (Elliott & Dweck, 1988; Erdley et al., 1997). Mastery-oriented children generally adopt **learning goals** by which they seek to *increase their abilities.* Their failures are actually diagnostic, telling them that they need to change their approach and keep working in order to master new skills. By contrast, children with a learned helplessness orientation generally adopt **performance goals:** They are motivated to *display their competencies* and will give up on experiencing difficulties because their performance goal has been immediately undermined. Would children who are prone to helplessness be more persistent at achievement tasks if they adopted a "learning goal" to *improve* their abilities—a goal that is not immediately undermined by an early mistake or two?

Research To test the plausibility of their goal-based model of helplessness, Elaine Elliott and Carol Dweck had fifth-graders perform a novel task, led them to believe they had either high or low ability at this kind of activity, and then told them they would soon be performing similar tasks, some of which would be rather difficult (thus leading the children to anticipate errors). Half the children worked under a *performance goal,* having been told that their performances were going to be compared with the performances of other kids and evaluated by an expert. The remaining children were induced to adopt a *learning goal* by instructions suggesting that although they would make many mistakes, working at the tasks would "sharpen the mind" and help them at school. As anticipated, children made many errors on the new tasks they performed. And also, as anticipated, the only children who displayed telltale signs of helplessness (that is, deteriorating performance,

low ability attributions) were those who thought they had low ability *and* were pursuing a *performance* goal. By contrast, even "low ability" students persisted after initial failures and showed remarkably little distress if they were pursuing a learning goal in which the focus was on *improving* their competencies rather than displaying them.

Applications As presently structured, most classrooms stress performance goals and foster the development of an *entity view* of ability—a notion that ability is stable and largely unchangeable. Students undertake the same assignments, their performances are compared, and they receive recognition (praise, gold stars, grades, and the like) that places undue attention on their relative abilities—information that seems to undermine many students' intrinsic interest in the subject matter (Butler 1989, 1990) and may seriously depress the perceived competencies and self-esteem of slower learners, who compare so unfavorably with their peers (Butler 1992; Pomerantz et al., 1995). Might we prevent these undesirable consequences by restructuring classroom goals—by emphasizing *individual mastery* of particular learning objectives (learning goals) rather than continuing to place children in direct competition (as teachers often do by saying "Let's see who can . . . finish first, come up with the best answer," and so on) and making comparative appraisals of their progress? Many developmentalists think so (see Butler, 1990, 1999; Stipek & Mac Iver, 1989). Such a focus on mastering new skills *for their own sake* should be particularly beneficial to the slower learners, who should begin to view their initial mistakes as evidence that they must change strategies and keep working to *improve* their competencies (an *incremental view* of ability) rather than treating these errors as proof that they have little ability and simply cannot master their assignments.

---

well-ingrained attributional styles affect children's *motivation* to persist at challenging tasks that they have initially failed to master. So, as we concluded when reviewing the various theories of attachment in Chapter 4, it makes no sense to brand any single achievement theory as "correct" and to ignore the others. Each of these theories has helped us to understand why children differ so dramatically when responding to the challenges they face.

learning goal: state of affairs in which one's primary objective in an achievement context is to increase one's skills or abilities.

performance goal: state of affairs in which one's primary objective in an achievement context is to display one's competencies (or to avoid looking incompetent).

Cultural and Subcultural Influences on Achievement

INDIVIDUALISTIC VERSUS COLLECTIVISTIC PERSPECTIVES ON ACHIEVEMENT

There is now ample evidence that a child's cultural heritage affects his or her orientation toward achievement. In *individualistic* societies such as the United States, Canada, and the countries of Western Europe, child-rearing practices promote self-reliance and individual assertion, and children are given a great deal of freedom to pursue *personal* (and often highly creative) objectives. By contrast, *collectivist* societies in Africa, Asia, and Latin America emphasize the importance of maintaining social harmony and pursuing goals that are considered honorable by other members of one's social network and/or that maximize *social* welfare (Berry et al., 1992; Triandis, 1995). How might these diverse cultural values affect people's reactions to achievement tasks?

Consider first a cross-cultural study that challenged people to make correct judgments about visual stimuli when access to social norms were available (Berry, 1967). Participants were Arctic Eskimos, members of an individualistic society who are forced by their geography to hunt and fish for a living, and the Temne of Sierra Leone, a collectivist people whose livelihood depends on their pulling together to successfully plant, harvest, and ration a single crop (rice). Individuals from each culture were asked to make comparisons among lines that differed in length. For each comparison, the participant was shown a standard line and eight test lines. The participant's task was to select the test line that was the same length as the standard. Before each judgment, the experimenter presented fictitious group norms by telling the subject "Most Temne (Eskimo) people say this line [an incorrect choice] is equal in length to the standard." The incorrect line that was five lines away from the correct one served as the contrived group norm for each trial (see Figure 7.4). The distance of the participant's choice away from the correct line and in the direction of the contrived norm served as a measure of conformity for that trial. A total conformity score was determined by simply adding across trials the number of lines a participant's choices were away from the correct lines.

The top line on the stimulus card is the standard. On each trial, the subject is informed that one of the other lines (designated here by the asterisk) was most often perceived to be the same length as the standard by members of a reference group. The correct choice for this card is the second line from the bottom.

FIGURE 7.4   A common method of measuring conformity to group norms. (Adapted from Berry, 1967.)

As expected, Berry found that the Temne largely conformed to the contrived group norms, whereas the Eskimos disregarded normative information and displayed their independence by selecting the correct lines (or lines very close to the correct ones). One Temne illustrated the cultural roots of his conformity by stating "When Temne people choose a thing, we must all agree with the decision—that is what we call cooperation" (Berry, 1967, p. 417). Eskimo participants spoke infrequently while making their judgments, although they sometimes flashed confident smiles as they rejected the group norm in favor of a line much nearer to the correct one.

Cultural differences in children's achievement orientations are especially clear in so-called *mixed-motive* contexts that pit self-interest against that of the group. A mixed-motive game is one in which participants can choose either to compete or to cooperate to earn enough points or credits to win a valuable prize; but unknown to them, the only way for any player to earn a prize is for all of them to begin to cooperate early on and to continue to cooperate until they reach their objective. Children from a collectivist society (Mexico), who are taught to cooperate, clearly outperform their more competitive Mexican-American and European-American age-mates at these mixed-motive challenges (Kagan & Masden, 1971, 1972). In fact, many 7- to 9-year-old American children are already so competitive in mixed-motive contexts that on discovering that they can't win a prize, they then seek to lower their partner's score (with the apparent objective of "beating" him or her at a personal contest).

We see, then, that people from different cultures do think of achievement in very different ways. To a person from a collectivist culture, achievement implies that one must suppress individualism and pull together with partners or co-workers to work for the greater good of the group. By contrast, people from more individualistic cultures are much more likely to stress individual accomplishments and evidence of *personal merit* as indications that one has achieved.

Of course, an emphasis on individualism or collectivism is only one of many general beliefs that vary across cultures and influence children's achievement orientations. To cite another example, there are clear cultural differences in the connections that people make between effort and achievement: Compared to American mothers, Chinese and Japanese mothers believe that scholastic achievement is far more dependent on the amount of effort a child expends than on his or her innate intelligence (Stevenson & Lee, 1990). In other words, Asian parents adopt more of an *incremental* perspective on ability than American parents do—a perspective that seems to carry over to their children and may prevent Asian youngsters from acting helpless when they experience difficulties with their lessons. We will explore this intriguing cultural difference in more detail when we consider the topic of schooling and scholastic influences in Chapter 12.

ETHNIC VARIATIONS IN ACHIEVEMENT

Several recent reviews of the literature suggest that there are clear ethnic variations in achievement—at least in the area of academic achievement, which has been most heavily studied. Although there are tremendous individual differences *within* any ethnic group, African-American, Native American, and Latino children tend to earn poorer grades at school and lower scores on standardized scholastic achievement tests than their European-American classmates, whereas Asian-Americans (particularly recent immigrants) tend to outperform European-Americans at school (Chen & Stevenson, 1995; Fuligni, 1997; Slaughter-Defoe et al., 1990). These racial and ethnic differences in academic achievement are reduced substantially when ethnic variations in socioeconomic status are controlled, but they are still detectable nonetheless (Alexander & Entwisle, 1988; Pungello et al., 1996; Sue & Okazaki, 1990). Why then, do such differences exist?

One early hypothesis was that ethnic differences in scholastic achievement reflect group differences in intelligence. Indeed, students from underachieving ethnic minority groups do perform at lower levels on IQ tests than European-American or Asian-American students (Neisser et al., 1996). But recent research suggests that much (perhaps a large majority) of ethnic variations in IQ-test performance is really a hidden social-class effect, and that minority and majority students raised in comparable environments score at about the same levels on IQ tests (Brooks-Gunn et al., 1996; Scarr & Weinberg, 1983; Waldman et al., 1994). And even when their tested cognitive abilities on entering school are comparable to their European-American classmates, children from underachieving ethnic minorities are often lagging behind in academic achievement by the end of the first grade (Alexander & Entwisle, 1988). So it seems that factors other than intellectual differences must figure prominently in explaining ethnic variations in academic achievement.

Yet another explanation for ethnic variations in achievement is that a larger percentage of students from underachieving ethnic minority groups are from lower socioeconomic backgrounds—a factor that we will see is associated with poorer academic performance. In other words, the argument was that ethnic variations in scholastic achievement, like ethnic variations in IQ, largely represent social-class effects. Consistent with this viewpoint, Charlotte Patterson and her associates (1990) found that variation in family income (an indicator of socioeconomic status) is a better predictor of the academic competencies of African-American and white school children than is race per se. Still, *even after controlling for social class,* African-American students did not perform as well academically as their white classmates. Why is this?

Certainly *not* because their parents devalue the importance of schooling or academic achievement. African-American and Latino-American parents seem to value education at least as much as (if not more than) European-American parents do (Galper, Wigfield, & Seefeldt, 1997; Steinberg et al., 1992), and they are actually more likely to appreciate the value of homework, competency testing, and a longer school day (Stevenson, Chen, & Uttal, 1990). Today many developmentalists believe that ethnic variations in academic achievement may be attributable not so much to differences in parental attitudes about the value of education as to (1) subtle subcultural differences in parenting practices, (2) differences across ethnic groups in peer endorsement of academics, and (3) the negative influence of social stereotypes on academic performance.

Ethnic Variations in Parenting   Subtle differences in parenting across ethnic groups may well influence children's propensity for achievement, even when the families studied are of the same socioeconomic status. Elsie Moore (1986), for example, found that African-American and European-American mothers from middle-class families clearly differed as they monitored their children's reactions to a tough cognitive challenge. In general, children from European-American homes seemed to enjoy testing sessions, whereas children from the African-American homes did not, often answering questions quickly, as if they hoped to escape from an unpleasant experience. These contrasting reactions appeared to be linked to parenting practices that mothers used while supervising their children's problem-solving activities. Compared with the African-American mothers, European-American mothers provided a great deal of *positive* encouragement. They joked to relieve tension, often cheered when their children showed some progress, and seemed to be conveying an attitude that mastering challenges can be fun. By contrast, African-American mothers were more inclined to try to urge their children onward by showing mild signs of *displeasure* at a child's *lack of progress* (perhaps conveying to the child that tackling challenges involves a risk of disapproval), and their evaluations of their children's performance were somewhat more negative than those of European-American mothers. Perhaps this is why their children were less comfortable during the problem-solving session. In sum, Moore's findings suggest that even when children from different ethnic backgrounds all grow up in advantaged homes, there may still be subtle differences in parenting styles that contribute to ethnic variations in scholastic achievement (see also Alexander & Entwisle, 1988; Slaughter-Defoe et al., 1990; & Stevenson et al., 1990 for further discussion of this point).

Interestingly, Asian-American students often experience a stringent style of parenting that is more similar to the pattern Moore observed of middle-class Black than of White mothers. However, this strict, controlling pattern of parenting, coupled with the *very strong* emphasis on education and *very high* achievement standards that many Asian-American parents set for their children, actually *fosters* academic success. Why? Probably because Asian-American families often retain at least some collectivist values from the family's culture of origin—especially those that specify to Asian-American children that they must remain *respectful* of and *obey* their elders, who have a duty to train them to be socially responsible and competent human beings (Chao, 1994).

Peer Group Influences   Peers are also an important influence on grade-school children and adolescents who may sometimes support and at other times undermine parents' attempts to encourage academic achievement. Peer pressures that interfere with academic achievement may be especially acute for many lower-income African-American and Latino students. Lawrence Steinberg and his colleagues (1992) found that the African-American and Latino peer cultures in many low-income areas actively *discourage* academic achievement, whereas European- and Asian-American peer groups are more inclined to value and encourage it. High-achieving African-American students in some inner city schools actually run the risk of being rejected by their African-American peers if their academic accomplishments cause them to be perceived as "acting white" (Ford & Harris, 1996; Fordham & Ogbu, 1986).

On the other hand, children whose parents value education highly and work hard to promote academic achievement tend to associate with peers who share those values. In his recent study of Latino, East Asian, Filipino, and European immigrant families, Andrew Fuligni (1997) found that immigrant adolescents tend to make higher grades at school than native-born U.S. adolescents do, despite the fact that their parents are not highly educated and often speak little English at home. Why? Because the parents of these high achievers strongly endorsed the value of academics, a value that was clearly reinforced by their friends, who often studied with them, shared class notes, and encouraged them to do well in school. This kind of peer support for parental values also fosters the academic achievement of talented African-American students (Ford & Harris, 1996) and preadolescents in Shanghai, China (Chen, Rubin, & Li, 1997), and is probably a strong contributor to the academic successes of students from any background. Clearly, it is easier to remain focused on academic goals if one is not receiving mixed messages about their value from parents and peers.

Finally, the recent research in Box 7.2 points to a subtle way that negative social stereotypes may undermine the scholastic performance of students from some ethnic minorities—even talented students who are highly motivated to achieve.

SOCIAL CLASS DIFFERENCES IN ACHIEVEMENT

In addition to their membership in particular racial or ethnic groups, children also differ in their social-class standing or **socioeconomic status (SES)**—that is, their positions within a society that is stratified according to status and power. In Western societies, the most common measures of a family's social class—family income, prestige of parents' occupations, and parents' educational levels—are based on the family's current or prior accomplishments. In these cultures, social class is clearly an achievement-related construct, and it is perhaps not surprising to find that children from middle- and upper-class backgrounds score higher in *n* Ach and are more likely to do well in school than children from the lower socioeconomic strata (see Hess, 1970; McLoyd, 1998; Patterson et al., 1990).

As was the case with ethnic variations in achievement, social-class differences in achievement were first attributed to group differences in intelligence. Middle- and upper-class children do tend to score somewhat higher on IQ tests than lower- and working-class youngsters do (Neisser et al., 1996), thus implying that children from the higher socioeconomic strata may have an "intellectual advantage" that contributes to their greater achievements. Nevertheless, most contemporary theorists believe that class-linked variations in parenting and family life are far more important than intelligence in explaining social-class differences in academic achievement. Indeed, it has been argued (and repeatedly shown) that economic hardship creates psychological distress—a strong discomfort and dissatisfaction with life's conditions that makes lower-income adults edgy and irritable and reduces their capacity to be sensitive, supportive, and highly involved in their children's learning activities, either as a direct participant or as a monitor of the child's (or adolescent's) educational progress (Conger et al., 1992, 1995; McLoyd, 1998). What's more, lower-SES homes

socioeconomic status (SES):
one's position within a society that is stratified according to status and power.

stereotype threat: a fear that one will be judged to have traits associated with negative social stereotypes about his or her racial or ethnic group.

Box 7.2   *Focus on Research*

A Threat in the Air: How Social Stereotypes Can Influence Academic Performance

Two students, one Black and the other White, sit next to each other in a college English class. Both are from middle-class families and attended top-flight high schools, where they earned good grades. Yet, the Black student is now flunking out of college, whereas the White student is not. Why is their performance so different?

Claude Steele (1997) believes that the answer may have little to do with race differences in genetics, parenting, social-class, or family dysfunction. Instead, he argues that any member of an ethnic group characterized by such negative stereotypes as "Blacks are less intelligent" or "Latinos are lazy" often experience **stereotype threat** in testing situations—an underlying suspicion that the stereotypes about his social group could be true and a fear that he will be judged to have traits associated with the negative stereotype. Once aroused, this stereotype threat creates a disruptive anxiety that impairs the student's ability to do his best in testing situations. So, according to Steele, a minority group member might still be influenced by a negative stereotype, even if he has publicly proclaimed it to be false.

To test his theory, Steele and Joshua Aronson (1995) administered a very difficult verbal-skills test to older adolescent females after telling them that these problems were either (1) designed to assess their abilities (which might trigger stereotype threat among stigmatized minorities) or (2) simply of interest to the researchers (no stereotype threat). As the figure indicates, African-Americans performed *poorly* when they thought their abilities were being assessed, but performed much better—in fact, *just as well as White students did*—when the test was portrayed as a nonevaluative exercise. In a second study, Steele and Aronson found that simply having Black students indicate their race on the test booklet is sufficient to trigger stereotype threat and undermine test performance.

So it appears that stereotype threat can handicap affected minority students and contribute most importantly to ethnic differences in academic performance. And there is more. Steele (1997) has shown that students who have substantial intrinsic interest in academics but who often experience stereotype threat (and resulting poor performances) can become extremely frustrated and actually *disidentify* with school or with those domains of schooling to which the stereotypes apply, coming to view them as less important to their own life outcomes. This disidentification may thus close the door on many career

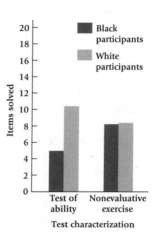

Average performance on a difficult verbal test as a function of race and test characterization. African-American students perform poorly on tests of mental abilities when they think they are taking a test that may result in their being stereotyped as unintelligent. (Adapted from Steele & Aronson, 1995.)

options and even contribute to a decision to drop out of school. How might these vulnerabilities to negative stereotypes be overcome?

One approach that Steele favors is a program in which Blacks and Whites regularly study together, discussing personal and social issues, as well as participating in mastery workshops in their academic subjects. By avoiding self-segregation, these cross-race collaborative programs can help minority students see that students from *all* racial and ethnic backgrounds must often struggle to master their lessons and that members of no race or ethnicity are inherently inferior intellectually to any other—perceptions that should surely go a long way toward defusing stereotype threat. Interestingly, both Black and White college students who have participated in such programs show increases in their grade-point averages, with the improvement being especially striking for Black students (Steele as cited in Woo, 1995). Steele also claims that schools might further reduce stereotype threat by (1) ending remedial programs that set only minimal goals and (2) relying less on those kinds of affirmative-action efforts that, in subtle ways, send minorities the message that they can't compete or succeed without assistance. If there is one single principle, Steele says, it is to "challenge [minorities], don't remediate them. Challenge conveys faith in their [own] potential" (as cited in Woo, 1995).

Box 7.3   *Applying Developmental Research*

Recipes for Effective Compensatory Interventions

Evaluations of compensatory education programs conducted over the past 30 years point strongly to two conclusions: Outcomes can be improved dramatically if (1) disadvantaged children are exposed to compensatory education earlier in life and for longer periods, and (2) ways are found to help parents become more involved in their children's learning activities.

The Importance of Parental Involvement

Regardless of their format, compensatory education programs are almost always more effective when they involve the parents of disadvantaged children in one way or another. Today, many developmentalists favor involving parents through *two-generation interventions* that not only provide disadvantaged children with high-quality preschool education but also provide parents with social support, information about child rearing and other family matters, and the educational and vocational training parents need to lift themselves out of poverty (Ramey & Ramey, 1998).

Victoria Seitz and Nancy Apfel (1994; Seitz et al., 1985) conducted such an intervention, targeting poverty-stricken mothers who had recently delivered their first-born children. Other impoverished mothers and their first-borns received no intervention and served as a control group. Ten years later, Seitz and her associates (1985) followed up on the first-born children of these families. They found that children who had received the compensatory intervention were much more likely than nonparticipants to be making normal scholastic progress

and were much *less* likely to have been retained in a grade or required costly remedial services such as special education. And there was more. In what might be called a *diffusion* effect, the younger siblings of the "intervention" and the "control" participants displayed precisely the same differences in scholastic outcomes that the first-borns did, even though these younger brothers and sisters of program participants had not been born *until after the intervention was over* (Seitz & Apfel, 1994). Apparently, this family intervention made disadvantaged mothers who participated more involved in their children's lives and more confident and effective in their parenting—a change that not only benefited their first-born child who received stimulating preschool care but all their subsequent children as well. It was an effective intervention indeed.

The Importance of Intervening Early

Critics of Head Start and other similar programs argue that it begins too late (often after age 3) and is too brief to have any lasting impact. Indeed, interventions that begin in infancy and last for several years produce more enduring gains in IQ and academic performance.

The Carolina Abecedarian project is one such program (Campbell & Ramey, 1994, 1995). Program children came from families on welfare in which mothers scored far below average in IQ tests. The project provided stimulating day care and (later) compensatory education for eight hours a day, five days a week, starting when partici-

are not as intellectually challenging, on average, as middle-class homes are; yet, when lower-SES parents encourage learning and provide many challenges to master, their children perform much better on IQ tests and later display as much intrinsic interest in scholastic achievement as middle-class youngsters do (Gottfried, Fleming, & Gottfried, 1998; Klebanov et al., 1998).

Influences from outside the family may also contribute to social class differences in academic achievement. For example, teachers often respond in stereotyped ways to children from lower socioeconomic backgrounds, subtly (or not so subtly) communicating that they do not expect them to accomplish as much as their middle-class age-mates (McLoyd, 1998). And as we will see in Chapter 12, even young grade-school children are aware of these teacher expectancies and may begin to perform in class so as to confirm them. So the very people who are charged with educating our youth may contribute to social-class differences in scholastic achievement.

What can be done to improve the educational, and ultimately, the occupational prospects of America's economically disadvantaged children? Perhaps the most enduring legacy of President Lyndon Johnson's War on Poverty of the 1960s is a vari-

Two-generation family interventions that target disadvantaged children and their parents lead to changes in parenting that benefit all children in the family.

pants were 6 to 12 *weeks* old and continuing to age 5. Other children from the same disadvantaged backgrounds did not participate and served as a control group. At regular intervals over the next 15 years, the progress of these two groups of high-risk children was assessed by administering periodic IQ tests and tests of academic achievement. The results were striking. The program participants began to outperform their counterparts in the control group on IQ tests, starting at age 18 months and maintaining this IQ advantage through age 15. Here, then is evidence that high-quality preschool interventions that

begin very early have *lasting* intellectual benefits. They can have lasting educational benefits too, for program participants outperformed the control group in all areas of academic achievement from the third year of school onward (see also Reynolds & Temple, 1998).

Two-generation family interventions and long-term programs such as the Abecedarian project are expensive to administer, and there are critics who claim that they would not be worth the high costs of providing them to all disadvantaged families. However, such an attitude may be "penny wise and pound foolish," for Victoria Seitz and her associates (1985) found that extensive two-generation interventions emphasizing quality day care often pay for themselves by (1) allowing more parents freedom from full-time child care to work, thereby reducing their need for public assistance, and (2) providing the foundation for cognitive growth that enables most disadvantaged children to avoid special education services that cost in excess of $1,500 per pupil per year. And when we consider the long-term economic benefits that could accrue later in life when gainfully employed adult graduates of highly successful interventions pay more taxes than disadvantaged nonparticipants, need less welfare, and are less often maintained at public expense in penal institutions, the net return on each dollar invested in compensatory education could be very impressive indeed.

ety of preschool **compensatory interventions** (*Head Start* being the best known) that were aimed at (1) compensating for the cognitive disadvantages that poverty-stricken children typically display on entering school (see, for example, Stipek & Ryan, 1997) and (2) placing them on a roughly equal footing with their middle-class peers. Long-term follow-ups of some of the better of the early compensatory interventions suggested that they rarely produced any permanent boosts in the IQs of disadvantaged children. However, this does not mean these programs failed, for intervention participants were much more likely than other low-SES nonparticipants to have more positive attitudes about school, to meet their school's basic requirements, and to graduate from high school, while also being less likely to be retained in grade or to require costly special educational services (Barnett, 1993; Darlington, 1991). Indeed, there is now ample reason to believe that the outcomes of compensatory education will be even better in the future (Ramey & Ramey, 1998), as we will see in examining some of the more effective of these programs in Box 7.3.

In sum, a person's propensity for achievement may indeed be influenced by the teachings, attitudes, and values that prevail within his or her culture, subculture, and

compensatory interventions: special educational programs designed to further the cognitive growth and scholastic achievements of disadvantaged children.

socioeconomic niche within society. Yet there are truly dramatic individual differences in achievement within any cultural, ethnic, or socioeconomic group—differences that are heavily influenced by variations in home and family lives.

Home and Family Influences on Achievement

As early as 6 months of age, infants already differ in their willingness to explore the environment and their attempts to control objects, situations, and the actions of other people (Yarrow et al., 1984). Moreover, these early differences in mastery behavior are better predictors of children's intellectual performance at age 2½ than are the children's own first-year scores on infant intelligence tests (Messer et al., 1986). Which infants are most "mastery oriented" early in life? Leon Yarrow and his associates (1984) found that those who scored highest in mastery motivation had parents who frequently provided *sensory stimulation* designed to amuse them and arouse their curiosity—experiences such as tickling, bouncing, games of pat-a-cake, and so on.

Important as these observations may be, instilling a strong will to achieve requires much more than tickling a child or bouncing her on one's knee. Over the years, researchers have identified three especially potent "home" influences on children's mastery/achievement motivation and actual achievement behavior: the quality of the child's attachments, the character of the home environment, and the child-rearing practices that parents use—practices that can either foster or inhibit a child's will to achieve.

QUALITY OF ATTACHMENTS AND ACHIEVEMENT

In Chapter 5, we reviewed a portion of the evidence suggesting that secure attachments to parents promote mastery behaviors. Recall that infants and toddlers who were securely attached to their primary caregivers at ages 12 to 18 months are more likely than those who were insecurely attached to solve problems successfully as 2-year-olds and to display a strong sense of curiosity, self-reliance, and eagerness to solve problems some three to five years later as they enter elementary school. And children whose attachments are secure on entering school tend to remain more self-assured and to do better in school than their insecurely attached peers through middle childhood and into adolescence—even when other factors known to affect academic achievement, such as IQ and social class, are held constant (Jacobsen & Hofmann, 1997). Interestingly, securely attached youngsters are not any more intellectually competent, on average, than their insecurely attached age-mates; instead, they seem more *eager* to *apply* their competencies to the challenges they encounter (Belsky, Garduque, & Hrncir, 1984). So children apparently need the "secure base" provided by a loving, responsive parent to feel comfortable about taking risks and *seeking* challenges.

THE HOME ENVIRONMENT

A young child's tendency to explore, to acquire new skills, and to solve problems will also depend on the character of the home environment and the challenges it provides. Bettye Caldwell and Robert Bradley have developed an instrument called the **HOME Inventory** (*Home Observation for Measurement of the Environment*) that allows a researcher to visit an infant, a toddler, or a preschool child at home and gain a good idea of just how challenging that home environment is (Caldwell & Bradley, 1984). The infant-toddler version of the HOME inventory consists of 45 statements, each of which is scored *yes* (the statement is true of this home) or *no* (the statement is not true of this home). To gather the information to complete the inventory, the researcher

HOME Inventory: a measure of the amount and type of intellectual stimulation provided by a child's home environment.

TABLE 7-3 Subscales and sample items from the HOME inventory (Infant version)

SUBSCALE 1: EMOTIONAL AND VERBAL RESPONSIVITY OF PARENT (11 ITEMS)

Sample Items:	Parent responds verbally to child's vocalizations or verbalizations.
	Parent's speech is distinct, clear, and audible.
	Parent caresses or kisses child at least once.

SUBSCALE 2: AVOIDANCE OF RESTRICTION AND PUNISHMENT (8 ITEMS)

Sample Items:	Parent neither slaps nor spanks child during visit.
	Parent does not scold or criticize child during visit.
	Parent does not interfere with or restrict child more than three times during visit.

SUBSCALE 3: ORGANIZATION OF PHYSICAL AND TEMPORAL ENVIRONMENT (6 ITEMS)

Sample Items:	Child gets out of house at least four times a week.
	Child's play environment is safe.

SUBSCALE 4: PROVISION OF APPROPRIATE PLAY MATERIALS (9 ITEMS)

Sample Items:	Child has a push or pull toy.
	Parent provides learning facilitators appropriate to age—mobile, table and chairs, highchair, playpen, and so on.
	Parent provides toys for child to play with during visit.

SUBSCALE 5: PARENTAL INVOLVEMENT WITH CHILD (6 ITEMS)

Sample Items:	Parent talks to child while doing household work.
	Parent structures child's play periods.

SUBSCALE 6: OPPORTUNITIES FOR VARIETY IN DAILY STIMULATION (5 ITEMS)

Sample Items:	Father provides some care daily.
	Child has three or more books in his or her room.

SOURCE: Adapted from Bradley, 1984.

---

will (1) ask the child's mother to describe her daily routine and child-rearing practices, (2) carefully observe the mother as she interacts with her child, and (3) note the kinds of play materials that the parent makes available for the child. The 45 bits of information collected are then grouped into the six categories, or subscales, in Table 7-3. The home then receives a score on each subscale. The higher the scores across all six subscales, the more challenging the home environment.

Does the quality of the home environment predict children's achievement behavior? To find out, William van Doorninck and his associates (1981) visited the homes of 50 12-month-old infants from economically disadvantaged backgrounds and used the HOME inventory to classify these settings as relatively stimulating (high HOME scores) or unstimulating (low HOME scores). Five to nine years later, the research team followed up on these children by looking at their standardized achievement test scores and the grades they had earned at school. As we see in Table 7-4, the quality of the home environment at age 12 months predicted children's academic achievement several years later. Two out of three children from stimulating homes were then performing quite well at school, whereas 70% of those from unstimulating homes were doing very poorly (see also Bradley, Caldwell, & Rock, 1988). Although White and Piaget may well be correct in claiming that the seeds of mastery motivation are inborn, it seems that the joy of discovery and problem solving is unlikely to blossom in a barren home environment where the child has few problems to solve and limited opportunities for learning.

TABLE 7-4 Relationship between quality of home environment at 12 months of age and children's grade-school academic achievement five to nine years later

QUALITY OF HOME ENVIRONMENT AT AGE 12 MONTHS	ACADEMIC ACHIEVEMENT	
	AVERAGE OR HIGH (TOP 70%)	LOW (BOTTOM 30%)
Stimulating	20 children	10 children
Unstimulating	6 children	14 children

SOURCE: Adapted from Doorninck, Caldwell, Wright, & Frankenberg, 1981.

Interestingly, the scores homes make on the HOME inventory predict the future scholastic motivations and academic achievements of children from all social classes and racial/ethnic groups (Bradley et al., 1989; Gottfried et al., 1998; Luster & Dubow, 1992). And which aspects of the early home environment contribute most to children's achievement propensities? Research consistently reveals that the home subscales measuring "variety of stimulation" the child receives and the "age-appropriateness of play materials" are strong predictors of children's later scholastic achievement—as strong as or stronger than the HOME subscale measuring "parental involvement" (Bradley & Caldwell, 1984b; Gottfried et al., 1994). Why should the variety and age-appropriateness of the child's stimulation be so important? Perhaps because young children who have many *age-appropriate* toys and experiences will acquire a strong sense of mastery as their attempts to control these objects and events regularly prove to be successful. By contrast, toys and activities that are too complex for the child may foster a sense of ineffectiveness and, eventually, a reluctance to try to master new challenges. Of course, these findings in no way minimize the importance of having warm and responsive parents; instead, they simply imply that the amount and variety of age-appropriate stimulation that the child receives at home have an effect on achievement above and beyond that predicted by factors related to parental involvement, such as the quality of the child's attachments.

Of course, the demands that parents make of their child and the ways they respond to her accomplishments can also influence the child's will to achieve. Let's now consider some of the child-rearing practices that seem to encourage (or discourage) the development of a healthy achievement orientation.

CHILD-REARING AND ACHIEVEMENT

What kinds of child-rearing practices foster achievement motivation? In their book *The Achievement Motive,* McClelland et al. (1953) proposed that parents who stress **independence training**—doing things on one's own—and who warmly reinforce such self-reliant behavior will contribute in a positive way to the growth of achievement motivation; and research bears this out (Grolnick & Ryan, 1989; Winterbottom, 1958).

However, Bernard Rosen and Ray D'Andrade (1959) were quick to suggest that direct **achievement training** (encouraging children to do things well) is at least as important to the development of achievement motivation as independence training. To evaluate their hypothesis, Rosen and D'Andrade visited the homes of boys who had tested either high or low in achievement motivation and asked these 9- to 11-year-olds to work at difficult and potentially frustrating tasks—for example, building a tower out of irregularly shaped blocks while blindfolded and using only one hand. To assess the kind of independence and achievement training the boys received at home, the investigators asked parents to watch their son work and give any encouragement or suggestions that they cared to. The results were clear. Both mothers and fathers of high need-achievers *set lofty standards* for their boys to accomplish and were noticeably concerned about the quality of their sons' performance. They gave many *helpful hints* and were *quick to praise* their sons for meeting one of their performance standards. By contrast, parents of low need-achievers (particularly fathers) stressed neither independence nor achievement training. They often told their sons how to perform the tasks and became rather irritated whenever the boys experienced any difficulty. Finally, the high need-achievers tended to outperform the low need-achievers, and they seemed to enjoy the tasks more as well. So it appears that self-reliance, achievement motivation, and achievement behavior are more likely to develop when parents encourage children to do things on their own (offering a hint now and then) and *to do them well*.

Finally, the patterns of praise (or punishment) that accompany the child's accomplishments are also important. Children who seek challenges and display high levels

independence training: encouraging children to become self-reliant by accomplishing goals without others' assistance.

achievement training: encouraging children to do things well—that is, to meet or exceed high standards as they strive to accomplish various objectives.

of achievement motivation have parents who *praise their successes and are not overly critical of an occasional failure;* by contrast, children who shy away from challenges and are low in achievement motivation have parents who are slow to acknowledge their successes (or who do so in a "matter-of-fact" way) and are inclined to *punish* their failures (Burhans & Dweck, 1995; Teeven & McGhee, 1972).

We see, then, that parents of youngsters high in achievement motivation possess three characteristics: (1) They are warm, accepting, and quick to praise the child's accomplishments; (2) they provide guidance and control by setting standards for the child to live up to and then monitoring her progress to ensure that she does; and (3) they permit the child some independence or autonomy, allowing her a say in deciding how best to master challenges and meet their expectations. Diana Baumrind (1973) calls this warm, firm, but democratic parenting an **authoritative parenting**

PHOTO 7.4 Parents who encourage achievement and who respond warmly to successes are likely to raise mastery-oriented children who enjoy challenges.

style—a style that she and others have found to foster positive attitudes about achievement and considerable academic success among grade-school children and adolescents, both in Western societies (Glasgow et al., 1997; Lamborn et al., 1991; Steinberg, Elmen, & Mounts, 1989) and in Asia (Lin & Fu, 1990). If children are encouraged and supported in a positive manner as they tackle their schoolwork, they are likely to enjoy new challenges and feel confident of mastering them (Connell, Spencer, & Aber, 1994). By contrast, parents can undermine a child's school performance and motivation to succeed if they (1) are uninvolved and offer little in the way of guidance or (2) are highly controlling and do such things as nag continually about homework, offer tangible bribes for good grades, or harp incessantly about bad ones (Ginsburg & Bronstein, 1993).

CONFIGURAL INFLUENCES: BIRTH ORDER, FAMILY SIZE, AND CHILDREN'S ACHIEVEMENT BEHAVIOR

We complete our review of home and family influences on achievement with a puzzle. Over the past 40 years, investigators have found that *birth order*—a person's ordinal position among his or her siblings—seems to affect achievement propensities. First-borns are overrepresented among populations of eminent people; they also tend to hold higher educational aspirations than later-borns and to score higher in *n* Ach and on standardized tests of scholastic achievement/aptitude as well (see Paulhus & Shaffer, 1981, and Zajonc & Mullally, 1997, for reviews). The puzzle: How might we explain these birth-order effects?

Carmi Schooler (1972) originally thought the birth-order effect was an artifact that reflected social-class differences in family size. Since low-SES families have more children, a greater percentage of later-borns would come from low-SES backgrounds, where achievement outcomes are not as good (Schooler, 1972). However, other investigators continued to find birth-order differences in achievement *even when the influence of family size and social class were controlled.* One interesting aspect of this latter research is that *family size* also has an effect: the more children in the family, the lower the child's attainments (see Breland, 1974; Kellaghan & MacNamara, 1972).

Why do you think first-borns and children from smaller families tend to outperform later-borns and those from larger families on tests of intellectual aptitude and scholastic achievement? Could it be that first-borns (and children from smaller

authoritative parenting: flexible, democratic style of parenting in which warm, accepting parents provide guidance and control while allowing the child some say in deciding how best to meet challenges and obligations.

families) are smarter than later-borns (and children from larger families)? Might they receive more direct achievement training from parents than later-borns (or children from large families) do? Let's consider this latter, or **parental socialization hypothesis**, first.

Evidence for Parental Socialization Effects   One finding consistent with the parental socialization hypothesis is that parents hold higher achievement expectancies for first-borns than for later-borns (Baskett, 1985). But do these expectancies influence the amount of stimulation and achievement training that parents provide? Indeed they may. Using the HOME inventory, Bradley and Caldwell (1984a) found that the early home environments of first-borns are more challenging and stimulating than those of later-borns. And consider what Mary Rothbart (1971) found when she asked mothers to supervise the performance of their 5-year-olds on a series of achievement tasks. Half the children were first-borns and half were later-borns; to control for family size, all were from two-child families. Rothbart discovered that mothers spent an equal amount of time interacting with first-born and later-born children. However, the quality of the interaction differed: mothers gave more complex technical explanations to the first-borns, put more pressure on first-borns to achieve, and were more concerned about the quality of their performance—perhaps explaining why first-borns outperformed later-borns on all but one of the experimental tasks. So it seems that first-borns are more likely to be challenged as infants and to receive more direct achievement training during the preschool years than later-borns do.

The Mental Mediation (or Confluence) Hypothesis   The **mental mediation hypothesis**—the notion that first-borns (and children from smaller families) may achieve more because they are smarter, on average, than later-borns (and children from large families)—was proposed by Robert Zajonc (1975; and see Zajonc & Mullally, 1997) to explain the remarkable findings of Belmont and Marolla (1973). Analyzing records from nearly 400,000 Dutch soldiers, Belmont and Marolla found that after controlling for social class, family size had a significant effect on IQ: As we see in Figure 7.5, the brightest soldiers tended to come *from smaller families.* When the researchers then looked at the effects of birth order within any given family size, there was a clear birth-order effect: *First-borns outperformed second-borns, who outperformed third-borns,* and so on down the line. These findings are not unique to Dutch soldiers, having now been replicated in samples of males and females from several countries (Zajonc et al., 1979).

Zajonc offers a most interesting explanation for these birth-order and family-size effects. According to his *confluence hypothesis,* a child's intellectual development depends on *the average intellectual level of all family members living at home.* First-borns have a clear advantage because they are initially exposed only to adults, whose intellectual levels are relatively high. By contrast, a second child experiences a less stimulating intellectual environment because she must deal with a cognitively immature older sibling as well as her parents. A third child is further disadvantaged by the presence of *two* relatively immature older siblings. So later-borns and children from larger families were said to achieve less than first-borns and children from small families for one very simple reason: They spend more time in a world of child-sized minds, less time with adults, and have fewer opportunities to maximize their intellectual potential (Zajonc, 1975; Zajonc & Mullally, 1997).

Zajonc's interesting theory has some merit in that studies using the HOME inventory reveal that a household's intellectual climate does seem to depreciate as family size increases (Bradley & Caldwell, 1984a; Gottfried et al., 1994).

parental socialization hypothesis: the notion that first-borns (and children from small families) achieve more than later-borns (and children from large families) because they receive more direct achievement training from their parents.

mental mediation (or confluence) hypothesis: the notion that first-borns (and children from small families) achieve more than later-borns (and children from large families) because their home environments are more conducive to the development of their intellectual potential.

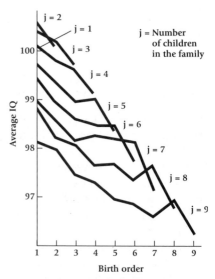

FIGURE 7.5   Average scores on a nonverbal measure of intelligence as a function of the examinee's birth order and the size of his family. Note that subjects from smaller families score higher on this test than subjects from large families. We also see that, within a given family size, children born early tend to obtain higher IQs than those born late. (Adapted from Belmont & Marolla, 1973.)

However other confluence predictions do not always ring true. To cite one example, children who live with only one parent rather than two do not always show the poorer intellectual or academic performances that confluence theory anticipates (Duncan et al., 1994; Entwisle & Alexander, 1990). Note also that the birth-order and family-size effects on IQ that confluence theory seeks to explain are relatively modest (accounting for 3 to 4 IQ points at best) and are detectable only when large numbers of families are compared. So the trends that emerge for the population as a whole may not apply to children within any particular family (such as your own).

Summing Up From our review of the literature, it seems reasonable to conclude that the slightly greater attainments of first-borns and children from small families occur, in part, because these youngsters often receive more *direct achievement training* than later-borns or children from large families. And although first-borns and children from smaller families do tend to score slightly higher in IQ than later-borns and children from large families, it remains for future research to determine whether these small variations in intellectual performance help to explain birth-order and family-size differences in *achievement*.

Now we come to an "achievement" question that will serve as a bridge topic to our next chapter (on sex differences and gender-role development): Are there sex differences in achievement?

On Sex Differences in Achievement and a Look Ahead

How often have you heard the maxims "That's a man's job," "Women are just not suited for this kind of work (activity) (study)," or "A woman's place is in the home"? In the vast majority of the world's societies, men are expected to pursue a career of some sort, while women, if not actively discouraged from harboring these aspirations, are at least trained for the tasks of child care and managing a household. Indeed, this differential gender-typing was one of the reasons that early studies of achievement motivation focused almost exclusively on males, with the assumption that girls, who are trained to be homemakers and mothers first, were simply less inclined than boys to seek challenges for the sheer joy of mastering them (Maccoby & Jacklin, 1974).

Are girls and women any less achievement-oriented than boys and men? The answer to this question really depends on how we define one's propensity for achievement. Let's first correct the myth that girls lack achievement motivation. In one review of studies including participants of both sexes, girls and women actually displayed equivalent or slightly higher scores on the McClelland fantasy measure of n Ach than boys did (Maccoby & Jacklin, 1974). Nor is there any evidence that girls lack the intellectual capacity or any other attribute that would enable them to achieve in the overwhelming majority of endeavors heretofore labeled "masculine" domains (see Halpern, 1997). Yet all too often, these arguments fall on deaf ears. In this regard, it is interesting to note that many girls and women (even college students) believe that they are less capable than men at succeeding in so-called masculine professions involving mathematical and scientific training and that the successes they do achieve in the "masculine" academic subjects are due to their hard work rather than their own abilities (Jacobs & Eccles, 1992; Parsons, Adler, & Kaczala, 1982). Indeed, grade-school girls consistently *underestimate* their academic competencies (particularly in mathematics), whereas boys consistently overestimate theirs (Crandall, 1969; Lummis & Stevenson, 1990).

So are there sex differences in achievement? Historically, there have been—if our criterion for "achieving" is success in traditionally masculine domains such as politics, medicine, law, and science. Yet, the most accurate conclusion we can draw about sex differences in achievement is that men and women have differed in their *areas* of achievement rather than in their needs or capacities for achieving. Even as we enter the 21st century, the occupational aspirations and attainments of young people are still reasonably traditional, with most boys and men pointing to or working at occupations dominated by men and most girls and women being more inclined to select traditionally feminine occupations (U.S. Bureau of the Census, 1997). Indeed, a major focus of our next chapter will be to carefully consider the many, many factors (some of which are subtle and some not so subtle) that underlie and help to perpetuate such gender-typed divisions of labor.

Summary

- A basic aim of socialization is to build on children's **mastery motivation** to encourage them to pursue important objectives and to take pride in their accomplishments.

THE CONCEPT OF ACHIEVEMENT MOTIVATION

- **Achievement motivation** has been conceptualized in very different ways. McClelland regarded it as a learned motive to compete and strive for success (that is the **need for achievement,** or *n* Ach). This viewpoint depicts the high achiever as having an **intrinsic orientation.** However, behavioral theorists view the motivation to achieve as a need to attain social approval and other external incentives; thus, the high achiever has an **extrinsic orientation.**

EARLY REACTIONS TO ONE'S ACCOMPLISHMENTS: FROM MASTERY TO SELF-EVALUATION

- Infants are guided by a mastery motive and take pleasure in their everyday accomplishments. By age 2, toddlers have begun to anticipate others' approval or disapproval of their performances, and children 3 and older evaluate their accomplishments against performance standards and can experience true pride or shame, depending on how successfully they match those standards. For 3½- to 5-year-olds, winning a competition is bliss, but losing is not yet considered a "failure."

THEORIES OF ACHIEVEMENT MOTIVATION AND ACHIEVEMENT BEHAVIOR

- Research testing McClelland's need-achievement theory demonstrated that people reliably differ in achievement motivation (*n* Ach). However, McClelland's notion that this one global motive would predict achievement behaviors in all contexts was badly overstated.

- Atkinson's revision of need-achievement theory pointed to two competing motives—**the motive to achieve success (M_s)** and the **motive to avoid failure (M_{af})**—that influence achievement behavior. Atkinson also broke new ground by stressing that two achievement-related cognitions—**achievement expectancies** and **achievement value**—are important determinants of achievement behaviors.

- Weiner's attribution theory grew out of earlier work on **locus of control** and focused on how the **causal attributions** we make for our successes and failures influence our achievement expectancies and the perceived value of success (or failure).

- Dweck's theory identified two contrasting achievement orientations. **Mastery-oriented** children and adolescents attribute their successes to stable, internal causes (such as high ability) and their failures to unstable causes (lack of effort). They adopt an **incremental view of ability;** consequently, they feel quite competent and will work hard to overcome failures. By contrast, **helpless children** often stop trying after a failure because they display an **entity view of ability** and attribute their failures to a lack of ability that they feel they can do little about. Children who are often criticized for their lack of ability and who feel pressured to adopt **performance goals** rather than **learning goals** are at risk of becoming helpless. Helpless children can become more mastery-oriented if they are taught (through **attribution training**) that their failures can and often should be attributed to unstable causes, such as a lack of effort, that they can overcome by trying harder.

CULTURAL AND SUBCULTURAL INFLUENCES ON ACHIEVEMENT

- One's cultural heritage can clearly affect one's orientation toward achievement. People from *collectivistic* societies are taught to suppress individualism and to work for the greater good of their social groups. By contrast, people from *individualistic* societies are taught to be more self-reliant and will come to stress personal accomplishments as indications of achievement.

- Academic achievement varies as a function of ethnicity and **socioeconomic status (SES).** Subtle differences in parenting style, as well as disruptive peer influences and **stereotype threat,** seem to contribute to the poor academic performances of underachieving ethnic minorities.

■ Regardless of ethnicity, children from disadvantaged backgrounds face serious risks of becoming academic underachievers. **Compensatory interventions,** especially two-generation interventions and/or those that start very early and last throughout the preschool period, can significantly reduce the academic risks that disadvantaged children face.

HOME AND FAMILY INFLUENCES ON ACHIEVEMENT

■ Infants and toddlers who are securely attached to primary caregivers are likely to become curious preschoolers who seek challenges and will later do well at school.

■ Research with the **HOME Inventory** reveals that stimulating home environments that provide young children with a variety of age-appropriate challenges will foster academic achievement in the years ahead.

■ Early **independence training** and **achievement training** promote achievement motivation, particularly if parents warmly reinforce successes and are not overly critical of occasional failures. Parents who combine all these practices into one parenting style (**authoritative parenting**) tend to raise children who achieve considerable academic success.

■ First-borns and children from smaller families display slightly higher n Ach and academic achievement than later-borns and children from large families. The **parental socialization hypothesis**—the notion that first-borns and children from small families receive more achievement training—has received some support. However, the **mental mediation (or confluence)** hypothesis—that later-borns and children from small families *achieve* more because they are smarter—is not strongly supported by existing research.

ON SEX DIFFERENCES IN ACHIEVEMENT AND A LOOK AHEAD

■ Males and females differ in their areas, or domains, of achievement but not in their motivation or their capacities for achievement.

Chapter Eight

Sex Differences, Gender-Role Development, and Sexuality

Categorizing Males and Females: Gender-Role Standards

Some Facts and Fictions About Sex Differences

Actual Psychological Differences Between the Sexes

Cultural Myths

Do Cultural Myths Contribute to Sex Differences in Ability (and Vocational Opportunity)?

Developmental Trends in Gender Typing

Development of the Gender Concept

Development of Gender-Role Stereotypes

Development of Gender-Typed Behavior

Subcultural Variations in Gender Typing

Theories of Gender Typing and Gender-Role Development

Money and Ehrhardt's Biosocial Theory

Freud's Psychoanalytic Theory

Social Learning Theory

Kohlberg's Cognitive-Developmental Theory

Gender Schema Theory

An Integrative Theory

Psychological Androgyny: A Prescription for the Future?

Do Androgynous People Really Exist?

Are There Advantages to Being Androgynous?

Applications: On Changing Gender-Role Attitudes and Behavior

Sexuality and Sexual Behavior

Cultural Influences on Sexuality

Adolescent Sexual Attitudes and Behaviors

Personal and Social Consequences of Adolescent Sexual Activity

Summary

ow important is a child's gender to his or her development? Many people would say "Very important!" Often the first bit of information that parents receive about their child is his or her sex, and the question "Is it a boy or a girl?" is the very first one that most friends and relatives ask when proud new parents telephone to announce the birth of their baby (Intons-Peterson & Reddel, 1984). Indeed, the ramifications of this gender labeling are normally swift in coming and rather direct. In the hospital nursery or delivery room, parents often call an infant son things like "big guy" or "tiger," and they are likely to comment on the vigor of his cries, kicks, or grasps. By contrast, infant daughters are more likely to be labeled "sugar" or "sweetie" and described as soft, cuddly, and adorable (Maccoby, 1980; MacFarlane, 1977). A newborn infant is usually blessed with a name that reflects his or her sex, and in many Western societies, children are immediately adorned in either blue or pink. Mavis Hetherington and Ross Parke (1975, pp. 354–355) describe the predicament of a developmental psychologist who "did not want her observers to know whether they were watching boys or girls":

> Even in the first few days of life some infant girls were brought to the laboratory with pink bows tied to wisps of their hair or taped to their little bald heads. . . . When another attempt at concealment of sex was made by asking mothers to dress their infants in overalls, girls appeared in pink and boys in blue overalls, and "Would you believe overalls with ruffles?"

This gender indoctrination continues during the first year as parents provide their children with "gender-appropriate" clothing, toys, and hairstyles (Pomerleau et al., 1990). They also play differently with and expect different reactions from their young sons and daughters (Caldera, Huston, & O'Brien, 1989). So it is clear that a child's companions view gender as an important attribute—one that often determines how they will respond to him or her.

Why do people react differently to males and females—especially *infant* males and females? One explanation centers on the biological differences between the sexes. Recall that fathers determine the sex of their offspring. A zygote that receives an X chromosome from each parent is a genetic (XX) female that will develop into a baby girl, whereas a zygote that receives a Y chromosome from the father is a genetic (XY) male that will normally assume the appearance of a baby boy. Could it be that this basic genetic difference between the sexes is ultimately responsible for *sex differences in behavior*—differences that might explain why parents often do not treat their sons and daughters alike? We explore this interesting idea in some detail in a later section of the chapter.

However, there is more to sex differences than biological heritage. Virtually all societies expect males and females to behave differently and to assume different roles. To conform to these expectations, the child must understand that he is a boy or that she is a girl and must incorporate this information into his or her self-concept. In this chapter we concentrate on the interesting and controversial topic of **gender typing**—the process by which children acquire not only a gender identity but also the motives, values, and behaviors considered appropriate in their culture for members of their biological sex.

We begin the chapter by summarizing what people generally believe to be true about sex differences in cognition, personality, and social behavior. As it turns out, some of these beliefs have an element of truth to them, although many others are best described

gender typing: the process by which a child becomes aware of his or her gender and acquires motives, values, and behaviors considered appropriate for members of that sex.

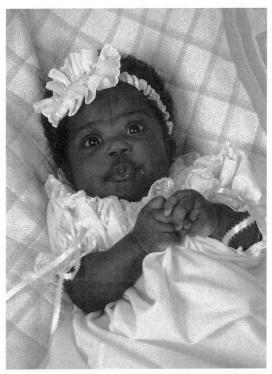

PHOTO 8.1 Gender-role socialization begins very early as parents provide their infants with "gender-appropriate" clothing, toys, and hairstyles.

as fictions or fables that are not supported by research. We then look at developmental trends in gender typing and see that youngsters are often well aware of gender-role stereotypes and are displaying gender-typed patterns of behavior long before they are old enough to go to kindergarten. And how do children learn so much about the sexes and gender roles at such an early age? We address this issue by reviewing several influential theories that specify how biological forces, social experiences, and cognitive development might combine or interact to influence the gender-typing process. And after examining a new perspective which asserts that traditional gender-roles have outlived their usefulness in today's modern society, we conclude by briefly considering another self-aspect that is central to our concept of self as male or female—human sexuality.

Categorizing Males and Females: Gender-Role Standards

Most of us have learned a great deal about males and females by the time we enter college. In fact, if you and your classmates were asked to jot down ten psychological dimensions on which men and women are thought to differ, it is likely that every member of the class could easily generate such a list. Here's a head start: Which gender is most likely to display emotions? to be tidy? to be competitive? to use harsh language?

A **gender-role standard** is a value, a motive, or a class of behavior that is considered more appropriate for members of one sex than the other. Taken together, a society's gender-role standards describe how males and females are expected to behave and reflect the stereotypes by which we categorize and respond to members of each sex.

The female's role as child bearer is largely responsible for the gender-role standards and stereotypes that have prevailed in many societies, including our own. Girls have typically been encouraged to assume an **expressive role** that involves being kind, nurturant, cooperative, and sensitive to the needs of others (Parsons, 1955). These psychological traits, it was assumed, will prepare girls to play the wife and mother roles—to keep the family functioning and to raise children successfully. By contrast, boys have been encouraged to adopt an **instrumental role,** for as a traditional husband and father, a male would face the tasks of providing for the family and protecting it from harm. Thus, young boys are expected to become dominant, assertive, independent, and competitive. Similar norms and role prescriptions are found in many, though certainly not all, societies (Williams & Best, 1990). In one rather ambitious project, Herbert Barry, Margaret Bacon, and Irving Child (1957) analyzed the gender-typing practices of 110 nonindustrialized societies, looking for sex differences in the socialization of five attributes: nurturance, obedience, responsibility, achievement, and self-reliance. As shown in Table 8-1, achievement and self-reliance were more strongly encouraged in young boys, whereas young girls were encouraged to become nurturant, responsible, and obedient.

Children in modern industrialized societies also face strong gender-typing pressures, though not always to the same extent and in the same ways that children in non-industrialized societies do. (For example, parents in many Western societies place roughly equal emphasis on achievement for sons and for daughters; Lytton & Romney, 1991). Furthermore, the findings in Table 8-1 do not imply that self-reliance in girls is frowned on or that dis-

gender-role standard: a behavior, value, or motive that members of a society consider more typical or appropriate for members of one sex.

expressive role: a social prescription, usually directed toward females, that one should be cooperative, kind, nurturant, and sensitive to the needs of others.

instrumental role: a social prescription, usually directed toward males, that one should be dominant, independent, assertive, competitive, and goal-oriented.

TABLE 8-1 Sex differences in the socialization of five attributes in 110 societies

ATTRIBUTE	PERCENTAGE OF SOCIETIES IN WHICH SOCIALIZATION PRESSURES WERE GREATER FOR	
	BOYS	GIRLS
Nurturance	0	82
Obedience	3	35
Responsibility	11	61
Achievement	87	3
Self-reliance	85	0

NOTE: The percentages for each attribute do not add to 100 because some of the societies did not place differential pressure on boys and girls with respect to that particular attribute. For example, 18% of the societies for which pertinent data were available did not differentiate between the sexes in the socialization of nurturance.

SOURCE: Adapted from Barry, Bacon, & Child, 1957.

Box 8.1   *Developmental Issues*

What Traits Characterize Males and Females?

Several recent surveys have asked college students to respond to lists of various mannerisms and personal characteristics by saying which of these traits characterize the "typical" man or "typical" woman (or by judging which are clearly "masculine" or clearly "feminine" attributes). Although you may not agree with peer consensus, see if you can anticipate how they have responded by indicating whether each trait in the list below is more characteristic of men or more characteristic of women. (The results of the survey are given at the bottom of the page.)

Trait	More characteristic of	
	Men	Women
1. Active	____	____
2. Aware of others' feelings	____	____
3. Adventurous	____	____
4. Considerate	____	____
5. Aggressive	____	____
6. Creative	____	____
7. Ambitious	____	____
8. Cries easily	____	____
9. Competitive	____	____
10. Other-oriented	____	____

Trait	Men	Women
11. Dominant	____	____
12. Emotional	____	____
13. Independent	____	____
14. Artistic	____	____
15. Displays leadership	____	____
16. Excitable	____	____
17. Mathematical	____	____
18. Empathic	____	____
19. Makes decisions easily	____	____
20. Feelings hurt easily	____	____
21. Mechanical	____	____
22. Gentle	____	____
23. Outspoken	____	____
24. Kind	____	____
25. Persistent	____	____
26. Neat	____	____
27. Self-confident	____	____
28. Seeks approval	____	____
29. Skilled in business	____	____
30. Tactful	____	____
31. Takes a stand	____	____
32. Understanding	____	____

Answers for Box 8.1: College students generally indicate that the even-numbered traits characterize women, whereas the odd-numbered ones are more characteristic of men. (Source for these traits: Ruble, 1983.)

obedience by young boys is acceptable. In fact, all five attributes that Barry et al. studied were encouraged of *both* boys and girls, but with different emphases on different attributes depending on the sex of the child (Zern, 1984; see also Pomerantz & Ruble, 1998). So it appears that the first goal of socialization is to encourage children to acquire those traits that will enable them to become well-behaved, contributing members of society. A second goal (but one that adults view as important nevertheless) is to "gender-type" the child by stressing the importance of relationship-oriented (or expressive) attributes for girls and individualistic (or instrumental) attributes for boys.

Because cultural norms specify that girls should assume an expressive role and boys an instrumental role, we may be inclined to assume that girls and women actually display expressive traits and that boys and men possess instrumental traits (Broverman et al., 1972; Williams & Best, 1990). If you are thinking that these stereotypes have disappeared as attention to women's rights has increased and as more women have entered the labor force, think again. Although some change has occurred, adolescents and young adults still endorse many traditional stereotypes about men and women (Bergen & Williams, 1991; Twenge, 1997; test yourself in Box 8.1). Might these beliefs about sex differences have any basis in fact? Let's see if they do.

Some Facts and Fictions About Sex Differences

The old French maxim "Vive la difference" reflects a fact that we all know to be true: Males and females are anatomically different. Adult males are typically taller, heavier, and more muscular than adult females, while females may be hardier in the sense that they live longer. But although these physical variations are fairly obvious, the evidence for sex differences in psychological functioning is not as clear as most of us might think.

ACTUAL PSYCHOLOGICAL DIFFERENCES BETWEEN THE SEXES

In a classic review of more than 1,500 studies comparing males and females, Eleanor Maccoby and Carol Jacklin (1974) concluded that few traditional gender stereotypes have much empirical support. In fact, their review pointed to only four *small* but reliable differences between the sexes that were consistently supported by research. Here are their conclusions, with some updates and amendments:

1. *Verbal ability.* Girls have greater verbal abilities than boys. Girls acquire language and develop verbal skills at an earlier age than boys and display a small but consistent verbal advantage on tests of reading comprehension and speech fluency throughout childhood and adolescence (Halpern, 1997; Hedges & Nowell, 1995).

2. *Visual/spatial abilities.* Boys outperform girls on tests of **visual/spatial abilities**—that is, the ability to draw inferences about or to otherwise mentally manipulate pictorial information (see Figure 8.1 for two kinds of visual/spatial tasks on which sex differences have been found). The male advantage in spatial abilities is not large, although it is detectable by middle childhood and persists across the life span (Kerns & Berenbaum, 1991; Voyer, Voyer, & Bryden, 1995).

3. *Mathematical ability.* Beginning in adolescence, boys show a small but consistent advantage over girls on tests of *arithmetic reasoning* (Halpern, 1997; Hyde, Fennema, & Lamon, 1990; see Figure 8.2). Girls actually exceed boys in computational skills; but boys have acquired more mathematical problem-solving strategies that enable them to outperform girls on complex word problems, geometry, and the mathematics portion of the Scholastic Assessment Test (SAT) (Byrnes & Takahira, 1993; Casey, 1996). The

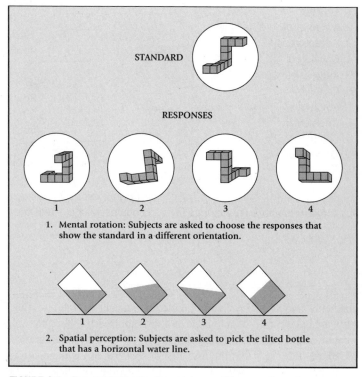

FIGURE 8.1 Two spatial tasks for which sex differences in performance have been found. From Linn & Petersen, 1985.

male advantage in mathematical problem solving is most apparent among high math achievers; more males than females are exceptionally talented in math (Stumpf & Stanley, 1996). And it seems that sex differences in visual/spatial abilities and the problem-solving strategies they support contribute to sex differences in arithmetic reasoning (Casey, Nuttall, & Pezaris, 1997). However, we will soon see that social forces—namely the messages boys and girls receive about their respective abilities—can also influence their mathematical, verbal, and visual/spatial reasoning skills.

4. *Aggression.* Finally, boys are more physically and verbally *aggressive* than girls, starting as early as age 2, and are about 10 times more likely than girls are to be in-

visual/spatial abilities: the ability to mentally manipulate or otherwise draw inferences about pictorial information.

volved in antisocial behavior and violent crime during adolescence (U.S. Department of Justice, 1995). However, girls are more likely than boys to display covert forms of hostility toward others by snubbing or ignoring them or by trying to undermine their relationships or social status (Crick et al., 1997; Crick & Grotpeter, 1995).

Other sex differences: Critics were quick to challenge Maccoby and Jacklin's review, claiming that the procedures they used to gather and tabulate their results led them to underestimate the number of sex differences that actually exist (Block, 1976; Huston, 1983). More recent research, which often combines the results of several studies and provides a better estimate of the reliability of sex-related differences, points to several additional sex differences in personality and social behavior. For example:

5. *Activity level.* Even before they are born, boys are more physically active than girls (DiPietro et al., 1996) and they remain more active throughout childhood, especially when interacting with peers (Eaton & Enns, 1986; Eaton & Yu, 1989). In fact, the heightened activity that boys display may help to explain why they are more likely than girls to initiate and to be receptive to bouts of nonaggressive, rough-and-tumble play (Humphreys & Smith, 1987).

6. *Fear, timidity, and risk taking.* As early as the first year of life, girls appear to be more fearful or timid in uncertain situations than boys are. They are also more cautious and less assertive in these situations than boys are, taking far fewer risks than boys do (Chrisopherson, 1989; Feingold, 1994).

7. *Developmental vulnerability.* From conception, boys are more physically vulnerable than girls to prenatal and perinatal birth hazards and to the effects of disease (Raz et al., 1994, 1995). Boys are also more likely than girls to display a variety of developmental problems, including reading disabilities, speech defects, hyperactivity, emotional disorders, and mental retardation (Halpern, 1997; Henker & Whalen, 1989).

8. *Emotional expressivity/sensitivity.* In some ways, females do appear to be more emotionally expressive than males. Two-year-old girls are already using more emotion-related words than 2-year-old boys do (Cervantes & Callanan, 1998), and parents of preschoolers talk more with daughters than with sons about emotions and memorable emotional events (Kuebli, Butler, & Fivush, 1995; Reese & Fivush, 1993). Indeed, this social support for reflecting on their feelings may help to explain why girls and women characterize their emotions as deeper, or more intense, and feel freer to express them than boys and men do (Diener, Sandvik, & Larson, 1985; Fuchs & Thelen, 1988; Saarni, 1993).

The evidence for sex differences in empathic sensitivities is mixed. Girls and women consistently *rate themselves* (and are described by others) as more nurturant and empathic than boys and men (Cohen & Strayer, 1996; Feingold, 1994). Yet boys often appear no less empathic or compassionate than girls when studied in naturalistic settings (Fabes, Eisenberg, & Miller, 1990; Zahn-Waxler et al., 1992). For example, boys display at least as much affection toward and concern for the welfare of their pets and older relatives as girls do (Melson, Peet, & Sparks, 1991).

9. *Compliance.* From early in the preschool period, girls are more compliant than boys to the requests and demands of parents, teachers, and other authority figures (Feingold, 1994; Maccoby, 1990). And when trying to persuade others to comply with them, girls are more likely to rely on tact and polite suggestions, whereas many boys are inclined to adopt more forceful or demanding strategies (Cowan & Avants, 1988; Maccoby, 1990).

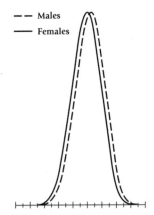

FIGURE 8.2 These two distributions of scores—one for males, one for females—give some idea of the size of the gap between the sexes in abilities for which sex differences are consistently found. Despite a small difference in average performance, the scores of males and females overlap considerably. (Adapted from Hyde, Fennema, & Lamon, 1990.)

PHOTO 8.2 Rough-and-tumble play is more common among boys than among girls.

In reviewing the evidence for "real" sex differences, we must keep in mind that the data reflect *group averages* that may or may not characterize the behavior of any particular individual. For example, gender accounts for about 5% of the variation children display in overt aggressive behaviors (Hyde, 1984), so the remaining 95% is due to differences between people other than their sex. Furthermore, the sex differences in verbal, spatial, and mathematical abilities that Maccoby and Jacklin identified are also small, are most apparent at the extreme (that is, very high or very low) ends of the ability distributions (Halpern, 1997), and may not be evident elsewhere (Daubman, Heatherington, & Ahn, 1992). For example, women do better on tests of mathematical ability, sometimes even outperforming men, in societies like Israel, where women have excellent opportunities in technical training and technical occupations (Baker & Jones, 1992). Findings such as these imply that most sex differences are not biologically inevitable and that cultural and other social influences play an important role in the development of males and females (Halpern, 1997).

What, then, should we conclude about psychological differences between the sexes? Although contemporary scholars may quibble at times about which sex differences are real or meaningful (Eagly, 1995; Hyde & Plant, 1995), most developmentalists can agree on this: *Males and females are far more psychologically similar than they are different,* and even the most well-documented differences seem to be modest. So it is impossible to accurately predict the aggressiveness, the mathematical skills, the activity level, or the emotional expressivity of any individual simply by knowing his or her gender. Only when group averages are computed do the sex differences emerge.

CULTURAL MYTHS

Another conclusion that most developmentalists now endorse is Maccoby and Jacklin's (1974) proposition that many (perhaps most) gender-role stereotypes are "cultural myths" that are simply not supported by the research currently available. Among the most widely accepted of these "myths" are those in Table 8-2.

TABLE 8-2 Some unfounded beliefs about sex differences

BELIEFS	FACTS
1. Girls are more "social" than boys.	The two sexes are equally interested in social stimuli, equally responsive to social reinforcement, and equally proficient at learning from social models. At certain ages, boys actually spend more time than girls with playmates.
2. Girls are more "suggestible" than boys.	Most studies of children's conformity find no sex differences. However, sometimes boys are more likely than girls to accept peer-group values that conflict with their own.
3. Girls have lower self-esteem than boys.	The sexes are highly similar in their overall self-satisfaction and self-confidence throughout childhood and adolescence. More boys than girls show gains in self-esteem over the course of adolescence, possibly reflecting the greater freedom and encouragement that males receive to pursue instrumental roles.
4. Girls are better at simple repetitive tasks, whereas boys excel at tasks that require higher-level cognitive processing.	The evidence does not support these assertions. Neither sex is superior at rote learning, probability learning, or concept formation.
5. Boys are more "analytic" than girls.	With the exception of the *small* sex differences in cognitive abilities that we have already discussed, boys and girls do *not* differ on tests of analytical or logical reasoning.
6. Girls lack achievement motivation.	No such differences exist! Perhaps the myth of lesser achievement motivation for females has persisted because males and females have generally directed their achievement strivings toward different goals.

SOURCE: Adapted from Maccoby & Jacklin, 1974.

Box 8.2   *Focus on Research*

Do Gender Stereotypes Color Children's Interpretations of Counterstereotypic Information?

Maccoby and Jacklin (1974) proposed that, once people learn gender stereotypes, they are more likely to attend to and remember events that are consistent with these beliefs than events that would disconfirm them. Carol Martin and Charles Halverson (1981) agree, arguing that gender stereotypes are well-ingrained schemes or naive theories that people use to organize and represent experience. Once established, these gender schemes should have at least two important effects on a child's (or an adult's) cognitive processes: (1) an *organizational* effect on memory, such that information consistent with the scheme will be easier to remember than counterstereotypic events, and (2) a *distortion* effect, such that counterstereotypic information will tend to be remembered as much more consistent with one's gender scheme than the information really is. For example, it should be easier for people to remember that they saw a girl at the stove cooking (gender-consistent information) than a boy partaking in the same activity (gender-inconsistent information). And if people were to witness the latter event, they might distort what they had seen to make it more consistent with their stereotypes—perhaps by remembering the actor as a girl rather than a boy or by reconstructing the boy's activities as *fixing* the stove rather than cooking.

Martin and Halverson (1983) tested their hypotheses in an interesting study with 5- and 6-year-olds. During a first session, each child was shown 16 pictures, half of which depicted a child performing *gender-consistent* activities (for example, a boy playing with a truck) and half

showing children displaying *gender-inconsistent* behaviors (for example, a girl chopping wood). One week later, children's memory for what they had seen was assessed.

The results of this experiment were indeed interesting. Children easily recalled the sex of the actor for scenes in which actors had performed gender-consistent activities. But when the actor's behavior was gender *inconsistent,* these youngsters often distorted the scene by saying that the actor's sex was consistent with the activity they recalled (for example, they were likely to say that it had been a boy rather than a girl who had chopped wood). As predicted, children's *confidence* about the sex of the actors was greater for gender-consistent scenes than for gender-inconsistent ones, suggesting that counterstereotypic information is harder to remember. But it was interesting to note that, when children actually distorted a gender-inconsistent scene, they were just as confident about the sex of the actor (which they recalled *incorrectly*) as they were for the gender-consistent scenes in which they correctly recalled the actor's sex. So it seems that children are likely to distort counterstereotypic information to be more consistent with their stereotypes and that these memory distortions are as "real" to them as stereotypical information that has not been distorted.

Why, then, do inaccurate gender stereotypes persist? Because we find disconfirming evidence harder to recall and, in fact, often distort that information in ways that will confirm our initial (and inaccurate) beliefs.

Why do these inaccuracies persist? Maccoby and Jacklin (1974) propose that

a . . . likely explanation for the perpetuation of "myths" is the fact that stereotypes are such powerful things. An ancient truth is worth restating here: if a generalization about a group of people is believed, whenever a member of the group behaves in the expected way the observer notes it and his belief is confirmed and strengthened; when a member of the group behaves in a way that is not consistent with the observer's expectations, the instance is likely to pass unnoticed, and the observer's generalized belief is protected from disconfirmation. . . . [This] well-documented [selective attention] . . . process . . . results in the perpetuation of myths that would otherwise die out under the impact of negative evidence. (p. 355)

In other words, gender-role stereotypes are well-ingrained cognitive schemes that we use to interpret and often to distort the behavior of males and females (Martin & Halverson, 1981; see also Box 8.2). People even use these schemes to classify the behavior of infants. In one study (Condry & Condry, 1976), college students watched a videotape of a 9-month-old child who was introduced as either a girl ("Dana") or a boy ("David"). As the students observed the child at play, they were asked to interpret his or her reactions to toys such as a teddy bear or a jack-in-the-box. The resulting impressions of the infant's behavior clearly depended on his or her presumed sex. For example, a strong reaction to the jack-in-the-box was labeled "anger" when the child was presumed to be a boy and "fear" when the child had been introduced as a girl (see also Burnham & Harris, 1992).

As it turns out, the persistence of unfounded or inaccurate gender-role stereotypes has important consequences for both boys and girls. Some of the more negative implications of these cultural myths are discussed in the following section.

DO CULTURAL MYTHS CONTRIBUTE TO SEX DIFFERENCES IN ABILITY (AND VOCATIONAL OPPORTUNITY)?

In 1968, Phillip Goldberg asked college women to judge the merits of several scientific articles that were attributed to a male author ("John McKay") or to a female author ("Joan McKay"). Although these manuscripts were identical in every other respect, participants judged the articles written by a male to be of higher quality than those by a female.

These young women were reflecting a belief, common to people in many societies, that girls and women lack the potential to excel in either math and science courses or in occupations that require this training. Kindergarten and first-grade girls already believe that they are not as good as boys are in arithmetic; and throughout the grade-school years, children increasingly come to regard reading, art, and music as girls' domains and mathematics, athletics, and mechanical subjects as more appropriate for boys (Eccles et al., 1990, 1993; Entwisle & Baker, 1983). Furthermore, an examination of the percentages of male and female practitioners in various occupations reveals that women are overrepresented in fields that call for verbal ability (for example, library science; elementary education) and are seriously underrepresented in most other professions, particularly the sciences and other technical fields (for example, engineering) that require a math/science background (U.S. Bureau of the Census, 1997). How do we explain these dramatic sex differences? Are the small sex-related differences in verbal, mathematical, and visual/spatial performances responsible? Or rather, do gender-role stereotypes create a **self-fulfilling prophecy**—one that *promotes* sex differences in cognitive performance and steers boys and girls along different career paths? Today many developmentalists favor the latter viewpoint. Let's take a closer look.

Home Influences   Parents may often contribute to sex differences in ability and self-perceptions by treating their sons and daughters differently. Jacquelynne Eccles and her colleagues (1990) have conducted a number of studies aimed at understanding why girls tend to shy away from math and science courses and are underrepresented in occupations that involve math and science. They find that parental expectations about sex differences in mathematical ability do become self-fulfilling prophecies. The plot goes something like this:

1. Parents, influenced by gender stereotypes, expect their sons to outperform their daughters in math. Even before their children have received any formal math instruction, mothers in the United States, Japan, and Taiwan express a belief that boys have more mathematical ability than girls (Lummis & Stevenson, 1990).
2. Parents attribute their sons' successes in math to ability but often credit their daughters' successes to hard work (Parsons, Adler, & Kaczala, 1982). These attributions further reinforce the belief that girls lack mathematical talent and turn in respectable performances only through plodding effort (see also Pomerantz & Ruble, 1998).

self-fulfilling prophecy: phenomenon whereby people cause others to act in accordance with the expectations they have about those others.

3. Children begin to internalize their parents' views, so that girls often come to believe that they are "no good" in math (Jacobs & Eccles, 1992).
4. Thinking they lack ability, girls become less interested in math, less likely to take math courses, and less likely than boys to pursue career possibilities that involve math after high school (Benbow & Arjimand, 1990; U.S. Bureau of the Census, 1997).

In short, those parents who expect their daughters to have trouble with numbers may get what they expect. In their research, Eccles and her colleagues have ruled out the possibility that parents (and girls themselves) expect less of girls because girls actually do worse in math than boys do. The negative effects of low parental expectancies on girls' self perceptions are evident even when boys and girls perform *equally well* on tests of math aptitude and attain similar grades in math (Eccles et al., 1990). Parental beliefs that girls excel in English and that boys excel in sports contribute to sex differences in interests and competencies in these areas as well (Eccles et al., 1990).

Scholastic Influences   Teachers also have stereotyped beliefs about the relative abilities of boys and girls in particular subjects. Sixth-grade math instructors, for example, believe that boys have more ability in math but that girls try harder at it (Jussim & Eccles, 1992). And even though these teachers often reward girls' greater efforts by assigning them equal or higher grades than they give to boys (Jussim & Eccles, 1992), their subtle message that girls must try harder to succeed in math may nonetheless convince many girls that their talents might be best directed toward other nonquantitative achievement domains for which they are better suited . . . like music or English.

In sum, unfounded beliefs about sex differences in cognitive abilities may indeed contribute to the small sex-related ability differences we have discussed and, ultimately, to the large underrepresentation of women in the sciences and other occupations requiring quantitative skills. Even as we approach the 21st century, most high school students continue to prepare for occupations dominated by members of their own sex (Associated Press, 1994a), and there is a clear need for programs to educate parents, teachers, and counselors about the subtle ways that gender stereotypes can undermine the educational and occupational aspirations of talented female students (Benbow & Arjimand, 1990). Fortunately, there are some hopeful signs that the times are changing. Although we still see few females among the engineering graduates of most colleges, women in 1990 earned 40% of all degrees conferred by law schools in the United States, and more than 30% of all medical degrees. The corresponding percentages in 1970 were about 9% for law and 5% for medicine (Bianchi, 1995). So there is reason to suspect that many of the constraining stereotypes about women's competencies will eventually crumble as women achieve, in ever-increasing numbers, in politics, professional occupations, and the sciences, skilled trades, and virtually all other walks of life. To oppose such a trend is to waste a most valuable resource: the abilities and efforts of more than half the world's population.

Now let's examine the gender-typing process to see why boys and girls may come to view themselves so differently and often choose to assume different roles.

Developmental Trends in Gender Typing

Gender-typing research has traditionally focused on three separate but interrelated topics: (1) the development of **gender identity,** or the knowledge that one is either a boy or a girl and that gender is an unchanging attribute, (2) the development of *gender-role stereotypes,* or ideas about what males and females are supposed to be like,

gender identity: one's awareness of one's gender and its implications.

and (3) the development of *gender-typed* patterns of *behavior*—that is, the child's tendency to favor same-sex activities over those normally associated with the other sex.

DEVELOPMENT OF THE GENDER CONCEPT

The first step in the development of a gender identity is to discriminate males from females and to place oneself into one of these categories. By 6 months of age, infants are using differences in vocal pitch to discriminate female speech from that of males (Miller, 1983); and by the end of the first year, they can reliably discriminate photographs of men and women (women are the long-haired ones) and are beginning to match male and female voices with faces in tests of intermodal perception (Leinbach & Fagot, 1993; Poulin-Dubois et al., 1994).[1]

Between ages 2 and 3, children begin to tell us what they know about gender as they acquire and correctly use such labels as "mommy" and "daddy" and (slightly later) "boy" and "girl" (Leinbach & Fagot, 1986). By ages 2½ to 3, almost all children can accurately label themselves as either boys or girls (Thompson, 1975), although it will take longer for them to grasp the fact that gender is a permanent attribute. Many 3- to 5-year-olds, for example, think that boys could become mommies or girls daddies if they really wanted to, or that a person who changes clothing and hairstyles can become a member of the other sex (Fagot, 1985b; Marcus & Overton, 1978). Children normally begin to understand that sex is an unchanging attribute between the ages of 5 and 7, so that most youngsters have a firm, future-oriented identity as a boy or a girl by the time they enter grade school.

DEVELOPMENT OF GENDER-ROLE STEREOTYPES

Remarkable as it may seem, toddlers begin to acquire gender-role stereotypes at about the same time that they become aware of their basic identities as boys or girls. Deanna Kuhn and her associates (1978) showed a male doll ("Michael") and a female doll ("Lisa") to 2½- to 3½-year-olds and then asked each child which of the two dolls would engage in gender-stereotyped activities such as cooking; sewing; playing with dolls, trucks, or trains; talking a lot; giving kisses; fighting; or climbing trees. Almost all the 2½-year-olds had some knowledge of gender-role stereotypes. For example, boys and girls agreed that girls talk a lot, never hit, often need help, like to play with dolls, and like to help their mothers with chores such as cooking and cleaning. By contrast, these young children felt that boys like to play with cars, like to help their fathers, like to build things, and are apt to make statements such as "I can hit you." The 2- to 3-year-olds who know the most about gender stereotypes are those who can correctly label photographs of other children as boys and girls (Fagot, Leinbach, & O'Boyle, 1992). So an understanding of gender labels seems to accelerate the process of gender stereotyping.

Over the preschool and early grade-school years, children learn more and more about the toys, activities, and achievement domains considered appropriate for boys and for girls (Serbin, Powlishta, & Gulko, 1993; Welch-Ross & Schmidt, 1996). Eventually, grade-school children draw sharp distinctions between the sexes on *psychological* dimensions, learning first the positive traits that characterize their own gender and the negative traits associated with the other sex (Serbin et al., 1993). By ages 10 to 11, children's stereotyping of personality traits is beginning to rival that of adults. In one well-known cross-cultural study, Deborah Best and her colleagues (1977) found that fourth- and fifth-graders in England, Ireland, and the United States

---

[1]*Intermodal perception* refers to one's ability to use one sensory channel (say, vision) to identify a stimulus that is already familiar through modality (such as audition, or hearing).

PHOTO 8.3 By age 2½ to 3, children know that boys and girls prefer different kinds of activities, and they have already begun to play in gender-stereotyped ways.

generally agree that women are weak, emotional, soft-hearted, sophisticated, and affectionate, whereas men are ambitious, assertive, aggressive, dominating, and cruel.

How seriously do children take the gender-role prescriptions they are rapidly learning? Do they believe that they must conform to these stereotypes? Many 3- to 7-year-olds do; they often reason like little chauvinists, treating gender-role standards as blanket rules that are not to be violated (Biernat, 1991; Ruble & Martin, 1998). Consider the reaction of one 6-year-old to a boy named George who likes to play with dolls:

> (*Why do you think people tell George not to play with dolls?*) Well, he should only play with things that boys play with. The things that he is playing with now is girls' stuff. . . . (*Can George play with Barbie dolls if he wants to?*) No sir! . . . (*What should George do?*) He should stop playing with girls' dolls and start playing with G.I. Joe. (*Why can a boy play with G.I. Joe and not a Barbie doll?*) Because if a boy is playing with a Barbie doll, then he's just going to get people teasing him . . . and if he tries to play more, to get girls to like him, then the girls won't like him either. (Damon, 1977, p. 255; italics added)

Why are young children so rigid and intolerant of gender-role transgressions? Possibly because gender-related issues are very important to them between the ages of 3 and 7. After all, this is the time when they are firmly classifying themselves as boys or girls and beginning to suspect that they will *always be* boys and girls. Thus, they may exaggerate gender-role stereotypes to "get them cognitively clear" so that they can live up to their self-images (Maccoby, 1980).

By ages 8 to 9, however, children are becoming more flexible and less chauvinistic in their thinking about gender (Damon, 1977; Levy, Taylor, & Gelman, 1995; Serbin et al., 1993). Notice how 9-year-old James makes a clear distinction between moral rules that people are obligated to obey and gender-role standards that are customary but *nonobligatory.*

> (*What do you think his parents should do?*) They should . . . get him trucks and stuff, and see if he will play with those. (*What if . . . he kept on playing with dolls? Do you think they would punish him?*) No. (*How come?*) It's not really doing anything bad. (*Why isn't it bad?*) Because . . . if he was breaking a window, and he kept on doing that, they could punish him, because you're not supposed to break windows. But if you want to you can play with dolls. (*What's the difference? . . .*) Well, breaking windows you're not supposed to do. And if you play with dolls, you can, but boys usually don't. (Damon, 1977, p. 263; italics added)

However, just because grade-school children say that boys and girls can legitimately pursue cross-sex interests and activities does not necessarily imply that they *approve* of those who do. When asked about whether they could be friends with a boy who wears lipstick or a girl who plays football and to evaluate such gender-role transgressions, grade-school children (and adults) were reasonably tolerant of violations by girls. However, participants (especially boys) came down hard on boys who behaved like girls, viewing these transgressions almost as bad as violating a moral rule. Here, then, is an indication of the greater pressure placed on boys to conform to gender roles (Levy et al., 1995).

Thinking about the traits that males and females might display and the hobbies and occupations they might pursue becomes increasingly flexible during early adolescence, as children make the transition from elementary school to junior high. But soon thereafter, gender-role prescriptions once again become less flexible, with both boys and girls showing a strong intolerance of cross-sex mannerisms displayed by either males or females (Alfieri, Ruble, & Higgins, 1996; Sigelman, Carr, & Begley, 1986; Signorella et al., 1993). How might we explain this second round of gender chauvinism?

Apparently, an adolescent's increasing intolerance of cross-sex mannerisms and behaviors is tied to a larger process of **gender intensification**—a magnification of sex differences that is associated with increased pressure to conform to gender roles as one reaches puberty (Boldizar, 1991; Galambos, Almieda, & Peterson, 1990; Hill & Lynch, 1983). Boys begin to see themselves as more masculine; girls emphasize their feminine side. Why might gender intensification occur? Parental influence is one contributor: As children enter adolescence, mothers become more involved in joint activities with daughters and fathers more involved with sons (Crouter, Manke, & McHale, 1995). However, peer influences may be even more important. For example, adolescents increasingly find that they must conform to traditional gender norms to succeed in the dating scene. A girl who was a tomboy and thought nothing of it may find during adolescence that she must dress and behave in more "feminine" ways to attract boys, and a boy may find that he is more popular if he projects a more sharply "masculine" image (Burn, O'Neil, & Nederend, 1996; Katz, 1979). Social pressures on adolescents to conform to traditional roles may even help explain why sex differences in cognitive abilities sometimes become more noticeable as children enter adolescence (Hill & Lynch, 1983; Roberts et al., 1990). Later in high school, teenagers become more comfortable with their identities as young men or women and more flexible once again in their thinking about gender (Urberg, 1979). Yet, even adults may remain highly intolerant of males who blatantly disregard gender-role prescriptions (Levy et al., 1995).

DEVELOPMENT OF GENDER-TYPED BEHAVIOR

The most common method of assessing the "gender-appropriateness" of children's behavior is to observe whom and what they like to play with. Sex differences in toy preferences develop very early—even before the child has established a clear gender identity or can correctly label various toys as "boy things" or "girl things" (Blakemore, LaRue, & Olejnik, 1979; Fagot, Leinbach, & Hagan, 1986; Weinraub et al., 1984). Boys of 14 to 22 months usually prefer trucks and cars to other objects, whereas girls of this age would rather play with dolls and soft toys (Smith & Daglish, 1977). In fact, 18- to 24-month-old toddlers will often refuse to play with cross-sex toys, even when there are no other objects available for them to play with (Caldera, Huston, & O'Brien, 1989).

Gender Segregation Children's preferences for same-sex playmates also develop very early. In nursery school, 2-year-old girls already prefer to play with other girls (La Freniere, Strayer, & Gauthier, 1984), and by age 3, boys are reliably selecting boys rather than girls as companions. This **gender segregation**, which has been observed in a variety of cultures (Leaper, 1994; Whiting & Edwards, 1988), becomes progres-

gender intensification: a magnification of sex differences early in adolescence; associated with increased pressure to conform to traditional gender roles.

gender segregation: children's tendency to associate with same-sex playmates and to think of the other sex as an outgroup.

sively stronger with each passing year (Serbin et al., 1993). Four- and 5-year-olds have already begun to actively *reject* playmates of the other sex (Ramsey, 1995), and by age 6½, children spend more than 10 times as much time with same-sex as with opposite-sex companions (Maccoby, 1988). Alan Sroufe and his colleagues find that those 10- to 11-year-olds who insist most strongly on maintaining clear gender boundaries and who avoid consorting with the "enemy" tend to be viewed as socially competent and popular, whereas children who violate gender segregation rules tend to be much less popular and less well adjusted. In fact, children who display a *preference* for cross-sex friendships are likely to be *rejected* by their peers (Kovacs, Parker, & Hoffman, 1996). However, gender boundaries and biases against other-sex companions decline in adolescence when the social and physiological events of puberty trigger an interest in members of the opposite sex (Serbin et al., 1993).

Why does gender segregation occur? Eleanor Maccoby (1990) believes that it largely reflects differences between boys' and girls' play styles—an incompatibility that may stem from boys' heightened levels of androgen, which fosters active, rambunctious behavior. In one study (Jacklin & Maccoby, 1978), an adult observer recorded how often pairs of same-sex and mixed-sex toddlers played together or played alone when placed in a playroom with several interesting toys. As we see in Figure 8.4, boys directed far more social responses to boys than to girls, whereas girls were more sociable with girls than with boys. Interactions between playmates in the same-sex pairings were lively and positive in character. By contrast, girls tended to withdraw from boys in the mixed-sex pairs. Boys were simply too boisterous and domineering to suit the taste of many girls, who prefer less roughhousing and would rather rely on polite negotiations rather than demands or shows of force when settling disputes with their playmates (see also Alexander & Hines, 1994; Moller & Serbin, 1996).

Cognitive and social-cognitive development also contribute to the increasing gender segregation children display. Once preschoolers label themselves boys or girls and begin to acquire gender stereotypes, they come to favor the group to which they belong and will eventually view the other sex as a homogeneous out-group with many negative characteristics (Martin, 1994; Powlishta, 1995). In fact, children who hold the more stereotyped views of the sexes are the ones most likely to maintain gender segregation in their own play activities and to make few if any opposite-sex friends (Kovacs et al., 1996; Martin, 1994).

Sex Differences in Gender-Typed Behavior   Many cultures, including our own, assign greater status to the male gender role (Turner & Gervai, 1995), and boys face stronger pressures than girls to adhere to gender-appropriate codes of conduct (Bussey & Bandura, 1992; Lobel & Menashri, 1993). Consider that fathers of baby girls are generally willing to offer a truck to their 12-month-old daughters, whereas fathers of baby boys are likely to withhold dolls from their sons (Snow, Jacklin, & Maccoby, 1983). And boys are quicker than girls to adopt gender-typed toy preferences. Judith Blakemore and her associates (1979), for example, found that 2-year-old boys clearly favor gender-appropriate toys whereas some 2-year-old girls may not. And by ages 3 to 5, boys (1) are much more likely than girls to say that they *dislike* opposite-sex toys (Bussey & Bandura, 1992; Eisenberg, Murray, & Hite, 1982) and (2) *may* even prefer a girl playmate who likes "boy" toys to a boy playmate who prefers girls' activities (Alexander & Hines, 1994).

Between the ages of 4 and 10, both boys and girls are becoming more aware of what is expected of them and conforming to these cultural prescriptions (Huston, 1983). Yet girls are more likely than boys to retain an interest in cross-sex toys, games, and activities. Consider what John Richardson and Carl Simpson (1982) found when recording the toy preferences of 750 5- to 9-year-olds as expressed in their letters to

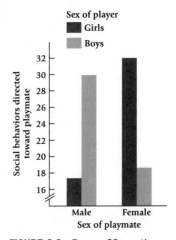

FIGURE 8.3   By age 33 months, toddlers already prefer playmates of their own sex: boys are much more sociable with boys than with girls, whereas girls are more outgoing with girls than with boys. (Adapted from Jacklin & Maccoby, 1978.)

Santa Claus. Although most requests were clearly gender-typed, we see in Table 8-3 that more girls than boys were asking for "opposite sex" items (see also Etaugh & Liss, 1992). With respect to their actual gender-role preferences, young girls often wish they were boys, and nearly half of today's college women claim that they were tomboys when they were young (Burn et al., 1996). Yet it is unusual for a boy to wish he were a girl (Martin, 1990).

There are probably several reasons that girls are drawn to male activities and the masculine role during middle childhood. For one thing, they are becoming increasingly aware that masculine behavior is more highly valued, and perhaps it is only natural that girls would want to be what is "best" (or at least something other than a second-class citizen) (Frey & Ruble, 1992). Furthermore, girls are given much more leeway than boys are to partake in cross-sex activities; it is acceptable to be a "tomboy" but a sign of ridicule and rejection should a boy be labeled a "sissy" (Martin, 1990). Finally, fast-moving masculine games and "action" toys may simply be more inherently interesting than the feminine playthings and pastimes (dolls, dollhouses, dish sets, cleaning and care-taking utensils) designed to encourage girls to adopt a nurturant, expressive orientation.

In spite of their earlier interest in masculine activities, most girls come to prefer (or at least to comply with) many of the prescriptions for the feminine role by early adolescence. Why? Probably for biological, cognitive, and social reasons. Once they reach puberty and their bodies assume a more womanly appearance (*biological growth*), girls often feel the need to become more "feminine" if they hope to be attractive to members of the other sex (Burn et al., 1996; Katz, 1979). Furthermore, these young adolescents are also attaining formal operations and advanced role-taking skills (*cognitive growth*), which may help to explain why (1) they become self-conscious about their changing body images (Von Wright, 1989), (2) so concerned about other people's evaluation of them (Elkind, 1981a; remember the *imaginary audience* phenomenon), and (3) more inclined to conform to the *social* prescriptions of the female role.

TABLE 8-3 Percentages of boys and girls who requested popular "masculine" and "feminine" items from Santa Claus

	PERCENTAGE OF BOYS REQUESTING	PERCENTAGE OF GIRLS REQUESTING
Masculine items		
Vehicles	43.5	8.2
Sports equipment	25.1	15.1
Spatial/temporal toys (construction sets, clocks, and so on)	24.5	15.6
Feminine items		
Dolls (adult female)	.6	27.4
Dolls (babies)	.6	23.4
Domestic accessories	1.7	21.7

SOURCE: Adapted from Richardson & Simpson, 1982.

SUBCULTURAL VARIATIONS IN GENDER TYPING

Although not extensive, research on social-class and ethnic variations in gender-typing reveals that (1) middle-class adolescents (but not children) hold more flexible gender-role attitudes than their low-SES peers (Bardwell, Cochran, & Walker, 1986; Canter & Ageton, 1984) and (2) African-American children hold less stereotyped views of women than European-American children do (Bardwell et al., 1986).

Researchers have attributed these social-class and ethnic variations in gender-typing to differences in education and family life. For example, people from middle-class backgrounds typically have a wider array of educational and occupational options available to them, perhaps explaining why they eventually adopt more flexible attitudes about the roles that men and women should play. And a greater percentage of African-American than European-American children are living in *single-parent* homes and have mothers who are *employed* outside the house (U.S. Bureau of the Census, 1997). So the less stereotyped portrayal of women observed among African-American youngsters may simply reflect the fact that their mothers are more likely than European-American mothers to be assuming both instrumental (male) and expressive (female) functions in their own roles as a parent.

TABLE 8-4 An overview of gender-typing

AGE IN YEARS	GENDER IDENTITY	GENDER STEREOTYPING	GENDER-TYPED BEHAVIOR
0–2½	• Ability to discriminate males from females emerges and improves. • Child accurately labels the self as a boy or a girl.		• Gender-typed toy/activity preferences emerge. • Preferences for same-sex playmates emerge (gender segregation).
3–6	• Conservation of gender (recognition that one's gender is unchanging) emerges.	• Gender stereotyping of interests, activities, and occupations emerges and becomes quite rigid.	• Gender-typed play/toy preferences become stronger, particularly for boys. • Gender segregation intensifies.
7–11		• Gender stereotyping of personality traits and achievement domains emerges. • Gender stereotyping becomes less rigid.	• Gender segregation continues to strengthen. • Gender-typed toy/activity preferences continue to strengthen for boys; girls develop (or retain) interests in some masculine activities.
12 & beyond	• Gender identity becomes more salient, reflecting gender intensification pressures.	• Intolerance of cross-sex mannerisms increases early in adolescence. • Gender stereotyping becomes more flexible in most respects later in adolescence.	• Conformity to gender-typed behaviors increases early in adolescence, reflecting gender intensification. • Gender segregation becomes less pronounced.

Finally, children raised in "countercultural" or "avant-garde" homes (in which parents strive to promote egalitarian sex-role attitudes) are indeed less gender-stereotyped than children from traditional families in their *beliefs* about which activities and occupations are appropriate for males and females (Weisner & Wilson-Mitchell, 1990). Nevertheless, these youngsters are quite aware of traditional gender stereotypes and are just as "gender-typed" in their own toy and activity preferences as children from traditional families.

In sum, gender-role development proceeds at a remarkable pace (Ruble & Martin, 1998; see Table 8-4 for a brief overview). By the time they enter school, children have long been aware of their basic gender identities, have acquired many, many stereotypes about how the sexes differ, and have come to prefer gender-appropriate activities and same-sex playmates. During middle childhood, their knowledge continues to expand as they learn more about gender-stereotyped *psychological* traits, and they become more flexible in their thinking about gender roles. Yet their *behavior,* especially if they are boys, becomes even more gender-typed, and they segregate themselves even more from the other sex. Now a most intriguing question: How does all this happen so fast?

Theories of Gender Typing and Gender-Role Development

Several theories have been proposed to account for sex differences and the development of gender roles. Some theories emphasize the role of biological differences between the sexes, whereas others emphasize *social* influences on children. Some emphasize what society does to children, others what children do to themselves as they try to understand gender and all its implications. Let's briefly examine a biologically oriented theory and then consider the more "social" approaches offered by psychoanalytic theory, social learning theory, cognitive-developmental theory, and gender schema theory.

"Once there was a baby named Chris . . . [who] went to live on a beautiful island . . . [where] there were only boys and men; Chris was the only girl. Chris lived a very happy life on this island, but she never saw another girl or woman" (Taylor, 1996, p. 1559). What would Chris be like?

When Marianne Taylor (1996) asked 4- to 10-year-olds to indicate Chris's toy preferences, occupational aspirations, and personality traits, 4- to 8-year-olds assigned stereotypically feminine attributes to her, despite the fact that she was raised in a masculinizing environment and never saw a girl or woman. In other words, preschool and young grade-school children display an *essentialist bias,* assuming that Chris's biological status as a girl will determine what she will become. Only the 9- to 10-year-olds in this study showed any awareness that Chris's masculinizing environment might influence her activities, aspirations, and personality characteristics.

Many scholars once displayed a similar essentialist bias by assuming that virtually all sex differences were largely attributable to biological variations between males and females. What biological differences might be so important? For one, males have a Y chromosome and hence, some genes that all females lack. For another, the sexes clearly differ in hormonal balance, with males having higher concentrations of androgens (including testosterone) and lower levels of estrogen than females do. But do these biological *correlates* of gender and gender differences actually cause sex differences in behavior? Do they predispose boys and girls to prefer and to adopt different gender roles?

Today, even biologically oriented theorists take a softer stance, arguing that biological and social influences *interact* to determine a person's behaviors and role preferences. Nowhere is this interactive emphasis any more apparent than in the *biosocial theory* proposed by John Money and Anke Ehrhardt (1972). Although biosocial theory concentrates on biological forces that may channel and constrain the development of boys and girls, it also acknowledges that early biological developments will affect other people's *reactions* to the child and suggests that these social forces play a major part in steering the child toward a particular gender role. Let's take a closer look at this influential theory.

An Overview of Gender Differentiation and Gender-Role Development   Money and Ehrhardt (1972) propose that there are a number of critical episodes or events that will affect a person's eventual preference for the masculine or the feminine gender role. The first critical event occurs at conception as the child inherits either an X or a Y chromosome from the father. Over the next six weeks, the developing embryo has only an undifferentiated gonad, and the sex chromosomes determine whether this structure becomes the male testes or the female ovaries. If a Y chromosome is present, the embryo develops testes; otherwise ovaries will form.

These newly formed gonads then determine the outcome of episode 2. The testes of a male embryo secrete two hormones—*testosterone,* which stimulates the development of a male internal reproductive system, and *mullerian inhibiting substance* (MIS), which inhibits the development of female organs. In the absence of these hormones, the embryo develops the internal reproductive system of a female.

At a third critical point, three to four months after conception, secretion of testosterone by the testes normally leads to the growth of a penis and scrotum. If testosterone is absent (as in normal females), or if the male fetus has inherited a rare recessive disorder, called **testicular feminization syndrome (TFS),** that makes his body insensitive to male sex hormones, female external genitalia (labia and clitoris) will form. Testosterone also alters the development of the brain and nervous system.

testicular feminization syndrome (TFS): a genetic anomaly in which a male fetus is insensitive to the effects of male sex hormones and will develop femalelike external genitalia.

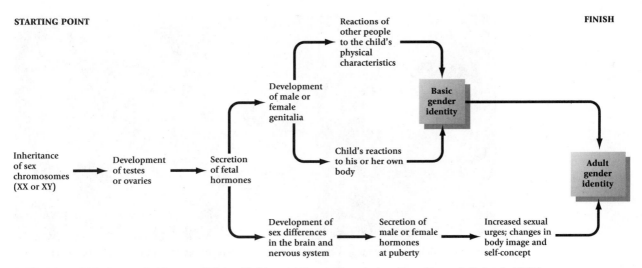

FIGURE 8.4 Critical events in Money and Ehrhardt's biosocial theory of sex typing. (From Money & Ehrhardt, 1972.)

For example, it signals the male brain to stop secreting hormones in a cyclical pattern so that males do not experience menstrual cycles at puberty.

Once a child is born, *social* factors immediately come into play. Parents and other people label and begin to react to the child based on the appearance of his or her genitals. If one's genitals are abnormal so that he or she is mislabeled a member of the other sex, this incorrect label can affect his or her future development. For example, if a biological male were consistently labeled and treated as a girl (as a boy with TFS syndrome and female external genitalia might be), he would, by about age 2½ to 3, acquire the gender identity (though not the biological characteristics) of a girl. Finally, biological factors enter the scene again at puberty when large quantities of hormones are released, stimulating the growth of the reproductive system, the appearance of secondary sex characteristics, and the development of sexual urges. These events, in combination with one's earlier self-concept as a male or a female, provide the basis for an adult gender identity and gender role preference (see Figure 8.5).

Evidence for Biological Influences on Gender-Role Development   How much influence *do* biological factors have on the behavior of males and females? To answer this question, we must consider what investigators have learned about genetic and hormonal influences.

Genetic Influences   Genetic factors may contribute to some sex differences in personality, cognitive abilities, and social behavior. Corrine Hutt (1972), for example, suspects that several of the developmental disorders more commonly seen among boys may be **X-linked recessive traits** for which their mother is a carrier (genetic [XX] females would have to inherit a recessive gene from each parent to show the same disorders). Furthermore, **timing of puberty**, a biological variable regulated in part by our genotypes, has a slight effect on visual/spatial performances. Both boys and girls who mature *late* tend to outperform early maturers of their own sex on some visual/spatial tasks, allegedly because slow maturation promotes increasing specialization of the brain's right hemisphere, which serves spatial functions (see Newcombe & Dubas, 1987). However, later research indicates that the spatial performances of both boys and girls are more heavily influenced by their *previous involvement* in spatial activities and their *self-concepts* than by the timing of puberty (Newcombe & Dubas, 1992;

X-linked recessive disorder: an attribute determined by a recessive gene that appears only on X chromosomes; since the gene determining these characteristics is recessive (that is, dominated by other genes that might appear at the same location on X chromosomes), such characteristics are more common among males, who have only one X chromosome; also called *sex-linked trait.*

timing of puberty effect: the finding that people who reach puberty late perform better on visual/spatial tasks than those who mature early.

PHOTO 8.4 Girls who often play with visual/spatial toys tend to perform better on tests of spatial ability.

Signorella, Jamison, & Krupa, 1989). Specifically, it appears that having a strong masculine self-concept and ample experience with spatial toys and activities will foster the growth of spatial skills in both boys and girls, whereas having restricted spatial experiences and a feminine self-concept seems to inhibit spatial abilities.

How closely are our masculine and feminine self-concepts related to the genes that we have inherited? Results from several behavioral genetics studies of adolescent twins suggest that genotype accounts for about 50% of the variability in people's masculine self-concepts but only 0% to 20% of the variability in their feminine self-concepts (Loehlin, 1992; Mitchell, Baker, & Jacklin, 1989). So even though genes determine our biological sex and may have some influence on the outcome of gender-typing, it appears that at least half the variability in people's masculine and feminine self-concepts is attributable to environmental influences.

Hormonal Influences Biological influences on development are also evident in studies of children who have been exposed to the "wrong" hormones during the prenatal period (Ehrhardt & Baker, 1974; Gandelman, 1992; Money & Ehrhardt, 1972). Before the consequences were known, some mothers who had problems carrying pregnancies to term were given drugs containing progestin, which are converted to the male hormone testosterone by the body. Other children with a condition known as **congenital adrenal hyperplasia (CAH)** have a genetic defect which causes their adrenal glands to produce unusually high levels of androgen from the prenatal period onward. These conditions usually have no effect on males; but female fetuses are often masculinized so that, despite their XX genetic endowment and female internal organs, they were born with external genitalia that resembled those of a boy (for example, a large clitoris that looked like a penis and fused labia that resembled a scrotum).

Money and Ehrhardt (1972; Ehrhardt & Baker, 1974) have followed several of these **androgenized females** whose external organs were surgically altered and who were then raised as girls. Compared with their sisters and other girls, many more androgenized girls were tomboys who often played with boys and who preferred boys' toys and activities to traditionally feminine pursuits (see also Berenbaum & Snyder, 1995; Hines & Kaufman, 1994). As adolescents, they began dating somewhat later than other girls and felt that marriage should be delayed until they had established their careers. A high proportion (37%) described themselves as homosexual or bi-

congenital adrenal hyperplasia (CAH): a genetic anomaly that causes one's adrenal glands to produce unusually high levels of androgen from the prenatal period onward; often has masculinizing effects on female fetuses.

androgenized females: females who develop malelike external genitalia because of exposure to male sex hormones during the prenatal period.

sexual (Money, 1985; see also Dittman, Kappes, & Kappes, 1992). Androgenized females also perform better than most girls and women on tests of spatial ability, further suggesting that early exposure to male hormones may have "masculinizing" effects on a female fetus's brain (Kimura, 1992; Resnick et al., 1986). Although a skeptic might wonder whether other family members had reacted to the girls' abnormal genitalia early in life, treating those girls more like boys, interviews with the girls' parents suggested that they had not (Ehrhardt & Baker, 1974). So we must seriously consider the possibilities that (1) many differences between males and females may be hormonally mediated and (2) prenatal exposure to male sex hormones can influence the attitudes, interests, and activities of human females.[2]

EVIDENCE FOR SOCIAL-LABELING INFLUENCES

Although biological forces may steer boys and girls toward different activities and interests, Money and Ehrhardt (1972) insist that social-labeling influences are also important—so important, in fact, that they can modify or even *reverse* biological predispositions. Indeed, some of the evidence for this provocative claim comes from Money's own work with androgenized girls.

Recall that Money's androgenized girls were born with the internal reproductive organs of a normal female even though their external genitalia resembled a penis and scrotum. These children are sometimes labeled boys at birth and raised as such until their abnormalities are detected. Money (1965) reports that the discovery and correction of this condition (by surgery and gender reassignment) presents few if any adjustment problems, provided that the sex change occurs *before age 18 months*. But after age 3, gender reassignment is exceedingly difficult because these genetic females have experienced prolonged masculine gender-typing and have already labeled themselves boys. These data led Money to conclude that there is a "critical period" between 18 months and 3 years of age for the establishment of gender identity. As illustrated in Box 8.3, it may be more accurate to call the first three years a *sensitive* period, for other investigators have claimed that it is possible under certain circumstances to assume a new identity later in adolescence. Nevertheless, Money's findings indicate that early social labeling and gender-role socialization can play a very prominent part in determining a child's gender identity and role preferences.

Cultural Influences   Because most societies promote instrumental traits in males and expressive traits in females, some theorists have concluded that traditional gender roles are part of the natural order of things—a product of our bioevolutionary history (Archer, 1996, 1997; Buss, 1995). Yet there are sizable differences across cultures in what people expect of boys and girls (Whiting & Edwards, 1988). Consider Margaret Mead's (1935) classic study of three tribal societies in New Guinea. *Both* males and females among the Arapesh were taught to be cooperative, nonaggressive, and sensitive to the needs of others. This behavioral profile would be considered "expressive" or "feminine" in Western cultures. By contrast, *both* men and women of the Mundugumor tribe were expected to be assertive, aggressive, and emotionally unresponsive in their interpersonal relationships—a masculine pattern of behavior by Western standards. Finally, the Tchambuli displayed a pattern of gender-role development

---

[2]It is still not entirely clear that the masculine interests and abilities these girls display are a direct result of their prenatal exposure to androgen. Many of those girls received cortisone therapy to control their androgen levels and prevent further masculinization of their bodies, and one side effect of cortisone is to dramatically increase a person's activity level. So, a plausible alternative interpretation is that the high-intensity "masculine" behaviors and the interest patterns androgenized girls display are really due more to the medical treatments they received than to their prenatal exposure to male sex hormones (Huston, 1983).

Box 8.3   *Current Controversies*

Is Biology Destiny?

When biological sex and social labeling conflict, which wins out? Consider the case of a male identical twin whose penis was damaged beyond repair during circumcision (Money & Tucker, 1975). After seeking medical advice and considering the alternatives, the parents agreed to a surgical procedure that made their 21-month-old son a girl anatomically. After the operation, the family began to actively gender-type this boy-turned-girl by changing her hairstyle; dressing her in frilly blouses, dresses, and the like; purchasing feminine toys for her to play with; and teaching such feminine behaviors as sitting to urinate. By age 5, the girl twin was quite different from her *genetically identical* brother: She knew she was a girl and was far neater and daintier than her brother. Here, then, was a case in which assigned sex and gender-role socialization seemed to overcome biological predispositions. Or did they?

Milton Diamond and Keith Sigmundson (1997) followed up on this "John" turned "Joan" and found that the story had a twist ending. Over time, Joan became quite uncomfortable with doll play and other traditionally feminine pursuits; she preferred to dress up in men's clothing, play with her twin brother's toys, and take things apart to see how they worked. Somewhere around the age of 10, she had the distinct feeling that she was not a girl: "I began to see how different I felt and was . . . I

thought I was a freak or something . . . but I didn't want to admit it. I figured I didn't want to wind up opening a can of worms" (pp. 299–300). Being rejected by other children because of her masculine looks and feminine dress also took their toll, as did continued pressure from psychiatrists to behave in a more feminine manner. Finally, at age 14 and years of inner turmoil and suicidal thinking, Joan had had it and simply refused to take female hormones and pretend to be a girl any longer. She then received male hormone shots, a mastectomy, and surgery to construct a penis and emerged as a quite handsome and popular young man who dated girls, married at age 25, and appears to be comfortable with his hard-won identity as a man. Perhaps, then, we should back off from the conclusion that early gender-role socialization is all that matters. Biology matters too.

A second source of evidence that biology matters is a study of 18 biological males in the Dominican Republic who had a genetic condition (TFS syndrome) that made them insensitive prenatally to the effects of male hormones (Imperato-McGinley et al., 1979). They had begun life with ambiguous genitals and were labeled and raised as girls. However, under the influence of male hormones produced at puberty, they sprouted beards and became masculine in appearance. How, in light of Money and Ehrhardt's critical-period hypothesis, could a person

---

opposite to that of Western societies: males were passive, emotionally dependent, and socially sensitive whereas females were dominant, independent, and assertive. So members of these three tribes developed in accordance with the gender roles that were *socially* prescribed by their culture—none of which matched the female/ expressive—male/instrumental pattern seen in Western societies. Clearly, social forces contribute heavily to gender-typing.

In sum, Money and Ehrhardt's biosocial theory stresses the importance of early biological developments that influence how parents and other social agents label a child at birth and that possibly also affect behavior more directly. However, the theory also holds that whether children are socialized as boys or girls strongly influences their gender-role development—in short, that biological and social forces *interact*. But how, exactly, do they interact?

A Psychobiosocial Viewpoint   Diane Halpern (1997) has recently proposed a *psychobiosocial model* to explain how nature and nurture might jointly influence the development of gender-typed attributes. Halpern agrees with Money and Ehrhardt that prenatal exposure to male or female hormones initially influences the organization of

adjust to becoming a man after leading an entire childhood as a girl?

Amazingly, 16 of these 18 individuals seemed able to accept their late conversion from female to male and to adopt masculine lifestyles, including the establishment of heterosexual relationships. One retained a female identity and gender role, and the remaining individual switched to a male gender identity but still dressed as a female. Clearly, this study also casts doubt on the notion that socialization during the first three years is absolutely critical to later gender-role development. Instead, it suggests that hormonal influences may be more important than social influences.

However, Imperato-McGinley's conclusions have been challenged (Ehrhardt, 1985). Little information was reported about how these individuals were raised, and it is quite possible that Dominican parents, knowing TFS syndrome was common in their society, treated these girls-turned-boys differently from other "girls" when they were young. Furthermore, the girls-turned-boys had genitals that were not completely normal in appearance, and the practice of river bathing in Dominican culture almost certainly means that these youngsters compared themselves to normal girls (and boys) and may have recognized early on that they were "different." So these children may not have received an exclusively feminine upbringing and may never have fully committed themselves to being girls. Nor should we automatically assume that their later incorporation of the masculine role was due to hormones. One study of TFS males raised as females among the Sambia of New Guinea found that *social pressures*—namely, the argument that they could not bear children—is what appeared most responsible for the gender switches that occurred after puberty (Herdt & Davidson, 1988).

Finally, another little Canadian boy, whose penis was damaged during circumcision and who was raised as a girl from 7 months of age, has now reached adulthood and continues to live quite comfortably within her *female* gender identity (Bradley et al., 1998). Clearly, biology is not destiny and social influences are important in shaping one's gender identity and gender-role preferences.

What studies like these of individuals with genital abnormalities appear to teach us is this: We are predisposed by our biology to develop as males or females; the first three years of life are a *sensitive period* perhaps, but not a critical period, for the establishment of gender identity; and *neither* biology nor social labeling can fully account for gender-role development.

PHOTO 8.5 Gender-role behaviors are often specific to one's culture. Like many Peruvian boys, this youngster routinely washes clothes and attends to household tasks.

male and female brains in ways that might make boys, for example, somewhat more receptive to spatial activities and girls somewhat more susceptible to quiet verbal exchanges. These heightened sensitivities, in concert with others' beliefs about the kinds of experiences most appropriate for boys and for girls, means that boys are likely to receive a richer array of spatial experiences than girls do, whereas girls will be exposed more often to verbal play activities.

Drawing on recent advances in the field of cognitive neuroscience, Halpern then proposes that the different experiences boys and girls have will influence the neural pathways laid down in their immature and highly *plastic* (that is, changeable) brains. Although the genetic code does impose constraints on brain development, it does not provide specific "wiring" instructions, and the precise architecture of the brain is heavily influenced by the early experiences one has (Johnson, 1997). So according to Halpern (1997), boys, who receive more early spatial experiences than girls do, may develop a richer array of neural pathways in areas of the brain that serve spatial functions which, in turn, may make them ever more receptive to spatial activities and to acquiring spatial skills. By contrast, girls may develop a richer array of neural interconnections in areas of the brain serving verbal functions, thereby becoming ever more receptive to verbal activities and to acquiring verbal skills. From a psychobiosocial perspective then, nature and nurture feed on each other and are a false dichotomy. In Halpern's words, "Biology and environment are as inseparable as conjoined twins who share a common heart" (p. 1097).

What both biosocial theory and the psychobiosocial model do *not* do is to specify the precise social processes that contribute most heavily to children's emerging gender identities and gender-typed patterns of behavior. Let's turn now to the social theories of gender-typing, the first of which was Sigmund Freud's psychoanalytic approach.

FREUD'S PSYCHOANALYTIC THEORY

Recall from Chapter 2 that Freud thought sexuality (the sex instinct) was inborn. However, he believed that one's preference for a particular gender role emerges during the **phallic stage** of psychosexual development as children begin to emulate and to **identify** with their same-sex parent. Specifically, Freud claimed that a 3- to 6-year-old boy will internalize masculine attributes and behaviors when he is forced to identify with his father as a means of renouncing his incestuous desire for his mother, reducing his **castration anxiety,** and thus resolving his **Oedipus complex.** However, Freud believed that gender-typing is more difficult for a young girl who lacks a penis, already feels castrated, and will experience no overriding fear that would compel her to strongly identify with her mother and resolve her **Electra complex.** Why, then, would a girl ever develop a preference for the feminine role? Freud offered several suggestions, one of which was that the object of a girl's affection, her father, was likely to encourage her feminine behavior—an act that increases the attractiveness of the mother, who serves as the girl's model of femininity. So by trying to please her father (or to prepare for relationships with other males after she recognizes the implausibility of possessing her father), a girl should be motivated to incorporate her mother's feminine attributes and will eventually become gender-typed (Freud, 1924/1961a).

Evaluating Freud's Theory Although children are rapidly learning gender stereotypes and developing gender-typed playmate and activity preferences at roughly the ages Freud says they should, his psychoanalytic theory of gender-typing has not fared well at all. Many 4- to 6-year-olds are so ignorant about differences between male and female genitalia that it is hard to see how most boys could fear castration or how most girls could feel castrated as Freud says they do (Bem, 1989; Katcher, 1955). Further-

phallic stage: Freud's third stage of psychosexual development (from 3 to 6 years of age) in which children gratify the sex instinct by fondling their genitals and developing an incestuous desire for the parent of the other sex.

identification: Freud's term for the child's tendency to emulate another person, usually the same-sex parent.

castration anxiety: in Freud's theory, a young boy's fear that his father will castrate him as punishment for his rivalrous conduct.

Oedipus complex: Freud's term for the conflict that 3- to 6-year-old boys were said to experience when they develop an incestuous desire for their mothers and a jealous and hostile rivalry with their fathers.

Electra complex: female version of the Oedipus complex, in which a 3- to 6-year-old girl was thought to envy her father for possessing a penis and would choose him as a sex object in the hope that he would share with her this valuable organ that she lacked.

more, Freud assumed that a boy's identification with his father is based on fear; but most researchers find that boys identify more strongly with fathers who are warm and nurturant rather than overly punitive and threatening (Hetherington & Frankie, 1967; Mussen & Rutherford, 1963). Finally, studies of parent/child resemblances reveal that school-age children and adolescents are not all that similar psychologically to either parent (Maccoby & Jacklin, 1974). Clearly, these findings are damaging to the Freudian notion that children acquire important personality traits by identifying with the same-sex parent.

Let's now consider the social-learning interpretation of gender-typing to see whether this approach looks any more promising.

SOCIAL LEARNING THEORY

According to social learning theorists such as Albert Bandura (1989) and Walter Mischel (1970), children acquire their gender identities and gender-role preferences in two ways. First, through **direct tuition** (or *differential reinforcement*), children are encouraged and rewarded for gender-appropriate behaviors and are punished or otherwise discouraged for behaviors considered more appropriate for members of the other sex. Second, through *observational learning,* children adopt the attitudes and behaviors of a variety of same-sex models.

Direct Tuition of Gender Roles   Are parents actively involved in teaching boys how to be boys and girls how to be girls? Yes, indeed (Leaper, Anderson, & Sanders, 1998; Lytton & Romney, 1991), and their shaping of gender-typed behaviors begins rather early. Beverly Fagot and Mary Leinbach (1989), for example, found that parents are already encouraging gender-appropriate activities and discouraging cross-gender play during the second year of life, *before* children have acquired their basic gender identities. Daughters are consistently reinforced for dancing, dressing up (as women), following parents around, asking for help, and playing with dolls; and they are generally discouraged from manipulating objects, running, jumping, and climbing. By contrast, sons are often reprimanded for such "feminine" behaviors as doll play or seeking help and are actively encouraged to play with masculine items such as blocks, trucks, and push-and-pull toys that require large muscle activity (Fagot, 1978).

Are children influenced by the "gender curriculum" their parents provide? They certainly are! In fact, parents who show the clearest patterns of differential reinforcement have children who are relatively quick to (1) label themselves as boys or girls, (2) develop strong gender-typed toy and activity preferences, and (3) acquire an understanding of gender stereotypes (Fagot & Leinbach, 1989; Fagot, Leinbach, & O'Boyle, 1992). And fathers are even more likely than mothers to encourage "gender-typed" behaviors and to discourage behavior considered more appropriate for the other sex (Leve & Fagot, 1997; Lytton & Romney, 1991). So it seems that children's earliest preferences for gender-typed toys and activities may well result from their parents' (particularly fathers') successful attempts to reinforce these interests.

Throughout the preschool period, parents become less and less inclined to carefully monitor and differentially reinforce their children's gender-typed activities (Fagot & Hagan, 1991; Lytton & Romney, 1991). Why? Because many other factors conspire to maintain these interests, not the least of which is the behavior of same-sex peers (Beal, 1994). Even before they have established their basic gender identities, 2-year-old boys will often belittle or disrupt each other for playing with girl toys or with girls, and 2-year-old girls are quite critical of other girls who choose to play with boys (Fagot, 1985a). So peers are beginning to differentially reinforce gender-typed attitudes and behaviors even as parents are becoming somewhat less likely to do so.

direct tuition: teaching young children how to behave by reinforcing "appropriate" behaviors and by punishing or otherwise discouraging inappropriate conduct.

Observational Learning   According to Bandura (1989), children acquire many of their gender-typed attributes and interests by observing and imitating a variety of same-sex models. The assumption is that boys will see which toys, activities, and behaviors are "for boys" and girls will learn which activities and behaviors are "for girls" by selectively attending to and imitating a variety of *same-sex* models, including peers, teachers, older siblings, and media personalities, as well as their mothers or their fathers.

Yet, there is some question of just how important *same-sex* modeling influences are during the *preschool* period, for researchers often find that 3- to 5-year-olds learn a great deal from models of both sexes. For example, children of employed mothers (who play the *masculine* instrumental role) or of fathers who routinely perform such *feminine* household tasks as cooking, cleaning, and child care are less aware of gender stereotypes than are children of more traditional parents (Serbin et al., 1993; Turner & Gervai, 1995). Furthermore, John Masters and his associates (1979) found that preschool children are much more concerned about the sex-appropriateness of the *behavior* they are observing than the sex of the model who displays it. Four- to 5-year-old boys, for example, will play with objects labeled "boys' toys" even after they have seen a girl playing with them. However, these youngsters are reluctant to play with "girls' toys" that boy models have played with earlier, and they think that other boys would also shun objects labeled as girls' toys (Martin, Eisenbud, & Rose, 1995). So children's toy choices are affected more by the labels attached to the toys than by the sex of the child who served as a model. But once they recognize that gender is an unchanging aspect of their personalities (at age 5 to 7), children do begin to attend more selectively to same-sex models and are now more likely to avoid toys and activities that other-sex models seem to enjoy (Frey & Ruble, 1992; Ruble et al., 1981).

Media Influences   Not only do children learn by observing other children and adult models with whom they interact, but they also learn about gender roles from reading stories and watching television. Although sexism in children's books has declined over the past 50 years, male characters are still more likely than female characters to engage in active, instrumental pursuits such as riding bikes or making things, whereas female characters are often depicted as passive and dependent individuals who spend much of their time playing quietly indoors and "creating problems that require masculine solutions" (Kortenhaus & Demorest, 1993; Turner-Bowker, 1996). It is similar in the world of television: Males are usually featured as the central characters who work at professions, make important decisions, respond to emergencies, and assume positions of leadership, whereas females are often portrayed as relatively passive and emotional creatures who manage a home or work at "feminine" occupations such as waitressing or nursing (Liebert & Sprafkin, 1988).

Apparently children are influenced by these highly sexist media portrayals, for those who watch a lot of commercial television are more likely to prefer gender-typed activities and to hold highly stereotyped views of men and women than are their classmates who watch little television (McGhee & Frueh, 1980; Signorielli & Lears, 1992). But as more women play detectives and more men raise families on television, children's perceptions of male and female roles are likely to change. In fact, children who regularly watch *The Cosby Show* and other relatively nonsexist programs do hold less stereotyped views of the sexes (Rosenwasser, Lingenfelter, & Harrington, 1989).

In sum, there is a lot of evidence that differential reinforcement and observational learning contribute to gender-role development. However, social learning theorists have often portrayed children as *passive pawns* in the process: Parents, peers, and TV characters show them what to do and reinforce them for doing it. Might this perspective miss something, namely the child's *own* contribution to gender-role socialization? Consider, for example, that children do not always receive gender-stereotyped Christmas presents because their sexist parents force these objects on them. Many parents who would rather buy gender-neutral or educational toys end up "giving in" to sons who beg for machine guns or daughters who want tea sets (Robinson & Morris, 1986).

KOHLBERG'S COGNITIVE-DEVELOPMENTAL THEORY

Lawrence Kohlberg (1966) has proposed a cognitive theory of gender-typing that is quite different from the other theories we have considered and helps to explain why boys and girls adopt traditional gender roles even when their parents may not want them to. Kohlberg's major themes are these:

1. Gender-role development depends on cognitive development; children must acquire certain understandings about gender before they will be influenced by their social experiences.
2. Children *actively socialize themselves*; they are not merely passive pawns of social influence.

According to both psychoanalytic theory and social learning theory, children first learn to do "boy" or "girl" things because their parents encourage these activities; then, they come to identify with or habitually imitate same-sex models, thereby acquiring a stable gender identity. By contrast, Kohlberg suggests that children *first* establish a stable gender identity and then *actively* seek out same-sex models and other information to learn how to act like a boy or a girl. To Kohlberg, it's not "I'm treated like a boy; therefore, I must be one" (social learning position). It's more like "Hey, I'm a boy; therefore, I'd better do everything I can to find out how to behave like one" (cognitive–self-socialization position).

Kohlberg believes that children pass through the following three stages as they acquire a mature understanding of what it means to be a male or a female:

1. **Basic gender identity.** By age 3, children have labeled themselves boys or girls.
2. **Gender stability.** Somewhat later, gender is perceived as *stable over time*. Boys invariably become men and girls grow up to be women.
3. **Gender consistency.** The gender concept is complete when the child realizes that one's sex is also *stable across situations*. Five- to 7-year-olds who have reached this stage are no longer fooled by appearances. They know, for example, that one's gender cannot be altered by cross-dressing or taking up cross-sex activities.

When do children become motivated to socialize themselves—that is, to seek out same-sex models and learn how to act like males and females? According to Kohlberg, self-socialization begins only after children reach *gender consistency*. So for Kohlberg, a mature understanding of gender (1) instigates true sex-typing and (2) is the *cause* rather than the consequence of attending to same-sex models.

Studies conducted in more than 20 different cultures reveal that preschool children do proceed through Kohlberg's three stages of gender identity in the sequence he describes and that attainment of gender consistency (or conservation of gender) is clearly associated with other relevant aspects of cognitive development, such as the conservation of liquids and mass (Marcus & Overton, 1978; Munroe, Shimmin, & Munroe, 1984). Furthermore, boys who have achieved gender consistency do begin to pay more attention to male than to female characters on television (Luecke-Aleska et al., 1995) and will now favor novel toys that male models prefer to those that female models like—even when the toys they are passing on are the *more attractive objects* (Frey & Ruble, 1992). So children with a mature gender identity (especially boys) often play it safe and select the toy or activity that other members of their gender view as more appropriate for them.

basic gender identity: the stage of gender identity in which the child first labels the self as a boy or a girl.

gender stability: the stage of gender identity in which the child recognizes that gender is stable over time.

gender consistency: the stage of gender identity in which the child recognizes that a person's gender is invariant despite changes in the person's activities or appearance (also known as gender constancy).

Criticisms of Kohlberg's Theory   The major problem with Kohlberg's theory is that gender-typing is well under way before the child acquires a mature gender identity. We have seen, for example, that 2-year-old boys prefer masculine toys before they have achieved a basic gender identity, and that 3-year-olds of each sex have learned many gender-role stereotypes and already prefer same-sex activities and playmates long before they begin to attend more selectively to same-sex models. Furthermore, we've noted that gender reassignment can be exceedingly difficult after children reach age 3 (Kohlberg's basic identity stage) and have initially categorized themselves as boys or girls. In fact, one's level of gender identity may rest as much on social experience as on cognitive development, for even 3- and 4-year-olds who have often seen members of the other sex naked may display gender consistency on gender-identity tests (Bem, 1989). Finally, measures of gender identity simply do not predict how much children know about gender stereotypes or how gender-typed their behaviors are (Bussey & Bandura, 1992; Lobel & Menashri, 1993; Martin & Little, 1990). So Kohlberg badly overstates the case in arguing that a mature understanding of gender is necessary for gender-typing to begin. As we will see in the next section, only a rudimentary understanding of gender permits children to acquire gender stereotypes and develop strong gender-typed toy and activity preferences.

GENDER SCHEMA THEORY

Carol Martin and Charles Halverson (1981, 1987) have proposed a somewhat different cognitive theory of gender-typing (actually, an information-processing theory) that appears quite promising. Like Kohlberg, Martin and Halverson believe that children are intrinsically motivated to acquire interests, values, and behaviors that are consistent with their "boy" or "girl" self-images. But unlike Kohlberg, they argue that this "self-socialization" begins as soon as the child acquires a *basic gender identity* at ages 2½ or 3 and is well under way by ages 6 to 7, when the child achieves gender consistency.

According to Martin and Halverson's "gender schema" theory, establishment of a basic gender identity motivates a child to learn about the sexes and to incorporate this information into **gender schemas**—that is, organized sets of beliefs and expectations about males and females that will influence the kinds of information he attends to, elaborates, and remembers. First, children acquire a simple "**in-group/out-group schema**" that allows them to classify some objects, behaviors, and roles as "for boys" and others as "for girls" (for example, trucks are for boys; dolls are for girls; girls can cry but boys should not, and so on). This is the kind of information that researchers normally tap when studying children's knowledge of gender stereotypes. And this initial categorization of objects and activities clearly affects children's thinking. In one research program, 4- and 5-year-olds were shown unfamiliar gender-neutral toys (for example, spinning bells; a magnet stand), were told that these objects were either "for boys" or "for girls," and were asked whether they and other boys or girls would like them. Children clearly relied on the labels to guide their thinking. Boys, for example, liked "boy" objects better than girls did, and children assumed that other boys would also like these objects better than other girls would. Just the opposite pattern of reasoning was observed when *these same objects* were labeled as "for girls." Even highly attractive toys soon lost their luster if they were labeled as being for the other gender (Martin et al., 1995).

In addition, children are said to construct an **own-sex schema,** which consists of detailed plans of action they will need in order to perform various gender-consistent behaviors and enact a gender role. So a girl who has a basic gender identity might first learn that sewing is "for girls" and building model airplanes is "for boys." Then, because she is a girl and wants to act consistently with her own self-concept, she will gather a

gender schemas: organized sets of beliefs and expectations about males and females that guide information processing.

"in-group/out-group" schema: one's general knowledge of the mannerisms, roles, activities, and behaviors that characterize males and females.

own-sex schema: detailed knowledge or plans of action that enable a person to perform gender-consistent activities and to enact his or her gender role.

great deal of information about sewing to add to her own-sex schema, while largely ignoring information about building model airplanes (see also Figure 8.5). To test this notion, 4- to 9-year-olds were given boxes of gender-neutral objects (for example, burglar alarms, pizza cutters) and told that these objects were either "boy" items or "girl" items (Bradbard et al., 1986). As predicted, boys subsequently explored "boy" items more than girls did, whereas girls explored more than boys when the objects were described as things girls enjoy. One week later, boys recalled much more in-depth information about "boy" items than girls did, whereas girls recalled more than boys about these very same objects if they had been labeled "girl" items. If children's information-gathering efforts are consistently guided by their own-sex schemas in this way, we can easily see how boys and girls might acquire very different stores of knowledge and develop different interests and competencies as they mature.

Once formed, gender schemas "structure" experience by providing a framework for processing social information. The idea here is that children are likely to encode and remember information consistent with their gender schemas and to forget schema-inconsistent information or to otherwise distort it so that it becomes more consistent with their stereotypes (Liben & Signorella, 1993; Martin & Halverson, 1983), especially if they have reached ages 6 to 7, when their own stereotyped knowledge and preferences have crystallized and are especially strong (Welch-Ross & Schmidt, 1996). Support for this idea was presented in Box 8.2; recall that children who heard stories in which actors performed gender-atypical behaviors (for example, a girl chopping wood) tended to recall the action but to alter the scene to conform to their gender stereotypes (saying that a boy had been chopping). Surely these strong tendencies to forget or to distort counterstereotypic information help to explain why unfounded beliefs about males and females are so slow to die.

In sum, Martin and Halverson's gender schema theory is an interesting "new look" at the gender-typing process. Not only does this model describe how gender-role stereotypes might originate and persist over time, but it also indicates how these emerging "gender schemas" might contribute to the development of strong gender-role preferences and gender-typed behaviors long before a child may realize that gender is an unchanging attribute.

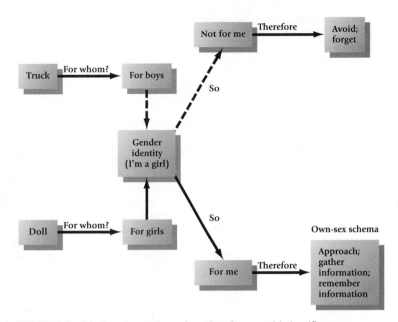

FIGURE 8.5 Gender-schema theory in action. A young girl classifies new information according to an "in-group/out-group schema" as either "for boys" or "for girls." Information about boys' toys and activities is ignored, but information about toys and activities for girls is relevant to the self and so is added to an ever-larger "own-sex schema." (Adapted from Martin & Halverson, 1987.)

AN INTEGRATIVE THEORY

Biological, social-learning, cognitive-developmental, and gender schema perspectives have each contributed in important ways to our understanding of sex differences and gender-role development (Ruble & Martin, 1998; Serbin et al., 1993). In fact, the processes that different theories emphasize seem to be especially important at different periods. Biological theories account for the major biological developments that occur before birth—the events that induce people to label the child as a boy or a girl and to treat him or her accordingly. The differential reinforcement

TABLE 8-5   An overview of the gender-typing process from the perspective of an integrative theorist

DEVELOPMENTAL PERIOD	EVENTS AND OUTCOMES	MOST PERTINENT THEORY(IES)
Prenatal period	The fetus develops male or female genitalia which others will react to once the child is born.	Biosocial/psychobiosocial
Birth to 3 years	Parents and other companions label the child a boy or a girl, frequently remind the child of his or her gender, and begin to encourage gender-consistent behavior while discouraging cross-sex activities. As a result of these social experiences, the neural developments they foster, and the development of very basic classification skills, the young child acquires gender-typed behavioral preferences and the knowledge that he or she is a boy or a girl (basic gender identity).	Social-learning (differential reinforcement) Psychobiosocial
3 to 6 years	Once children acquire a basic gender identity, they begin to seek information about sex differences, form gender schemas, and become intrinsically motivated to perform those acts that are viewed as "appropriate" for their own sex. When acquiring gender schemas, children attend to *both* male and female models. Once their gender schemas are well established, these youngsters are likely to imitate behaviors considered appropriate for their sex, regardless of the gender of the model who displays them.	Gender schema
7 to puberty	Children finally acquire a sense of gender consistency—a firm, future-oriented image of themselves as boys who must necessarily become men or girls who will obviously become women. At this point they begin to rely less exclusively on gender schemas and begin to look to the behavior of same-sex models to acquire those mannerisms and attributes that are consistent with their firm categorization of self as a male or female.	Cognitive-developmental (Kohlberg)
Puberty and beyond	The biological upheavals of adolescence, in conjunction with new social expectations (gender intensification), cause teenagers to reexamine their self-concepts, forming an adult gender identity.	Biosocial/psychobiosocial Social-learning Gender schema Cognitive-developmental

process that social-learning theorists emphasize seems to account rather well for early gender-typing: Young children display gender-consistent behaviors largely because other people encourage these activities and will often discourage behaviors considered more appropriate for members of the other sex. As a result of this early socialization and the growth of categorization skills, 2½- to 3-year-olds acquire a basic gender identity and begin to form *gender schemas* which tell them (1) what boys and girls are like and (2) how they, as boys and girls, are supposed to think and act. And when they finally understand, at age 6 or 7, that their gender will never change, children begin to focus less exclusively on gender schemas and to pay more and more attention to same-sex models to decide which attitudes, activities, interests, and mannerisms are most appropriate for members of their own sex (Kohlberg's viewpoint). Of course, summarizing developments in an integrative model such as this one (see Table 8-5 for an overview) does not mean that biological forces play no further role after the child is born or that differential reinforcement ceases to affect development once the child acquires a basic gender identity. But an integrative theorist would emphasize that from age 3 on, children are active, *self-socializers* who will try very hard to acquire the masculine or feminine attributes they view as consistent with their male or female self-images. This is why parents who hope to discourage their children from adopting traditional gender roles are often amazed that their sons and daughters seem to become little "sexists" all on their own.

One more point: All theories of gender-role development would agree that what children actually learn about being a male or a female will depend greatly on what their society offers them in the way of a "gender curriculum." In other words, we must view gender-role development through an *ecological* lens and appreciate that there is nothing inevitable about the patterns of male and female development that we see in our society today. (Indeed, recall the gender-role reversals that Mead observed among the Tchambuli tribe of New Guinea.) In another era, in another culture, the gender-typing process can produce very different kinds of boys and girls.

Should we in Western cultures be trying to raise different kinds of boys and girls? As we will see in our next section, some theorists would answer this question with a resounding YES!

Psychological Androgyny: A Prescription for the Future?

Throughout this chapter, we have used the term *gender appropriate* to describe the mannerisms and behaviors that societies consider more suitable for members of one sex than the other. Today many developmentalists believe that these rigidly defined gender-role standards are actually harmful because they constrain the behavior of both males and females. Sandra Bem (1978), for example, has stated that her major purpose in studying gender roles is "to help free the human personality from the restrictive prison of sex-role stereotyping and to develop a conception of mental health that is free from culturally imposed definitions of masculinity and femininity."

For many years, psychologists assumed that masculinity and femininity were at opposite ends of a single dimension. If one possessed highly masculine traits, one must be very unfeminine; being highly feminine implied being unmasculine. Bem (1974) challenged this assumption by arguing that individuals of either sex can be characterized by psychological **androgyny**—that is, by a balancing or blending of *both* desirable masculine-stereotyped traits (for example, being assertive, analytical, forceful, and independent) and desirable feminine-stereotyped traits (for example, being affectionate, compassionate, gentle, and understanding). In Bem's model, then, masculinity and femininity are *two separate dimensions* of personality. A male or female who has many desirable masculine-stereotyped traits and few feminine ones is defined as a *masculine gender-typed* person. One who has many feminine- and few masculine-stereotyped traits is said to be *feminine gender-typed*. The androgynous person possesses both masculine and feminine traits, whereas the *undifferentiated* individual lacks both of these kinds of attributes (see Figure 8.6).

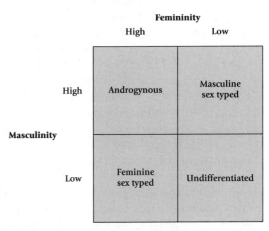

FIGURE 8.6 Categories of sex-role orientation based on viewing masculinity and femininity as separate dimensions of personality.

DO ANDROGYNOUS PEOPLE REALLY EXIST?

Bem (1974) and other investigators (Spence & Helmerich, 1978) have developed self-perception inventories that contain both a masculinity (or instrumentality) scale and a femininity (or expressivity) scale. In one large sample of college students (Spence & Helmreich, 1978), roughly 66% of the test takers proved to be either "masculine" men or "feminine" women, about 30% were androgynous, and the remaining 7% to 8% were either undifferentiated or "sex-reversed" (masculine gender-typed females or feminine gender-typed males). Janet Boldizar (1991) has developed a similar gender-role inventory for grade-school children and found that approximately 25% to 30% of third- through seventh-graders can be classified as androgynous. So androgynous individuals do exist, and in sizable numbers.

androgyny: a gender-role orientation in which the individual has incorporated a large number of both masculine and feminine attributes into his or her personality.

ARE THERE ADVANTAGES TO BEING ANDROGYNOUS?

When we think about the idea that a person can be both assertive and sensitive, both independent and understanding, we can't help but think that being androgynous is psychologically healthy. Is it? Bem (1975, 1978) demonstrated that androgynous men and women behave more flexibly than traditionally gender-typed individuals. For example, androgynous people, like masculine gender-typed people, can display the "masculine," instrumental trait of *independence* by resisting social pressure to judge very unamusing cartoons as funny just because their companions do. Yet they are as likely as feminine gender-typed individuals to display the "feminine," expressive quality of *nurturance* by interacting positively with a baby. Androgynous people do seem to be more highly adaptable, more able to adjust their behavior to the demands of the situation at hand (Harter, Waters, Whitesell, & Kastelic, 1998; Shaffer, Pegalis, & Cornell, 1992). Furthermore, androgynous children and adolescents appear to enjoy higher self-esteem and are perceived as more likable and better adjusted than their traditionally gender-typed peers (Allgood-Merten & Stockard, 1991; Boldizar, 1991; O'Heron & Orlofsky, 1990). It has also become clear that androgynous men can still feel quite masculine and androgynous women appropriately feminine even though they sometimes express traits traditionally associated with the other sex (Spence, 1993).

But before we conclude that androgyny is a thoroughly desirable attribute, let's note that it is the possession of "masculine" traits rather than androgyny per se that is most strongly associated with good adjustment and high self-esteem (Spence & Hall, 1996; Whitley, 1983). This finding should not surprise us, for people in many societies value masculine characteristics more highly than feminine attributes (Turner & Gervai, 1995). But even so, there are signs that the times may be changing. In her study of grade-school children, Boldizar (1991) found that (1) androgyny was by far the best single predictor of children's impressions of their global self-worth, and (2) femininity predicted some aspects of self-esteem (physical attractiveness; behavioral conduct) just as well as or better than masculinity did. And other recent research (reviewed by Mayer & Sutton, 1996) finds that androgynous couples are more satisfied with their intimate relationships than gender-typed couples are and that it was the feminine component of androgyny that contributed most to their relationship satisfaction.

In sum, it may be premature to conclude that one is better off in *all* respects to be androgynous rather than masculine or feminine in orientation. But given the behavioral flexibility that androgynous people display and the strong contribution that androgyny makes to children's and adolescents' perceived self-worth, we can safely assume that it is probably adaptive and certainly not harmful for girls and women to become a little more "masculine," and for boys and men to become a little more like women.

APPLICATIONS: ON CHANGING GENDER-ROLE ATTITUDES AND BEHAVIOR

Today many people believe that the world would be a better place if sexism were eliminated and if boys and girls were no longer steered toward adopting the confining "masculine" or "feminine" roles. In a nonsexist culture, women would no longer suffer from a lack of assertiveness and confidence in the world of work, and men would be freer to display their sensitive, nurturant sides that many now suppress in the interest of appearing "masculine." How might we reduce sexism and encourage children to be more flexible about the interests and attributes they might display?

Bem (1983, 1989) believes that parents must take an active role by (1) teaching their young children about genital anatomy as part of a larger lesson that one's biological sex is unimportant outside the domain of reproduction, and (2) delaying children's exposure to gender stereotypes by encouraging cross-sex as well as same-sex play and by dividing household chores more equitably (with fathers sometimes cooking and cleaning and mothers gardening or making repairs). If preschoolers come to think of sex as a purely biological attribute and often see themselves and their parents pursuing cross-sex interests and activities, they should be less inclined to construct the rigid gender stereotypes that might otherwise evolve in a highly sexist early environment. Research suggesting that androgynous parents tend to raise androgynous children is consistent with Bem's prescriptions for change (Orlofsky, 1979). So, too, are findings that children whose mothers work or whose fathers routinely perform "feminine" household and child-care tasks are less aware of gender stereotypes and are more likely to be androgynous themselves, compared with youngsters whose mothers are not employed and whose fathers display more traditional patterns of gender-typed behavior (Hoffman, 1989; Turner & Gervai, 1995).

How might we reach children from more traditional backgrounds, who have already received thousands of gender-stereotyped messages from family members, television, and their peers? Apparently, interventions that simply show children the benefits of cross-gender cooperation or that praise them for playing with other-sex toys and play partners have no lasting effect: Children soon retreat to same-sex play and continue to prefer same-sex peers after the interventions are over (Maccoby, 1988). One particularly ambitious program (Guttentag & Bray, 1976) exposed kindergarten, fifth-grade, and ninth-grade students to age-appropriate readings and activities designed to teach them about the capabilities of women and about the problems created by stereotyping and sexism. This program worked quite well with the younger children, particularly the girls, who often became outraged by what they had learned about sexism. However, it actually had a boomerang effect among ninth-grade boys, who seemed to resist the new ideas they were being taught and actually expressed more stereotyped views after the training than before. And although ninth-grade girls took many of the lessons to heart, they still tended to cling to the idea that women should run the family and that men should be the primary breadwinners.

This study and others (see Katz & Walsh, 1991, for a review) suggest that efforts to change gender-role attitudes are more effective with younger children than with older ones and possibly with girls than with boys. It makes some sense that it is easier to alter children's thinking early on, before their stereotypes have become fully crystallized; and many researchers now favor *cognitive interventions* that either attack the stereotypes directly or remove constraints on children's thinking that permit them to construct these rigid gender schemas. As we see in Box 8.4 on page 262, these cognitive interventions can be quite effective indeed.

Finally, there is some evidence that programs designed to modify children's gender-stereotyped attitudes and behaviors may be more effective when the adult in charge is a man (Katz & Walsh, 1991). Why? Possibly because men normally make stronger distinctions between "gender-appropriate" and "gender-inappropriate" behaviors than women do; thus men may be particularly noteworthy as *agents of change.* In other words, children may feel that cross-gender activities and aspirations are quite legitimate indeed if a man encourages (or fails to discourage) these pursuits.

So new gender-role attitudes can be taught, although it remains to be seen whether such change will persist and generalize to new situations should these attitudes not be reinforced at home or in the culture at large. Sweden is one culture that has made a strong commitment to gender equality: Men and women have the same opportunities to pursue traditionally masculine (or traditionally feminine) careers, and fathers and mothers are viewed as equally responsible for housework and child care. Swedish adolescents still value masculine attributes more highly than feminine characteristics.

Box 8.4   *Applying Developmental Research*

Combating Gender Stereotypes with Cognitive Interventions

During the preschool period when children are constructing gender schemas, their thinking tends to be intuitive and one-dimensional. As we have seen, children who encounter a violation of their gender schemas—learning of a boy who likes to cook, for example—are unlikely to process and retain this information. After all, their one-dimensional, intuitive thinking makes it extremely hard to separate the gender-typed activity (cooking) from the gender category (for girls). So the information doesn't compute and is likely to be distorted or forgotten.

Rebecca Bigler and Lynn Liben (1990, 1992) have devised and compared two cognitive interventions aimed at reducing children's gender schematic thinking about the occupations that men and women might pursue. The 5- to 11-year-olds who participated in this research were assigned to one of three conditions:

1. *Rule training.* Through a series of problem-solving discussions, children were taught (1) that the most important considerations in deciding who would perform well at such traditionally masculine and feminine occupations as construction worker and beautician are the person's interests and willingness to learn, and (2) that the person's gender was irrelevant.

2. *Classification training.* Children were given multiple classification tasks that required them to sort objects into two categories at once (for example, men and women engaged in masculine and feminine activities). This training was designed to illustrate that objects can be classified in many ways—knowledge that would help children to see that occupations can be classified independent of the kinds of people who normally enact these roles.

3. *Control group.* Children were simply given lessons on the contributions of various occupations to the community.

Compared to children in the control group, those who either received rule training or who improved in classification skills showed clear declines in occupational stereotyping. Furthermore, later tests of information processing provided further evidence for the weakening of children's stereotypes. Specifically, children who received rule training or who had gained in classification skills after the classification training were much more likely than "control" children to remember counterstereotypic information in stories (for example, recalling that the garbage man in

Interventions that show men and women participating side by side at traditionally "masculine" or traditionally "feminine" occupations can be highly effective at combating rigid gender stereotypes.

a story was actually a woman). It seems, then, that gender stereotypes can be modified by directly attacking their accuracy (rule training) or by promoting the cognitive skills (classification training) that help children to see the fallacies in their own rigid gender schemas.

Unfortunately, teachers may unwittingly foster gender-schematic thinking should they group children on the basis of gender and emphasize gender differences during the first few years of school. In a recent experiment, Bigler (1995) randomly assigned some 6- to 11-year-old summer school students to "gender classrooms" in which teachers created separate boy and girl bulletin boards, seated boys with boys and girls with girls, and often made statements that distinguished boys from girls (for example, "All the boys should be sitting down"; "All the girls put their bubble-makers in the air"). Other children were assigned to classrooms in which teachers were instructed to refer to their pupils only by name and to treat the entire class as a unit. After only four weeks, children in the "gender classrooms" endorsed more gender stereotypes than those in control classrooms, particularly if they were one-dimensional thinkers who have trouble understanding that a person can belong to more than one social category at the same time. So it seems that teachers can help to combat gender stereotyping by not grouping pupils on the basis of gender during the early grades, when young one-dimensional thinkers are otherwise prone to construct rigid gender schemas.

However, they are much less adamant about it than American adolescents are, and are much more inclined to view gender roles as acquired domains of expertise rather than as biologically programmed duties (Intons-Peterson, 1988).

Although our society has not made the commitment to gender equality that Sweden has, it is slowly becoming more egalitarian, and some people believe that these changes are having an impact on children (Etaugh, Levine, & Mennella, 1984). Judith Lorber (1986) sees much hope in her 13-year-old's response to her inquiry about whether a pregnant acquaintance of theirs had delivered a boy or girl: "Why do you want to know?" this child of a new era asked (p. 567).

Sexuality and Sexual Behavior

The biological upheaval of puberty brings about major hormonal changes, one of which is increased production of androgens in both boys and girls, which dramatically increases one's sex drive (Udry, 1990). Although grade-school children do indulge in masturbation and such other forms of sexual experimentation as kiss-and-chase games and playing "doctor" that help to groom them for heterosexual relationships later in life (Thorne, 1993), the new urges they feel make adolescents increasingly aware of their own **sexuality**—an aspect of development that will greatly influence their self-concepts. One major hurdle adolescents face is figuring out how to properly manage and express their sexual feelings, an issue that is heavily influenced by the social and cultural contexts in which they live.

CULTURAL INFLUENCES ON SEXUALITY

Societies clearly differ in the education they provide children about sexual matters and in their attempts to encourage them to prepare for their roles as mature sexual beings (Ford & Beach, 1951). Some societies are rather *permissive* about childhood sexuality. On the island of Ponape, for example, 4- and 5-year-olds receive a thorough "sex education" from adults and are encouraged to experiment with one another. Among the Chewa of Africa, parents believe that practice makes perfect; so, with the blessings of their parents, older boys and girls build huts and play at being husbands and wives in trial marriages. By contrast, *restrictive cultures* view sexuality as a taboo subject and vigorously suppress its expression. In New Guinea, for example, Kwoma children are punished for sex play and are not allowed to touch themselves. In fact, a Kwoma boy caught having an erection is likely to have his penis beaten with a stick!

Where do the United States and other Western societies fall on this continuum of sexual permissiveness-restrictiveness? Most can be classified as relatively restrictive. If you are like many Western children and adolescents, the "facts of life" may have come as a shock to you, having been related not by your parents, but by an older sibling or peer; in fact, you may have had trouble imagining your parents ever having done what it takes to conceive a child (Walters, 1997). American parents generally discourage overt sex play and often find ways to elude the sexually explicit questions their children may ask (Thorne, 1993). Mainly, adults leave the task of preparing for sexual relations up to children themselves, and many children and adolescents end up learning from their peers how they should relate to members of the other sex (Whitaker & Miller, 1999).

ADOLESCENT SEXUAL ATTITUDES AND BEHAVIORS

How, then, do Western adolescents, who receive so little guidance from adults, ever learn to manage sexual urges and to incorporate their sexuality into their self-concepts? These tasks have never been easy and, as we see in Box 8.5, can be especially trying

sexuality: aspect of self referring to erotic thoughts, actions, and orientation.

Box 8.5   *Current Controversies*

On Sexual Orientation and the Origins of Homosexuality

Much of the task of establishing one's sexual identity is becoming aware of one's *sexual orientation*—one's preference for sexual partners of the same or other sex. Sexual orientation exists on a continuum and not all cultures categorize sexual preferences as ours does (Paul, 1993), but we commonly describe people as having primarily heterosexual, homosexual, or bisexual orientations. Most adolescents establish a heterosexual orientation without much soul-searching. For the 3% to 6% of youths who are attracted to members of their own sex, the process of accepting that they have a homosexual orientation and establishing a positive identity in the face of negative societal attitudes can be a long and torturous one (Hershberger & D'Augelli, 1995; Patterson, 1995c). It is not that homosexual youths are especially critical of themselves, for their levels of general self-esteem are quite comparable to those of heterosexual peers (Savin-Williams, 1995). Yet, they may be anxious or even depressed about their gay or lesbian orientation, often because they fear rejection from family members or physical and verbal abuse from peers were their orientation to become known (Baumrind, 1995; Hershberger & D'Augelli, 1995). Consequently, many gay or lesbian youth do not gather the courage to "come out" until their mid-20s, if they come out at all (Garnets & Kimmel, 1991; Miller, 1995).

How do adolescents become homosexual or heterosexual? In addressing this issue, John Money (1988) emphasizes that sexual orientation is not a choice we make but, rather, something that happens to us. In other words, we do not prefer to be gay or straight; we simply turn out that way. Yet not everyone agrees with this viewpoint: As Diana Baumrind (1995) has noted, many bisexual individuals may actively choose to adopt a heterosexual identity, even though they have been sexually attracted to members of both sexes. Similarly, Celia Kitzinger and Sue Wilkinson (1995) find that many women with more than 10 years of heterosexual experience, and who had always viewed themselves as heterosexuals, make a transition to lesbianism later in adulthood (see also Diamond, 1998), and it now appears that some men become gay later in life after having thought of themselves as (and having lived as) heterosexuals (Savin-Williams, 1998). Clearly these findings imply that at least some homosexual individuals were not predestined to be homosexual and had at least some say in the matter.

Concordance rates for homosexuality among male and among female identical and fraternal twin pairs

	IDENTICAL TWINS	FRATERNAL TWINS
Both male twins are gay/bisexual if one is	52%	22%
Both female twins are gay/bisexual if one is	48%	16%

SOURCE: Male figures are from Bailey & Pillard, 1991. Female figures are from Bailey et al., 1993.

How, then, might homosexual individuals become homosexual? Part of the answer lies in the genetic code, it seems. Michael Bailey and his colleagues (Bailey & Pillard, 1991; Bailey et al., 1993) find that identical twins are more alike in sexual orientation than fraternal twins are. But as we see in the table, only about half of identical twin pairs share the same sexual orientation. This means that environment contributes *at least as much as genes* to the development of sexual orientation.

What environmental factors might help to determine whether a person with a genetic predisposition toward homosexuality comes to be attracted to same-sex companions? We really don't know as yet. The old psychoanalytic view that male homosexuality stems from having a domineering mother and a weak father has received little support (LeVay, 1996). Nor is there any compelling evidence for the long-standing "seduction hypothesis"—the idea that homosexuals have been lured into the lifestyle by an older same-sex companion. Even the once popular notion that fathers who reject their sons will make them effeminate and push them toward homosexuality has failed to gain much support (Bell et al., 1981; Green, 1987). And growing up with a gay or lesbian parent also seems to have little impact on later sexual orientation (Bailey et al., 1995; Golombok & Tasker, 1996). A more promising hypothesis is that hormonal influences during the prenatal period may be important. For example, women exposed before birth to heightened levels of androgen are more likely than other women to express a bisexual or lesbian orientation—a finding which suggests that high doses of sex hormones prenatally may dispose at least some females to homosexuality (Dittman et al., 1992; Meyer-Bahlberg et al., 1995). However, the fact is that no one yet knows exactly which factors in the prenatal or postnatal environment contribute, along with genes, to a homosexual orientation (Berenbaum & Snyder, 1995; Paul, 1993).

for these teenagers who find themselves attracted to members of their own sex. Judging from letters to advice columns, adults seem to think that modern adolescents, driven by raging hormones, are almost obsessed with sex and feel quite free to express their sexuality. How accurate is this portrayal?

Sexual Attitudes   Adolescents have become increasingly liberal in their thinking about sex throughout the 20th century, with recent attitudes reverting only slightly in a more conservative direction due to fears of contracting AIDS (McKenna, 1997). Yet, it is clear that today's youth have changed some of their attitudes about sex while retaining many of the same views held by their parents and grandparents.

What has changed? For one thing, adolescents now firmly believe that premarital *sex with affection* is acceptable, although like people of earlier eras, they think that casual or exploitative sex is wrong, even if they have had such experiences (Astin et al., 1994). Still, only a minority of sexually active individuals in one survey (25% of the males and 48% of the females) cited affection for the partner as the reason they first had intercourse (Laumann et al., 1994).

A second major change in adolescent attitudes about sex is the decline of the **double standard**—the idea that many sexual practices viewed as appropriate for males (for example, premarital sex, promiscuity) are less appropriate for females. The double standard hasn't completely disappeared, for college students of the early 1990s still believed that a woman who has many sexual partners is more immoral than an equally promiscuous man (Robinson et al., 1991). But Western societies are rapidly moving toward a single standard of sexual behavior for both males and females.

Finally, sexual attitudes today are highly variable and seem to reflect an *increased confusion about sexual norms*. As Philip Dreyer (1982) notes, the "sex with affection" idea is very ambiguous: Must one truly be in love, or is mere liking enough to justify sexual intercourse? It is now up to the individual(s) to decide. Yet these decisions are tough because adolescents receive mixed messages from many sources. On the one hand, they are often told by parents, the clergy, and advice columnists to value virginity and to avoid such consequences as pregnancy and sexually transmitted diseases. On the other hand, adolescents are strongly encouraged to be popular and attractive, and the more than 12,000 glamorous sexual innuendos and behaviors that they see annually on television (many of which depict promiscuity in a favorable way and occur between *unmarried* couples) may convince them that sexual activity is one means to these ends (Associated Press, 1999). Apparently the behavior of older siblings adds to the confusion, for younger brothers and sisters of a sexually active sibling tend to be sexually active themselves, often at an earlier age than the older siblings were (East, 1996; Rodgers & Rowe, 1988). One young adolescent, lamenting the strong social pressures she faced to become sexually active, offered this amusing definition of a virgin: "An awfully ugly third-grader" (Gullotta, Adams, & Alexander, 1986, p. 109). In years gone by, the norms of appropriate behavior were much simpler: Sex was fine if you were married (or perhaps engaged), but it should otherwise be avoided. This is not to say that our parents or grandparents always resisted the temptations they faced; but they probably had a lot less difficulty than today's adolescents in deciding whether what they were doing was acceptable or unacceptable.

Sexual Behavior   Not only have sexual attitudes changed over the years, but so have patterns of sexual behavior. Generally, today's adolescents are involved in more intimate forms of sexual activity (masturbation, petting, and intercourse) at earlier ages than adolescents of earlier eras (Bingham & Crockett, 1996; Forrest & Singh, 1990). Figure 8.7 shows the percentages of high school students from different historical periods who reported ever having experienced premarital intercourse. Notice that the

double standard: the view that sexual behavior that is appropriate for members of one sex is less appropriate for the other.

long-term increase in sexual activity at the high school level may have peaked, for the most recent data available (for 1995) indicates that about half of high school girls (down from 55% in 1990) and 55% of high school boys (down from 60% in 1990) have ever had intercourse (McKenna, 1997). (By comparison, some 70% to 80% of college students have had sexual intercourse.) Notice also from the figure that the sexual behavior of girls has changed more than that of boys—so much so that sex differences in adolescent sexual activity have all but disappeared. Finally, it is clearly a myth to assume that today's youth are having sex as early and as often as circumstances permit. Only about 30% of U.S. adolescents have had sex by age 15, and their experiences are usually limited to one partner (Hendrick, 1994). Girls are more likely than boys to insist that sex and love—physical and emotional intimacy—go together, and they are more likely than boys to have been in a steady relationship with their first sexual partner (Darling, Davidson, & Passarello, 1992). This attitudinal gap between the sexes can sometimes create misunderstandings and hurt feelings, and it may partially explain why girls are less likely than boys to describe their first sexual experience as satisfying (Darling et al., 1992; de Gaston, Jensen, & Weed, 1995).

In sum, both the sexual attitudes and the sexual behaviors of adolescents have changed dramatically in this century—so much so that some kind of sexual involvement is now part of the average adolescent's experience (McKenna, 1997). This is true of all major ethnic groups and social classes, and differences in sexual activity among social groups are shrinking dramatically (Forrest & Singh, 1990; Hendrick, 1994).

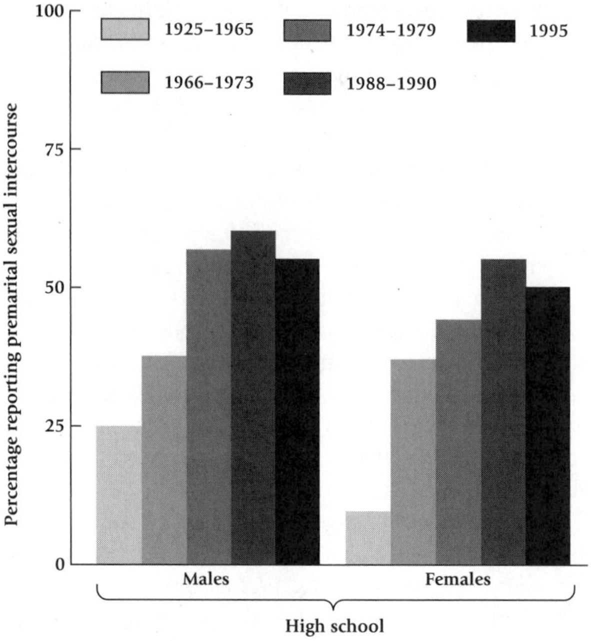

FIGURE 8.7 Historical changes in the percentages of high school students reporting premarital sexual intercourse. (Data for first three time periods adapted from Dreyer, 1982; data for more recent periods from Baier, Rosenzweig, & Whipple, 1991; Centers for Disease Control, 1992; Reinisch et al., 1992; McKenna, 1997.)

PERSONAL AND SOCIAL CONSEQUENCES OF ADOLESCENT SEXUAL ACTIVITY

Who is most inclined to become sexually active early in adolescence and how risky is this activity? Research has identified a number of factors that contribute to early sexual involvement. Teenagers who have intercourse very early tend to be early maturers from low-income families, who are having difficulties at home and at school, whose friends are sexually active, and who are already involved in such delinquent activities as alcohol or substance abuse (Bingham & Crockett, 1996; Capaldi, Crosby, & Stoolmiller, 1996; Fagot et al., 1998; Scaramella et al., 1998). Indeed, the finding that African-American, Native American and Latino-American adolescents are more likely than adolescents of other ethnicities to be sexually involved at earlier ages probably reflects the fact that more teenagers from those social groups are living in poverty, having difficulties at school, and have friends or older siblings who are sexually active (Coley & Chase-Lansdale, 1998; East, 1996).

Sadly, large numbers of sexually active adolescents fail to use contraception, largely because they (1) are uninformed

PHOTO 8.6 Some kind of sexual involvement is now part of the average adolescent's experience.

about reproductive issues, (2) are too cognitively immature to take seriously the possibility that their behavior could have serious long-term consequences, and (3) are concerned that other people (including their partners) will think negatively of them if they appear prepared and thus "ready" to have sex (Coley & Chase-Lansdale, 1998; Walters, 1997). Of course, such unsafe sex places them at risk of experiencing two serious consequences: sexually transmitted disease and teenage pregnancy.

Sexually Transmitted Disease　In the United States, approximately one in five sexually active adolescents will contract a sexually transmitted disease (STD)—syphilis, gonorrhea, chlamydia, genital herpes, or AIDS (acquired immune deficiency syndrome)—that, left untreated, can cause problems ranging from sterility to death in the infected individual to birth defects and other complications for his or her children (Cates, 1995). Clearly, risk of STD is highest for teenagers who fail to use condoms regularly and for those who have sex with multiple partners.

As the number of cases of AIDS has grown, so too have efforts to educate children and adolescents about how to prevent this deadly disease. The incidence of AIDS in the United States is growing fastest among 13- to 19-year-olds, particularly African-American and Latino adolescents from urban backgrounds (Centers for Disease Control and Prevention, 1994; Faden & Kass, 1996). Most states now require some form of AIDS education in the public schools, and there is evidence that these programs can increase grade-school children's knowledge about this disease and its prevention (Gill & Beazley, 1993; Sigelman et al., 1996). Indeed, AIDS education programs are particularly effective when they are tailored to the cultural traditions, beliefs, and values of the children targeted by the program (Sigelman et al., 1996).

Teenage Pregnancy and Childbearing　Adolescents who are sexually active face another important consequence: Each year in the United States more than *one million* unmarried teenage girls become pregnant. And although as many as 70% of these pregnancies end in miscarriage or abortion, over the next four years, *two million* U.S. babies will be born to adolescent mothers (Miller et al., 1996). The incidence of teenage pregnancy is about twice as high in the United States as in Canada and most European nations, ranging from a high of 16 pregnancies per 100 teenage girls in California to 6 pregnancies per 100 girls in North Dakota (Allan Guttmacher Foundation, as cited by McKenna, 1997). Though a problem among teenagers of all ethnicities, out-of-wedlock births are more common among such economically disadvantaged groups as African Americans, Latinos, and Native Americans, and about two-thirds of these adolescent mothers choose to keep their babies rather than place them for adoption.

Consequences for Adolescent Mothers　Unfortunately for the adolescent who gives birth, the consequences are likely to include an interrupted education, a loss of contact with her social network, and if she is one of the 50% who drop out of school, a life of low-paying (or no) jobs that perpetuates her economic disadvantage (Coley & Chase-Lansdale, 1998). In addition, many adolescent girls, particularly younger ones, are not prepared psychologically to become parents, a fact that can greatly affect their babies' developmental outcomes.

Consequences for Babies of Adolescent Mothers　Teenage mothers, especially those from economically disadvantaged backgrounds, are more likely than older mothers to be poorly nourished, to use alcohol and drugs while pregnant, and to fail to obtain adequate prenatal care. Consequently, many adolescent mothers experience more prenatal and birth complications than older mothers do and are more likely to deliver premature or low birth weight babies (Seitz & Apfel, 1994).

Not only are their babies at risk for getting off to a rocky start, but so too are many adolescent mothers, who are ill prepared intellectually for the responsibilities of motherhood and who rarely receive adequate financial or social support from a teenage father (Coley & Chase-Lansdale, 1998; Fagot et al., 1998). Compared to older mothers, adolescent mothers know less about child development, view their infants as more difficult, experience greater parenting stress, and respond to their babies with less sensitivity and affection (Miller et al., 1996; Sommer et al., 1993). It is not completely clear at this point whether the poor parenting practices that seem to characterize adolescent mothers occur because these mothers are so young or because the adolescent mothers studied come from extremely disadvantaged backgrounds in which parenting (regardless of the parent's age) is generally less sensitive and stimulating (Coley & Chase-Lansdale, 1998). But regardless of how we choose to interpret it, this pattern of parenting can have long-term consequences, for children born to teenagers often show sizable intellectual deficits and emotional disturbances during the preschool years, and poor academic achievement, poor peer relations, and delinquent behaviors later in childhood (Coley & Chase-Lansdale, 1998; Hardy et al., 1998; Miller et al., 1996). A teenage mother's life situation and her child's developmental progress may improve later on, especially if she returns to school and avoids having more children; nevertheless, she (and her children) are at risk of remaining economically disadvantaged compared to peers who postpone parenthood until their 20s (Hardy et al., 1998; Hoffman, Foster, & Furstenberg 1993).

Dealing with the Problem of Teenage Sexuality   How might we delay the onset of sexual behavior and reduce the incidence of teenage pregnancies and STDs? Many developmentalists now believe that the critical first steps to accomplishing these aims should begin at home. Parents consistently underestimate the sexual activity of their teens (particularly younger teens) and are reluctant to communicate just how strongly opposed they are to sexual activity by their teenagers (Jaccard & Dittus, 1991; Jaccard, Dittus, & Gordon, 1998). Yet, it is becoming quite clear that early and frank discussions about sexual matters between parents and their teens (or even preteens) can be a helpful preventive strategy. Recent research from the U.S. Centers for Disease Control and Prevention (Miller et al., 1998; Whitaker & Miller, 1999) reveals that parent-child communications about sexual risks and condom use, undertaken *before* teens initiate sex, appear to (1) delay the onset of adolescent sexual relations and (2) promote regular condom use once teens do become sexually active—outcomes that clearly lessen the likelihood that adolescents will conceive a child or contract STDs (see also Jaccard et al., 1998).

Promising interventions from outside the family are also beginning to emerge. One such approach is the privately funded *Teen Outreach* program now underway at nearly 50 locales around the United States. Adolescents in *Teen Outreach* perform volunteer service activities (for example, peer tutoring, hospital work) and take part in regular classroom discussions centering on such topics as their volunteer work, future career options, and current and future relationship decisions. A recent evaluation of *Teen Outreach* at 25 sites nationwide revealed that the incidence of pregnancy among female participants was less than half that of girls from similar social and family backgrounds who had not participated in the program (Allen et al., 1997). Apparently, productively engaged adolescents who have reason to be optimistic about their futures and their abilities to manage personal relationships are much less likely to become pregnant.

Finally, formal sex education that goes beyond the biological facts of reproduction can be an effective intervention indeed. Programs that are most successful at delaying sexual activity and at increasing contraceptive use among older sexually active adolescents generally rely on a two-pronged approach of (1) teaching that abstinence is best for preteens and young adolescents, and (2) providing to older teens ample information about contraceptives and about strategies they can use to resist pressures to have sex (Frost & Forrest, 1995). And in light of evidence from Western Europe that free distribution of condoms does *not* encourage sexually inactive teenagers to become sexually active, many educators in this country are calling for similar contraceptive programs in the United States (Pollack, 1997). Those who favor earlier and more extensive sex education and free access to contraception believe there is little chance of preventing the harmful consequences of teenage sexuality unless more adolescents either postpone sex or practice safer sex.

Summary

- **Gender typing** is the process by which children acquire a gender identity as well as the motives, values, and behaviors considered appropriate in their society for members of their biological sex.

CATEGORIZING MALES AND FEMALES: GENDER-ROLE STANDARDS

- A **gender-role standard** is a motive, value, or behavior considered more appropriate for members of one sex than the other. Many societies are characterized by a gender-based division of labor in which females are encouraged to adopt an **expressive role** and males an **instrumental role.**

SOME FACTS AND FICTIONS ABOUT SEX DIFFERENCES

- Girls outperform boys in many assessments of verbal ability and are more emotionally expressive, compliant, and timid than boys are. Boys are more active and more physically and verbally aggressive than girls and tend to outperform girls on tests of arithmetic reasoning and **visual/spatial skills.** In all, however, these sex differences are small, and males and females are far more psychologically similar than they are different.

- Of the many traditional gender-role stereotypes that are not supported by research are the notions that females are more sociable, suggestible, and illogical and less analytical and achievement oriented than males. The persistence of these "cultural myths" can create **self-fulfilling prophecies** that promote sex differences in cognitive performance and steer males and females along different career paths.

DEVELOPMENTAL TRENDS IN GENDER TYPING

- By ages 2½ to 3, children firmly label themselves as boys or girls, taking their first step in the development of **gender identity.** Between ages 5 and 7, they come to realize that gender is an unchanging aspect of self.

- Children begin to learn gender-role stereotypes about the same age that they display a basic gender identity. By ages 10 to 11, children's stereotyping of male and female personality traits rivals that of an adult. At first, stereotypes are viewed as obligatory prescriptions, but children become more flexible in their thinking about gender during middle childhood before becoming somewhat more rigid once again during the adolescent period of **gender intensification.**

- Even before reaching basic gender identity, many toddlers are displaying gender-typed toy and activity preferences. By age 3, they display **gender segregation** by preferring to spend time with same-sex associates and developing clear prejudices against members of the other sex. Boys face stronger gender-typing pressures than girls do and are quicker to develop gender-typed toy and activity preferences.

THEORIES OF GENDER TYPING AND GENDER-ROLE DEVELOPMENT

- Money and Ehrhardt's biosocial theory emphasizes biological developments that occur before birth and influence the way a child is socialized. The behavior of **androgenized females** implies that prenatal androgen levels may contribute to sex differences in play styles and activity preferences. Yet, the development of children raised as members of the other sex (for example, those with **testicular feminization syndrome**) illustrates that social labeling and gender-role socialization play a crucial role in determining one's gender identity and role preferences.

- Freud believed that children become gender-typed as they **identify** with the same-sex parent during the **phallic stage** of development in order to resolve their **Oedipus** or **Electra complexes.** However, several lines of research have failed to support Freud's theory.

- Consistent with social learning theory, children acquire many of their earliest gender-typed toy and activity preferences through **direct tuition** (or differential reinforcement). *Observational learning* also contributes to gender typing as preschool children attend to models of *both sexes* and become increasingly aware of gender stereotypes.

■ Kohlberg's cognitive-developmental theory claims that children are self-socializers who must pass through **basic gender identity** and **gender stability** before reaching **gender consistency,** the point at which they begin to selectively attend to same-sex models and become gender-typed. However, research consistently reveals that gender typing begins much earlier than Kohlberg thought and that measures of gender consistency do not predict the strength of gender typing.

■ According to Martin and Halverson's *gender schema* theory, children who have established a basic gender identity construct "**in-group/out group**" and **own-sex gender schemas,** which serve as scripts by which they process gender-related information and socialize themselves into a gender role. Schema-consistent information is gathered and retained, whereas schema-inconsistent information is ignored or distorted, thus perpetuating gender stereotypes that have no basis in fact.

■ The best account of gender typing is an eclectic, integrative theory that recognizes that processes emphasized in biosocial, psychobiosocial, social-learning, cognitive-developmental, and gender schema theories all contribute to gender-role development.

PSYCHOLOGICAL ANDROGYNY: A PRESCRIPTION FOR THE FUTURE?

■ The psychological attributes *masculinity* and *femininity* are generally considered to be at opposite ends of a single dimension. However, one "new look" at gender roles proposes that masculinity and femininity are two separate dimensions and that the **androgynous** person is someone who possesses a fair number of masculine *and* feminine characteristics. Recent research shows that androgynous people do exist, are relatively popular and well adjusted, and may be adaptable to a wider variety of environmental demands than people who are traditionally gender-typed.

■ Parents and teachers (particularly males) may prevent rigid gender typing by emphasizing that one's sex is largely irrelevant outside the domain of reproduction, by encouraging and modeling other-sex as well as same-sex activities, and by highlighting and discussing the many exceptions to any unfounded gender stereotypes children may have acquired.

SEXUALITY AND SEXUAL BEHAVIOR

■ The hormonal changes of puberty bring about an increase in sex drive and the need to properly manage one's **sexuality**—a task that may be particularly difficult for teenagers who are sexually attracted to same-sex peers. Sexual attitudes have become increasingly liberal over the years, as a majority of adolescents now think that sex with affection is acceptable and are rejecting the **double standard** for sexual behavior. Teenage sexual activity has also increased, although the sexual behavior of girls has changed more than that of boys.

■ Large numbers of sexually active teenagers fail to use contraception regularly, thus placing themselves at risk of contracting sexually transmitted diseases (STDs) or becoming pregnant.

■ Adolescent pregnancy and childbearing represent a major social problem in the United States. Teenage mothers, most of whom are poor and ill-prepared psychologically to be parents, often drop out of school and perpetuate their economic disadvantage. And their poor parenting contributes to the emotional problems and cognitive deficiencies their children often display. Improved sex education and contraceptive services, coupled with effective preventive programs such as *Teen Outreach,* can help to reduce teenage pregnancy and its undesirable consequences.

Chapter Nine

Aggression and Antisocial Conduct

What Is Aggression?

Aggression as an Instinct

Behavioral Definitions of Aggression

Aggression as a Social Judgment

Theories of Aggression

Instinct Theories

Learning Theories

Dodge's Social Information-Processing Theory

Developmental Trends in Aggression

Early Conflict and the Origins of Aggression

Age-Related Changes in the Nature of Aggression

Is Aggression a Stable Attribute?

Sex Differences in Aggression

The Biological Viewpoint

The Social-Learning Viewpoint

The Interactive Viewpoint

Cultural and Subcultural Influences on Aggression

Family Influences on Aggression

Parental Child-Rearing Practices and Children's Aggression

Family Climate and Children's Aggression

Methods of Controlling Aggression and Antisocial Conduct

Catharsis: A Dubious Strategy

Creating Nonaggressive Environments

Eliminating the Payoffs for Aggression

Social-Cognitive Interventions

Summary

*O*n a clear afternoon in early May 1970, I suddenly found myself lying on the ground, coughing from tear gas and hoping that I would survive the ordeal of the moment. The scene: Kent State University. Just seconds before, a column of Ohio National Guardsmen had turned and fired on a group of bystanders, killing four and wounding several others. Surprisingly, the mood of many people around me was not one of terror but one of retribution. Within minutes there was talk of locating weapons and extracting revenge from the guardsmen. The potential for an even stronger confrontation was apparent, and it is fortunate, I think, that school administrators quickly closed the university before additional blood could be spilled.

Human aggression and other forms of antisocial conduct are pervasive phenomena. We need not look beyond the evening news to observe instances of brutality, for rapes, kidnappings, shoot-outs, and murders are everyday items for Dan Rather and his colleagues in the network and local news bureaus. Elliot Aronson (1976) has described a book that surely qualifies as the shortest capsule history of the world, a 10- to 15-page chronological listing of the most important events in human history. Perhaps you can guess how it reads. That's right: one war after another, with a few other happenings such as the birth of Jesus Christ and invention of the printing press sandwiched in-between. If an extraterrestrial being somehow obtained a copy and deciphered it, he or she would be forced to conclude that we are extremely hostile, antisocial creatures who should probably be avoided.

What makes humans aggressive? Most vertebrates do not try to kill members of their own species as we sometimes do. Is an inclination to aggress a part of human nature or something that children must acquire? Is there any hope for peaceful coexistence among people with conflicting interests? If so, how can aggression and other forms of antisocial behavior be modified or controlled? These are but a few of the issues that we consider in the pages that follow.

What Is Aggression?

Most of us have an implicit definition of aggression. Rape is an act that almost everyone would consider violent and aggressive. But the vigorous and passionate lovemaking of consenting partners is generally considered nonaggressive behavior. When I introduce the topic of aggression in my classes, I often ask students to define the term in their own words. As I write these definitions on the board, classmates invariably begin to argue about the meaning of aggression and the kinds of behavior that should be considered aggressive. These debates are hardly surprising in view of the fact that social scientists have argued the very same issues for 60 to 70 years. At this point it may be useful to look at some of the more common definitions of aggression.

AGGRESSION AS AN INSTINCT

Could aggression be an instinct—a basic component of human nature? Freud thought so, describing the **Thanatos** (or death instinct) as the factor responsible for the generation of aggressive energy in all human beings. Freud held a "hydraulic" view of aggression: hostile, aggressive energy would build up to a critical level and then be discharged through some form of violent, destructive behavior.

Psychoanalytic theorists are not the only ones who have adopted this viewpoint. The famous ethologist Konrad Lorenz (1966) described aggression as a fighting instinct triggered by certain "eliciting" cues in the environment. In his book *African Genesis,* Robert Ardrey (1967) even implied that the human being "is a predator whose natural instinct is to kill with a weapon" (p. 322). Although there are several important differences between psychoanalytic and ethological perspectives on ag-

Thanatos: Freud's name for inborn, self-destructive instincts, which were said to characterize all human beings.

gression, both schools of thought maintain that aggressive, antisocial conduct results from an inborn propensity for violence.

BEHAVIORAL DEFINITIONS OF AGGRESSION

Most behavioral (learning) theorists have rejected an instinctual explanation for violent and destructive acts, choosing instead to think of human aggression and antisocial conduct as a particular category of goal-driven behaviors. Among the more frequently cited "**behavioral" definitions of aggression** is that of Arnold Buss (1961), who characterized an aggressive act as "a response that delivers noxious stimuli to another organism" (p. 3).

Notice that Buss's definition emphasizes the *consequences of action* rather than the intentions of the actor. According to Buss, any act that delivers pain or discomfort to another creature has to be considered aggressive. Yet how many of us consider our dentists aggressive when they drill on our teeth, producing some pain in the process? Is a klutzy dance partner being aggressive when he or she steps on our toes? And is a sniper who misses his target any less aggressive just because no physical harm has been done?

Although you are certainly free to disagree, most people would consider the sniper's behavior aggressive while viewing the dentist's and the dance partner's actions as careless or accidental. In making this pattern of attributions, people are relying on an **intentional definition of aggression,** which implies that an aggressive act is *any form of behavior designed to harm or injure another living being who is motivated to avoid such treatment* (Baron & Richardson, 1994). Note that this intentional definition would classify as aggressive all acts in which harm is intended but not done (for example, a violent kick that misses its target) while excluding accidental injuries or activities such as rough-and-tumble play in which participants are enjoying themselves with no harmful intent.

Aggressive acts are often divided into two categories: **hostile aggression** and **instrumental aggression.** If an actor's major goal is to harm or injure a victim (either physically, psychologically, or by destroying his work or property), his or her actions qualify as hostile aggression. By contrast, instrumental aggression describes those situations in which one person harms another as a means to a nonaggressive end (for example, knocking a playmate down to obtain his candy). Clearly, the same overt act could be classified as either hostile or instrumental aggression, depending on the circumstances. If a young boy hit his sister and teased her for crying, we might consider this hostile aggression. But these same actions might be labeled instrumental aggression (or a mixture of hostile or instrumental aggression) had the boy also grabbed a toy that his sister was using.

Although we will see that the distinction between hostile and instrumental aggression has proved useful to those who study young children, it is often very difficult to tell whether the aggressive behavior of older children, adolescents, or adults is hostile or instrumental in character. Bandura (1973), for example, describes a teenage gang that routinely assaulted innocent victims on the street. But gang members did not necessarily attack others for kicks (hostile motives); they were required to rough up at least 10 individuals to become full-fledged members of the group (an instrumental goal). So even behaviors that appear to be clear instances of hostile aggression may actually be controlled by hidden reinforcement contingencies.

In sum, the distinction between hostile and instrumental aggression is not as sharp as many would have us believe. Even if we consider these forms conceptually distinct, we must still note that both are common and both have important consequences for victims and aggressors. Bandura (1973) reflects the sentiment of many in calling for a comprehensive theory of aggression and antisocial conduct—one that embraces both hostile and instrumental aggression.

behavioral definition of aggression: any action that delivers noxious stimuli to another organism.

intentional definition of aggression: any action intended to harm or injure another living being who is motivated to avoid such treatment.

hostile aggression: aggressive acts for which the perpetrator's major goal is to harm or injure a victim.

instrumental aggression: aggressive acts for which the perpetrator's major goal is to gain access to objects, space, or privileges.

AGGRESSION AS A SOCIAL JUDGMENT

Although we have talked as if there were a class of intentional behaviors that almost everyone would label "aggressive," such a viewpoint is simply incorrect. Bandura and others (for example, Parke & Slaby, 1983) argue convincingly that "aggression" is really a social label that we apply to various acts, guided by our judgments about the meaning of those acts to us. Presumably, our interpretation of an act as aggressive or nonaggressive will depend on a variety of social, personal, and situational factors such as our own beliefs about aggression (which may vary as a function of our gender, culture, social class, and prior experiences), the context in which the response occurs, the intensity of the response, and the identities and reactions of the people involved, to name a few. Accordingly, a high-intensity response such as a hard right hand to someone's jaw is more likely to be labeled aggressive than a milder version of the same action, which we might interpret as a playful prompt or even as a sign of affection (Costabile et al., 1991). Shooting a deer may be seen as much more violent and aggressive by a pacifist vegetarian than by a carnivorous card-carrying member of the National Rifle Association. Scuffles between children are more likely to be labeled aggressive if someone is hurt in the process (Costabile et al., 1991). And as we see in Box 9.1, the identities of the people involved in an incident can play a major role in determining our impressions of their aggressive intent.

In sum, aggression is to no small extent a *social judgment* that we make about the seemingly injurious or destructive behaviors that we observe or experience. Clearly, we can continue to think of aggression as behavior that is *intended* to frustrate, harm, injure, or deprive someone, as long as we recognize that the basis for inferring whether an actor has a harmful intent can vary dramatically across perceivers, perpetrators, victims, contexts, and situations, thereby ensuring that people will often disagree about what has happened and whether it qualifies as aggression.

Theories of Aggression

By now you may have guessed that each of the preceding definitions of aggression is based on a theory of some sort. In the pages that follow we consider several theories that have been offered as explanations of human aggression.

INSTINCT THEORIES

Freud's Psychoanalytic Theory   Freud believed that we are all born with a death instinct (Thanatos) that seeks the cessation of life and underlies all acts of violence and destruction. His view was that energy derived from food is continually being converted to aggressive energy and that these aggressive urges must be discharged periodically to prevent them from building to dangerous levels. According to Freud, aggressive energy can be discharged in a socially acceptable fashion through vigorous work or play, or through less desirable activities such as insulting others, fighting, or destroying property. An interesting Freudian notion is that aggressive urges are occasionally directed inward, resulting in some form of self-punishment, self-mutilation, or perhaps even suicide.

Most contemporary psychoanalytic theorists continue to think of aggression as an instinctual drive but reject Freud's notion that we harbor a self-directed death instinct. Presumably, an instinctual tendency to aggress occurs whenever we are frustrated in our attempts at need satisfaction or face some other threat that hinders the functioning of the ego (Feshbach, 1970). Viewed in this way, aggressive drives are *adaptive*: they help the individual to satisfy basic needs and thus serve to promote life rather than self-destruction.

Box 9.1 Focus on Research

Adult Reactions to Roughhousing: Boys Will Be Boys, but Girls Are Aggressors

Imagine that you are walking down the street on a snowy winter afternoon and you happen to notice a child hitting, jumping on, and throwing snowballs at an age-mate. How might you interpret this event? Would your judgment be affected by the identities of the actor and the recipient? What would you think if the children were both boys? Both girls? A boy and a girl?

John Condry and David Ross (1985) conducted an interesting experiment to determine how adults might interpret the rough-and-tumble activities of children they thought to be boys or girls. Subjects first watched a videotape in which two children, whose genders were concealed by snowsuits, played together in the snow. The play soon became quite rough as one child (the target) hit, jumped on, and hurled snowballs at the other (the recipient). Before watching the video, participants were told that these children were both boys, both girls, a boy target and girl recipient, or a girl target and boy recipient. After the video was over, participants were asked to rate the behavior of the target child along two dimensions:

(1) the amount of aggression the target displayed toward the recipient and (2) the extent to which the target's behavior was merely active, playful, and affectionate.

The results were indeed interesting. As we see in scanning the figure, the rough-and-tumble behavior of the target child was much less likely to be interpreted as aggressive, and tended to be seen instead as a display of affection, when both the target child and the recipient were said to be boys. So, if we see two children "roughhousing" and think that the two are boys, we say "Boys will be boys" and may fail to intervene. By contrast, boys' roughhousing with girls was definitely interpreted as aggressive behavior. And notice that the high-intensity antics of the girl targets were also seen as highly aggressive, regardless of whether the recipient of those actions was a boy or a girl! In summarizing these data, Condry and Ross say, "It may not be fair, and it certainly is not equal, but from the results of this study, it looks as if boys and girls really are judged differently in terms of what constitutes aggression" (p. 230).

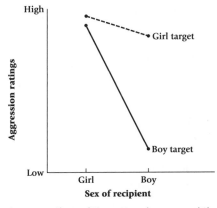
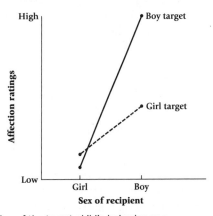

Average ratings of the aggressiveness and the affection of the target child's behavior as a function of the gender of the target and the recipient. (Adapted from Condry & Ross, 1985.) © 1985 by The Society for Research in Child Development. Reprinted by permission.

Lorenz's Ethological Theory of Aggression   A second instinct theory of aggression stems from the work of ethologist Konrad Lorenz. Lorenz (1966) argues that humans and animals have a basic fighting (aggressive) instinct that is directed against members of the same species. Like psychoanalytic theorists, Lorenz views aggression as a hydraulic system that generates its own energy. But he believes that aggressive urges continue to build until relieved by an appropriate *releasing stimulus*.

What kinds of stimuli are likely to trigger aggressive behavior? What functions might these displays of aggression serve? According to Lorenz, all instincts, including aggression, serve a basic evolutionary purpose: *to ensure the survival of the individual and the species.* Thus, fights that occur when one animal enters another's territory are said to be adaptive; they disperse individuals over a wider area, thereby preventing large numbers of animals from congregating in the same locale, exhausting all sources of food, and starving. An animal may also fight off an intruder to protect its young, thereby allowing them to live, to mature, and eventually to reproduce. Finally, fighting among the males of a species determines which males will mate with available females. Since the stronger males usually win these battles, intraspecies aggression helps to ensure that the hardiest members of the lot will be the ones to reproduce.

From an ethological perspective, aggression can help most species survive because they have evolved various "instinctual inhibitions" that prevent them from killing members of their own kind. For example, many species of fish engage in "threat" displays or ritualized aggressive ceremonies in which one of the participants will "win" without seriously injuring an adversary. Birds of the same species could easily kill each other (or peck each other's eyes out) but rarely do so. Wolves normally refrain from killing each other when the loser of a battle "signals" that it has had enough by offering its unprotected throat to the teeth of the victor.

According to Lorenz, human beings kill members of their own species because their aggressive instinct is poorly

"Of course, we'll never actually __use__ it against a potential enemy, but it will allow us to negotiate from a position of strength."

According to Lorenz, humans are "lethal" creatures because their aggressive instinct is so poorly controlled.

controlled. Because Homo sapiens in prehistoric times lacked the innate equipment to kill (such as claws or fangs), there was little need for the evolution of instinctual inhibitions against maiming or killing other human beings. But humans did evolve intellectually, developed weapons of destruction, and, lacking innate inhibitions, showed little reluctance to use this lethal weaponry to defeat human adversaries. Lorenz points out that this lack of aggressive inhibitions, coupled with the recent development of doomsday weapons, presents a crucial challenge to humanity: We must now work very hard to channel our aggressive urges into socially acceptable pursuits or face the very real possibility of becoming an endangered species.

A Critique of Instinct Theories   It is often argued that instinct theories of aggression are of limited explanatory value. For example, the notion that all aggression stems from inborn, instinctual forces cannot easily explain why some societies are more aggressive than others. Cultures such as the Arapesh of New Guinea, the Lepchas of the Himalayas, and the Pygmies of the Congo all use weapons to procure food but rarely show any kind of intraspecies aggression. When invaded by outsiders, these peace-loving people retreat to inaccessible regions rather than stand and fight (Gorer, 1968). Although these observations do not rule out the possibility of biological influences on aggression, they present a strong challenge to any theory that humans are *instinctively* aggressive.

To date, there is no neurophysiological evidence that the body generates or accumulates aggressive energy (Scott, 1966, 1972). John Scott believes that the instigation of aggression derives from external rather than internal forces. The mere fact that animals fight doesn't mean they are expending pent-up aggressive energy. To assume so is like assuming that "most people find the odor of roses pleasant [because] there is spontaneous internal stimulation to go out and smell the flowers" (Scott, 1966, p. 696).

Now recall one of the central arguments of instinct theory: Human aggression is so widespread because it stems from recurring internal forces for which we have no inborn or instinctual inhibitions. Critics scoff at this assertion. It is true that human beings do not bare their throats or rely on other such signals of aggressive appeasement in exactly the same way that animals do. However, Bandura (1973) points out that these primitive gestures are unnecessary for humans, who have evolved a much more intricate system—namely, language—for controlling aggression.

Indeed, *human* ethologists are nowhere near as pessimistic about the prospect of controlling human aggression as Lorenz and Freud were. Ethological studies of children's play groups (Sluckin & Smith, 1977; Strayer, 1980) reveal that even 3- to 5-year-olds form reasonably stable *dominance hierarchies* (determined on the basis of who dominates whom in conflict situations) and know which of their playmates is likely to dominate or submit to them during a conflict. Strayer (1980) proposes that the function of these dominance hierarchies is to *minimize* aggression, just as similar hierarchies minimize fighting and promote the social adaptation of apes and other species. And apparently he is right. In play groups characterized by such dominance hierarchies, children who are attacked or otherwise dominated rarely counterattack or enlist the aid of teachers and peers. Instead, the nondominant child usually terminated the incident by stepping away or making some sort of conciliatory gesture to the dominant peer, such as offering to be his friend, offering to share a disputed possession, or even touching the former adversary in a friendly manner (Sackin & Thelen, 1984). So not only can children successfully end most disputes before they escalate into violent, aggressive exchanges, but they are remarkably proficient at doing so at an early age.

And even if human beings were instinctively aggressive, it is likely that an individual's aggressive inclinations would soon be affected by social experiences. If we look at the animal literature, we find that cats will normally kill rats, a behavior that many people have called instinctive. In one ingenious experiment, Kuo (1930) raised kittens either by themselves, with rat-killing mothers, or with rats as companions. Of the kittens raised with rat-killing mothers, 85% became regular rat killers. But only 45% of the isolated kittens ever killed a rat, and few of those reared with rats (17%) became rat killers. When Kuo later exposed the pacifistic kittens to adult rat-killing models, 82% of the isolated pacifists became vigorous rat killers. However, only 7% of the pacifists that had been reared with rats followed the model's example and attacked rats.

Kuo's study nicely illustrates the importance of environmental influences as determinants of aggressive behavior. It appears that aggressive responses that are often labeled instinctive can be modified substantially or even eliminated through social learning. Largely for this reason, many theorists now believe that human aggressive behaviors, whatever their basic origins, have been so modified by learning that it is simply not helpful to spend much time speculating about their possible bioevolutionary significance (Bandura, 1973; Baron & Richardson, 1994).

LEARNING THEORIES

Disenchanted by instinctual theories of aggression, John Dollard and his associates at Yale University proposed an early and highly influential learning theory of human aggression that came to be known as the **frustration-aggression hypothesis** (Dollard et al., 1939). This model had two basic propositions: (1) Frustration (the thwarting of goal-directed behavior) always produces some form of aggression, and (2) aggression is always caused by some form of frustration.

The problems with this very simple theory soon become apparent. To cite one example, we learned in Chapter 4 that young infants who are frustrated to tears over losing their ability to control objects will become very *angry* and flail their limbs without necessarily intending to harm anyone (Feshbach, 1964; Sullivan et al., 1992).

frustration/aggression hypothesis: early learning theory of aggression, holding that frustration triggers aggression and that all aggressive acts can be traced to frustrations.

Simply stated, frustration does not invariably result in aggression (see also Geen, 1998). Even frustrated 3-year-olds are more inclined to get angry and to display unfocused temper tantrums than they are to commit aggressive responses (Goodenough, 1931). And must we assert that all acts of aggression are instigated by some kind of frustration. Leonard Berkowitz certainly didn't think so.

Berkowitz's Revised Frustration-Aggression Hypothesis Like Seymour Feshbach (1964) and other early critics of the original frustration hypothesis, Berkowitz (1965, 1989) believes that frustration creates only a "readiness for aggressive acts," which we may think of as *hostility* or anger. However, he adds that a variety of other causes that might produce negative affect or trigger hostile thoughts—events such as being attacked or even one's previously acquired *aggressive habits*—may also heighten a person's readiness to aggress. Finally, Berkowitz argues that an angered or otherwise hostile person who is "ready to aggress" will not necessarily commit an aggressive response!

> Aggressive responses will not occur, even given [a readiness to aggress], unless there are suitable cues, stimuli associated with the present or previous anger instigators. . . . These cues *evoke aggressive responses* from [a person who] is "primed" to make them. The strength of the aggressive response made to the [eliciting] cue is . . . a function of (1) the aggressive cue value of this stimulus—the strength of the association between the eliciting stimulus and the past or present determinants of aggression—and (2) the degree of aggression readiness. (1965, p. 308; italics added)

So the earliest version of Berkowitz's theory made a bold assertion—namely, that aggressive cues must be present before an aggressive act will occur. However, Berkowitz (1974) eventually modified his position to allow for the possibility that an extremely angry person may behave aggressively even when aggressive cues are not present. A schematic representation of Berkowitz's theory appears in Figure 9.1.

Notice that Berkowitz's theory anticipates individual differences in aggression: When exposed to aggressive cues, children with well-ingrained aggressive habits should be more inclined to behave aggressively than those whose aggressive habits are not well established. But by far the most provocative of Berkowitz's ideas is the "**aggressive cues" hypothesis,** which implies that exposure to any object or event previously associated with aggression will serve a cuing function and increase the likelihood of aggressive exchanges among young children. Would toys such as guns, tanks, rubber soldiers, and other symbolic implements of destruction have such an effect?

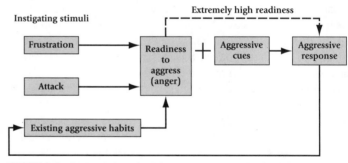

FIGURE 9.1 Berkowitz's revised frustration/aggression hypothesis. (Adapted from Berkowitz, 1974.) Adapted by permission of the American Psychological Assn.

Apparently they can. In one study, Seymour Feshbach (1956) exposed 5- to 8-year-olds to structured play sessions in the classroom; these sessions revolved around *aggressive* themes such as pirates and soldiers or *neutral* themes such as circuses, farm activities, and running a store. Then, during periods of free play, an adult observer noted any aggressive interactions among these children and labeled each as *thematic aggression*—action that was appropriate in the context of earlier play, such as challenging an enemy pirate—or *inappropriate* aggression—verbal taunts or physical blows that were clearly outside the context of the previous play session. Not surprisingly, thematic aggression was highest for the children who had played with aggressive toys. However, these children were also involved in a greater number of inappropriate aggressive exchanges than classmates who had played with neutral toys (see also Turner & Goldsmith, 1976; Watson & Peng, 1992). So it appears that toys that encourage the

"aggressive cues" hypothesis: Berkowitz's notion that the presence of stimuli previously associated with aggression can evoke aggressive responses from an angry individual.

enactment of aggressive themes can indeed increase the likelihood of hostile, aggressive interactions in children's play groups.

In sum, Berkowitz's revised frustration/aggression hypothesis views aggressive behavior as stemming from a combination of *internal forces* (anger; dispositional hostility) and external stimuli (aggressive cues). Although this theory may help to explain how aggressive responses are evoked from a person who is angry at the moment, it has little to say about the development of aggressive habits or about how various stimuli become "aggressive cues." Furthermore, other theorists have criticized Berkowitz's model on the grounds that many aggressive acts are committed not out of a sense of anger or outrage but merely as a means to nonaggressive ends. And as we will see, the impact of aggressive cues on children's behavior seems to depend more on children's *interpretations* of those stimuli and events (cognitive factors) than on the mere presence of the cues themselves.

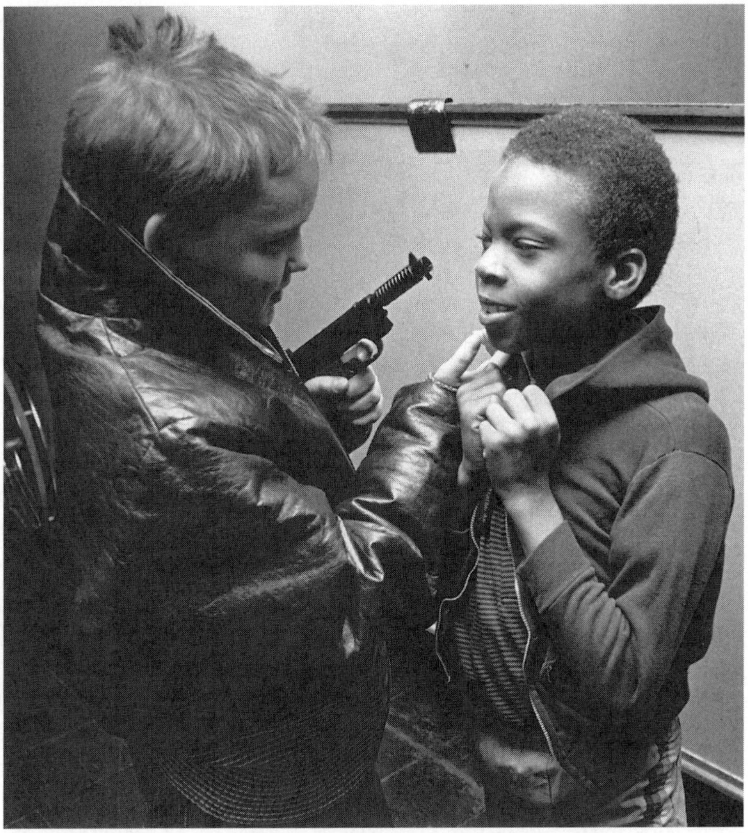

Bandura's Social-Learning Theory   Bandura's (1973, 1989) social-learning theory of aggression is noteworthy in several respects. It is the first model to stress cognitive influences on aggression. It treats aggression as a class of social behaviors that are acquired

PHOTO **9.1** Although these young boys seem to be enjoying themselves, toys that encourage the enactment of aggressive themes do increase the likelihood of hostile interactions in children's play groups.

through the same processes as any other type of social behavior. And whereas most theorists concentrate on factors that instigate aggression, Bandura proceeds a step further by seeking to explain how aggressive behaviors are *acquired* and *maintained.*

According to Bandura, aggressive responses are acquired in either of two ways. The first and most important method is *observational learning*—a cognitive process by which children attend to and retain in memory the aggressive responses they see others commit. The now-classic Bandura (1965) experiment that we discussed in Chapter 2 clearly illustrates his point. Recall that children who witnessed an adult model beat up a Bobo Doll clearly *learned* the aggressive responses they had observed and were likely to direct similar acts toward Bobo, as long as they had not seen the model punished for aggression.

Children may also acquire aggressive responses (or aggressive habits) through *direct experience.* A child who is reinforced for aggressive behavior will be more likely to resort to aggression in the future. Consider, for example, a preschool child who discovers that he can easily gain access to attractive toys by simply overpowering his nursery-school classmates, who cave in to his forceful demands. Clearly, this child's bullying has been reinforced by his control of the desired objects he sought.

How Is Aggression Maintained?   According to Bandura (1973), aggressive behaviors are often maintained (and may become habitual) if they are frequently instrumental in procuring benefits for the aggressor or otherwise satisfying his or her objectives. In other words, highly aggressive children have presumably learned that the use of force is an effective and efficient means to other ends.

Indeed, aggressive children do tend to have more positive *expectancies* about the outcomes of aggression; compared to nonaggressive peers, they are (1) more confident that aggression will yield tangible rewards (such as control of a disputed toy), (2) more certain that aggression will be easy for them and successful at terminating others' noxious behavior, and (3) more inclined to believe that aggression will enhance their self-esteem and will not cause their victims any permanent harm (Crick & Dodge, 1996; Quiggle et al., 1992; Slaby & Guerra, 1988). In addition, aggressive children are more likely than nonaggressive children to *value* the outcomes of aggression; that is, they attach much significance to their ability to dominate and control their victims, and they are not particularly concerned about the suffering they may cause or the possibility of being rejected by their peers (Boldizar, Perry, & Perry, 1989; Crick & Dodge, 1996; Zakriski & Coie, 1996). Furthermore, highly aggressive children tend to cluster together in cliques that encourage and *reinforce* aggressive solutions to conflict (Cairns et al., 1988; Dishion, Andrews, & Crosby, 1995), and they may become so accustomed to dominating others (or attempting to dominate others) that aggression becomes habitual and especially satisfying. In the language of Bandura's theory, these aggressive individuals "have . . . adopted a *self*-reinforcement system in which aggressive actions are a source of personal pride" (1973, p. 208). A passage from Toch (1969) illustrates how violence can be self-reinforcing:

> And he said "F—— you man." And the dude got up and we were both on him, man. And we beat him to a pulp. . . . Once we got going we just wasted the dude. . . . Sent him on down to the hospital. And after that I felt like a king, man. It felt like you know, "I'm the man. You're not going to mess with me." . . . I felt like everybody looking up to me (pp. 91–92)

In sum, Bandura claims that aggressive habits often persist because they are (1) instrumental to the satisfaction of nonaggressive goals, (2) useful as a means of terminating others' noxious behaviors, (3) socially sanctioned by aggressive peers, and (4) even intrinsically rewarding for the aggressor.

Internal Arousal and Aggressive Behavior   Notice that Bandura differs from other aggression theorists in a very important way: He depicts human beings as basically rational creatures who typically aggress in order to *satisfy important personal objectives* rather than as reactive creatures who are "driven" to aggress by such "internal" forces as instincts, frustrations, or anger. Yet, Bandura concedes that internal arousal *of any kind* can increase the likelihood of aggression if cues available in a situation might cause one to *interpret* that arousal as frustration or anger. And the available evidence is consistent with Bandura's views. Compared with participants who have not been aroused, those who have experienced nonhostile forms of arousal from exercising, or even from viewing erotica, are likely to display heightened aggression if exposed to insults or some other provocation (Geen, 1998; Zillmann, 1989). So it seems that any kind of internal arousal may be more a catalyst for rather than an instigator of aggression.

Evaluating Bandura's Theory   Bandura is a learning theorist who, like all other learning theorists, views aggression as a class of behaviors that have some instrumental value for the aggressor. His major contributions to the study of human aggression are his focus on (1) the processes by which aggressive responses are acquired and maintained, and (2) the *cognitive* contributors to aggressive behavior, particularly the notion that one's *interpretation* of the social situation (including situational cues to the possible meaning of any arousal one may be experiencing) plays an important role in determining whether he or she will respond aggressively to that situation. However, it appears that Bandura may overstate the case in arguing that virtually all highly aggressive children are highly aggressive because they *value* aggression as an effective *instrumental* strategy for attaining other objectives.

To illustrate, recent research points to two kinds of highly aggressive children: *proactive aggressors* and *reactive aggressors.* Compared to nonaggressive youngsters, **proactive aggressors** are quite confident that aggression will "pay off" in tangible benefits (such as control of a disputed toy), and they are included to believe that they can enhance their self-esteem by dominating other children, who will generally submit to them before any serious harm has been done (Crick & Dodge, 1996; Quiggle et al., 1992; Slaby & Guerra, 1988). So for proactive aggressors, who sound very much like the highly aggressive youngsters that Bandura describes, shows of force are an *instrumental* strategy by which they achieve personal goals.

By contrast, **reactive aggressors** display high levels of *hostile,* retaliatory aggression. These youngsters are quite suspicious and wary of other people, often viewing them as belligerent adversaries who *deserve* to be dealt with in a forceful manner (Astor, 1994; Crick & Dodge, 1996). These hostile individuals do not as easily fit the mold for a highly aggressive child from the framework of Bandura's social-learning theory, which focuses so heavily on the *instrumental* value of aggression.

Interestingly, both groups of highly aggressive children display distinct biases in their processing of social information that contribute to their high levels of aggression. And one recent theory of children's aggression—the *social information-processing* approach—anticipates and easily explains these variations in aggressive behavior. Let's take a closer look.

DODGE'S SOCIAL INFORMATION-PROCESSING THEORY

Kenneth Dodge (1986; Crick & Dodge, 1994) has formulated a social information-processing model that seeks to explain how children come to favor aggressive or nonaggressive solutions to social problems. To illustrate, imagine that you are an 8-year-old who is harmed under somewhat ambiguous circumstances: A peer walks by, nudges your work table with his leg and says "Oops!" as he scatters a puzzle you have been working on for a long time and had nearly completed. As you quickly assess the damage, you really have little information about why this incident may have occurred, although you are certainly aroused by it. So how would you respond?

Dodge proposes that a child's response to this situation will depend on the outcome of six cognitive steps or processes that are illustrated in Figure 9.2 on page 282. As shown in the figure, the youngster who is harmed will first *encode* and *interpret* the immediate cues (How exactly was the damage done? What was the harmdoer's reaction? Did he mean to do it?). After interpreting the cues, the child must then *formulate a goal* (to resolve the incident), *generate* and *evaluate* possible strategies for achieving this goal, and finally, *select and enact* a response. Notice the model proposes that a child's *mental state*—his past social experiences (especially those involving harmdoing), social expectancies, and knowledge of social rules—can influence any of the theory's six phases of information processing.

According to Dodge, the mental states of *reactive aggressors,* who have a history of bickering with peers, are likely to include an expectancy that "others are hostile to me." So when harmed under ambiguous circumstances (such as having their puzzle scattered by a careless peer), they are much more inclined than nonaggressive children to (1) search for and find cues compatible with this expectancy, (2) attribute hostile intent to the harmdoer, and (3) become very angry and quickly retaliate in a hostile manner without generating or carefully considering the probable effectiveness of other nonaggressive solutions to this problem. Not only does research consistently indicate

proactive aggressors: highly aggressive children who find aggressive acts easy to perform and who rely heavily on aggression as a means of solving social problems or achieving other personal objectives.

reactive aggressors: children who display high levels of hostile, retaliatory aggression because they overattribute hostile intents to others and can't control their anger long enough to seek nonaggressive solutions to social problems.

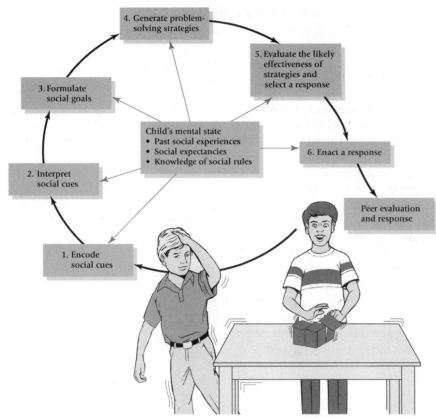

FIGURE 9.2 Dodge's social information-processing model of the steps children take when deciding how to respond to harmdoing or other social problems. The boy whose creation is destroyed by the other boy's nudging the table must first encode and interpret the social cues (i.e., did he mean it or was it accidental?) and then proceed through the remaining steps to formulate and enact a response to this harmdoing. (Adapted from Crick & Dodge, 1994.)

that reactive aggressors do overattribute hostile intent to peers (Crick & Dodge, 1996; Dodge, 1980), but by virtue of their own hostile retaliations, these children will have many negative experiences with teachers and peers (Dodge et al., 1990; Trachtenberg & Viken, 1994), who come to dislike them, thereby reinforcing their expectancy that "others are hostile to me" (see Figure 9.3). Interestingly, girls can be as reactively aggressive as boys, displaying the same kind of **hostile attributional bias** and a strong readiness to react aggressively to ambiguous harmdoing (Crick & Dodge, 1996; Guerra & Slaby, 1990).

Proactive aggressors, by contrast, display a very different pattern of social information processing. Since these youngsters do not feel especially disliked (Zakriski & Coie, 1996), they are not so inclined to quickly attribute hostile intent to a person who causes them some harm under ambiguous circumstances. However, this does not mean that the proactive aggressor is inclined to let the incident pass. In fact, these youngsters are much more inclined than nonaggressive children to formulate an *instrumental goal* (for example, I'll teach the careless so-and-so to be more careful around me) and to *coolly and consciously decide* that an aggressive response is likely to be most effective at achieving this aim. The "mental states" of proactive aggressors favor aggressive solutions to conflict because they expect positive outcomes to result from their use of force and they feel quite capable about the prospect of dominating their targets (Crick & Dodge, 1996).

hostile attributional bias: tendency to view harm done under ambiguous circumstances as having stemmed from a hostile intent on the part of the harmdoer; characterizes reactive aggressors.

A Preliminary Evaluation The research cited above provides impressive support for Dodge's social-cognitive theory of aggression. Like Bandura, social information-processing theorists stress that children's behavioral responses to provocations and other harmdoing depend more on their own cognitive interpretations of the situation than on the amount of objective harm done. However, the social information-processing viewpoint goes far beyond this basic premise to illustrate that children with different mental states and social information-processing biases may interpret and respond to provocations and other harmdoing in very different ways.

Yet, the social information-processing approach is relatively new, and as is often true of newer theories, it leaves many questions unanswered. For example, the model aptly describes variations in the information-processing strategies of children already known to be proactively aggressive, reactively aggressive, or nonaggressive, but it does not address the issues of how these children came to be aggressive or nonaggressive or why they have different information-processing biases in the first place. Fortunately, social-developmentalists are learning more about the origins of children's attributional biases. For example, we will see later in the chapter how the hostile attributional bias that characterizes reactive aggressors can emerge very early and often originates at home.

You may also have noticed that Dodge's theory pays little attention to how various *emotional reactions* (for example, anger) might color children's interpretations of social cues and/or influence their behavioral reactions to harmdoing. Sandra Graham and her associates (1992) have addressed this issue. They believe that the attributions we make about a harmdoer's intent influence how angry we become, and that it is the *amount of anger we experience* (rather than our attributions about intent) that best predicts how we will respond to the harmdoer (see Figure 9.4 for an overview of this model). Indeed, Graham's study of aggressive and nonaggressive adolescents revealed that (1) perceptions of others' intent does predict how angry participants become about harmdoing and (2) that participants' anger was a better predictor of their preferred *behavioral* responses to harmdoing than were their attributions of intent. Nevertheless, the data also revealed that anger may have colored the attributions of many *highly aggressive* adolescents, making them more likely to believe that ambiguous harmdoing was intentional (see also Downey et al., 1998). So even though Graham's data do not answer all the questions we may have about the links between cognitive processing biases, anger, and aggression, they reinforce Parke and Slaby's (1983) earlier assessment of social information-processing theory, which held that "the extent to which cognitive models of aggression [are able to] incorporate other dimensions such as affect [or emotional arousal] will determine their ultimate usefulness; it is unlikely that simple cognitive models alone will suffice" (p. 573).

Our survey of the major theories points mainly to factors that motivate and maintain aggression and that account for individual differences in aggressive behavior.

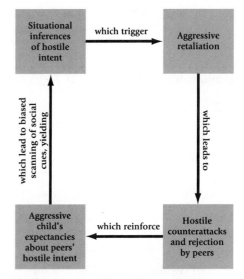

FIGURE 9.3 A social-cognitive model of the reactive aggressor's biased attributions about ambiguous harmdoing and their behavioral outcomes.

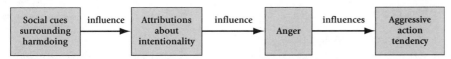

FIGURE 9.4 A mediational model of the relationship among attributions of intentionality, anger, and aggressive behavior. The model predicts that our inferences about a harmdoer's intentionality are the major influence on how angry we become about harmdoing and that our anger (rather than our attributions about intent) most directly influences our behavioral reactions to harmdoing. (Adapted from Graham, Hudley, & Williams, 1992.) © 1992 by the American Psychological Assn. Reprinted by permission.

Now let's look more carefully at age-related changes in aggression and the social contexts in which aggressive behaviors are acquired and maintained.

Developmental Trends in Aggression

Although children have served as participants in many studies of aggression, relatively few of these studies have addressed developmental issues. In this section of the chapter we examine what is known about the origins and changing character of children's aggressive behavior.

EARLY CONFLICT AND THE ORIGINS OF AGGRESSION

Although very young infants do get angry and may occasionally strike people, it is difficult to think of these actions as having an aggressive intent. Piaget (1952) describes an incident in which he frustrated 7-month-old Laurent by placing his hand in front of an interesting object that Laurent was trying to reach. The boy then smacked Piaget's hand, as if it merely represented an obstruction that must be removed.

However, the picture soon changes. Marlene Caplan and her associates (1991) found that even 1-year-olds can be quite forceful with each other when one child controls a toy that the other desires. It seemed to Caplan and her associates that one child's possession of a toy makes that object a more valuable commodity in the eyes of other infants (a clear social influence), for even when duplicate toys were readily available, 12-month-olds would occasionally ignore these objects and try to overpower a peer in order to control the *other child's* plaything. Clearly the intimidators in these tussles were treating other children as adversaries rather than inanimate obstacles—a finding which implies that the seeds of instrumental aggression may have already been sown by the end of the first year.

Although 2-year-olds have just as many (or more) **conflicts** over toys as 1-year-olds, conflict and aggression are hardly synonymous terms, even for toddlers. In fact, Caplan found that 2-year-olds were much more likely than 1-year-olds to resolve their disputes by negotiating with an adversary or by sharing resources than by fighting with each other, especially when toys were in short supply. So it seems that early conflicts need not be training grounds for aggression and can even be adaptive, serving as a context in which infants, toddlers, and preschool children can learn to negotiate and achieve their aims without resorting to shows of force—especially when adults intervene and encourage harmonious means of conflict resolution (Perlman & Ross, 1997). Indeed, Japanese mothers are especially intolerant of harmdoing and encourage their children to suppress anger in the interest of promoting social harmony. As a result, Japanese *preschoolers* are already less angered by interpersonal conflicts and less likely to respond aggressively to them than American children are (Zahn-Waxler et al., 1996).

AGE-RELATED CHANGES IN THE NATURE OF AGGRESSION

Determining whether children become any more or less aggressive over time is not always easy because the aggressive or antisocial acts that 2-year-olds display are not directly comparable to those of a 5-year-old, an 8-year-old, or an adolescent. As a result, researchers have chosen to study age-related changes in both the form of aggressive behavior and the situations that elicit aggressive or antisocial conduct.

Aggression During the Preschool Period   Much of what we know about changes in aggression among preschool children comes from a handful of studies. One is a proj-

conflict: circumstances in which two (or more) persons have incompatible needs, desires, or goals.

ect conducted by Florence Goodenough (1931), who asked mothers of 2- to 5-year-olds to keep diaries recording each angry outburst displayed by their children, its apparent causes, and its consequences. A second longitudinal study conducted by Mark Cummings and his associates (1989) recorded the squabbles that occurred among pairs of children at play, once when these children were 2 years old, and again at age 5. Finally, Willard Hartup (1974) conducted an observational study in which he analyzed the causes and consequences of aggressive acts that occurred over a five-week period in groups of 4- to 5-year-olds and 6- to 7-year-olds. Taken together, these studies indicate the following:

PHOTO 9.2 The squabbles of young children usually center around toys, candy, or other treasured resources and qualify as acts of instrumental aggression.

1. Unfocused temper tantrums diminish during the preschool period and are uncommon after age 4.
2. The tendency to retaliate in response to attack or frustration increases dramatically for children over age 3.
3. *The primary instigators of aggression vary with the age of the child.* At ages 2 to 3, children are most often aggressive after parents have thwarted or angered them by exerting authority; older children are much more likely to aggress after conflicts with siblings or peers.
4. The *form* of aggression also changes over time. Two- and 3-year-olds are likely to hit or kick an adversary. Most of the squabbles among children this young concern toys and other possessions, so that their aggression is usually *instrumental* in character. Older nursery schoolers (and young grade-school children) show less and less physical aggression as they choose instead to tease, taunt, tattle, and call their victims uncomplimentary names. And although older children continue to fight over objects, an increasing percentage of their aggressive outbursts are *hostile* in character—designed primarily to harm another person.
5. Apparently, the frequency of aggressive interactions declines with age, for pairs of 5-year-olds squabble less often (and have conflicts of shorter duration) than was true of these same children when observed three years earlier, as 2-year-olds.

Why are aggressive exchanges less common among 5-year-olds than among 2-, 3-, and 4-year-olds? One possibility is that parents, day-care providers, and nursery school teachers are actively preparing older preschoolers for a structured kindergarten environment by refusing to tolerate antisocial conduct and encouraging such alternative prosocial responses as cooperation and sharing (Emmerich, 1966). Of course, older children may have also learned from their own experiences that negotiation can be a relatively painless and efficient method of achieving objectives that they used to attempt through shows of force without undermining their relationships with playmates (Fabes & Eisenberg, 1992; Shantz, 1987).

PHOTO 9.3 As children mature, an increasing percentage of their aggressive acts qualify as examples of hostile aggression.

Aggression During the Grade-School Years Over the course of middle childhood, physical aggression and other forms of overt antisocial conduct (for example, disobedience) continue to decline as children become increasingly proficient at settling disputes more amicably (Loeber & Stouthamer-Loeber, 1998; Trembley et al., 1996). Yet, hostile aggression (especially among boys) shows a slight increase with age, even as instrumental aggression and other forms of disorderly conduct are becoming less frequent. Why is there an increase in hostile aggression? Hartup's (1974) explanation is remarkably straightforward: Older children are becoming more proficient role-takers and thus, are better able to infer the motives and intentions of other people. So if a companion behaves in a deliberately harmful way, a grade-school child is more likely than a preschooler to detect the aggressive intent and to retaliate in a hostile manner against the harmdoer.

Research on children's perceptions of harmdoing is generally consistent with Hartup's point of view. Although 3- to 5-year-olds may appropriately infer an actor's aggressive intentions if the relevant cues are clear and made *very obvious* to them, they are nowhere near as proficient at interpreting such information as older children or adolescents are (Nelson-LeGall, 1985). In one study (Dodge et al., 1984), kindergartners, second-graders, and fourth-graders were asked to judge the intentions of a child who had destroyed a peer's tower of blocks accidentally or while portraying either a hostile, a benign, or a prosocial intent. The results were clear: kindergartners correctly discriminated the actor's true intentions less than half the time (42%). Second-graders were more accurate (57% correct) but not nearly as skilled at detecting intentional cues as the fourth-graders (72% correct).

Yet it is important to note that 7- to 12-year-olds, who can easily discriminate accidental from deliberate harmdoing (see Dodge, 1980), may react aggressively to almost any provocation, even one they know was unintentional (Sancilio et al., 1989). Why? Because grade-school children (particularly boys) are reluctant to condemn **retaliatory aggression,** often viewing it as a normal (though not necessarily moral) response to provocation (Astor, 1994; Coie et al., 1991). So another reason hostile aggression increases with age is that peers informally sanction the practice of *fighting back*; they view it as a normal reaction to harmdoing (Sancilio et al., 1989).

Perpetrators and Victims of Childhood Aggression Finally, it is interesting to note that while most children become less involved in aggressive exchanges over the course of childhood, a minority of youngsters become even more frequent participants in fights and other aggressive interactions (Loeber & Stouthamer-Loeber, 1998). In fact, by ages 8 to 12, a small minority of youngsters are involved in a large majority of the conflicts. Who is involved? In many groups, the participants are a handful of highly aggressive instigators and the 10% to 15% of their classmates who are regularly abused by these bullies (Olweus, 1984; Perry, Kusel, & Perry, 1988).

Each of us has probably known at least one victimized peer—a youngster who repeatedly serves as a target for other children's hostile acts. Who are these children and who singles them out for abuse?

Research with Swedish male adolescents (Olweus, 1984, 1993) and with American grade-school children of both sexes (Egan & Perry, 1998; Kochenderfer & Ladd, 1996; Perry et al., 1988) provides some clues. Based on teacher ratings, about 10% of Olweus's adolescent sample could be described as habitual bullies who regularly subjected another 10% of the sample (their whipping boys) to physical and verbal harassment. Victimization rates are even higher among younger children; about one child in five reports moderate to high levels of victimization in kindergarten (Kochenderfer & Ladd, 1996), and grade-school girls bully other girls and are victimized (usually in verbally aggressive ways) about as often as grade-school boys are

retaliatory aggression: aggressive acts elicited by real or imagined provocations.

(Egan & Perry, 1998; Pepler & Craig, 1995). Habitual bullies have often observed adult conflict and aggression (for example, spouse abuse) at home but have rarely themselves been the target of aggression or abuse (Schwartz et al., 1997). Their home experiences suggest that aggression pays off for the perpetrator, and they come to view victims as "easy marks" who will surrender tangible resources or otherwise submit to their dominance without putting up much of a fight. So bullies appear to harass their victims for personal or instrumental reasons (Olweus, 1993) and are usually classifiable as *proactive* aggressors.

Chronic victims are generally disliked by their peers (Boivin & Hymel, 1997) and are usually low in self-esteem (particularly in social self-esteem), physically weak, and highly anxious (Olweus, 1993). Of these factors, low social self-regard appears to be particularly important at inviting victimization, for many otherwise anxious youngsters who are physically weak are never chronically victimized if they have high social self-regard and communicate assertively that attacks on them are will not be tolerated (Egan & Perry, 1998). Yet, even though chronic victims share certain characteristics, they are not all alike. Most are **passive victims** who are socially withdrawn and appear to do little (other than be "easy marks") to invite the hostilities they receive (Olweus, 1993). These victimized children often have demanding but somewhat aloof and unresponsive parents who allow them little autonomy and foster passive, nonassertive social behavior. What's more, passively victimized boys often have had very close, even overprotective, relationships with their mothers in which they have been encouraged to voice their fears, anxieties, and self-doubts as a means of attracting attention—practices that are often discouraged of boys as part of masculine gender typing and which are not well received by the male peer group (Ladd & Kochenderfer Ladd, 1998). By contrast, a smaller number in both Olweus's Swedish sample and Perry's American samples could be described as **provocative victims**—that is, oppositional, restless, and hot-tempered individuals who often irritated peers, were inclined to fight back (unsuccessfully), and who displayed the hostile attributional bias that characterizes reactive aggressors. Provocative victims have often been physically abused or otherwise victimized at home and may have learned from these experiences to view other people as hostile adversaries (Schwartz et al., 1997).

Unfortunately, many children (and adolescents who become chronic victims will continue to be victimized, especially if they blame themselves for their victimization and have no friends or other regular associates who are capable of sticking up for them when they are harassed (Graham & Juvonen, 1998; Hodges et al., 1997, 1999). What's more, becoming a victim places these youngsters at risk for a variety of adjustment problems, including anxiety, depression, further erosion of self-esteem, and a growing dislike for and avoidance of school (Downey et al., 1998; Egan & Perry, 1998; Hodges et al., 1999; Ladd, Kochenderfer, & Coleman, 1997; Olweus, 1993). And when we consider that as many as 10% to 20% of children in a typical elementary school class face these problems because they are victimized, there is clearly a pressing need for programs to stop the abuse—for interventions that not only take strong measures to discourage bullying but that also help victimized children to build self-esteem and to develop social skills and supportive friendships that will improve their standing among peers and make them less inviting targets for their tormentors (Egan & Perry, 1998; Hodges et al., 1997, 1999).

Aggression and Antisocial Conduct in Adolescence In a recent review of developmental trends in aggression and antisocial conduct, Rolf Loeber and Magda Stouthamer-Loeber (1998) concluded that the incidence of fighting and other overt, easily detectable forms of aggression continues to decline from middle childhood throughout adolescence—a trend that holds for both boys and girls (Stanger, Achenbach, &

passive victims (of aggression): socially withdrawn and anxious children whom bullies torment, even though they appear to have done nothing to trigger such abuse.

provocative victims (of aggression): restless, hot-tempered, and oppositional children who are victimized because they often irritate their peers.

Verhulst, 1997). How, then, might we explain the dramatic increase in juvenile arrests for assault and other forms of serious violence in late adolescence and early adulthood (Cairns & Cairns, 1986; Loeber & Farrington, 1998)? These seemingly inconsistent findings seem to suggest that (1) the most violent of young adolescents often show an *increase* rather than a decline in physical aggression as they progress through their teenage years (Loeber & Stouthamer-Loeber, 1998), and (2) these undercontrolled individuals are growing larger and stronger, and they have greater access to weapons than was true during childhood. Thus, they become ever more likely to inflict *serious* injuries when they act on their aggressive inclinations (Cairns et al., 1989).

One final point: Although most adolescents become notably less aggressive with age, they are not necessarily becoming any better behaved. Not only do more covert forms of social ostracism increase dramatically, especially among girls as they enter adolescence (Cairns et al., 1989; Galen & Underwood, 1997), but teenage boys become much more inclined to express their anger and frustrations indirectly, through such acts as theft, truancy, substance abuse, malicious destruction of property, and sexual misconduct (Loeber & Stouthamer-Loeber, 1998; U.S. Department of Justice, 1995). So it seems that adolescents who are becoming less *overtly* aggressive may simply turn to other forms of antisocial conduct to express their discontents.

IS AGGRESSION A STABLE ATTRIBUTE?

We have seen that the kinds of aggression/antisocial conduct that children display clearly change over time. But what about aggressive (or antisocial) dispositions? Do aggressive preschoolers remain highly aggressive throughout the grade-school years? Do highly combative grade-school children become aggressive, antisocial adolescents and young adults?

Apparently, aggression is a reasonably stable attribute. Not only are aggressive toddlers likely to remain relatively aggressive as 5-year-olds (Cummings, Iannotti, & Zahn-Waxler, 1989), but longitudinal research conducted in Iceland, New Zealand, and the United States reveals that the amount of moody, ill-tempered, and aggressive behavior children display between ages 3 and 10 is a fairly good predictor of their aggressive or other antisocial inclinations later in life (Hart et al., 1997; Henry et al., 1996; Newman et al., 1997). Rowell Huesmann and his associates (1984), for example, tracked one group of 600 participants for 22 years. As we see in Figure 9.5, highly aggressive 8-year-olds often became relatively hostile 30-year-olds who were likely to batter their spouses and children and to be convicted of criminal offenses.

Of course, these findings reflect group trends and do not imply that all highly aggressive children will remain highly aggressive over time. In fact, there is a great deal of variability at the individual level, with some youngsters (called *limited-duration types*) being highly aggressive earlier in life and outgrowing it, whereas others (called *late-onset types*) become more aggressive (even violent) during adolescence after a relatively tranquil childhood (Windle & Windle, 1995). However, we should not be surprised to find that aggression is a reasonably stable attribute for many individuals. Shortly we will see how some home settings can serve as "breeding grounds" for the development

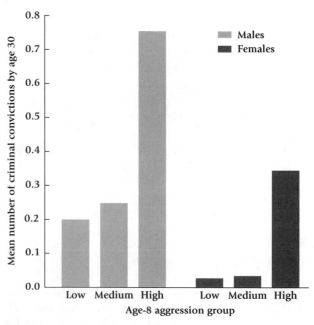

FIGURE 9.5 Aggression in childhood predicts criminal behavior in adulthood for both males and females. (From Huesmann, Eron, Lefkowitz, & Walder, 1984.)

of aggressive habits. And when children who have learned to react aggressively to conflicts at home later face similar problems at school, they may try their forceful tactics on classmates, thereby inviting snubs, rejections, or counterattacks, which lead them to assume that peers are hostile toward them. Before long, these children may find themselves in the vicious cycle portrayed earlier in Figure 9.3—a pattern that seems likely to perpetuate their aggressive inclinations.

In addition, certain biological predispositions may help to explain the stability of aggression over time. For example, Philippe Rushton and his associates (1986) found that even after living apart for several years, male identical twins were still more alike in their self-reported levels of aggression ($r= +.40$) than were male fraternal twins ($r = +.04$). Clearly some caution is required in interpreting these findings. The data are simply verbal reports that may or may not accurately reflect the twins' actual levels of aggressive behavior, and not all twin studies of aggression have reported such dramatic results (see Geen, 1998). Nevertheless, Rushton's findings imply that our aggressive inclinations are influenced to some extent by the genes we have inherited.

How might one's genotype contribute to aggression and, specifically, to the stability of aggression over time? Perhaps in many ways. For example, a child with a genetically influenced active and impetuous temperament may regularly *elicit* negative reactions from other people, which, in turn, may engender hostility and aggression (see, for example, O'Connor et al., 1998). And recall the concept of active *genotype/environment* correlations (discussed in Chapter 3)—that individuals create or select environmental niches that best suit their genotypes. Perhaps children who are genetically predisposed to be aggressive and who have begun to develop some aggressive habits will choose to associate with people like themselves (that is, aggressive peers). If so, they will have created an environment for themselves that could easily perpetuate their aggressive inclinations (Rushton et al., 1986).

Sex Differences in Aggression

Although aggression is a reasonably stable attribute for members of each sex, data from more than 100 countries around the world reveal that boys and men are more *overtly* (that is, physically *and* verbally) aggressive than girls and women are (Harris, 1992; Maccoby & Jacklin, 1974). Furthermore, the magnitude of these sex differences in aggression is greater in studies conducted in the naturalistic environment than in laboratory investigations of aggressive behavior (Hyde, 1984). Why do males and females differ in aggression? Let's consider three complementary points of view, as well as a recent program of research which implies that researchers who study sex differences may have underestimated the aggressive inclinations of girls and women.

THE BIOLOGICAL VIEWPOINT

According to Maccoby and Jacklin (1974, 1980), there are at least four reasons to suspect that biological factors contribute heavily to sex differences in aggression. First, males are more aggressive than females in almost every society that has been studied. Second, reliable sex differences in aggression appear so early (about ages 2 to 2½) that it is difficult to attribute them solely to social learning or to parental child-rearing practices. Third, males tend to be the more aggressive gender among our closest phylogenetic relatives—species such as baboons and chimpanzees. Finally, there is evidence to suggest a link, in both animals and humans, between male hormones such as testosterone and aggressive behavior. Let's take a closer look at these proposed hormonal influences.

Might the heightened aggression of males be attributable to their higher levels of *testosterone*—the male sex hormone that is thought to promote heightened activity, a readiness to anger, and hence, a predisposition to behave aggressively (Archer, 1991)? The evidence seems quite convincing when experiments are conducted with animals. Female rhesus monkeys exposed prenatally to the male hormone testosterone later display patterns of social behavior more characteristic of males: They often threaten other monkeys, initiate rough-and-tumble play, and try to "mount" a partner as males do at the beginning of a sexual encounter (Wallen, 1996; Young, Goy, & Phoenix, 1964). By contrast, genetically male rat pups that are castrated and cannot produce testosterone tend to be passive and to display feminine sexual behavior (Beach, 1965).

What about humans? Dan Olweus and his associates (1980) found that 16-year-old bullies who view themselves as physically and verbally aggressive do have higher testosterone levels than boys who view themselves as nonaggressive, and men with extremely high testosterone levels tend to display higher rates of delinquency, abusiveness, and violence (Dabbs et al., 1995; Dabbs & Morris, 1990). Yet we must be extremely cautious in interpreting these correlational data, because a person's hormonal level may depend on his or her experiences. To illustrate, Irwin Bernstein and his associates (Rose, Bernstein, & Gordon, 1975) found that the testosterone levels of male rhesus monkeys rose after they had won a fight but fell after they had been defeated. Similarly, human participants who "beat" their opponent at competitive games show an increase in testosterone, whereas losers show a clear decline (see Geen, 1998). What these findings imply is that higher concentrations of male sex hormones might be either a cause or an effect of oppositional behavior, and it is difficult to establish conclusively that these hormones either cause one to act aggressively or explain sex differences in aggression (Archer, 1991).

THE SOCIAL-LEARNING VIEWPOINT

Proponents of a social-learning viewpoint are not only critical of the hormonal evidence for sex differences in aggression but also point out that very young boys are not always more aggressive than girls. In fact, Marlene Caplan and her associates (1991) found that forceful, aggressive resolutions of disputes over toys were actually more numerous among 1-year-olds when the play groups were dominated *by girls!* Even at age 2, groups dominated by boys were more likely than those dominated by girls to negotiate and share when toys were scarce. Not until ages 2½ to 3 are sex differences in aggression reliable—and this is clearly enough time for social influences to have steered boys and girls in different directions (Fagot, Leinbach, & O'Boyle, 1992; Loeber & Stouthamer-Loeber, 1998).

What social influences might conspire to make boys more aggressive than girls? For one, parents play rougher with boys than with girls and react more negatively to the aggressive behaviors of daughters than to those of sons (Mills & Rubin, 1990; Parke & Slaby, 1983). Furthermore, the ray-guns, tanks, missile launchers, and other symbolic implements of destruction that boys often receive as gifts encourage the enactment of aggressive themes—and actually promote aggressive behavior (Feshbach, 1956; Watson & Peng, 1992). During the preschool years, children come to view aggression as a male attribute in their gender schemas; and by middle childhood, boys expect aggressive acts to provide them with more tangible benefits and to elicit less disapproval from either parents or peers than girls do (Hertzberger & Hall, 1993; Perry, Perry, & Weiss, 1989). So even though biological factors may contribute, sex differences in aggression clearly depend to no small extent on gender typing and gender differences in social learning.

Finally, proponents of an interactive viewpoint believe that sex-linked constitutional factors (biology) interact with social-environmental influences to promote sex differences in aggression. Consider some of the constitutional differences between infant males and females. Female infants tend to mature faster, to talk sooner, and to be more sensitive to pain than male infants, whereas males tend to be larger and more muscular, to sleep less, to cry more, and to be somewhat more active, more irritable, and harder to comfort than female infants (Hutt, 1972; Maccoby, 1980; Tanner, 1990). Clearly these (and other) sex-linked constitutional differences could have *direct* effects on a child's behavior; but a more likely possibility is that they have *indirect,* or interactive, effects by influencing the behavior of the child's companions (Tieger, 1980). For example, parents may find that they can play more vigorously with an active, muscular son who may be somewhat less sensitive to pain than with a docile, less muscular daughter who seems to enjoy these activities less. Or perhaps they are apt to become more impatient with irritable and demanding sons who are difficult to quiet or to comfort. In the first case, parents would be encouraging boys to partake in the kinds of fast-paced, vigorous activities from which aggressive outbursts often emerge. In the second case, parents' greater impatience or irritability with sons than with daughters could push males in the direction of becoming quicker to anger and/or somewhat more hostile or resentful toward other people. So it is unlikely that sex differences in aggression (or in any other form of social behavior) are automatic or "biologically programmed." Instead it seems as if a child's biological predispositions are likely to affect the *behavior* of caregivers and other close companions, which, in turn, will elicit certain reactions from the child and influence the activities and interests that the child is likely to display. The implication then is that biological factors and social influences are intertwined in complex ways and are both important contributors to sex differences in aggression.

One final point: Some investigators now believe that boys may appear so much more aggressive than girls because researchers have focused on *overt,* easily detectable aggressive behaviors and have failed to consider *covertly* hostile acts that may be more common among girls than boys. The research in Box 9.2 on page 292 clearly supports this point of view.

To this point, we've noted that one's genotype and other biological correlates of gender can influence one's propensity for aggressive, antisocial conduct. However, Albert Bandura, Seymour Feshbach, and many other aggression theorists believe that a person's *absolute* level of aggression—that is, how aggressive and antisocial an individual is likely to become—will depend very critically on the social environment in which he or she is raised. We now consider two important sets of social influences that help to explain why some children and adolescents are more aggressive than others: (1) the norms and values endorsed by their societies and subcultures, and (2) the family settings in which they are raised.

Cultural and Subcultural Influences on Aggression

Cross-cultural and ethnographic studies consistently indicate that some societies and subcultures are more violent and aggressive than others. Earlier, we referred to such cultures as the Arapesh of New Guinea and the Lepchas of Sikkim—passive, nonaggressive social orders that actively preach collectivist values, strongly discourage fighting and other forms of interpersonal conflict and will flee rather than fight when their territory is invaded by outsiders (Gorer, 1968). In marked contrast to these groups

Box 9.2   Focus on Research

How Girls Are More Aggressive Than Boys

Recently, Nicki Crick and Jennifer Grotpeter (1995) proposed that both boys and girls can be quite hostile and aggressive, but they display their aggression in very different ways. Boys, who often pursue competitive, instrumental goals, are likely to strike, insult, or display other *overt* forms of aggression toward others who displease them or who interfere with their objectives. Girls, by contrast, are more likely to focus on *expressive* or *relational* goals—on establishing close, intimate connections with others rather than attempting to compete with or dominate their associates. So Crick and Grotpeter proposed that girls' aggressive behavior would be more consistent with the *social* goals they pursue, consisting largely of covert forms of **relational aggression**—actions such as withdrawing acceptance of an adversary, excluding her from one's social network, or taking some sort of action (for example, spreading rumors) that might damage her friendships or general status in the peer group.

To test this hypothesis, third- through sixth-graders were asked to nominate classmates who often displayed (1) overtly aggressive acts (for example, hitting or insulting others) and (2) *relationally manipulative* acts (for example, withdrawing acceptance; snubbing or excluding others). As we see in the figure, far more boys than girls were viewed as high in overt aggression—a finding that replicates past research. However, far more girls than boys were perceived to be high in relational aggression. Clearly, such subtle or indirect expressions of hostility may be difficult at times for victims to detect and may thus allow the perpetrator to behave aggressively while avoiding open conflict. Even 3- to 5-year-old girls are learning this lesson, for they are already more inclined than preschool boys are to try to exclude rather than hit a peer who provokes them (Crick, Casas, & Mosher, 1997; Crick et al., 1998), and to victimize certain peers in relationally manipulative ways (Crick, Casas, & Ku, 1999).

Do other children perceive these attempts to undermine a person's status or the quality of his or her personal relationships as clear examples of aggression?

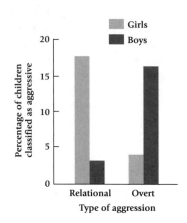

Percentage of girls and boys nominated by classmates as high in relationally manipulative behaviors and overt aggression (physical or verbal assaults) by a sample of 3rd- through 6th-graders. (Adapted from Crick & Grotpeter, 1995.)

Crick and her associates (1996) addressed this issue by asking 9- to 12-year-olds to indicate the ways in which peers of each sex try to get back at or "to be mean to" someone who makes them mad. Overwhelmingly, children said that boys will hit or insult their adversaries, whereas they felt that the most likely response for girls was to try to undermine an adversary's social standing. So children clearly do view these relationally manipulative acts as harmful and "aggressive"—a viewpoint that grows even stronger among adolescents (Galen & Underwood, 1997). Furthermore, girls who frequently display relational aggression are often lonely and are rejected by their peers in much the same way that boys high in overt aggression are at risk of poor peer relations (McNeilly-Choque et al., 1996; Tomada & Schneider, 1997).

In sum, boys and girls often tend to express their hostilities in very different ways. Since most prior research on children's aggression has focused on physical and verbal assaults and has largely ignored relationally manipulative acts, it clearly underestimates girls' aggressive inclinations.

are the Gebusi of New Guinea, who teach their children to be combative and emotionally unresponsive to the needs of others and who show a murder rate that is more than 50 times higher than that of any industrialized nation (Scott, 1992). The United States is also an "aggressive" society. On a percentage basis, the incidence of rape, homicide, and assault is higher in the United States than in any other industrialized

relational aggression: acts such as snubbing, exclusion, withdrawing acceptance, or spreading rumors that are aimed at damaging an adversary's self-esteem, friendships, or social status.

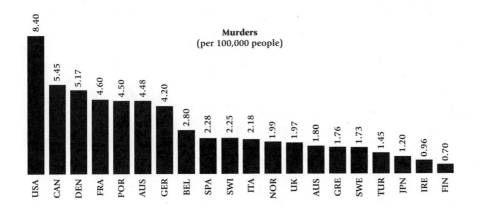

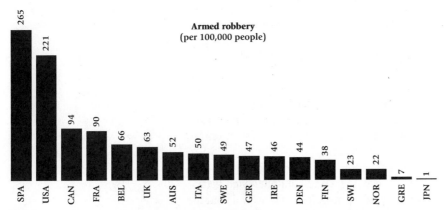

FIGURE 9.6 Frequencies of two major violent crimes in modern industrialized societies. (Adapted from Wolff, Rutten, & Bayer, 1992.) © 1992 by Michael Wolff & Company, Inc. Originally appeared in *Where We Stand* by Michael Wolff et al., originally published by Bantam Books. Reprinted by permission of Curtis Brown, Ltd.

nation, and it ranks a close second to Spain (and far above third-place Canada) in the incidence of armed robbery (Wolff, Rutten, & Bayer, 1992) (see Figure 9.6).

There are also cross-cultural variations in the patterns of aggression displayed by men and women. Among the Mundugumor of New Guinea, both boys and girls are socialized to be aggressive and insensitive to other's needs—as if their society is actively trying to suppress empathic responses. These are practices that serve the Mundugumor well. During some periods of their history, the Mundugumor were cannibals who routinely killed human beings as prey and considered almost anyone other than close kinfolk to be fair game (Mead, 1935). Even within Western societies, there are cross-cultural variations in the patterning of aggression by boys and girls. For example, rural Italian boys are similar to boys in other cultures in showing more overt aggression than girls; however, they also show more relational aggression than Italian girls, perhaps reflecting their heavy exposure to relational (rather than more physical) forms of aggression in their close-knit extended families (Tomada & Schneider, 1997).

Studies conducted in England, Canada, and the United States also point to subcultural or social-class differences in aggression: Children and adolescents from the lower socioeconomic strata (particularly males from larger urban areas) exhibit more aggressive behavior and higher levels of delinquency than their age-mates from the middle class (see Atwater, 1992, and Feshbach, 1970, for reviews). African-American males, in particular, are overrepresented among school-age children labeled as aggressive and among juveniles arrested for delinquency—so much so that researchers who study childhood aggression often include large numbers of black males in their samples (Graham et al., 1992). Yet, this finding may simply reflect the reality that more African-Americans live in poverty, for other researchers are finding that economically disadvantaged white children and adolescents are every bit as aggressive and are just as inclined to commit violent crimes as disadvantaged African-Americans are (Dodge, Pettit, & Bates, 1994; Farrington, 1987).

Several factors contribute to social class differences in aggression and antisocial conduct. For example, parents from lower-income families are more likely than middle-class parents to rely on physical punishment to discipline aggression and noncompliance, thereby *modeling aggression* even as they are trying to suppress it (Dodge et al., 1994; Patterson, DeBaryshe, & Ramsey, 1989; Sears et al., 1957). Lower-income parents are also more inclined to endorse aggressive solutions to conflict and to encourage their children to respond forcefully when provoked by peers (Dodge et al., 1994; Jagers, Bingham, & Hans, 1996)—practices that may foster the development of the hostile attributional bias that highly aggressive youngsters so often display. Finally, economic frustrations faced by poor people can promote antisocial conduct. One study found that crimes of larceny (minor theft) increased dramatically among poorer members of society soon after the introduction of television to their communities (Hennigan et al., 1982). The authors explained this finding by arguing that the poor felt a sense of frustration or "*relative deprivation*" after viewing mostly affluent people on television; consequently, they turned to larceny to obtain some of the good things in life they were lacking. And now it appears that these same feelings of relative deprivation are contributing to the rise of more violent crimes (muggings, armed robberies) as well (Wolff et al., 1992).

In sum, people's aggressive or antisocial inclinations will depend, in part, on the extent to which their culture (or subculture) encourages and condones such behavior. Yet not all people in pacifistic societies are kind, cooperative, and helpful, and the vast majority of people raised in relatively "aggressive" societies or subcultures are not especially prone to violence. One reason for the dramatic differences in aggression within any social order is that children are raised in very different families. In our next section, we see how the home setting can sometimes serve as a breeding ground for hostile, antisocial conduct.

Family Influences on Aggression

How might one's family and the family setting contribute to violent and aggressive behavior? In the pages that follow, we consider two interrelated avenues of influence: (1) the effects of particular child-rearing practices and (2) the more global impact of the family environment on children's aggressive inclinations.

PARENTAL CHILD-REARING PRACTICES AND CHILDREN'S AGGRESSION

When investigators began to study the development of aggression, they operated under the assumption that parents' attitudes and child-rearing strategies play a major role in shaping children's aggressive inclinations. Clearly, there is some truth to this assumption. Some of the most reliable findings in the child-rearing literature are that *cold* and *rejecting* parents who apply **power-assertive discipline** (particularly physical punishment) in an *erratic* fashion and often *permit* their child to express aggressive impulses are likely to raise hostile, aggressive children (Dishion, 1990; Dodge et al., 1994; Olweus, 1980). Surely these findings make good sense. Cold and rejecting parents are frustrating their children's emotional needs and modeling a lack of con-

power-assertion: a form of discipline in which an adult relies on his or her superior power (for example, by administering spankings or withholding privileges) to modify or control a child's behavior.

cern for others by virtue of their aloofness. By ignoring many of the child's aggressive outbursts, the permissive parent is legitimizing combative activities and failing to provide many opportunities for the child to control his or her aggressive urges. And when aggression escalates to the point that the parent spanks the child, the adult is serving as a model for the very behavior that he or she is trying to suppress. So it is hardly surprising to find that parents who rely on physical coercion to discipline aggression have children who are highly aggressive outside the home (DeKlyen et al., 1998; Patterson et al., 1989; Weiss et al., 1992). A child who learns that he will be hit, kicked, or shoved when he displeases his parents will probably direct the same kind of responses toward playmates who displease him (Hart, Ladd, & Burleson, 1990).

PHOTO 9.4 Children who are hit when they displease others are likely to hit others who displease them.

Might the Child Be Influencing the Parent? Although parental attitudes and child-rearing practices certainly contribute to children's aggression and antisocial conduct, the direction of influence may also flow in the opposite direction, from child to parent. In Dan Olweus's (1980) child-rearing study, the best predictors of aggression among young adolescent males were (1) the mothers' permissiveness toward, or willingness to tolerate, the boys' aggressive behavior earlier in childhood and (2) the mothers' cold and rejecting attitudes toward their sons. However, the next best predictor was not a child-rearing variable at all but rather a measure of the boys' own temperamental impulsivity (highly active, impulsive boys tended to be the most aggressive). According to Olweus, a boy with an active and impetuous temperament may simply "exhaust his mother, resulting in her becoming more permissive of aggression in the boy" (p. 658). And should the impetuous child really anger his mother so that she can no longer ignore his conduct, she may express her negative feelings openly or resort to physical punishment as a control tactic, thereby increasing the likelihood that her boy will behave in a surly and belligerent manner. Although contemporary theorists disagree about just how much temperament contributes to aggressive, antisocial conduct (see, for example, Dodge, 1990; Lytton, 1990), it seems that children (by virtue of their temperaments) have a hand in creating the very child-rearing environments that will influence their propensities for aggression (O'Connor et al., 1998 Vucinich, Bank, & Patterson, 1992).

Parents as Managers Another way that parents may influence their children's aggression and antisocial conduct is through their management and monitoring of the child's whereabouts, activities, and choice of friends. Gerald Patterson and his associates (Capaldi & Patterson, 1991; Patterson et al., 1989; Patterson & Stouthamer-Loeber, 1984) consistently find that lack of parental monitoring is associated with such aggressive or delinquent adolescent behaviors as fighting, sassing teachers, destroying property, using drugs, and general rule breaking outside the home, especially when the members of a child's or an adolescent's peer group are inclined to endorse antisocial conduct (Mason et al., 1996). According to Patterson, this lack of parental monitoring often reflects an uninvolved and almost uncaring (unattached?) attitude on the parent's part.

However, not all parents who fail to monitor their children can be described as uncaring or unconcerned. Sanford Dornbusch and his associates (1985) found that a parent's ability to influence children depends in part on the composition of the family. Specifically, Dornbusch et al. found that the heads of *mother-only* households have a particularly difficult time managing the activities of adolescent sons and daughters without the support of a spouse or some other adult in the home (see also Steinberg, 1987). And given the association between lack of parental monitoring and deviant adolescent behavior in their own (and other) studies, Dornbusch et al. concluded that "the raising of adolescents is not a task that can easily be borne by a mother alone" (p. 340).

In sum, it appears that parental awareness of and control over a child's activities may be just as important in determining an adolescent's aggressive inclinations as the particular child-rearing practices that parents have used. Furthermore, Dornbusch's finding that the structure of the family affects parental control suggests another interesting conclusion: To understand how aggression develops within the home setting, one must think of the family as a *social system* in which interactions among *all* family members (or the lack thereof) will affect the child's developmental outcomes. We will see just how true this conclusion is in the pages that follow.

FAMILY CLIMATE AND CHILDREN'S AGGRESSION

Developmentalists have long suspected that the emotional climate of the home can and often does influence children's adjustment. One major contributor to a disruptive home environment is a strife-ridden parental relationship.

Parental Conflict and Children's Aggression   How are children influenced by their exposure to parental conflict? A growing body of evidence indicates that they often become extremely distressed when parents fight and that continuing conflict at home increases the likelihood that children will have hostile, aggressive interactions with siblings and peers (Cummings & Davies, 1994; Davies & Cummings, 1998; Harold et al., 1997). As noted earlier, youngsters who have often witnessed their parents fight without being abused themselves often learn that aggression pays off (for the victor) and are more likely to become *proactive aggressors,* whereas those youngsters who were themselves victimized at home as well are more inclined to distrust and to be suspicious of other people, becoming more *reactively aggressive* (Schwartz et al., 1997).

How exactly might a hostile climate at home promote such strong aggressive tendencies in children—particularly among those youngsters who are never seriously battered or mistreated by their parents? Let's see what developmentalists have learned by conceptualizing families as complex social systems.

Coercive Home Environments as "Breeding Grounds" for Aggression   Over the past 20 years, Gerald Patterson (1982; Patterson, Reid, & Dishion, 1992) has observed patterns of interaction in families that have at least one highly aggressive child. The aggressive children in Patterson's sample seemed "out of control"—they fought a lot at home and at school and were generally unruly and defiant. These families were then compared with other families of the same size and socioeconomic status that had no problem children.

Patterson soon discovered that he could not explain "out-of-control" behavior by merely focusing on the child-rearing practices that parents use. Instead, it seemed that highly aggressive children were living in rather atypical family environments that were characterized by a social climate that *they had helped to create.* Unlike most homes, where people frequently display approval and affection, the highly aggressive problem child usually lives in a setting in which family members are constantly bickering with one another: They are reluctant to initiate conversations, and when they do talk, they tend to needle, threaten, or otherwise irritate other family members rather than converse amiably. Patterson called these settings **coercive home environments** because a high percentage of interactions centered on one family member's attempts to force another to stop irritating him or her. He also noted that **negative reinforcement** was important in maintaining these coercive interactions: When one family member is making life unpleasant for another, the second will learn to whine, yell, scream, tease, or hit because these actions often force the antagonist to stop (and thus are reinforced). Consider the following sequence of events, which may be fairly typical in a coercive home environment:

1. A girl teases her older brother, who makes her stop teasing by yelling at her (yelling is negatively reinforced).
2. A few minutes later, the girl calls her brother a nasty name. The boy then chases and hits her.
3. The girl stops calling him names (which negatively reinforces hitting). She then whimpers and hits him back, and he withdraws (negatively reinforcing her hits). The boy then approaches and hits his sister again, and the conflict escalates.
4. At this point the mother intervenes. However, her children are too emotionally disrupted to listen to reason, so she finds herself applying punitive and coercive tactics to make them stop fighting.
5. The fighting stops (thus reinforcing the mother for using coercive methods). However, the children soon begin to whine, cry, or yell at the mother. These counter-coercive techniques are then reinforced if the mother backs off and accepts peace at any price. Unfortunately, backing off is only a temporary solution. The next time the children antagonize each other and become involved in an unbearable conflict, the mother is likely to use even more coercion to get them to stop. The children once again apply their own methods of countercoercion to induce her to "lay off," and the family atmosphere becomes increasingly unpleasant for everyone.

Mothers of problem children rarely use social approval as a means of behavior control, choosing instead to largely ignore prosocial conduct, to interpret many innocuous acts as antisocial, and to rely almost exclusively on coercive tactics to deal with perceived misconduct (Patterson et al., 1992; Strassberg, 1995). Perhaps the overwhelmingly negative treatment that these problem children receive at home (including parents' tendency to label ambiguous events as antisocial) helps to explain why they generally mistrust other people and display the *hostile attributional bias* so commonly observed among highly aggressive children (Dishion, 1990; Weiss et al., 1992). And ironically, children from highly coercive home environments eventually become resistant to punishment. They have learned to fight coercion with countercoercion and will often do so by defying the parent and *repeating the very act that she is trying to suppress.* Why? Because this is one of the few ways that the child can successfully command the attention of an adult who rarely offers praise or shows any signs of affection. No wonder Patterson calls these children "out of control"! By contrast, children from noncoercive families receive much more positive attention from siblings and parents, so they don't have to irritate other family members to be noticed (Patterson, 1982).

So we see that the flow of influence in the family setting is *multidirectional:* Coercive *interactions* between parents and their children and the children themselves will affect the behavior of *all* parties and contribute to the development of a hostile family environment—a true breeding ground for aggression. Unfortunately, these problem families may never break out of this destructive pattern of attacking and counterattacking one another unless they receive help. In Box 9.3 we consider one particularly effective approach to this problem—a method that necessarily focuses on the family as a social system rather than simply on the aggressive child who has been referred for treatment.

coercive home environment: a home in which family members often annoy one another and use aggressive or otherwise antisocial tactics as a method of coping with these aversive experiences.

negative reinforcer: any stimulus whose removal or termination as the consequence of an act will increase the probability that the act will recur.

Box 9.3 *Applying Developmental Research*

Helping Children (and Parents) Who Are "Out of Control"

How does one treat a problem child who is hostile, defiant, and "out of control"? Rather than focusing on the problem child, Gerald Patterson's (1981, 1982) approach is to work with the entire family. Patterson begins by carefully observing the family's interactions and determining just how family members are reinforcing one another's coercive activities. The next step is to describe the nature of the problem to parents and to teach them a new approach to managing their children's behavior. Some of the principles, skills, and procedures that Patterson stresses are the following:

1. Don't give in to the child's coercive behavior.
2. Don't escalate your own coercion when the child becomes coercive.
3. Control the child's coercion with the time-out procedure—a method of discipline in which the child is sent to her room (or some other location) until she calms down and stops using coercive tactics.
4. Identify those of the child's behaviors that are most irritating, and then establish a point system in which the child can earn credits (rewards, privileges) for acceptable conduct or lose them for unacceptable behavior. Parents with older problem children are taught how to formulate "behavioral contracts" that specify how the child is expected to behave at home and at school, as well as how deviations from this behavioral code will be punished. Whenever possible, children should have a say in negotiating these contracts.

5. Be on the lookout for occasions when you can respond to the child's prosocial conduct with warmth and affection. Although this is often difficult for parents who are accustomed to snapping at their children and accentuating the negative, Patterson believes that parental affection and approval will reinforce good conduct and eventually elicit displays of affection from the child—a clear sign that the family is on the road to recovery.

A clear majority of problem families respond quite favorably to these methods. Not only do problem children become less coercive, defiant, and aggressive, but the mother's depression fades as she gradually begins to feel better about herself, her child, and her ability to resolve family crises (Patterson, 1981). Some problem families show an immediate improvement. Others respond more gradually to the treatment and may require periodic "booster shots"—that is, follow-up treatments in which the clinician visits the family, determines why progress has slowed (or broken down), and then retrains the parents or suggests new procedures to correct the problems that are not being resolved. Clearly, this therapy works because it recognizes that "out of control" behavior stems from a *family system* in which both parents and children are influencing each other and contributing to the development of a hostile family environment. Therapies that focus exclusively on the problem child are not enough!

Coercive Home Environments as Contributors to Chronic Delinquency   How serious are the risks faced by "out-of-control" children who grow up in a coercive home environment? Patterson and his associates (1989) have addressed this issue by reviewing the literature on problem children and drawing some strong conclusions. As shown in Figure 9.7, coercive parenting early in childhood contributes to the development of children's hostile attributional biases, defiant, aggressive behaviors, and general lack of self-restraint which, by middle childhood, can cause these youngsters to be rejected by grade-school peers, criticized by teachers, and to founder academically (Birch & Ladd, 1998; Coie & Dodge, 1998). These poor outcomes may then cause parents to feel less invested in their children and less inclined to closely monitor their activities (Patterson et al., 1989; Vuchinich et al., 1992).

Furthermore, the rejection that problem children experience from peers, coupled with their likely placement in classes or study groups with other academically deficient children, often means that they will have ample exposure to other relatively defiant, aggressive, and socially unskilled youngsters like themselves. By ages 11 to 14, these youngsters are associating mainly with other hostile, antisocial classmates, banding together to form *deviant peer cliques* that tend to devalue academics, endorse aggressive solutions to conflict, and promote such dysfunctional adolescent activities as sexual misconduct, substance abuse, dropping out of school, and a variety of other kinds of antisocial or delinquent behaviors (Cairns et al., 1988; Coie & Dodge, 1998; Dishion et al., 1991, 1995). So, to return to the question raised earlier, Patterson claims that living in a coercive home environment poses serious risks indeed, for such an experience is often a crucial first step along the road to chronic aggression and delinquency.

Of course, not all chronically delinquent or antisocial individuals are products of coercive home environments. In their study of more than 4,000 Vietnam veterans, Windle and Windle (1995) found that about one veteran in five of those who were classified as highly aggressive were *late-onset types*—men who become aggressive in adulthood without having a history of aggression or a disordered home life earlier in childhood. Furthermore, some juvenile and adult offenders who commit mostly *covert* offenses (theft, fraud, etc.) are apparently not the products of coercive home environments. Yet most violent offenders do progress from minor aggression early in childhood to more serious fighting during the middle school and high school years to such truly violent acts as criminal assault, rape, robbery, and murder later in adolescence and young adulthood, following a pathway consistent with Patterson's coercion model (see Loeber & Stouthhamer-Loeber, 1998).

Although boys are more likely than girls to take the developmental path described in Figure 9.7 (McFadyen-Ketchum et al., 1996), the delinquency "gender gap" is narrowing. Male delinquents still dominate the violent crime statistics; but females are about as likely as males to be involved in larcenies, sexual misconduct, and substance abuse, and they are more likely than males to be arrested for such status offenses as running away from home and engaging in prostitution (*Uniform Crime Reports,* 1997). It may take a more disordered home environment to push girls along the path to delinquency, but, girls can become just as chronically antisocial as boys (Loeber & Stouthamer-Loeber, 1998).

Not surprisingly, antisocial male adolescents tend to pair up with antisocial females. Not only are these antisocial couples at risk of experiencing hostile and even abusive romantic relationships (Capaldi & Clark, 1998; Patterson, 1998), they are also inclined to make an early entry into parenthood, a role that they are ill-prepared to handle. In fact, these young, antisocial parents frequently rely on the same unresponsive and coercive child-rearing practices that their parents used with them (Fagot et al., 1998; Serbin et al., 1998), thus exposing their own offspring to a home environment that fosters irritable, coercive child behaviors, hostile attributional biases, and all their concomitants (that is, peer rejection, academic difficulties, and identification with

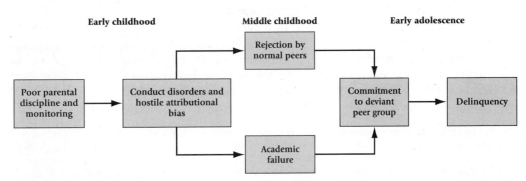

FIGURE 9.7 A model of the development of chronic antisocial behavior. (Adapted from Patterson, DeBaryshe, & Ramsey, 1989.) © 1989 by the American Psychological Assn. Reprinted by permission.

deviant peers). Here, then is one way in which hostile, antisocial inclinations are transmitted from generation to generation (Patterson, 1998).

Family interventions of the kind described in Box 9.3 can be quite effective at modifying the antisocial tendencies of preadolescent (and younger) children. However, once early antisocial patterns continue into adolescence, so many factors conspire to maintain them that interventions are usually unsuccessful (Kazdin, 1995).[1] Note the implication here: To cope with the problem of chronic aggression and delinquency, we must think in terms of *preventive* interventions—ideally, programs that would (1) teach parents more effective child-management techniques, (2) foster children's social skills to prevent them from being rejected by their peers, and (3) provide any academic remediation that may be necessary to keep children on track at school and to lessen the likelihood that they will fall in with deviant peer groups and/or become high school dropouts. Of course, any intervention that makes aggressive, antisocial conduct a less viable or attractive option would be a step in the right direction. Let's now consider some of the procedures that developmentalists have used in attempting to control children's hostilities.

Methods of Controlling Aggression and Antisocial Conduct

What methods other than family therapy might help parents and teachers suppress the aggressive antics of young children so that antisocial approaches to conflict do not become habitual? Over the years, a variety of solutions have been offered, including procedures to eliminate the payoffs for aggression, modeling and coaching strategies, creation of nonaggressive play environments, and training to help children empathize with victims of harmdoing. But few solutions have been so highly touted as the recommendation that we offer children harmless ways to express their anger or frustrations. Let's consider this "popular" alternative first.

CATHARSIS: A DUBIOUS STRATEGY

Sigmund Freud believed that hostile, aggressive urges build over time, and he urged people to find harmless ways to release them every now and then (that is, to experience catharsis) before they reach dangerous levels and trigger a truly violent outburst. The implications of this **catharsis hypothesis** are clear: If we encourage young children to vent their anger or frustrations on inanimate objects such as Bobo dolls, they should drain away their aggressive energies and become less inclined to harm other people.

Popular as this **cathartic technique** has been, it does not work and *may even backfire*. In one study (Walters & Brown, 1963), children who had been encouraged to slap, punch, and kick an inflatable Bobo doll were found to be much more aggressive in their later interactions with peers than were classmates who had not had an opportunity to beat on the doll. Other investigators have noted that children who are first angered by a peer and then given an opportunity to aggress against an inanimate object become no less aggressive toward the peer who had angered them in the first place (Mallick & McCandless, 1966). So cathartic techniques do not reduce aggressive urges (Geen & Quantry, 1977). In fact, they may imply to impressionable

catharsis hypothesis: the notion that aggressive urges are reduced when people witness or commit real or symbolic acts of aggression.

cathartic technique: a strategy for reducing aggression by encouraging children to vent their anger or frustrations on inanimate objects.

---

[1]This conclusion applies to *early-onset* aggression and delinquency among youngsters who are truly the products of coercive home environments. By contrast, many late-onset delinquents, who engage in mischievous, antisocial acts in the context of normal peer-group activities, are not products of coercive homes, are not as closely intertwined with a deviant peer culture, and are much more inclined to simply drop out of delinquent activities over time (Patterson, Capaldi, & Bank, 1991).

youngsters that hitting and kicking are acceptable methods of expressing their anger or frustrations.

CREATING NONAGGRESSIVE ENVIRONMENTS

One simple but effective approach for reducing children's aggression is to create play areas that minimize the likelihood of conflict. For example, parents and teachers might remove (or refuse to buy) such "aggressive" toys as guns, tanks, and rubber knives that are known to provoke hostilities (Watson & Peng, 1992). Providing ample space for vigorous play also helps to eliminate the accidental bumps, shoves, and trips that often escalate into full-blown hostilities (Hartup, 1974). Finally, shortages of play materials sometimes contribute to conflicts and aggression; but children are likely to play quite harmoniously if adults have provided enough balls, slides, swings, and other toys to keep them from having to compete for scarce resources (Smith & Connolly, 1980).

How might one reach children who have already become highly aggressive? Developmentalists now recognize that different forms of aggression require different kinds of interventions (Coie & Koeppl, 1990; Crick & Dodge, 1996). Recall that proactive aggressors rely on forceful strategies because these tactics are easy for them to enact and often enable these youngsters to achieve personal goals. An effective intervention for those children might teach them that aggression doesn't pay and that alternative prosocial responses, such as cooperation or sharing, are better ways to achieve their objectives. By contrast, hot-headed reactive aggressors may profit more from social-cognitive interventions that teach them to control their anger and to suppress their tendency to overattribute hostile intentions to companions who displease them. Let's take a closer look at these two kinds of intervention.

ELIMINATING THE PAYOFFS FOR AGGRESSION

Parents and teachers can reduce the incidence of *proactive aggression* by identifying and eliminating its reinforcing consequences and by encouraging alternative means of achieving one's objectives. For example, if 4-year-old Lennie were to hit his 3-year-old sister Gail in order to take possession of a toy, Lennie's mother could teach him that this instrumental aggression doesn't pay by simply returning the toy to Gail and denying him his objective. However, this strategy wouldn't work if Lennie is an insecure child who feels neglected and has attacked his sister *in order to attract his mother's attention*; under these circumstances, the mother would be reinforcing Lennie's aggression if she attended to it at all! So what is she to do?

One proven method that she might use is the **incompatible-response technique**—a strategy of ignoring all but the most serious of Lennie's aggressive antics (thereby denying him an "attentional" reward) while reinforcing such acts as cooperation and sharing that are incompatible with aggression. Teachers who have tried this strategy find that it quickly produces an increase in children's prosocial conduct and a corresponding decrease in their hostilities (Brown & Elliot, 1965; see also Slaby & Crowley, 1977).

And how might adults handle *serious* acts of harmdoing without "reinforcing" them with their attention? One effective approach is the **time-out technique** that Patterson favors—a technique in which the adult removes the offender from the situation in which his aggression is reinforced (for example, by sending him to his room until he is ready to exert some self-control and behave appropriately). Although this approach may generate some resentment, the adult in charge is not physically abusing the child, is not serving as an aggressive model, and is not likely to unwittingly reinforce the child who misbehaves as a means of attracting attention. The time-out procedure is

incompatible-response technique: a nonpunitive method of behavior modification in which adults ignore undesirable conduct while reinforcing acts that are incompatible with these responses.

time-out technique: a form of discipline in which children who misbehave are removed from the setting until they are prepared to act more appropriately.

most effective at controlling children's hostilities when adults also reinforce cooperative or helpful acts that are incompatible with aggression (Parke & Slaby, 1983).

Responses incompatible with aggression may also be instilled by modeling or by coaching strategies. When children see a model choose a nonaggressive solution to a conflict or are explicitly coached in the use of nonaggressive methods of problem solving, they become more likely to select and enact similar solutions to their own problems (Shure, 1989; Zahavi & Asher, 1978).

SOCIAL-COGNITIVE INTERVENTIONS

Highly aggressive youngsters—particularly those high in *reactive aggression*—can profit from social-cognitive interventions that help them to

PHOTO 9.5 Time-out can be a most effective means of controlling children's aggression and other misconduct, particularly when adults also strive to reinforce behaviors that are incompatible with aggression.

(1) regulate their anger and (2) to become more skilled at empathizing with and taking others' perspectives so they will not be so likely to overattribute hostile intentions to their peers (Crick & Dodge, 1996; Rabiner, Lenhart, & Lochman, 1990). In one study (Guerra & Slaby, 1990), a group of violent adolescent offenders were coached in such skills as (1) looking for nonhostile cues that might be associated with harmdoing, (2) controlling their impulses (or anger), and (3) generating nonaggressive solutions to conflict. Not only did these violent offenders show dramatic improvements in their social problem-solving skills, but they also became less inclined to endorse beliefs supporting aggression and less aggressive in their interactions with authority figures and other inmates. Michael Chandler (1973) found a similar reduction in the hostile social cognitions and aggressive behaviors of a group of 11- to 13-year-old delinquents who had participated in a 10-week program designed specifically to make them more aware of other people's intentions and feelings.

Some researchers now believe that the best interventions are likely to be comprehensive ones that minimize the rewards for aggression, replace aggressive with prosocial responses, and include all the elements of successful social-cognitive training programs (Gibbs, Potter, & Goldstein, 1995). Yet it is important to note that any reduction in hostilities that results from successful interventions of any kind could be short-lived if lessons participants have learned are quickly undermined in a coercive home environment (Pettit, Dodge, & Brown, 1988) or in the company of chronically aggressive friends who value and endorse aggression (Dishion et al., 1995). Indeed, two years after their release, the "trained offenders" in Guerra and Slaby's (1990) study were only slightly less likely to have stayed clean and not violated their parole (34% had violated parole) than other offenders who had not been trained (46% were parole violators). Although these long-term outcomes are in the right direction, the program likely would have had much better long-term results if it had been instituted earlier, before these offenders had made a strong commitment to a deviant peer culture to which they often return, receiving little if any support for their new ways of thinking.

Finally, highly aggressive children are often found to be deficient in **empathy** (Cohen & Strayer, 1996)—a social-cognitive attribute that successful social-cognitive interventions usually try to foster. Indeed, empathy is an attribute that parents and teachers who have no special training in intervention techniques can nevertheless promote in young children *from toddlerhood on*. How? By simply modeling empathic

empathy: the ability to experience the same emotions that someone else is experiencing.

concern for their children (Barnett, 1987; Eisenberg, Fabes et al., 1991) and by using disciplinary techniques that (1) point out the harmful consequences of their own child's harmdoing while (2) encouraging him to put himself in the victim's place and imagine how the victim feels (Zahn-Waxler, Radke-Yarrow, & King, 1979; Zahn-Waxler, Radke-Yarrow, et al., 1992). In our next chapter, we will see that parents who often display empathy and who rely heavily on rational, nonpunitive disciplinary techniques tend to raise relatively nonaggressive and sympathetic youngsters who seem genuinely concerned about the welfare of others.

Summary

WHAT IS AGGRESSION?

- Human aggression is a pervasive phenomenon that has been defined in many different ways. Freud used the term **Thanatos** to describe what he considered to be an inborn aggressive and destructive instinct, whereas ethologists also view aggression as a basic part of human nature.

- Learning theorists have rejected instinct definitions in favor of the **behavioral definition of aggression** and, more recently, an **intentional definition of aggression.** Aggressive acts are often further subdivided into two categories: **hostile aggression** and **instrumental aggression.** Yet people often disagree on whether particular acts are truly aggressive, thus reflecting the notion that aggression is largely a social judgment individuals make about injurious acts, based on the meaning of those acts *to them.*

THEORIES OF AGGRESSION

- Freud proposed that humans are driven by a destructive instinct, the *Thanatos,* which he considered responsible for the generation of aggressive impulses. Ethologists describe aggression as a fighting instinct triggered by certain eliciting cues in the environment. Thus, both schools of thought view humans as instinctively aggressive.

- From the early and rather simple **frustration/aggression hypothesis** sprang other learning theories of aggression. Berkowitz's revised frustration-aggression theory contends that frustration as well as attack and previously acquired aggressive habits increase one's readiness to aggress. But aggressive responses may not occur unless **aggressive cues** are present to evoke them. Bandura's social learning theory describes how aggressive responses are acquired through direct experience and observational learning and are maintained to become habits. He also broke new ground by claiming that (1) any form of arousal can promote aggression and (2) our cognitive interpretation of harmdoing is more important in determining our reactions than is the amount of objective harm done.

- Dodge's social-information processing theory extends Bandura's cognitive emphasis, describing six information-processing phases that children pass through to interpret harm done and formulate a response. This model has helped us to discriminate **proactive aggressors,** for whom aggression is usually a means to other ends, from **reactive aggressors,** who display a **hostile attributional bias** and quickly retaliate after real or imagined provocations.

DEVELOPMENTAL TRENDS IN AGGRESSION

- Instrumental aggression emerges by the end of the first year as infants begin to quarrel with siblings and peers over toys and other possessions.

- Over the course of childhood, aggression becomes less physical and increasingly verbal, and somewhat less instrumental and increasingly hostile or **retaliatory** in nature. By middle childhood, a small number of youngsters are responsible for a majority of aggressive incidents. The participants in these exchanges are often bullies and their **passive** and/or **provocative victims.**

- Overt aggression continues to decline in adolescence, except for the most highly aggressive individuals, who can become truly violent. However, many adolescents, while showing less aggression, are turning to other covert or indirect methods to express their anger or discontent.

- Aggressive dispositions tend to be stable over time for both boys and girls. Both genetic influences and environmental factors contribute to this stability.

SEX DIFFERENCES IN AGGRESSION

- On an absolute level, males are more *overtly* (physically and verbally) aggressive than females. This well-established sex difference reflects the interactive influence of biological and social forces. However, this research may underestimate female proclivities for aggression, for girls are often found to exceed boys in **relational aggression.**

CULTURAL AND SUBCULTURAL INFLUENCES ON AGGRESSION

■ A person's aggressive inclinations will depend, in part, on the cultural and subcultural settings in which he or she is raised. Due in part to social class differences in parenting, children and adolescents from disadvantaged backgrounds are more aggressive and display higher rates of delinquency than their middle-class peers.

FAMILY INFLUENCES ON AGGRESSION

■ Cold and rejecting parents who rely on **power assertion** and who often permit aggression are likely to raise highly aggressive children. However, the socialization of aggression is a two-way street, for characteristics of the child (such as temperament or reactions to discipline) can affect parental attitudes and child-rearing practices.

■ Strife-ridden homes appear to be breeding grounds for aggression and violence. Highly aggressive "out-of-control" youngsters often live in **coercive home environments** in which such hostile behaviors as bickering and fighting are **negatively reinforced.** Family therapy is often necessary to help these out-of-control children who otherwise are at risk of alienating teachers and peers, falling in with deviant peers, and becoming chronic delinquents.

METHODS OF CONTROLLING AGGRESSION AND ANTISOCIAL CONDUCT

■ Contrary to the **catharsis hypothesis, cathartic techniques** are not effective means of reducing children's hostilities. Creating "nonaggressive" play environments is a more fruitful approach. *Proactive* aggressors can benefit when adults rely on such control procedures as **time out** and the **incompatible-response technique,** which teaches them that aggression doesn't pay and that nonaggressive means of problem solving are better ways to achieve their objectives. And all aggressive youngsters, particularly hot-headed *reactive aggressors,* can benefit from social-cognitive interventions that help them to regulate their anger and to become more skilled at empathizing with and taking other's perspectives, thus becoming less inclined to attribute hostile intents to other people.

Chapter Ten

Altruism and Moral Development

What Are Altruism and Prosocial Behavior?

The Motivational (or Intentional) Definition of Altruism

A Behavioral Definition of Altruism

Theories of Altruism and Prosocial Development

Biological Theories: Are We Programmed for Prosocial Conduct?

Psychoanalytic Theory: Let Your Conscience (Superego) Be Your Guide

Social-Learning Theory: What's in It for Me?

Cognitive Theories of Altruism: Maturity Is the Medium

Developmental Trends in Altruism

Origins of Prosocial Behavior

Age-Related Changes in Altruism

Cognitive and Affective Contributors to Altruism

Role-Taking and Altruism

Prosocial Moral Reasoning

Empathy: An Important Affective Contributor to Altruism

Viewing Oneself as Altruistic

Cultural and Social Influences on Altruism

Cultural Influences

Reinforcing Altruism

Modeling Influences: Practicing and Preaching Altruism

Who Raises Altruistic Children?

What Is Morality?

How Developmentalists Look at Morality

Psychoanalytic Explanations of Moral Development

Freud's Theory of Oedipal Morality

Evaluating Freud's Theory and Newer Psychoanalytic Ideas About Morality

Cognitive-Developmental Theory: The Child as a Moral Philosopher

Piaget's Theory of Moral Development

An Evaluation of Piaget's Theory

Kohlberg's Theory of Moral Development

Support for Kohlberg's Theory

Criticisms of Kohlberg's Approach

Morality as a Product of Social Learning (and Social Information Processing)

How Consistent Are Moral Conduct and Moral Character?

Learning to Resist Temptation

Who Raises Children Who Are Morally Mature?

Summary

ωhat would you say is the most important aspect of a child's social development? Surely this is a question that might generate any number of answers. But when one sample of new parents encountered this item in a child-rearing survey conducted by one of my laboratory classes, 74% of them indicated that they hoped, above all, that their child would acquire a strong sense of *morality*—right and wrong—to guide their transactions with other people.

When asked what sort of moral principles they hoped to instill, these new parents provided many answers. However, most of their responses fit into one of the following three categories:

1. *Avoid hurting others.* Parents generally hoped their children could learn to become appropriately autonomous and to serve their needs without harming others. In fact, unprovoked and intentional acts of harmdoing—or *aggression*—was one class of behavior that most parents said they would try to suppress as they try to instill the principle that it is inappropriate and a violation of another person's rights to purposely attempt to harm that person.
2. *Prosocial concern.* Another value that many parents hoped to instill was a sense of *altruism*—that is, a selfless concern for the welfare of other people and a willingness to act on that concern. In fact, it is not at all unusual for parents to encourage such altruistic acts as sharing, comforting, or helping others while their children are still in diapers.
3. *A personal commitment to abide by rules.* Finally, almost all our survey respondents mentioned the importance of persuading children to comply with socially condoned rules of conduct and of monitoring their behavior to ensure that these rules are followed. They felt that the ultimate goal of this *moral socialization* is to help the child acquire a set of *personal* values, or ethical principles, that will enable her to distinguish right from wrong and to do the "right" things, even when there may be no one else present to monitor and evaluate her conduct.

Having covered the topic of aggression in Chapter 9, we now consider the other two interrelated aspects of social development that people often consider when making judgments about a person's moral character. We begin by exploring the development of an attribute that is seemingly incompatible with aggression—prosocial concern (or altruism)—as we consider how young and reputedly selfish children might come to make personal sacrifices to benefit others. We then examine the broader issue of moral development and trace the child's evolution from a seemingly self-indulgent creature who appears to respect no rules to a moral philosopher of sorts who has internalized certain ethical principles to evaluate her own and others' conduct.

Let's now consider how children might become prosocially inclined.

What Are Altruism and Prosocial Behavior?

Prosocial behavior is *any action that benefits other people,* such as sharing with someone less fortunate than oneself, comforting or rescuing a distressed person, cooperating with someone or helping him or her to achieve an objective, or even simply making others feel good by complimenting them on their appearance or accomplishments. Now before proceeding further, briefly scan the following four statements:

1. John S., a millionaire, makes a $50,000 contribution to AIDS research.
2. Odell W. intervenes to help a young female mugging victim and is stabbed to death.

prosocial behavior: actions, such as sharing, helping, or comforting, that benefit other people.

3. Juan K. donates a pint of blood, receiving $15 for his donation.
4. Sam P. repays his friend Jim for a previous favor by offering to help Jim paint his garage.

Most of us would undoubtedly agree that these acts are examples of *prosocial* behavior. But would you consider each to be *altruistic?* My own students often disagree on whether one or more of these four acts qualify as **altruism.** So, too, do developmentalists interested in the growth of prosocial concern, as we see in examining the two most common definitions of altruism.

The Motivational (or Intentional) Definition of Altruism

Those who favor a **motivational/(intentional) definition of altruism** focus on the motives, or intentions, that underlie prosocial acts. According to this motivational perspective, an act of kindness can be labeled "altruistic" if the actor's *primary* motive or intent is to provide positive consequences for another person. In other words, the true altruist acts more out of a concern for others than for any positive outcomes he or she may anticipate as a result of helping, sharing with, or comforting them.

Over the years, a clear majority of my own students have favored a motivational definition of altruism. They usually say that scenarios 1 and 2 seem to reflect a selfless concern for promoting the welfare of other people, whereas scenarios 3 and 4, while clearly examples of prosocial behavior, do not qualify as altruism because the actors are reaping personal gains from their benevolence (scenario 3) or simply repaying the recipient for a favor (scenario 4). Yet, the more skeptical minority seriously doubts that any form of helping is motivated *solely* out of a concern for others without regard for the self. And these skeptics may have a point, for it is often difficult to determine exactly what motivates a prosocial act. For example, John S. of scenario 1 could be considered altruistic if we conclude that his donation was truly prompted by a desire to help humankind find a cure for AIDS. But what would you think about the same behavior had you learned that John has AIDS or if you decided that his large donation was intended as a tax write-off? Even Odell W., who made the supreme sacrifice in scenario 2, could conceivably be seeking the adulation of the female victim or "doing the right thing" in order to maintain his own self-respect. If so, his behavior might not qualify as "altruism" under a strict interpretation of the motivational definition. And suppose you found a wallet containing a large sum of money, returned it to its owner, and subsequently declined a monetary offering with the statement "Your thanks is my reward." Is this "thank you" a sufficient reward to render your behavior nonaltruistic? Clearly, the problems involved in inferring a helper's true intentions have led some developmentalists to conclude that altruism is best defined behaviorally.

A Behavioral Definition of Altruism

According to the **behavioral definition of altruism,** an altruistic act is one that benefits another person, *regardless of the actor's motives.* In other words, altruism and prosocial behavior are viewed as roughly synonymous concepts, so that any and all of the acts depicted the four scenarios above could be labeled "altruistic."

What kinds of behaviors do children view as altruistic? How do their views differ from those of adults? Lizette Peterson and Donna Gelfand (1984) addressed these issues by asking college students and first-, fourth-, and sixth-graders to rate the altruistic motivation of different children who had helped adults (1) out of empathy, (2) to obtain a tangible reward, (3) to win praise, (4) to repay a favor, or (5) to avoid

altruism: a concern for the welfare of others that is expressed through such prosocial acts as sharing, cooperating, and helping.

motivational/intentional definition of altruism: beneficial acts for which the actor's primary motive or intent was to address the needs of others.

behavioral definition of altruism: behavior that benefits another person, regardless of the actor's motives.

criticism. Even the first-graders knew that an actor who helped in order to avoid criticism was not displaying an altruistic motive. However, they felt that all the other actors were about equally altruistic. Surprisingly, perhaps, fourth- and sixth-graders showed roughly the same pattern of results as first-graders—thus indicating that even 9- to 12-year-olds often fail to discriminate the motives underlying prosocial acts and seem to favor a *behavioral* definition of altruism. By contrast, the adults in this study favored the motivational definition, for they attributed greater altruism to helpers who had empathized with the recipient than to those who were simply repaying a favor or who had something to gain (praise or a tangible reward) from their assistance.

Yet even though adults generally favor a motivational definition of altruism, neither they nor most developmentalists make sharp distinctions between altruism and prosocial behavior when referring (or responding to) the benevolence of young children. One reason they don't is that people in Western societies (even those as young as second-graders) generally perceive themselves as having less of an obligation to do something nice for others (the positive side of morality) than to inhibit harmdoing and antisocial conduct (the negative side of morality; cf. Grusec, 1991; Kahn, 1992). In other words, benevolent acts, while socially sanctioned, often have a *discretionary* quality about them and thus, are often *not* viewed as mandatory.[1] So in the interest of promoting such nonobligatory behaviors, parents and other socialization agents are likely to view a variety of benevolent acts as "good" and worthy of praise (even if not solely altruistic).

Nevertheless, there are developmentalists who continue to argue that the motivational bases of children's early acts of kindness have important implications for predicting future conduct. David Rosenhan (1972b), for example, has proposed that we distinguish **autonomous altruism**—those prosocial acts motivated by a concern for others—from **normative altruism**—those acts of kindness given in expectation of receiving personal benefits or avoiding criticism for failing to act. Later in the chapter, we will see that this distinction may indeed be useful, for these two kinds of prosocial conduct may just evolve along separate developmental paths.

Theories of Altruism and Prosocial Development

Several theorists have debated the issue of whether the bases for altruism are innate or learned. *Ethologists* believe that a sense of prosocial concern is a preadapted, genetically programmed attribute—a basic component of human nature—that helps to ensure the survival of the species. By contrast, *psychoanalytic* and *social-learning* theorists argue that a child's prosocial inclinations derive not from his or her genes or evolutionary history but from experiences with social agents (altruism is acquired). *Cognitive-developmental* theorists can certainly agree with the latter point of view. However, they would add that both the form and the frequency of a child's prosocial conduct will depend, in part, on his or her cognitive skills and level of intellectual development.

BIOLOGICAL THEORIES: ARE WE PROGRAMMED FOR PROSOCIAL CONDUCT?

In 1965, Donald Campbell argued that altruism is, in part, instinctive—a basic component of human nature. His argument hinged on the assumption that individuals, be they animal or human, are more likely to receive protection from natural enemies

autonomous altruism: prosocial acts motivated by a concern for others with no expectations of being repaid for such favors.

normative altruism: prosocial acts that are performed with the expectation of receiving some personal benefit for acting or avoiding criticism for failing to act.

---

[1]As we see later in the chapter, people from collectivist societies and subcultures are much more inclined to view prosocial conduct as obligatory or mandatory than are Westerners from individualistic societies.

and to satisfy their basic needs if they live together in cooperative social units. If this assumption is correct, then cooperative, altruistic individuals would be most likely to survive and to pass along "altruistic genes" to their offspring. Thus, over thousands of years evolutionary processes would favor the development of innate prosocial motives.[2] Campbell notes that "the tremendous survival value of being social makes innate social motives as likely on *a priori* grounds as self-centered ones" (1965, p. 301).

How exactly have we humans evolved that might make us prosocially inclined? Martin Hoffman (1981, 1993) proposes that the capacity for *empathy*—our tendency to become aroused by and to vicariously experience the emotions of others—is the biological substrate for altruistic concern. Why else, Hoffman asks, would we set aside our own selfish motives to aid other people or to avoid harming them unless we had the capacity to share their emotions and experience their distress?

Indeed, we noted in Box 3.1 that newborn infants may be displaying a primitive empathic response when they become distressed at the sound of another infant's cries; and we also learned in Chapter 3 that empathy is a genetically influenced attribute, for identical twins are much more alike in empathic concern than fraternal twins are (Matthews et al., 1981; Zahn-Waxler, Robinson, & Emde, 1992). And we will soon see that there is a meaningful relationship between a person's empathic sensitivities and his or her prosocial behavior. However, an inborn capacity for empathy does *not* imply that altruism is "automatic" or biologically programmed, for as Hoffman (1981) has argued, empathy is subject to environmental influence and may be fostered or dramatically inhibited by the social environments in which children are raised. With that comment in mind, let us turn to other theories that stress environmental contributions to children's prosocial development.

PSYCHOANALYTIC THEORY: LET YOUR CONSCIENCE (SUPEREGO) BE YOUR GUIDE

Recall from our discussion of psychoanalytic theory in Chapter 2 that Sigmund Freud described the young, unsocialized child as a self-serving creature constantly driven by id-based, hedonistic impulses. This characterization of human nature might seem to suggest that the concept of altruism offers a severe challenge to a psychoanalytic account of personality development: How is it possible for a selfish, egoistic child to acquire a sense of altruistic concern that will occasionally dictate that he or she make self-sacrificing responses to benefit others?

The challenge is not as formidable as it first appears. According to proponents of psychoanalytic theory, prosocial norms and principles—for example, the **norm of social responsibility** and the Golden Rule—are but a few of the many parental prescriptions and values that may be internalized during the period of childhood in which the superego develops. We will examine the process of superego development as we take up Freud's theory of Oedipal morality later in the chapter.

SOCIAL-LEARNING THEORY: WHAT'S IN IT FOR ME?

Altruism presents an interesting paradox for social-learning theory (Rosenhan, 1972a). A central premise of the social-learning approach is that people repeat behaviors that are reinforced and avoid repeating responses that prove costly or punishing. Yet many prosocial acts seem to defy this view of human nature: Altruists occasionally choose to take dangerous risks, forgo personal rewards, and donate their

norm of social responsibility: the principle that we should help others who are in some way dependent on us for assistance.

---

[2]One such motive might be *reciprocal altruism*—the idea that people are genetically programmed to help others because one day these recipients of aid will reciprocate by aiding the original benefactor and/or his genetic relatives, thus serving to ensure their survival (Trivers, 1983).

own valuable resources (thereby incurring a loss) in order to benefit others. The challenge for social-learning theorists is to explain how these self-sacrificial tendencies are acquired and maintained.

Responses to the challenge have been many and varied. On a conceptual level, several reinforcement theorists have taken the position that all prosocial acts, even those that prove extremely costly to the benefactor, are prompted by some form of subtle reward or self-gain. For example, we could argue that the German citizens who risked their lives to rescue Jews from their Nazi tormentors did so in order to increase their self-esteem, to win a favorable evaluation from future generations, or to reap the benefits afforded morally righteous people in the afterlife. The major problem with this explanation is its circularity: It assumes that because helping behavior occurred, the consequences of this behavior must have been reinforcing (Sigelman, 1984).

Although tangible rewards do not always follow altruistic responses, altruism may still be a function of social learning and reinforcement. Let's consider three ways in which children might learn that altruism "pays off."

Conditioning of Empathic Responses   Our capacity for empathy may help to explain why we might help, comfort, or share with others in situations where there are no obvious tangible rewards to sustain helping behavior. For example, a person who empathizes with a suffering victim and vicariously experiences the victim's distress may have learned from past experience that if she helps or comforts the victim, she will not only relieve the victim's pain and suffering but her own distress as well. So prosocial responses may often appear to be self-sacrificing when, in fact, they *reinforce* the helper by making her feel good or by relieving empathic distress. Eleanor Maccoby (1980) has even proposed that such empathic mediation of prosocial behavior often begins early in life:

> With empathic distress the process would work in the following way: A twelve-month-old has cried on hundreds of different occasions and the sound of crying has repeatedly been associated with the child's own distress. And so by a process of [classical conditioning], the sound of crying—anyone's crying—can now evoke feelings of distress . . . and even tears. If the young listener thinks of a way to make the other person stop crying, he or she will feel better. From the standpoint of simple self-interest, then, we should expect children to learn to perform such "altruistic" actions. (p. 347)

Direct Tuition of Altruism   Learning theorists argue that we come to behave prosocially without expecting immediate or tangible benefits because previous rewards for similar acts of kindness have made such behavior intrinsically reinforcing. The process might work this way. Parents, teachers, and other socializing agents often preach the virtues of prosocial conduct and reward children who behave accordingly. Over a period of time (and reinforcements), some of the positive affect stemming from these rewards becomes associated with the prosocial acts that are rewarded, so that altruistic gestures eventually become conditioned, or secondary, reinforcers that, when enacted, make the child feel good. And because individuals in most cultures receive periodic praise, recognition, or other forms of extrinsic reinforcement for their benevolence, we can imagine how prosocial acts might retain their "satisfying" qualities and even become resistant to extinction.

Observational Learning of Altruism   Finally, Albert Bandura (1989) believes that the most pervasive influence on children's prosocial concern is the behavior of other people—the social models to whom they are exposed. And he may be right, for as we will see, children who witness the charitable acts of altruistic models often become more prosocially inclined, even when the models incur personal costs and receive no

PHOTO **10.1** Children learn many prosocial lessons by observing the behavior of altruistic models.

tangible benefits for their kindness (see Radke-Yarrow, Zahn-Waxler, & Chapman, 1983, for a review).

Why might children imitate the seemingly costly acts of altruistic models? The answer may lie in the ways in which children process the relevant social information and interpret what they have seen. For example, Kohlberg (1969) argued that the model's behavior merely informs the child of what older, more competent people consider the "appropriate" or mature response under the circumstances. Presumably, the child then follows the model's example as part of his attempt to emulate the behavior of competent others; that is, imitating competent people is intrinsically reinforcing. A second possibility is that the model's prosocial acts simply remind children of the norm of social responsibility, which they may have already internalized. Finally, children may learn that altruism is *self-reinforcing* if altruistic models "reinforce" themselves by expressing happiness or some other form of positive affect when they help others. Indeed, Midlarsky and Bryan (1972) discovered that models who express positive affect while helping—for example, "Giving to the poor makes me feel *good*"—elicit more prosocial behavior from fourth- and fifth-grade children than equally charitable models who express positive affect that is unrelated to their acts of kindness (such as "This game is fun").

In sum, learning theorists have offered several plausible explanations for children's willingness to perform prosocial acts that promise few if any tangible rewards and may even be costly. In a later section of the chapter, we follow up on these ideas by taking a closer look at the contributions of reinforcement, empathy, and social modeling influences to children's prosocial development.

COGNITIVE THEORIES OF ALTRUISM: MATURITY IS THE MEDIUM

Both cognitive-developmental theorists and social information-processing theorists assume that prosocial responses such as cooperation, sharing, giving reassurance and comfort, and volunteering to help others should become increasingly apparent over the course of childhood (Eisenberg, Lennon, & Roth, 1983; Kohlberg, 1969; Chapman et al., 1987). The basis for this prediction is straightforward: As children develop intellectually, they will acquire important cognitive skills that will affect both their reasoning about prosocial issues and their motivation to act in the interests of others.

Cognitive theorists have proposed that there are four broad phases of prosocial development. The first phase, in which some sharing and demonstrations of sympathy are observed, begins in the second year of life and is thought to be tied to the infant's ability to recognize himself or herself and to differentiate the self from other people (Hoffman, 1988; Zahn-Waxler, Radke-Yarrow, et al., 1992). As we will see in our next section, this is the period when infants begin to react more reliably to others' distress, often becoming distressed themselves (that is, empathizing) and occasionally trying to cheer a distressed companion. The second broad phase of development roughly coincides with Piaget's preoperational period (ages 3 to 6). Presumably, young preschool children are still relatively egocentric, and their thinking about prosocial issues (as well as their actual behavior) is often self-serving, or hedonistic: Acts that benefit others are considered worth performing if those acts will also benefit oneself. During middle childhood and preadolescence (or Piaget's concrete-operational stage)—children are becoming less egocentric, are acquiring important role-taking skills, and should now begin to focus on the legitimate needs of others as a justification for prosocial behavior. This is the period when children begin to think that any act of kindness that most people would condone is probably "good" and should be performed. It is also the phase at which empathic or sympathetic responses should become an important contributor to altruism. Finally, adolescents who have reached formal operations have begun to understand and appreciate the implications of abstract prosocial norms—universal principles such as the norm of social responsibility or the Golden Rule that (1) would encourage them to direct their acts of kindness to a wider range of prospective recipients and (2) may also trigger strong attributions of personal responsibility for prosocial conduct and feelings of guilt or self-condemnation should they callously ignore their obligations (Chapman et al., 1987; Eisenberg et al., 1983).

Most cognitively oriented researchers have chosen to explore the links between particular cognitive skills (for example, role-taking) and children's prosocial behaviors rather than trying to identify broad stages of prosocial development. Yet Nancy Eisenberg and her associates have charted age-related changes in children's reasoning about prosocial issues, and her results are indeed interesting. We review both these lines of inquiry in a later section of the chapter.

A Final Comment Although research on children's moral *transgressions* and the development of moral inhibitions has a long and storied history, only within the past 25 to 30 years have social developmentalists taken a strong interest in altruism and the growth of prosocial concern. And even though ethologists and behavior geneticists have called our attention to possible biological bases of prosocial conduct and have proposed a number of intriguing ideas that are definitely worth pursuing, most of the existing work on prosocial development stems from either the social-learning or the cognitive approaches. What's more, these theories are often viewed as more conflicting or contradictory than they really are. In truth, they emphasize *different* aspects of development:

> The social learning approach emphasizes the role of antecedent and consequent environmental events (e.g., the presence or absence of a model or reinforcement), [whereas] the cognitive-developmental approach emphasizes the role of cognitive structures as measured, for example, by role-taking tasks and moral judgement stories. (Rushton, 1976, p. 909)

I will simply add that predictions derived from both theories have received ample support, sometimes in the same experiment! For example, Rushton (1975) found that children exposed to charitable models were later more charitable themselves than age-mates exposed to selfish models—a finding consistent with social-learning theory. However, closer inspection of the data revealed that children who had tested relatively high (that is, mature) in their levels of moral reasoning were much more charitable overall and were more likely to criticize the stinginess of a selfish model than those who had tested lower (or less mature) in their moral reasoning—findings that are clearly anticipated by cognitive-developmental theory. So in light of these results and other empirical evidence that we will examine, it seems wise to consider the social-learning and the cognitive perspectives as complementary, rather than contradictory, statements about the origins and development of prosocial concern.

Developmental Trends in Altruism

As we noted in opening this chapter, a genuine concern about the welfare of other people and a willingness to act on this concern are attributes that most adults hope their children will acquire—to an extent that many parents are already encouraging altruistic acts such as sharing, cooperating, or helping while their children are still in diapers! Until recently, experts in child development would have claimed that these well-intentioned adults were wasting their time, for infants and toddlers were thought so egocentric as to be incapable of considering the needs of anyone other than themselves. But the experts were wrong!

ORIGINS OF PROSOCIAL BEHAVIOR

Long before children receive any formal moral or religious training, they may act in ways that resemble the prosocial behavior of older people. Twelve- to 18-month-olds, for example, will occasionally offer toys to their companions (Hay et al., 1991) and even attempt to help their mothers with such household chores as sweeping or dusting (Rheingold, 1982). And the prosocial conduct of very young children even has a certain "rationality" about it. For example, 2-year-olds are more likely to offer toys to a peer when playthings are scarce than when they are plentiful (Hay et al., 1991). Moreover, a type of *reciprocity* appears by the end of the third year. In one study (Levitt et al., 1985), 29- to 36-month-old toddlers who had previously received a toy from a peer when they had had none of their own typically returned the favor when they later found themselves with several toys to play with and the peer without any. Yet, if that peer had earlier refused to share, the toddlers almost invariably hoarded the toys when it was their turn to control them.

Are toddlers capable of expressing sympathy and behaving compassionately toward their companions? Yes indeed, and these displays of prosocial concern are not all that uncommon (Eisenberg & Fabes, 1998; Radke-Yarrow et al., 1983; Zahn-Waxler, Radke-Yarrow, et al., 1992). Consider the reaction of 21-month-old John to his distressed playmate Jerry:

> Today Jerry was kind of cranky; he just started . . . bawling and he wouldn't stop. John kept coming over and handing Jerry toys, trying to cheer him up. . . . He'd say things like "Here Jerry," and I said to John "Jerry's sad; he doesn't feel good; he had a shot today." John would look at me with his eyebrows wrinkled together like he really understood that Jerry was crying because he was unhappy. . . . He went over and rubbed Jerry's arm and said "Nice Jerry," and continued to give him toys. (Zahn-Waxler, Radke-Yarrow, & King, 1979, pp. 321–322)

Clearly, John was concerned about his little playmate and did what he could to make him feel better.

Although some toddlers will often try to comfort distressed companions, others rarely do. These individual differences are due, in part, to cognitive development, for

23- to 25-month-olds who have achieved self-recognition (as assessed by the rouge test and other similar measures) are more likely than those who haven't to display some sympathy for and to try to comfort a victim of distress (Zahn-Waxler, Radke-Yarrow, et al., 1992). By contrast, younger toddlers often become *personally distressed* (rather than concerned) by others' distress and less inclined to show compassion—sometimes even behaving aggressively.

Individual differences in early compassion may also depend on parents' reactions to occasions in which their toddler has harmed another child. Carolyn Zahn-Waxler and her associates (1979) found that mothers of less compassionate toddlers typically used coercive tactics such as verbal rebukes or physical punishment to discipline harmdoing. By contrast, mothers of highly compassionate toddlers frequently disciplined harmdoing with simple **affective explanations** that may foster sympathy (and perhaps some remorse) by helping the child to see the relation between his or her own acts and the distress they have caused (for example, "You made Doug cry; it's not nice to bite!").

AGE-RELATED CHANGES IN ALTRUISM

Although many 2- to 3-year-olds will show some sympathy and compassion toward distressed companions, they are not particularly eager to make truly *self-sacrificial* responses, such as sharing a treasured cookie with a peer. Sharing and other benevolent acts are more likely if adults instruct a toddler to consider others' needs (Levitt et al., 1985), or if a peer should actively elicit sharing through a request or a threat of some kind, such as "I won't be your friend if you won't gimme some" (Birch & Billman, 1986). But on the whole, acts of *spontaneous* self-sacrifice in the interest of others are relatively infrequent among toddlers and young preschool children (Eisenberg & Fabes, 1998). Is this because toddlers are largely oblivious to others' needs and to the good they might do by sharing or helping their companions? Probably not, for at least one observational study in a nursery school setting found that 2½- to 3½-year-olds often took pleasure in performing acts of kindness for others during *pretend play;* by contrast, 4- to 6-year-olds performed more *real* helping acts and rarely "play-acted" the role of an altruist (Bar-Tal, Raviv, & Goldberg, 1982).

PHOTO 10.2 Young children are not very altruistic and often must be coaxed to share.

Many studies conducted in cultures from around the world find that sharing, helping, and most other forms of prosocial conduct become more and more common from the early elementary school years onward (see, for example, Underwood & Moore, 1982; Whiting & Edwards, 1988). In one early study conducted in Turkey (Ugurel-Semin, 1952), each child in a group of 4- to 12-year-olds was asked to divide an odd number of treats between himself or herself and another known child of the same age. Children were then classified as *altruistic* if they either gave more treats than they kept (or shared equally by refusing to assign the odd item) or as *selfish* if they kept more than they gave. Sharing clearly increased with age. Only 33% of the 4- to 6-year-old children chose an altruistic division of resources, compared with 69% of the 6- to 7-year-olds, 81% of the 7- to 9-year-olds, and 96% of the 9- to 12-year-olds.

Seeking to determine whether aspects of prosocial concern other than sharing might increase with age, Green and Schneider (1974) gave boys from four age groups—5 to 6, 7 to 8, 9 to 10, and 11 to 12—opportunities to (1) share candy with classmates who would not otherwise receive any, (2) help an experimenter who had "accidentally" dropped some pencils on the floor, and (3) volunteer to work on a proj-

affective explanations: discipline which focuses a child's attention on the harm or distress that his or her conduct has caused others.

TABLE 10-1 Prosocial behavior of boys from four age groups

ALTRUISTIC RESPONSE	AGE GROUP			
	5–6	7–8	9–10	13–14
Average number of candy bars shared	1.36 (60%)	1.84 (92%)	2.88 (100%)	4.24 (100%)
Percentage of children who picked up pencils	48%	76%	100%	96%
Percentage of children who volunteered to work for needy children	96%	92%	100%	96%

NOTE: Figures in parentheses indicate percentage of children sharing at least one candy bar.

SOURCE: Adapted from Green & Schneider, 1974. © 1974 by The Society for Research in Child Development. Reprinted by permission.

ect that would benefit poor children. The age trends for these three types of prosocial conduct appear in Table 10-1. The sharing data are consistent with previous literature indicating that generosity increases over the course of middle childhood. Furthermore, this developmental increase in prosocial concern apparently generalized to at least one measure of helping—picking up pencils for the experimenter. There were no age differences on the volunteering-to-work index; over 90% of the boys in each age group were willing to sacrifice some of their play time to help needy children. This lack of age differences may be due to an inability of the younger children to anticipate or understand the costs that they would incur (giving up play time) as a result of their helpfulness.

Much of the research that we will examine seeks to explain *why* older children and adolescents tend to become more prosocially inclined. But before turning to this research, let's address one other issue social developmentalists have pondered: Are there sex differences in altruism?

Although people commonly assume that girls are (or will become) more helpful, generous, or compassionate than boys (see Shigetomi, Hartmann, & Gelfand, 1981), there is little evidence for this notion in either laboratory experiments or survey studies (Grusec, Goodnow, & Cohen, 1996; Radke-Yarrow et al., 1983). Girls sometimes emit stronger *facial* expressions of sympathy than boys do (Eisenberg et al., 1992a). However, the vast majority of studies find that girls and women do not differ appreciably from boys and men in either the amount of sympathy they *say* they experience or in their willingness to comfort, help, or share resources with people in need (Eisenberg & Fabes, 1998). Nor is there much evidence for the idea that girls are more likely than boys to reliably *seek* assistance. From first through fifth grade, children of both sexes become less and less dependent on others to accomplish tasks for them, and they are equally likely to favor indirect help (such as hints) that will enable them to master tasks on their own (Shell & Eisenberg, 1996). So the notions that girls are any more altruistic than boys or any less capable of accomplishing tasks without direct assistance are probably best described as cultural myths that have little basis in fact.

Cognitive and Affective Contributors to Altruism

As we noted earlier, cognitive theories of altruism contend that increases in prosocial behavior throughout middle childhood and early adolescence are closely linked to the development of such attributes as role-taking skills, prosocial moral reasoning, empathy, and even a better understanding of the responsibilities implied should we come to view ourselves as helpful, compassionate, or otherwise altruistic individuals. Let's see if there is any support for these ideas.

ROLE-TAKING AND ALTRUISM

It makes some sense to assume that proficient role-takers might be more altruistic than poor role-takers if their role-taking skills help them to recognize and appreciate the factors that contribute to another person's distress or misfortune. And there is some support for this notion. In one study (Hudson, Forman, & Brian-Meisels, 1982), second-graders who had previously tested high or low in role-taking skills tutored kindergartners at an arts-and-crafts task and were filmed to see how they responded should their younger pupils experience any difficulties. Both the good and the poor role-takers were quite helpful if the younger children *explicitly* asked for help. But if the younger children's needs were *subtle* or their requests *indirect* (for example, frequent glances at the tutor accompanied by frowns), good role-takers recognized them and provided the necessary assistance whereas poor role-takers usually smiled at their young charges and resumed their own activities without helping.

Other reviewers have found that measures of *physical perspective-taking* (that is, imagining what another person can see or sense) do *not* predict children's prosocial behavior very well, whereas measures of **social perspective-taking** (inferring what another is thinking or the goals that he is pursuing) are reliable predictors of prosocial conduct (Carlo et al., 1991; Underwood & Moore, 1982). Indeed, evidence for a *causal* link between social perspective-taking and altruism is quite clear in studies showing that children and adolescents who receive training that bolsters these role-taking skills subsequently become more charitable, more cooperative, and more concerned about the needs of others when compared with age-mates who receive no training (Chalmers & Townsend, 1990; Iannotti, 1978). However, role-taking is only one of several personal attributes that play a part in the development of altruistic behavior. Three other important contributors are children's level of **prosocial moral reasoning**, their empathic reactions to the distress of other people, and their emerging self-concepts as altruistic individuals.

PROSOCIAL MORAL REASONING

Over the past 20 years, researchers have charted the development of children's reasoning about prosocial issues and its relationship to altruistic behavior. Nancy Eisenberg and her colleagues, for example, have presented children with stories in which the central character has to decide whether to help or comfort someone when the prosocial act would be personally costly to the help giver. The following story illustrates the kinds of dilemmas children were asked to resolve (Eisenberg-Berg & Hand, 1979):

> One day a girl named Mary was going to a friend's birthday party. On her way she saw a girl who had fallen down and hurt her leg. The girl asked Mary to go to her house and get her parents so that [they] could come and take her to a doctor. But if Mary did . . . , she would be late to the party and miss the ice-cream, cake, and all the games. What should Mary do?

As illustrated in Table 10-2, reasoning about these prosocial dilemmas may progress through as many as five levels between early childhood and adolescence. Notice that preschoolers' responses are frequently *self-serving:* These youngsters often say that Mary should go to the party so as not to miss out on the fun and games. But as children mature, they tend to become increasingly responsive to the needs and wishes of others; so much so that some high school students feel that they could no longer respect themselves were they to ignore the appeal of a person in need in order to pursue their own interests (Eisenberg et al., 1983; Eisenberg, Miller, et al., 1991).

Does a child's or adolescent's level of prosocial moral reasoning predict his or her altruistic behavior? Apparently so. Preschoolers who have progressed beyond the

social perspective-taking: the ability to infer others' thoughts, intentions, motives, and attitudes.

prosocial moral reasoning: the thinking that people display when deciding whether to help, share with, or comfort others when these actions could prove costly to themselves.

TABLE 10-2 Eisenberg's levels of prosocial moral reasoning

LEVEL	APPROXIMATE AGE	BRIEF DESCRIPTION AND TYPICAL RESPONSE
Hedonistic	Preschool, early elementary school	Concern is for one's own needs. Giving help is most likely if it will benefit the self. *Example:* "I wouldn't help 'cause I'd miss the party."
Needs oriented	Elementary school and a few preschoolers	Others' needs are recognized as a legitimate basis for helping, but there is little evidence of sympathy or guilt for failing to help. *Example:* "I'd help because she needs help."
Stereotyped, approval oriented	Elementary school and some high school students	Concern for approval and stereotyped images of good and bad heavily influence one's thinking. *Example:* "My mother would hug me for helping."
Empathic orientation	Older elementary school and high school students	Judgments now include evidence of sympathetic feelings; vague references are sometimes made to duties and values. *Example:* "I'd feel good about helping because she was in pain."
Internalized values orientation	A small minority of high school students; no elementary school students	Justifications for helping (or not helping) are based on internalized values, norms, convictions, and responsibilities; violating these principles could undermine self-respect. *Example:* "I refused to make a donation because the [charity] wastes too much money fundraising and gives little to its intended recipients."

SOURCE: Adapted from Eisenberg, Lennon, & Roth, 1983.

hedonistic level of prosocial moral reasoning are more likely to help and to *spontaneously* share valuable commodities with their peers than are those who still reason in a self-serving way (Eisenberg-Berg & Hand, 1979; Miller et al., 1996). Studies of older participants tell a similar story. Mature moral reasoners among a high school sample often said they would help someone they *disliked* if that person really needed their help, whereas immature moral reasoners were apt to ignore the needs of a person they disliked (Eisenberg, 1983; Eisenberg, Miller, et al., 1991). Another study conducted recently in Brazil found that adolescents rated high by their peers in prosocial behavior were more likely than those who were less prosocially inclined to reason at Eisenberg's highest levels of prosocial moral reasoning (Carlo et al., 1996).

Why are mature moral reasoners so sensitive to the needs of others—even *disliked* others? Eisenberg's view is that the child's growing ability to *sympathize* with others contributes heavily to mature prosocial reasoning and to the development of a selfless concern for promoting the welfare of *whoever* might require his assistance (Eisenberg et al., 1987; Eisenberg, Miller, et al., 1991). Let's now consider what researchers have learned about the relationship between empathy and altruism.

EMPATHY: AN IMPORTANT AFFECTIVE CONTRIBUTOR TO ALTRUISM

Although infants and toddlers do seem to recognize and often react to (that is, empathize with) the distress of their companions (Zahn-Waxler et al., 1979; Zahn-Waxler, Radke-Yarrow et al., 1992; and see Box 3.1), their responses are not always helpful ones. In fact, many young children exhibit clear signs of *personal distress* on witnessing the distress or misfortunes of others (this may be the predominant response early in life) and may turn away from a person in need, or even attack him or her, in an attempt to relieve their *own* discomfort. Other children (even some young ones) are more inclined to interpret their empathic arousal as concern, or sympathy, for distressed others, and it is this **sympathetic empathic arousal**, rather than **self-oriented distress**, that should eventually come to promote altruism (Batson, 1991; Hoffman, 1993; Miller et al., 1996).

Socialization of Empathy As we noted earlier when discussing the origins of compassion in toddlers, parents can help to promote sympathetic empathic arousal by (1) modeling empathic concern and (2) by relying on affectively oriented forms of

sympathetic empathic arousal: feelings of sympathy or compassion that may be elicited when we experience the emotions of (that is, empathize with) a distressed other; thought to become an important mediator of altruism.

self-oriented distress: feeling of *personal* discomfort or distress that may be elicited when we experience the emotions of (that is, empathize with) a distressed other; thought to inhibit altruism.

discipline that help young children understand the harmful effects of any distress they may have caused others (Barnett, 1987; Eisenberg, Fabes, et al., 1991; Zahn-Waxler et al., 1979, 1992). Interestingly, mothers who use more *positive* facial expressions while modeling sympathy and who explicitly verbalize their own sympathetic feelings have children who act more sympathetically—probably because the mother's positivity and her affective explanations help to *counteract* the negative reactions that so many young children would otherwise have to others' misfortunes, thus making them less inclined to interpret their own arousal as *personal* distress (Fabes et al., 1994).

Age Trends in the Empathy-Altruism Relationship   So what is the relationship between empathy and altruism? The answer depends, in part, on how empathy is measured and how old the research participants are. In studies that assess empathy by having children report their own feelings about the misfortunes of story characters, researchers have found little association between empathy and altruism. However, teacher ratings of children's empathic sensitivities and children's own *facial* expressions of emotion in response to others' misfortunes are better predictors of prosocial behavior (Chapman et al., 1987; Eisenberg et al., 1990). Overall, the evidence for a link between empathy and altruism seems to be modest at best for preschool and young grade-school children but stronger for preadolescents, adolescents, and adults (Underwood & Moore, 1982).

One possible explanation for these age trends is that it simply takes some time for children to become better at regulating negative emotionality and suppressing personal distress to others' misfortunes so they can respond more sympathetically (Eisenberg, Fabes, et al., 1998). And it is likely that social-cognitive development plays an important part in this process, for younger children may lack the role-taking skills and insight about their own emotional experiences to fully understand and appreciate (1) *why* others are distressed, and thus, (2) *why* they are feeling aroused (Roberts & Strayer, 1996). For example, when kindergartners see a series of slides showing a boy becoming depressed after his dog runs away, they usually attribute his sadness to an external cause (the dog's disappearance) rather than to a more "personal" or internal one, such as the boy's longing for his pet (Hughes, Tingle, & Sawin, 1981). And, although kindergartners report that they too feel sad after seeing the slides, they usually provide egocentric explanations for their empathic arousal—explanations that seem to reflect *personal distress* (for example, "I might lose my dog"). However, 7- to 9-year-olds are beginning to associate their own empathic emotions with those of the story character as they put themselves in his place and infer the *psychological* basis for his sadness (for example, I'm sad because he's sad . . . because, if he really liked the dog, then . . ."). So empathy may become a stronger contributor to altruism once children become better at inferring others' points of view (role-taking) and understanding the psychological bases of their own empathic emotions—information that can help them feel *sympathy* for distressed or needy companions (Roberts & Strayer, 1996).

The Felt-Responsibility Hypothesis   Now an important question: *How* exactly does empathy promote altruism? Clearly, people can feel sympathy for distressed others without feeling compelled to help. So how might empathy promote altruistic *behavior*?

PHOTO 10.3   As children mature and develop better role-taking skills, they are more likely to sympathize with distressed companions and to provide them with comfort or assistance.

One possibility is that a child's *sympathetic* empathic arousal causes him to reflect on altruistic lessons he has learned—lessons such as the Golden Rule, the *norm of social responsibility,* or even the knowledge that other people approve of helping behavior. As a result of this reflection, the child is likely to assume some personal *responsibility* for aiding a victim in distress (see Figure 10.1) and would now feel guilty for callously ignoring that obligation (Chapman et al., 1987; Williams & Bybee, 1994). Notice that this "**felt responsibility**" **hypothesis** is reflected in Eisenberg's higher levels of prosocial moral reasoning (see Table 10-2) and may help to explain why the link between empathy and altruism becomes stronger with age. Since older children are likely to have learned (and internalized) more altruistic principles than younger children, they should have much more to reflect on as they experience empathic arousal. Consequently, they are more likely than younger children to feel responsible for helping a distressed person and to follow through by rendering the necessary assistance.

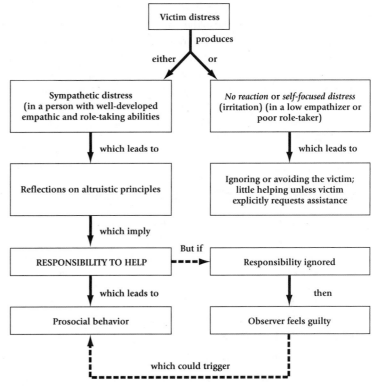

FIGURE 10.1 How empathy promotes altruism: a "felt responsibility" interpretation.

VIEWING ONESELF AS ALTRUISTIC

A person's willingness to sacrifice in order to benefit others may also hinge very critically on how altruistic she believes herself to be. Although researchers have been largely unsuccessful at identifying a definable set of altruistic personality traits (Myers, 1999), it nevertheless appears that adolescents and adults who view prosocial concern as an important part of their self-concepts do tend to be more prosocially inclined than those who do not view themselves as particularly compassionate, charitable, or helpful (Clary & Snyder, 1991; Hart & Fegley, 1995; Wuthnow, 1994). Could we then promote altruism by persuading youngsters to think of themselves as generous or helpful individuals?

Joan Grusec and Erica Redler (1980) sought to answer these questions by first urging 5- and 8-year-olds to (1) donate marbles to poor children, (2) share colored pencils with classmates who hadn't any, and (3) help an experimenter with a dull and repetitive task. Once children had donated, shared, or begun to work on the repetitive task, either they were told that they were "nice" or "helpful" persons for the good that they had done (self-concept training condition) or nothing was said (control condition). One to two weeks later, the children were asked by another adult to donate drawings and craft materials to help cheer up sick children at a local hospital.

Grusec and Redler found that self-concept training had a much greater effect on the 8-year-olds than the 5-year-olds. The 8-year-olds who were told they were "nice" or "helpful" were more likely than those in the control condition to make drawings for and to share their possessions with sick children. Why was the self-concept training so effective with 8-year-olds but not with 5-year-olds? The research we reviewed in Chapter 6 provides a strong clue. Recall that 8-year-olds are just beginning to describe the self in psychological terms and to see these "traits" as *stable* aspects of their

"felt responsibility" hypothesis: the theory that empathy may promote altruism by causing one to reflect on altruistic norms and, thus, to feel some obligation to help others who are distressed.

character. Thus, when told that they were "nice" or "helpful," Grusec and Redler's 8-year-olds (but not the 5-year-olds) apparently incorporated these traitlike attributions into their self-concepts and were later trying to live up to this new, more altruistic self-image by generously volunteering assistance when help was needed.

So encouraging youngsters to think of themselves as altruistic is one way to promote acts of kindness—at least among children old enough to understand and fully appreciate the implications of traitlike attributions. In our next section, we consider a number of other social and cultural influences that have a bearing on how altruistic children are likely to become.

Cultural and Social Influences on Altruism

According to prominent social-learning theorists (for example, Bandura, 1989), our altruistic inclinations are heavily influenced by the company we keep. We now consider how such "social" influences as cultural values and the behaviors and child-rearing practices of parents and other socialization agents might help to explain why some of us are more prosocially inclined than others.

CULTURAL INFLUENCES

Cultures clearly differ in their endorsement or encouragement of altruism. In one interesting cross-cultural study, Beatrice and John Whiting (1975) observed the altruistic behavior of 3- to 10-year-olds in six cultures—Kenya, Mexico, the Philippines, Okinawa, India, and the United States. As we see in Table 10-3, the cultures in which children were most altruistic were the less industrialized societies where people tend to live in large families and children *routinely contribute to the family welfare* by processing food, preparing meals, fetching wood and water, or caring for younger brothers or sisters. Although children in Western industrialized societies are involved in relatively few family-maintenance activities, those who are assigned housework or other tasks that *benefit all family members* are more prosocially inclined than age-mates whose responsibilities consist mainly of *self*-care routines, such as cleaning their own rooms (Grusec et al., 1996).

Another factor contributing to the low altruism scores of children from Western industrialized nations is the tremendous emphasis these *individualistic societies* place on competition and on individual rather than group goals. By contrast, children from *collectivist societies* (and such collectivist subcultures as Native American tribes in North America or kibbutz-reared children in Israel) are taught to suppress individualism, to cooperate with others for the greater good of the group, and to avoid inter-

TABLE 10-3 Prosocial behavior in six cultures: percentages of children in each culture who scored above the median altruism score for the cross-cultural sample as a whole

TYPE OF SOCIETY	PERCENTAGE SCORING HIGH IN ALTRUISM	TYPE OF SOCIETY	PERCENTAGE SCORING HIGH IN ALTRUISM
Nonindustrialized		*Industrialized*	
Kenya	100	Okinawa	29
Mexico	73	India	25
Philippines	63	United States	8

SOURCE: Based on Whiting & Whiting, 1975.

personal conflicts (Triandis, 1994, 1995). The impact of these cultural teachings can be seen in a number of contexts. For example, Anne Marie Tietjen (1986) found that children from a collectivist subculture in New Guinea typically become less other-oriented and more self-centered in their thinking about prosocial issues once they have spent three years attending Westernized schools. And even within the same society (Israel), communally reared kibbutz children are much more inclined to co-operate with one another and to *seek* each others' assistance than are their city-dwelling age-mates, whose environment stresses typical Western attitudes calling for self-reliance and individual achievement (Nadler, 1986, 1991).

For children in many of the world's collectivist societies, then, prosocial behavior does not have the same "discretionary" quality about it that is true of individualistic societies; instead, giving of oneself for the greater good of the group is every bit as much an *obligation* as resolving not to break moral rules (Lee et al., 1997; Triandis, 1995). And as we'll see in Box 10.1 on pages 321–322, children from one collectivist society (People's Republic of China) become so attuned to their culture's prosocial ideals that they think it quite inappropriate to call attention to their own good deeds—and may even deny responsibility for their acts of kindness!

Although cultures may differ in the emphasis they place on altruism, most people in most societies endorse the norm of social responsibility—the rule of thumb prescribing that one should help others who need help. Let's now consider some of the ways adults might persuade young children to adopt this important value and to become more concerned about the welfare of other people.

REINFORCING ALTRUISM

Might we promote altruism by offering children tangible rewards for their generous or helpful acts? Probably not. Although the practice of giving children toys or bubble gum for acts of kindness does increase the frequency of such behavior in the short run (Fischer, 1963), rewarded children are actually *less likely* than other "nonrewarded" peers to make sacrifices for others once the rewards stop (Fabes et al., 1989). What seems to be happening is that children who are "bribed" with tangible incentives for prosocial conduct are apt to attribute their acts of kindness to the rewards rather than to the recipient's needs or to their own inclinations to be kind to others. Consequently, tangible rewards can undermine any altruistic motivation that children already have. Apparently parents understand that a strong concern for others is not easily established through bribery, for mothers of 4- to 7-year-olds report that they rarely use tangible rewards to promote prosocial behavior (Grusec, 1991); and the mothers who are most likely to do so have children who are the least prosocially inclined (Fabes et al., 1989).

On the other hand, *verbal reinforcement* can promote altruistic behavior if it is administered by a *warm* and *charitable* person whom children *respect* and *admire* (Mills & Grusec, 1989; Yarrow, Scott, & Waxler, 1973). Perhaps verbal approval is effective under these circumstances because children hope to live up to standards set by a liked and respected person, and praise that accompanies their kindly acts suggests that they are accomplishing that objective.

However, there is an important qualifier. Elizabeth Midlarsky and associates (1973) found that praise administered by an adult that children know to be *selfish* will usually backfire and make youngsters who receive it *less* inclined to share or to perform other acts of kindness in the future. Why? Because an adult who praises a child's good deeds after behaving selfishly calls attention to the inconsistency between his words and deeds, thus prompting many children to wonder "Well, why should I sacrifice

Box 10.1 Cultural Influences

Cultural Differences in Thinking About Prosocial Conduct

In Western individualistic societies such as Canada and the United States, children are taught that prosocial acts are laudable and that they should feel good and even take credit for their self-sacrificial behaviors. By contrast, children in the collectivist Peoples Republic of China not only learn that prosocial conduct is necessary and an obligation; they are also taught to be modest, to avoid self-aggrandizement, and thus, not to seek praise or personal recognition for their own good deeds. In fact, admitting or seeking credit for prosocial conduct is viewed as a violation of both traditional Chinese cultural norms and the government's communist-collectivist doctrine.

How might these teachings affect Chinese children's thinking about prosocial issues? Would they truly seek to downplay their good deeds? Would they be so modest and self-effacing that they might even deny responsibility for (that is, lie about) having performed altruistic acts?

To address these issues, Kang Lee and associates (1997) conducted an interesting cross-cultural study in which 7-, 9-, and 11-year-old children from Canada and the Peoples Republic of China evaluated four brief stories. To compare Canadian and Chinese children's thinking about *prosocial* issues, two stories involved a child who first carried out a good deed (for example, anonymously donating money to a classmate who otherwise could not go on a field trip) and who then either *truthfully admitted* this prosocial act or who *lied about it* (saying "I did not do it") when the teacher asked, "Do you know [who is responsible for this act of kindness]?" For comparative purposes, children's thinking about *antisocial* conduct was also assessed. Each participant heard two stories in which the actor committed a misdeed (for example, injuring a classmate by knocking him down) and who then either *truthfully admitted* or who *lied* about this act when questioned by a teacher. After hearing each story, participants evaluated the goodness or naughtiness of both the actor's behavior and his or her statement about that behavior when questioned by the teacher.

Interestingly, there were no major cultural differences in evaluation of either the actor's *antisocial* conduct (which was considered very bad) or evaluations of the actor's statements about it. Both Chinese and Canadian children felt that it was very good for harmdoers to tell the truth about committing transgressions and very bad to lie about them. Similarly, both Chinese and Canadian children evaluated *prosocial* acts quite positively. However, their thinking about lying and telling the truth about prosocial conduct diverged sharply.

As the figure illustrates, Canadian children at all three ages thought that altruists should readily admit (that is, tell the truth and take credit for) their good deeds and that denying responsibility for (lying about) them was bad (or perhaps stupid). By contrast, we see that as Chinese

for others when he hasn't?" The implications for parents are obvious: Praise given for prosocial conduct is likely to promote altruism only if the person providing it lives by the same principles that he or she finds so praiseworthy.

MODELING INFLUENCES: PRACTICING AND PREACHING ALTRUISM

Social-learning theorists have assumed that adults who encourage altruism and who practice what they preach will affect children in two ways. By behaving altruistically, the adult model may induce the child to perform similar acts of kindness. In addition, regular exposure to the model's **altruistic exhortations** provides the child with opportunities to internalize principles such as the norm of social responsibility that should contribute to the development of an altruistic orientation.

Laboratory experiments consistently indicate that young children who observe charitable or helpful models become more charitable or helpful themselves, especially if the model has established a warm relationship with them and provides a compelling justification (rationale) for his acts of kindness (Rushton, 1980; Yarrow et al., 1973). Indeed, these modeling effects can be long-lasting, for children who observe

altruistic exhortations: verbal encouragements to help, comfort, share, or cooperate with others.

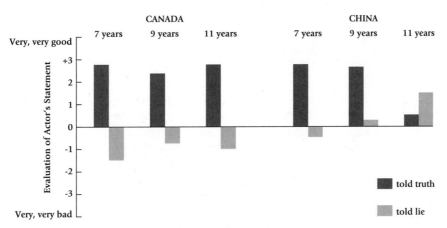

CANADA   CHINA

Ratings by Canadian and Chinese children of actors who told the truth or lied about committing good deeds. (Adapted from Lee et al., 1997.)

children grow older, they increasingly come to view taking credit for prosocial acts in *less* positive terms and denying responsibility for them much *more* positively. For Chinese children, prosocial conduct is *expected,* not discretionary, and is *not* viewed as worthy of individual praise or recognition in the same way that Canadian children think it is. In fact, the strong emphasis on self-effacement and modesty in Chinese culture eventually overrides children's reluctance to lie, so that Chinese children come to view acting modest about performing behavior expected of them to be more praiseworthy than boldly telling the truth and calling undue attention to acts that any good child should perform (Lee et al., 1997).

In sum, Lee's study clearly illustrates that the values that shape people's thinking about prosocial behavior (as well as the circumstances under which "little white lies" might be appropriate) can vary dramatically from culture to culture.

charitable models are subsequently more generous than those who observe selfish models, even when tested *two to four months later* (Rice & Grusec, 1975; Rushton, 1980). So it seems that encounters with altruistic models may indeed foster the development of prosocial habits and altruistic values.

Finally, it is important to note that *altruistic exhortations*—a form of verbal modeling—are likely to be far more effective at promoting prosocial conduct when the person who provides them lives by these same values. In one study (Midlarsky & Bryan, 1972), children were exposed to an adult model who took 10 turns at a game, winning five times and losing five times. On winning trials, the model either behaved *charitably,* by donating some of his winnings to a needy children's fund, or *selfishly,* by keeping all his winnings for himself. On losing trials, the model either preached *charity* and emphasized the positive impact of charitable acts on recipients ("I know that I don't have to give, but it would make some children very happy") or preached *greed* and stressed the undesirable aspects of charity ("I could really use some spending money this week; it makes some children feel bad to get charity"). The child then played the game, won five times, and thus had five opportunities to donate money anonymously to needy children.

TABLE 10-4 Average percentage of winnings donated by children exposed to charitable or selfish models who preached charity or greed

MODEL'S BEHAVIOR	MODEL'S VERBAL PREACHING		ROW AVERAGES
	CHARITY	GREED	
Charitable	44.0	27.5	35.8
Selfish	17.5	10.5	14.0
Column Averages	30.8	19.0	

SOURCE: Adapted from Midlarsky & Bryan, 1972. © 1972 by Academic Press. Reprinted by permission.

Table 10-4 summarizes the results. As expected, children who observed a charitable model donated a larger percentage of their winnings (35.8%) than did children who observed a selfish model (14%). Furthermore, the model's verbal exhortations had a significant effect; models who exhorted charity elicited larger donations from the children (30.8%) than models who exhorted greed (19%). So charitable exhortations can increase children's generosity if they are strongly stated and justified in terms of the needs of prospective recipients. However, the relatively large donations prompted by the charitable model who preached charity serve as a reminder that our altruistic exhortations are most effective when we practice what we preach.

Now let's turn to the child-rearing literature to see whether the variables that promote altruism in the laboratory have similar effects on children in the natural environment.

WHO RAISES ALTRUISTIC CHILDREN?

Studies of Prosocial Activists   Studies of unusually charitable adults indicate that these "altruists" have enjoyed a warm and affectionate relationship with parents who themselves were highly concerned about the welfare of others. For example, Christians who risked their lives to save Jews from the Nazis during World War II reported that they had had close ties to moralistic parents (and other confidants) who always acted in accordance with their ethical principles (London, 1970; Oliner & Oliner, 1988).

David Rosenhan's (1970; 1972b) interviews of White "freedom riders" from the U.S. civil rights movement of the 1960s suggested that there were two kinds of prosocial activists. *Fully committed activists* seemed to display a selfless commitment Rosenhan called *autonomous altruism:* These volunteers had put their careers on hold and some had even given up their homes to work full-time promoting the civil rights of others. By contrast, *partially committed activists* were less behaviorally committed to the cause and did not alter the course of their lives in any significant way. It seemed to Rosenhan that their part-time participation was motivated by "group esprit" among freedom riders and social conformity—that is, by *personal considerations* that qualified their actions as *normative altruism.*

Interestingly, these two groups held similar attitudes about racial equality and civil rights and seemed to differ in only two important ways. First, fully committed activists had enjoyed warmer relationships with their parents than partially committed activists had. Second, fully committed activists had parents who often advocated altruism *and* who backed up these exhortations by performing many kind and compassionate deeds. By contrast, parents of partially committed activists had often preached but rarely practiced altruism (Rosenhan, 1970).

Rosenhan then concluded that the antecedents of a strong selfless sense of autonomous altruism are having a *warm relationship with parents who themselves were outstanding models of prosocial concern*—the same pattern that characterized Christians taking great risks to save Jews during World War II, and which is also reminiscent of the laboratory evidence indicating that warm and nurturant models who practice what they preach are especially effective at eliciting prosocial responses from young children.

Unfortunately, one disadvantage of interview data such as Rosenhan's is that they could well be inaccurate. For example, were the parents of the fully committed activists really that altruistic, or were these altruistic activists simply being charitable in their memories of their parents? One way to assess the merits of Rosenhan's ideas about the antecedents of altruism would be to identify groups of people who had had the same kinds of childhood experiences as Rosenhan's fully committed and partially committed activists and then see whether the former group is *subsequently* more altruistic than the latter group.

Gil Clary and Jude Miller (1986) conducted such a **prospective study** of volunteers for a crisis counseling center in Minneapolis, Minnesota. During the training period, volunteers completed an extensive questionnaire, and based on Rosenhan's criteria, were classified as probable autonomous altruists or probable normative altruists. As the volunteers were being trained, the cohesiveness or "esprit de corps" of their training group was also assessed and classified as high or low. The question was straightforward: Who among these volunteers would complete the 6-month obligation to the counseling center that they had promised to fulfill when they volunteered? The results provided dramatic support for Rosenhan's earlier conclusions. The majority of those classified as normative altruists completed their obligation only if their group's *esprit de corps* was high and they were obtaining *personal benefits* from their participation. By contrast, the major-

PHOTO 10.4 Children who are committed to performing prosocial acts often have parents who have encouraged altruism and who have practiced what they preach.

ity of those classified as autonomous altruists completed their commitment, regardless of whether their group's esprit de corps was high or low. So here is clear evidence that having a warm relationship with altruistic parents forecasts *future* altruism—prosocial acts that seem to be internally motivated and reflect a genuine concern for others' welfare rather than any personal benefits one might obtain.

Parental Disciplinary Practices Parental reactions to a child's harmdoing also play an important role in the development of altruism. Recall that mothers of less compassionate infants and toddlers react to harmdoing in punitive or forceful ways, whereas mothers of compassionate toddlers rely more heavily on nonpunitive, affective explanations in which they persuade the child to accept personal responsibility for her harmdoing and urge her to direct some sort of comforting or helpful response toward the victim (Zahn-Waxler, Radke-Yarrow, et al., 1979, 1992). Research with older children paints a similar picture: parents who continue to rely on rational, nonpunitive disciplinary techniques in which they regularly display sympathy and concern for others tend to raise children who are sympathetic and self-sacrificing, whereas frequent use of forceful and punitive discipline appears to inhibit altruism and lead to the development of self-centered values (Brody & Shaffer, 1982; Eisenberg et al., 1992; Krevans & Gibbs, 1996).

There are probably several reasons that rational affectively oriented discipline that is heavy on reasoning might inspire children to become more altruistic. First, it encourages the child to assume another person's perspective (role-taking) and to experience that person's distress (empathy training). It also teaches the child to perform helpful or comforting acts that make both himself and the other person feel better. Finally, these reparative responses might convince children that they can be "caring"

prospective study: study in which the suspected causes of or contributors to an outcome are assessed earlier to see whether they are actually associated with the developments they are presumed to influence.

or "helpful" people, thereby fostering a *prosocial self-concept* that children may try to live up to by performing other acts of kindness in the future.

We are now ready to turn to what Sigmund Freud and many other early theorists (for example, McDougall, 1908) claimed to be the most important aspect of socialization—the establishment of a mature sense of morality. In truth, we have been considering the topic of morality since we began Chapter 9, for the process of moral development encompasses both the growth of prosocial values and the inhibition of hostile, antisocial impulses.

What Is Morality?

During the course of development, most of us arrive at a point at which we wish to behave responsibly and to think of ourselves (and be thought of by others) as moral individuals (Blasi, 1990; Hoffman, 1988). What is **morality**? College students generally agree that morality implies a capacity (1) to *distinguish right from wrong,* (2) *to act on this distinction,* and (3) *to experience pride in virtuous conduct and guilt or shame over acts that violate one's standards* (Quinn, Houts, & Grasser, 1994; Shaffer, 1994). When asked to indicate the particular attributes that *morally mature* individuals display, adults in one Western society (Canada) generally agreed on six aspects, or dimensions, of moral maturity that appear in Table 10-5.

Implicit in college students' consensual definition of morality and the character traits that define moral maturity for adults is the idea that morally mature individuals do not submit to society's dictates because they expect tangible rewards for complying or fear punishments for transgressing. Rather, they eventually internalize the moral principles they have learned and will conform to these ideals, even when authority figures are not present to enforce them. As we will see, virtually all contemporary theorists consider **internalization**—the shift from externally controlled actions to conduct that is governed by internal standards and principles—to be a most crucial milestone along the road to moral maturity.

HOW DEVELOPMENTALISTS LOOK AT MORALITY

Developmental theorizing and research have centered on the same three moral components that college students mention in their global definition of morality:

1. An *affective,* or emotional, component that consists of the feelings (guilt, concern for others' feelings, and so on) that surround right or wrong actions and that motivate moral thoughts and actions.
2. A *cognitive* component that centers on the way we conceptualize right and wrong and make decisions about how to behave.

TABLE 10-5 Six dimensions of character that define moral maturity for Canadian adults

CHARACTER DIMENSION	SAMPLE TRAITS
1. Principled-Idealistic	Has clear values; Concerned about doing right; Ethical; Highly developed conscience; Law-abiding
2. Dependable-Loyal	Responsible; Loyal; Reliable; Faithful to spouse; Honorable
3. Has Integrity	Consistent; Conscientious; Rational; Hard-working
4. Caring-Trustworthy	Honest; Trustful; Sincere; Kind; Considerate
5. Fair	Virtuous; Fair; Just
6. Confident	Strong; Self-assured; Self-confident

SOURCE: Walker & Pitts, 1998.

morality: a set of principles or ideals that help the individual to distinguish right from wrong, to act on this distinction, and to feel pride in virtuous conduct and guilt (or shame) for conduct that violates one's standards.

internalization: the process of adopting the attributes or standards of other people—taking these standards as one's own.

3. A *behavioral component* that reflects how we actually behave when we experience the temptation to lie, cheat, or violate other moral rules.

As it turns out, each of the major theories of moral development has focused on a different component of morality. Psychoanalytic theorists emphasize the affective component, or powerful **moral affects.** They believe that children are motivated to act in accordance with their ethical principles to experience positive affects such as pride and to avoid such negative moral emotions as guilt and shame. Cognitive-developmental theorists have concentrated on the cognitive aspects of morality, or **moral reasoning,** and have found that the ways children think about right and wrong may change rather dramatically as they mature. Finally, the research of social-learning and social information-processing theorists has helped us to understand how children learn to resist temptation and to practice **moral behavior,** inhibiting actions such as lying, stealing, and cheating that violate moral norms.

In examining each of these theories and the research it has generated, we will look at the relationships among moral affect, moral reasoning, and moral behavior. This information should help us decide whether a person really has a *unified* "moral character" that is stable over time and across situations. Then we will take an in-depth look at how various child-rearing practices may affect a child's moral development and, in so doing, will attempt to integrate much of the information we have reviewed.

PHOTO 10.5 Resisting temptation is a difficult feat for young children, particularly when there is no one around to help them exercise willpower.

Psychoanalytic Explanations of Moral Development

In Chapter 2, we learned that psychoanalysts view the mature personality as having three components: an irrational *id,* which seeks the immediate gratification of instinctual needs; a rational *ego* that formulates *realistic* plans for meeting these needs; and a moralistic *superego* (or conscience) that monitors the acceptability of the ego's thoughts and deeds. Freud claimed that infants and toddlers lack a superego and will act on their selfish impulses unless parents control their behavior. But once the superego emerges, it was said to function as an *internal* censor—one that has the power to make a child feel proud of his virtuous conduct and guilty or shameful about committing moral transgressions. So children who are morally mature should generally resist temptation to violate moral norms in order to maintain self-esteem and avoid experiencing negative moral affects.

FREUD'S THEORY OF OEDIPAL MORALITY

According to Freud (1935/1960), the superego develops during the phallic stage (ages 3 to 6), when children were said to experience an emotional conflict with the same-sex parent that stemmed from their incestuous desire for the other-sex parent. To resolve this *Oedipus complex,* a boy was said to *identify* with and pattern himself after his father, particularly if his father is a threatening figure who arouses fear. Not only does he learn his masculine role in this manner, but he also internalizes his father's moral standards. Similarly, a girl resolves her *Electra complex* by identifying with her mother and internalizing her mother's moral standards. However, Freud claimed that because girls do not experience the intense fear of castration that boys experience, they will develop weaker superegos than boys do.

moral affect: the emotional component of morality, including feelings such as guilt, shame, and pride in ethical conduct.

moral reasoning: the cognitive component of morality; the thinking that people display when deciding whether various acts are right or wrong.

moral behavior: the behavioral component of morality; actions that are consistent with one's moral standards in situations in which one is tempted to violate them.

We might credit Freud for pointing out that moral emotions such as pride, shame, and guilt are potentially important determinants of ethical conduct and that the internalization of moral principles is a crucial step along the way to moral maturity. Yet, the "specifics" of his theory are largely unsupported. For example, threatening and punitive parents do not raise children who are morally mature. Quite the contrary; parents who rely on harsh forms of discipline tend to have children who often misbehave and who rarely express feelings of guilt, remorse, shame, or self-criticism (Brody & Shaffer, 1982; Kochanska, 1997b). Furthermore, there is simply no evidence that boys develop stronger superegos than girls. Finally, Freud's proposed age trends for moral development are actually rather pessimistic. As early as 13 to 15 months of age, some toddlers are already complying with some prohibitions in the absence of external surveillance (Kochanska, Tjebkes, & Forman, 1998). By age 2, more toddlers are beginning to show clear signs of distress if they violate rules (Kochanska et al., 1995), and they will sometimes try to correct any mishaps they think they have caused—*even when no one else is present to tell them to* (Cole, Barrett, & Zahn-Waxler, 1992). In addition, 3-year-olds are already displaying complex emotions that look very much like *pride* when they live up to a standard and *shame* when they fail to do so (Lewis et al., 1992; Stipek et al., 1992). These observations imply that the process of moral internalization may have already begun long before young children would have even experienced much of an Oedipus or Electra complex, much less having resolved it. So even though Freud's broader themes about the significance of moral emotions have some merit, perhaps it is time to lay his theory of **oedipal morality** to rest.

This is precisely what modern psychoanalytically oriented theorists have done. They argue that children may begin to form a conscience *as toddlers* if they are *securely attached* to warm and responsive parents who have often cooperated with their wishes during joint play and have shared many positive emotional experiences with them. Within the context of a warm, mutually responsive emotional relationship (rather than a fear-provoking one), toddlers are likely to display the kind of *committed compliance* we discussed in Chapter 6—an orientation in which they are (1) highly motivated to embrace the parent's agenda and to comply with her rules and requests, (2) sensitive to a parent's emotional signals indicating whether they have done right or wrong, and (3) beginning to internalize these parental reactions to their triumphs and transgressions, coming to experience the pride, shame, and (later) guilt that will help them to evaluate and regulate their own conduct (Emde et al., 1991; Kochanska, 1997b). Although data to evaluate those newer psychoanalytic ideas are not extensive, Grazyna Kochanska (1997b) reports that preschoolers who had earlier enjoyed warm, mutually responsive emotional relationships with their mothers as 2- to 3-year-olds show more signs of having a strong internalized conscience (for example, a reluctance to break rules) at ages 3½ to 5 than do age-mates whose earlier mother-toddler relationships had been less warm and mutually responsive.

Unfortunately, modern psychoanalytic theorists have had less to say about moral development beyond the preschool period or about children's *moral reasoning*—the very issue that cognitive-developmentalists emphasize.

Cognitive-Developmental Theory: The Child as a Moral Philosopher

Cognitive-developmentalists study morality by charting the development of *moral reasoning*—the thinking children display when deciding whether various acts are right or wrong. According to cognitive theorists, both cognitive growth and social ex-

oedipal morality: Freud's theory that moral development occurs during the phallic period (ages 3 to 6) when children internalize the moral standards of the same-sex parent as they resolve their Oedipus or Electra conflicts.

periences help children develop progressively richer understandings of the meaning of rules, laws, and interpersonal obligations. As children acquire these new understandings, they are said to progress through an *invariant sequence* of moral stages, each of which evolves from and replaces its predecessor and represents a more advanced or "mature" perspective on moral issues. In this portion of the chapter, we first examine Jean Piaget's early theory of moral development before turning to Lawrence Kohlberg's revision and extension of Piaget's approach.

PIAGET'S THEORY OF MORAL DEVELOPMENT

Piaget's early work on children's moral judgments focused on two aspects of moral reasoning. He studied children's developing *respect for rules* by rolling up his sleeves and playing marbles with Swiss children ages 5 to 13. As they played, Piaget would ask questions such as "Where do these rules come from? Must everyone obey a rule? Can these rules be changed?" To study children's conceptions of *justice*, Piaget gave them moral-decision stories to ponder. Here is one example:

> *Story A.* A little boy who is called John is in his room. He is called to dinner. He goes into the dining room. But behind the door there was a chair, and on the chair there was a tray with 15 cups on it. John couldn't have known that there was all this behind the door. He goes in, the door knocks against the tray, bang go the 15 cups, and they all get broken.

> *Story B.* Once there was a little boy whose name was Henry. One day when his mother was out he tried to reach some jam out of the cupboard. He climbed onto a chair and stretched out his arm. But the jam was too high up, and he couldn't reach it. . . . While he was trying to get it, he knocked over a cup. The cup fell down and broke. (Piaget, 1932/1965, p. 122)

Having heard the stories, participants were asked such questions as "Which child is naughtier? Why?" and "How should the naughtier child be punished?" Using these research techniques, Piaget formulated a theory of moral development that included a premoral period and two moral stages.

The Premoral Period According to Piaget, preschool children show little concern for or awareness of rules. In a game of marbles, these **premoral** children do not play systematically with the intent of winning. Instead, they seem to make up their own rules, and they think the point of the game is to take turns and have fun.

The Stage of Moral Realism, or Heteronomous Morality Between the ages of 5 and 10, children develop a strong respect for rules as they enter Piaget's stage of **heteronomous morality** ("heteronomous" means "under the rule of another"). Children now believe that rules are laid down by powerful authority figures such as God, the police, or their parents, and they think these regulations are sacred and unalterable. Try breaking the speed limit with a 6-year-old at your side and you may see what Piaget was talking about. Even if you are rushing to the hospital in a medical emergency, the young child may note that you are breaking a "rule of the road" and consider your behavior unacceptable conduct that deserves to be punished. Heteronomous children think of rules as *moral absolutes*. They believe there is a "right" side and a "wrong" side to any moral issue, and right always means following the rules.

Heteronomous children are also likely to judge the naughtiness of an act by its objective consequences rather than the actor's intent. For example, many 5- to 9-year-olds judged John, who broke 15 cups while performing a well-intentioned act, to be naughtier than Henry, who broke one cup while stealing jam.

Heteronomous children also favor *expiatory punishment*—punishment for its own sake with no concern for its relation to the nature of the forbidden act. So a 6-year-old

premoral period: in Piaget's theory, the first 5 years of life, when children have little respect for or awareness of socially defined rules.

heteronomous morality: Piaget's first stage of moral development, in which children view the rules of authority figures as sacred and unalterable.

might favor spanking a boy who had broken a window rather than making the boy pay for the window from his allowance. Furthermore, the heteronomous child believes in **immanent justice**—the idea that violations of social rules will invariably be punished in one way or another (see, for example, Dennis's warning to Joey in the cartoon). So if a 6-year-old boy were to fall and skin his knee while stealing cookies, he might conclude that this injury was the punishment he deserved for his transgression. Life for the heteronomous child is fair and just.

"HEY, CAREFUL, JOEY! GOD SEES EVERYTHING WE DO, THEN HE GOES AN' TELLS SANTA CLAUS!"

The Stage of Moral Relativism, or Autonomous Morality   By ages 10 or 11, most children have reached Piaget's second moral stage—moral relativism, or **autonomous morality**. Older, autonomous children now realize that social rules are arbitrary agreements that can be challenged and even changed with the consent of the people they govern. They also feel that rules can be violated in the service of human needs. Thus, a driver who speeds during a medical emergency will no longer be considered immoral, even though she is breaking the law. Judgments of right and wrong now depend more on the actor's intent to deceive or to violate social rules than on the objective consequences of the act itself. So 10-year-olds reliably say that Henry, who broke one cup while stealing some jam (bad intent), is naughtier than John, who broke 15 cups while coming to dinner (good or neutral intent).

When deciding how to punish transgressions, the morally autonomous child usually favors reciprocal punishments—that is, treatments that tailor punitive consequences to the "crime" so that the rule breaker will understand the implications of a transgression and perhaps be less likely to repeat it. Therefore, an autonomous child may decide that the boy who deliberately breaks a window should pay for it out of his allowance (and learn that windows cost money) rather than simply submit to a spanking. Finally, autonomous youngsters no longer believe in immanent justice because they have learned from experience that violations of social rules often go undetected and unpunished.

Moving from Heteronomous to Autonomous Morality   According to Piaget, both *cognitive maturation* and *social experience* play a role in the transition from heteronomous to autonomous morality. The cognitive advances that are necessary for this shift are a general decline in egocentrism and the development of role-taking skills that will enable the child to view moral issues from several perspectives. The kind of social experience that Piaget considered important is *equal status* contact with peers. As we noted in Chapter 6, peers must learn to take each other's perspectives and resolve their disagreements in mutually beneficial ways, often without any adult intervention, if they are to play cooperatively or accomplish other group goals. So equal-status contacts with peers may lead to a more flexible, autonomous morality because they (1) lessen the child's respect for adult authority, (2) increase his or her self-respect and respect for peers, and (3) illustrate that rules are arbitrary agreements that can be changed with the consent of the people they govern.

And what role do parents play? Interestingly, Piaget claimed that unless parents relinquish some of their power, they may *slow* the progress of moral development by reinforcing the child's exaggerated respect for rules and authority figures. If, for example, a parent enforces a demand with a threat or a statement such as "Do it because I told you to!" it is easy to see how the young child might conclude that rules are "absolutes" that derive their "teeth" from the parent's power to enforce them.

immanent justice: the notion that unacceptable conduct will invariably be punished and that justice is ever-present in the world.

autonomous morality: Piaget's second stage of moral development, in which children realize that rules are arbitrary agreements that can be challenged and changed with the consent of the people they govern.

AN EVALUATION OF PIAGET'S THEORY

Many researchers in many cultures have replicated Piaget's findings when they rely on his research methods. For example, younger children around the world are more likely than older ones to display such aspects of heteronomous morality as a belief in immanent justice or a tendency to emphasize consequences more than intentions when judging how wrong an act is (Jose, 1990; Lapsley, 1996). In addition, the maturity of children's moral judgments is related to such indications of cognitive development as IQ and role-taking skills (Ambron & Irwin, 1975; Lapsley, 1996). There is even some support for Piaget's "peer participation" hypothesis: Popular children who often take part in peer-group activities and who assume positions of leadership tend to make mature moral judgments (Bear & Rys, 1994; Keasey, 1971).

Nevertheless, there is ample reason to believe that Piaget's theory clearly underestimates the moral capacities of preschool and grade-school children.

Do Younger Children Ignore an Actor's Intentions? Consider Piaget's claim that children younger than 9 or 10 judge acts as right or wrong based on the consequences the acts produce rather than the intentions that guided them. Unfortunately, Piaget's moral-decision stories were flawed in that they (1) confounded intentions and consequences by asking whether a person who caused little harm with a bad intent was naughtier than one who caused a larger amount of harm while serving good intentions, and (2) made information about the consequences of an act *much clearer* than information about the actor's intentions.

FIGURE 10.2 Example of drawings used by Nelson to convey an actor's intentions to preschool children. (Adapted from Nelson, 1980.) © 1980 by the Society for Research in Child Development. Reprinted by permission.

Sharon Nelson (1980) overcame these flaws in an interesting experiment with 3-year-olds. Each child listened to stories in which a character threw a ball to a playmate. The actor's motive was described as *good* (his friend had nothing to play with) or *bad* (the actor was mad at his friend), and the consequences of his act were either *positive* (the friend caught the ball and was happy to play with it) or *negative* (the ball hit the friend in the head and made him cry). To ensure that her 3-year-olds would understand the actor's intentions, Nelson showed them drawings such as Figure 10-2, which depicts a negative intent.

Not surprisingly, the 3-year-olds in this study judged acts that had positive consequences more favorably than those that caused harm. However, as Figure 10-3 shows, they also judged the well-intentioned child who had wanted to play much more favorably than the child who intended to hurt his friend, *regardless of the consequences of his actions.* Moreover, 3- to 5-year-olds can discriminate (and will react more negatively to) blatant *lies,* in which the actor presents false information while *intending* to deceive, from honest mistakes on an actor's part (Siegal & Peterson, 1998). So even *preschool* children will consider an actor's intentions when making moral judgments; in fact, young children often attempt to escape punishment through such *intentional* pleas as "I didn't *mean* to, mommy!" But Piaget was right in one respect: Younger children do assign more weight to consequences and less weight to intentions than older children do, even though both younger and older children consider both sources of information when evaluating others' conduct (Lapsley, 1996; Zelazo, Helwig, & Lau, 1996).

Do Younger Children Respect All Rules (and Adult Authority)? According to Piaget, young children think of rules as sacred and obligatory prescriptions that are laid down by respected authority figures

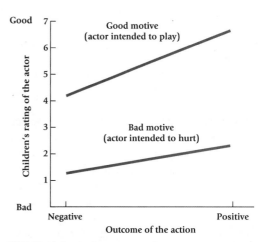

FIGURE 10.3 Average ratings of an actor's behavior for actors who produced positive or negative outcomes while serving either good or bad intentions. (Adapted from Nelson, 1980.) © 1980 by the Society for Research in Child Development. Reprinted by permission.

and are not to be questioned or changed. However, Elliot Turiel (1983) notes that children actually encounter two kinds of rules. **Moral rules** focus on the welfare and basic rights of individuals and include prescriptions against hitting, stealing, lying, cheating, or otherwise harming others or violating their rights. By contrast, **social-conventional rules** are determined by social consensus and regulate conduct in particular social situations. These standards are more like rules of social etiquette and include the rules of games as well as school rules that forbid snacking in class or using the restroom without permission. Do children treat these two kinds of rules as equivalent?

Apparently not. Judith Smetana (1981, 1985, Smetana, Schlagman, & Adams, 1993) finds that even 2½- to 3-year-olds consider moral transgressions such as hitting, stealing, and refusing to share to be much more serious and more deserving of punishment than social-conventional violations such as snacking in class or not saying "please" when requesting a toy. When asked whether a violation would be acceptable if there were no rule against it, children said that moral transgressions are always wrong but social-conventional violations are all right in the absence of any explicit rule. Clearly, parents view themselves as responsible for enforcing both moral and social-conventional rules. However, they attend more closely to moral violations and place much more emphasis on the harm such violations do to others (Nucci & Smetana, 1996; Nucci & Weber, 1995), perhaps explaining why children understand the need for and importance of *moral* prescriptions by age 2½ to 3—much sooner than Piaget had assumed they would.

Furthermore, Piaget's theory predicts that 6- to 10-year-old heteronomous children should be even more inclined than younger children are to respect pronouncements laid down by adults. Yet children of this age are quite capable of questioning adult authority. They believe that parents are justified in enforcing rules against stealing and other *moral* transgressions; but they feel that a parent is clearly abusing authority should he arbitrarily impose rules that restrict their choice of friends or leisure activities—areas that they perceive as under their own *personal* jurisdiction (Tisak & Tisak, 1990). In addition, they increasingly recognize that adult authority may be limited to certain contexts, acknowledging, for example, that teachers have a right to regulate smoking at school but not in the neighborhood (Smetana & Bitz, 1996). Perhaps the best illustration that older heteronomous children are not totally cowed by adult authority is this: Ten-year-olds who are relatively religious believe that not even the endorsement of the ultimate authority figure—God—would make a *moral* transgression (such as stealing) morally right (Nucci & Turiel, 1993). So 6- to 10-year-olds, even those in cultures like Korea where respect for authority is so highly stressed, have ideas about what constitutes *legitimate* authority, and those ideas are not based solely on an unwavering respect for the sanctity or wisdom of adults, as Piaget had assumed (Kim, 1998).

Do Parents Impede Children's Moral Development?   Finally, Piaget was partially right and partially wrong in his views of parents as agents of moral socialization. He was right in assuming that parents can impede moral growth by adopting a heavy-handed, authoritarian approach in which they *challenge* the child's moral reasoning and present their own ideas in a lecture like format as lessons to be learned (Walker & Taylor, 1991a). But he was very wrong in assuming that parents typically operate in this way when discussing moral issues with their children. Consider that 6- to 7-year-olds, who should be at Piaget's heteronomous stage, often make *autonomous* moral judgments—*as long as their parents do* (Leon, 1984). How is this possible? Research by Lawrence Walker and John Taylor (1991a) suggests an answer: By carefully tailoring their own reasoning to the child's ability to understand, and by presenting new moral perspectives in a supportive (rather than challenging) way, parents may often *promote* their children's moral development.

moral rules: standards of acceptable and unacceptable conduct that focus on the rights and privileges of individuals.

social-conventional rules: standards of conduct determined by social consensus that indicate what is appropriate within a particular social context.

Developmentalists are indebted to Piaget for suggesting that children's moral reasoning develops in stages that are closely tied to cognitive growth. Even today, his theory continues to stimulate research and new insights—including the findings above, which reveal that children younger than 10 are considerably more sophisticated in their moral reasoning than Piaget made them out to be. But is moral reasoning fully developed by ages 10 to 11, as Piaget had assumed? Lawrence Kohlberg certainly didn't think so.

KOHLBERG'S THEORY OF MORAL DEVELOPMENT

Kohlberg (1963, 1984; Colby & Kohlberg, 1987) has refined and extended Piaget's theory of moral development by asking 10-, 13-, and 16-year-old boys to resolve a series of "moral dilemmas." Each dilemma challenged the respondent by requiring him to choose between (1) obeying a rule, law, or authority figure and (2) taking some action that conflicts with these rules and commands while serving a human need. The following story is the best known of Kohlberg's moral dilemmas:

> In Europe, a woman was near death from a special kind of cancer. There was one drug that doctors thought might save her. It was a form of radium that a druggist in the same town had recently discovered. The drug was expensive to make, but the druggist was charging $2,000, or 10 times the cost of the drug, for a small (possibly life-saving) dose. Heinz, the sick woman's husband, borrowed all the money he could, about $1,000, or half of what he needed. He told the druggist that his wife was dying and asked him to sell the drug cheaper or to let him pay later. The druggist replied "No, I discovered the drug, and I'm going to make money from it." Heinz then became desperate and broke into the store to steal the drug for his wife. Should Heinz have done that?

Kohlberg was actually less interested in the respondent's decision (that is, what Heinz should have done) than in the underlying rationale, or "thought structures," that the individual used to justify his decision. So, if a participant says "Heinz should steal the drug to save his wife's life," it is necessary to determine why her life is so important. Is it because she cooks and irons for Heinz? Because it's a husband's duty to save his wife? Or because the preservation of life is among the highest of human values? To determine the "structure" of a person's moral reasoning, Kohlberg asked probing questions: Does Heinz have an obligation to steal the drug? If Heinz doesn't love his wife, should he steal it for her? Should Heinz steal the drug for a stranger? Is it important for people to do everything they can to save another life? Is it against the law to steal? Does that make it morally wrong? The purpose of these probes is to clarify how individual participants reason about obedience and authority on the one hand and about human needs, rights, and privileges on the other.

Through his use of these elaborate *clinical interviews,* Kohlberg's first discovery was that moral development is far from complete when the child reached age 10 to 11, or Piaget's autonomous stage. Indeed, moral reasoning seemed to evolve and become progressively more complex throughout adolescence and into young adulthood. Careful analyses of his participants' responses to several dilemmas led Kohlberg to conclude that moral growth progresses through an *invariant sequence* of three moral levels, each of which is composed of two distinct moral stages. According to Kohlberg, the order of these moral levels and stages is invariant because they depend on the development of certain cognitive abilities that evolve in an invariant sequence. Like Piaget, Kohlberg assumed that each succeeding stage evolves from and replaces its predecessor; once the individual has attained a higher stage of moral reasoning, he or she should never regress to earlier stages.

PHOTO 10.6 Lawrence Kohlberg (1927–1987) formulated a highly influential theory that changed the way developmentalists looked at the growth of moral reasoning.

As an alternative to conducting time-consuming clinical interviews, John Gibbs and his associates have developed a questionnaire measure of moral reasoning called the Sociomoral Reflection Measure—Short Form (SRM-SF). This instrument asks participants to (1) rate the importance of values pertaining to human needs (for example, saving a life) and to rules, laws, and authority (for example, obeying laws) and (2) to briefly explain these ratings. The explanations are then scored for thinking that reflects Kohlberg's moral stages. Because the scores people make on this instrument do correspond to those obtained from clinical interviews (Basinger, Gibbs, & Fuller, 1995), the SRM-SF is a versatile alternative to conducting clinical interviews which, for untrained researchers, can be very difficult to interpret (Shaffer, 1988).

Before examining Kohlberg's moral stages, we should emphasize that each stage represents a particular perspective, or *method of thinking* about moral dilemmas, rather than a particular type of moral decision. As we will see, decisions are not very informative in themselves, because people at each moral stage might well endorse either of the alternative courses of action (for example, steal or not steal) when resolving one of these ethical dilemmas. (However, participants at Kohlberg's highest moral level do generally favor serving human needs over complying with rules or laws that would compromise others' welfare.) The basic themes and defining characteristics of Kohlberg's three moral levels and six stages are as follows.

Level 1: Preconventional Morality   Rules are truly external to the self rather than internalized. The child conforms to rules imposed by authority figures to avoid punishment or obtain personal rewards. Morality is self-serving: What is right is what one can get away with or what is personally satisfying.

Stage 1: Punishment-and-Obedience Orientation   The goodness or badness of an act depends on its consequences. The child will obey authorities to avoid punishment, but may not consider an act wrong if it will not be detected and punished. The greater the harm done or the more severe the punishment is, the more "bad" the act is. The following two responses reflect a "punishment-and-obedience" orientation to the Heinz dilemma:

Protheft: It isn't really bad to take the drug—he did ask to pay for it first. He wouldn't do any other damage or take anything else, and the drug he'd take is only worth $200, not $2,000.
Antitheft: Heinz doesn't have permission to take the drug. He can't just go and break through a window. He'd be a bad criminal doing all that damage . . . and stealing anything so expensive would be a big crime.

Stage 2: Naive Hedonism   A person at this second stage conforms to rules in order to gain rewards or satisfy personal objectives. There is some concern for the perspective of others, but other-oriented behaviors are ultimately motivated by the hope of benefiting in return. "You scratch my back and I'll scratch yours" is the guiding philosophy. Here are two samples of this hedonistic, self-serving morality (see also Calvin's moral philosophy in the cartoon):

Protheft: Heinz isn't really doing any harm to the druggist, and he can always pay him back. If he doesn't want to lose his wife, he should take the drug.
Antitheft: Hey, the druggist isn't wrong, he just wants to make a profit like everybody else. That's what you're in business for, to make money.

Level 2: Conventional Morality   The individual now strives to obey rules and social norms in order to win others' approval or to maintain social order. Social praise and the avoidance of blame have now replaced tangible rewards and punishments as

preconventional morality: Kohlberg's term for the first two stages of moral reasoning, in which moral judgments are based on the tangible punitive consequences (Stage 1) or rewarding consequences (Stage 2) of an act for the actor rather than on the relationship of that act to society's rules and customs.

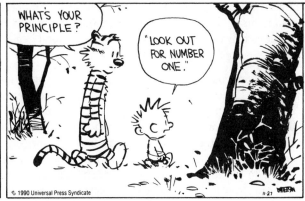

CALVIN AND HOBBES copyright 1990 UNIVERSAL PRESS SYNDICATE. Reprinted with permission. All rights reserved.

motivators of ethical conduct. The perspectives of other people are clearly recognized and given careful consideration.

Stage 3: "Good Boy" or "Good Girl" Orientation   Moral behavior is that which pleases, helps, or is approved of by others. Actions are evaluated on the basis of the actor's intent. "He means well" is a common expression of moral approval at this stage. As we see in the responses below, the primary objective of a Stage 3 respondent is to be thought of as a "good" person.

Protheft: Stealing is bad, but Heinz is only doing something that is natural for a good husband to do. You can't blame him for doing something out of love for his wife. You'd blame him if he didn't save her.

Antitheft: If Heinz's wife dies, he can't be blamed. You can't say he is heartless for failing to commit a crime. The druggist is the selfish and heartless one. Heinz tried to do everything he really could.

Stage 4: Social-Order—Maintaining Morality   At this stage, the individual considers the perspectives of the generalized other—that is, the will of society as reflected in law. Now what is right is what conforms to the rules of *legal* authority. The reason for conforming is not a fear of punishment but a belief that rules and laws maintain a social order that is worth preserving. As we see in the following responses, laws ultimately transcend special interests:

Protheft: The druggist is leading the wrong kind of life if he just lets somebody die; so it's Heinz's duty to save [his wife]. But Heinz just can't go around breaking laws—he must pay the druggist back and take his punishment for stealing.

Antitheft: It's natural for Heinz to want to save his wife, but it's still always wrong to steal. You have to follow the rules regardless of your feelings or the special circumstances.

Level 3: Postconventional (or Principled) Morality   A person at this third level of moral reasoning now defines right and wrong in terms of broad principles of justice that could conflict with written laws or with the dictates of authority figures. Morally right and legally proper are not always the same.

Stage 5: The Social-Contract Orientation   At Stage 5, the individual now views laws as instruments for expressing the will of the majority and furthering human values. Laws that accomplish these ends and are impartially applied are viewed as social

conventional morality:
Kohlberg's term for the third and fourth stages of moral reasoning, in which moral judgments are based on a desire to gain approval (Stage 3) or to uphold laws that maintain social order (Stage 4).

postconventional morality:
Kohlberg's term for the fifth and sixth stages of moral reasoning, in which moral judgments are based on social contracts and democratic law (Stage 5) or on universal principles of ethics and justice (Stage 6).

contracts that one has an obligation to follow; but imposed laws that compromise human rights or dignity are considered unjust and worthy of challenge. Notice how distinctions between what is legal and what is moral begin to appear in the following Stage 5 responses to Heinz's dilemma:

Protheft: Before you say stealing is morally wrong, you've got to consider this whole situation. Of course, the laws are quite clear about breaking into a store. And . . . Heinz would know that there were no *legal* grounds for his actions. Yet it would be reasonable for anybody, in that kind of situation, to steal the drug.

Antitheft: I can see the good that would come from illegally taking the drug. But the ends don't justify the means. The law represents a consensus of how people have agreed to live together, and Heinz has an obligation to respect these agreements. You can't say Heinz would be completely wrong to steal the drug, but even these circumstances don't make it right.

Stage 6: Morality of Individual Principles of Conscience   At this "highest" moral stage, the individual defines right and wrong on the basis of the self-chosen ethical principles of his or her own conscience. These principles are not concrete rules such as the Ten Commandments. They are abstract moral guidelines or principles of universal justice (and respect for the rights of *all* human beings) that *transcend* any law or social contract that may conflict with them. Kohlberg (1981) described Stage 6 thinking as a kind of "moral musical chairs" in which the person facing a moral dilemma is able to take the perspective of *every person* who could potentially be affected by a decision and arrive at a solution that would be regarded as "just" by all. Here are two Stage 6 responses to the Heinz dilemma:

Protheft: When one must choose between disobeying a law and saving a human life, the higher principle of preserving life makes it morally *right* to steal the drug.

Antitheft: With many cases of cancer and the scarcity of the drug, there may not be enough to go around to everybody who needs it. The correct course of action can only be the one that is "right" by all people concerned. Heinz ought to act not on emotion or the law, but according to what he thinks an ideally just person would do in this case.

Stage 6 is Kohlberg's vision of ideal moral reasoning. But because it is so very rare and virtually no one functions consistently at this level, Kohlberg came to view it as a hypothetical construct—that is, the stage to which people would progress were they to develop beyond Stage 5. In fact, the later versions of Kohlberg's manual for scoring moral judgments no longer attempt to measure Stage 6 reasoning (Colby & Kohlberg, 1987).

SUPPORT FOR KOHLBERG'S THEORY

Although Kohlberg believed that his stages form an invariant and universal sequence of moral growth that is closely tied to cognitive development, he also claimed that cognitive growth, by itself, is not sufficient to guarantee moral development. In order to move beyond the preconventional level of moral reasoning, children must be exposed to persons or situations that introduce *cognitive disequilibria*—that is, conflicts between existing moral concepts and new ideas that will force them to reevaluate their viewpoints. So, like Piaget, Kohlberg believed that both cognitive development and *relevant social experiences* underlie the growth of moral reasoning.

How much support is there for these ideas? Let's review the evidence, starting with data bearing on Kohlberg's invariant-sequence hypothesis.

Are Kohlberg's Stages an Invariant Sequence?   If Kohlberg's stages represent a true developmental sequence, we should find a strong positive correlation between age and maturity of moral reasoning. This is precisely what researchers have found in studies conducted in the United States, Mexico, the Bahamas, Taiwan, Turkey, Honduras, India, Nigeria, and Kenya (Colby & Kohlberg, 1987). So it seems that Kohlberg's levels and stages of moral reasoning are "universal" structures that are age-related—just as we would expect them to be if they formed a developmental sequence. But do these studies establish Kohlberg's stages as a fixed, or *invariant* sequence?

No, they do not! The problem is that participants at each age level were *different* people, and we cannot be certain that a 25-year-old at Stage 5 has progressed through the various moral levels and stages in the order specified by Kohlberg's theory.

Clearly the most compelling evidence for Kohlberg's invariant-sequence hypothesis would be a demonstration that individual children progress through the moral stages in precisely the order that Kohlberg said they should. Ann Colby and her associates (1983) have conducted a 20-year longitudinal study of Kohlberg's original research participants, who were reinterviewed five times at three- to four-year intervals. As shown in Figure 10.4, moral reasoning developed very gradually, with use of preconventional reasoning (Stages 1 and 2) declining sharply in adolescence—the same period in which conventional reasoning (Stages 3 and 4) is on the rise. Conventional reasoning remained the dominant form of moral expression in adulthood, with very few participants ever moving beyond it to postconventional morality (Stage 5). But even so, Colby et al. found that participants proceeded through the stages they did attain in precisely the order Kohlberg predicted and that no one ever skipped a stage. Similar results have been reported in a nine-year longitudinal study of adolescents in Israel and a twelve-year longitudinal project conducted in Turkey (Colby & Kohlberg, 1987). So Kohlberg's moral stages do seem to represent an invariant sequence (see also Rest, Thoma, & Edwards, 1997). Let's note, however, that people progress in an orderly fashion to *their* highest stage of reasoning and that Stage 3 or 4 is the end of this developmental journey for most individuals worldwide (Snarey, 1985).

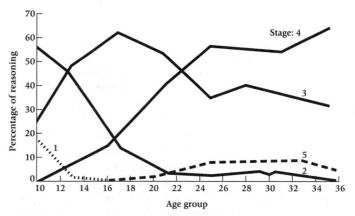

FIGURE 10.4   Use of Kohlberg's moral stages at ages 10 through 36 by male participants studied longitudinally over a 20-year period. (Adapted from Colby, Kohlberg, Gibbs, & Lieberman, 1983.) © 1983 by The Society for Research in Child Development. Reprinted by permission.

Cognitive Prerequisites for Moral Growth   According to Kohlberg (1963), the young, preconventional child reasons about moral issues from an egocentric point of view. At Stage 1 the child thinks that certain acts are bad because they are punished. At Stage 2 the child shows a limited awareness of the needs, thoughts, and intentions of others but still judges *self-serving* acts as appropriate. However, conventional reasoning clearly requires some role-taking abilities. A person at Stage 3, for example, must necessarily recognize others' points of view before she will evaluate intentions that would win their approval as "good" or morally acceptable. Furthermore, Kohlberg proposed that postconventional moral reasoning requires *formal operations*. A Stage 5 individual who bases moral judgments on abstract principles must be able to reason abstractly rather than simply adhering to the rule of law or concrete moral norms.

These hypotheses have received ample support. Lawrence Walker (1980), for example, found that all 10- to 13-year-olds who had reached Kohlberg's Stage 3 ("good boy-good girl" morality) were quite proficient at mutual role-taking, although not all proficient role-takers had reached Stage 3 in their moral reasoning. Similarly, Carolyn

Tomlinson-Keasey and Charles Keasey (1974) and Deanne Kuhn and her associates (1977) found that (1) all participants who showed any evidence of postconventional (Stage 5) moral reasoning had reached formal operations but that (2) most formal operators had not reached Kohlberg's postconventional level of moral reasoning. What these findings imply is that role-taking skills are *necessary but not sufficient* for the development of conventional morality, and that formal operations are *necessary but not sufficient* for the emergence of postconventional morality. This pattern is precisely what Kohlberg had expected, as he viewed cognitive growth as only one prerequisite for moral development. The other prerequisite is *relevant social experience*—that is, exposure to persons or situations that force a person to reevaluate and alter his current moral perspectives.

Evidence for Kohlberg's "Social-Experience" Hypothesis Does research support the proposition that social experience contributes to moral development? Yes, indeed, and we've already discussed an important example—that parents can promote the growth of moral reasoning if they are sensitive to the child's viewpoint when discussing moral issues and present their own perspectives in a supportive (and nonthreatening) way.

Peer Interactions Like Piaget, Kohlberg felt that interactions with peers probably contribute more to moral growth than one-sided discussions with adult authority figures. And they were right to call attention to the role peers play as agents of moral socialization. Children do seem to think more actively and deeply about their own and their partners' moral ideas in discussions with peers than in talks with their mothers or other adults; what's more, discussions with peers are more likely to stimulate moral growth (Kruger, 1992; Kruger & Tomasello, 1986).

Interestingly, the participants who seem to benefit most from peer discussions are those whose moral reasoning was least mature before the discussions began. And the changes in moral reasoning that they display are not merely a modeling effect. Berkowitz and Gibbs (1983) report that change is unlikely to occur unless the discussions include **transactive interactions**—exchanges in which each discussant performs mental operations on the reasoning of his or her partner (for example, "Your reasoning misses an important distinction"; "Here's an elaboration of your position"; "We can combine our positions into a common view"). This is an important finding,

transactive interactions: verbal exchanges in which individuals perform mental operations on the reasoning of their discussion partners.

for it reinforces Kohlberg's idea that social experiences promote moral growth by introducing cognitive challenges to a person's current reasoning—challenges to which the *less mature* individual will adapt by assimilating and accommodating to the other person's logic. Why do the more mature discussants not move in the direction of their less mature partners? Because the challenges introduced by their less mature partners are based on reasoning they have already rejected. In fact, their failure to regress in the face of such logic provides additional support for Kohlberg's invariant-sequence hypothesis.

Now an important issue. We've seen that parents who *directly contest* a child's moral judgments through the kinds of challenges that Berkowitz and Gibbs (1983) describe do *not* seem to foster growth; but peers do! How might we explain this inconsistency? Walker and Tay-

PHOTO 10.7 Discussing weighty ethical issues with peers often promotes the growth of moral reasoning.

lor (1991a) believe there is a simple explanation. Cognitive conflict introduced in a challenging way by a parent (who then offers his or her own discrepant point of view) is likely to be perceived as hostile criticism and thus to arouse defensiveness in a child or adolescent. By contrast, the same kind of criticism is less likely to be perceived as threatening when voiced by a social equal; in fact, adolescents may be especially inclined to listen carefully and to accommodate to a peer's position because they are so highly motivated to establish and maintain good relations with peers. Although more research is needed to confirm this explanation, it seems that parents and peers do promote moral growth in very different ways.

Advanced Education   Another kind of social experience that promotes moral growth is receiving an advanced education. Consistently, adults who go on to college and receive many years of education exhibit more complex reasoning about moral issues than those who are less educated (Speicher, 1994), and differences in the moral reasoning between college students and their nonstudent peers become greater with each successive year of school that the college students complete (Rest & Thoma, 1985). Advanced education may foster moral growth in two ways: (1) by contributing to cognitive growth and (2) by exposing students to diverse moral perspectives that produce cognitive conflict and soul-searching (Kohlberg, 1984; Mason & Gibbs, 1993).

Cultural Influences   Finally, simply living in a complex, diverse, and democratic society can stimulate moral development. Just as we learn the give-and-take of mutual perspective-taking by discussing issues with our friends, we learn in a diverse democracy that the opinions of many groups must be weighed and that laws reflect a consensus of the citizens rather than the arbitrary rulings of a dictator. Cross-cultural studies suggest that postconventional moral reasoning emerges primarily in Western democracies and that people in rural villages in many nonindustrialized countries show no signs of it (Boyes & Walker, 1988; Harkness, Edwards, & Super, 1981; Snarey & Keljo, 1991). People in these homogeneous communities may have less experience with the kinds of political conflicts and compromises that take place in a more diverse society and so may never have any need to question conventional moral standards. By adopting a contextual perspective on development, we can appreciate that the conventional (mostly Stage 3) reasoning typically displayed by adults in these societies—with its collectivist emphasis on cooperation and loyalty to the immediate social group—is adaptive and mature within their own social systems (Harkness et al., 1981).

In sum, Kohlberg has described an invariant sequence of moral stages and has identified some of the cognitive factors and major environmental influences that determine how far an individual progresses in this sequence. Yet critics have offered many reasons for suspecting that Kohlberg's theory is far from a complete account of moral development.

CRITICISMS OF KOHLBERG'S APPROACH

Many of the criticisms of Kohlberg's theory have centered on the possibilities that it is biased against certain groups of people, that it underestimates the moral sophistication of young children, and that it says much about moral reasoning but little about moral affect and moral behavior.

Is Kohlberg's Theory Biased?

Cultural Bias   Although research indicates that children and adolescents in many cultures proceed through the first three or four of Kohlberg's stages in order, we have seen that postconventional morality as Kohlberg defines it simply does not exist in

Box 10.2 *Cultural Influences*

Cultural Differences in Moral Reasoning

Is each of the following acts wrong? If so, how serious a violation is it?

1. A young married woman is beaten black and blue by her husband after going to a movie without his permission despite having been warned not to do so again.
2. A brother and sister decide to get married and have children.
3. The day after his father dies, the oldest son in a family has a haircut and eats chicken.

These are three of 39 acts presented by Richard Shweder, Manamahan Mahapatra, and Joan Miller (1987) to children ages 5 to 13 and adults in India and the United States. You may be surprised to learn that Hindu children and adults rated the son's having a haircut and eating chicken after his father's death as among the more very morally offensive of the 39 acts they rated, and the husband's beating of his disobedient wife as not wrong at all. American children and adults, of course, viewed wife beating as far more serious than breaking seemingly arbitrary rules about appropriate mourning behavior. Although Indians and Americans could agree that a few acts like brother-sister incest were serious moral violations, they did not agree on much else.

Furthermore, Indian children and adults viewed the Hindu ban against behavior disrespectful of one's dead father as a *universal moral rule;* they thought it would be best if *everyone in the world* followed it and strongly disagreed that it would be acceptable to change the rule if most people in their society wanted to change it. Hindus also believed that it is a serious moral offense for a widow to eat fish or wear brightly colored clothes or for a woman to cook food for her family during her menstrual period. To orthodox Hindus, rules against such behavior are required by natural law; they are not just arbitrary social conventions created by members of society. Hindus also regard it as morally necessary for a man to beat his disobedient wife in order to uphold his obligations as head of the family.

What effects do cultural beliefs of this sort have on moral development? The developmental trend in moral thinking that Shweder detected in India was very different from the developmental trend he observed in the United States, as the figure shows. With age, Indian children saw more and more issues as matters of universal moral principle, whereas American children saw fewer and fewer issues in the same light (and more and more as matters of arbitrary social convention that can legitimately differ from society to society).

Based on these cross-cultural findings, Shweder calls into question Kohlberg's claims that all children everywhere construct similar moral codes at similar ages and that certain universal moral principles exist. Shweder also questions Turiel's claim that children everywhere distinguish from an early age between moral rules and social-conventional rules, for the concept of social-conventional rules was simply not very meaningful to Indians of any age. Instead, Shweder believes that culture defines for a child exactly what is morally acceptable or unacceptable and then assists the young to adopt that conceptual framework. Indeed, we saw evidence of this very process in Box 10.1: children from the collectivist

some societies. Critics have charged that Kohlberg's highest stages reflect a Western ideal of justice, and that his stage theory is therefore biased against people who live in non-Western collectivist societies or who otherwise do not value individualism and individual rights highly enough to want to challenge society's rules (Gibbs & Schnell, 1985; Shweder, Mahapatra, & Miller, 1990). People in collectivist societies that emphasize social harmony and place the good of the group ahead of the good of the individual may be viewed as conventional moral thinkers in Kohlberg's system but may actually have very sophisticated concepts of justice (Shweder, 1997; Snarey & Keljo, 1991; Vasudev & Hummel, 1987). Although there are some aspects of moral development that do seem to be common to all cultures, the research presented in Box 10.2 indicates that other aspects of moral growth can vary considerably from society to society.

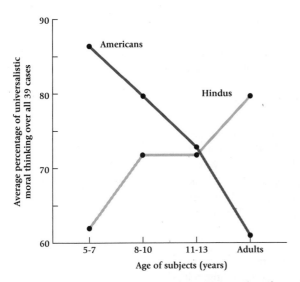

Universalistic moral thinking—the tendency to view rules of behavior as universally valid and unalterable—increases with age among Hindu children in India but decreases with age in the United States. The course of moral development is likely to be different in different societies. (Adapted from Shweder, Mahapatra, & Miller, 1987.) Reprinted by permission of the University of Chicago Press.

Peoples Republic of China gradually adopt their society's communist-collectivist ideals of behaving prosocially and remaining modest or humble about it—to the point that they think it better to *lie* and deny *personal* responsibility for a good deed than to boldly claim responsibility or seek recognition for their acts of kindness.

Interestingly, there are also important *subcultural* influences on moral reasoning. For example, individuals who occupy a subordinate position within their societies (for example, Arab women and Brazilian children from the lower socioeconomic strata) are more inclined than agemates of higher status to view themselves as having relatively few personal choices about how to behave and as under greater moral obligation to submit to authority (Nucci, Camino, & Sapiro, 1996; Wainryb & Turiel, 1994).

Clearly, these findings challenge the cognitive-developmental position that *all* important aspects of moral growth are universal. Instead, they tend to support a *contextual* perspective on moral development by suggesting that children's moral judgments are shaped by the culture and subculture in which they live. In Canada, for example, one need not display a strong sense of religiosity or spiritualism to be considered morally mature (Walker & Pitts, 1998), whereas a strong sense of spiritualism and adherence to an "ethics of divinity" is of central importance to Hindus—and seems to explain their tendency to view so many cultural prescriptions as universal moral laws (Shweder, 1997). What then should we conclude about culture and moral reasoning? Perhaps children all over the world do think in more *cognitively complex* ways about issues of morality and justice as they get older, as Kohlberg claimed, but at the same time adopt different notions about *what* is right and *what* is wrong (or a personal choice versus a moral obligation) as Shweder and others claim.

Gender Bias   Critics have also charged that Kohlberg's theory, which was developed from responses provided by male participants to dilemmas involving male characters, does not adequately represent female moral reasoning. Carol Gilligan (1977, 1982, 1993), for example, has been disturbed by her observation that in some early studies, women seemed to be the moral inferiors of men, typically reasoning at Kohlberg's Stage 3 while men usually reasoned at Stage 4. Her response was to argue that differential gender typing causes boys and girls to adopt different moral orientations. According to Gilligan, the strong independence and assertiveness training that boys receive encourages them to view moral dilemmas as inevitable conflicts of interest between *individuals* that laws and other social conventions are designed to resolve. She calls this orientation the **morality of justice**—a perspective that approximates Stage 4 in Kohlberg's scheme. By contrast, girls are taught to be nurturant,

morality of justice: Gilligan's term for what she presumes to be the dominant moral orientation of males, focusing more on socially defined justice as administered through law than on compassionate concerns for human welfare.

empathic, and concerned about others—in short, to define their sense of "goodness" in terms of their interpersonal *relationships*. So for females, morality implies a sense of caring or compassionate concern for human welfare—a **morality of care** that may seem to represent Stage 3 in Kohlberg's scheme. However, Gilligan insists that the morality of care that females adopt can become quite abstract or "principled," even though Kohlberg's scheme might place it at Stage 3 because of its focus on interpersonal obligations.

Gilligan then derived stages in the development of a morality of care by analyzing interviews with 29 women facing the difficult dilemma of deciding whether to have an abortion. In the first stage, *self-interest* guides moral decisions—a position similar to Kohlberg's preconventional morality. Women said they would do whatever was best for them personally. At a second, or *self-sacrificing* stage (akin to Kohlberg's conventional morality), a woman would consider her partner's needs rather than her own in deciding whether to have or abort a baby. Finally, Gilligan detected a third "postconventional" stage—one in which the abstract principle of *nonviolence* causes a woman to try to avoid hurting anyone. This mature morality of care is reflected in the thinking of one 25-year-old: "I would not be doing myself or the child a favor by having this child. . . . I don't need to pay off my imaginary debts to the world through this child, and I don't think it is right to bring a child into the world and use it for that purpose" (Gilligan, 1977, p. 505).

Has research supported Gilligan's claims that there are sex differences in moral reasoning, moral orientations, and moral development? Not very convincingly, it hasn't. At this point, there is little support for the claim that Kohlberg's theory is biased against women. Most studies indicate that women's reasoning about moral issues is just as complex as men's when their answers are scored by Kohlberg's criteria (Jadack et al., 1995; Walker, 1995). Nor is there much evidence for sex differences in moral orientations: When reasoning about *real-life* dilemmas they have faced, both males and females raise issues of compassion and interpersonal responsibility about as often as or more often than they talk about issues of law, justice, and individual rights (Walker, 1995; Wark & Krebs, 1996). In fact, participants of both sexes generally view both justice-related and care-related attributes as central elements of moral maturity (Walker & Pitts, 1998; and review Table 10-5), and justice and care orientations tend to be better integrated among relatively mature moral reasoners (Walker, de Vries, & Trevethan, 1987). Although there are some indications that females do tend to raise care issues more than males do (Wark & Krebs, 1996) and to place somewhat more emphasis on the interpersonal aspects of everyday problem solving (Strough, Berg, & Sansone, 1996; Williams & Bybee, 1994), it has become quite clear that the "justice" and the "care" orientations are *not* sex-specific moralities, as Gilligan had claimed.

Nevertheless, Gilligan's theory and the research designed to test it have broadened our view of morality by illustrating that both men and women often think about moral issues—especially real-life as opposed to hypothetical moral issues—in terms of their responsibilities for the welfare of other people. Kohlberg emphasized only one way, a very legalistic way, of thinking about right and wrong. There seems to be merit in tracing the development of *both* a morality of justice and a morality of care in both males and females (Brabeck, 1983; Gilligan, 1993).

Is Kohlberg's Theory Incomplete?   Another common criticism of Kohlberg's theory is that it focuses too heavily on moral reasoning and neglects moral affect and behavior. Yet Kohlberg did assume that mature moral reasoners should be more inclined to behave morally and that the links between moral reasoning and moral behavior would become stronger as individuals progress toward higher levels of moral understanding (Blasi, 1990).

morality of care: Gilligan's term for what she presumes to be the dominant moral orientation for females—an orientation focusing more on compassionate concerns for human welfare than on socially defined justice as administered through law.

Does Moral Reasoning Predict Moral Conduct? Most of the available data are consistent with Kohlberg's viewpoint. With few exceptions (for example, Kochanska, Padavich, & Koening, 1996), most researchers have found that the moral judgments of young children do *not* predict their behavior in situations where they are induced to cheat or violate other moral norms (Nelson, Grinder, & Biaggio, 1969; Santrock, 1975; Toner & Potts, 1981). However, studies of older grade-school children, adolescents, and young adults often do find that individuals at higher stages of moral reasoning are more likely than those at lower stages to behave altruistically and conscientiously, and they are less likely to cheat or take part in delinquent or criminal activity (Colby & Kohlberg, 1987; Rest et al., 1997). Kohlberg (1975), for example, found that only 15% of college students who reasoned at the postconventional level actually cheated on a test when given an opportunity, compared with 55% of the "conventional" students and 70% of those at the preconventional level. Yet the relationship between stage of moral reasoning and moral behavior is only moderate at best (Bruggerman & Hart, 1996). Why? Largely because people at any stage will occasionally revert to lower stages of moral reasoning (that is, regress), especially when resolving dilemmas in which strong punishment for wrongdoing is a distinct possibility (Sobesky, 1983; Wark & Krebs, 1996). So it seems that personal qualities other than moral reasoning, and many situational factors as well, may also influence a person's moral conduct in daily life (Thoma, Rest, & Davison, 1991). One such influence is moral affect.

Kohlberg Ignores Moral Emotions Norma Haan and her associates (1985) point out that moral dilemmas in everyday life arouse powerful emotions (moral affects). We care about moral issues and how our decisions will affect other people; we agonize about what to do and want to feel that we are moral beings; and we do often feel guilty or remorseful when we violate moral norms. These moral emotions play a central role in morality by influencing our thoughts and motivating our actions, and any theory that overlooks the role of emotions, as Kohlberg's tends to, would seem to be woefully incomplete (Hart & Chmiel, 1992; LeCapitaine, 1987).

Kohlberg Underestimates Young Children Finally, Kohlberg's focus on legalistic dilemmas that laws were designed to address caused him to overlook other "nonlegalistic" forms of moral reasoning that influence the behavior of grade-school children. For example, we've seen that young elementary school children do often consider the needs of others or will do whatever they think people will approve of when resolving Eisenberg's *prosocial* moral dilemmas— even though these youngsters are hopelessly mired in Stage 1 (or Stage 2) when tested on Kohlberg's dilemmas. Furthermore, 8- to 10-year-old Stage 1 reasoners have often developed some sophisticated notions about *distributive justice*—deciding what is a "fair and just" allocation of limited resources (toys, candies, etc.) among a group of deserving recipients (see Damon, 1988; Sigelman & Waitzman, 1991)—reasoning not adequately represented in Kohlberg's theory. Interestingly, fear of punishment, deference to authority, and other legalistic themes that Kohlberg believed to characterize the moral judgments of 8- to 10-year-olds do not even appear in children's distributive-

PHOTO 10.8 Although children this young usually display preconventional moral reasoning on Kohlberg's legalistic dilemmas, they actually have some reasonably sophisticated standards of distributive justice.

justice reasoning. So by focusing so heavily on legalistic concepts, Kohlberg has clearly underestimated the moral sophistication of grade-school children.

In sum, Kohlberg's theory of moral development has become prominent for good reason. It does indeed describe a universal sequence of changes in moral reasoning extending from childhood through adulthood. Furthermore, the evidence supports Kohlberg's view that both cognitive growth and social experiences contribute to moral development. However, there is also some merit to the criticisms. Kohlberg's theory does not fully capture the morality of people who live in many collectivist societies or who choose to emphasize a spiritual or a care orientation rather than an orientation centering on individual rights and justice, and it clearly underestimates the moral reasoning of young children. And because Kohlberg concentrated so heavily on moral reasoning, we must rely on other perspectives to help us to understand how moral affect and moral behavior develop, and how thought, emotions, and behavior interact to make us the moral beings that most of us ultimately become.

In our next section, we turn to the social-learning and social information-processing perspectives—approaches that attempt to specify some of the important cognitive, social, and emotional influences on children's moral behavior.

Morality as a Product of Social Learning (and Social Information Processing)

Social-learning theorists such as Albert Bandura (1986, 1991) and Walter Mischel (1974) have been interested primarily in the behavioral component of morality—in what we actually do when faced with temptation. They claim that moral behaviors are learned in the same way that other social behaviors are: through the processes of differential reinforcement and observational learning. They also consider moral behavior to be strongly influenced by the specific situations in which people find themselves. It is not at all surprising, they say, to see a person behave morally in one situation but transgress in another situation or to proclaim that nothing is more important than honesty but then lie or cheat.

HOW CONSISTENT ARE MORAL CONDUCT AND MORAL CHARACTER?

Perhaps the most extensive study of children's moral conduct is one of the oldest—the Character Education Inquiry reported by Hugh Hartshorne and Mark May (1928–1930). The purpose of this five-year project was to investigate the moral "character" of 10,000 children ages 8 to 16 by tempting them to lie, cheat, or steal in a variety of situations. The most noteworthy finding of this massive investigation was that children tended *not* to be consistent in their moral behavior; a child's willingness to cheat in one situation did not predict his willingness to lie, cheat, or steal in other situations. Of particular interest was the finding that children who cheated in a particular setting were just as likely as those who did not to state that cheating is wrong! Hartshorne and May concluded that "honesty" is largely specific to the situation rather than a stable character trait.

This "**doctrine of specificity**" has been questioned by other researchers. Roger Burton (1963; 1976) reanalyzed Hartshorne and May's data using newer and more sophisticated statistical techniques. His analyses provide some support for behavioral consistency. For example, a child's willingness to cheat or not cheat in one context (for example, on tests in class) is reasonably consistent, although the same child might behave very differently in highly unrelated contexts (for example, at competitive games on the playground). Other investigators have since discovered that moral

doctrine of specificity: a viewpoint shared by many social-learning theorists which holds that moral affect, moral reasoning, and moral behavior may depend on the situation one faces as much as or more than on an internalized set of moral principles.

behaviors of a *particular kind* (for example, sharing, refusing to break rules) are reasonably consistent over time and across situations (Kochanska et al., 1996; Rushton, 1980). Finally the correlations among measures of moral affect, moral reasoning, and moral behavior become progressively stronger with age (Blasi, 1980, 1990).

So the "doctrine of specificity" is clearly an overstatement. However, the finding that all three moral components become more consistent and more highly interrelated with age does not mean that morality ever becomes a wholly stable and unitary attribute; one's willingness to lie, cheat, or violate other moral norms may always depend to some extent on contextual factors, such as the importance of the goal one might achieve by transgressing or the amount of encouragement provided by peers for deviant conduct (Burton, 1976). In other words, the moral character of even the most mature of adults is unlikely to be perfectly consistent across all situations.

LEARNING TO RESIST TEMPTATION

From society's standpoint, one of the more important indexes of morality is the extent to which an individual is able to resist pressures to violate moral norms, *even when the possibility of detection and punishment is remote* (Hoffman, 1970). A person who resists temptation in the absence of external surveillance not only has learned a moral rule but is *internally* motivated to abide by that rule. How do children acquire moral standards, and what motivates them to obey these learned codes of conduct? Social-learning theorists have attempted to answer these questions by studying the effects of reinforcement, punishment, and social modeling on children's moral behavior.

Reinforcement as a Determinant of Moral Conduct
We have seen on several occasions that the frequency of many behaviors can be increased if these acts are reinforced. Moral behaviors are certainly no exception. When warm, accepting parents set clear and reasonable standards for their children and often *praise* them for behaving well, even toddlers are likely to meet their expectations and to display strong evidence of an internalized conscience by ages 4 to 5 (Kochanska, 1997b; Kuczynski & Kochanska, 1995). Children are generally motivated to comply with the wishes of a warm, socially reinforcing adult, and the praise that accompanies their desirable conduct tells them that they are accomplishing that objective.

PHOTO **10.9** Sometimes it is difficult to tell whether children are working together, helping each other, or using each other's work. Although there is some consistency to children's moral behavior, a child's conduct in any particular situation is likely to be influenced by factors such as the importance of the goal that might be achieved by breaking a moral rule and the probability of being caught should he or she commit a transgression.

The Role of Punishment in Establishing Moral Prohibitions Although reinforcing acceptable behaviors is an effective way to promote desirable conduct, adults will often fail to recognize that a child has *resisted* a temptation and is deserving of praise. By contrast, people are quick to inform a child of his or her misdeeds by *punishing* moral transgressions. Is punishment an effective way to foster the development of **inhibitory controls**? As we will see, the answer depends very critically on the child's *interpretation* of these aversive experiences.

Early Research Ross Parke (1977) used the *"forbidden toy" paradigm* to study the effects of punishment on children's resistance to temptation. During the first phase of a typical experiment, participants are punished (by hearing a noxious buzzer) whenever they touch an attractive toy; however, nothing happens when they play with

inhibitory control: an ability to display acceptable conduct by resisting the temptation to commit a forbidden act.

TABLE 10-6　Characteristics of punishment and the punitive context that influence a child's resistance to temptation

Timing of punishment	Punishment administered as children initiate deviant acts is more effective than punishment given after the acts have been performed. Early punishment makes children apprehensive as they prepare to commit a transgression, so that they are less likely to follow through. By contrast, late punishment makes children apprehensive *after* the act is completed, so that they may perform the act again and only then feel anxious.
Intensity of punishment	High-intensity punishment (a loud buzzer or a forceful *no!*) is more effective at inhibiting undesirable conduct than milder forms of the same punitive consequences. However, a caution is in order. Although the high-intensity punishments used in this research were certainly discomforting, they were probably a lot less aversive than a forceful spanking or a week's restriction to one's room. If high-intensity punishments are perceived as "cruel and unusual," children may become hostile toward the punitive agent and/or concerned only with not getting caught—hence they may be willing to commit the prohibited acts, perhaps "out of spite," when the disciplinarian is not around to oversee their activities.
Consistency of punishment	To be effective, punishment must be administered *consistently.* As most prohibited acts are themselves satisfying to the child, he or she will experience positive outcomes on those occasions when transgressions are not punished. In other words, inconsistent punishment may result in the *partial reinforcement* of unacceptable behavior, which strengthens these responses and makes them extremely resistant to extinction—even after the disciplinarian begins to punish them on a regular basis.
Relationship to the punitive agent	Punishment is more effective in establishing moral prohibitions when administered by someone who has previously established a warm and friendly (rewarding) relationship with the child. Children who are punished by a warm, caring person may perceive the reprimand as a loss of affection and may inhibit the punished act as a means of regaining approval. However, children who are punished by a cold, rejecting adult should not be highly motivated to inhibit forbidden acts, because they have no expectation of reestablishing a warm relationship with this cool or aloof disciplinarian.

unattractive toys. Once the child has learned the prohibition, the experimenter leaves and the child is surreptitiously observed to determine whether he or she plays with the forbidden toys.

Parke soon discovered that not all punishments were equally effective at promoting the development of moral controls. As illustrated in Table 10-6, *firm* (rather than mild) punishments, administered *immediately* (rather than later) and *consistently* by a *warm* (rather than an aloof) disciplinarian proved most effective at inhibiting a child's undesirable conduct. Yet Parke's most important discovery was that all forms of punishment became more effective if accompanied by a cognitive rationale that provides the transgressor with reasons for inhibiting a forbidden act.

Why Are Rationales Important? An Information-Processing Analysis　Why do rationales increase the effectiveness of punishment, even mild or delayed punishments that produce little moral restraint by themselves? According to Martin Hoffman's (1988) information-processing viewpoint, rationales are effective because they specify the reasons a punished act was wrong and why the transgressor should feel guilty, shameful, or otherwise less than virtuous were she to repeat it. So when youngsters who have received such rationales think about committing the forbidden act in the future, they should experience a general uneasiness (stemming from previous disciplinary encounters), should be inclined to make an *internal attribution* for this arousal (for example, "I'd feel guilty were I to deviate"; "I'd violate my positive self-image"), and should now be more likely to inhibit the forbidden act and to feel rather good about their "mature and responsible" conduct (see Figure 10-5). By contrast, children who receive no rationales or who have been exposed to reasoning that focuses their attention on the negative consequences *they* can expect for future transgressions (for example, "You'll be spanked again if you do it") will experience just as much uneasiness when they think about committing the forbidden act. However, these youngsters

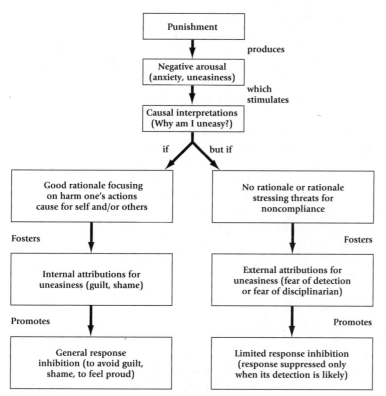

FIGURE 10.5 The social information-processing model of the suppressive effects of punishment.

should tend to make *external attributions* for their emotional arousal (for example, "I'm worried about getting caught and punished")—attributions that might make them comply with moral norms in the presence of authority figures but should do little to inhibit deviant conduct if there is no one around to detect their transgressions.

Of course, it may take many disciplinary encounters that include good rationales before young children come to connect the uneasiness they are experiencing with the information they receive and begin to make the kinds of internal attributions the model anticipates. Nevertheless, it is important to note that a fear of detection and punishment per se is not enough to persuade children to resist temptations in the *absence* of external surveillance. In order to establish truly internalized, *self*-controls, adults must structure disciplinary encounters to include an appropriate rationale—one that tells the child why the prohibited act is wrong and why she should feel guilty or otherwise less than virtuous were she to repeat it (Hoffman, 1988). Clearly, true self-restraint is largely under *cognitive* control—it depends more on what's in children's heads rather than on the amount of fear or uneasiness in their guts.

Moral Self-Concept Training   If making internal attributions about one's feelings or one's conduct truly promotes moral self-restraint, then we should be able to convince children that they can resist the temptation to break rules or violate moral norms *because* they are "good," "honest," or otherwise "responsible" persons. This kind of *moral self-concept training* really does work. William Casey and Roger Burton (1982) found that 7- to 10-year-olds became much more honest while playing games if being "honest" was stressed and the players had learned to remind themselves to follow the rules. Yet when honesty was *not* stressed, players often cheated. Furthermore, David Perry and his associates (1980) found that when 9- to 10-year-olds were told they were especially good at carrying out instructions and following rules (moral self-concept training), their behavior after succumbing to a nearly irresistible temptation (leaving a boring task to watch an exciting TV show) was very different from the behavior of peers who had not been told they were especially good. Specifically, children who had heard positive attributions about themselves were more inclined than control participants to *punish their own transgressions* by giving back many of the valuable prize tokens they had been paid for working at the boring task. So it seems that labeling children as "good" or "honest" may not only increase the likelihood that they will resist temptations but may also contribute to children's feelings of guilt or remorse should they behave inappropriately and violate their positive self-images.

In sum, moral self-concept training, particularly when combined with praise for desirable conduct, can be a most effective alternative to punishment as a means of establishing inhibitory controls—one that should help convince the child that "I'm resisting temptation because I want to" and lead to the development of truly *internalized* controls rather than a response inhibition based on a fear of detection and punishment. Furthermore, this positive, nonpunitive approach should produce none of the undesirable side effects (for example, resentment) that often accompany punishment.

Effects of Social Models on Children's Moral Behavior   Might children be influenced by rule-following models who exhibit moral behaviors in a "passive" way by failing to commit forbidden acts? Indeed they may, as long as they are aware that the "passive" model is resisting the temptation to violate a rule. Joan Grusec and her associates (1979) found that a rule-following model can be particularly effective at inspiring children to behave in kind if he clearly verbalizes that he is following a rule *and* states a rationale for not committing the deviant act. Furthermore, rule-following models whose rationales match the child's customary level of moral reasoning are more influential than models whose rationales are well beyond that level (Toner & Potts, 1981).

Finally, consider what Nace Toner and his associates (1978) found: 6- to 8-year-olds who were persuaded to *serve* as models of moral restraint for other children became more likely than age-mates who had not served as rule-following models to obey other rules during later tests of resistance to temptation. It was almost as if serving as a model had produced a change in children's self-concepts, so that they now defined themselves as "people who follow rules." The implications for child rearing are clear: Perhaps parents could succeed in establishing inhibitory controls in their older children by appealing to their maturity and persuading them to act as models of self-restraint for their younger brothers and sisters.

Who Raises Children Who Are Morally Mature?

Many years ago, Martin Hoffman (1970) reviewed the child-rearing literature to see whether the disciplinary techniques that *parents* actually use have any effect on the moral development of their children. He compared three major approaches:

1. **Love withdrawal:** withholding attention, affection, or approval after a child misbehaves—in other words, creating anxiety over a loss of love.
2. **Power assertion:** using superior power to control the child's behavior (such as forceful commands, physical restraint, spankings, and withdrawal of privileges—techniques that may generate fear, anger, or resentment).
3. **Induction:** explaining why a behavior is wrong and should be changed by emphasizing how it affects other people; often suggesting how the child might undo any harm done.

TABLE 10-7 Relationships between parents' use of three disciplinary strategies and children's moral development

DIRECTION OF RELATIONSHIP BETWEEN PARENT'S USE OF A DISCIPLINARY STRATEGY AND CHILDREN'S MORAL MATURITY	TYPE OF DISCIPLINE		
	POWER-ASSERTION	LOVE WITHDRAWAL	INDUCTION
+ (positive correlation)	7	8	38
− (negative correlation)	32	11	6

NOTE: Table entries represent the number of occasions on which a particular disciplinary technique was found to be associated (either positively or negatively) with a measure of children's moral affect, reasoning, or behavior.

SOURCE: Adapted from Brody & Shaffer, 1982.

Suppose little Suzie has just terrorized the family cat by chasing him with a lit sparkler during a Fourth of July celebration. Using *love withdrawal,* a parent might say "How could you! Get away; I can't bear to look at you." Using *power assertion,* a parent might spank Suzie or say "That's it! No movie for you this Saturday." Using *induction,* the parent might say, "Suzie, look how scared Frank is. You could have set him on fire, and you know how sad we'd all be if he was burned." Induction, then, is a matter of providing rationales that focus special attention on the consequences of one's wrongdoing for other people (or cats, as the case may be).

Although only a limited number of child-rearing studies had been conducted by 1970, their results suggested that (1) neither love withdrawal nor power assertion were particularly effective at promoting moral maturity, but that (2) induction seemed to foster the development of all three aspects of morality—moral emotions, moral reasoning, and moral behavior (Hoffman, 1970). Table 10-7 summarizes the relationships among the three patterns of parental discipline and various measures of children's moral maturity that emerged from a later review of the literature that included many more studies (Brody & Shaffer, 1982). Clearly these data confirm Hoffman's conclusions: Parents who rely on inductive discipline tend to have children who are morally mature, whereas frequent use of power assertion is more often associated with moral *immaturity* than with moral maturity. The few cases in which induction was not associated with moral maturity all involved children under age 4. However, recent research indicates that induction can be highly effective with 2- to 5-year-olds, reliably promoting sympathy and compassion for others as well as a willingness to comply with parental requests; by contrast, use of such high-intensity power-assertive tactics as becoming angry and physically restraining or spanking the child is already associated with and seems to promote noncompliance, defiance, and a lack of concern for others (Crockenberg & Litman, 1990; Kochanska; 1997b; Kochanska et al., 1996; Zahn-Waxler et al., 1979).

Why is inductive discipline effective? Hoffman cites several reasons. First, it provides children with *cognitive standards* (or rationales) that children can use to evaluate their conduct. Second, this form of discipline helps children to sympathize with others (Krevans & Gibbs, 1996) and allows parents to talk about such *moral affects* as pride, guilt, and shame that are not easily discussed with a child who is made emotionally insecure by love-withdrawal, or angry and resentful by power-assertive techniques. Third, parents who use inductive discipline are likely to explain to the child (1) what he or she *should have done* when tempted to violate a prohibition and (2) what he or she *can now do* to make up for a transgression. So induction

love withdrawal: a form of discipline in which an adult withholds attention, affection, or approval in order to modify or control a child's behavior.

power-assertion: a form of discipline in which an adult relies on his or her superior power (for example, by administering spankings or withholding privileges) to modify or control a child's behavior.

induction: a nonpunitive form of discipline in which an adult explains why a child's behavior is wrong and should be changed by emphasizing its effects on others.

"IF YOU'RE TRYIN' TO GET SOMETHING INTO MY HEAD, YOU'RE WORKIN' ON THE WRONG END!"

Dennis the Menace®used by permission of Hank Ketcham and © by North American Syndicate.

may be an effective method of moral socialization because it calls attention to the cognitive, affective, and behavioral aspects of morality and may help the child to integrate them.

Finally, it is important to note that few if any parents are totally inductive, love-oriented, or power-assertive in their approach to discipline; most make at least some use of all three disciplinary techniques. Although parents classified as "inductive" rely heavily on inductive methods, they will occasionally take punitive measures whenever punishment is necessary to command the child's attention or to discipline repeated transgressions. So the style of parenting that Hoffman calls induction may be very similar to the "rationale + mild punishment" treatment that Parke (1977) found most effective in laboratory studies of resistance to temptation.

Criticisms of Hoffman's Ideas about Discipline   Several investigators have wondered whether Hoffman's conclusions about the effectiveness of inductive discipline might not be overstated. For example, inductive discipline used by White, middle-class mothers is consistently associated with measures of children's moral maturity; however, the same findings don't always hold for fathers or for parents from other socioeconomic backgrounds (Brody & Shaffer, 1982; Grusec & Goodnow, 1994). Furthermore, one recent study found that the positive association between parents' use of power-assertive discipline and children's aggressive, antisocial conduct held for European-American but not for African-American children (Deater-Deckard & Dodge, 1997). Clearly more research is needed to establish how culturally specific Hoffman's ideas may be.

Other critics have raised the *direction-of-effects* issue: Does induction promote moral maturity, or do morally mature children elicit more inductive forms of discipline from their parents? Since child rearing studies are based on correlational data, either of these possibilities can explain Hoffman's findings. Hoffman (1975) responds by claiming that parents exert far more control over their children's behavior than children exert over parents. In other words, he believes that parental use of inductive discipline promotes moral maturity rather than the other way around. And there is some *experimental* support for Hoffman's claim in that induction is much more effective than other forms of discipline at persuading children to keep their promises and to comply with rules imposed by *unfamiliar* adults (Kuczynski, 1983). What's more, parents' *preexisting* attitudes about child rearing and the goals *they* pursue on deciding to discipline play a major role in determining the techniques they use (Dix, 1991). For example, parents who value strict obedience are likely to use more coercive forms of discipline, particularly if they also make dispositional attributions (for example, "He did that out of meanness") about a child's misconduct. By contrast, parents who view discipline more as a means of teaching children important lessons while maintaining harmonious family relationships are likely to avoid dominating their child, to communicate their acceptance and concern for his welfare, and to rely more on reasoning (Hastings & Grusec, 1998).

Nevertheless, children clearly have a hand in determining how they are disciplined by their parents. For example, the research presented in Box 10.3 reveals that a child's *temperament* can influence how he or she reacts to different kinds of discipline which, in turn, may affect how he or she is treated. Other research indicates that children who react unfavorably to discipline by acting out or by repeating their transgressions often drive adults to use more and more power-assertive (and less and less effective) means of discipline over time (Anderson, Lytton, & Romney, 1986; Lytton, 1990).

So moral socialization at home is a two-way street: although inductive discipline does indeed promote moral maturity, children who respond more favorably to these rational, nonpunitive techniques are the ones who are most likely to be treated this way by their parents.

Box 10.3 Focus on Research

Temperament, Discipline, and Moral Internalization

Recently, Grazyna Kochanska (1993, 1997a) proposed that the kind of parenting most likely to foster moral internalization depends on a child's temperament. Some children are temperamentally *fearful*—that is, prone to become highly anxious and to burst into tears when they receive a sharp reprimand from their parents. According to Kochanska, fearful children respond much more favorably to gentle, psychological forms of discipline that deemphasize power assertion—something akin to Hoffman's induction. Other children are highly impulsive and temperamentally *fearless*. Kochanska believes that these emotionally nonreactive youngsters may not be sufficiently aroused by mild psychological forms of discipline to internalize parental rules or even to stop performing the behavior for which they are being reprimanded! Although their parents may be inclined to become forceful with them when gentle forms of discipline do not work, Kochanska claims that resorting to power assertion proves no more effective with a fearless child than with a fearful one. Instead, she proposes that the route to moral internalization for a fearless child is warm, sensitive parenting of the kind that promotes secure attachments and a mutually cooperative parent–child relationship. Her view is that a secure and mutually positive orientation fosters *committed compliance* from the child, who wants to cooperate with and please his parents.

To test her theory, Kochanska (1995, 1997a) classified a sample of 2- to 3-year-olds as temperamentally fearful or fearless. She then observed each of them interacting with their mothers to assess the mothers' warmth and responsiveness to social signals and the kinds of discipline that the mother used. Data on the security of the child's attachment to his or her mother were also available. The strength of children's moral internalization was assessed at three times: ages 2 to 3, 4, and 5. Measures of moral internalization included complying with requests and following rules (that is, refusing to touch prohibited toys) at age 2 to 3, as well as refusing to cheat at games and maturity of moral reasoning at ages 4 and 5.

The results of this longitudinal study provided clear support for Kochanska's theory. For the *fearful* children, use of gentle, inductive discipline that was low in power assertion predicted higher levels of moral internalization at all three ages. Yet this same discipline bore no relationship to the levels of moral internalization that *fearless* participants displayed. Instead, a secure attachment to a mother who was highly responsive to their social signals is what predicted strength of conscience among fearless children.

Here, then, is another example of how "goodness of fit" between parenting practices and children's temperaments foster adaptive outcomes. Judging from the child-rearing literature, most children probably are sufficiently aroused by gentle, inductive disciplinary techniques to learn moral lessons, although this approach may be essential to foster moral internalization among especially fearful youngsters. However, continued reliance on this same discipline constitutes a poor fit for highly fearless children, who are more likely to internalize moral lessons in the context of a secure relationship with a parent whose discipline is firm and reminds the child of the desirability of maintaining the warm, mutually cooperative relationship they have enjoyed. Finally, Kochanska and her associates (1996) find that mothers' frequent use of power assertion consistently *inhibits* children's moral internalization and represents a poor fit with all temperaments.

A Child's-Eye View of Discipline   What do children think about various disciplinary strategies? Do they feel (as many developmentalists do) that physical punishment and love withdrawal are ineffective methods of promoting moral restraint? Would they favor inductive techniques, or perhaps prefer that their parents adopt more permissive attitudes about transgressions?

Michael Siegal and Jan Cowen (1984) addressed these issues by asking children and adolescents between the ages of 4 and 18 to listen to stories describing different kinds of misdeeds and to evaluate strategies that mothers had used to discipline these antics. Five kinds of transgressions were described: (1) simple disobedience (the child refused to clean his room), (2) causing physical harm to others (the child punched a playmate), (3) causing physical harm to oneself (ignoring an order not to touch a hot stove), (4) causing psychological harm to others (making fun of a physically disabled person), and (5) causing physical damage (breaking a lamp while roughhousing). The four disciplinary techniques on which mothers were said to have relied were *induction,* (reasoning with the culprit by pointing out the harmful consequences of his or her actions), *physical punishment* (striking the child), *love withdrawal* (saying she wanted nothing more to do with the culprit), and *permissive nonintervention* (ignoring the incident and assuming that the child would learn important lessons on his or her own). Each participant heard 20 stories that resulted from pairing each of the four maternal disciplinary strategies with each of the five kinds of transgressions. After listening to or reading each story, the participant indicated whether the mother's approach to the problem was "very wrong," "wrong," "half right-half wrong," "right," or "very right."

Although the perceived appropriateness of each disciplinary technique varied somewhat across transgressions, the most interesting findings overall were that (1) induction was the most preferred disciplinary strategy for participants of all ages (even preschoolers), and (2) physical punishment was the next most favorably evaluated technique. So all participants seemed to favor a rational disciplinarian who relies heavily on reasoning that is occasionally backed by power assertion. By contrast, love withdrawal and permissiveness were favorably evaluated by no age group. In fact, the 4- to 9-year-olds in the sample favored any form of discipline, even love withdrawal, over a permissive attitude on the mother's part (which they viewed as "wrong" or "very wrong"). Apparently young children see the need for adults to step in and restrain their inappropriate conduct, for they were disturbed by stories in which youngsters were generally free to do their own thing, largely unencumbered by adult constraints.

In sum, the disciplinary style that children favor (induction backed by occasional use of power assertion) is the one most closely associated with measures of moral maturity in the child-rearing studies and with resistance to temptation in the laboratory. Perhaps another reason that inductive discipline may promote moral maturity is simply that children view this approach as the "right" way to deal with transgressions and they may be highly motivated to accept influence from a disciplinarian whose "worldview" matches their own. By contrast, children who favor induction but are usually disciplined in other ways may see little justification for internalizing the values and exhortations of a disciplinarian whose very methods of inducing compliance seem unwise, unjust, and hardly worthy of their respect.

Summary

WHAT ARE ALTRUISM AND PROSOCIAL BEHAVIOR?

■ **Prosocial behavior** consists of actions that benefit other people. **Altruism,** a form of prosocial behavior, has been defined in two ways. The **motivational, or intentional, definition** contends that an act is altruistic if the helper is acting more out of a concern for others than for any personal benefits that might accrue (compare with **autonomous altruism**). By contrast, proponents of a **behavioral definition** think of altruism as any act that benefits others, regardless of the helper's motives (compare with **normative altruism**).

THEORIES OF ALTRUISM AND PROSOCIAL DEVELOPMENT

■ Evolutionary theorists argue that altruism is a preadapted, genetically programmed motive that evolved because it promotes the survival of the individual and the species. By contrast, proponents of psychoanalytic, social-learning, and cognitive-developmental theories believe that children must *acquire* a sense of altruistic concern. Psychoanalytic theorists assume that altruistic values are internalized and become a part of one's superego. Social-learning theorists believe that altruistic habits are acquired and maintained because children learn that prosocial behavior is in some way reinforcing. Cognitive-developmental theorists argue that the growth of altruistic concern depends on fundamental cognitive changes that occur during childhood, including (1) a gradual decline in egocentrism, (2) the development of role-taking skills, and (3) the growth of empathic concern and prosocial moral reasoning.

DEVELOPMENTAL TRENDS IN ALTRUISM

■ Early indications of prosocial conduct, such as sharing toys and comforting distressed companions, appear in infancy and toddlerhood, particularly among youngsters whose mothers emphasize **affective explanations** as part of their disciplinary strategies.

■ Sharing, helping, and other forms of prosocial behavior become more and more common from the preschool period onward. Contrary to widely held stereotypes, girls are neither more altruistic than boys nor any less capable than boys are of accomplishing tasks without seeking assistance.

COGNITIVE AND AFFECTIVE CONTRIBUTORS TO ALTRUISM

■ The growth of altruistic concern is linked to the development of **social perspective-taking skills, prosocial moral reasoning, sympathetic empathic arousal,** and establishment of an altruistic self-concept. Although young children often interpret empathic arousal as personal, or **self-oriented distress,** they eventually acquire the role-taking skills to interpret their reactions as sympathy for others, which promotes altruism by making them feel responsible for others' welfare (the "**felt responsibility" hypothesis**).

CULTURAL AND SOCIAL INFLUENCES ON ALTRUISM

■ Prosocial conduct is much more apparent in *collectivist* societies, where strongly stressed social goals make it almost obligatory, than in *individualistic* societies, where it has more of a discretionary quality about it.

■ Many other social influences affect one's propensity for altruism. Parents can promote altruistic behavior through their **altruistic exhortations,** by praising their child's kindly deeds, and by practicing themselves the prosocial lessons they have preached. Furthermore, parents who discipline harmdoing with nonpunitive, affective explanations that point out the negative effects of one's misconduct on victims are likely to raise children who become sympathetic, self-sacrificing, and concerned about the welfare of others.

WHAT IS MORALITY?

■ **Morality** has been defined in many ways, although almost everyone agrees that it implies a set of internalized principles or ideals that help the individual to distinguish right from wrong and to act on this distinction. Morality has three basic components: **moral affect, moral reasoning,** and **moral behavior.**

PSYCHOANALYTIC EXPLANATIONS OF MORAL DEVELOPMENT

■ According to Freud's theory of **Oedipal morality,** children internalize the moral standards of the same-sex parent during the phallic stage as they resolve their Oedipus or Electra complexes and form a conscience or superego.

■ Research has consistently discredited Freud's theory. However, newer psychoanalytic ideas that the conscience forms earlier in toddlerhood in the context of a warm supportive (rather than fear-provoking) parent-child relationship has received some support.

COGNITIVE-DEVELOPMENTAL THEORY: THE CHILD AS A MORAL PHILOSOPHER

■ Cognitive-developmental theorists have emphasized the cognitive component of morality by studying the development of moral reasoning. Jean Piaget formulated a two-stage model of moral development based on changes that occur in children's conceptions of rules and their sense of social justice. From a **premoral period** in which children allegedly respect no rules, they progress to **heteronomous morality,** in which they view rules as moral absolutes and believe in **immanent justice,** and finally, to **autonomous morality,** in which they regard rules as flexible and justice as relative rather than absolute.

■ Piaget clearly identified some important trends in the development of moral reasoning. However, shortcomings of his research methods and his failure to capture children's distinctions between **moral rules** and **social conventional rules** caused him to underestimate the moral sophistication of preschool and young grade-school children.

■ Lawrence Kohlberg's revision and extension of Piaget's theory views moral reasoning as progressing through an invariant sequence of three levels, (**preconventional, conventional,** and **postconventional moralities**), each composed of two distinct stages. According to Kohlberg, the order of progression through the levels and stages is invariant because each of these modes of thinking depends, in part, on the development of cognitive abilities that evolve in a fixed sequence. Yet Kohlberg also claimed that no moral growth occurs in the absence of social experiences that would cause a person to reevaluate her existing moral concepts.

■ Research indicates that Kohlberg's stages do form an invariant sequence. Furthermore, both cognitive development and such relevant social experiences as exposure to divergent moral perspectives in the context of **transactive interactions** with parents, peers, and other participants in higher education or democratic activities do contribute to the growth of moral reasoning. However, Kohlberg's theory may not adequately describe the morality of people who live in many non-Westernized societies or who emphasize a **morality of care** rather than a **morality of justice;** and like Piaget, Kohlberg clearly underestimates the moral reasoning of young children. Critics also claim the theory says too little about moral affect and moral behavior.

MORALITY AS A PRODUCT OF SOCIAL LEARNING (AND SOCIAL INFORMATION PROCESSING)

- Although their **doctrine of specificity** is clearly an overstatement, social learning theorists have helped to explain how children come to resist temptation and inhibit acts that violate moral norms. Among the factors that promote the development of **inhibitory controls** are praise given for virtuous conduct, punishments that include appropriate rationales, and exposing the child to (or having children serve as) models of moral restraint. Other nonpunitive techniques, such as moral self-concept training, are also quite effective at promoting moral behavior.

WHO RAISES CHILDREN WHO ARE MORALLY MATURE?

- Child-rearing studies consistently imply that use of **inductive discipline** promotes moral maturity, whereas **love withdrawal** has little effect, and **power-assertion** is associated with moral *immaturity.* The effectiveness of induction may vary, however, depending on the child's temperament. But children generally prefer inductive discipline to other approaches, and most seem highly motivated to accept influence from an inductive adult whose methods they can respect.

Chapter Eleven

The Family

Functions of the Family

The Family as a Social System
Direct and Indirect Influences
Families Are Developing Systems
Families Are Embedded Systems
A Changing Family System in a Changing World

Parental Socialization During Childhood and Adolescence
Two Major Dimensions of Parenting
Four Patterns of Parenting
Social Class and Ethnic Variations in Child Rearing
The Quest for Autonomy: Renegotiating the Parent/Child Relationship During Adolescence

The Influence of Siblings and Sibling Relationships
Changes in the Family System When a New Baby Arrives
Sibling Relationships over the Course of Childhood
Positive Contributions of Sibling Relationships
Characteristics of Only Children

Diversity in Family Life
Adoptive Families
Gay and Lesbian Families
The Impacts of Family Conflict and Divorce
Remarriage and Blended Families
Maternal Employment Revisited

When Parenting Breaks Down: The Problem of Child Abuse
Who Are the Abusers?
Who Is Abused?
Social-Situational Triggers: The Ecology of Child Abuse
Consequences of Abuse and Neglect
How Can We Solve the Problem?

Reflections on the Family

Summary

*I*n April of 1995, at the age of 95 and on the day after her own 75th wedding anniversary, Cora Shaffer attended the 50th wedding anniversary party of her eldest son (then aged 73). Also present at that gathering was Cora's other surviving child, four of her eight grandchildren, eight of her 11 great-grandchildren, and nine of her 11 great-great grandchildren. Remarkably, Cora could easily recite the most notable dates (birthdays, wedding anniversaries) of *all* of her descendants and could give you a pretty fair account of the most notable current events (for example, recent occupational, education, or personal attainments) of all these relatives as well. When I asked her how she managed to keep up with all the family doings, she laughed, said she had ample time for family matters since her retirement in 1985 (at age 85!), and quipped that "Alexander Graham Bell must have had folks like me in mind when he invented the telephone." And yet, this woman could also expound at length about the lives and times of departed relatives *she had known,* some of whom had been born in the early 1840s, before the telephone (or even the pony express) had been invented. Clearly, Cora Shaffer valued her ties to past, present, and future generations of Shaffers.

Most of us will never have the opportunity to know and care about as many generations of relatives as my grandmother did, but her emphasis on family ties is not at all unusual. More than 99% of children in the United States are raised in a family of one kind or another (U.S. Bureau of the Census, 1997), and the vast majority of children in all societies grow up in a home setting with at least one biological parent or other relative. So virtually all of us are bound to families. We are born into them, work our way toward adulthood in them, start our own as adults, and remain connected to them in old age. We are part of our families, and they are part of us.

Our focus in this chapter is on the family as a *social system*—an institution that both influences and is influenced by its young. What is a family and what functions do families serve? How does the birth of a child affect other family members? Do the existing (or changing) relationships among other members of the family have any effect on the care and training that a young child receives? Are some patterns of parenting better than others? Do parents decide how they will raise their children—or might children be influencing their parents? Does the family's cultural heritage and socioeconomic status affect parenting and parent/child interactions? How important are siblings as socialization agents? How are children affected by the increasing diversity of family life we see today—by growing up with gay or lesbian parents, or by having to adjust to maternal employment, divorce, or a return to the two-parent family when a single parent remarries? And why do some parents abuse their offspring? These are some of the major issues that we will consider as we look at the important roles that families play in the cognitive, social, and emotional development of children and adolescents.

Functions of the Family

Families serve society in many ways. They produce and consume goods and services, thereby playing a role in the economy. Traditionally, the family has served as an outlet for the sexual urges of its adult members and as the means of replenishing the population. Families provide social and emotional supports that help family members cope with crises. They also care for their elderly, although this function in Western societies is often shared with such institutions as Social Security, Medicare (or other kinds of socialized medicine), and nursing homes. But perhaps the most widely recognized functions of the family—functions families serve in all societies—are the caregiving and training that parents and other family members provide for their young.

Socialization is the process by which children acquire the beliefs, values, and behaviors deemed significant and appropriate by the older members of their society.

The socialization of each generation serves society in at least three ways. First, it is a means of regulating children's behavior and controlling their undesirable or anti-social impulses. Second, socialization promotes the personal growth of the individual. As children interact with and become like other members of their culture, they acquire the knowledge, skills, motives, and aspirations that should enable them to adapt to their environment and function effectively within their communities. Finally, socialization perpetuates the social order: Appropriately socialized children become competent, adaptive, prosocial adults who will impart what they have learned to their own children.

After studying the child-rearing practices of many diverse cultures, Robert LeVine (1974, p. 238) concluded that families in all societies have *three basic goals* for their children:

1. The **survival goal**—to promote the physical survival and health of the child, ensuring that the child will live long enough to have children of his or her own.
2. The **economic goal**—to foster the skills and behavioral capacities that the child will need for economic self-maintenance as an adult.
3. The **self-actualization goal**—to foster behavioral capabilities for maximizing other cultural values (for example, morality, religion, achievement, wealth, prestige, and a sense of personal satisfaction).

According to LeVine, these universal goals of parenting form a hierarchy. Parents and other caregivers are initially concerned about maximizing the child's chances of survival, and all higher-order goals are placed on the back burner until it is clear that the youngster is healthy and is likely to survive. When physical health and security can be taken for granted, then parents begin to encourage those characteristics that are necessary for economic self-sufficiency. Only after survival and the attributes necessary for economic productivity have been established do parents begin to encourage the child to seek status, prestige, and self-fulfillment.

LeVine's ideas stem from observations of child-rearing practices in societies where infants often die before their second birthday. Regardless of whether one is observing African Bushmen, South American Indians, or Indonesian tribes, parents in societies where infant mortality is high tend to maintain close contact with their infants 24 hours a day, often carrying them on their hips or their backs in some sort of sling or cradleboard. These practices increase infants' chances of survival by reducing the likelihood of their becoming ill or dehydrated, crawling into the river or the campfire, or ambling off to be captured by a predator. Sleeping with parents at night is also a common practice in these societies (Whiting & Edwards, 1988)—one that may promote survival by sensitizing parents to infants' breathing control errors which, if not corrected, could otherwise result in *sudden infant death syndrome* (cf. McKenna, 1986; Morelli et al., 1992).[1] Although infants are kept close at all times, their parents rarely chat with or smile at them, and may seem almost uninterested in their future psychological development. Could this pattern of psychologically aloof yet competent physical caregiving be a defensive maneuver that prevents parents from becoming overly attached to a very young infant who might well die? Perhaps so, for many cultures in which infant mortality is high still institutionalize practices such as not speaking to newborns as if they were human beings or not naming them until late in the first year, when it is more probable that they will survive (Brazelton, 1979).

socialization: the process by which children acquire the beliefs, values, and behaviors considered desirable or appropriate by their culture or subculture.

survival goal: LeVine's first priority of parenting—to promote the physical health and safety (survival) of young children.

economic goal: LeVine's second priority of parenting—to promote skills that children will need for economic self-sufficiency.

self-actualization goal: LeVine's third priority of parenting—to promote the child's cognitive and behavioral capacity for maximizing such cultural values as morality, achievement, prestige, and personal satisfaction.

---

[1]Sudden infant death syndrome (SIDS; also known as "crib death") refers to the silent death of a seemingly healthy baby who, without apparent cause, simply stops breathing (usually at night while sleeping). In the United States, this mysterious affliction accounts for as many as one-third of infant deaths that occur between the second week of life and the end of the first year (Wise, 1995).

The next task parents face is to promote those characteristics and competencies that will enable children to care for themselves and their own future families. Anthropologist John Ogbu (1981) points out that the economy of a culture (that is, the way in which people support themselves or subsist) will determine how families socialize their young. To illustrate his point, he cites a well-known cross-cultural study by Herbert Barry and his associates (1959), who hypothesized that societies that depend on an agricultural or pastoral economy (those that accumulate food) would stress obedience, cooperation, and responsibility when raising their children. By contrast, groups that do not accumulate food (hunting, trapping, and fishing societies) were expected to train their children to be independent, assertive, and venturesome. In other words, both types of society were expected to emphasize the values, competencies, and attributes that are necessary to maintain their way of life. Barry et al. used existing anthropological records to review the economic characteristics and child-rearing techniques of 104 preliterate societies all over the world. As predicted, they found that agricultural and pastoral societies did place strong pressures on their children to be cooperative and obedient, whereas hunting and fishing societies stressed assertiveness, self-reliance, and individual accomplishments.

Even in industrial societies such as the United States, a family's social position or socioeconomic status affects their child-rearing practices. For example, parents from the lower socioeconomic strata, who typically work for a boss and must defer to his or her authority, tend to stress obedience, neatness, cleanliness, and respect for power—attributes that should enable their children to function effectively within a blue-collar economy. By contrast, middle-class parents, particularly those who work for themselves or who are professionals, are more likely to stress ambition, curiosity, creativity, and independence when raising their children (Arnett, 1995; Kohn, 1979). The latter finding would hardly surprise LeVine, who would argue that middle-class parents who have the resources to promote their child's eventual economic security are freer to encourage his or her initiative, achievement, and personal self-fulfillment (the third set of parenting goals) at a very early age.

PHOTO 11.1 In many cultures, parents increase their babies' chances of survival by keeping them close at all times.

Of course, families are only one of many institutions involved in the socialization process. Religious institutions, for example, provide important emotional supports and moral socialization that often increase family cohesion and promote healthy developmental outcomes (Brody, Stoneman, & Flor, 1996). And as we will see in Chapter 12, such institutions as the schools, the mass media, and children's groups (for example, Boy and Girl Scouts) frequently supplement the training and emotional support functions served by families. Nevertheless, many children have limited exposure to people outside the family until they are placed in day care or nursery school or begin their formal schooling. So the family has a clear head start on other institutions when it comes to socializing a child. And since the events of the early years are so very important to the child's social, emotional, and intellectual development, it is appropriate to think of the family as society's primary instrument of socialization.

The Family as a Social System

When developmentalists began to study socialization in the 1940s and 1950s, they focused almost entirely on the mother/child relationship, operating under the assumption that mothers (and to a lesser extent fathers) were the agents who molded children's conduct and character (Ambert, 1992). However, modern family researchers have rejected this simple unidirectional model in favor of a more comprehensive "systems" approach (Minuchin, 1988)—one that is similar to Urie Bronfenbrenner's (1993, 1995) ecological systems theory that we discussed in Chapter 3. The systems approach recognizes that parents influence their children. But it also stresses that (1) children influence the behavior and child-rearing practices of their parents, and (2) that families are complex social systems. The **family social system** is a network of *reciprocal* relationships and alliances that are constantly evolving and are greatly affected by community and cultural influences. Now consider some implications of this systems perspective.

DIRECT AND INDIRECT INFLUENCES

What does it mean to say that a family is a social system? To Jay Belsky (1981), it means that the family, much like the human body, is a *holistic structure* consisting of interrelated parts, each of which affects and is affected by every other part, and each of which contributes to the functioning of the whole.

To illustrate, let's consider the simplest of **traditional nuclear families,** consisting of a mother, a father, and a first-born child. According to Belsky (1981), even this man-woman-infant "system" is a complex entity. An infant interacting with his or her mother is already involved in a process of reciprocal influence, as is evident when we notice that the infant's smile is likely to be greeted by the mother's smile or that a mother's concerned expression often makes her infant wary. These influences, in which any pair of family members affects and is affected by each other's behavior, are called **direct effects.** And what happens when Dad arrives? As shown in Figure 11.1, the mother-infant-dyad is suddenly transformed into a *"family system [comprising] a husband-wife as well as mother-infant and father-infant relationships"* (Belsky, 1981, p. 17).

One implication of viewing the family as a system is that interactions between any two family members are likely to be influenced by attitudes and behaviors of a third family member—a phenomenon known as an **indirect, or third party, effect.** To illustrate, fathers clearly influence the mother/infant relationship: Happily married mothers who have close, supportive relationships with their husbands tend to interact much more patiently and sensitively with their infants than mothers who experience marital tension and feel that they are raising their children on their own (Cox et al., 1989, 1992). Meanwhile, mothers directly influence the father/infant relationship: Fathers tend to be more involved with their infants when their wives believe that a father should play an important role in a child's life (Palkovitz, 1984) and when the two parents talk frequently about the baby (Belsky, Gilstrap, & Rovine, 1984; Levy-Shiff, 1994). Overall, children fare best when couples **coparent**—that is, mutually support each other's parenting efforts and function as a cooperative (rather than an antagonistic) team. Unfortunately, effective coparenting is difficult for couples experiencing marital discord and other life stress (Belsky, Crnic, & Gable, 1995; McHale, 1995), and disputes between parents over child-rearing issues can be particularly harmful, often forecasting increases in childhood and adolescent adjustment problems over and above those attributable to other aspects of marital conflict (Jouriles et al., 1991; Vaughn et al., 1988). Clearly, both mothers and fathers can influence their children *indirectly* through their interactions with their spouses.

Of course, children also exert direct and indirect effects on their parents. A highly impulsive toddler who shows little inclination to comply with requests may drive a mother to punitive coercive methods of discipline (direct "child to mother" effect; Kochanska, 1993), which, in turn, may make the child more defiant than ever (a direct "mother-to-child" effect; Crockenberg & Litman, 1990). Alarmed by this state of affairs, the exasperated mother may then criticize her husband for his nonintervention,

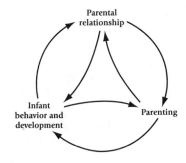

FIGURE 11.1 A model of the family as a social system. As implied in the diagram, a family is bigger than the sum of its parts. Parents affect infants, who affect each parent and the marital relationship. Of course, the marital relationship may affect the parenting the infant receives, the infant's behavior, and so on. Clearly, families are complex social systems. As an exercise, you may wish to rediagram the patterns of influence within a family after adding a sibling or two. (Belsky, 1981.) © 1981 by The American Psychological Assn. Reprinted by permission.

family social system: the complex network of relationships, interactions, and patterns of influence that characterize a family with three or more members.

traditional nuclear family: a family unit consisting of a wife/mother, a husband/father, and their dependent child(ren).

direct effect: instances in which any pair of family members affects and is affected by the other's behavior.

indirect, or third party, effect: instances in which the relationship between two individuals in a family is modified by the behavior or attitudes of a third family member.

coparenting: circumstance in which parents mutually support each other and function as a cooperative parenting team.

thereby precipitating an unpleasant discussion about parental obligations and responsibilities (an indirect effect of the child's impulsivity on the husband-wife relationship).

In short, every person and every relationship within the family affects every other person and relationship through pathways of reciprocal influence illustrated in Figure 11.1. Now we begin to see why it was rather naive to think we might understand how families influence children by concentrating exclusively on the mother/child relationship.

Now think about how complex the family system becomes with the birth of a second child and the addition of sibling/sibling and sibling/parent relationships. Or consider the complexity of an **extended family** household, a nearly universal practice in some cultures in which parents and their children live with (or in very close proximity to) other kin—grandparents or aunts, uncles, nieces, and nephews. It turns out that living in extended families is a fairly common arrangement for African Americans—an adaptive one in that large numbers of economically disadvantaged Black mothers must work, are often supporting their offspring without the father, and can surely use the assistance they receive from grandparents, siblings, uncles, aunts, and cousins who may live with them and serve as alternative caregivers for young children (Pearson et al., 1990; Wilson, 1989).

Until recently, family researchers had largely ignored extended families or had viewed them as *unhealthy* contexts for development, due largely to the fact that so many of these families were raising children without a father living at home (Wilson, 1989). This view is rapidly changing because of research showing how support from members of extended families (for example, grandmothers, aunts and uncles, and even fathers residing elsewhere) can help economically disadvantaged mothers to cope with the many stresses they face and to become more sensitive, responsive parents (Burton, 1990; Coley, 1998; Taylor & Roberts, 1995). Regardless of whether their kin live in their homes, disadvantaged African-American schoolchildren and adolescents whose families receive ample kinship support usually receive competent parenting at home which, in turn, is associated with such positive outcomes as a strong sense of self-reliance, good psychological adjustment, solid academic performance, and fewer behavioral problems (Taylor, 1996; Taylor & Roberts, 1995; Zimmerman, Salem, & Maton, 1995). And in cultures such as the Sudan, where social life is governed by collectivist ideals stressing communal interdependence and intergenerational harmony, children routinely display better patterns of psychological adjustment if raised in extended-family households rather than in Westernized, two-parent nuclear families (Al Awad & Sonuga-Barke, 1992). So it seems that the healthiest family contexts for development will depend very heavily on both the needs of individual families and the values that families (within particular cultural and subcultural contexts) are trying to promote.

PHOTO 11.2 Older members of extended families serve many useful functions. In addition to providing information and emotional support to young parents, grandmothers, and even great-grandmothers may figure prominently in the care and guidance of the family's children.

FAMILIES ARE DEVELOPING SYSTEMS

Not only are families complex social systems, they are dynamic systems as well. Consider that every family member is a *developing* individual and that relationships between husband and wife, parent and child, and sibling and sibling will also change in ways that can influence the development of each family member (Klein & White, 1996). Many such changes are planned, as when parents allow toddlers to do more things on their own as a means of encouraging autonomy and the development of individual initiative. Yet, a host of unplanned or unforeseen changes (such as the death of a sibling or the souring of the husband-wife relationship) can greatly affect family interactions and growth of its children. So the family is not only a system in which developmental change takes place; its dynamics also change with development of its members.

extended family: a group of blood relatives from more than one nuclear family (for example, grandparents, aunts, uncles, nieces, and nephews) who live together, forming a household.

FAMILIES ARE EMBEDDED SYSTEMS

The social systems perspective also emphasizes that all families are embedded within larger cultural and subcultural contexts and that the ecological niche a family occupies (for example, the family's religion, its socioeconomic status, and the values that prevail within a subculture, a community, or even a neighborhood) can affect family interactions and the development of a family's children (Bronfenbrenner, 1993, 1995). As we will see later in the chapter, economic hardship exerts a strong influence on parenting: Parents often become depressed over their financial situation which, in turn, can cause them to become less nurturant toward and involved with their children (Conger et al., 1992, 1995; McLoyd, 1998). And yet, economically distressed parents who have close ties to a "community"—a church group, a volunteer organization, or a circle of close friends and other confidants—experience far less stress and less disruption of their parenting routines (Burchinal, Follmer, & Bryant, 1996; Hashima & Amato, 1994). Clearly the broader social contexts that families experience can greatly affect the ways that family functions are carried out.

In sum, even the simplest of families is a true social system that is much bigger than the sum of its parts. Not only does each family member influence the behavior of every other, but the relationship between any two family members can affect the interactions and relationships of all other family members. And when we consider that family members develop, relationships change, and that all family dynamics are influenced by the broader social contexts in which families are embedded, it becomes quite clear that socialization within the family is best described not as a two-way street between parents and children, but as the busy intersection of many, many avenues of influence.

A CHANGING FAMILY SYSTEM IN A CHANGING WORLD

Not only is the family a complex, developing system, but it exists and develops in a world that is constantly changing. During the last half of the 20th century, several dramatic social changes have affected the makeup of the typical family and the character of family life. Drawing on U.S. census data and other surveys, we highlight the following changes:

1. *More single adults.* More adults are living as singles today than in the past. Marriage isn't "out," however, as about 90% of young adults will eventually marry (Chadwick & Heaton, 1992).
2. *Active postponement of marriage.* Many young singles are postponing marriage to pursue educational and career goals. Although the average age of first marriage actually decreased during the first half of this century, it has risen again to about 24 for women and 26 for men (U.S. Bureau of the Census, 1997).
3. *Decreased childbearing.* Today's adults are not only waiting longer after they marry to have children, they are having fewer of them—about 1.8 on average (U.S. Bureau of the Census, 1997). The Baby Boom period after World War II was an unusual departure from an otherwise consistent trend toward smaller family sizes. Today, about 12% of married women remain childless, many by choice (U.S. Bureau of the Census, 1997).
4. *More women are employed.* In 1950, 12% of married women with children under age 6 worked outside the home; now the figure is 63%, a truly dramatic social change (U.S. Bureau of the Census, 1997). Although women still carry the lion's share of child-rearing and housework responsibilities, fewer and fewer children have a mother whose full-time job is to be a mother.
5. *More divorce.* The divorce rate has been increasing over the past several decades, to the point that an additional one *million* children each year are affected by their

parents' divorce (Hetherington, Bridges, & Insabella, 1998). By one estimate, up to 60% of newly married couples can expect to divorce (Bumpass, 1990).

6. *More single-parent families.* Nearly 60% of all children born in the 1980s and 1990s will spend some time in a **single-parent family** (Teegartin, 1994). In 1960, only 9% of children lived with one parent, usually a widowed one; now 24% live with a single parent, usually a never-married or divorced one (see Figure 11.2). Father-headed single-parent homes are more common than they used to be, now accounting for about 17% of all single-parent families (U.S. Bureau of the Census, 1997).

7. *More children living in poverty.* Unfortunately, the increase in the number of single-parent families has contributed to an increase in the proportion of children living below the poverty line; 54% of children living in female-headed homes live in poverty, compared to 10% of children in two-parent homes (Eggebeen & Lichter, 1991). Spending at least some time living in poverty is the rule rather than the exception for African-American children (Brooks-Gunn, Klebanov, & Duncan, 1996), 65% of whom have spent some time in single-parent homes (Teegartin, 1994).

8. *More remarriage.* Because more married couples are divorcing, more adults (about 66% of divorced mothers and 75% of divorced fathers) are remarrying, forming **blended (or reconstituted) families** that involve at least one child, his or her biological parent, and a stepparent, and that often blend multiple children from two families into a new family system (Hetherington et al., 1998). About 25% of American children will spend some time in a stepparent family (Hetherington & Jodl, 1994).

What these changes tell us is that modern families are much more diverse than ever. Our stereotyped image of the model family—the *Leave It to Beaver* nuclear aggregation with a breadwinning father, a housewife mother, and at least two children—

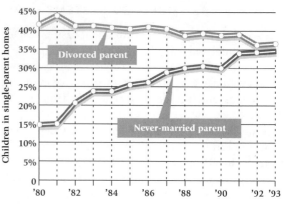

(The remaining 28% of children in single-parent households are with a widowed parent, a parent who is separated, a single grandparent, or in some other arrangement.)

FIGURE 11.2 The single-parent, postdivorce family is a common phenomenon of the past two decades; now, however, the number of children living with single parents who never married is almost equal to the number living with single parents who are divorced. In 1970, just 7% of American children in single-parent homes had a never-married parent. (From U.S. Census data cited in Teegartin, 1994.)

PHOTO 11.3 Because divorce and remarriage are so common, many children now live in blended (stepparent) families with stepsiblings.

single-parent family: a family system consisting of one parent (either the mother or the father) and the parent's dependent child(ren).

blended (or reconstituted) families: new families resulting from cohabitation or remarriage that include a parent, one or more children, and step-relations.

is just that: a stereotype. By one estimate, this "typical" family represented about 50% of American households in 1960, but only 12% in 1995 (Hernandez, 1997). Although the family is by no means dying, we must broaden our image of it to include the many dual-career, single-parent, and blended families that exist today and are influencing the development of the *majority* of our children. Bear that in mind as we begin our excursion into family life, seeking to determine how families influence the development of their children.

Parental Socialization During Childhood and Adolescence

In previous chapters, we considered the results of a large body of research aimed at understanding how parents might affect the social, emotional, and intellectual development of their infants and toddlers. Recall that this work was remarkably consistent in its implications: Warm and sensitive parents who often talk to their infants and try to stimulate their curiosity are contributing in a positive way to the establishment of secure emotional attachments as well as to the children's curiosity and willingness to explore, their sociability, and their intellectual development. It also helps if *both* parents are sensitive, responsive caregivers who can agree on how their infant should be raised and support each other in their roles as parents. Indeed, Jay Belsky (1981) has argued that parental warmth/sensitivity "is the most influential dimension of [parenting] in infancy. It not only fosters healthy psychological functioning during this developmental epoch, but also . . . lays the foundation on which future experience will build" (p. 8).

During the second year, parents continue to be caregivers and playmates, but they also become more concerned with teaching children how to behave (or how *not* to behave) in a variety of situations (Fagot & Kavanaugh, 1993). According to Erik Erikson (1963), this is the period when socialization begins in earnest. Parents must now manage the child's budding autonomy in the hope of instilling a sense of social propriety and self-control, while taking care not to undermine his or her curiosity, initiative, and feelings of personal competence.

TWO MAJOR DIMENSIONS OF PARENTING

Erikson and others (for example, Maccoby & Martin, 1983) claim that two aspects of parenting are especially important throughout childhood and adolescence: *parental acceptance/responsiveness* and *parental demandingness/control* (sometimes called "permissiveness-restrictiveness").

Acceptance/responsiveness refers to the amount of support and affection a parent displays. Parents classified as accepting and responsive often smile at, praise, and encourage their children, expressing a great deal of warmth, even though they can become quite critical when a child misbehaves. By contrast, less accepting and relatively unresponsive parents are often quick to criticize, belittle, punish, or ignore a child; they rarely communicate to children that they are valued or loved. Throughout the text, we have discussed a wealth of evidence suggesting that parental affection/responsiveness is a powerful contributor to such healthy developmental outcomes as secure attachments and the problem-solving and social skills that such attachments foster (see Chapters 4 and 5) high self-esteem, good role-taking skills, and positive identity outcomes (see Chapter 6), competent intellectual and academic performances during the grade-school years (Pettit, Bates, & Dodge, 1997, and see Chapter 7), more flexible and androgynous gender identities (see Chapter 8), and a strong conscience coupled with a healthy sense of prosocial concern (see Chapter 10).

Now compare this behavioral profile with that of the "unwanted" Czechoslovakian children we met in Chapter 5, whose mothers had tried repeatedly without success

acceptance/responsiveness: a dimension of parenting that describes the amount of responsiveness and affection that a parent displays toward a child.

to gain permission to abort them (David, 1994). Compared with "wanted" children from similar family backgrounds, the unwanted children had less stable family ties; were described as anxious, emotionally frustrated, and irritable; had more physical health problems; made poorer grades in school (even though they were comparable in IQ to the "wanted" children); were less popular with peers; and were more likely to require psychiatric attention for serious behavior disorders throughout childhood, adolescence, and young adulthood. Other investigators are also finding that a primary contributor to poor peer relations, clinical depression and other psychosocial problems later in life is a family setting in which one or both parents have treated the child as if he or she was unworthy of their attention and affection (Ge, Best, et al., 1996; MacKinnon-Lewis et al., 1997; MacDonald, 1992). Children simply do not thrive when they are often ignored or rejected; nor are they apt to become happy, well-adjusted adults (MacDonald, 1992).

PHOTO 11.4 Warmth and affection are crucial components of effective parenting.

Demandingness/control refers to the amount of regulation or supervision parents undertake with their children. Controlling/demanding parents place limits on their children's freedom of expression by imposing many demands and actively surveying their children's behavior to ensure that these rules and regulations are followed. Uncontrolling/undemanding parents are much less restrictive; they make fewer demands and allow children considerable freedom to pursue their interests and to make decisions about their own activities.

Is it better for parents to be highly controlling; or rather, should they impose few restrictions and grant their children considerable autonomy? To answer these questions, we need to be more specific about the degrees of control that parents display and to look carefully at patterns of parental acceptance.

demandingness/control: a dimension of parenting that describes how restrictive and demanding parents are.

FOUR PATTERNS OF PARENTING

It turns out that the two major parenting dimensions are reasonably independent, so that we find parents who display each of the few possible combinations of acceptance/responsiveness and control/demandingness shown in Figure 11.3. How are these four parenting styles related to a child's or an adolescent's social, emotional, and intellectual development?

Baumrind's Early Research   Perhaps the best-known research on parenting styles is Diana Baumrind's (1967, 1971) early studies of preschool children and their parents. Each child in Baumrind's sample was observed on several occasions in nursery school and at home. These data were used to rate the child on such behavioral dimensions as sociability, self-reliance, achievement, moodiness, and self-control. Parents were also interviewed and observed while interacting with their children at home. When Baumrind analyzed the parental data, she found that individual parents generally used one of three parenting

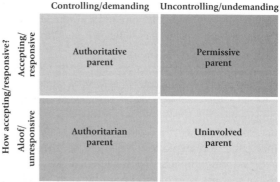

FIGURE 11.3 Two major dimensions of parenting. When we cross the two dimensions, we come up with four parenting styles: accepting/controlling (or "authoritative"); accepting/uncontrolling (or "permissive"); aloof/controlling (or "authoritarian"); and aloof/uncontrolling (or "uninvolved"). Which parenting style do you think would be associated with the most favorable outcomes? The least favorable outcomes? (From Maccoby & Martin, 1983.)

styles shown in Figure 11.3 (none of her parents could be classified as "uninvolved"). These three patterns of parenting were described as follows:

Authoritarian parenting: A very restrictive pattern of parenting in which adults impose many rules, expect strict obedience, will rarely if ever explain to the child why it is necessary to comply with all these regulations, and will often rely on punitive, forceful tactics (that is, power-assertion or love withdrawal) to gain compliance. Authoritarian parents are not sensitive to a child's conflicting viewpoints, expecting instead for the child to accept their word as law and to respect their authority.

Authoritative parenting: A more flexible style of parenting in which parents make many reasonable demands of their children. They are careful to provide rationales for complying with the limits they set and will ensure that their children follow those guidelines. However, they are much more accepting of and responsive to their children's points of view than authoritarian parents are and will often seek their children's participation in family decision making. So, authoritative parents exercise control in a *rational, democratic* (rather than a heavy-handed, overbearing) way that recognizes and respects their children's perspectives.

Permissive parenting: An accepting but lax pattern of parenting in which adults make relatively few demands, permit their children to freely express their feelings and impulses, do not closely monitor their children's activities, and rarely exert firm control over their behavior.

When Baumrind (1967) linked these three parenting styles to the characteristics of the preschool children who were exposed to each style, she found that children of authoritative parents were developing rather well. They were cheerful, socially responsible, self-reliant, achievement oriented, and cooperative with adults and peers. By contrast, children of authoritarian parents tended to be moody and seemingly unhappy much of the time, easily annoyed and unfriendly, relatively aimless, and generally not very pleasant to be around. Finally, children of permissive parents were often impulsive and aggressive, especially if they were boys. They tended to be bossy and self-centered, lacking in self-control, and quite low in independence and achievement.

Although Baumrind's findings clearly favor authoritative parenting, one might legitimately wonder whether children of authoritarian or permissive parents might eventually "outgrow" whatever shortcomings they displayed as preschoolers. Seeking to answer this question, Baumrind (1977) observed her participants (and their parents) again when the children were 8 to 9 years old. As we see in Table 11-1, children of authoritative parents were still relatively high in both *cognitive competencies*

TABLE 11-1 Relationships between child-rearing patterns and developmental outcomes in middle childhood and adolescence

CHILD-REARING PATTERN	OUTCOMES	
	CHILDHOOD	ADOLESCENCE
Authoritative	High cognitive and social competencies	High self-esteem, excellent social skills, strong moral/prosocial concern, high academic achievement
Authoritarian	Average cognitive and social competencies	Average academic performance and social skills; more conforming than adolescents of permissive parents
Permissive	Low cognitive and social competencies	Poor self-control and academic performance; more drug use than adolescents of authoritative or authoritarian parents

SOURCES: Baumrind, 1977, 1991; Steinberg et al., 1994.

(that is, shows originality in thinking, has high achievement motivation, likes intellectual challenges) and *social skills* (for example, is sociable and outgoing, participates actively and shows leadership in group activities), whereas children of authoritarian parents were generally average to below average in cognitive and social skills and children of permissive parents were relatively unskilled in both areas. Indeed, the strengths of children exposed to authoritative parenting were still evident in adolescence: Compared to teenagers raised by either permissive or authoritarian parents, those raised by authoritative parents were relatively confident, achievement oriented, and socially skilled, and they tended to stay clear of drug abuse and other problem behaviors (Baumrind, 1991). The link between authoritative parenting and positive developmental outcomes seems to hold for all racial and ethnic groups studied to date in the United States (Glasgow et al., 1997; Lamborn et al., 1991; Luster & McAdoo, 1996; Steinberg et al., 1994) and in a variety of different cultures as well (Pinto, Folkers, & Sines, 1991; Scott, Scott, & McCabe, 1991).

Uninvolved Parenting   In recent years it has become quite clear that the least successful parenting style is what might be termed **uninvolved parenting**—an extremely lax and undemanding approach displayed by parents who have either *rejected* their children or are so overwhelmed with their own stresses and problems that they haven't much time or energy to devote to child rearing (Maccoby & Martin, 1983). By age 3, children of uninvolved parents are already relatively high in aggression and such externalizing behaviors as temper tantrums (Miller et al., 1993). Furthermore, they tend to perform very poorly in the classroom later in childhood (Eckenrode, Laird, & Doris, 1993) and often become hostile, selfish, and rebellious adolescents who lack meaningful long-range goals and are prone to commit such antisocial and delinquent acts as alcohol and drug abuse, sexual misconduct, truancy, and a wide variety of criminal offenses (Lamborn et al., 1991; Kurdek & Fine, 1994; Patterson et al., 1992; Weiss & Schwarz, 1996). In effect, these youngsters have neglectful, "detached" parents whose actions (or lack thereof) seem to be saying "I don't care about you or about what you do"—a message that undoubtedly breeds resentment and willingness to strike back at these aloof, uncaring adversaries or at other authority figures.

Explaining the Effectiveness of Authoritative Parenting   Why is authoritative parenting so consistently associated with positive social, emotional, and intellectual outcomes? Probably for several reasons. First, authoritative parents are warm and accepting—they communicate a sense of *caring concern* that may motivate their children to comply with the directives they receive in a way not seen in children of more aloof and demanding (authoritarian) parents. Then there is the issue of how control is exercised. Unlike the authoritarian parent who sets *inflexible* standards and *dominates* the child, allowing little if any freedom of expression, the authoritative parent exercises control in a *rational* way, carefully explaining his or her point of view while also considering the child's viewpoint. Demands that come from a warm, accepting parent and that appear to be fair and reasonable rather than arbitrary and dictatorial are likely to elicit *committed compliance* rather than complaining or defiance (Kochanska, 1997b). Finally, authoritative parents are careful to tailor their demands to the child's ability to regulate his or her own conduct. In other words, they set standards that children can *realistically* achieve and allow the child some freedom, or *autonomy,* in deciding how best to comply with these expectations. This kind of treatment carries a most important message—something like "You are a capable human being whom I trust to be self-reliant and accomplish important objectives." Of course, we've seen in earlier chapters that feedback of this sort fosters the growth of self-reliance, achievement motivation, and high self-esteem in childhood and is the kind of sup-

uninvolved parenting: a pattern of parenting that is both aloof (or even hostile) and overpermissive, almost as if parents neither cared about their children nor about what they may become.

port that adolescents need to feel comfortable about exploring various roles and ideologies to forge a personal identity.

In sum, it appears that authoritative parenting—warmth combined with *moderate* and *rational* parental control—is the parenting style most consistently associated with positive developmental outcomes. Children apparently need love *and* limits—a set of rules that help them to structure and to evaluate their conduct. Without such guidance, they may not learn self-control and may become quite selfish, unruly, and lacking in clear achievement goals, particularly if their parents are also aloof or uncaring (Steinberg et al., 1994). But if they receive too much guidance and are hemmed in by inflexible restrictions, they may have few opportunities to become self-reliant and may lack confidence in their own decision-making abilities (Grolnick & Ryan, 1989; Steinberg et al., 1994).

The Direction-of-Effects Issue Does authoritative parenting really foster positive traits in children? Or do easygoing, manageable children cause parents to be authoritative? Baumrind (1983, 1993) insists that authoritative parenting causes children to be well behaved rather than the other way around. She notes that children of authoritative parents often resist parental demands at first; but they eventually come around *because* parents are firm in their demands and sufficiently patient to allow their children time to comply without caving in to the children's unreasonable demands or turning to power-assertive tactics. Indeed, longitudinal studies of early parental control strategies used by mothers with their $1\frac{1}{2}$- to 3-year-olds clearly supports Baumrind's "parental influence" hypothesis. Specifically, authoritative mothers who demanded that their children perform competent actions (or do's) and who dealt firmly *but patiently* with noncompliance had toddlers who became more compliant over time and who displayed few problem behaviors. By contrast, authoritarian mothers whose demands emphasized don'ts (don't touch; don't yell) and who used arbitrary, power-assertive control strategies had children who were less competent and cooperative, and who displayed an increase in problem behaviors over time (Crockenberg & Litman, 1990; Kuczynski & Kochanska, 1995).

Yet it is also true that extremely stubborn and impulsive children who show little self-control do tend to elicit more coercive forms of parenting (Kuczynski & Kochanska, 1995; O'Connor et al., 1998; Ritchie, 1999) and may eventually wear their parents out, causing them to become more lax, less affectionate, and possibly even hostile and uninvolved (Lytton, 1990; Stice & Barrera, 1995). So as we concluded when considering the impact of discipline on moral development in Chapter 10, socialization within the family is a matter of *reciprocal* influence: Parents certainly influence their children; but children can have some influence on the kind of parenting they receive.

SOCIAL CLASS AND ETHNIC VARIATIONS IN CHILD-REARING

Associations between authoritative parenting and healthy psychological development have been found in many cultures and subcultures. Yet people from different social strata and ethnic backgrounds face different kinds of problems, pursue different goals, and adopt different values about what it takes to adapt to their environments, and these ecological considerations often affect their approaches to child rearing.

Social Class Differences in Child Rearing How, then, do parenting styles differ by social class? Compared to middle-class parents, economically disadvantaged and working-class parents tend to:

1. Stress obedience and respect for authority more and to place somewhat less emphasis on fostering independence, curiosity, and creativity

2. Be more restrictive and authoritarian, more frequently using power-assertive discipline
3. Talk to and reason with their children less frequently
4. Show less warmth and affection (Maccoby, 1980; McLoyd, 1998)

According to Eleanor Maccoby (1980), these class-linked differences in parenting have been observed in many cultures and across racial and ethnic groups in the United States. However, we should keep in mind that what we are talking about here are *group trends* rather than absolute contrasts: Some middle-class parents are highly restrictive, power-assertive, and aloof in their approach to child rearing, whereas many lower- and working-class parents function more like their counterparts in the middle class (Kelly, Power, & Wimbush, 1992; Laosa, 1981). But on average it appears that lower-SES and working-class parents are somewhat more critical, more punitive, and more intolerant of disobedience than parents from the middle and upper socioeconomic strata.

Explaining Social Class Differences in Child Rearing Undoubtedly, many factors contribute to social-class differences in child rearing, and economic considerations seem to head the list. Consider that a low income may mean that living quarters are crowded; that family members must occasionally make do without adequate food, clothing, or medical care; and that parents are constantly tense or anxious about living under these marginal conditions. Eleanor Maccoby (1980) suggests that low-income living is probably much more *stressful* for parents and that stress affects the ways parental functions are carried out. Vonnie McLoyd (1989, 1998) agrees. Her reviews of the literature suggest that economic hardship creates its own psychological distress—a most pervasive discomfort that makes economically disadvantaged adults more edgy and irritable and more vulnerable to all negative life events (including the daily hassles associated with child rearing), thereby diminishing their capacity to be warm, supportive parents who are highly involved in their children's lives.

Recently, Rand Conger and his associates (1992, 1994, 1995; see also Bolger et al., 1995) offered support for this "economic distress" hypothesis by finding clear links between family economic hardships, nonnurturant/uninvolved parenting, and poor child-rearing outcomes. The causal sequence, shown in Figure 11.4, goes like this: Parents who are experiencing economic pressure or feeling that they cannot cope with their financial problems tend to become depressed, which increases marital conflict. Marital conflict, in turn, disrupts each parent's ability to be a supportive, involved parent—largely, perhaps, by undermining parents' beliefs that they can handle child-rearing problems in an efficacious manner (see Gondoli & Silverberg, 1997). And parents may have reason for such concern, because their children and adolescents often react negatively to the marital strife and the insensitive parenting they receive, experiencing a loss of *emotional security,* which contributes to such child and adolescent problems as low self-esteem, poor school performance, poor peer relations, and such adjustment problems as depression, hostility, and antisocial conduct (see Davies & Cummings, 1998). Many conflicts that economically distressed parents have with their adolescents center on money matters—a highly sensitive topic that can make a financially strapped parent feel downright hostile toward his or her children (Conger et al., 1994). And the adjustment problems and antisocial conduct that nonnurturant/insensitive parenting helps to create may further exasperate parents, causing them to back away and become even less nurturant and less involved in the lives of their children (Rueter & Conger, 1998; Vuchinich, Bank, & Patterson, 1992). Of course, we should keep in mind that many, many low-income adults are able to cope with their problems and parent quite effectively, particularly if their economic and/or marital distresses are not prolonged, they feel highly efficacious about

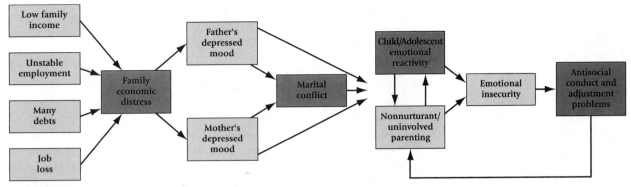

FIGURE 11.4 A model of the relationships among family economic distress, patterns of parenting, and child/adolescent adjustment. (Adapted from Conger et al., 1992; Davies & Cummings, 1998.)

parenting, and they receive emotional and parenting support from kin, friends, and other adults living outside the home (McLoyd, 1998). Nevertheless, it appears that Maccoby and McLoyd were quite correct in assuming that economic hardships are a very important contributor to the relatively aloof and coercive style of parenting often observed in low-income, economically distressed families.

Another explanation for the link between social class and parenting styles focuses on the skills needed by workers in white-collar and blue-collar jobs (Arnett, 1995; Kohn, 1979). A large percentage of lower-SES and working-class breadwinners are blue-collar workers who must please a supervisor and defer to his or her authority. For this reason, many lower-income parents may emphasize obedience and respect for authority because these are precisely the attributes they view as critical for success in the blue-collar economy. By contrast, middle- and upper-class parents may reason and negotiate more with their children while emphasizing individual initiative, curiosity, and creativity because these are the skills, attributes, and abilities that matter in their own occupations as business executives, white-collar workers, or professionals (Greenberger, O'Neil, & Nagel, 1994).

Finally, many contextual factors other than parenting conspire to differentiate economically disadvantaged children from their more advantaged middle- and working-class peers. The research presented in Box 11.1 on page 370, for example, illustrates how children from impoverished families can be negatively influenced by their life circumstances, regardless of the type of parenting they have received.

Ethnic Variations in Child Rearing   Parents of different ethnicities may also hold distinct child-rearing beliefs and values that are products of their cultural backgrounds or the ecological niches they occupy in society (MacPhee, Fritz, & Miller-Heyl, 1996). For example, Native American and Hispanic parents, whose cultural backgrounds stress communal rather than individual goals, are more inclined than European-American parents to (1) maintain close ties to a variety of kin and (2) insist that their children display calm, proper, and polite behaviors and a strong respect for others, as opposed to independence, competitiveness, and the pursuit of individual goals (Harwood et al., 1996; MacPhee et al., 1996). These parents foster such attributes by displaying ample warmth and affection while teaching their children to respect parental authority, particularly the father's legitimate right to set limits and to promote their welfare (Harrison et al., 1994).

Asian and Asian-American parents also tend to stress self-discipline and interpersonal harmony and, if anything, are even more rigidly controlling than parents of other ethnicities (Greenberger & Chen, 1996; Uba, 1994). Yet, this seemingly authoritarian parenting may mean something quite different for children of East Asian

Box 11.1 *Developmental Issues*

Family Instability, Homelessness, and Child Development

As we have noted throughout the text, children raised in economically disadvantaged families, particularly those who have experienced poverty for long periods, are at greater risk than children whose economic needs are met of displaying a variety of substandard developmental outcomes: cognitive deficiencies and poor academic achievement, anxiety and depression, low self-worth, conduct disorders during childhood, and aggressive/antisocial behaviors by early adolescence. Clearly, the nonnurturent/uninvolved parenting often seen in economically distressed families helps to explain these outcomes. Yet, there are other correlates of economic disadvantage that may be implicated as well.

Family Instability

One such correlate is *family instability*. When developmentalists talk about family instability, they are referring to circumstances that challenge the daily continuity and cohesiveness of a child's family life—such factors as (1) many changes in residence, (2) a primary caregiver's having had many intimate partners, (3) living in many family arrangements (for example, with a parent, with grandparents, in foster care, etc.), and (4) experiencing many negative life events (for example, serious illnesses, deaths of close relatives, job losses by parents). Although families within any social class vary with respect to how "stable" they are, all the above indicators of family instability are more commonly experienced by the economically disadvantaged segments of society (Coll et al., 1996).

Recently, Brian Ackerman and his associates (1999) used the above indexes to assess the stability/instability of more than 300 economically disadvantaged families. They were seeking to determine whether family instability was associated with any emotional problems and conduct disorders displayed by the families' 5-year-old preschool and 7-year-old first-grade children, even after controlling for the type of parenting these children had received. The results clearly implicated family instability as a potential contributor to developmental difficulties. Specifically, children from the more unstable families displayed more *externalizing* problems (for example, aggression and disobedient/antisocial conduct) as 5-year-olds and more *internalizing* disorders (for example, anxiety, depression, social withdrawal) as 7-year-olds. So even when economically disadvantaged children receive adequate parenting, they remain at risk of displaying behavioral problems if their family lives are otherwise highly unstable.

Homelessness

One kind of family instability that may seem horrifying to those of us who grew up in stable families is the plight of those who do not have a place of their own to call "home." In any given year, nearly 750,000 school-age American children are homeless at least part of the time (U.S. Department of Education, 1995). Although we have all seen televised examples of homeless nuclear families living in cars or camped out in parks or highway rest stops, the typical homeless family is a single mother in her 20s and her one or two children who are residing in a public shelter. How does homelessness affect developing children and adolescents?

To date, we have little research bearing on this question. However, John Buckner and his associates (1999) have recently compared the behavioral profiles of homeless children age 6 and older to those of other economically disadvantaged age-mates who had never been homeless. After controlling for other variables that might influence the type of parenting children had received (for example, maternal stress), Brucker and associates found that homeless children living in shelters scored notably higher on such *internalizing* behaviors as anxiety/depression, socially withdrawn behavior, and somatic complaints than did other impoverished children who had never been homeless. It is likely that homelessness contributes to these internalizing disorders because children living in shelters may be painfully aware of the negative social stigma associated with homelessness, are shamed by being homeless, and are ostracized by peers, thus coming to feel depressed, self-critical, and low in self-worth.

In sum, family instabilities (including homelessness) may clearly contribute to the less than optimal patterns of development that economically disadvantaged children often display. Unfortunately, many U.S. public assistance programs have recently been cut back in the name of welfare reform—an action that raises the threat of increased economic distress, family instabilities, and homelessness among poor families, particularly those headed by single mothers. As Buckner and associates (1999) point out, adequate economic assistance to needy families (for example, food stamps, housing subsidies, and child care that would allow parents to hold jobs) is absolutely essential if poor children are to have stable homes and/or to avoid the many harmful consequences of growing up under extreme conditions of poverty.

ancestry than for European-Americans. Ruth Chao (1994) notes, for example, that Chinese children perform very well in school even though their parents are highly authoritarian rather than authoritative. In Chinese culture, parents believe that strictness is the best way to express love for children and to train them properly; and children accept long-standing cultural values specifying that they obey elders and honor their families. Thus, an "authoritarian" style that may be too controlling to work well for European-Americans appears highly effective indeed in China (and among Asian immigrant families in the United States; see Fuligni, 1997; Huntsinger, Jose, & Larson, 1998).

Although it is difficult to summarize the diversity of child-rearing practices that characterize African-American families, research suggests that young Black mothers (particularly if they are single and less educated) are inclined to demand strict obedience from their children and to use coercive forms of discipline to ensure that they get it (Kelley et al., 1992; Ogbu, 1994). Were we to quickly assume (as researchers did for years) that one particular pattern of parenting (authoritative) is superior to all others, then we might be tempted to conclude that the *no nonsense* style often seen in Black families is maladaptive. Yet, this somewhat coercive and controlling pattern of parenting may actually be *highly adaptive* for many young mothers who lack caregiving support if it protects children who reside in dangerous neighborhoods from becoming victims of crime (Ogbu, 1994) or from associating with antisocial peers (Mason et al., 1996). In fact, use of coercive discipline within the normal range does not foster heightened aggression and antisocial conduct in African-American youth in the same way it does for European-Americans, possibly because it may be viewed by African-American children as a sign of caring and concern rather than a symptom of parental hostility (Deater-Deckard & Dodge, 1997). Furthermore, this "no nonsense" parenting, which falls somewhere in between the authoritarian and authoritative styles, is adaptive in other ways, for African-American children who are treated in this way tend to be cognitive and socially competent youngsters who display little anxiety, depression, or other internalizing disorders (Brody & Flor, 1998).

Considering the findings we have reviewed, one must be careful *not* to assume that a "middle-class" pattern of authoritative parenting that seems to promote favorable outcomes in many contexts is necessarily the most adaptive pattern for all ecological niches. In fact, an authoritative style that fosters curiosity, independence, and individual accomplishments may actually represent "incompetent" parenting among the Temne of Sierra Leone, a collectivist society in which everyone must pull together and suppress individualism if the community is to successfully plant, harvest, and ration the meager crops on which its livelihood absolutely depends (Berry, 1967). And since many children from Western societies will choose a career within the so-called blue-collar economy, it hardly seems reasonable to conclude that a lower-SES pattern of child rearing that prepares them for this undertaking is in some way deficient or "incompetent."

In sum, development always takes place in a cultural or subcultural context, and no single pattern of child rearing is the optimal pattern for all cultures and subcultures. Louis Laosa (1981, p. 159) makes this same point, noting that "indigenous patterns of child care throughout the world represent largely successful adaptations to conditions of life that have long differed from one people to another. [Adults] are 'good [parents]' by the only relevant standards, those of their own culture."

THE QUEST FOR AUTONOMY: RENEGOTIATING THE PARENT/CHILD RELATIONSHIP DURING ADOLESCENCE

One of the most important developmental tasks that adolescents face is to achieve a mature and healthy sense of **autonomy.** This complex attribute has two major components: (1) *emotional autonomy,* or an ability to serve as one's own source of emotional strength rather than childishly depending on parents to provide comfort, reassurance, and emotional security, and (2) *behavioral autonomy,* or an ability to make one's own decisions, to govern one's own affairs, and to take care of oneself (Steinberg, 1996). If adolescents are to "make it" as adults, they can't be rushing home for loving hugs after every little setback. Nor can they continue to rely on parents to get them to work on time or to remind them of their duties and obligations.

So what happens within the family system as children mature and begin to act more autonomously? Sparks fly! In cultures as diverse as China and the United States, conflicts between parents and children about self-governance issues become much more common early in adolescence and gradually decline in frequency (though not necessarily in intensity) throughout the teenage years (Holmbeck & Hill, 1991; Laursen, Coy, & Collins, 1998; Yau & Smetana, 1996). These squabbles, which occur about equally often in families that have immigrated from collectivist cultures as in European-American homes (see Fuligni, 1998), are usually neither prolonged nor severe, often centering around such issues as the adolescent's physical appearance, her choice of friends, or her neglect of schoolwork and household chores. And much of the friction stems from the different perspectives that parents and adolescents adopt. Parents view conflicts through a moral or *social-conventional* lens, feeling that they have a responsibility to monitor and regulate their child's conduct, whereas the adolescent, locked in his quest for autonomy, views his nagging parents as infringing on *personal* rights and choices (Smetana, 1995; Yau & Smetana, 1996). As teenagers continue to assert themselves and parents slowly loosen the reins, the parent/child relationship gradually evolves from an enterprise in which the parent was dominant to one in which parents and adolescents are on a more equal footing (Feldman & Gehring, 1988; Furman & Burhmester, 1992). Yet Chinese and Asian-American parents tend to exert their authority far longer than European-American parents do (Greenberger & Chen, 1996; Yau & Smetana, 1996), a practice that often bothers and may depress Asian-American adolescents (Greenberger & Chen, 1996).

Researchers once believed that the most adaptive route to establishing autonomy was for adolescents to separate from parents by cutting the emotional cords. Indeed, teenagers who perceive their relationships with parents to be very conflictual and nonsupportive do appear to be better adjusted when they distance themselves from their families and become emotionally autonomous (Fuhrman & Holmbeck, 1995). Yet adolescents who are warmly received at home would be ill-advised to cut the emotional cords, for those who gradually achieve more autonomy while maintaining *close attachments* to family members display the best overall pattern of psychosocial adjustment (Lamborn & Steinberg, 1993; Steinberg, 1996).

PHOTO 11.5 As adolescents begin their quest for autonomy, conflicts with parents become more commonplace.

Encouraging Autonomy How might parents successfully promote adolescent autonomy and healthy psychological outcomes? It seems that parents of well-adjusted adolescents gradually relinquish control as their teenagers display a readiness to accept more responsibility; but they also continue to monitor their adolescents' conduct and demand more in the way of self-governance as well (Lamborn et al., 1991; Youniss & Smoller, 1985). Furthermore, parents of well-adjusted adolescents keep their rules and regulations to a reasonable minimum, strive to explain them, and continue to be

autonomy: the capacity to make decisions independently, to serve as one's own source of emotional strength, and to otherwise manage one's life tasks without depending on others for assistance; an important developmental task of adolescence.

warm and supportive, even in the face of the inevitable conflicts that arise (Steinberg, 1996). Does this parenting style sound familiar? It should, for this winning combination of parental acceptance and a pattern of flexible control that is neither too lax nor overly restrictive is an *authoritative* approach—the same style that fosters high self-esteem and solid academic performances in childhood and healthy identity outcomes later in adolescence. (Indeed, becoming appropriately autonomous seems to be a necessary prerequisite for achieving a stable personal identity). It is mainly when parents react negatively to a teenager's push for autonomy and become overly strict or overly permissive that adolescents are likely to experience personal distress or to rebel and to get into trouble (Barber, Olsen, & Shagle, 1994; Fuhrman & Holmbeck, 1995; Lamborn et al., 1991). Of course, we must remind ourselves that socialization within the family is a matter of reciprocal influence, and that it may be much easier for a parent to respond authoritatively to a responsible, levelheaded adolescent than to one who is rude, hostile, and unruly.

In sum, conflicts and power struggles are an almost inevitable consequence of an adolescent's quest for autonomy. Yet most teenagers and their parents are able to resolve these differences while maintaining positive feelings for one another as they renegotiate their relationship so that it becomes more equal (Furman & Buhrmester, 1992). As a result, young autonomy seekers become more self-reliant while also developing a more "friendlike" attachment to their parents.

Might an adolescent's experiences in the world of work help to foster a healthy sense of autonomy? Box 11.2 on pages 374–375 explores this issue.

The Influence of Siblings and Sibling Relationships

Although families are getting smaller, the majority of American children still grow up with at least one sibling, and there is certainly no shortage of speculation about the roles that brothers and sisters play in a child's life. Many parents, distressed by the fighting and bickering that their children display, often fear that such rivalrous conduct will undermine the growth of children's prosocial concern and their ability to get along with others. At the same time, the popular wisdom is that only children are likely to be lonely, overindulged "brats" who would profit both socially and emotionally from having siblings to teach them that they are not nearly as "special" as they think they are (Falbo, 1992).

Although rivalries among siblings are certainly commonplace, we will see that siblings can play some very positive roles in a child's life, often serving as caregivers, teachers, playmates, and confidants. And yet, we will also see that only children may not be nearly as disadvantaged by their lack of sibling relationships as people have commonly assumed.

CHANGES IN THE FAMILY SYSTEMS WHEN A NEW BABY ARRIVES

Judy Dunn and Carol Kendrick (1982; see also Dunn, 1993) have studied how firstborn children adapt to a new baby, and the account they provide is not an entirely cheerful one. After the baby arrives, mothers typically devote less warm and playful attention to their older child, who may respond to this perceived "neglect" by becoming difficult and disruptive and less securely attached, particularly if he or she is 2 years of age or older and can more readily appreciate that an "exclusive" relationship with caregivers has been undermined by the baby's birth (Teti et al., 1996). Clearly, older children often resent losing the mother's attention and may harbor animosities toward

Box 11.2 *Developmental Issues*

Does Part-Time Employment Foster a Healthy Sense of Autonomy (and Positive Developmental Outcomes)?

More than 60% of high school students in the United States work part time, and it is reasonable to assume that their work experiences could have any number of effects on their development. On the positive side, Michael Shanahan and his associates (1996) find that the money teenagers make often fosters a sense of self-efficacy and economic autonomy. Other investigators have reported that working youth feel they have become more punctual, dependable, responsible, and self-reliant as a result of having held a job (see Mortimer et al., 1996, for a review). However, some potential disadvantages of adolescent employment have been reported as well.

Lawrence Steinberg and his associates have compared working and nonworking youth on such outcome measures as their autonomy from parents, academic performances, psychological adjustment, and involvement in delinquent activities (Greenberger & Steinberg, 1986; Steinberg & Dornbusch, 1991; Steinberg, Fegley, & Dornbusch, 1993). Overall, this research reports far more bad news than good about teenagers who work, particularly about those who work more than 20 hours per week during the school year. Specifically, adolescents who worked such long hours had much more autonomy over day-to-day decisions than age-mates who worked 10 hours a week or less. Yet, this greater autonomy seemed to be directed toward "cutting the cords" to parents, for teenagers who were heavily invested in work were much less involved in family activities and were monitored less

closely by older family members. And the psychological and behavioral correlates of all this freedom were downright gloomy. Compared with peers who worked 10 hours a week or less, teenagers who worked 20 or more hours a week were lower in self-esteem, made lower grades at school, and reported higher levels of anxiety, depression, and somatic complaints (for example headaches, stomachaches), and more frequent involvement in alcohol and drug use and other delinquent activities. So would adolescents be better off by avoiding employment, if possible, and by concentrating on their schooling?

Not necessarily. Critics have argued that working may look like such a negative influence because the adolescents who worked long hours in the earlier reports often came from nonsupportive home environments or were already experiencing academic (or other) difficulties that may have *caused* them to separate from parents and to seek greater involvement in the world of work. In other words, their preexisting problems, rather than their heavy work involvement, could have been the primary contributor to their poor psychosocial outcomes. In agreement with earlier reports, Michael Shanahan and his associates (1996) found that younger (7th to 10th grade) working youth spent less time with their families and were monitored less closely than were nonworking peers. Yet, within this rural sample, adolescent employment was associated with more sharing of advice with older family members and with *improved* emotional relationships with

the baby for stealing it; their own difficult behavior may make matters worse by alienating their parents.

Thus, **sibling rivalry**—a spirit of competition, jealousy, or resentment between siblings—often begins as soon as a younger brother or sister arrives. How can it be minimized? The adjustment process is easier if the first-born had secure relationships with both parents before the baby arrived and continues to enjoy close ties afterward (Dunn & Kendrick, 1982; Volling & Belsky, 1992). Parents are advised to continue to provide love and attention to their older children and to maintain their normal routines as much as possible. It also helps to encourage older children to become aware of the baby's needs and assist in the care of their new brother or sister (Dunn & Kendrick, 1982; Howe & Ross, 1990). Yet Dunn and Kendrick (1982) find that parents may have to walk a thin line between two traps: becoming so attentive to the new baby that they deprive the older child of attention, and becoming so indulgent

sibling rivalry: the spirit of competition, jealousy, and resentment that may arise between two or more siblings.

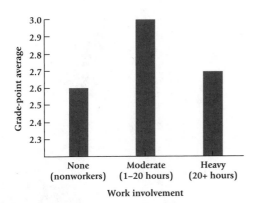

Grade-point averages of high school seniors as a function of work involvement. Notice that students who worked a moderate amount made the best grades and that even the students who were heavily invested in work performed just as well as their nonworking peers. (Adapted from Mortimer et al., 1996.)

them. In another four-year longitudinal study of 1,000 high school students that controlled for such other variables as family background and prior academic performance that might influence developmental outcomes, Jeylen Mortimer and associates (1996) found that working 20 hours or more per week did *not* undermine teenagers' academic achievement, self-esteem, or other aspects of their psychological adjustment. In fact, the figure shows that high school seniors who worked a moderate number (1 to 20) of hours per week actually made better grades than those who didn't work. The sole cause

for concern was that high school seniors who worked more than 20 hours a week used alcohol more frequently than those who were not employed.

Clearly, the question of whether adolescents are affected positively or negatively by their working experiences is a complex one, although it now seems that even a heavy work involvement need not be harmful. Some developmentalists believe that adolescents are much more likely to benefit from challenging jobs that provide opportunities for self-direction and decision making than from menial, repetitive fast-food or manual labor positions that require few academic skills and do little to foster a sense of self-efficacy or self-esteem. Indeed, Michael Shanahan and his associates (1991; Call, Mortimer, & Shanahan, 1995) found that adolescent boys displayed clear increases in mastery motivation and became less depressed when the work they performed offered opportunities for advancement and provided skills that would be useful in the future. By contrast, boys showed declines in mastery motivation and became more depressed while working menial jobs with demands that conflicted with their involvement in school. So whether working fosters a healthy sense of autonomy and has positive or negative effects on adolescent adjustment may depend far more on the *quality* of adolescents' work experiences than the quantity of work they perform.

of the first-born that he or she becomes a "spoiled brat" who resents any competition from the younger sibling.

SIBLING RELATIONSHIPS OVER THE COURSE OF CHILDHOOD

Fortunately, most older siblings adjust fairly quickly to having a new brother or sister, becoming much less anxious and less inclined to display the problem behaviors that they showed early on. But even in the best of sibling relationships, conflict is normal. Indeed, Judy Dunn (1993) reports that the number of minor skirmishes between very young siblings can range as high as 56 per hour! Actual confrontations often become more frequent and intense once the younger sib reaches 18 to 24 months of age and is better at "holding his own" by hitting or teasing the older sib or by directing a parent's attention to the older sib's misconduct (Dunn & Munn, 1985).

Although rivalrous conduct among siblings occurs throughout the preschool and grade-school years, researchers who have observed siblings at home find that their interactions are more often positive and supportive than oppositional and conflictual (Abramovitch et al., 1986; Baskett & Johnson, 1982). There are some reliable differences in the behavior of older and younger siblings, with older siblings often becoming the more domineering and aggressive parties, and younger siblings the more compliant ones (Abramovitch et al., 1986; Erel, Margolin, & John, 1998). Yet, older sibs also initiate more helpful, playful, and other prosocial behaviors, a finding that may reflect the pressure parents place on them to demonstrate their maturity by caring for a younger brother or sister.

In some ways, sibling relationships are truly paradoxical because they are often both *close* and *conflictual* (Furman & Buhrmester, 1985). Grade-school siblings who are similar in age report more warmth and closeness than other sibling pairs—but, at the same time, more friction and conflict! Yet grade-school children consistently say that their sibling relationships are as important or more important to them than their relationships with friends (Furman & Buhrmester, 1985), and highly aggressive children or those who are otherwise socially unskilled are much better adjusted if they have maintained close ties with their siblings (Dunn et al., 1994; East & Rook, 1992; Stormshak et al., 1996).

PHOTO 11.6 Coercive and rivalrous conduct between siblings is a normal aspect of family life.

Parents clearly influence just how smooth or stormy the sibling relationship becomes. Brothers and sisters are more likely to get along if their parents get along (Dunn, 1993). Indeed, marital conflict is most likely to predict conflictual interactions among siblings if (1) the older child already has a shaky, insecure relationship with his or her mother who (2) is inclined to use power-assertive discipline (Erel et al., 1998). Marital conflict may put children on edge and contribute directly to emotional insecurity (Davies & Cummings, 1998), whereas parental use of power-assertive discipline may communicate to more powerful older sibs that dominating or other forceful strategies are the way one deals with associates (particularly smaller, less powerful associates) who displease them.

Sibling relationships are also friendlier and less conflictual if mothers and fathers respond warmly and sensitively to *all* their children and do not consistently favor one child over the other (Brody, Stoneman, & McCoy, 1994; McHale et al., 1995). Younger siblings are particularly sensitive to unequal treatment, often reacting negatively and displaying adjustment problems if they perceive that the older sib is favored by parents (McHale et al., 1995; Tarullo et al., 1995). It is not that older siblings are unaffected by differential treatment; but because they are older, they are usually better able to understand that siblings may have different needs and that unequal treatment may be justified, even if that means parents may sometimes favor a younger sib in certain respects (Kowal & Kramer, 1997).

As is true of parent/child relationships, sibling relationships become much more egalitarian during the adolescent years. Siblings now quarrel less frequently and their relationships otherwise become less intense, probably because teenagers are spending less time with brothers and sisters who are, after all, part of the family from whom they want to develop some autonomy (Furman & Buhrmester, 1992; Larson et al., 1996). But even though they are immersing themselves in close friendships and romantic relationships, adolescents continue to perceive their siblings as important and intimate associates—people to whom they can turn for support and companionship, despite the fact that relations with them have often been rather stormy (Buhrmester & Furman, 1990; Furman & Buhrmester, 1992).

Perhaps these seemingly paradoxical data make perfectly good sense if we reexamine the findings on the nature of sibling/sibling interactions. Yes, rivalries and conflicts among siblings are a very normal part of family life, but the observational record consistently shows that brothers and sisters often do nice things for one another and that these acts of kindness and affection are typically much more common than hateful or rivalrous conduct (Abramovitch et al., 1986; Baskett & Johnson, 1982).

POSITIVE CONTRIBUTIONS OF SIBLING RELATIONSHIPS

What positive roles might siblings play in one another's lives? One important contribution that older siblings make is to provide *caretaking* services for younger brothers and sisters. Indeed, one survey of child-rearing practices in 186 societies found that older children were the principal caregivers for infants and toddlers in 57% of the groups studied (Weisner & Gallimore, 1977). Even in industrialized societies such as the United States, older siblings (particularly girls) are often asked to look after their younger brothers and sisters (McHale & Gamble, 1989). Of course, their role as caregivers provides older children opportunities to influence their younger siblings in many ways, by serving as their teachers, playmates, and advocates, and as important sources of emotional security.

Siblings as Attachment Objects   Do infants become attached to older brothers and sisters, viewing them as providers of security? To find out, Robert Stewart (1983) exposed 10- to 20-month-old infants to a variation of Ainsworth's "Strange Situation." Each infant was left with a 4-year-old sibling in a strange room that a strange adult soon entered. The infants typically showed signs of distress as their mothers departed, and they were wary in the company of the stranger. Stewart noted that these distressed infants would often approach their older brother or sister, particularly when the stranger first appeared. And most of the 4-year-olds offered some sort of comforting or caregiving to their baby brothers and sisters. Other investigators have replicated these findings and shown that the older children who are most inclined to comfort a distressed infant or toddler sibling are those who are securely attached to their mothers (Teti & Ablard, 1989) and have developed the role-taking skills to understand why their younger brother or sister is distressed (Garner, Jones, & Palmer, 1994; Stewart & Marvin, 1984). Furthermore, infants are likely to venture much farther away to explore a strange environment if an attentive older sibling is nearby to serve as a "secure base" for exploration (Samuels, 1980; Stewart & Marvin, 1984). So it does seem as if older siblings can become important sources of emotional support who help younger sibs to cope with uncertain situations when parents are not around. And these sibling attachments can be quite meaningful over the long run, for as we have noted, a secure tie to a sibling can help to prevent the anxiety and adjustment problems that grade-school children often display if they are ignored or rejected by their peers (East & Rook, 1992; Stormshak et al., 1996).

Siblings as Models and Tutors   In addition to the caretaking and emotional support they may provide, older siblings often teach new skills to younger brothers and sisters, either by modeling these competencies or by providing direct instruction. Even toddlers are quite attentive to older sibs, often choosing to imitate their behaviors or taking over toys that they have abandoned (Abramovitch, Corter, & Pepler, 1980). Younger children tend to admire their older siblings, who continue to serve as important models and tutors throughout childhood (Buhrmester & Furman, 1990). Given a problem to master, children are likely to learn more when they have an older sibling available to guide them than when they have access to an equally competent older peer (Azmitia & Hesser, 1993). Why? Because (1) older siblings feel a greater responsibility to teach if the pupil is a younger *sibling,* (2) they provide more detailed instructions and encouragement than older peers do, and (3) younger children are more inclined to seek the older sibling's guidance. This kind of informal instruction clearly pays off: When older siblings play school with younger brothers and sisters, teaching them such lessons as the ABCs, younger siblings have an easier time learning to read (Norman-Jackson, 1982). And older siblings who often tutor younger ones may profit as well, for they score higher on tests of academic aptitude than peers who have not had these tutoring experiences (Paulhus & Shaffer, 1981; Smith, 1990).

Siblings as Contributors to Social-Cognitive Understandings   Finally, the sheer frequency and intensity of sibling interactions imply that these contacts may foster the growth of many social-cognitive competencies. In Chapter 6, for example, we learned that playful interactions among siblings contribute to children's understanding of false beliefs and to the emergence of a belief-desire theory of mind. Furthermore, siblings are not at all shy about communicating their wants, needs, and emotional reactions to conflict, thus providing each other with information that fosters the growth of perspective-taking skills, emotional understanding, a capacity for negotiation and compromise, and more mature forms of moral reasoning (Dunn et al., 1995; Herrera & Dunn, 1997; Howe, Petrakos, & Rinaldi, 1998). Clearly, there are many ways in which children may benefit from their experiences with siblings.

PHOTO 11.7   Older siblings often serve as teachers for their younger brothers and sisters.

CHARACTERISTICS OF ONLY CHILDREN

Are "only" children who grow up without siblings the spoiled, selfish, overindulged brats that people often presume them to be? Hardly! Two major reviews of hundreds of pertinent studies found that only children are (1) relatively high, on average, in self-esteem and achievement motivation, (2) more obedient and slightly more intellectually competent than children with siblings, and (3) likely to establish very good relations with peers (Falbo, 1992; Falbo & Polit, 1986). Since only children enjoy an exclusive relationship with their parents, they may receive more quality time from adults and more direct achievement training than children with siblings do, perhaps explaining their tendency to be relatively friendly, well-behaved, and instrumentally competent (Baskett, 1985). Furthermore, these singletons have no younger sibs that they can dominate and may soon learn that they must negotiate and be accommodating if they hope to play successfully with *peer* playmates, most of whom are probably at least as powerful as they are.

Might these findings simply reflect the fact that parents who choose to have only one child differ systematically from those who have more children? Probably not. In 1979, the People's Republic of China implemented a one-child family policy in an attempt to control its burgeoning population. Regardless of the number of children parents may have wanted, most Chinese couples, in urban areas at least, have been limited to one child. Contrary to the fears of many critics, there is no evidence that China's one-child policy has produced a generation of spoiled, self-centered brats who behave like "little emperors." Only children in China closely resemble only children in Western countries, scoring slightly higher than children with siblings on measures of intelligence and academic achievement and showing few meaningful differences in personality (Falbo & Posten, 1993; Jaio, Ji, & Jing, 1996). In fact, only children in China actually report less anxiety and depression than children with siblings do, a finding that may reflect China's social condemnation of multichild families and only children's tendency to taunt children with siblings with such remarks as "You shouldn't be here" or "Your parents should have only one child" (Yang et al., 1995).

So evidence from very different cultural settings suggests that only children are hardly disadvantaged by having no brothers and sisters. Apparently, many singletons are able to gain through their friendships and peer alliances whatever they may miss by not having siblings at home.

Diversity in Family Life

As we noted earlier in the chapter, modern families are more diverse today than ever before: The *majority* of our children are growing up in dual-career, single-parent, or blended families that may be very different from the two-parent, single-breadwinner aggregation with two or more children that people often think of as the typical family unit. So let's examine some of these variations in family life.

ADOPTIVE FAMILIES

If one member of the pair is infertile, couples who hope to become parents often seek to adopt a child. Yet those who are successful in adopting may face many challenges. For example, adults who remain distressed about their own infertility may have some difficulties relating to adoptive children (Burns, 1990; Humphrey & Humphrey, 1988). However, the clear majority of adoptive parents develop strong emotional ties to their adoptees (Levy-Shiff et al., 1991), and it now appears as if an adult's desire to be a parent is much more important to a child's outcomes than the adult's genetic ties (or lack thereof) to his or her children (Golombok et al., 1995). Nevertheless, since adoptive parents and their children share no genes, the rearing environments adoptive parents provide may not be as closely compatible with an adoptee's own genetic predispositions as they are for a biological child. These environmental incompatibilities, coupled with the fact that many adoptees have been neglected or abused prior to their adoptions, or have other special needs (Kirchner, 1998), may help to explain why adoptees display more learning difficulties and emotional problems than their nonadopted peers later in childhood and adolescence (Sharma, McGue, & Benson, 1998; Verhulst & Versluis-Den Bieman, 1995).

Don't misunderstand. Adopted children typically fare much better in adoptive homes than in foster care, where their foster parents may not be very invested in them or their long-range prospects (Bohman & Sigvardsson, 1990). Even *transracially adopted* children from lower-socioeconomic backgrounds usually fare quite well intellectually and academically and often display healthy patterns of psychosocial adjustment when raised in supportive, relatively affluent middle-class adoptive homes (Brodzinsky et al., 1987; DeBerry et al., 1996; Sharma et al., 1998). So adoption is a quite satisfactory arrangement for most adoptive parents and their adoptees.

Adoption practices in the United States are changing from a confidential system, in which the identities of the birth mother and adoptive parents are withheld from each other, to a more open system that allows for varying amounts of direct or indirect contact between birth mothers and members of adoptive families. Since adoptees are often curious about their biological origins and may be upset about the prospect of never knowing their birth parents, more open arrangements may prove beneficial to them. Preliminary research with 5- to 13-year-old adoptees reveals that children (particularly the older ones) are both more curious and more satisfied with information about their roots when they could share information or even have contact with their birth mothers (Wrobel et al., 1996); yet there was no evidence in this study that providing information about birth mothers had such harmful effects as confusing children about the meaning of adoption or undermining their self-esteem, as some critics of open adoption policies had feared.

GAY AND LESBIAN FAMILIES

In the United States, several million gay men or lesbians are parents, most through previous heterosexual marriages, although some have adopted children or conceived through donor insemination (Flaks et al., 1995; Chan, Raboy, & Patterson, 1998). Historically, many courts have been so opposed to the prospect of lesbians and gay men raising children that they have denied the petitions of homosexual parents in child custody hearings solely on the basis of these parents' sexual orientations. Among the concerns people have are that gay and lesbian parents may be less mentally healthy or that they will molest their children who, in turn, are at risk of being stigmatized by peers because of their parents' sexual orientations. But perhaps the greatest concern is the fear that children raised by gay or lesbian parents are likely to become gay or lesbian themselves (Bailey et al., 1995).

Interestingly, there is virtually no basis for any of these speculations. As shown in Figure 11.5, more than 90% of adult children of lesbian mothers or gay fathers develop a heterosexual orientation—a figure that is not significantly different from the percentages of heterosexuals raised by heterosexual parents. Furthermore, children of gay and lesbian parents are just as cognitively, emotionally, and morally mature, on average, and are otherwise as well adjusted as children of heterosexual parents (Chan et al., 1998; Flaks et al., 1995; Patterson, 1995b). Finally, gay fathers and lesbian mothers are every bit as knowledgeable about effective child-rearing techniques as heterosexual parents are (Bigner & Jacobsen, 1989; Flaks et al., 1995), and partners of homosexual parents are usually attached to the children and assume some caregiving responsibilities. In fact, lesbian mothers are happiest and their children somewhat better adjusted when child-care responsibilities are more evenly distributed between the biological parent and her partner (Patterson, 1995a).

In sum, there is no credible scientific evidence that would justify denying a person's rights of parenthood on the basis of his or her sexual orientation. Aside from the possibility of being stigmatized by their parent's lifestyle, children raised in gay and lesbian families are virtually indistinguishable from those of heterosexual couples.

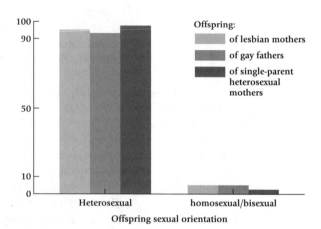

FIGURE 11.5 Sexual orientation of adult children raised by lesbian mothers, gay fathers, and single-parent heterosexual mothers. (Notice that children with homosexual parents are just as likely to display a heterosexual orientation as children raised by heterosexuals.) (Adapted from Bailey et al., 1995; Golombok & Tasker, 1996.)

THE IMPACTS OF FAMILY CONFLICT AND DIVORCE

Earlier we noted that about half of today's marriages will end in divorce and that as many as 60% of all children born in the 1980s and 1990s will spend some time (about five years, on average) in a single-parent home—usually one headed by the mother (Hetherington et al., 1998; Teegartin, 1994). What effects might a divorce have on developing children? As we address this issue, let's first note that divorce is *not* a singular life event; instead, it represents a series of stressful experiences for the entire family that often begins with marital conflict before the actual separation and includes a multitude of life changes afterward. As Mavis Hetherington and Kathleen Camara (1984) see it, families must often cope with "the diminution of family resources, changes in residence, assumption of new roles and responsibilities, establishment of new patterns of [family] interaction, reorganization of routines . . . , and [possibly] the introduction of new relationships [that is, stepparent/child and stepsibling relationships] into the existing family" (p. 398).

Before the Divorce: Exposure to Marital Conflict The period prior to divorce is often accompanied by a dramatic rise in family conflict that may include many heated verbal arguments and even physical violence between parents. How are children influenced by their exposure to marital conflict? A growing body of evidence indicates that they often become extremely distressed and that continuing conflict at home increases the likelihood that children will have hostile, aggressive interactions with siblings and peers (Cummings & Davies, 1994). Furthermore, regular exposure to marital discord is a contributor to a number of other child and adolescent adjustment problems, including anxiety, depression, and externalizing conduct disorders (Davies & Cummings, 1998; Fincham, 1998; Harold et al., 1997; McCloskey, Figueredo, & Koss, 1995). Marital discord can have both *direct effects* on children and adolescents, by putting them on edge emotionally and undermining the maturity of their behavior, and *indirect effects,* by undermining parental acceptance/sensitivity and the quality of the parent-child relationship (Erel & Burman, 1995; Harold et al., 1997). So conflict-ridden homes are not healthy contexts for child or adolescent development, and longitudinal research indicates that children in strife-ridden homes will often fare better in the long run if their parents separate or divorce (Amato, Loomis, & Booth, 1995; Hetherington et al., 1998). Nevertheless, we will see that divorce can be a highly unsettling experience that has its own effects on the well-being of all family members. Indeed, this family transition often strikes hardest at children who had rarely been exposed to overt conflict prior to their parent's separation (Hetherington et al., 1998; Simons, 1996).

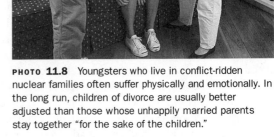

PHOTO 11.8 Youngsters who live in conflict-ridden nuclear families often suffer physically and emotionally. In the long run, children of divorce are usually better adjusted than those whose unhappily married parents stay together "for the sake of the children."

Immediate Effects of Divorce: Crisis and Reorganization Most families going through a divorce experience a *crisis period* of a year or more in which the lives of all family members are seriously disrupted (Booth & Amato, 1991; Hetherington, Cox, & Cox, 1982; Hetherington & Stanley-Hagan, 1997; Simons, et al., 1996). Typically, both parents experience emotional as well as practical difficulties. The mother, who obtains custody of any children in about 83% of divorcing families, may feel angry, depressed, lonely, or otherwise distressed, although often relieved as well. The father is also likely to be distressed, particularly if he did not seek the divorce and feels shut off from his children. Having just become single adults, both parents often feel isolated from former married friends and other bases of social support on which they relied as marrieds. Divorced women with children usually face the added problem of getting by with less money—about 50% to 75% of the family income they had before, on average (Bianchi, Subaiya, & Kahn, 1997). And life may seem especially difficult if they must move to a lower-income neighborhood and try to work and raise young children single-handedly (Emery & Forehand, 1994).

As you might suspect, psychologically distressed adults do not make the best parents. Hetherington and her associates (1982, 1998) find that custodial mothers, overwhelmed by responsibilities and by their own emotional reactions to divorce, often become edgy, impatient, and insensitive to their children's needs; as a result, they frequently begin to rely on coercive methods of child rearing. Indeed, divorced mothers often appear (to their children, at least) to have been transformed into more hostile, less caring parents (Fauber et al., 1990). Meanwhile, noncustodial fathers are likely to change in a different way, becoming somewhat overpermissive and indulging during visits with their children.

Perhaps you can imagine how these changes in parenting are likely to be received. Children of divorce, who are often anxious, angry, or depressed by the family breakup, may react by becoming whiney and argumentative, disobedient, and downright disrespectful. Parent/child relationships during this crisis phase are best described as a vicious circle in which the child's emotional distress and problem behaviors and the adult's ineffective parenting styles feed on each other and make everyone's life unpleasant (Baldwin & Skinner, 1989). However, children's initial reactions to divorce vary somewhat as a function of their ages, temperaments, and sex.

Children's Age   Younger, cognitively immature preschool and early grade-school children often display the most visible signs of distress as a divorce unfolds. They may not understand why their parents have divorced and are even inclined to feel guilty if they think they are somehow responsible for the breakup of their families (Hetherington, 1989). Older children and adolescents are better able to understand the personality conflicts and lack of caring that may lead distressed parents to divorce and to resolve any loyalty conflicts that may arise; however, they often remain highly distressed over their parents' divorce and may react by withdrawing from family members and becoming more involved in such undesirable peer-sponsored activities as truancy, sexual misconduct, substance abuse, and other forms of delinquent behavior (Amato, 1993; Hetherington et al., 1998). So even though they are better able to comprehend the reasons for the parents' divorce and to feel less responsible for having caused it, older children and adolescents seem to suffer no less than younger children do (Amato, 1993; Hetherington & Clingempeel, 1992).

Children's Temperament and Sex   The stresses associated with parental conflict and divorce hit particularly hard at temperamentally difficult children, who display more immediate and long-range adjustment problems to these events than easygoing children do (Henry et al., 1996; Hetherington & Clingempeel, 1992). Often the highly volatile behavior of a temperamentally difficult child elicits more coercive forms of parenting from his impatient and highly distressed caregiver which, in turn, represents an extremely "poor fit" with a difficult child's reactive demeanor and contributes substantially to his adjustment difficulties.

Although the finding is by no means universal (see Allison & Furstenberg, 1989), many investigators report that the impact of marital strife and divorce is more powerful and enduring for boys than for girls. Even before a divorce, boys are already displaying more overt behavioral problems than girls are (Block, Block, & Gjerde, 1986, 1988). And at least two early longitudinal studies found that girls had largely recovered from their social and emotional disturbances two years after a divorce, whereas boys, who improved dramatically over this same period, were nevertheless continuing to show signs of emotional stress and problems in their relationships with parents, siblings, teachers, and peers (Hetherington et al., 1982; Wallerstein & Kelly, 1980).

Why might marital turmoil and dissolution strike harder at boys? One explanation is that boys may feel closer to fathers than girls do, so they experience more frustration and a deeper sense of loss when the father is no longer readily available to them (Clarke-Stewart & Hayward, 1996; Lamb, 1997). And because boys are normally more active and less compliant than girls are (see Chapter 8), they may respond more negatively and vigorously to new restrictions imposed by the custodial parent—reactions that often elicit the kinds of coercive discipline that are likely to perpetuate their whiney, surly, and defiant behavior (Hetherington et al., 1982). However, some developmentalists believe that boys look so poorly adjusted because investigators have focused more on overt behavior problems that are easy to detect than on other, more subtle adjustment measures, such as covert psychological distress. Indeed, at least three studies suggest that even prior to a divorce (and for up to 10 years afterward), girls experience more *covert* distress than boys do (Allison & Furstenberg, 1989; Chase-Lansdale, Cherlin, & Kiernan, 1995; Doherty & Needle, 1991). What's more, a disproportionate number of girls from divorced families show precocious sexual activity at adolescence and a persistent lack of self-confidence in their relationships with boys and men (Cherlin, Kiernan, & Chase-Lansdale, 1995; Fernandez, 1997). So divorce seems to affect boys and girls in different ways.

Yet another reason that boys may look bad is that most researchers have limited their studies to the most common custodial arrangement—mother-headed households. Interestingly, those boys whose fathers assume custody fare much better than boys who live with their mothers; in fact, some research even implies that children of both sexes have fewer problems in the custody of fathers than in mother-custody homes (Amato & Keith, 1991; Clarke-Stewart & Hayward, 1996). However, these findings in no way suggest that the typical father is better suited for child-care responsibilities than mothers are. Instead, they probably imply that (1) custodial fathers are a select group of men who are more child-oriented than noncustodial fathers, (2) homes headed by a custodial father are less likely to suffer severe economic declines, and (3) effective coparenting may be more likely in father-custody homes, simply because noncustodial mothers are more inclined than noncustodial fathers to remain actively involved in parenting (Hetherington et al., 1998). The latter point is particularly important, for children in mother-custody homes also fare particularly well if their noncustodial fathers remain involved in their lives and guide them in an authoritative manner (Coley, 1998).

In sum, a divorce can strike very hard at children of either sex. Clearly, we would be overstating the case (not to mention being insensitive to girls) were we to conclude that this disruptive life experience is anything but a struggle for the majority of boys *and* girls.

Long-Term Reactions to Divorce Although many of the emotional and behavioral disturbances that accompany a divorce will diminish considerably over the next two years, there may be aftereffects. Compared to children in harmonious, two-parent families, some children of divorce are still showing signs of academic difficulties and psychological distress through adolescence and into young adulthood (Fernandez, 1997; Chase-Lansdale et al., 1995; Jonsson & Gahler, 1997). However, the vast majority of children from divorced families (approximately 75% to 80%) improve dramatically over time and display healthy patterns of psychological adjustment (Chase-Lansdale et al., 1995; Hetherington et al., 1998).[2]

Nevertheless, even the well-adjusted children of divorce may show some residual effects. In one longitudinal study, children from divorced families were still rather negative in their assessments of the impact of divorce on their lives when interviewed more than 20 years after the breakup of their families (Wallerstein & Lewis, as cited by Fernandez, 1997). Another interesting long-term reaction is that adolescents from divorced families are more likely than those from nondivorced families to fear that their own marriages will be unhappy (Franklin, Janoff-Bulman, & Roberts, 1990; Wallerstein & Blakeslee, 1989). There may well be some basis for this concern, for adults whose parents divorced are more likely than adults from intact families to experience an unhappy marriage and a divorce themselves (Amato, 1996).

In sum, divorce tends to be a most unsettling and troubling life event—one that few children feel very positive about, even after 20 years have elapsed. But despite the gloomy portrait of divorce we have painted here, there are some more encouraging

---

[2]The corresponding percentage of children who show no long-term adjustment problems when reared in nondivorcing homes is 90%—a finding indicating that predivorce family conflict and the experience of a divorce do present significant developmental risks (Hetherington et al., 1998).

Box 11.3 *Applying Developmental Research*

Smoothing the Rocky Road to Recovery from a Divorce

Some individuals adjust rather well to a divorce, whereas others may suffer negative and long-lasting effects. Who is likely to fare well and what factors make the process of adjustment easier for members of divorcing families?

Adequate Financial Support

Divorcing families fare better if they have adequate finances (Hetherington, 1989; Simons et al., 1993). Unfortunately, many mother-headed families experience a precipitous drop in income, which may necessitate a move to a lower-income neighborhood and a mother's return to work at precisely the time her children need stability and increased attention. Furthermore, a lack of money for trips, treats, and other amenities to which children may be accustomed can be a significant contributor to family quarrels and bickering. Unfortunately, only about half of noncustodial fathers pay any child support (Sorenson, 1997), and recent efforts to require noncustodial parents to pay their fair share are a step in the right direction.

Adequate Parenting by the Custodial Parent

The custodial parent obviously plays a crucial role in the family's adjustment to divorce. If he or she can continue to respond in a warm, consistent, and authoritative manner, children are much less likely to experience serious problems (Hetherington & Clingempeel, 1992; Kline et al., 1989). Of course, it is difficult to be an effective parent when one is highly stressed or depressed. Yet both the custodial parent and the children can benefit immensely

from receiving outside social support—not the least important of which is that provided by the *noncustodial* parent.

Social/Emotional Support from the Noncustodial Parent

If divorced parents continue to squabble and are hostile to each other, both are likely to be upset, the custodial parent's parenting is likely to suffer, and children will likely feel "caught in the middle" and torn in their loyalties; these children will probably have difficulties adjusting (Amato, 1993; Buchanan, Maccoby, & Dornbusch, 1991). Recently, the state of Arizona passed a law requiring couples hoping to divorce to complete a 4½-hour seminar to understand the impact of the divorce on their children before their divorce action may proceed (Associated Press, 1996). The purpose of the seminar is to make parents aware that (1) their children are likely to be more traumatized by the parents' postdivorce wrangling than by the separation itself, and (2) *regular contact* with a noncustodial parent who *supports* the custodial guardian in his or her parenting role is a strong contributor to children's positive adjustment to life in a single-parent home (see also Hetherington et al., 1998). Ideally, then, children should be permitted to maintain close, affectionate ties with *both* parents and shielded from any continuing conflict between them (Amato, 1993; Coley, 1998).

Is *joint physical custody* the answer? Obviously, living part of the time in each parent's home does prevent loss of contact with noncustodial fathers, which happens all too often and can be very upsetting to children (Kline et

messages. First, researchers are consistently finding that children in stable, single-parent (or stepparent) homes are usually better adjusted than those who remain in conflict-ridden two-parent families. Indeed, many of the behavior problems that children display after a divorce are actually evident well *before* the divorce and may often be more closely related to long-standing family conflict than to the divorce itself (Amato & Booth, 1996; Cherlin et al., 1991). Take away the marital discord and the breakdown in parenting often associated with divorce, and the experience, while always stressful, need not always be damaging (Amato, 1993). So today's conventional wisdom holds that unhappily married couples who have unreconcilable differences might well *divorce* for the good of the children; that is, children are likely to *benefit* if the ending of a stormy marriage ultimately reduces the stress they experience and enables either or both parents to be more sensitive and responsive to their needs (Amato et al., 1995; Hetherington et al., 1998).

A second encouraging message is that not all divorcing families experience all the difficulties we have described. In fact, some adults and children manage this transi-

al., 1989). Yet, this "contact advantage" may be offset by new kinds of instability (that is, changes in residence, and sometimes, in schools and peer groups) that can leave some children distressed and confused (Kline et al., 1989). It may not really matter whether parents obtain joint custody if they both maintain high-quality relationships with their children (Emery & Tuer, 1993; Kline et al., 1989). But when parents' relationship is hostile and conflictual, living in dual residences may heighten children's perceptions of being "caught in the middle"—an impression associated with high levels of stress and poor adjustment outcomes (Buchanan et al., 1991).

Additional Social Support

Divorcing adults are less depressed if they participate in support groups such as *Parents Without Partners* (a national organization with local chapters that attempt to help single parents cope with their problems) or if they have relatives or close confidants to whom they can turn (Emery, 1988; Hetherington, 1989). Children also benefit from the support they receive from close friends (Lustig, Wolchik, & Braver, 1992) as well as from participating in peer-support groups at school, in which they and other children of divorce are encouraged to share their feelings, correct their misconceptions, and learn positive coping skills (Grych & Fincham, 1992; Pedro-Carroll & Cowen, 1985). In sum, friends, peers, school personnel, and other sources of social support outside the nuclear family can do much to help families adjust to divorce.

Minimizing Additional Stresses

Generally, families respond more positively to divorce if additional disruptions are kept to a minimum—for example, if parents do not have to go through messy divorce trials and custody hearings, seek new jobs or residences, cope with the loss of their children, and so on. One way to accomplish some of these aims is through *divorce mediation*—meetings prior to the divorce in which a trained professional tries to help divorcing parents reach amicable agreements on disputed issues such as child custody and property settlements. Divorce mediation does appear to be an effective intervention—one that not only increases the likelihood of out-of-court settlements but also promotes better feelings between divorcing adults and increases the likelihood that a noncustodial father will pay child support and remain involved in the lives of his children (Dillon & Emery, 1996).

Here, then, we have some effective first steps in the path toward a positive divorce experience—as well as a better understanding of why divorce is more disruptive for some families than for others. This research also serves as yet another excellent sample of the family as a social system embedded in larger social systems. Mother, father, and children will all influence each other's adjustment to divorce, and the family's experience will also depend on the supports available within the neighborhood, the schools, the community, and family members' own social networks.

tion quite well and may even grow psychologically as a result of it. Who are these survivors? Box 11.3 provides some clues by exploring the factors that seem to promote a positive adjustment to divorce.

REMARRIAGE AND BLENDED FAMILIES

Within three to five years after a divorce, about 70% to 75% of single-parent families experience yet another major change when the parent remarries or *cohabits* with a partner outside of marriage and the children acquire a stepparent—and perhaps new siblings as well (Hetherington et al., 1998; U.S. Bureau of the Census, 1997). Remarriage often improves the financial and other life circumstances of custodial parents, and most newly remarried adults report that they are satisfied with their second marriages. Yet these blended families introduce many new challenges for children, who must now adjust not only to the parenting of an unfamiliar adult but also to the behavior of stepsiblings (if any) and to the possibility of receiving less attention from both their custodial and noncustodial parents (Hetherington et al., 1998). In fact, the restabilizing of family roles after the custodial parent remarries often takes considerably longer than was true after a divorce (Cherlin & Furstenberg, 1994). Furthermore, second marriages are somewhat more likely to end in divorce than first marriages are (Booth & Edwards, 1992). Imagine, then, the stresses experienced by families that find themselves in a recurring cycle of marriage, marital conflict, divorce, single parenthood, and remarriage. Indeed, recent studies reveal that the more marital transitions grade-school children have experienced, the poorer are their academic performances and the less well-adjusted they are (Capaldi & Patterson, 1991; Kurdek, Fine, & Sinclair, 1995; and see Figure 11.6).

So how do children fare in relatively *stable* blended families? The answer depends in part on their ages and gender and on whether their mother or father has formed the new family.

Mother/Stepfather Families   After an initial period of disruption and confusion that occurs as new family roles iron themselves out, boys seem to benefit more than girls by gaining a *stepfather*. Stepfathers who are warm and accepting offer relief from the coercive cycles that boys may have experienced with a custodial mother, so that these stepsons often enjoy a boost in self-esteem and will eventually overcome many of the adjustment problems they displayed before their mothers remarried (Hetherington, 1989; Vucinich et al., 1991). Why do girls not fare as well? Certainly *not* because stepfathers are treating stepdaughters any worse than stepsons; in fact, just the opposite is true during the early stages of remarried life, and that no matter how hard stepfathers try, their stepdaughters often remain rather cool and aloof. Girls often view stepfathers as threats to their relationships with their mothers and may even resent their mothers for remarrying and becoming less attentive to their needs (Hetherington, 1989; Vucinich et al., 1991).

Father/Stepmother Families   Less is known about children's reactions to *stepmothers* because stepmother families are still relatively uncommon (recall that fathers currently receive custody of their children in only about 17% of all divorcing families). What research there is indicates that introduction of a stepmother into the family system is somewhat more disruptive initially than the introduction of a stepfather, in part because (1) fathers granted custody typically have very close relations with their children that stepmothers may disrupt (Mekos, Hetherington, & Reiss, 1996), and (2) stepmothers play more active roles as behavior monitors and disciplinarians than stepfathers do (Hetherington et al., 1998). Furthermore, the transition from a father-custody single-parent home to a two-parent *stepmother* family is once again more disruptive and difficult for girls than for boys, particularly if the biological mother maintains frequent contact with her children (Brand, Clingempeel, & Bowen-Woodward, 1988; Clingempeel & Segal, 1986). Girls are often so closely allied with their mothers that they are bothered by either a stepfather competing for their mother's attention or a stepmother attempting to play a substitute-mother role. But the emotional disruption and resentment that daughters may initially experience in stepmother families is often overcome, for most girls eventually warm up to their stepmothers and may benefit from the support of a second mother figure (Brand et al., 1988).

Age and Family Constellation   The structure, or composition, of a blended family can influence how well children adjust to it. Problems are more common when each adult brings a child into the family, in part because parents tend to be warmer and more involved with their biological offspring than with their stepchild, and children pick up on this differential treatment and react negatively to it (Mekos et al., 1996). In addition, changes in parenting not only disrupt parent-child relationships but re-

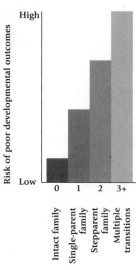

FIGURE 11.6   Grade-school boys' risk for poor adjustment outcomes (that is, antisocial behavior, low self-esteem, peer rejection, drug use, depression, poor academic performance, and deviant peer associations) as a function of number of marital transitions experienced. (From Capaldi & Patterson, 1991.)

lationships among *biological* siblings as well; and these negative sibling interactions can undermine a child's social competencies and contribute substantially to any problem behaviors that he or she may exhibit (Hetherington et al., 1998).

Interestingly, preadolescent and young adolescent children of both sexes find it more difficult to adjust to life in a blended family than younger children or older adolescents do. In fact, Mavis Hetherington and Glenn Clingempeel (1992) found that even after spending more than two years in a blended family, many younger adolescents were less well adjusted than age-mates from nondivorced families and had shown little improvement over the 26-month course of the study. Of course, many early adolescents in blended families adjust quite well, and authoritative parenting within these homes is associated with more favorable adjustment outcomes (Hetherington & Clingempeel, 1992). Nevertheless, a fair number (perhaps one-third) of adolescents disengage from their blended families, and the incidence of sexual misconduct, dropping out of high school, and a host of other deviant or delinquent behaviors is higher among adolescents in stepparent homes than among age-mates from nondivorced families (Capaldi & Patterson, 1991; Demo & Acock, 1996; Simons & Chao, 1996; Whitbeck, Simons, & Goldberg, 1996).

How might we explain this latter finding? One possibility that has received some support (see Fine & Kurdek, 1994; Mekos et al., 1996) is that many stepparents are hesitant to impose restrictions on adolescents or to carefully monitor their activities, preferring to leave these tasks to the biological parent. And because grandparents often become less involved in their grandchildren's lives once a custodial parent remarries (Clingempeel et al., 1992), the biological parent may now have little social support for the rules she imposes and may find it extremely difficult to adequately monitor the activities of younger, autonomy-seeking adolescents on her own (Hetherington & Jodl, 1994). But before we get too carried away about the antisocial tendencies of adolescents in blended families, an important truth should be stated here: The vast majority of adolescents who experience this marital transition turn out to be perfectly normal teenagers who may experience some initial problems adjusting but are unlikely to display any prolonged psychopathological tendencies (Emery & Forehand, 1994). In fact, disengagement from a blended family may even be beneficial if a teenager's time away from home is spent at a job or at extracurricular activities that foster constructive, supportive relationships with adult mentors or peers (Hetherington et al., 1998).

MATERNAL EMPLOYMENT REVISITED

In Chapter 5, we learned that a clear majority of American mothers now work outside the home and that this arrangement need not undermine the emotional security of their children. Infants and toddlers are likely to become or to remain securely attached to their working parents if their mothers (and fathers) have favorable attitudes about both working and parenting, and if they receive sensitive responsive care at home.

Looking beyond primary attachments, research with older children suggests that maternal employment, in itself, is unlikely to impede a child's social or intellectual development (Harvey, 1999). In fact, the opposite may be true, for children of working mothers (particularly daughters) tend to be more independent, to enjoy higher self-esteem, and to hold higher educational and occupational aspirations and less stereotyped views of men and women than those whose mothers are not employed (Hoffman, 1989; Richards & Duckett, 1994). Indeed, one large study of a national sample of *low-income* families linked maternal employment to children's cognitive *competence*: second-graders whose mothers had worked a great deal outperformed those whose mothers had worked less (if at all) in mathematics, reading, and language achievement (Vandell & Ramanan, 1992; see also Williams & Radin, 1993).

Parenting of Employed Mothers   One reason that children of employed mothers often experience favorable (rather than unfavorable) developmental outcomes and look so socially mature is that employed mothers are more inclined than unemployed mothers to grant their children independence and autonomy when their youngsters are ready for it (Hoffman, 1989). And when mothers have stimulating jobs, receive adequate social support from their husbands or partners and other close associates, and are highly committed to being a parent, they have generally favorable impressions of their children, rely less on power assertion to control their behavior, and are inclined to take an authoritative approach to child rearing—precisely the parenting style that is so often associated with favorable cognitive, social, and emotional outcomes (Crockenberg & Litman, 1991; Greenberger & Goldberg, 1989; Greenberger, O'Neil, & Nagel, 1994). Of course, employed mothers may be less effective parents if they are dissatisfied with their jobs, are not highly committed to parenting, or receive little support in their parenting role (Greenberger & Goldberg, 1989; Greenberger & O'Neil, 1993).

Against this backdrop of generally favorable outcomes associated with maternal employment is a recurring finding that has caused some concern: *Middle-class boys* (but not girls) of working mothers tend to score lower in intelligence and academic achievement than boys whose mothers are not employed (Bronfenbrenner, 1986; Gold & Andres, 1978), particularly when their mothers work long hours (Goldberg, Greenberger, & Nagel, 1996; Gottfried, Gottfried, & Bathurst, 1988). Yet even these results must be qualified, for Ann Crouter and her associates (1990) found that maternal employment is associated with lower academic achievement only when a boy's working parents failed to carefully monitor his behavior. Indeed, boys in dual-earner families are just as competent academically as boys (and girls) with nonemployed mothers when parents monitor their activities and ensure that they devote sufficient attention to schoolwork (Crouter et al., 1990; see also Moorehouse, 1991).

PHOTO 11.9   Children fare rather well, both socially and academically, if their working parents are authoritative and carefully monitor their activities.

So it seems that maternal employment may often foster the development of daughters without impeding that of sons, as long as working mothers are motivated to work, are highly committed to parenting, and have the supports they need to be effective parents.

The Importance of Good Day Care   As we noted in Chapter 5, one of the strongest supports working parents could hope for is *high-quality* day care for their children. Recall that children who enter high-quality day care centers early in life tend to display positive social, emotional, and intellectual outcomes from infancy through early adolescence (Andersson, 1989, 1992; Broberg et al., 1997). Much of the research that points to the long-term benefits of excellent day care comes from Western European countries, where day care for infants, toddlers, and preschool children is often government subsidized, staffed with trained, well-paid child-care professionals, and widely available to all citizens at a modest fee (usually less than 10% of an average woman's wages (Scarr, 1998). By comparison, day care in the United States is often woefully inadequate. Typically run as a for-profit enterprise, U.S. day-care centers and day-care homes are generally staffed by poorly compensated caregivers who have little training or experience in early childhood education and who rarely stay in the profession long enough to gain much expertise (Zigler & Gilman, 1993). Furthermore, American day care is expensive; providing one child with what is often far less than optimal care can run $3,200 to $4,500 per year, or about 25% to 30% of the annual income of a minimum-wage worker (U.S. Bureau of the Census, 1997). In 1990, the U.S. Congress passed a bill granting some tax relief to parents to help offset the cost of day care, but the absence of a national day-care policy that would ensure the availability of *high-quality* care at a *reasonable cost* to *all* who may need it means that many American workers will have to struggle to find and finance the kind of alternative care that would help them to optimize the development of their children (Scarr, 1998).

Self-Care The importance of adequate alternative care raises another employment-related issue: the after-school care of children whose mothers work. In the United States, some 2 to 4 *million* grade-school students between the ages of 6 and 13 qualify as **self-care (or latchkey) children**—those who care for themselves after school with little or no adult supervision (Zigler & Finn-Stevenson, 1993). Are these children at risk of being victimized, led astray by peers, or experiencing other less than desirable outcomes?

Research designed to answer these questions is often contradictory. Some studies find that self-care children do display higher levels of anxiety, poor academic performance, and more delinquent or antisocial conduct than supervised youngsters do (Marshall et al., 1997; Pettit et al., 1997); other studies find no such effects (Galambos & Maggs, 1991; Vandell & Corasantini, 1988). Why the inconsistencies? Let's begin by noting that the risks of self-care do seem to be greater for lower-income children in urban neighborhoods—settings that may present many opportunities for unsupervised children to associate with deviant peer groups and to take part in antisocial conduct (Posner & Vandell, 1994; Vandell & Ramanan, 1991). And regardless of the neighborhood, the way self-care children spend their time is crucial. Grade-school children and adolescents who have received authoritative parenting, who are required to come home after school to complete homework or other chores, and who are monitored at a distance by telephone calls are generally responsible and well-adjusted. By contrast, unmonitored age-mates who are allowed to "hang out" after school are more inclined to be influenced by peers and to engage in delinquent or antisocial conduct (Galambos & Maggs, 1991; Steinberg, 1986).

So it appears that there are steps working parents can take to minimize some of the potential risks of leaving schoolchildren to care for themselves—namely, by requiring them to go home after school, by supervising them *in absentia* to ensure that they do, and by parenting them in an authoritative manner. Nevertheless, leaving children younger than 8 or 9 to fend for themselves may be asking for trouble (Pettit, Laird, et al., 1997). Not only is the practice illegal in many states, but 5- to 7-year-olds often lack the cognitive skills to avoid high-risk hazards such as swimming pools or heavy traffic or to cope with such emergencies as personal injuries or fires (Peterson, Ewigman, & Kivlahan, 1993). Younger children in self-care also appear to be more vulnerable to sexual abuse and to harm at the hands of burglars as well (Zigler & Finn-Stevenson, 1993).

Fortunately, organized after-school care for school-age children is becoming more common in American communities, now serving an estimated 2½ million children nationwide (Rosenthal & Vandell, 1996). These programs differ in quality, ranging from "social addresses," where children gather, largely unsupervised, to well-run programs with trained staff, reasonable child-to-staff ratios, and curricula that include a variety of age-appropriate activities including sports, games, dance, art projects, music, computer activities, and academic assistance. Not only do children prefer the higher-quality after-school care programs (Rosenthal & Vandell, 1996), but they fare

self-care (or latchkey) children: children who care for themselves after school or in the evenings while their parents are working.

better in these programs as well. Jill Posner and Deborah Vandell (1994), for example, found that 9-year-olds from high-risk neighborhoods who attended *closely supervised* after-school care programs providing ample recreational opportunities and/or academic assistance were more academically competent, were rated as better adjusted by teachers, and were much *less* likely to be involved in antisocial activities than agemates who were not supervised after school by an adult. However, the same benefits of after-school care are not found if the programs children attend are primarily custodial and provide little stimulation or adult guidance (Vandell & Corasantini, 1990). So the *quality* of day care that children receive is important at all ages. Given the success of the publicly funded programs that Posner and Vandell (1994) evaluated, we might encourage politicians and community leaders to look carefully at them as a potentially affordable means of (1) optimizing developmental outcomes and (2) preventing more children of working mothers from having to face the risks of being alone in the afternoon and early evening.

When Parenting Breaks Down: The Problem of Child Abuse

Family relationships can be our greatest source of nurturance and support, but they can also be a powerful source of anguish. Nowhere is this more obvious than in cases of **child abuse.** Every day, thousands of infants, children, and adolescents are burned, bruised, beaten, starved, suffocated, sexually molested, or otherwise mistreated by their caregivers. Other children are not targets of these "physical" forms of abuse, but they are victims of such *psychological abuse* as rejection, ridicule, or even being terrorized by their parents (Wiehe, 1996). Still others are *neglected* and deprived of the basic care and stimulation they need to develop normally. Although instances of severe battering are the most visible forms of child abuse and are certainly horrible, many investigators now believe that strong and recurrent psychological abuse and neglect may prove to be even more harmful to children in the long run (Erickson & Egeland, 1996; Grusec & Walters, 1991).

Child abuse is a very serious problem. About 3 *million* reports of child maltreatment are filed each year in the United States, and about a third of these (or one *million*) are substantiated as abuse cases by child protection agencies (Emery & Laumann-Billings, 1998). Since many cases of child abuse are never reported or detected, these figures may represent only the tip of the iceberg. Indeed, one national sampling of families in the United States found that 11% of the children had reportedly been kicked, bitten, punched, beaten up, hit with an object, or threatened with a knife or a gun by their parents in the past year (Wolfner & Gelles, 1993). What's more, surveys of sexual abuse find that more than 400,000 American children a year are coerced into oral, anal, or genital intercourse (Finkelhor & Dziuba-Leatherman, 1994), usually by a stepfather, an older sibling, or another male relative or family friend (Trickett & Putnam, 1993; Wiehe, 1996). It is not a pretty picture, is it? And reports of child abuse have increased over the past 20 years due, in part, to increased awareness of the problem and a greater willingness of citizens to report suspected cases, but also to true increases in family violence associated with increased use of illegal drugs, greater poverty, and the disintegration of family-oriented residential areas (Emery & Laumann-Billings, 1998; Garbarino, 1995).

As you might expect, many, many factors contribute to a social problem as widespread as child abuse. Fortunately, we are gaining a better understanding of why abuse occurs by adopting a social systems perspective and recognizing that (1) some adults may be more inclined than others to abuse children, (2) some children may be more likely than others to be abused, and (3) abuse may be more likely to occur in some contexts, communities, and cultures than in others.

child abuse: term used to describe any extreme maltreatment of children, involving physical battering, sexual molestations, psychological insults such as persistent ridicule, rejection, and terrorization, and physical or emotional neglect.

WHO ARE THE ABUSERS?

Researchers have found that there is no single "abusive personality syndrome" that accurately characterizes adults who commit child abuse (Wiehe, 1996). Child abusers come from all races, ethnic groups, and social classes, and many of them even appear on the surface to be rather typical, loving parents who would never harm their children.

Yet there are at least some differences between parents who abuse their children and those who do not. Let's note first that some 20% to 40% of abusive parents are alcoholics or drug users, thus suggesting that alcoholism or drug dependence may often play a role in precipitating abusive incidents (Emery & Laumann-Billings, 1998; Windom, 1992). Moreover, although most maltreated children do not abuse their own children when they become parents, roughly 30% do (Kaufman & Zigler, 1989). In other words, abusive parenting is often passed from generation to generation (Simons et al., 1991; van IJzendoorn, 1992). In addition, abusive mothers are often battered women—victims of abuse in their own romantic relationships (Coohey & Braun, 1997; McClosky et al., 1995). They may have learned through their experiences as a child and a romantic partner that violence is a common reaction to frustrations. Abusive mothers are also often young, poverty-stricken, and poorly educated; frequently, they are raising children without a partner to share their burdens (Wiehe, 1996; Wolfner & Gelles, 1993). And many abusive parents of each sex are *emotionally insecure* individuals who are likely to interpret a child's irritability or independence in the face of an autonomy conflict as signs that their children are *disrespectful* or are *rejecting* them. Finally, abusive parents generally favor authoritarian control over authoritative techniques (which they view as largely ineffective). Although abusive parents do not report using physical punishment any more *often* than nonabusive parents do, they do admit to relying heavily on the most severely punitive tactics—actions such as yanking children's hair, hitting them in the face, or striking them with objects (Trickett & Susman, 1988).

In sum, abusive parents are often highly stressed, younger caregivers with little social support who have a history of abuse, who believe that coercive discipline is more effective than reasoning, and who find parenting more unpleasant and ego-threatening than nonabusive parents do. Still, there are many, many *nonabusive* parents who display all these characteristics, and it has been difficult to specify, in advance, exactly who will or will not become a child abuser (Trickett et al., 1991).

WHO IS ABUSED?

Abusive parents often single out only one child in the family as a target, thus implying that some children may bring out the worst in their parents (Gil, 1970). No one is suggesting that children are to *blame* for this abuse, but some children do appear to be at more risk than others. For example, infants who are emotionally unresponsive, hyperactive, irritable, temperamentally impulsive, or ill are far more likely to be abused than quiet, healthy, and responsive babies who are easy to care for (Ammerman & Patz, 1996; Belsky, 1993). Yet it is important to emphasize that most "difficult" children are never abused, while many cheerful and seemingly easygoing children will be mistreated. Just as caregiver characteristics cannot fully predict or explain why abuse occurs, neither can characteristics of children, although it is likely that the combination of a high-risk parent and a high-risk child spells trouble (Bugental, Blue, & Cruzcosa, 1989).

But even the match between high-risk child and caregiver does not invariably result in child abuse. The broader social contexts in which families are embedded matter too.

SOCIAL-SITUATIONAL TRIGGERS: THE ECOLOGY OF CHILD ABUSE

Child abuse is most likely to occur in families under stress. Such significant life changes as a divorce, the death of a family member, the loss of a job, or a move to a new home can disrupt social and emotional relationships within a family and contribute to neglectful or abusive parenting (Bronfenbrenner, 1986; Emery & Laumann-Billings, 1998; Wolfner & Gelles, 1993). Children are also much more likely to be abused or neglected if their parents are unhappily married (Belsky, 1993; Egeland et al., 1988).

High-Risk Neighborhoods   Families are also embedded in broader social contexts (that is, a neighborhood, a community, and a culture) that can affect a child's chances of being abused. Some residential areas can be labeled **high-risk neighborhoods** because they have much higher rates of child abuse than other neighborhoods with similar demographic characteristics (Coulton et al., 1995). What are these high-risk areas like? According to James Garbarino (Garbarino & Kostelny, 1992; Garbarino & Sherman, 1980), they tend to be impoverished and deteriorating neighborhoods that offer struggling parents little in the way of *community services,* such as parks, recreation centers, preschool programs, and churches, or *informal support systems,* such as contacts with friends and relatives. Consequently, socially isolated parents who live in these neighborhoods have nowhere to turn for advice and assistance during particularly stressful periods, and they often end up taking out their frustrations on their children.

Cultural Influences   Finally, the broader cultural contexts in which families live can affect the likelihood that children will be abused. Some developmentalists believe that child abuse is rampant in the United States because people in this society (1) have a permissive attitude about violence and (2) generally sanction the use of physical punishment as a means of controlling children's behavior (Whipple & Richey, 1997). There may well be some truth to these assertions, for cross-cultural studies reveal that children are less often abused in societies that discourage the use of physical punishment and advocate nonviolent ways of resolving interpersonal conflicts (Belsky, 1993; Gilbert, 1997). In fact, several Scandinavian countries, where children are rarely abused, have *outlawed* the use of corporal punishment (spanking), even by parents (Finkelhor & Dziuba-Leatherman, 1994).

Clearly, child abuse is a very complex phenomenon with many causes and contributing factors (see Table 11-2 for a brief review). It is not easy to specify who will

PHOTO 11.10   The incidence of child abuse is relatively high in deteriorating neighborhoods that offer few services and little if any social support to financially troubled families.

high-risk neighborhood: a residential area in which the incidence of child abuse is much higher than in other neighborhoods with the same demographic characteristics.

TABLE 11-2   Factors contributing to child abuse and neglect

CONTRIBUTING FACTOR	EXAMPLES
Parental characteristics	Younger age (under 25); low educational level; depression or other psychological disturbance; history of rejection or abuse; belief in effectiveness of coercive discipline; general insecurity or low ego strength; alcoholism and/or illegal drug use
Child characteristics	Irritable or impulsive temperament; hyperactivity; prematurity; inattentiveness; sickliness or other chronic developmental problems
Family characteristics	Financial strain or poverty; job loss; frequent moves; marital instability; lack of spousal support; many children to care for; divorce.
Neighborhood	High-risk areas characterized by few community services and little opportunity for informal social support from friends and relatives.
Culture	Approval of coercive methods of resolving conflicts and use of corporal punishment to discipline children

abuse their children and who will not, but we know that abuse is most likely to occur when a psychologically vulnerable parent faces overwhelming stress with insufficient social support (Wolfner & Gelles, 1993).

CONSEQUENCES OF ABUSE AND NEGLECT

Children who are neglected or abused tend to display a number of serious problems, including intellectual deficits, academic difficulties, depression, social anxiety, low self-esteem, and disturbed relationships with teachers and peers (Bagley, 1995; Bolger, Patterson, & Kupersmidt, 1998; Trickett & McBride-Chang, 1995; and see Box 11.4 on pages 394–395 for some noteworthy consequences of childhood sexual abuse). The behavioral correlates of physical abuse differ somewhat from those of neglect. Neglected children are more likely than those who are physically and sexually abused to founder academically and to have to repeat a grade (Eckenrode et al., 1993). Victims of neglect may receive very little stimulation from nurturing adults that would foster their intellectual or academic competencies. By contrast, hostility, aggression, and disordered social relationships are more common among physically abused youngsters, who often create disciplinary problems at school (Eckenrode et al., 1993) and are likely to be rejected by peers (Bolger et al., 1998; Haskett & Kistner, 1991; Salzinger et al., 1993).[3]

One particularly disturbing correlate of physical abuse is a lack of normal empathy in response to the distress of peers. When Mary Main and Carol George (1985) observed the responses of abused and nonabused toddlers to the fussing and crying of peers, they found that nonabused children typically attended carefully to the distressed child, showed concern, or even attempted to provide comfort. But as shown in Figure 11.7, not one abused child showed appropriate concern; instead, abused toddlers were likely to become angry and attack the crying child (see also Klimes-Dougan & Kistner, 1990). So it seems that physically abused children are likely to become abusive companions who have apparently learned from their own experiences at home that distress signals are particularly irritating to others and will often elicit angry responses rather than displays of sympathy. Other forms of domestic violence (for example, spouse battering) are also common in families that abuse children (McCloskey et al., 1995), so that victims of abuse may have few occasions to learn to respond compassionately to others' distress but many opportunities to learn aggressive solutions to conflict. No wonder these children are often rejected by their peers.

Unfortunately, the harmful social and emotional consequences of abuse and neglect can be long lasting, and some adolescents will try to escape their pain, anxieties, self-doubts, and disordered social lives by attempting to take their own lives (Bagley, 1995; Sternberg et al., 1993). Furthermore, adults who were abused as children are prone to violence, both inside and outside the family, and they show higher-than-average rates of criminal activity, substance abuse, depression, and other psychological disturbances (Bagley, 1995; Malinosky-Rummell & Hansen, 1993).

The good news is that many abused or neglected youngsters are remarkably resilient, especially if they are able to establish a warm, secure, and supportive relationship with a nonabusive parent, a grandparent, or some other member of the family (Egeland et al., 1988). And even though abused children are at risk of becoming abusive parents, it is worth emphasizing once again that the majority of abuse victims do *not* abuse their own children. Abused parents who succeed at breaking the cycle of

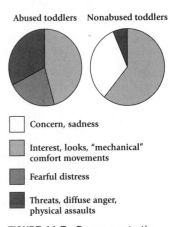

Abused toddlers   Nonabused toddlers

☐ Concern, sadness

▨ Interest, looks, "mechanical" comfort movements

▨ Fearful distress

■ Threats, diffuse anger, physical assaults

FIGURE 11.7 Responses to the distress of peers observed in abused and nonabused toddlers in the day-care setting. (The figures show the mean proportion of responses falling in each category for the nine abused and nine nonabused toddlers.) (Adapted from Main & George, 1985.)

---

[3]It should be noted, however, that all the above consequences of abuse and neglect may appear in any particular child who is the victim of *prolonged* maltreatment, regardless of the type(s) of maltreatment he or she has experienced (Bolger et al., 1998; Manley, Cicchetti, & Barnett, 1994).

Box 11.4 *Developmental Issues*

Childhood Sexual Abuse

In the 1970s, developmentalists began to discover that the sexual abuse of children was far more common than they had thought. We noted earlier that approximately 400,000 children a year are sexually abused in the United States. And if we count all those individuals who report that they were *ever* molested as children, as David Finkelhor and his associates (1990) did in a national survey, 27% of the women and 16% of the men had experienced some form of sexual abuse, ranging from being fondled in ways they considered inappropriate to actually being raped. About 25% of the victims were first victimized before age 8, usually by a father, stepfather, grandfather, uncle, teacher, or other male authority figure whom the victim knew well and trusted (Burkhardt & Rotatori, 1995; Wiehe, 1996). Women also commit sexual abuse, although female-initiated sex offenses are often underreported because boys are less likely than girls to disclose their abuse (Rudin, Zalewski, & Bodmer-Turner, 1995).

Sexual abuse is more common in poverty-stricken families, particularly those in which parents are unhappily married and one or both of them abuse alcohol or drugs and were molested themselves as children (Burkhardt & Rotatori, 1995). Yet sexual abuse can and does occur (and is probably underreported) in middle-class families that display none of these risk factors. In many cases, the perpetrator entices and entraps the victim by implying that the child is special and that their sexual activity will be a mutual secret. This pretext is then reinforced by the offender giving the victim gifts, special favors, or privileges (Wiehe, 1996). And often the victim has little choice but to comply because he or she either did not understand what was happening or was operating under threats of reprisal for noncompliance.

Effects of Abuse

After reviewing 45 studies, Kathleen Kendall-Tackett and her associates (1993) concluded that there is no one distinctive "syndrome" of psychological disorders that characterizes all who experience sexual abuse. Instead, these victims display any number of problems commonly seen in emotionally disturbed individuals, including anxiety, depression, low self-esteem, acting out, aggression, withdrawal, and academic difficulties. Roughly 20% to 30% of sexual abuse victims experience each of these problems, and boys seem to display the same types and degrees of disturbance as girls do.

Many of these after-effects boil down to feelings of shame, a lack of self-worth, and a strong reluctance to trust other people (Bolger et al., 1998; Cole & Putnam, 1992; Wiehe, 1996). And there are two problems that seem to be uniquely associated with sexual abuse. First, about a third of the victims engage in "sexualized behav-

abuse are more likely than those who do not (1) to have received emotional support from a nonabusive parent (or parent substitute), a therapist, or a spouse and (2) to have avoided severe stress as adults (Egeland et al., 1988; Vondra & Belsky, 1993).

Despite our better understanding of the causes of child abuse and observations that its often severe consequences can be lessened or even overcome, we are still a long way from solving the problem. Rather than conclude on that depressing note, let's consider some of the methods that have been used to assist the abused child and his or her abusers.

HOW CAN WE SOLVE THE PROBLEM?

It can be discouraging to realize that so many factors contribute to the maltreatment of children. Where do we begin to intervene? Just how many problems must we correct before we can prevent or stop the violence and discourage the neglect? Despite the complexity of the problem, progress has been made.

Preventing Abuse and Neglect   Let's first consider the task of preventing child maltreatment before it starts. This requires identifying high-risk families—a task that is

iors"—acting out sexually by placing objects in their vaginas, masturbating in public, behaving seductively, or if they are older, becoming sexually promiscuous (Kendall-Tackett et al., 1993). Perhaps it is not surprising, then, that adults who were sexually abused as children are more likely than nonabused individuals to be sexually victimized as adults and to report dissatisfaction with their sexual relationships and marriages (Bagley, 1995). Second, about a third of abuse victims show the symptoms of *posttraumatic stress disorder*—a clinical syndrome that includes nightmares, flashbacks to the traumatizing events, and feelings of helplessness and anxiety in the face of danger (Kendall-Tackett et al., 1993; McNew & Abell, 1995). Victims who are extremely traumatized are also at risk of displaying such self-destructive acts as drug and alcohol abuse, reckless behavior, and suicide attempts (Wiehe, 1996). And yet, about half of all sexually abused children and adolescents display no long-term psychological symptoms as young adults (Bagley, 1995; Kilpatrick, 1992).

Preventing and Treating Child Abuse
Overcoming the harmful effects of sexual abuse can be very difficult, particularly if it occurred frequently over a long period, if the perpetrator was a close relative such as the father or an older sibling, and if the child's mother looked the other way, refused to believe the child's story, or becomes hostile toward the victim for making such accusations (Kendall-Tackett et al., 1993; Trickett et al., 1993). Yet many symptoms fade within a year or two and recovery may proceed particularly well if the nonabusing parent believes the child's story, puts a stop to the abuse, and provides a stable and loving home environment thereafter (Kendall-Tackett et al., 1993). Psychotherapy aimed at treating the anxiety, depression, and self-blame many victims experience and at teaching them not to be revictimized can also contribute to the healing process (O'Donohue & Elliott, 1992).

Perhaps the best way to combat child sexual abuse is to identify it early and to prevent it from continuing. Sex education programs at school are one promising strategy: When children learn how to recognize inappropriate "touches" and other sexual advances, they are more inclined to report them to teachers (Bagley, 1995). It is also important that teachers be trained to recognize the signs of sexual abuse and how to report any child disclosures or their own suspicions to the appropriate child protection or law enforcement agencies (Burkhardt & Rotatori, 1995). Early identification of a possible problem is crucial to limit the amount of pain and suffering abuse victims experience and to ensure that they get the help they need.

greatly aided by the kinds of studies we have reviewed. For example, once neonatal assessment indicates that an infant may be at risk of abuse or neglect because he or she is particularly irritable or unresponsive, it makes some sense to help the child's parents to appreciate and evoke the baby's positive qualities. These interventions, which are often implemented through *home-visitor programs,* are particularly effective when targeted at high-risk parents who are experiencing high levels of stress or otherwise living under very difficult circumstances (for example, in poverty without much social support). Home visitations are aimed at addressing a high-risk parent's *material* needs (for example, cribs, transportation, and child care), *psychological* needs (parenting education; techniques for reducing stress), and *educational* needs (providing job skills), and they do seem both to improve parents' well-being and to reduce the incidence of child abuse (Emery & Laumann-Billings, 1998).

Indeed, the demonstrated success of home visitations and other similar interventions has led child welfare agencies in several states to develop family support and education programs designed to prevent child abuse (Zigler & Finn Stevenson, 1993). For example, the *Ounce of Prevention program,* a collaborative effort of the Illinois Department of Children and Family Services and the Pittway Corporation, attempts to head off child abuse by offering parent-education classes that teach effective child-management techniques and by providing such support services (through churches, medical clinics, and schools) as child-care programs, medical assistance, and job training. Other similar family support systems, which are regularly evaluated to ensure that they are meeting families' needs, are now available in Arkansas, Iowa, Massachusetts, Oregon, and Vermont (Wiehe, 1996; Zigler & Finn Stevenson, 1993).

At the community level, steps might be taken to assess the probable impact on children of actions undertaken by the government or by industry. For example, a local planning board's decision to rezone a stable residential area or to locate a highway there can create a high-risk neighborhood by causing property values to decline, destroying play areas, and ultimately isolating families from friends, community services (which may no longer exist), or other bases of social support. James Garbarino (1992, 1995) is one of many theorists who believe that significant numbers of American children are likely to be mistreated because of political or economic decisions that undermine the health and stability of low-risk, family-oriented neighborhoods.

Controlling Abuse   How do we deal with parents who are already abusive? What does seem clear is that a visit or two from a social worker is unlikely to solve the problem. Kempe and Kempe (1978) report that a fair percentage of abusive parents will stop physically maltreating their children if they can be persuaded to use certain services, such as 24-hour "hot lines" or crisis nurseries, that will enable them to discuss their hostile feelings with a volunteer or to get away from their children for a few hours when they are about to lose control. However, these are only stopgap measures that will probably not work for long unless the abuser also takes advantage of other services—such as **Parents Anonymous** or family therapy—that are designed to help the caregiver understand his or her problem while providing the friendship and emotional support that an abusive parent so often lacks.[4] Ultimately, however, a comprehensive approach is likely to be most effective. Abusive parents need emotional support *and* opportunities to learn more effective parenting and coping skills, whereas the victims of abuse and neglect need stimulating day-care programs *and* specialized training to help them overcome the cognitive, social, and emotional problems associated with abuse (Culp et al., 1991; Oates & Bross, 1995; Wiehe, 1996). In short, the ultimate goal in attempting to prevent or control child abuse must be to convert a pathological family system into a healthy one.

It is important to note that some family systems are more pathological than others and may not respond to supportive interventions of the kind we've discussed. Indeed, it may shock you to learn that between 35% and 50% of all fatalities due to child abuse or neglect occur in cases of *severe* and *repeated* maltreatment of which law enforcement and child protection agencies are already aware (Lung & Daro, 1996)! According to Robert Emery and Lisa Laumann-Billings (1998), cases of severe abuse or neglect—those in which a child's physical or psychological welfare is immediately and profoundly compromised—call for *coercive* rather than supportive interventions. One such control tactic becoming increasingly common involves arresting and prosecuting parents for acts that would qualify as criminal or sexual assault if they occurred between strangers. Yet even severe abuse is often difficult to prove (beyond the reasonable doubt required for criminal conviction) and American courts are quite hesitant to take children from abusive parents, even when there is reason to suspect a child has been repeatedly abused (Gelles, 1996). One reason for this reluctant attitude is that, historically, children have been treated as their parents' possessions (Hart

Parents Anonymous: an organization of reformed child abusers (modeled after Alcoholics Anonymous) that functions as a support group and helps parents to understand and overcome their abusive tendencies.

---

[4]Fortunately these services are often free. Chapters of Parents Anonymous are now located in many cities and towns in the United States (for the location of a nearby chapter, one can consult a telephone directory or write to Parents Anonymous, 675 W. Foothill Blvd., Suite 220, Claremont, CA 91711). In addition, many cities and counties provide free family therapy to abusive parents.

& Brassard, 1987). Another is that abused children and their parents are often attached to each other, so that neither the abusive adult nor the mistreated child wishes to be separated. And, unfortunately, many abused children may be left with their families because satisfactory placements in foster homes are often in short supply. However, it is essential that we carefully weigh the child's rights against the rights and wishes of parents, for it bears repeating that some severely abusive adults will go so far as to kill their children, regardless of the counseling or other supportive interventions they may receive (Emery & Laumann-Billings, 1998; Wiehe, 1996).

Although some people may disagree, developmentalists the world over have argued that no caregiver has the right to abuse a child (Hart, 1991). And in cases of severe abuse or neglect, developmentalists generally agree that our first priority must be to provide for the health and safety of mistreated children, even if that means terminating the abusers' legal rights of parenthood and placing their children in foster care or adoptive homes. The challenge we now face is to become much more successful at preventing and controlling child abuse so that the difficult decision of whether to separate children from their parents will need to be made less frequently than it is at present.

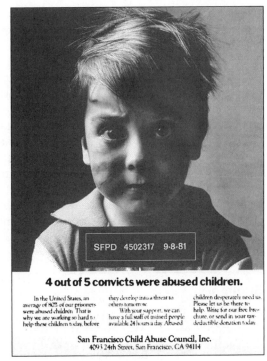

4 out of 5 convicts were abused children.

In the United States, an average of 80% of our prisoners were abused children. That is why we are working so hard to help these children today, before they develop into a threat to others tomorrow.

With your support, we can have a full staff of trained people available 24 hours a day. Abused children desperately need us. Please let us be there to help. Write for our free brochure, or send in your tax-deductible donation today.

San Francisco Child Abuse Council, Inc.
4093 24th Street, San Francisco, CA 94114

PHOTO **11.11** Many programs attempt to prevent and control the problem of child abuse.

Reflections on the Family

James Garbarino (1992) characterizes the family as "the basic unit of human experience" (p. 7). To fully appreciate the awesome significance of the family for children and adolescents, think for a moment on how very badly things can go when the family does not fulfill its important functions. Start with a neglected infant who not only may fail to thrive physically (see Chapter 5) but does not experience anything faintly resembling warm, sensitive, and responsive parenting. How is this child to form the secure attachments that serve as foundations for later social and intellectual competencies? Or think about the child whose parents are downright hostile—and who either provide no guidance at all or who hem the child in with rules and punish his every misstep. How is this child to learn how to care about other people, to become appropriately autonomous, and to fit into society?

Regina Campos and her associates (1994) have studied homeless street youths in Brazil whose families have failed them by neglecting, abusing, or otherwise dismissing them as unimportant. What were these homeless youngsters like? Compared to age-mates who worked on the streets but lived at home, youths "of the street" are faring very poorly. They struggle daily to survive, often begging if necessary to get by. What's more, they live in constant fear of being victimized and are themselves heavily involved in such antisocial behaviors as prostitution, drug abuse, thievery, and a host of other criminal activities. In short, these youngsters who have no family life are pursuing a highly atypical and deviant lifestyle that might seem to place them on the fast track to psychopathology, as we see in one 16-year-old's account of his daily routine:

> When you go to sleep it's about 5 in the morning; we wake up around 2 or 3 in the afternoon . . . get up, wash your face, if you have money you have breakfast [then] go out to steal, then you start to sell the stuff and the money all goes on drugs, because in the street it's all drugs! . . . Then, you get high, you're all set, then you come down and sleep. (Campos et al., 1994, p. 322)

What happens to these homeless street youths when they grow up? Clearly, there is reason to suspect that their outcomes are likely to be grim, considering fact that 80% of the prison population of one major Brazilian city consisted of former street youth (Campos et al., 1994).

You get the picture. It is often easier to illustrate the grave importance of families by accentuating the negative; and fortunately, most of us have fared much better than this, even though we do not always acknowledge just how significant our families may have been in underwriting our developmental successes. So think about what you have learned in this chapter the next time you gather with the closest members of your own family. Chances are you will understand why children and adults who are asked to reflect on what or who is most important in their lives almost invariably speak of their families (Furman & Buhrmester, 1992; Whitbourne, 1986). Although we change and our families change as we get older, it seems that we never cease to affect, or to be affected by, those folks we call "family."

Summary

FUNCTIONS OF THE FAMILY

■ The family is the primary agent of **socialization**—the context in which children begin to acquire the beliefs, attitudes, values, and behaviors considered appropriate in their society. Basic objectives of parenting in all societies are the (1) **survival goal**, (2) **economic goal**, and (3) **self-actualization goal.**

THE FAMILY AS A SOCIAL SYSTEM

■ Whether a **traditional nuclear family** or an **extended family**, families are best viewed as **social systems** in which each family member has **direct effects** and **indirect**, or **third party, effects** on all other family members. Children fare better when adult members of the family can effectively **coparent**, mutually supporting each others' parenting efforts.

■ Families are also developing social systems embedded in community and cultural contexts that affect how family functions are carried out.

■ Social changes affecting family life today include greater numbers of single adults, later marriages; a decline in childbearing; more female participation in the work force, and more divorces, **single-parent families**, and **blended** or **reconstituted families**, and greater numbers of families living in poverty.

PARENTAL SOCIALIZATION DURING CHILDHOOD AND ADOLESCENCE

■ Parents differ along two broad child-rearing dimensions —**acceptance/responsiveness** and **demandingness/ control**—that, when considered together, yield four patterns of parenting. Generally, accepting and demanding (or **authoritative**) parents who appeal to rea-son to enforce their demands tend to raise highly competent, well-adjusted children. Children of less-accepting but highly demanding (or **authoritarian**) parents and accepting but undemanding (or **permissive**) parents display somewhat less favorable developmental outcomes, and children of unaccepting, unresponsive, and undemanding (or **uninvolved**) parents are often deficient in virtually all aspects of psychological functioning.

■ Parents from different cultures, subcultures, and social classes have different values, concerns, and outlooks on life that influence their child-rearing practices. Yet parents from all social backgrounds emphasize the characteristics that contribute to *success as they know it* in their own ecological niches, and it is inappropriate to conclude that one particular style of parenting is somehow "better" or more competent than all others.

■ Parent/child relationships are renegotiated as adolescents begin to seek **autonomy.** Although family conflict escalates during this period, adolescents are likely to become appropriately autonomous if their parents willingly grant them more freedom, explain the rules and restrictions that they impose, and continue to be loving and supportive guides.

THE INFLUENCE OF SIBLINGS AND SIBLING RELATIONSHIPS

■ **Sibling rivalry** is a normal aspect of family life that may begin as soon as a younger sibling arrives; yet there is a positive side to having siblings. Siblings are typically viewed as intimate associates who can be counted on for support. Older sibs frequently serve as caregivers, security objects, models, and teachers for their younger siblings, and they often profit themselves from the instruction and guidance they provide. Yet sibling relationships are not essential for normal development, for only children are just as socially, emotionally, and intellectually competent (or slightly more so), on average, than children with siblings are.

DIVERSITY IN FAMILY LIFE

■ Infertile couples and single adults who desire to be parents often adopt to start a family. Although adoptees display more emotional and learning problems than biological children do, adoption is a highly satisfactory arrangement for the vast majority of adoptive parents and their children. Adopted children are often more satisfied with their family lives in open adoption systems that permit them to learn about their biological roots.

■ Gay and lesbian parents are just as effective as heterosexual parents are. Their children tend to be well adjusted and are overwhelmingly heterosexual in orientation.

■ Divorce represents a major transition in family life that is stressful and unsettling for children and their parents. Children's initial reactions often include anger, fear, depression, and guilt—feelings that may last more than a year. The emotional upheaval that follows a divorce often influences the parent/child relationship. Children often become cranky, disobedient, or otherwise difficult, while the custodial parent may suddenly become more punitive and controlling. The stresses resulting from a divorce and this new coercive lifestyle often affect the child's peer relations and schoolwork. Visible signs of distress may be most apparent in younger children and those with difficult temperaments, and girls adjust better than boys to life in a single-parent, mother-headed home. Although some aftereffects of divorce can be seen even after 10 to 20 years have elapsed, children of divorce are usually better adjusted than those who remain in conflict-ridden two-parent families. Among the factors that help children to make positive adjustments to divorce are adequate financial and emotional support from the noncustodial parent, additional social support (from friends, relatives, and the community) for custodial parents and their children, and a minimum of additional stressors surrounding the divorce itself.

■ Forming a blended family after a single parent remarries (or cohabits) is often a stressful transition for all family members. Boys seem to adjust better than girls to having a stepparent, and younger children and older adolescents adjust better than preadolescents and young adolescents do. Although the incidence of antisocial conduct and delinquency is higher in stepparent than in intact homes, the vast majority of children and adolescents successfully negotiate this family transition and show no psychopathological tendencies.

■ As long as working mothers are satisfied with their jobs, are committed to parenting, and receive adequate support from their spouses or partners and other close associates, their employment is associated with such favorable child outcomes as self-reliance, sociability, competent intellectual and academic performances, and less stereotyped views of men and women. One of the strongest supports that working parents could hope for is stimulating day care for their children—a support system that is woefully inadequate in the United States, compared to that provided by many other Western industrialized nations. Large numbers of American grade-school children whose mothers work must care for themselves after school. When monitored from a distance by authoritative parents, these **self-care** (or **latchkey**) **children** fare well. After-school care programs are becoming more common in the United States, and well-managed ones that offer children meaningful activities can help to optimize developmental outcomes and lessen the chances that children of working mothers will engage in antisocial conduct.

WHEN PARENTING BREAKS DOWN: THE PROBLEM OF CHILD ABUSE

■ **Child abuse** is related to conditions within the family, the community, and the larger culture. Abusers come from all social strata, although many of them are young, highly stressed caregivers who favor coercive forms of discipline and were themselves abused as children. Highly impulsive children and those who are irritable, emotionally unresponsive, or ill are more vulnerable to abuse than healthy, even-tempered children who are easy to care for. The incidence of child abuse is highest when stressed caregivers are living in **high-risk neighborhoods** where they are isolated from sources of social support and the broader culture approves of force as a means of resolving conflicts. The long-term consequences of abuse are often severe and long-lasting. Programs designed to assist abused children and their abusive parents have achieved some noteworthy success. However, we are still a long way from solving the problem.

Chapter Twelve

Extrafamilial Influences I:

TELEVISION, COMPUTERS, AND SCHOOLING

The Early Window: Effects of Television on Children and Adolescents

Television and Children's Lifestyles

Development of Television Literacy

Effects of Televised Violence

Other Potentially Undesirable Effects of Television

Television as an Educational Tool

Should Television Be Used to Socialize Children?

Child Development in the Computer Age

Computers in the Classroom

Concerns About Computers

The School as a Socialization Agent

Does Schooling Promote Cognitive Development?

Determinants of Effective (and Ineffective) Schooling

The Teacher's Influence

Do Our Schools Meet the Needs of All Our Children?

How Well-Educated Are Our Children? Cross-Cultural Comparisons

Summary

*I*n Chapter 11, we considered the family as an agent of socialization, looking at the ways that parents and siblings affect developing children. Although families have an enormous impact on their young, it is only a matter of time before other societal institutions begin to exert their influence. For example, infants, toddlers, and preschool children are often exposed to alternative caregivers and a host of new playmates when their working parents place them in some kind of day care or nursery school. Yet even those toddlers who remain at home soon begin to learn about a world beyond the family once they develop an interest in television. And by ages 6 to 7, virtually all children in Western societies are going to elementary school, a setting that requires them to interact with other little people who are similar to themselves and to adjust to rules and practices that may be very dissimilar to those they follow at home.

So as they mature, children are becoming increasingly familiar with the outside world and spend much less time under the watchful of their parents. How do these experiences affect their lives? The next two chapters explore this issue as we consider the impacts of four **extrafamilial influences** on development: television, computers, and the schools (in this chapter) and the society of one's peers (in Chapter 13).

The Early Window: Effects of Television on Children and Adolescents

It seems almost incomprehensible that the average American of only 50 years ago had never seen a television set. Now more than 98% of American homes have one or more TV sets, and children between the ages of 3 and 11 watch an average of three to four hours of TV a day (Comstock, 1993; Huston et al., 1992). As we see in Figure 12.1, TV viewing begins in infancy, increases until about age 12, and then declines somewhat during adolescence—a trend that holds in Australia, Canada, and several European countries as well as in the United States. By age 18, a child born today will have spent more time watching television than in any other single activity except sleeping (Liebert & Sprafkin, 1988). Boys watch more TV than girls do, and ethnic minority children living in poverty are especially likely to be heavy viewers (Signorielli, 1991). Is all this time in front of the tube damaging to children's cognitive, social, and emotional development, as many critics have feared? Let's explore this issue by first considering what effects television might have on children's lifestyles.

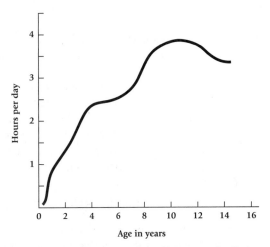

FIGURE 12.1 Average number of hours per day that American children and adolescents spent watching television in 1987. (From Liebert & Sprafkin, 1988.) © 1988 by Allyn & Bacon. Reprinted by permission.

TELEVISION AND CHILDREN'S LIFESTYLES

Has television changed children's lifestyles and the character of family life? In some ways it has. One early survey found that a majority of families altered their sleeping patterns and mealtimes once they had purchased a television set (Johnson, 1967). The presence of TV at home also had the effect of decreasing the amount of time parents spend with their youngsters in non-TV related leisure activities such as games and family outings, and most parents at least occasionally used television as an "electronic baby-sitter." Although family members may spend many hours in close proximity as they watch television together, many critics believe that this form of family interaction is not very meaningful for the younger set—particularly if they are told to sit still or keep their mouths shut until the commercials come on. Urie Bronfenbrenner (1970b) has argued:

extrafamilial influences: social agencies other than the family that influence a child's or an adolescent's cognitive, social, and emotional development.

The primary danger of . . . television . . . lies not so much in the behavior it produces—although there is danger there—as in the behavior that it prevents: the talks, games, the family festivities and arguments through which much of the child's learning takes place and through which his character is formed. Turning on the television can turn off the process that transforms children into people.

So is TV viewing as harmful to family life and social development as the early critics maintained? One way to assess the global impact of television is to see whether children who have access to the medium differ systematically from those who live in remote areas not served by television. And one such study of Canadian children gave some cause for concern. Prior to the introduction of television to the isolated town, "Notel," children living there tested higher in creativity and reading proficiency than did age-mates in comparable Canadian towns served by television. Yet two to four years after television was introduced, the children of Notel showed declines in their reading skills and creativity (to levels shown by peers in other towns), less community involvement, and dramatic increases in aggression and gender stereotyping (Corteen & Williams, 1986; Harrison & Williams, 1986).

Although sobering, these findings may be somewhat atypical. Other investigators report that the biggest impact of the coming of television is to persuade children to substitute TV watching for such other leisure activities as listening to the radio, reading comics, or going to movies (Huston et al., 1992; Liebert & Sprafkin, 1988). And as long as TV viewing is not excessive, children and adolescents exposed to the medium show no significant cognitive or academic deficiencies, are no less interested in schooling or their future careers, and spend no less time socializing with peers (Hagborg, 1995; Liebert & Sprafkin, 1988). In fact, one review of the literature found that children may actually learn a great deal of useful information from television, particularly educational programming (Anderson & Collins, 1988).

So in moderate doses, television neither deadens young minds nor impairs children's social development. Yet we will see that this medium does have the potential to do good or harm, depending on what children are watching and their ability to understand and interpret what they have seen.

DEVELOPMENT OF TELEVISION LITERACY

Television literacy refers to one's ability to understand how information is conveyed on the small screen. It involves the ability to process program content to construct a story line from characters' activities and the sequencing of scenes. It also involves an ability to interpret the *form* of the message—production features such as zooms, fade-outs, split-screens, and sound effects that are often essential to understanding a program's content (Fitch, Huston, & Wright, 1993).

Prior to ages 8 or 9, children process program content in a piecemeal fashion. They are likely to be captivated by zooms, fast-paced action, loud music, and children's (or cartoon characters') voices, and will often direct their attention elsewhere during slower scenes that contain quiet dialogue (Anderson et al., 1981). Consequently, preschool children are usually unable to construct a causal chain of events leading from the beginning to the end of a story. Even 6-year-olds have trouble recalling a coherent story line due, in part, to their tendency to remember the *actions* that characters perform rather than the motives or goals that characters pursue and the events that shaped these goals (McKenna & Ossoff, 1998; van den Broek, Lorch, & Thurlow, 1996). Furthermore, children younger than 7 do not fully grasp the fictional nature of television programming, often thinking that characters retain their roles (and scripted characteristics) in real life (Wright et al., 1994). And even though 8-year-olds may know that TV programming is fiction, they may still view it as an *accurate* portrayal of everyday events (Wright et al., 1995).

television literacy: one's ability to understand how information is conveyed in television programming and to interpret this information properly.

Comprehension of TV programming increases sharply from middle childhood throughout adolescence. Experience watching TV helps children to properly interpret the zooms, fade-outs, musical scores, and other production features that help viewers to infer characters' motives and to connect nonadjacent scenes. Furthermore, older children and adolescents are increasingly able to draw accurate inferences about scenes that are widely separated in time (van den Broek, 1997). So if a character were to act nice and gain someone's trust in order to dupe him later, a 10-year-old would eventually recognize the character's deceptive intent and evaluate him negatively. By contrast, a 6-year-old, who focuses more on concrete behaviors than on subtle intentions, will often brand this con artist a "nice guy" and be likely to evaluate his later self-serving acts much more positively (van den Broek et al., 1996).

Does their strong focus on actions and general lack of television literacy increase the likelihood that younger children will imitate the particularly vivid behaviors that TV characters display? Yes, indeed; and whether these imitations are beneficial or harmful depends very critically on what children happen to be viewing (Liebert & Sprafkin, 1988).

EFFECTS OF TELEVISED VIOLENCE

As early as 1954, complaints raised by parents, teachers, and experts in child development prompted Senator Estes Kefauver, then chairman of the Senate Subcommittee on Juvenile Delinquency, to question the need for violence in television programming. Yet more than 40 years later, the National Television Violence Study, a two-year survey of the frequency, nature, and context of TV violence, revealed that American television programming remains incredibly violent (Mediascope, 1996; Seppa, 1997). Fifty-eight percent of programs broadcast between 6 A.M. and 11 P.M. contained *repeated* acts of overt aggression, and 73% contained violence in which the perpetrator neither displayed any remorse nor received any penalty or criticism. In fact, the most violent TV programs are those intended for children, especially cartoons, and nearly 40% of the violence on TV is initiated by such heroes as "*The Mighty Morphin Power Rangers*" or other characters portrayed as attractive role models for children (Seppa, 1997). Furthermore, nearly two-thirds of the violent incidents in children's programming are couched in humor.

Theoretical Perspectives on Media Violence   Does a heavy exposure to media violence encourage spectators to behave aggressively or to partake in other kinds of antisocial conduct? Proponents of the *catharsis hypothesis* say no. In fact, Seymour Feshbach (1970) argued that people may often experience *catharsis* (that is, a draining away of aggressive energy) by merely thinking aggressive thoughts (fantasy aggression). If this is the case, exposure to televised violence should *reduce* aggressive impulses by providing fantasy material that viewers can use for cathartic purposes.

By contrast, *social-learning theorists* such as Albert Bandura (1973) offer several reasons to explain why media violence might *enhance* the aggressive or antisocial inclinations of children who watch it. First, there is physiological evidence that children become *emotionally aroused* when they see others fight (Cline, Croft, & Courrier, 1973; Osborn & Endsley, 1971)—arousal that might be reinterpreted as anger and thereby promote aggressive behavior if children should soon experience a situation that seems to suggest an aggressive response. Second, actors who portray violence on television serve as *aggressive models* who teach children a variety of violent acts that they may not know about or would not otherwise have considered performing. Robert Liebert and Joyce Sprafkin (1988) provide several dramatic illustrations of how children have acquired and performed unusual aggressive responses after watching similar actions on television. Here is one example:

In Los Angeles, a housemaid caught a seven-year-old boy in the act of sprinkling ground glass into the family's lamb stew. There was no malice behind the act. It was purely experimental, having been inspired by curiosity to learn whether it would really work as well as it did on television. (p. 9)

Finally, televised violence may reduce children's *inhibitions* about aggression if people in the story approve (or do not disapprove) of the actor's aggressive behavior. I am reminded of the "Thanks!" that townspeople typically shouted to the Lone Ranger as he rode into the sunset after shooting the villain of that particular episode or conspiring with Tonto to beat him to a pulp. If an actor's aggressive behavior is "legitimized" by social approval, observers may assume that aggressive solutions to conflict are acceptable or even socially condoned.

In sum, Bandura's position on the effects of TV violence is diametrically opposed to that of Feshbach and other proponents of the catharsis hypothesis. Who is right? Attempts to resolve this theoretical controversy include three types of research: (1) *correlational surveys* that assess the relationship between children's television viewing habits and aggressive behavior, (2) *laboratory investigations* in which participants are exposed to aggressive films and then immediately faced with a situation where they may choose to behave aggressively, and (3) *field experiments* in which the content of television programming is manipulated over a period of time in a real-world setting to measure the effects of the manipulation on viewers' aggressive inclinations. We briefly consider examples of each type of research as we evaluate the relative merits of the catharsis and the social learning hypotheses.

Results of Correlational Surveys   The vast majority of correlational surveys conducted to date find that children and adolescents who watch a lot of televised violence tend to be more hostile and aggressive than their peers who watch little violence. This positive relationship between exposure to TV violence and aggressive behavior in naturalistic settings has been documented over and over with preschool, grade-school, high school, and adult participants in the United States and with grade-school boys and girls in Australia, Canada, Finland, Israel, Great Britain, and Poland (Geen, 1998; Liebert & Sprafkin, 1988; Parke & Slaby, 1983). Furthermore, longitudinal studies suggest that the link between TV violence and aggression is *reciprocal*: Watching TV violence increases children's aggressive tendencies, which stimulates interest in violent programming, which promotes further aggression (Eron, 1982; Huesmann et al., 1984). Although longitudinal surveys are correlational research and do *not* demonstrate causality, their results are at least consistent with the argument that early exposure to a heavy diet of televised violence can lead to the development of hostile, antisocial habits that persist over time. Indeed, when Rowell Huesmann (1986) followed up on boys from an earlier study when they were 30 years old, he found that their earlier preferences for violent television at age 8 predicted not only their aggressiveness as adults, but their involvement in serious criminal activities as well (see Figure 12.2).

Results of Laboratory Experiments   One method of assessing whether televised violence really can instigate (or reduce) aggression is to expose children to violent programming and then give them an opportunity to commit aggressive acts. By 1972, 18 such laboratory experiments had been conducted, and 16 of them found that children became more aggressive after watching violent sequences on television (Liebert & Baron, 1972).[1]

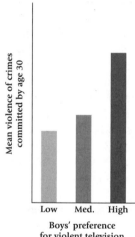

FIGURE 12.2   Relationship between boys' preference for violent TV programming at age 8 and mean violence of crimes committed by age 30. (Adapted from Huesmann, 1986.)

---

[1] A well-controlled and rather dramatic example of this research (Liebert & Baron, 1972) was used in Chapter 1 to illustrate the strengths of laboratory experimentation.

Despite the consistency of this early experimental research, the laboratory findings have been criticized as resulting from highly artificial viewing experiences. Critics claim that children are encouraged to give their *undivided attention* to program clips that have been edited to contain mostly violent incidents, then immediately offered a tailor-made opportunity to behave aggressively in an atypical laboratory setting. Is it possible that the instigating effects of TV violence are extremely short-lived and thus are a problem only in a laboratory setting where subjects are "encouraged" to be aggressive by the requirements of the task they face soon after observing unusually violent programming? Liebert, Neale, and Davidson (1973) acknowledge this possibility, noting that "we know from laboratory studies what type of relationship can exist between television violence and aggression, but cannot be wholly certain that this relationship does exist in the complex world of free-ranging behavior" (p. 69). And yet, as Box 12.1 on page 406 illustrates, boys who watch an unedited and highly violent program *designed for children* do subsequently become more aggressively inclined when interacting with peers in their natural environment.

Results of Field Experiments The field experiment would seem to be an excellent method of assessing the impact of televised violence on spectators' behavior because it combines the naturalistic approach of a correlational survey with the more rigorous control of an experiment. In other words, well-conducted field experiments can determine whether real-life exposure to violent television increases the incidence of aggressive behavior in natural settings.

An Experiment with Preschool Children In one well-known field experiment, Lynette Friedrich and Aletha Stein (1973; Stein & Friedrich, 1972) carefully observed a sample of nursery school children to establish a baseline level of aggression for each child. Then for the next month at school, children were exposed daily to either a violent TV show (for example, *Batman* or *Superman*) or to a nonviolent program (for example, *Mr. Rogers' Neighborhood*). Following these month-long television diets, the children were observed daily for two additional weeks to measure the effects of the programming. The results were clear: Children who had watched violent programming were subsequently more aggressive in their interactions with nursery school classmates than were those who had watched nonviolent programming. Although the impact of violent programming was statistically significant only for those youngsters who were above average in aggression on the initial baseline measure, these "initially aggressive" children were by no means extreme or deviant. They simply represented the more aggressive members of a normal nursery-school peer group. Stein and Friedrich remind us that "these effects occurred in [a naturalistic context] that was removed both in time and environmental setting from the viewing experience. They occurred with a small amount of exposure . . . and they endured during the post viewing period" (1972, p. 247).

An Experiment with Adolescents Earlier in Box 1.2 (on page 25), we discussed a similar field experiment conducted with Belgian delinquents. Recall that for a period of one week, half these delinquent inmates saw a different violent movie (for example, *Bonnie & Clyde, The Dirty Dozen*) each evening whereas the other half watched relatively nonviolent movies (for example, *Lily, La Belle Americaine*). Compared to their baseline levels of aggression, inmates who watched violent movies become more physically aggressive; those who watched nonviolent movies did not. And in agreement with the Friedrich and Stein (1973) experiment, violent movies promoted larger increases in aggression among inmates who were already relatively high in aggression before the movies were shown. In fact, these highly aggressive inmates who had watched violent fare continued to show elevations in verbal aggression throughout

Box 12.1 Focus on Research

Do "The Mighty Morphin Power Rangers" Promote Children's Aggression?

Currently, one of the most popular and most violent TV shows for children is *"The Mighty Morphin Power Rangers"*—a program that airs five to six times a week in many markets and contains in excess of 200 violent acts per hour. The *Power Rangers* are a racially diverse group of adolescents who are ordered by Zordon, their elderly leader, to transform, or "morph," into super heroes to battle monsters sent to earth by an evil Asian woman bent on taking control of the planet. Violence occurs not only in battles between the forces of good and evil but in nonbattle scenes in which the adolescent heroes practice martial arts on each other. The National Coalition on Television Violence says that *"Power Rangers"* is the most violent TV program for children it has ever studied (Kiesewetter, 1993)—and most of its violence is *hostile,* being intended to harm or kill another character. Do *unedited* versions of this immensely popular program increase the likelihood of aggression among its young viewers as they play in their *natural* environment?

Chris Boyatzis and associates (1995) sought to answer this question in an interesting experiment with 5- to 7-year-olds. Half the children in this study had been randomly assigned to watch a randomly selected, unedited episode of *"The Mighty Morphin Power Rangers"* at school whereas the remaining children in a control group engaged in other activities and did not view the program. After the program had been shown, children in the experimental group were each observed for a set length of time as they played in their classrooms, and instances of aggressive behavior (for example, physical and verbal aggression; taking objects by force) were recorded. Their behavior was then compared to that of children in the control group, who had not viewed the program.

The dramatic results appear in the figure. Notice that watching *"Power Rangers"* had no effect on the girls, probably because the majority of the "Rangers" are boys and young boys identify more strongly with aggressive TV characters than young girls do. However, we see that boys who had watched the show committed seven times the number

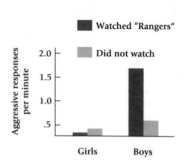

Average number of aggressive responses per minute in the free play of girls and boys who either had or had not watched an episode of *"The Mighty Morphin Power Rangers."* (Adapted from Boyatzis et al., 1995.)

of aggressive acts during free play compared with their male counterparts who had not watched this episode.

Here, then, is dramatic evidence that exposure to an *unedited* and *randomly selected* episode of a violent children's show featuring male characters dramatically increases the likelihood of aggression among young male playmates in the *natural environment*. Furthermore, it is worth emphasizing that the boys who become more aggressive had been *randomly assigned* to watch "Power Rangers" and were not merely the most aggressive boys in their classes. Later research suggests that a lack of TV literacy may have contributed strongly to these results, for children younger than 8 or 9 tend not to recall any prosocial causes the *Power Rangers* are pursing and usually say "the fights" when asked what they do remember (McKenna & Ossoff, 1998). Clearly, the Boyatzis et al. (1995) experiment may have somewhat overdramatized the impact of *"Power Rangers"* on young boys by observing their play *immediately* after they viewed the show. Nevertheless, the results certainly imply that *repeated exposure* of young, non-TV-literate audiences to this popular and highly accessible program can and probably does increase the frequency of aggressive peer interactions in the natural environment and may lead children (particularly boys) to favor aggressive solutions to conflict as well.

the week following the presentation of violent movies (Leyens et al., 1975; and see Parke et al., 1977 for similar results reported in other field experiments conducted on adolescents in the United States).

Despite these impressive results, critics have had a field day with field experiments on the impacts of TV violence. Results, though usually in the anticipated direction, are very weak in many studies (Geen, 1998), and the strongest effects often come from "captive" audiences in correctional institutions—precisely the populations that one might expect to be more heavily influenced by programming that advocates and displays violence (see, for example, Freedman, 1984). Yet one might anticipate less dramatic results in "non-captive" audiences, whatever their background, simply because it is not always possible to control precisely what they watch. Researchers in the Friedrich and Stein (1973) experiment, for example, could specify what nursery school children watched at school but not what they watched at home. Their results could well have been even stronger had they had more precise control over the home viewing practices of the children they studied.

Televised Violence as a Desensitizing Agent Even if young viewers do not act out the aggression they observe on television, they may be influenced by it nonetheless. For example, a steady diet of televised violence can instill **mean-world beliefs**—a tendency to view the world as a violent place inhabited by people who typically rely on aggressive solutions to their interpersonal problems (Comstock, 1993; Slaby et al., 1995). In fact, 7- to 9-year-olds who show the strongest preferences for violent television are the ones most likely to believe that violent shows are an accurate portrayal of everyday life.

In a similar vein, prolonged exposure to televised violence can *desensitize* children—that is, make them less emotionally upset by violent acts and more willing to tolerate them in real life. Margaret Thomas and her colleagues (1977; Drabman & Thomas, 1974) tested this **desensitization hypothesis** with 8- to 10-year-olds. Participants watched either a violent detective show or a nonviolent but exciting sporting event while hooked up to a physiograph that recorded their emotional reactions. Then each participant was told to watch over two kindergartners, visible in the next room on a TV monitor, and to come get the experimenter should *anything* go wrong. A prepared film then showed the two kindergartners getting into an intense battle that escalated until the video went dead. Participants who had earlier watched the violent program were now less physiologically aroused by the fight they observed and were more inclined to tolerate it (by being much slower to intervene) than their counterparts who had watched an equally arousing but nonviolent sporting event. Apparently TV violence can desensitize viewers to real-world instances of aggression.

PHOTO 12.1 Heavy exposure to media violence may blunt children's emotional reactions to real-life aggression and convince them that the world is a violent place populated mainly by hostile and aggressive people.

What Can We Conclude About Exposure to TV Violence? So, does exposure to violent TV fare instigate aggression and cultivate aggressive and antisocial tendencies in young children? Even after more than 40 years of research, there is far from unanimous agreement on this issue. Some critics, for example, have tended to dismiss all the evidence because of the weaknesses that characterize particular studies or a particular research method. And few social developmentalists today would blame our social ills on the fact that our violent and antisocial adults may have watched *Batman* or the *Untouchables* as youth or would claim that heavy exposure to media violence, by itself, will transform an otherwise well-adjusted viewer into a violent sociopath. Nevertheless, investigators who have carefully conducted large-scale reviews of the correlational, experimental, and field experimental literatures—three approaches to the question that have different strengths that largely offset the other methods' weaknesses—note that the data *converge* on the conclusions that the aggression-instigating effects of TV violence are (1) observed among *both* boys and girls, (2) strongest when the violence appears justified, and (3) sufficiently powerful to desensitize viewers to

mean-world belief: a belief, fostered by televised violence, that the world is a more dangerous and frightening place than is actually the case.

desensitization hypothesis: the notion that people who watch a lot of media violence will become less aroused by aggression and more tolerant of violent and aggressive acts.

aggression, create mean-world beliefs, and to cultivate aggressive habits and antisocial behavior among heavy viewers (see Coie & Dodge, 1998; Geen, 1998; Hearold, 1986; Rosenthal, 1986). Of course we should heed the cautions expressed by these researchers, who have stressed that televised violence is only one of many contributors to children's hostile, antisocial conduct and may be nowhere near as strong a contributor as growing up in a coercive home environment or identifying with deviant and antisocial peers (Geen, 1998; Huesmann & Miller, 1994). However, it is difficult to argue that a heavy exposure to TV violence has salutary long-term effects on anyone, and its capacity to do harm is substantial (Coie & Dodge, 1998). Finally, let's note that there is virtually no support for the notion that exposure to media violence leads to a reduction of viewers' aggressive impulses through catharsis.

OTHER POTENTIALLY UNDESIRABLE EFFECTS OF TELEVISION

Aside from its potential for instigating aggressive behavior and cultivating hostile, antisocial attitudes, TV might teach young viewers several other undesirable lessons. Let's briefly consider two such influences that often annoy or even anger many adults.

Television as a Source of Social Stereotypes   Another unfortunate effect that television may have on children is to reinforce a variety of potentially harmful social stereotypes (Huston et al., 1992). In Chapter 8, for example, we noted that gender-role stereotyping is common on television and that children who watch a lot of commercial TV are likely to hold more traditional views of men and women than their classmates who watch little television. Yet television might also be employed to counter gender stereotypes. Early attempts to accomplish this aim by showing males performing competently at traditionally feminine activities and females excelling at traditionally masculine pursuits enjoyed some limited success (Johnston & Ettema, 1982; Rosenwasser et al., 1989). However, these programs would undoubtedly become more effective if they were combined with the kinds of cognitive training procedures, described in Chapter 8, that undermine the inflexible and erroneous *beliefs* on which gender stereotypes rest (Bigler & Liben, 1990, 1992).

Stereotyped views of minorities are also common on television. Largely because the influence of the civil rights movement, African Americans now appear on television in a much wider range of occupations, and their numbers equal or exceed their proportions in the population. However, Latinos and other ethnic minorities remain underrepresented. And when non-Black minorities do appear, they are usually portrayed in an unfavorable light, often cast as villains or victims (Associated Press, 1994b; Liebert & Sprafkin, 1988).

Although the evidence is limited, it seems that children's ethnic and racial attitudes are influenced by televised portrayals of minority groups. Earlier depictions of African Americans as comical, inept, or lazy led to negative racial attitudes (Graves, 1975; Liebert & Sprafkin, 1988) whereas positive portrayals of minorities in cartoons and on such educational programs as *Sesame Street* appear to reduce children's racial and ethnic stereotypes and increase their likelihood of having ethnically diverse friends (Graves, 1993; Gorn, Goldberg, & Kanungo, 1976). Apparently television has the power to bring people of different racial and ethnic backgrounds closer together—or to drive them further apart—depending on the ways these social groups are depicted on the small screen.

Children's Reactions to Commercial Messages   In the United States, the average child is exposed to nearly 20,000 television commercials each year—many of which extol the virtues of toys, fast foods, and sugary treats that adults may not wish to purchase. Nevertheless, young children continue to ask for products that they have seen on television, and conflicts often ensue when parents refuse to honor their requests (Atkin, 1978; Kunkel & Roberts, 1991). Young children may be so persistent because they rarely understand the manipulative (selling) intent of ads, often treating them like public service announcements that are intended to be helpful and informative (Liebert & Sprafkin, 1988). By ages 9 to 11, most children realize that ads are designed to persuade and sell, and by 13 to 14, they will have acquired a healthy skepticism about advertising and product claims (Linn, de Benedictis, & Delucchi, 1982; Robertson & Rossiter, 1974). Nevertheless, even adolescents are often persuaded by the ads they see, particularly if the product endorser is a celebrity or the appeals are deceptive and misleading (Huston et al., 1992).

Is it any wonder, then, that many parents are concerned about the impact of commercials on their children? Not only do children's ads often push products that are unsafe or have poor nutritional value, but the many ads for over-the-counter drugs and glamorous depictions of alcohol use could cause children to underestimate the consequences of such risky behaviors as drinking, self-medication, and drug use (Tinsley, 1992). *Action for Children's Television*—an organization of parents that monitors and tries to change television's impact on children—considers the potentially harmful influence of TV commercials to be an even greater problem than televised violence! And policymakers are beginning to respond to the outcries, as evidenced by a recent law limiting the number of commercials on children's programs and requiring broadcasters to offer more educational programming or risk losing their licenses (Zigler & Finn Stevenson, 1993).

Reducing the Harmful Effects of Television Exposure How might concerned parents limit the potentially harmful effects of commercial television? Table 12-1 lists several effective strategies recommended by experts, including monitoring children's home viewing habits to limit their exposure to highly violent or otherwise offensive fare while trying to interest them in programs with prosocial or educational themes. Information about programs that experts consider inappropriate for children can be obtained from *The National Foundation to Improve Television,* 60 State Street, Boston, MA 02109 (phone: [617] 523-6353).

Although each of the guidelines in Table 12-1 is excellent, the suggestion that parents help their young, non-TV-literate viewers to evaluate what they are watching is particularly important. One reason that younger children are so responsive to aggressive

TABLE 12-1 Effective strategies for regulating children's exposure to television

STRATEGY	IMPLEMENTATION
Limit TV viewing	Set clear rules that limit times when children may watch TV. Don't use the medium as an electronic baby-sitter or increase its attractiveness by withholding TV privileges as a punishment.
Encourage appropriate viewing	Encourage children to watch child-appropriate informational or prosocial programs. Use lock-out features available on cable or satellite systems to restrict child access to channels with excessive violent or sexual content.
Explain televised information to children	Watch TV with children and point out subtleties they may miss, such as an aggressor's antisocial motives and the unpleasant consequences that perpetrators may suffer as a result of their violent acts. Critical discussions centering on the violence and negative social stereotypes portrayed on television help children to evaluate what they see and to view it as less "real."
Model good viewing habits	Parental viewing practices influence children's viewing practices so avoid watching too much television, particularly programs that are inappropriate for children.
Parent authoritatively	Warmth coupled with reasonable and rational limit setting make children more responsive to parental control, including restrictions on TV viewing.

SOURCES: Slaby et al., 1995; Seppa, 1997.

models on TV is that they don't always interpret the violence they see in the same way adults do, often missing subtleties such as an aggressor's inappropriate motives and intentions or the unpleasant consequences that perpetrators may suffer as a result of their aggressive acts (Collins, Sobol, & Westby, 1981; Slaby et al., 1995). When adults highlight this information while strongly disapproving of a perpetrator's conduct, children gain a much better understanding of media violence and are less affected by what they have seen—particularly if the adult commentator also suggests how these perpetrators might have approached their problems in a more constructive way (cf. Collins, 1983; Liebert & Sprafkin, 1988). Unfortunately, this may be an underutilized strategy, for as Michele St. Peters and her associates (1991) have noted, parent/child co-viewing at home most often occurs *not* during action/adventure shows or other highly violent fare, but during the evening news, sporting events, or prime-time dramas—programming that is not particularly captivating for young children.

TELEVISION AS AN EDUCATIONAL TOOL

Thus far, we've cast a wary eye at television, talking mostly about its capacity to do harm. Yet this "early window" could become a most effective way of teaching a number of valuable lessons if only its content were altered to convey such information. Let's examine some of the evidence to support this claim.

Educational Television and Children's Prosocial Behavior   Many TV programs—especially offerings such as *Sesame Street* and *Mister Rogers' Neighborhood* broadcast on public television—are designed, in part, to illustrate the benefits of such prosocial activities as cooperation, sharing, and comforting distressed companions. One major review of the literature found that young children who often watch prosocial programming do become more prosocially inclined (Hearold, 1986). However, it is important to emphasize that these programs may have few if any lasting benefits unless an adult monitors the broadcasts and encourages children to rehearse and enact the prosocial lessons they have learned (Friedrich & Stein, 1975; Friedrich-Cofer et al., 1979). Furthermore, young children are more likely to process and enact any prosocial lessons that are broadcast when the programming is free of violent acts that will otherwise compete for their attention. But despite these important qualifications, it seems that the positive effects of prosocial programming greatly outweigh the negatives and that prosocial television actually promotes prosocial behavior to a greater extent than violent television promotes aggression! Hearold (1986) believes that these findings have important and far-reaching policy implications:

> Many organizations and groups have chosen to work for the removal of . . . violence in television programs. It is a defensive position: eliminate the negative. Alternatively, I would recommend accentuating the positive: apply money and effort to creating new entertainment programs with prosocial themes. . . . Although fewer studies exist on prosocial effects, the effect size[2] [of prosocial programming] is so much larger [than that of violent programming], holds up better under more stringent experimental conditions, and is consistently higher for boys and girls, that the potential for prosocial effects overrides the smaller but persistent negative effects of antisocial programs. (p. 116)

Television as a Contributor to Cognitive Development   In 1968, the U.S. government and a number of private foundations provided funds to create *Children's Television Workshop (CTW),* an organization committed to producing TV programs that would

---

[2]An "effect size" is a statistical term that indicates the strength of a relationship between variables (for example, between exposure to prosocial television programming and subsequent prosocial behavior) when results of many different studies are combined.

hold children's interest and foster their intellectual development. CTW's first production, *Sesame Street,* became the world's most popular children's series—seen an average of three times a week by about half America's preschool children and broadcast to nearly 50 other countries around the world (Liebert & Sprafkin, 1988). Targeted at 3- to 5-year-olds, *Sesame Street* attempts to foster important cognitive skills such as counting, recognizing and discriminating numbers and letters, ordering and classifying objects, and solving simple problems. A major aim of the program was for children from disadvantaged backgrounds to be much better prepared for school after viewing it on a regular basis.

Evaluating Sesame Street   During the first season *Sesame Street* was broadcast, its impact was assessed by the Educational Testing Service. About 950 3- to 5-year-olds from five areas of the United States took a

PHOTO 12.2   Children learn many valuable lessons from educational TV programs such as *Sesame Street.*

pretest that measured their cognitive skills and determined what they knew about letters, numbers, and geometric forms. At the end of the season, they took this test again to see what they had learned.

When the data were analyzed, it was clear that *Sesame Street* was achieving its objectives. As shown in Figure 12.3, children who watched *Sesame Street* the most (groups Q3 and Q4, who watched four or more times a week) were the ones who showed the biggest improvements in their total test scores (panel A), their scores on the alphabet test (panel B), and their ability to write their names (panel C). The 3-year-olds posted bigger gains than the 5-year-olds, probably because the younger children knew less to begin with. The results of a second similar study which included only urban disadvantaged preschoolers paralleled those of the original study

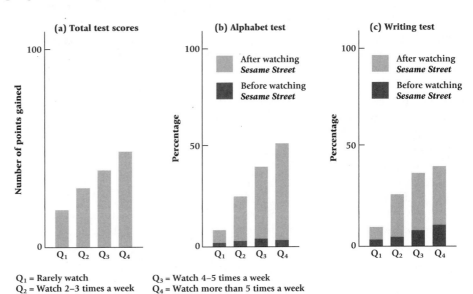

Q₁ = Rarely watch
Q₂ = Watch 2–3 times a week
Q₃ = Watch 4–5 times a week
Q₄ = Watch more than 5 times a week

FIGURE 12.3   Relationship between amount of viewing of *Sesame Street* and children's abilities: (a) improvement in total test scores for children grouped into different quartiles according to amount of viewing; (b) percentage of children who recited the alphabet correctly, grouped according to quartiles of amount of viewing; (c) percentage of children who wrote their first names correctly, grouped according to quartiles of amount of viewing. (From Liebert & Sprafkin, 1988.)

(Bogatz & Ball, 1972), and others have found that regular exposure to *Sesame Street* is associated with impressive gains in preschoolers' vocabularies and prereading skills as well (Rice et al., 1990). Finally, disadvantaged children who had been heavy viewers of *Sesame Street* were later rated by their first-grade teachers as better prepared for school and more interested in school activities than classmates who had rarely watched the program (Bogatz & Ball, 1972).

Other Educational Programs   The success of *Sesame Street* has prompted CTW and other noncommercial producers to create programs that teach children subjects such as reading skills (*The Electric Company*), math (*Square One*), logical reasoning (*Think About*), science (*3-2-1 Contact*), and social studies (*Big Blue Marble*). Designed for first- through fourth-graders, *The Electric Company* does produce gains in reading skills, but only when children watch at school where teachers can help them to apply what they have learned (Ball & Bogatz, 1973).[3] Unfortunately, recent educational programs produced by commercial networks and aimed at older children have largely failed to attract a wide viewership, although such offerings as ABC's *Science Court* and the syndicated show *Popular Mechanics for Kids* rate as qualified successes (Farhl, 1998).

Criticisms of Educational Programming   One recurring criticism of educational television is that it is essentially a one-way medium in which the pupil is a passive recipient of information rather than an active constructor of knowledge. Critics fear that heavy TV viewing (be it educational TV or otherwise) will blunt children's curiosity, and they believe that a child's viewing time would be more profitably spent in active, imaginative activities under the guidance of an adult (Singer & Singer, 1990). Indeed, we've seen that programs such as *The Electric Company* (as well as those stressing prosocial behavior) are unlikely to achieve their objectives unless children watch *with an adult* who encourages them to apply what they have learned. Perhaps John Wright and Aletha Huston (1983) were correct in arguing that television's potential as a teaching device will be greatly enhanced once it becomes *computer-integrated* and interactive, thereby allowing the viewer to be more actively involved in the learning process.

Although *Sesame Street* was targeted primarily at disadvantaged preschoolers in an attempt to narrow the intellectual gap between these youngsters and their advantaged peers, early research suggested that children from advantaged backgrounds were the ones who were more likely to watch the program. Thus, it was feared that *Sesame Street* might actually end up *widening* the intellectual and academic gaps between advantaged and disadvantaged youth (Cook et al., 1975). Yet this particular concern now appears unfounded. Later research suggests that children from disadvantaged backgrounds are not only watching *Sesame Street* about as often as their advantaged peers (Pinon, Huston, & Wright, 1989) but are learning just as much from it (Rice et al., 1990). What's more, children benefit from viewing this series even when they watch it alone (Rice et al., 1990). So viewing *Sesame Street* appears to be a potentially valuable experience for all preschool children—and a true educational bargain that only costs about a penny a day per viewer (Palmer, 1984). The formidable task lies ahead: convincing more parents that *Sesame Street* (and other educational programs) are valuable resources that they and their children should not be missing.

SHOULD TELEVISION BE USED TO SOCIALIZE CHILDREN?

Although television is often criticized as an instigator of violence or an "idiot box" that undermines the intellectual curiosity of our young, we have seen that the

---

[3]In 1985 *The Electric Company* went off the air. However, episodes are still available to schools on video-cassette for classroom use.

medium can have many positive effects on children's social, emotional, and intellectual development. Should we now work at harnessing television's potential—at using this "early window" as a means of socializing our children? Many developmentalists think so, although not everyone agrees, as we see in the following newspaper account of a conference on behavioral control through the media. To set the stage, the conference participants were reacting to the work of Dr. Robert M. Liebert, a psychologist who had produced some 30-second TV spots to teach children cooperative solutions to conflict. Here is part of the account that appeared in the *New York Times:*

> The outburst that followed Liebert's presentation flashed around the conference table. Did he believe that he had a right to . . . impose values on children? Should children . . . be taught cooperation? Did ghetto kids perhaps need to be taught to slug it out in order to survive in this society? Was it not . . . immoral to create a TV ad . . . to influence kids' behavior? Liebert was accused of . . . manipulation and even brainwashing. One would have thought he had proposed setting up Hitler Youth Camps on Sesame Street.
>
> However, I understand why the hackles had gone up around the . . . table. I am one of those people who [are] terrified of manipulation. A Skinnerian world filled with conditioned people scares the daylights out of me—even if those people do hate war and . . . love their fellow man. [Behavior control through technology may come] . . . at the cost of our freedom. (Rivers, 1974, quoted in Liebert & Sprafkin, 1988, pp. 243–44)

The concern of those conference participants is perhaps understandable, for television is often used as a means of political indoctrination in many countries. And is the use of television for socialization not a subtle form of brainwashing? Perhaps it is. However, one could argue that television in this country is already serving as a potent agent of socialization and that much of what children see in the media helps to create attitudes and to instigate actions that the majority of us may not condone. Perhaps the question we should be asking is, "Can we somehow alter television to make it a more effective agent of socialization—one that teaches attitudes, values, and behaviors that more accurately reflect the mores of a free society?" Surely we can, although it remains to be seen whether we will.

Child Development in the Computer Age

Like television, the computer is a modern technology that has the potential to influence children's learning and lifestyles. But in what ways? If we take our cues from Hollywood, we might be led to believe that young computer "hackers" will grow up to be *brainy* but socially inept misfits like those curiously lovable characters from the movie *Revenge of the Nerds*. Indeed, most educators believe that the microcomputer has salutary effects on children's education by serving as an effective supplement to classroom instruction—a tool that helps children learn more and have more fun learning. By 1996, over 98% of American public schools were using computers as instructional tools, and more than 35 million machines were available for use in American homes (U.S. Bureau of the Census, 1997). So computers are now widely accessible; but do they really help children to learn, to think, or to create? Is there a danger that young "hackers" will become so enamored of computer technology and so reclusive or socially unskilled that they risk being ostracized by their peers?

COMPUTERS IN THE CLASSROOM

The results of literally hundreds of studies reveal that classroom use of computers produces many, many benefits. For example, elementary school students do learn more and report that they enjoy school more when they receive at least some **computer-assisted instruction (CAI)** (Clements & Nastasi, 1992; Collis, 1996;

computer-assisted instruction (CAI): Use of computers to teach new concepts and practice academic skills.

Lepper & Gurtner, 1989). Many CAI programs are simply drills that start at a student's current level of mastery and present increasingly difficult problems, often intervening with hints or clues when progress breaks down. Other, more elaborate forms of CAI are guided tutorials that rely less on drill and more on the discovery of important concepts and principles in the context of highly motivating, thought-provoking games. Regular use of drill programs during the early grades does seem to improve children's basic reading and math skills—particularly for disadvantaged students and other low achievers (Clements & Nastasi, 1992; Fletcher-Flinn & Gravatt, 1995; Lepper & Gurtner, 1989). However, the benefits of CAI are greatest when children receive at least some exposure to highly involving guided tutorials as well as simple drills.

Word Processing   Aside from their drill function, computers are also tools that can further children's basic writing and communication skills (Clements, 1995). Once they can read and write, children can be introduced to word-processing programs that eliminate much of the drudgery of handwriting and increase the likelihood that the young composers will revise, edit, and polish their writing (Clements & Nastasi, 1992). Furthermore, computer-prompted cognitive strategies also help students to think about what they wish to say and to organize their thoughts into more coherent essays (Lepper & Gurtner, 1989).

Computer Programming and Cognitive Growth   Finally, it seems that teaching students to *program* (and thus *control*) a computer can have such important benefits as fostering mastery motivation and self-efficacy, as well as promoting novel modes of thinking that are unlikely to emerge from computer-assisted academic drills. In his own research, Douglas Clements (1991, 1995) trained first- and third-graders in Logo, a computer language that allows children to take drawings they've made and translate them into input statements so that they eventually succeed at reproducing their creations on the computer monitor. Although Clements's "Logo" children performed no better on achievement tests than age-mates who participated in the more usual kinds of computer-assisted academic exercises, Logo users scored higher on tests of Piagetian concrete-operational abilities, mathematical problem-solving strategies, and creativity (Clements, 1995; Nastasi & Clements, 1994). And because children must detect errors and debug their Logo programs to get them to work, programming fosters thinking about one's own thinking and is associated with gains in **metacognitive knowledge** (Clements, 1990). Clearly these findings are important, for they suggest that computers are useful not only for teaching children academic lessons but for helping them to *think* in new ways as well.

metacognition: one's knowledge about cognition and about the regulation of cognitive activities.

Social Impacts   Are young computer users at risk of becoming reclusive, socially unskilled misfits as some people have feared? Hardly! Children often use home computers as a toy to *attract* playmates (Crook, 1992; Kee, 1986). And research conducted in classrooms reveals that students who are learning to solve problems by computer or to program a computer (1) are likely to seek collaborative solutions to the challenges they face and (2) are more inclined to persist after experiencing problems when they are collaborating with a peer (Nastasi & Clements, 1993, 1994; Weinstein, 1991). Con-

PHOTO 12.3 Learning by computer is an effective complement to classroom instruction and an experience that can teach young children to collaborate.

flicts may arise should collaborators disagree about how to approach a problem; yet the strong interest that collaborators frequently display when facing a programming challenge often supersedes their differences and encourages amiable methods of conflict resolution (Nastasi & Clements, 1993). So computers seem to promote (rather than impede) peer interactions—contacts that are often lively and challenging, and that appear to foster the growth of socially skilled behaviors.

CONCERNS ABOUT COMPUTERS

What are the danger signs of exposing children to computer technology? Three concerns are most often raised.

Concerns About Video Games   The results of one recent survey revealed that more than 80% of U.S. adolescents spend two or more hours a week playing computer video games (Williams, 1998). It is not that this activity necessarily diverts children from schoolwork and peer activities, as many parents have assumed; time spent playing at the computer is usually a substitute for other leisure activities, most notably TV viewing. Nevertheless, critics have feared (and early evidence suggests) that heavy exposure to such popular and incredibly violent video games as *Alien Intruder* and *Mortal Kombat* can instigate aggression and cultivate aggressive habits in the same ways that televised violence does (Fling et al., 1992; Williams, 1998).

Concerns About Social Inequalities   Other critics are convinced that the computer revolution may leave some groups of children behind, lacking in skills required in our increasingly computer-dependent society. For example, children from economically disadvantaged families may be exposed to computers at school but are unlikely to have them at home (Rocheleau, 1995). Also, boys are far more likely than girls to take an interest in computers and to sign up for computer camps. Why? Probably because computers are often viewed as involving mathematics, a traditionally masculine subject, and many available computer games are designed with boys in mind (Lepper, 1985; Ogletree & Williams, 1990). Yet this gender gap is narrowing, largely due to the increasing use of computers to foster cooperative classroom learning activities that girls typically enjoy (Collis, 1996; Rocheleau, 1995).

Concerns About Internet Exposure   The proliferation of home computers and on-line services means that literally millions of children and adolescents around the world may now have unsupervised access to the internet and the *World Wide Web*. Clearly, exposure to information available on the Web can be a boon to students researching topics pertinent to their school assignments. Nevertheless, many parents and teachers are alarmed about potentially unsavory Web influences. For example, children and adolescents chatting with acquaintances on-line have been drawn into cybersexual relationships and, occasionally, to meetings with and exploitation by their adult chat mates (Williams, 1998). Furthermore, the Web is (or has been) a primary recruiting tool for such cults as *Heaven's Gate,* as well as hate organizations such as the *Ku Klux Klan* (Downing, 1999). So there are reasons to suspect that unrestricted Web access could prove harmful to some children and adolescents, and additional research aimed at estimating these risks is sorely needed.

Like television sets, then, computers may prove to be either a positive or a negative force on development, depending on how they are used. Outcomes may be less than positive if a young person's primary uses of the machine are to fritter away study time chatting about undesirable topics on-line, or to hole up by himself, zapping mutant aliens from space. But the news may be rather positive indeed for youngsters who use computers to learn, to create, and to collaborate amicably with siblings and peers.

The School as a Socialization Agent

Of all the formal institutions that children encounter in their lives away from home, few have as much opportunity to influence their development as the schools they attend. Starting at age 5 or 6, the typical child in the United States spends about five hours of each weekday at school. And children are staying there longer than ever before. In 1870 there were only 200 public high schools in the United States, and only half of all American children were attending during the three to five months that school was in session. Today the school term is about nine months long (180 school days); more than 75% of American youth are still attending high school at age 17; and nearly 50% of U.S. high school graduates enroll in some form of higher education (U.S. Bureau of the Census, 1997).

If asked to characterize the mission of the schools, we are likely to think of them as the place where children acquire basic knowledge and academic proficiencies: reading, writing, arithmetic, computer skills, and later, foreign languages, social studies, higher math, and science. But schools also expose children to an **informal curriculum** that teaches them how to fit into their culture. Students are expected to obey rules, cooperate with their classmates, respect authority, and become good citizens. And much of the influence that peers may have on developing children occurs in the context of school-related activities and may depend very critically on the type of school a child attends and the quality of a child's school experiences. So it is quite proper to think of the school as an agent of socialization that is likely to affect children's social and emotional development as well as to impart knowledge and help prepare students for a job and economic self-sufficiency.

In this section of the chapter, we focus on the ways schools influence children. First, we consider whether formal classroom experiences are likely to promote children's intellectual development. Then we see that schools clearly differ in "effectiveness"—that is, the ability to accomplish both curricular goals and noncurricular objectives that contribute to what educators often call "good citizenship." After reviewing the characteristics of effective and less effective schools, we examine some of the ways teachers might influence the social behavior and academic progress of their pupils. Finally, we discuss a few of the obstacles that handicapped students and disadvantaged youth may encounter at school as we consider whether our educational system is currently meeting the needs of our children.

DOES SCHOOLING PROMOTE COGNITIVE DEVELOPMENT?

If you have completed the first two years of college, you may already know far more biology, chemistry, and physics than many of the brightest college professors of only 100 years ago. Clearly, students acquire a vast amount of knowledge about their world from the schooling they receive. But when developmentalists ask, "Do schools promote cognitive growth?" they want to know whether formal education hastens intellectual development or encourages modes of thinking and methods of problem solving that are less likely to develop in the absence of schooling.

To address these issues, investigators have typically studied the intellectual growth of children from developing countries where schooling is not compulsory or not yet available throughout the society. Studies of this type generally find that children who attend school are quicker to reach certain Piagetian milestones (for example, conservation) and will perform better on tests of memory and metacognitive knowledge than age-mates from similar backgrounds who do not go to school (see Rogoff, 1990; Sharp, Cole, & Lave, 1979). And it seems that the more schooling children complete, the better their cognitive performance. Consider what Frederick Morrison and his associates (1995, 1997) found when comparing the cognitive performance of children

informal curriculum: noncurricular objectives of schooling such as teaching children to cooperate, to respect authority, to obey rules, and to become good citizens.

who had just made the age cutoff for entering first grade with that of youngsters who had just missed the cutoff and had spent the year in kindergarten. When tested at the end of the school year, the youngest first-graders clearly outperformed the nearly *identically aged* kindergartners in reading, memory, language, and arithmetic skills. In another study of fourth-, fifth-, and sixth-graders in Israel (Cahan & Cohen, 1989), children at any given grade performed at higher levels on a variety of intellectual tests than their chronological *age-mates* in the next lower grade. Finally, one recent study found that U.S. school children on an *extended-year* (210 day) calendar tested higher in academic achievement and general cognitive competencies in the fall of the next school year than did peers who were equally competent at the beginning of the study but who had attended school on a normal 180-day calender (Frazier & Morrison, 1998). Taken together, these findings clearly indicate that children's intellectual performances are influenced, in part, by the *amount* of schooling they have had.

So schooling does seem to promote cognitive growth, both by transmitting general knowledge and by teaching children a variety of rules, principles, strategies, and problem-solving skills (including an ability to concentrate and an appreciation for abstraction) that they can apply to many different kinds of information (Ceci, 1991; Ceci & Williams, 1997).

Interestingly, the vast majority of U.S. children now begin their schooling well before age 6—attending kindergarten as 5-year-olds and, in many cases, going to nursery school or day care before that (National Center for Educational Statistics, 1995). Is this a healthy trend? As we see in Box 12.2 on p. 418, there are advantages as well as some possible disadvantages associated with early entry into a school-like environment.

DETERMINANTS OF EFFECTIVE (AND INEFFECTIVE) SCHOOLING

One of the first questions parents often ask when searching for a residence in a new town is, "Where should we live so that our children will get the best education?" This concern reflects the common belief that some schools are "better" or "more effective" than others. But are they?

Michael Rutter (1983) certainly thinks so. According to Rutter, **effective schools** are those that promote academic achievement, social skills, polite and attentive behavior, positive attitudes toward learning, low absenteeism, continuation of education beyond the age at which attendance is mandatory, and acquisition of skills that will enable students to find and hold a job. Rutter argues that some schools are more successful than others at accomplishing these objectives, regardless of the students' racial, ethnic, or socioeconomic backgrounds. Let's examine the evidence for this claim.

In one large study, Rutter and his associates (1979) conducted extensive interviews and observations in 12 high schools serving lower- to lower-middle income populations in London, England. As the children entered these schools, they were given a battery of achievement tests to measure their prior academic accomplishments. At the end of high school, the pupils took another major exam to assess their academic progress. Other information, such as attendance records and teacher ratings of classroom behavior, was also available. When the data were analyzed, Rutter found that the 12 schools clearly differed in "effectiveness": students from the "better" schools exhibited fewer problem behaviors, attended school more regularly, and made more academic progress than students from the less effective schools. We get some idea of the importance of these "schooling effects" from Figure 12.4. The

effective schools: schools that are generally successful at achieving curricular and noncurricular objectives, regardless of the racial, ethnic, or socioeconomic background of the student population.

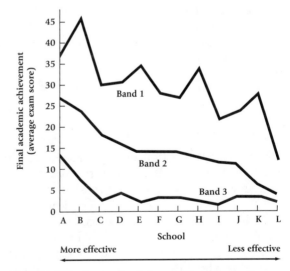

FIGURE 12.4 Average level of academic achievement in secondary school as a function of initial achievement at the time of entry (bands 1–3) and the school that pupils were attending (schools A–L). Note that pupils in all three bands performed at higher levels on this final academic assessment if they attended the more effective schools. Moreover, students in band 2 performed like band-1 students in the more effective schools but like band-3 students in the least effective schools. From Rutler et al., 1979.

Box 12.2   Current Controversies

Should Preschoolers Attend School?

In recent years, children in the United States have begun their schooling at increasingly younger ages. Not only is kindergarten for 5-year-olds compulsory in most states, but there is talk of requiring school for 4-year-olds (Zigler, 1987). And already many preschoolers spend 4- to 8-hour days in day-care settings or nursery schools that have a strong academic emphasis and attempt to ready them for the classroom.

Is attending preschool beneficial? Developmentalists such as Edward Zigler (1987) and David Elkind (1981b), author of *The Hurried Child,* express some concerns that the current push for earlier and earlier education may be going too far. They feel that many young children today are not given enough time simply to be children—to play and socialize as they choose. Elkind even worries that children may lose their self-initiative and enjoyment of learning if their lives are orchestrated by parents who incessantly push them to achieve.

Three recent studies seem to confirm Elkind's concerns (Hart, Burts, et al., 1998; Hyson, Hirsch-Pasek, & Rescorla, 1989; Stipek et al., 1995). Three- to 6-year-olds in academically oriented preschools or kindergartens displayed an initial advantage in such basic academic competencies as a knowledge of letters and reading skills but had lost it by the end of kindergarten. What's more, students in these highly structured, academically oriented programs proved to be *less creative, more stressed, and more anxious about tests, less prideful* about their successes, *less confident* about succeeding in the future, and generally *less enthusiastic* about school than children who attended preschool or kindergarten programs that emphasized child-centered social agendas and flexible hands-on, discovery-based learning. So there may well be dangers in overemphasizing academics during the preschool period, after all.

On the other hand, preschool programs that offer a healthy mix of play and basic skill-building activities can be very beneficial to young children, especially to disadvantaged children. Children who attend high-quality preschools often develop social skills at an earlier age than those who remain at home (Clarke-Stewart, 1993). And, although most children who attend preschool classes are no more or less intellectually advanced than those who remain at home, *disadvantaged* preschoolers who attend programs designed to prepare them for school display more cognitive growth and achieve more success in school than other disadvantaged youngsters (Burchinal et al., 1997; Ramey & Ramey, 1998). So as long as preschool programs allow plenty of time for play and for skill building in the context of group social interactions, they can help children from all social backgrounds acquire social and communication skills, as well as an appreciation of rules and routines, that will smooth the transition from individual learning at home to group learning in an elementary school classroom (Zigler & Finn-Stevenson, 1993).

"bands" on the graph refer to the pupils' academic accomplishments *at the time they entered* high school (band 3, low achievers; band 1, high achievers). In all three bands, students attending the "more effective" schools outperformed those in the "less effective" schools on the final assessment of academic achievement. Even more revealing is the finding that the initially poor students (band 3) who attended the "better" schools ended up scoring just as high on this final index of academic progress as the initially good (band 1) students who attended the least effective schools. Similar findings were obtained in other large studies of elementary and high schools in the United States. Even after controlling for important variables such as the racial composition and socioeconomic backgrounds of the student bodies and the type of communities served, some elementary schools were found to be much more "effective" than others (Brookover et al., 1979; Hill, Foster, & Gendler, 1990).

So the school that children attend can make a difference. And you may be surprised by some of the factors that do and do not have a bearing on how "effective" a school is.

Some Misconceptions About Effective Schooling

Monetary Support   Surprising as it may seem, a school's level of support has little to do with the quality of education students receive. Seriously inadequate funding can undermine the quality of education; but as long as a school has qualified teachers and a reasonable level of support, the precise amount of money spent per pupil, the number of books in the school library, teachers' salaries, and teachers' academic credentials play only a minor role in determining student outcomes (Rutter, 1983).

School and Class Size   Another factor that has relatively little to do with a school's effectiveness is average class size: In typical elementary and secondary school classes ranging from 20 to 40 students, class size has little or no effect on academic achievement (Odden, 1990; Toch & Streisand, 1997). However, classes smaller than 15 to 20 pupils are beneficial in the primary grades (kindergarten through grade 3) (Finn & Achilles, 1990), and primary students in larger classes—especially disadvantaged or low-ability students—do much better in reading and math when they are tutored part of the day in smaller study groups (Odden, 1990; Slavin, 1989; Toch & Streisand, 1997). So if a school district has money available to hire additional instructors, the wisest course might be to devote these "personnel resources" to the primary grades—precisely the settings in which smaller classes promote academic achievement.

There is some evidence that the size of one's school affects older students' participation in structured extracurricular activities—settings in which such aspects of the "informal curriculum" as cooperation, fair play, and healthy attitudes toward competition are likely to be stressed. Although larger high schools offer a greater number of extracurricular activities, students in the smaller schools tend to be (1) more heavily involved, (2) more likely to hold positions of responsibility of leadership, and (3) more satisfied with extracurricular experiences (Barker & Gump, 1964; Jacobs & Chase, 1989). Why? One reason is that students in larger schools receive much less encouragement to participate, often becoming lost in the crowd and feeling a sense of alienation and a lack of connectedness with peers and the academic culture. This is indeed unfortunate, for one recent longitudinal study that tracked adolescents from the seventh through the twelfth grade found that high school students—particularly less competent students with poor social skills—were much less likely to drop out of school if they had maintained a voluntary connection to their school environments by participating in one or more extracurricular activities (Mahoney & Cairns, 1997; see Figure 12.5). The implications of these findings are clear: To better accomplish their mission of educating students and properly preparing them for adult life, middle and secondary schools—large and small—might do more to encourage all students to participate in extracurricular activities and not be so quick to deny them these opportunities because of marginal academic performances (Mahoney & Cairns, 1997).

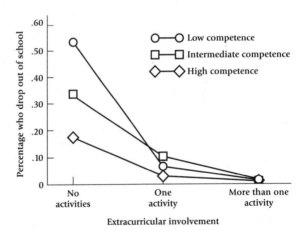

FIGURE 12.5 Rates of high school dropout as a function of student social/academic competencies and participation in extracurricular activities. Clearly, students of low or intermediate competence are more likely to stay in school if they participate in extracurricular activities and maintain a positive and voluntary connection to peers and the school environment. (Mahoney & Cairns, 1997.)

Ability Tracking   The merits of **ability tracking**—a procedure in which students are grouped by IQ or academic achievement and then taught in classes made up of students of comparable "ability"—have been debated for years. Some educators believe that students learn more when surrounded by peers of equal ability. Others argue that ability tracking undermines the self-esteem of lower-ability students and contributes to their poor academic achievement and high dropout rate.

In his early review of the literature, Rutter (1983) found that neither ability tracking nor mixed-ability teaching has decisive advantages: Both procedures are common in highly effective and less effective schools. Yet recent research suggests some qualifications. Apparently, ability tracking does widen the gap between high and low achievers (Dornbush, Glasgow, & Lin, 1996; Slavin, 1987), whereas mixed-ability instruction in elementary and middle schools seems to promote the academic achievement of less capable students without undermining the performance of their more capable peers (Kulik & Kulik, 1992). Ability tracking *can* be beneficial to high-ability students, *if* they are exposed to a curriculum tailored to their learning needs (Fuligni, Eccles, & Barber, 1995; Kulik & Kulik, 1992). However, lower ability students are unlikely to benefit and may well suffer if they are stigmatized as "dummies" and are not challenged academically, or if they are denied access to the more effective instructors who might help them to master such challenges (Fuligni et al., 1995; Kulik & Kulik, 1992).

Classroom Organization   Chances are that you were educated in a **traditional classroom** with seats arranged in neat rows facing the teacher, who lectured or gave demonstrations at a desk or a chalkboard. In a traditional classroom, the curriculum is highly structured: Normally, everybody will be studying the same subject, and students are expected to interact with the teacher rather than with each other.

In an **open classroom**, children are viewed as active, autonomous agents who learn better by becoming more actively involved in their education. Rarely are children in open classrooms all doing the same thing at once. A more typical scenario is for students to distribute themselves around the room, working individually or in small groups at reading stories, playing word games, solving math puzzles, creating art, or working on the class's science project. And rather than being centers of attention or central authority figures, teachers in open classrooms help children to decide what they will learn about and will circulate around the room, guiding and instructing students in response to their individual needs (Minuchin & Shapiro, 1983).

There are some clear social and emotional advantages associated with open classrooms: Students express more positive attitudes about school, are more self-directed in pursuing learning objectives, and display a greater ability to cooperate with classmates while creating fewer disciplinary problems than students in traditional classrooms (Minuchin & Shapiro, 1983). However, many investigators find no difference in the academic performance of students in open and traditional classrooms (Minuchin & Shapiro, 1983), and others have concluded that students actually learn more in a *traditional* classroom whenever the subject matter requires them to learn abstract concepts that may be difficult for them to grasp on their own (Good, 1979; Slavin, as cited in Associated Press, 1994a). Clearly, each of these classroom arrangements has its advantages and disadvantages, and both are common in effective (and in less effective) schools (Associated Press 1994a; Rutter, 1983).

ability tracking: the educational practice of grouping students according to ability and then educating them in classes with students of comparable educational or intellectual standing.

traditional classroom: a classroom arrangement in which all pupils sit facing an instructor, who normally teaches one subject at a time by lecturing or giving demonstrations.

open classroom: a less structured classroom arrangement in which there is a separate area for each educational activity and children distribute themselves around the room, working individually or in small groups.

PHOTO 12.4   Children at work in an open classroom.

Factors That Do Contribute to Effective Schooling

Composition of the Student Body   To some extent, the "effectiveness" of a school is a function of what it has to work with. On average, academic achievement is lowest in schools with a preponderance of economically disadvantaged students, and it appears that *any* child is likely to make more academic progress if taught in a school with a higher concentration of intellectually capable peers (Brookover et al., 1979; Portes & MacLeod, 1996). However, this *does not* mean that a school is only as good as the students it serves, for many schools that draw heavily from disadvantaged minority populations are highly effective at motivating students and preparing them for jobs or higher education (Reynolds, 1992).

The Scholastic Atmosphere of Successful Schools   So what is it about the learning environment of some schools that allows them to accomplish so much? Reviews of the literature (Phillips, 1997; Reynolds, 1992; Rutter, 1983) point to the following values and practices that characterize effective schools:

1. *Academic emphases.* Effective schools have a clear focus on academic goals. Children are regularly assigned homework, which is checked, corrected, and discussed with them.
2. *Classroom management.* In effective schools, teachers waste little time getting activities started or dealing with distracting disciplinary problems. Lessons begin and end on time. Pupils are told exactly what is expected of them and receive clear and unambiguous feedback about their academic performance. The classroom atmosphere is comfortable; all students are actively encouraged to work to the best of their abilities, and ample praise acknowledges good work.
3. *Discipline.* In effective schools, the staff is firm in enforcing rules and does so on the spot rather than sending offenders off to the principal's office. Rarely do instructors resort to physical sanctions (slapping or spanking), which contribute to truancy, defiance, and a tense classroom atmosphere.
4. *Teamwork.* Effective schools have faculties that work as a team, jointly planning curricular objectives and monitoring student progress, under the guidance of a principal who provides active, energetic leadership.

In sum, the effective school environment is a comfortable but businesslike setting in which academic successes are expected and students are motivated to learn (Phillips, 1997; Rutter, 1983).

The "Goodness of Fit" Between Students and Schools   There is another important point to make about effective schooling: Characteristics of the student and of the school environment often interact to affect student outcomes—a phenomenon Lee Cronbach and Richard Snow (1977) call **aptitude-treatment interaction (ATI).** Over the years, much educational research has been based on the assumption that a particular teaching method, philosophy of education, or organizational system will prove superior for all students, regardless of their abilities, personalities, and cultural backgrounds. This assumption is often wrong. Instead, many approaches to education are highly effective with some kinds of students but quite ineffective with others. The secret to being effective is to find an appropriate fit between learners and educational practices.

For example, teachers tend to get the most out of *high-ability, middle-class* students by moving at a quick pace and insisting on high standards of performance—that is, by challenging these students. By contrast, *low-ability* and *disadvantaged* students often respond more favorably to a teacher who motivates them by providing truly engaging learning exercises and remaining warm and encouraging rather than intrusive and demanding (Good & Brophy, 1994; Sachs & Mergendoller, 1997).

Sensitivity to students' *cultural* traditions is also crucial for designing an effective instructional program. European-American students come from cultures that stress individual accomplishments, perhaps making them especially well suited for the individual mastery expectations that are emphasized in traditional classrooms. By contrast, ethnic Hawaiians and other students from collectivist cultures that stress cooperation

aptitude-treatment interaction (ATI): phenomenon whereby characteristics of the student and of the school environment interact to affect student outcomes, such that any given educational practice may be effective with some students but not with others.

and collaborative approaches to learning often founder in traditional Western class-rooms. They pay little attention to the teacher or their lessons and spend a lot of time seeking the attention of classmates—behaviors that are perceived by teachers as re-flecting their lack of interest in school (Tharp, 1989). Yet when instruction is made more culturally compatible for these youngsters, by having teachers circulate among small groups, instructing each group and encouraging group members to pull together and assist each other to achieve learning objectives, Hawaiian children become much more enthusiastic about school and achieve much more as well (see Figure 12.6).

Unfortunately, young adolescents from any social background may begin to lose interest in academics should they experience a mismatch between their school envi-ronments and their changing developmental needs—a point well illustrated by the findings presented in Box 12.3 on pages 424–425.

In sum, the "goodness of fit" between students and their classroom environments is a crucial aspect of effective schooling. Education that is carefully tailored to stu-dents' cultural backgrounds, personal characteristics, and developmental needs is much more likely to succeed.

THE TEACHER'S INFLUENCE

Once they reach school age, many children spend nearly as much time around their teachers as they do around their parents. Indeed, teachers are often the first adults outside the immediate family to play a major role in a child's life, and the functions that teachers serve will change rather dramatically as children progress through the educational system (Minuchin & Shapiro, 1983). Preschool and kindergarten classes are in some ways similar to home life: teachers serve as companions or substitute caregivers who provide reassurance if needed while striving to help their pupils achieve the objectives of the preschool curriculum. Elementary school classrooms are more structured: Teachers are focusing mainly on curricular goals, and grade-school children are now more inclined to perceive their instructors as evaluators and au-thority figures rather than pals. During the adolescent years, teachers continue to serve as evaluators and authority figures. But since high school and college students change classes hourly and have many different teachers, it is less likely that any sin-gle instructor will exert as much influence as was true during the grade-school years.

Much of the research on teacher influences has focused on two very broad topics: (1) influences stemming from the teacher's evaluation of students and (2) the effects of teaching styles on pupil outcomes.

Teachers as Appraisers and Evaluators

Teacher Expectancy Effects   Teachers form distinct impressions of their students' scholastic abilities, and these expectancies can clearly affect children's academic progress. In a landmark study, Robert Rosenthal and Lenore Jacobson (1968) pro-posed that a teacher's expectancies about a student can influence the child's achieve-ment through what they called the **Pygmalion effect**: A student should perform better when expected to do well than when expected to do poorly, so teacher ex-pectancies may become *self-fulfilling prophecies*. To demonstrate this, Rosenthal and Jacobson gave each elementary school teacher in their study a list of five students who were supposed to be "rapid bloomers." In fact, the so-called rapid bloomers had been randomly selected from class rosters. The only way they differed from other students is that their teachers expected more of them. Yet planting these high expectancies in the minds of first- and second-grade teachers was sufficient to cause the so-called rapid bloomers to show greater gains in IQ and reading achievement than their un-labeled classmates.

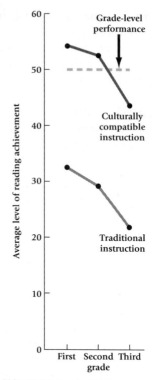

FIGURE 12.6   Reading achievement of ethnic Hawaiian first- through third-grade students who received traditional or culturally compatible classroom instruction. The students who received culturally compatible instruction read at grade level, whereas those receiving traditional instruction read far below grade level. (Adapted from Tharp & Gallimore, 1988.)

Pygmalion effect: the tendency of teacher expectancies to become self-fulfilling prophecies, causing students to perform better or worse depending on their teacher's estimation of their potential.

Although some investigators have failed to replicate Rosenthal and Jacobson's results (Cooper, 1979), many others have reported similar findings, showing that (1) students expected by teachers to do well are likely to live up to these positive expectancies, whereas (2) those expected to perform poorly often do earn lower grades and score lower on standardized tests than classmates of comparable ability for whom the teacher has no negative expectancies (see Harris & Rosenthal, 1986; Weinstein et al., 1987). Clearly, the positive or negative expectancies that most teachers form often reflect *real* differences between students: Those expected to perform well (or poorly) in the future have typically performed well (or poorly) in the past (Jussim & Eccles, 1992). Still, even if two students have equal aptitude and motivation, the one whose teacher expects great things is likely to outperform the one whose teacher expects less (Jussim & Eccles, 1992).

How exactly does the Pygmalion effect work? It seems that teachers expose high-expectancy students to more challenging materials, demand better performances from them, and are more likely to praise these youngsters for answering questions correctly (perhaps leading them to infer that they have high ability). And when high-expectancy students do not answer correctly, they often hear the question rephrased so that they can get it right, thus implying that failures can be overcome by persisting and trying harder (Dweck & Elliot, 1983). Meanwhile, low expectancy students are not often challenged and are more likely to be criticized when they answer questions incorrectly—a practice that may convince them that they have *little ability* and undermine their motivation to achieve (Brophy, 1983; Dweck & Elliott, 1983). Even first-graders are becoming aware of their teachers' expectations, and between first and fifth grade, they increasingly expect of themselves the kind of performance that their teachers expect of them (Weinstein et al., 1987).

Many now believe that teachers should be made aware of how their expectancies and associated classroom behaviors can influence their students. Indeed, the clever instructor might even use this knowledge to get the most out of nearly every child in his or her class by (1) setting *mastery* goals that the child can realistically achieve, (2) communicating these *positive* expectancies to the child, and (3) praising the *ability* the child has shown upon reaching these academic milestones (Butler, 1990; Dweck & Elliot, 1983).

Impacts of Testing Procedures   Teachers often hear students make such statements as "I knew the material but froze during the test" or "I worried so much about finishing that I made stupid mistakes." Are these kinds of statements merely rationalizations for poor marks?

Probably not, in many cases. A sizable minority of children and adolescents (even very capable ones) become highly anxious during tests, and this **test anxiety** can interfere with their academic performance, *particularly if the test is timed*. In one well-known study (Hill & Eaton, 1977), highly anxious and less anxious grade-schoolers took an arithmetic test under one of two conditions. Some children had all the time they needed to complete the test, whereas the remaining youngsters had a time limit imposed on them—one ensuring that they would fail to finish. The results were clear. On the timed test, highly anxious children made three times as many errors and spent twice as much time per problem as their low-anxious classmates. But if time pressures were removed, the highly anxious students worked just as quickly and performed just as well on the test as their less anxious peers. We see, then, that the way teachers structure their evaluative procedures can have a major impact on the academic performance of students high in test anxiety. Although any test has the potential to elicit some concern from students about being evaluated, it appears that teachers who favor and use highly stressful evaluative techniques may inadvertently

test anxiety: a concern about being evaluated that can undermine performance, especially under highly stressful, competitive testing procedures.

Box 12.3 Developmental Issues

On the Difficult Transition to Secondary Schools

For some time now, educators have been concerned about a number of undesirable changes that often occur when students make the transition from elementary school to junior high school: loss of self-esteem and interest in school, declining grades, and increased troublemaking, to name a few (Eccles, Midgley et al., 1993, 1996; Seidman et al., 1994). Why is this a treacherous move?

One reason that the transition is difficult is because young adolescents, particularly girls, are often experiencing major physical and psychological changes at the same time that they are required to change schools. Roberta Simmons and Dale Blyth (1987), for example, found that girls who were reaching puberty as they were making the transition from sixth grade in an elementary school to seventh grade in a junior high school were more likely to experience drops in self-esteem and other negative changes than girls who remained in a kindergarten–eighth grade (K-8) school during this vulnerable period. Adolescents at greatest risk of academic and emotional difficulties are those who must also cope with other life transitions, such as family turmoil or a change in residence, at about the time they change schools (Flanagan & Eccles, 1993). Could it be, then, that more adolescents would remain interested in academics and show better adjustment outcomes if they weren't forced to change schools at the precise time that they are experiencing many other changes often associated with puberty? This has been part of the rationale for the development of *middle schools,* serving grades 6 through 8, which are now more common than junior high schools in the United States (Braddock & McPartland, 1993).

Yet Jacquelynne Eccles and her colleagues (Eccles, Lord, & Midgley, 1991; Eccles, Midgley et al., 1993) report that students do not necessarily find the transition to middle school any easier than the transition to junior high school. This has led them to suspect that it is not as important *when* adolescents make a school change as *what* their new school is like. Specifically, they have proposed a "goodness of fit" hypothesis stating that the transition to a new school is likely to be especially difficult when that school, whether a junior high or middle school, is ill-matched to the developmental needs of early adolescents.

Eccles and her associates have found that the transition to junior high school often involves going from a small school with close student–teacher relationships, a good deal of choice regarding learning activities, and reasonable discipline to a larger, more bureaucratized environment where student–teacher relationships are impersonal, good grades are harder to come by, opportunities for choice are limited, assignments are not very intellectually stimulating, and discipline is rigid—all this at a time when adolescents are seeking *more,* rather than less, autonomy and are more intellectually capable.

Eccles and others have demonstrated that the "fit" between developmental needs and school environment is indeed an important influence on adolescent adjustment to school. In one study (Mac Iver & Reuman, 1988), the transition to junior high brought about a decline in intrinsic interest in learning mainly among students who wanted more involvement in classroom decisions but ended up with fewer such opportunities than they had in elementary school. Furthermore, the lack of close, supportive relations with teachers makes many autonomy-seeking adolescents in impersonal secondary schools much more susceptible to peer values and influences,

underrate the scholastic abilities and perhaps undermine the achievement motivation of their more anxious pupils.

Teacher's Evaluations of Children's Conduct   Finally, it seems that the ways in which teachers evaluate and respond to the nonacademic aspects of a child's conduct can clearly influence that child's standing among peers. In one interesting experiment (White & Kistner, 1992), kindergartners, first-graders, and second-graders watched a videotape in which a child responded appropriately in class much of the time but was disruptive (giggling and flying paper airplanes) at other times. The teacher's

Moving from small, close-knit elementary schools to highly bureaucratic and impersonal secondary schools is stressful for adolescents, many of whom lose interest in academics and become more susceptible to peer-group influences.

The message? Declines in academic motivation and performance are not inevitable as students move from elementary to secondary schools. These declines occur primarily when the fit between student and school environment goes from good to poor. How might we improve the fit? Parents can help by recognizing how difficult school transitions can be and communicating this understanding to their teens. Indeed, one study found that adolescents whose parents were in tune with their developmental needs and who fostered autonomy in decision making generally adjusted well to the transition to junior high and posted *gains* in self-esteem (Lord, Eccles, & McCarthy, 1994). Teachers can also help by seeking parents' opinions about scholastic matters and keeping them involved during this transitional period—a time when collaborative relations between parents and teachers normally decline and adolescents often feel that they are facing the stresses of this new, impersonal academic atmosphere with little social support (Eccles & Harold, 1993). Finally, The Carnegie Council on Adolescent Development (1989) advises secondary schools to reorganize into smaller communities for learning in order to provide young adolescents with more social support and to make them feel less anonymous. The key elements of this "communities" approach involve forming (1) "schools within schools," in which subsets of students and teachers grouped together as "teams" become more familiar with (and, hopefully, supportive of) each other, and (2) small group advisories, or homerooms, to ensure that every student has access to at least one adult who knows him or her well.

which they often perceived as antisocial (Seidman et al., 1994). Finally, a third study illustrates just how important a *good* fit between students and school environments can be. Students experienced negative changes in their attitudes toward mathematics if their transition to junior high resulted in less personal and supportive relations with math teachers; but for those few students whose transition to junior high involved gaining more supportive teachers than they had in elementary school, interest in academics actually *increased* (Midgley, Feldlaufer, & Eccles, 1989).

responses to this child varied in different versions of the videotape. Some children saw the teacher accentuate the positive by praising the child's appropriate behaviors. Others saw the teacher accentuate the negative by *derogating* the offender (saying, for example, "I've had just about enough, Billy"). Finally, children in a control condition heard the teacher make neutral statements to the entire class without responding either positively or negatively to the target child's conduct. After viewing one of the above videotapes, participants judged the target child's likability and were asked to indicate whether the target child was apt to display such prosocial behaviors as helping others and such antisocial behaviors as pushing and shoving other kids.

The results, which appear in Figure 12.7, were interesting. Compared to the target child in the control condition, the target child who was praised for appropriate conduct was judged to be more likable and more inclined to display prosocial behaviors such as helping, whereas the child who received *derogatory* feedback was deemed significantly less likable and much more inclined to display antisocial acts such as hitting and shoving. In a similar vein, Sandra Birch and Gary Ladd (1998) found that disruptive kindergartners, who often required discipline and who established *conflictual* relationships with their teachers, came to display more and more aggression and less and less prosocial behavior toward peers as they made the transition from kindergarten to first grade.

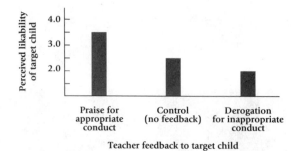

FIGURE 12.7 Average likability ratings for a disruptive child as a function of the type of verbal feedback the teacher provides. (Adapted from White & Kistner, 1992.)

So it seems that elementary school teachers may either promote a child's status in the eyes of peers (by praising appropriate conduct) or undermine it (by derogating inappropriate behavior). And this kind of influence is potentially important, for as we will see in Chapter 13, children who are rejected by peers early in the grade-school years often retain their "rejectee" status and are at risk for experiencing a variety of adjustment problems later in life. Although teachers may find it impossible not to react to the behavior of an habitually disruptive pupil, they may be doing both themselves and the disruptive child a favor by *correcting* rather than derogating inappropriate conduct, and by looking for opportunities to praise such children for their appropriate behaviors.[4]

Teaching Styles and Instructional Techniques Earlier we learned that teachers in "effective" schools set clear-cut standards for their students to achieve, emphasize successes more than failures, firmly enforce rules without derogating an offender or becoming overly punitive, and use praise rather than threats to encourage each child to work to the best of his or her ability. Perhaps you have noticed that these managerial characteristics are in some ways similar to the pattern of control that Diana Baumrind calls authoritative parenting. Indeed, Baumrind (1972) believes that the three major patterns of control that characterize parent/child interactions are also found in the classroom. Teachers who use an **authoritarian** style tend to dominate their pupils, relying on power-assertive methods to enforce their demands. The **authoritative** teacher is also controlling but will rely on reason to explain his or her demands, encourage verbal give-and-take, and value autonomy and creative expression so long as the child is willing to live within the rules that the teacher has established. Finally, the **laissez-faire** (or permissive) instructor makes few demands of students and provides little or no active guidance. Baumrind believes that teachers who use an authoritative style will promote children's intellectual curiosity, their academic achievement, and their social and emotional development.

A classic study by Kurt Lewin and his associates (Lewin, Lippitt, & White, 1939) supports Baumrind's viewpoint. Eleven-year-old boys who met after school to participate in hobby activities, such as making papier-mâché theater masks, were supervised by adults who functioned (1) as *authoritarian* leaders (by rigidly assigning jobs and work partners and by dictating policies without providing rationales for these edicts), (2) as authoritative, or *democratic,* leaders (by guiding the boys as they chose their own

authoritarian instruction: a restrictive style of instruction in which the teacher makes absolute demands and uses threats or force (if necessary) to ensure that students comply.

authoritative instruction: a controlling style of instruction in which the teacher makes many demands but also allows some autonomy and individual expression as long as students are staying within the guidelines that the teacher has set.

laissez-faire instruction: a permissive style of instruction which the teacher makes few demands of students and provides little or no active guidance.

---

[4]Indeed, derogatory feedback may even *reinforce* inappropriate conduct if the child is disrupting the class as a means of seeking attention. By contrast, corrective feedback (perhaps backed by "time out," if necessary) provides less attention to a disruptive child and, coupled with the use of praise for appropriate on-task behaviors, is an example of the *incompatible-response technique* that has often proved effective in modifying children's aggressive inclinations (see Chapter 9).

jobs and work partners and participated in policymaking), or (3) as *laissez-faire* leaders (by providing little or no guidance and remaining noncommittal for the most part). How did the boys react to these supervisory styles? Authoritarian leadership produced tension, restlessness, hostile outbursts, and a general dissatisfaction with the group experience. Productivity (as indexed by the number of theater masks constructed) was high under authoritarian leadership while the leader was present. But when the leader left the room, work patterns disintegrated. Democratic leadership was more effective; the boys were friendly toward one another and happier with the leader. Although productivity was not as high under democratic supervision, the boys continued working in the leader's absence and the work they completed was of higher quality than that produced under authoritarian or laissez-faire leaders. Finally, the laissez-faire approach resulted in an apathetic group atmosphere and very low productivity. All but 1 of the 20 boys in this experiment clearly favored democratic supervision.

These findings also hold in the classroom, where students prefer a democratic atmosphere (Rosenthal, Underwood, & Martin, 1969; U.S. Department of Education, 1996) and often achieve more under a flexible, nondictatorial instructional style as well (Minuchin & Shapiro, 1983). And even among preschool children, lax, permissive supervision is highly ineffective at keeping children on task and often results in high levels of misconduct (Arnold, McWilliams, & Arnold, 1998). So authoritative instruction does seem to promote a climate that is highly conducive to academic achievement. Yet, we should keep in mind that there are many ways in which authoritative instructors might attempt to motivate their pupils and the techniques that work best will largely depend on the "goodness of fit" between the instructor's methods and the type of student that he or she is trying to reach.

DO OUR SCHOOLS MEET THE NEEDS OF ALL OUR CHILDREN?

Public education in the United States arose not so much from a desire to educate a workforce (most 19th century workers were farmers or unskilled laborers who required little education) as from the need to "Americanize" a nation of immigrants—to bring them into the mainstream of American society (Rudolph, 1965). So our public schools have traditionally been majority-culture, middle-class institutions staffed by White instructors who promote middle-class values.

However, more and more of the students educated in our public schools come from non-White social backgrounds; in fact, a *majority* of students in California's public schools now belong to various "minority" groups (Garcia, 1993). How well are minority students being served by our schools? And how well are today's schools meeting the needs of students with developmental disabilities and other special needs?

Educational Experiences of Ethnic Minorities In his book *Dark Ghetto,* Kenneth Clark (1965) argued that the American public school classroom represents a "clash of cultures" in which teachers who have adopted middle-class values fail to appreciate the difficulties that minority students face in trying to adjust to the quiet, orderly, Eurocentric atmosphere of the schools. To cite one example of clashing language customs, African-American children are asked fewer questions at home than White children are, and the questions they are asked are typically open-ended prompts that call for them to recount their knowledge or experiences through long, elaborate verbal responses (Brice-Heath, 1982, 1989). Consequently, these youngsters are often hesitant to answer what, for them, are "unusual" knowledge-training questions (requiring brief, factually correct answers) at school and may thus be branded by teachers as unknowledgeable or uncooperative.

Indeed, many lower-income children from ethnic minority groups do have problems at school. We noted in Chapter 7, for example, that these children tend to be academic underachievers, making poorer grades and lower scores on standardized achievement tests than European-American classmates. And they are also more likely than their European-American peers to be disciplined by the staff, to be "held back" in one or more grades, and to drop out before completing high school (Dusek, 1991; U.S. Bureau of Census, 1997). Why is this? Let's consider three possibilities.

Parental Involvement   Although it was once fashionable to attribute the academic underachievement of ethnic minorities to a failure on their parents' part to value education or to encourage academic achievement, we learned in Chapter 7 that this is a serious misconception.[5] Recall that African-American and Latino-American parents value education at least as much as European-American parents do (Galper et al., 1997), and they are actually more inclined to favor such reforms as competency testing for students and a longer school day (Stevenson et al., 1990). However, minority parents are often less knowledgeable about the school system and less heavily involved in parent/teacher conferences, PTA meetings, and other school-sponsored activities, and this lack of involvement may partially counteract their message that schooling is important. Yet when minority parents *are* highly involved in school activities, their children feel more confident about mastering academic challenges and tend to do well in school (Connell, Spencer, & Aber, 1994; Luster & McAdoo, 1996). So active parental involvement can make a big difference.

PHOTO 12.5   Children are more likely to do well in school if their parents value education and are interested and involved in school activities.

Interfacing Parent and Peer Influences   Although minority parents play a crucial role in fostering their children's scholastic competencies, we cannot fully appreciate their impact without also understanding how peers influence academic achievement. Lawrence Steinberg and his colleagues (1992) have conducted a large-scale study of school achievement among African-, Latino-, Asian-, and European-American high school students. They found that academic success and good personal adjustment are usually associated with *authoritative* parenting. However, this positive parental influence on academic achievement can easily be undermined by African-American peers, who often devalue academic achievement and pressure many African-American students to choose between academic success and peer acceptance (see also Ogbu, 1994).

Latino parents tend to be strict and somewhat authoritarian rather than flexible and authoritative. As a result, many Latino students may have relatively few opportunities at home to act autonomously and acquire decision-making skills that would serve them well in the individualistic context of our schools (Steinberg et al., 1992). Furthermore, Latino students from low-income areas also tend to associate with peers who do not strongly value academics and who may undercut their parents' efforts to promote academic achievement. By contrast, European-American students are more likely than either African-American or Latino students to have a combination of authoritative parenting *and* peer support for education working in their favor.

Interestingly, high-achieving Asian-American students often experience restrictive, authoritarian parenting at home. However, this highly controlling pattern, coupled

---

[5]Let's also recall from Chapter 7 that the underachievements displayed by ethnic minorities are *not* simply attributable to intellectual deficiencies. Even when intelligence (that is, IQ test performance) is equivalent, African-American, Native American, and Latino-American students tend to make lower grades and lower scores on standardized achievement tests than European-American and Asian-American students do.

with a *very strong* emphasis on education and the *very high* achievement standards that many Asian-American parents set for their children actually *fosters* academic success. Why? Because as we noted in Chapter 7, Asian-American children are also taught from a very early age to be respectful and to obey their elders, who have a duty to train them to be socially responsible and competent human beings (Chao, 1994; Huntsinger et al., 1998). Given this kind of socialization in Asian-American homes, it is hardly surprising that the Asian-American peer group strongly endorses education and encourages academic success (Fuligni, 1997). The result? Asian-American students typically spend more hours studying, often with their supportive friends, than other students do, which undoubtedly accounts for much of their academic success (Fuligni, 1997; Steinberg et al., 1992).

Teacher Expectancies   Finally, we must consider another hypothesis about ethnic differences in school achievement: the possibility that underachievement by some minority students is rooted in subtle stereotyping and discrimination on the part of teachers. According to social stereotypes, Asian-Americans are expected to be bright and hard-working whereas African-American, Native American, and Latino students from low-income neighborhoods are expected to perform poorly in school. And teachers are hardly immune to these stereotypes. Minority students often feel that White teachers do not understand them and that they could do better in school were they given more respect and understanding (Ford & Harris, 1996). Consistent with this viewpoint, teachers in one study were asked to select from a checklist those attributes that best described their lower-income, minority pupils. Teachers consistently selected adjectives such as *lazy, fun-loving,* and *rebellious,* thus implying that they did not expect much of these students (Gottlieb, 1966).

Perhaps you can see how teachers who form expectancies based on these stereotypes might unwittingly contribute to ethnic variations in academic achievement. For example, they may subtly communicate to an Asian-American student that she is expected to do well by rephrasing questions the child has missed or by giving helpful hints if she looks indecisive, thus sending the message that failures can be overcome by *persisting* and *trying harder.* By contrast, a Mexican-American or African-American student from a low-income neighborhood might be tagged by the teacher as a low-ability student, who is then rarely challenged and is even criticized for errors in ways that cause him to doubt his abilities. Even minority students who are doing well at school are at risk of becoming underachievers if negative stereotypes about their ethnicity are subtly communicated to them and they begin to experience the *stereotype threat* we discussed in Box 7.2, which can clearly undermine their academic performances (Steele, 1997).

In sum, parents' values and styles of parenting, peers' level of support for academic achievement, and teacher expectancies probably all contribute to racial and ethnic differences in school achievement. Some theorists believe that children from lower-income, minority subcultures are at an immediate disadvantage when they enter a middle-class scholastic setting and that schools must change dramatically if they are to motivate and better educate these children. Researchers have known for years that underachieving ethnic minorities fare much better at school if the experiences they have in class (or read about in their textbooks) include more information about people of their own ethnicity (Kagan & Zahn, 1975; Stevenson et al., 1990), and this knowledge is a large part of the rationale behind recent efforts to make the school experience more culturally relevant for these youngsters. Among the positive changes we see today are stronger bilingual education programs designed to meet the needs of children from the over 100 distinct language groups in the United States (Garcia, 1993), and multicultural education programs that bring the perspectives of many cultural and subcultural groups into the classroom so that all students feel more welcome there (Banks, 1993).

Educating Students with Special Needs   One major challenge educators face is successfully teaching students with special needs—learning disabilities, mental retardation, physical and sensory handicaps, and other developmental disorders. These youngsters were once placed in separate schools or classrooms—or in some cases, were rejected as unteachable by public schools—until the U.S. Congress passed the *Education for All Handicapped Children Act* in 1975. Revised in 1990, this law requires school districts to provide an education comparable to that received by other children to all youngsters with special needs. The intent of the law was to better prepare children with special needs to participate in society by ensuring that their educational experiences were as similar as possible to those of pupils in typical public school classrooms. How might the law be served? Many school districts opted for **mainstreaming**—the practice of integrating special-needs children into regular classrooms for all or large parts of the day, as opposed to segregating them in special schools or classrooms.

Has mainstreaming accomplished its objectives? Not very well. Compared with other special-needs children who attend segregated special education classes, mainstreamed youngsters sometimes fare better academically and socially, but often they do not (Buysse & Bailey, 1993; Hunt & Goetz, 1997; Manset & Semmel, 1997). Furthermore, their self-esteem often declines because classmates tend to ridicule them and are reluctant to choose them as friends or playmates (Guralnick & Groom, 1988; Hunt & Goetz, 1997; Taylor, Asher, & Williams, 1987).

Do these findings imply that mainstreaming has failed? In one sense, it has, for we have learned that simply putting special-needs students into regular classrooms accomplishes little by itself. To work, mainstreaming must seek to ensure that students from diverse backgrounds and ability levels do, in fact, interact in positive ways and learn what they are supposed to be learning. How might we accomplish these objectives?

Robert Slavin and his colleagues (1991, 1996; Stevens & Slavin, 1995a; 1995b) have had much success with **cooperative learning methods** in which a mainstreamed child and several classmates are assigned to work teams and are reinforced for performing well *as a team*. For example, each member of a math team is given problems to solve that are appropriate to his or her ability level. Yet members of a work team also monitor one another's progress and offer one another aid when needed. To encourage this cooperation, the teams that complete the most math units are rewarded—for example, with special certificates that designate them as "superteams." Similarly, the "jigsaw method" of instruction developed by Elliot Aronson and his colleagues (1978) to facilitate racial integration involves giving each member of a small learning team one portion of the material to be learned and requiring him or her to teach it to teammates. Here, then, is a formula for ensuring that children of different social backgrounds and ability levels will interact in a context where the efforts of even the least capable team members are important to the *group's* success.

Clearly, these cooperative learning methods work. Mainstreamed second- through sixth-graders in classrooms stressing cooperative learning come to like school better and to outperform mainstreamed peers in traditional classrooms in vocabulary, reading and language skills, and tests of metacognitive knowledge, posting even bigger advan-

mainstreaming: the educational practice of integrating developmentally disabled students with special needs into regular classrooms rather than placing them in segregated special education classes.

cooperative learning methods: an educational practice whereby children of different races or ability levels are assigned to teams; each team member works on problems geared to his or her ability level, and all members are reinforced for "pulling together" and performing well as a team.

PHOTO 12.6 By stressing teamwork to achieve shared goals, cooperative learning activities make mainstreaming a more fruitful experience for children of all ability levels.

tages in the second year of cooperative learning than in the first (Stevens & Slavin, 1995a). What's more, both special-needs children and gifted children thrive in the cooperative learning classrooms, often displaying clear gains in self-esteem and becoming more fully accepted by peers (Stevens & Slavin, 1995b). So mainstreaming can succeed if educators deliberately design learning experiences that encourage students from different backgrounds or ability levels to pool their efforts in order to achieve common goals.

HOW WELL-EDUCATED ARE OUR CHILDREN? CROSS-CULTURAL COMPARISONS

How successful are our schools at imparting academic skills to their pupils? Large surveys of the reading, writing, and mathematical achievement of 9- to 17-year-old American students reveal that most of them do learn to read during the elementary school years and have acquired such mathematical proficiencies as basic computational skills and graph reading abilities by the time they finish high school (Dossey et al., 1988; National Education Goals Panel, 1992). Yet only about one American student in four could be described as truly proficient in reading and mathematics achievement (National Assessment of Educational Progress, as cited in Greene, 1997). Furthermore, American youth do not write very well; in fact, more than one-third of all 17-year-olds could not produce a well-formed and coherent paragraph. Are these findings cause for alarm?

Many educators think so (Short & Talley, 1997; Tirozzi & Uro, 1997), especially in view of the results of several cross-national surveys of children's academic achievement—studies indicating that the average scores obtained by American schoolchildren in mathematics, science, and verbal skills are consistently lower, and sometimes much lower, than those made by students in many other industrialized nations (National Education Goals Panel, 1992; Stevenson, Chen, & Lee, 1993).

Cross-cultural research conducted by Harold Stevenson and his colleagues (Chen & Stevenson, 1995; Stevenson, Lee, & Stigler, 1986; Stevenson et al., 1993) leaves no doubt that schoolchildren in Taiwan, the People's Republic of China, and Japan outperform students in the United States in math, reading, and other school subjects. The gap in math performance is especially striking; in recent testings of fifth-graders, for example, only 4% of Chinese children and 10% of Japanese students had scores on a math achievement test as low as those of the *average* American child (Stevenson et al., 1993). Achievement differences of this sort are evident from the time children enter school and grow larger each year as children progress from first to fifth to eleventh grade (Geary et al., 1996; Stevenson et al., 1993). Why do these differences exist, and what can they tell us about improving American education?

The problem is not that American students are any less intelligent, for they enter school performing just as well on IQ tests as their Asian counterparts (Stevenson et al., 1985), and they score at least as well as Japanese and Chinese students on general information tests covering material not typically covered in school (Stevenson et al.,1993). Indeed, most of the achievement gap between American and Asian students seems to reflect cultural differences in the following educational attitudes and practices.

Classroom Instruction   Asian students spend more time being educated than American students do. Elementary school teachers in Asian countries devote more class time to core academic subjects—for example, two to three times as many hours a week on math instruction. The Asian classroom is a comfortable but businesslike setting where little time is wasted; Asian students spend about 95% of their time on "on task" activities such as listening to the teacher and completing assignments, whereas

PHOTO 12.7 Children in traditional Asian classrooms are required to stay in their seats working on assignments or paying close attention to their teacher.

American students spend only about 80% of their time "on task" (Stigler, Lee, & Stevenson, 1987). Asian students also attend school for more hours per day and more days per year (often attending half the day on Saturdays) than American students do (Fuligni & Stevenson, 1995; Stevenson et al., 1986).

Parental Involvement Asian parents are strongly committed to the educational process. They hold higher achievement expectancies for their children than American parents do, and even though their children are excelling by American standards, Asian parents are much less likely than American parents to be satisfied with their children's current academic performance (Chen & Stevenson, 1995; Stevenson et al., 1993). Asian parents think that homework is more important than American parents do, and they also receive frequent communications from their children's teachers in notebooks children carry to and from school each day. These communications enable Asian parents to keep close tabs on how their children are progressing and to follow teachers' suggestions about how they can encourage and assist their children at home (Stevenson & Lee, 1990). By contrast, communications between U.S. parents and teachers are often limited to brief annual parent-teacher conferences.

Student Involvement Not only do Asian students spend more days in class and more class time on academic assignments than American children do, but they are assigned and complete more homework as well (Stevenson et al., 1993). During the high school years, Asian students continue to devote more time to scholastic activities and spend much less time working, dating, or socializing with friends than American students do (Fuligni & Stevenson, 1995).

A Strong Emphasis on Effort A major reason that Asian students apply themselves so diligently to academic activities is that their parents, teachers, and they, themselves, share the strong belief that all youngsters have the potential to master their studies if they work hard enough; by contrast, their American counterparts are more inclined to believe that academic success reflects other factors such as the quality of the child's teachers (see Figure 12.8) or one's native intelligence (Chen & Stevenson, 1995; Stevenson et al., 1993). Asian students face especially strong pressures to excel in the classroom because their prospects for obtaining a college education largely depend on the results of a competitive exam they take in high school. Yet, their strong belief that effort will ultimately pay off in better learning (and higher test scores) helps to explain why Asian youngsters are no more anxious about school or otherwise psychologically maladjusted than American students are (Chen & Stevenson, 1995; Crystal et al., 1994).

So the formula for more effective education may not be so mysterious after all, judging from the success of the Chinese and Japanese educational systems. The secret is to get teachers, students, and parents working together to make education a top priority for youth, to set high achievement goals, and to invest the day-by-day effort required to attain those objectives. In response to evidence that American schools are being outclassed by those in other countries, the U.S. Congress passed *Goals 2000: Educate America Act of 1994,* which proclaimed that U.S. students will be first in the world in science and mathematics achievement by the year 2000 (Short & Talley, 1997). Although this goal will not be met that soon (Greene, 1997), many states and local school districts have taken up the challenge. How? By strengthening curricula, tightening standards for teacher certification, raising standards for graduation and promotion from grade to grade, implementing alternative academic calendars to shorten summer vacations and increase student retention of previously learned material, and, most important, seeking ways to involve parents as partners with teachers at both the elementary and secondary school levels to create more supportive learning environments and foster higher standards of academic achievement (Tirozzi & Uro, 1997; Zigler, Finn-Stevenson, & Stern, 1997). These educational reformers are well aware that improving the scholastic and vocational preparation of America's youth is crucial if Americans are to maintain a leadership role in an ever-changing and ever more competitive world.

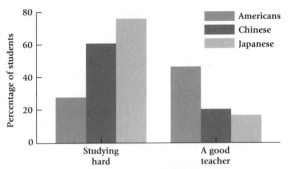

FIGURE 12.8 Percentages of Chinese, Japanese, and American high school students who picked "studying hard" or having "a good teacher" as the most important factor influencing their performance in mathematics. (Adapted from Chen & Stevenson, 1995.)

Summary

- This chapter focuses on three **extrafamilial influences** on developing children and adolescents: Television, computers, and the schools.

THE EARLY WINDOW: EFFECTS OF TELEVISION ON CHILDREN AND ADOLESCENTS

- Although children spend more time watching television than in any other waking activity, TV viewing, in moderate doses, is unlikely to impair their cognitive growth, academic achievement, or peer relations.

- Prior to age 8 or 9, children are most captivated by visual production features of TV programming and may have difficulty inferring characters' motives and intentions or reconstructing a coherent story line. However, cognitive development and experience watching television leads to increases in **television literacy** during middle childhood and adolescence.

- Three lines of evidence—correlational surveys, laboratory experiments, and field experiments—*converge* on the conclusions that heavy exposure to televised violence can instigate aggressive behavior, cultivate aggressive habits and **mean-world beliefs**, and **desensitize** viewers to instances of real-world aggression. Taken together, this evidence supports the social-learning viewpoint on the effects of televised violence and provides no support for the catharsis hypothesis.

- In addition to the potentially harmful impacts of televised violence, commercial TV programs also present negative stereotypes that influence viewers' beliefs about ethnicity, race, and gender, and children are easily manipulated by TV commercials that push products parents are reluctant to purchase.

- On the positive side, children are likely to learn prosocial lessons and to put them into practice after watching acts of kindness on television. Parents can help by watching shows such as *Mister Rogers' Neighborhood* with their children and then encouraging them to verbalize or role-play the prosocial lessons they have observed. Educational programs such as *Sesame Street* have been quite successful at fostering basic cognitive skills, particularly when children watch with an adult who discusses the material with them and helps them to apply what they have learned.

CHILD DEVELOPMENT IN THE COMPUTER AGE

■ Children seem to benefit, both intellectually and socially, from their use of computers. **Computer-assisted instruction (CAI)** often improves children's basic academic skills; word processing programs foster the growth of writing skills; and computer programming facilitates cognitive and **metacognitive** development. Furthermore, computers promote rather than inhibit social interactions with peers.

■ Despite the demonstrated advantages associated with children's use of computers, critics fear that (1) disadvantaged children and girls may reap fewer of these benefits, (2) violent computer games may instigate aggression and antisocial behavior and (3) harm may result from youngsters' unrestricted access to the Internet and the World Wide Web.

THE SCHOOL AS A SOCIALIZATION AGENT

■ Schools influence many aspects of development. Formal scholastic curricula are intended to impart academic knowledge, and schooling promotes cognitive and metacognitive development by teaching rules and problem-solving strategies that can be applied to many different kinds of information. Schools also pursue an **informal curriculum** that teaches children culturally valued social skills that help them become good citizens.

■ Some schools are more "effective" than others at producing positive outcomes such as low absenteeism, an enthusiastic attitude about learning, academic achievement, occupational skills, and socially desirable patterns of behavior. What makes a school effective is not its physical characteristics, **open** or **traditional classroom** structure, whether students experience **ability tracking**, or the amount of money spent per pupil. Instead, **effective schools** are those in which (1) students are motivated to learn, (2) teachers create a classroom environment that is comfortable, engaging, and task-focused, and (3) there are positive **aptitude-treatment interactions**—that is, a "good fit" between students' personal or cultural characteristics and the kinds of instruction they receive.

■ Teachers may influence their pupils' progress in many ways. Teacher expectancies can create self-fulfilling prophecies (or a **Pygmalion effect**), whereby students who are expected to do well or poorly actually perform better or worse than they otherwise would had their teacher had no prior expectations about their likely outcomes. Furthermore, teachers who emphasize competition in the classroom and who favor stressful evaluative procedures are likely to undermine the academic performance of their slower students and those high in **test anxiety**. And teachers' reactions to a child's appropriate and inappropriate classroom behaviors can even influence a child's popularity with peers. In particular, elementary school teachers who tend to *derogate* inappropriate conduct (rather than correcting it) may undermine the offender's status in the peer group, whereas giving *praise* for *appropriate* behavior seems to promote peer acceptance. Finally, teaching styles can also affect pupil outcomes. **Authoritative instruction** is more likely than either **authoritarian** or **laissez-faire instruction** to motive students to do their best. Yet, even the authoritative teacher may have to use different instructional techniques with different children to get the most out of each pupil.

■ Racial and ethnic differences in academic achievement can often be traced to parental and peer influences and to teacher expectancies. At best, **mainstreaming** has produced modest improvements in the academic performance of students with developmental disabilities while failing to enhance their peer acceptance or self-esteem. Among the steps that might be taken to better meet the educational needs of all our students are creating stronger bilingual and multicultural educational programs and making greater use of **cooperative learning methods** in the classroom.

■ Cross-national surveys of academic achievement clearly brand American students as "underachievers," especially in math and science. The achievement gap that exists between American schoolchildren and those in other industrialized societies centers around cultural differences in educational attitudes, educational practices, and the involvement of both parents and students in the learning process.

Chapter Thirteen

Extrafamilial Influences II:

PEERS AS SOCIALIZATION AGENTS

Who Is a Peer and What Functions Do Peers Serve?

The Significance of Peer Interaction

Frequency of Peer Contacts

Peers as Promoters of Positive Developmental Outcomes

The Development of Peer Sociability

Peer Sociability in Infancy and Toddlerhood

Sociability During the Preschool Period

Peer Sociability in Middle Childhood and Adolescence

Personal and Social Influences on Sociability

Peer Acceptance and Popularity

Measuring Children's Popularity with Peers

Why Are Children Accepted, Rejected, or Neglected by Peers?

On Improving the Social Skills of Rejected Children

Children and Their Friends

On the Development of Friendship

Social Interactions among Friends and Acquaintances

Are There Distinct Advantages to Having Friends?

How Do Peers Exert Their Influence?

Peer Reinforcement and Modeling Influences

Peers as Critics and Agents of Persuasion

The Normative Function of Peer Groups

Peer Versus Adult Influences and the Question of Cross-Pressures

Summary

*T*hroughout this text we have concentrated on adults as the major source of influence on developing children. In their various roles as parents, teachers, coaches, scoutmasters, and religious leaders, adults clearly represent the power, authority, and expertise of a society. But grown-ups are by no means the sole influence on the social development of children—even very young children. In this chapter, we examine the impacts of yet another critically important agent of socialization: other children and the society of one's peers.

Although youngsters spend an enormous amount of time and energy socializing with each other, only within the past 30 years have developmentalists given much thought to how contacts with peers might influence developing children. What roles do peers play in a child's or an adolescent's development? If we allow ourselves to be influenced by popular novels and films such as *Lord of the Flies* and *Dead Poets Society*, we might conclude that peers are subversive agents who often undermine the best laid plans of adults and lead the child into a life of delinquency and antisocial conduct. However, developmentalists now know that this perspective on peer influences is highly distorted and unnecessarily negative (Hartup, 1983). Yes, peers are occasionally "bad influences"; but they clearly have the potential to affect their playmates in a number of positive ways. Consider the viewpoint of a lonely farmer from the Midwestern United States whose own life experiences convinced him that normal peer interactions foster healthy and adaptive developmental outcomes.[1]

> Dear Dr. Moore:
>
> I read the report in the Oct. 30 issue of _____ about your study of only children. I am an only child, now 57 years old, and I want to tell you some things about my life. Not only was I an only child, but I grew up in the country where there were no nearby children to play with . . . [And] from the first year of school, I was teased and made fun of . . . I dreaded to get on the school bus and go to school because the other children on the bus called me "Mommy's baby." In about the second grade I heard the boys use a vulgar word. I asked what it meant and they made fun of me. So I learned a lesson—don't ask questions. This can lead to a lot of confusion to hear talk one doesn't understand and not be able to learn what it means.
>
> I never went out with a girl while I was in school—in fact I hardly talked to them. In our school the boys and girls did not play together. Boys were sent to one part of the playground and girls to another. So I didn't learn anything about girls. When we got into high school and boys and girls started dating, I could only listen to their stories about their experiences.
>
> I could tell you a lot more, but the important thing is I have never married or had any children. I have not been very successful in an occupation or vocation. I believe my troubles are not all due to being an only child . . . but I do believe you are right in recommending playmates for . . . school agers and not have them strictly supervised by adults. . . . Parents of only children should make special efforts to provide playmates for them.
>
> Sincerely yours,

If we assume that peers are important agents of socialization, a number of questions remain to be answered. For example, who qualifies as a peer? How do peers influence one another? What is it about peer influence that is unique? What are the consequences (if any) of poor peer relations? Is it important to have special peer alliances or friendships? Do peers eventually become a more potent source of influence than parents or other adults. These are some of the issues that we will explore in the pages that follow.

---

[1]This letter appears with the permission of its author and its recipient, Dr. Shirley G. Moore.

Who Is a Peer and What Functions Do Peers Serve?

Webster's New Collegiate Dictionary defines a **peer** as "one that is of equal standing with another." Developmentalists also think of peers as "*social equals*" or as individuals *who, for the moment at least, are operating at similar levels of behavioral complexity* (Lewis & Rosenblum, 1975). According to this *activity-based* definition, children who differ somewhat in age could still be considered "peers"—as long as they can adjust their behaviors to suit one another's capabilities as they pursue common interests or goals.

THE SIGNIFICANCE OF PEER INTERACTION

Contemporary research on peer influence has been heavily influenced by theorists from the *ethological* tradition, who have sought to determine the *adaptive significance* of child-child interactions. You may recall from Chapters 9 and 10 that conflicts among peers when resources (toys) are scarce can help youngsters learn how to resolve their differences amicably by fostering the growth of prosocial modes of conflict resolution, such as sharing (cf. Caplan et al., 1991). We also noted that even blatantly hostile exchanges among 3- to 5-year-olds may prove adaptive by helping to create *dominance hierarchies* that establish the relative power and status of individual group members and thereby *minimize* the likelihood of future aggression within the peer group (cf. Sackin & Thelen, 1984; Strayer, 1980). Based on such observations, ethologists propose that peer interaction may be a special form of social behavior that has been "selected" over the centuries to promote the development of adaptive patterns of social conduct in each successive generation. Let's now consider some of the specific functions that child-child interactions might serve.

Same-Age (or Equal-Status) Interactions We gain some idea of why contacts among age-mates may be important by contrasting them to exchanges that occur at home. A child's interactions with parents and older siblings are rarely equal-status contacts; typically young children are placed in a subordinate position by an older member of the family who is instructing them, issuing orders, or otherwise overseeing their activities. By contrast, age-mates are much less critical and directive, and children are freer to try out new roles, ideas, and behaviors when interacting with someone of similar status. And in so doing, they are likely to learn important lessons about themselves and others—lessons such as "She quits when I don't take turns," "He hits me when I push him," or "Nobody likes a cheater." Many theorists believe that peer contacts are important precisely because they are *equal-status* contacts—that is, they teach children to understand and appreciate the perspectives of people *just like themselves* and will thereby contribute to the development of social competencies that may be difficult to acquire in the nonegalitarian atmosphere of the home.

Mixed-Age Interactions According to Hartup (1983), interaction among children of *different* ages is also a critically important context for social and personality development. Although **mixed-age peer interactions** tend to be somewhat *asymmetrical,* with one child (typically the elder) possessing more power than the other, these asymmetries may help children to acquire certain social competencies. One cross-cultural survey revealed that the presence of younger peers may foster the development of compassion, caregiving and prosocial inclinations, assertiveness, and leadership skills in older children (Whiting & Edwards, 1988). At the same time, younger children may benefit from mixed-age interactions by acquiring a variety of new skills from older playmates and by learning how to seek assistance and how to defer gracefully to the wishes and directives of these more powerful associates. Older children usually took

peers: two or more persons who are operating at similar levels of behavioral complexity.

mixed-age peer interaction: interactions among children who differ in age by a year or more.

charge of mixed-age interactions and adjusted their behavior to the competencies of their younger companions (see also Brody, Graziano, & Musser, 1983; Graziano et al., 1976). Even 2-year-olds show such powers of leadership and accommodation, for they are more inclined to take the initiative and to display simpler and more repetitive play routines when paired with an 18-month-old toddler than with an age-mate (Brownell, 1990).

By the time children enter grade school, they know that same-age and mixed-age interactions serve different purposes, and their preferences for associating with older, younger, or same-age peers clearly depends on the goals they are pursuing (French, 1984). Six- to 9-year-olds, for example, prefer age-mates to younger or older children if their objective is to pick a friend. However, older children are preferred over age-mates if the child feels the need for sympathy or guidance, whereas younger children are the ones participants choose if the

PHOTO **13.1** Both older and younger children benefit from mixed-age interactions.

situation calls for them to display compassion or to teach another child what they already know. The latter finding implies that peers may often serve as "expert" guides, teaching important skills to their younger (or less competent) associates through the kinds of collaborative exchanges that Vygotsky (1978) stressed in his sociocultural theory of human development. As we saw in Chapter 11, elder siblings are more likely than unrelated older peers to assume such a tutorial role; but recent research nevertheless indicates that children can (and do) learn much and acquire many new skills through their transactions with older (or more competent) peers (Rubin, Bukowski, & Parker, 1998).

Perhaps you have noticed that mixed-age peer interactions are presumed to benefit older and younger children in many of the same ways that sibling interactions benefit older and younger siblings (see Chapter 11). But there is a crucial difference between sibling and peer contacts, for one's status as either a younger or an older sibling is *fixed* by order of birth, whereas one's peer status is *flexible*, depending on whom he is associating with. So mixed-age *peer* interactions may provide children with experiences they might otherwise miss in their sibling interactions and, in fact, may be the primary context in which (a) an habitually domineering elder sibling learns to be more accommodating (when interacting with older peers), (b) an oppressed younger sib learns to lead and to show compassion (when dealing with even younger children), and (c) an only child (who has no sibs) acquires both sets of social competencies. Viewed in this way, mixed-age peer interactions may be important experiences indeed.

FREQUENCY OF PEER CONTACTS

Between the ages of 2 and 12, children spend more and more time with peers and less and less time with adults (Rubin et al., 1998). This trend is well illustrated in Figure 13.1, which summarizes what Sherri Ellis and her colleagues (1981) found while observing 436 children playing in their homes and around the neighborhood. Interestingly this same study revealed that youngsters of all ages spend *less* time with age-mates (defined as children whose ages were within a year of their own) than with children who were more than a year older or younger than they were. And it is likely that Ellis's neighborhood study underestimates the sheer amount of contact that so many of today's young children have with both same-age and mixed-age peers as they receive alternative care in group settings.

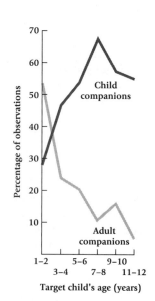

FIGURE **13.1** Developmental changes in children's companionship with adults and other children. (Adapted from Ellis, Rogoff, & Cromer, 1981.)

Another finding of Ellis's study is a familiar one: Even 1- to 2-year-olds played more often with same-sex companions than with other-sex companions, and this *gender segregation* became increasingly apparent with age. Once in their sex-segregated worlds, boys and girls experience different kinds of social relationships. Boys tend to form "packs," whereas girls form "pairs"; that is, a boy often plays competitive games or team sports in groups; a girl more often establishes a longer and more cooperative relationship with one or two playmates (Archer, 1992; Benenson, Apostoleris, & Parnass, 1997; Lansford & Parker, 1999).

Overall, then, children spend an increasing amount of time with peers, and those peers are typically *same sex* children who are only *roughly similar* in age but who enjoy the same kinds of gender-typed activities.

PEERS AS PROMOTERS OF POSITIVE DEVELOPMENTAL OUTCOMES

To this point, we have speculated that peer interactions may promote the development of many social and personal competencies that are not easily acquired within the decidedly nonegalitarian parent-child relationship. Is there truly any basis for such a claim? And if so, just how important are these peer influences? Developmentalists became very interested in these questions once they learned of Harry Harlow's research with rhesus monkeys.

Harlow's Work with Monkeys Will youngsters who have little or no contact with peers turn out to be abnormal or maladjusted? To find out, Harlow and his associates (Alexander & Harlow, 1965; Suomi & Harlow, 1978) raised groups of rhesus monkeys with their mothers and denied them the opportunity to play with peers. These "**mother-only**" **monkeys** failed to develop normal patterns of social behavior. When finally exposed to age-mates, the peer-deprived youngsters preferred to avoid them. On those occasions when they did approach a peer, these social misfits tended to be highly (and inappropriately) aggressive, and their antisocial tendencies often persisted into adulthood.

Is peer contact, then, the key to normal social development? Not entirely. In later experiments, Harlow and his colleagues separated rhesus monkeys from their mothers and raised them so that they had continuous exposure to their peers. These "**peer-only**" **monkeys** were observed to cling tenaciously to one another and to form strong mutual attachments. Yet their social development was somewhat atypical in that they became highly agitated over minor stresses or frustrations (see also Higley et al., 1992), and as adults they were unusually aggressive toward monkeys from outside their peer groups.

A Human Parallel In 1951, Anna Freud and Sophie Dann reported a startling human parallel to Harlow's peer-only monkeys. During the summer of 1945, six 3-year-olds were found living by themselves in a Nazi concentration camp. By the time these children were 12 months old, their parents had been put to death. Although they received minimal caregiving from a series of inmates who were periodically executed, these children had, in effect, reared themselves.

When rescued at the war's end, the six orphans were flown to a special treatment center in England, where attempts were made to "rehabilitate" them. How did these "peer-only" children respond to this treatment? They began by breaking nearly all their toys and

"mother-only" monkeys: monkeys who are raised with their mothers and denied any contact with peers.

"peer-only" monkeys: monkeys who are separated from their mothers (and other adults) soon after birth and raised with peers.

PHOTO 13.2 Monkeys raised only with peers form strong mutual attachments and will often attack other monkeys from outside their peer group.

damaging their furniture. Moreover, they often reacted with cold indifference or open hostility toward the staff at the center. And like Harlow's monkeys, these children had no other wish than to be together and became extremely agitated when they were separated . . . even for short periods. They also showed a remarkable prosocial concern for one another:

> There was no occasion to urge the children to "take turns"; they did it spontaneously. They were extremely considerate of each other's feelings. . . . At mealtimes handing food to one's neighbor was of greater importance than eating oneself. (Freud & Dann, 1951, pp. 131–133)

Although these youngsters displayed many signs of anxiety and were highly suspicious of outsiders, they eventually established positive relationships with their adult caregivers and acquired a new language during the first year at the center. The story even has a happy ending, for 35 years later, these orphans were leading effective, productive lives as middle-aged adults (Hartup, 1983).

Taken together, Harlow's monkey research and Freud and Dann's observations of their war orphans suggest that parents and peers each contribute something different and perhaps unique to a child's (or a monkey's) social development. Regular contacts with sensitive, responsive parents not only permit infants to acquire some basic interactive skills but also provide a sense of *security* that enables them to venture forth to explore the environment and to discover that other individuals can be interesting companions (Hartup, 1989; Rubin et al., 1998). By contrast, contacts with peers may allow children (and young monkeys) to elaborate their basic interactive routines and to develop competent and adaptive patterns of social behavior with associates who are more or less similar to themselves. Indeed, Harlow's "peer-only" monkeys lacked the security of a mother-infant relationship, perhaps explaining why they clutched at one another, were reluctant to explore, and were terrified by (and aggressive toward) outsiders. But *within their own peer groups,* they developed competent interactive routines and displayed normal patterns of social and sexual behavior (Suomi & Harlow, 1978).

Just how important is it for human beings to establish and maintain *harmonious* relations with their peers? Apparently it is very important. Recent reviews of more than 30 studies reveal that youngsters who had been rejected by their peers during grade school are much more likely than those who had enjoyed good peer relations to drop out of school, to become involved in delinquent or criminal activities, and to display serious psychological difficulties later in adolescence and young adulthood (Parker & Asher, 1987; Parker et al., 1995; see also Crick, 1996, 1997; Rubin et al., 1998). So, merely having contact with peer associates is not enough to ensure normal developmental outcomes; getting along with peers is important, too.

In sum, peers do seem to be important agents of socialization, and the task of becoming *appropriately* sociable with peers is a most important developmental hurdle. In our next section, we will focus on the growth of peer sociability and on some of the factors that influence how appropriately (or inappropriately) sociable a child turns out to be.

The Development of Peer Sociability

Sociability is a term that describes the child's willingness to engage others in social interaction and to seek their attention or approval. In Chapter 4, we noted that even young infants are sociable creatures: Months before forming their first attachments, they are already smiling, cooing, or otherwise trying to attract the attention of caregivers and are likely to protest whenever any *adult* puts them down or walks off and

sociability: one's willingness to interact with others and to seek their attention or approval.

leaves them alone (Schaffer & Emerson, 1964). But would they be so positively disposed to a peer—that is, an infant or a toddler companion?

PEER SOCIABILITY IN INFANCY AND TODDLERHOOD

Although babies show an interest in other babies from the first months of life, they do not really *interact* until about the middle of the first year. By then, infants will often smile or babble at their tiny companions, vocalize, offer toys, and gesture to one another (Vandell & Mueller, 1995; Vandell, Wilson & Buchanan, 1980). By the end of the first year, infants may even imitate a peer's simple actions with a toy, thus implying that they are trying to share meaning with or to understand the intentions of a peer (Rubin et al., 1998). Nevertheless, many friendly gestures among children this young go unnoticed and unreciprocated.

Between 12 and 18 months of age, toddlers begin to react more appropriately to each other's behavior, often partaking in more complex exchanges in which participants appear to take turns. Here is one example:

> Larry sits on the floor and Bernie turns and looks toward him. Bernie waves his hand and says "da," still looking at Larry. He repeats the vocalization three more times before Larry laughs. Bernie vocalizes again and Larry laughs again. This same sequence is repeated twelve more times before Bernie . . . walks off. (Mueller & Lucas, 1975, p. 241)

Yet, there is some question about whether these "action/reaction" episodes qualify as true social discourse, for 12- to 18-month-olds often seem to treat peers as particularly responsive "toys" that they can control by making them look, gesture, smile, and laugh (Brownell, 1986).

By 18 months of age, however, almost all infants are beginning to display *coordinated interactions* with age-mates that are clearly social in character. They now take a great delight in *imitating* each other and will often gaze and smile at their partners as they turn their imitative sequences into social games (Eckerman & Stein, 1990; Howes & Matheson, 1992). By ages 20 to 24 months, toddlers' play has a strong verbal

PHOTO 13.3 With age, toddlers' interactions with one another become increasingly skilled and reciprocal.

component: Playmates often describe their ongoing play activities to each other ("I fall down!" "Me too, I fall down") or attempt to influence the role their partner should assume ("You go in playhouse") (Eckerman & Didow, 1996). This coordinated social speech makes it easier for 2- to 2½-year-olds to assume *complementary roles,* such as chaser and chasee in a game of tag, or to cooperate to achieve a shared goal, as illustrated by one child's operating a handle, thereby enabling the second to retrieve attractive toys from a container (Brownell & Carriger, 1990).

Both social and cognitive developments contribute to the growth of peer sociability over the first two years. In Chapter 5, we learned that toddlers who are securely attached to their caregivers are generally more outgoing and more attractive as playmates than those who are insecurely attached, thus implying that the sensitive, responsive caregiving that securely attached infants receive contributes in a positive way to development of **social skills.** And 18- to 24-month-olds are beginning to display truly coordinated, reciprocal interactions at precisely the time they first display self-awareness on the rouge test and can discriminate photographs of themselves from those of peers (see Chapter 6). This may be no accident. Celia Brownell and Michael Carriger (1990) propose that toddlers must first realize that both they and their companions are autonomous causal agents who can make things happen before they are likely to play complementary games or try to coordinate their actions to accomplish a goal. And consistent with their reasoning, they found that toddlers who cooperated successfully to achieve a goal did score higher on a test of self–other differentiation than their less-cooperative age-mates, thus implying that early interactive skills may depend very heavily on their social-cognitive development. Indeed, a sense of *intersubjectivity*—the ability to share meaning with a social partner—is absolutely essential for the emergence of intricate *pretend play* activities that unfold and become progressively more complex throughout the preschool period (Rubin et al., 1998).

SOCIABILITY DURING THE PRESCHOOL PERIOD

Between the ages of 2 and 5, children not only become more outgoing but also direct their social gestures to a wider audience. Observational studies suggest that 2- to 3-year-olds are more likely than older children to remain near an adult and to seek physical affection, whereas the sociable behaviors of 4- to 5-year-olds normally consist of playful bids for attention or approval that are directed at *peers* rather than adults (Harper & Huie, 1985; Hartup, 1983).

As children become more peer oriented during the preschool years, the character of their interactions changes as well. In a classic study, Mildred Parten (1932) observed 2½- to 4-year-olds during free-play periods at nursery school, looking for developmental changes in the *social complexity* of peer interactions. She found that preschoolers' play activities could be placed into four categories, arranged from least to most socially complex:

1. **Nonsocial activity**—children watch others play or engage in their own solitary play and largely ignore what others are doing.
2. **Parallel play**—children play side by side but interact very little and do not try to influence the behavior of other players.
3. **Associative play**—children now share toys and swap materials, but pursue their own agendas and do not cooperate to achieve shared goals.
4. **Cooperative play**—children now act out make-believe themes, assume reciprocal roles, and collaborate to achieve shared goals.

As we see in Figure 13.2, solitary and parallel play declined with age whereas associative and cooperative play became more common. Parten concluded that her data

social skills: thoughts, actions, and emotional regulatory activities that enable children to achieve personal or social goals while maintaining harmony with their social partners.

nonsocial activity: onlooker behavior and solitary play.

parallel play: largely noninteractive play in which players are in close proximity but do not often attempt to influence each other.

associative play: form of social discourse in which children pursue their own interests but will swap toys or comment on each other's activities.

cooperative play: true social play in which children cooperate or assume reciprocal roles while pursing shared goals.

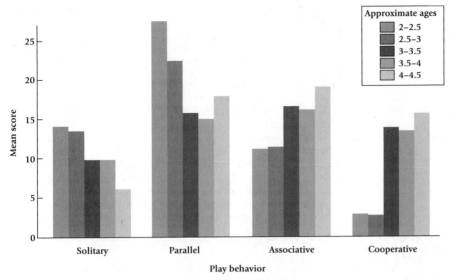

FIGURE 13.2 Frequency of activities engaged in by preschool children of different ages. With age, solitary and parallel play occur less frequently whereas associative and cooperative play occur more frequently. (Adapted from Parten, 1932.)

reflect a three-step developmental sequence in which solitary play emerges first and is least mature, followed by a parallel play, which eventually gives way to more mature forms of associative and cooperative play.

Other researchers have challenged Parten's conclusions, noting that solitary play is actually quite common throughout the preschool period and need not be considered immature (Hartup, 1983; Rubin et al., 1983). If solitary play is *functional* in character, involving such cognitively simplistic and repetitive actions as rolling a ball back and forth or running around a room, then it might be properly labeled "immature." However, most of the solitary play of the preschool period is more cognitively complex and *constructive* in nature, as children work alone to build towers of blocks, draw pictures, or complete puzzles. And preschoolers who spend much of their playtime in such constructive solitary pursuits are often bright youngsters who have few if any difficulties interacting with peers.

Could it be, then, that the "maturity" of preschool play depends as much (or more) on its *cognitive complexity* as on its social or nonsocial character? Indeed, it could and the cognitive and social characteristics of preschool play are clearly interrelated. In a longitudinal study in which the play activities of a group of 1- to 2-year-olds were observed at six-month intervals for three years, Carollee Howes and Catherine Matheson (1992) found that play became more and more cognitively complex with age, as described by the six-category sequence in Table 13-1 on page 444. What's more, there was a clear relationship between the complexity of a child's play and the child's social competence with peers: Children whose play was more complex at any given age were rated as more outgoing and prosocially inclined and as less aggressive and withdrawn at the next observation period six months later. So it seems that the *cognitive complexity* of a child's play (particularly pretend play) is a reliable predictor of his or her future social competencies with peers (see also Doyle et al., 1992; Rubin et al., 1983, 1998).

How important are the pretend-play activities of the preschool period? Carolee Howes (1992) claims that they serve at least three crucial developmental functions. First, pretend play helps children master ways of sharing meaning with their social

TABLE 13-1 Changes in play activities from infancy through the preschool period

PLAY TYPE	AGE OF APPEARANCE	DESCRIPTION
Parallel play	6–12 months	Two children perform similar activities without paying any attention to each other.
Parallel aware play	By age 1	Children engage in parallel play while occasionally looking at each other or monitoring each other's activities.
Simple pretend play	1–1½ years	Children engage in similar activities while talking, smiling, sharing toys, or otherwise interacting.
Complementary and reciprocal play	1½–2 years	Children display action-based role reversals in social games such as run-and-chase or peekaboo.
Cooperative social pretend play	2½–3 years	Children play complementary *nonliteral,* or "pretend," roles (for example, mommy and baby), but without any planning or discussion about the meaning of these roles or about the form the play will take.
Complex social pretend play (or sociodramatic play)	3½–4 years	Children actively *plan* their pretend play. They name and explicitly assign roles for each player and propose a play script, and may stop playing to modify the script if play breaks down.

SOURCE: Adapted from Howes & Matheson, 1992.

equals. In addition, play provides opportunities for young children to learn to *compromise* as they negotiate the roles they will enact in their play and the rules that guide these pretend episodes. Last, social pretext is a context that permits children to display feelings that may bother them, thereby allowing them opportunities to better understand their own (or their partner's) emotional crises, to receive social support from (or provide it to) playmates, and to develop a sense of trust and even intimate ties to these associates. So pretend play may be a major contributor to the growth of communication skills, emotional understanding, social perspective-taking, and an enhanced capacity for caring. Viewed in this way, it is hardly surprising that preschoolers who are relatively proficient at pretend-play activities tend to be favorably received by their peers (Rubin et al., 1998).

PEER SOCIABILITY IN MIDDLE CHILDHOOD AND ADOLESCENCE

Peer interactions become increasingly sophisticated throughout the grade-school years. Not only do cooperative forms of complex social pretend play become more commonplace, but by ages 6 to 10, children have become enthusiastic participants in games (such as Tee-Ball and Monopoly) that are governed by formal sets of rules (Hartup, 1983; Piaget, 1965).

Another very noticeable way that peer interactions change during middle childhood is that contacts among 6- to 10-year-olds more often occur in true **peer groups.** When psychologists talk about peer groups, they are referring not merely to a collection of playmates but, rather, to a true confederation that (1) interacts on a regular basis; (2) defines a sense of belonging; (3) formulates its own *norms* that specify how members are supposed to dress, think, and behave; and (4) develops a structure or hierarchical organization (for example, leader and other roles) that enables group members to work together toward the accomplishment of shared goals. Furthermore, elementary school children now clearly *identify* with their groups; to be a "Brownie," a "Blue Knight," or "one of Smitty's gang" is often a source of great personal pride. So between ages 6 and 10, children are exposing themselves to a most potent social context—the *peer group*—in which they are likely to discover the value of teamwork, develop a sense of commitment and loyalty to shared goals, and learn a number of other important lessons about how social organizations pursue their objectives (Hartup, 1983; Sherif et al., 1961).

peer group: a confederation of peers that interact regularly, defines a sense of membership, and formulates norms that specify how members are supposed to look, think, act.

Under what conditions are a collection of individuals likely to coalesce, forming a true group? Obviously, one prerequisite is that the members of an aggregation be in a setting that permits and in some way encourages them to interact regularly. But interaction alone does not necessarily imply the formation of a group. Groups are composed of people who are drawn together by common goals or motives.

The importance of proximity and shared goals to the formation and functioning of children's groups has been demonstrated by Muzafer Sherif and his associates (1961) in an elaborate field experiment known as the "Robber's Cave" study. There were three distinct phases to this classic piece of research, and as we see in Box 13.1 on pages 446–447, the results of each phase have taught us important lessons about children's experiences in peer groups.

By early adolescence, youngsters are spending more than twice as much time with peers—particularly with small groups of close friends known as **cliques**—as with parents, siblings, or any other agent of socialization (Berndt, 1989; Larson & Richards, 1991). Early peer cliques usually consist of four to eight *same-sex* members who share similar values and activity preferences; but by mid-adolescence, boy cliques and girl cliques begin to interact more frequently, eventually forming *heterosexual cliques* (Dunphy, 1963). Once formed, cliques often develop distinct and colorful dress codes, dialects, and behaviors—norms that set cliques apart from each other and help clique members to establish a firm sense of belongingness or a group identity (Cairns et al., 1995).

Often several cliques with similar norms and values become identifiable as larger, more loosely organized aggregations known as **crowds.** Crowds do not replace cliques; membership in a crowd is based on reputation rather than active choice, and individual members within a particular clique may even belong to different crowds (Urberg et al., 1995). Crowds are defined by the attitudes and activities their members share, and they come into play mainly as a mechanism for defining an adolescent's niche within the larger social structure of a high school and, occasionally, for organizing such social activities as parties, trips to the football game, and so on. The names may vary, but most schools have crowds of "brains," "populars," "jocks," "druggies," "grungers", and "burnouts," each consisting of a loose aggregation of adolescents who are similar to one another in some fundamental way and different from the adolescents in other crowds (Brown, Mory, & Kinney, 1994; Brown & Lohr, 1987). And everyone in the high school seems to recognize these differences: "[the brains] all wear glasses and 'kiss up' to teachers" (Brown et al., 1994, p. 128); "the partyers goof off a lot more than the jocks do, but they don't come to school stoned like the burnouts do" (p. 133).

Not only do cliques and crowds permit adolescents to express their values and to try out new roles as they begin to forge an identity apart from their families, but they also pave the way for the establishment of dating relationships (Brown, 1990; Dunphy, 1963). Gender segregation usually breaks down early in adolescence as members of boys' and girls' cliques begin to interact. Same-sex cliques provide what amounts to a "secure base" for exploring ways to behave with members of the other sex: Talking to girls when your buddies are there is far less threatening than doing so on your own. And as heterosexual cliques and crowds take shape, adolescents are likely to have many opportunities to get to

clique: a small group of friends that interacts frequently.

crowd: a large, reputationally based peer group made up of individuals and cliques that share similar norms, interests, and values.

PHOTO 13.4 Young adolescents spend more time socializing with their peers than with their parents or siblings. Much time is spent with small numbers of same-sex associates who genuinely like each other and prefer similar activities. These same-sex cliques often evolve into mixed-sex (heterosexual) cliques by mid-adolescence.

Box 13.1   Focus on Research

Robber's Cave: An Experimental Analysis of Group Formation and Intergroup Conflict

Many years ago, Muzafer Sherif and his colleagues (Sherif, 1956; Sherif et al., 1961) designed an ingenious field experiment to study the formation and functioning of children's peer groups. The three phases of this experiment and the lessons learned from each are described below.

Phase 1: Group Formation

The 22 subjects who participated in the "Robber's Cave" experiment were 11-year-old boys at a summer camp in Oklahoma. Initially the campers were divided into two sets and housed in different areas of a large, woodsy preserve. Neither aggregation was aware of the other's presence.

The boys in each aggregation lived closely together and participated in many enjoyable activities, such as hiking, crafts, organized games, and the building of "hideouts." To encourage the formation of group structures, camp counselors arranged for the boys to work at tasks requiring them to assume different roles and to coordinate their efforts in order to accomplish shared goals. For example, one evening the boys came to dinner, only to discover that the staff had not prepared the meal. However, the ingredients (for example, raw meat, Kool-Aid, watermelon) were available. Under these circumstances, the hungry boys soon divided the labor: Some cooked, others sliced watermelon or mixed drinks, and others either served food or cleaned up. This and other such cooperative activities soon led to the development of cohesive groups. Leaders emerged, individual members assumed different statuses, and each group developed rules or norms to govern its daily activities. The groups even assumed names, becoming the "Eagles" and the "Rattlers."

Let's now summarize this first phase. When previously unacquainted children were thrust together and encouraged to work cooperatively at necessary and/or attractive tasks, they formed cohesive groups, assumed different roles, and developed norms to regulate their interactions and accomplish group goals. But interesting questions remained. For example, what would happen to "group *esprit*" should the Eagles and Rattlers come in conflict with each other?

Phase 2: Intergroup Conflict

Next the investigators chose to study intergroup rivalry and its effects on the structure of a peer group. They first arranged for the Eagles and Rattlers to "accidentally" discover each other and then talked the groups into a series of competitions—baseball games, tugs-of-war, and the like. Prizes were to be awarded to the winners (for example, money, trophies, pocket knives), and the boys practiced intently for the coming events.

Once the competitions began, the investigators were careful to observe the boys' reactions to success and failure. The immediate effect of failure was internal friction, mutual accusation, and blame—in short, decreased group cohesion and a shake-up in the group structure. So, when the Rattlers emerged victorious from the first baseball game, Mason (the Eagles' best athlete) threatened to "beat up" certain Eagles if they "didn't try harder" in the future. Craig, the Eagle leader, was eventually deposed for failing to give his all at athletic competition.

As the competitions progressed and boys in each group assumed new statuses, both the Eagles and the Rattlers became more cohesive than ever before. New norms emerged, and increased solidarity within each group was apparent from the hostilities these rival factions displayed toward each other. At first these exchanges were limited to verbal taunts such as "You're not Eagles—you're pigeons." But, after losing a series of contests, the Eagles vented their frustrations by securing the Rattlers' flag and burning it. The Rattlers then lost two consecutive contests, endured the verbal scoffs of the Eagles, and suffered internal disharmony. They finally decided that the Eagles had used unfair tactics in the most recent tug-of-war, and they reacted by staging a raid on the Eagles' cabin, stealing comic books and a pair of jeans belonging to the Eagle leader. The jeans were painted orange and displayed as a flag by the Rattlers. Armed with rocks, the Eagles started on a retaliatory raid, but the counselors stopped them before any serious injuries could result.

So the second phase of the experiment revealed that intergroup conflict may bring about changes in the internal structures of rival groups, particularly within the group that is placed in a subordinate position by losing. As conflict continues, members of opposing groups develop strong "we versus them" attitudes that help to reestablish a sense of ingroup solidarity and to maintain the group's animosity toward its rivals.

Phase 3: Reducing Intergroup Hostility

Sherif and his associates had created a monster. By the end of phase 2 the Eagles and Rattlers had reached a point at which their contacts with each other invariably resulted in name calling, threats, and fisticuffs. The third phase of the experiment was designed to reduce these hostilities.

It soon became apparent that intergroup conflicts were easier to create than to reduce. One of the first strategies was to bring the boys together in a pleasant, noncompetitive setting—for example, at the movies. This plan failed miserably: The boys used these occasions to call each other names and squabble, and, if anything, the hostilities became even more intense. Several other ploys were tried and found ineffective. For example, both groups attended religious services emphasizing cooperation and brotherly love, but the boys reverted to their rivalrous conduct immediately after the services were over. "Summit" meetings between the two group leaders were not attempted, for it was felt that any concessions made by the leaders would be interpreted by followers as traitorous behavior.

Finally, Sherif et al. devised a strategy that they thought would work. If the two groups were to face common problems that could not be solved by either group working alone, they would be forced to "pull together," which should decrease intergroup hostilities. The counselors then cleverly engineered a series of these problems, or "**superordinate goals.**" On one occasion, when everyone was hungry and the camp truck would not start, the boys combined their efforts to get the truck going so they would have supplies for dinner that night. As a result of these and other cooperative exchanges, the two groups became much less antagonistic toward each other. In fact, friendships developed across group lines, and the Eagles, who had won a monetary prize in the previous athletic competition, ended up using the money to treat their former rivals. Sherif has summarized these results in the following way:

> What our limited experiments have shown is that the possibilities for achieving harmony are greatly enhanced when groups are brought together to work toward common ends. Then favorable information about a disliked group is seen in a new light, and leaders are in a position to take bolder steps toward cooperation. In short, hostility gives way when groups pull together to achieve overriding goals that are real and compelling to all concerned. (Sherif, 1956, p. 58)

Notice, then, that the same factors that promote *within-group* cohesion—namely, working toward a common goal—can also help to reduce *between-group* hostilities. Surely the results of phase 3 are applicable far beyond the camp setting in which they were obtained. Although feelings have waxed and waned over the years, Americans and Russians have been much more positive in their impressions of each other whenever their governments were actively pressing for the attainment of a shared goal—halting the arms race. And perhaps the only way to reduce well-ingrained animosities between rivalrous, inner-city adolescent gangs or between such ethnic groups as Arabs and Israelis, English and French Canadians, and South African blacks and whites is for leaders of these rival factions to identify common problems that must be solved and that neither group is likely to resolve without the other's cooperation. The challenge, of course, is to identify superordinate goals that are attractive and will be received enthusiastically by members of different groups. But, in any case, the search for a common ground will surely prove far less costly in terms of both economic and human resources than a continuation and possible escalation of intense intergroup conflicts.

superordinate goals: important objectives that cannot be achieved unless rivaling groups or factions set their differences aside and pull together to work as a team.

know members of the other sex in casual social situations, without having to be intimate. Eventually, strong cross-sex friendships develop and couples form, often double-dating or spending time with a small number of other couples. At this point, the old cliques and crowds may gradually begin to disintegrate, having served their purposes of helping adolescents establish a social identity and bringing the boys and girls together (Brown, 1990; Dunphy, 1963).

PERSONAL AND SOCIAL INFLUENCES ON SOCIABILITY

Were you to carefully observe children of any age, you would soon discover that some of them are drawn to peers and seem to thrive on social interaction whereas others appear rather unsociable, or even withdrawn. How might we account for these individual differences in peer sociability?

Sociability as a Heritable Attribute   Let's first note that one's genotype can clearly influence his or her responsiveness to other people. Over the first year, identical twins are much more similar than fraternal twins in their frequency of social smiling and their fear of strangers (Freedman, 1974), and these differences in sociability are still apparent when pairs of identical and fraternal twins are retested at 18 and 24 months of age (Matheny, 1983). In fact, Sandra Scarr's (1968) study of 6- to 10-year-old twin pairs suggests that genetic influences on sociability are often detectable well into middle childhood. Even when identical twins have been *mistakenly reared* as fraternals, they are still (1) as similar as identical twins who have been raised as identical on aspects of sociability such as friendliness and shyness and (2) much more similar on these same measures than are pairs of true fraternal twins.

Although sociability appears to be a genetically influenced attribute, environmental factors play a major role in its expression. For example, Denise Daniels and Robert Plomin (1985b) found a significant correlation between the shyness of adopted toddlers and the sociability of their *biological* mothers: Shy toddlers tended to have mothers who were low in sociability, whereas non-shy toddlers had mothers who were more outgoing. This finding argues for a genetic influence on sociability, since biological mothers and their adopted-away toddlers have genes in common. Yet Daniels and Plomin also found a significant correlation between the shyness of adopted toddlers and the sociability of their *adoptive* mothers, and the magnitude of this relationship was nominally greater than that between the toddlers and their biological mothers! Since adoptive mothers and their adopted children have no genes in common, environmental factors must have been responsible for their resemblance on these sociability measures.

What environmental experiences are likely to influence a child's responsiveness to peers? Let's consider the direct and the indirect roles that *parents* play in fostering (or inhibiting) peer interactions.

Direct Parental Effects on Peer Interaction   There are several ways that parents directly influence the sheer amount of contact their children have with peers. Their choice of a residence is one such influence. If parents choose to live in a neighborhood where there are parks, playgrounds, and many young children, their own sons and daughters will have ample opportunities to interact with peers. By contrast, a decision to reside in a neighborhood with big yards, widely spaced houses, and few playgrounds or available playmates could seriously restrict children's access to peers (Medrich et al., 1982).

When young children cannot easily get together on their own, their contact with peers will depend very heavily on whether their parents serve as "booking agents" for peer interaction—whether parents arrange visits by playmates, enroll their children in day care or nursery school, or encourage their participation in other organized activities for children (Hart et al., 1997; Parke & Kellum, 1994). Of course, parents who arrange home visits by peer playmates are also in a position to influence their child by monitoring his or her peer interactions to ensure that play proceeds smoothly and amiably, without major conflicts. This brings us to an interesting issue.

Should parents closely monitor or intrude on playful interactions between young children? Gary Ladd and Beckie Golter (1988) attempted to answer this question by asking parents of preschool children how they had supervised any recent interactions their child had had with peers at home. Some parents reported that they had closely watched over the children or had even participated in their play activities (direct monitoring); others said they had checked occasionally on the children without often intruding or becoming involved as a playmate (indirect monitoring). Which form of monitoring is associated with successful and harmonious peer interactions? Ladd and Golter's findings clearly favor indirect parental monitoring. As we see in Figure 13.3, preschoolers whose parents had indirectly monitored their peer interactions were much better liked (and less often disliked) by their nursery school classmates than those whose parents closely monitored and often intruded on their play activities.

Interestingly, it is mothers who believe that their children are not very socially skilled who are most likely to intrude in their children's play activities—a finding which implies that conflictual peer interactions may promote direct monitoring rather than the other way around (Mize, Pettit, & Brown, 1995). Nevertheless, the quality of monitoring and intervention that parents provide clearly matters. If a parent's coaching is supportive and optimistic, and it focuses heavily on prosocial strategies, the child will often display more harmonious interactions with peers (Mize & Pettit, 1997; Russell & Finnie, 1990). By contrast, parents who become agitated and who issue commands rather than constructive solutions usually elicit negative responses from their children, who continue to display poor social skills and nonharmonious peer interactions (Carson & Parke, 1996; Russell & Finnie, 1990). A negative and controlling parent who is always barking orders may inhibit sociability by simply taking all the fun out of play activities. Alternatively, these parents may be teaching their children to be bossy and dictatorial themselves—a style that is likely to elicit negative reactions from playmates and convince the child that contacts with peers are not all that pleasant (Kochanska, 1992; Russell & Finney, 1990).

Let's note, however, that findings favoring indirect, nonintrusive monitoring of children's peer interactions in no way imply that adults should simply butt out and leave their children to resolve all difficulties they may have with peers on their own. Recall from our discussion in Chapter 9 that parents who consistently fail to monitor their children's (or adolescents') whereabouts, activities, and associates tend to raise surly and aggressive youngsters who are often rejected by peers (Dishion, 1990). Furthermore, children in day care are occasionally found to be more aggressive and disobedient than those reared at home—although these "negative returns" are typically limited to those youngsters who receive extremely low-quality day care in which interactions with peers are often *not* monitored by their day-care providers (Clarke-Stewart, 1993; Howes, 1990).

Taken together, then, the findings we have reviewed imply that parents can foster the development of social skills and positive peer relations by (1) teaching their youngsters how to initiate and maintain harmonious social interactions (Mize & Pettit, 1997; Landry et al., 1998), (2) indirectly monitoring their children's transactions with peers to ensure that they comply with the rules of social etiquette they have learned, and (3) allowing playmates considerable freedom to structure their own play activities and to resolve most minor disputes on their own (Ladd & Hart, 1992; Rubin et al., 1998).

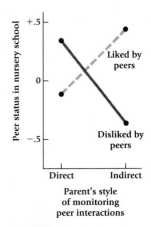

FIGURE 13.3 Nursery school children enjoy a more favorable status with peers when parents have indirectly monitored their interactions with playmates. (Based on Ladd & Golter, 1988.)

Effects of Structured Preschool Activities   Another way parents might directly influence their young children's contacts with peers is to enroll them in structured activities for preschoolers. In Chapter 12, we noted that a major objective of many nursery schools is to prepare preschoolers for a formal scholastic environment by introducing them to a "social" curriculum that fosters the growth of communicative and interactive skills and an appreciation for rules of social etiquette. Does nursery school have any noticeable effect on children's sociability with peers? Does the amount of nursery school experience children have make a difference?

John Shea (1981) addressed these issues by observing 3- and 4-year-olds as they entered nursery school and attended classes two, three, or five days a week. As children mingled on the playground, their behavior was videotaped, and individual acts were classified on five dimensions: aggression, rough-and-tumble play, distance from the nearest child, distance from the teacher, and frequency of peer interaction. Over a 10-week observation period, children gradually ventured farther from the teacher as they became much more playful and outgoing with one another and much less forceful and aggressive. Furthermore, these changes were most noticeable for the children who attended school five days a week and least apparent (but detectable nevertheless) for those who attended twice a week. Shea concluded that nursery school attendance has a very positive effect on young children's reactions to other children.

Most of the research published since Shea's early study supports his conclusion. As we saw in Box 12.2, children who receive high-quality day care or who attend nursery schools that emphasize a social curriculum do tend to be more outgoing with peers and to develop social skills at an earlier age than children who remain at home. Why? Probably for at least three reasons. First, guidance offered by nursery school teachers and knowledgeable day-care providers undoubtedly plays a part in improving children's social skills (Howes, Hamilton, & Matheson, 1994). Furthermore, children often become securely attached to warm and responsive teachers and day-care providers, and their positive working models of these individuals may encourage them to be more outgoing with other people in the nursery school or day-care setting (that is, with their classmates). Carolee Howes and her associates (1998) recently found that children who had established a secure rather than insecure attachment with a preschool teacher were not only inclined to form close friendships during the preschool period but were also more likely to have close (as opposed to shaky, nonsupportive) friendships five to seven years later in elementary school. Finally, we must not overlook the possibility that nursery school children may often become more sociable because they have become more familiar with their classmates and feel more comfortable with them. Indeed, play among preschoolers is much more cooperative, complex, and socially skilled when playmates are familiar companions rather than strangers (Brody, Graziano, & Musser, 1983; Harper & Huie, 1985; Rubin et al., 1998). So for any or all these reasons, it seems that parents may indeed foster their children's social competence with peers by arranging for them to receive care in a high-quality child-care program.

Indirect Parental Effects on Peer Sociability   In addition to their roles as initiators and monitors of peer interactions, parents may indirectly influence their children's reactions to peers by virtue of their behavior as caregivers, authority figures, and disciplinarians.

Parents as Caregivers   In Chapter 5, we learned that different patterns of caregiving during the first year are reliably associated with the development of different kinds of attachments. Although attachment behaviors and peer sociability represent different social systems, attachment theorists (Ainsworth, 1979; Bowlby, 1988) argue that the quality of a child's primary attachments will influence his or her reactions to other people later in life. Specifically, they believe that children who are insecurely attached to one or more unresponsive caregivers may be rather anxious and inhibited in the presence of unfamiliar companions and much less sociable than children who are securely attached.

The available evidence is generally consistent with this notion. Recall from our discussion in Chapter 5 that infants who were securely attached to their mothers at 12 to 18 months of age are more likely than those who were insecurely attached to display socially competent behaviors and to be attractive to peers as playmates throughout the toddler, preschool, and elementary school periods (see Rubin et al., 1998, for a recent review). Furthermore, securely attached 3½- to 6-year-olds already *perceive* peers in more positive ways and have established more friendships with them than children who are insecurely attached (Cassidy et al., 1996), and adults who recall their early attachments as secure are less lonely and are more likely to receive social support from peers than those who portray their childhood attachments as insecure (Berscheid & Reis, 1998; Kobak & Sceery, 1988).

Why might secure attachments foster peer sociability and positive peer relations? Bowlby's (1988) viewpoint (see also Bretherton, 1995) was that securely attached youngsters have formed positive working models of their sensitive, responsive caregivers, and these perceptions, in turn, predispose them to have positive views of other people and to assume that others will welcome their sociable gestures. However, links between attachment security and peer sociability are correlational data that are subject to alternative interpretation. One such interpretation is that children with easy temperaments or who are otherwise socially skilled are the ones who are most likely to establish secure attachments and to be appropriately sociable with peers. Yet, a recent study of 3- to 4-year-olds by Kelly Bost and associates (1998) revealed that (1) the security of children's attachments clearly predicted their later social competencies with peers, whereas (2) measures of children's earlier social competencies with peers did *not* predict the quality of their attachments with their mothers in a later follow-up assessment. So it appears that secure attachments do indeed promote social competencies (and favorable relations with peers) rather than the other way around.

Patterns of Child Rearing and Peer Sociability   Perhaps you have gleaned from our discussion thus far that parents of appropriately sociable children tend to be warm, sensitive companions who both teach and model effective social skills and who monitor their children in a nonintrusive way, thereby allowing them considerable autonomy to properly apply the guidelines they have learned in the context of playful interactions with peers. Clearly this pattern of warmth, sensitivity, and moderate control sounds very much like the *authoritative* pattern of child rearing we have commented on favorably throughout the text—a pattern that is consistently associated with children's socially skilled behaviors and acceptance by peers (Baumrind, 1971; Hinshaw et al., 1997; Mize & Pettit, 1997). By contrast, highly authoritarian (or uninvolved) parents who rely heavily on power assertion as a control tactic tend to raise youngsters who are often aggressive or otherwise socially unskilled when interacting with other children and are likely to be *rejected* by peers (Dekovic & Janssens, 1992; Hart et al., 1998; Rubin et al., 1998). So there is ample evidence that the path to positive (or negative) peer interactions often begins at home. As Putallaz and Heflin have noted:

> Parental involvement, warmth, and moderate control appear to be important [to] children's social competence. Within the social context of the family, children appear to learn certain interactional skills and behaviors that they then transfer to their interactions with peers. (1990, p. 204)

One final point and an important one: Although authoritative parenting seems to promote good social skills and positive peer relations, Box 13.2 reveals that the particular skills it fosters can vary dramatically from culture to culture.

Box 13.2 Cultural Influences

A Cross-Cultural Examination of Parenting and Children's Social Skills

As we learned in Box 4.1, shyness and socially inhibited behaviors have very different meanings in different cultures. In *individualistic* societies such as the United States and Canada, children are encouraged to become autonomous, outwardly confident, and properly assertive, whereas shyness and a corresponding inability to assert oneself in social situations are taken as indications of social immaturity and considered psychologically maladaptive. By contrast, children in such *collectivist* societies as China, Taiwan, and Korea are encouraged to restrain their personal desires in favor of pursuing group goals. Indeed, both Confucian and Taoist Chinese philosophies seek to instill this communal orientation by stressing that self-restraint and socially inhibited behaviors are crucially important social *skills* rather than weaknesses. So if authoritative parenting or its components (that is, warmth, guidance, and a generally nonpunitive orientation to child rearing) promote socially skilled behaviors, then Western parents who display this profile should tend to raise children who are not at all shy or socially inhibited, whereas Chinese parents who display the same pattern of parenting should produce children who are generally reserved or inhibited.

These hypotheses were recently tested by Xinyin Chen and associates (1998) in a cross-cultural study of 2-year-olds and their mothers from Canada and the People's Republic of China. Each of the toddlers was observed in an unfamiliar play room containing novel toys (for example, a big robot that moved and made strange noises) as well as a friendly stranger wearing a mask, who encouraged the child to join her in play. These observations permitted the researchers to note how wary the child seemed of unfamiliar stimuli and thus, to assign him or her a score for behavioral inhibition. In addition, the mothers of these toddlers each completed a questionnaire to assess their child-rearing attitudes and behaviors. Among the dimensions of interest were (1) the mother's acceptance of her child (warmth), her encouragement of mastery or achievement behavior, and her orientation to punishment (that is, favoritism of power-assertive discipline).

As might be expected from the value placed on social restraint in Chinese culture and its devaluation in Canada, Chinese toddlers proved to be significantly more inhibited than their Canadian counterparts. But there was more. When Chen et al. correlated mothers' scores on the three child-rearing dimensions with their children's scores on the behavioral inhibition measure, strikingly different patterns emerged across cultures. As the correlations in the table indicate, warm, accepting mothers who actively encourage achievement and are reluctant to use power assertion had the more *inhibited* 2-year-olds in China, where inhibition is valued, but the more *uninhibited* toddlers in Canada, where inhibition is *not* a strength but self-assertion is. Not only are these results consistent with the researchers' cross-cultural hypotheses, but they serve as a rather dramatic reminder that even though the parenting styles that foster good social skills may be similar in many respects across cultures, the particular skills they foster may vary dramatically from culture to culture.

Correlations between child-rearing attitudes/behaviors and toddlers' behavioral inhibition in a Chinese and a Canadian sample

CHILD-REARING VARIABLE	CHINA	CANADA
Acceptance of child	.17	−.22
Encouragement of achievement	.18	−.21
Punitiveness	−.15	.22

Note: A positive correlation means that mothers high on that child-rearing variable tended to have behaviorally inhibited toddlers, whereas a negative correlation indicates that mothers scoring high on that dimension had relatively *un*inhibited toddlers. (Adapted from Chen et al., 1998.)

Peer Acceptance and Popularity

Perhaps no other aspect of children's social lives has received more attention than **peer acceptance**—the extent to which a child is viewed by peers as a worthy or likable companion. As you might expect, many factors determine one's worthiness in the eyes of peers, some of which are specific to a particular group or setting. For example, toughness, hostility, and an ability to handle a motorcycle may make you a valued Hell's Angel, but these qualities would probably not enhance your standing among the members of your monthly investment club. Clearly, different groups value

peer acceptance: a measure of a person's likability (or dislikability) in the eyes of the peers.

different attributes, and those who are accepted possess the characteristics that are valued by *their* peer groups. Nevertheless, there are a number of factors that seem to affect a person's social standing in many kinds of groups, regardless of the age, sex, or sociocultural backgrounds of the members. These are the qualities on which we focus as we review the determinants of one's standing with his or her peers.

MEASURING CHILDREN'S POPULARITY WITH PEERS

Developmentalists generally rely on **sociometric techniques** to assess a child's status in the peer group. These techniques require children to state their preferences for other group members with respect to some specific criterion. If you wanted to measure popularity, for example, you might use the *rating-scale technique* and ask each child to rate every other child in the group on a 5-point likeability scale (ranging from "really like to play with" to "really don't like to play with"). Other investigators favor a *paired-comparison* approach in which the child is presented with the names of two group members at a time and asked to pick the one he or she likes better. Because all pairs of group members are eventually presented, this technique yields an overall measure of popularity for each child in the group. However, the approach that many investigators favor (and that seems to provide the sharpest distinctions between different categories of peer acceptance (cf. Terry & Coie, 1991) is the **nominations technique**: each child is asked to name a specific number of peers (often 3) whom he or she *really likes* (or would prefer as playmates) and the same number of peers whom he or she *likes least* (or would not want as play partners). Even 3- to 5-year-olds can respond appropriately to sociometric surveys, for they already know who among their nursery school classmates is perceived as liked or disliked (Denham et al., 1990; Howes, 1988). And lest you wonder, the sociometric classifications that children receive from these measures (1) are positively correlated with teacher ratings of peer popularity and (2) accurately predict the character of children's peer interactions as well (Green et al., 1980; Howes, 1988; Hymel, 1983). So it seems that sociometric surveys provide *valid* assessments of children's social standing in their peer groups.

How is a child's social standing determined? With the often-used nominations technique, the number of positive and negative nominations that each child receives determines his or her standing along two sociometric dimensions. First, the number of negative nominations (as a disliked peer) is subtracted from the number of positive nominations (as a liked peer) to locate the child on a *social preference* dimension. Children who receive more positive than negative nominations have positive social preference scores, whereas those receiving more negative than positive nominations fall toward the negative end of this dimension. Then the child's *total number* of positive and negative nominations are added to locate him or her on a *social impact* dimension. Children high in social impact thus receive many nominations and are quite noticeable to their peers whereas those who receive few nominations (and are low in social impact) do not stand out and may seem almost invisible in the peer group.

Categories of Peer Acceptance After a child is located on the social preference and the social impact dimensions, he or she can usually be assigned to one of five sociometric categories. As shown in Figure 13.4, children classified as **popular** are high in both social preference and social impact,

sociometric techniques: procedures that ask children to identify those peers whom they like or dislike or to rate peers for their desirability as companions; used to measure children's peer acceptance (or nonacceptance).

nominations technique: sociometric measures in which children are asked to nominate a specific number of peers as liked and the same number as disliked. The number and patterning of positive and negative nominations a child receives determine his or her sociometric status.

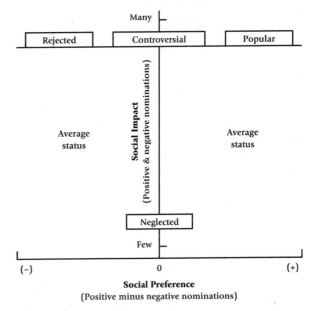

FIGURE 13.4 Five sociometric classifications (statuses) that children might attain based on the number and patterning of nominations each receives as a "liked" or a "disliked" peer. (Adapted from Berndt, 1992.)

having received many positive nominations and few negative ones from their peers. By contrast, **rejected children** are high in social impact but low in social preference; they are disliked by many children and liked by few. Children classified as **neglected** receive very few positive or negative nominations; they are low in social impact and intermediate (neither high nor low) on the social preference dimension. Children labeled **controversial** receive many positive and many negative nominations. Like neglected children, they score intermediate on the social preference dimension; they differ from neglectees, however, in that they are high in social impact. Together, these four types of children make up about two-thirds of the pupils in a typical elementary school classroom. The remaining one-third are of **average status,** having received moderate numbers of positive and/or negative nominations (Coie, Dodge, & Coppotelli, 1982).

A note or two about these sociometric classifications is in order. First, controversial children have not been studied extensively because they make up only about 5% of the students in a typical elementary school classroom and they often do not remain controversial for long. In fact, one study found that nearly 60% of children initially classified as controversial had achieved another status in the peer group over intervals as brief as one month (Newcomb & Bukowski, 1984). Second, longitudinal studies reveal that the popular and average status classifications are moderately stable over time but that the rejection classification is highly stable, with rejectees often retaining this status from year to year (Rubin et al., 1998). One reason for this persistence is that the peers come to react quite unfavorably when assessing the causes of a rejectee's prosocial and antisocial conduct. That is, they tend to attribute a rejectee's *antisocial* behavior to stable dispositional causes (for example, "She's mean and nasty"), while attributing *prosocial* behaviors to unstable situational factors (for example, "His mother made him invite me to the party"). By contrast, the prosocial behaviors of liked children are attributed to dispositional causes ("He invited me because he likes me"), whereas their *antisocial* acts are attributed to unstable, situational factors ("He didn't invite me because he ran out of invitations") (Hymel, 1986; Hymel et al., 1990). So liked children receive the benefit of the doubt should they respond negatively to their peers, but disliked children are assigned personal responsibility for their negative antics without receiving any credit for any acts of kindness that might help them to overcome their bad reputations and low social status. This social-cognitive bias on the part of peers, coupled with the fact that rejectees do often annoy or anger their peer associates (see below) seem to explain why rejectees often remain rejected over the long run.

Finally, let's note that both neglected children and rejected children are not well received by their peers. Yet it is not nearly as bad to be ignored by other children as to be rejected by them. Neglectees do not feel as lonely as rejectees do (Cassidy & Asher, 1992; Crick & Ladd, 1993), and they are much more likely than rejected children to eventually attain a more favorable sociometric status should they enter a new class at school or a new play group (Coie & Dodge, 1983). Furthermore, rejected children are the ones who face the greater risk of displaying deviant, antisocial behavior and other serious adjustment problems later in life (Parker & Asher, 1987; Parker et al., 1995; Rubin et al., 1998).

WHY ARE CHILDREN ACCEPTED, NEGLECTED, OR REJECTED BY PEERS?

At several points throughout the text, we have discussed factors that seem to contribute to children's popularity or social status. By way of review:

Parenting Styles As noted earlier in the chapter, warm, sensitive, and authoritative caregivers who rely on reasoning rather than power to guide and control children's

popular children: children who are liked by many members of their peer group and disliked by very few.

rejected children: children who are disliked by many peers and liked by few.

neglected children: children who receive few nominations as either a liked or a disliked individual from members of their peer group.

controversial children: children who receive many nominations as a liked and many as a disliked individual.

average-status children: children who receive a moderate number of nominations as a liked and/or a disliked individual from members of their peer group.

Calvin and Hobbes

by Bill Watterson

conduct tend to raise youngsters who are securely attached and who are liked by both adults and peers. By contrast, highly authoritarian and/or emotionally unresponsive parents who rely heavily on power assertion as a control tactic often have insecurely attached youngsters who are uncooperative, aggressive, or disruptive, and who are actively disliked by peers.

The fact that parents influence their children's social skills implies that the *long-term* adjustment problems many rejected children display may stem as much from a rejectee's disordered home life as from poor peer relations. Nevertheless, we will see that rejected youngsters' patterns of thinking and social interaction often alienate peers, thereby eliciting negative reactions that perpetuate and even intensify the problems these children exhibit.

Temperamental Characteristics   Certain aspects of children's temperaments are correlated with and undoubtedly contribute to their sociometric statuses. For example, we learned in Chapter 4 that difficult children who are often irritable and impulsive are at risk for having nonharmonious interactions with peers that could cause them to become rejected. In addition, relatively passive children who are behaviorally inhibited or slow to warm up are at risk (in Western societies, at least) of being neglected or even rejected by peers (see also Eisenberg et al., 1998).

Cognitive Skills   Both cognitive and social-cognitive skills predict children's peer acceptance. Among groups of third- through eighth-graders, the most popular children are those who have well-developed role-taking skills (Kurdek & Krile, 1982; Pellegrini, 1985), and children who have established intimate friendships score higher on tests of role-taking than classmates without close friends (McGuire & Weisz, 1982). In addition, popular, average-status, and neglected youngsters also tend to perform better academically and to score higher on IQ tests than rejected children and adolescents do (Bukowski et al., 1993; Chen, Rubin, & Li, 1997; Wentzel & Asher, 1995).

At least two additional sets of characteristics seem to reliably predict children's and adolescents' standing among their peers: their physical attributes and their patterns of interpersonal behavior.

Physical Correlates of Peer Acceptance

Facial Attractiveness   Despite the maxim that "beauty is only skin deep," many of us seem to think otherwise. Even 6-month-old infants can easily discriminate attractive from unattractive faces (Langlois et al., 1991), and 12-month-old infants already prefer to interact with attractive rather than unattractive strangers (Langlois, Roggman, & Rieser-Danner, 1990). By the preschool period, attractive youngsters are often described in more favorable ways (that is, friendlier, smarter) than their less attractive classmates by both teachers and peers (Adams & Crane, 1980; Langlois, 1986), and attractive children are generally more popular than unattractive children from elementary school onward (Langlois, 1986). This link between facial attractiveness and peer acceptance even begins to make some sense when we consider how attractive and unattractive children interact with their playmates. Although attractive and unattractive 3-year-olds do not yet differ a great deal in the character of their social behaviors, by age 5, unattractive youngsters are more likely than attractive ones to be active and boisterous during play sessions and to respond aggressively toward peers (Langlois & Downs, 1979). So unattractive children do seem to develop patterns of social interaction that could alienate other children.

Why might this happen? Some theorists have argued that parents, teachers, and other children may contribute to a self-fulfilling prophecy by subtly (or not so subtly) communicating their expectancies to attractive youngsters, letting them know they are smart and are supposed to do well in school, behave pleasantly, and be likable. Information of this sort undoubtedly has an effect on children: Attractive youngsters may become progressively more confident, friendly, and outgoing, whereas unattractive children may resent the less favorable feedback they receive and become more defiant and aggressive. This is precisely how a "beautiful is good" stereotype could become a reality (Langlois & Downs, 1979).

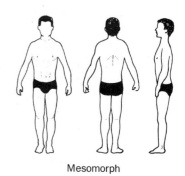

Mesomorph

Body Build   Body build (or physique) is another physical attribute that can affect a child's self-concept and popularity with peers. In one study (Staffieri, 1967), 6- to 10-year-olds were shown full-length silhouettes of *ectomorphic* (thin, linear), *endomorphic* (soft, rounded, chubby), and *mesomorphic* (athletic and muscular) physiques (see Figure 13.5). After stating which body type they preferred, the children were given a list of adjectives and asked to select those that applied to each body type. Finally, each child listed the names of five classmates who were good friends and three classmates whom he or she didn't like very well.

The results were clear. Not only did children prefer the mesomorphic silhouette, they attributed positive adjectives—for example, brave, strong, neat, and helpful—to this figure while assigning much less favorable adjectives to the ectomorphic and endomorphic figures. Among the children themselves, there was a definite relationship between body build and popularity: The mesomorphs in the class turned out to be the most popular children, whereas endomorphic classmates were least popular (see also Sigelman, Miller, & Whitworth, 1986).

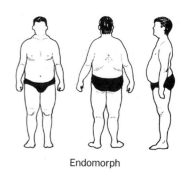

Endomorph

Timing of Puberty   Although physique continues to play a part in determining one's sociometric status beyond childhood (Clauser, 1975), a variable that seems to have even more impact on the social fortunes of preadolescents and young adolescents is the age at which they reach puberty, and the impacts of pubertal timing differ somewhat for boys and girls.

Longitudinal research conducted at the University of California suggests that boys who mature early enjoy a number of social advantages over boys who mature late. One study followed the development of 16 early maturing and 16 late maturing male adolescents over a six-year period and found late maturers to be more eager, anxious, and attention-seeking (and were also rated by teachers as less masculine and less physically attractive) than early maturers (Jones & Bayley, 1950). Early maturers tended to be poised and confident in social settings and were more likely to win athletic honors and election to student offices. Although this study was based on only 32 boys in

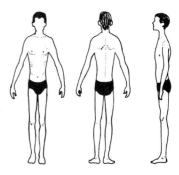

Ectomorph

FIGURE 13.5 The three body types used in Staffieri's experiment.

California, other researchers have found that late maturing boys do tend to feel somewhat socially inadequate and inferior (Duke et al., 1982; Livson & Peskin, 1980). Late maturing boys also have lower educational aspirations than early maturers do, and they even score lower early in adolescence on school achievement tests (Dubas, Graber, & Petersen, 1991).

Why is the early maturing boy so advantaged? One reason may be that his greater size and strength often make him a more capable athlete, which in turn is apt to bring social recognition from adults and peers (Simmons & Blyth, 1987). The early maturer's adultlike appearance may also prompt others to overestimate his competencies and to grant him privileges and responsibilities normally reserved for older individuals. Indeed, parents hold higher educational and achievement aspirations for early maturing than for late maturing sons (Duke et al., 1982), and they have fewer conflicts with early maturers about issues such as acceptable curfews and the boy's choice of friends (Savin-Williams & Small, 1986). Perhaps you can see how this generally positive, harmonious atmosphere might promote the poise or self-confidence that enables early maturers to become popular and to assume positions of leadership within the peer group.

PHOTO 13.5 Early maturing boys tend to be poised and confident in social settings and popular with their peers.

For girls, maturing early may be something of a *disadvantage*. Several studies have found that early maturing girls are somewhat less outgoing and less popular than their prepubertal classmates (Aro & Taipale, 1987; Clausen, 1975; Faust, 1960) and are likely to report more symptoms of anxiety and depression as well (Ge, Conger, & Elder, 1996; Hayward et al., 1997). Intuitively, these findings make some sense. A girl who matures very early may look very different from female classmates, who may tease her, and from boys in the class, who will not mature for two to three years and are not yet all that enthusiastic about the early maturer's more womanly attributes (Caspi et al., 1993). As a result, early maturing girls often seek (or are sought out by) older companions, particularly boys, who will often steer them away from academic pursuits and into less desirable activities, such as smoking, drinking, drug use, and sex, that they are not yet prepared to handle (Caspi et al., 1993; Stattin & Magnusson, 1990). Indeed, risks of psychological distress among early maturing girls are much higher when they attend coed schools and have lots of boys as friends (Caspi et al., 1993; Ge et al., 1996).

Overall, then, both the advantages of maturing early and the disadvantages of maturing late are greater for boys than for girls. However, it is important to note that differences in peer acceptance between early and late maturers are not large and are highly variable from child to child; also many factors other than timing of puberty influence whether this period of life goes smoothly.

Behavioral Correlates of Peer Acceptance Although one's physical characteristics and cognitive/scholastic/athletic prowess are all meaningfully related to peer acceptance, even the brightest and most attractive children may be unpopular if peers consider their behavior inappropriate or antisocial (Dodge, 1983). What behavioral characteristics are most important in influencing a child's standing with peers?

Several studies of preschool, elementary school, and middle school (young adolescent) children report pretty much the same findings. Popular children are observed to be relatively calm, outgoing, friendly, and supportive companions who can successfully initiate and maintain interactions and can resolve disputes amicably (Coie, Dodge, & Kupersmidt, 1990; Denham et al., 1990; Ladd, Price, & Hart, 1988). Stated another way, these "sociometric stars" are warm, cooperative, and compassionate individuals who display many prosocial behaviors and are seldom disruptive or aggressive (Newcomb, Bukowski, & Pattee, 1993; Rubin et al., 1998).

Neglected children, by contrast, often appear passive and shy. They are not very talkative; they make fewer attempts than children of average status to enter play groups; and they seldom call attention to themselves (Coie et al., 1990; Harrist et al., 1997). Nevertheless, these "neglectees" are no less socially skilled than children of average status; nor are they any more lonely or more distressed about the character of their social relationships (Cassidy & Asher, 1992; Wentzel & Asher, 1995). Their passive and less sociable behavior appears to stem more from their beliefs that they are not socially skilled than from any active ostracism or exclusion by their peer groups (Cassidy & Asher, 1992; Rubin et al., 1998).

There are at least two kinds, or categories, of *rejected* children, each with a distinct behavioral profile. **Rejected-aggressive children** often alienate peers by using forceful means to dominate them or their resources. These disruptive braggarts tend to be uncooperative and critical of peer group activities and to display very low levels of prosocial behavior (Newcomb et al., 1993; Parkhurst & Asher, 1992). Rejected-aggressive children are prone to interpret others' behavior as hostile, even when it isn't; yet, they clearly overestimate their social standing, often saying that they are liked just as well as, or better than, most children (Zakriski & Coie, 1996). These are the youngsters who display the greatest risk of becoming chronically hostile and displaying externalizing conduct disorders and even criminal acts of violence later in adolescence and adulthood (Parker et al., 1995; Rubin et al., 1998).

Rejected-withdrawn children, on the other hand, are typically socially awkward companions who display many unusual and immature behaviors and are insensitive to peer group expectations. Unlike rejected-aggressive children, they expect to be rebuffed, are well aware that other children do not like them, and eventually begin to withdraw as peers actively exclude them from their activities (Downey et al., 1998; Harrist et al., 1997: Hymel, Bowker, & Woody, 1993; Zakriski & Coie, 1996). These withdrawn rejectees feel especially lonely and are at risk of experiencing low self-esteem, depression, and other emotional disorders (Hymel et al., 1993; Rabiner, Keane, & MacKinnon-Lewis, 1993). And because of their unusual behaviors, their hypersensitivity to criticism, and their lack of close friends to stick up for them, they are particularly inviting targets for abuse at the hands of bullies (Hodges et al., 1997; Parkhurst & Asher, 1992).

The Direction of Effects Issue   Now let's consider a thorny interpretive problem: Do the behavioral profiles that children display really *cause* them to become popular, rejected, or neglected by peers? Do popular children, for example, become popular because they are friendly, cooperative, and nonaggressive? Or is it that children become friendlier, more cooperative, and less aggressive after achieving their popularity? One way to test these competing hypotheses is to place children in play groups with *unfamiliar* peers and then see whether the behaviors they display will predict their eventual status in the peer group. Several studies of this type have been conducted (Coie & Kupersmidt, 1983; Dodge, 1983; Dodge et al., 1990; Ladd et al., 1988) and the results are reasonably consistent: The patterns of behavior that children display do predict the statuses they will achieve with their peers. Children who are ultimately accepted by unfamiliar peers are highly effective at initiating social interactions and at responding positively to others' bids for attention. When they want to join a group activity, for example, these socially skilled, *soon-to-be-accepted* children will first watch and attempt to understand what is going on, and then comment pleasantly and con-

rejected-aggressive children: a subgroup of rejected children who display high levels of hostility and aggression in their interactions with peers.

rejected-withdrawn children: a subgroup of rejected children who are often passive, socially unskilled, and insensitive to peer-group expectations.

structively about the proceedings as they blend smoothly into the group. By contrast, children who are ultimately *rejected* are pushy and self-serving: They will often criticize or disrupt group activities and may even threaten reprisals if they are not allowed to join in. Other children who end up being neglected by their peers tend to hover around the edges of a group, initiating few interactions and shying away from other children's bids for attention. Interestingly, some children who are neglected by familiar playmates will suddenly become quite sociable with *unfamiliar* peers (Coie & Kupersmidt, 1983), whereas other extremely withdrawn neglectees are apt to retain this status or to eventually even become rejected (French, 1988; Rubin et al., 1998).

In sum, peer popularity is affected by many factors. It may help to have a pleasant temperament, an attractive face, and academic competencies, but it is even more important to display good social-cognitive skills and to behave in socially competent ways. Definitions of desirable social behavior, of course, may vary from culture to culture and change over time. In Box 4.1, for example, we learned that shyness, which may undermine one's popularity in Western societies, actually promotes peer acceptance in China, where being quiet and reserved are more socially desirable attributes. The ingredients of popularity also change with age: Although establishing close relationships with members of the other sex enhances popularity during adolescence, frequent consorting with "the enemy" violates norms of gender segregation during childhood and detracts from one's popularity (Kovacs et al., 1996; Sroufe et al., 1993). In short, contextual factors clearly play a part in determining who is popular and who is not.

Unfortunately, children who are rejected by peers are likely to retain their rejected status from grade to grade and are at risk of experiencing any (or all) of the adjustment problems associated with peer rejection (Cillessen et al., 1992; Coie et al., 1990). Let's now examine some of the programs that can help rejected children to improve their social skills and their prospects for experiencing healthier psychological outcomes.

ON IMPROVING THE SOCIAL SKILLS OF REJECTED CHILDREN

The finding that peer rejection is a strong predictor of current and future psychological difficulties has prompted many investigators to devise interventions aimed at improving the social skills of unpopular children. Here are some of the more effective techniques.

Reinforcement and Modeling Therapies   Many early approaches to social-skills training were based on learning theory and involved (1) reinforcing children (with tokens or praise) for displaying such socially appropriate behaviors as cooperation and sharing, or (2) exposing children to social models who display a variety of socially skilled acts. Both approaches have been successful at increasing the frequency of children's socially skilled behaviors. And when teachers and peers participate in the intervention, they are much more likely to notice changes in the rejected child's behavior and are more inclined to change their opinion of him or her (Bierman & Furman, 1984; White & Kistner, 1992). There are several ways for teachers and other adults to structure play environments so that it becomes easier to reinforce children for their appropriate social conduct. For example, they might persuade youngsters to work at tasks or strive for superordinate goals that require cooperation among *all* present (see Box 13.1). Even simple strategies such as giving children "social" toys to play with (cards, checkers, and the like) should provide ample opportunities for adults to reinforce examples of appropriate social behavior.

Similarly, some modeling therapies are more effective than others. Modeling programs work best when the model is similar to the target child and when his socially skillful actions are accompanied by some form of commentary that directs the child's attention to the purposes and benefits of behaving appropriately toward peers (Asher, Renshaw, & Hymel, 1982).

Cognitive Approaches to Social-Skills Training   The fact that modeling strategies work better when accompanied by verbal rationales and explanations implies that interventions prompting the child to imagine the positive consequences of skillful social overtures are likely to be effective. Why? Because the child's active cognitive involvement in the social-skills training may increase her understanding and appreciation of the principles that are taught, thereby persuading her to internalize and then rely on these lessons when interacting with peers.

   Coaching is a cognitive social-learning technique in which the therapist displays one or more social skills, carefully explains the rationales for using them, allows children to practice such behavior, and then suggests how the children might improve on their performances. Sherri Oden and Steven Asher (1977) coached third- and fourth-grade social isolates on four important skills: how to participate in play activities, how to take turns and share, how to communicate effectively, and how to give attention and help to peers. Not only did the children who were coached become more outgoing and positive, but follow-up measures a year later revealed that these former isolates had achieved even further gains in social status (see also Bierman, 1986; Mize & Ladd, 1990; Schneider, 1992). Coaching is particularly effective at improving social skills and sociometric standings when it is combined with other forms of social-skills training, such as encouraging children to work together toward the attainment of cooperative goals (Bierman & Furman, 1984).

PHOTO 13.6   Coaching can be effective at improving the social skills of rejected children.

   Other cognitive interventions, firmly grounded in cognitive-developmental theory, include attempts to improve children's *role-taking* skills and *social problem-solving abilities* (Chandler, 1973; Rabiner, Lenhart, & Lochman, 1990). These techniques can be especially effective with rejected-aggressive children who often display a *hostile attributional bias* (a tendency to overattribute hostile intentions to their companions) that has been acquired at home from coercive parents who mistrust other people and endorse aggression (Keane, Brown, & Crenshaw, 1990; Pettit, Dodge, & Brown, 1988). In order to help these aggressive rejectees, the training must not only emphasize that aggression is inappropriate but also help them to generate nonaggressive solutions to conflict. One approach that looks promising is the **social problem-solving training** that Myrna Shure and George Spivack (1978; Shure, 1989) devised to help preschoolers generate and then evaluate amicable solutions to interpersonal problems. Over a 10-week period, children role-played conflict scenarios with puppets and were encouraged to discuss the impact of their solutions on the feelings of all parties involved in a conflict. Shure and Spivack found that the longer the children had participated in the program, the fewer aggressive solutions they offered. Furthermore, the children's classroom adjustment (as rated by teachers) improved as they became better able to think through the social consequences of their own actions (see also Hudley & Graham, 1995).

coaching: method of social-skills training in which an adult displays and explains various socially skilled behaviors, allows the child to practice them, and provides feedback aimed at improving the child's performances.

social problem-solving training: method of social-skills training in which an adult helps children (through role-playing or role-taking training) to make less hostile attributions about harm-doing and to generate nonaggressive solutions to conflict.

Academic Skills Training   Children who are failing miserably at school are often rejected by their classmates (Dishion et al., 1995). Might we elevate their social status by improving their academic skills and bringing them back into the mainstream of school activities? One research team tried this approach, providing extensive academic skills training to low-achieving, socially rejected fourth-graders (Coie & Krehbiel, 1984). This training not only improved the children's reading and math achievement, but their social standing improved as well. One year after the intervention ended, these former rejectees enjoyed average status in their peer group.

So there is a variety of techniques adults might use to improve the social skills of unpopular children and help them to establish a more favorable standing among their peers. Yet a caution is in order, for the long-term success of any intervention could easily be compromised if the new social skills and problem-solving strategies children have acquired are likely to be undermined by highly aggressive friends or by coercive, mistrusting parents who endorse aggressive solutions to conflict. For these reasons, Gregory Pettit and his associates (1988) favor *preventive* therapies—family-based interventions in which parents who value and encourage aggression are identified early and retrained themselves, thus possibly preventing their children from ever being rejected by peers. Academic skills training is also a preventive strategy: Children who gain in scholastic competence not only become better liked but are also less likely to select highly aggressive children as friends or to become members of deviant peer cliques (Dishion et al., 1995). Today we are seeing a much stronger emphasis on preventive interventions—programs that are undertaken as soon as a child's problems with peers become apparent. And such an emphasis is clearly warranted, for (as we learned in Chapter 9) social-skills training programs rarely succeed once a child's deviant, antisocial conduct has continued beyond the first few grades at school (Kazdin, 1995).

Children and Their Friends

As young children become more outgoing and are exposed to a wider variety of peers, they typically form close ties to one or more playmates—bonds that we call **friendships.** Recall from Chapter 6 that children have some pretty firm ideas about what qualifies someone as a friend. Before age 8, the principal basis for friendship is *common activity:* Children view a friend as someone who likes them and who enjoys similar kinds of play activities. By contrast, 8- to 10-year-olds, equipped with more sophisticated social perspective-taking skills, begin to see friends as individuals who are *psychologically similar* and who can be trusted to be loyal, kind, cooperative, and sensitive to each other's feelings and needs (Berndt, 1996; Pataki, Shapiro, & Clark, 1994). And although adolescents continue to think that loyalty and shared psychological attributes are characteristics that friends display, their conceptions of friendship now focus more on *reciprocal emotional commitments.* That is, friends are viewed as intimate associates who truly understand each other's strengths, can accept each other's weaknesses, and are willing to share their innermost thoughts and feelings (Hartup, 1996).

ON THE DEVELOPMENT OF FRIENDSHIP

Although young children may have many playmates, few of these companions become close friends. How do friendships develop? One way to find out is to randomly pair unacquainted children as playmates and then observe their play over a period of weeks for clues as to why some pairs become friends and others do not. John Gottman (1983) tried this approach with pairs of initially unacquainted 3- to 9-year-olds. Each pair of playmates met in the home of one of the children for several play sessions over a period of four weeks. At the end of the study, mothers responded to a questionnaire on which they indicated whether their children had become friends

friendship: a strong and often enduring relationship between two individuals, characterized by loyalty, intimacy, and mutual affection.

with their new playmates. Furthermore, observers had recorded children's behavior during the play sessions, hoping to use these observations as a way of determining how the interactions of children who become friends differ from those of eventual nonfriends.

As expected, Gottman found that some of the playmate pairs became fast friends whereas others did not. He also found several important differences in the play activities of eventual friends and nonfriends. First, even though eventual friends didn't always initially agree on which play activities to pursue, they were much more successful than eventual nonfriends at *resolving conflicts* and establishing a *common-ground activity*—that is, at agreeing on what and how to play. Eventual friends were also the more successful at *communicating clearly* with each other and *exchanging information*. And some of the information exchanged was very personal in nature, for eventual friends were more likely than children who did not become friends to engage in **self-disclosure**. So it seemed to Gottman as if children who generally agreed about play activities early on simply "hit it off," thus becoming more inclined to show affection and approval toward their partners and to reveal personal information about themselves—processes that allowed their relationship to gel as a friendship. Do these same processes that help to create friendships also characterize interactions among longer-term friends? Let's see whether they do.

SOCIAL INTERACTIONS AMONG FRIENDS AND ACQUAINTANCES

As early as ages 1 to 2, children may become attached to a preferred play partner and respond very differently to these "friends" than to other playmates (Ross et al., 1992). For example, friends display more advanced forms of pretend play than acquaintances do—as well as more affection and more approval (Howes, Droege, & Matheson, 1994; Whaley & Rubenstein, 1994). Friends often do nice things for each other, and many altruistic behaviors may first appear within these early alliances of the preschool era. Frederick Kanfer and his associates (1981), for example, found that 3- to 6-year-olds were generally willing to give up their own valuable play time to perform a dull task if their efforts would benefit a friend; yet, this same kind of self-sacrifice was almost never made for a mere acquaintance (see also Zarbatany et al., 1996). Young children also express more sympathy in response to the distress of a friend than to that of an acquaintance, and they are more inclined to try to relieve the friend's distress as well (Costin & Jones, 1992; Farver & Branstetter, 1994).

It is often said that there is a "chemistry" to close friendships and that best friends seem to be "in tune" with each other. Research clearly supports this notion. Casual conversations among pairs of sixth-graders are much more cheerful, playful, and relaxed when the members of these pairings are good friends rather than mere acquaintances (Field et al., 1992). In fact, a measure of participants' saliva cortisol levels (a physiological correlate of stress) taken after the conversations suggested that casual interactions between acquaintances are more stressful than those between friends. Even when collaborating on school assignments, friends tend to be more "in synch," agreeing more readily with each other and spending more time "on task" than collaborating acquaintances do (Hartup, 1996). One reason that interactions among friends may be so synchronous and productive is that friends are more similar than acquaintances are in sociometric status as well as in their levels of shyness and prosocial behaviors (Haselager et al., 1998). So perhaps it is fair to say that interactions between friends are often characterized by a sense of mutuality, positive regard, and many other relevant points of similarity, and do, indeed, have a favorable "chemistry" about them.

How long do children's friendships last? It may surprise you to learn that even preschool friendships can be highly stable. Carollee Howes (1988), for example,

self-disclosure: the act of revealing private or intimate information about oneself to another person.

found that children who attend the same day-care center for several years often keep the same close friends for more than a year. Although they may wax and wane in strength, close friendships often remain stable from year to year during middle childhood (Berndt & Hoyle, 1985; Cairns et al., 1995). However, friendship networks (the list of all individuals that a child might nominate as "friends") tend to shrink in size as children approach adolescence (Berndt, Hawkins, & Hoyle, 1986; Berndt & Hoyle, 1985). This loss of friends may simply reflect the young adolescent's growing awareness that the obligations of friendship—which now include the exchange of intimate information and the provision of emotional support—are easier to live up to if one selects a smaller circle of very close friends.

ARE THERE DISTINCT ADVANTAGES TO HAVING FRIENDS?

Do friends play a unique role in shaping a child's development? Do children who have established adequate peer relations but no close friends turn out any differently from those who have one or more of these special companions? Although few well-controlled longitudinal studies that would be needed to answer these questions have yet been conducted (Hartup, 1996), we can draw some tentative conclusions about the roles friends play as socializing agents.

Friends as Providers of Security and Social Support   One strong clue that friends play an important role in children's lives is the finding that having at least one supportive friend can go a long way toward reducing the loneliness and the victimization unpopular children experience when they are excluded from the larger peer group (Hodges et al., 1997, 1999; Parker & Asher, 1993; Parker & Seal, 1996). A close relationship with one or more friends may provide an emotional safety net—a kind of security that not only helps children deal more constructively with new challenges but may also help them bear more easily almost any other form of life stress (for example, coping with a divorce or with a rejecting parent). Indeed, Gary Ladd and his associates (1987, 1990, 1997) found that children who enter kindergarten along with their friends seem to like school better and have fewer adjustment problems than those who enter school without many friends. Furthermore, we saw in Chapter 11 that children who respond most constructively to their parents' divorce are often those who have the support of friends, particularly those whose parents are also divorced. Close supportive friendships play an especially important role in promoting the social competencies and self-esteem of children from nonnurturant, noncohesive families; and should youngsters from such nonsupportive family environments lose a particularly close friend, they often experience sizable declines in their feelings of self-worth (Gauze et al., 1996).

PHOTO 13.7   Sometimes nothing is as reassuring as the affection and encouragement of a friend.

So friends are potentially important sources of security and **social support,** and they become increasingly important in fulfilling this role as children grow older. Fourth-graders, for example, say that their parents are their primary sources of social support; however, friends are perceived to be (1) as supportive as parents by seventh-graders and (2) the most frequent providers of social support by tenth-grade adolescents (Buhrmester, 1996; Furman & Buhrmester, 1992).

Friends as Contributors to Social Problem-Solving Skills   Since friendships are usually described as pleasant and rewarding relationships that are worth preserving,

social support: tangible and intangible resources provided by other people in times of uncertainty or stress.

children should be highly motivated to resolve any conflicts with these "special" companions (Hartup, 1996). And apparently they are: From the preschool period onward, disagreeing friends are more likely than disagreeing acquaintances to step away before the squabbles become intense, to make concessions by accepting equal outcomes, and to continue their interactions after the conflict is over (Hartup et al., 1988; Laursen, Hartup, & Koplas, 1996). By middle childhood, friends are much more inclined than acquaintances are to follow the rules (and not cheat) while playing competitive games and to respect the opinions, needs, and wishes of their partner while negotiating to settle a dispute (Fonzi et al., 1997; Nelson & Aboud, 1985). These experiences of amicably resolving conflicts with a friend are undoubtedly important contributors to the growth of mature social problem-solving skills—one of the strongest predictors of a healthy sociometric status with peers (Rubin et al., 1998).

Friendships as Preparation Positive Adult Adjustment   We've seen that close friendships are characterized by increasing intimacy and mutuality from middle childhood through adolescence. Could these relatively intense and intimate ties to what are overwhelmingly same-sex companions be necessary for the development of the deep interpersonal sensitivity and commitment so often observed in stable adult love relationships? Harry Stack Sullivan (1953) thought so. Sullivan reported that many of his lonely, mentally disturbed patients had failed to form close friendships when they were young, and he concluded that the close reciprocal bonds that develop between same-sex friends (or "chums") during preadolescence provide the foundation for a strong sense of self-worth and the growth of caring and compassionate attitudes that a person needs to establish and maintain intimate love relationships later in life. Consistent with Sullivan's ideas, preadolescents who have established *intimate* same-sex friendships are more likely than their friendless age-mates to have broken through the gender segregation barrier and begun to forge closer ties with members of the opposite sex (George & Hartmann, 1996).

However, a critic could argue that a strong test of Sullivan's theory would require a *prospective* longitudinal study to see whether preadolescents who are friendless really do turn out any different as adults from age-mates who have at least one close chum. Recently, such a study was conducted. And as we see in Box 13.3, its results not only confirm some of the central premises of Sullivan's theory but also illustrate that having a close friend has long-term advantages over and above those associated with having established a favorable sociometric status with peers.

Does Quality of Friendships Matter?   One more point—and an important one: Friendships clearly differ in quality, and the very children who tend to have poor social skills—those who are insecurely attached to their parents, who have highly controlling or uninvolved parents, or who are rejected by peers—also tend to have friendships that are nonsupportive and lacking in trust (Dishion et al., 1995; Kerns et al., 1996; Parker & Asher, 1993; Youngblade & Belsky, 1992). Indeed, low-quality friendships are often highly conflictual alliances in which children respond to disagreements by seeking revenge and behaving in a hostile rather than a conciliatory manner toward a friend (Rose & Asher, 1999). Does the *quality* of a child's friendships influence his or her adjustment and developmental outcomes?

Apparently so. Studies of both kindergartners (Ladd, Kochenderfer, & Coleman, 1996) and 7th- and 8th-grade preadolescents (Berndt & Keefe, 1995) reveal that children who enter a school year with close, supportive friendships typically showed an increase in their liking for or involvement with school, whereas students whose friendships are more rivalrous and conflictual displayed poorer attitudes toward school, often becoming less engaged in scholastic activities and increasingly disruptive. Furthermore, children who are insecurely attached to their parents or who are

Box 13.3 *Developmental Issues*

A Longitudinal Analysis of the Benefits of Chumships

Recently, Catherine Bagwell, Andrew Newcomb, and William Bukowski (1998) conducted a *prospective* longitudinal study to test Sullivan's (1953) hypothesis that children who establish close, intimate friendships as preadolescents will show some strengths as adults (that is, very positive mental health, a strong sense of self-worth, and solid ties to romantic partners) that their chumless peers are less likely to display. Participants were 15 males and 15 females who, as 11-year-old fifth-graders, had completed sociometric measures that enabled the researchers to determine (1) their levels of general peer acceptance and (2) whether they had established a close, reciprocal tie with a best friend. Twelve years later, these participants (now age 23) completed an extensive packet of questionnaires that assessed such adjustment indexes as their general self-worth, school and job performance, levels of aspiration for the future, perceived competence in romantic relationships and relationships with family members, and depressive as well as other measures of psychopathological symptomatology.

The results of this study were most interesting indeed. First, let's note that the results provided impressive support for Sullivan's theory. That is, preadolescents who had established close ties to a best friend were found as young adults to feel more competent with one group of intimate associates (family members), to have a stronger sense of self-worth, and to report less depressive symptomatology than their counterparts who had been chumless as preadolescents. What's more, these findings were *uniquely attributable* to participants' earlier *friendship* status rather than to their general levels of peer acceptance.

Although friended preadolescents did not view themselves as any more competent 12 years later in their adult romantic relationships than did their chumless age-mates, it is possible that the results may have differed had the assessments of romantic competence come from the romantic partners rather than the participants themselves (after all, who among 23-year-olds would like to admit that they are incompetent romantics?).

As might be expected, one's level of general peer acceptance also predicted later adjustment outcomes, but the outcomes it predicted differed from those forecast by participants' earlier status as a friended or a chumless preadolescent. Specifically, participants who had been rejected in the fifth grade had lower levels of aspiration 12 years later and viewed themselves as less competent in their school and job performances than their counterparts who had enjoyed more favorable sociometric statuses. Finally, *both* earlier peer acceptance and earlier friendship status made important contributions to participants' general mental health, such that young adults who had been rejected and chumless as preadolescents reported the higher levels of psychopathological symptoms.

In sum, this study clearly implies that close, supportive friendships with a preadolescent chum promote many of the very competencies that Sullivan emphasized in his earlier theorizing. And although the study is like many others in suggesting that general peer acceptance is a potent contributor to healthy adult adjustment outcomes, its strength lies in its illustration that close supportive friendships can have salutary effects on social development *over and above* those stemming from one's general acceptance by peers.

rejected by the larger peer group are more likely to display poor adjustment outcomes if their social support is provided mainly by their friends (Booth, Rubin, & Rose-Krasnor, 1998; Rubin et al., 1998). This finding seems to reflect the fact that the friendship networks of these children are often made up of other socially unskilled and antisocial individuals who (1) are not particularly supportive companions and (2) are inclined to encourage maladaptive patterns of behavior (Dishion et al., 1995; Rubin et al., 1998). Indeed, it seems that only when best friendships *are* close and nonconflictual do they foster the social competencies and self-esteem of children from nonnurturant and disordered families (Gauze et al., 1996). Clearly, these findings have an important practical implication: In view of the crucial roles that harmonious and *supportive* friendships can play in a child's life, perhaps our interventions for at-risk, unpopular children should be broadened to include lessons in how to establish and maintain these intimate ties as well as the more general kinds of social skills training (Asher, Parker, & Walker, 1996; Rose & Asher, 1999).

How Do Peers Exert Their Influence?

To this point, we have seen that it is important for children to establish good peer relations and close supportive friendships because they will acquire many competent and adaptive patterns of social behavior through their interactions with peers. How do peers exert their influence? In many of the same ways that parents do: by reinforcing, modeling, discussing, and even pressuring one another to comply with the values and behaviors they condone.

PEER REINFORCEMENT AND MODELING INFLUENCES

It is easy to see that parents, teachers, and other powerful authority figures are in a position to reward or punish the behavior of children. But can a peer, who shares a similar status with the child, truly become an effective reinforcing agent?

Yes indeed. Recall from Chapter 8 that 22- to 24-month-old toddlers have already begun to encourage gender-appropriate play and to criticize or disrupt a playmate's cross-sex activities. And playmates are influenced by these reactions: Children who receive peer approval for gender-appropriate play tend to keep playing, whereas those who are criticized by peers for cross-sex play usually stop such activity in less than a minute (Lamb, Easterbrooks, & Holden, 1980).

Many of the reinforcers that peers provide one another are quite subtle or unintentional. For example, a child who "caves in" to a bully has not only reinforced the bully's aggressive tactics without meaning to but has also set herself up to be victimized again. Yet, when a potential victim "punishes" a tormentor by fighting back, she may persuade him to seek other victims and possibly even learn that fighting "pays off," thus becoming more aggressive herself (Patterson, Littman, & Bricker, 1967).

So peers *are* important sources of social reinforcement. Although we have sampled but two studies from a voluminous literature, the evidence clearly indicates that children's social behaviors are often strengthened, maintained, or virtually eliminated by the favorable or unfavorable reactions they elicit from peers.

Modeling Influences   Peers also influence one another by serving as social models for a multitude of behaviors—some good, and some not so good. Among the attributes and activities that are easily acquired by observing peer models are socially skilled behaviors (Cooke & Apolloni, 1976), achievement behaviors (Sagotsky & Lepper, 1982), mature moral judgments (Kruger, 1992), an ability to delay gratification (Stumphauzer, 1972), and gender-typed attitudes and behaviors (Frey & Ruble, 1992), to name a few. You may recall that several of these findings were discussed at length in earlier chapters.

Finally, peers clearly influence each other by serving as objects for social comparison. You may recall from our discussion in Chapter 6 that grade-school children often reach conclusions about their competencies and sense of self-worth by comparing their behaviors and accomplishments to those displayed by peers.

PEERS AS CRITICS AND AGENTS OF PERSUASION

Another way that peers influence each other is by discussing and debating issues on which they disagree. Typically, both parties to these discussions (which can become rather heated) are invested in their own points of view and are trying to persuade their partner to adopt (or at least move toward) the position they are advocating. Indeed, we learned in Chapter 10 that older children and young adolescents can be persuaded to change their perspectives on moral issues should a peer challenge their existing viewpoints (that is, induce cognitive disequilibria) and present a more sophisticated set of arguments for them to assimilate and adopt as their own. Furthermore, peers may be the *most effective* agents of persuasion-via-cognitive conflict, for you may recall from our earlier discussion of moral development that cognitive challenges from *authority figures* (parents) are often perceived by children as heavy-handed criticism and are generally less successful than other methods at inducing youngsters to change their viewpoints. By contrast, a peer is an equal-status associate whose well-reasoned challenges are (1) less likely to be perceived as derisive and (2) should carry some weight in that most children and adolescents are very interested in establishing or maintaining good peer relations (Walker & Taylor, 1991a).

THE NORMATIVE FUNCTION OF PEER GROUPS

A major reason that peers become increasingly important as agents of socialization is that, from middle childhood onward, an increasing percentage of peer interactions occur in true *peer groups*—confederations that influence their members by setting **norms** specifying how group members are supposed to look, dress, think, and act. And children do become increasingly responsive to normative peer pressures as they grow older, although they are hardly the blind conformists people commonly assume them to be.

In his classic study of **peer conformity,** Thomas Berndt (1979) asked third- through twelfth-graders to indicate the likelihood that they would bend to peer pressure when peers were advocating various prosocial or antisocial acts. He found that conformity to peer pressure for prosocial behaviors did not change much with age. Instead, the most striking developmental change was a sharp increase in conformity to peers urging *antisocial* behavior. This receptivity to peer-sponsored misconduct peaked in the ninth grade (or about age 15; see Figure 13.6) and then declined throughout the high school years (see also Brown, Clasen, & Elcher, 1986; Steinberg & Silverberg, 1986). So parents may have some grounds for worrying that their 13- to 15-year-olds could wind up in trouble by going along with the crowd. Peer pressure of all kinds is especially strong at this age (Gavin & Furman, 1989), and there is nothing worse than being viewed as a "dweeb" who does not fit in (Kinney, 1993).

Why does conformity to peer-sponsored misconduct *decrease* by the end of high school? Perhaps this trend reflects the progress older adolescents have made in their quest for autonomy: They are now better able to make their own decisions and are less dependent on the opinions of *either* parents or peers. According to Lawrence Steinberg and Susan Silverberg (1986), strong conformity to peer pressure early in adolescence may even be a necessary step in the development of autonomy: Young adolescents who are struggling to become less dependent on their parents may need the security that peer acceptance provides before they will develop the confidence to take their own stands and stick by them. And they are unlikely to gain such acceptance if they conform too closely to adult rules and values without taking a chance and going along with peers every now and then (Allen, Weissberg, & Hawkins, 1989). Although the parent whose teenager is nabbed with his friends for cherry-bombing mailboxes or deflating tires may not be totally comforted by this thought, it does seem that a period of heavy peer influence may pave the way for later independence.

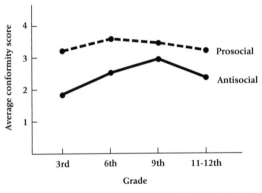

FIGURE 13.6 Average scores by grade for conformity to peer pressure for prosocial and antisocial behaviors. (Adapted from Berndt, 1979.) © 1979 by the American Psychological Assn. Reprinted by permission.

norms: group-defined rules or expectations about how the members of that group are to think or behave.

peer conformity: the tendency to go along with the wishes of peers or to yield to peer group pressures.

Cultural Influences   As we learned in Chapter 11, early adolescence is also the period when children in many cultures experience heightened conflicts with parents as they begin their quest for autonomy. Do younger adolescents around the world suddenly become more susceptible to peer-sponsored misconduct as they begin to experience more hassles with their parents at home?

Although the data on this point are sparse, the answer is apparently not. In their recent study of misconduct reported by early (seventh and eighth grade) adolescents in the United States, Taiwan, and the People's Republic of China, Chuansheng Chen and associates (1998) found that participants in all three cultures reported *similar levels* of general misconduct such as cheating on tests, lying to parents, fighting, destroying property, smoking and drinking alcohol, and so on. This was true even though the Chinese peer groups in this study were found to be much *less* inclined than Chinese-American and European-American peer groups to endorse this kind of behavior. So it seems that Chinese and Taiwanese adolescents are no better behaved than their American counterparts, even though their peers are less likely than American peers are to encourage antisocial conduct. One limitation of this study is that it sampled middle-class youngsters in all three cultures who reported only low to moderate levels of misconduct. Nonetheless, the finding that Chinese youth could be just as mischievous and antisocial as Americans, despite experiencing *lower levels* of conflict at home and fewer peer pressures, suggests that much of the blame placed on *peers* for triggering adolescent misconduct may be overstated. Indeed, we now conclude our discussion of peer influences by examining yet another body of research that makes this same point in a different way.

PEER VERSUS ADULT INFLUENCES AND THE QUESTION OF CROSS-PRESSURES

In years gone by, adolescence was often characterized as a stormy period when all youths experience **cross-pressures**—strong conflicts that stem from differences in the values or practices advocated by parents and those favored by peers. What's more, there are theorists today (most notably Harris, 1995) who claim that peers eventually become the major source of influence on developing adolescents and that the patterns of child rearing that parents have used *will matter little in the long run*. How accurate are these "life portraits" of the teenage years?

At first glance, these assertions may seem to have some merit for some youths, particularly those "rejected" youths who form deviant peer cliques and endorse antisocial behaviors that are likely to alienate their parents, teachers, and most other peers (Dishion et al., 1991, 1995; Patterson et al., 1989; Vitaro et al., 1997). These youngsters do experience strong cross-pressures, which they often resolve by rejecting mainstream values in favor of those advocated by their deviant peers. Yet as we will see, (1) the exaggerated susceptibility of these antisocial youth to peer influence largely reflects a hidden *parental* influence, and (2) the cross-pressures "problem" is simply not much of a problem for most adolescents.

Perhaps the major reason that parent/peer warfare is typically kept to a minimum is that parents, by virtue of their parenting styles, have a good deal of influence on the company their adolescents keep. Authoritative parents who are warm, neither too controlling nor too lax, and who are consistent in their discipline generally find that their adolescents are closely attached to them and have internalized their values. These adolescents have little need to rebel or to desperately seek acceptance from peers when they are so warmly received at home (Brown et al., 1993; Fuligni & Eccles, 1993). In fact, they tend to associate with friends who share their values, which largely protects them from unhealthy peer influences (Bogenschneider et al., 1998; Chassin et al., 1998; Fletcher et al., 1995).

cross-pressures: conflicts stemming from differences in the values and practices advocated by parents and those favored by peers.

Interestingly, problems for youths who *do* "fall in with the wrong crowd" and display antisocial behavior usually begin at home. One way parents can go wrong is by being too strict, failing to adjust to an adolescent's needs for greater autonomy. This may cause adolescents to become alienated from parents and overly susceptible to negative peer influences, to the point that they would let schoolwork slide or break parental rules to please their friends (Fuligni & Eccles, 1993). Parents can also go wrong by failing to provide enough discipline and by not monitoring their children's activities closely enough (Barber et al., 1994; Brown et al., 1993; Dishion et al., 1991, 1995). So parents have a good deal of power to influence, *through their parenting,* whether their adolescents will end up in "good" or "bad" crowds and are exposed to healthy or unhealthy peer pressures.

Another reason that parent/peer conflicts are kept to a minimum is that parents and peers tend to exert their influence in different domains. Hans Sebald (1986), for example, has asked adolescents whether they would seek the advice of their parents or the advice of their peers on a number of different issues. Peers were likely to be more influential than parents on such issues as what styles to wear and which clubs, social events, hobbies, and other recreational activities to choose. By contrast, adolescents claimed that they would depend more on their *parents* when the issue involved scholastic or occupational goals or other *future-oriented* decisions. Teenagers are unlikely to be torn between parent and peer pressures as long as parents and peers have different primary areas of influence.

Of course, there are some issues for which parental opinions are likely to conflict with those of many peers (for example, opinions about acceptable conduct on dates or about the harm involved in experimenting with tobacco, alcohol, or marijuana). Yet, peer group values are rarely as deviant as adults commonly assume; even at midadolescence, when negative peer pressures are greatest, most teenagers report that their friends and associates are more likely to *discourage* antisocial behavior than to condone it (Brown et al., 1986). And on many issues for which parental and peer norms might seem to be in conflict, the adolescent's behavior is actually a product of both parental and peer influences. Consider the following example. Denise Kandel (1973) studied a group of adolescents whose best friends either did or did not smoke marijuana and whose parents either did or did not use psychoactive drugs. Among those teenagers whose parents used drugs but whose friends did not, only 17% were marijuana users. When parents did not use drugs but best friends did, 56% of the adolescents used marijuana. From these findings, we might conclude that the peer group is more influential than parents over marijuana use. However, the highest rate of marijuana smoking (67%) occurred among teenagers whose parents and peers *both* used psychoactive drugs, and a similar pattern emerges when we look at parental and peer influences on use of alcohol, tobacco, and other illicit drugs (Bogenschneider et al., 1998; Chassin et al., 1996, 1998; Newcomb & Bentler, 1989).

In sum, adolescent socialization is not a continual war of parents *versus* peers; instead, these two important sources of influence combine to influence one's development (Bogenschneider et al., 1998; Mounts & Steinberg, 1995). Most adolescents have cordial relationships with their parents, accept many of their parents' values, and are reluctant to stray too far from these guidelines and undermine their parents' approval. And most parents know how important it is for their children and adolescents to establish close

PHOTO 13.8 Although teenagers are often characterized as wild and rebellious, typically their norms and values are a reflection of adult society.

relationships with their social equals. They seem to appreciate what the lonely farmer whose letter opened this chapter has learned the hard way: Many of the social competencies that serve people well are the fruits of their alliances with close friends and peers.

Summary

WHO IS A PEER AND WHAT FUNCTIONS DO PEERS SERVE?

- **Peer** contacts represent a second world for children—a world of equal-status interactions that is very different from the nonegalitarian environment of the home. However, **mixed-age peer interactions** are also crucially important socialization contexts that have benefits for both younger and older peer associates.

- Contacts with peers increase dramatically with age, and during the preschool or early elementary school years, children are spending at least as much of their leisure time with peers as with adults. The "peer group" consists mainly of same-sex associates of somewhat different ages.

- Research with **mother-only** and **peer-only monkeys** and young children indicates that peer contacts are important for the development of competent and adaptive patterns of social behavior. Children who fail to establish and maintain adequate relations with their peers will run the risk of experiencing any number of serious adjustment problems later in life.

THE DEVELOPMENT OF PEER SOCIABILITY

- **Sociability** between peers emerges by the middle of the first year. By ages 18 to 24 months, toddlers' sociable interactions are becoming much more complex and coordinated as they reliably imitate each other, assume complementary roles in simple social games, and occasionally coordinate their actions to achieve shared goals.

- During the preschool years, **nonsocial activities** and **parallel play** become less common, whereas **associative play** and **cooperative play** become more common. Pretend play contributes in many ways to the growth of **social skills,** and the maturity of a preschooler's play activities predict his or her present and future and popularity with peers.

- During middle childhood, more peer interactions occur in true peer groups—confederations that associate regularly, define a sense of group membership, and formulate **norms** that specify how group members are supposed to behave. By early adolescence, youngsters are spending even more time with peers—particularly with their closest friends in small **cliques,** and in larger confederations of like-minded cliques, known as **crowds.** Cliques and crowds help adolescents to forge an identity apart from their families and pave the way for the establishment of dating relationships.

- Several factors contribute to individual differences in peer sociability, and among the more important influences are the child's genotype, the security of the child's attachments, and the child-rearing practices that parents employ. Parents influence their children's sociability with peers by virtue of the neighborhood in which they choose to live, their willingness to serve as "booking agents" for peer contacts, and their monitoring of peer interactions. Warm, sensitive, authoritative parents tend to raise appropriately sociable children who establish good relations with peers, whereas highly authoritarian or uninvolved parents—particularly those who rely on power-assertion as a control tactic—tend to raise disruptive, aggressive youngsters whom peers often dislike.

PEER ACCEPTANCE AND POPULARITY

- Children clearly differ in **peer acceptance**—the extent to which other youngsters view them as likable (or dislikable) companions. Using **sociometric techniques,** developmentalists find that there are five categories of peer acceptance: (1) **popular children** (liked by many and disliked by few), (2) **rejected children** (disliked by many and liked by few), (3) **controversial children** (liked by many and disliked by many), (4) **neglected children** (seldom nominated by others as likable or dislikable), and (5) **average-status children** (those who are liked or disliked by a moderate number of peers). Neither neglected children nor rejected children are well received by peers; however, it is the rejected child who is typically the lonelier of the two and at greater risk of displaying serious adjustment problems later in life.

- Although physical characteristics, cognitive prowess, and the parenting one has received may contribute to a child's popularity with peers, one's patterns of social behavior are the strongest predictor of peer acceptance. Popular children are generally warm, cooperative, and compassionate companions who display many prosocial behaviors and are rarely disruptive or aggressive. Neglected children often have adequate social skills, but they appear shy and reserved and tend to hover at the edge of peer-group activities. Rejected children display many unpleasant and annoying behaviors and few prosocial ones. **Rejected-aggressive** children are hostile, impulsive, highly, uncooperative, and aggressive, whereas **rejected-withdrawn** children are socially awkward and immature companions who are hypersensitive to criticism and have actively isolated themselves from peers.

- Programs to improve the social skills of rejected children include reinforcement and modeling therapies, such social-cognitive interventions as **coaching** and **social problem-solving training,** and even academic remediation, which keeps children on track at school and reduces their exposure to hostile, antisocial peers. Social-skills training programs work better (1) with younger children than with adolescents, and (2) when the target children's teachers and classmates also participate in the intervention.

CHILDREN AND THEIR FRIENDS

- Children typically form close ties, or **friendships,** with one or more members of their play groups. Younger children view a friend as a harmonious playmate, whereas older children and adolescents come to think of friends as close companions who share similar interests and values and are willing to provide them with intimate social and emotional support.

- Interactions among friends are warmer, more cooperative, more compassionate, and more synchronous (though not necessarily less conflictual) than those among nonfriend acquaintances.

- Close friendships appear to promote positive developmental by (1) providing children and adolescents with security and **social support,** (2) promoting the growth of social problem-solving skills and an ability to compromise, and (3) fostering a strong sense of self-worth and caring and compassionate attitudes that are the foundation of intimate love relationships later in life. The benefits of friendship occur over and above those attributable to positive peer relations. However, friendships differ in quality, and only close, supportive friendships seem to foster adaptive developmental outcomes.

HOW DO PEERS EXERT THEIR INFLUENCE?

- Peers influence a child in many of the same ways that parents do—by modeling, reinforcing, discussing, and pressuring associates to conform to the behaviors and values they condone. **Peer conformity** pressures peak at mid-adolescence, when teenagers are most susceptible to peer-sponsored misconduct. Yet, severe **cross-pressures** are not a problem for most adolescents, who have established warm relations with their parents and have generally internalized many of their parents' values. What's more, peer-group values are often very similar to those of parents, and peers are more likely to discourage than to condone antisocial conduct. So adolescent socialization is not a continual battle between parents and peers; instead, these two important influences combine to affect one's development.

Chapter Fourteen

Epilogue

Major Themes in Human Social and Personality Development

Human Development Is a Holistic Enterprise

We Are Active Contributors
to Our Own Development

There Is Both Continuity
and Discontinuity in Development

There Is Much Plasticity in Human Development

The Nature–Nurture Distinction
Is a False Dichotomy

Both Normative and Idiosyncratic
Developments Are Important

We Develop in a Cultural and Historical Context

Development Is Best Viewed
from Multiple Perspectives

Patterns of Parenting (and Adult Guidance)
Clearly Matter

Many Social Forces Conspire
to Shape Development

We've Come a Long Way, Baby . . .
But Have So Far to Go

We have now concluded our survey of the major theories and empirical issues that make up the discipline known as social and personality development. The content of this book is based on more than 10,000 empirical studies of developing children and adolescents, and your knowledge base was undoubtedly expanded further by other writings that your instructor asked you to read or presented as part of classroom exercises. Now that you have reached this point in the course, it may be helpful to reflect for a moment on what you have learned and what all this knowledge implies for your role as a parent, prospective parent, or aspiring child-care professional who may one day influence the lives of developing persons.

Were we to fast-forward to one year from today, you might find that you recall fewer than 50% of the "facts" you had at your command when you took the final exam in this course. Psychologists who study long-term learning and memory tell us that this is to be expected and in no way implies that you haven't profited from taking the class. In fact, I usually mention this to my own students as we near the end of the course and say to them that I'd feel I had succeeded as their instructor (and textbook author) if they now see the "bigger picture" and can retain and use this knowledge to their own advantage in the years ahead. And what is this bigger picture? I like to define it as a set of broad principles about human development that are relatively timeless and extremely important to keep in mind if we hope to optimize the development of the children and adolescents under our direction. The principles I discuss below are not intended as an exhaustive list. In fact, one useful exercise that you and your classmates may wish to do is to generate your own list of important principles about human social and personality development and see how closely your list matches the points discussed below. It is likely that you will have some insights that do not appear on my list and that should be there. In that event, I'd like to hear from you so that I (and future student cohorts) might benefit from your reasoning.

Major Themes in Human Social and Personality Development

HUMAN DEVELOPMENT IS A HOLISTIC ENTERPRISE

Although this is a second-level or "specialty" course focusing on social and personality development, I hope it is quite obvious by now that human development is truly a holistic endeavor. For example, the fact that a 7-month-old infant becomes attached to her caregivers is not just a milestone in social development. This infant has developed *cognitive schemes* for the faces of familiar companions and can discriminate them from unfamiliar individuals. She has also developed the *motor capabilities* that permit her to crawl to her attachment objects to maintain the proximity she desires. She protests separations from loved ones, in part because of the growth of *object permanence* which makes her aware that departing companions continue to exist when they pass from view (and therefore can be summoned). And the emergence of attachment bonds affect development in many other ways—for example, by providing the *security* and social skills that allow toddlers to (1) confidently explore the world around them, thereby developing their problem-solving capabilities and promoting a sense of self-efficacy as well as (2) encouraging them to strike up social relationships with new associates, which can lead to new attachments that take the form of friendships. In sum, we are at once physical, cognitive, social, and emotional beings, and all these developmental threads are interwoven in the whole developing self.

WE ARE ACTIVE CONTRIBUTORS TO OUR OWN DEVELOPMENT

Early developmental theorists tended to view human beings as passively shaped by influences beyond their control. Sigmund Freud saw the child as driven by biological forces but *molded* by early experiences in the family. John B. Watson and other early learning theorists portrayed young human beings as *tabulae rasae* who develop in positive or negative directions, based primarily on how their parents choose to raise them. Jean Piaget did much to alter this view of child development by emphasizing how children *actively* explore their environments and *actively* construct new understandings of the objects, events, and people they encounter. His viewpoint was echoed (in a different way) by Albert Bandura, who was among the first to claim that children, by virtue of their own behavior, *actively* influence how they are treated by their parents, and by behavioral geneticists, who claim that we *actively* select environmental niches that are "comfortable" for us because they are compatible with our own genetic predispositions. Certainly, we are affected by many people with whom we might not ordinarily choose to interact (for example, day-care providers, teachers, unfriendly classmates, etc.). But just as certainly we create our own environments, influence those around us, and by so doing, contribute to our own development. It is this ongoing transaction between an active person and a changing environment, each influencing the other in a reciprocal way, that steers development.

THERE IS BOTH CONTINUITY AND DISCONTINUITY IN DEVELOPMENT

Developmentalists have long grappled with the issue of continuity and discontinuity in human development. Is development stagelike, or does it occur in small, orderly steps? Do early traits carry over into later life, or do they not?

PHOTO 14.1 Humans actively contribute to their own development by selecting environmental niches that suit their genetic predispositions and by influencing the character of the social environments that they experience.

Although some research supports the claims of theorists such as Piaget and Kohlberg, who contend that we progress through qualitatively distinct stages of cognitive development, moral development, and gender identity, we now know that advances in these domains occur gradually, so that transitions from one "stage" to another do not unfold abruptly. Moreover, the rate at which children progress through a series of developmental milestones often depends heavily on their environment. (Recall from Chapter 8, for example, that children who have often seen people of both sexes naked may achieve a mature sense of gender constancy two to three years before those who lack this experience.) Today, many developmentalists are quite comfortable assuming that development, within particular domains, may be sequential (or even stagelike), with earlier milestones serving as prerequisites for those that follow. Yet they recognize that the "transitions" we see (and take as stage markers) reflect the culmination of a large number of smaller, incremental changes that prepare a child or adolescent to make these transitions. Viewed in this way, human development seems to be both continuous and discontinuous.

Of course, another important variation on the continuity–discontinuity debate is the issue of whether early developments carry over and have implications for the kinds of persons we become later in life. Here again, the literature points to developmental continuities and discontinuities. In Chapter 4, for example, we learned that the temperamental attribute of *behavioral inhibition* is moderately stable over the course of childhood, such that inhibited youngsters often remained inhibited over a period of 8 to 10 years, whereas their uninhibited counterparts often remained relatively uninhibited. And yet, we also learned that this developmental continuity was most apparent for the 20% to 25% of children who were most highly inhibited (or highly uninhibited) to begin with, and that the remaining 75% to 80% often displayed sizable fluctuations in their behavioral inhibition over time—a developmental *discontinuity.* So if we look at population trends, development often seems continuous, with earlier traits, or earlier developments, predicting later life outcomes. Yet at the *individual* level, development is often discontinuous, and trying to predict the characterological attributes that a particular adult will display from a knowledge of his or her childhood traits remains a risky business.

THERE IS MUCH PLASTICITY IN HUMAN DEVELOPMENT

One reason that earlier traits or earlier developments often do *not* forecast later life outcomes is that human beings are resilient organisms who display much *plasticity*— a remarkable capacity to change in response to experience. Thus, infants who have failed to thrive and who show stunted social and intellectual development can "catch up" if provided with adequate diets *and* the affection and guidance of a sensitive caregiver. A hostile grade-school child who has alienated peers and is foundering academically can often be helped to get back on track at school and to achieve a more favorable sociometric status with the assistance of the academic remediation and social-skills training programs that we discussed in Chapter 13. Evidence of such plasticity and change in later life is especially heartening to all of us who would hope to foster healthy development. Contrary to what Freud believed, early experiences in themselves rarely make or break us. Instead, there are opportunities throughout life to undo the damage done by early traumas, to teach new skills, and to redirect young lives along more fruitful pathways. True, adverse early experiences that continue or are followed by other adverse experiences are likely to produce maladaptive developmental outcomes. But if potentially damaging early experiences are offset by favorable later experiences, we can expect plastic and resilient young humans to display a strong self-righting tendency and *adaptive* developmental outcomes.

THE NATURE-NURTURE DISTINCTION IS A FALSE DICHOTOMY

In a very important sense, the nature/nurture issue has been resolved. It is now clear that multiple causal forces, representing *both* nature and nurture, and ranging from changes in cell chemistry to changes in the global economy or the values of one's culture, conspire to direct human development.

Indeed, we learned in Chapter 3 that the genes each of us inherits play a most important role in influencing the environments each of us experiences. That is, we each display genetically influenced attributes that may *evoke* particular kinds of responses from other people (environmental influences) that will affect our development. Furthermore, we tend to actively seek out experiences, or environmental niches, that are most compatible with our genetically influenced characteristics—niches that clearly influence our development. At the same time, our environments can influence the course of biological development. In Chapter 8, for example, we noted that the different experiences young boys and girls may have as part of early gender-role socialization can affect the "wiring" of the immature brain: Boys who receive ample visual/spatial experiences, for example, may develop more synaptic connections than girls do in areas of the brain that process spatial information, whereas girls, who tend to receive more varied verbal experiences than boys, may develop more extensive synaptic connections in the areas of the brain that process verbal information. So how much of the sex differences we've observed in visual/spatial skills or in verbal skills is attributable to nature and how much to nurture? We now know that this question is nearly impossible to answer, for the forces of nature and nurture on these (and virtually all other aspects of social and personality development) are complexly intertwined and difficult to disentangle. Diane Halpern's (1997) compelling conclusion certainly bears repeating here: When it comes to explaining many aspects of human development, "biology and environment are as inseparable as conjoined twins who share a common heart" (p. 1097).

Having drawn this conclusion, I would certainly hope that no one who has taken this course would ever attribute the behavior of an oppositional or defiant young son (or pupil) to "bad seed." Yes, genes may influence our reactions to environmental stimulation and, ultimately, our social conduct—but they hardly *determine* that conduct. Social behavior often reflects an intricate interplay that unfolds as other people react to a child's genetically influenced attributes in ways that promote either adaptive or maladaptive responses. Stated another way, nature needs nurture to be expressed behaviorally, and nurture always acts on nature. There would be no development at all without the ongoing contribution of *both*.

BOTH NORMATIVE AND IDIOSYNCRATIC DEVELOPMENTS ARE IMPORTANT

In any human development textbook, there is a tendency to emphasize normative developments that are shared by nearly all individuals—that is, to highlight developmental regularities and commonalities. And we each do share a great deal with our fellow developing humans. But let's not forget that each of us is truly one of a kind who will also display a unique (or idiosyncratic) pattern of development. In fact, the developmental diversities we display are so impressive that it often seems impossible to characterize them accurately.

Individuality is apparent starting at birth if we look closely at each infant's temperament, daily rhythms, and rate of development. Yet young infants are not nearly as diverse as they will become, for early development is strongly channeled by a species-wide maturational blueprint that unfolds in remarkably predictable ways (McCall, 1981). For example, the vast majority of infants worldwide proceed through a predictable sequence of motor skills over the first 10 months, take their first steps and utter their first meaningful word at about age 1 year, and begin to respond more reciprocally to peer playmates and to combine words into simple sentences at about age 18 months. Yet late in toddlerhood, our unique genetic endowments, in concert with our individualized rearing environments, begin to express themselves more fully. The result? We can tell a good deal about an individual 2-year-old just by knowing his age, whereas we know much less about a person simply by knowing that he or she is an 8-year-old. And because diversity increases with age, adolescents are much less alike than 8-year-olds or 11-year-olds are.

In sum, no child should ever be expected to emerge as a carbon copy of his parents, an especially competent older sibling, or even a genetically identical twin. Development *always* proceeds in normative *and* idiosyncratic directions, and such diversity is even adaptive from an evolutionary point of view because species with highly diverse characteristics are more likely to survive catastrophic changes in their environments. To truly explain human development, then, we must recognize and appreciate developmental diversities and must seek to understand the forces that underlie both the normative and the idiosyncratic changes that children and adolescents display. Only by doing so will we ever accomplish the aim of that perceptive young sophomore we met in Chapter 1, who claimed that her reason for taking this course was to learn how we all turn out so similar and, at the same time, so different from each other.

WE DEVELOP IN A CULTURAL AND HISTORICAL CONTEXT

We have also seen throughout the text that children and adolescents are embedded in a sociocultural context that affects their development. Social and personality development simply takes different forms in different cultures, social classes, and racial and ethnic groups. Furthermore, development in the 12th or 18th century was different from development in the 20th century; and each person's development is influenced by social changes and historical events occurring *during his or her lifetime*. The implication? Our current knowledge of human development is largely culture bound and time bound, for it is most often based on studies of children and adolescents in Western societies in the latter half of the 20th century—and often white, middle-class participants at that!

The more developmentalists study cultural, subcultural, and historical variations in development, the more they appreciate the importance of *contextual influences* and the usefulness of such theories as Bronfenbrenner's (1993, 1995) *ecological systems model* and Vygotsky's (1978) *sociocultural theory* that emphasize these influences. We know, for example, that shyness is a social strength rather than a social liability, in cultures such as China that stress communal rather than individualistic goals and seek to inhibit self-aggrandizement. We now know that the somewhat coercive, "no-nonsense" parenting often seen in lower-SES African-American families may be more adaptive than other parenting styles if it helps to shield youngsters from negative peer influences that would undermine academic achievement or promote antisocial conduct. What's more, we should also recognize that changes in the family and in men's and women's roles, not to mention technological and social innovations yet to come, may conspire to make human development in the mid-21st century very different from what it is today. Clearly, then, we should disabuse ourselves of the rather dogmatic and ethnocentric notions that a particular set of values, style of child rearing, or pattern of developmental outcomes is "optimal" for everyone. What qualifies as adaptive patterns of development—and the forces that foster or inhibit them—can vary dramatically across cultures and subcultures and is *always* time bound.

PHOTO 14.2 This Guatemalan girl will spend hundreds of hours learning to weave because the livelihood of her people depends on this craft. However, it would be far less sensible for children from industrialized societies to set aside their schoolwork to acquire weaving skills that are unnecessary for their economic self-maintenance. Clearly, what qualifies as adaptive development may vary dramatically from culture to culture.

DEVELOPMENT IS BEST VIEWED FROM MULTIPLE PERSPECTIVES

As we have seen at many points throughout the text, many disciplines have something to contribute to a comprehensive understanding of social and personality development. Behavioral geneticists and endocrinologists, for example, have helped us to understand how genes and hormones might influence our behavior and other people's reactions to it, thereby creating a social "environment" in which the personality develops. Psychologists and family theorists have contributed immensely to our understanding of the relationships and family social systems that influence and are influenced by developing children and adolescents. Meanwhile, anthropologists, sociologists, historians, and even economists have taught us much about the impacts of changing economic and varying sociocultural contexts in which individuals develop.

Not surprisingly, then, the task of understanding something as complex as human social and personality development requires that we take an eclectic approach and recognize that many theories have something to offer and that none has a monopoly on the truth. To illustrate, I once asked Carol Lynn Martin (co-author of the gender schema theory we reviewed in Chapter 8) if she thought her new ideas about preschoolers' schematic processing of gender-related information pretty much explained how they come to prefer masculine and feminine gender roles. She replied "Heavens no!" and proceeded to tell me that while she thought her ideas were somewhat innovative and worth pursuing, she had benefited immensely from the earlier theories of Bandura, Kohlberg, and people in the social information-processing camp, and that our knowledge of gender typing would actually be quite impoverished if all we knew was what she had demonstrated in her own research. My own impression was that Dr. Martin was being somewhat self-effacing and modest in assessing her contributions; yet she was quite correct that biosocial, psychobiosocial, social-learning, and cognitive-developmental theorists have all contributed, and contributed substantially, along with gender schema theorists, to what we now know about the development of gender roles (review Table 8-5, on page 258). And so it goes for every domain of development we have studied: Our knowledge is *always* enriched by integrating the contributions of researchers from many disciplines and diverse theoretical viewpoints.

PATTERNS OF PARENTING (AND ADULT GUIDANCE) CLEARLY MATTER

In Box 3.3, we touched on an interesting debate concerning the importance of parenting and child-rearing practices in shaping children's and adolescents' developmental outcomes. Behavioral geneticist Sandra Scarr (1992) argued that patterns of parenting are not all that important. Presumably, humans have evolved in ways that make them responsive and adaptable to a wide range of environments. Thus, given an "average expectable" home environment—that is, one that falls within the broad range of those typical of the human species—children will display normal, adaptive developmental outcomes, regardless of the child-rearing practices their parents (or other guardians) employ. By contrast, environmentalists such as Diana Baumrind (1993), Martin Hoffman (1988), and Kenneth Dodge (see Coie & Dodge, 1998) claim that patterns of parenting and adult guidance do matter and that different child-rearing styles and practices can produce *very large differences* in children's and adolescents' developmental outcomes. So which viewpoint should we accept?

Quite frankly, my biases are showing here, but the empirical record clearly suggests to me that parenting *does* matter and exerts a most important influence on developing children and adolescents. In fact, the research we have reviewed throughout the text points to two broad conclusions that are strongly supported by existing research.

Children Need Love, Guidance . . . and Limits At several points, we have noted that developing individuals fare much better if they are warmly received by their caregivers, and that a cool, aloof (or rejecting) attitude on caregivers' part often forecasts poor developmental outcomes. Warmth is clearly a crucial component of effective parenting (and effective alternative caregiving and effective instruction during the preschool and early grade-school years). Yet warmth and acceptance alone are not sufficient to guarantee developmental successes. We need only recall the far less than optimal outcomes displayed by children of *permissive* parents, who generally accept their children but provide them with few standards to govern and evaluate their behavior, and do not carefully monitor their conduct.

The pattern of parenting that is most closely associated with adaptive developmental outcomes is one characterized by warm acceptance, provision of guidance or standards for children to live up to, and a monitoring of the child's or the adolescent's behavior, to ensure that he or she is complying with parental guidelines or otherwise meeting those expectations. In other words, developing persons seem to fare best when they receive love, guidance . . . and limits from involved parents who are highly concerned with helping to underwrite their developmental successes. For many ethnic groups in Western democracies, the *authoritative* pattern of child rearing, with its emphasis on granting youngsters some autonomy in deciding how to satisfy parental expectations, is a particularly effective method of combining love and guidance with reasonable limitations to promote adaptive outcomes. However, this winning combination of love, guidance, and limits can be embodied in other ways that are equally (or more) effective for families within other cultures, subcultures, or ecological niches. For example, the "no-nonsense" parenting often observed in lower-SES African-American families—a style in-between Baumrind's authoritative and authoritarian patterns of parenting—is highly effective in shielding youngsters who live in dangerous neighborhoods from deviant peer influences and other forms of harm. And even though no-nonsense parenting is somewhat power-assertive and coercive by white middle-class standards, it does not predict aggression and antisocial conduct in the same way for African-American youth as it does for whites—possibly because it is interpreted as a sign of concern and caring (rather than aloofness and hostility) by African-American children (Deater-Deckard & Dodge, 1997). Similarly, the highly restrictive pattern of parenting displayed by Chinese and immigrant Chinese-American parents would be considered authoritarian by Western standards. And yet it forecasts highly favorable developmental outcomes because of Chinese cultural values (accepted by both parents and their offspring) stressing that (1) caring, concerned parents have an obligation to be highly controlling and restrictive so as to train their children to become well-socialized members of a collectivist order, and (2) children are obligated to honor their concerned parents by accepting and living up to the guidelines and limitations their parents set for them. So a pattern of child rearing that is too rigid to work very well among families highly acculturated into Western, individualistic democracies is most effective in other contexts, largely because it skillfully interfaces the love, guidance, and limits that developing persons need with other important values that prevail within these contexts.

The message? Yes, love and the provision of guidance . . . and limits are all crucial components of effective parenting. However, there are many ways to incorporate these elements into the caregiving that parents (and other adults) provide, and the pattern that works best largely depends on one's culture and/or the ecological niche occupied by one's family. There is clearly much truth to Louis Laosa's (1981) observation that "indigenous patterns of child care throughout the world represent largely successful adaptations to conditions of life that have long differed from one people to another. [Adults] are good [parents] by the only *relevant* standards, those of their own culture" (p. 159, italics added).

Parents Must Themselves Be Adaptable   Let's also note that raising a child successfully is hard work and that there are no magic formulas that provide absolute guarantees of fostering developmental successes. Why not? Perhaps the main reason is because children and adolescents are each unique beings, and practices that work well for one individual may fail miserably with another, even if the two youngsters are siblings raised in the same home by the same adult caregivers!

One clear example of this point is Grazyna Kochanska's (1997a) research on temperament and moral internalization that we discussed in Box 10.3. Recall that temperamentally *fearful* youngsters showed greater evidence of acquiring a strong internalized conscience if their parents used gentle, psychological forms of inductive discipline and deemphasized power assertion. However, this same kind of discipline was less effective with highly impulsive, temperamentally *fearless* youngsters, who responded much better to parents who fostered compliance by establishing a warm, mutually cooperative relationship with the child, thus making the fearless youngster eager to cooperate with and please his parents and concerned about undermining a highly satisfying parent–child alliance.

What this study (and many, many others we have reviewed) clearly illustrates is this: Favorable outcomes are more likely to result when parents successfully adapt to *their* child, thereby creating a "goodness of fit" between their parenting practices and their child's unique characteristics. Of course, establishing such "goodness of fit" may sometimes require the patience of a saint, particularly if the child is often cranky, oppositional, or otherwise difficult. And yet, we have seen that parents who can set their preconceived opinions aside and sensitively adapt their caregiving to their own child's difficult demeanor tend to have youngsters who become securely attached to them (van den Boom, 1995) and may no longer be perceived as difficult later in childhood (Chess & Thomas, 1984). By contrast, difficult children are likely to remain that way if their parents fail to adapt to their oppositional demeanor, choosing instead to be impatient, demanding, and forceful with them.

In sum, effective parents are those who can sensitively adjust to their own child, creating a good fit between their parenting practices and the child's unique characteristics. As we noted in Chapter 4, one of the reasons that caregiver *sensitivity* predicts attachment security (and many other adaptive outcomes) is that the very notion of *sensitive* care implies an ability to tailor one's routines to whatever characteristics a child (or an adolescent) might display.

MANY SOCIAL FORCES CONSPIRE TO SHAPE DEVELOPMENT

Perhaps the major strength of recent contextualist models of social and personality development is their calling our attention to the many extrafamilial influences on developing children and adolescents. We now know that schools are a crucial agent of socialization and that children can be influenced by the goodness of fit between their own background or developmental needs and the characteristics of the schools they attend. We also have learned that such cultural and technological forces as the content of television programming and exposure to personal computers have the capacity to influence developing persons in many ways—some good, and some not so good. And we have learned over the past 30 years that the society of one's peers is another important developmental context, not only for acquiring social skills that are valued by one's equals but also for the growth of such attributes as prosocial concern, cooperation and teamwork, healthy attitudes about competition, a sense of identity and belongingness apart from one's family, and self-esteem (to name a few). So although the family may be the primary agent of socialization, each of us is exposed, either directly or indirectly, to a variety of extrafamilial contexts and experiences that can play a major part in shaping our personalities and social behaviors.

PHOTO 14.3 Although families may be the primary agent of socialization, each of us is exposed to a variety of extrafamilial contexts that play meaningful roles in shaping our personalities and social conduct.

WE'VE COME A LONG WAY, BABY . . . BUT HAVE SO FAR TO GO

In 1979, I dedicated the first edition of this text "to those researchers who have made the study of social and personality development an exciting endeavor" and expressed my belief that this discipline had "come of age." Among the most exciting new thrusts then were (1) emergence of the Bowlby-Ainsworth ethological theory of attachment and of research seeking to identify the long-term implications (if any) of secure and insecure attachments, and (2) the movement afoot among many other social developmentalists to pinpoint the significance (if any) of peers as socializing agents. This was also the time at which Bronfenbrenner's (1979) early version of *ecological systems theory* appeared. And as social-developmentalists began to increasingly incorporate contextual assumptions into their thinking, they started asking new questions that might not have occurred to them in the past. For example, early returns suggesting that good peer relations promoted adaptive developmental outcomes and that peer rejection spelled trouble prompted many investigators to go beyond peer acceptance to see whether establishing special peer alliances, or *friendships,* had any unique impacts on one's social and personality development (such as protecting a child with a negative sociometric status against the maladaptive outcomes associated with peer rejection). At the same time, Bronfenbrenner's emphasis on *mesosystem* influences—the connections among microsystems such as the family and peer groups—prompted researchers to explore such links and to learn that the pathways to positive peer relations and high-quality intimate friendships often begin at home. And the current emphasis on cultural influences on development, which has come to the forefront of our discipline in the past 10 years, largely stemmed from Bronfenbrenner's writings about the developmental significance of *macrosystems,* as well as from empirical observations that the forces that produce one set of outcomes for white, middle-class youngsters in Western societies didn't always have the same effects elsewhere—and from researchers' desire to determine why this is so.

Clearly, we have come a long way since 1979. In fact, a sizable majority of the research citations in this fourth edition of the text date from 1985 to the present and represent knowledge that simply was not available at the time the first edition of this book was written. As we enter the 21st century, there can be little doubt that the field of social and personality development is an extremely dynamic one, with our knowledge increasing almost exponentially every few years or so. Yet as a developing entity, the field is far from mature.

Why do I say this, given that we have learned so much about social and personality development in the past 10 to 15 years? Simply because it often seems to social developmentalists that the more they learn about a topic, the more they recognize how much more there is to learn. Were you to read articles from our leading journals (and I hope you will), you would find that all of them provide some sort of "answer" for the questions they have raised. And yet, the discussion sections of these same articles usually raise many more interesting questions that their data do *not* address, along with a call for additional research to explore these issues.

For developmentalists, then, there are always more questions than answers. I find this to be both a humbling and inspiring thought. I hope that you too will feel inspired as we complete our introduction to social and personality development, for much as you may have learned, there is much, much more to be discovered. And I sincerely hope that you will use what you have learned (and may learn should you take additional courses) to observe more closely your own development and that of those around you, and will seek to steer your own and others' lives in healthier directions.

ability tracking: the educational practice of grouping students according to ability and then educating them in classes with students of comparable educational or intellectual standing.

acceptance/responsiveness: a dimension of parenting that describes the amount of responsiveness and affection that a parent displays toward a child.

accommodation: Piaget's term for the process by which children modify their existing schemes in order to incorporate or adapt to new experiences.

achievement expectancies: cognitive expectations of succeeding or failing at a particular achievement-related activity.

achievement motivation: a willingness to strive to succeed at challenging tasks and to meet high standards of accomplishment.

achievement training: encouraging children to do things well—that is, to meet or exceed high standards as they strive to accomplish various objectives.

achievement value: perceived value of attaining a particular goal should one strive to achieve it.

active genotype/environment correlations: the notion that our genotypes affect the types of environments that we prefer and seek out.

activity/passivity issue: debate among developmental theorists about whether children are active contributors to their own development or passive recipients of environmental influence.

adaptation: inborn tendency to adjust to the demands of the environment.

adoption design: study in which adoptees are compared with their biological relatives and their adoptive relatives to estimate the heritability of an attribute.

"aggressive cues" hypothesis: Berkowitz's notion that the presence of stimuli previously associated with aggression can evoke aggressive responses from an angry individual.

altruism: a concern for the welfare of others that is expressed through such prosocial acts as sharing, cooperating, and helping.

altruistic exhortations: verbal encouragements to help, comfort, share, or cooperate with others.

androgenized females: females who develop malelike external genitalia because of exposure to male sex hormones during the prenatal period.

androgyny: a gender-role orientation in which the individual has incorporated a large number of both masculine and feminine attributes into his or her personality.

aptitude-treatment interaction (ATI): phenomenon whereby characteristics of the student and of the school environment interact to affect student outcomes, such that any given educational practice may be effective with some students but not with others.

asocial phase (of attachment): approximately the first six weeks of life, in which infants respond in an equally favorable way to interesting social and nonsocial stimuli.

assimilation: Piaget's term for the process by which children interpret new experiences by incorporating them into their existing schemes.

associative play: form of social discourse in which children pursue their own interests but will swap toys or comment on each other's activities.

attachment: a close emotional relationship between two persons, characterized by mutual affection and a desire to maintain proximity.

Attachment Q-set: alternative method of assessing attachment security that is based on observations of the child's attachment-related behaviors at home; can be used with infants, toddlers, and preschool children.

attribution retraining: therapeutic intervention in which helpless children are persuaded to attribute failures to their lack of effort rather than a lack of ability.

authoritarian instruction: a restrictive style of instruction in which the teacher makes absolute demands and uses threats or force (if necessary) to ensure that students comply.

authoritarian parenting: a restrictive pattern of parenting in which adults set many rules for their children, expect strict obedience, and rely on power rather than reason to elicit compliance.

authoritative instruction: a controlling style of instruction in which the teacher makes many demands but also allows some autonomy and individual expression as long as students are staying within the guidelines that the teacher has set.

authoritative parenting: flexible, democratic style of parenting in which warm, accepting parents provide guidance and control while allowing the child some say in deciding how best to meet challenges and obligations.

autonomous altruism: prosocial acts motivated by a concern for others with no expectations of being repaid for such favors.

autonomous morality: Piaget's second stage of moral development, in which children realize that rules are arbitrary agreements that can be challenged and changed with the consent of the people they govern.

autonomy: the capacity to make decisions independently, to serve as one's own source of emotional strength, and to otherwise manage one's life tasks without depending on others for assistance; an important developmental task of adolescence.

autonomy versus shame and doubt: the second of Erikson's psychosocial stages, in which toddlers either assert their wills and attend to their own basic needs or become passive, dependent, and lacking in self-confidence.

average-status children: children who receive a moderate number of nominations as a liked and/or a disliked individual from members of their peer group.

avoidant attachment: an insecure infant/caregiver bond, characterized by little separation protest and a tendency of the child to avoid or ignore the caregiver.

baby biography: a detailed record of an infant's growth and development over a period of time.

basic gender identity: the stage of gender identity in which the child first labels the self as a boy or a girl.

behavioral comparisons phase: the tendency to form impressions of others by comparing and contrasting their overt behaviors.

behavioral definition of altruism: behavior that benefits another person, regardless of the actor's motives.

behavioral definition of aggression: any action that delivers noxious stimuli to another organism.

behavioral genetics: the scientific study of how genotype interacts with environment to determine behavioral attributes such as intelligence, personality, and mental health.

behavioral inhibition: a temperamental attribute reflecting one's tendency to withdraw from unfamiliar people or situations.

behavioral schemes: organized patterns of behavior that are used to represent and respond to objects and experiences.

behaviorism: a school of thinking in psychology that holds that conclusions about human development should be based on controlled observations of overt behavior rather than speculation about unconscious motives or other unobservable phenomena; the philosophical underpinning for social-learning theories.

belief-desire theory: theory of mind that develops between ages 3 and 4; the child now realizes that both beliefs and desires may determine behavior and that people will often act on their beliefs, even if they are inaccurate.

blended (or reconstituted) families: new families resulting from cohabitation or remarriage that include a parent, one or more children, and step-relations.

caregiving hypothesis: Ainsworth's notion that the type of attachment an infant develops with a particular caregiver depends primarily on the kind of caregiving he has received from that person.

case study: a research method in which the investigator gathers extensive information about the life of an individual and then tests developmental hypotheses by analyzing the events of the person's life history.

castration anxiety: in Freud's theory, a young boy's fear that his father will castrate him as punishment for his rivalrous conduct.

categorical self: a person's classification of the self along socially significant dimensions such as age and sex.

catharsis hypothesis: the notion that aggressive urges are reduced when people witness or commit real or symbolic acts of aggression.

cathartic technique: a strategy for reducing aggression by encouraging children to vent their anger or frustrations on inanimate objects.

causal attributions: conclusions drawn about the underlying causes of our own or another person's behavior.

centered thinking (centration): the tendency to focus on only one aspect of a problem when two or more aspects are relevant.

child abuse: term used to describe any extreme maltreatment of children, involving physical battering, sexual molestation, psychological insults such as persistent ridicule, rejection, and terrorization, and physical or emotional neglect.

chronosystem: in ecological systems theory, changes in the individual or the environment that occur over time and influence the direction development takes.

clinical method: a type of interview in which a participant's response to each successive question (or problem) determines what the investigator will ask next.

clique: a small group of friends that interacts frequently.

coaching: method of social-skills training in which an adult displays and explains various socially skilled behaviors, allows the child to practice them, and provides feedback aimed at improving the child's performances.

coercive home environment: a home in which family members often annoy one another and use aggressive or otherwise antisocial tactics as a method of coping with these aversive experiences.

cognitive development: age-related changes that occur in mental activities such as attending, perceiving, learning, thinking, and remembering.

cognitive operation: an internal mental activity that one performs on objects of thought.

cohort effect: age-related difference among cohorts that is attributable to cultural/historical differences in cohorts' growing-up experiences rather than to true developmental change.

collectivist (or communal) society: society that values cooperative interdependence, social harmony, and adherence to group norms. These societies generally hold that the group's well-being is more important than that of the individual.

committed compliance: compliance based on an eagerness or readiness to cooperate with a responsive parent who has been willing to cooperate with the child.

compensation: the ability to consider more than one aspect of a problem at a time (also called decentration).

compensatory interventions: special educational programs designed to further the cognitive growth and scholastic achievements of disadvantaged children.

compliance: the act of obeying the requests or commands of others.

computer-assisted instruction (CAI): use of computers to teach new concepts and allow students to practice academic skills.

concordance rate: the percentage of cases in which a particular attribute is present for one member of a twin pair if it is present for the other.

concrete-operational stage: Piaget's third stage of cognitive development, lasting from about age 7 to age 11, when children are acquiring cognitive operations and thinking more logically about tangible objects and experiences.

"conditioned anxiety" hypothesis: notion that infants fear separations from caregivers (and strangers who might cause such separations) because prior discomforts have been especially intense when caregivers were not present to relieve them.

conflict: circumstances in which two or more persons have incompatible needs, desires, or goals.

confounding variable: some factor other than the independent variable which, if not controlled by the experimenter, could explain any differences across treatment conditions in participants' performance on the dependent variable.

congenital adrenal hyperplasia (CAH): a genetic anomaly that causes one's adrenal glands to produce unusually high levels of androgen from the prenatal period onward; often has masculinizing effects on female fetuses.

conservation: the recognition that the properties of an object or substance do not change when its appearance is altered in some superficial way.

consistency schema: attributional heuristic implying that actions that a person consistently performs are likely to be internally caused (reflecting a dispositional characteristic).

constructivist: one who gains knowledge by acting or otherwise operating on objects or events to discover their properties.

contextual model: view of children as active entities whose developmental paths represent a continuous, dynamic interplay between internal forces (nature) and external influences (nurture).

continuity/discontinuity issue: debate among theorists about whether developmental changes are best characterized as gradual and quantitative or abrupt and qualitative.

controversial children: children who receive many nominations as a liked and many as a disliked individual.

conventional morality: Kohlberg's term for the third and fourth stages of moral reasoning, in which moral judgments are based on a desire to gain approval (Stage 3) or to uphold laws that maintain social order (Stage 4).

cooperative learning methods: an educational practice whereby children of different races or ability levels are assigned to teams; each team member works on problems geared to his or her ability level, and all members are reinforced for "pulling together" and performing well as a team.

cooperative play: true social play in which children cooperate or assume reciprocal roles while pursing shared goals.

coparenting: circumstance in which parents mutually support each other and function as a cooperative parenting team.

correlational design: a type of research design that indicates the strength of associations among variables; though correlated variables are systematically related, these relationships are not necessarily causal.

correlation coefficient: a numerical index, ranging from −1.00 to + 1.00, of the strength and direction of the relationship between two variables.

cross-cultural comparison: a study that compares the behavior and/or development of people from different cultural or subcultural backgrounds.

cross-generational problem: the fact that long-term changes in the environment may limit conclusions of a longitudinal project to that generation of children who were growing up while the study was in progress.

cross-pressures: conflicts stemming from differences in the values and practices advocated by parents and those favored by peers.

cross-sectional design: a research design in which subjects from different age groups are studied at the same point in time.

crowd: a large, reputationally based peer group made up of individuals and cliques that share similar norms, interests, and values.

deferred imitation: reproduction of a modeled activity that has been witnessed at some point in the past.

defiance: active resistance to others' requests or demands; noncompliant acts that are accompanied by anger and an intensification of ongoing behavior.

delay of gratification: a form of self-control that involves the capacity to inhibit impulses to seek small rewards available immediately in the interest of obtaining larger, delayed incentives.

demandingness/control: a dimension of parenting that describes how restrictive and demanding parents are.

dependent variable: the aspect of behavior that is measured in an experiment and assumed to be under the control of the independent variable.

deprivation dwarfism: a childhood growth disorder triggered by emotional deprivation and characterized by decreased production of growth hormone (GH), slow growth, and small stature.

desensitization hypothesis: the notion that people who watch a lot of media violence will become less aroused by aggression and more tolerant of violent and aggressive acts.

desire theory: an early theory of mind in which a person's actions are thought to be a reflection of her desires rather than other mental states such as beliefs.

developmental stage: a distinct phase within a larger sequence of development; a period characterized by a particular set of abilities, motives, behaviors, or emotions that occur together and form a coherent pattern.

difficult temperament: temperamental profile in which the child is irregular in daily routines and adapts slowly to new experiences, often responding negatively and intensely.

direct effect: instances in which any pair of family members affects and is affected by the other's behavior.

direct tuition: teaching young children how to behave by reinforcing "appropriate" behaviors and by punishing or otherwise discouraging inappropriate conduct.

disequilibriums: imbalances or contradictions between one's thought processes and environmental events. By contrast, *equilibrium* refers to a balanced, harmonious relationship between one's cognitive structures and the environment.

disorganized/disoriented attachment: an insecure infant/caregiver bond, characterized by the infant's dazed appearance on reunion or a tendency to first seek and then abruptly avoid the caregiver.

doctrine of specificity: a viewpoint shared by many social-learning theorists which holds that moral affect, moral reasoning, and moral behavior may depend on the situation one faces as much or more than on an internalized set of moral principles.

double standard: the view that sexual behavior that is appropriate for members of one sex is less appropriate for the other.

"early experience hypothesis": the notion that the social and emotional events of infancy are very influential in determining the course of one's future development.

easy temperament: temperamental profile in which the child quickly establishes regular routines, is generally good natured, and adapts easily to novelty.

eclectics: those who borrow from many theories in their attempts to predict and explain human development.

ecological systems theory: Bronfenbrenner's model emphasizing that the developing person is embedded in a series of environmental systems that interact with one another and with the person to influence development.

ecological validity: state of affairs in which the findings of one's research are an accurate representation of processes that occur in the natural environment.

economic goal: LeVine's second priority of parenting—to promote skills that children will need for economic self-sufficiency.

effective schools: schools that are generally successful at achieving curricular and noncurricular objectives, regardless of the racial, ethnic, or socioeconomic background of the student population.

ego: psychoanalytic term for the rational component of the personality.

egocentrism: the tendency to view the world from one's own perspective while failing to recognize that others may have different points of view.

electra complex: female version of Oedipus complex, in which a 3- to 6-year-old girl was believed to envy her father for possessing a penis and to seek him as a sex object in the hope of sharing the organ that she lacks.

emotional bonding: term used to describe the strong affectional ties that parents may feel toward a neonate; some theorists believe that the strongest bonding occurs shortly after birth, during a sensitive period.

emotional display rules: culturally defined rules specifying which emotions should or should not be expressed under which circumstances.

emotional self-regulation: strategies for managing emotions or adjusting emotional arousal to a comfortable level of intensity.

empathic concern: a measure of the extent to which an individual recognizes the needs of others and is concerned about their welfare.

empathy: the ability to experience the same emotions that someone else is experiencing.

engrossment: paternal analogue of maternal emotional bonding; term used to describe fathers' fascination with their neonates, including their desire to touch, hold, caress, and talk to the newborn baby.

entity view of ability: belief that one's ability is a highly stable trait that is not influenced much by effort or practice.

environmental determinism: the notion that children are passive creatures who are molded by their environments.

eros: Freud's name for instincts such as respiration, hunger, and sex that help the individual (and the species) to survive.

ethnography: method in which the researcher seeks to understand the unique values, traditions, and social processes of a culture or subculture by living with its members and making extensive observations and notes.

ethology: the study of the bioevolutionary bases of behavior and development.

evocative genotype/environment correlations: the notion that our heritable attributes affect others' behavior toward us and thus influence the social environment in which development takes place.

exosystem: social systems that children and adolescents do not directly experience but that may nonetheless influence their development; the third of Bronfenbrenner's environmental layers, or contexts.

experimental control: steps taken by an experimenter to ensure that all extraneous factors that could influence the dependent variable are roughly equivalent in each experimental condition; these precautions must be taken before an experimenter can be reasonably certain that observed changes in the dependent variable were caused by the manipulation of the independent variable.

experimental design: a research design in which the investigator introduces some change in the participant's environment and then measures the effect of that change on the participant's behavior.

expressive role: a social prescription, usually directed toward females, that one should be cooperative, kind, nurturant, and sensitive to the needs of others.

extended family: a group of blood relatives from more than one nuclear family (for example, grandparents, aunts, uncles, nieces, and nephews) who live together, forming a household.

extrafamilial influences: social agencies other than the family that influence a child's or an adolescent's cognitive, social, and emotional development.

extrinsic orientation: a desire to achieve in order to earn external incentives such as grades, prizes, or the approval of others.

false-belief task: method of assessing one's understanding that people can hold inaccurate beliefs which can influence their conduct, wrong as these beliefs may be.

false self behavior: acting in ways that do not reflect one's true self or the "true me."

falsifiability: a criterion for evaluating the scientific merit of theories; a theory is falsifiable when it is capable of generating predictions that could be disconfirmed.

family social system: the complex network of relationships, interactions, and patterns of influence that characterize a family with three or more members.

"felt responsibility" hypothesis: the theory that empathy may promote altruism by causing one to reflect on altruistic norms and, thus, to feel some obligation to help distressed others.

field experiment: an experiment that takes place in a naturalistic setting such as the home, the school, or a playground.

fixation: arrested development at a particular psychosexual stage; often occurs as a means of coping with existing conflicts and preventing movement to the next stage, where stress may be even greater.

foreclosure: identity status characterizing individuals who have prematurely committed themselves to occupations or ideologies without really thinking about these commitments.

formal-operational stage: Piaget's fourth and final stage of cognitive development, from ages 11 to 12 and beyond, when the individual begins to think more rationally and systematically about abstract concepts and hypothetical events.

friendship: a strong and often enduring relationship between two individuals, characterized by loyalty, intimacy, and mutual affection.

frustration/aggression hypothesis: early learning theory of aggression, holding that frustration triggers aggression and that all aggressive acts can be traced to frustrations.

gender consistency: the stage of gender identity in which the child recognizes that a person's gender is invariant despite changes in the person's activities or appearance (also known as gender constancy).

gender identity: one's awareness of one's gender and its implications.

gender intensification: a magnification of sex differences early in adolescence; associated with increased pressure to conform to traditional gender roles.

gender-role standard: a behavior, value, or motive that members of a society consider more typical or appropriate for members of one sex.

gender schemas: organized sets of beliefs and expectations about males and females that guide information processing.

gender segregation: children's tendency to associate with same-sex playmates and to think of the other sex as an outgroup.

gender stability: the stage of gender identity in which the child recognizes that gender is stable over time.

gender typing: the process by which a child becomes aware of his or her gender and acquires motives, values, and behaviors considered appropriate for members of that sex.

genotype: the genetic endowment that an individual inherits.

"goodness-of-fit" model: Thomas and Chess's notion that development is likely to be optimized when parents' child-rearing practices are sensitively adapted to the child's temperamental characteristics.

growth hormone (GH): a pituitary hormone that stimulates the growth and development of body cells.

habits: well-learned associations between stimuli and responses that represent the stable aspects of one's personality.

heritability: the amount of variability in a trait that is attributable to hereditary factors.

heritability coefficient: a numerical estimate, ranging from .00 to +1.00, of the amount of variation in an attribute that is due to hereditary factors.

heteronomous morality: Piaget's first stage of moral development, in which children view the rules of authority figures as sacred and unalterable.

heuristic value: a criterion for evaluating the scientific merit of theories. A heuristic theory is one that continues to stimulate new research and new discoveries.

high-risk neighborhood: a residential area in which the incidence of child abuse is much higher than in other neighborhoods with the same demographic characteristics.

holistic perspective: a unified view of the developmental process that emphasizes the interrelationships among the physical/biological, mental, social, and emotional aspects of human development.

HOME inventory: a measure of the amount and type of intellectual stimulation provided by a child's home environment.

hostile aggression: aggressive acts for which the perpetrator's major goal is to harm or injure a victim.

hostile attributional bias: tendency to view harm done under ambiguous circumstances as having stemmed from a hostile intent on the part of the harmdoer; characterizes reactive aggressors.

hypothesis: a theoretical prediction about some aspect of experience.

hypothetico-deductive reasoning: a style of problem solving in which all possible solutions to a problem are generated and then systematically evaluated to determine the correct answer(s).

id: psychoanalytic term for the inborn component of the personality that is driven by the instincts.

identification: Freud's term for the child's tendency to emulate another person, usually the same-sex parent.

identity: a mature self-definition; a sense of who one is, where one is going in life, and how one fits into society.

identity achievement: identity status characterizing individuals who have carefully considered identity issues and have made firm commitments to an occupation and ideologies.

identity crisis: Erikson's term for the uncertainty and discomfort that adolescents experience when they become confused about their present and future roles in life.

identity diffusion: identity status characterizing individuals who are not questioning who they are and have not yet committed themselves to an identity.

imaginary audience: allegedly a form of adolescent egocentrism that involves confusing one's own thoughts with those of a hypothesized audience and concluding that others share your preoccupations.

immanent justice: the notion that unacceptable conduct will invariably be punished and that justice is ever-present in the world.

imprinting: an innate or instinctual form of learning in which the young of certain species will follow and become attached to moving objects (usually their mothers).

incompatible-response technique: a nonpunitive method of behavior modification in which adults ignore undesirable conduct while reinforcing acts that are incompatible with these responses.

incremental view of ability: belief that one's ability can be improved through increased effort and practice.

independence training: encouraging children to become self-reliant by accomplishing goals without others' assistance.

independent variable: the aspect of the environment that an experimenter modifies or manipulates in order to measure its impact on behavior.

indirect, or third party, effect: instances in which the relationship between two individuals in a family is modified by the behavior or attitudes of a third family member.

individualistic society: society that values personalism and individual accomplishments, which often take precedence over group goals. These societies tend to emphasize ways in which individuals differ from each other.

induction: a nonpunitive form of discipline in which an adult explains why a child's behavior is wrong and should be changed by emphasizing its effects on others.

informal curriculum: noncurricular objectives of schooling such as teaching children to cooperate, to respect authority, to obey rules, and to become good citizens.

"in-group/out-group" schema: one's general knowledge of the mannerisms, roles, activities, and behaviors that characterize males and females.

inhibitory control: an ability to display acceptable conduct by resisting the temptation to commit a forbidden act.

innate purity: the idea that infants are born with an intuitive sense of right and wrong that is often misdirected by the demands and restrictions of society.

inner experimentation: the ability to solve simple problems on a mental, or symbolic, level without having to rely on trial-and-error experimentation.

inner speech: internalized private speech; covert verbal thought.

instinct: an inborn biological force that motivates a particular response or class of responses.

instrumental aggression: aggressive acts for which the perpetrator's major goal is to gain access to objects, space, or privileges.

instrumental role: a social prescription, usually directed toward males, that one should be dominant, independent, assertive, competitive, and goal-oriented.

intentional definition of aggression: any action intended to harm or injure another living being who is motivated to avoid such treatment.

internalization: the process of adopting the attributes or standards of other people—taking these standards as one's own.

internal working models: cognitive representations of self, others, and relationships that infants construct from their interactions with caregivers.

intimacy versus isolation: the sixth of Erikson's psychosocial conflicts, in which young adults must commit themselves to a shared identity with another person (that is, intimacy) or else remain aloof and unconnected to others.

intrinsic orientation: a desire to achieve in order to satisfy one's personal needs for competence or mastery.

introversion/extroversion: the opposite poles of a personality dimension: Introverts are shy, anxious around others, and tend to withdraw from social situations; extroverts are highly sociable and enjoy being with others.

intuitive thought: Piaget's term for reasoning that is dominated by appearances (or perceptual characteristics of objects and events) rather than by rational thought processes.

invariant developmental sequence: a series of developments that occur in one particular order because each development in the sequence is a prerequisite for the next.

kinship: the extent to which two individuals have genes in common.

laissez-faire instruction: a permissive style of instruction which the teacher makes few demands of students and provides little or no active guidance.

learned helplessness: the failure to learn how to respond appropriately in a situation because of previous exposures to uncontrollable events in the same or similar situations.

learned helplessness orientation: a tendency to give up or to stop trying after failing because these failures have been attributed to a lack of ability that one can do little about.

learning goal: state of affairs in which one's primary objective in an achievement context is to increase one's skills or abilities.

locus of control: personality dimension distinguishing people who assume that they are personally responsible for their life outcomes (internal locus) from those who believe that their outcomes depend more on circumstances beyond their control (external locus).

looking-glass self: the idea that a child's self-concept is largely determined by the ways other people respond to him or her.

longitudinal design: a research design in which one group of subjects is studied repeatedly over a period of months or years.

love withdrawal: a form of discipline in which an adult withholds attention, affection, or approval in order to modify or control a child's behavior.

macrosystem: the larger cultural or subcultural context in which development occurs; Bronfenbrenner's outermost environmental layer, or context.

mainstreaming: the educational practice of integrating developmentally disabled students with special needs into regular classrooms rather than placing them in segregated special education classes.

mastery motivation: an inborn motive to explore, understand, and control one's environment.

mastery orientation: a tendency to persist at challenging tasks because of a belief that one has high ability and/or that earlier failures can be overcome by trying harder.

maternal deprivation hypothesis: the notion that socially deprived infants develop abnormally because they have failed to establish attachments to a primary caregiver.

mean-world belief: a belief, fostered by televised violence, that the world is a more dangerous and frightening place than is actually the case.

mechanistic model: view of children as passive entities whose developmental paths are primarily determined by external (environmental) influences.

mental mediation (or confluence) hypothesis: the notion that firstborns (and children from small families) achieve more than laterborns (and children from large families) because their home environments are more conducive to the development of their intellectual potential.

mesosystem: the interconnections among an individual's immediate settings, or microsystems; the second of Bronfenbrenner's environmental layers, or contexts.

metacognition: one's knowledge about cognition and about the regulation of cognitive activities.

microsystem: the immediate settings (including role relationships and activities) that the person actually encounters; the innermost of Bronfenbrenner's environmental layers, or contexts.

mixed-age peer interaction: interactions among children who differ in age by a year or more.

moral affect: the emotional component of morality, including feelings such as guilt, shame, and pride in ethical conduct.

moral behavior: the behavioral component of morality; actions that are consistent with one's moral standards in situations in which one is tempted to violate them.

morality: a set of principles or ideals that help the individual to distinguish right from wrong, to act on this distinction, and to feel pride in virtuous conduct and guilt (or shame) for conduct that violates one's standards.

morality of care: Gilligan's term for what she presumes to be the dominant moral orientation for females—an orientation focusing more on compassionate concerns for human welfare than on socially defined justice as administered through law.

morality of justice: Gilligan's term for what she presumes to be the dominant moral orientation of males, focusing more on socially defined justice as administered through law than on compassionate concerns for human welfare.

moral reasoning: the cognitive component of morality; the thinking that people display when deciding whether various acts are right or wrong.

moral rules: standards of acceptable and unacceptable conduct that focus on the rights and privileges of individuals.

moratorium: identity status characterizing individuals who are currently experiencing an identity crisis and are actively exploring occupational and ideological positions in which to invest themselves.

"mother-only" monkeys: monkeys who are raised with their mothers and denied any contact with peers.

motivational/intentional definition of altruism: beneficial acts for which the actor's primary motive or intent was to address the needs of others.

motive to achieve success (M_s): Atkinson's term for the disposition describing one's tendency to approach challenging tasks and to take pride in mastering them; analogous to McClelland's need for achievement.

motive to avoid failure (M_{af}): Atkinson's term for the disposition describing one's tendency to shy away from challenging tasks so as to avoid the embarrassment of failing.

naturalistic observation: a method in which the scientist tests hypotheses by observing people as they engage in everyday activities in their natural habitats (for example, at home, at school, or on the playground).

natural (or quasi) experiment: a study in which the investigator measures the impact of some naturally occurring event that is assumed to affect people's lives.

natural selection: an evolutionary process, proposed by Charles Darwin, stating that individuals with characteristics that promote adaptation to the environment will survive, reproduce, and pass these adaptive characteristics to offspring; those lacking these adaptive characteristics will eventually die out.

nature versus nurture issue: debate within developmental psychology over the relative importance of biological predispositions (nature) and environmental influences (nurture) as determinants of human development.

need for achievement (n Ach): McClelland's depiction of achievement motivation as a learned motive to compete and to strive for success in situations in which one's performance can be evaluated against some standard of excellence.

negative reinforcer: any stimulus whose removal or termination as the consequence of an act will increase the probability that the act will recur.

neglected children: children who receive few nominations as either a liked or a disliked individual from members of their peer group.

neonate: a newborn infant from birth to approximately one month of age.

nominations technique: sociometric measures in which children are asked to nominate a specific number of peers as liked and the same number as disliked. The number and patterning of positive and negative nominations a child receives determine his or her sociometric status.

nonorganic failure to thrive: an infant growth disorder, caused by lack of attention and affection (and associated undernutrition) that causes growth to slow dramatically or stop.

nonrepresentative sample: a subgroup that differs in important ways from the larger group (or population) to which it belongs.

nonshared environmental influence (NSE): an environmental influence that people living together do not share and should make these individuals different from one another.

nonsocial activity: onlooker behavior and solitary play.

normative altruism: prosocial acts that are performed with the expectation of receiving some personal benefit for acting or avoiding criticism for failing to act.

norm of social responsibility: the principle that we should help others who are in some way dependent on us for assistance.

norms: group-defined rules or expectations about how the members of that group are to think or behave.

object permanence: the realization that objects continue to exist when they are no longer visible or detectable through the other senses.

observational learning: learning that results from observing the behavior of others.

observer influence: tendency of participants to react to an observer's presence by behaving in unusual ways.

oedipal morality: Freud's theory that moral development occurs during the phallic period (ages 3 to 6) when children internalize the moral standards of the same-sex parent as they resolve their Oedipus or Electra conflicts.

oedipus complex: Freud's term for the conflict that 3- to 6-year-old boys experience when they develop an incestuous desire for their mothers and, at the same time, a jealous and hostile rivalry with their fathers.

open classroom: a less structured classroom arrangement in which there is a separate area for each educational activity and children distribute themselves around the room, working individually or in small groups.

operant learning: a form of learning in which voluntary acts (or operants) become either more or less probable, depending on the consequences they produce.

operational schemes: Piaget's term for schemes that utilize cognitive operations, or mental "actions of the head," that enable one to transform objects of thought and to reason logically.

organismic model: view of children as active entities whose developmental paths are primarily determined by forces from within themselves.

organization: an inborn tendency to combine and integrate available schemes into coherent systems or bodies of knowledge.

original sin: the idea that children are inherently negative creatures who must be taught to rechannel their selfish interests into socially acceptable outlets.

own-sex schema: detailed knowledge or plans of action that enable a person to perform gender-consistent activities and to enact his or her gender role.

parallel play: largely noninteractive play in which players are in close proximity but do not often attempt to influence each other.

parental socialization hypothesis: the notion that first-borns (and children from small families) achieve more than later-borns (and children from large families) because they receive more direct achievement training from their parents.

Parents Anonymous: an organization of reformed child abusers (modeled after Alcoholics Anonymous) that functions as a support group and helps parents to understand and overcome their abusive tendencies.

parsimony: a criterion for evaluating the scientific merit of theories; a parsimonious theory is one that uses relatively few explanatory principles to explain a broad set of observations.

particularistic development: developmental outcomes that vary from person to person.

passive genotype/environment correlations: the notion that the rearing environments that biological parents provide are influenced by the parents' own genes, and hence are correlated with the child's own genotype.

passive victims (of aggression): socially withdrawn and anxious children whom bullies torment, even though they appear to have done nothing to trigger such abuse.

peer acceptance: a measure of a person's likability (or dislikability) in the eyes of the peers.

peer conformity: the tendency to go along with the wishes of peers or to yield to peer-group pressures.

peer group: a confederation of peers who interact regularly, that defines a sense of membership, and that formulates norms that specify how members are supposed to look, think, and act.

"peer-only" monkeys: monkeys who are separated from their mothers (and other adults) soon after birth and raised with peers.

peers: two or more persons who are operating at similar levels of behavioral complexity.

performance goal: state of affairs in which one's primary objective in an achievement context is to display one's competencies (or to avoid looking incompetent).

permissive parenting: a pattern of parenting in which otherwise accepting adults make few demands of their children and rarely attempt to control their behavior.

personal agency: the recognition that one can be the cause of an event or events.

personal fable: allegedly a form of adolescent egocentrism in which the individual thinks that he and his thoughts and feelings are special or unique.

phallic stage: Freud's third stage of psychosexual development (from 3 to 6 years of age) in which children gratify the sex instinct by fondling their genitals and developing an incestuous desire for the parent of the other sex.

phase of indiscriminate attachments: period between 6 weeks and 6 to 7 months of age in which infants prefer social to nonsocial stimulation and are likely to protest whenever any adult puts them down or leaves them alone.

phase of multiple attachments: period when infants are forming attachments to companions other than their primary attachment object.

phase of specific attachment: period between 7 and 9 months of age when infants are attached to one close companion (usually the mother).

phenotype: the ways in which a person's genotype is expressed in observable or measurable characteristics.

popular children: children who are liked by many members of their peer group and disliked by very few.

postconventional morality: Kohlberg's term for the fifth and sixth stages of moral reasoning, in which moral judgments are based on social contracts and democratic law (Stage 5) or on universal principles of ethics and justice (Stage 6).

power-assertion: a form of discipline in which an adult relies on his or her superior power (for example, by administering spankings or withholding privileges) to modify or control a child's behavior.

preadapted characteristic: an innate attribute that is a product of evolution and serves some function that increases the chances of survival for the individual and the species.

preconventional morality: Kohlberg's term for the first two stages of moral reasoning, in which moral judgments are based on the tangible punitive consequences (Stage 1) or rewarding consequences (Stage 2) of an act for the actor rather than on the relationship of that act to society's rules and customs.

premoral period: in Piaget's theory, the first five years of life, when children have little respect for or awareness of socially defined rules.

preoperational stage: Piaget's second stage of cognitive development, lasting from about age 2 to age 7, when children are thinking at a symbolic level but are not yet using cognitive operations.

primary circular reaction: a pleasurable response, centered on the infant's own body, that is discovered by chance and performed over and over.

primary (or basic) emotions: the set of emotions present at birth or emerging early in the first year that some theorists believe to be biologically programmed.

private self (or I): those inner, or subjective, aspects of self that are known only to the individual and are not available for public scrutiny.

private speech: Vygotsky's term for the subset of a child's verbal utterances that serve a self-communicative function and guide the child's activities.

proactive aggressors: highly aggressive children who find aggressive acts easy to perform and who rely heavily on aggression as a means of solving social problems or achieving other personal objectives.

proprioceptive feedback: sensory information from the muscles, tendons, and joints that helps one to locate the position of one's body (or body parts) in space.

prosocial behavior: actions, such as sharing, helping, or comforting, that benefit other people.

prosocial moral reasoning: the thinking that people display when deciding whether to help, share with, or comfort others when these actions could prove costly to themselves.

prospective study: study in which the suspected causes or contributors to an outcome are assessed earlier to see whether they are actually associated with the developments they are presumed to influence.

provocative victims (of aggression): restless, hot-tempered, and oppositional children who are victimized because they often irritate their peers.

psychological comparisons phase: tendency to form impressions of others by comparing and contrasting these individuals on abstract psychological dimensions.

psychological constructs phase: tendency to base one's impressions of others on the stable traits these individuals are presumed to have.

psychosexual theory: Freud's theory which states that maturation of the sex instinct underlies stages of personality development, and that how parents manage children's instinctual impulses will determine the traits children come to display.

psychosocial theory: Erikson's revision of Freud's theory which emphasizes sociocultural (rather than sexual) determinants of development and posits a series of eight psychosocial conflicts that people must resolve successfully to display healthy psychological adjustment.

public self (or me): those aspects of self that others can see or infer.

punisher: any consequence of an act that suppresses that act and/or decreases the probability that it will recur.

Pygmalion effect: the tendency of teacher expectancies to become self-fulfilling prophecies, causing students to perform better or worse depending on their teacher's estimation of their potential.

random assignment: a control technique in which participants are assigned to experimental conditions through an unbiased procedure so that the members of the groups are not systematically different from one another.

reactive aggressors: children who display high levels of hostile, retaliatory aggression because they overattribute hostile intents to others and can't control their anger long enough to seek nonaggressive solutions to social problems.

reactive attachment disorder: inability to form secure attachment bonds with other people; characterizes many victims of early social deprivation and/or abuse.

reciprocal determinism: the notion that the flow of influence between children and their environments is a two-way street; the environment may affect the child, but the child's behavior will also influence the environment.

reinforcer: any consequence of an act that increases the probability that the act will recur.

rejected-aggressive children: a subgroup of rejected children who display high levels of hostility and aggression in their interactions with peers.

rejected children: children who are disliked by many peers and liked by few.

rejected-withdrawn children: a subgroup of rejected children who are often passive, socially unskilled, and insensitive to peer-group expectations.

relational aggression: acts such as snubbing, exclusion, withdrawing acceptance, or spreading rumors that are aimed at damaging an adversary's self-esteem, friendships, or social status.

relational self-worth: feelings of self-worth within a particular relationship context (for example, with parents; with male classmates); may differ across relationship contexts.

reliability: The extent to which a measuring instrument yields consistent results, both over time and across observers.

repression: a type of motivated forgetting in which anxiety-provoking thoughts and conflicts are forced out of conscious awareness.

resistant attachment: an insecure infant/caregiver bond, characterized by strong separation protest and a tendency of the child to remain near but resist contact initiated by the caregiver, particularly after a separation.

retaliatory aggression: aggressive acts elicited by real or imagined provocations.

reversibility: the ability to reverse, or negate, an action by mentally performing the opposite action.

role-taking: the ability to assume another person's perspective and understand his or her thoughts, feelings, and behaviors.

rouge test: test of self-recognition that involves marking a toddler's face and observing his or her reaction to the mark when the child is placed before a mirror.

scaffolding: process by which an expert, when instructing a novice, responds contingently to the novice's behavior in a learning situation, so that the novice gradually increases his or her understanding of a problem.

scheme: an organized pattern of thought or action that a child constructs to make sense of some aspect of his or her experience; Piaget sometimes uses the term *cognitive structures* as a synonym for schemes.

schizophrenia: a serious form of mental illness characterized by disturbances in logical thinking, emotional expression, and interpersonal behavior.

scientific method: an attitude or value about the pursuit of knowledge that dictates that investigators must be objective and must allow their data to decide the merits of their theorizing.

secondary circular reaction: a pleasurable response, centered on an object external to the self, that is discovered by chance and performed over and over.

secondary (or complex) emotions: self-conscious or self-evaluative emotions that emerge in the second year and depend, in part, on cognitive development.

secondary reinforcer: an initially neutral stimulus that acquires reinforcement value by virtue of its repeated association with other reinforcing stimuli.

secure attachment: an infant/caregiver bond in which the child welcomes contact with a close companion and uses this person as a secure base from which to explore the environment.

secure base: use of a caregiver as a base from which to explore the environment and to which to return for emotional support.

selective attrition: nonrandom loss of participants during a study which results in a nonrepresentative sample.

selective breeding experiment: a method of studying genetic influences by determining whether traits can be bred in animals through selective mating.

self: the combination of physical and psychological attributes that is unique to each individual.

self-actualization goal: LeVine's third priority of parenting—to promote the child's cognitive and behavioral capacity for maximizing such cultural values as morality, achievement, prestige, and personal satisfaction.

self-assertion: noncompliant acts that are undertaken by children in the interest of doing things for themselves or otherwise establishing autonomy.

self-care (or latchkey) children: children who care for themselves after school or in the evenings while their parents are working.

self-concept: one's perceptions of one's unique combination of attributes.

self-control: ability to regulate one's conduct and to inhibit actions that are unacceptable or that conflict with a goal.

self-disclosure: the act of revealing private or intimate information about oneself to another person.

self-esteem: one's evaluation of one's worth as a person based on an assessment of the qualities that make up the self-concept.

self-fulfilling prophecy: phenomenon whereby people cause others to act in accordance with the expectations they have about those others.

self-oriented distress: feeling of *personal* discomfort or distress that may be elicited when we experience the emotions of (that is, empathize with) a distressed other; thought to inhibit altruism.

self-recognition: the ability to recognize oneself in a mirror or a photograph, coupled with the conscious awareness that the mirror or photographic image is a representation of "me."

sensitive period: period of time that is optimal for the development of particular capacities, or behaviors, and in which the individual is particularly sensitive to environmental influences that would foster these attributes.

sensorimotor stage: Piaget's first stage of cognitive development, from birth to 2 years, when infants are relying on behavioral schemes to adapt to the environment.

separation anxiety: a wary or fretful reaction that infants and toddlers often display when separated from the person(s) to whom they are attached.

sequential design: a research design in which subjects from different age groups are studied repeatedly over a period of months or years.

seriation: a cognitive operation that allows one to order a set of stimuli along a quantifiable dimension such as height or weight.

sexuality: aspect of self referring to one's erotic thoughts, actions, and orientation.

shared environmental influences (SE): an environmental influence that people living together share and should make these individuals similar to one another.

sibling rivalry: the spirit of competition, jealousy, and resentment that may arise between two or more siblings.

single-parent family: a family system consisting of one parent (either the mother or the father) and the parent's dependent child(ren).

situational compliance: compliance based primarily on the parent's power to control the child's conduct.

slow-to-warm-up temperament: temperamental profile in which the child is inactive and moody and displays mild passive resistance to new routines and experiences.

sociability: one's willingness to interact with others and to seek their attention or approval.

social cognition: the thinking that people display about the thoughts, feelings, motives, and behaviors of themselves and other people.

social comparison: the process of defining and evaluating the self by comparing oneself to other people.

social-conventional rules: standards of conduct determined by social consensus that indicate what is appropriate within a particular social context.

social information-processing (or attribution) theory: social-cognitive theory stating that the explanations we construct for social experiences largely determine how we react to those experiences.

socialization: the process by which individuals acquire the beliefs, values, and behaviors considered desirable or appropriate by their culture or subculture.

social perspective-taking: the ability to infer others' thoughts, intentions, motives, and attributes.

social problem-solving training: method of social-skills training in which an adult helps children (through role-playing or role-taking training) to make less hostile attributions about harmdoing and to generate nonaggressive solutions to conflict.

social referencing: the use of others' emotional expressions to infer the meaning of otherwise ambiguous situations.

social skills: thoughts, actions, and emotional regulatory activities that enable children to achieve personal or social goals while maintaining harmony with their social partners.

social stimulation hypothesis: the notion that socially deprived infants develop abnormally because they have had little contact with companions who respond contingently to their social overtures.

social support: tangible and intangible resources provided by other people in times of uncertainty or stress.

sociocultural theory: Vygotsky's perspective on development, in which children acquire their culture's values, beliefs, and problem-solving strategies through collaborative dialogues with more knowledgeable members of society.

socioeconomic status (SES): one's position within a society that is stratified according to status and power.

sociometric techniques: procedures that ask children to identify those peers whom they like or dislike or to rate peers for their desirability as companions; used to measure children's peer acceptance (or nonacceptance).

stereotype threat: a fear that one will be judged to have traits associated with negative social stereotypes about his or her racial or ethnic group.

stranger anxiety: a wary or fretful reaction that infants and toddlers often display when approached by an unfamiliar person.

Strange-Situation: a series of eight separation and reunion episodes to which infants are exposed in order to determine the quality of their attachments.

structured interview or structured questionnaire: a technique in which all participants are asked the same questions in precisely the same order so that the responses of different participants can be compared.

structured observation: an observational method in which the investigator cues the behavior of interest and observes participants' responses in a laboratory.

superego: psychoanalytic term for the component of the personality that consists of one's internalized moral standards.

superordinate goals: important objectives that cannot be achieved unless rivaling groups or factions set their differences aside and pull together to work as a team.

survival goal: LeVine's first priority of parenting—to promote the physical health and safety (survival) of young children.

symbolic function: the ability to use symbols (for example, images and words) to represent objects and experiences.

symbolic representations: the images and verbal labels that observers generate in order to retain the important aspects of a model's behavior.

symbolic schemes: internal mental symbols (such as images or verbal codes) that one uses to represent aspects of experience.

sympathetic empathic arousal: feelings of sympathy or compassion that may be elicited when we experience the emotions of (that is, empathize with) a distressed other; thought to become an important mediator of altruism.

synchronized routines: generally harmonious interactions between two persons in which participants adjust their behavior in response to the partner's actions.

tabula rasa: the idea that the mind of an infant is a "blank slate" and that all knowledge, abilities, behaviors, and motives are acquired through experience.

television literacy: one's ability to understand how information is conveyed in television programming and to properly interpret this information.

temperament: a person's characteristic modes of emotional and behavioral responding to environmental events, including such attributes as activity level, irritability, fearfulness, and sociability.

temperament hypothesis: Kagan's view that the Strange-Situation measures individual differences in infants' temperaments rather than the quality of their attachments.

tertiary circular reaction: an exploratory scheme in which infants devise new methods of acting on objects to reproduce interesting results.

test anxiety: a concern about being evaluated that can undermine performance, especially under highly stressful, competitive testing procedures.

testicular feminization syndrome (TFS): a genetic anomaly in which a male fetus is insensitive to the effects of male sex hormones and will develop femalelike external genitalia.

Thanatos: Freud's name for inborn, self-destructive instincts that were said to characterize all human beings.

theory: a set of concepts and propositions designed to organize, describe, and explain an existing set of observations.

theory of mind: an understanding that people are cognitive beings with mental states that are not always accessible to others and that often guide their behavior.

time-out technique: a form of discipline in which children who misbehave are removed from the setting until they are prepared to act more appropriately.

"timing of puberty" effect: the finding that people who reach puberty late perform better on visual/spatial tasks than those who mature early.

tools of intellectual adaptation: Vygotsky's term for methods of thinking and problem-solving strategies that children internalize from their interactions with more competent members of society.

traditional classroom: a classroom arrangement in which all pupils sit facing an instructor, who normally teaches one subject at a time by lecturing or giving demonstrations.

traditional nuclear family: a family unit consisting of a wife/mother, a husband/father, and their dependent child(ren).

transactive interactions: verbal exchanges in which individuals perform mental operations on the reasoning of their discussion partners.

transitivity: the ability to infer relations among elements in a serial order (for example, if A > B and B > C, then A > C).

trust versus mistrust: the first of Erikson's eight psychosocial stages, in which infants must learn to trust their closest companions or else run the risk of mistrusting other people later in life.

twin design: study in which sets of twins that differ in zygosity (kinship) are compared to determine the heritability of an attribute.

unconscious motives: Freud's term for feelings, experiences, and conflicts that influence a person's thinking and behavior but lie outside the person's awareness.

uninvolved parenting: a pattern of parenting that is both aloof (or even hostile) and overpermissive, almost as if parents neither cared about their children nor about what they might become.

universal development: normative developments that all individuals display.

validity: the extent to which a measuring instrument accurately reflects what the researchers intended to measure.

visual/spatial abilities: the ability to mentally manipulate or otherwise draw inferences about pictorial information.

X-linked recessive disorder: an attribute determined by a recessive gene that appears only on X chromosomes; since the gene determining these characteristics is recessive (that is, dominated by other genes that might appear at the same location on X chromosomes), such characteristics are more common among males, who have only one X chromosome; also called *sex-linked trait.*

younger-peer therapy: a method of rehabilitating emotionally withdrawn individuals by regularly exposing them to younger but socially responsive companions.

zone of proximal development: Vygotsky's term for the range of tasks that are too complex to be mastered alone but can be accomplished with guidance and encouragement from a more skillful partner.

Aboud, F. E. (1988). *Children and prejudice.* New York: Blackwell.

Abramovitch, R., Corter, C., & Pepler, D. J. (1980). Observations of mixed-sex sibling dyads. *Child Development, 51,* 1268–1271.

Abramovitch, R., Corter, C., Pepler, D. J., & Stanhope, L. (1986). Sibling and peer interaction: A final follow-up and a comparison. *Child Development, 57,* 217–229.

Abravanel, E., & Sigafoos, A. D. (1984). Exploring the presence of imitation during early infancy. *Child Development, 55,* 381–392.

Ackerman, B. P., Kogos, J., Youngstrom, E., Schoff, K., & Izard, C. (1999). Family instability and the problem behaviors of children from economically disadvantaged families. *Developmental Psychology, 35,* 258–268.

Adams, G. R., Abraham, K. G., & Markstrom, C. A. (1987). The relations among identity development, self-consciousness, and self-focusing during middle and late adolescence. *Developmental Psychology, 23,* 292–297.

Adams, R. E., & Passman, R. H. (1980, March). *The effects of advance preparation upon children's behavior during brief separation from their mother.* Paper presented at annual meeting of the Southeastern Psychological Association, Washington, DC.

Adams, R. E., & Passman, R. H. (1981). The effects of preparing two-year-olds for brief separations from their mothers. *Child Development, 52,* 1068–1071.

Adams, G. R., & Crane, P. (1980). An assessment of parents' and teachers' expectations of preschool children's social preference for attractive or unattractive children and adults. *Child Development, 51,* 224–231.

Adler, A. (1964). *Problems of neurosis.* New York: Harper & Row. (Original work published 1929)

Ainsworth, M. D. S. (1967). *Infancy in Uganda: Infant care and the growth of love.* Baltimore: Johns Hopkins University Press.

Ainsworth, M. D. S. (1979). Attachment as related to mother-infant interaction. In J. S. Rosenblatt, R. A. Hinde, C. Beer, & M. Busnel (Eds.), *Advances in the study of behavior* (Vol. 9). Orlando, FL: Academic Press.

Ainsworth, M. D. S. (1989). Attachments beyond infancy. *American Psychologist, 44,* 709–716.

Ainsworth, M. D. S., Blehar, M. C., Waters, E., & Wall, S. (1978). *Patterns of attachment: A psychological study of the strange situation.* Hillsdale, NJ: Erlbaum.

Al Awad, A. M. H., & Sonuga-Barke, E. J. S. (1992). Childhood problems in a Sudanese city: A comparison of extended and nuclear families. *Child Development, 63,* 906–914.

Alessandri, S. M., & Lewis, M. (1996). Differences in pride and shame in maltreated and nonmaltreated toddlers. *Child Development, 67,* 1857–1869.

Alexander, B. K., & Harlow, H. F. (1965). Social behavior in juvenile rhesus monkeys subjected to different rearing conditions during the first 6 months of life. *Zoologische Jahrbucher Physiologie, 60,* 167–174.

Alexander, G. M., & Hines, M. (1994). Gender labels and play styles: Their relative contribution to children's selection of playmates. *Child Development, 65,* 869–879.

Alexander, K. L., & Entwisle, D. R. (1988). Achievement in the first two years of school: Patterns and processes. *Monographs of the Society for Research in Child Development, 53,* (2, Serial No. 218).

Alfieri, T., Ruble, D. N., & Higgins, E. T. (1996). Gender stereotypes during adolescence: Developmental changes and the transition to junior high school. *Developmental Psychology, 32,* 1129–1137.

Allen, J. P., Moore, C., Kuperminc, G., & Bell, K. (1998). Attachment and adolescent psychosocial functioning. *Child Development, 69,* 1406–1419.

Allen, J. P., Philliber, S., Herrling, S., & Kuperminc, G. P. (1997). Preventing teen pregnancy and academic failure: Experimental evaluation of a developmentally based approach. *Child Development, 68,* 729–742.

Allen, J. P., Weissberg, R. P., & Hawkins, J. A. (1989). The relation between values and social competence in early adolescence. *Developmental Psychology, 25,* 458–464.

Alley, T. R. (1981). Head shape and the perception of cuteness. *Developmental Psychology, 17,* 650–654.

Allgood-Merten, B., & Stockard, J. (1991). Sex role identity and self-esteem: A comparison of children and adolescents. *Sex Roles, 25,* 129–139.

Allison, P. D., & Furstenberg, F. F., Jr. (1989). How marital dissolution affects children: Variations by age and sex. *Developmental Psychology, 25,* 540–549.

Amato, P. R. (1993). Children's adjustment to divorce: Theories, hypotheses, and empirical support. *Journal of Marriage and the Family, 55,* 23–38.

Amato, P. R. (1996). Explaining the intergenerational transmission of divorce. *Journal of Marriage and the Family, 58,* 628–640.

Amato, P. R., & Booth, A. (1996). A prospective study of divorce and parent–child relationships. *Journal of Marriage and the Family, 58,* 356–365.

Amato, P. R., & Keith, B. (1991). Parental divorce and the well-being of children: A meta-analysis. *Psychological Bulletin, 110,* 26–46.

Amato, P. R., Loomis, L. S., & Booth, A. (1995). Parental divorce, marital conflict, and offspring well-being during early childhood. *Social Forces, 73,* 895–915.

Ambert, A. (1992). *The effect of children on parents.* New York: Haworth.

Ambron, S. R., & Irwin, D. M. (1975). Role-taking and moral judgment in five- and seven-year-olds. *Developmental Psychology, 11,* 102.

American Academy of Pediatrics. (1986). Sexuality, contraception, and the media. *Pediatrics, 71,* 535–536.

Ammerman, R. T., & Patz, R. J. (1996). Determinants of child abuse potential: Parent and child factors. *Journal of Clinical Child Psychology, 25,* 300–307.

Anderson, D. R., & Collins, P. A. (1988). *The impact on children's education: Television's influence on cognitive development.* Washington, DC: U.S. Department of Education.

Anderson, D. R., Lorch, E. P., Field, D. E., & Sanders, J. (1981). The effects of TV program comprehensibility on preschool children's visual attention to television. *Child Development, 52,* 151–157.

Anderson, K. E., Lytton, H., & Romney, D. M. (1986). Mothers' interactions with normal and conduct-disordered boys: Who affects whom? *Developmental Psychology, 22,* 604–609.

Andersson, B. (1989). Effects of public day-care: A longitudinal study. *Child Development, 60,* 857–866.

Andersson, B. (1992). Effects of day-care on cognitive and socioemotional competence of thirteen-year-old Swedish schoolchildren. *Child Development, 63,* 20–36.

Archer, J. (1991). The influence of testosterone on human aggression. *British Journal of Psychology, 92,* 1–28.

Archer, J. (1992a). Childhood gender roles: Social context and organization. In H. McGurk (Ed.), *Childhood social development: Contemporary perspectives.* Hove, England: Erlbaum.

Archer, J. (1992b). *Ethology and human development.* Hertfordshire, England: Harvester Wheatsheaf.

Archer, J. (1996). Sex differences in social behavior: Are the social role and evolutionary explanations compatible? *American Psychologist, 51,* 909–917.

Archer, J. (1997). On the origins of sex differences in social behavior: Darwinian and non-Darwinian accounts. *American Psychologist, 52,* 1383–1384.

Archer, S. L. (1982). The lower age boundaries of identity development. *Child Development, 53,* 1551–1556.

Archer, S. L. (1992). A feminist's approach to identity research. In G. R. Adams, T. P. Gullotta, & R. Montemayor (Eds.), *Adolescent identity formation* (Advances in Adolescent Development, Vol. 4). Newbury Park, CA: Sage.

Archer, S. L. (1994). *Interventions for adolescent identity development.* Thousand Oaks, CA: Sage.

Ardrey, R. (1967). *African genesis.* New York: Dell.

Aries, P. (1962). *Centuries of childhood.* New York: Knopf.

Arnett, J. J. (1995). Broad and narrow socialization: The family in the context of a cultural theory. *Journal of Marriage and the Family, 57,* 617–628.

Arnett, J.J., & Balle-Jensen, L. (1993). Cultural bases of risk behavior: Danish adolescents. *Child Development, 64,* 1842–1855.

Arnold, D. H., McWilliams, L., & Arnold, E. H. (1998). Teacher discipline and child misbehavior in day-care: Untangling causality with correlational data. *Developmental Psychology, 34,* 267–287.

Aro, H., & Taipale, V. (1987). The impact of timing of puberty on psychosomatic symptoms among fourteen- to sixteen-year-old Finnish girls. *Child Development, 58,* 261–268.

Aronson, E. (1976). *The social animal.* New York: W. H. Freeman.

Aronson, E., Blaney, N., Stephan, C., Sikes, J., & Snapp, M. (1978). *The jigsaw classroom.* Beverly Hills, CA: Sage.

Arsenio, W. F., & Kramer, R. (1992). Victimizers and their victims: Children's conception of mixed emotional consequences of moral transgressions. *Child Development, 63,* 915–927.

Asendorph, J. B., & Baudonniere, P. (1993). Self-awareness and other-awareness: Mirror self-recognition and synchronic imitation among unfamiliar peers. *Developmental Psychology, 29,* 88–95.

Asendorph, J. B., Warkentin, V., & Baudonniere, P. (1996). Self-awareness and other awareness II: Mirror self-recognition, social contingency awareness, and synchronic imitation. *Developmental Psychology, 32,* 313–321.

Asher, S. R., Parker, J. G., & Walker, D. L. (1996). Distinguishing friendship from acceptance: Implications for intervention and assessment. In W. M. Bukowski, A. F. Newcomb, & W. W. Hartup (Eds.), *The company they keep: Friendship during childhood and adolescence* (pp. 366–405). New York: Cambridge University Press.

Asher, S. R., Renshaw, P. D., & Hymel, S. (1982). Peer relations and the development of social skills. In S. G. Moore (Ed.), *The young child: Reviews of research* (Vol. 3). Washington, DC: National Association for the Education of Young Children.

Associated Press. (1994a, July 30). Science: A man's domain. *Atlanta Constitution,* p. A6.

Associated Press. (1994b, September 7). Study: TV ignores, maligns Hispanics. *Fresno Bee,* F1, F4.

Associated Press. (1994c, August 24). Which practices work best in today's schools? *Atlanta Constitution,* p. A1, A14.

Associated Press. (1996, December 30). Arizona to require divorcing parents to study impact on children. *Dallas Morning News,* p. 18a.

Associated Press. (1999, January 10). TV sex rampant, critics say. *Atlanta Constitution,* D1, D3.

Astin, A. W., Korn, W. S., Sax, L. J., & Mahoney, K. M. (1994). *The American freshman: National norms for fall 1994.* Los Angeles, CA: Higher Education Research Institute, University of California at Los Angeles.

Astor, R. A. (1994). Children's moral reasoning about family and peer violence: The role of provocation and retribution. *Child Development, 65,* 1054–1067.

Atkin, C. (1978). Observation of parent-child interaction in supermarket decision-making. *Journal of Marketing, 42,* 41–45.

Atkinson, J. W. (1964). *An introduction to motivation.* Princeton, NJ: Van Nostrand.

Atwater, E. (1992). *Adolescence* (2nd ed.). Englewood Cliffs, NJ: Prentice Hall.

Azmitia, M. (1988). Peer interaction and problem-solving: When are two heads better than one? *Child Development, 59,* 87–96.

Azmitia, M. (1992). Expertise, private speech, and the development of self-regulation. In R. M. Diaz & L. E. Berk (Eds.), *Private speech: From social interaction to self-regulation.* Hillsdale, NJ: Erlbaum.

Azmitia, M., & Hesser, J. (1993). Why siblings are important agents of cognitive development: A comparison of siblings and peers. *Child Development, 64,* 430–444.

Bagley, C. (1995). *Child sexual abuse and mental health in adolescents and adults.* Aldershot, England: Ashgate Publishing Company.

Bagwell, C. L., Newcomb, A. F., & Bukowski, W. M. (1998). Preadolescent friendship and peer rejection as predictors of adult adjustment. *Child Development, 69,* 140–153.

Baier, J. L., Rosenzweig, M. G., & Whipple, E. (1991). Patterns of sexual behavior, coercion, and victimization of university students. *Journal of College Student Development, 32,* 310–322.

Bailey, J. M., Bobrow, D., Wolfe, M., & Mikach, S. (1995). Sexual orientation of adult sons of gay fathers. *Developmental Psychology, 31,* 124–129.

Bailey, J. M., & Pillard, R. C. (1991). A genetic study of male sexual orientation. *Archives of General Psychiatry, 48,* 1089–1096.

Bailey, J. M., Pillard, R. C., Neale, M. C., & Agyei, Y. (1993). Heritable factors influence sexual orientation in women. *Archives of General Psychiatry, 50,* 217–223.

Baker, D. P., & Jones, D. P. (1992). Opportunity and performance: A sociological explanation for gender differences in academic mathematics. In J. Wrigley (Ed.), *Education and gender equality.* London: The Falmer Press.

Baker, L. A., & Daniels, D. (1990). Nonshared environmental influences and personality differences in adult twins. *Journal of Personality and Social Psychology, 58,* 103–110.

Baker, L. A., Mack, W., Moffitt, T. E., & Mednick, S. (1989). Sex differences in property crime in a Danish adoption cohort. *Behavior Genetics, 19,* 355–370.

Baldwin, D. A., & Moses, L. J. (1996). The ontogeny of social information gathering. *Child Development, 67,* 1915–1939.

Baldwin, D. V., & Skinner, M. L. (1989). Structural model for antisocial behavior: Generalization to single-mother families. *Developmental Psychology, 25,* 45–50.

Ball, S., & Bogatz, C. (1970). *The first year of Sesame Street: An evaluation.* Princeton, NJ: Educational Testing Service.

Ball, S., & Bogatz, C. (1973). *Reading with television: An evaluation of The Electric Company.* Princeton, NJ: Educational Testing Service.

Bandura, A. (1965). Influence of models' reinforcement contingencies on the acquisition of imitative responses. *Journal of Personality and Social Psychology, 1,* 589–595.

Bandura, A. (1973). *Aggression: A social learning analysis.* Englewood Cliffs, NJ: Prentice Hall.

Bandura, A. (1977). *Social learning theory.* Englewood Cliffs, NJ: Prentice Hall.

Bandura, A. (1978). The self system in reciprocal determinism. *American Psychologist, 33,* 344–358.

Bandura, A. (1986). *Social foundation of thought and action: A social cognitive theory.* Englewood Cliffs, NJ: Prentice Hall.

Bandura, A. (1989). Social cognitive theory. In R. Vasta (Ed.), *Annals of child development* (Vol. 6, pp. 1–60). Greenwich, CT: JAI Press.

Bandura, A. (1991). Social cognitive theory of moral thought and action. In Kurtines, W. M., & Gewirtz, J. L. (Eds.), *Handbook of moral behavior and development* (Vol. 1, pp. 45–103). Hillsdale, NJ: Erlbaum.

Bandura, A. (1992). Perceived self-efficacy in cognitive development and functioning. *Educational Psychologist, 28,* 117–148.

Banks, J. A. (1993). Multicultural education: Historical development, dimensions, and practice. *Review of Educational Research, 19,* 3–49.

Barber, B. K., Olsen, J. E., & Shagle, S. C. (1994). Associations between parental psychological and behavioral control and youth internalized and externalized behaviors. *Child Development, 65,* 1120–1136.

Barden, R. C., Ford, M. E., Jensen, A G., Rogers-Salyer, M., & Salyer, K. E. (1989). Effects of craniofacial deformity in infancy on the quality of mother-infant interactions. *Child Development, 60,* 819–824.

Bardwell, J. R., Cochran, S. W., & Walker, S. (1986). Relation of parental education, race, and gender to sex-role stereotyping in five-year-old kindergartners. *Sex Roles, 15,* 275–281.

Barenboim, C. (1981). The development of person perception in childhood and adolescence: From behavioral comparisons to psychological constructs to psychological comparisons. *Child Development, 52,* 129–144.

Barker, R. G., & Gump, P. V. (1964). *Big school, small school.* Stanford, CA: Stanford University Press.

Barnett, M. A. (1987). Empathy and related responses in children. In N. Eisenberg & J. Strayer (Eds.), *Empathy and its development.* Cambridge, England: Cambridge University Press.

Barnett, W. S. (1993). Benefit-cost analysis of preschool education: Findings from a 25-year follow-up. *American Journal of Orthopsychiatry, 63,* 500–508.

Baron, R. A., & Richardson, D. (1994). *Human aggression.* New York: Wiley.

Barry, H., III, Bacon, M. K., & Child, I. L. (1957). A cross-cultural survey of some sex differences in socialization. *Journal of Abnormal and Social Psychology, 55,* 327–332.

Barry, H., Child, I. L., & Bacon, M. K. (1959). The relation of child training to subsistence economy. *American Anthropologist, 61,* 51–63.

Bar-Tal, D., Raviv, A., & Goldberg, M. (1982). Helping behavior among preschool children: An observational study. *Child Development, 53,* 396–402.

Bartholomew, K., & Horowitz, L. M. (1991). Attachment styles among young adults: A test of a four-category model. *Journal of Personality and Social Psychology, 61,* 226–244.

Basinger, K. S., Gibbs, J. C., & Fuller, D. (1995). Context and the measurement of moral judgment. *International Journal of Behavioral Development, 18,* 537–556.

Baskett, L. M. (1985). Sibling status effects: Adult expectations. *Developmental Psychology, 21,* 441–445.

Baskett, L. M., & Johnson, S. M. (1982). The young child's interaction with parents versus siblings: A behavioral analysis. *Child Development, 53,* 643–650.

Batson, C. D. (1991). *The altruism question: Toward a social-psychological answer.* Hillsdale, NJ: Erlbaum.

Battle, E. S. (1966). Motivational determinants of academic competence. *Journal of Personality and Social Psychology, 4,* 634–642.

Bauer, P. J., & Mandler, J. M. (1989). One thing follows another: Effects of temporal structure on 1- to 2-year-olds' recall of events. *Developmental Psychology, 25,* 197–206.

Baumrind, D. (1967). Child care practices anteceding three patterns of preschool behavior. *Genetic Psychology Monographs, 75,* 43–88.

Baumrind, D. (1971). Current patterns of parental authority. *Developmental Psychology Monographs, 4*(1, Part 2).

Baumrind, D. (1972). From each according to her ability. *School Review, 80,* 161–197.

Baumrind, D. (1973). The development of instrumental competence through socialization. In A. Pick (Ed.), *Minnesota symposium on child psychology* (Vol. 7). Minneapolis: University of Minnesota Press.

Baumrind, D. (1977, March). *Socialization determinants of personal agency.* Paper presented at the biennial meeting of the Society for Research in Child Development, New Orleans.

Baumrind, D. (1983). Rejoinder to Lewis's reinterpretation of parental firm control effects: Are authoritative families really harmonious? *Psychological Bulletin, 94,* 132–142.

Baumrind, D. (1991). Effective parenting during the early adolescent transition. In P. A. Cowan & E. M. Hetherington (Eds.), *Family transitions.* Hillsdale, NJ: Erlbaum.

Baumrind, D. (1993). The average expectable environment is not good enough: A response to Scarr. *Child Development, 64,* 1299–1317.

Baumrind, D. (1995). Commentary on sexual orientation: Research and social policy implications. *Developmental Psychology, 31,* 130–136.

Beach, F. A. (1965). *Sex and behavior.* New York: Wiley.

Beal, C. R. (1994). *Boys and girls: The development of gender roles.* New York: McGraw-Hill.

Bear, G. G., & Rys, G. S. (1994). Moral reasoning, classroom behavior, and sociometric status among elementary school children. *Developmental Psychology, 30,* 633–638.

Beckwith, L., Rodning, C., & Cohen, S. (1992). Preterm children at early adolescence and continuity and discontinuity in maternal responsiveness from infancy. *Child Development, 63,* 1198–1208.

Beilin, H. (1992). Piaget's enduring contribution to developmental psychology. *Developmental Psychology, 28,* 191–204.

Bell, A. P., Weinberg, M. S., & Hammersmith, S. K. (1981). *Sexual preference: Its development in men and women.* Bloomington: Indiana University Press.

Bell, R. Q. (1979). Parent, child, and reciprocal influences. *American Psychologist, 34,* 821–826.

Belmont, L., & Marolla, F. A. (1973). Birth order, family size, and intelligence. *Science, 182,* 1096–1101.

Belsky, J. (1981). Early human experience: A family perspective. *Developmental Psychology, 17,* 3–23.

Belsky, J. (1993). Etiology of child maltreatment: A developmental ecological analysis. *Psychological Bulletin, 114,* 413–434.

Belsky, J. (1996). Parent, infant, and social-contextual antecedents of father-son attachment security. *Developmental Psychology, 32,* 905–913.

Belsky, J., Crnic, K., & Gable, S. (1995). The determinants of coparenting in families with toddler boys: Spousal differences and daily hassles. *Child Development, 66,* 629–642.

Belsky, J., Garduque, L., & Hrncir, E. (1984). Assessing performance, competence, and executive capacity in infant play: Relations to home environment and security of attachment. *Developmental Psychology, 20,* 406–417.

Belsky, J., Gilstrap, B., & Rovine, M. (1984). The Pennsylvania Infant and Family Development Project I: Stability and change in mother-infant and father-infant interaction in a family setting. *Child Development, 55,* 692–705.

Belsky, J., Rosenberger, K., & Crnic, K. (1995). Maternal personality, marital quality, social support, and infant temperament: Their significance for mother-infant attachment in human families. In C. Pryce, R. Martin, & D. Skuse (Eds.), *Motherhood in human and nonhuman primates* (pp. 115–124). Basel, Switzerland: Kruger.

Belsky, J., & Rovine, M. (1988). Nonmaternal care in the first year of life and the security of infant-parent attachment. *Child Development, 59,* 157–167.

Belsky, J., Rovine, M., & Taylor, D. G. (1984). The Pennsylvania Infant and Family Development Project, III: The origins of individual differences in infant-mother attachment—maternal and infant contributions. *Child Development, 55,* 718–728.

Belsky, J., Spritz, B., & Crnic, K. (1996). Infant attachment security and affective-cognitive information processing at age 3. *Psychological Science, 7,* 111–114.

Bem, S. L. (1974). The measurement of psychological androgyny. *Journal of Consulting and Clinical Psychology, 42,* 155–162.

Bem, S. L. (1975). Sex-role adaptability: One consequence of psychological androgyny. *Journal of Personality and Social Psychology, 31,* 634–643.

Bem, S. L. (1978). Beyond androgyny: Some presumptuous prescriptions for a liberated sexual identity. In J. A. Sherman & F. L. Denmark (Eds.), *The psychology of women: Future directions in research.* New York: Psychological Dimensions.

Bem, S. L. (1983). Gender schema theory and its implications for child development: Raising gender aschematic children in a gender-schematic society. *Signs: Journal of Women in Culture and Society, 8,* 598–616.

Bem, S. L. (1989). Genital knowledge and gender constancy in preschool children. *Child Development, 60,* 649–662.

Benbow, C. P., & Arjimand, O. (1990). Predictors of high academic achievement in mathematics and science by mathematically talented students: A longitudinal study. *Journal of Educational Psychology, 82,* 430–441.

Bendig, A. W. (1958). Predictive and postdictive validity of need achievement measures. *Journal of Educational Research, 52,* 119–120.

Benenson, J. F., Apostoleris, N. H., & Parnass, J. (1997). Age and sex differences in dyadic and group interaction. *Developmental Psychology, 33,* 538–543.

Benoit D., & Parker, K. C. H. (1994). Stability and transmission of attachment across three generations. *Child Development, 65,* 1444–1456.

Berenbaum, S. A., & Snyder, A. (1995). Early hormonal influences on childhood sex-typed activity and playmate preferences: Implications for the development of sexual orientation. *Developmental Psychology, 31,* 31–42.

Bergen, D. J., & Williams, J. E. (1991). Sex stereotypes in the United States revisited: 1972–1988. *Sex Roles, 24,* 413–424.

Berkowitz, L. (1965). The concept of aggressive drive: Some additional considerations. In L. Berkowitz (Ed.), *Advances in experimental social psychology* (Vol. 2). Orlando, FL: Academic Press.

Berkowitz, L. (1974). Some determinants of impulsive aggression: Role of mediated association with reinforcement for aggression. *Psychological Review, 81,* 165–176.

Berkowitz, L. (1989). The frustration-aggression hypothesis: An examination and reformulation. *Psychological Bulletin, 106,* 59–73.

Berkowitz, M., & Gibbs, J. C. (1983). Measuring the developmental features of moral discussion. *Merrill-Palmer Quarterly, 29,* 399–410.

Berman, A. L., & Jobes, D. A. (1991). *Adolescent suicide: Assessment and intervention.* Washington, DC: American Psychological Association.

Bernal, M. E., & Knight, G. P. (1997). Ethnic identity of Latino children. In J. G. Garcia & M. C. Zea (Eds.), *Psychological interventions and research with Latino populations.* Boston: Allyn & Bacon.

Berndt, T. J. (1979). Developmental changes in conformity to peers and parents. *Developmental Psychology, 15,* 608–616.

Berndt, T. J. (1989). Friendships in childhood and adolescence. In W. Damon (Ed.), *Child development today and tomorrow.* San Francisco: Jossey-Bass.

Berndt, T. J. (1996). Friendship quality affects adolescents' self-esteem and social behavior. In W. M. Bukowski, A. F. Newcomb, & W. W. Hartup (Eds.), *The company they keep: Friendship during childhood and adolescence* (pp. 346–365). New York: Cambridge University Press.

Berndt, T. J., Hawkins, J. A., & Hoyle, S. G. (1986). Changes in friendship during a school year: Effects on children's and adolescents' impressions of friendship and sharing with friends. *Child Development, 57,* 1284–1297.

Berndt, T. J., & Hoyle, S. G. (1985). Stability and change in childhood and adolescent friendships. *Developmental Psychology, 21,* 1007–1015.

Berndt, T. J., & Keefe, K. (1995). Friends' influence on adolescents' adjustment to school. *Child Development, 66,* 1312–1329.

Berndt, T. J., & Perry, T. B. (1990). Distinctive features and effects of early adolescent friendships. In R. Montemayor, G. R. Adams, & T. P. Gulotta (Eds.), *From childhood to adolescence: A transitional period.* Newbury Park, CA: Sage.

Berry, J. W. (1967). Independence and conformity in subsistence-level societies. *Journal of Personality and Social Psychology, 7,* 415–418.

Berry, J. W., Poortinga, Y. H., Segall, M. H., & Dasen, P. R. (1992). *Cross-cultural psychology: Research and applications.* New York: Cambridge University Press.

Berscheid, E., & Reis, H. T. (1998). Attraction and close relationships. In D. T. Gilbert, S. T. Fiske, & G. Lindzey (Eds.), *Handbook of social psychology* (Vol. 2, pp. 193–281). New York: McGraw-Hill.

Best, D. L., Williams, J. E., Cloud, J. M., Davis, S. W., Robertson, L. S., Edwards, J. R., Giles, H., & Fowlkes, J. (1977). Development of sex-trait stereotypes among young children in the United States, England, and Ireland. *Child Development, 48,* 1375–1384.

Beyth-Marom, R., Austin, L., Fischoff, B., Palmgren, C., & Jacobs-Quadrel, M. (1993). Perceived consequences of risky behaviors: Adolescents and adults. *Developmental Psychology, 29,* 549–563.

Bianchi, S. M. (1995). The changing economic roles of women and men. In R. Farley (Ed.), *State of the union: America in the 1990s.* New York: Russell Sage.

Bianchi, S. M., Subaiya, L., & Kahn, J. (1997, March). *Economic well-being of husbands and wives after marital disruption.* Paper presented at the annual meeting of the Population Association of America, Washington, DC.

Bierman, K. L. (1986). Process of change during social skills training with preadolescents and its relation to treatment outcome. *Child Development, 57,* 230–240.

Bierman, K. L., & Furman, W. (1984). The effects of social skills training and peer involvement on the social adjustment of preadolescents. *Child Development, 55,* 157–162.

Biernat, M. (1991). Gender stereotypes and the relationship between masculinity and femininity: A developmental analysis. *Journal of Personality and Social Psychology, 61,* 351–365.

Bigler, R. S. (1995). The role of classification skill in moderating environmental influences on children's gender stereotyping: A study of the functional use of gender in the classroom. *Child Development, 66,* 1072–1087.

Bigler, R. S., & Liben, L. S. (1990). The role of attitudes and interventions in gender-schematic processing. *Child Development, 61,* 1440–1452.

Bigler, R. S., & Liben, L. S. (1992). Cognitive mechanisms in children's gender stereotyping: Theoretical and educational implications of a cognitive-based intervention. *Child Development, 63,* 1351–1363.

Bigler, R. S., & Liben, L. S. (1993). A cognitive-developmental approach to racial stereotyping and reconstructive memory in Euro-American children. *Child Development, 64,* 1507–1518.

Bigner, J. J., & Jacobsen, R. B. (1989). Parenting behaviors of homosexual and heterosexual fathers. *Journal of Homosexuality, 18,* 173–186.

Biller, H. B. (1993). *Fathers and families: Paternal factors in child development.* Westport, CT: Auburn House.

Bingham, C. R., & Crockett, L. J. (1996). Longitudinal adjustment patterns of boys and girls experiencing early, middle, and later sexual intercourse. *Developmental Psychology, 32,* 647–658.

Birch, L. L., & Billman, J. (1986). Preschool children's food sharing with friends and acquaintances. *Child Development, 57,* 387–395.

Birch, S. H., & Ladd, G. W. (1998). Children's interpersonal behaviors and the teacher-child relationship. *Developmental Psychology, 34,* 934–946.

Biringen, Z. (1990). Direct observation of maternal sensitivity and dyadic interactions in the home: Relations to maternal thinking. *Developmental Psychology, 26,* 278–284.

Bjorklund, D. F. (2000). *Children's thinking: Developmental function and individual differences* (3rd ed.). Pacific Grove, CA: Brooks/Cole.

Bjorklund, D. F., & Bjorklund, B. R. (1992). *Looking at children: An introduction to child development.* Pacific Grove, CA: Brooks/Cole.

Black-Gutman, D., & Hickson, F. (1996). The relationship between racial attitudes and social-cognitive development in children: An Australian study. *Developmental Psychology, 32,* 448–456.

Blakemore, J. E. O., LaRue, A. A., & Olejnik, A. B. (1979). Sex-appropriate toy preference and the ability to conceptualize toys as sex-role related. *Developmental Psychology, 15,* 339–340.

Blasi, A. (1980). Bridging moral cognition and moral action: A critical review of the literature. *Psychological Bulletin, 88,* 1–45.

Blasi, A. (1990). Kohlberg's theory and moral motivation. In D. Schrader (Ed.), *New directions for child development* (No. 47, pp. 51–57). San Francisco: Jossey-Bass.

Block, J., & Robins, R. W. (1993). A longitudinal study of consistency and change in self-esteem from early adolescence to early adulthood. *Child Development, 64,* 909–923.

Block, J. H. (1976). Issues, problems, and pitfalls in assessing sex differences: A critical review of The psychology of sex differences. *Merrill-Palmer Quarterly, 27,* 283–308.

Block, J. H., Block, J., & Gjerde, P. F. (1986). The personality of children prior to divorce: A prospective study. *Child Development, 57,* 827–840.

Block, J. H., Block, J., & Gjerde, P. F. (1988). Parental functioning and the home environment of families of divorce: Prospective and current analyses. *Journal of the American Academy of Child and Adolescent Psychiatry, 27,* 207–213.

Blount, R. (1986, May 4). "I'm about five years ahead of my age." *Atlanta Journal and Constitution,* p. C17.

Bogatz, G. A., & Ball, S. (1972). *The second year of Sesame Street: A continuing evaluation.* Princeton, NJ: Educational Testing Service.

Bogenschneider, K., Wu, M., Rafaelli, M., & Tsay, J. C. (1998). Parental influences on adolescent peer orientation and substance use: The interface of parenting practices and values. *Child Development, 69,* 1672–1688.

Bohlin, G., & Hagekull, B. (1993). Stranger wariness and sociability in the early years. *Infant Behavior and Development, 16,* 53–67.

Bohman, M., & Sigvardsson, S. (1990). Outcome in adoption: Lessons from longitudinal studies. In D. M. Brodzinsky (Ed.), *The psychology of adoption* (pp. 93–106). New York: Oxford University Press.

Boivin, M., & Hymel, S. (1997). Peer experiences and social self-perceptions: A sequential model. *Developmental Psychology, 33,* 135–145.

Boldizar, J. P. (1991). Assessing sex-typing and androgyny in children: The children's sex-role inventory. *Developmental Psychology, 27,* 505–515.

Boldizar, J. P., Perry, D. G., & Perry, L. C. (1989). Outcome values and aggression. *Child Development, 60,* 571–579.

Bolger, K. E., Patterson, C. J., & Kupersmidt, J. B.(1998). Peer relationships and self-esteem among children who have been maltreated. *Child Development, 69,* 1171–1197.

Bolger, K. E., Patterson, C. J., Thompson, W. W., & Kupersmidt, J. B. (1995). Psychosocial adjustment among children experiencing persistent intermittent family economic hardship. *Child Development, 66,* 1107–1129.

Boone, R. T., & Cunningham, J. G. (1998). Children's decoding of emotion in expressive body movement: The development of cue attunement. *Developmental Psychology, 34,* 1007–1016.

Booth, A., & Amato, P. (1991). Divorce and psychological stress. *Journal of Health and Social Behavior, 32,* 396–407.

Booth, A., & Edwards, J. N. (1992). Starting over: Why remarriages are more unstable. *Journal of Family Issues, 13,* 179–194.

Booth, C. L., Rubin, K. H., & Rose-Krasnor, L. (1998). Perceptions of emotional support from mother and friend in middle childhood: Links with social-emotional adaptation and preschool attachment security. *Child Development, 69,* 427–442.

Borstelmann, L. J. (1983). Children before psychology: Ideas about children from antiquity to the late 1800s. In P. H. Mussen (Ed.), *Handbook of child psychology* (Vol. 1). New York: Wiley.

Bost, K. K., Vaughn, B. E., Washington, W. N., Gielinski, K. L., & Bradbard, M. R. (1998). Social competence, social support, and attachment: Demarcation of construct domains, measurement, and paths of influence for preschool children attending Head Start. *Child Development, 69,* 192–218.

Bouchard, T. J., Jr., Lykken, D. T., McGue, M., Segal, N. L., & Tellegen, A. (1990). Sources of human psychological differences: The Minnesota study of twins reared apart. *Science, 250,* 223–228.

Bouchard, T. J., Jr., & McGue, M. (1981). Family studies of intelligence: A review. *Science, 212,* 1055–1059.

Bower, T. G. R. (1982). *Development in infancy.* New York: W. H. Freeman.

Bowlby, J. (1960). Separation anxiety. *International Journal of Psychoanalysis, 41,* 89–113.

Bowlby, J. (1969). *Attachment and loss. Vol. 1: Attachment.* London: Hogarth Press.

Bowlby, J. (1973). *Attachment and loss. Vol. 2: Separation: Anxiety and anger.* London: Hogarth Press.

Bowlby, J. (1980). *Attachment and loss. Vol. 3: Loss, sadness, and depression.* New York: Basic Books.

Bowlby, J. (1988). *A secure base: Clinical applications of attachment theory.* London: Routledge.

Boyatzis, C. J., Matillo, G. M., & Nesbitt, K. M. (1995). Effects of the "Mighty Morphin Power Rangers" on children's aggression with peers. *Child Study Journal, 25,* 44–55.

Boyes, M. C., & Chandler, M. (1992). Cognitive development, epistemic doubt, and identity formation in adolescence. *Journal of Youth and Adolescence, 21,* 277–304.

Boyes, M. C., & Walker, L. J. (1988). Implications of cultural diversity for the universality claims of Kohlberg's theory of moral reasoning. *Human Development, 31,* 44–59.

Brabeck, M. (1983). Moral judgment: Theory and research on differences between males and females. *Developmental Review, 3,* 274–291.

Bradbard, M. R., Martin, C. L., Endsley, R. C., & Halverson, C. F. (1986). Influence of sex stereotypes on children's exploration and memory: A competence versus performance distinction. *Developmental Psychology, 22,* 481–486.

Braddock, J. H., II, & McPartland, J. M. (1993). Education of early adolescents. *Review of Educational Research, 19,* 135–170.

Bradley, R. H., & Caldwell, B. M. (1984a). The HOME inventory and family demographics, *Developmental Psychology, 20,* 315–320.

Bradley, R. H., & Caldwell, B. M. (1984b). The relation of infants' home environments to achievement test performance in the first grade: A follow-up study. *Child Development, 55,* 803–809.

Bradley, R. H., Caldwell, B. M., & Rock, S. L. (1988). Home environment and school performance: A 10-year follow-up and examination of three models of environmental action. *Child Development, 59,* 852–867.

Bradley, R. H., Caldwell, B. M., Rock, S. L., Ramey, C. T., Barnard, K. E., Gray, C., Hammond, M. A., Mitchell, S., Gottfried, A. W., Siegel, L., & Johnson, D. L. (1989). Home environment and cognitive development in the first 3 years of life: A collaborative study involving six sites and three ethnic groups in North America. *Developmental Psychology, 25,* 217–235.

Bradley, S. J., Oliver, G. D., Chernick, A. B., & Zucker, K. J. (1998). Experiment of nurture: Ablatio penis at 2 months, sex reassignment at 7 months, and a psychosexual follow-up in young adulthood. *Pediatrics, 102,* 132–133.

Brand, E., Clingempeel, W. G., & Bowen-Woodward, K. (1988). Family relationships and children's psychological adjustment in stepmother and stepfather families: Findings and conclusions from the Philadelphia Stepfamily Research Project. In E. M. Hetherington & J. D. Arasteh (Eds.), *Impact of divorce, single-parenting, and stepparenting on children.* Hillsdale, NJ: Erlbaum.

Braungart, J. M., Plomin, R., DeFries, J. C., & Fulker, D. W. (1992). Genetic influence on tester-rated infant temperament as assessed by Bayley's Infant Behavior Record: Nonadoptive and adoptive siblings and twins. *Developmental Psychology, 28,* 40–47.

Brazelton, T. B. (1979). Behavioral competence of the newborn infant. *Seminars in Perinatology, 3,* 35–44.

Breland, H. M. (1974). Birth order, family configuration, and verbal achievement. *Child Development, 45,* 1011–1019.

Bretherton, I. (1985). Attachment theory: Retrospect and prospect. In I. Bretherton & E. Waters (Eds.), Growing points of attachment theory and research. *Monographs of the Society for Research in Child Development, 50* (Serial No. 209).

Bretherton, I. (1990). Open communication and internal working models: Their role in the development of attachment relationships. In R. A. Thompson (Ed.), Socioemotional development. *Nebraska Symposium on Motivation* (Vol. 36). Lincoln: University of Nebraska Press.

Bretherton, I. (1995). A communication perspective on attachment relationships and internal working models. In E. Waters, B. E. Vaughn, G. Posada, & K. Kondo-Ikemura (Eds.), Caregiving, cultural, and cognitive perspectives on secure-base behavior and working models: New growing points of attachment theory and research. *Monographs of the Society for Research in Child Development, 60,* (2–3, Serial No. 244).

Bretherton, I., Stolberg, U., & Kreye M. (1981). Engaging strangers in proximal interaction: Infants' social initiative. *Developmental Psychology, 17,* 746–755.

Brice-Heath, S. (1982). Questioning at home and at school: A comparative study. In G. Spindler (Ed.), *Doing the ethnography of schooling: Educational anthropology in action.* New York: Holt, Rinehart & Winston.

Brice-Heath, S. (1989). Oral and literate traditions among black Americans living in poverty. *American Psychologist, 44,* 367–373.

Bridges, L. J., & Grolnick, W. J. (1995). The development of emotional self-regulation in infancy and early childhood. In N. Eisenberg (Ed.), *Social development: Vol 15. Review of personality and social psychology.* Thousand Oaks, CA: Sage.

Broberg, A. G., Wessels, H., Lamb, M. E., & Hwang, C. P. (1997). Effects of day care on the cognitive development of 8-year-olds: A longitudinal study. *Developmental Psychology, 33,* 62–69.

Brockington, I. (1996). *Motherhood and mental health.* Oxford, England: Oxford University Press.

Brody, G. H., & Flor, D. L. (1998). Maternal resources, parenting practices, and child competence in rural single-parent African American families. *Child Development, 69,* 803–816.

Brody, G. H., Graziano, W. G., & Musser, L. M. (1983). Familiarity and children's behavior in same-age and mixed-age peer groups. *Developmental Psychology, 19,* 568–576.

Brody, G. H., & Shaffer, D. R. (1982). Contributions of parents and peers to children's moral socialization. *Developmental Review, 2,* 31–75.

Brody, G. H., Stoneman, Z., & Flor, D. (1996). Parental religiosity, family processes, and youth competence in rural, two-parent African-American families. *Developmental Psychology, 32,* 696–706.

Brody, G. H., Stoneman, Z., & McCoy, J. K. (1994). Forecasting sibling relationships in early adolescence from child temperaments and family processes in middle childhood. *Child Development, 65,* 771–784.

Brodzinsky, D. M., Radice, C., Huffman, L., & Merkler, K. (1987). Prevalence of clinically significant symptomatology in nonclinical samples of adopted and nonadopted children. *Journal of Clinical Child Psychology, 16,* 350–356.

Bronfenbrenner, U. (1970a). *Two worlds of childhood: U.S. and U.S.S.R.* New York: Russell Sage Foundation.

Bronfenbrenner, U. (1970b). *Who cares for America's children?* Invited address presented at the Conference of the National Association for the Education of Young Children, Washington, DC.

Bronfenbrenner, U. (1977). Toward an experimental ecology of human development. *American Psychologist, 32,* 513–531.

Bronfenbrenner, U. (1979). *The ecology of human development.* Cambridge, MA: Harvard University Press.

Bronfenbrenner, U. (1986). Ecology of the family as a context for human development: Research perspectives. *Developmental Psychology, 22,* 723–742.

Bronfenbrenner, U. (1989). Ecological systems theory. In R. Vasta (Ed.), *Annals of child development: Theories of child development: Revised formulations and current issues* (Vol. 6, pp. 187–251). Greenwich, CT: JAI Press.

Bronfenbrenner, U. (1993). The ecology of cognitive development: Research models and fugitive findings. In R. H. Wozniak & K. W. Fisher (Eds.), *Development in context* (pp. 3–44). Hillsdale, NJ: Erlbaum.

Bronfenbrenner, U. (1995). The bioecological model from a life course perspective: Reflections of a participant observer. In P. Moen, G. H. Elder, Jr., & K. Luscher (Eds.), *Examining lives in context* (pp. 599–618). Washington, DC: American Psychological Association.

Bronfenbrenner, U., & Ceci, S. J. (1994). Nature-nurture reconceptualized in developmental perspective: A bioecological model. *Psychological Review, 101,* 568–586.

Bronfenbrenner, U., & Neville, P. R. (1995). America's children and families: An international perspective. In S. L. Kagan & B. Weissbourd (Eds.), *Putting families first* (pp. 3–27). San Francisco: Jossey-Bass.

Brookover, W., Beady, C., Flood, P., Schweitzer, J., & Wisenbaker, J. (1979). *School social systems and student achievement: Schools can make a difference.* New York: Praeger.

Brooks-Gunn, J., Klebanov, P. K., & Duncan, G. J. (1996). Ethnic differences in children's intelligence test scores: Role of economic deprivation, home environment, and maternal characteristics. *Child Development, 67,* 396–408.

Brophy, J. E. (1983). Research on the self-fulfilling prophecy and teacher expectations. *Journal of Educational Psychology, 75,* 631–661.

Broverman, I. K., Vogel, S. R., Clarkson, F. E., & Rosenkrantz, P. S. (1972). Sex-role stereotypes: A current appraisal. *Journal of Social Issues, 28,* 59–78.

Brown, B. B. (1990). Peer groups. In S. Feldman & G. Elliott (Eds.), *At the threshold: The developing adolescent.* Cambridge, MA: Cambridge University Press.

Brown, B. B., Clasen, D. R., & Eicher, S. A. (1986). Perceptions of peer pressure, peer conformity dispositions, and self-reported behavior among adolescents. *Developmental Psychology, 22,* 521–530.

Brown, B. B., & Lohr, M. J. (1987). Peer-group affiliation and adolescent self-esteem: An integration of ego-identity and symbolic-interaction theories. *Journal of Personality and Social Psychology, 52,* 47–55.

Brown, B. B., Mory, M. S., & Kinney, D. (1994). Casting adolescent crowds in a relational perspective: Caricature, channel, and context. In R. Montemayor, G. R. Adams, & T. P. Gulotta (Eds.), *Personal relationships during adolescence.* Thousand Oaks, CA: Sage.

Brown, B. B., Mounts, N., Lamborn, S. D., & Steinberg, L. (1993). Parenting practices and peer group affiliation in adolescence. *Child Development, 64,* 467–482.

Brown, J. D. (1998). *The self.* New York: McGraw-Hill.

Brown, J. R., & Dunn, J. (1996). Continuities in emotion understanding from three to six years. *Child Development, 67,* 789–802.

Brown, P., & Elliot, R. (1965). Control of aggression in a nursery school class. *Journal of Experimental Child Psychology, 2,* 103–107.

Brownell, C. A. (1986). Convergent developments: Cognitive-developmental correlates of growth in infant/toddler peer skills. *Child Development, 57,* 275–286.

Brownell, C. A. (1990). Peer social skills in toddlers: Competencies and constraints illustrated by same-age and mixed-age interaction. *Child Development, 61,* 838–848.

Brownell, C. A., & Carriger, M. S. (1990). Changes in cooperation and self/other differentiation during the second year. *Child Development, 61,* 1164–1174.

Bruggerman, E. L., & Hart, K. J. (1996). Cheating, lying, and moral reasoning by religious and secular high school students. *Journal of Educational Research, 89,* 340–344.

Bruner, J. (1997). Celebrating divergence: Piaget and Vygotsky. *Human Development, 40,* 63–73.

Buchanan, C. M., Maccoby, E. E., & Dornbusch, S. M. (1991). Caught between parents: Adolescents' experiences in divorced homes. *Child Development, 62,* 1008–1029.

Buckner, J. C., Bassuk, E. L., Weinreb, L. F., & Brooks, M. G. (1999). Homelessness and its relation to the mental health and behavior of low-income school-age children. *Developmental Psychology, 35,* 246–257.

Bugental, D. B., Blue, J., & Cruzcosa, M. (1989). Perceived control over caregiving outcomes: Implications for child abuse. *Developmental Psychology, 25,* 532–539.

Buhrmester, D. (1990). Intimacy of friendship, interpersonal competence, and adjustment during preadolescence and adolescence. *Child Development, 61,* 1101–1111.

Buhrmester, D. (1996). Need fulfillment, interpersonal competence, and the developmental contexts of friendship. In. W. M. Bukowski, A. F. Newcomb, & W. M. Hartup (Eds.) *The company they keep: Friendship during childhood and adolescence* (pp. 158–185). New York: Cambridge University Press.

Buhrmester, D., & Furman, W. (1990). Perceptions of sibling relationships during middle childhood and adolescence. *Child Development, 61,* 1387–1398.

Bukowski, W. M., Gauze, C., Hoza, B., & Newcomb, A. F. (1993). Differences and consistency between same-sex and other-sex peer relationships during early adolescence. *Developmental Psychology, 29,* 253–263.

Bullock, M., & Lutkenhaus, P. (1990). Who Am I? Self understanding in toddlers. *Merrill-Palmer Quarterly, 36,* 217–238.

Bumpass, L. L. (1990). What's happening to the family? Interactions between demographic and institutional change. *Demography, 27,* 483–498.

Burchinal, M. R., Campbell, F. A., Bryant, D. M., Wasik, B. H., & Ramey, C. T. (1997). Early intervention and mediating processes in the cognitive performance of low-income African American families. *Child Development, 68,* 933–954.

Burchinal, M. R., Follmer, A., & Bryant, D. M. (1996). The relations of maternal social support and family structure with maternal responsiveness and child outcomes among African-American families. *Developmental Psychology, 32,* 1073–1083.

Burhans, K. K., & Dweck, C. S. (1995). Helplessness in early childhood: The role of contingent worth. *Child Development, 66,* 1719–1738.

Burkhardt, S. A., & Rotatori, A. F. (1995). *Treatment and prevention of childhood sexual abuse: A child-generated model.* Washington, DC: Taylor & Francis.

Burn, S., O'Neil, A. K., & Nederend, S. (1996). Childhood tomboyishness and adult androgeny. *Sex Roles, 34,* 419–428.

Burnette, E. (1997). Talking openly about race thwarts racism in children. *Monitor of the American Psychological Association, 28*(6), 33.

Burnham, D. K., & Harris, M. B. (1992). Effects of real gender and labeled gender on adults' perceptions of infants. *Journal of Genetic Psychology, 153,* 165–183.

Burns, L. H. (1990). An exploratory study of perceptions of parenting after infertility. *Family Systems Medicine, 8,* 177–189.

Burton, L. M. (1990). Teenage childrearing as an alternative life-course strategy in multigenerational black families. *Human Nature, 1,* 123–143.

Burton, R. V. (1963). The generality of honesty reconsidered. *Psychological Review, 70,* 481–499.

Burton, R. V. (1976). Honesty and dishonesty. In T. Lickona (Ed.), *Moral development and behavior.* New York: Holt, Rinehart & Winston.

Buss, A. H. (1961). *The psychology of aggression.* New York: Wiley.

Buss, A. H., & Plomin, R. (1984). *Temperament: Early developing personality traits.* Hillsdale, NJ: Erlbaum.

Buss, D. M. (1995). Psychological sex differences: Origins through sexual selection. *American Psychologist, 50,* 164–168.

Buss, K. A., & Goldsmith, H. H. (1998). Fear and anger regulation in infancy: Effects on temporal dynamics of affective expression. *Child Development, 69,* 359–374.

Bussey, K. (1992). Lying and truthfulness: Children's definitions, standards, and evaluative reactions. *Child Development, 63,* 129–137.

Bussey, K., & Bandura, A. (1992). Self-regulatory mechanisms governing gender development. *Child Development, 63,* 1236–1250.

Butler, R. (1989). Mastery versus ability appraisal: A developmental study of children's observations of peers' work. *Child Development, 60,* 1350–1361.

Butler, R. (1990). The effects of mastery and competitive conditions on self-assessment at different ages. *Child Development, 61,* 201–210.

Butler, R. (1992). What young people want to know and when: Effects of mastery and ability goals on different kinds of social comparison. *Journal of Personality and Social Psychology, 62,* 934–943.

Butler, R. (1999). Information seeking and achievement motivation in middle childhood and adolescence: The role of conceptions of ability. *Developmental Psychology, 35,* 146–163.

Butler, R., & Ruzany, N. (1993). Age and socialization effects on the development of social comparison motives and normative ability assessment in kibbutz and urban children. *Child Development, 64,* 532–543.

Butterworth, G. (1992). Origins of self-perception in infancy. *Psychological Inquiry, 3,* 103–111.

Buysse, V., & Bailey, D. B. (1993). Behavioral and developmental outcomes in young children with disabilities in integrated and segregated settings: A review of comparative studies. *Journal of Special Education, 26,* 434–461.

Bynner, J., O'Malley, P., & Bachman, J. (1981). Self-esteem and delinquency revised. *Journal of Youth and Adolescence, 10,* 407–441.

Byrnes, J. P., & Takahira, S. (1993). Explaining gender differences on SAT-math items. *Developmental Psychology, 29,* 805–810.

Cahan, S., & Cohen, N. (1989). Age versus schooling effects on intelligence development. *Child Development, 60,* 1239–1249.

Cairns, R. B., & Cairns, B. D. (1986). The developmental-interactional view of social behavior: Four issues of adolescent aggression. In D. Olweus, J. Block, & M. Radke-Yarrow (Eds.), *Development of antisocial and prosocial behavior: Research, theories, and issues.* New York: Academic Press.

Cairns, R. B., Cairns, B. D., Neckerman, H. J., Ferguson, L. L., & Gariepy, J. (1989). Growth and aggression: 1. Childhood to early adolescence. *Developmental Psychology, 25,* 320–330.

Cairns, R. B., Cairns, B. D., Neckerman, H. J., Gest, S. D., & Gariepy, J. (1988). Social networks and aggressive behavior: Peer support or peer rejection. *Developmental Psychology, 24,* 815–823.

Cairns, R. B., Leung, M., Buchanan, L., & Cairns, B. D. (1995). Friendships and social networks in childhood and adolescence: Fluidity, reliability, and interrelations. *Child Development, 66,* 1330–1345.

Caldera, Y. M., Huston, A. C., & O'Brien, M. (1989). Social interactions and play patterns of parents and toddlers with feminine, masculine, and neutral toys. *Child Development, 60,* 70–76.

Caldwell, B. M., & Bradley, R. H. (1984). *Manual for the Home Observation for Measurement of the Environment.* Little Rock: University of Arkansas Press.

Calkins, S. D., Fox, N. A., & Marshall, T. R. (1996). Behavioral and physiological antecedents of inhibited and uninhibited behavior. *Child Development, 67,* 523–540.

Call, K. T., Mortimer, J. T., & Shanahan, M. (1995). Helpfulness and the development of competence in adolescence. *Child Development, 66,* 129–138.

Campbell, D. T. (1965). Ethnocentric and other altruistic motives. In D. Levine (Ed.), *Nebraska Symposium on Motivation* (Vol. 13). Lincoln: University of Nebraska Press.

Campbell, F. A., & Ramey, C. T. (1994). Effects of early intervention on intellectual and academic achievement: A follow-up study of children from low-income families. *Child Development, 65,* 684–698.

Campbell, F. A., & Ramey, C. T. (1995). Cognitive and school outcomes for high-risk African-American students at middle adolescence: Positive effects of early intervention. *American Educational Research Journal, 32,* 743–772.

Campbell, S. B., Cohn, J. F., & Meyers, T. (1995). Depression in first-time mothers: Mother-infant interaction and depression chronicity. *Developmental Psychology, 31,* 349–357.

Campos, R., Raffaelli, M., Ude, W., Greco, M., Ruff, A., Rolf, J., Antunes, C., M., Halsley, N., Greco, D., & Associates (1994). Social networks and daily activities of street youth in Belo Horizonte, Brazil. *Child Development, 65,* 319–330.

Camras, L. A., Oster, H., Campos, J. J., Miyake, K., & Bradshaw, D. (1992). Japanese and American infants' responses to arm restraint. *Developmental Psychology, 28,* 578–583.

Canter, R. J., & Ageton, S. S. (1984). The epidemiology of adolescent sex-role attitudes. *Sex Roles, 11,* 657–676.

Capaldi, D. M., & Clark, S. (1998). Prospective family predictors of aggression toward female partners for at-risk young men. *Developmental Psychology, 34,* 1175–1188.

Capaldi, D. M., Crosby, L., & Stoolmiller, M. (1996). Predicting the timing of first sexual intercourse for at-risk adolescent males. *Child Development, 67,* 344–359.

Capaldi, D. M., & Patterson, G. R. (1991). Relation of parental transitions to boys' adjustment problems: I. A linear hypothesis. II. Mothers at risk for transition and unskilled parenting. *Developmental Psychology, 27,* 489–504.

Caplan, M., Vespo, J., Pedersen, J., & Hay, D. F. (1991). Conflict and its resolution in small groups of one- and two-year-olds. *Child Development, 62,* 1513–1524.

Carlo, G., Knight, G. P., Eisenberg, N., & Rotenberg, K. J. (1991). Cognitive processes and prosocial behaviors among children: The role of affective attributions and reconciliations. *Developmental Psychology, 27,* 456–461.

Carlo, G., Koller, S. H., Eisenberg, N., Da Silva, M. S., & Frohloch, C. B. (1996). A cross-national study on the relations between prosocial moral reasoning, gender role orientations, and prosocial behaviors. *Developmental Psychology, 32,* 231–240.

Carlson, E. A. (1998). A prospective longitudinal study of attachment disorganization/disorientation. *Child Development, 69,* 1107–1128.

Carlson, V., Cicchetti, D., Barnett, D., & Braunwald, K. (1989). Disorganized/ disoriented attachment relationships in maltreated infants. *Developmental Psychology, 25,* 525–531.

Carnegie Council on Adolescent Development. (1989). *Turning points: Preparing American youth for the 21st century.* Washington, DC: Carnegie Council on Adolescent Development.

Carson, J. L., & Parke, R. D. (1996). Reciprocal negative affect on parent-child interactions and children's peer competency. *Child Development, 67,* 2217–2226.

Casey, M. B. (1996). Understanding individual differences in spatial ability within females: A nature/nurture interactions framework. *Developmental Review, 16,* 241–260.

Casey, M. B., Nuttall, R. L., & Pezaris, E. (1997). Mediators of gender differences in mathematics college entrance test scores: A comparison of spatial skills with internalized beliefs and anxieties. *Developmental Psychology, 33,* 669–680.

Casey, W. M., & Burton, R. V., (1982). Training children to be consistently honest through verbal self-instructions. *Child Development, 53,* 911–919.

Caspi, A., Elder, G. H., Jr., & Bem, D. J. (1988). Moving away from the world: Life-course patterns of shy children. *Developmental Psychology, 24,* 824–831.

Caspi, A., Lynam, D., Moffitt, T. E., & Silva, P. A. (1993). Unraveling girls' delinquency: Biological, dispositional, and contextual contributors to adolescent misbehavior. *Developmental Psychology, 29,* 19–30.

Caspi, A., & Silva, P. A. (1995). Temperamental qualities at age three predict personality traits in young adulthood: Longitudinal evidence from a birth cohort. *Child Development, 66,* 486–498.

Cassidy, J., & Asher, S. R. (1992). Loneliness and peer relations in young children. *Child Development, 63,* 350–365.

Cassidy, J., & Berlin, L. J. (1994). The insecure/ambivalent pattern of attachment: Theory and research. *Child Development, 65,* 971–991.

Cassidy, J., Kirsh, S. J., Scolton, K. L., & Parke, R. D. (1996). Attachment and representations of peer relationships. *Developmental Psychology, 32,* 892–904.

Cassidy, J., Parke, R. D., Butkovsky, L., & Braungart, J. M. (1992). Family-peer connections: The roles of emotional expressiveness within the family and children's understanding of emotions. *Child Development, 63,* 603–618.

Cassidy, K. W. (1998). Preschoolers' use of desires to solve theory of mind problems in a pretense context. *Developmental Psychology, 34,* 503–511.

Cates, W., Jr. (1995). Sexually transmitted diseases. In B. P. Sachs, R. Beard, E. Papiernik, & C. Russell (Eds.), *Reproductive health care for women and babies* (pp. 57–84). New York: Oxford University Press.

Ceci, S. J. (1991). How much does schooling influence general intelligence and its cognitive components? A reassessment of the evidence. *Developmental Psychology, 27,* 703–722.

Ceci, S. J., & Williams, W. W. (1997). Schooling, intelligence, and income, *American Psychologist, 52,* 1051–1058.

Centers for Disease Control and Prevention. (1994). *HIV/AIDS Surveillance Report, 6*(1). Washington, DC: U.S. Government Printing Office.

Cervantes, C. A., & Callanan, M. A. (1998). Labels and explanations in mother-child emotion talk: Age and gender differentiation. *Developmental Psychology, 34,* 88–98.

Chadwick, B. A., & Heaton, T. B. (1992). *Statistical handbook on the American family.* Phoenix, AZ: Onyx Press.

Chalmers, J. B., & Townsend, M. A. R. (1990). The effects of training in social perspective taking on socially maladjusted girls. *Child Development, 61,* 178–190.

Chan, R. W., Raboy, B., & Patterson, C. J. (1998). Psychosocial adjustment among children conceived via donor insemination by lesbian and heterosexual mothers. *Child Development, 69,* 443–457.

Chandler, M. J. (1973). Egocentrism and antisocial behavior: The assessment and training of social perspective taking skills. *Developmental Psychology, 9,* 326–332.

Chandler, S., & Field, P. A. (1997). Becoming a father: First-time fathers' experience of labor and delivery. *Journal of Nurse-Midwifery, 42,* 17–24.

Chao, R. K. (1994). Beyond parental control and authoritarian parenting style: Understanding Chinese parenting through the cultural notion of training. *Child Development, 65,* 1111–1119.

Chapman, M., Zahn-Waxler, C., Cooperman, G., & Iannotti, R. J. (1987). Empathy and responsibility in the motivation of children's helping. *Developmental Psychology, 23,* 140–145.

Charlesworth, W. R. (1992). Darwin and developmental psychology: Past and present. *Developmental Psychology, 28,* 5–16.

Chase-Lansdale, P. L., Cherlin, A. J., & Kiernan, K. E. (1995). The long-term effects of parental divorce on the mental health of young adults: A developmental perspective. *Child Development, 66,* 1614–1634.

Chassin, L., Curran, P. J., Hussong, A. M., & Colder, C. R. (1996). The relation of parent alcoholism to adolescent substance use: A longitudinal follow-up study. *Journal of Abnormal Psychology, 105,* 70–80.

Chassin, L., Presson, C. C., Todd, M., Rose, J. S., & Sherman, S. J. (1998). Maternal socialization of adolescent smoking: The intergenerational transmission of parenting and smoking. *Developmental Psychology, 34,* 1189–1201.

Chen, C., Greenberger, E., Lester, J., Dong, Q., & Guo, M. (1998). A cross-cultural study of family and peer correlates of adolescent misconduct. *Developmental Psychology, 34,* 770–781.

Chen, C., & Stevenson, H. W. (1995). Motivation and mathematics achievement: A comparative study of Asian-American, Caucasian-American, and East Asian high school students. *Child Development, 66,* 1215–1234.

Chen, X., Hastings, P. D., Rubin, K. H., Chen, H., Cen, G., & Stewart, S. L. (1998). Child-rearing attitudes and behavioral inhibition in Chinese and Canadian toddlers: A cross-cultural study. *Developmental Psychology, 34,* 677–686.

Chen, X., Rubin, K. H., & Li, Z. (1995). Social functioning and adjustment in Chinese children: A longitudinal study. *Developmental Psychology, 31,* 531–539.

Chen, X., Rubin, K. H., & Li, D. (1997). Relation between academic achievement and social adjustment: Evidence from Chinese children. *Developmental Psychology, 33,* 518–525.

Chen, X., Rubin, K. H., & Sun, Y. (1992). Social reputation in Chinese and Canadian children: A cross-cultural study. *Child Development, 63,* 1336–1343.

Cherlin, A. J., & Furstenberg, F. F. (1994). Stepfamilies in the United States: A reconsideration. In J. Blake & J. Hagen (Eds.), *Annual review of sociology* (pp. 359–381). Palo Alto, CA: Annual Reviews.

Cherlin, A. J., Furstenberg, F. F., Jr., Chase-Lansdale, P. L., Kiernan, K. E., Robins, P. K., Morrison, D. R., & Teitler, J. O. (1991). Longitudinal studies of effects of divorce on children in Great Britain and the United States. *Science, 252,* 1386–1389.

Cherlin, A. J., Kiernan, K. E., & Chase-Lansdale, P. L. (1995). Parental divorce in childhood and demographic outcomes in young adulthood. *Demography, 32,* 299–318.

Chess, S., & Thomas, R. (1984). *Origins and evolution of behavior disorders.* New York: Brunner/Mazel.

Child, I. L. (1954). Socialization. In G. Lindzey (Ed.), *Handbook of social psychology.* Reading, MA: Addison-Wesley.

Chisholm, K. (1998). A three year follow-up of attachment and indiscriminate friendliness in children adopted from Romanian orphanages. *Child Development, 69,* 1092–1106.

Christopherson, E. R. (1989). Injury control. *American Psychologist, 44,* 237–241.

Cillessen, A. H. N., van IJzendoorn, H. W., van Lieshout, C. F. M., & Hartup, W. W. (1992). Heterogeneity among peer-rejected boys: Subtypes and stabilities. *Child Development, 63,* 893–905.

Clark, E. A., & Hanisee, J. (1982). Intellectual and adaptive performance of Asian children in adoptive American settings. *Developmental Psychology, 18,* 595–599.

Clark, K. B. (1965). *Dark ghetto.* New York: Harper & Row.

Clark, R., Hyde, J. S., Essex, M. J., & Klein, M. H. (1997). Length of maternity leave and quality of mother-infant interactions. *Child Development, 68,* 364–383.

Clarke, A. M., & Clarke, A. D. B. (1976). *Early experience: Myth and evidence.* New York: Free Press.

Clarke-Stewart, K. A. (1978). And daddy makes three: The father's impact on the mother and young child. *Child Development, 49,* 466–478.

Clarke-Stewart, A. (1989). Infant day care: Maligned or malignant. *American Psychologist, 44,* 266–273.

Clarke-Stewart, K. A. (1980). The father's contribution to children's cognitive and social development in early childhood. In F. A. Pedersen (Ed.), *The father-infant relationship: Observational studies in the family setting.* New York: Praeger.

Clarke-Stewart, A. (1993). *Daycare.* Cambridge, MA: Harvard University Press.

Clarke-Stewart, K. A., & Hayward, C. (1996). Advantages of father custody and contact for the psychological well-being of school-age children. *Journal of Applied Developmental Psychology, 17,* 239–270.

Clary, E. G., & Miller, J. (1986). Socialization and situational influences on sustained altruism. *Child Development, 57,* 1358–1369.

Clary, E. G., & Snyder, M. (1991). A functional analysis of altruism and prosocial behavior: The case of volunteerism. *Review of Personality and Social Psychology, 12,* 119–148.

Clausen, J. A. (1975). The social meaning of differential physical maturation. In D. Drugastin & G. H. Elder (Eds.), *Adolescence in the life cycle.* New York: Halsted Press.

Clements, D. H. (1990). Metacomponential development in a Logo programming environment. *Journal of Educational Psychology, 82,* 141–149.

Clements, D. H. (1991). Enhancement of creativity in computer environments. *American Educational Research Journal, 28,* 173–187.

Clements, D. H. (1995). Teaching creativity with computers. *Educational Psychology Review, 7,* 141–161.

Clements, D. H., & Nastasi, B. K. (1992). Computers and early childhood education. In M. Gettinger, S. N. Elliott, & T. R. Kratochwill (Eds.), *Advances in school psychology: Preschool and early childhood treatment directions.* Hillsdale, NJ: Erlbaum.

Cline, V. E., Croft, R. G., & Courrier, S. (1973). Desensitization of children to television violence. *Journal of Personality and Social Psychology, 27,* 360–365.

Clingempeel, W. G., Colyar, J. J., Brand, E., & Hetherington, E. M. (1992). Children's relationships with maternal grandparents: A longitudinal study of family structure and pubertal status effects. *Child Development, 63,* 1404–1422.

Clingempeel, W. G., & Segal, S. (1986). Stepparent-stepchild relationships and the psychological adjustment of children in stepmother and stepfather families. *Child Development, 57,* 474–484.

Coates, B., & Hartup, W. W. (1969). Age and verbalization in observational learning. *Developmental Psychology, 1,* 556–562.

Cohen, D., & Strayer, J. (1996). Empathy in conduct disordered and comparison youth. *Developmental Psychology, 32,* 988–998.

Cohen, P., Kasen, S., Brook, J. S., & Hartmark, C. (1998). Behavior patterns of young children and their offspring: A two-generation study. *Developmental Psychology, 34,* 1202–1208.

Coie, J. D., & Dodge, K. A. (1983). Continuities and changes in children's social status: A five-year longitudinal study. *Merrill-Palmer Quarterly, 19,* 261–282.

Coie, J. D., & Dodge, K. A., (1998). Aggression and antisocial behavior. In W. Damon (Series Ed.) & N. Eisenberg (Vol. Ed.), *Handbook of child psychology: Vol. 3. Social, emotional, and personality development* (5th ed., pp. 779–862). New York: Wiley.

Coie, J. D., Dodge, K. A., & Coppotelli, H. (1982). Dimensions and types of social status: A cross-age perspective. *Developmental Psychology, 18,* 557–570.

Coie, J. D., Dodge, K. A., & Kupersmidt, J. B. (1990). Peer group behavior and social status. In S. R. Asher & J. D. Coie (Eds.), *Peer rejection in childhood.* Cambridge, England: Cambridge University Press.

Coie, J. D., Dodge, K. A., Terry, R., & Wright, V. (1991). The role of aggression in peer relations: An analysis of aggression episodes in boys' play groups. *Child Development, 62,* 812–826.

Coie, J. D., & Koeppl, G. K. (1990). Adapting intervention to the problems of aggressive and disruptive rejected children. In S. R. Asher & J. D. Coie (Eds.), *Peer rejection in childhood.* New York: Cambridge University Press.

Coie, J. D., & Krehbiel, G. (1984). Effects of academic tutoring on the social status of low-achieving, socially rejected children. *Child Development, 55,* 1465–1478.

Coie, J. D., & Kupersmidt, J. B. (1983). A behavioral analysis of emerging social status in boys' groups. *Child Development, 54,* 1400–1416.

Colby, A., & Kohlberg, L. (1987). *The measurement of moral judgment* (Vol. 1): *Theoretical foundations and research validation.* Cambridge: Cambridge University Press.

Colby, A., Kohlberg, L., Gibbs, J., & Lieberman, M. (1983). A longitudinal study of moral judgment. *Monographs of the Society for Research in Child Development, 48* (Nos. 1–2, Serial No. 200).

Cole, P. M., Barrett, K. C., & Zahn-Waxler, C. (1992). Emotion displays in two-year-olds during mishaps. *Child Development, 63,* 314–324.

Cole, P. M., Michel, M. K., & Teti, L. O. (1994). The development of emotion regulation and dysregulation: A clinical perspective. In N. Fox (Ed.), The development of emotion regulation: Biological and behavioral considerations. *Monographs of the Society for Research in Child Development, 59* (Nos. 2–3, Serial No. 240).

Cole, P. M., & Putnam, F. W. (1992). Effect of incest on self and social functioning: A developmental psychopathology perspective. *Journal of Consulting and Clinical Psychology, 60,* 174–184.

Coleman, J. S., Campbell, E. Q., Hobson, C. J., McPartland, J., Mood, A. M., Weinfeld, F. D., & York, R. L. (1966). *Equality of educational opportunity.* Report from U.S. Office of Education. Washington, DC: U.S. Government Printing Office.

Coley, R. L. (1998). Children's socialization experiences and functioning in single-mother households: The importance of fathers and other men. *Child Development, 69,* 219–230.

Coley, R. L., & Chase-Lansdale, P. L. (1998). Adolescent pregnancy and parenthood: Recent evidence and future directions. *American Psychologist, 53,* 152–166.

Coll, C. G., Crnic, K., Lamberty, G., Wasik, B. H., Jenkins, R., Garcia, H. V., & McAdoo, H. P. (1996). An integrative model for the study of developmental competencies in minority children. *Child Development, 67,* 1891–1914.

Collins, W. A. (1983). Interpretation and inference in children's television viewing. In J. R. Bryant & D. R. Anderson (Eds.), *Children's understanding of television: Research on attention and comprehension.* New York: Academic Press.

Collins, W. A., Sobol, B. L., & Westby, S. (1981). Effects of adult commentary on children's comprehension and inferences about a televised aggressive portrayal. *Child Development, 52,* 158–163.

Collis, B. A. (1996). *Children and computers at school.* Mahwah, NJ: Erlbaum.

Committee on Adolescence. (1996). *Adolescent Suicide.* (Group for the Advancement of Psychiatry, Report No. 140). Washington, DC: American Psychiatric Press.

Comstock, G. A. (1993). *The medium and society: The role of television in American life.* In G. L. Berry & J. K. Asamen (Eds.), Children and television: Images in a changing sociocultural world (pp. 117–131). Newbury Park, CA: Sage.

Condry, J., & Condry, S. (1976). Sex differences: A study in the eye of the beholder. *Child Development, 47,* 812–819.

Condry, J. C., & Ross, D. F. (1985). Sex and aggression: The influence of gender label on the perception of aggression in children. *Child Development, 56,* 225–233.

Conger, R. D., Conger, K. J., Elder, G. H., Jr., Lorenz, F. O., Simons, R. L., & Whitbeck, L. B. (1992). A family process model of economic hardship and adjustment of early adolescent boys. *Child Development, 63,* 527–541.

Conger, R. D., Ge, X., Elder, G. H., Jr., Lorenz, F. O., & Simons, R. L. (1994). Economic stress, coercive family processes, and developmental problems of adolescents. *Child Development, 65,* 541–561.

Conger, R. D., Patterson, G. R., & Ge, X. (1995). It takes two to replicate: A mediational model for the impact of parents' stress on adolescent adjustment. *Child Development, 66,* 80–97.

Connell, J. P., Spencer, M. B., & Aber, J. L. (1994). Educational risk and resilience in African-American youth: Context, self, action, and outcomes in school. *Child Development, 65,* 493–506.

Connolly, J. A., & Doyle, A. (1984). Relation of social fantasy play to social competence in preschoolers. *Developmental Psychology, 20,* 797–806.

Coohey, C., & Braun, N. (1997). Toward an integrated framework for understanding child physical abuse. *Child Abuse and Neglect, 21,* 1081–1094.

Cook, T. D., Appleton, H., Conner, R. F., Shaffer, A., Tabkin, G., & Weber, J. S. (1975). *Sesame Street revisited.* New York: Russell Sage Foundation.

Cooke, T., & Apolloni, T. (1976). Developing positive social-emotional behaviors: A study of training and generalization effects. *Journal of Applied Behavior Analysis, 9,* 65–78.

Cooley, C. H. (1902). *Human nature and the social order.* New York: Scribner's.

Cooper, H. M. (1979). Pygmalion grows up: A model for teacher expectation, communication, and performance influence. *Review of Educational Research, 49,* 389–410.

Cooper, R. P., & Aslin, R. N. (1990). Preference for infant-directed speech in the first month after birth. *Child Development, 61,* 1585–1595.

Coopersmith, S. (1967). *The antecedents of self esteem.* New York: W.H. Freeman.

Corteen, R. S., & Williams, T. (1986). Television and reading skills. In T. Williams (Ed.), *The impact of television: A natural experiment in three communities.* Orlando, FL: Academic Press.

Corter, C. M., Zucker, K. J., & Galligan, R. F. (1980). Patterns in the infant's search for mother during brief episodes. *Developmental Psychology, 16,* 62–69.

Costabile, A., Smith, P. K., Matheson, L., Aston, J., Hunter, T., & Boulton, M. (1991). Cross-national comparison of how children distinguish serious and playful fighting. *Developmental Psychology, 27,* 881–887.

Costin, S. E., & Jones, D. C. (1992). Friendship as a facilitator of emotional responsiveness and prosocial interventions among young children. *Developmental Psychology, 28,* 941–947.

Cote, J. E., & Levine, C. (1988). A critical examination of the ego identity status paradigm. *Developmental Review, 8,* 147–184.

Coulton, C. J., Korbin, J. E., Su, M., & Chow, J. (1995). Community level factors and child maltreatment rates. *Child Development, 66,* 1262–1276.

Cousins, S. D. (1989). Culture and self-perception in Japan and the United States. *Journal of Personality and Social Psychology, 56,* 124–131.

Cowan, G., & Avants, S. K. (1988). Children's influence strategies: Structure, sex differences, and bilateral mother-child influences. *Child Development, 59,* 1303–1313.

Cox, M. J., Owen, M. T., Henderson, V. K., & Margand, N. A. (1992). Prediction of infant-father and infant-mother attachment. *Developmental Psychology, 28,* 474–483.

Cox, M. J., Owen, M. T., Lewis, J. M., & Henderson, V. K. (1989). Marriage, adult adjustment, and early parenting. *Child Development, 60,* 1015–1024.

Crain, R. M. (1996). The influence of age, race, and gender on child and adolescent multidimensional self-concept. In B. A. Bracken (Ed.), *Handbook of self-concept: Developmental, social, and clinical considerations.* New York: Wiley.

Crandall, V. C. (1967). Achievement behavior in young children. In *The young child: Reviews of research.* Washington, DC: National Association for the Education of Young Children.

Crandall, V. C. (1969). Sex differences in expectancy of intellectual and academic reinforcement. In C. P. Smith (Ed.), *Achievement-related motives in children.* New York: Russell Sage Foundation.

Crandall, V. C., Katkovsky, W., & Preston, A. A. (1960). A conceptual formulation of some research on children's achievement development. *Child Development, 31,* 787–797.

Crews, F. (1996). The verdict on Freud [Review of *Freud evaluated: The completed arc*]. *Psychological Science, 7,* 63–68.

Crick, N. R. (1996). The role of overt aggression, relational aggression, and prosocial behavior in the prediction of children's future social adjustment. *Child Development, 67,* 2317–2327.

Crick, N. R. (1997). Engagement in gender normative versus nonnormative forms of aggression: Links to social-psychological adjustment. *Developmental Psychology, 33,* 610–617.

Crick, N. R., Bigbee, M. A., & Howes, C. (1996). Gender differences in children's normative beliefs about aggression: How do I hurt thee? Let me count the ways. *Child Development, 67,* 1003–1014.

Crick, N. R., Casas, J. F., & Ku, H. (1999). Relational and physical forms of peer victimization in preschool. *Developmental Psychology, 35,* 376–385.

Crick, N. R., Casas, J. F., & Mosher, M. (1997). Relational and overt aggression in preschool. *Developmental Psychology, 33,* 579–588.

Crick, N. R., & Dodge, K. A., (1994). A review and reformulation of social information processing mechanisms in children's social adjustment. *Psychological Bulletin, 115,* 74–101.

Crick, N. R., & Dodge, K. A., (1996). Social information-processing mechanisms in reactive and proactive aggression. *Child Development, 67,* 993–1002.

Crick, N. R., & Grotpeter, J. K. (1995). Relational aggression, gender, and social-psychological adjustment. *Child Development, 66,* 710–722.

Crick, N. R., & Ladd, G. W. (1993). Children's perceptions of their peer experiences: Attributions, loneliness, social anxiety, and social avoidance. *Developmental Psychology, 29,* 244–254.

Crick, N. R., Wellman, N. E., Casas, J. F., O'Brien, K. M., Nelson, D. A., Grotpeter, J. K., & Markon, K. (1998). Childhood aggression and gender: A new look at an old problem. In D. Bernstein (Ed.), *Nebraska Symposium on Motivation:* Vol. 44. Lincoln: University of Nebraska Press.

Crockenberg, S., & Litman, C. (1990). Autonomy as competence in 2-year-olds: Maternal correlates of child defiance, compliance, and self-assertion. *Developmental Psychology, 26,* 961–971.

Crockenberg, S., & Litman, C. (1991). Effects of maternal employment on maternal and two-year-old child behavior. *Child Development, 61,* 930–953.

Cronbach, L. J., & Snow, R. E. (1977). *Aptitude and instructional methods: A handbook for research on interactions.* New York: Irvington.

Crook, C. (1992). Cultural artifacts in social development: The case of computers. In H. McGurk (Ed.), *Childhood social development: Contemporary perspectives.* Hove, England: Erlbaum.

Cross, W. E. (1985). Black identity: Rediscovering the distinction between personal identity and reference group orientation. In M. B. Spencer, G. K. Brookins, & W. R. Allen (Eds.), *Beginnings: The social and affective development of black children.* Hillsdale, NJ: Erlbaum.

Crouter, A. C., MacDermid, S. M., McHale, S. M., & Perry-Jenkins, M. (1990). Parental monitoring and perceptions of children's school performance and conduct in dual- and single-career families. *Developmental Psychology, 26,* 649–657.

Crouter, A. C., Manke, B. A., & McHale, S. M. (1995). The family context of gender intensification in early adolescence. *Child Development, 66,* 317–329.

Crowell, J. A., & Feldman, S. S. (1991). Mothers' working models of attachment relationships and mother and child behavior during separation and reunion. *Developmental Psychology, 27,* 597–605.

Crystal, D. S., Chen, C., Fuligni, A. J., Stevenson, H. W., Hsu, C., Ko, H., Kitamura, S., & Kimura, S. (1994). Psychological maladjustment and academic achievement: A cross-cultural study of Japanese, Chinese, and American high school students. *Child Development, 65,* 738–753.

Crystal, D. S., Watanabe, H., Weinfert, K., & Wu, C. (1998). Concepts of human differences: A comparison of American, Japanese and Chinese children and adolescents. *Developmental Psychology, 34,* 714–722.

Culp, R. E., Little, V., Letts, D., & Lawrence, H. (1991). Maltreated children's self-concept: Effects of a comprehensive treatment program. *American Journal of Orthopsychiatry, 61,* 114–121.

Cummings, E. M., & Davies, P. T. (1994). *Children and marital conflict: The impact of family dispute and resolution.* New York: Guilford Press.

Cummings, E. M., Iannotti, R. J., & Zahn-Waxler, C. (1989). Aggression between peers in early childhood: Individual continuity and developmental change. *Child Development, 60,* 887–895.

Dabbs, J. M., Jr., Carr, T. S., Frady, F. L., & Riad, J. K. (1995). Testosterone, crime, and misbehavior among 692 male prison inmates. *Personality and Individual Differences, 18,* 627–633.

Dabbs, J. M., & Morris, R. (1990). Testosterone, social class, and antisocial behavior in a sample of 4,462 men. *Psychological Science, 1,* 209–211.

Damon, W. (1977). *The social world of the child.* San Francisco: Jossey-Bass.

Damon, W. (1988). *The moral child.* New York: Free Press.

Damon, W., & Hart, D. (1988). *Self-understanding in childhood and adolescence.* New York: Cambridge University Press.

Daniels, D. (1986). Differential experiences of siblings in the same family as predictors of adolescent sibling personality differences. *Journal of Personality and Social Psychology, 51,* 339–346.

Daniels, D., & Plomin, R. (1985a). Differential experience of siblings in the same family. *Developmental Psychology, 21,* 747–760.

Daniels, D., & Plomin, R. (1985b). Origins of individual differences in infant shyness. *Developmental Psychology, 21,* 118–121.

Darling, C. A., Davidson, J. K., & Passarello, L. C. (1992). The mystique of first intercourse among college youth: The role of partners, contraceptive practices, and psychological reactions. *Journal of Youth and Adolescence, 21,* 97–117.

Darlington, R. B. (1991). The long-term effects of model preschool programs. In L. Okagaki & R. J. Sternberg (Eds.), *Directors of development. Influences on the development of children's thinking.* Hillsdale, NJ: Erlbaum.

Darwin, C. A. (1877). A biographical sketch of an infant. *Mind, 2,* 285–294.

Das Eiden, R., Teti, D. M., & Corns, K. M. (1995). Maternal working models of attachment, marital adjustment, and the parent-child relationship. *Child Development, 66,* 1504–1518.

Daubman, K., Heatherington, L., & Ahn, A. (1992). Gender and the self-presentation of academic achievement. *Sex Roles, 27,* 187–204.

David, H. P. (1992). Born unwanted: Long-term developmental effects of denied abortion. *Journal of Social Issues, 48,* 163–181.

David, H. P. (1994). Reproductive rights and reproductive behavior: Clash or convergence of private values and public policies. *American Psychologist, 49,* 343–349.

Davies, P. T., & Cummings, E. M. (1998). Exploring children's emotional insecurity as a mediator of the link between marital relations and child adjustment. *Child Development, 69,* 124–139.

Davis, T. L. (1995). Gender differences in masking negative emotions: Ability or motivation? *Developmental Psychology, 31,* 660–667.

DeAngelis, T. (1997a). Chromosomes contain clues on schizophrenia. *Monitor of the American Psychological Association, 28*(1), 26.

DeAngelis, T. (1997b). When children don't bond with parents. *Monitor of the American Psychological Association, 28*(6), 10–12.

Deater-Deckard, K., & Dodge, K. A. (1997). Externalizing behavior problems and discipline revisited: Nonlinear effects and variation by culture, context, and gender. *Psychological Inquiry, 8,* 161–175.

DeBerry, K. M., Scarr, S., & Weinberg, R. (1996). Family racial socialization and ecological competence: Longitudinal assessments of African-American transracial adoptees. *Child Development, 67,* 2375–2399.

de Gaston, J. P., Jensen, L., & Weed, S. (1995). A closer look at adolescent sexual activity. *Journal of Youth and Adolescence, 24,* 465–479.

DeKlyen, M., Biernbrum, M. A., Speltz, M. L., & Greenberg, M. T. (1998). Fathers and preschool behavior problems. *Developmental Psychology, 34,* 264–275.

Dekovic, M., & Janssens, J. M. A. M. (1992). Parents' child-rearing style and children's sociometric status. *Developmental Psychology, 28,* 925–932.

deMause, L. (1974). The evolution of childhood. In L. deMause (Ed.), *The history of childhood.* New York: Harper & Row.

Demo, D. H., & Acock, A. C. (1996). Family structure, family process, and adolescent well-being. *Journal of Research on Adolescence, 6,* 457–488.

Denham, S. A., McKinley, M., Couchoud, E. A., & Holt, R. (1990). Emotional and behavioral predictors of preschool peer ratings. *Child Development, 61,* 1145–1152.

Denham, S. A., Zoller, D., & Couchoud, E. A. (1994). Socialization of preschoolers' emotion understanding. *Developmental Psychology, 30,* 928–936.

Despert, J. L. (1965). *The emotionally disturbed child: Then and now.* New York: Brunner/Mazel.

Dewsbury, D. A. (1992). Comparative psychology and ethology: A reassessment. *American Psychologist, 47,* 208–215.

De Wolff, M. S., & van IJzendoorn, M. H. (1997). Sensitivity and attachment: A meta-analysis of parental antecedents of infant attachment. *Child Development, 68,* 571–591.

Diamond, L. M. (1998). Development of sexual orientation among adolescent and young adult women. *Developmental Psychology, 34,* 1085–1095.

Diamond, M., & Sigmundson, H. K. (1997). Sex reassignment at birth: Long-term review and clinical implications. *Archives of Pediatric and Adolescent Medicine, 151,* 298–304.

Diener, E., Sandvik, E., & Larsen, R. J. (1985). Age and sex effects for emotional intensity. *Developmental Psychology, 21,* 542–546.

DiLalla, L. F., Kagan, J., & Reznick, J. S. (1994). Genetic etiology of behavioral inhibition among 2-year-old children. *Infant Behavior and Development, 17,* 405–412.

Dillon, P. A., & Emery, R. E. (1996). Divorce mediation and resolution of child custody disputes: Long-term effects. *American Journal of Orthopsychiatry, 66,* 131–140.

DiPietro, J. A., Hodgson, D. M., Costigan, K. A., Hilton, S. C., & Johnson, T. R. B. (1996). Fetal neurobehavioral development. *Child Development, 67,* 2553–2567.

Dishion, T. J. (1990). The family ecology of boys' peer relations in middle childhood. *Child Development, 61,* 874–892.

Dishion, T. J., Andrews, D. W., & Crosby, L. (1995). Antisocial boys and their friends in early adolescence: Relationship characteristics, quality, and interactional processes. *Child Development, 66,* 139–151.

Dishion, T. J., Patterson, G. R., Stoolmiller, M., & Skinner, M. L. (1991). Family, school, and behavioral antecedents to early adolescent involvement with antisocial peers. *Developmental Psychology, 27,* 172–180.

Dittman, R. W., Kappes, M. E., & Kappes, M. H. (1992). Sexual behavior in adolescent and adult females with congenital adrenal hyperplasia. *Psychoneuroendocrinology, 17,* 153–170.

Dix, T. H. (1991). The affective organization of parenting: Adaptive and maladaptive processes. *Psychological Bulletin, 110,* 3–25.

Dodge, K. A. (1980). Social cognition and children's aggressive behavior. *Child Development, 51,* 162–170.

Dodge, K. A. (1983). Behavioral antecedents of peer social status. *Child Development, 54,* 1386–1399.

Dodge, K. A. (1986). A social information processing model of social competence in children. In M. Perlmutter (Ed.), *Minnesota symposia on child psychology* (Vol. 18). Hillsdale, NJ: Erlbaum.

Dodge, K. A. (1990). Nature versus nurture in childhood conduct disorder: It is time to ask a different question. *Developmental Psychology, 26,* 698–701.

Dodge, K. A. (1998). Emotion and social information-processing. In J. Garber & K. A. Dodge (Eds.), *The development of emotion regulation and deregulation.* New York: Cambridge University Press.

Dodge, K. A., Coie, J. D., Pettit, G. S., & Price, J. M. (1990). Peer status and aggression in boys' groups: Developmental and contextual analyses. *Child Development, 61,* 1289–1309.

Dodge, K. A., Murphy, R. R., & Buchsbaum, K. (1984). The assessment of intention-cue detection skills in children: Implications for developmental psychopathology. *Child Development, 55,* 163–173.

Dodge, K. A., Pettit, G. S., & Bates, J. E. (1994). Socialization mediators of the relation between socioeconomic status and child conduct problems. *Child Development, 65,* 649–665.

Doherty, W. J., & Needle, R. H. (1991). Psychological adjustment and substance abuse among adolescents before and after a parental divorce. *Child Development, 62,* 328–337.

Dollard, J., Doob, L. W., Miller, N. E., Mowrer, O. H., & Sears, R. R. (1939). *Frustration and aggression.* New Haven, CT: Yale University Press.

Dornbusch, S. M., Carlsmith, J. M., Bushwall, S. J., Ritter, P. L., Leiderman, H., Hastorf, A. H., & Gross, R. T. (1985). Single parents, extended households, and the control of adolescents. *Child Development, 56,* 326–341.

Dornbusch, S. M., Glasgow, K. L., & Lin, I. (1996). The social structure of schooling. *Annual Review of Psychology, 47,* 401–429.

Dossey, J. A., Mullis, I. V. S., Lindquist, M. M., & Chambers, D. L. (1988). *The Mathematics Report Card: Are we measuring up?* Princeton, NJ: Educational Testing Service.

Downey, G., Lebolt, A., Rincon, C., & Freitas, A. L. (1998). Rejection sensitivity and children's interpersonal difficulties. *Child Development, 69,* 1074–1091.

Downing, L. L. (1999). *Fragile realities: Conversion and commitment in cults and other powerful groups.* State University of New York at Oneonta.

Doyle, A. B., & Aboud, F. E. (1995). A longitudinal study of white children's racial prejudice as a social-cognitive development. *Merrill-Palmer Quarterly, 41,* 209–228.

Doyle, A. B., Doehring, P., Tessier, O., de Lorimier, S., & Shapiro, S. (1992). Transitions in children's play: A sequential analysis of states preceding and following social pretense. *Developmental Psychology, 28,* 137–144.

Drabman, R. S., & Thomas, M. H. (1974). Does media violence increase children's toleration of real-life aggression? *Developmental Psychology, 10,* 418–421.

Dreyer, P. H. (1982). Sexuality during adolescence. In B. B. Wolman (Ed.), *Handbook of developmental psychology.* New York: Wiley.

Droege, K. L., & Stipek, D. J. (1993). Children's use of dispositions to predict classmates' behavior. *Developmental Psychology, 29,* 646–654.

Drotar, D. (1992). Personality development, problem solving, and behavior problems among preschool children with early histories of nonorganic failure-to-thrive. *Developmental and Behavioral Pediatrics, 13,* 266–273.

Dubas, J. S., Graber, J. A., & Petersen, A. C. (1991). The effects of pubertal development on achievement during adolescence. *American Journal of Education, 99,* 444–460.

Duke, P. M., Carlsmith, J. M., Jennings, D., Martin, J. A., Dornbusch, S. M., Gross, R. T., & Siegel-Gorelick, B. (1982). Educational correlates of early and late sexual maturation in adolescence. *Journal of Pediatrics, 100,* 633–637.

Duncan, G. J., Brooks-Gunn, J., & Klebanov, P. K. (1994). Economic deprivation and early childhood development. *Child Development, 65,* 296–318.

Dunn, J., & Plomin, R. (1990). *Separate lives: Why siblings are so different.* New York: Basic Books.

Dunn, J. (1993). *Young children's close relationships. Beyond attachment.* Newbury Park, CA: Sage.

Dunn, J. (1994). Changing minds and changing relationships. In C. Lewis & P. Mitchel (Eds.), *Children's early understanding of mind: Origins and development* (pp. 297–310). Hove: Erlbaum.

Dunn, J., Brown, J., & Beardsall, L. (1991). Family talk about feeling states and children's later understanding of children's emotions. *Developmental Psychology, 27,* 448–455.

Dunn, J., Brown, J. R., & Maguire, M. (1995). The development of children's moral sensibility: Individual differences and emotional understanding. *Developmental Psychology, 31,* 649–659.

Dunn, J., & Kendrick, C. (1982). *Siblings: Love, envy, and understanding.* Cambridge, MA: Harvard University Press.

Dunn, J., & Munn, P. (1985). Becoming a family member: Family conflict and the development of social understanding in the second year. *Child Development, 56,* 480–492.

Dunn, J., Slomkowski, C., & Beardsall, L. (1994). Sibling relationships from the preschool period through middle childhood and early adolescence. *Developmental Psychology, 30,* 315–324.

Dunphy, D. C. (1963). The social structure of urban adolescent peer groups. *Sociometry, 26,* 230–246.

Dusek, J. B. (1991). *Adolescent development and behavior* (2nd ed.). Englewood Cliffs, NJ: Prentice-Hall.

Dweck, C. S. (1975). The role of expectations and attributions in the alleviation of learned helplessness. *Journal of Personality and Social Psychology, 31,* 674–685.

Dweck, C. S. (1978). Achievement. In M. E. Lamb (Ed.), *Social and personality development.* New York: Holt, Rinehart and Winston.

Dweck, C. S., Davidson, W., Nelson, S., & Enna, B. (1978). Sex differences in learned helplessness: II. The contingencies of evaluative feedback in the classroom; III. An experimental analysis. *Developmental Psychology, 14,* 268–276.

Dweck, C. S., & Elliott, E. S. (1983). Achievement motivation. In P. H. Mussen (Ed.), *Handbook of child psychology. Vol. 4: Socialization, personality, and social development.* New York: Wiley.

Dweck, C. S., & Leggett, E. L. (1988). A social-cognitive approach to motivation and personality. *Psychological Review, 95,* 256–273.

Eagly, A. H. (1995). The science and politics of comparing men and women. *American Psychologist, 50,* 145–158.

East, P. L. (1996). The younger sisters of childbearing adolescents: Their attitudes, expectations, and behaviors. *Child Development, 67,* 267–282.

East, P. L., & Rook, K. S. (1992). Compensatory patterns of support among children's peer relationships: A test using school friends, nonschool friends, and siblings. *Developmental Psychology, 28,* 163–172.

Easterbrooks, M. A., & Goldberg, W. A. (1984). Toddler development in the family: Impact of father involvement and parenting characteristics. *Child Development, 55,* 740–752.

Eaton, W. O., & Enns, L. R. (1986). Sex differences in human motor activity level. *Psychological Bulletin, 100,* 19–28.

Eaton, W. O., & Yu, A. P. (1989). Are sex differences in child motor activity level a function of sex differences in maturational status? *Child Development, 60,* 1005–1011.

Eccles, J. S., Flanagan, C., Lord, S., & Midgley, C. (1996). Schools, families, and early adolescents: What are we doing wrong and what can we do instead? *Journal of Developmental and Behavioral Pediatrics, 17,* 267–276.

Eccles, J. S., & Harold, R. D. (1993). Parent-school involvement during the early adolescent years. *Teachers College Record, 94,* 568–587.

Eccles, J. S., Jacobs, J. E., & Harold, R. D. (1990). Gender role stereotypes, expectancy effects, and parents' socialization of gender differences. *Journal of Social Issues, 46,* 183–201.

Eccles, J. S., Lord, S., & Midgley, C. (1991). What are we doing to early adolescents? The impact of educational contexts on early adolescents. *American Journal of Education, 99,* 521–542.

Eccles, J. S., Midgley, C., Wigfield, A., Buchanan, C. M., Reuman, D., Flanagan, C., & Mac Iver, D. (1993). Development during adolescence: The impact of stage-environment fit on young adolescents' experiences in schools and in families. *American Psychologist, 48,* 90–101.

Eccles, J. S., Wigfield, A., Harold, R. D., & Blumefeld, P. (1993). Age and gender differences in children's self- and task perceptions during elementary school. *Child Development, 64,* 830–847.

Eckenrode, J., Laird, M., & Doris, J. (1993). School performance and disciplinary problems among abused and neglected children. *Developmental Psychology, 29,* 53–62.

Eckerman, C. O., & Didow, S. M. (1996). Nonverbal imitation and toddlers' mastery of verbal means of achieving coordinated action. *Developmental Psychology, 32,* 141–152.

Eckerman, C. O., & Stein, M. R. (1990). How imitation begets imitation and toddlers' generation of games. *Developmental Psychology, 26,* 370–378.

Eder, R. A. (1989). The emergent personalogist: The structure and content of 3½-, 5½-, and 7½-year-olds' concepts of themselves and other persons. *Child Development, 60,* 1218–1228.

Eder, R. A. (1990). Uncovering young children's psychological selves: Individual and developmental differences. *Child Development, 61,* 849–863.

Egan, S. K., & Perry, D. G. (1998). Does low self-regard invite victimization? *Developmental Psychology, 34,* 299–309.

Egeland, B., Jacobvitz, D., & Sroufe, L. A. (1988). Breaking the cycle of abuse. *Child Development, 59,* 1080–1088.

Eggebeen, D. J., & Lichter, D. T. (1991). Race, family structure, and changing poverty among American children. *American Sociological Review, 56,* 801–817.

Ehrhardt, A. A. (1985). The psychobiology of gender. In A. S. Rossi (Ed.), *Gender and the life course.* New York: Aldine.

Ehrhardt, A. A., & Baker, S. W. (1974). Fetal androgens, human central nervous system differentiation, and behavioral sex differences. In R. C. Friedman, R. M. Rickard, & R. L. Van de Wiele (Eds.), *Sex differences in behavior.* New York: Wiley.

Eisenberg, N. (1983). Children's differentiations among potential recipients of aid. *Child Development, 54,* 594–602.

Eisenberg, N., & Fabes, R. A. (1998). Prosocial development. In W. Damon (Series Ed.), & N. Eisenberg (Vol. Ed.), *Handbook of child psychology:* Vol. 3. *Social, emotional, and personality development* (5th ed., pp. 701–778). New York: Wiley.

Eisenberg, N., Fabes, R. A., Carlo, G., Troyer, D., Speer, A. L., Karbon, M., & Switzer, G. (1992). The relations of maternal practices and characteristics to children's vicarious emotional responsiveness. *Child Development, 63,* 583–602.

Eisenberg, N., Fabes, R. A., Miller, P. A., Shell, R., Shea, C., & May-Plumlee, T. (1990). Preschoolers' vicarious emotional responding and their situational and dispositional prosocial behavior. *Merrill-Palmer Quarterly, 36,* 507–529.

Eisenberg, N., Fabes, R. A., Murphy, B., Maszk, P., Smith, M., & Karbon, M. (1995). The role of emotionality and regulation in children's social functioning: A longitudinal study. *Child Development, 66,* 1360–1384.

Eisenberg, N., Fabes, R. A., Schaller, M., Carlo, G., & Miller, P. A. (1991). The relations of parental characteristics and practices in children's vicarious emotional responding. *Child Development, 62,* 1393–1408.

Eisenberg, N., Fabes, R. A., Shepard, S. A., Murphy, B. C., Jones, S., & Guthrie, I. K. (1998). Contemporaneous and longitudinal prediction of children's sympathy from dispositional regulation and emotionality. *Developmental Psychology, 34,* 910–924.

Eisenberg, N., Guthrie, I. K., Fabes, R. A., Reiser, M., Murphy, B. C., Holgren, R., Maszk, P., & Losoya, S. (1997). The relations of regulation and emotionality to resiliency and competent social functioning in elementary school children. *Child Development, 68,* 295–311.

Eisenberg, N., Lennon, R., & Roth, K. (1983). Prosocial development: A longitudinal study. *Developmental Psychology, 19,* 846–855.

Eisenberg, N., Miller, P. A., Shell, R., McNalley, S., & Shea, C. (1991). Prosocial development in adolescence: A longitudinal study. *Developmental Psychology, 27,* 849–857.

Eisenberg, N., Murray, E., & Hite, T. (1982). Children's reasoning regarding sex-typed toy choices. *Child Development, 53,* 81–86.

Eisenberg, N., Schaller, M., Fabes, R. A., Bustamante, D., Mathy, R. M., Shell, R., & Rhodes, K. (1988). Differentiation of personal distress and sympathy in children and adolescents. *Developmental Psychology, 24,* 766–775.

Eisenberg, N., Shell, R., Pasternack, J., Lennon, R., Beller, R., & Mathy, R. M. (1987). Prosocial development in middle childhood: A longitudinal study. *Developmental Psychology, 23,* 712–718.

Eisenberg, N., Shepard, S. A., Fabes, R. A., Murphy, B. C., & Guthrie, I. K. (1998). Shyness and children's emotionality, regulation, and coping: Contemporaneous, longitudinal, and cross-context relations. *Child Development, 69,* 767–790.

Eisenberg-Berg, N., & Hand, M. (1979). The relationship of preschoolers' reasoning about prosocial moral conflicts to prosocial behavior. *Child Development, 50,* 356–363.

Elder, G. H., Liker, J. K., & Cross, C. E. (1984). Parent-child behavior in the Great Depression: Life course and intergenerational influences. In P. B. Baltes & O. G. Brim (Eds.), *Life-span development and behavior* (Vol. 6). New York: Academic Press.

Elicker, J., Englund, M., & Sroufe, L. A. (1992). Predicting peer competence and peer relationships in childhood from early parent-child relationships. In R. D. Parke & G. W. Ladd (Eds.), *Family-peer relationships: Modes of linkage.* Hillsdale, NJ: Erlbaum.

Elkind, D. (1967). Egocentrism in adolescence. *Child Development, 38,* 1025–1033.

Elkind, D. (1981a). *Children and adolescents: Interactive essays on Jean Piaget* (3rd ed.). New York: McGraw-Hill.

Elkind, D. (1981b). *The hurried child: Growing up too fast too soon.* Reading, MA: Addison-Wesley.

Elliott, E. S., & Dweck, C. S. (1988). Goals: An approach to motivation and achievement. *Journal of Personality and Social Psychology, 54,* 5–12.

Ellis, S., Rogoff, B., & Cromer, C. C. (1981). Age segregation in children's social interactions. *Developmental Psychology, 17,* 399–407.

Ellsworth, C. P., Muir, D. W., & Hains, S. M. J. (1993). Social competence and person-object differentiation: An analysis of the still-face effect. *Developmental Psychology, 29,* 63–73.

Emde, R. N. (1992). Individual meaning and increasing complexity: Contributions of Sigmund Freud and Rene Spitz to developmental psychology. *Developmental Psychology, 28,* 347–359.

Emde, R. N., Biringen, Z., Clyman, R. B., & Oppenheim, D. (1991). The moral self of infancy: Affective core and procedural knowledge. *Developmental Review, 11,* 251–270.

Emde, R. N., Plomin, R., Robinson, J., Corley, R., DeFries, J., Fulker, D. W., Reznick, J. S., Campos, J., Kagan, J., & Zahn-Waxler, C. (1992). Temperament, emotion, and cognition at fourteen months: The MacArthur longitudinal twin study. *Child Development, 63,* 1437–1455.

Emery, R. E. (1988). *Marriage, divorce, and children's adjustment*. Beverly Hills, CA: Sage.

Emery, R. E., & Forehand, R. (1994). Parental divorce and children's well-being: A focus on resilience. In R. J. Haggerty, L. R. Sherrod, N. Garmezy, & M. Rutter (Eds.), *Stress, risk, and resilience in children and adolescents* (pp. 64–99). New York: Cambridge University Press.

Emery, R. E., & Laumann-Billings, L. (1998). An overview of the nature, causes, and consequences of abusive family relationships: Toward differentiating maltreatment and violence. *American Psychologist, 53,* 121–135.

Emery, R. E., & Tuer, M. (1993). Parenting and the marital relationship. In T. Luster & L. Okagaki (Eds.), *Parenting. An ecological perspective*. Hillsdale, NJ: Erlbaum.

Emmerich, W. (1966). Continuity and stability in early social development: II. Teacher's ratings. *Child Development, 37,* 17–27.

Entwisle, D. R., & Alexander, K. L. (1990). Beginning school math competence: Minority and majority considerations. *Child Development, 61,* 454–471.

Entwisle, D. R., & Baker, D. P. (1983). Gender and young children's expectations for performance in arithmetic. *Developmental Psychology, 19,* 200–209.

Erdley, C. A., Cain, K. M., Loomis, C. C., Dumas-Hines, F., & Dweck, C. S. (1997). Relations among children's social goals, implicit personality theories, and responses to social failure. *Developmental Psychology, 33,* 263–272.

Erel, O., & Burman, B. (1995). Interrelatedness of marital relations and parent-child relations: A meta-analytic review. *Psychological Bulletin, 118,* 108–132.

Erel, O., Margolin, G., & John, R. S. (1998). Observed sibling interaction: Links with the marital and the mother-child relationship. *Developmental Psychology, 34,* 288–298.

Erickson, M. F., & Egeland, B. J. (1996). Child neglect. In J. Biere, L. Berliner, J. Bulkey, C. Jenny, & T. Reid (Eds.), *The APSAC handbook on child maltreatment* (pp. 4–20). Thousand Oaks, CA: Sage.

Erikson, E. H. (1963). *Childhood and society* (2nd ed.). New York: Norton.

Erikson, E. H. (1982). *The life cycle completed: A review*. New York: Norton.

Eron, L. D. (1982). Parent-child interaction, television violence, and aggression of children. *American Psychologist, 37,* 197–211.

Etaugh, C., Levine, D., & Mennella, A. (1984). Development of sex biases in children: 40 years later. *Sex Roles, 10,* 911–922.

Etaugh, C., & Liss, M. B. (1992). Home, school, and playroom: Training grounds for adult gender roles. *Sex Roles, 26,* 129–147.

Eyer, D. E. (1992). *Mother-infant bonding. A scientific fiction*. New Haven, CT: Yale University Press.

Fabes, R. A., & Eisenberg, N. (1992). Young children's coping with interpersonal anger. *Child Development, 63,* 116–128.

Fabes, R. A., Eisenberg, N., Karbon, M., Bernzweig, J., Speer, A. L., & Carlo, G. (1994). Socialization of children's vicarious emotional responding and prosocial behavior: Relations with mothers' perceptions of children's emotional reactivity. *Developmental Psychology, 30,* 44–55.

Fabes, R. A., Eisenberg, N., & Miller, P. A. (1990). Maternal correlates of children's vicarious emotional responsiveness. *Developmental Psychology, 26,* 639–648.

Fabes, R. A., Eisenberg, N., Nyman, M., & Michealieu, Q. (1991). Young children's appraisals of others' spontaneous emotional reactions. *Developmental Psychology, 27,* 858–866.

Fabes, R. A., Fultz, J., Eisenberg, N., May-Plumlee, T., & Christopher, F. S. (1989). Effects of rewards on children's prosocial motivation: A socialization study. *Developmental Psychology, 25,* 509–515.

Faden, R. R., & Kass, N. E. (1996). *HIV/AIDS, and childbearing*. New York: Oxford University Press.

Fagot, B. I. (1978). The influence of sex of child on parental reactions to toddler children. *Child Development, 49,* 459–465.

Fagot, B. I. (1985a). Beyond the reinforcement principle: Another step toward understanding sex-role development. *Developmental Psychology, 21,* 1097–1104.

Fagot, B. I. (1985b). Changes in thinking about early sex-role development. *Developmental Review, 5,* 83–98.

Fagot, B. I. (1997). Attachment, parenting, and peer interactions of toddler children. *Developmental Psychology, 33,* 489–499.

Fagot, B. I., & Hagan, R. I. (1991). Observations of parent reactions to sex-stereotyped behaviors: Age and sex effects. *Child Development, 62,* 617–628.

Fagot, B. I., & Kavanagh, K. (1990). The prediction of antisocial behavior from avoidant attachment classification. *Child Development, 61,* 864–873.

Fagot, B. I., & Kavanaugh, K. (1993). Parenting during the second year: Effects of children's age, sex, and attachment classification. *Child Development, 64,* 258–271.

Fagot, B. I., & Leinbach, M. D. (1989). The young child's gender schema: Environmental input, internal organization. *Child Development, 60,* 663–672.

Fagot, B. I., & Leinbach, M. D. (1993). Gender-role development in young children: From discrimination to labeling. *Developmental Review, 13,* 205–224.

Fagot, B. I., Leinbach, M. D., & Hagan, R. (1986). Gender labeling and the adoption of sex-typed behaviors. *Developmental Psychology, 22,* 440–443.

Fagot, B. I., Leinbach, M. D., & O'Boyle, C. (1992). Gender labeling, gender stereotyping, and parenting behaviors. *Developmental Psychology, 28,* 225–230.

Fagot, B. I., Pears, K. C., Capaldi, D. M., Crosby, L., & Leve, C. S. (1998). Becoming an adolescent father: Precursors and parenting. *Developmental Psychology, 34,* 1209–1219.

Falbo, T. (1992). Social norms and the one-child family: Clinical and policy implications. In F. Boer & J. Dunn (Eds.), *Children's sibling relationships* (pp. 71–82). Hillsdale, NJ: Erlbaum.

Falbo, T., & Polit, D. F. (1986). Quantitative review of the only child literature: Research evidence and theory development. *Psychological Bulletin, 100,* 176–189.

Falbo, T., & Poston, D. L., Jr. (1993). The academic, personality, and physical outcomes of only children in China. *Child Development, 64,* 18–35.

Farber, S. L. (1981). *Identical twins reared apart: A reanalysis*. New York: Basic Books.

Farhl, P. (1998, January 10). "Educational" TV programs are flunking in viewership. *Washington Post* report as cited in the *Athens Banner-Herald,* pp. A1, A14.

Farrington, D. P. (1987). Epidemiology. In H. C. Quay (Ed.), *Handbook of juvenile delinquency*. New York: Wiley.

Farver, J. M., & Branstetter, W. H. (1994). Preschoolers' prosocial responses to their peers' distress. *Developmental Psychology, 30,* 334–341.

Fauber, R., Forehand, R., Thomas, A. M., & Wierson, M. (1990). A mediational model of the impact of marital conflict on adolescent adjustment in intact and divorced families: The role of disrupted parenting. *Child Development, 61,* 1112–1123.

Faust, M. S. (1960). Developmental maturity as a determinant of prestige in adolescent girls. *Child Development, 31,* 173–184.

Fein, G. G. (1986). The affective psychology of play. In A. W. Gottfried & C. C. Brown (Eds.), *Play interactions: The contributions of play material and parental involvement to children's development*. Lexington, MA: Lexington Books.

Feingold, A. (1994). Gender differences in personality: A meta-analysis. *Psychological Bulletin, 116,* 429–456.

Feinman, S. (1992). *Social referencing and the social construction of reality in infancy*. New York: Plenum.

Feldman, R., Greenbaum, G. W., & Yirmiya, N. (1999). Mother-related affect synchrony as an antecedent of the emergence of self-control. *Developmental Psychology, 35,* 223–231.

Feldman, S. S., & Gehring, T. M. (1988). Changing perceptions of family cohesion and power across adolescence. *Child Development, 59,* 1034–1045.

Fernald, A., & Mazzie, C. (1991). Prosody and focus in speech to infants and adults. *Developmental Psychology, 27,* 209–221.

Fernandez, E. (1997, June 3). The grim legacy of divorce. *The Atlanta Constitution,* p. F5.

Feshbach, S. (1956). The catharsis hypothesis and some consequences of interaction with aggressive and neutral play objects. *Journal of Personality, 24,* 449–461.

Feshbach, S. (1964). The function of aggression and the regulation of aggressive drive. *Psychological Review, 71,* 257–272.

Feshbach, S. (1970). Aggression. In P. H. Mussen (Ed.), *Carmichael's manual of child psychology* (Vol. 2). New York: Wiley.

Field, T. M. (1987). Affective and interactive disturbances in infants. In J. D. Osofsky (Ed.), *Handbook of infant development* (2nd ed.). New York: Wiley.

Field, T. M., Greenwald, P., Morrow, C., Healy, B., Foster, T., Guthertz, M., & Frost, P. (1992). Behavior state matching during interactions of preadolescent friends versus acquaintances. *Developmental Psychology, 28,* 242–250.

Field, T. M., Healy, B., Goldstein, S., Perry, S., Bendell, D., Schanberg, S., Zimmerman, E. A., & Kuhn, C. (1988). Infants of depressed mothers show "depressed" behavior even with nondepressed adults. *Child Development, 59,* 1569–1579.

Field, T. M., Woodson, R., Greenberg, R., & Cohen, D. (1982). Discrimination and imitation of facial expressions by neonates. *Science, 218,* 179–181.

Fincham, F. D. (1998). Child development and marital relations. *Child Development, 69,* 543–574.

Fincham, F. D., Hokoda, A., & Sanders, R., Jr. (1989). Learned helplessness, test anxiety, and academic achievement: A longitudinal analysis. *Child Development, 60,* 138–145.

Findley, M. J., & Cooper, H. M. (1983). Locus of control and academic achievement: A literature review. *Journal of Personality and Social Psychology, 44,* 419–427.

Fine, M. A., & Kurdek, L. A. (1994). Parenting cognition in stepfamilies: Differences between parents and stepparents and relations to parenting satisfaction. *Journal of Social and Personal Relationships, 11,* 95–112.

Finkelhor, D., & Dziuba-Leatherman, J. (1994). Victimization of children. *American Psychologist, 49,* 173–183.

Finkelhor, D., Hotaling, G. T., Lewis, I., & Smith, C. (1990). Sexual abuse in a national survey of adult men and women: Prevalence, characteristics, and risk factors. *Child Abuse & Neglect, 14,* 14–28.

Finkelstein, N. W., & Ramey, C. T. (1977). Learning to control the environment in infancy. *Child Development, 48,* 806–819.

Finn, J. D., & Achilles, C. M. (1990). Answers and questions about class size: A statewide experiment. *Educational Research Journal, 27,* 557–577.

Fischer, K. W., & Bidell, T. (1998). Dynamic development of psychological structures in action and thought. In R. M. Lerner (Ed.), *Theoretical models of human development,* Vol. 1 of W. Damon (Gen. Ed.), *Handbook of child psychology* (pp. 467–561). New York: Wiley.

Fischer, W. F. (1963). Sharing in pre-school children as a function of the amount and type of reinforcement. *Genetic Psychology Monographs, 68,* 215–245.

Fisher, L., Ames, E. W., Chisholm, K., & Savoie, L. (1997). Problems reported by parents of Romanian orphans adopted to British Columbia. *International Journal of Behavioral Development, 20,* 67–82.

Fitch, M., Huston, A. C., & Wright, J. C. (1993). From television forms to gender schemata: Children's perceptions of television reality. In G. L. Berry & J. K. Asamen (Eds.), *Children and television: Images in a changing sociocultural world* (pp. 38–52). Newbury Park, CA: Sage.

Fitch, S. A., & Adams, G. R. (1983). Ego identity and intimacy status: Replication and extension. *Developmental Psychology, 19,* 839–845.

Flaks, D. K., Ficher, I., Masterpasqua, F., & Joseph, G. (1995). Lesbians choosing motherhood: A comparative study of lesbian and heterosexual parents and their children. *Developmental Psychology, 31,* 105–114.

Flanagan, C. A., & Eccles, J. S. (1993). Changes in parents' work status and adolescents' adjustment to school. *Child Development, 64,* 246–257.

Flavell, J. H. (1963). *The developmental psychology of Jean Piaget.* New York: Van Nostrand Reinhold.

Flavell, J. H. (1996). Piaget's legacy. *Psychological Science, 7,* 200–203.

Flavell, J. H., Miller, P. H., & Miller, S. A. (1993). *Cognitive development* (3rd ed.). Englewood Cliffs, NJ: Prentice Hall.

Fletcher, A. C., Darling, N. E., Steinberg, L., & Dornbusch, S. M. (1995). The company they keep: Relation of adolescents' adjustment and behavior to their friends' perceptions of authoritative parenting in the social network. *Developmental Psychology, 31,* 300–310.

Fletcher-Flinn, C. M., & Gravatt, B. (1995). The efficacy of computer-assisted instruction (CAI): A meta-analysis. *Journal of Educational Computing Research, 12,* 219–242.

Fling, S., Smith, L., Rodriguez, T., Thornton, D., Atkins, E., & Nixon, K. (1992). Video games, aggression, and self-esteem: A survey. *Social Behavior and Personality, 20,* 39–46.

Florsheim, P., Tolan, P., & Gorman-Smith, D. (1998). Family relationships, parenting practices, the availability of male family members, and the behavior of inner-city boys in single-mother and two-parent families. *Child Development, 69,* 1437–1447.

Fogel, A. (1995). Relational narratives of the prelinguistic self. In P. Rochat (Ed.), *The self in infancy: Theory and research* (pp. 117–139). Amsterdam: North Holland-Elsevier.

Fonagy, P., Steele, H., & Steele, M. (1991). Maternal representations of attachment during pregnancy predict the organization of infant-mother attachment at one year of age. *Child Development, 62,* 891–905.

Fonzi, A., Schneider, B. H., Tani, F., & Tomada, G. (1997). Predicting children's friendship status from their dyadic interaction in structured situations of potential conflict. *Child Development, 68,* 496–506.

Ford, C. S., & Beach, F. A. (1951). *Patterns of sexual behavior.* New York: Harper.

Ford, D. Y., & Harris, J. J., III (1996). Perceptions and attitudes of black students toward school, achievement, and other educational variables. *Child Development, 67,* 1141–1152.

Fordham, S., & Ogbu, J. (1986). Black students' school success: Coping with the "burden of 'acting white.'" *Urban Review, 18,* 176–206.

Forrest, J. D., & Singh, S. (1990). The sexual and reproductive behavior of American women, 1982–1988. *Family Planning Perspectives, 22,* 206–214.

Fox, N. A., Bell, M. A., & Jones, N. A. (1992). Individual differences in response to stress and cerebral asymmetry. *Developmental Neuropsychology, 8,* 161–184.

Fox, N. A., Kimmerly, N. L., & Schafer, W. D. (1991). Attachment to mother/attachment to father: A meta-analysis. *Child Development, 62,* 210–225.

Frankel, K. A., & Bates, J. E. (1990). Mother-toddler problem-solving: Antecedents in attachment, home behavior, and temperament. *Child Development, 61,* 810–819.

Franklin, K. M., Janoff-Bulman, R., & Roberts, J. E. (1990). Long-term impact of parental divorce on optimism and trust: Changes in general assumptions or narrow beliefs? *Journal of Personality and Social Personality, 59,* 743–755.

Frazier, J. A., & Morrison, F. J. (1998). The influence of extended-year schooling on the growth of achievement and perceived competence in early elementary school. *Child Development, 69,* 495–517.

Freedman, D. G. (1965). Hereditary control of early social behaviors. In B. M. Foss (Ed.), *Determinants of infant behavior* (Vol. 3). London: Methuen.

Freedman, D. G. (1974). *Human infancy: An evolutionary perspective.* Hillsdale, NJ: Erlbaum.

Freedman, J. L. (1984). Effect of television violence on aggressiveness. *Psychological Bulletin, 96,* 227–246.

French, D. C. (1984). Children's knowledge of the social functions of younger, older, and same-age peers. *Child Development, 55,* 1429–1433.

French, D. C. (1988). Heterogenity of peer-rejected boys: Aggressive and nonaggressive subtypes. *Child Development, 59,* 976–985.

Freud, A., & Dann, S. (1951). An experiment in group upbringing. In R. Eisler, A. Freud, H. Hartmann, & E. Kris (Eds.), *The psychoanalytic study of the child* (Vol. 6). New York: International Universities Press.

Freud, S. (1930). *Three contributions to the theory of sex.* New York: Nervous and Mental Disease Publishing Co. (Original work published 1905)

Freud, S. (1933). *New introductory lectures in psychoanalysis.* New York: Norton.

Freud, S. (1960). *A general introduction to psychoanalysis.* New York: Washington Square Press. (Original work published 1935)

Freud, S. (1961a). Some physical consequences of the anatomical distinction between the sexes. In J. Strachey (Ed.), *The standard edition of the complete psychological works of Sigmund Freud* (Vol. 19). London: Hogarth Press. (Originally published 1924)

Freud, S. (1961b). The dissolution of the Oedipus complex. In J. Strachey (Ed. & Trans.). *The standard edition of the complete psychological works of Sigmund Freud* (Vol. 19). London: Hogarth Press. (Original work published 1924)

Freud, S. (1964). An outline of psychoanalysis. In J. Strachey (Ed. & Trans.). *The standard edition of the complete psychological works of Sigmund Freud* (Vol. 23). London: Hogarth Press. (Original work published 1940)

Frey, K. S., & Ruble, D. N. (1985). What children say when the teacher is not around: Conflicting goals in social comparison and performance assessment in the classroom. *Journal of Personality and Social Psychology, 48,* 550–562.

Frey, K. S., & Ruble, D. N. (1992). Gender constancy and the cost of sex-typed behavior: A test of the conflict hypothesis. *Developmental Psychology, 28,* 714–721.

Friedrich, L. K., & Stein, A. H. (1973). Aggressive and prosocial television programs and the natural behavior of preschool children. *Monographs of the Society for Research in Child Development, 38* (4, Serial No. 51).

Friedrich, L. K., & Stein, A. H. (1975). Prosocial television and young children: The effects of verbal labeling and role-playing on learning and behavior. *Child Development, 46,* 27–38.

Friedrich-Cofer, L. K., Huston-Stein, A., Kipnis, D. M., Susman, E. J., & Clewett, A. S. (1979). Environmental enhancement of prosocial television content: Effects on interpersonal behavior. *Developmental Psychology, 15,* 637–646.

Friend, M., & Davis, T. L. (1993). Appearance-reality distinction: Children's understanding of the physical and affective domains. *Developmental Psychology, 29,* 907–914.

Frost, J. J., & Forrest, J. D. (1995). Understanding the impact of effective teenage pregnancy prevention programs. *Family Planning Perspectives, 27,* 188–195.

Fuchs, D., & Thelen, M. H. (1988). Children's expected interpersonal consequences of communicating their affective state and reported likelihood of expression. *Child Development, 59,* 1314–1322.

Fuhrman, T., & Holmbeck, G. N. (1995). A contextual-moderator analysis of emotional anatomy and adjustment in adolescence. *Child Development, 66,* 793–811.

Fuligni, A. J. (1997). The academic achievement of adolescents from immigrant families: The roles of family background, attitudes, and behavior. *Child Development, 68,* 351–363.

Fuligni, A. J. (1998). Authority, autonomy, and parent-adolescent conflict and cohesion: A study of adolescents from Mexican, Chinese, Filipino, and European backgrounds. *Developmental Psychology, 34,* 782–792.

Fuligni, A. J., & Eccles, J. S. (1993). Perceived parent-child relationships and early adolescents' orientation toward peers. *Developmental Psychology, 29,* 622–632.

Fuligni, A. J., Eccles, J. S., & Barber, B. K. (1995). The long-term effects of seventh-grade ability grouping in mathematics. *Journal of Early Adolescence, 15,* 58–69.

Fuligni, A. J., & Stevenson, H. W. (1995). Time use and mathematics achievement among American, Chinese, and Japanese high school students. *Child Development, 66,* 830–842.

Fuller, B., Holloway, S. D., & Liang, X. (1996). Family selection of child-care centers: The influence of household support, ethnicity, and parental practices. *Child Development, 67,* 3320–3337.

Furman, W., & Buhrmester, D. (1985). Children's perceptions of the qualities of sibling relationships. *Child Development, 56,* 448–461.

Furman, W., & Buhrmester, D. (1992). Age and sex differences in perceptions of networks of personal relationships. *Child Development, 63,* 103–115.

Fyans, L. J., Jr., Salili, F., Maehr, M. L., & Desai, K. A. (1983). A cross-cultural exploration into the meaning of achievement. *Journal of Personality and Social Psychology, 44,* 1000–1013.

Galambos, N. L., Almeida, D. M., & Petersen, A. C. (1990). Masculinity, femininity, and sex role attitudes in early adolescence: Exploring gender intensification. *Child Development, 61,* 1905–1914.

Galambos, N. L., & Maggs, J. L. (1991). Out-of-school care of young adolescents and self-reported behavior. *Developmental Psychology, 27,* 644–655.

Galen, B. R., & Underwood, M. K. (1997). A developmental investigation of social aggression among children. *Developmental Psychology, 33,* 589–600.

Gallup, G. G., Jr. (1979). Self-recognition in chimpanzees and man: A developmental and comparative perspective. In M. Lewis & L. A. Rosenblum (Eds.), *Genesis of behavior. Vol. 2: The child and its family.* New York: Plenum.

Galper, A., Wigfield, A., & Seefeldt, C. (1997). Head Start parents' beliefs about their children's abilities, task values, and performances on different activities. *Child Development, 68,* 897–907.

Gandelman, R. (1992). *Psychobiology of behavioral development.* New York: Oxford University Press.

Garbarino, J. (1992). *Children and families in the social environment* (2nd ed.). New York: Aldine de Gruyter.

Garbarino, J. (1995). Growing up in a socially toxic environment: Life for children and families in the 1990s. In G. B. Melton (Ed.), *Nebraska Symposium on Motivation: Vol. 42. The individual, the family, and the social good: Personal fulfillment in times of change* (pp. 1–20). Lincoln: University of Nebraska Press.

Garbarino, J., & Kostelny, K. (1992). Child maltreatment as a community problem. *Child Abuse & Neglect, 16,* 455–464.

Garbarino, J., & Sherman, D. (1980). High-risk neighborhoods and high-risk families: The human ecology of child maltreatment. *Child Development, 51,* 188–198.

Garcia, E. E. (1993). Language, culture, and education. *Review of Educational Research, 19,* 51–98.

Gardner, L. J. (1972). Deprivation dwarfism. *Scientific American, 277,* 76–82.

Garland, A., & Zigler, E. (1993). Adolescent suicide prevention: Current research and social policy implications. *American Psychologist, 48,* 169–182.

Garner, P. W., Jones, D. C., & Miner, J. L. (1994). Social competence among low-income preschoolers: Emotion socialization practices and social cognitive correlates. *Child Development, 65,* 622–637.

Garner, P. W., Jones, D. C., & Palmer, D. J. (1994). Social-cognitive correlates of preschool children's sibling caregiving behavior. *Developmental Psychology, 30,* 905–911.

Garner, P. W., & Power, T. G. (1996). Preschoolers' emotional control in the disappointment paradigm and its relation to temperament, emotional knowledge, and family expressiveness. *Child Development, 67,* 1406–1419.

Garnets, L., & Kimmel, D. (1991). Lesbian and gay male dimensions of the psychological study of human diversity. In J. D. Goodchilds (Ed.), *Psychological perspectives on human diversity in America.* Washington, DC: American Psychological Association.

Gauze, C., Bukowski, W. M., Aquan-Assee, J., & Sippola, L. K. (1996). Interactions between family environment and friendship and associations with well-being during early adolescence. *Child Development, 67,* 2201–2216.

Gavin, L. A., & Furman, W. (1989). Age differences in adolescents' perceptions of their peer groups. *Developmental Psychology, 25,* 827–834.

Gavin, L. N., & Furman, W. (1996). Adolescent girls' relationships with mothers and best friends. *Child Development, 67,* 375–386.

Ge, X., Best, K. M., Conger, R. D., & Simons, R. L. (1996). Parenting behaviors and the occurrence and co-occurrence of adolescent depressive symptoms and conduct problems. *Developmental Psychology, 32,* 717–731.

Ge, X., Conger, R. D., & Elder, G. H., Jr. (1996). Coming of age too early: Pubertal influences on girls' vulnerability to psychological distress. *Child Development, 67,* 3386–3400.

Geary, D. C., Bow-Thomas, C. C., Liu, F., & Siegler, R. S. (1996). Development of arithmetical competencies in Chinese and American children: Influence of age, language, and schooling. *Child Development, 67,* 2022–2044.

Geen, R. G. (1998). Aggression and antisocial behavior. In D. T. Gilbert, S. T. Fiske, & G. Lindzey (Eds.), *Handbook of Social Psychology* (Vol. 2, pp. 317–356). New York: McGraw-Hill.

Geen, R. G., & Quanty, M. B. (1977). The catharsis of aggression: An evaluation of a hypothesis. In L. Berkowitz (Ed.), *Advances in experimental social psychology* (Vol. 10). New York: Academic Press.

Gelles, R. J. (1996). *The book of David: How preserving families can cost children's lives.* New York: Basic Books.

George, C., Kaplan, N., & Main, M. (1985). *Attachment interview for adults.* Unpublished manuscript, University of California, Berkeley.

George, T. P., & Hartmann, D. P. (1996). Friendship networks of unpopular, average, and popular children. *Child Development, 67,* 2301–2316.

Gesell, A. (1933). Maturation and the patterning of behavior. In C. Murchison (Ed.), *A handbook of child psychology.* Worcester, MA: Clark University Press.

Gewirtz, J. L., & Pelaez-Nogueras, M. (1992). Skinner, B. F: Legacy to human infant behavior and development. *American Psychologist, 47,* 1411–1422.

Gewirtz, J. L., & Petrovich, S. B. (1982). Early social and attachment learning in the frame of organic and cultural evolution. In T. M. Field, A. Huston, H. C. Quav, L. Troll, & G. E. Finley (Eds.), *Review of human development.* New York: Wiley.

Gibbs, J. C., Potter, G. B., & Goldstein, A. P. (1995). *The EQUIP program: Teaching youth to think and act responsibly through a peer-helping approach.* Champaign, IL: Research Press.

Gibbs, J. C., & Schnell, S. V. (1985). Moral development "versus" socialization. A critique. *American Psychologist, 40,* 1071–1080.

Gil, D. G. (1970). *Violence against children.* Cambridge, MA: Harvard University Press.

Gilbert, N. (1997). *Combatting child abuse: International perspectives and trends.* New York: Oxford University Press.

Gill, N. J., & Beazley, R. P. (1993). Grade 6 students benefit from learning about AIDS. *Canadian Journal of Public Health, 94* (Suppl. 1), 524–527.

Gilligan, C. (1977). In a different voice: Women's conceptions of self and morality. *Harvard Educational Review, 47,* 481–517.

Gilligan, C. (1982). *In a different voice: Psychological theory and women's development.* Cambridge, MA: Harvard University Press.

Gilligan, C. (1993). Adolescent development reconsidered. In A. Garrod (Ed.), *Approaches to moral development: New research and emerging themes.* New York: Teachers College Press.

Ginsburg, G. S., & Bronstein, P. (1993). Family factors related to children's intrinsic/extrinsic motivational orientation and academic performance. *Child Development, 64,* 1461–1474.

Girard, C. (1993). Age, gender, and suicide: A cross-national analysis. *American Sociological Review, 58,* 553–574.

Glasgow, K. L., Dornbusch, S. M., Troyer, L., Steinberg, L., & Ritter, P. L. (1997). Parenting style, adolescents' attributions, and educational outcomes in nine heterogeneous high schools. *Child Development, 68,* 507–529.

Gnepp, J. (1989). Personalized inferences of emotions and appraisals: Component processes and correlates. *Developmental Psychology, 25,* 277–288.

Gnepp, J., & Klayman, J. (1992). Recognition of uncertainty in emotional inferences: Reasoning about emotionally equivocal situations. *Developmental Psychology, 28,* 145–158.

Gold, D., & Andres, D. (1978). Developmental comparisons between 10-year-old children with employed and nonemployed mothers. *Child Development, 49,* 75–84.

Goldberg, P. (1968). Are women prejudiced against women? *Trans/Action, 5,* 28–30.

Goldberg, S. (1983). Parent-infant bonding: Another look. *Child Development, 54,* 1355–1382.

Goldberg, S., Perrotta, M., Minde, K., & Corter, C. (1986). Maternal behavior and attachment in low-birth-weight twins and singletons. *Child Development, 57,* 34–46.

Goldberg, W. A., Greenberger, E., & Nagel, S. K. (1996). Employment and achievement: Mothers' work involvement in relation to children's achievement behaviors and mothers' parenting behaviors. *Child Development, 67,* 1512–1527.

Goldfarb, W. (1943). The effects of early institutional care on adolescent personality. *Journal of Experimental Education, 12,* 107–129.

Goldfarb, W. (1947). Variations in adolescent adjustment in institutionally reared children. *Journal of Orthopsychiatry, 17,* 449–457.

Goldsmith, H. H., & Alansky, J. A. (1987). Maternal and infant temperamental predictors of attachment: A meta-analytic review. *Journal of Consulting and Clinical Psychology, 55,* 805–816.

Goldsmith, H. H., Buss, K. A., & Lemery, K. S. (1997). Toddler and childhood temperament: Expanded content, stronger genetic evidence, new evidence for the importance of environment. *Developmental Psychology, 33,* 891–905.

Goldsmith, H. H., Buss, A. H., Plomin, R., Rothbart, M. K., Thomas, A., Chess, S., Hinde, R. A., & McCall, R. B. (1987). Roundtable: What is temperament? Four approaches. *Child Development, 58,* 505–529.

Golombok, S., Cook, R., Bish, A., & Murray, C. (1995). Families created by new reproductive technologies: Quality of parenting and social and emotional development of the children. *Child Development, 66,* 285–298.

Golombok, S., & Tasker, F. (1996). Do parents influence the sexual orientation of their children: Findings from a longitudinal study of lesbian families. *Developmental Psychology, 32,* 3–11.

Gondoli, D. M., & Silverberg, S. B. (1997). Maternal emotional distress and diminished responsiveness: The mediating role of parenting efficacy and parental perspective taking. *Developmental Psychology, 33,* 861–868.

Good, T. L. (1979). Teacher effectiveness in the elementary school: What do we know about it now? *Journal of Teacher Education, 30,* 52–64.

Good, T. L., & Brophy, J. E. (1994). *Looking in classrooms* (6th ed.). New York: HarperCollins.

Goodenough, F. L. (1931). *Anger in young children.* Minneapolis: University of Minnesota Press.

Goossens, F. A., & van IJzendoorn, M. H. (1990). Quality of infants' attachments to professional caregivers: Relation to infant-parent attachment and day-care characteristics. *Child Development, 61,* 832–837.

Gorer, G. (1968). Man has no "killer" instinct. In M. F. A. Montague (Ed.), *Man and aggression.* New York: Oxford University Press.

Gorn, G. J., Goldberg, M. E., & Kanungo, R. N. (1976). The role of educational television in changing the intergroup attitudes of children. *Child Development, 47,* 277–280.

Gottesman, I. I., & Shields, J. (1982). *Schizophrenia: The epigenetic puzzle.* Cambridge, England: Cambridge University Press.

Gottfried, A. E., Fleming, J. S., & Gottfried, A. W. (1998). Role of cognitively stimulating home environment in children's academic intrinsic motivation: A longitudinal study. *Child Development, 69,* 1448–1460.

Gottfried, A. E., Gottfried, A. W., & Bathurst, K. (1988). Maternal employment, family environment and children's development: Infancy through the school years. In A. E. Gottfried & A. W. Gottfried (Eds.), *Maternal employment and children's development: Longitudinal research* (pp. 11–58). New York: Plenum.

Gottfried, A. W., Gottfried, A. E., Bathurst, K., & Guerin, D. W. (1994). *Gifted IQs: Early developmental aspects: The Fullerton Longitudinal Study.* New York: Plenum.

Gottlieb, D. (1966). Teaching and students: The views of Negro and white teachers. *Sociology of Education, 37,* 344–353.

Gottlieb, G. (1991). Experimental canalization of behavioral development: Results. *Developmental Psychology, 27,* 35–39.

Gottlieb, G. (1996). Commentary: A systems view of psychobiological development. In D. Magnusson (Ed.), *The lifespan development of individuals: Behavioral, neurobiological, and psychosocial perspectives: A synthesis.* Cambridge, England: Cambridge University Press.

Gottman, J. M. (1983). How children become friends. *Monographs of the Society for Research in Child Development, 48* (3, Serial No. 201).

Gould, S. J. (1978). Sociobiology: The art of story telling. *New Scientist, 80,* 530–533.

Graham, S., Hudley, C., & Williams, E. (1992). Attributional and emotional determinants of aggression among African-American and Latino young adolescents. *Developmental Psychology, 28,* 731–740.

Graham, S., & Juvonen, J. (1998). Self-blame and peer victimization in middle school: An attributional analysis. *Developmental Psychology, 34,* 587–599.

Graves, S. B. (1975, April). *How to encourage positive racial attitudes.* Paper presented at the biennial meeting of the Society for Research in Child Development, Denver.

Graves, S. B. (1993). Television, the portrayal of African Americans, and the development of children's attitudes. In G. L. Berry & J. K. Asamen (Eds.), *Children and television: Images in a changing sociocultural world* (pp. 179–190). Newbury Park, CA: Sage.

Gray, W. M., & Hudson, L. M. (1984). Formal operations and the imaginary audience. *Developmental Psychology, 20,* 619–627.

Graziano, W. G., French, D., Brownell, C. A., & Hartup, W. W. (1976). Peer interaction in same- and mixed-age triads in relation to chronological age and incentive condition. *Child Development, 47,* 707–714.

Green, F. P., & Schneider, F. W. (1974). Age differences in the behavior of boys on three measures of altruism. *Child Development, 45,* 248–251.

Green, K. D., Forehand, R., Beck, S. J., & Vosk, B. (1980). An assessment of the relationship among measures of children's social competence and children's academic achievement. *Child Development, 51,* 1149–1156.

Green, M. (1987). *Theories of human development: A comparative approach.* Englewood Cliffs, NJ: Prentice-Hall.

Green, R. (1987). *The "sissy boy syndrome" and the development of homosexuality.* New Haven, CT: Yale University Press.

Greenberg, M. T., & Morris, N. (1974). Engrossment: The newborn's impact upon the father. *American Journal of Orthopsychiatry, 44,* 520–531.

Greenberger, E., & Chen, C. (1996). Perceived family relationships and depressed mood in early and late adolescence: A comparison of European and Asian Americans. *Developmental Psychology, 32,* 707–716.

Greenberger, E., & Goldberg, W. A. (1989). Work, parenting, and the socialization of children. *Developmental Psychology, 25,* 22–35.

Greenberger, E., & O'Neil, R. (1993). Spouse, parent, worker: Role commitments and role-related experiences in the construction of adults' well-being. *Developmental Psychology, 29,* 181–197.

Greenberger, E., O'Neil, R., & Nagel, S. K. (1994). Linking workplace and homeplace: Relations between the nature of adults' work and their parenting behavior. *Developmental Psychology, 30,* 990–1002.

Greenberger, E., & Steinberg, L. (1986). *When teenagers work: The psychological and social costs of adolescent employment.* New York: Basic Books.

Greene, R. (1997, February 28). U.S. students' scores getting better, but few performing above basic level. *The Atlanta Constitution,* C3.

Grieser, D. L., & Kuhl, P. K. (1988). Maternal speech to infants in a tonal language: Support for the universal prosodic features in motherese. *Child Development, 59,* 14–20.

Grolnick, W. S., Bridges, L. J., & Connell, J. P. (1996). Emotion regulation in two-year-olds: Strategies and emotional expression in four contexts. *Child Development, 67,* 928–941.

Grolnick, W. S., & Ryan, R. M. (1989). Parent styles associated with self-regulation and competence in school. *Journal of Educational Psychology, 81,* 143–154.

Gross, A. L., & Ballif, B. (1991). Children's understanding of emotion from facial expressions and situations: A review. *Developmental Review, 11,* 368–398.

Grossman, F. K., Eichler, L. S., Winickoff, S. A., & Associates (1980). *Pregnancy, birth, and parenthood: Adaptations of mothers, fathers, and infants.* San Francisco: Jossey-Bass.

Grossmann, K., Grossmann, K. E., Spangler, S., Suess, G., & Unzner, L. (1985). Maternal sensitivity and newborn responses as related to quality of attachment in Northern Germany. In I. Bretherton & E. Waters, Growing points of attachment theory. *Monographs of the Society for Research in Child Development, 50,* (1–2, Serial No. 209).

Grotevant, H. D., & Cooper, C. R. (1986). Individuation in family relations: A perspective on individual differences in the development of identity and role-taking skills in adolescence. *Human Development, 29,* 82–100.

Grusec, J. E. (1991). Socializing concern for others in the home. *Developmental Psychology, 27,* 338–342.

Grusec, J. E. (1992). Social learning theory and developmental psychology: The legacies of Robert Sears and Albert Bandura. *Developmental Psychology, 28,* 776–786.

Grusec, J. E., & Goodnow, J. J. (1994). Impact of parental discipline methods on the child's internalization of values: A reconceptualization of current points of view. *Developmental Psychology, 30,* 4–19.

Grusec, J. E., Goodnow, J. J., & Cohen, L. (1996). Household work and the development of concern for others. *Developmental Psychology, 32,* 999–1007.

Grusec, J. E., Kuczynski, L., Rushton, J. P., & Simutis, Z. (1979). Learning resistance to temptation through observation. *Developmental Psychology, 15,* 233–240.

Grusec, J. E., & Redler, E. (1980). Attribution, reinforcement, and altruism: A developmental analysis. *Developmental Psychology, 16,* 525–534.

Grusec, J. E., & Walters, G. C. (1991). Psychological abuse and childrearing belief systems. In R. H. Starr, Jr., & D. A. Wolfe (Eds.), *The effects of child abuse and neglect* (pp. 186–202). New York: Guilford.

Grych, J. H., & Fincham, F. D. (1992). Interventions for children of divorce: Toward greater integration of research and action. *Psychological Bulletin, 111,* 434–454.

Guerra, N. G., & Slaby, R. G. (1990). Cognitive mediators of aggression in adolescent offenders: 2. Intervention. *Developmental Psychology , 26,* 269–277.

Gullota, T. P., Adams, G. R., & Alexander, S. J. (1986). *Today's marriages and families. A wellness approach.* Monterey, CA: Brooks/Cole.

Gunnar, M. R., Larson, M. C., Hertsgaard, L., Harris, M. L., & Brodersen, L. (1992). The stressfulness of separation among 9-month-old infants: Effects of social context variables and infant temperament. *Child Development, 63,* 290–303.

Guralnick, M. J., & Groom, J. M. (1988). Friendships of preschool children in mainstreamed playgroups. *Developmental Psychology, 24,* 595–604.

Gurucharri, C., & Selman, R. L. (1982). The development of interpersonal understanding during childhood, preadolescence, and adolescence: A longitudinal follow-up study. *Child Development, 53,* 924–927.

Guttentag, M., & Bray, H. (1976). *Undoing sex stereotypes. Research and resources for educators.* New York: McGraw-Hill.

Haan, N., Aerts, E., & Cooper, B. A. B. (1985). *On moral grounds. The search for practical morality.* New York: New York University Press.

Hagborg, W. J. (1995). High school student television viewing time: A study of school performance and adjustment. *Child Study Journal, 25,* 155–167.

Hala, S., & Chandler, M. (1996). The role of strategic planning in accessing false-belief understanding. *Child Development, 67,* 2948–2966.

Hall, G. S. (1891). The contents of children's minds on entering school. *Pedagogical Seminary, 1,* 139–173.

Hall, G. S. (1904). *Adolescence.* New York: Appleton-Century-Crofts.

Halpern, D. F. (1997). Sex differences in intelligence: Implications for education. *American Psychologist, 52,* 1091–1102.

Hardy, J. B., Astone, N. M., Brooks-Gunn, J., Shapiro, S., & Miller, T. L. (1998). Like mother, like child: Intergenerational patterns of age at first birth and associations with childhood and adolescent characteristics and adult outcomes in the second generation. *Developmental Psychology, 34,* 1220–1232.

Harkness, S., Edwards, C. P., & Super, C. M. (1981). Social roles and moral reasoning: A case study in a rural African community. *Developmental Psychology, 17,* 595–603.

Harlow, H. F. (1962). The heterosexual affectional system in monkeys. *American Psychologist, 17,* 1–9.

Harlow, H. F., & Harlow, M. K. (1977). The young monkeys. In *Readings in developmental psychology today* (2nd ed.). Del Mar, CA: CRM Books.

Harlow, H. F., & Zimmerman, R. R. (1959). Affectional responses in the infant monkey. *Science, 130,* 421–432.

Harold, G. T., Fincham, F. D., Osborne, L. M., & Conger, R. D. (1997). Mom and dad are at it again: Adolescent perceptions of marital conflict and adolescent psychological distress. *Developmental Psychology, 33,* 333–350.

Harper, L. V., & Huie, K. S. (1985). The effects of prior group experience, age, and familiarity on the quality and organization of preschoolers' social relationships. *Child Development, 56,* 704–717.

Harris, J. R. (1995). Where is the child's environment? A group socialization theory of development. *Psychological Review, 102,* 458–489.

Harris, M. J., & Rosenthal, R. (1986). Four factors in the mediation of teacher expectancy effects. In R. S. Feldman (Ed.), *The social psychology of education. Current research and theory.* Cambridge, England: Cambridge University Press.

Harris, N. B. (1992). Sex, race, and the experience of aggression. *Aggressive Behavior, 18,* 201–217.

Harris, P. L. (1989). *Children and emotion: The development of psychological understanding.* Oxford: Basil Blackwell.

Harrison, A. O., Wilson, M. N., Pine, C. J., Chan, S. Q., & Buriel, R. (1994). Family ecologies of ethnic minority children. In G. Handel & G. G. Whitchurch (Eds.), *The psychosocial interior of the family* (pp. 187–210). New York: Aldine De Gruyter.

Harrison, L. F., & Williams, T. (1986). Television and cognitive development. In T. Williams (Ed.), *The impact of television: A natural experiment in three communities.* Orlando, FL: Academic.

Harrist, A. W., Zaia, A. F., Bates, J. E., Dodge, K. A., & Pettit, G. S. (1997). Subtypes of social withdrawal in early childhood: Sociometric status and social-cognitive differences across four years. *Child Development, 68,* 278–294.

Hart, C. H., Burts, D. C., Durland, M. A., Charlesworth, R., DeWolf, M., & Fleege, P. O. (1998). Stress behaviors and activity type participation of preschoolers in more or less developmentally appropriate classrooms: SES and sex differences. *Journal of Research in Childhood Education,* Vol. 12(2), pp. 176–196.

Hart, C. H., De Wolf, D. M., Wozniak, P., & Burts, D. C. (1992). Maternal and paternal disciplinary styles: Relations with preschoolers' playground behavioral orientations and peer status. *Child Development, 63,* 879–892.

Hart, C. H., Ladd, G. W., & Burleson, B. R. (1990). Children's expectations of the outcomes of social strategies: Relations with socioeconomic status and maternal disciplinary styles. *Child Development, 61,* 127–137.

Hart, C. H., Nelson, D., Robinson, C. C., Olsen, S. F., & McNeilly-Choque, M. K. (1998). Overt and relational aggression in Russian nursery-school-age children: Parenting style and marital linkages. *Developmental Psychology, 34,* 687–697.

Hart, C. H., Olsen, S. F., Robinson, C. C., & Mandleco, B. L. (1997). The development of social and communicative competence in childhood: Review and a model of personal, familial, and extrafamilial processes. *Communication Yearbook, 20,* 305–373.

Hart, D., & Chmiel, S. (1992). Influence of defense mechanisms on moral judgment development: A longitudinal study. *Developmental Psychology, 28,* 722–730.

Hart, D., & Fegley, S. (1995). Prosocial behavior and caring in adolescence: Relations to self-understanding and social judgment. *Child Development, 66,* 1346–1359.

Hart, D., Hofmann, V., Edelstein, W., & Keller, M. (1997). The relation of childhood personality types to adolescent behavior and development: A longitudinal study of Icelandic children. *Developmental Psychology, 33,* 195–205.

Hart, S. N. (1991). From property to person status: Historical perspective on children's rights. *American Psychologist, 46,* 53–59.

Hart, S. N., & Brassard, M. R. (1987). A major threat to children's mental health. Psychological maltreatment. *American Psychologist, 42,* 160–165.

Harter, S. (1981). A new self-report scale of intrinsic versus extrinsic orientation in the classroom: Motivational and informational components. *Developmental Psychology, 17,* 300–312.

Harter, S. (1982). The perceived competence scale for children. *Child Development, 53,* 87–97.

Harter, S. (1983). Developmental perspectives on the self-system. In P. H. Mussen (Ed.), *Handbook of child psychology. Vol. 4: Socialization, personality and social development.* New York: Wiley.

Harter, S. (1986). Cognitive-developmental processes in the integration of concepts about emotions and the self. *Social Cognition, 4,* 119–151.

Harter, S. (1988) Developmental processes in the construction of the self. In T.D. Yawkey & J. E. Johnson (Eds.), *Integrative processes and socialization: Early to middle childhood.* Hillsdale, NJ: Erlbaum.

Harter, S. (1990). Issues in the assessment of the self-concept of children and adolescents. In A. M. LaGreca (Ed.), *Through the eyes of the child: Obtaining self-reports from children and adolescents.* Boston: Allyn & Bacon.

Harter, S. (1996). Historical roots of contemporary issues involving self-concept. In B. A. Bracken (Ed.), *Handbook of self-concept: Developmental, social, and clinical considerations.* New York: Wiley.

Harter, S. (1998). The development of self-representations. In William Damon (Series Ed.) & N. Eisenberg (Vol. Ed), *Handbook of Child Psychology: Vol 3, Social, emotional, and personality development* (5th ed.). New York: Wiley.

Harter, S., Marold, D. B., Whitesell, N. R., & Cobbs, G. (1996). A model of the effects of perceived parent and peer support on adolescent false self behavior. *Child Development, 67,* 360–374.

Harter, S., & Monsour, A. (1992). Developmental analysis of conflict caused by opposing attributes in the adolescent self-portrait. *Developmental Psychology, 28,* 251–260.

Harter, S., & Pike, R. (1984). The pictorial scale of perceived competence and social acceptance for young children. *Child Development, 55,* 1969–1982.

Harter, S., Waters, P., & Whitesell, N. R. (1998). Relational self-worth: Differences in perceived worth as a person across interpersonal contexts among adolescents. *Child Development, 69,* 756–766.

Harter, S., Waters, P. L., Whitesell, N. R., & Kastelic, D. (1998). Level of voice among female and male high school students: Relational context, support, and gender orientation. *Developmental Psychology, 34,* 892–901.

Harter, S., & Whitesell, N. (1989). Developmental changes in children's understanding of simple, multiple, and blended emotion concepts. In C. Saarni & P. Harris (Eds.), *Children's understanding of emotion.* Cambridge, England: Cambridge University Press.

Hartshorne, H., & May, M. S. (1928–1930). *Studies in the nature of character. Vol. 1: Studies in deceit. Vol. 2: Studies in self control. Vol. 3: Studies in the organization of character.* New York: Macmillan.

Hartung, B., & Sweeney, K. (1991). Why adult children return home. *Social Science Journal, 28,* 467–480.

Hartup, W. W. (1974). Aggression in childhood: Developmental perspectives. *American Psychologist, 29,* 336–341.

Hartup, W. W. (1983). Peer relations. In P. H. Mussen (Ed.), *Handbook of child psychology. Vol. 4: Socialization, personality, and social development* (pp. 103–196). New York: Wiley.

Hartup, W. W. (1989). Social relationships and their developmental significance. *American Psychologist, 44,* 120–126.

Hartup, W. W. (1992). Friendships and their developmental significance. In H. McGurk (Ed.), *Childhood social development: Contemporary perspectives.* Hove, England: Erlbaum.

Hartup, W. W. (1996). The company they keep: Friendships and their developmental significance. *Child Development, 67,* 1–13.

Hartup, W. W., Laursen, B., Stewart, M. I., & Eastenson, A. (1988). Conflict and friendship relations of young children. *Child Development, 59,* 1590–1600.

Harvey, E. (1999). Short-term and long-term effects of early parental employment on children of the National Longitudinal Survey of Youth. *Developmental Psychology, 35,* 445–459.

Harwood, R. L., Schoelmerich, A., Ventura-Cook, E., Schulze, P. A., & Wilson, S. P. (1996). Culture and class influences on Anglo and Puerto Rican mothers' beliefs regarding long-term socialization goals and child behavior. *Child Development, 67,* 2446–2461.

Haselager, G. J. T., Hartup, W. W., van Lieshout, C. F. M., & Riksen-Walraven, J. M. A. (1998). Similarities between friends and nonfriends in middle childhood. *Child Development, 69,* 1198–1208.

Hashima, P. Y., & Amato, P. R. (1994). Poverty, social support, and parental behavior. *Child Development, 65,* 394–403.

Haskett, M. E., & Kistner, J. A. (1991). Social interactions and peer perceptions of young physically abused children. *Child Development, 62,* 979–990.

Hastings, P. D., & Grusec, J. E. (1998). Parenting goals as organizers of responses to parent-child disagreement. *Developmental Psychology, 34,* 465–479.

Hausen-Corn, P. (1995). Mastery motivation in toddlers with developmental disabilities. *Child Development, 66,* 236–248.

Haviland, J. M., & Lelwica, M. (1987). The induced affect response: 10-week-old infants' responses to three emotion expressions. *Developmental Psychology, 23,* 97–104.

Hay, D. F., Caplan, M., Castle, J., & Stimson, C. A. (1991). Does sharing become increasingly "rational" in the second year of life? *Developmental Psychology, 27,* 987–993.

Hayward, C., Killen, J. D., Wilson, D. M., Hammer, L. D., Litt, I. F., Kraemer, H. C., Haydel, F., Varady, M., & Taylor, C. B. (1997). Psychiatric risk associated with puberty in adolescent girls. *Journal of the American Academy of Child and Adolescent Psychiatry, 36,* 255–262.

Hazan, C., & Shaver, P. (1987). Romantic love conceptualized as an attachment process. *Journal of Personality and Social Psychology, 52,* 511–524.

Hearold, S. (1986). A synthesis of 1043 effects of television on social behavior. In G. Comstock (Ed.), *Public communications and behavior: Volume I* (pp. 65–133). New York: Academic Press.

Hebb, D. O. (1980). *Essay on mind.* Hillsdale, NJ: Erlbaum.

Heckhausen, J., & Dweck, C. S. (1999). *Motivation and self-regulation across the life-span.* New York: Cambridge University Press.

Hedges, L. V., & Nowell, A. (1995, July 7). Sex differences in mental test scores, variability, and numbers of high-scoring individuals. *Science, 269,* 41–45.

Heider, F. (1958). *The psychology of interpersonal relations.* New York: Wiley.

Heinicke, C. M., & Westheimer, I. (1965). *Brief separations.* New York: International Universities Press.

Hendrick, B. (1994, June 7). Teen sexual activity increases, as does use of condoms. *Atlanta Constitution,* pp. A1, A6.

Henker, B., & Whalen, C. K. (1989). Hyperactivity and attention deficits. *American Psychologist, 44,* 216–223.

Hennigan, K. M., Del Rosario, M. L., Heath, L., Cook, T. D., Wharton, J. D., & Calder, B. J. (1982). Impact of the introduction of television on crime in the United States: Empirical findings and theoretical implications. *Journal of Personality and Social Psychology, 42,* 461–477.

Henry, B., Caspi, A., Moffitt, T. E., & Silva, P. A. (1996). Temperamental and familial predictors of violent and nonviolent criminal convictions: Age 3 to age 18. *Developmental Psychology, 32,* 614–623.

Herdt, G. H., & Davidson, J. (1988). The Sambia "turnim-man": Sociocultural and clinical aspects of gender formation in male pseudohermaphrodites with 5-alpha-reductase deficiency in Papua New Guinea. *Archives of Sexual Behavior, 17,* 33–56.

Hernandez, D. J. (1997). Child development and the social demography of childhood. *Child Development, 68,* 149–169.

Herrera, C., & Dunn, J. (1997). Early experiences with family conflict: Implications for arguments with a close friend. *Developmental Psychology, 33,* 869–881.

Hershberger, S. L., & D'Augelli, A. R. (1995). The impact of victimization on the mental health and suicidality of lesbian, gay, and bisexual youths. *Developmental Psychology, 31,* 65–74.

Hertsgaard, L., Gunnar, M., Erickson, M. F., & Nachmias, M. (1995). Adrenocortical responses to the Strange Situation in infants with disorganized/disoriented attachment relationships. *Child Development, 66,* 1100–1106.

Hertzberger, S. D., & Hall, J. A. (1993). Consequences of retaliatory aggression against siblings and peers: Urban minority children's expectations. *Child Development, 64,* 1773–1785.

Hess, R. D. (1970). Social class and ethnic influences upon socialization. In P. H. Mussen (Ed.), *Carmichael's manual of child psychology* (Vol. 2), New York: Wiley.

Hetherington, E. M. (1989). Coping with family transitions: Winners, losers, and survivors. *Child Development, 60,* 1–14.

Hetherington, E. M., Bridges, M., & Insabella, G. M. (1998). What matters? What does not? Five perspectives on the association between marital transitions and children's adjustment. *American Psychologist, 53,* 167–184.

Hetherington, E. M., & Camara, K. A. (1984). Families in transition: The processes of dissolution and reconstitution. In R. D. Parke (Ed.), *Review of child development research. Vol. 7: The family.* Chicago: University of Chicago Press.

Hetherington, E. M., & Clingempeel, W. G. (1992). Coping with marital transitions. *Monographs of the Society for Research in Child Development, 57,* (2–3, Serial No. 227).

Hetherington, E. M., Cox, M., & Cox, R. (1982). Effects of divorce on parents and children. In M. E. Lamb (Ed.), *Nontraditional families.* Hillsdale, NJ: Erlbaum.

Hetherington, E. M., & Frankie, G. (1967). Effect of parental dominance, warmth, and conflict on imitation in children. *Journal of Personality and Social Psychology, 6,* 119–125.

Hetherington, E. M., & Jodl, K. M. (1994). Stepfamilies as settings for child development. In A. Booth & J. Dunn (Eds.), *Stepfamilies: Who benefits? Who does not?* (pp. 55–79). Hillsdale, NJ: Erlbaum.

Hetherington, E. M., & Parke, R. D. (1975). *Child psychology: A contemporary viewpoint.* New York: McGraw-Hill.

Hetherington, E. M., & Stanley-Hagan, M. S. (1997). The effects of divorce on fathers and their children. In M. Bornstein (Ed.), *The role of the father in child development* (pp. 191–211). New York: Wiley.

Heyman, G. D., Dweck, C. S., & Cain, K. M. (1992). Young children's vulnerability to self-blame and helplessness: Relationship to beliefs about goodness. *Child Development, 63,* 401–415.

Heyman, G. D., & Gelman, S. A. (1998). Young children use motive information to make trait inferences. *Developmental Psychology, 34,* 310–321.

Higgins, E. T., & Parsons, J. E. (1983). Stages as subcultures: Social-cognitive development and the social life of the child. In E. T. Higgins, W. W. Hartup, and D. N. Ruble (Eds.), *Social cognition and social development: A sociocultural perspective.* New York: Cambridge University Press.

Higley, J. D., Hopkins, W. D., Thompson, W. W., Byrne, E. A., Hirsh, R. M., & Suomi, S. J. (1992). Peers as primary attachment sources in yearling rhesus monkeys. *Developmental Psychology, 28,* 1163–1171.

Hill, J. P., & Lynch, M. E. (1983). The intensification of gender-related role expectations during early adolescence. In J. Brooks-Gunn & A. C. Petersen (Eds.), *Girls at puberty. Biological and psychosocial perspectives.* New York: Plenum.

Hill, K. T., & Eaton, W. O. (1977). The interaction of test anxiety and success-failure experiences in determining children's arithmetic performances. *Developmental Psychology, 13,* 205–211.

Hill, P. T., Foster, G. E., & Gendler, T. (1990). *High schools with character: Alternatives to bureaucracy.* CA: Rand Corporation.

Hill, S. D., & Tomlin, C. (1981). Self-recognition in retarded children. *Child Development, 53,* 1320–1329.

Hinde, R. A. (1989). Ethological and relationships approaches. In R. Vasta (Ed.), *Annals of child development: Vol. 6. Theories of child development: Revised formulations and current issues.* Greenwich, CT: JAI Press.

Hines, M., & Kaufman, F. R. (1994). Androgen and the development of human sex-typical behavior: Rough-and-tumble play and sex of preferred playmates in children with congenital adrenal hyperplasia. *Child Development, 65,* 1042–1053.

Hinshaw, S. P., Zupan, B. A., Simmel, C., Nigg, J. T., & Melnick, S. (1997). Peer status in boys with attention-deficit hyperactivity disorder: Predictions from overt and covert antisocial behavior, social isolation, and authoritative parenting beliefs. *Child Development, 68,* 880–896.

Hobbes, T. (1904). *Leviathan.* Cambridge: Cambridge University Press. (Original work published 1651)

Hock, E., & DeMeis, D. K. (1990). Depression in mothers of infants: The role of maternal employment. *Developmental Psychology, 26,* 285–291.

Hodges, E. V. E., Boivin, M., Vitaro, F., & Bukowski, W. M. (1999). The power of friendship: Protection against an escalating cycle of peer victimization. *Developmental Psychology, 35,* 94–104.

Hodges, E. V. E., Malone, M. J., & Perry, D. G. (1997). Individual risk and social risk as interacting determinants of victimization in the peer group. *Developmental Psychology, 33,* 1032–1039.

Hodges, J., & Tizard, B. (1989). IQ and behavioral adjustment of ex-institutional adolescents. *Journal of Child Psychology and Psychiatry, 30,* 53–75.

Hofferth, S. (1996). Child care in the United States today. *The Future of Children, 6* (2), 41–61.

Hoffman, L. W. (1989). Effects of maternal employment in the two-parent family. *American Psychologist, 44,* 283–292.

Hoffman, L. W. (1991). The influence of the family environment on personality: Accounting for sibling differences. *Psychological Bulletin, 108,* 187–203.

Hoffman, L. W. (1994). Commentary on Plomin, R. (1994): A proof and a disproof questioned. *Social Development, 3,* 60–63.

Hoffman, M. L. (1970). Moral development. In P. H. Mussen (Ed.), *Carmichael's manual of child psychology* (Vol. 2). New York: Wiley.

Hoffman, M. L. (1975). Moral internalization, parental power, and the nature of parent-child interaction. *Developmental Psychology, 11,* 228–239.

Hoffman, M. L. (1981). Is altruism part of human nature? *Journal of Personality and Social Psychology, 40,* 121–137.

Hoffman, M. L. (1988). Moral development. In M. H. Bornstein & M. E. Lamb (Eds.), *Developmental Psychology: An advanced textbook* (2nd ed., pp. 497–548). Hillsdale, NJ: Erlbaum.

Hoffman, M. L. (1993). Empathy, social cognition, and moral education. In A. Garrod (Ed.), *Approaches to moral development: New research and emerging themes.* New York: Teachers College Press.

Hoffman, S. D., Foster, E. M., & Furstenberg, F. F., Jr. (1993). Reevaluating the costs of teenage childbearing. *Demography, 30,* 1–13.

Hoffner, C., & Badzinski, D. M. (1989). Children's integration of facial and situational cues to emotion. *Child Development, 60,* 411–422.

Holden, C. (1996, November 15). Small refugees suffer the effects of early neglect. *Science, 274,* 1076–1077.

Holmbeck, G. N., & Hill, J. P. (1991). Conflictive engagement, positive affect, and menarche in families with seventh-grade girls. *Child Development, 62,* 1030–1048.

Horney, K. (1967). *Feminine psychology.* New York: Norton. (Original work published 1923–1937)

Hornik, R., & Gunnar, M. R. (1988). A descriptive analysis of social referencing. *Child Development, 59,* 626–634.

Horowitz, F. D. (1992). John B. Watson's legacy: Learning and environment. *Developmental Psychology, 28,* 360–367.

Howard-Pitney, B., LaFromboise, T. D., Basil, M., September, B., & Johnson, M. (1992). Psychological and social indicators of suicide ideation and suicide attempts in Zuni adolescents. *Journal of Consulting and Clinical Psychology, 60,* 473–476.

Howe, N., Petrakos, H., & Rinaldi, C. M. (1998). "All the sheeps are dead. He murdered them": Sibling pretense, negotiation, internal state language, and relationship quality. *Child Development, 69,* 182–191.

Howe, N., & Ross, H. S. (1990). Socialization, perspective-taking, and the sibling relationship. *Developmental Psychology, 26,* 160–165.

Howes, C. (1988). Peer interaction of young children. *Monographs of the Society for Research in Child Development, 53* (1, Serial No. 217).

Howes, C. (1990). Can the age of entry into child care and the quality of child care predict adjustment in kindergarten? *Developmental Psychology, 26,* 292–303.

Howes, C. (1992). *The collaborative construction of pretend.* Albany: State University of New York Press.

Howes, C., Droege, K., & Matheson, C. C. (1994). Play and communicative processes within long-term and short-term friendship dyads. *Journal of Social and Personal Relationships, 11,* 401–410.

Howes, C., Hamilton, C. E., & Matheson, C. C. (1994). Children's relationships with peers: Differential associations with aspects of the parent-child relationship. *Child Development, 65,* 253–263.

Howes, C., Hamilton, C. E., & Philipsen, L. C. (1998). Stability and continuity of child-caregiver and child-peer relationships. *Child Development, 69,* 418–426.

Howes, C., & Matheson, C. C. (1992). Sequences in the development of competent play with peers: Social and social pretend play. *Developmental Psychology, 28,* 961–974.

Howes, C., Phillips, D. A., & Whitebrook, M. (1992). Thresholds of quality: Implications for the social development of children in center-based child care. *Child Development, 63,* 449–460.

Howes, P., & Markman, H. J. (1989). Marital quality and child functioning: A longitudinal investigation. *Child Development, 60,* 1044–1051.

Hudley, C., & Graham, S. (1995). School-based interventions for aggressive African-American boys. *Applied and Preventive Psychology, 4,* 185–195.

Hudson, L. M., Forman, E. R., & Brion-Meisels, S. (1982). Role-taking as a predictor of prosocial behavior in cross-age tutors. *Child Development, 53,* 1320–1329.

Huesmann, L. R. (1986). Psychological processes promoting the relation between exposure to media violence and aggressive behavior by the viewer. *Journal of Social Issues, 42,* 125–139.

Huesmann, L. R., Eron, L. D., Lefkowitz, M. M., & Walder, L. O. (1984). Stability of aggression over time and generations. *Developmental Psychology, 20,* 1120–1134.

Huesmann, L. R., Lagerspitz, K., & Eron, L. D. (1984). Intervening variables in the TV violence-aggression relation: Evidence from two countries. *Developmental Psychology, 20,* 746–775.

Huesmann, L. R., & Miller, L. S. (1994). Long-term effects of repeated exposure to media violence in childhood. In L. R. Huesmann (Ed.), *Aggressive behavior: Current perspectives.* New York: Plenum.

Hughes, C., & Dunn, J. (1998). Understanding mind and emotion: Longitudinal associations with mental-state talk between young friends. *Developmental Psychology, 34,* 1026–1037.

Hughes, R., Jr., Tingle, B. A., & Sawin, D. B. (1981). Development of empathic understanding in children. *Child Development, 52,* 122–128.

Humphrey, M., & Humphrey, H. (1988). *Families with a difference: Varieties of surrogate parenthood.* London: Routledge.

Humphreys, A. P., & Smith, P. K. (1987). Rough and tumble, friendship, and dominance in school children: Evidence for continuity and change with age. *Child Development, 58,* 201–212.

Hunt, P., & Goetz, L. (1997). Research on inclusive educational programs, practices, and outcomes for students with severe disabilities. *Journal of Special Education, 31,* 3–29.

Hunter, J. E., & Hunter, R. F. (1984). Validity and utility of alternative predictors of job performance. *Psychological Bulletin, 96,* 72–98.

Huntsinger, C. S., Jose, P. E., & Larson, S. L. (1998). Do parent practices to encourage academic competence influence the social adjustment of young European American and Chinese American children? *Developmental Psychology, 34,* 747–756.

Huston, A. C. (1983). Sex-typing. In P. H. Mussen (Ed.), *Handbook of child psychology: Vol. 4. Socialization, personality, and social development* (4th ed., pp. 387–467). New York: Wiley.

Huston, A. C., Donnerstein, E., Fairchild, H., Feshbach, N. D., Katz, P. A., Murray, J. P., Rubinstein, E. A., Wilcox, B. L., & Zuckerman, D. (1992). *Big world, small screen.* Lincoln: University of Nebraska Press.

Hutt, C. (1972). *Males and females.* Baltimore: Penguin Books.

Hwang, C. P. (1986). Behavior of Swedish primary and secondary caretaking fathers in relation to mother's presence. *Developmental Psychology, 22,* 749–751.

Hyde, J. S. (1984). How large are sex differences in aggression? A developmental meta-analysis. *Developmental Psychology, 20,* 722–736.

Hyde, J. S., Fennema, E., & Lamon, S. J. (1990). Gender differences in mathematics performance: A meta-analysis. *Psychological Bulletin, 107,* 139–155.

Hyde, J. S., & Plant, E. A. (1995). Magnitude of psychological gender differences: Another side to the story. *American Psychologist, 50,* 159–161.

Hymel, S. (1983). Preschool children's peer relations: Issues in sociometric assessment. *Merrill-Palmer Quarterly, 19,* 237–260.

Hymel, S. (1986). Interpretations of peer behavior: Affective bias in childhood and adolescence. *Child Development, 57,* 431–445.

Hymel, S., Bowker, A., & Woody, E. (1993). Aggressive versus withdrawn unpopular children: Variations in peer and self-perceptions in multiple domains. *Child Development, 64,* 879–896.

Hymel, S., Rubin, K. H., Rowden, L., & Le Mare, L. (1990). Children's peer relationships: Longitudinal prediction of internalizing and externalizing problems from middle to late childhood. *Child Development, 61,* 2004–2021.

Hyson, M. C., Hirsch-Pasek, K., & Rescorla, L. (1989). *Academic environments in early childhood: Challenge or pressure?* Summary report to the Spencer Foundation.

Iannotti, R. J. (1978). Effect of role-taking experiences on role-taking, empathy, altruism, and aggression. *Developmental Psychology, 14,* 119–124.

Imperato-McGinley, J., Peterson, R. E., Gautier, T., & Sturla, E. (1979). Androgyns and the evolution of male gender identity among male pseudohermaphrodites with 5a-reductase deficiency. *New England Journal of Medicine, 300,* 1233–1237.

Inhelder, B., & Piaget, J. (1958). *The growth of logical thinking from childhood to adolescence.* New York: Basic Books.

Intons-Peterson, M. J. (1988). *Gender concepts of Swedish and American youth.* Hillsdale, NJ: Erlbaum.

Intons-Peterson, M. J., & Reddel, M. (1984). What do people ask about a neonate? *Developmental Psychology, 20,* 358–359.

Isabella, R. A. (1993). Origins of attachment: Maternal interactive behavior across the first year. *Child Development, 64,* 605–621.

Isabella, R. A., & Belsky, J. (1991). Interactional synchrony and the origins of infant-mother attachment. *Child Development, 62,* 373–384.

Isberg, R. S., Hauser, S. I., Jacobson, A. M., Powers, S. I., Noam, G., Weiss-Perry, B., & Follansbee, D. (1989). Parental contexts of adolescent self-esteem: A developmental perspective. *Journal of Youth and Adolescence, 18,* 1–23.

Izard, C. E. (1982). *Measuring emotions in infants and children.* New York: Cambridge University Press.

Izard, C. E. (1993). Four systems for emotion activation: Cognitive and noncognitive processes. *Psychological Review, 100,* 68–90.

Izard, C. E., Fantauzzo, C. A., Castle, J. M., Haynes. O. M., Rayias, M. F., & Putnam, P. H. (1995). The ontogeny and significance of infants' facial expressions in the first 9 months of life. *Developmental Psychology, 31,* 997–1013.

Izard, C. E., Hembree, E. A., & Heubner, R. R. (1987). Infants' emotion expressions to acute pain: Developmental change and stability of individual differences. *Developmental Psychology, 23,* 105–113.

Jaccard, J., & Dittus, P. (1991). *Parent-teen communication: Toward the prevention of unintended pregnancies.* New York: Springer-Verlag.

Jaccard, J., Dittus, P. J., & Gordon, V. V. (1998). Parent-adolescent congruency in reports of adolescent sexual behavior and in communications about sexual behavior. *Child Development, 69,* 247–261.

Jacklin, C. N., & Maccoby, E. E. (1978). Social behavior at 33 months in same-sex and mixed-sex dyads. *Child Development, 49,* 557–569.

Jackson, J. F. (1993). Human behavioral genetics, Scarr's theory and her views on intervention: A critical review and commentary on their implications for African-American children. *Child Development, 63,* 1318–1332.

Jacobs, J. E., & Eccles, J. S. (1992). The impact of mothers' gender-role stereotypic beliefs on mothers' and children's ability perceptions. *Journal of Personality and Social Psychology, 63,* 932–944.

Jacobs, L. C., & Chase, C. I. (1989). Student participation in and attitudes toward high school activities. *The High School Journal, 22,* 175–181.

Jacobson, J. L., & Wille, D. E. (1986). The influence of attachment pattern on developmental changes in peer interaction from the toddler to the preschool period. *Child Development, 57,* 338–347.

Jacobsen, T., & Hofmann, V. (1997). Children's attachment representations: Longitudinal relations to school behavior and academic competency in middle childhood and adolescence. *Developmental Psychology, 33,* 703–710.

Jadack, R. A., Hyde, J. S., Moore, C. F., & Keller, M. L. (1995). Moral reasoning about sexually transmitted diseases. *Child Development, 66,* 167–177.

Jagers, R. J., Bingham, K., & Hans, S. L. (1996). Socialization and social judgments among inner-city African-American kindergartners. *Child Development, 67,* 140–150.

Jaio, S., Ji, G., & Jing, Q. (1996). Cognitive development of Chinese urban only children and children with siblings. *Child Development, 67,* 387–395.

Johnson, D. W., & Johnson, R. T. (1989). *Cooperation and competition: Theory and research.* Edina, MN: Interaction.

Johnson, M. H. (1997). *Developmental cognitive neuroscience: An introduction.* Cambridge, MA: Blackwell.

Johnson, N. (1967). *How to talk back to your television.* Boston: Little, Brown.

Johnson, W., Emde, R. N., Pannabecker, B., Stenberg, C., & Davis, M. (1982). Maternal perception of infant emotion from birth through 18 months. *Infant Behavior and Development, 5,* 313–322.

Johnston, J., & Ettema, J. S. (1982). *Positive images.* Newbury Park, CA: Sage.

Jones, D. C., Abbey, B. B., & Cumberland, A. (1998). The development of display rule knowledge: Linkage with family expressiveness and social competence. *Child Development, 69,* 1209–1222.

Jones, M. C., & Bayley, N. (1950). Physical maturing among boys as related to behavior. *Journal of Educational Psychology, 41,* 129–148.

Jones, R. A., Hendrick, C., & Epstein, Y. (1979). *Introduction to social psychology.* Sunderland, MA: Sinauer.

Jones, S. S. (1996). Imitation or exploration? Young children's matching of adults' oral gestures. *Child Development, 67,* 1952–1969.

Jonsson, J. O., & Gahler, M. (1997). Family dissolution, family reconstitution, and children's educational careers: Recent evidence for Sweden. *Demography, 34,* 277–293.

Jose, P. M. (1990). Just world reasoning in children's immanent justice arguments. *Child Development, 61,* 1024–1033.

Jouriles, E. N., Murphy, C. M., Farris, A. M., Smith, D. A., Richters, J. E., & Waters, E. (1991). Marital adjustment, parental disagreements about child rearing and behavior problems in boys: Increasing the specificity of the marital assessment. *Child Development, 62,* 1424–1433.

Juffer, F., & Rosenboom, L. G. (1997). Infant-mother attachment of internationally adopted children in the Netherlands. *International Journal of Behavioral Development, 20,* 93–107.

Jussim, L., & Eccles, J. S. (1992). Teacher expectations II: Construction and reflection of student achievement. *Journal of Personality and Social Psychology, 63,* 947–961.

Kagan, J. (1972). Do infants think? *Scientific American, 226,* 74–82.

Kagan, J. (1976). Emergent themes in human development. *American Scientist, 64,* 186–196.

Kagan, J. (1984). *The nature of the child.* New York: Basic Books.

Kagan, J. (1989). *Unstable ideas: Temperament, cognition. and self.* Cambridge, MA: Cambridge University Press.

Kagan, J. (1991). Continuity and discontinuity. In S. E. Brauth, W. S. Hall, & R. J. Dooling (Eds.), *Plasticity of development.* Cambridge, MA: Bradford/MIT Press.

Kagan, J. (1992). Behavior, biology, and the meaning of temperamental constructs. *Pediatrics, 90,* 510–513.

Kagan, J., Kearsley, R. B., & Zelazo, P. R. (1978). *Infancy: Its place in human development.* Cambridge, MA: Harvard University Press.

Kagan, J., & Moss, H. A. (1962). *Birth to maturity.* New York: Wiley.

Kagan, S., & Masden, M. C. (1971). Cooperation and competition of Mexican, Mexican-American, and Anglo-American children of two ages and four instructional sets. *Developmental Psychology, 5,* 32–39.

Kagan, S., & Masden, M. C. (1972). Rivalry in Anglo-American and Mexican children of two ages. *Journal of Personality and Social Psychology, 24,* 214–220.

Kagan, S., & Zahn, G. L. (1975). Field dependence and the school achievement gap between Anglo-American and Mexican-American children. *Journal of Educational Psychology, 67,* 643–650.

Kahn, P. H., Jr. (1992). Children's obligatory and discretionary moral judgements. *Child Development, 63,* 416–430.

Kaitz, M., Meschulach-Safaty, O., Auerbach, J., & Eidelman, A. (1988). A reexamination of newborns' ability to imitate facial expressions. *Developmental Psychology, 24,* 3–7.

Kandel, D. (1973). Adolescent marijuana use: Role of parents and peers. *Science, 181,* 1067–1070.

Kanfer, F. H., Stifter, E., & Morris, S. J. (1981). Self-control and altruism: Delay of gratification for another. *Child Development, 52,* 674–682.

Kaplan, P. S., Jung, P. C., Ryther, J. S., & Zarlengo-Strouse, P. (1996). Infant-directed versus adult-directed speech as signals for faces. *Developmental Psychology, 32,* 880–891.

Katcher, A. (1955). The discrimination of sex differences by young children. *Journal of Genetic Psychology, 87,* 131–143.

Katz, P. A. (1979). The development of female identity. *Sex Roles, 5,* 155–178.

Katz, P. A., & Walsh, P. V. (1991). Modification of children's gender-stereotyped behavior. *Child Development, 62,* 338–351.

Kaufman, A. S., & Zigler, E. (1989). The intergenerational transmission of child abuse. In D. Cicchetti & V. Carlson (Eds.), *Child maltreatment: Theory and research on the causes and consequences of child abuse and neglect* (pp. 129–150). New York: Cambridge University Press.

Kazdin, A. E. (1995). *Conduct disorders in childhood and adolescence* (2nd ed.). Thousand Oaks, CA: Sage.

Kean, A. W. G. (1937). The history of the criminal liability of children. *Law Quarterly Review, 3,* 364–370.

Keane, S. P., Brown, K. P., & Crenshaw, T. M. (1990). Children's intention-cue detection as a function of maternal social behavior: Pathways to social rejection. *Developmental Psychology, 26,* 1004–1009.

Keasey, C. B. (1971). Social participation as a factor in the moral development of preadolescents. *Developmental Psychology, 5,* 216–220.

Keating, D., & Clark, L. V. (1980). Development of physical and social reasoning in adolescence. *Developmental Psychology, 16,* 23–30.

Kee, D. W. (1986). Computer play. In A. W. Gottfried & C. C. Brown (Eds.), *Play interactions: The contribution of play materials and parental involvement to children's development.* Lexington, MA: Lexington Books.

Keith, J. (1985). Age in anthropological research. In R. H. Binstock & E. Shanus (Eds.), *Handbook of aging and the social sciences* (2nd ed.). New York: Van Nostrand Reinhold.

Kellaghan, T., & MacNamara, J. (1972). Family correlates of verbal reasoning ability. *Developmental Psychology, 7,* 49–53.

Keller, A., Ford, L. H., Jr., & Meachum, J. A. (1978). Dimensions of self-concept in preschool children. *Developmental Psychology, 14,* 483–489.

Keller, H., & Scholmerich, A. (1987). Infant vocalizations and parental reactions during the first four months of life. *Developmental Psychology, 23,* 62–67.

Kelley, H. H. (1973). The process of causal attribution. *American Psychologist, 28,* 107–128.

Kelley, M. L., Power, T. G., & Wimbush, D. D. (1992). Determinants of disciplinary practices in low-income Black mothers. *Child Development, 63,* 573–582.

Kempe, R. S., & Kempe, C. H. (1978). *Child abuse.* Cambridge, MA: Harvard University Press.

Kendall-Tackett, K. A., Williams, L. M., & Finkelhor, D. (1993). Impact of sexual abuse on children: A review and synthesis of recent empirical studies. *Psychological Bulletin, 113,* 164–180.

Kennell, J. H., Voos, D. K., & Klaus, M. H. (1979). Parent-infant bonding. In J. D. Osofsky (Ed.), *Handbook of infant development.* New York: Wiley.

Kerns, K. A., & Berenbaum, S. A. (1991). Sex differences in spatial ability in children. *Behavior Genetics, 21,* 383–396.

Kerns, K. A., Klepec, L., & Cole, A. (1996). Peer relationships and preadolescents' perceptions of security in the child-mother relationship. *Developmental Psychology, 32,* 457–466.

Kerr, M., Lambert, W. W., & Bem, D. J. (1996). Life course sequelae of childhood shyness in Sweden: Comparison with the United States. *Developmental Psychology, 32,* 1100–1105.

Kerr, M., Lambert, W. W., Stattin, H., & Klackbengerg-Larsson, I. (1994). Stability of inhibition in a Swedish longitudinal sample. *Child Development, 65,* 138–146.

Kerwin, C., Ponterotto, J. G., Jackson, B. L., & Harris, A. (1993). Racial identity in biracial children: A qualitative investigation. *Journal of Counseling Psychology, 40,* 221–231.

Kessen, W. (1975). *Childhood in China.* New Haven, CT: Yale University Press.

Kett, J. F. (1977). *Rites of passage. Adolescence in America, 1790 to the present.* New York: Basic Books.

Kiesewetter, J. (1993, December 17). Top kids show also ranks as most violent. *The Cincinnati Enquirer,* p. A1.

Kilpatrick, A. (1992). *Long-range effects of child and adolescent sexual experiences: Myths, mores, and menaces.* Hillsdale, NJ: Erlbaum.

Kim, J. M. (1998). Korean children's concepts of adult and peer authority and moral reasoning. *Developmental Psychology, 34,* 947–955.

Kim, U., & Choi, S. H. (1994). Individualism, collectivism, and child development: A Korean perspective. In P. M. Greenfield & R. R. Cocking (Eds.), *Cross cultural roots of minority child development.* Hillsdale, NJ: Erlbaum.

Kimura, D. (1992). Sex differences in the brain. *Scientific American, 267,* 119–125.

Kinney, D. A. (1993). From nerds to normals: The recovery of identity among adolescents from middle school to high school. *Sociology of Education, 44,* 21–40.

Kirchner, J. (1998, January 25). State making adoption process easier. Associated Press, as reported in the *Athens Banner Herald,* p. 4A.

Kitzinger, C., & Wilkinson, S. (1995). Transitions from heterosexuality to lesbianism: The discursive production of lesbian identities. *Developmental Psychology, 31,* 95–104.

Klaus, M. H., & Kennell, J. H. (1976). *Maternal-infant bonding.* St. Louis: Mosby.

Klaus, M. H., & Kennell, J. H. (1982). *Parent-infant bonding.* St. Louis: Mosby.

Klebanov, P. K., Brooks-Gunn, J., McCarton, C., & McCormick, M. C. (1998). The contribution of neighborhood and family income to developmental test scores over the first three years of life. *Child Development, 69,* 1420–1436.

Klein, D. M., & White, J. M. (1996). *Family theories: An introduction.* Thousand Oaks, CA: Sage.

Klimes-Dougan, B., & Kistner, J. (1990). Physically abused preschoolers' responses to peers' distress. *Developmental Psychology, 26,* 599–602.

Kline, M., Tschann, J. M., Johnston, J. R., & Wallerstein, J. S. (1989). Children's adjustment to joint and sole physical custody families. *Developmental Psychology, 25,* 430–438.

Klinnert, M. D., Emde, R. N., Butterfield, P., & Campos, J. J. (1986). Social referencing: The infant's use of emotional signals from a friendly adult with mother present. *Developmental Psychology, 22,* 427–432.

Kobak, R. R., & Sceery, A. (1988). Attachment in late adolescence: Working models, affect regulation and representation of self and others. *Child Development, 59,* 135–146.

Kochanska, G. (1991). Socialization and temperament in the development of guilt and conscience. *Child Development, 62,* 1379–1392.

Kochanska, G. (1992). Children's interpersonal influence with mothers and peers. *Developmental Psychology, 28,* 491–499.

Kochanska, G. (1993). Toward a synthesis of parental socialization and child temperament in early development of conscience. *Child Development, 64,* 325–347.

Kochanska, G. (1995). Children's temperament, mothers' discipline, and the security of attachment: Multiple pathways to emerging internalization. *Child Development, 66,* 597–615.

Kochanska, G. (1997a). Multiple pathways to conscience for children with different temperaments: From toddlerhood to age 5. *Developmental Psychology, 33,* 228–240.

Kochanska, G. (1997b). Mutually responsive orientation between mothers and their young: Implications for early socialization. *Child Development, 68,* 94–112.

Kochanska, G. (1998). Mother-child relationship, child fearfulness, and emerging attachment: A short-term longitudinal study. *Developmental Psychology, 34,* 480–490.

Kochanska, G., & Aksan, N. (1995). Mother-child mutually positive affect, the quality of child compliance to requests and prohibitions, and mater-

nal control as correlates of early internalization. *Child Development, 66,* 236–254.

Kochanska, G., Casey, R. J., & Fukumoto, A. (1995). Toddlers' sensitivity to standard violations. *Child Development, 66,* 643–656.

Kochanska, G., Padavich, D. L., & Koenig, A. L. (1996). Children's narratives about hypothetical moral dilemmas and objective measures of their conscience: Mutual relations and socialization antecedents. *Child Development, 67,* 1420–1436.

Kochanska, G., Tjebkes, T. L., & Forman, D. R. (1998). Children's emerging regulation of conduct: Restraint, compliance, and internalization from infancy to the second year. *Child Development, 69,* 1378–1389.

Kochenderfer, B. J., & Ladd, G. W. (1996). Peer victimization: Cause or consequence of school maladjustment? *Child Development, 67,* 1305–1317.

Kohlberg, L. (1963). The development of children's orientations toward a moral order: I. Sequence in the development of moral thought. *Vita Humana, 6,* 11–33.

Kohlberg, L. (1966). A cognitive-developmental analysis of children's sex-role concepts and attitudes. In E. E. Maccoby (Ed.), *The development of sex differences.* Stanford, CA: Stanford University Press.

Kohlberg, L. (1969). Stage and sequence: The cognitive-developmental approach to socialization. In D. A. Goslin (Ed.), *Handbook of socialization theory and research.* Skokie, IL: Rand McNally.

Kohlberg, L. (1975, June). The cognitive-developmental approach to moral education. *Phi Delta Kappan,* pp. 670–677.

Kohlberg, L. (1981). *Essays on moral development.* Vol. 1. *The philosophy of moral development.* San Francisco: Harper & Row.

Kohlberg, L. (1984). *Essays on moral development.* Vol. 2. *The psychology of moral development.* San Francisco: Harper & Row.

Kohn, M. L. (1979). The effects of social class on parental values and practices. In D. Reiss & H. A. Hoffman (Eds.), *The American family: Dying or developing?* (pp. 49–68). New York: Plenum.

Kopp, C. B. (1987). The growth of self-regulation: Caregivers and children. In N. Eisenberg (Ed.), *Contemporary topics in developmental psychology.* New York: Wiley.

Kopp, C. B. (1989). Regulation of distress and negative emotions: A developmental view. *Developmental Psychology, 25,* 343–354.

Kortenhaus, C. M., & Demarest, J. (1993). Gender role stereotyping in children's literature: An update. *Sex Roles, 28,* 219–232.

Kovacs, D. M., Parker, J. G., & Hoffman, L. W. (1996). Behavioral, affective, and social correlates of involvement in cross-sex friendships in elementary school. *Child Development, 67,* 2269–2286.

Kowal, A., & Kramer, L. (1997). Children's understanding of parental differential treatment. *Child Development, 68,* 113–126.

Krevans, J., & Gibbs, J. C. (1996). Parents' use of inductive discipline: Relations to children's empathy and prosocial behavior. *Child Development, 67,* 3263–3277.

Kroger, J. (1995). The differentiation of "firm" and "developmental" foreclosure identity statuses: A longitudinal study. *Journal of Adolescent Research, 10,* 317–337.

Kroger, J. (1996). Identity, regression, and development. *Journal of Adolescence, 19,* 203–222.

Kruger, A. C. (1992). The effect of peer and adult-child transductive discussions on moral reasoning. *Merrill-Palmer Quarterly, 38,* 191–211.

Kruger, A. C., & Tomasello, M. (1986). Transactive discussions with peers and adults. *Developmental Psychology, 22,* 681–685.

Kuchuk, A., Vibbert, M., & Bornstein, M. H. (1986). The perception of smiling and its experiential correlates in three-month-old infants. *Child Development, 57,* 1054–1061.

Kuczynski, L. (1983). Reasoning, prohibitions, and motivations for compliance. *Developmental Psychology, 19,* 126–134.

Kuczynski, L., & Kochanska, G. (1995). Function and content of maternal demands: Developmental significance of early demands for competent action. *Child Development, 66,* 616–628.

Kuczynski, L., Zahn-Waxler, C., & Radke-Yarrow, M. (1987). Development and content of imitation in the second and third years of life: A socialization perspective. *Developmental Psychology, 23,* 276–282.

Kuebli, J., Butler, S., & Fivush, R. (1995). Mother-child talk about past emotions: Relations of maternal language and child gender over time. *Cognition and Emotion, 9,* 265–283.

Kuhn, D. (1992). Cognitive development. In M. H. Bornstein & M. E. Lamb (Eds.), *Developmental psychology: An advanced textbook* (3rd ed.). Hillsdale, NJ: Erlbaum.

Kuhn, D., Kohlberg, L., Langer, J., & Haan, N. (1977). The development of formal operations in logical and moral judgment. *Genetic Psychology Monographs, 95,* 97–188.

Kuhn, D., Nash, S. C., & Brucken, L. (1978). Sex-role concepts of two- and three-year-olds. *Child Development, 49,* 445–451.

Kulik, J. A., & Kulik, C. C. (1992). Meta-analytic findings on grouping programs. *Gifted Child Quarterly, 36,* 73–77.

Kunkel, D., & Roberts, D. (1991). Young minds and marketplace value: Issues in children's advertising. *Journal of Social Issues, 47*(1), 57–72.

Kuo, Z. Y. (1930). The genesis of the cat's response to the rat. *Journal of Comparative and Physiological Psychology, 11,* 1–35.

Kurdek, L. A., & Fine, M. A. (1994). Family acceptance and family control as predictors of adjustment in young adolescents: Linear, curvilinear, or interactive effects? *Child Development, 65,* 1137–1146.

Kurdek, L. A., Fine, M. A., & Sinclair, R. J. (1995). School adjustment in sixth graders: Parenting transitions, peer climate, and peer norm effects. *Child Development, 66,* 430–445.

Kurdek, L. A., & Krile, D. (1982). A developmental analysis of the relation between peer acceptance and both interpersonal understanding and perceived social self-competence. *Child Development, 53,* 1485–1491.

La Barbera, J. D., Izard, C. E., Vietze, P., & Parisi, S. A. (1976). Four- and six-month-old infants' visual responses to joy, anger, and neutral expressions. *Child Development, 47,* 535–538.

Ladd, G. W. (1990). Having friends, keeping friends, making friends, and being liked by peers in the classroom: Predictors of children's early school adjustment. *Child Development, 61,* 1081–1100.

Ladd, G. W., & Golter, B. S. (1988). Parents' management of preschoolers' peer relations: Is it related to children's social competence? *Developmental Psychology, 24,* 109–117.

Ladd, G. W., & Hart, C. H. (1992). Creating informal play opportunities: Are parents' and preschoolers' initiations related to children's competence with peers? *Developmental Psychology, 28,* 1179–1187.

Ladd, G. W., Kochenderfer, B. J., & Coleman, C. C. (1996). Friendship quality as a predictor of young children's early school adjustment. *Child Development, 67,* 1103–1118.

Ladd, G. W., Kochenderfer, B. J., & Coleman, C. C. (1997). Classroom peer acceptance, friendship, and victimization: Distinct relational systems that contribute uniquely to children's school adjustment. *Child Development, 68,* 1181–1197.

Ladd, G. W., & Kochenderfer Ladd, B. (1998). Parenting behaviors and parent-child relationships: Correlates of peer victimization in kindergarten? *Developmental Psychology, 34,* 1450–1458.

Ladd, G. W., & Price, J. M. (1987). Predicting children's social and school adjustment following the transition from preschool to kindergarten. *Child Development, 58,* 1168–1189.

Ladd, G. W., Price, J. M., & Hart, C. H. (1988). Predicting preschoolers' play status from their playground behaviors. *Child Development, 59,* 986–992.

La Freniere, P., Strayer, F. F., & Gauthier, R. (1984). The emergence of same-sex affiliative preferences among preschool peers: A developmental ethological perspective. *Child Development, 55,* 1958–1965.

Lamb, M. E. (1975). Fathers: Forgotten contributors to child development. *Human Development, 18,* 245–266.

Lamb, M. E. (1981). The development of father-infant relationships. In M. E. Lamb (Ed.), *The role of the father in child development.* New York: Wiley.

Lamb, M. E. (1997). *The role of the father in child development* (rev. ed.). New York: Wiley.

Lamb, M. E., Easterbrooks, M. A., & Holden, G. W. (1980). Reinforcement and punishment among preschoolers: Characteristics, effects, and correlates. *Child Development, 51,* 1230–1236.

Lamb, M. E., & Oppenheim, D. (1989). Fatherhood and father-child relations. Five years of research. In S. H. Cath, A. Gurwitt, & L. Gunsberg (Eds.), *Fathers and their families.* Hillsdale, NJ: Erlbaum.

Lamborn, S. D., Mounts, N. S., Steinberg, L., & Dornbusch, S. M. (1991). Patterns of competence and adjustment among adolescents from authoritative, authoritarian, indulgent, and neglectful families. *Child Development, 62,* 1049–1065.

Lamborn, S. D., & Steinberg, L. (1993). Emotional autonomy redux: Revising Ryan and Lynch. *Child Development, 64,* 483–499.

Landry, S. H., Smith, K. E., Miller-Loncar, C. L., & Swank, P. R. (1998). The relation of change in maternal interactive styles to the developing social competence of full-term and preterm children. *Child Development, 69,* 105–123.

Langlois, J. H. (1986). From the eye of the beholder to behavioral reality: Development of social behaviors and social relations as a function of physical attractiveness. In C. P. Herman, M. P. Zanna, & E. T. Higgins (Eds.), *Physical appearance, stigma, and social behavior: The Ontario Symposium* (Vol. 3). Hillsdale, NJ: Erlbaum.

Langlois, J. H., & Downs, A. C. (1979). Peer relations as a function of physical attractiveness: The eye of the beholder or behavioral reality. *Child Development, 50,* 409–418.

Langlois, J. H., Ritter, J. M., Casey, R. J., & Sawin, D. B. (1995). Infant attractiveness predicts maternal behaviors and attitudes. *Developmental Psychology, 31,* 464–472.

Langlois, J. H., Ritter, J. M., Roggman, L. A., & Vaughn, L. S. (1991). Facial diversity and infant preferences for attractive faces. *Developmental Psychology, 27,* 79–84.

Langlois, J. H., Roggman, L. A., & Rieser-Danner, L. A. (1990). Infants' differential social responses to attractive and unattractive faces. *Developmental Psychology, 26,* 153–159.

Lansford, J. E., & Parker, J. G. (1999). Children's interactions in triads: Behavioral profiles and effects of gender and patterns of friendship among members. *Developmental Psychology, 35,* 80–93.

Laosa, L. M. (1981). Maternal behavior: Sociocultural diversity in modes of family interaction. In R. W. Henderson (Ed.), *Parent-child interaction: Theory, research, and prospects.* Orlando, FL: Academic Press.

Lapsley, D. K. (1996). *Moral psychology.* Boulder, CO: Westview.

Lapsley, D. K., Milstead, M., Quintana, S. M., Flannery, D., & Buss, R. R. (1986). Adolescent egocentrism and formal operations: Tests of a theoretical assumption. *Developmental Psychology, 22,* 800–807.

Larson, R., & Ham, M. (1993). Stress and "storm and stress" in early adolescence: The relationship of negative events with dysphoric affect. *Developmental Psychology, 29,* 130–140.

Larson, R. W., & Richards, M. H. (1991). Daily companionship in late childhood and early adolescence: Changing developmental contexts. *Child Development, 62,* 284–300.

Larson, R. W., Richards, M. H., Moneta, G., Holmbeck, G., & Duckett, E. (1996). Changes in adolescents' daily interactions with their families from ages 10 to 18: Disengagement and transformation. *Developmental Psychology, 32,* 744–753.

Laumann, E. O., Gagnon, J. H., Michael, R. T., & Michaels, S. (1994). *The social organization of sexuality: Sexual practices in the United States.* Chicago: University of Chicago Press.

Laursen, B., Coy, K. C., & Collins, W. A. (1998). Reconsidering changes in parent-child conflict across adolescence: A meta-analysis. *Child Development, 69,* 817–832.

Laursen, B., Hartup, W. W., & Koplas, A. L. (1996). Towards understanding peer conflict. *Merrill-Palmer Quarterly, 42,* 76–102.

Leaper, C. (1994). *New directions for child development: Vol. 65. Childhood gender segregation: Causes and consequences.* San Francisco: Jossey-Bass.

Leaper, C., Anderson, K. J., & Sanders, P. (1998). Moderators of gender effects on parents' talk to their children. *Developmental Psychology, 34,* 3–27.

LeCapitaine, J. E. (1987). The relationship between emotional development and moral development and the differential impact of three psychological interventions on children. *Psychology in the Schools, 24,* 372–378.

Lee, K., Cameron, C. A., Xu, F., Fu, G., & Board, J. (1997). Chinese and Canadian children's evaluation of lying and truth telling: Similarities and differences in the context of pro- and antisocial behaviors. *Child Development, 68,* 924–934.

Legerstee, M., Anderson, D., & Schaffer, A. (1998). Five- and eight-month-old infants recognize their faces and voices as familiar social stimuli. *Child Development, 69,* 37–50.

Leinbach, M. D., & Fagot, B. I. (1986). Acquisition of gender labeling: A test for toddlers. *Sex Roles, 15,* 655–666.

Leinbach, M. D., & Fagot, B. I. (1993). Categorical habituation to male and female faces: Gender schematic processing in infancy. *Infant Behavior and Development, 16,* 317–322.

LeMare, L. J., & Rubin, K. H. (1987). Perspective taking and peer interaction: Structural and developmental analyses. *Child Development, 58,* 306–315.

Lemery, K. S., Goldsmith, H. H., Klinnert, M. D., & Mrazek, D. A. (1999). Developmental models of infant and childhood temperament. *Developmental Psychology, 35,* 189–204.

Leon, M. (1984). Rules mothers and sons use to integrate intent and damage information in their moral judgments. *Child Development, 55,* 2106–2113.

Lepper, M. R. (1985). Microcomputers in education: Motivation and social issues. *American Psychologist, 40,* 1–18.

Lepper, M. R., & Gurtner, J. (1989). Children and computers: Approaching the twenty-first century. *American Psychologist, 44,* 170–178.

Lerner, R. M. (1991). Changing organism-context relations as the basic process of development: A developmental contextual perspective. *Developmental Psychology, 27,* 27–32.

Lerner, R. M. (1996). Relative plasticity, integration, temporality, and diversity in human development: A developmental contextual perspective about theory, process, and method. *Developmental Psychology, 32,* 781–786.

Lerner, R. M., & von Eye, A. (1992). Sociobiology and human development: Arguments and evidence. *Human Development, 35,* 12–33.

Lester, B. M., Corwin, M. J., Sepkoski, C., Seifer, R., Peucker, M., McLaughlin, S., & Golub, H. L. (1991). Neurobehavioral syndrome in cocaine-exposed newborn infants. *Child Development, 62,* 694–705.

Lester, B. M., Kotelchuck, M., Spelke, E., Sellers, M. J., & Klein, R. E. (1974). Separation protest in Guatemalan infants: Cross-cultural and cognitive findings. *Developmental Psychology, 10,* 79–85.

LeVay, S. (1996). *Queer science: The use and abuse of research into homosexuality.* Cambridge, MA: The MIT Press.

Leve, L. D., & Fagot, B. I. (1997). Gender-role socialization and discipline processes in one- and two-parent families. *Sex Roles, 36,* 1–21.

Levin, I., & Druyan, S. (1993). When sociocognitive transaction among peers fails: The case of misconceptions in science. *Child Development, 64,* 1571–1591.

LeVine, R. A. (1974). Parental goals: A cross-cultural view. *Teachers College Record, 76,* 226–239.

LeVine, R. A. (1989). Cultural environments in child development. In W. Damon (Ed.), *Child development today and tomorrow.* San Francisco: Jossey-Bass.

LeVine, R. A., Dixon, S., LeVine, S., Richman, A., Liederman, P. H., Keefer, C. H., & Brazelton, T. B. (1994). *Child care and culture: Lessons from Africa.* New York: Cambridge University Press.

Levinson, D. (1989). *Family violence in cross-cultural perspective.* Newbury Park, CA: Sage.

Levitt, M. J., Weber, R. A., Clark, M. C., & McDonnell, P. (1985). Reciprocity of exchange in toddler sharing behavior. *Developmental Psychology, 21,* 122–123.

Levy, G. D., Taylor, M. G., & Gelman, S. A. (1995). Traditional and evaluative aspects of flexibility in gender roles, social conventions, moral rules, and physical laws. *Child Development, 66,* 515–531.

Levy-Shiff, R. (1994). Individual and contextual correlates of marital change across the transition to parenthood. *Developmental Psychology, 30,* 591–601.

Levy-Shiff, R., Goldshmidt, I., & Har-Even, D. (1991). Transition to parenthood in adoptive families. *Developmental Psychology, 27,* 131–140.

Lewin, K., Lippitt, R., & White, R. K. (1939). Patterns of aggressive behavior in experimentally created "social climates." *Journal of Social Psychology, 10,* 271–299.

Lewin, L. M., Hops, H., Davis, B., & Dishion, T. J. (1993). Multimethod comparison of similarity in school adjustment of siblings and unrelated children. *Developmental Psychology, 24,* 963–969.

Lewis, C., Freeman, N. H., Kyriakidou, C., Maridaki-Kassotaki, K., & Berridge, D. M. (1996). Social influences on false belief access: Specific sibling influences or general apprenticeship? *Child Development, 67,* 2930–2947.

Lewis, M., Alessandri, S. M., & Sullivan, M. W. (1990). Violation of expectancy, loss of control and anger expressions in young infants. *Developmental Psychology, 26,* 745–751.

Lewis, M., Alessandri, S. M., & Sullivan, M. W. (1992). Differences in shame and pride as a function of children's gender and task difficulty. *Child Development, 63,* 630–638.

Lewis, M., & Brooks-Gunn, J. (1979). *Social cognition and the acquisition of self.* New York: Plenum Press.

Lewis, M., & Rosenblum, M. A. (1975). *Friendship and peer relations.* New York: Wiley.

Lewis M., Stanger, C., & Sullivan, M. W. (1989). Deception in 3-year-olds. *Developmental Psychology, 24,* 434–440.

Lewis, M., Sullivan, M. W., Stanger, C., & Weiss, M. (1989). Self-development and self-conscious emotions. *Child Development, 60,* 146–156.

Leyens, J. P., Parke, R. D., Camino, L., & Berkowitz, L. (1975). Effects of movie violence on aggression in a field setting as a function of group dominance and cohesion. *Journal of Personality and Social Psychology, 32,* 346–360.

Liben, L. S., & Signorella, M. L. (1993). Gender-schematic processing in children: The role of initial interpretations of stimuli. *Developmental Psychology, 29,* 141–149.

Liebert, R. M., & Baron, R. A. (1972). Some immediate effects of televised violence on children's behavior. *Developmental Psychology, 6,* 469–475.

Liebert, R. M., Neale, J. M., & Davidson, E. S. (1973). *The early window: Effects of television on children and youth.* New York: Pergamon Press.

Liebert, R. M., & Sprafkin, J. (1988). *The early window: Effects of television on children and youth* (3rd ed.). New York: Pergamon Press.

Lin, C. C., & Fu, V. R. (1990). A comparison of child-rearing practices among Chinese, immigrant Chinese, and Caucasian-American parents. *Child Development, 61,* 429–433.

Linn, M. C., de Benedictis, T., & Delucchi, K. (1982). Adolescent reasoning about advertisements: Preliminary investigations. *Child Development, 53,* 1599–1613.

Linn, M. C., & Petersen, A. C. (1985). Emergence and characterization of sex differences in spatial ability: A meta-analysis. *Child Development, 56,* 1479–1498.

Littenberg, R., Tulkin, S., & Kagan, J. (1971). Cognitive components of separation anxiety. *Developmental Psychology, 4,* 387–388.

Livesley, W. J., & Bromley, D. B. (1973). *Person perception in childhood and adolescence.* London: Wiley.

Livson, N., & Peskin, H. (1980). Perspectives on adolescence from longitudinal research. In J. Adelson (Ed.), *Handbook of adolescent psychology.* New York. Wiley.

Lobel, T. E., & Menashri, J. (1993). Relations of conceptions of gender-role transgressions and gender constancy to gender-typed toy preferences. *Developmental Psychology, 29,* 150–155.

Locke, J. (1913). *Some thoughts concerning education.* Sections 38 and 40. London: Cambridge University Press. (Original work published 1690)

Loeber, R., & Farrington, D. P. (1998). *Serious and violent juvenile offenders: Risk factors and successful interventions.* Thousand Oaks, CA: Sage.

Loeber, R,. & Stouthamer-Loeber, M. (1998). Development of juvenile aggression and violence: Some common misconceptions and controversies. *American Psychologist, 53,* 242–259.

Loehlin, J. C. (1992). *Genes and environment in personality development* (Individual Differences and Development Series, Vol. 2). Newbury Park, CA: Sage.

London, P. (1970). The rescuers: Motivational hypotheses about Christians who saved Jews from the Nazis. In J. Macaulay & L. Berkowitz (Eds.), *Altruism and helping behavior.* Orlando, FL: Academic Press.

Lorber, J. (1986). Dismantling Noah's ark. *Sex Roles, 14,* 567–580.

Lord, S. E., Eccles, J. S., & McCarthy, K. A. (1994). Surviving the junior high school transition: Family processes and self-perceptions as protective and risk factors. *Journal of Early Adolescence, 14,* 162–199.

Lorenz, K. Z. (1937). The companion in the bird's world. *Auk, 54,* 245–273.

Lorenz, K. Z. (1943). Die angeboren Formen moglicher Erfahrung [The innate forms of possible experience]. *Zeitschrift für Tierpsychologie, 5,* 233–409.

Lorenz, K. (1966). *On aggression.* San Diego: Harcourt Brace Jovanovich.

Lorenz, K. Z. (1981). *The foundations of ethology.* New York: Springer-Verlag.

Lozoff, B. (1989). Nutrition and behavior. *American Psychologist, 44,* 231–236.

Ludemann, P. M. (1991). Generalized discrimination of positive facial expressions by seven- and ten-month-old infants. *Child Development, 62,* 55–67.

Luecke-Aleksa, D., Anderson, D. R., Collins, P. A., & Schmitt, K. L. (1995). Gender constancy and television viewing. *Developmental Psychology, 31,* 773–780.

Lummis, M., & Stevenson, H. W. (1990). Gender differences in beliefs and achievement: A cross-cultural study. *Developmental Psychology 26,* 254–263.

Lung, C. T., & Daro, D. (1996). *Current trends in child abuse reporting and fatalities: The results of the 1995 annual fifty state survey.* Chicago: National Committee to Prevent Child Abuse.

Luster, T., & Dubow, E. (1992). Home environment and maternal intelligence as predictors of verbal intelligence: A comparison of preschool and school-age children. *Merrill-Palmer Quarterly, 38,* 151–175.

Luster, T., & McAdoo, H. (1996). Family and child influences on educational attainment: A secondary analysis of the High/Scope Perry preschool data. *Developmental Psychology, 32,* 26–39.

Lustig, J. L., Wolchik, S. A., & Braver, S. L. (1992). Social support in chumships and adjustment in children of divorce. *American Journal of Community Psychology, 20,* 393–399.

Lyons-Ruth, K., Alpern, L., & Repacholi, B. (1993). Disorganized infant attachment classification and maternal psychosocial problems as predictors of hostile-aggressive behavior in the preschool classroom. *Child Development, 64,* 572–585.

Lyons-Ruth, K., Connell, D. B., Grunebaum, H. U., & Botein, S. (1990). Infants at social risk: Maternal depression and family support services as mediators of infant development and security of attachment. *Child Development, 61,* 85–98.

Lyons-Ruth, K., Easterbrooks, M. A., & Cibelli, C.D. (1997). Infant attachment strategies, infant mental lag, and maternal depressive symptoms: Predictors of internalizing and externalizing problems at age 7. *Developmental Psychology, 33,* 681–692.

Lytton, H. (1990). Child and parent effects in boys' conduct disorder. A reinterpretation. *Developmental Psychology, 26,* 683–697.

Lytton, H., & Romney, D. M. (1991). Parents' differential socialization of boys and girls: A meta-analysis. *Psychological Bulletin, 109,* 267–296.

Maccoby, E. E. (1980). *Social development: Psychological growth and the parent-child relationship.* San Diego, CA: Harcourt Brace Jovanovich.

Maccoby, E. E. (1988). Gender as a social category. *Developmental Psychology, 24,* 755–765.

Maccoby, E. E. (1990). Gender and relationships: A developmental account. *American Psychologist, 45,* 513–520.

Maccoby, E. E., & Jacklin, C. N. (1974). *The psychology of sex differences.* Stanford, CA: Stanford University Press.

Maccoby, E. E., & Jacklin, C. N. (1980). Sex differences in aggression: A rejoinder and reprise. *Child Development, 51,* 964–980.

Maccoby, E. E., & Martin, J. A. (1983). Socialization in the context of the family: Parent-child interaction. In E. M. Hetherington (Ed.; P. H. Mussen, General Ed.), *Handbook of child psychology: Vol. 4. Socialization, personality, and social development* (4th ed.). New York: Wiley.

MacDonald, K. (1992). Warmth as a developmental construct: An evolutionary analysis. *Child Development, 63,* 753–773.

MacFarlane, A. (1977). *The psychology of childbirth.* Cambridge, MA: Harvard University Press.

Mac Iver, D., & Reuman, D. A. (1988, April). *Decision-making in the classroom and early adolescents' valuing of mathematics.* Paper presented at the annual meeting of the American Educational Research Association, New Orleans, LA.

MacKinnon-Lewis, C., Starnes, R., Volling, B., & Johnson, S. (1997). Perceptions of parenting as predictors of boys' sibling and peer relations. *Developmental Psychology, 33,* 1024–1031.

MacPhee, D., Fritz, J., & Miller-Heyl, J. (1996). Ethnic variations in personal social networks and parenting. *Child Development, 67,* 3278–3295.

Mahler, M. S., Pine, F., & Bergman, A. (1975). *The psychological birth of the infant.* New York: Basic Books.

Mahoney, J. L., & Cairns, R. B. (1997). Do extracurricular activities protect against early school dropout? *Developmental Psychology, 33,* 241–253.

Main, M., & Cassidy, J. (1988). Categories of response to reunion with the parent at age 6: Predictable from infant attachment classifications and stable over a 1-month period. *Developmental Psychology, 24,* 415–426.

Main, M., & George, C. (1985). Responses of abused and disadvantaged toddlers to distress in agemates: A study in the day-care setting. *Developmental Psychology, 21,* 407–412.

Main, M., & Goldwyn, R. (1994). *Interview-based adult attachment classifications: Related to infant-mother and infant-father attachment.* Unpublished manuscript, University of California, Berkeley.

Main, M., & Solomon, J. (1990). Procedures for identifying infants as disorganized/disoriented during the Ainsworth Strange Situation. In M. T. Greenberg, D. Cicchetti, & E. M. Cummings (Eds.), *Attachment in the preschool years: Theory, research, and intervention.* Chicago: University of Chicago Press.

Main, M., & Weston, D. R. (1981). The quality of the toddler's relationship to mother and to father: Related to conflict and the readiness to establish new relationships. *Child Development, 52,* 932–940.

Malatesta, C. Z., Culver, C., Tesman, J. R., & Shepard, B. (1989). The development of emotion expression during the first two years of life. *Monographs of the Society for Research in Child Development, 54,* (1–2, Serial No. 219).

Malatesta, C. Z., Grigoryev, P., Lamb, C., Albin, M. & Culver, C. (1986). Emotional socialization and expressive development in preterm and full-term infants. *Child Development, 57,* 316–330.

Malatesta, C. Z., & Haviland, J. M. (1982). Learning display rules: The socialization of emotion expression in infancy. *Child Development, 53,* 991–1003.

Malinosky-Rummell, R., & Hansen, D. J. (1993). Long-term consequences of childhood physical abuse. *Psychological Bulletin, 114,* 68–79.

Mallick, S. K., & McCandless, B. R. (1966). A study of the catharsis of aggression. *Journal of Personality and Social Psychology, 4,* 591–596.

Mangelsdorf, S. C. (1992). Developmental changes in infant-stranger interaction. *Infant Behavior and Development, 15,* 191–208.

Mangelsdorf, S. C., Gunnar, M., Kestenbaum, R., Lang, S., & Andreas, D. (1990). Infant proneness-to-distress temperament, maternal personality, and mother-infant attachment: Associations and goodness of fit. *Child Development, 61,* 820–831.

Mangelsdorf, S. C., Plunkett, J. W., Dedrick, C. F., Berlin, M., Meisels, S. J., McHale, J. L., & Dichtellmiller, M. (1996). Attachment security in very low birth weight infants. *Developmental Psychology, 32,* 914–920.

Mangelsdorf, S. C., Shapiro, J. R., & Marzolf, D. (1995). Developmental and temperamental differences in emotion regulation in infancy. *Child Development, 66,* 1817–1828.

Manley, J. T., Cicchetti, D., & Barnett, D. (1994). The impact of subtype, frequency, chronicity, and severity of child maltreatment on social competence and behavior problems. *Development and Psychopathology, 6,* 121–143.

Manset, G., & Semmel, M. I. (1997). Are inclusive programs for students with mild disabilities effective? A comparative review of model programs. *Journal of Special Education, 31,* 155–180.

Marcia, J. E. (1980). Identity in adolescence. In J. Adelson (Ed.), *Handbook of adolescent psychology.* New York: Wiley.

Marcia, J. E., Waterman, A. S., Matteson, D., Archer, S. C., & Orlofsky, J. L. (1993). *Ego identity: A handbook for psychosocial research.* New York: Springer-Verlag.

Marcus, D. E., & Overton, W. F. (1978). The development of cognitive gender constancy and sex-role preferences. *Child Development, 49,* 434–444.

Markstrom-Adams, C. (1992). A consideration of intervening factors in adolescent identity formation. In G. R. Adams, T. P. Gullotta, & R. Montemayer (Eds.), *Adolescent identity formation* (Advances in Adolescent Development, Vol. 4). Newbury Park, CA: Sage.

Markstrom-Adams, C., & Adams, G. R. (1995). Gender, ethnic group, and grade differences in psychosocial functioning during middle adolescence. *Journal of Youth and Adolescence, 24,* 397–417.

Markus, H., & Kitayama, S. (1994). A collective fear of the collective: Implications for selves and theories of selves. *Personality and Social Psychology Bulletin, 20,* 568–579.

Marsh, H. W. (1989). Age and sex effects in multiple dimensions of self-concept: Preadolescence to early adulthood. *Journal of Educational Psychology, 81,* 417–430.

Marsh, H. W., Craven, R., & Debus, R. (1998). Structure, stability, and development of children's self-concepts: A multicohort-multioccasion study. *Child Development, 69,* 1030–1053.

Marsh, H. W., & Hattie, J. (1996). Theoretical perspectives on the structure of self-concept. In B. A. Bracken (Ed.), *Handbook of self-concept: Developmental, social, and clinical considerations.* New York: Wiley.

Marshall, N. L., Coll, C. G., Marx, F., McCartney, K., Keefe, N., & Ruh, J. (1997). After-school time and children's behavioral adjustment. *Merrill-Palmer Quarterly, 43*, 497–514.

Martin, C. L. (1989). Children's use of gender-related information in making social judgments. *Developmental Psychology, 25*, 80–88.

Martin, C. L. (1990). Attitudes and expectations about children with non-traditional gender roles. *Sex Roles, 22*, 151–165.

Martin, C. L. (1994). Cognitive influences on the development and maintenance of gender segregation. *New Directions for Child Development, 65*, 35–51.

Martin, C. L., Eisenbud, L., & Rose, H. (1995). Children's gender-based reasoning about toys. *Child Development, 66*, 1453–1471.

Martin, C. L., & Halverson, C. F., Jr. (1981). A schematic processing model of sex typing and stereotyping in children. *Child Development, 52*, 1119–1134.

Martin, C. L., & Halverson, C. F., Jr. (1983). The effects of sex-typing schemas on young children's memory. *Child Development, 54*, 563–574.

Martin, C. L., & Halverson, C. F., Jr. (1987). The roles of cognition in sex-roles and sex-typing. In D. B. Carter (Ed.), *Current conceptions of sex roles and sex-typing: Theory and research*. New York: Praeger.

Martin, C. L., & Little, J. K. (1990). The relation of gender understanding to children's sex-typed preferences and gender stereotypes. *Child Development, 61*, 1429–1439.

Martin, G. B., & Clark, R. D., III. (1982). Distress crying in neonates: Species and peer specificity. *Developmental Psychology, 18*, 3–9.

Martin, N. G., & Jardine, R. (1986). Eysenck's contributions to behavior genetics. In S. Modgil & C. Modgil (Eds.), *Hans Eysenck: Consensus and controversy*. Philadelphia: Falmer.

Masden, A. S., Coatsworth, J. D., Neeman, J., Gest, J. D., Tellegen, A., & Garmezy, N. (1995). The structure and coherence of competence from childhood through adolescence. *Child Development, 66*, 1635–1659.

Mason, C. A., Cauce, A. M., Gonzales, N., & Hiraga, Y. (1996). Neither too sweet nor too sour: Problem peers, maternal control, and problem behavior in African-American adolescents. *Child Development, 67*, 2115–2130.

Mason, M. G., & Gibbs, J. C. (1993). Social perspective taking and moral judgment among college students. *Journal of Adolescent Research, 8*, 109–123.

Masters, J. C., Ford, M. E., Arend, R., Grotevant, H. D., & Clark, L. V. (1979). Modeling and labeling as integrated determinants of children's sex-typed imitative behavior. *Child Development, 50*, 364–371.

Matejcek, Z., Dytrych, Z., & Schuller, V. (1979). The Prague study of children born from unwanted pregnancies. *International Journal of Mental Health, 7*, 63–74.

Matheny, A. P. (1983). A longitudinal twin study of the stability of components from Bayley's Infant Behavior Record. *Child Development, 54*, 356–360.

Matias, R., & Cohn, J. F. (1993). Are Max-specified infant facial expressions during face-to-face interaction consistent with differential emotions theory? *Developmental Psychology, 29*, 524–531.

Matsumoto, D. (1990). Cultural similarities and differences in display rules. *Motivation and Emotion, 14*, 195–214.

Matthews, K. A., Batson, C. D., Horn, J., & Rosenman, R. H. (1981). "Principles in his nature which interest him in the fortune of others": The heritability of empathic concern for others. *Journal of Personality, 49*, 237–247.

Matula, K. E., Huston, T. L., Grotevant, H. D., & Zamutt, A. (1992). Identity and dating commitment among women and men in college. *Journal of Youth and Adolescence, 21*, 339–356.

Mayer, F. S., & Sutton, K. (1996). *Personality: An integrative approach*. Upper Saddle River, NJ: Prentice-Hall.

Mayes, L. C., & Zigler, E. (1992). An observational study of the affective concomitants of mastery in infants. *Journal of Psychology and Psychiatry, 4*, 659–667.

McCall, R. B. (1977). Challenges to a science of developmental psychology. *Child Development, 48*, 333–344.

McCall, R. B. (1981). Nature-nurture and the two realms of development: A proposed integration with respect to mental development. *Child Development, 52*, 1–12.

McCartney, K., Harris, M. J., & Bernieri, F. (1990). Growing up and growing apart: A developmental meta-analysis of twin studies. *Psychological Bulletin, 107*, 226–237.

McClelland, D. C. (1961). *The achieving society*. New York: Free Press.

McClelland, D. C., Atkinson, J. W., Clark, R. A., & Lowell, E. L. (1953). *The achievement motive*. New York: Appleton-Century-Crofts.

McCloskey, L. A., Figueredo, A. J., & Koss, M. P. (1995). The effects of systematic family violence on children's mental health. *Child Development, 66*, 1239–1261.

McConaghy, M. (1979). Gender permanence and the genital basis of gender: Stages in the development of constancy and gender identity. *Child Development, 50*, 1223–1226.

McDougall, W. (1908). *An introduction to social psychology*. London: Methuen.

McFadyen-Ketchum, S. A., Bates, J. E., Dodge, K. A., & Pettit, G. S. (1996). Patterns of change in early childhood aggressive-disruptive behavior: Gender differences in predictions from early coercive and affectionate mother-child interactions. *Child Development, 67*, 2417–2433.

McGhee, P. E., & Frueh, T. (1980). Television viewing and the learning of sex-role stereotypes. *Sex Roles, 6*, 179–188.

McGue, M., Sharma, A., & Benson, P. (1996). The effect of common rearing on adolescent adjustment: Evidence from a U.S. adoption cohort. *Developmental Psychology, 32*, 604–613.

McGuire, K. D., & Weisz, J. R. (1982). Social cognition and behavioral correlates of preadolescent chumship. *Child Development, 53*, 1478–1484.

McHale, J. P. (1995). Coparenting and triadic interactions during infancy: The roles of marital distress and child gender. *Developmental Psychology, 31*, 985–996.

McHale, S. M., Crouter, A. C., McGuire, S. A., & Updegraff, K. A. (1995). Congruence between mothers' and fathers' differential treatment of siblings: Links with family relations and children's well-being. *Child Development, 66*, 116–128.

McHale, S. M., & Gamble, W. C. (1989). Sibling relationships of children with disabled and nondisabled brothers and sisters. *Developmental Psychology, 25*, 421–429.

McKenna, J. (1986). An anthropological perspective on the Sudden Infant Death Syndrome (SIDS): The role of parental breathing cues and speech breathing adaptations. *Medical Anthropology, 10*, 90–92.

McKenna, M. A. J. (1997, May 2). U.S., Georgia get welcome news on teenagers and sex. *Atlanta Constitution*, p. D1.

McKenna, M. W., & Ossoff, E. P. (1998). Age differences in children's comprehension of a popular television program. *Child Study Journal, 28*, 53–68.

McLoyd, V. C. (1989). Socialization and development in a changing economy: The effects of paternal job and income loss on children. *American Psychologist, 44*, 293–302.

McLoyd, V. C. (1998). Socioeconomic disadvantage and child development. *American Psychologist, 53*, 185–204.

McNeilly-Choque, M. K., Hart, C. H., Robinson, C. C., Nelson, L. J., & Olsen, S. F. (1996). Overt and relational aggression on the playground: Correspondence among different informants. *Journal of Research in Childhood Education, 11*, 47–67.

McNew, J., & Abell, N. (1995). Posttraumatic stress symptomatology: Similarities and differences between Vietnam veterans and adult survivors of childhood sexual abuse. *Social Work, 40*, 115–126.

Mead, G. H. (1934). *Mind, self, and society*. Chicago: University of Chicago Press.

Mead, M. (1935). *Sex and temperament in three primitive societies*. New York: William Morrow.

Measelle, J. R., Albow, J. C., Cowan, P., & Cowan, C. P. (1998). Assessing young children's views of their academic, social, and emotional lives: An evaluation of the self-perception scales of the Berkeley Puppet Interview. *Child Development, 69*, 1556–1576.

Mediascope, Inc. (1996). *National Television Violence Study: Executive summary 1994–1995*. Studio City, CA: Author.

Medrich, E. A., Rosen, J., Rubin, V., & Buckley, S. (1982). *The serious business of growing up*. Berkeley: University of California Press.

Meilman, P. W. (1979). Cross-sectional age changes in ego identity status during adolescence. *Developmental Psychology, 15*, 230–231.

Mekos, D., Hetherington, E. M., & Reiss, D. (1996). Sibling differences in problem behavior and parental treatment in nondivorced and remarried families. *Child Development, 67,* 2148–2165.

Melson, G. F., Peet, S., & Sparks, C. (1991). Children's attachments to their pets: Links to socioemotional development. *Children's Environmental Quarterly, 8,* 55–65.

Meltzoff, A. N. (1988a). Imitation of televised models by infants. *Child Development, 59,* 1221–1229.

Meltzoff, A. N. (1988b). Infant imitation after a 1-week delay: Long-term memory for novel acts and multiple stimuli. *Developmental Psychology, 24,* 470–476.

Meltzoff, A. N. (1988c). Infant imitation and memory: Nine-month-olds in immediate and deferred tests. *Child Development, 59,* 217–225.

Meltzoff, A. N. (1990a). Foundations for developing a concept of self: The role of imitation in relating self to other and the value of social mirroring, social modeling, and self-practice in infancy. In D. Cicchetti & M. Beeghly (Eds.), *The self in transition: Infancy to childhood* (pp. 139–164), Chicago: University of Chicago Press.

Meltzoff, A. N. (1990b). Towards a developmental cognitive science. *Annals of the New York Academy of Sciences, 608,* 1–37.

Meltzoff, A. N. (1995). Understanding the intentions of others: Re-enactment of intended acts by 18-month-old children. *Developmental Psychology, 31,* 838–850.

Meltzoff, A. N., & Moore, M. K. (1977). Imitation of facial and manual gestures by human neonates. *Science, 198,* 75–78.

Meltzoff, A. N., & Moore, M. K. (1989). Imitation in newborn infants: Exploring the range of gestures imitated and the underlying mechanisms. *Developmental Psychology, 25,* 954–962.

Meltzoff, A. N., & Moore, M. K. (1992). Early imitation within a functional framework: The importance of person, identity, movement, and development. *Infant Behavior and Development, 15,* 479–505.

Messer, D. J., McCarthy, M. E., McQuiston, S., MacTurk, R. H., Yarrow, L. W., & Vietze, P. M. (1986). Relation between mastery behavior in infancy and competence in early childhood. *Developmental Psychology, 22,* 366–372.

Meyer-Bahlberg, H. F. L., Ehrhardt, A. A., Rosen, L. R., Gruen, R. S., Veridiano, N. P., Vann, F. H., & Neuwalder, H. F. (1995). Prenatal estrogens and the development of homosexual orientation. *Developmental Psychology, 31,* 12–21.

Midgley, C., Feldlaufer, H., & Eccles, J. S. (1989). Student/teacher relations and attitudes toward mathematics before and after the transition to junior high school. *Child Development, 60,* 981–992.

Midlarsky, E., & Bryan, J. H. (1972). Affect expressions and children's imitative altruism. *Journal of Experimental Research in Personality, 6,* 195–203.

Midlarsky, E., Bryan, J. H., & Brickman, P. (1973). Aversive approval: Interactive effects of modeling and reinforcement on altruistic behavior. *Child Development, 44,* 321–328.

Miller, C. L. (1983). Developmental changes in male/female voice classification by infants. *Infant Behavior and Development, 6,* 313–330.

Miller, C. L., Miceli, P. J., Whitman, T. L., & Borkowski, J. G. (1996). Cognitive readiness to parent and intellectual-emotional development in children of adolescent mothers. *Developmental Psychology, 32,* 533–541.

Miller, G. V. (1995). *The gay male's odyssey in the corporate world.* Binghamton, NY: Haworth Press.

Miller, K. S., Levin, M. L., Whitaker, D. J., & Xu, X. (1998). Patterns of condom use among adolescents: The impact of mother-adolescent communication. *American Journal of Public Health, 88,* 1542–1544.

Miller, N. B., Cowan, P. A., Cowan, C. P., Hetherington, E. M., & Clingempeel, W. G. (1993). Externalizing in preschoolers and early adolescents: A cross-study replication of a family model. *Developmental Psychology, 29,* 3–18.

Miller, P. A., Eisenberg, N., Fabes, R. A., & Shell, R. (1996). Relations of moral reasoning and vicarious emotion to young children's prosocial behavior toward peers and adults. *Developmental Psychology, 32,* 210–219.

Miller, P. H., & Aloise, P. A. (1989). Young children's understanding of the psychological causes of behavior: A review. *Child Development, 60,* 257–285.

Mills, R. S. L., & Grusec, J. E. (1989). Cognitive, affective, and behavioral consequences of praising altruism. *Merrill-Palmer Quarterly, 35,* 299–326.

Mills, R. S. L., & Rubin, K. H. (1990). Parental beliefs about problematic social behaviors in early childhood. *Child Development, 61,* 138–151.

Minor, C. A., & Neel, R. G. (1958). The relationship between achievement motive and occupational preference. *Journal of Counseling Psychology, 5,* 39–43.

Minuchin, P. P. (1988). Relationships within the family: A systems perspective on development. In R. A. Hinde & J. Stevenson-Hinde (Eds.), *Relationships within families: Mutual influences* (pp. 7–26). New York: Oxford University Press.

Minuchin, P. P., & Shapiro, E. K. (1983). The school as a context for social development. In P. H. Mussen (Ed.), *Handbook of child psychology. Vol. 4: Socialization, personality, and social development* (4th ed., pp. 197–274). New York: Wiley.

Mischel, H. N., & Mischel, W. (1983). The development of children's knowledge of self-control strategies. *Child Development, 53,* 603–619.

Mischel, W. (1970). Sex-typing and socialization. In P. H. Mussen (Ed.), *Carmichael's manual of child psychology* (Vol. 2). New York: Wiley.

Mischel, W. (1974). Processes in the delay of gratification. In L. Berkowitz (Ed.), *Advances in experimental social psychology* (Vol. 7). New York: Academic.

Mischel, W. (1986). *Introduction to personality* (4th ed.). New York: Holt, Rinehart & Winston.

Mischel, W., & Baker, N. (1975). Cognitive appraisals and transformations in delay behavior. *Journal of Personality and Social Psychology, 31,* 254–261.

Mischel, W., & Ebbesen, E. B. (1970). Attention in delay of gratification. *Journal of Personality and Social Psychology, 16,* 329–337.

Mischel, W., & Patterson, C. J. (1976). Substantive and structural elements of effective plans for self-control. *Journal of Personality and Social Psychology, 34,* 942–950.

Mischel, W., Shoda, Y., & Peake, P. K. (1988). The nature of adolescent competencies predicted by preschool delay of gratification. *Journal of Personality and Social Psychology, 54,* 687–696.

Mitchell, J. E., Baker, L. A., & Jacklin, C. N. (1989). Masculinity and femininity in twin children: Genetic and environmental factors. *Child Development, 60,* 1475–1485.

Mize, J., & Ladd, G. W. (1990). A cognitive-social learning approach to social skill training with low-status preschool children. *Developmental Psychology, 26,* 388–397.

Mize, J., & Pettit, G. S. (1997). Mother's social coaching, mother-child relationship style, and children's peer competence: Is the medium the message? *Child Development, 68,* 312–322.

Mize, J., Pettit, G. S., & Brown, E. G. (1995). Mothers' supervision of their children's peer play: Relations with beliefs, perceptions, and knowledge. *Developmental Psychology, 31,* 311–321.

Moller, L. C., & Serbin, L. A. (1996). Antecedents of toddler gender segregation: Cognitive consonance, gender-typed toy preferences and behavioral compatibility. *Sex Roles, 35,* 445–460.

Money, J. (1965). Psychosexual differentiation. In J. Money (Ed.), *Sex research: New developments.* New York: Holt, Rinehart and Winston.

Money, J. (1985). Pediatric sexology and hermaphrodism. *Journal of Sex and Marital Therapy, 11,* 139–156.

Money, J. (1988). *Gay, straight, and in-between: The sexology of erotic orientation.* New York: Oxford University Press.

Money, J., & Ehrhardt, A. (1972). *Man and woman, boy and girl.* Baltimore: Johns Hopkins University Press.

Money, J., & Tucker, P. (1975). *Sexual signatures: On being a man or a woman.* Boston: Little, Brown.

Montemayor, R., & Eisen, M. (1977). The development of self-conceptions from childhood to adolescence. *Developmental Psychology, 13,* 314–319.

Moore, E. G. J. (1986). Family socialization and the IQ test performance of traditionally and transracially adopted black children. *Developmental Psychology, 22,* 317–326.

Moorehouse, M. J. (1991). Linking maternal employment patterns to mother-child activities and children's school competence. *Developmental Psychology, 27,* 295–303.

Morelli, G. A., Rogoff, B., Oppenheim, D., & Goldsmith, D. (1992). Cultural variation in infants' sleeping arrangements: Questions of independence. *Developmental Psychology, 28,* 604–613.

Morgan, G. A., & Ricciuti, H. N. (1969). Infants' responses to strangers during the first year. In B. M. Foss (Ed.), *Determinants of infant behavior* (Vol. 4). London: Methuen.

Morrison, F. J., Griffith, E. M., & Alberts, D. M. (1997). Nature-nurture in the classroom: Entrance age, school readiness, and learning in children. *Developmental Psychology, 33,* 254–262.

Morrison, F. J., Smith, L., & Dow-Ehrensberger, M. (1995). Education and cognitive development: A natural experiment. *Developmental Psychology, 31,* 789–799.

Mortimer, J. T., Finch, M. D., Ryu, S., Shanahan, M. J., & Call, K. T. (1996). The effects of work intensity on adolescent mental health, achievement, and behavioral adjustment: New evidence from a prospective study. *Child Development, 67,* 1243–1261.

Mounts, N. S., & Steinberg, L. (1995). An ecological analysis of peer influence on adolescent grade point average and drug use. *Developmental Psychology, 31,* 915–922.

Mueller, E., & Lucas, T. (1975). A developmental analysis of peer interactions among toddlers. In M. Lewis & L. Rosenblum (Eds.), *Friendship and peer relations.* New York: Wiley.

Mullis, A. K., Mullis, R. L., & Normandin, D. (1992). Cross-sectional and longitudinal comparisons of adolescent self-esteem. *Adolescence, 27,* 51–61.

Mumme, D. L., Fernald, A., & Herrera, C. (1996). Infants' responses to facial and vocal emotional signals in a social referencing paradigm. *Child Development, 67,* 3219–3237.

Munro, G., & Adams, G. R. (1977). Ego-identity formation in college students and working youth. *Developmental Psychology, 13,* 523–524.

Munroe, R. H., Shimmin, H. S., & Munroe, R. L. (1984). Gender understanding and sex-role preferences in four cultures. *Developmental Psychology, 20,* 673–682.

Murray, H. (1938). *Explorations in personality.* New York: Oxford University Press.

Murray, L., Fiori-Cowley, A., Hooper, R., & Cooper, P. (1996). The impact of postnatal depression and associated adversity on early mother-infant interactions and later infant outcome. *Child Development, 67,* 2512–2526.

Mussen, P. H., & Rutherford, E. (1963). Parent-child relations and parental personality in relation to young children's sex-role preferences. *Child Development, 34,* 589–607.

Myers, B. J. (1987). Mother-infant bonding as a critical period. In M. H. Bornstein (Ed.), *Sensitive periods in development: Interdisciplinary perspectives.* Hillsdale, NJ: Erlbaum.

Myers, D. G. (1999). *Social psychology* (6th ed.). New York: McGraw-Hill.

Nadler, A. (1986). Help-seeking as a cultural phenomenon: Differences between city and kibbutz dwellers. *Journal of Personality and Social Psychology, 51,* 976–982.

Nadler, A. (1991). Help-seeking behavior: Psychological costs and instrumental benefits. In M. S. Clark (Ed.), *Prosocial behavior.* Newbury Park, CA: Sage.

Nastasi, B. K., & Clements, D. H. (1993). Motivational and social outcomes of cooperative computer education environments. *Journal of Computing in Childhood Education, 4,* 15–43.

Nastasi, B. K., & Clements, D. H. (1994). Effectance motivation, perceived scholastic competence, and higher-order thinking in two cooperative computer environments. *Journal of Educational Computing Research, 10,* 249–275.

National Center for Educational Statistics. (1995). *Digest of educational statistics.* Washington, DC: U.S. Government Printing Office.

National Education Goals Panel. (1992). *The National Education Goals Report. 1992.* Washington, DC: U.S. Department of Education.

Neisser, U., Boodoo, G., Bouchard, T. J., Jr., Boykin, A. W., Brody, N., Ceci, S. J., Halpern, D. F., Loehlin, J. C., Perloff, R., Sternberg, R. J., & Urbina, S. (1996). Intelligence: Knowns and unknowns. *American Psychologist, 51,* 77–101.

Nelson, C. A. (1987). The recognition of facial expressions in the first two years of life: Mechanisms of development. *Child Development, 58,* 889–909.

Nelson, E. A., Grinder, R. E., & Biaggio, A. M. B. (1969). Relationships between behavioral, cognitive-developmental, and self-report measures of morality and personality. *Multivariate Behavioral Research, 4,* 483–500.

Nelson, J., & Aboud, F. E. (1985). The resolution of social conflict among friends. *Child Development, 56,* 1009–1017.

Nelson, K. (1993). The psychological and social origins of autobiographical memory. *Psychological Science, 4,* 1–8.

Nelson, S. A. (1980). Factors influencing young children's use of motives and outcomes as moral criteria. *Child Development, 51,* 823–829.

Nelson-LeGall, S. (1985). Motive-outcome matching and outcome foreseeability: Effects on attribution of intentionality and moral judgments. *Developmental Psychology, 21,* 332–337.

Nelson-LeGall, S., & Jones, E. (1990). Cognitive-motivational influences on the task-related help-seeking behavior of Black children. *Child Development, 61,* 581–589.

Newcomb, A. F., & Bukowski, W. M. (1984). A longitudinal study of the utility of social preference and social impact sociometric classification schemes. *Child Development, 55,* 1434–1447.

Newcomb, A. F., Bukowski, W. M., & Pattee, L. (1993). Children's peer relations: A meta-analytic review of popular, rejected, neglected, controversial, and average sociometric status. *Psychological Bulletin, 113,* 99–128.

Newcomb, M. D., & Bentler, P. M. (1989). Substance use and abuse among children and teenagers. *American Psychologist, 44,* 242–248.

Newcombe, N., & Dubas, J. S. (1987). Individual differences in cognitive ability: Are they related to timing of puberty? In R. M. Lerner & T. T. Foch (Eds.), *Biological-psychosocial interactions in early adolescence: A life-span perspective.* Hillsdale, NJ: Erlbaum.

Newcombe, N., & Dubas, J. S. (1992). A longitudinal study of predictors of spatial ability in adolescent females. *Child Development, 63,* 37–46.

Newman, D. L., Caspi, A., Moffitt, T. E., & Silva, P. A. (1997). Antecedents of adult interpersonal functioning: Effects of individual differences in age 3 temperament. *Developmental Psychology, 33,* 206–217.

NICHD Early Child Care Research Network. (1997). The effects of infant child care on mother-infant attachment security: Results of the NICHD study of early child care. *Child Development, 68,* 860–879.

NICHD Early Child Care Research Network. (1998a). Early child care and self-control, compliance, and problem behavior at twenty-four and thirty-six months. *Child Development, 69,* 1145–1170.

NICHD Early Child Care Research Network. (1998b). Relations between family predictors and child outcomes: Are they weaker for children in child care? *Developmental Psychology, 34,* 1119–1128.

Nicholls, J. G. (1989). *The competitive ethos and democratic education.* Cambridge, MA: Harvard University Press.

Nicholls, J. G., & Miller, A. T. (1984). Reasoning about the ability of self and others: A developmental study. *Child Development, 55,* 1990–1999.

Nichols, M. R. (1993). Parental perspectives on the childbirth experience. *Maternal-Child Nursing Journal, 21,* 99–108.

Ninio, A., & Rinott, N. (1988). Fathers' involvement in the care of their infants and their attributions of cognitive competence to infants. *Child Development, 59,* 652–663.

Norman-Jackson, J. (1982). Family interactions, language development, and primary reading achievement of Black children in families of low income. *Child Development, 53,* 349–358.

Nottelmann, E. D. (1987). Competence and self-esteem during transition from childhood to adolescence. *Developmental Psychology, 23,* 441–450.

Novak, M. A. (1979). Social recovery of monkeys isolated for the first year of life: II. Long-term assessment. *Developmental Psychology, 15,* 50–61.

Nucci, L., Camino, C., & Sapiro, C. M. (1996). Social class effects on northeastern Brazilian children's conceptions of areas of personal choice and social regulation. *Child Development, 67,* 1223–1242.

Nucci, L., & Smetana, J. G. (1996). Mothers' concepts of young children's areas of personal freedom. *Child Development, 67,* 1870–1886.

Nucci, L., & Turiel, E. (1993). God's word, religious rules, and their relation to Christian and Jewish children's concepts of morality. *Child Development, 64,* 1475–1491.

Nucci, L., & Weber, E. K. (1995). Social interactions in the home and the development of young children's conceptions within the personal domain. *Child Development, 66,* 1438–1452.

Oates, R. K., & Bross, D. C. (1995). What have we learned about treating child physical abuse? A literature review of the last decade. *Child Abuse and Neglect, 19,* 463–473.

O'Conner, B. P. (1995). Identity development and perceived parental behavior as sources of adolescent egocentrism. *Journal of Youth and Adolescence, 24,* 205–227.

O'Connor, B. P., & Nikolic, J. (1990). Identity development and formal operations as sources of adolescent egocentrism. *Journal of Youth and Adolescence, 19,* 149–158.

O'Connor, T. G., Deater-Deckard, K., Fulker, D., Rutter, M., & Plomin, R. (1998). Genotype-environment correlations in late childhood and early adolescence: Antisocial behavior problems and coercive parenting. *Developmental Psychology, 34,* 970–981.

Odden, A. (1990). Class size and student achievement: Research-based policy alternatives. *Educational Evaluation and Policy Analysis, 12,* 213–227.

Oden, S., & Asher, S. R. (1977). Coaching children in social skills for friendship making. *Child Development, 48,* 495–506.

O'Donohue, W. T., & Elliott, A. N. (1992). Treatment of the sexually abused child: A review. *Journal of Clinical Child Psychology, 21,* 218–228.

Ogbu, J. U. (1981). Origins of human competence: A cultural-ethological perspective. *Child Development, 52,* 413–429.

Ogbu, J. U. (1988). Black education: A cultural-ecological perspective. In H. P. McAdoo (Ed.), *Black families.* Beverly Hills: Sage.

Ogbu, J. U. (1994). From cultural differences to differences in cultural frames of reference. In P. M. Greenfield & R. R. Cocking (Eds.), *Cross-cultural roots of minority child development* (pp. 365–391). Hillsdale, NJ: Erlbaum.

Ogletree, S. M., & Williams, S. W. (1990). Sex and sex-typing effects on computer attitudes and aptitude. *Sex Roles, 23,* 703–712.

O'Heron, C. A., & Orlofsky, J. L. (1990). Stereotypic and nonstereotypic sex role trait and behavior orientations, gender identity, and psychological adjustment. *Journal of Personality and Social Psychology, 58,* 134–143.

Oliner, S. P., & Oliner, P. M. (1988). *The altruistic personality: Rescuers of Jews in Nazi Europe.* New York: Free Press.

Olson, G. M., & Sherman, T. (1983). A conceptual framework for the study of infant mental processes. In L. P. Lippitt (Ed.), *Advances in infancy research* (Vol. 3). Norwood, NJ: Ablex.

Olweus, D. (1980). Familial and temperamental determinants of aggressive behavior in adolescent boys: A causal analysis. *Developmental Psychology, 16,* 644–660.

Olweus, D. (1984). Aggressors and their victims: Bullying at school. In H. Frude & H. Gault (Eds.), *Disruptive behaviors in schools.* New York: Wiley.

Owleus, D. (1993). *Bullying at school.* Oxford: Blackwell.

Olweus, D., Mattsson, A., Schalling, D., & Low, H. (1980). Testosterone, aggression, physical and personality dimensions in normal adolescent males. *Psychosomatic Medicine, 42,* 253–269.

O'Mahoney, J. F. (1989). Development of thinking about things and people: Social and nonsocial cognition during adolescence. *Journal of Genetic Psychology, 150,* 217–224.

O'Neill, D. K. (1996). Two-year-old children's sensitivity to a parent's knowledge state when making requests. *Child Development, 67,* 659–667.

Oppenheim, D., Nir, A., Warren, S., & Emde, R. N. (1997). Emotion regulation in mother-child narrative co-construction: Associations with children's narratives and adaptation. *Developmental Psychology, 33,* 284–294.

Oppenheim, D., Sagi, A., & Lamb, M. E. (1988). Infant-adult attachments on the kibbutz and their relation to socioemotional development 4 years later. *Developmental Psychology, 24,* 427–433.

Orlofsky, J. L. (1979). Parental antecedents of sex-role orientation in college men and women. *Sex Roles, 5,* 495–512.

Osborn, D. K., & Endsley, R. C. (1971). Emotional reactions of young children to TV violence. *Child Development, 42,* 321–331.

Overton, W. F. (1984). World views and their influence on psychological theory and research: Kuhn-Lakotes-Lunden. In H. W. Reese (Ed.), *Advances in child development and behavior* (Vol. 18). New York: Academic.

Paikoff, R. L., & Brooks-Gunn, J. (1991). Do parent-child relationships change at puberty? *Psychological Bulletin, 110,* 47–66.

Palkovitz, R. (1984). Parental attitudes and fathers' interactions with their 5-month-old infants. *Developmental Psychology, 20,* 1054–1060.

Palmer, E. L. (1984). Providing quality television for America's children. In J. P. Murray & G. Salomon (Eds.), *The future of children's television.* Boys Town, NE: Boys Town Center.

Park, S., Belsky, J., Putnam, S., & Crnic, K. (1997). Infant emotionality, parenting, and 3-year inhibition: Exploring stability and lawful discontinuity in a male sample. *Developmental Psychology, 33,* 218–227.

Parke, R. D. (1977). Some effects of punishment on children's behavior—revisited. In E. M. Hetherington & R. D. Parke (Eds.), *Contemporary readings in child psychology.* New York: McGraw Hill.

Parke, R. D. (1995). Fathers and families. In M. Bornstein (Ed.), *Handbook of parenting* (Vol. 3, pp. 27–63). Hillsdale, NJ: Erlbaum.

Parke, R. D., Berkowitz, L., Leyens, J., West, S., & Sebastian, R. J. (1977). Some effects of violent and nonviolent movies on the behavior of juvenile delinquents. In L. Berkowitz (Ed.), *Advances in experimental social psychology* (Vol. 10). Orlando, FL: Academic Press.

Parke, R. D., & Kellum, S. G. (1994). *Exploring family relationships with other social contexts.* Hillsdale, NJ. Erlbaum.

Parke, R. D., & Slaby, R. G. (1983). The development of aggression. In P. H. Mussen (Ed.), *Handbook of child psychology. Vol. 4: Socialization, personality, and social development* (pp. 547–641). New York: Wiley.

Parker, J. G., & Asher, S. R. (1987). Peer relations and later adjustment: Are low-accepted children "at risk"? *Psychological Bulletin, 102,* 357–389.

Parker, J. G., & Asher, S. R. (1993). Friendship and friendship quality in middle childhood: Links with peer group acceptance and feelings of loneliness and social dissatisfaction. *Developmental Psychology, 29,* 611–621.

Parker, J. G., Rubin, K. H., Price, J., & DeRosier, E. (1995). Peer relationships, child development, and adjustment. A developmental psychopathology perspective. In D. Cicchetti & E. Cohen (Eds.), *Developmental psychopathology: Vol. 2 Risk, disorder, and adaptation* (pp. 96–161). New York: Wiley.

Parker, J. G., & Seal, J. (1996). Forming, losing, renewing, and replacing friendships: Applying temporal parameters to the assessment of children's friendship experiences. *Child Development, 67,* 2248–2268.

Parkhurst, J. T., & Asher, S. R. (1992). Peer rejection in middle school: Subgroup differences in behavior, loneliness, and interpersonal concerns. *Developmental Psychology, 28,* 231–241.

Parsons, J. E., Adler, T. F., & Kaczala, C. M. (1982). Socialization of achievement attitudes and beliefs: Parental influences. *Child Development, 53,* 310–321.

Parsons, T. (1955). Family structure and the socialization of the child. In T. Parsons & R. F. Bales (Eds.), *Family socialization and interaction processes.* New York: Free Press.

Parten, M. (1932). Social participation among preschool children. *Journal of Abnormal and Social Psychology, 27,* 243–269.

Passman, R. H., & Longeway, K. P. (1982). The role of vision in maternal attachment: Giving 2-year-olds a photograph of their mother during separation. *Developmental Psychology, 18,* 530–533.

Passman, R. H., & Weisberg, P. (1975). Mothers and blankets as agents for promoting play and exploration by young children in a novel environment: The effects of social and nonsocial attachment objects. *Developmental Psychology, 11,* 170–177.

Pataki, S. P., Shapiro, C., & Clark, M. S. (1994). Children's acquisition of appropriate norms for friendships and acquaintances. *Journal of Social and Personal Relationships, 11,* 427–442.

Patel, N., Power, T. G., & Bhavnagri, N. P. (1996). Socialization values and practices of Indian immigrant parents: Correlates of modernity and acculturation. *Child Development, 67,* 303–313.

Patterson, C. J. (1995a). Families of the lesbian baby boom: Parent's division of labor and children's adjustment. *Developmental Psychology, 31,* 115–123.

Patterson, C. J. (1995b). Lesbian mothers, gay fathers, and their children. In A. R. D'Augelli & C. J. Patterson (Eds.), *Lesbian, gay, and bisexual identities over the lifespan: Psychological perspectives* (pp. 262–290). New York: Oxford University Press.

Patterson, C. J. (1995c). Sexual orientation and human development: An overview. *Developmental Psychology, 31,* 3–11.

Patterson, C. J., Kupersmidt, J. B., & Vaden, N. A. (1990). Income level, gender, ethnicity, and household composition as predictors of children's school-based competence. *Child Development, 61,* 485–494.

Patterson, G. R. (1981). Mothers: The unacknowledged victims. *Monographs of the Society for Research in Child Development, 45*(5, Serial No. 186).

Patterson, G. R. (1982). *Coercive family processes.* Eugene, OR: Castilia Press.

Patterson, G. R. (1998). Continuities—A search for causal mechanisms: Comment on the special section. *Developmental Psychology, 34,* 1263–1268.

Patterson, G. R., Capaldi, D., & Bank, L. (1991). An early starter model for predicting delinquency. In D. Pepler & K. H. Rubin (Eds.), *The development and treatment of childhood aggression* (pp. 139–168). Hillsdale, NJ: Erlbaum.

Patterson, G. R., DeBaryshe, B. D., & Ramsey, E. (1989). A developmental perspective on antisocial behavior. *American Psychologist, 44,* 329–335.

Patterson, G. R., Littman, R. A., & Bricker, W. (1967). Assertive behavior in children: A step toward a theory of aggression. *Monographs of the Society for Research in Child Development, 32*(5, Serial No. 113).

Patterson, G. R., Reid, J. B., & Dishion, T. J. (1992). *Antisocial boys.* Eugene, OR: Castalia.

Patterson, G. R., & Stouthamer-Loeber, M. (1984). The correlation of family management practices and delinquency. *Child Development, 55,* 1299–1307.

Patterson, S. J., Sochting, I., & Marcia, L. E. (1992). The inner space and beyond: Women and identity. In G. R. Adams, T. P. Gullotta, & R. Montemayor (Eds.), *Adolescent identity formation* (Advances in Adolescent Development, Vol. 4). Newbury Park, CA: Sage.

Paul, J. P. (1993). Childhood cross-gender behavior and adult homosexuality: The resurgence of biological models of sexuality. *Journal of Homosexuality, 24,* 41–54.

Paulhus, D., & Shaffer, D. R. (1981). Sex differences in the impact of number of younger and number of older siblings on scholastic aptitude. *Social Psychology Quarterly, 44,* 363–368.

Pearson, J. L., Hunter, A. G., Ensminger, M. E., & Kellam, S. G. (1990). Black grandmothers in multigenerational households: Diversity in family structure and parenting involvement in the Woodlawn community. *Child Development, 61,* 434–442.

Pederson, D. R., Gleason, K. E., Moran, G., & Bento, S. (1998). Maternal attachment representations, maternal sensitivity, and the mother-infant attachment relationship. *Developmental Psychology, 34,* 925–933.

Pederson, D. R., & Moran, G. (1995). A categorical description of infant-mother relationships in the home and its relation to Q-sort measures of mother infant interaction. In E. Waters, B. E. Vaughn, G. Posada, & K. Kondo-Ikemura (Eds.), Caregiving, cultural, and cognitive perspectives on secure base behavior and working models: New growing points of attachment theory and research. *Monographs of the Society for Research in Child Development, 60* (2–3, Serial No. 244).

Pederson, D. R., & Moran, G. (1996). Expressions of the attachment relationship outside of the Strange Situation. *Child Development, 67,* 915–929.

Pedlow, R., Sanson, A., Prior, M., & Oberklaid, F. (1993). Stability of maternally reported temperament from infancy to 8 years. *Developmental Psychology, 29,* 998–1007.

Pedro-Carroll, J. L., & Cowen, E. L. (1985). The children of divorce intervention program: An investigation of the efficacy of a school-based prevention program. *Journal of Consulting and Clinical Psychology, 53,* 603–611.

Peevers, B. H., & Secord, P. F. (1973). Developmental changes in attribution of descriptive concepts to persons. *Journal of Personality and Social Psychology, 27,* 120–128.

Pellegrini, D. S. (1985). Social cognition and competence in middle childhood. *Child Development, 56,* 253–264.

Pepler, D. J., & Craig, W. M. (1995). A peek behind the fence: Naturalistic observations of aggressive children with remote audiovisual recording. *Developmental Psychology, 31,* 548–553.

Perlman, M., & Ross, H. S. (1997). The benefits of parent intervention in children's disputes: An examination of concurrent changes in children's fighting styles. *Child Development, 68,* 690–700.

Perry, D. G., Kusel, S. J., & Perry, L. C. (1988). Victims of peer aggression. *Developmental Psychology, 24,* 807–814.

Perry, D. G., Perry, L. C., Bussey, K., English, D., & Arnold, G. (1980). Processes of attribution and children's self-punishment following misbehavior. *Child Development, 51,* 545–551.

Perry, D. G., Perry, L. C., & Weiss, R. J. (1989). Sex differences in the consequences that children anticipate for aggression. *Developmental Psychology, 25,* 312–319.

Peskin, J. (1992). Ruse and representations: On children's ability to conceal information. *Developmental Psychology, 28,* 84–89.

Petersen, A. C., Compas, B. E., Brooks-Gunn, J., Stemmler, M., Ey, S., & Grant, K. E. (1993). Depression in adolescence. *American Psychologist, 48,* 155–164.

Peterson, L., Ewigman, B., & Kivlahan, C. (1993). Judgments regarding appropriate child supervision to prevent injury: The role of environmental risk and child age. *Child Development, 64,* 934–950.

Peterson, L., & Gelfand, D. M. (1984). Causal attributions of helping as a function of age and incentives. *Child Development, 55,* 504–511.

Pettit, G. S., Bates, J. E., & Dodge, K. A. (1997). Supportive parenting, ecological context, and children's adjustment: A seven-year longitudinal study. *Child Development, 68,* 908–923.

Pettit, G. S., Dodge, K. A., & Brown, M. M. (1988). Early family experience, social problem solving patterns, and children's social competence. *Child Development, 59,* 107–120.

Pettit, G. S., Laird, R. D., Bates, J. E., & Dodge, K. A. (1997). Patterns of after-school care in middle childhood: Risk factors and developmental outcomes. *Merrill-Palmer Quarterly, 43,* 515–538.

Phillips, D. (1984). The illusion of incompetence among academically competent children. *Child Development, 55,* 2000–2016.

Phillips, D. A., Voran, M., Kisker, E., Howes, C., & Whitebook, M. (1994). Child care for children in poverty: Opportunity or inequity? *Child Development, 65,* 472–492.

Phillips, M. (1997). What makes schools effective? A comparison of the relationships of communitarian climate and academic climate to mathematics achievement and attendance during middle school. *American Educational Research Journal, 34,* 633–662.

Phinney, J. S. (1993). A three-stage model of ethnic identity development in adolescence. In M. E. Bernal & G. P. Knight (Eds.), *Ethnic identity: Formation and transmission among Hispanics and other minorities.* Albany: State University of New York Press.

Phinney, J. S. (1996). When we talk about American ethnic groups, what do we mean? *American Psychologist, 51,* 918–927.

Phinney, J. S., Ferguson, D. L., & Tate, J. D., (1997). Intergroup attitudes among ethnic minority adolescents: A casual model. *Child Development, 68,* 955–969.

Phinney, J. S., & Rosenthal, D. A. (1992). Ethnic identity in adolescence: Process, context, and outcome. In G. R. Adams, T. P. Gullotta, & R. Montemayor (Eds.), *Adolescent identity formation* (Advances in Adolescent Development, Vol. 4). Newbury Park, CA: Sage.

Piaget, J. (1950). *The psychology of intelligence.* San Diego, CA: Harcourt Brace Jovanovich.

Piaget, J. (1951). *Play, dreams, and imitation in childhood.* New York: Norton.

Piaget, J. (1952). *The origins of intelligence in children.* New York: International Universities Press.

Piaget, J. (1954). *The construction of reality in the child.* New York: Basic Books.

Piaget, J. (1965). *The moral judgment of the child.* New York: Free Press. (Original work published 1932)

Piaget, J. (1970). Piaget's theory. In P. H. Mussen (Ed.), *Carmichael's manual of child psychology* (Vol. 1). New York: Wiley.

Piaget, J., & Inhelder, B. (1969). *The psychology of the child.* New York: Basic Books.

Pickens, J., & Field, T. (1993). Facial expressivity in infants of depressed mothers. *Developmental Psychology, 29,* 986–988.

Pike, A., McGuire, S., Hetherington, E. M., Reiss, D., & Plomin, R. (1996). Family environment and adolescent depressive symptoms and antisocial behavior: A multivariate genetic analysis. *Developmental Psychology, 32,* 590–603.

Pinon, M., Huston, A. C., & Wright, J. C. (1989). Family ecology and child characteristics that predict young children's educational television viewing. *Child Development, 60,* 846–856.

Pinto, A., Folkers, E., & Sines, J. O. (1991). Dimensions of behavior and home environment in school-age children: India and the United States. *Journal of Cross-Cultural Psychology, 22,* 491–508.

Pipp, S., Easterbrooks, M. A., & Harmon, R. J. (1992). The relation between attachment and knowledge of self and mother in one-year-old infants to three-year-old infants. *Child Development, 63,* 738–750.

Pipp-Siegel, S., & Foltz, C. (1997). Toddlers' acquisition of self/other knowledge: Ecological and interpersonal aspects of self and other. *Child Development, 68,* 69–79.

Pleck, J. H. (1997). Paternal involvement: Levels, sources, and consequences. In M. E. Lamb (Ed.), *The role of the father in child development* (3rd ed, pp. 66–103). New York: Wiley.

Plomin, R. (1990). *Nature and nurture.* Pacific Grove, CA: Brooks/Cole.

Plomin, R. (1994). *Genetics and experience: The interplay between nature and nurture.* Thousand Oaks, CA: Sage.

Plomin, R., & DeFries, J. C. (1985). *Origins of individual differences in infancy.* Orlando, FL: Academic Press.

Plomin, R., DeFries, J. C., McClearn, G. E., & Rutter, M. (1997). *Behavioral genetics* (3rd ed.). New York: W. H. Freeman.

Plomin, R., Reiss, D., Hetherington, E. M., & Howe, G. W. (1994). Nature and nurture: Genetic contributions to measures of the family environment. *Developmental Psychology, 30,* 32–43.

Plomin, R., & Rende, R. (1991). Human behavioral genetics. *Annual Review of Psychology, 42,* 161–190.

Plomin, R., & Rutter, M. (1998). Child development, molecular genetics, and what to do with genes once they are found. *Child Development, 69,* 1223–1242.

Pollack, R. H. (1997, March). *Personal communication.*

Pomerantz, E. M., & Ruble, D. N. (1997). Distinguishing multiple dimensions and conceptions of ability: Implications for self-evaluation. *Child Development, 68,* 1165–1180.

Pomerantz, E. M., & Ruble, D. N. (1998). The role of maternal control in the development of sex differences in child self-evaluative factors. *Child Development, 69,* 458–478.

Pomerantz, E. M., Ruble, D. N., Frey, K. S., & Grenlich, F. (1995). Meeting goals and confronting conflict: Children's changing perceptions of social comparison. *Child Development, 66,* 723–738.

Pomerleau, A., Bolduc, D., Malcuit, G., & Cossette, L. (1990). Pink or blue: Environmental gender stereotypes in the first two years of life. *Sex Roles, 22,* 359–367.

Portes, A., & MacLeod, D. (1996). Educational progress of children of immigrants: The roles of class, ethnicity, and school context. *Sociology of Education, 69,* 255–275.

Posada, G., Gao, Y., Wu, F., Posada, R., Tascon, M., Schoelmerich, A., Sagi, A., Kondo-Ikemura, K., Haaland, W., & Synnevang, B. (1995). The secure base phenomenon across cultures: Children's behavior, mothers' preferences, and experts' concepts. In E. Waters, B. E. Vaughn, G. Posada, & K. Kondo-Ikemura (Eds.), Caregiving, cultural, and cognitive perspectives on secure-base behavior and working models: New growing points of attachment theory and research. *Monographs of the Society for Research in Child Development, 60* (2–3, Serial No. 244).

Posner, J. K., & Vandell, D. L. (1994). Low-income children's after-school care: Are there beneficial effects of after-school programs? *Child Development, 65,* 440–456.

Poulin-Dubois, D., Serbin, L. A., Kenyon, B., & Derbyshire, A. (1994). Infants' intermodal knowledge about gender. *Developmental Psychology, 30,* 436–442.

Povinelli, D. J., Landau, K. R., & Perilloux, H. K. (1996). Self-recognition in young children using delayed versus live feedback: Evidence of a developmental asynchrony. *Child Development, 67,* 1540–1554.

Povinelli, D. J., & Simon, B. B., (1998). Young children's understanding of briefly versus extremely delayed images of the self: Emergence of the autobiographical stance. *Developmental Psychology, 34,* 188–194.

Powlishta, K. K. (1995). Intergroup processes in childhood: Social categorization and sex role development. *Developmental Psychology, 31,* 781–788.

Powlishta, K. K., Serbin, L. A., Doyle, A., & White, D. R. (1994). Gender, ethnic, and body type biases: The generality of prejudice in childhood. *Developmental Psychology, 30,* 526–536.

Priel, B., & deSchonen, S. (1986). Self-recognition: A study of a population without mirrors. *Journal of Experimental Child Psychology, 41,* 237–250.

Provence, S., & Lipton, R. C. (1962). *Infants in institutions.* New York: International Universities Press.

Pungello, E. P., Kupersmidt, J. B., Burchinal, M. R., & Patterson, C. J. (1996). Environmental risk factors and children's achievement from middle childhood to early adolescence. *Developmental Psychology, 32,* 755–767.

Putallaz, M., & Heflin, A. H. (1990). Parent-child interactions. In S. R. Asher & J. D. Coie (Eds.), *Peer rejection in childhood* (pp. 189–216). Cambridge, England: Cambridge University Press.

Quiggle, N. L., Garber, J., Panak, W. F., & Dodge, K. A. (1992). Social information processing in aggressive and depressed children. *Child Development, 63,* 1305–1320.

Quinn, R. A., Houts, A. C., & Graesser, A. C. (1994). Naturalistic conceptions of morality: A question-answering approach. *Journal of Personality, 62,* 260–267.

Rabiner, D. L., Keane, S. P., & MacKinnon-Lewis, C. (1993). Children's beliefs about familiar and unfamiliar peers in relation to their sociometric status. *Developmental Psychology, 29,* 236–243.

Rabiner, D. L., Lenhart, L., & Lochman, J. E. (1990). Automatic versus reflective social problem solving in relation to children's sociometric status. *Developmental Psychology, 26,* 1010–1016.

Radke-Yarrow, M., Cummings, E. M., Kuczynski, L., & Chapman, M. (1985). Patterns of attachment in two- and three-year-olds in normal families and families with parental depression. *Child Development, 56,* 884–893.

Radke-Yarrow, M., Zahn-Waxler, C., & Chapman, M. (1983). Children's prosocial dispositions and behavior. In E. M. Hetherington (Ed.), *Handbook of child psychology* (Vol. 4): *Socialization, personality, and social development.* New York: Wiley.

Ramey, C. T., & Ramey, S. L. (1998). Early intervention and early experience. *American Psychologist, 53,* 109–120.

Ramsey, P. G. (1995). Changing social dynamics in early childhood classrooms. *Child Development, 66,* 764–773.

Raynor, J. O. (1970). Relationships between achievement-related motives, future orientation, and academic performance. *Journal of Personality and Social Psychology, 15,* 28–33.

Raz, S., Goldstein, R., Hopkins, T. L., Lauterbach, M. D., Shah, F., Porter, C. L., Riggs, W. W., Magill, L. H., & Sander, C. J. (1994). Sex differences in early vulnerability to cerebral injury and their neurobehavioral implications. *Psychobiology, 22,* 244–253.

Raz, S., Lauterbach, M. D., Hopkins, T. L., Glogowski, B. K., Porter, C. L., Riggs, W. W., & Sander, C. J. (1995). A female advantage in cognitive recovery from early cerebral insult. *Developmental Psychology, 31,* 958–966.

Reese, E., & Fivush, R. (1993). Parental styles of talking about the past. *Developmental Psychology, 29,* 546–606.

Reinisch, J. M., Sanders, S. A., Hill, C. A., & Ziemba-Davis, M. (1992). High-risk sexual behavior among heterosexual undergraduates at a midwestern university. *Family Planning Perspectives, 24,* 116.

Reissland, N. (1988). Neonatal imitation in the first hour of life: Observations in rural Nepal. *Developmental Psychology, 24,* 464–469.

Remley, A. (1988, October). The great parental value shift: From obedience to independence. *Psychology Today,* pp. 56–59.

Repacholi, B. M., & Gopnik, A. (1997). Early reasoning about desires: Evidence from 14- and 18-month-olds. *Developmental Psychology, 33,* 12–21.

Resnick, S. M., Berenbaum, S. A., Gottesman, I. I., & Bouchard, T. J. (1986). Early hormonal influences on cognitive functioning in congenital adrenal hyperplasia. *Developmental Psychology, 22,* 191–198.

Rest, J. R., & Thoma, S. J. (1985). Relation of moral judgment development to formal education. *Developmental Psychology, 21,* 709–714.

Rest, J. R., Thoma, S. J., & Edwards, L. (1997). Designing and validating a measure of moral judgment: Stage preference and stage consistency approaches. *Journal of Educational Psychology, 89,* 5–28.

Reynolds, A. J., & Temple, J. A. (1998). Extended early childhood intervention and school achievement: Age thirteen findings from the Chicago Longitudinal Study. *Child Development, 69,* 231–246.

Reynolds, D. (1992). School effectiveness and school improvement: An updated review of the British literature. In D. Reynolds & P. Cuttance (Eds.), *School effectiveness: Research, policy, and practice.* London, England: Cassell.

Rheingold, H. L. (1982). Little children's participation in the work of adults, a nascent prosocial behavior. *Child Development, 53,* 114–125.

Rholes, W. S., Jones, M., & Wade, C. (1988). Children's understanding of personal disposition and its relationship to behavior. *Journal of Experimental Child Psychology, 45,* 1–17.

Rholes, W. S., & Ruble, D. N. (1984). Children's understanding of dispositional characteristics of others. *Child Development, 55,* 550–560.

Ribble, M. (1943). *The rights of infants.* New York: Columbia University Press.

Rice, M. E., & Grusec, J. E. (1975). Saying and doing: Effects on observer performance. *Journal of Personality and Social Psychology, 32,* 584–593.

Rice, M. L., Huston, A. C., Truglio, R., & Wright, J. (1990). Words from "Sesame Street": Learning vocabulary while viewing. *Developmental Psychology, 26,* 421–428.

Richards, M. H., Crowe, P. A., Larson, R., & Swarr, A. (1998). Developmental patterns and gender differences in the experience of peer companionship during adolescence. *Child Development, 69,* 154–163.

Richards, M. H., & Duckett, E. (1994). The relationship of maternal employment to early adolescent daily experience with and without parents. *Child Development, 65,* 225–236.

Richardson, J. G., & Simpson, C. H. (1982). Children, gender, and social structure: An analysis of the contents of letters to Santa Claus. *Child Development, 53,* 429–436.

Rinkoff, R. F., & Corter, C. M. (1980). Effects of setting and maternal accessibility on the infant's response to brief separation. *Child Development, 51,* 603–606.

Ritchie, K. L. (1999). Maternal behaviors and cognitions during discipline episodes: A comparison on power bouts and single acts of noncompliance. *Developmental Psychology, 35,* 580–589.

Roberts, L. R., Sarigiani, P. A., Petersen, A. C., & Newman, J. L. (1990). Gender differences in the relationship between achievement and self-image during early adolescence. *Journal of Early Adolescence, 10,* 159–175.

Roberts, W., & Strayer, J. (1996). Empathy, emotional expressiveness, and prosocial behavior. *Child Development, 67,* 449–470.

Robertson, T. S., & Rossiter, J. R. (1974). Children and commercial persuasion: An attribution theory analysis. *Journal of Consumer Research, 1,* 13–20.

Robinson, C. C., & Morris, J. T. (1986). The gender-stereotyped nature of Christmas toys received by 36-, 48-, and 60-month-old children: A comparison between nonrequested vs. requested toys. *Sex Roles, 15,* 21–32.

Robinson, I., Ziss, K., Ganza, B., Katz, S., & Robinson, E. (1991). Twenty years of sexual revolution, 1965–1985: An update. *Journal of Marriage and the Family, 53,* 216–220.

Robinson, J. L., Kagan, J., Reznick, J. S., & Corley, R. (1992). The heritability of inhibited and uninhibited behavior: A twin study. *Developmental Psychology, 28,* 1030–1037.

Rochat, P., & Morgan, R. (1995). Spatial determinants of the perception of self-produced leg movements by 3- to 5-month-old infants. *Developmental Psychology, 31,* 626–636.

Rocheleau, B. (1995). Computer use by school-age children: Trends, patterns, and predictors. *Journal of Educational Computing Research, 12,* 1–17.

Rodgers, J. L., & Rowe, D. C. (1988). Influence of siblings on adolescent sexual behavior. *Developmental Psychology, 24,* 722–728.

Rogoff, B. (1990). *Apprenticeship in thinking: Cognitive development in social context.* New York: Oxford University Press.

Rogoff, B. (1998). Cognition as a collaborative process. In D. Kuhn & R. S. Siegler (Eds.), *Cognition, language, and perceptual development,* Vol. 2. In W. Damon (Gen. Ed.), *Handbook of child psychology* (pp. 679–744). New York: Wiley.

Rogoff, B., Mistry, J., Goncu, A., & Mosier, C. (1993). Guided participation in cultural activity by toddlers and caregivers. *Monographs of the Society for Research in Child Development, 58* (8, Serial No. 236).

Roithmaier, A., Kiess, W., Kopecky, M., Fuhrmann, G., & Butenandt, O. (1988). Psychosozialer Minderwuchs. *Monatschift für Kinderheilkunde, 133,* 760–763.

Roopnarine, J. L., Talukder, E., Jain, D., Joshi, P., & Srivastave, P. (1990). Characteristics of holding, patterns of play, and social behaviors between parents and infants in New Delhi, India. *Developmental Psychology, 26,* 667–673.

Rose, A. J., & Asher, S. R. (1999). Children's goals and strategies in response to conflicts within a friendship. *Developmental Psychology, 35,* 69–79.

Rose, R. M., Bernstein, I. S., & Gordon, T. P. (1975). Consequences of social conflict on plasma testosterone levels in rhesus monkeys. *Psychosomatic Medicine, 37,* 50–61.

Rosen, B. C., & D'Andrade, R. (1959). The psychological origins of achievement motivation. *Sociometry, 22,* 185–218.

Rosen, K. S., & Rothbaum, F. (1993). Quality of parental caregiving and security of attachment. *Developmental Psychology, 29,* 358–367.

Rosen, W. D., Adamson, L. B., & Bakeman, R. (1992). An experimental investigation of infant social referencing: Mothers' messages and gender differences. *Developmental Psychology, 28,* 1172–1178.

Rosenberg, M. (1979). *Conceiving the self.* New York: Basic Books.

Rosenhan, D. L. (1970). The natural socialization of altruistic autonomy. In J. Macaulay & L. Berkowitz (Eds.), *Altruism and helping behavior.* New York: Academic Press.

Rosenhan, D. L. (1972a). Learning theory and prosocial behavior. *Journal of Social Issues, 28,* 151–163.

Rosenhan, D. L. (1972b). Prosocial behavior of children. In W. W. Hartup (Ed.), *The young child* (Vol. 2). Washington, DC: National Association for the Education of Young Children.

Rosenholtz, S. J., & Simpson, C. (1984). The formation of ability conceptions: Developmental trend or social construction? *Review of Educational Research, 54,* 31–63.

Rosenthal, D. A., & Feldman, S. S. (1992). The relationship between parenting behavior and ethnic identity in Chinese-American and Chinese-Australian adolescents. *International Journal of Psychology, 27,* 19–31.

Rosenthal, R. (1986). Media violence, antisocial behavior, and the social consequences of small effects. *Journal of Social Issues, 42,* 141–154.

Rosenthal, R., & Jacobson, L. (1968). *Pygmalion in the classroom.* New York: Holt, Rinehart and Winston.

Rosenthal, R., & Vandell, D. L. (1996). Quality of care at school-aged child-care programs: Regulatable features, observed experiences, child perspectives, and parent perspectives. *Child Development, 67,* 2434–2445.

Rosenthal, T., Underwood, B., & Martin, M. (1969). Assessing classroom incentive practices. *Journal of Educational Psychology, 60,* 370–376.

Rosenwasser, S. M., Lingenfelter, M., & Harrington, A. F. (1989). Nontraditional gender role portrayals and children's gender role perceptions. *Journal of Applied Developmental Psychology, 10,* 97–105.

Ross, H. S., Conant, C., Cheyne, C. A., & Alevizos, E. (1992). Relationships and alliances in the social interactions of kibbutz toddlers. *Social Development, 1,* 1–17.

Rothbart, M. K. (1971). Birth order and mother-child interaction in an achievement situation. *Journal of Personality and Social Psychology, 17,* 113–120.

Rothbart, M. K. (1981). Measurement of temperament in infancy. *Child Development, 52,* 569–578.

Rothbart, M. K., & Bates, J. E. (1998). Temperament. In W. Damon (Series Ed.), & N. Eisenberg (Vol. Ed.), *Handbook of child psychology: Vol. 3, Social, emotional, and personality development* (5th ed., pp. 105–176), New York: Wiley.

Rousseau, J. J. (1955). *Emile.* New York: Dutton. (Original work published 1762)

Rovee-Collier, C. (1995). Time windows in cognitive development. *Developmental Psychology, 31,* 147–169.

Rowe, D. C. (1994). *The limits of family influence: Genes, experience, and behavior.* New York: Guilford.

Rowe, D. C., & Plomin, R. (1981). The importance of nonshared (E_1) environmental influences in behavioral development. *Developmental Psychology, 17,* 517–531.

Rubenstein, J. L., Heeren, T., Housman, D., Rubin, C., & Stechler, G. (1989). Suicidal behavior in normal adolescents: Risks and protective factors. *American Journal of Orthopsychiatry, 59,* 59–71.

Rubin, K. H., Bukowski, W. M., & Parker, J. G. (1998). Peer interactions, relationships, and groups. In W. Damon (Series Ed.) and N. Eisenberg (Vol. Ed.), *Handbook of child psychology: Vol 3. Social, emotional, and personality development* (5th ed., pp. 619–700). New York: Wiley.

Rubin, K. H., Fein, G., & Vandenberg, B. (1983). Play. In E. M. Hetherington (Ed.), *Handbook of child psychology. Vol. 4: Socialization, personality, and social development* (pp. 693–744). New York: Wiley.

Ruble, D. N. (1988). Sex-role development. In M. H. Bornstein & M. E. Lamb (Eds.), *Developmental psychology: An advanced textbook* (2nd ed.). Hillsdale, NJ: Erlbaum.

Ruble, D. N., Balaban, T., & Cooper, J. (1981). Gender constancy and the effects of sex-typed televised toy commercials. *Child Development, 52,* 667–673.

Ruble, D. N., & Dweck, C. S. (1995). Self-conceptions, person conceptions, and their development. In N. Eisenberg (Ed.), *Social development*. Thousand Oaks, CA: Sage.

Ruble, D. N., & Martin, C. L. (1998). Gender development. In N. Eisenberg (Vol. Ed.), & W. Damon (Series Ed.), *Handbook of child psychology: Vol. 3, Social, emotional, and personality development* (5th ed., pp. 933–1016). New York: Wiley.

Ruble, T. L. (1983). Sex stereotypes: Issues of change in the 1970s. *Sex Roles, 9,* 397–402.

Rudin, M., Zalewski, C., & Bodmer-Turner, J. (1995). Characteristics of child sexual abusive victims according to perpetrator gender. *Child Abuse & Neglect, 19,* 963–973.

Rudolph, F. (1965). *Essays on early education in the republic.* Cambridge, MA: Harvard University Press.

Rueter, M. A., & Conger, R. D. (1998). Reciprocal influences between parenting and adolescent problem-solving behavior. *Developmental Psychology, 34,* 1470–1482.

Ruff, H. A., Lawson, K. R., Parrinello, R., & Weissberg, R. (1990). Long-term stability of individual differences in sustained attention in the early years. *Child Development, 61,* 60–75.

Ruffman, T. K., Olson, D. R., Ash, T., & Keenan, T. (1993). The ABCs of deception: Do young children understand deception in the same way as adults? *Developmental Psychology, 29,* 74–87.

Ruffman, T., Perner, J., Naito, M., Parkin, L., & Clements, W. A. (1998). Older (but not younger) siblings facilitate false belief understanding. *Developmental Psychology, 34,* 161–174.

Rushton, J. P. (1975). Generosity in children: Immediate and long term effects of modeling, preaching, and moral judgement. *Journal of Personality and Social Psychology, 31,* 459–466.

Rushton, J. P. (1976). Socialization and the altruistic behavior of children. *Psychological Bulletin, 83,* 898–913.

Rushton, J. P. (1980). *Altruism, socialization, and society.* Englewood Cliffs, NJ: Prentice-Hall.

Rushton, J. P., Fulker, D. W., Neale, M. C., Nias, K. K. B., & Eysenck, H. J. (1986). Altruism and aggression. The heritability of individual differences. *Journal of Personality and Social Psychology, 50,* 1192–1198.

Russell, A., & Finnie, V. (1990). Preschool children's social status and maternal instructions to assist group entry. *Developmental Psychology, 26,* 600–611.

Rutter, M. (1979). Protective factors in children's responses to stress and disadvantage. In M. W. Kent & J. E. Rolf (Eds.), *Primary prevention of psychopathology. Vol. 3: Social competence in children.* Hanover, NH: University Press of New England.

Rutter, M. (1981). *Maternal deprivation revisited* (2nd ed.). New York: Penguin Books.

Rutter, M. (1983). School effects on pupil progress: Research findings and policy implications. *Child Development, 54,* 1–29.

Rutter, M., Maughan, B., Mortimore, P., Ouston, J., & Smith, A. (1979). *Fifteen thousand hours: Secondary schools and their effects on children.* Cambridge, MA: Harvard University Press.

Saarni, C. (1984). An observational study of children's attempts to monitor their expressive behavior. *Child Development, 55,* 1504–1513.

Saarni, C. (1990). Emotional competence: How emotions and relationships become integrated. In R. A. Thompson (Ed.), Socioemotional development. *Nebraska Symposium on Motivation* (Vol 36). Lincoln: University of Nebraska Press.

Saarni, C. (1993). Socialization of emotion. In M. Lewis & J. M. Haviland (Eds.), *Handbook of emotions* (pp. 435–446). New York: Guilford.

Sabbagh, M. A., & Callanan, M. A. (1998). Metarepresentation in action: 3-, 4-, and 5-year olds' developing theories of mind in parent-child conversations. *Developmental Psychology, 34,* 491–502.

Sackin, S., & Thelen, E. (1984). An ethological study of peaceful associative outcomes to conflict in preschool children. *Child Development, 55,* 1098–1102.

Sacks, C. H., & Mergendoller, J. R. (1997). The relationship between teachers' theoretical orientation toward reading and student outcomes in kindergarten children with different initial reading abilities. *American Educational Research Journal, 34,* 721–739.

Sagi, A., & Hoffman, M. L. (1976). Empathic distress in newborns. *Developmental Psychology, 12,* 175–176.

Sagi, A., van IJzendoorn, M. H., Aviezer, O., Donnell, F., & Mayseless, O. (1994). Sleeping out of home in a kibbutz communal arrangement: It makes a difference for mother-infant attachment. *Child Development, 65,* 992–1004.

Sagotsky, G., & Lepper, M. R. (1982). Generalization of changes in children's preferences for easy or difficult goals induced through peer modeling. *Child Development, 53,* 372–375.

Salzinger, S., Feldman, R. S., Hammer, M., & Rosario, M. (1993). The effects of physical abuse on children's social relationships. *Child Development, 64,* 169–187.

Samuels, C. (1986). Bases for the infant's development of self-awareness. *Human Development, 29,* 36–48.

Samuels, H. R. (1980). The effect of older siblings on infant locomotor exploration of a new environment. *Child Development, 51,* 607–609.

Sancilio, M. F. M., Plumert, J. M., & Hartup, W. W. (1989). Friendship and aggressiveness as determinants of conflict outcomes in middle childhood. *Developmental Psychology, 25,* 812–819.

Santrock, J. W. (1975). Moral structure: The interrelations of moral behavior, moral judgment, and moral affect. *Journal of Genetic Psychology, 127,* 201–213.

Savin-Williams, R. C. (1995). An exploratory study of pubertal maturation timing and self-esteem among gay and bisexual male youths. *Developmental Psychology, 31,* 56–64.

Savin-Williams, R. C. (1998). *And then I became gay: Young men's stories.* New York: Routledge.

Savin-Williams, R. C., & Demo, D. H. (1984). Developmental change and stability in adolescent self-concept. *Developmental Psychology, 20,* 1100–1110 .

Savin-Williams, R. C., & Small, S. A. (1986). The timing of puberty and its relationship to adolescent and parent perceptions of family interactions. *Developmental Psychology, 22,* 342–347.

Scaramella, L. V., Conger, R. D., Simons, R. L., & Whitbeck, L. B. (1998). Predicting risk for pregnancy by late adolescence: A social-contextual perspective. *Developmental Psychology, 34,* 1233–1245.

Scarr, S. (1968). Environmental bias in twin studies. *Eugenics Quarterly, 15,* 34–40.

Scarr, S. (1992). Developmental theories for the 1990s: Development and individual differences. *Child Development, 63,* 1–19.

Scarr, S. (1998). American child care today. *American Psychologist, 53,* 95–108.

Scarr, S., & McCartney, K. (1983). How people make their own environments: A theory of genotype-environment effects. *Child Development, 54,* 424–435.

Scarr, S., Webber, P. L., Weinberg, R. A., & Wittig, M. A. (1981). Personality resemblance among adolescents and their parents in biologically related and adoptive families. *Journal of Personality and Social Psychology, 40,* 885–898.

Scarr, S., & Weinberg, R. A. (1978). The influence of family background on intellectual attainment. *American Sociological Review, 43,* 674–692.

Scarr, S., & Weinberg, R. A. (1983). The Minnesota adoption studies: Genetic differences and malleability. *Child Development, 54,* 260–267.

Schaffer, H. R. (1971). *The growth of sociability.* Baltimore: Penguin Books.

Schaffer, H. R. (1977). *Mothering.* Cambridge, MA: Harvard University Press.

Schaffer, H. R. (1990). *Making decisions about children: Psychological questions and answers.* Cambridge, MA: Basil Blackwell.

Schaffer, H. R., & Emerson, P. E. (1964). The development of social attachments in infancy. *Monographs of the Society for Research in Child Development, 29* (3, Serial No. 94).

Schaie, K. W. (1986). Beyond calendar definitions of age, time, and cohort: The general developmental model revisited. *Developmental Review, 6,* 252–277.

Schaie, K. W. (1990). Intellectual development in adulthood. In E. J. Birren & K. W. Schaie (Eds.). *The handbook of the psychology of aging* (3rd ed.). San Diego, CA: Academic Press.

Schmitz, S., Saudino, K. J., Plomin, R., Fulker, D. W., & DeFries, J. C. (1996). Genetic and environmental influences on temperament in middle childhood: Analyses of teacher and tester ratings. *Child Development, 67,* 409–422.

Schneider, B. H. (1992). Didactic methods for enhancing children's peer relations: A quantitative review. *Clinical Psychology Review, 12,* 363–382.

Schooler, C. (1972). Birth order effects: Not here, not now! *Psychological Bulletin, 78,* 161–175.

Schwartz, D., Dodge, K. A., Pettit, G. S., & Bates, J. E. (1997). The early socialization of aggressive victims of bullying. *Child Development, 68,* 665–675.

Scott, J. P. (1962). Critical periods in behavior development. *Science, 138,* 949–957.

Scott, J. P. (1966). Agonistic behavior in mice and rats: A review. *American Zoologist, 6,* 683–701.

Scott, J. P. (1968). *Early experience and the organization of behavior.* Pacific Grove, CA: Brooks/Cole.

Scott, J. P. (1972). Hostility and aggression. In B. Wolman (Ed.), *Handbook of genetic psychology.* Englewood Cliffs, NJ: Prentice-Hall.

Scott, J. P. (1992). Aggression: Functions and control in social systems. *Aggressive Behavior, 18,* 1–20.

Scott, W. A., Scott, R., & McCabe, M. (1991). Family relationships and children's personality: A cross-cultural, cross-source comparison. *British Journal of Social Psychology, 30,* 1–20.

Sears, R. R. (1963). Dependency motivation. In M. Jones (Ed.), *Nebraska Symposium on Motivation* (Vol. 11). Lincoln: University of Nebraska Press.

Sears, R. R., Maccoby, E. E., & Levin, H. (1957). *Patterns of child rearing.* New York: Harper & Row.

Sebald, H. (1986). Adolescents' shifting orientation toward parents and peers: A curvilinear trend over recent decades. *Journal of Marriage and the Family, 48,* 5–13.

Secord, P. H., & Peevers, D. H. (1974). The development and attribution of person concepts. In T. Mischel (Ed.), *Understanding other persons.* Totowa, NJ: Rowman & Littlefield.

Segal, U. A. (1991). Cultural variables in Asian Indian families. *Families in Society: The Journal of Contemporary Human Services, 72,* 233–242.

Seidman, E., Allen, L., Aber, J. L., Mitchell, C., & Feinman, J. (1994). The impact of school transitions in early adolescence on the self-system and perceived social context of poor urban youth. *Child Development, 65,* 507–522.

Seifer, R., Schiller, M., Sameroff, A. J., Resnick, S., & Riordan, K. (1996). Attachment, maternal sensitivity, and infant temperament during the first year of life. *Developmental Psychology, 32,* 12–25.

Seitz, V., & Apfel, N. H. (1994). Parent-focused intervention: Diffusion effects on siblings. *Child Development, 65,* 677–683.

Seitz, V., Rosenbaum, L. K., & Apfel, N. H. (1985). Effects of family support intervention: A ten-year follow-up. *Child Development, 56,* 376–391.

Selman, R. L. (1976). Social-cognitive understanding: A guide to educational and clinical practice. In T. Lickona (Ed.), *Moral development and behavior: Theory, research, and social issues.* New York: Holt, Rinehart and Winston.

Selman, R. L. (1980). *The growth of interpersonal understanding.* Orlando, FL: Academic Press.

Seppa, N. (1997). Children's TV remains steeped in violence. *Monitor of the American Psychological Association, 28*(6), 36.

Serbin, L. A., Cooperman, J. M., Peters, P. L., Lehoux, P. M., Stack, D. M., & Schwartzman, A. E. (1998). Intergenerational transfer of psychosocial risk in women with childhood histories of aggression, withdrawal, or aggression and withdrawal. *Developmental Psychology, 34,* 1246–1262.

Serbin, L. A., Powlishta, K. K., & Gulko, J. (1993). The development of sex typing in middle childhood. *Monographs of the Society for Research in Child Development, 58*(2, Serial No. 232).

Shaffer, D. R. (1973). *Children's responses to a hypothetical proposition.* Paper presented at the annual meeting of the Midwestern Psychological Association: Chicago.

Shaffer, D. R. (1988). On the measurement of moral judgments. *Journal of Research and Development in Education, 21,* 100–107.

Shaffer, D. R. (1994). Do naturalistic conceptions of morality provide any [novel] answers? *Journal of Personality, 62,* 263–268.

Shaffer, D. R. (1999). *Developmental psychology* (5th ed.). Pacific Grove, CA: Brooks/Cole.

Shaffer, D. R., Pegalis, L. J., & Cornell, D. P. (1992). Gender and self-disclosure revisited: Personal and contextual variations in self-disclosure to same-sex acquaintances. *Journal of Social Psychology, 132,* 307–315.

Shanahan, M. J., Elder, G. H., Jr., Burchinal, M., & Conger, R. D. (1996). Adolescent paid labor and relationships with parents: Early work-family linkages. *Child Development, 67,* 2183–2200.

Shanahan, M. J., Finch, M. D., Mortimer, J. T., & Ryu, S. (1991). Adolescent work experience and depressive affect. *Social Psychology Quarterly, 54,* 299–317.

Shantz, C. U. (1983). Social cognition. In P. H. Mussen (Ed.), *Handbook of child psychology. Vol. 3: Cognitive development.* New York: Wiley.

Shantz, C. U. (1987). Conflicts between children. *Child Development, 58,* 283–305.

Sharma, A. R., McGue, M. K., & Benson, P. L. (1998). The psychological adjustment of United States adopted adolescents and their nonadopted siblings. *Child Development, 69,* 791–802.

Sharp, D., Cole, M., & Lave, C. (1979). Education and cognitive development: The evidence from experimental research. *Monographs of the Society for Research in Child Development, 44* (1–2, Serial No. 178).

Shaw, D. S., Keenan, K., & Vondra, J. I. (1994). Developmental precursors of externalizing behavior: Ages 1 to 3. *Developmental Psychology, 30,* 355–364.

Shea, J. D. C. (1981). Changes in interpersonal distances and categories of play behavior in the early weeks of preschool. *Developmental Psychology, 17,* 417–425.

Shell, R. M., & Eisenberg, N. (1996). Children's reactions to the receipt of direct and indirect help. *Child Development, 67,* 1391–1405.

Sherif, M. (1956). Experiments in group conflict. *Scientific American, 195,* 54–58.

Sherif, M., Harvey, O. J., White, B. J., Hood, W. R., & Sherif, C. W. (1961). *Intergroup conflict and cooperation: The Robber's Cave experiment.* Norman: University of Oklahoma Press.

Shigetomi, C. C., Hartmann, D. P., & Gelfand, D. M. (1981). Sex differences in children's altruistic behavior and reputations for helpfulness. *Developmental Psychology, 17,* 434–437.

Shoda, Y., Mischel, W., & Peake, P. K. (1990). Predicting adolescent cognitive and self-regulatory competencies from preschool delay of gratification: Identifying diagnostic conditions. *Developmental Psychology, 26,* 978–986.

Short, R. J., & Talley, R. C. (1997). Rethinking psychology and the schools: Implications of recent national policy. *American Psychologist, 52,* 234–240.

Shulman, S., Elicker, J., & Sroufe, A. (1994). Stages of friendship growth in preadolescence as related to attachment history. *Journal of Social and Personal Relationships, 11,* 341–361.

Shultz, T. R., & Wells, D. (1985). Judging the intentionality of action-outcomes. *Developmental Psychology, 21,* 83–89.

Shure, M. B. (1989). Interpersonal competence training. In W. Damon (Ed.), *Child development today and tomorrow.* San Francisco: Jossey-Bass.

Shure, M. B., & Spivack, G. (1978). *Problem-solving techniques in childrearing.* San Francisco: Jossey-Bass.

Shweder, R. A. (1997, April). Varieties of moral intelligence: Autonomy, community, divinity. In L. A. Jensen (Chair), *Shweder's ethics of autonomy, community, and divinity: Theory and research.* Symposium presented at the biennial meeting of the Society for Research in Child Development, Washington, DC.

Shweder, R. A., Mahapatra, M., & Miller, J. G. (1987). Culture and moral development. In J. Kagan & S. Lamb (Eds.), *The emergence of morality in young children* (pp. 1–83). Chicago: University of Chicago Press.

Shweder, R. A., Mahapatra, M., & Miller, J. G. (1990). Culture and moral development. In J. W. Stigler, R. A. Shweder, & G. Herdt (Eds.), *Cultural psychology. Essays on comparative human development.* Cambridge, England: Cambridge University Press.

Siegal, M., & Cowen, J. (1984). Appraisals of intervention: The mother's versus the culprit's behavior as determinants of children's evaluations of discipline techniques. *Child Development, 55,* 1760–1766.

Siegal, M., & Peterson, C. C. (1998). Preschoolers' understanding of lies and innocent and negligent mistakes. *Developmental Psychology, 34,* 332–341.

Sigelman, C. K. (1984). Prosocial behavior. In K. Deaux & L. S. Wrights-man, *Social Psychology in the 80s* (4th ed.). Monterey, CA: Brooks/Cole.

Sigelman, C. K. (1999). *Life-span human development* (3rd ed.). Pacific Grove, CA: Brooks/Cole.

Sigelman, C. K., Carr, M. B., & Begley, N. L. (1986). Developmental changes in the influence of sex-role stereotypes on person perception. *Child Study Journal, 16,* 191–205.

Sigelman, C. K., Derenowski, E., Woods, T., Makai, T., Alfred-Livo, L., Durazo, O., & Maddock, A. (1996). Mexican-American and Anglo-American children's responsiveness to a theory-centered AIDS education program. *Child Development, 67,* 253–266.

Sigelman, C. K., Miller, T. E., & Whitworth, L. A. (1986). The early development of stigmatizing reactions to physical differences. *Journal of Applied Developmental Psychology, 7,* 17–32.

Sigelman, C. K., & Waitzman, K. A. (1991). The development of distributive justice orientations: Contextual influences on children's resource allocations. *Child Development, 62,* 1367–1378.

Signorella, M. L., Bigler, R. S., & Liben, L. S. (1993). Developmental differences in children's gender schemata about others: A meta-analytic review. *Developmental Review, 13,* 147–183.

Signorella, M. L., Jamison, W., & Krupa, M. H. (1989). Predicting spatial performance from gender stereotyping in activity preferences and in self-concept. *Developmental Psychology, 25,* 89–95.

Signorielli, N. (1991). *A sourcebook on children and television.* Westport, CT: Greenwood Press.

Signorielli, N., & Lears, M. (1992). Children, television, and conceptions about chores: Attitudes and behaviors. *Sex Roles, 27,* 157–170.

Simmons, R. G., & Blyth, D. A. (1987). *Moving into adolescence: The impact of pubertal change in school context.* New York: Aldine de Gruyter.

Simmons, R. G., Burgeson, R., Carlton-Ford, S., & Blyth, D. A. (1987). The impact of cumulative change in early adolescence. *Child Development, 58,* 1220–1234.

Simons, R. L. (1996). The effect of divorce on adult and child adjustment. In R. L. Simons & Associates (Eds.), *Understanding differences between divorced and intact families: Stress, interaction, and child outcome* (pp. 3–20). Thousand Oaks, CA: Sage.

Simons, R. L., Beaman, J., Conger, R. D., & Chao, W. (1993). Stress, support, and antisocial behavior trait as determinants of emotional well-being and parenting practices among single mothers. *Journal of Marriage and the Family, 55,* 385–398.

Simons, R. L., & Chao, W. (1996). Conduct problems. In R. L. Simons & Associates (Eds.), *Understanding differences between divorced and intact families: Stress, interaction, and child outcome* (pp. 125–143). Thousand Oaks, CA: Sage.

Simons, R. L., Johnson, C., & Lorenz, F. O. (1996). Family structural differences in stress and behavioral predispositions. In R. L. Simons & Associates (Eds.), *Understanding differences between divorced and intact families: Stress, interaction, and child outcome* (pp. 45–63). Thousand Oaks, CA: Sage.

Simons, R. L., Whitebeck, L. B., Conger, R. D., & Wu, C. (1991). Intergenerational transmission of harsh parenting. *Developmental Psychology, 27,* 159–171.

Singelis, T. M. (1994). The measurement of independent and interdependent self-construals. *Personality and Social Psychology Bulletin, 20,* 580–591.

Singer, D. G., & Singer, J. L. (1990). *The house of make-believe: Children's play and the developing imagination.* Cambridge, MA: Harvard University Press.

Singer, L. M., Brodzinsky, D. M., Ramsay, D., Steir, M., & Waters, E. (1985). Mother-infant attachments in adoptive families. *Child Development, 56,* 1543–1551.

Skinner, B. F. (1953). *Science and human behavior.* New York: Macmillan.

Slaby, R. G., & Crowley, C. G. (1977). Modification of cooperation and aggression through teacher attention to children's speech. *Journal of Experimental Child Psychology, 23,* 442–458.

Slaby, R. G., & Frey, K. S. (1975). Development of gender constancy and selective attention to same-sex models. *Child Development, 46,* 849–856.

Slaby, R. G., & Guerra, N. G. (1988). Cognitive mediators of aggression in adolescent offenders: 1. Assessment. *Developmental Psychology, 24,* 580–588.

Slaby, R. G., Roedell, W. C., Arezzo, D., & Hendrix, K. (1995). *Early violence prevention.* Washington, DC: National Association for the Education of Young Children.

Slaughter-Defoe, D. T., Nakagawa, K., Takanishi, R., & Johnson, D. L. (1990). Toward cultural/ecological perspectives on schooling and achievement in African- and Asian-American children. *Child Development, 61,* 363–383.

Slavin, R. E. (1987). Ability grouping and student achievement in elementary schools: A best evidence synthesis. *Review of Educational Research, 57,* 293–336.

Slavin, R. E. (1989). Class size and student achievement: Small effects of small classes. *Educational Psychologist, 24,* 99–110.

Slavin, R. E. (1991). Cooperative learning and group contingencies. *Journal of Behavioral Education, 1,* 105–115.

Slavin, R. E. (1996). Research on cooperative learning and achievement: What we know, what we need to know. *Contemporary Educational Psychology, 21,* 43–69.

Sluckin, A. M., & Smith, P. K. (1977). Two approaches to the concept of dominance in preschool children. *Child Development, 48,* 917–923.

Smetana, J. G. (1981). Preschool children's conceptions of moral and social rules. *Child Development, 52,* 1333–1336.

Smetana, J. G. (1985). Preschool children's conceptions of transgressions: Effects of varying moral and conventional domain-related attributes. *Developmental Psychology, 21,* 18–29.

Smetana, J. G. (1995). Parenting styles and conceptions of parental authority during adolescence. *Child Development, 66,* 299–316.

Smetana, J. G., & Bitz, B. (1996). Adolescents' conceptions of teachers' authority and their relations to rule violations at school. *Child Development, 67,* 1153–1172.

Smetana, J. G., Schlagman, N., & Adams, P. W. (1993). Preschool children's judgments about hypothetical and actual transgressions. *Child Development, 64,* 202–214.

Smith, P. K., & Connolly, K. J. (1980). *The ecology of preschool behavior.* New York: Cambridge University Press.

Smith, P. K., & Daglish, L. (1977). Sex differences in parent and infant behavior in the home. *Child Development, 48,* 1250–1254.

Smith, T. W. (1990). Academic achievement and teaching younger siblings. *Social Psychology Quarterly, 53,* 352–363.

Snarey, J. R. (1985). Cross-cultural universality of social-moral development: A critical review of Kohlbergian research. *Psychological Bulletin, 97,* 202–232.

Snarey, J. R., & Keljo, K. (1991). In a gemeinschaft voice: The cross-cultural expansion of moral development theory. In W. M. Kurtines & J. L. Gewirtz (Eds.), *Handbook of moral behavior and development* (Vol. 1, pp. 395–424). Hillsdale, NJ: Erlbaum.

Snidman, N., Kagan, J., Riordan, L., & Shannon, D. C. (1995). Cardiac function and behavioral reactivity. *Psychophysiology, 32,* 199–207.

Snow, M. E., Jacklin, C. N., & Maccoby, E. E. (1983). Sex-of-child differences in father-child interaction at one year of age. *Child Development, 54,* 227–232.

Sobesky, W. E. (1983). The effects of situational factors on moral judgments. *Child Development, 54,* 575–584.

Sodian, B., Taylor, C., Harris, P. L., & Perner, J. (1991). Early deception and the child's theory of mind: False trails and genuine markers. *Child Development, 62,* 468–483.

Sommer, K., Whitman, T. L., Borkowski, J. G., Schellenbach, C., Maxwell, S., & Kerugh, D. (1993). Cognitive readiness and adolescent parenting. *Developmental Psychology, 29,* 389–398.

Sorensen, E. (1997). A national profile of nonresident fathers and their ability to pay child support. *Journal of Marriage and the Family, 59,* 785–797.

Speicher, B. (1994). Family patterns of moral judgment during adolescence and early adulthood. *Developmental Psychology, 30,* 624–632.

Speltz, M. L., Endriga, M. C., Fisher, P. A., & Mason, C. A. (1997). Early predictors of attachment in infants with cleft lip/or palate. *Child Development, 68,* 12–25.

Spence, J. T. (1993). Gender-related traits and gender ideology: Evidence for a multifactorial theory. *Journal of Personality and Social Psychology, 64,* 624–635.

Spence, J. T., & Hall, S. K. (1996). Children's gender-related self-perceptions, activity preferences, and occupational stereotypes: A test of three models of gender constructs. *Sex Roles, 35,* 659–691.

Spence, J. T., & Helmreich, R. L. (1978). *Masculinity and femininity: Their psychological dimensions, correlates, and antecedents.* Austin: TX: University of Texas Press.

Spencer, M. B. (1988). Self-concept development. In D. T. Slaughter (Ed.), *Black children in poverty: Developmental perspectives.* San Francisco: Jossey-Bass.

Spencer, M. B., & Markstrom-Adams, C. (1990). Identity processes among racial and ethnic minority children in America. *Child Development, 61,* 290–310.

Spitz, R. A. (1945). Hospitalism: An inquiry into the genesis of psychiatric conditions in early childhood. In A. Freud (Ed.), *The psychoanalytic study of the child* (Vol. 1). New York: International Universities Press.

Spitz, R. A. (1965). *The first year of life: A psychoanalytic study of normal and deviant object relations.* New York: International Universities Press.

Spitze, G. (1988). Women's employment and family relations: A review. *Journal of Marriage and the Family, 50,* 595–618.

Sroufe, L. A. (1977). Wariness of strangers and the study of infant development. *Child Development, 48,* 1184–1199.

Sroufe, L. A. (1985). Attachment classification from the perspective of infant-caregiver relationships and infant temperament. *Child Development, 56,* 1–14.

Sroufe, L. A., Bennett, C., Englund, M., Urban, J., & Shulman, S. (1993). The significance of gender boundaries in preadolescence: Contemporary correlates and antecedents of boundary violation and maintenance. *Child Development, 64,* 455–466.

Sroufe, L. A., Egeland, B., & Kreutzer, T. (1990). The fate of early experience following developmental change: Longitudinal approaches to individual adaptation in childhood. *Child Development, 61,* 1363–1373.

Sroufe, L. A., Waters, E., & Matas, L. (1974). Contextual determinants of infant affectional response. In M. Lewis & L. A. Rosenblum (Eds.), *The origins of fear.* New York: Wiley.

Staffieri, J. R. (1967). A study of social stereotype of body image in children. *Journal of Personality and Social Psychology, 7,* 101–104.

Stanger, C., Achenbach, T. M., & Verhulst, F. C. (1997). Accelerated longitudinal comparisons of aggressive versus delinquent syndromes. *Development and Psychopathology, 9,* 43–58.

Stattin, H., & Magnusson, D. (1990). *Paths through life: Vol. 2. Pubertal maturation in female development.* Hillsdale, NJ: Erlbaum.

Steele, B. F., & Pollack, C. B. (1974). A psychiatric study of parents who abuse infants and small children. In R. E. Helfer & C. H. Kempe (Eds.), *The battered child.* Chicago: University of Chicago Press.

Steele, C. M. (1997). A threat in the air: How stereotypes shape intellectual identity and performance. *American Psychologist, 52,* 613–629.

Steele, C. M., & Aronson, J. (1995). Stereotype threat and the intellectual test performance of African Americans. *Journal of Personality and Social Psychology, 69,* 797–811.

Steele, H., Steele, M., & Fonagy, P. (1996). Associations among attachment classifications of mothers, fathers, and their infants. *Child Development, 67,* 541–555.

Stein, A. H., & Friedrich, L. K. (1972). Television content and young children's behavior. In J. P Murray, E. A. Rubinstein, & G. A. Comstock (Eds.), *Television and social behavior.* Vol. 2: *Television and social learning.* Washington, DC: U.S. Government Printing Office.

Steinberg, L. (1986). Latchkey children and susceptibility to peer pressure: An ecological analysis. *Developmental Psychology, 22,* 433–439.

Steinberg, L. (1987). Single parents, stepparents, and the susceptibility of adolescents to antisocial peer pressure. *Child Development, 58,* 269–275.

Steinberg, L. (1996). *Adolescence* (4th ed.), New York: McGraw-Hill.

Steinberg, L., & Dornbusch, S. M. (1991). Negative correlates of part-time employment during adolescence: Replication and elaboration. *Developmental Psychology, 27,* 304–313.

Steinberg, L., Dornbusch, S. M., & Brown, B. B. (1992). Ethnic differences in adolescent achievement: An ecological perspective. *American Psychologist, 47,* 723–729.

Steinberg, L., Elmen, J. D., & Mounts, N. S. (1989). Authoritative parenting, psychosocial maturity, and academic success among adolescents. *Child Development, 60,* 1424–1436.

Steinberg, L., Fegley, S., & Dornbusch, S. M. (1993). Negative impact of part-time work on adolescent adjustment: Evidence from a longitudinal study. *Developmental Psychology, 29,* 171–180.

Steinberg, L., Lamborn, S. D., Darling, N., Mounts, N. S., & Dornbusch, S. M. (1994). Over-time changes in adjustment and competence among adolescents from authoritative, authoritarian, indulgent, and neglectful families. *Child Development, 65,* 754–770.

Steinberg, L., & Silverberg, S. B. (1986). The vicissitudes of autonomy in early adolescence. *Child Development, 57,* 841–851.

Stern, D. (1977). *The first relationship: Infant and mother.* Cambridge, MA: Harvard University Press.

Stern, D. N. (1985). *The interpersonal world of the infant.* New York: Basic Books.

Stern, D. N. (1995). Self/other differentiation in the domain of intimate socio-affective interaction: Some considerations. In P. Rochat (Ed.), *The self in infancy: Theory and research* (pp. 419–429). Amsterdam: North Holland-Elsevier.

Sternberg, K. J., Lamb, M. E., Greenbaum, C., Cicchetti, D., Dawud, S., Cortes, R. M., Krispin, O., & Lorey, F. (1993). Effects of domestic violence on children's behavior problems and depression. *Developmental Psychology, 29,* 44–52.

Stevens, R. J., & Slavin, R. E. (1995a). Effects of a cooperative learning approach in reading and writing on academically handicapped and non-handicapped students. *Elementary School Journal, 95,* 241–262.

Stevens, R. J., & Slavin, R. E. (1995b). The cooperative elementary school: Effects on students' achievement, attitudes, and social relations. *American Educational Research Journal, 32,* 321–351.

Stevenson, H. W., Chen, C., & Lee, S. (1993). Mathematics achievement of Chinese, Japanese, and American children: Ten years later. *Science, 259,* 53–58.

Stevenson, H. W., Chen, C., & Uttal, D. H. (1990). Beliefs and achievement: A study of Black, White, and Hispanic children. *Child Development, 61,* 508–523.

Stevenson, H. W., & Lee, S. Y. (1990). Contexts of achievement: A study of American, Chinese, and Japanese children. *Monographs of the Society for Research in Child Development, 55,* (1–2, Serial No. 221).

Stevenson, H. W., Lee, S. Y., & Stigler, J. W. (1986). Mathematics achievement of Chinese, Japanese, and American children. *Science, 231,* 693–699.

Stevenson, H. W., Stigler, J. W., Lee, S. Y., Lucker, G. W., Litamura, S., & Hsu, C. (1985). Cognitive performance and academic achievement of Japanese, Chinese, and American children. *Child Development, 56,* 718–734.

Stewart, R. B. (1983). Sibling attachment relationships: Child-infant interactions in the strange situation. *Developmental Psychology, 19,* 192–199.

Stewart, R. B., & Marvin, R. S. (1984). Sibling relations: The role of conceptual perspective-taking in the ontogeny of sibling caregiving. *Child Development, 55,* 1322–1332.

Stice, E., & Barrera, M., Jr. (1995). A longitudinal examination of the reciprocal relations between perceived parenting and adolescents' substance use and externalizing behaviors. *Developmental Psychology, 31,* 322–334.

Stigler, J. W., Lee, S. Y., & Stevenson, H. W. (1987). Mathematics classrooms in Japan, Taiwan, and the United States. *Child Development, 58,* 1272–1285.

Stipek, D., Feiler, R., Daniels, D., & Milbern, S. (1995). Effects of different instructional approaches on young children's achievement and motivation. *Child Development, 66,* 209–233.

Stipek, D., Gralinski, H., & Kopp, C. (1990). Self-concept development in the toddler years. *Developmental Psychology, 26,* 972–977.

Stipek, D., & Mac Iver, D. (1989). Developmental change in children's assessment of intellectual competence. *Child Development, 60,* 521–538.

Stipek, D., Recchia, A., & McClintic, S. (1992). Self-evaluation in young children. *Monographs of the Society for Research in Child Development, 57*(1, Serial No. 226).

Stipek, D. J., & Ryan, R. H. (1997). Economically disadvantaged preschoolers: Ready to learn but further to go. *Developmental Psychology, 33,* 711–723.

Stormshak, E. A., Bellanti, C. J., Bierman, K. L., and the Conduct Problems Prevention Research Group. (1996). The quality of sibling relationships and the development of social competence and behavioral control in aggressive children. *Developmental Psychology, 32,* 79–89.

St. Peters, M., Fitch, M., Huston, A. C., Wright. J. C., & Eakins, D. J. (1991). Television and families: What do young children watch with their parents? *Child Development, 62,* 1409–1423.

Strassberg, Z. (1995). Social information processing in compliance situations by mothers of behavior-problem boys. *Child Development, 66,* 376–389.

Strayer, F. F. (1980). Social ecology of the preschool peer group. In W. A. Collins (Ed.), *Minnesota Symposia on Child Psychology. Vol. 13: Development of cognition, affect, and social relations.* Hillsdale, NJ: Erlbaum.

Streitmatter, J. (1993). Gender differences in identity development: An examination of longitudinal data. *Adolescence, 28,* 55–66.

Strough, J., Berg, C. A., & Sansone, C. (1996). Goals for solving everyday problems across the life span: Age and gender differences in the salience of interpersonal concerns. *Developmental Psychology, 32,* 1106–1115.

Stumpf, H., & Stanley, J. C. (1996). Gender-related differences on the College Board's Advanced Placement and Achievement Tests, 1982–1992. *Journal of Educational Psychology, 88,* 353–364.

Stumphauzer, J. S. (1972). Increased delay of gratification in young inmates through imitation of high-delay peer models. *Journal of Personality and Social Psychology, 21,* 10–17.

Sue, S., & Okazaki, S. (1990). Asian-American educational achievements: A phenomenon in search of explanation. *American Psychologist, 45,* 913–920.

Sui-Chu, E. H., & Willms, J. D. (1996). Effects of parental involvement on eighth-grade achievement. *Sociology of Education, 69,* 126–141.

Sullivan, H. S. (1953). *The interpersonal theory of psychiatry.* New York: Norton.

Sullivan, M. W., Lewis, M., & Alessandri, S. M. (1992). Cross-age stability in emotional expressions during learning and extinction. *Developmental Psychology, 28,* 58–63.

Suomi, S. J., & Harlow, H. F. (1972). Social rehabilitation of isolate reared monkeys. *Developmental Psychology, 6,* 487–496.

Suomi, S. J., & Harlow, H. F. (1978). Early experience and social development in rhesus monkeys. In M. E. Lamb (Ed.), *Social and personality development.* New York: Holt, Rinehart and Winston.

Tanner, J. M. (1990). *Foetus into man: Physical growth from conception to maturity* (2nd ed.). Cambridge, MA: Harvard University Press.

Tarullo, L. B., DeMudler, E. K., Ronsaville, D. S., Brown, E., & Radke-Yarrow, M. (1995). Maternal depression and maternal treatment of siblings as predictors of child psychopathology. *Developmental Psychology, 31,* 395–405.

Taylor, A. R., Asher, S. R., & Williams, G. A. (1987). The social adaptation of mainstreamed mildly retarded children. *Child Development, 58,* 1321–1334.

Taylor, M., & Carlson, S. M. (1997). The relation between individual differences in fantasy and theory of mind. *Child Development, 68,* 436–455.

Taylor, M. G. (1996). The development of children's beliefs about social and biological aspects of gender differences. *Child Development, 67,* 1555–1571.

Taylor, R. D. (1996). Adolescents' perceptions of kinship support and family management practices: Association with adolescent adjustment in African-American families. *Developmental Psychology, 32,* 687–695.

Taylor, R. D., & Roberts, D. (1995). Kinship support and maternal and adolescent well-being in economically disadvantaged African-American families. *Child Development, 66,* 1585–1597.

Teegartin, C. (1994, July 25). Never-marrieds soar among single parents. *Atlanta Constitution,* pp. A1, A7.

Teeven. R. C., & McGhee, P. E. (1972). Childhood development of fear of failure motivation. *Journal of Personality and Social Psychology, 21,* 345–348.

Terry, R., & Coie, J. D. (1991). A comparison of methods for defining sociometric status among children. *Developmental Psychology, 27,* 867–880.

Teti, D. M., & Ablard, K. E. (1989). Security of attachment and infant-sibling relationships: A laboratory study. *Child Development, 60,* 1519–1528.

Teti, D. M., Gelfand, D. M., Messinger, D. S., & Isabella, R. (1995). Maternal depression and the quality of early attachment: An examination of infants, preschoolers, and their mothers. *Developmental Psychology, 31,* 364–376.

Teti, D. M., Sakin, J. W., Kucera, E., Corns, K. M., & Das Eiden, R. (1996). And baby makes four: Predictors of attachment security among preschool-age first-borns during the transition to siblinghood. *Child Development, 67,* 579–596.

Tharp, R. G. (1989). Psychocultural variables and constants: Effects on teaching and learning in schools. *American Psychologist, 44,* 349–359.

Tharp, R. G., & Gallimore, R. (1988). *Rousing minds to life: Teaching. learning, and schooling in social context.* Cambridge, England: Cambridge University Press.

Thoma, S. J., Rest, J. R., & Davison, M. L. (1991). Describing and testing a moderator of the moral judgment and action relationship. *Journal of Personality and Social Psychology, 61,* 659–669.

Thomas, A., & Chess, S. (1977). *Temperament and development.* New York: Brunner/Mazel.

Thomas, A., & Chess, S. (1986). The New York longitudinal study: From infancy to early adult life. In R. Plomin & J. Dunn (Eds.). *The study of temperament: Changes, continuities, and challenges.* Hillsdale, NJ: Erlbaum.

Thomas, A., Chess, S., & Birch, H. G. (1970). The origin of personality. *Scientific American, 223,* 102–109.

Thomas, A., Chess, S., & Korn, S. (1982). The reality of difficult temperament. *Merrill-Palmer Quarterly, 28,* 1–20.

Thomas, M. H., Horton, R. W., Lippincott, E. C., & Drabman, R. S. (1977). Desensitization to portrayals of real-life aggression as a function of exposure to television violence. *Journal of Personality and Social Psychology, 35,* 450–458.

Thompson, R. A. (1994). Emotion regulation: A theme in search of definition. In N. A. Fox (Ed.), The development of emotion regulation: Biological and behavioral considerations. *Monographs of the Society for Research in Child Development, 59* (Nos. 2–3, Serial No. 240).

Thompson, R. A. (1998). Early sociopersonality development. In N. Eisenberg (Ed.), & W. Damon (Series Ed.), *Handbook of child psychology: Vol. 3: Social emotional. and personality development* (5th ed.). New York: Wiley.

Thompson, R. A., Lamb, M. E., & Estes, D. (1982). Stability of infant-mother attachment and its relationship to changing life circumstances in an unselected middle-class sample. *Child Development, 53,* 144–148.

Thompson, S. K. (1975). Gender labels and early sex-role development. *Child Development, 46,* 339–347.

Thompson, W. R., & Melzack, R. (1956). Early environment. *Scientific American, 114,* 38–42.

Thorne, A., & Michaelieu, Q. (1996). Situating adolescent gender and self-esteem with personal memories. *Child Development, 67,* 1374–1390.

Thorne, B. (1993). *Gender play. Girls and boys in school.* New Brunswick, NJ: Rutgers University Press.

Thurber, C. A. (1995). The experience and expression of homesickness in preadolescent and adolescent boys. *Child Development, 66,* 1162–1178.

Tieger, T. (1980). On the biological bases of sex differences in aggression. *Child Development, 51,* 943–963.

Tietjen, A. M. (1986). Prosocial reasoning among children and adults in a Papua New Guinea society. *Developmental Psychology, 22,* 861–868.

Tinbergen, N. (1973). *The animal in its world: Explorations of an ethologist, 1932–1972* (Vols. 1 & 2). Cambridge, MA: Harvard University Press.

Tinsley, B. J. (1992). Multiple influences on the acquisition and socialization of children's health attitudes and behavior: An integrative review. *Child Development, 63,* 1043–1069.

Tirozzi, G. N., & Uro, G. (1997). Education reform in the United States: National policy in support of local efforts for school improvement. *American Psychologist, 52,* 241–249.

Tisak, M. S., & Tisak, J. (1990). Children's conceptions of parental authority, friendship, and sibling relations. *Merrill-Palmer Quarterly, 36,* 347–368.

Toch, H. (1969). *Violent men.* Hawthorne, NY: Aldine.

Toch, T., & Streisands, B. (1997, October 13). Does class size matter? *U.S. News & World Report, 123,* 22–29.

Tomada, G., & Schneider, B. H. (1997). Relational aggression, gender, and peer acceptance: Invariance across culture, stability over time, and concordance among informants. *Developmental Psychology, 33,* 601–609.

Tomlinson-Keasey, C., & Keasey, C. B. (1974). The mediating role of cognitive development in moral judgment. *Child Development, 45,* 291–298.

Toner, I. J. (1981). Role involvement and delay maintenance behavior in preschool children. *Journal of Genetic Psychology 138,* 245–251.

Toner, I. J., Moore, L. P., & Ashley, P. K. (1978). The effect of serving as a model of self-control on subsequent resistance to deviation in children. *Journal of Experimental Child Psychology, 26,* 85–91.

Toner, I. J., Moore, L. P., & Emmons, B. A. (1980). The effect of being labeled on subsequent self-control in children. *Child Development, 51,* 618–621.

Toner, I. J., & Potts, R. (1981). Effect of modeled rationales on moral behavior, moral choice, and level of moral judgment in children. *Journal of Psychology, 107,* 153–162.

Trachtenberg, S., & Viken, R. J. (1994). Aggressive boys in the classroom: Biased attributions or shared perceptions. *Child Development 65,* 829–835.

Tremblay, R. E., Boulerice, B., Harden, P. W., McDuff, P., Perusse, D., Pihl, R. O., & Zoccolillo, M. (1996). Do children in Canada become more aggressive as they approach adolescence? In Human Resources Development Canada & Statistics Canada (Eds.), *Growing up in Canada: National Longitudinal Survey of Children and Youth* (pp. 127–137). Ottawa, Ontario, Canada: Statistics Canada.

Triandis, H. C. (1994). *Culture and social behavior.* New York: McGraw-Hill.

Triandis, H. C. (1995). *Individualism and collectivism.* Boulder, CO: Westview Press.

Trickett, P. K., Aber, J. L., Carlson, V., & Cicchetti, D. (1991). Relationship of socioeconomic status to the etiology and developmental sequelae of physical child abuse. *Developmental Psychology, 27,* 148–158.

Trickett, P. K., & McBride-Chang, C. (1995). The developmental impact of different forms of child abuse and neglect. *Developmental Review, 15,* 311–337.

Trickett, P. K., & Putnam, F. W. (1993). Impact of child sexual abuse on females: Toward a developmental, psychobiological integration. *Psychological Science, 4,* 81–87.

Trickett, P. K., & Susman, E. J. (1988). Parental perceptions of child-rearing practices in physically abusive and nonabusive families. *Developmental Psychology, 24,* 270–276.

Trivers, R. L. (1983). The evolution of cooperation. In D. L. Bridgeman (Ed.), *The nature of prosocial development.* New York: Academic Press.

Tronick, E. Z. (1989). Emotions and emotional communications in infants. *American Psychologist, 44,* 112–119.

Tronick, E. Z., Morelli, G. A., & Ivey, P. K. (1992). The Efe forager infant and toddler's pattern of social relationships: Multiple and simultaneous. *Developmental Psychology, 28,* 568–577.

Tryon, R. C. (1940). Genetic differences in maze learning in rats. *Yearbook of the National Society for Studies in Education, 39,* 111–119.

Tubman, J. G., Windle, M., & Windle, R. C. (1996). The onset and cross-temporal patterning of sexual intercourse in middle adolescence: Prospective relations with behavioral and emotional problems. *Child Development, 67,* 327–343.

Tudge, J. R. H. (1992). Processes and consequences of peer collaboration: A Vygotskian analysis. *Child Development, 63,* 1364–1379.

Turiel, E. (1983). *The development of social knowledge: Morality and convention.* Cambridge, England: Cambridge University Press.

Turner, C. W., & Goldsmith, D. (1976). Effects of toy guns and airplanes on children's antisocial free play behavior. *Journal of Experimental Child Psychology, 21,* 303–315.

Turner, P. J., & Gervai, J. (1995). A multidimensional study of gender typing in preschool children and their parents: Personality, attitudes, preferences, behavior, and cultural differences. *Developmental Psychology, 31,* 759–772.

Turner-Bowker, D. M. (1996). Gender stereotyped descriptions in children's picture books: Does "curious Jane" exist in the literature? *Sex Roles, 35,* 461–488.

Twenge, J. M. (1997). Changes in masculine and feminine traits over time: A meta-analysis. *Sex Roles, 36,* 305–325.

Tyson, P., & Tyson, R. L. (1990). *Psychoanalytic theories of development: An integration.* New Haven, CT: Yale University Press.

Uba, L. (1994). *Asian Americans: Personality patterns, identity, and mental health.* New York: Guilford.

Udry, J. R. (1990). Hormonal and social determinants of adolescent sexual initiation. In J. Bancroft & J. M. Reinisch (Eds.), *Adolescence and puberty* (pp. 70–87). New York: Oxford University Press.

Ugurel-Semin, R. (1952). Moral behavior and moral judgment of children. *Journal of Abnormal and Social Psychology, 47,* 463–474.

Underwood, B., & Moore, B. (1982). Perspective-taking and altruism. *Psychological Bulletin, 91,* 143–173.

Underwood, M. K., Coie, J. D., & Herbsman, C. R. (1992). Display rules for anger and aggression in school-age children. *Child Development, 63,* 366–380.

Uniform Crime Reports for the United States. 1997. Federal Bureau of Investigation. Washington, DC: U.S. Government Printing Office.

Urberg, K. A. (1979). Sex-role conceptualization in adolescents and adults. *Developmental Psychology, 15,* 90–92.

Urberg, K. A., Degirmencioglu, S. M., Tolson, J. M., & Halliday-Scher, K. (1995). The structure of adolescent peer networks. *Developmental Psychology, 31,* 540–547.

U.S. Bureau of the Census. (1996). *Statistical abstract of the United States: 1996* (116th ed.). Washington, DC: U.S. Government Printing Office.

U.S. Bureau of the Census. (1997). *Statistical abstract of the United States* (117th ed.). Washington, DC: U.S. Government Printing Office.

U.S. Department of Education (1995). *Reports to Congress: A compilation and analysis of reports submitted by states in accordance with Section 722(d) (3) of the Education for Homeless Children and Youth Program.* Washington, DC: U.S. Department of Education, Office of Elementary and Secondary Education.

U.S. Department of Education (1996). *Report to Congress: Goals 2000: Increasing student achievement through state and local initiatives.* Washington, DC: U.S. Government Printing Office.

U.S. Department of Justice. (1995). *Crime in the United States.* Washington, DC: U.S. Government Printing Office.

Vandell, D. L., & Corasantini, M. A. (1988). The relation between third graders' after-school care and social, academic, and emotional functioning. *Child Development, 59,* 868–875.

Vandell, D. L., & Corasantini, M. A. (1990). Variations in early child care: Do they predict subsequent social, emotional, and cognitive differences? *Early Childhood Research Quarterly, 5,* 555–572.

Vandell, D. L., Henderson, V. K., & Wilson, K. S. (1988). A longitudinal study of children with day-care experiences of varying quality. *Child Development, 59,* 1286–1292.

Vandell, D. L., & Mueller, E. C. (1995). Peer play and friendships during the first two years. In H. C. Smith, A. J. Chapman, & J. R. Smith (Eds.), *Friendship and social relations in children* (pp. 181–208). New Brunswick, NJ: Transaction.

Vandell, D. L., & Ramanan, J. (1991). Children of the National Longitudinal Survey of Youth: Choices in after-school care and child development. *Developmental Psychology, 27,* 637–643.

Vandell, D. L., & Ramanan, J. (1992). Effects of early and recent maternal employment on children from low-income families. *Child Development, 63,* 938–949.

Vandell, D. L., Wilson, K. S., & Buchanan, N. R. (1980). Peer interaction in the first year of life: An examination of its structure, content, and sensitivity to toys. *Child Development, 51,* 481–488.

van den Boom, D. C. (1995). Do first-year intervention effects endure? Follow-up during toddlerhood of a sample of Dutch irritable infants. *Child Development, 66,* 1798–1816.

van den Boom, D. C. (1997). Sensitivity and attachment: New steps for developmentalists. *Child Development, 68,* 592–594.

van den Broek, P. W. (1997). Discovering the element of the universe: The development of event comprehension from childhood to adulthood. In P. van den Broek, P. Bauer, & T. Bourg (Eds.), *Developmental spans in event comprehension: Bridging fictional and actual events* (pp. 321–342). Mahwah, NJ: Erlbaum.

van den Broek, P., Lorch, E. P., & Thurlow, R. (1996). Children's and adults' memory for television stories: The role of causal factors, story-grammar categories, and hierarchial level. *Child Development, 67,* 3010–3028.

van Doorninck, W. J., Caldwell, B. M., Wright, C., & Frankenberg, W. K. (1981). The relationship between twelve-month home stimulation and school achievement. *Child Development, 52,* 1080–1083.

van IJzendoorn, M. H. (1992). Intergenerational transmission of parenting: A review of studies in nonclinical populations. *Developmental Review, 12,* 76–99.

van IJzendoorn, M. H. (1995). Adult attachment representations, parental responsiveness, and infant attachment: A meta-analysis on the predictive validity of the Adult Attachment Interview. *Psychological Bulletin, 117,* 387–403.

van IJzendoorn, M. H., & De Wolff, M. S. (1997). In search of the absent father—meta-analysis of infant-father attachment: A rejoinder to our discussants. *Child Development, 68,* 604–609.

van IJzendoorn, M. H., Goldberg, S., Kroonenberg, P. M., & Frenkel, O. J. (1992). The relative effects of maternal and child problems on the quality of attachment: A meta-analysis of attachment in clinical samples. *Child Development, 63,* 840–858.

van IJzendoorn, M. H., & Kroonenberg, P. M. (1988). Cross-cultural patterns of attachment: A meta-analysis of the Strange Situation. *Child Development, 59,* 147–156.

Vannatta, R. A. (1996). Risk factors related to suicidal behavior among male and female adolescents. *Journal of Youth and Adolescence, 25,* 149–160.

Vartanian, L. R., & Powlishta, K. K. (1996). A longitudinal examination of the social-cognitive foundations of adolescent egocentrism. *Journal of Early Adolescence, 16,* 157–178.

Vasudev, J., & Hummel, R. C. (1987). Moral stage sequence and principled reasoning in an Indian sample. *Human Development, 30,* 105–118.

Vaughn, B., Block, J., & Block, J. (1988). Parental agreement on child rearing during early childhood and the psychological characteristics of adolescents. *Child Development, 59,* 1020–1033.

Vaughn, B. E., Kopp, C. B., & Krakow, J. B. (1984). The emergence and consolidation of self-control from eighteen to thirty months of age: Normative trends and individual differences. *Child Development, 55,* 990–1004.

Vaughn, B. E., Stevenson-Hinde, J., Waters, E., Kotsaftis, A., Lefever, G. B., Shouldice, A., Trudel, M., & Belsky, J. (1992). Attachment security and temperament in infancy and early childhood: Some conceptual clarification. *Developmental Psychology, 28,* 463–473.

Vaughn, B. E., & Waters, E. (1990). Attachment behavior at home and in the lab: Q-sort observations and Strange Situation classifications of 1-year-olds. *Child Development, 61,* 1965–1973.

Verhulst, F. C., & Versluis-Den Bieman, H. J. (1995). Developmental course of problem behaviors in adolescent adoptees. *Journal of the American Academy of Child and Adolescent Psychiatry, 34,* 151–159.

Verschueren, K., Marcoen, A., & Schoefs, V. (1996). The internal working model of self, attachment, and competence in five-year-olds. *Child Development, 67,* 2493–2511.

Vinden, P. G. (1996). Junín Quechua children's understanding of mind. *Child Development, 67,* 1707–1716.

Vinter, A. (1986). The role of movement in eliciting early imitations. *Child Development, 57,* 66–71.

Vitaro, F., Tremblay, R. E., Kerr, M., Pagani, L., & Bukowski, W. M. (1997). Disruptiveness, friends' characteristics, and delinquency in early adolescence: A test of two competing models of development. *Child Development, 68,* 676–689.

Vobejda, B. (1991, September 15). The future deferred. Longer road from adolescence to adulthood often leads back through parents' home. *The Washington Post,* pp. A1, A29.

Volling, B. L., & Belsky, J. (1992). The contribution of mother-child and father-child relationships to the quality of sibling interaction: A longitudinal study. *Child Development, 63,* 1209–1222.

Vondra, J., & Belsky, J. (1993). Developmental origins of parenting: Personality and relationship factors. In T. Luster & L. Okagaki (Eds.), *Parenting. An ecological perspective.* Hillsdale, NJ: Erlbaum.

Von Wright, M. R. (1989). Body image satisfaction in adolescent boys and girls: A longitudinal study. *Journal of Youth and Adolescence, 18,* 71–83.

Voyer, D., Voyer, S., & Bryden, M. P. (1995). Magnitude of sex differences in spatial abilities: A meta-analysis and consideration of critical variables. *Psychological Bulletin, 117,* 250–270.

Vuchinich, S., Bank, L., & Patterson, G. R. (1992). Parenting, peers, and the stability of antisocial behavior in preadolescent boys. *Developmental Psychology, 28,* 510–521.

Vuchinich, S., Hetherington, E. M., Vuchinich, R. A., & Clingempeel, W. G. (1991). Parent-child interaction and gender differences in early adolescents' adaptation to stepfamilies. *Developmental Psychology, 27,* 618–626.

Vygotsky, L. S. (1962). *Thought and language* (E. Hanfmann & G. Vakar, Eds. & Trans.). Cambridge, MA: MIT Press. (Original work published in 1934)

Vygotsky, L. S. (1978). *Mind in society: The development of higher mental processes* (M. Cole, V. John-Steiner, S. Scribner, & E. Souberman, Eds.). Cambridge, MA: Harvard University Press. (Original work published 1930, 1933, 1935)

Wachs, T. D. (1992). *The nature of nurture.* Newbury Park, CA: Sage.

Wagner, B. M. (1997). Family risk factors for child and adolescent suicidal behavior. *Psychological Bulletin, 121,* 246–298.

Wainryb, C., & Turiel, E. (1994). Dominance, subordination, and concepts of personal entitlements in cultural contexts. *Child Development, 65,* 1701–1722.

Walden, T. A., & Baxter, A. (1989). The effect of context and age on social referencing. *Child Development, 60,* 1511–1518.

Waldman, I. D., Weinberg, K. A., & Scarr, S. (1994). Racial-group differences in IQ in the Minnesota Transracial Adoption Study: A reply to Levin and Lynn. *Intelligence, 19,* 29–44.

Walker, L. J. (1980). Cognitive and perspective-taking prerequisites for moral development. *Child Development, 51,* 131–139.

Walker, L. J. (1995). Sexism in Kohlberg's moral psychology: In W. M. Kurtines & J. L. Gewirtz (Eds.), *Moral development: An introduction* (pp. 83–107). Boston: Allyn & Bacon.

Walker, L. J., de Vries, B., & Trevethan, S. D. (1987). Moral stages and moral orientations in real-life and hypothetical dilemmas. *Child Development, 58,* 842–858.

Walker, L. J., & Pitts, R. C. (1998). Naturalistic conceptions of moral maturity. *Developmental Psychology, 34,* 403–419.

Walker, L. J., & Taylor, J. H. (1991a). Family interactions and the development of moral reasoning. *Child Development, 62,* 264–283.

Walker, L. J., & Taylor, J. H. (1991b). Stage transitions in moral reasoning: A longitudinal study of developmental processes. *Developmental Psychology, 27,* 330–337.

Wallen, K. (1996). Nature needs nurture: The interaction of hormonal and social influences on the development of behavioral sex differences in rhesus monkeys. *Hormones and Behavior 30,* 364–378.

Wallerstein, J. S., & Blakeslee, S. (1989). *Second chances: Men, women, and children a decade after divorce.* New York: Ticknor and Fields.

Wallerstein, J. S., & Kelly, J. B. (1980). *Surviving the breakup: How children and parents cope with divorce.* New York: Basic Books.

Walters, A. S. (1997). *Survey of 500 adolescents' discoveries about the facts of life.* Unpublished data, University of Georgia.

Walters, R. H., & Brown, M. (1963). Studies of reinforcement of aggression: Transfer of responses to an interpersonal situation. *Child Development, 34,* 562–571.

Ward, M. J., & Carlson, E. A. (1995). Associations among adult attachment representations, maternal sensitivity, and infant-mother attachment in a sample of adolescent mothers. *Child Development, 66,* 69–79.

Wark, G. R., & Krebs, D. L. (1996). Gender and dilemma differences in real-life moral judgments. *Developmental Psychology, 32,* 220–230.

Wartner, U. G., Grossmann, K., Fremmer-Bombik, E., & Suess, G. (1994). Attachment patterns at age six in south Germany: Predictability from infancy and implications for preschool behavior. *Child Development, 65,* 1014–1027.

Waterman, A. S. (1982). Identity development from adolescence to adulthood: An extension of theory and a review of research. *Developmental Psychology, 18,* 341–358.

Waterman, A. S. (1992). Identity as an aspect of optimal psychological functioning. In G. R. Adams, T. P. Gullotta, & R. Montemayor (Eds.), *Adolescent identity formation* (Advances in Adolescent Development, Vol. 4). Newbury Park, CA: Sage.

Waterman, A. S., & Archer, S. L. (1990). A life-span perspective on identity formation: Developments in form, function, and process. In P. B. Baltes, D. L. Featterman, & R. M. Lerner (Eds.), *Life-span development and behavior: Vol. 10.* Hillsdale, NJ: Erlbaum.

Waters, E., Vaughn, B. E., & Egeland, B. R. (1980). Individual differences in mother-infant attachment relationships at age one: Antecedents in neonatal behavior in an urban, economically disadvantaged sample. *Child Development, 51,* 208–216.

Waters, E., Vaughn, B. E., Posada, G., & Kondo-Ikemura, K. (1995). Caregiving, cultural, and cognitive perspectives on secure-base behavior and working models: New growing points of attachment theory and research. *Monographs of the Society for Research in Child Development, 60,* (2–3, Serial No. 244).

Waters, E., Wippman, J., & Sroufe, L. A. (1979). Attachment, positive affect, and competence in the peer group: Two studies in construct validation. *Child Development, 50,* 821–829.

Watson, J. B. (1913). Psychology as the behaviorist views it. *Psychological Review, 20,* 158–177.

Watson, J. B. (1925). *Behaviorism.* New York: Norton.

Watson, J. B. (1928). *Psychological care of infant and child.* New York: Norton.

Watson, J. B., & Raynor, R. (1920). Conditioned emotional reactions. *Journal of Experimental Psychology, 3,* 1–14.

Watson, J. S., Hayes, L. A., Vietze, P., & Becker, J. (1979). Discriminative infant smiling to orientations of talking faces of mother and stranger. *Journal of Experimental Child Psychology, 28,* 92–99.

Watson, M. W., & Peng, Y. (1992). The relation between toy gun play and children's aggressive behavior. *Early Education and Development, 3,* 370–389.

Weinberg, M. K., Tronick, E. A., Cohn, J. F., & Olson, K. L. (1999). Gender differences in emotional expressivity and self-regulation during early infancy. *Developmental Psychology, 35,* 175–188.

Weiner, B. (1974). *Achievement and attribution theory.* Morristown, NJ: General Learning Press.

Weiner, B. (1982). An attribution theory of motivation and emotion. In H. Krohne & L. Laux (Eds.), *Achievement, stress, and anxiety,* Washington, DC: Hemisphere.

Weiner, B. (1986). *An attributional theory of motivation and emotion.* New York: Springer-Verlag.

Weinraub, M., Clemens, L. P., Sockloff, A., Ethridge, T., Gracely, E., & Myers, B. (1984). The development of sex-role stereotypes in the third year: Relationships to gender labeling, gender identity, sex-typed toy preferences, and family characteristics. *Child Development, 55,* 1493–1503.

Weinraub, M., & Lewis, M. (1977). The determinants of children's responses to separation. *Monographs of the Society for Research in Child Development, 42,* (4, Serial No. 172).

Weinstein, C. S. (1991). The classroom as a social context for learning. *Annual Review of Psychology, 42,* 493–525.

Weinstein, R. S., Marshall, H. H., Sharp, L., & Botkin, M. (1987). Pygmalion and the student: Age and classroom differences in children's awareness of teacher expectations. *Child Development, 58,* 1079–1093.

Weisner, T. S., & Gallimore, R. (1977). My brother's keeper: Child and sibling caretaking. *Current Anthropology, 18,* 169–190.

Weisner, T. S., & Wilson-Mitchell, J. E. (1990). Nonconventional family lifestyles and sex typing in six-year-olds. *Child Development, 61,* 1915–1933.

Weiss, B., Dodge, K. A., Bates, J. E., & Pettit, G. S. (1992). Some consequences of early harsh discipline: Child aggression and a maladaptive social information processing style. *Child Development, 63,* 1321–1335.

Weiss, L. H., & Schwarz, J. C. (1996). The relationship between parenting types and older adolescents' personality, academic achievement, adjustment, and substance use. *Child Development, 67,* 2101–2114.

Weisz, J. R., Chaiyasit, W., Weiss, B., Eastman, K. L., & Jackson, E. W. (1995). A multimethod study of problem behavior among Thai and American children in school: Teacher reports versus direct observations. *Child Development, 66,* 402–415.

Welch-Ross, M. K., & Schmidt, C. R. (1996). Gender-schema development and children's constructive story memory: Evidence for a developmental model. *Child Development, 67,* 820–835.

Wellman, H. M. (1990). *The child's theory of mind.* Cambridge, MA: MIT Press.

Wellman, H. M., Hollander, M., & Schult, C. A. (1996). Young children's understanding of thought bubbles and of thoughts. *Child Development, 67,* 768–788.

Wellman, H. M., & Woolley, J. (1990). From simple desires to ordinary beliefs: The early development of everyday psychology. *Cognition, 35,* 245–275.

Wells, L. E. (1989). Self-enhancement through delinquency: A conditional test of self-derogation theory. *Journal of Research in Crime and Delinquency, 26,* 226–252.

Wentzel, K. R., & Asher, S. R. (1995). The academic lives of neglected, rejected, popular, and controversial children. *Child Development, 66,* 754–763.

Wertsch, J. V., & Tulviste, P. (1992). L. S. Vygotsky and contemporary developmental psychology. *Developmental Psychology, 28,* 548–557.

Whaley, K. L., & Rubenstein, T. S. (1994). How toddlers "do" friendship: A descriptive analysis of naturally occurring friendships in a group child care setting. *Journal of Social and Personal Relationships, 11,* 383–400.

Whipple, E. E., & Richey, C. A. (1997). Crossing the line between physical discipline and child abuse: How much is too much? *Child Abuse & Neglect, 21,* 431–444.

Whitaker, D. J., & Miller, K. S. (1999). Parent-adolescent discussion about sex and condoms: Input on peer influences of sexual risk behavior. *Journal of Adolescent Research,* in press.

Whitbeck, L. B., Simons, R. L., & Goldberg, E. (1996). Adolescent sexual intercourse. In R. L. Simons & Associates (Eds.), *Understanding differences between divorced and intact families: Stress, interaction, and child outcome* (pp. 144–156). Thousand Oaks, CA: Sage.

Whitbourne, S. K. (1986). *The me I know: A study of adult identity.* New York: Springer-Verlag.

White, K. J., & Kistner, J. (1992). The influence of teacher feedback on young children's peer preferences and perceptions. *Developmental Psychology, 28,* 933–940.

White, R. W. (1959). Motivation reconsidered: The concept of competence. *Psychological Review, 66,* 297–333.

White, S. H. (1992). G. Stanley Hall: From philosophy to developmental psychology. *Developmental Psychology, 28,* 25–34.

Whiting, B. B., & Edwards, C. P. (1988). *Children of different worlds: The formation of social behavior.* Cambridge, MA: Harvard University Press.

Whiting, B. B., & Whiting, J. W. M. (1975). *Children of six cultures.* Cambridge, MA: Harvard University Press.

Whitley, B. E., Jr. (1983). Sex-role orientation and self-esteem: A critical meta-analytic review. *Journal of Personality and Social Psychology, 44,* 765–778.

Wichstrom, L. (1999). The emergence of gender differences in depressed mood during adolescence: The role of intensified gender socialization. *Developmental Psychology, 35,* 232–245.

Wiehe, V. R. (1996). *Working with child abuse and neglect.* Thousand Oaks, CA: Sage.

Wiggam, A. E. (1923). *The new decalogue of science.* Indianapolis: Bobbs-Merrill.

Willems, E. P., & Alexander, J. L. (1982). The naturalistic perspective in research. In B. B. Wolman (Ed.), *Handbook of developmental psychology.* Englewood Cliffs, NJ: Prentice-Hall.

Williams, B. (1998, January 19). Stricter controls on internet access sorely needed, parents fear. *Atlanta Constitution,* pp. A1, A15.

Williams, C., & Bybee, J. (1994). What do children feel guilty about? Developmental and gender differences. *Developmental Psychology, 30,* 617–623.

Williams, E., & Radin, N. (1993). Parental involvement, maternal employment, and adolescents' academic achievement: An 11-year follow-up. *American Journal of Orthopsychiatry, 63,* 306–312.

Williams, J. E., Bennett, S. M., & Best, D. L. (1975). Awareness and expression of sex-stereotypes in young children. *Developmental Psychology, 11,* 635–642.

Williams, J. E., & Best, D. L. (1990). *Measuring sex stereotypes: A multination study* (rev. ed.). Newbury Park, CA: Sage.

Wilson, M. N. (1989). Child development in the context of the Black extended family. *American Psychologist, 44,* 380–385.

Windle, R. C., & Windle, M. (1995). Longitudinal patterns of physical aggression: Associations with adult social, psychiatric, and personality functioning and testosterone levels. *Development and Psychopathology, 7,* 563–585.

Windle, R. C., & Windle, M. (1997). An investigation of adolescents' substance abuse behaviors, depressed affect, and suicidal behaviors. *Journal of Child Psychology and Psychiatry and Allied Disciplines, 38,* 921–929.

Windom, C. S. (1992, June). *Child abuse and alcohol use.* Paper presented for the Working Group on Alcohol-Related Violence, Washington, DC.

Winter, D. G. (1996). *Personality: Analysis and interpretation of lives.* New York: McGraw-Hill.

Winterbottom, M. (1958). The relation of need for achievement to learning experiences in independence and mastery. In J. Atkinson (Ed.), *Motives in fantasy, action, and society.* Princeton, NJ: Van Nostrand.

Wise, P. H. (1995). Infant mortality: Confronting disciplinary fragmentation in research and policy. In B. E. Sachs, R. Beard, E. Papiernik, & C. Russell (Eds.), *Reproductive health care for women and babies* (pp. 375–390). New York: Oxford University Press.

Wolff, M., Rutten, P., & Bayer, A. F., III. (1992). *Where we stand: Can America make it in the race for health, wealth, and happiness?* New York: Bantam Books.

Wolfner, G. D., & Gelles, R. J. (1993). A profile of violence toward children: A national study. *Child Abuse and Neglect, 17,* 197–212.

Woo, E. (1995, December 11). Can racial stereotypes psych out students? *Los Angeles Times.*

Wright, J. C., & Huston, A. C. (1983). A matter of form: Potentials of television for young viewers. *American Psychologist, 38,* 835–843.

Wright, J. C., Huston, A. C., Reitz, A. L., & Piemyat, S. (1994). Young children's perception of television reality: Determinants and developmental differences. *Developmental Psychology, 30,* 229–239.

Wright, J. C., Huston, A. C., Truglio, R., Fitch, M., Smith, E., & Piemyat, S. (1995). Occupational portrayals on television: Children's role schemata, career aspirations, and perceptions of reality. *Child Development, 66,* 1706–1718.

Wrobel, G. M., Ayers-Lopez, S., Grotevant, H. D., McRoy, R. G., & Friedrich, M. (1996). Openness in adoption and level of child participation. *Child Development, 67,* 2358–2374.

Wuthnow, R. (1994). *God and mammon in America.* New York: Free Press.

Yang, B., Ollendick, T. H., Dong, Q., Xia, Y., & Lin, L. (1995). Only children and children with siblings in the People's Republic of China: Levels of fear, anxiety, and depression. *Child Development, 66,* 1301–1311.

Yarrow, L. J., MacTurk, R. H., Vietze, P. M., McCarthy, M. E., Klein, R. P., & McQuiston, S. (1984). Developmental course of parental stimulation and its relationship to mastery motivation during infancy. *Developmental Psychology, 20,* 492–503.

Yarrow, M. R., Scott, P. M., & Waxler, C. Z. (1973). Learning concern for others. *Developmental Psychology, 8,* 240–260.

Yau, J., & Smetana, J. G. (1996). Adolescent-parent conflict among Chinese adolescents in Hong Kong. *Child Development, 67,* 1262–1275.

Yeates, K. O., & Selman, R. L. (1989). Social competence in the schools: Toward an integrative developmental model for intervention. *Developmental Review, 9,* 64–100.

Young, W. C., Goy, R. W., & Phoenix, C. H. (1964). Hormones and sexual behavior. *Science, 143,* 212–218.

Youngblade, L. M., & Belsky, J. (1992). Parent-child antecedents of 5-year-olds' close friendships: A longitudinal analysis. *Developmental Psychology, 28,* 700–713.

Youngblade, L. M., & Dunn, J. (1995). Individual differences in children's pretend play with mother and sibling: Links to relationships and to other people's feelings and beliefs. *Child Development, 66,* 1472–1492.

Youniss, J., & Smollar, J. (1985). *Adolescent relations with mothers, fathers, and friends.* Chicago: University of Chicago Press.

Yuill, N., & Pearson, A. (1998). The development of bases for trait attribution: Children's understanding of traits as casual mechanisms based on desire. *Developmental Psychology, 34,* 574–586.

Zahavi, S., & Asher, S. R. (1978). The effect of verbal instructions on preschool children's aggressive behavior. *Journal of School Psychology, 16,* 146–153.

Zahn-Waxler, C., Friedman, R. J., Cole, P. M., Mizuta, I., & Himura, N. (1996). Japanese and United States preschool children's responses to conflict and distress. *Child Development, 67,* 2462–2477.

Zahn-Waxler, C., Radke-Yarrow, M., & King, R. A. (1979). Child rearing and children's prosocial initiations towards victims of distress. *Child Development, 50,* 319–330.

Zahn-Waxler, C., Radke-Yarrow, M., Wagner, E., & Chapman, M. (1992). Development of concern for others. *Developmental Psychology, 28,* 126–136.

Zahn-Waxler, C., Robinson, J. L., & Emde, R. N. (1992). The development of empathy in twins. *Developmental Psychology, 28,* 1038–1047.

Zajonc, R. B. (1975, August). Birth order and intelligence. Dumber by the dozen. *Psychology Today,* pp. 39–43.

Zajonc, R. B., Markus, H., & Markus, G. B. (1979). The birth order puzzle. *Journal of Personality and Social Psychology, 37,* 1325–1341.

Zajonc, R. B., & Mullally, P. R. (1997). Birth order: Reconciling conflicting effects. *American Psychologist, 52,* 685–699.

Zakriski, A. L., & Coie, J. D. (1996). A comparison of aggressive-rejected and nonaggressive-rejected children's interpretations of self-directed and other-directed rejection. *Child Development, 67,* 1048–1070.

Zarbatany, L., Brunschot, M. V., Meadows, K., & Pepper, S. (1996). Effects of friendship and gender on peer group entry. *Child Development, 67,* 2287–2300.

Zelazo, P. D., Helwig, C. C., & Lau, A. (1996). Intention, act, and outcome in behavioral prediction and moral judgment. *Child Development, 67,* 2478–2492.

Zeman, J., & Garber, J. (1996). Display rules for anger, sadness, and pain: It depends on who is watching. *Child Development, 67,* 957–973.

Zeman, J., & Shipman, K. (1997). Social-contextual influences on expectancies for managing anger and sadness: The transition from middle childhood to adolescence. *Developmental Psychology, 33,* 917–924.

Zern, D. S. (1984). Relationships among selected child-rearing variables in a cross-cultural sample of 110 societies. *Developmental Psychology, 20,* 683–690.

Zigler, E. F. (1987). Formal schooling for four-year-olds? No. *American Psychologist, 42,* 254–260.

Zigler, E., & Finn Stevenson, M. F. (1993). *Children in a changing world: Developmental and social issues.* Pacific Grove, CA: Brooks/Cole.

Zigler, E. F., & Finn-Stevenson, M. (1996). Funding child care and public education. *The Future of Children, 6,* 104–121.

Zigler, E., Finn-Stevenson, M., & Stern, B. M. (1997). Supporting children and families in the schools: The school of the 21st century. *American Journal of Orthopsychiatry, 67,* 396–407.

Zigler, E. F., & Gilman, E. (1993). Day care in America: What is needed? *Pediatrics, 91,* 175–178.

Zillman, D. (1989). Aggression and sex: Independent and joint operations. In H. L. Wagner & S. R. Manstead (Eds.), *Handbook of psychophysiology: Emotion and social behavior.* Chichester: John Wiley.

Zimmerman, M. A., Salem, D. A., & Maton, K. I. (1995). Family structure and psychosocial correlates among urban African-American adolescent males. *Child Development, 66,* 1598–1613.

Zupan, B. A., Hammen, C., & Jaenicke, C. (1987). The effects of current mood and prior depressive history on self-schematic processing in children. *Journal of Experimental Child Psychology 43,* 149–158.

Abbey, B. B., 109, 110
Abel, N., 395
Aber, J. L., 176, 177, 211, 225, 391, 424, 428
Ablard, K. E., 377
Aboud, F. E., 190, 196, 464
Abraham, K. G., 185
Abramovitch, R., 376, 377
Abravanel, E., 47, 55
Achenbach, T. M., 287–288
Achilles, C. M., 419
Ackerman, B. P., 370
Acock, A. C., 387
Adams, G. R., 185, 186, 188, 265, 456
Adams, P. W., 332
Adams, R. E., 132
Adamson, L. B., 112
Adler, A., 43, 227, 238
Adler, T. F., 238
Aerts, E., 343
Ageton, S. S., 244
Agyei, Y., 265, 380
Ahn, A., 236
Ainsworth, M. D. S., 70, 121, 125, 127, 130, 136, 139, 140, 143, 450
Aksan, N., 180
Alansky, J. A., 143
Al Awad, A. M. H., 360
Alberts, D. M., 416
Albin, M., 108
Albow, J. C., 174
Alessandri, S. M., 107, 165, 277, 328
Alevizos, E., 462
Alexander, B. K., 439
Alexander, G. M., 243
Alexander, J. L., 18
Alexander, K. L., 216, 217, 227
Alexander, S. J., 265
Alfieri, T., 242
Alfred-Livo, L., 267
Allen, J. P., 148, 268, 467
Allen, L., 176, 177, 211, 424
Alley, T. R., 125
Allgood-Merten, B., 260
Allison, P. D., 382, 383
Almeida, D. M., 242
Aloise, P. A., 95
Alpern, L., 147
Amato, P., 381

Amato, P. R., 361, 381, 382, 383, 384
Ambert, A., 358
Ambron, S. R., 331
Ames, E. W., 154
Ammerman, R. T., 391
Anderson, D., 166
Anderson, D. R., 255, 402
Anderson, K. E., 350
Anderson, K. J., 253
Andersson, B., 159, 388
Andreas, D., 144
Andres, D., 388
Andrews, D. W., 280, 302, 460, 465, 469
Antunes, C. M., 397, 398
Apfel, N. H., 220, 267
Apolloni, T., 466
Apostoleris, N. H., 439
Appleton, H., 412
Aquan-Assee, J., 463, 465
Archer, J., 68, 187, 249, 290
Archer, S. C., 185
Archer, S. L., 184, 185, 186, 439
Ardrey, R., 272
Arend, R., 254
Arezzo, D., 407, 409
Aries, P., 7
Arjimand, O., 239
Arnett, J. J., 63, 358, 369
Arnold, D. H., 427
Arnold, E. H., 427
Arnold, G., 347
Aro, H., 457
Aronson, E., 272, 430
Aronson, J., 219
Arsenio, W. F., 112
Asendorph, J. B., 166, 167
Ash, T., 58, 109
Asher, S. R., 302, 430, 440, 454, 455, 458, 460, 463, 464, 466
Ashley, P. K., 348
Aslin, R. N., 110
Associated Press, 239, 265, 384, 408
Astin, A. W., 265
Aston, J., 274
Astone, N. M., 268
Astor, R. A., 281, 286
Atkin, C., 409
Atkins, E., 415

Atkinson, J. W., 201, 204, 205, 206, 224
Atwater, E., 293
Auerbach, J., 47, 55
Austin, L., 63
Avants, S. K., 235
Aviezer, O., 139
Ayers-Lopez, S., 379
Azmitia, M., 93, 377

Bachman, J., 186
Bacon, M. K., 232, 233, 358
Badzinski, D. M., 112
Bagley, C., 395
Bagwell, C. L., 465
Baier, J. L., 266
Bailey, D. B., 430
Bailey, J. M., 75, 265, 380
Bakeman, R., 112
Baker, D. P., 236, 238
Baker, L. A., 80, 81, 248
Baker, N., 182
Balaban, T., 254
Baldwin, D. A., 111
Baldwin, D. V., 382
Ball, S., 412
Balle-Jensen, L., 63
Ballif, B., 107
Bandura, A., 45, 46, 48, 49, 73, 86, 98, 178, 243, 253, 254, 256, 273, 277, 279, 280, 291, 311, 320, 344, 403
Bank, L., 295, 300, 368
Banks, J. A., 429
Barber, B. K., 373, 420, 469
Barden, R. C., 125
Bardwell, J. R., 244
Barenboim, C., 189, 191
Barker, R. G., 419
Barnard, K. E., 224
Barnett, D., 140, 393
Barnett, M. A., 303, 318
Barnett, W. S., 221
Baron, R. A., 23, 24, 25, 273, 277, 404
Barrera, M. Jr., 367
Barrett, K. C., 180, 328
Barry, H., 232, 233, 358
Bar-Tal, D., 314
Bartholomew, K., 138, 148, 150
Basil, M., 178

Basinger, K. S., 334
Baskett, L. M., 376, 377
Bassuk, E. L., 370
Bates, J. E., 115, 147, 287, 295, 296, 299, 363, 389, 458
Bathurst, K., 226, 388
Batson, C. D., 79, 309, 317
Battle, E. S., 207
Baudonniere, P., 166, 167
Bauer, P. J., 95
Baumrind, D., 86, 87, 225, 264, 364, 365, 366, 367, 426, 451, 478
Baxter, A., 110
Bayer, A. F. III, 293, 294
Bayley, N., 456
Beach, F. A., 263, 290
Beady, C., 418, 421
Beal, C. R., 253
Beaman, J., 384
Bear, G. G., 331
Beardsall, L., 111, 376
Beazley, R. P., 267
Beck, S. J., 453
Becker, J., 121
Beckwith, L., 183
Begley, N. L., 242
Beilin, H., 63
Bell, A. P., 264
Bell, K., 148
Bell, M. A., 115
Bell, R. Q., 49
Bellanti, C. J., 376
Beller, R., 317
Belmont, L., 226
Belsky, J., 88, 89, 114, 121, 140, 142, 143, 145, 148, 159, 222, 359, 363, 374, 391, 392, 394, 464
Bem, D. J., 117
Bem, S. L., 40, 252, 256, 259, 260
Benbow, C. P., 239
Bendell, D., 144
Bendig, A. W., 204
Benenson, J. F., 439
Bennett, C., 459
Bennett, S. M., 16
Benoit, D., 150
Benson, P., 81
Benson, P. L., 379
Bentler, P. M., 469
Bento, S., 150
Berenbaum, S. A., 236, 248, 249, 264
Berg, C. A., 342
Bergen, D. J., 233
Bergman, A., 165
Berkowitz, L., 25, 278, 406
Berkowitz, M., 338
Berlin, L. J., 140
Berlin, M., 142
Berman, A. L., 178, 179
Bernal, M. E., 186, 187
Berndt, T. J., 194, 445, 453, 460, 463, 464, 467
Bernieri, F., 83

Bernstein, I. S., 290
Bernzweig, J., 318
Berridge, D. M., 171
Berry, J. W., 215, 371
Berscheid, E., 148, 451
Best, D. L., 16, 232, 233, 240
Best, K. M., 364, 457
Beyth-Marom, R., 63
Bhavnagri, N. P., 20
Biaggio, A. M. B., 343
Bianchi, S. M., 239, 381
Bidell, T., 63, 64
Bierman, K. L., 376, 459, 460
Biernat, M., 241
Biernbrum, M. A., 295
Bigbee, M. A., 292
Bigler, R. S., 168, 190, 242, 262, 408
Bigner, J. J., 380
Biller, H. B., 146
Billman, J., 314
Bingham, C. R., 265, 266
Bingham, K., 294
Birch, H. G., 115
Birch, L. L., 314
Birch, S. H., 298, 426
Biringen, Z., 114, 141, 179, 328
Bish, A., 379
Bitz, B., 332
Bjorklund, B. R., 7, 160
Bjorklund, D. F., 7, 54, 64, 160
Black-Gutman, D., 190
Blakemore, J. E. O., 242, 243
Blakeslee, S., 383
Blaney, N., 430
Blasi, A., 326, 342
Blehar, M. C., 125, 136, 143
Block, J., 359, 382
Block, J. H., 177, 235, 382
Blount, R., 164
Blue, J., 391
Blumefeld, P., 211
Blyth, D. A., 176, 424, 457
Bobrow, D., 380
Bodmer-Turner, J., 394
Bogatz, C., 412
Bogatz, G. A., 412
Bogenschneider, K., 468, 469
Bohlin, G., 128
Bohman, M., 379
Boivin, M., 287, 463
Boldizar, J. P., 242, 259, 260, 280
Bolduc, D., 231
Bolger, K. E., 368, 393, 394
Booth, A., 381, 384, 386
Booth, C. L., 465
Booth, R. T., 111
Borkowski, J. G., 267, 268
Bornstein, M. H., 110
Borstelmann, L. J., 7
Bost, K. K., 148, 451
Botein, S., 90, 141, 142
Botkin, M., 423

Bouchard, T. J. Jr., 76, 83, 207, 216, 249
Boulerice, B., 286
Boulton, M., 274
Bowen-Woodward, K., 386
Bower, T. G. R., 54
Bowker, A., 458
Bowlby, J., 69, 70, 116, 118, 124, 125, 129, 130, 131, 133, 136, 139, 147, 148, 150, 155, 173, 450, 451
Bow-Thomas, C. C., 431
Bowker, A., 458
Boyatzis, C. J., 406
Boyes, M. C., 187, 339
Boykin, A. W., 207, 216, 218
Brabeck, M., 342
Bradbard, M. R., 148, 257, 451
Braddock, J. H. II, 424
Bradley, R. H., 222, 223, 224, 226
Bradley, S. J., 251
Bradshaw, D., 106, 107
Brand, E., 386, 387
Branstetter, W. H., 462
Brassard, M. R., 396–397
Braun, N., 391
Braungart, J. M., 112, 113–114
Braunwald, K., 140
Braver, S. L., 385
Bray, H., 261
Brazelton, T. B., 20, 108, 139, 357
Breland, H. M., 225
Bretherton, I., 122, 129, 139, 148, 451
Brice-Heath, S., 427
Bricker, W., 466
Brickman, P., 321
Bridges, L. J., 108
Bridges, M., 89, 362, 380, 381, 382, 383, 384, 385, 386, 387
Brion-Meisels, S., 316
Broberg, A. G., 158, 159
Brobow, D., 380
Brockington, I., 156
Brodersen, L., 132
Brody, G. H., 325, 328, 349, 350, 358, 371, 376, 438, 450
Brody, N., 207, 216, 218
Brodzinsky, D. M., 119, 379
Bromley, D. B., 171, 189
Bronfenbrenner, U., 24, 85, 86, 87, 88, 90, 99, 138, 155, 359, 361, 388, 392, 401, 477, 481
Bronstein, P., 225
Brook, J. S., 115
Brookover, W., 418, 421
Brooks, M. G., 370
Brooks-Gunn, J., 89, 150, 166, 185, 216, 220, 227, 268, 362
Brophy, J. E., 421, 423
Bross, D. C., 396
Broverman, I. K., 233
Brown, B. B., 89, 428, 429, 445, 448, 467, 468
Brown, E., 376
Brown, E. G., 449

Brown, J., 111
Brown, J. D., 165, 173, 175
Brown, J. R., 109, 111, 112, 378
Brown, K. P., 460
Brown, M., 300
Brown, M. M., 302, 460, 461
Brown, P., 301
Brownell, C. A., 167, 438, 441, 442
Brucken, L., 240
Bruggerman, E. L., 343
Bruner, J., 64
Brunschot, M. V., 462
Bryan, J. H., 311, 321, 323, 324
Bryant, D. M., 361, 418
Bryden, M. P., 236
Buchanan, C. M., 238, 384, 385, 424
Buchanan, L., 445, 463
Buchanan, N. R., 441
Buchsbaum, K., 286
Buckley, S., 448
Buckner, J. C., 370
Bugental, D. B., 391
Buhrmester, D., 194, 372, 373, 376, 377,
    398, 463
Bukowski, W. M., 287, 440, 441, 443, 444,
    449, 450, 451, 454, 455, 458, 459, 463,
    464, 465, 468
Bullock, M., 180
Bumpass, L. L., 362
Burchinal, M. R., 361, 374, 418
Burgeson, R., 176
Burhans, K. K., 212, 213, 225
Buriel, R., 369
Burkhardt, S. A., 394, 395
Burleson, B. R., 295
Burman, B., 381
Burn, S., 242, 244
Burnette, E., 187, 190
Burnham, D. K., 238
Burns, L. H., 279
Burton, L. M., 360
Burton, R. V., 183, 344, 345, 347, 360
Burts, D. C., 418
Bushwall, S. J., 295, 296
Buss, A. H., 112, 113, 273
Buss, D. M., 71
Buss, K. A., 108, 109, 114
Buss, R. R., 63
Bussey, K., 107, 243, 256, 347
Butenandt, O., 156
Butkovsky, L., 112
Butler, R., 177, 211, 212, 214, 423
Butler, S., 235
Butterfield, P., 110
Butterworth, G., 165
Buysse, V., 430
Bybee, J., 318, 342
Bynner, J., 186
Byrne, E. A., 439
Byrnes, J. P., 234

Cahan, S., 417
Cain, K. M., 212, 214

Cairns, B. D., 280, 288, 299, 445, 463
Cairns, R. B., 280, 288, 299, 419, 445, 463
Calder, B. J., 294
Caldera, Y. M., 231, 242
Caldwell, B. M., 222, 223, 224
Calkins, S. S., 115
Call, K. T., 375, 376
Callanan, M. A., 170, 235
Camara, K. A., 380
Cameron, C. A., 321, 322, 323
Camino, C., 341
Camino, L., 25, 406
Campbell, S. B., 141
Campbell, D. T., 308
Campbell, E. Q., 208
Campbell, F. A., 158, 220, 418
Campbell, S. B., 141
Campos, J. J., 106, 107, 110
Campos, R., 397, 398
Camras, L. A., 106, 107
Canter, R. J., 244
Capaldi, D., 300
Capaldi, D. M., 266, 295, 299, 386, 387
Caplan, M., 84, 290, 313, 437
Carlo, G., 303, 316, 317, 318
Carlsmith, J. M., 295, 296, 457
Carlson, E. A., 140, 148, 150
Carlson, S. M., 170
Carlson, V., 140, 391
Carlton-Ford, S., 176
Carnegie Council on Adolescent
    Development, 425
Carr, M. B., 242
Carr, T. S., 290
Carriger, M. S., 167, 442
Carson, J. L., 449
Casas, J. F., 236, 292
Casey, M. B., 234
Casey, R. J., 125, 180
Casey, W. M., 183, 347
Caspi, A., 28, 112, 114, 183, 288, 382, 457
Cassidy, J., 112, 138, 140, 148, 150, 451,
    454, 458
Cassidy, K. W., 170
Castle, J., 313
Castle, J. M., 106, 107
Cates, W. Jr., 267
Cauce, A. M., 371
Ceci, S. J., 85, 207, 216, 218, 417
Cen, G., 468
Center for Disease Control and Prevention,
    266, 267, 268, 420
Cervantes, C. A., 235
Chadwick, B. A., 361
Chaiyasit, W., 117, 297
Chalmers, J. B., 316
Chambers, D. L., 431
Chan, R. W., 380
Chan, S. Q., 369
Chandler, M., 58, 170, 187
Chandler, M. J., 302, 460
Chandler, S., 118
Chao, R. K., 217, 371, 429

Chao, W., 384, 387
Chapman, M., 141, 235, 303, 311, 312, 313,
    314, 315, 317, 318, 319, 325
Charlesworth, R., 418
Charlesworth, W. R., 7
Chase, C. I., 419
Chase-Lansdale, P. L., 266, 267, 268, 370,
    383, 384
Chassin, L., 468, 469
Chen, C., 89, 175, 216, 217, 218, 369, 372,
    428, 429, 431, 432, 433, 452
Chen, H., 468
Chen, X., 117, 218
Cherlin, A. J., 383, 384, 386
Chernick, A. B., 251
Chess, S., 112, 113, 115, 116, 142, 143,
    144
Cheyne, C. A., 462
Child, I. L., 2, 232, 233, 358
Chisholm, K., 154, 155, 157
Chmiel, S., 343
Christopher, F. S., 321
Christopherson, E. R., 235
Cibelli, C. D., 147
Cicchetti, D., 140, 391, 393
Cillessen, A. H. N., 459
Clark, E. A., 157
Clark, K. B., 427
Clark, L. V., 194, 254
Clark, M. C., 313, 314
Clark, M. S., 461
Clark, R., 90, 160
Clark, R. D. III, 72
Clark, S., 299
Clarke, A. D. B., 157
Clarke, A. M., 157
Clarke-Stewart, K. A., 146, 150, 158, 382,
    383, 418, 449
Clarkson, F. E., 233
Clary, E. G., 319, 325
Clasen, D. R., 467
Clausen, J. A., 456, 457
Clemens, L. P., 242
Clements, D. H., 413, 414, 415
Clements, W. A., 170
Clewett, A. S., 410
Cline, V. E., 403
Clingempeel, W. G., 89, 298, 366, 382, 384,
    386, 387
Cloud, J. M., 240
Clyman, R. B., 114, 179, 328
Coates, B., 48
Coatsworth, J. D., 176
Cobbs, G., 172
Cochran, S. W., 244
Cohen, D., 47, 55, 57, 235, 302
Cohen, L., 315, 320
Cohen, N., 417
Cohen, P., 115
Cohen, S., 183
Cohn, J. F., 106, 108, 141
Coie, J. D., 110, 280, 282, 298, 299, 301,
    408, 453, 454, 458, 459, 461, 478

Colby, A., 333, 337, 343
Colder, C. R., 469
Cole, A., 89, 464
Cole, M., 416
Cole, P. M., 108, 180, 284, 328, 394
Coleman, C. C., 287, 463, 464
Coleman, J. S., 208
Coley, R. L., 146, 196, 266, 267, 268, 383, 384
Coll, C. G., 208, 370, 389
Collins, P. A., 255, 402
Collins, W. A., 372, 410
Collis, B. A., 413, 415
Colyar, J. J., 387
Committee on Adolescence, 178
Compas, B. E., 150, 185
Comstock, G. A., 401, 407
Conant, C., 462
Condry, J., 237
Condry, J. C., 275
Condry, S., 237
Conger, K. J., 361, 368, 369
Conger, R. D., 218, 266, 296, 361, 364, 368, 369, 374, 381, 384, 391, 457
Connell, D. B., 90, 141, 142
Connell, J. P., 108, 225, 428
Conner, R. F., 412
Connolly, J. A., 57
Connolly, K. J., 301
Coohey, C., 391
Cook, R., 379
Cook, T. D., 294, 412
Cooke, T., 466
Cooley, C. H., 164, 174, 360
Cooper, B. A. B., 343
Cooper, C. R., 188
Cooper, H. M., 208, 423
Cooper, J., 254
Cooper, P., 141
Cooper, R. P., 110
Cooperman, G., 311; 312, 318, 319
Cooperman, J. M., 240, 241, 299
Coopersmith, S., 177
Coppotelli, H., 454
Corasantini, M. A., 389, 390
Corley, R., 115
Cornell, D. P., 260
Corns, K. M., 150, 373
Corteen, R. S., 402
Corter, C., 142, 376, 377
Corter, C. M., 128, 130
Cortes, R. M., 393
Corwin, M. J., 142
Cossette, L., 231
Costabile, A., 274
Costigan, K. A., 235
Costin, S. E., 462
Cote, J. E., 188
Couchoud, E. A., 111, 453, 458
Coulton, C. J., 392
Courrier, S., 403
Cousins, S. D., 175
Cowan, C. P., 174, 366

Cowan, G., 235
Cowan, P., 174
Cowan, P. A., 366
Cowen, E. L., 385
Cowen, J., 351
Cox, M., 381, 382
Cox, M. J., 89, 142, 145, 146, 359
Cox, R., 381, 382
Coy, K. C., 372
Craig, W. M., 287
Crain, R. M., 177
Crandall, V. C., 201, 205, 206, 207, 208, 227
Crane, P., 456
Craven, R., 174
Crenshaw, T. M., 460
Crews, F., 40
Crick, N. R., 22, 28, 235, 236, 280, 281, 292, 301, 302, 440, 454
Crnic, K., 88, 114, 148, 208, 359
Crockenberg, S., 159, 180, 349, 359, 367, 388
Crockett, L. J., 265, 266
Croft, R. G., 403
Cromer, C. C., 438
Cronbach, L. J., 421
Crook, C., 414
Crosby, L., 266, 280, 299, 302, 460, 465, 469
Cross, C. E., 9
Cross, W. E., 168
Crouter, A. C., 242, 388
Crowe, P. A., 176
Crowell, J. A., 141
Crowley, C. G., 301
Cruzcosa, M., 391
Crystal, D. S., 175, 433
Culp, R. E., 396
Culver, C., 107, 108
Cumberland, A., 109, 110
Cummings, E. M., 141, 285, 288, 296, 368, 369, 376, 381
Cunningham, J. G., 111
Curran, P. J., 469

Dabbs, J. M. Jr., 290
Daglish, L., 242
Damon, W., 168, 171, 191, 194, 241, 343
D'Andrade, R., 224
Daniels, D., 80, 418, 448
Dann, S., 4, 439, 440
Darling, C. A., 266
Darling, N., 218, 365, 366, 367
Darling, N. E., 414, 468
Darlington, R. B., 221
Daro, D., 396
Darwin, C. A., 7, 8, 37, 68
Das Eiden, R., 150, 373
Dasen, P. R., 215
Da Silva, M. S., 317
Daubman, K., 236
D'Augelli, A. R., 264
David, H. P., 141, 364
Davidson, E. S., 405

Davidson, J., 251, 266
Davidson, W., 212
Davies, P. T., 296, 368, 369, 376, 381
Davis, B., 77
Davis, M., 105
Davis, S. W., 240
Davis, T. L., 109, 112
Davison, M. L., 343
Dawud, S., 393
DeAngelis, T., 81, 133, 153, 155, 157
Deater-Deckard, K., 289, 295, 350, 367, 371, 479
DeBaryshe, B. D., 294, 295, 298, 299, 468
De Benedictis, T., 409
DeBerry, K. M., 187, 379
Debus, R., 174
Dedrick, C. F., 142
DeFries, J. C., 75, 81, 82, 85, 113–114, 114
De Gaston, J. P., 266
Degirmencioglu, S. M., 445
DeKlyen, M., 295
Dekovic, M., 451
De Lorimier, S., 443
Del Rosario, M. L., 294
Delucchi, K., 409
Demarest, J., 254
DeMause, L., 7
DeMeis, D. K., 159
Demo, D. H., 177, 387
DeMudler, E. K., 376
Denham, S. A., 111, 453, 458
Derbyshire, A., 240
Derenowski, E., 267
DeRosier, E., 440, 454, 458
Desai, K. A., 200
DeSchonen, S., 166
Despert, J. L., 7
De Vries, B., 342
DeWolf, M., 418
De Wolff, M. S., 140, 145, 146
Dewsbury, D. A., 68
Diamond, L. M., 265
Diamond, M., 250
Dichtellmiller, M., 142
Didow, S. M., 442
Diener, E., 235
DiLalla, L. F., 113, 115
Dillon, P. A., 385
DiPietro, J. A., 235
Dishion, T. J., 77, 280, 294, 296, 297, 299, 302, 366, 449, 460, 461, 465, 468, 469
Dittman, R. W., 249, 264
Dittus, P., 268
Dix, T. H., 350
Dixon, S., 20, 108, 139
Dodge, K. A., 28, 280, 281, 282, 286, 287, 294, 295, 296, 298, 299, 301, 302, 350, 363, 371, 389, 408, 454, 457, 458, 459, 460, 461, 478, 479
Doehring, P., 443
Doherty, W. J., 383
Dollard, J., 277
Dong, Q., 378, 452

Donnell, F., 139
Donnerstein, E., 408, 409
Doob, L. W., 277
Doris, J., 366, 393
Dornbusch, S. M., 89, 177, 218, 225, 295,
    296, 365, 366, 367, 372, 374, 384, 385,
    414, 420, 428, 429, 457, 468
Dossey, J. A., 431
Dow-Ehrensberger, M., 416
Downey, G., 283, 287
Downing, L. L., 415
Downs, A. C., 456
Doyle, A., 57
Doyle, A. B., 190, 443
Drabman, R. S., 407
Dreyer, P. H., 265, 266
Droege, K., 462
Droege, K. L., 189, 210
Drotar, D., 156
Druyan, S., 94
Dubas, J. S., 247, 457
Dubow, E., 224
Duckett, E., 376, 387
Duke, P. M., 457
Dumas-Hines, F., 214
Duncan, G. J., 216, 227, 362
Dunn, J., 80, 109, 111, 112, 170, 373, 375,
    376, 378
Dunphy, D. C., 445, 448
Durazo, O., 267
Durland, M. A., 418
Dusek, J. B., 428
Dweck, C. S., 189, 207, 210, 211, 212, 213,
    214, 225, 423
Dziuba-Leatherman, J., 390, 392

Eagly, A. H., 236
Eakins, D. J., 410
East, P. L., 265, 266, 376
Eastenson, A., 464
Easterbrooks, M. A., 146, 147, 167, 466
Eastman, K. L., 117, 297
Eaton, W. O., 235, 423
Ebbesen, E. B., 181
Eccles, J. S., 211, 227, 238, 239, 420, 423,
    424, 425, 468, 469
Eckenrode, J., 366, 393
Eckerman, C. O., 421, 442
Edelstein, W., 288
Eder, R. A., 168, 169, 189
Edwards, C. P., 242, 249, 314, 339, 357, 437
Edwards, J. N., 386
Edwards, J. R., 240
Edwards, L., 337, 343
Egan, S. K., 286, 287
Egeland, B., 151, 392, 393, 394
Egeland, B. J., 390
Egeland, B. R., 140
Eggebeen, D. J., 362
Ehrhardt, A., 246, 247, 248, 249, 251
Eicher, S. A., 467
Eichler, L. S., 117, 119
Eidelman, A., 47, 55

Eisen, M., 172
Eisenberg, N., 109, 111, 235, 243, 267, 268,
    285, 303, 311, 312, 313, 314, 315, 316,
    317, 318, 321, 325, 455
Eisenberg-Berg, N., 316, 317
Eisenbud, L., 254, 256
Elder, G. H. Jr., 9, 218, 361, 368, 369, 374,
    457
Elicker, J., 89, 148
Elkind, D., 244, 418
Elliot, R., 301
Elliott, A. N., 395
Elliott, E. S., 211, 214, 423
Ellis, S., 438
Ellsworth, C. P., 121
Elmen, J. D., 225
Emde, R. N., 79, 105, 110, 111, 114, 179,
    309, 312, 328
Emerson, P. E., 121, 122, 123, 124, 127, 441
Emery, R. E., 381, 385, 387, 390, 391, 392,
    395, 396, 397
Emmerich, W., 285
Emmons, B. A., 182
Endriga, M. C., 125
Endsley, R. C., 257, 403
English, D., 347
Englund, M., 148, 459
Enna, B., 212
Enns, L. R., 235
Ensminger, M. E., 360
Entwisle, D. R., 216, 217, 227, 238
Epstein, Y., 3
Erdley, C. A., 214
Erel, O., 376, 381
Erickson, M. F., 137, 390
Erikson, E. H., 40, 41, 98, 122, 136, 147,
    148, 168, 176, 180, 183, 185, 363
Eron, L. D., 288, 404
Essex, M. J., 90, 160
Estes, D., 150
Etaugh, C., 244, 263
Ethridge, T., 242
Ettema, J. S., 408
Ewigman, B., 389
Ey, S., 150, 185
Eyer, D. E., 119
Eysenck, H. J., 289

Fabes, R. A., 109, 111, 235, 267, 268, 285,
    303, 313, 314, 315, 317, 318, 321, 455
Faden, R. R., 267
Fagot, B. I., 147, 151, 163, 240, 242, 253,
    266, 290, 299, 363
Fairchild, H., 408, 409
Falbo, T., 373, 378
Fantauzzo, C. A., 106, 107
Farber, S. L., 83
Farhl, P., 412
Farrington, D. P., 288, 294
Farris, A. M., 359
Farver, J. M., 462
Fauber, R., 381
Faust, M. S., 457

Fegley, S., 319, 374
Feiler, R., 418
Fein, G. G., 57, 443
Feingold, A., 235
Feinman, J., 176, 177, 211, 424
Feinman, S., 110, 128
Feldlaufer, H., 425
Feldman, R., 180
Feldman, R. S., 393
Feldman, S. S., 141, 187, 372
Fennema, E., 234, 235
Ferguson, D. L., 187
Ferguson, L. L., 288
Fernald, A., 110, 111
Fernandez, E., 383
Feshbach, N. D., 408, 409
Feshbach, S., 274, 277, 278, 290, 291, 293,
    403
Ficher, I., 380
Field, D. E., 402
Field, P. A., 118
Field, T., 141
Field, T. M., 47, 55, 57, 142, 144, 462
Figueredo, A. J., 381, 391, 393
Finch, M. D., 375
Fincham, F. D., 212, 296, 381, 385
Findley, M. J., 208
Fine, M. A., 366, 386, 387
Finkelhor, D., 390, 392, 394, 395
Finkelstein, N. W., 155, 394
Finn, J. D., 419
Finnie, V., 449
Finn Stevenson, M. F., 161, 389, 395, 396,
    408, 418, 433
Fiori-Cowley, A., 141
Fischer, K. W., 63, 64
Fischoff, B., 63
Fisher, L., 154
Fisher, P. A., 125
Fisher, W. F., 321
Fitch, M., 402, 410
Fitch, S. A., 185
Fivush, R., 235
Flaks, D. K., 380
Flanagan, C., 238, 424
Flannery, D., 63
Flavell, J. H., 58, 59, 63, 64, 169, 170
Fleege, P. O., 418
Fleming, J. S., 220, 224
Fletcher, A. C., 414, 468
Fletcher-Flinn, C. M., 414
Fling, S., 415
Flood, P., 418, 421
Flor, D., 358
Flor, D. L., 371
Florsheim, P., 146
Fogel, A., 166
Folkers, E., 366
Follansbee, D., 177
Follmer, A., 361
Fonagy, P., 150
Fonzi, A., 464
Ford, C. S., 263

Ford, D. Y., 218, 429
Ford, L. H. Jr., 168
Ford, M. E., 125, 254
Fordham, S., 218
Forehand, R., 381, 387, 453
Forman, D. R., 328
Forman, E. R., 316
Forrest, J. D., 265, 266, 269
Foster, E. M., 268
Foster, G. E., 418
Foster, T., 462
Fowlkes, J., 240
Fox, N. A., 115, 146
Frady, F. L., 290
Frankel, K. A., 147, 383
Frankenberg, W. K., 223
Frankie, G., 253
Frazier, J. A., 417
Freedman, D. G., 448
Freedman, J. L., 407
Freeman, N. H., 171
Freemer-Bombik, E., 148
Freitas, A. L., 283, 287
French, D. C., 438, 459
Frenkel, O. J., 143, 144
Freud, A., 4, 439, 440
Freud, S., 8, 19, 37, 38, 40, 63, 76, 98, 122,
    136, 147, 178, 252, 327
Frey, K. S., 59, 177, 210, 214, 244, 254, 255,
    466
Friedman, R. J., 284
Friedrich, L. K., 25, 405, 407, 410
Friedrich-Cofer, L. K., 410
Friedrick, M., 379
Friend, M., 112
Fritz, J., 369
Frohlock, C. B., 317
Frost, J. J., 269
Frost, P., 462
Frueh, T., 254
Fu, G., 321, 322, 323
Fu, V. R., 225
Fuchs, D., 235
Fuhrman, T., 372, 373
Fuhrmann, G., 156
Fukumoto, A., 180
Fuligni, A. J., 175, 216, 218, 371, 372, 420,
    429, 432, 433, 468, 469
Fulker, D. W., 113–114, 289, 295, 367
Fuller, B., 159
Fuller, D., 334
Fultz, J., 321
Furman, W., 89, 194, 372, 373, 376, 377,
    398, 459, 460, 467
Furstenberg, F. F., 384, 386
Furstenberg, F. F. Jr., 268, 382, 383
Fyans, L. J . Jr., 200

Gable, S., 359
Gagnon, J. H., 265
Gahler, M., 383
Galambos, N. L., 242, 389
Galen, B. R., 288, 292

Galligan, R. F., 130
Gallimore, R., 377, 422
Gallup, G. G. Jr., 167
Galper, A., 217, 428
Gamble, W. C., 377
Gandelman, R., 248
Ganza, B., 265
Gao, Y., 130, 139
Garbarino, J., 390, 392, 396, 397
Garber, J., 110, 280, 281
Garcia, E. E., 427, 429
Garcia, H. V., 208, 370
Gardner, L. J., 156
Garduque, L., 140, 222
Gariepy, J., 280, 288, 299
Garland, A., 178
Garmezy, N., 176
Garner, P. W., 109, 111, 377
Garnets, L., 264
Gauthier, R., 242
Gautier, T., 250
Gauze, C., 455, 463, 465
Gavin, L. A., 89, 467
Ge, X., 218, 364, 457
Geary, D. C., 431
Geen, R. G., 278, 280, 281, 290, 300, 404,
    407, 408
Gehring, T. M., 372
Gelfand, D. M., 141, 307, 315
Gelles, R. J., 390, 391, 392, 393, 396
Gelman, S. A., 188, 189, 241, 242
Gendler, T., 418
George, C., 138, 393
George, T. P., 464
Gervai, J., 243, 254, 260, 261
Gesell, A., 68
Gest, J. D., 176
Gest, S. D., 280, 299
Gewirtz, J. L., 45, 125
Gibbs, J. C., 295, 302, 325, 334, 337, 338,
    339, 340, 349
Gielinski, K. L., 148, 451
Gil, D. G., 391
Gilbert, N., 392
Giles, H., 240
Gill, N. J., 267
Gilligan, C., 341, 342
Gilman, E., 158, 388
Gilstrap, B., 145, 359
Ginsburg, G. S., 225
Girard, C., 178
Gjerde, P. F., 382
Glasgow, K. L., 225, 366, 420
Gleason, K. E., 150
Glogowski, B. K., 235
Gnepp, J., 111, 196
Goetz, L., 430
Gold, D., 388
Goldberg, E., 387
Goldberg, M., 314
Goldberg, M. E., 408
Goldberg, P., 238
Goldberg, S., 119, 142, 143, 144, 388

Goldberg, W. A., 146, 388
Goldfarb, W., 153, 154
Goldsmith, D., 278, 357
Goldsmith, H. H., 108, 109, 112, 113, 114,
    143
Goldstein, A. P., 302, 334
Goldstein, R., 235
Goldstein, S., 144
Goldwyn, R., 138, 150
Golombok, S., 264, 379, 380
Golter, B. S., 449, 458
Golub, H. L., 142
Goncu, A., 93
Gondoli, D. M., 368
Gonzales, N., 371
Good, T. L., 420, 421
Goodenough, F. L., 278, 285
Goodnow, J. J., 315, 320, 350
Goossens, F. A., 143
Gopnik, A., 169
Gordon, T. P., 290
Gordon, V. V., 268
Gorer, G., 276, 291
Gorman-Smith, D., 146
Gorn, G. J., 408
Gottesman, I. I., 81, 249
Gottfried, A. E., 220, 224, 226, 388
Gottfried, A. W., 220, 224, 226, 388
Gottlieb, D., 429
Gottlieb, G., 73, 85
Gottman, J. M., 461
Gould, S. J., 72
Goy, R. W., 290
Graber, J. A., 457
Gracely, E., 242
Graesser, A. C., 326
Graham, S., 283, 287, 294, 460
Gralinski, H., 167–168
Grant, K. E., 150, 185
Gravatt, B., 414
Graves, S. B., 408
Gray, C., 224
Gray, W. M., 63
Graziano, W. G., 438, 450
Greco, D., 397, 398
Greco, M., 397, 398
Green, F. P., 314, 315
Green, K. D., 453
Green, M., 10, 264
Green, R., 264
Greenbaum, C., 393
Greenbaum, G. W., 180
Greenberg, M. T., 118, 295
Greenberg, R., 47, 55, 57
Greenberger, E., 89, 369, 372, 374, 388, 452
Greene, R., 431, 433
Greenwald, P., 462
Grenlich, F., 177, 210, 214
Grieser, D. L., 110
Griffith, E. M., 416
Grigoryev, P., 108
Grinder, R. E., 343
Grolnick, W. J., 108

Grolnick, W. S., 108, 224, 367
Groom, J. M., 430
Gross, A. L., 107
Gross, R. T., 295, 296, 457
Grossman, F. K., 117, 119
Grossmann, K., 139, 148
Grossmann, K. E., 139
Grotevant, H. D., 185, 188, 254, 379
Grotpeter, J. K., 235, 236, 292
Grunebaum, H. U., 90, 141, 142
Grusec, J. E., 49, 308, 315, 319, 320, 321, 323, 348, 350, 390
Grych, J. H., 385
Guerin, D. W., 226
Guerra, N. G., 280, 281, 282, 302, 407, 409
Gulko, J., 243, 254, 257
Gullota, T. P., 265
Gump, P. V., 419
Gunnar, M. R., 111, 132, 137, 144
Guo, M., 452
Guralnick, M. J., 430
Gurtner, J., 414
Gurucharri, C., 194
Guthertz, M., 462
Guthrie, I. K., 109, 318, 455
Guttentag, M., 261

Haaland, W., 130, 139
Haan, N., 338, 343
Hagan, R., 242
Hagan, R. I., 253
Hagborg, W. J., 402
Hagekull, B., 128
Hains, S. M. J., 121
Hala, S., 58, 170
Hall, G. S., 8, 9
Hall, J. A., 290
Hall, S. K., 260
Halliday-Scher, K., 445
Halpern, D. F., 207, 216, 218, 227, 234, 235, 236, 250, 252, 476
Halsley, N., 397, 398
Halverson, C. F. Jr., 237, 256, 257
Ham, M., 177
Hamilton, C. E., 450
Hammen, C., 173
Hammer, L. D., 457
Hammer, M., 393
Hammersmith, S. K., 264
Hammond, M. A., 224
Hand, M., 316, 317
Hanisee, J., 157
Hans, S. L., 294
Hansen, D. J., 393
Harden, P. W., 286
Hardy, J. B., 268
Har-Even, D., 119, 379
Harkness, S., 339
Harlow, H. F., 123, 136, 152, 153, 439, 440
Harlow, M. K., 152
Harmon, R. J., 147, 167
Harold, G. T., 296, 381
Harold, R. D., 211, 239, 424, 425

Harper, L. V., 442, 445
Harrington, A. F., 254, 408
Harris, A., 187
Harris, J. R., 468
Harris, J. J. III, 218, 429
Harris, M. B., 238
Harris, M. J., 83, 423
Harris, M. L., 132
Harris, N. B., 289
Harris, P. L., 107, 170
Harrison, A. O., 369
Harrison, L. F., 402
Harrist, A. W., 458
Hart, C. H., 288, 292, 295, 418, 449, 451, 458
Hart, D., 168, 171, 191, 288, 319, 343
Hart, K. J., 343
Hart, S. N., 396–397
Harter, S., 107, 166, 171, 172, 173, 174, 176, 184, 202, 207, 260
Hartmann, D. P., 315, 464
Hartmark, C., 115
Hartshorne, H., 344
Hartung, B., 9
Hartup, W. W., 48, 194, 285, 286, 301, 436, 437, 438, 440, 442, 443, 444, 459, 461, 462, 464
Harvey, E., 387
Harvey, O. J., 444, 446
Harwood, R. L., 369
Haselager, G. J. T., 462
Hashima, P. Y., 361
Haskett, M. E., 18, 19, 393
Hastings, P. D., 350, 468
Hastorf, A. H., 295, 296
Hattie, J., 173
Hausen-Corn, P., 200
Hauser, S. I., 177
Haviland, J. M., 108, 110
Hawkins, J. A., 463, 467
Hay, D. F., 84, 290, 313, 437
Haydel, F., 457
Hayes, L. A., 121
Haynes, O. M., 106, 107
Hayward, C., 382, 383, 457
Hazan, C., 138, 148
Healy, B., 144, 462
Hearold, S., 408, 410
Heath, L., 294
Heatherington, L., 236
Heaton, T. B., 361
Hebb, D. O., 85
Heckhausen, J., 207
Hedges, L. V., 236
Heeren, T., 178
Heflin, A. H., 451
Heider, F., 94
Heinicke, C. M., 133
Helmreich, R. L., 259
Helwig, C. C., 331
Hembree, E. A., 106
Henderson, V. K., 89, 142, 145, 146, 159, 359
Hendrick, C., 3, 13

Hendrix, K., 407, 409
Henker, B., 235
Hennigan, K. M., 294
Henry, B., 114, 183, 288, 382
Herbsman, C. R., 110
Herdt, G. H., 251, 266
Hernandez, D. J.
Herrera, C., 111, 378
Herrling, S., 268
Hershberger, S. L., 264
Hertsgaard, L., 132, 137
Hertzberger, S. D., 290
Hess, R. D., 218
Hesser, J., 377
Hetherington, E. M., 31, 80, 81, 253, 298, 362, 366, 380, 381, 382, 383, 384, 385, 386, 387
Heubner, R. R., 106
Heyman, G. D., 188, 189, 212
Hickson, F., 190
Higgins, E. T., 196, 242
Higley, J. D., 439
Hill, C. A., 266
Hill, J. P., 242, 372
Hill, K. T., 423
Hill, S. D., 167
Hills, P. T., 418
Hilton, S. C., 235
Himura, N., 284
Hinde, R. A., 69, 112, 113
Hines, M., 243, 248
Hinshaw, S. P., 451
Hiraga, Y., 371
Hirsch-Pasek, K., 418
Hirsh, R. M., 439
Hite, T., 243
Hobbes, T., 11, 15, 37
Hobson, C. J., 208
Hock, E., 159
Hodges, E. V. E., 287, 458, 463
Hodges, J., 157
Hodgson, D. M., 235
Hofferth, S., 157
Hoffman, L. W., 81, 243, 261, 350, 387, 388, 459
Hoffman, M. L., 72, 309, 312, 317, 326, 345, 346, 347, 348, 349, 478
Hoffman, S. D., 268
Hoffner, C., 112
Hofmann, V., 150, 222, 288
Hokoda, A., 212
Holden, C., 154
Holden, G. W., 466
Hole, S. G., 463
Holgren, R., 109
Hollander, M., 170
Holloway, S. D., 159
Holmbeck, G., 376
Holmbeck, G. N., 372, 373
Holt, R., 453, 458
Hood, W. R., 444, 446
Hooper, R., 141
Hopkins, T. L., 235

Hopkins, W. D., 439
Hops, H., 77
Horn, J., 79, 309
Horney, K., 43
Hornik, R., 111
Horowitz, F. D., 43, 49
Horowitz, L. M., 138, 148, 150
Horton, R. W., 407
Hotaling, G. T., 394
Housman, D., 178
Houts, A. C., 326
Howard-Pitney, B., 178
Howe, G. W., 80
Howe, N., 374, 378
Howes, C., 28, 33, 158, 159, 160, 292, 443, 449, 450, 453, 462
Howes, P., 90, 142
Hoyle, S. G., 194, 463
Hoza, B., 455
Hrncir, E., 140, 222
Hsu, C., 175, 217, 428, 431, 433
Hudley, C., 283, 294, 460
Hudson, L. M., 63, 316
Huesmann, L. R., 288, 404, 408
Huffman, L., 379
Hughes, C., 170
Hughes, R. Jr., 318
Huie, K. S., 442, 445
Hummel, R. C., 340
Humphrey, H., 379
Humphrey, M., 379
Humphreys, A. P., 235
Hunder, T., 274
Hunt, P., 430
Hunter, A. G., 360
Hunter, J. E., 183
Hunter, R. F., 183
Huntsinger, C. S., 371, 429
Hussong, A. M., 469
Huston, A. C., 231, 235, 242, 243, 249, 401, 402, 408, 409, 410, 412
Huston, T. L., 185
Huston-Stein, A., 410
Hutt, C., 247, 291
Hwang, C. P., 145, 158, 159
Hyde, J. S., 90, 160, 234, 235, 236, 289, 342
Hymel, S., 287, 453, 454, 458, 466
Hyson, M. C., 418

Iannotti, R. J., 285, 288, 311, 312, 316, 318, 319
Imperato-McGinley, J., 250
Inhelder, B., 57, 60
Insabella, G. M., 362, 380, 381, 382, 383, 384, 385, 386, 387
Intons-Peterson, M. J., 230, 263
Irwin, D. M., 331
Isabella, R., 141
Isabella, R. A., 121, 140
Isard, C., 370
Isberg, R. S., 177
Ivey, P. K., 155
Izard, C. E., 105, 106, 107, 110

Jaccard, J., 268
Jacklin, C. N., 227, 234, 236, 237, 243, 248, 252, 289
Jackson, B. L., 187
Jackson, E. W., 117, 297
Jackson, J. F., 87
Jacobs, J. E., 227, 239
Jacobs, L. C., 419
Jacobsen, J. L., 147
Jacobsen, R. B., 380
Jacobsen, T., 150, 222
Jacobson, A. M., 177
Jacobson, L., 422
Jacobs-Quadrel, M., 63
Jacobvitz, D., 392, 393, 394
Jadack, R. A., 342
Jaenicke, C., 173
Jagers, R. J., 294
Jain, D., 145
Jaio, S., 378
Jamison, W., 248
Janoff-Bulman, R., 383
Janssens, J. M. A. M., 451
Jardine, R., 79
Jenkins, R., 208, 370
Jennings, D., 457
Jensen, A. G., 125
Jensen, L., 266
Ji, G., 378
Jing, Q., 378
Jobes, D. A., 178, 179
Jodl, L. M., 362, 387
John, R. S., 376
Johnson, C., 381
Johnson, D. L., 216, 217, 224
Johnson, D. W., 93
Johnson, M., 178
Johnson, M. H., 252
Johnson, N., 401
Johnson, R. T., 93
Johnson, S., 364
Johnson, S. M., 376, 377
Johnson, T. R. B., 235
Johnson, W., 105
Johnston, J., 408
Johnston, J. R., 384, 385
Jones, D. C., 109, 110, 111, 377, 462
Jones, D. P., 236
Jones, E., 202, 286
Jones, M., 97
Jones, M. C., 456
Jones, N. A., 115
Jones, R. A., 3
Jones, S., 318, 455
Jones, S. S., 55
Jonsson, J. O., 383
Jose, P. E., 371, 429
Jose, P. M., 331
Joseph, G., 380
Joshi, P., 145
Jouriles, E. N., 359
Juffer, F., 154
Jung, P. C., 110

Jussim, L., 239, 423
Juvonen, Jr., 287

Kaczala, C. M., 227, 238
Kagan, J., 13, 28, 113, 114, 115, 127, 129, 130, 142, 158
Kagan, S., 215, 429
Kahn, J., 381
Kahn, P. H. Jr., 308
Kaitz, M., 47, 55
Kandel, D., 469
Kanfer, F. H., 462
Kanungo, R. N., 408
Kaplan, N., 138
Kaplan, P. S., 110
Kappes, M. E., 249, 264
Kappes, M. H., 249, 264
Karbon, M., 109, 318
Kasen, S., 115
Kass, N. E., 267
Kastelic, D., 260
Katcher, A., 252
Katkovsky, W., 201
Katz, P. A., 242, 244, 261, 408, 409
Katz, S., 265
Kaufman. A. S., 391
Kaufman, F. R., 248
Kavanaugh, K., 151, 363
Kazdin, A. E., 300, 461
Kean, A. W. G., 7
Keane, S. P., 458, 460
Keasey, C. B., 331, 338
Keating, D., 194
Kee, D. W., 414
Keefe, K., 464
Keefe, N., 389
Keefer, C. H., 20, 108, 139
Keenan, K., 183
Keenan, T., 58, 109
Keith, B., 383
Keith, J., 9
Keljo, K., 340
Kellaghan, T., 225
Kellam, S. G., 360
Keller, A., 168
Keller, H., 106, 125
Keller, M., 288
Keller, M. L., 342
Kelley, H. H., 95
Kelley, M. L., 368, 371
Kellum, S. G., 449
Kelly, J. B., 382
Kempe, C. H., 396
Kempe, R. S., 396
Kendall-Tackett, K. A., 394, 395
Kendrick, C., 373
Kennell, J. H., 117, 118, 119
Kenyon, B., 240
Kerns, K. A., 89, 236, 464
Kerr, M., 115, 117, 468
Kerugh, D., 268
Kerwin, C., 187
Kessen, W., 155

Kestenbaum, R., 144
Kett, J. F., 9
Kiernan, K. E., 383, 384
Kiesewetter, J., 406
Kiess, W., 156
Killen, J. D., 457
Kilpatrick, A., 395
Kim, J. M., 326
Kimmel, D., 264
Kimmerly, N. L., 146
Kimura, D., 249
Kimura, S., 175, 433
King, R. A., 303, 313, 314, 317, 318, 325
Kinney, D., 445, 467
Kipnis, D. M., 410
Kirchner, J., 379
Kirsh, S. J., 150, 451
Kisker, E., 160
Kistner, J. A., 18, 19, 393, 424, 425, 426, 459
Kitamura, S., 175, 433
Kitayama, S., 175
Kitzinger, C., 264
Kivlahan, C., 389
Klackbengerg-Larsson, I., 115
Klaus, M. H., 117, 118, 119
Klayman, J., 111
Klebanov, P. K., 216, 220, 227, 362
Klein, D. M., 360
Klein, M. H., 90, 160
Klein, R. E., 124
Klein, R. P., 222, 322
Klepec, L., 89, 464
Klimes-Dougan, B., 393
Kline, M., 384, 385
Klinnert, M. D., 110, 114
Knight, G. P., 186, 187, 316
Ko, H., 175, 433
Kobak, R. R., 451
Kochanska, G., 109, 143, 144, 180, 181, 328, 343, 345, 349, 351, 366, 367, 449, 480
Kochenderfer, B. J., 286, 287, 463, 464
Kochenderfer Ladd, B., 287
Koenig, A. L., 343, 345, 349, 351
Koeppl, G. K., 301
Kogos, J., 370
Kohlberg, L., 63, 255, 311, 333, 334, 335, 336, 337, 338, 339, 340, 341, 342, 343, 344, 353, 354
Kohn, M. L., 369
Koller, S. H., 317
Kondo-Ikemura, K., 130, 138, 139
Kopecky, M., 156
Koplas, A. L., 464
Kopp, C. B., 108, 167–168, 178, 179, 181
Korbin, J. E., 392
Korn, S., 115
Korn, W. S., 265
Kortenhaus, C. M., 254
Koss, M. P., 381, 391, 393
Kostelny, K., 392
Kotelchuck, M., 124
Kotsaftis, A., 143
Kovacs, D. M., 243, 459

Kowal, A., 376
Kraemer, H. C., 457
Krakow, J. B., 181
Kramer, L., 376
Kramer, R., 112
Krebs, D. L., 342, 343
Krehbiel, G., 461
Kreutzer, T., 151
Krevans, J., 325, 349
Kreye, M., 129
Krile, D., 455
Krispin, O., 393
Kroger, J., 184, 185, 188
Kroonenberg, P. M., 139, 143, 144
Kruger, A. C., 338, 466
Krupa, M. H., 248
Kucera, E., 373
Kuchuk, A., 110
Kuczynski, L., 19, 47, 141, 345, 348, 350, 367
Kuebli, J., 235
Kuhl, P. K., 110
Kuhn, C., 144
Kuhn, D., 64, 240, 338
Kulik, C. C., 420
Kulik, J. A., 420
Kunkel, D., 409
Kuo, Z. Y., 277
Kuperminc, G., 148, 268
Kupersmidt, J. B., 217, 218, 368, 393, 394, 458, 459
Kurdek, L. A., 366, 386, 387, 455
Kusel, S. J., 286
Kyriakidou, C., 171

La Barbera, J. D., 110
Ladd, G. W., 286, 287, 295, 298, 426, 449, 454, 458, 460, 463, 464
LaFromboise, T. D., 178
La Freniere, P., 242
Lagerspitz, K., 404
Laird, M., 366, 393
Laird, R. D., 389
Lamb, C., 108
Lamb, M. E., 122, 145, 150, 155, 158, 159, 382, 393, 466
Lambert, W. W., 115, 117
Lamberty, G., 208, 370
Lamborn, S. D., 177, 218, 225, 365, 366, 367, 372, 468
Lamon, S. J., 234, 235
Landau, K. R., 167
Landry, S. H., 449
Lang, S., 144
Langer, J., 338
Langlois, J. H., 125, 456
Lansford, J. E., 439
Laosa, L. M., 368, 371, 479
Lapsley, D. K., 63, 331
Larsen, R. J., 235
Larson, M. C., 132
Larson, R., 176, 177, 376, 445
Larson, S. L., 371, 429

LaRue, A. A., 242, 243
Lau, A., 331
Laumann, E. O., 265
Laumann-Billings, L., 390, 391, 392, 395, 396, 397
Laursen, B., 372, 464
Lauterbach, M. D., 235
Lave, C., 416
Lawrence, H., 396
Lawson, K. R., 114
Leaper, C., 242, 253
Lears, M., 254
Lebolt, A., 283, 287
LeCapitaine, J. E., 343
Lee, K., 321, 322, 323
Lee, S., 89, 431, 432, 433
Lee, S. Y., 216, 217, 428, 431, 432
Lefever, G. B., 143
Lefkowitz, M. M., 288, 404
Legerstee, M., 166
Leggett, E. L., 210, 211
Lehoux, P. M., 240, 241, 299
Leiderman, H., 295, 296
Leinbach, M. D., 240, 242, 253, 290
Lelwica, M., 110
LeMare, L. J., 196
Lemery, K. S., 114
Lenhart, L., 302, 460
Lennon, R., 311, 312, 316, 317
Leon, M., 332
Lepper, M. R., 414, 415, 466
Lerner, R. M., 30, 71, 99
Lester, B. M., 124, 142
Lester, J., 452
Letts, D., 396
Leung, M., 445, 463
LeVay, S., 264
Leve, C. S., 266, 299
Leve, L. D., 253
Levin, H., 294
Levin, I., 94
Levin, M. L., 268
Levine, C., 188
Levine, D., 263
LeVine, R. A., 20, 108, 139, 357
LeVine, S., 20, 108, 139
Levinson, D., 89
Levitt, M. J., 313, 314
Levy, G. D., 241, 242
Levy-Shiff, R., 119, 359, 379
Lewin, K., 426
Lewin, L. M., 77
Lewis, C., 171
Lewis, I., 394
Lewis, M., 107, 109, 127, 132, 165, 166, 277, 328, 437
Lewis, M. M., 89, 142, 145, 359
Leyens, J., 406
Leyens, J. P., 25, 406
Li, D., 218
Liang, X., 159
Liben, L. S., 168, 190, 242, 257, 262, 408
Lichter, D. T., 362

Lieberman, M., 337
Liebert, R. M., 22, 23, 24, 25, 254, 312, 401, 402, 403, 404, 405, 408, 409, 410, 411
Liederman, P. H., 20, 108, 139
Liker, J. K., 9
Lin, C. C., 225
Lin, I., 420
Lin, L., 378
Lindquist, M. M., 431
Lingenfelter, M., 254, 408
Linn, M. C., 234, 409
Lippincott, E. C., 407
Lippitt, R., 426
Lipton, R. C., 153, 154
Liss, M. B., 244
Litamura, S., 217, 428, 431
Litman, C., 159, 180, 349, 359, 367, 388
Litt, I. F., 457
Littenberg, R., 130
Little, J. K., 256
Little, V., 396
Littman, R. A., 466
Liu, F., 431
Livesley, W. J., 171, 189
Livson, N., 457
Lobel, T. E., 243, 256
Lochman, J. E., 302, 460
Locke, J., 2, 11, 15
Loeber, R., 286, 287, 288, 290, 299
Loehlin, J. C., 78, 79, 81, 207, 216, 218, 248
Lohr, M. J., 445
London, P., 324
Longeway, K. P., 132
Loomis, C. C., 214
Loomis, L. S., 381, 384
Lorber, J., 263
Lorch, E. P., 402, 403
Lord, S., 424
Lord, S. E., 425
Lorenz, F. O., 218, 361, 368, 369, 381
Lorenz, K., 68, 69, 125, 272, 275, 276
Lorey, F., 393
Losoya, S., 109
Low, H., 290
Lozoff, B., 156
Lucas, T., 441
Lucker, G. W., 217, 428, 431
Ludemann, P. M., 110
Luecke-Aleksa, D., 255
Lummis, M., 227, 228
Lung, C. T., 396
Luster, T., 89, 224, 366, 428
Lustig, J. L., 385
Lutkenhaus, P., 180
Lykken, D. T., 83
Lynam, D., 457
Lynch, M. E., 242
Lyons-Ruth, K., 90, 141, 142, 147
Lytton, H., 115, 232, 253, 295, 350, 367

Maccoby, E. E., 227, 231, 234, 235, 236, 237, 241, 243, 252, 261, 289, 291, 294, 310, 363, 364, 366, 368, 369, 384, 385

MacDermid, S. M., 388
MacDonald, K., 364
MacFarlane, A., 231
Mac Iver, D., 210, 214, 238, 424
Mack, W., 81
MacKinnon-Lewis, C., 364, 458
MacLeod, D., 421
MacNamara, J., 225
MacPhee, D., 369
MacTurk, R. H., 222, 322
Maddock, A., 267
Maehr, M. L., 200
Maggs, J. L., 389
Magill, L. H., 235
Magnusson, D., 457
Maguire, M., 109, 378
Mahapatra, M., 340
Mahler, M. S., 165
Mahoney, J. L., 419
Mahoney, K. M., 265
Main, M., 137, 138, 140, 146, 148, 150, 393
Makai, T., 267
Malatesta, C. Z., 107, 108
Malcuit, G., 231
Malinosky-Rummell, R., 393
Mallick, S. K., 300
Malone, M. J., 287, 458, 463
Mandleco, B. L., 288, 449
Mandler, J. M., 95
Mangelsdorf, S. C., 108, 129, 142, 144
Manke, B. A., 242
Manley, J. T., 393
Manset, G., 430
Marcia, J. E., 184, 185
Marcia, L. E., 185, 297
Marcoen, A., 173
Marcus, D. E., 240, 255
Margand, N. A., 89, 145, 146, 359
Margolin, G., 376
Maridaki-Kassotaki, K., 171
Markman, H. J., 90, 142
Markon, K., 236, 292
Markstrom, C. A., 185
Markstrom-Adams, C., 168, 186, 187
Markus, G. B., 226
Markus, H., 175, 226
Marold, D. B., 172
Marolla, F. A., 226
Marsh, H. W., 173, 174, 177
Marshall, H. H., 423
Marshall, N. L., 389
Marshall, T. R., 115
Mrthy, K. A., 425
Martin, C. L., 237, 241, 243, 244, 245, 254, 256, 257, 438, 478
Martin, G. B., 72
Martin, J. A., 363, 364, 366, 457
Martin, M., 427
Martin, N. G., 79
Marvin, R. S., 377
Marx, F., 389
Marzolf, D., 108
Masden, A. S., 176

Masden, M. C., 215
Mason, C. A., 125, 371
Mason, M. G., 295, 339
Masterpasqua, F., 380
Masters, J. C., 254
Maszk, P., 109
Matas, L., 128
Matejcek, Z., 141
Matheny, A. P., 448
Matheson, C. C., 450, 462
Matheson, L., 274
Mathy, R. M., 317
Matias, R., 106
Matillo, G. M., 406
Maton, K. I., 360
Matsumoto, D., 110
Matteson, D., 185
Matthews, K. A., 79, 309
Mattsson, A., 290
Matula, K. E., 185
Maughan, B., 417
Maxwell, S., 268
May, M. S., 344
Mayer, F. S., 260
Mayes, L. C., 200
May-Plumlee, T., 318, 321
Mayseless, O., 139
Mazzie, C., 110
McAdoo, H. P., 208, 370
McBride-Chang, C., 393
McCabe, M., 177, 366
McCall, R. B., 24, 112, 113, 476
McCandless, B. R., 300
McCarthy, M. E., 222, 322
McCartney, K., 82, 83, 84, 85, 389
McCarton, C., 220
McClearn, G. E., 75, 81, 82, 85, 114
McClelland, D. C., 201, 204, 205, 224
McClintic, S., 95, 107, 202
McCloskey, L. A., 381, 391, 393
McConaghy, M., 59
McCormick, M. C., 220
McCoy, J. K., 376
McDonnell, P., 313, 314
McDougall, W., 326
McDuff, P., 286
McFadyen-Ketchum, S. A., 299
McGhee, P. E., 225, 254
McGue, M., 76, 81, 83
McGue, M. K., 379
McGuire, K. D., 455
McGuire, M., 92
McGuire, S., 81
McHale, J. L., 142
McHale, J. P., 376
McHale, S. M., 242, 377, 388
McKenna, J., 357
McKenna, M. A. J., 265, 266, 267, 357
McKenna, M. W., 402, 406
McKinley, M., 453, 458
McLaughlin, S., 142
McLoyd, V. C., 218, 220, 368, 369
McNalley, S., 316, 317

McNeilly-Choque, M. K., 292, 451
McNew, J., 395
McPartland, J., 208
McPartland, J. M., 424
McQuiston, S., 222, 322
McRoy, R. G., 379
McWilliams, L., 427
Meachum, J. A., 168
Mead, G. H., 164, 196
Mead, M., 32, 249, 293
Meadows, K., 462
Measelle, J. R., 174
Mediascope, Inc., 403
Mednick, S., 81
Medrich, E. A., 448
Meilman, P. W., 184
Meisels, S. J., 142
Mekos, D., 386, 387
Melnick, S., 451
Melson, G. F., 235
Meltzoff, A. N., 47, 55, 57, 165, 169, 170,
  189
Melzack, R., 151
Menashri, J., 243, 256
Mennella, A., 263
Mergendoller, J. R., 421
Merkler, K., 379
Meschulach-Safaty, O., 47, 55
Messer, D. J., 222
Messinger, D. S., 141
Meyer-Bahlberg, H. F. L., 264
Meyers, T., 141
Miceli, P. J., 267, 268
Michael, R. T., 265
Michaelieu, Q., 111, 176, 177, 178
Michaels, S., 265
Michel, M. K., 108
Midgley, C., 238, 424, 425
Midlarsky, E., 311, 321, 323, 324
Mikach, S., 380
Milbern, S., 418
Miller, A. T., 210
Miller, C. L., 240, 267, 268
Miller, G. V., 264
Miller, J., 325
Miller, J. G., 340
Miller, K. S., 263, 268
Miller, L. S., 408
Miller, N. B., 366
Miller, N. E., 277
Miller, P. A., 235, 267, 268, 303, 316, 317,
  318
Miller, P. H., 59, 95, 169, 170
Miller, S. A., 59, 169, 170
Miller, T. E., 456
Miller, T. L., 268
Miller-Heyl, J., 369
Miller-Loncar, C. L., 449
Mills, R. S. L., 290, 321
Milstead, M., 63
Minde, K., 142
Miner, J. L., 111
Minor, C. A., 204

Minuchin, P. P., 359, 420, 422, 427
Mischel, H. N., 182
Mischel, W., 178, 181, 182, 183, 253, 344
Mistry, J., 93
Mitchell, C., 176, 177, 211, 424
Mitchell, J. E., 248
Mitchell, S., 224
Miyake, K., 106, 107
Mize, J., 449, 451, 460
Mizuta, I., 284
Moffitt, T. E., 28, 81, 114, 183, 288, 382, 457
Moller, L. C., 243
Moneta, G., 376
Money, J., 246, 247, 248, 249, 250, 264
Monroe, R. H., 255
Monsour, A., 171, 172
Montemayor, R., 172
Moo, H., 89, 366, 428
Mood, A. M., 208
Moore, B., 316, 318
Moore, C., 148
Moore, C. F., 342
Moore, E. G. J., 217, 314
Moore, L. P., 182, 348
Moore, M. K., 47, 55, 57
Moorehouse, M. J., 388
Moran, G., 138, 142, 150
Morelli, G. A., 155, 357
Morgan, G. A., 128
Morgan, R., 165
Morris, J. T., 255
Morris, N., 118
Morris, R., 290
Morris, S. J., 462
Morrison, D. R., 384
Morrison, F. J., 416, 417
Morrow, C., 462
Mortimer, J. T., 375, 376
Mortimore, P., 417
Mory, M. S., 445
Moses, L. J., 111
Mosher, M., 292
Mosier, C., 93
Moss, H. A., 28
Mounts, N., 468
Mounts, N. S., 177, 218, 225, 365, 366, 367,
  372, 469
Mowrer, O. H., 277
Mrazek, D. A., 114
Mueller, E., 441
Mueller, E. C., 441
Muir, D. W., 121
Mullally, P. R., 225, 226
Mullis, A. K., 177
Mullis, I. V. K., 431
Mullis, R. L., 177
Mumme, D. L., 111
Munn, P., 375
Munro, G., 188
Munroe, R. H., 255
Munroe, R. L., 255
Murphy, B., 109, 318, 455
Murphy, C. M., 359

Murphy, R. R., 286
Murray, C., 379
Murray, E., 243
Murray, H., 204
Murray, J. P., 408, 409
Murray, L., 141
Mussen, P. H., 253
Musser, L. M., 438, 450
Myers, B., 242
Myers, B. J., 119
Myers, D. G., 71, 318

Nachmias, M., 137
Nadler, A., 321
Nagel, S. K., 89, 369, 388
Naito, M., 170
Nakagawa, K., 216, 217
Nash, S. C., 240
Nastasi, B. K., 413, 414, 415
National Education Goals Panel, 431
Neale, J. M., 405
Neale, M. C., 265, 289, 380
Neckerman, H. J., 280, 288, 299
Nederend, S., 242, 244
Needle, R. H., 383
Neel, R. G., 204
Neeman, J., 176
Neisser, U., 207, 216, 218
Nelson, C. A., 110
Nelson, D., 451
Nelson, D. A., 236, 292
Nelson, E. A., 343
Nelson, J., 196, 464
Nelson, K., 167
Nelson, L. J., 292
Nelson, S., 212
Nelson, S. A., 331
Nelson-LeGall, S., 95, 202, 286
Nesbitt, K. M., 406
Neville, P. R., 90
Newcomb, A. F., 454, 455, 465
Newcomb, M. D., 469
Newcombe, N., 247
Newman, D. L., 28, 114, 183, 288
Newman, J. L., 242
Nias, K. K. B., 289
NICHD Early Child Care Research Network,
  141, 158, 159
Nicholls, J. G., 210
Nicholls, M. R., 145
Nichols, R. C., 79
Nigg, J. T., 451
Nikolic, J., 63
Ninio, A., 145
Nir, A., 111
Nixon, K., 415
Noam, G., 177
Normandin, D., 177
Norman-Jackson, J., 378
North American Syndicate, 349
Nottelmann, E. D., 177
Novak, M. A., 153
Nowell, A., 236

Nucci, L., 326, 341
Nuttall, R. L., 234
Nyman, M., 111

Oates, R. K., 396
Oberklaid, F., 114
O'Boyle, C., 240, 253, 290
O'Brien, K. M., 236, 292
O'Brien, M., 231, 242
O'Connor, B. P., 63, 185
O'Connor, T. G., 289, 295, 367
Odden, A., 419
Oden, S., 460
O'Donohue, W. T., 395
Ogbu, J. U., 187, 218, 358, 371, 428
O'Heron, C. A., 260
Okazaki, S., 216
Olejnik, A. B., 242, 243
Olgetree, S. M., 415
Oliner, P. M., 324
Oliner, S. P., 324
Oliver, G. D., 251
Ollendick, T. H., 378
Olsen, J. E., 373, 469
Olsen, S. F., 288, 292, 449, 451
Olson, D. R., 58, 109
Olson, G. M., 55
Olson, K. L., 108
Olweus, D., 286, 287, 290, 294, 295
O'Mahoney, J. F., 192
O'Malley, P., 186
O'Neil, A. K., 242, 244
O'Neil, R., 89, 369, 388
O'Neill, D. K., 169
Oppenheim, D., 111, 114, 145, 155, 179,
    328, 357
Orlofsky, J. L., 185, 260, 261
Osborn, D. K., 403
Osborne, L. M., 296, 381
Ossoff, E. P., 402, 406
Ouston, J., 417
Overton, W. F., 98, 240, 255
Owen, M. T., 89, 142, 145, 146, 359

Padavish, D. L., 343, 345, 349, 351
Pagani, L., 468
Paikoff, R. L., 89
Palkovitz, R., 145, 359
Palmer, D. J., 377
Palmer, E. L., 412
Palmgren, C., 63
Panak, W. F., 280, 281
Pannabecker, B., 105
Parisi, S. A., 110
Park, S., 114
Parke, R. D., 25, 31, 112, 150, 274, 283,
    290, 302, 345, 350, 404, 406, 449, 451
Parker, J. G., 243, 439, 440, 441, 443, 444,
    449, 450, 451, 454, 458, 459, 463, 464,
    465, 466
Parker, K. C. H., 150
Parkhurst, J. T., 440, 458

Parkin, L., 170
Parnass, J., 439
Parrinello, R., 114
Parsons, J. E., 196, 238
Parsons, T., 227, 232
Parten, M., 442, 443
Passarello, L. C., 266
Passman, R. H., 132
Pasternack, J., 317
Pataki, S. P., 461
Patel, N., 20
Pattee, L., 458
Patterson, C. J., 182, 217, 218, 264, 368,
    380, 393, 394
Patterson, G. R., 218, 294, 295, 296, 297,
    298, 299, 300, 366, 368, 386, 387, 461,
    464, 466, 468, 469
Patterson, S. J., 185, 297
Patz, R. J., 391
Paul, J. P., 264
Paulhus, D., 225, 378
Peake, P. K., 183
Pears, K. C., 266, 299
Pearson, A., 189, 192
Pearson, J. L., 360
Pedersen, J., 84, 290, 437
Pederson, D. R., 138, 142, 150
Pedlow, R., 114
Pedro-Carroll, J. L., 385
Peet, S., 235
Peevers, B. H., 95, 189
Pegalis, L. J., 260
Pelaez-Nogueras, M., 45
Pellegrini, D. S., 195, 455
Peng, Y., 278, 290, 301
Pepler, D. J., 287, 376, 377
Pepper, S., 462
Perilloux, H. K., 167
Perlman, M., 284
Perloff, R., 207, 216, 218
Perner, J., 170
Perrotta, M., 142
Perry, D. G., 280, 286, 287, 290, 347, 458,
    463
Perry, L. C., 280, 286, 290, 347
Perry, S., 144
Perry, T. B., 194
Perry-Jenkins, M., 388
Perusse, D., 286
Peskin, H., 457
Peskin, J., 109
Peters, P. L., 240, 241, 299
Petersen, A. C., 150, 185, 234, 242, 457
Peterson, C. C., 331
Peterson, L., 307, 389
Peterson, R. E., 250
Petrakos, H., 378
Petrovich, S. B., 125
Pettit, G. S., 282, 287, 294, 295, 296, 299,
    302, 363, 389, 449, 451, 458, 460, 461
Peucker, M., 142
Pezaris, E., 234

Philipsen, L. C., 450
Philliber, S., 268
Phillips, D., 207
Phillips, D. A., 158, 160
Phillips, M., 212, 421
Phinney, J. S., 186, 187
Phoenix, C. H., 290
Piaget, J., 17, 18, 37, 47, 50, 51, 52, 54, 55,
    57, 58, 59, 60, 61, 62, 63, 68, 91, 93,
    98, 195, 284, 328, 329, 330, 331, 332,
    333, 353, 444
Pickens, J., 141
Piemyat, S., 402
Pihl, R. O., 286
Pike, A., 81
Pike, R., 174
Pillard, R. C., 75, 265, 380
Pine, C. J., 369
Pine, F., 165
Pinon, M., 412
Pinto, A., 366
Pipp, S., 147, 167
Pitts, R. C., 326, 341, 342
Plant, E. A., 236
Pleck, J. H., 145, 146
Plomin, R., 75, 77, 78, 79, 80, 81, 82, 85,
    112, 113, 114, 289, 295, 367, 448
Plumert, J. M., 286
Plunkett, J. W., 142
Polit, D. F., 378
Pollack, C. B., 141
Pollack, R. H., 269
Pomerantz, E. M., 177, 210, 212, 214, 233,
    238
Pomerleau, A., 231
Ponterotto, J. G., 187
Poortinga, Y. H., 215
Porter, C. L., 235
Portes, A., 421
Posada, G., 130, 138, 139
Posada, R., 130, 139
Posner, J. K., 390
Poston, D. L., Jr., 378
Potter, G. B., 302, 334
Potts, R., 343, 348
Poulin-Dubois, D., 240
Povinelli, D. J., 167
Power, T. G., 20, 109, 368, 371
Powers, S. I., 177
Powlishta, K. K., 63, 243, 254, 257
Presson, C. C., 468
Preston, A. A., 201
Price, J., 440, 454, 458
Price, J. M., 282, 458, 463
Priel, B., 166
Prior, M., 114
Provence, S., 153, 154
Pungello, E. P., 216
Putallaz, M., 451
Putnam, F. W., 390, 394
Putnam, P. H., 106, 107
Putnam, S., 114

Quanty, M. B., 300, 404, 407, 408
Quiggle, N. L., 280, 281
Quinn, R. A., 326
Quintana, S. M., 63

Rabiner, D. L., 302, 458, 460
Raboy, B., 380
Radice, C., 379
Radin, N., 387
Radke-Yarrow, M., 47, 141, 235, 303, 311, 312, 313, 314, 315, 317, 318, 325, 376
Raffaelli, M., 397, 398, 468, 469
Ramanan, J., 387
Ramey, C. T., 155, 158, 220, 221, 224, 394, 418
Ramsay, D., 119
Ramsey, E., 294, 295, 298, 299, 468
Ramsey, P. G., 243
Raviv, A., 314
Rayias, M. F., 106, 107
Raynor, J. O., 44, 206
Raynor, R., 44
Raz, S., 235
Recchia, A., 95, 107, 202
Redler, E., 319
Reese, E., 235
Reid, J. B., 296, 366
Reinisch, M. M., 266
Reis, H. T., 148, 451
Reiser, M., 109
Reiss, D., 80, 81, 386, 387
Reissland, N., 55
Reitz, L., 402
Remley, A., 9
Rende, R., 81
Renshaw, P. D., 466
Repacholi, B., 147, 169
Rescorla, L., 418
Resnick, S., 143
Resnick, S. M., 249
Rest, J. R., 339, 343
Reuman, D., 238, 424
Reynolds, A. J., 221
Reynolds, D., 421
Reznick, J. S., 113, 115
Rheingold, H. L., 313
Rholes, W. S., 96, 97, 189
Riad, J. K., 290
Ribble, M., 153
Ricciuti, H. N., 128
Rice, M. E., 323
Rice, M. L., 412
Richards, M. H., 176, 376, 387, 445
Richardson, D., 273, 277
Richardson, J. G., 243, 244
Richey, C. A., 392
Richman, A., 20, 108, 139
Richters, J. E., 359
Rieser-Danner, L. A., 456
Riggs, W. W., 235
Riksen-Walraven, J. M. A., 462

Rinaldi, C. M., 378
Rincon, C., 283, 287
Rinkoff, R. F., 128
Rinott, N., 145
Riordan, L., 114
Riordon, K., 143
Ritchie, K. L., 367
Ritter, J. M., 125, 456
Ritter, P. L., 225, 295, 296, 366
Roberts, D., 360, 409
Roberts, J. E., 383
Roberts, L. R., 242
Roberts, W., 318
Robertson, L. S., 240
Robertson, T. S., 409
Robins, P. K., 384
Robins, R. W., 177
Robinson, C. C., 255, 288, 292, 449, 451
Robinson, E., 265
Robinson, I., 265
Robinson, J. L., 79, 115, 309, 312
Rochat, P., 165
Rocheleau, B., 415
Rock, S. L., 223, 224
Rodgers, J. L., 265
Rodning, C., 183
Rodrigues, T., 415
Roedell, W. C., 407, 409
Rogers-Salyer, M., 125
Roggman, L. A., 456
Rogoff, B., 48, 91, 92, 93, 357, 416, 438
Roithmaier, A., 156
Rolf, J., 397, 398
Romney, D. M., 232, 253, 350
Ronsaville, D. S., 376
Rook, K. S., 376
Roopnarine, L. L., 145
Rosario, M., 393
Rose, A. J., 464, 466
Rose, H., 254, 256
Rose, J. S., 468
Rose, R. M., 290
Rose-Krasnor, L., 465
Rosen, B. C., 224
Rosen, J., 448
Rosen, K. S., 146
Rosen, W. D., 112
Rosenbaum, L. K., 220
Rosenberg, M., 182
Rosenberger, K., 88
Rosenblum, M. A., 437
Rosenboom, L. G., 154
Rosenhan, D. L., 308, 324
Rosenholtz, S. J., 210
Rosenkrantz, P. S., 233
Rosenman, R. H., 79, 309
Rosenthal, D. A., 186, 187
Rosenthal, R., 389, 408, 422, 423
Rosenthal, T., 427
Rosenwasser, S. M., 254, 408
Rosenzweig, M. G., 266
Ross, D. F., 275

Ross, H. S., 284, 374, 462
Rossiter, J. R., 409
Rotatori, A. F., 394, 395
Rotenberg, K. J., 316
Roth, K., 311, 312, 316, 317
Rothbart, M. K., 112, 113, 115, 226
Rothbaum, F., 146
Rousseau, J. J., 11, 15
Rovee-Collier, C., 165
Rovine, M., 145, 159, 359
Rowe, D. C., 77, 79, 81, 265
Rubenstein, J. L., 178
Rubenstein, T. S., 462
Rubin, C., 178
Rubin, K. H., 117, 196, 218, 290, 440, 441, 443, 444, 449, 450, 451, 454, 455, 458, 459, 464, 465, 468
Rubin, V., 448
Rubinstein, E. A., 408, 409
Ruble, D. N., 96, 97, 177, 189, 210, 212, 214, 233, 234, 238, 241, 242, 244, 245, 254, 255, 257, 438, 466
Ruble, T. L., 233
Rudin, M., 394
Rudolph, F., 427
Ruff, A., 397, 398
Ruff, H. A., 114
Ruffman, T. K., 58, 109, 170
Ruh, J., 389
Rusany, N., 177
Rushton, J. P., 289, 312, 322, 323, 345, 348
Russell, A., 449
Rutherford, E., 253
Rutten, P., 293, 294
Rutter, M., 75, 81, 82, 85, 114, 119, 133, 157, 289, 295, 367, 368, 417, 419, 420, 421
Ryan, R. H., 221
Ryan, R. M., 224, 367
Rys, G. S., 331
Ryther, J. S., 110
Ryu, S., 375

Saarni, C., 110, 235
Sabbagh, M. A., 170
Sackin, S., 437
Sacks, C. H., 421
Sagi, A., 72, 130, 139, 155
Sagotsky, G., 466
St. Peters, M., 410
Sakin, J. W., 373
Salem, D. A., 360
Salili, F., 200
Salyer, K. E., 125
Salzinger, S., 393
Sameroff, A. J., 143
Samuels, C., 165, 166
Samuels, H. R., 377
Sancilio, M. F. M., 286
Sander, C. J., 235
Sanders, J., 402
Sanders, P., 253

Sanders, R. Jr., 212
Sanders, S. A., 266
Sandvik, E., 235
Sanson, A., 114
Sansone, C., 342
Santrock, J. W., 343
Sapiro, C. M., 341
Sarigiani, P. A., 242
Saudino, K. J., 114
Savin-Williams, R. C., 177, 264, 457
Savoie, L., 154
Sawin, D. B., 125, 318
Sax, L. J., 265
Scaramella, L. V., 266
Scarr, S., 82, 83, 84, 85, 86, 87, 157, 160, 187, 216, 379, 388, 389, 448, 478
Sceery, A., 451
Schafer, W. W., 146
Schaffer, A., 166
Schaffer, H. R., 56, 121, 122, 123, 124, 127, 133, 441
Schaie, K. W., 27
Schaller, M., 303, 318
Schalling, D., 290
Schanberg, S., 144
Schellenbach, C., 268
Schiller, M., 143
Schlagman, N., 332
Schmidt, C. R., 257
Schmitt, K. L., 255
Schmitz, S., 114
Schneider, B. H., 293, 460, 464
Schneider, F. W., 314, 315
Schnell, S. V., 340
Schoefs, V., 173
Scholmerich, A., 369
Schoff, K., 370
Scholmerich, A., 106, 125, 139
Schooler, C., 225
Schuller, V., 141
Schult, C. A., 170
Schulze, P. A., 369
Schwartz, D., 287, 296
Schwartzman, A. E., 240, 241, 299
Schwarz, J. C., 366
Schweitzer, J., 418, 421
Scolton, K. L., 150, 451
Scott, J. P., 152, 276, 292
Scott, P. M., 321
Scott, R., 177, 366
Scott, W. A., 177, 366
Seal, J., 463
Sears, R. R., 122, 136, 277, 294
Sebald, H., 469
Sebastian, R. J., 406
Secord, P. F., 95, 189
Seefeldt, C., 217, 428
Segal, N. L., 83
Segal, S., 386
Segal, U. A., 20
Segall, M. H., 215
Seidman, E., 176, 177, 211, 424

Seifer, R., 142, 143
Seitz, V., 220, 267
Sellers, M. J., 124
Selman, R. L., 63, 192, 193, 194
Semmel, M. I., 430
Sepkoski, C., 142
Seppa, N., 403, 409
September, B., 178
Serbin, L. A., 240, 241, 243, 254, 257, 299
Shaffer, A., 412
Shaffer, D. R., 61, 225, 260, 325, 326, 328, 334, 349, 350, 378
Shagle, S. C., 373, 469
Shah, F., 235
Shanahan, M. J., 374, 375, 376
Shannon, D. C., 114
Shantz, C. U., 195, 285
Shapiro, C., 461
Shapiro, E. K., 420, 422, 427
Shapiro, J. R., 108
Shapiro, S., 268, 443
Sharma, A., 81
Sharma, A. R., 379
Sharp, D., 416
Sharp, L., 423
Shaver, P., 138, 148
Shaw, D. S., 183
Shea, C., 316, 317, 318
Shea, J. D. C., 450
Shell, R., 267, 268, 316, 317, 318
Shell, R. M., 315
Shepard, B., 107, 108
Shepard, S. A., 318, 455
Sherif, C. W., 444, 446
Sherif, M., 444, 446
Sherman, D., 392
Sherman, S. J., 468
Sherman, T., 55
Shields, J., 81
Shigetomi, C. C., 315
Shimmin, H. S., 255
Shipman, K., 109
Shoda, Y., 183
Short, R. J., 341, 433
Shouldice, A., 143
Shulman, S., 89, 148, 459
Shultz, T. R., 95
Shure, M. B., 302, 460
Shweder, R. A., 340, 341
Siegal, M., 331, 351
Siegel, L., 224
Siegel-Gorelick, B., 457
Siegler, R. S., 431
Sigafoos, A. D., 47, 55
Sigelman, C. K., 242, 267, 310, 343, 456
Sigmundson, H. K., 250
Signorella, M. L., 242, 248, 254, 257, 401
Signorielli, N., 254, 401
Sigvardsson, S., 379
Sikes, J., 430
Silva, P. A., 28, 112, 114, 183, 288, 382, 457
Silverberg, S. B., 368, 467

Simmel, C., 451
Simmons, R. G., 176, 424, 457
Simon, B. B., 167
Simons, R. L., 218, 266, 361, 364, 369, 381, 384, 387, 391, 457
Simpson, C., 210
Simpson, C. H., 243, 244
Simutis, Z., 348
Sinclair, R. J., 386
Sines, J. O., 366
Singelis, T. M., 175
Singer, D. G., 412
Singer, J. L., 412
Singer, L. M., 119
Singh, S., 265, 266
Sippola, L. K., 463, 465
Skinner, B. F., 44, 45, 86, 98
Skinner, M. L., 299, 382, 461, 464, 468, 469
Slaby, R. G., 59, 274, 280, 281, 282, 283, 290, 301, 302, 404, 407, 409
Slaughter-Defoe, D. T., 216, 217
Slavin, R. E., 419, 420, 430, 431
Slomkowski, C., 376
Sluckin, A. M., 277
Small, S. A., 457
Smetana, J. G., 326, 332, 372
Smith, A., 417
Smith, C., 394
Smith, D. A., 359
Smith, E., 402
Smith, K. E., 449
Smith, L., 415, 416
Smith, P. K., 235, 242, 274, 277, 301
Smith, T. W., 378
Smollar, J., 372
Snapp, M., 430
Snarey, J. R., 340
Snidman, N., 114
Snow, M. E., 243
Snow, R. E., 421
Snyder, A., 248, 264
Snyder, M., 319
Sobesky, W. E., 343
Sobol, B. L., 410
Sochting, I, 185, 297
Society for Research in Child Development, 331
Sockloff, A., 242
Sodian, B., 170
Solomon, J., 137, 140
Sommer, K., 268
Sonuga-Barke, E. J. S., 360
Sorensen, E., 384
Spangler, S., 139
Sparks, C., 235
Speer, A. L., 318
Speicher, B., 339
Spelke, E., 124
Speltz, M. L., 125, 295
Spence, J. T., 259, 260
Spencer, M. B., 168, 186, 187, 225, 428
Spitz, R. A., 153, 155

Spitze, G., 159
Spivack, G., 460
Sprafkin, J., 22, 254, 401, 402, 403, 404,
    408, 409, 410, 411, 413
Spritz, B., 148
Srivastave, P., 145
Sroufe, L. A., 89, 127, 128, 129, 144, 147,
    148, 151, 243, 392, 393, 394, 459
Stack, D. M., 240, 241, 299
Staffieri, J. R., 456
Stanger, C., 107, 109, 287–288
Stanhope, L., 376, 377
Stanley, J. C., 234
Stanley-Hagan, M. S., 381
Starnes, R., 364
Stattin, H., 115, 457
Stechler, G., 178
Steele, B. F., 141
Steele, C. M., 219, 429
Steele, H., 150
Steele, M., 150
Stein, A. H., 25, 405, 407, 410
Stein, M. R., 441
Steinberg, L., 89, 177, 218, 225, 296, 365,
    366, 367, 372, 373, 374, 389, 414, 428,
    429, 467, 468, 469
Steir, M., 119
Stemmler, M., 150, 185
Stenberg, C., 105
Stephan, C., 430
Stern, B. M., 433
Stern, D., 119, 220
Stern, D. N., 165
Sternberg, K. J., 393
Sternberg, R. J., 207, 216, 218
Stevens, R. J., 430, 431
Stevenson, H. W., 89, 175, 216, 217, 227,
    228, 428, 429, 431, 432, 433
Stevenson-Hinde, J., 143
Stewart, M. I., 464
Stewart, R. B., 377
Stewart, S. L., 468
Stice, E., 367
Stifter, E., 462
Stigler, J. W., 217, 428, 431, 432
Stimson, C. A., 313
Stipek, D., 95, 107, 167–168, 202, 210, 214,
    221, 418
Stipek, D. J., 189, 210
Stockard, J., 260
Stolberg, U., 129
Stoneman, Z., 358, 376
Stoolmiller, M., 266, 299, 461, 464, 468, 469
Stormshak, E. A., 376
Stouthamer-Loeber, M., 286, 287, 288, 290,
    295, 299
Strassberg, Z., 297
Strayer, F. F., 242, 277, 437
Strayer, J., 235, 302, 318
Streisands, B., 419
Streitmatter, J., 184
Strough, J., 342

Stumpf, H., 234
Stumphauzer, J. S., 466
Sturla, E., 250
Su, M., & Chow, J., 392
Subaiya, L., 381
Sue, S., 216
Suess, G., 139, 148
Sullivan, H. S., 43, 464
Sullivan, M. W., 107, 109, 165, 277, 328
Sun, Y., 117
Suomi, S. J., 153, 439, 440
Super, C. M., 339
Susman, E. J., 391, 410
Sutton, K., 260
Swank, P. R., 449
Swarr, A., 176
Sweeney, K., 9
Synnevang, B., 130, 139

Tabkin, G., 412
Taipale, V., 457
Takahira, S., 234
Takanishi, R., 216, 217
Talley, R. C., 341, 433
Talukder, E., 145
Tani, F., 464
Tanner, J. M., 22, 156, 291
Tarullo, L. B., 376
Tascon, M., 130, 139
Tasker, F., 264, 380
Tate, J. D., 187
Taylor, A. R., 430
Taylor, C., 170, 457
Taylor, J. H., 332, 338–339, 467
Taylor, M., 170
Taylor, M. G., 241, 242, 246
Taylor, R. D., 360
Teegartin, C., 362, 380
Teeven, R. C., 225
Teitler, J. O., 384
Tellegen, A., 83, 176
Temple, J. A., 221
Terry, R., 453
Tesman, J. R., 107, 108
Tessier, O., 443
Teti, D. M., 141, 150, 373, 377
Teti, L. O., 108
Tharp, R. G., 422
Thelan, M. H., 235
Thelen, E., 437
Thoma, S. J., 337, 339, 343
Thomas, A., 112, 113, 115, 142, 143, 144
Thomas, A. M., 381
Thomas, M. H., 407
Thomas, R., 115, 116
Thompson, R. A., 108, 109, 150
Thompson, S. K., 240
Thompson, W. R., 151
Thompson, W. W., 368, 393, 394, 439
Thorne, A., 176, 177, 178
Thorne, B., 263
Thornton, D., 415

Thurber, C. A., 127
Thurlow, R., 402, 403
Tieger, T., 291
Tietjen, A. M., 321
Tinbergen, N., 68, 69
Tingle, B. A., 318
Tinsley, B. J., 409
Tirozzi, G. N., 431, 433
Tisak, J., 332
Tisak, M. S., 332
Tizard, B., 157
Tjebkes, T. L., 328
Toch, H., 280
Toch, T., 419
Todd, M., 468
Tolan, P., 146
Tolson, J. M., 445
Tomada, G., 293, 464
Tomasello, M., 338
Tomlin, C., 167
Tomlinson-Keasey, C., 338
Toner, I. J., 182, 343, 348
Townsend, M. A. R., 316
Trachtenberg, S., 282
Tremblay, R. E., 286, 468
Trevethan, S. D., 342
Triandis, H. C., 175, 201, 321
Trickett, P. K., 390, 391, 393
Trivers, R. L., 309
Tronick, E. A., 108
Tronick, E. Z., 110, 112, 119, 120, 155
Troyer, L., 225, 366
Trudel, M., 143
Truglio, R., 402, 412
Tryon, R. C., 74
Tsay, J. C., 468, 469
Tschann, J. M., 384, 385
Tucker, P., 250
Tudge, J. R. H., 93, 94
Tuer, M., 385
Tulkin, S., 130
Tulviste, P., 91, 93
Turiel, E., 326, 332, 341
Turner, C. W., 278
Turner, P. J., 243, 254, 260, 261
Turner-Bowker, D. M., 254
Twenge, J. M., 233
Tyson, P., 43
Tyson, R. L., 43

Uba, L., 369
Ude, W., 397, 398
Udry, J. R., 263
Ugurel-Semin, R., 314
Underwood, B., 316, 318, 427
Underwood, M. K., 110, 288, 292
Uniform Crime Reports, 299
Universal Press Syndicate, 335, 454
Unzner, L., 139
Urban, J., 459
Urberg, K. A., 242, 445
Urbina, S., 207, 216, 218

Uro, G., 431, 433
U.S. Bureau of the Census, 178, 179, 228, 238, 239, 244, 356, 361, 362, 385, 389, 414, 416, 428
U.S. Department of Education, 427
U.S. Department of Justice, 235, 288
Uttal, D. H., 217, 428, 429

Vaden, N. A., 217, 218
Vandell, D. L., 159, 387, 389, 390, 441
Vandenberg, B., 443
Van den Boom, D. C., 116, 142, 143, 144
Van den Broek, P. W., 402, 403
Van Doorninck, W. J., 223
Van IJzendoorn, H. W., 459
Van IJzendoorn, M. H., 139, 140, 143, 144, 145, 146, 150, 391
Van Lieshout, C. F. M., 459, 462
Vannatta, R. A., 63, 178
Varady, M., 457
Vasudev, J., 340
Vaugh, L. S., 456
Vaughn, B., 138, 140, 143, 148, 181, 359, 451
Ventura-Cook, E., 369
Verhulst, F. C., 287–288, 377
Verschueren, K., 173
Versluis-Den Bieman, H. J., 377
Vespo, J., 84, 290, 437
Vibbert, M., 110
Vietze, P., 110, 121, 222, 322
Viken, R. J., 282
Vinden, P. G., 171
Vinter, A., 47
Vitaro, F., 287, 463, 468
Vobejda, B., 9
Vogel, S. R., 233
Volling, B., 364, 374
Vondra, J., 183, 394
von Eye, A., 71
Von Wright, M. R., 244
Voos, D. K., 118
Voran, M., 160
Vosk, B., 453
Voyer, D., 236
Voyer, S., 236
Vuchinich, R. A., 298, 386
Vuchinich, S., 295, 298, 368
Vygotsky, L. S., 64, 91, 92, 93, 99, 108, 181, 438, 477

Wachs, T. D., 179
Wade, C., 97
Wagner, B. M.
Wagner, E., 235, 303, 312, 314, 317, 318, 325
Wainryb, C., 341
Waitzman, K. A., 343
Walden, T. A., 110
Walder, L. O., 288, 404
Waldman, I. D., 216
Walker, D. L., 466
Walker, L. J., 326, 332, 337, 339, 341, 342, 467
Walker, S., 244

Wall, S., 136, 143
Wallen, K., 290
Wallerstein, J. S., 382, 383, 384, 385
Walsh, P. V., 261
Walters, A. S., 263, 267
Walters, G. C., 390
Walters, R. H., 300
Ward, M. J., 150
Wark, G. R., 342, 343
Warkentin, V., 166, 167
Warren, S., 111
Wartner, U. G., 148
Washington, W. N., 148, 451
Wasik, B. H., 208, 370, 418
Watanabe, H., 175
Waterman, A. S., 185, 186, 188
Waters, E., 119, 128, 136, 138, 140, 143, 147, 359
Waters, P., 176
Waters, P. L., 260
Watson, J. B., 11, 43, 44, 63, 68, 86, 98
Watson, J. S., 121
Watson, M. W., 278, 290, 301
Waxler, C. Z., 321
Webber, P. L., 83
Weber, E. K., 326
Weber, J. S., 412
Weber, R. A., 313, 314
Weed, S., 266
Weinberg, K. A., 216
Weinberg, M. K., 108
Weinberg, M. S., 264
Weinberg, R. A., 83, 187, 379
Weiner, B., 207, 210
Weinfeld, F. D., 208
Weinfert, K., 175
Weinraub, M., 127, 132, 242
Weinreb, L. F., 370
Weinstein, C. S., 414
Weinstein, R. S., 423
Weisberg, P., 132
Weisner, T. S., 245, 377
Weiss, B., 117, 295, 297
Weiss, L. H., 366
Weiss, M., 107
Weiss, R. J., 290
Weissberg, R., 114
Weissberg, R. P., 467
Weiss-Perry, B., 177
Weisz, J. R., 117, 297, 455
Welch-Ross, M. K., 257
Wellman, H. M., 169, 170
Wellman, N. E., 236, 292
Wells, D., 95
Wells, L. E., 186
Wentzel, K. R., 455
Wertsch, J. V., 91, 93
Wessels, H., 158, 159
West, S., 406
Westby, S., 410
Westheimer, I., 133
Weston, D. R., 146
Whalen, C. K., 235

Whaley, K. L., 462
Wharton, J. D., 294
Whipple, E., 266
Whipple, E. E., 392
Whitaker, D. J., 263, 268
Whitbeck, L. B., 266, 361, 368, 369, 387
Whitbourne, S. K., 398
White, B. J., 444, 446
White, J. M., 360
White, K. J., 424, 425, 426, 459
White, R. K., 426
White, R. W., 200, 203
White, S. H., 8
Whitebeck, L. B., 391
Whitebrook, M., 158, 160
Whitesell, N. R., 107, 172, 176, 260
Whiting, B. B., 242, 249, 314, 320, 357, 437
Whiting, J. W. M., 320
Whitley, B. E. Jr., 260
Whitman, T. L., 267, 268
Whitworth, L. A., 456
Wiehe, V. R., 390, 391, 394, 396, 397
Wierson, M., 381
Wigfield, A., 211, 217, 238, 424, 428
Wiggam, A. E., 11
Wilcox, B. L., 408, 409
Wilkinson, S., 264
Wille, D. E., 147
Willems, E. P., 18
Williams, B., 415
Williams, C., 318, 342
Williams, E., 283, 294, 387
Williams, G. A., 430
Williams, J. E., 16, 232, 233, 240
Williams, L. M., 394, 395
Williams, S. W., 415
Williams, T., 402
Williams, W. W., 417
Wilson, D. M., 457
Wilson, K. S., 159, 441
Wilson, M. N., 360, 369
Wilson, S. P., 369
Wilson-Mitchell, J. E., 245
Wimbush, D. D., 368, 371
Windle, M., 178, 288, 299
Windle, R. C., 178, 288, 299
Windom, C. S., 391
Winickoff, S. A., 117, 119
Winter, D. G., 205
Winterbottom, M., 224
Wippman, J., 147
Wise, P. H., 357
Wisenbaker, J., 418, 421
Wittig, M. A., 83
Wolchik, S. A., 385
Wolfe, M., 380
Wolff, M., 293, 294
Wolfner, G. D., 390, 391, 392, 393
Woo, E., 219
Woodey, E., 458
Woods, T., 267
Woodson, R., 47, 55, 57
Woody, E., 458

Woolley, J., 170
Wright, C., 223
Wright, J., 412
Wright, J. C., 402, 410, 412
Wrobel, G. M., 379
Wu, C., 175, 391
Wu, F., 130, 139
Wu, M., 468, 469
Wuthnow, R., 319

Xia, Y., 378
Xu, X., 268

Yang, B., 378
Yarrow, L. J., 222, 322
Yarrow, M. R., 321
Yau, J., 372
Yeates, K. O., 192
Yirmiya, N., 180

York, R. L., 208
Young, W. C., 290
Youngblade, L. M., 170, 464
Youngstrom, E., 370
Youniss, J., 372
Yu, A. P., 235
Yuill, N., 189, 192

Zahavi, S., 302
Zahn, G. L., 429
Zahn-Waxler, C., 47, 79, 180, 235, 284, 285, 288, 303, 309, 311, 312, 313, 314, 315, 317, 318, 319, 325, 328
Zaia, A. F., 458
Zajonc, R. B., 225, 226
Zakriski, A. L., 280, 282, 458
Zalewski, C., 394
Zamutt, A., 185
Zarbatany, L., 462

Zarlengo-Strouse, P., 110
Zelazo, P. D., 331
Zelazo, P. R., 127, 158
Zelizer, 9
Zeman, J., 109, 110
Zern, D. S., 233
Ziemba-Davis, M., 266
Zigler, E. F., 158, 161, 198, 200, 388, 389, 391, 395, 396, 409, 418, 433
Zillman, D., 280
Zimmerman, E. A., 144
Zimmerman, M. A., 360
Zimmerman, R. R., 123
Ziss, K., 265
Zoccolillo, M., 286
Zoller, D., 111
Zucker, K. J., 130, 251
Zuckerman, D., 408, 409
Zupan, B. A., 173, 451

Ability
  entity view of, 210
  incremental view of, 210
  tracking, 419–420
Abstract ideation, 182
Abused children
  as parents, 141
Academic achievement
  amount of schooling and, 417
  cross-cultural studies of, 431
  effective schools and, 417–418
  of middle-class boys of working mothers,
    389
  parental influences on, 428–429
  peer influences on, 428–429
Academic competence, 174
Academic performance, social stereotypes and,
    219
Academic skills training, for rejected children,
    460–461
Acceptance, peer. *See* Peer, acceptance
Acceptance/responsiveness, in parenting,
    363–364
Accommodation, 52
Achievement
  academic. *See* Academic achievement
  attachment quality and, 222
  behavior, 201–202
    achievement motivation and, 204
    configural influences on, 225–227
    expectancies in, 206–207
    locus of control and, 208–209
    stability to classify causal attributions
      and, 208–209
  birth order and, 225–226
  child-rearing and, 224–225
  emotional reactions to, 205
  ethnic variations in, 216–218
  expectancies, 207, 209
  extrinsic orientation, 202
  failure, 203
  family/home influences on, 222–227
  family size and, 225
  goals, restructuring, 214
  individual, 200
  individualistic vs. collectivistic perspectives,
    215–216
  infants reactions to, 202–203

intrinsic orientation, 202
mental mediation or confluence hypothesis
    and, 226–227
in mixed-motive context, 215
motivational view of, 201 . *See also*
    Achievement motivation
outcomes, causes of, 208–209
parental socialization hypothesis and, 226
sex/gender differences in, 227–228
social class differences in, 218, 220–222
theories, 213
training
    definition of, 224
    direct, 227
value, 206
Achievement motivation
  achievement behavior and, 204
  measuring, 201
  theories
    of attribution, 207–211
    of learned helplessness, 212–213
    of McClelland, 204–205
    of need, 205–207
Achieving Society, The (McClelland), 204–205
Acquaintances, social interactions among,
    462–463
Active gene influences, 84
Active genotype/environment correlations, 82
Activity level, gender differences in, 235
Activity/passivity issue, in development, 12
Adaptation, 52
Adjustment
  positive adult, friends and, 464
  temperamental profiles and, 115
Adolescence, 10. *See also* Adolescents
Adolescents
  antisocial conduct of, aggression and,
    287–288
  delay of gratification and, 181–183
  minority, identity formation of, 186–187
  parent/child relationship and, 371–373
  peer sociability and, 444–448
  self concept of, 171–172
  self-worth and, 176–177
  sexual activity of
    interventions for, 268–269
    personal/social consequences of,
      266–269

sexual attitudes/behaviors of, 265–266
suicide and, 178–179
television violence and, 405–407
Adoptees, 379
Adoption study
  design, 74, 75
  of sociability, 448
Adoptive family, 379
Adult Attachment Interview, 138, 148, 150
Adult authority/guidance. *See also* Parenting
  importance of, 478–480
  young children and, 331–332
Affection, adolescent sexual attitudes and, 265
Affective explanations, in disciplining, 314
African-Americans
  child-rearing practices of, 371
  peer influences on schooling and, 428
  stereotype threat and, 219
Age, of children
  in achievement-related attributions,
    210–211
  in blended family, 386–387
  in empathy-altruism relationship, 318
  impact of divorce and, 382
  peer interactions and, 437–438
  in person perception, 189, 191
  television literacy and, 402–403
  television viewing and, 401
Aggression
  antisocial conduct in adolescence and,
    287–288
  behavioral definitions of, 273–274
  childhood
    perpetrators of, 286–287
    victims of, 286–287
  controlling, 300–303, 307
  cultural influences on, 291–294
  definition of, 272–274
  developmental trends in, 284–289
  early-onset, 300n
  family influences on, 294–300
  forms, age and, 285
  gender differences in, 234–235, 289–291
  during grade-school years, 286
  hostile, 273, 285
  in humans vs. animals, 73
  inhibitions, television violence and, 404
  as instinct, 272–273

instrumental, 273, 285
intentional definition of, 273
internal arousal and, 280
late-onset children and, 288
limited-duration children and, 288
maintenance of, 279–280
modeling, 294
nature of, age-related changes in, 284–288
observational learning of, 46
origins of, early conflict and, 284
payoffs, elimination of, 301–302
primary instigators of, 285
proactive, 301
reactive, 302
of rejected children, 458
relational, 292
retaliatory, 286
as social judgment, 274, 275
as stable attribute, 288–289
subcultural influences, 291–294
television violence and, 22–24, 403, 406,
    407–408
theories
    information-processing, 281–284
    instinct, 274–277
    learning, 277–281
    social information-processing,
        281–284
victims of
    in childhood, 286–287
    passive, 287
    proactive, 287
    provocative, 287
"Aggressive cues" hypothesis, 278
Aggressors
    late-onset, 299
    proactive, 287, 296
    reactive, 296
Altruism
    age-related changes in, 314–314
    autonomous, 308
    cognitive/affective contributors, 315–320
    cognitive theories of, 311–313
    cultural influences on, 320–321
    definition of, 307
        behavioral, 307–308
        motivational or intentional, 307
    developmental trends in, 313–315
    direct tuition of, 310
    evolution of, 72
    genetic influences, 72–73
    modeling influences, 322–323
    normative, 308, 324
    reciprocal, 309n
    reinforcing, 321–322
    role-taking and, 316
    in self-concept, 319–320
    theories, 308–313
    vs. prosocial behavior, 308
Altruistic exhortations, 322–323
Anal phase, 39
Androgenized females, 248–249

Androgyny
    advantages of, 260
    definition of, 259
Anger, 282
Antisocial behavior
    in adolescence, aggression and, 287–288
    controlling, 300–303
    development of, 298–300
    peer pressure and, 467
Approval-seeking, 203
Aptitude-treatment interaction (ATI), 421–422
AQS (Attachment Q-set), 138, 161
Arithmetic reasoning, gender differences in, 234
Arousal, from television violence, 403
Asian-Americans
    child-rearing and, 369, 371
    parental authority and, 372
    peer influences on schooling and, 428–429
Asocial phase of attachment, 121
Assimilation, 52
Associative play, 442
ATI (aptitude-treatment interaction), 421–422
Attachment
    asocial phase of, 121
    avoidant. See Avoidant attachment
    to caregivers, 136
    cultural variations in, 139
    definition of, 116–117
    in humans, 125–126
    indiscriminate, phase of, 121
    infants and, 121–122
    insecure
        long-term correlates of, 147–148
        with mother, offsetting, 150
    integrative theory of, 144
    later development and, 147–151, 161
    multiple, phase of, 122
    objects, fathers as, 145–147
    parents' internal working models and, 150
    quality
        achievement and, 222
        differences in, 161
        forecasting later outcomes and, 148–150
        individual differences in, 136–139
        sociability and, 450–451
    security
        assessment of, 136–138
        base for, 121–122
        committed compliance and, 328
        infant characteristics and, 142–145
        infant temperament and, 142–145
        influencing factors on, 139–145, 161
    specific, phase of, 121
    theories, 122–126
    therapy, 157, 161
Attachment object loss, reactions to, 131–133
Attachment Q-set (AQS), 138, 161
Attributional retraining, 213
Attributional theory
    of achievement, 207–211
    of social and personality development,
        94–97

Attributions
    achievement-related, age differences in,
        210–211
    external, 347
    internal, 346
    trait like, understanding, 96–97
Authoritarian instruction, 426–427
Authoritarian parenting
    definition of, 365
    outcome from, 479
    peer sociability and, 451
Authoritative instruction, 426–427
Authoritative parenting
    academic achievement and, 428
    definition of, 225, 365
    effectiveness of, 366–367
    outcome from, 479
    peer sociability and, 451
Autonomous altruism, 308
Autonomous morality, 330
Autonomy
    definition of, 371
    encouraging, 372–373
    part-time employment and, 374–375
    quest for, 371–372
    versus shame and doubt, 42, 180
Average-status children, 454
Avoidant attachment
    culture and, 139
    definition of, 137
    risk factors for, 140
    temperament and, 144

Baby biographies, 7–8
Basic gender identity, 255
Behavior
    aggressive. See Aggression
    antisocial. See Antisocial behavior
    evolutionary basis for. See Ethology
    gender-typed, 243–245
    goal-directed or intentional, 53–54
    regulation, socialization and, 2
    sex differences in, 231
Behavioral comparisons phase, 191
Behavioral consistency, 189
Behavioral definition
    of aggression, 273
    of altruism, 307–308
Behavioral genetics, 73–85
    contextual worldview and, 99
    contributions/criticisms of, 84–85
    definition of, 73–74
    summary of, 100
Behavioral inhibition, 114–115
Behavioral schemes, 51
Behavioral view, of achievement, 201–202
Behavior disorders, genetic contributions to,
    81
Behaviorism, 43–44
Belief-desire theory of mind, 169–171
Biological factors, in sex differences in
    aggression, 289–290

Biological growth, 244
Biological theories, of altruism/prosocial
        behavior development, 308–309
Biosocial theory, of gender-role development,
        246–249
Birth order, achievement and, 225–226
Bisexuals, 264
Blank slate (*tabulae rasa*), 2, 11, 44, 72, 474
Blended families, 362, 385–387
Body build, peer acceptance and, 456
Breeding, selective, 74

CAH (congenital adrenal hyperplasia), 248
CAI (computer-assisted instruction),
        413–414
Career identity, 184–185
Caregivers
        easing separation pain and, 132
        fathers as, 145
        insensitive
                interventions for, 142
                risk factors for, 141
        in marital relationship, effect on caregiving
                sensitivity, 141–142
        as secure base, 136
Caregiving. *See also* Parenting
        hypothesis, 141, 161
        inconsistent, 140
        quality of, attachment security and,
                141–142
        sensitivity, ecological constraints on,
                141–142
Caretaking, by siblings, 377
Carolina Abecedarian project, 220–221
Case study, 19–20, 21
Castration anxiety, 252
Categorical self, 167–168
Catharsis hypothesis
        definition of, 300
        television violence and, 403
Cathartic technique, 300
Causal attributions, 94, 207
Centered thinking, 58
Character dimensions, in defining moral
        maturity, 326
Child abuse
        consequences of, 393–394
        cultural influences, 392–393
        definition of, 390
        preventing/treating, 394–397
        psychological, 390
        scope of problem, 390
        sexual, 394–395
        social-situational triggers, 392–393
        victims, 391
Child abusers, characteristics of, 391
Childbearing, decreased, 361
Child custody, 384–385
Childhood
        delay of gratification in, 181–183
        middle, self concept in, 171–172
        in premodern times, 6–7

Child neglect. *See also* Neglected children
        as child abuse, 390
        consequences of, 393–394
        cultural influences, 392–393
Child-rearing
        achievement and, 224–225
        ethnic variations in, 369, 371
        in high infant mortality societies, 357
        patterns, peer sociability and, 451
        social class differences in, 367–369
        temperament and, 115–116
Children
        abused, as parents, 141
        acceptance of, reasons for, 455–459
        adopted, 379
        age of. *See* Age, of children
        altruistic, parents of, 324–326
        average-status, 454
        behaviorally inhibited, 144
        behaviorally uninhibited, 144
        conduct of, teacher's influence on, 424–426
        desensitization to violence, 407
        development of, *See* Development
        fearless, 144
        homeless street, 397–398
        hostile/out-of-control, dealing with, 298
        latch-key, 389–390
        neglected. *See* Neglected children
        newborn. *See* Neonates (newborns)
        only, characteristics of, 378–379
        "peer-only," 439–440
        popular, 453–454
        in poverty, 362
        poverty and, 362
        preschool. *See* Preschool children
        racial categorization and racism in, 190
        rejected. *See* Rejected children
        special-needs, education of, 430–431
        television viewing
                hours per day, 401
                lifestyle changes from, 401–402
        toddlers
                peer sociability and, 441–442
                racial categorization and racism in, 190
        unwanted, insensitive caregiving and, 141
        young
                actors' intention and, 331
                moral reasoning of, 343–344
                respect for rules, 331–332
Children's Television Workshop, 410–412
China, one-child family policy, 378
Chronosystem, 89
Chumships, 43
Circular reactions
        primary, 53
        secondary, 53
        tertiary, 53–54
Classification training, in combating gender
        stereotypes, 262
Classrooms. *See* School, classrooms
Clinical method, 17–18, 21
Cliques, 445

Close friendships, 43
Coaching, 458, 460
Coercive home environment, 296–297
Cognitive approaches, for social-skills
        training, 460–461
Cognitive competencies, 365–366
Cognitive development
        computer programming and, 414
        concrete-operational stage, 59–60
        definition of, 50
        description of, 64
        educational television and, 410–412
        formal-operational stage, 60–63
        preoperational stage, 56–59
        promotion, in school, 416–417
        sensorimotor stage, 53–56, 57
        stages, 52–63
Cognitive-developmental theory
        of altruism, 311–313
        of attachment, 124
        contributions to, 63–64
        criticisms of, 63–64
        of gender-typing, 255–256
        of morality, 328–344
        of separation and stranger anxiety, 130–131
        of social cognition, 191–192
        summary of, 100
Cognitive disequilibria, 336
Cognitive growth, 244
Cognitive immaturity, 98
Cognitive interventions, 261
Cognitive maturation, in morality
        development, 330
Cognitive operations, 56
Cognitive prerequisites, for moral growth,
        337–338
Cognitive schemes, 51, 473
Cognitive skills, popularity and, 455
Cognitive standards, for moral development,
        349
Cognitive theories, of altruism, 311–313
Cohort effect, 27
Collaborative learning, 92, 94
Collectivist or communal society, 174, 175
Collectivist societies
        achievement motivation and, 200–201, 215
        children's social skills and, 452
Committed compliance, 180
Communal societies. *See* Collectivist societies
Compensation, 59
Compensatory education programs, 220–221
Compensatory interventions, 221
Competencies, cognitive, 365–366
Competition, 200
Compliance
        definition of, 180
        gender differences in, 235
Computer-assisted instruction (CAI), 413–414
Computers
        classroom usage of, 413–415
        educational programming and, 412
        Internet exposure and, 415

programming, cognitive growth and, 414
  social impact of, 414–415
  social inequalities and, 415
  videogames and, 415
Conceptual perspective-taking, 58
Concordance rate, 74, 75
Concrete-operational stage, 59–60, 63
Concrete operators, 192
Concrete referents, 192
"Conditioned anxiety" hypothesis, 127–128
Conduct, of child, teacher's evaluations of,
  424–426
Confidence, gender-consistent activities and,
  237
Conflict
  early, aggression and, 284
  marital, impact on family, 380–381
  parent/peer, 468–470
Confounding variable, 24
Congenital adrenal hyperplasia (CAH), 248
Conscience, morality and, 336
Conscious motivation, 40
Conservation, 58–59, 192
Consistency schema, 96
Constructivist, 51
Contact comfort, 123
Contextual model, 99
Continuity/discontinuity issue, 12–13
Control group, 262
Conventional morality, 334–335
Cooperative learning methods, 430–431
Cooperative play, 442
Coparenting, 359
Correlational survey method
  design, 21–23
  strengths/limitations of, 27
  on television violence, 404
Correlation coefficient, 22, 75
Crib death, 357n
Critical period
  definition of, 70
  for gender identity establishment, 249
  imprinting and, 124
Critical-period hypothesis, 250–251
Cross-cultural studies
  of academic achievement, 431
  of aggression, 291–294
  of child development, 30–32
  of classroom instruction, 431–432
  of parental educational involvement, 432
  of parenting and children's social skills, 452
  of prosocial behavior, 322–323
Cross-generational problem, 29
Cross-pressures, 468
Cross-sectional design
  definition of, 26–28
  strengths/limitations of, 31
Crowds, 445
Cultural bias, in Kohlberg's morality theory,
  339–340
Culture
  achievement motivation and, 200–201
  cognitive development and, 64

gender-role attitudes and, 261, 263
  individualistic, 200
  influences
    on academic achievement, 431
    on achievement, 215–222
    on aggression, 291–294
    on altruism, 320–321
    on attachment, 139
    on belief-desire theory of mind, 171
    on child abuse/neglect, 392–393
    on gender-role development, 249–250
    on human development, 477
    on identity formation, 186–187, 188
    on moral growth, 339
    on moral reasoning, 340–341
    on peer-sponsored misconduct, 468
    on prosocial conduct, 322–323
    on schooling, 421–422
    on sexuality, 263
    on student effort, 432–433
    on survival characteristics, 356–357
  in intellectual development, 91
  masculinity/femininity concept and, 259
  myths, of sex differences, 236–238
  shyness and, 117
  socialization and, 2, 3

Data gathering methods, 15–21
Day care
  effect on infants/children, 157–158
  good, importance of, 388–389
  high-quality
    benefits of, 158–159
    characteristics of, 158
Death instinct, 272–273
Decentering, from perceptual illusions, 192
Deferred imitation, 47–48, 54
Defiance, 180, 183
Delay of gratification, in childhood and
  adolescence, 181–183
Delinquency
  early-onset, 300n
  gender gap in, 299
Demandingness/control, 364
Dependent variable, 23, 26
Depression, parental, insensitive caregiving
  and, 141
Deprivation dwarfism, 156, 157
Desensitization hypothesis, 407
Desire theorists, 169
Despair phase, in separation, 131
Detachment phase, in separation, 131
Development. See also specific aspects of
  activity/passivity issue, 12
  continuity/discontinuity issue, 12–13
  emotional. See Emotional development
  ethology and, 69–71
  family instability and, 370
  genotype/environment correlation influence
    on, 83–84
  homelessness and, 370
  later, attachment and, 147–151
  major issues, 14

nature versus nurture issue, 11–12
  optimal, emotional bonding and, 119
  parenting influences on, 86–87
  post hoc, 73
  research
    consumers of, 32–33
    fact-finding methods for, 15–21
    strengths/limitations of methods, 31
    study designs, 26–30
  stages of, 13
  theories, 68, 98–99. See also specific
    developmental theories
Developmental psychology, founder of, 8
Developmental vulnerability, gender
  differences in, 235
Deviant peer cliques, 299
Differential reinforcement, 253
Difficult temperament, 115
Diffusion effect, in compensatory education,
  220
Direct effects, 359
Direction-of-effects issue
  in moral development, 350
  in parenting, 367
  in peer acceptance, 458–459
Direct tuition
  of altruism, 310
  of gender roles, 253
Discipline
  child's-eye view of, 350–351
  parental, in moral development, 348–349
  in schools, 421
  temperament and, 350–351
Disequilibrium
  cognitive, 336
  in intellectual growth, 52
Disorganized/disoriented attachment
  caregiving quality and, 140–141
  definition of, 137
Dispositional attributes, inferring, 95–96
Distortion effect, 237
Distributive justice, 343
Divorce
  immediate effects of, 381–383
  impact on family, 380–385
  long-term reactions to, 383–385
  marital conflict before, 381
  rates, 361–362
  recovery from, 384–385
Doctrine of specificity, 344–345
Dogs, social isolation effects on, 151–152
Dominance hierarchies
  in minimization of aggression, 277
  peer interaction and, 437
Double standard, 265
Dropouts, school, 419
Dwarfism, deprivation, 156, 157

"Early experience" hypothesis, 136, 161
Eastern culture, prosocial conduct and,
  322–323
Easy temperament, 115
Eclectics, 101

Ecological systems, 101
Ecological systems theory, 50, 86–90
Ecological validity, 24–25
Economic distress hypothesis, 368
Economic goal, 357
Ectomorph, 456
Education
    advanced, moral growth and, 339
    in-school. See School
    interventions
        compensatory, 221
        discovery-based, 63
        two-generation, 220–221
Educational television
    and cognitive development, 410–412
    criticisms of, 412
    prosocial behavior and, 410
Education for all Handicapped Children Act
    (1975), 430
Effectance motivation, 200n
Effective school. See School, effective
Ego, 38
Egocentrism
    in adolescence, 62–63
    definition of, 57–58
Ego integrity, vs. despair, 42
Electra complex, 39, 76, 252, 327
The Electric Company, 412
Emotional autonomy, 371–372
Emotional bonding, early, 118–119
Emotional deprivation, failure to thrive and,
    156
Emotional development
    early, 105–113
        day care and, 157–158
        maternal employment and, 157–158
        maternal employment/day care and, 162
    father's contributions to, 146–147
    overview of, 113
Emotional display rules
    acquiring, 109–110
    definition of, 107–108
    self-regulation and, 108–109
Emotional expressions
    gender differences in, 235
    regulation of, 105–110
Emotional relationships, internal working
    models and, 148–150
Emotional self-regulation, 108–109
Emotions
    conversations about, 111
    displaying, 105–110
    early social development and, 112–113
    expression of. See Emotional expressions
    moral, 343
    primary or basic, 106–107
    recognizing/interpreting, 110–112
    secondary or complex, 107
    sensitivity to, gender differences in, 235
    socialization of, 107–110
    understanding, later milestones in,
        111–112
Empathic concern, 79

Empathy
    altruism and, 317–319
    definition of, 72, 111, 302
    in mediation of prosocial behavior, 310
    prosocial behavior development and, 309
    socialization of, 317–318
Employers
    family-friendly, 160–161
    parental-leave policies of, 160
Employment
    of mothers, 387–390
        effect on infants/children, 157–158
    part-time, sense of autonomy and, 374–375
Encoding, observations, 45–47
Endomorph, 456
Engrossment, 118–119
Entity view of ability, 210
Environment
    developmental influences, 85
    development and, 11–12
    ecological systems theory and, 86–90
    estimating contributions of, 76–77
    and heredity, as co-conspirators, 82–84
    influence
        on aggression, 277
        on temperament, 114
    nonaggressive, creation of, 301
Environmental determinism, 48–49
Epistemology, 50
Eros, 38
Ethnic identity, 186–187
Ethnic minorities
    achievement and, 216–218, 428n
    child-rearing and, 369, 371
    educational experiences and, 427–428
    gender typing and, 244–245
    stereotypes of, television depiction of, 408
    students
        parental influences on, 428–429
        peer influences on, 428–429
        teacher's expectancies of, 429
Ethnography, 20–21
Ethological theory
    of aggression, 275–276
    of attachment, 124–126, 148–150
Ethology
    classical, assumptions of, 69
    contextual worldview and, 99
    definition of, 68
    human development and, 69–71
    summary of, 100
    vs. modern evolutionary theory, 70–71
    vs. other theoretical approaches, 126
Eurocentric view, of achievement, 200
Evidence, converging, 31
Evocative genotype-environment correlations,
    82
Evolutionary theory, modern,
    contributions/criticisms of, 71–73
Exosystem, 89, 90
Experimental control, 24
Experimental design, 23–25
Expiatory punishment, 329–330

Expressive role, 232
Extended family, 360
External stimuli, 45
Extrafamilial influences
    computers. See Computers
    definition of, 401
    school. See School
    television. See Television
Extrinsic orientation, 202
Extroversion, 78–79

Facial attractiveness, peer acceptance and,
    455–456
Facial expressions
    emotions and, 106
    prosocial behavior and, 315, 318
Failure
    attributing to unstable causes, 213
    externalizing blame for, 211
    internalizing blame for, 212
Failure-to-thrive syndrome, emotional
    deprivation and, 156
False-belief task, 169–170
False self behaviors, 172
Falsifiability, 10
Families
    adoptive, 379
    blended, 385–387
    characterization of, 397
    conflict, impact of, 380–381
    as developing system, 360
    as embedded system, 360
    externalizing problems, 370
    father/stepmother, 386
    functions of, 356–358
    gay or lesbian, 380
    impact of divorce on, 380–385
    influences
        on aggression, 294–300
        from television viewing, 401–402
    instability, 370
    internalizing problems, 370
    mother/stepfather, 386
    siblings influence on, 373–379
    size of, achievement and, 225
    social changes in, 360–363
    as social system, 356, 358–363
    system, changes, when new baby arrives,
        373–375
Family Leave and Medical Act of 1993, 160
Family social system, 358
Family studies, 74–75
Father
    as attachment objects, 145–147
    as caregivers, 145
    contributions, to early social/emotional
        development, 146–147
    influence, on early intellectual
        development, 146
    influence on mother/infant relationship,
        359
    stepfathers, 386
Fear, gender differences in, 235

Fearfulness, 144
Fear of separation hypothesis, 127–128
Felt-responsibility hypothesis, 318–319
Females
  androgenized, 248–249
  categorizing, 232–233
Field experiment
  definition of, 24, 25
  strengths/limitations of, 27
  of television violence, 404, 405–407
Financial support, for divorcing families,
  384
Fixation, 39
"Forbidden toy" paradigm, 345–346
Forced choice statements, 168
Foreclosure, 184
Formal-operational stage, 60–63
Formal thought, personal and social
  consequences of, 62–63
Friendships
  advantages of, 463–466
  benefits, longitudinal study of, 465
  close, 43
  common activity and, 194
  definition of, 461
  development of, 461–462
  disagreements in, 196
  as preparation for positive adult
    adjustment, 464
  quality of, 464–466
  security from, 463
  social interactions and, 462–463
  social problem-solving skills from,
    463–464
  as social support, 463
Frustration-aggression hypothesis, 277–279

Gay families, 380
Gender
  appropriateness, 259
  bias, in Kohlberg's morality theory,
    341–342
  concept, development of, 240
  consistency, 237, 255
  identity, 239–240, 245
  indoctrination, 231
  intensification, 242
Gender-consistent activities, 237
Gender-role attitudes, changing, 260–263
Gender-role behavior, changing, 260–263
Gender roles
  biological influences on, 247–249
  cross-cultural comparison, 32
  cultural influences, 32, 249–250
  developmental theories, 245–259
    biosocial, 244–249
    cognitive-developmental, 255–256
    gender schema, 256–257
    integrative, 257–259
    psychobiosocial, 251–252
    psychoanalytic, 252–253
    social learning, 253–255

direct tuition of, 253
social-labeling influences on, 249–252
social values/customs and, 5
Gender-role standard, 232–233
Gender schema theory, 256–257
Gender segregation, 242–243
Gender stability, 255
Gender stereotypes
  combating with cognitive interventions,
    262
  interpretation of counterstereotypic
    information and, 237
  overview of, 245
Gender-typed behavior
  definition of, 245
  development of, 242–244
  sex differences in, 243–244
Gender typing
  definition of, 231–232
  developmental trends in, 239–245
  subcultural variations in, 244–245
  theories, 245–259
    biosocial, 244–249
    cognitive-developmental, 255–256
    integrative, 257–259
    psychoanalytic, 252–253
    psychobiosocial, 251–252
    social learning, 253–255
Generalizability, 20
Generativity, vs. stagnation, 42
Genes, estimating contributions of, 76–77
Genetic influences, on gender-role
  development, 247–248
Genital abnormalities, gender identity and,
  250–251
Genital phase, 39
Genotype, 73
Genotype/environment correlation, influence
  on human development, 83–84
GH (growth hormone), 156, 157
Goal-directed behavior, growth of, 53–54
Goals 2000: Educate America Act of 1994, 433
Golden Rule, 309, 319
"Good boy" orientation, 335
"Good girl" orientation, 335
Goodness-of-fit model, 116, 144
Group trends, 368
Growth, cognitive, 244
Growth hormone (GH), 156, 157
Guided (collaborative) learning, 92, 94

Habits, 44
Harter's Self-Perception Profile for Children,
  173–174
Hedonism, naive, 334
Heredity
  contributions to personality/mental health,
    78–81
  development and, 11–12
  and environment, as co-conspirators,
    82–84
  influences on temperament, 113–114

Heritability
  coefficient, 76–77
  definition of, 74
  estimates, misconceptions about, 78
  influences, estimating, 74–75
  of sociability, 448
Heteronomous morality, 329–330
Heterosexuality
  of children of gay/lesbian parents, 380
  establishing, 264
Heuristic, 8
Heuristic value, 10
High-risk neighborhoods, child abuse and,
  392
Historical influences
  on human development, 477
  on identity formation, 188
  on social-personality development, 6–7
Holistic perspective, 100
Home environment
  achievement and, 222–224
  coercive
    as breeding ground for aggression,
      296–297
    chronic delinquency and, 298–300
  influences
    on aggression, 288–289
    on sex differences, 238–239
HOME inventory, 222–224
Homelessness, child development and, 370
Homeless street children, 397–398
Home-visitor programs, 395
Homosexuality
  of children of gay/lesbian parents, 380
  concordance rates, 75
  origins of, 264
Hormones
  aggression and, 289–290
  gender-role development and, 248–249
  homosexuality and, 264
Hostile aggression, 273
Hostile attributional bias, 282, 297
Human nature
  altruism and, 72
  early philosophical perspectives on, 11–14
Hypothesis, 10
Hypothetical propositions, children's reactions
  to, 60, 61
Hypothetico-deductive reasoning, 60, 62

I (private self), 169
Id, 38
Identification, 39, 252
Identity
  achievement, 184
  crisis, 184
  definition of, 183–184
  diffusion, 184
  formation
    cognitive influences on, 186–187
    developmental trends in, 184–185
    of minority adolescents, 186–187

painfulness of, 185–186
    personal/social influences on, 186–188
  vs. role confusion, 42
Imaginary audience phenomenon, 62, 244
Imitation
  deferred, 54
  development of, 54
  origins of, 47–48
Immanent justice, 330
Immaturity, cognitive, 98
Imprinting, 69, 124–125
Incompatible-response technique, 301
Incremental view of ability, 210
Independence training, 224
Independent variable, 23, 26
Indirect or third party effect, 359
Individualistic societies
  children's social skills and, 452
  definition of, 174, 175
Individuality, development of, 50
Induction, 348–350
Industry, *vs.* inferiority, 42
Infants
  of adolescent mothers, 267–268
  attachment-related fears of, 126–131
  attachments and, 121–122
  characteristics, attachment security and, 142–145
  crying, 69
  with easy temperament, attachment and, 143
  peer sociability and, 441–442
  sleeping with parents, 357
  slow-to-warm up, attachment and, 143
  temperament, attachment security and, 142–145
  temperamentally difficult
    attachment and, 143
    improving sensitivity toward, 142
  unattached, 151, 153–157
Inferiority, *vs.* industry, 42
Informal curriculum, 416
Information-processing analysis, 346–347
In-group/out-group schema, 256, 257
Inhibitory control, 345
Initiative
  self-concept and, 168
  vs. guilt, 42
Innate purity, 11
Inner experimentation, 54
Inner speech, 94
Insecure attachment
  long-term correlates of, 147–148
  with mother, offsetting, 150
Instinct, 38
Instinct theories, of aggression, 274–277
Instrumental aggression, 273
Instrumental behavior, 48
Instrumental role, 232
Integrative theory, 257–259
Intellectual Achievement Responsibility
  Questionnaire, 208

Intellectual growth, 51–52
Intellectual performance. *See* IQ
Intellectual schemes, 51
Intelligence, 51–52, 389
Intentional behavior, growth of, 53–54
Intentional definition
  of aggression, 273
  of altruism, 307
Interactional synchrony, 119–121
Interactionist theory, 37
Interactive viewpoint, of sex differences in
  aggression, 291
Intermodal perception, 240n
Internal forces, in frustration/aggression
  hypothesis, 278
Internalization, 326
Internal working models, 148–150, 161
International Journal of Psychoanalysis, 8
Internet, 415
Interpersonal relationships, early, 5
Interrater reliability, 16
Interviews
  strengths/weaknesses of, 21
  structured, 16–17
Intimacy, *vs.* isolation, 42, 185
Intrinsic orientation, 202
Introversion, 78–79
Intuitive thought, 58
Invariant developmental sequence, 52–53
Invariant-sequence hypothesis of morality,
  336–337
Involuntary reflexive scheme, 55
IQ (intellectual performance)
  academic achievement and, 207
    genetic influences on, 76
    testing
      socioeconomic status and, 218
    middle-class boys of working mothers and,
    389

Joint physical custody, 384–385
Joy in mastery, 203
Justice, 329
"Just-so" stories, 72–73

Kinship, 74

Laboratory experiments
  strengths/limitations of, 27
  television violence, 404–405
Laissez-faire instruction, 426–427
Latch-key children, 389–390
Latency phase, 39
Latinos, peer influences on schooling, 428
Law of recapitulation, 7
Learned helplessness
  definition of, 155
  minimizing, 214
  theory of, 211–213
Learning goals, 214, 215
Learning theory, 43–50
  of aggression, 277–281

of altruism, 309–311
of attachment, 122–123
of gender-typing, 253–255
of moral development, 344–348
of stranger/separation anxiety, 127–128
summary of, 100
Lesbian families, 380
Lifestyle changes, from television viewing,
  401–402
Literacy, television, 402–403
Locus of control, achievement behavior and,
  207–209
Longitudinal design
  definition of, 28–29
  strengths/limitations, 31
Looking-glass self, 164, 175
Love withdrawal, 348–349

Macrosystem, 89
M_{af} (motive to avoid failure), 205–206
Mainstreaming, 430
Males, categorizing, 232–233
Manic-depressive psychosis, 81
Marital relationship
  conflict, effect on sibling conflict, 376
  effect on caregiving sensitivity, 141–142
Marriage, active postponement of, 361
Mastery motivation, 200
Mastery orientation, 211
Mastery success, 203
Maternal deprivation hypothesis, 155, 161
Maternal employment, 162
Mathematical ability, gender differences in, 234
Mating preferences, 71
Maturation, peer acceptance and, 456–457
Me (public self), 169
Mean-world beliefs, 407
Mechanistic model, 98
Media
  influence on gender-role development,
  254–255
  violence, 403–404 . *See also* Television,
  violence
Mental functions
  elementary, 91
  higher, 91
Mental illness
  genetic contributions to, 81
  predisposition to, 81
Mental states, understandings of, 169
Mesomorph, 456
Mesosystem, 89
Metacognitive knowledge, 414
Microsystem, 88–89
Middle childhood, self concept in, 171–172
Minorities. *See also* Ethnicity; Race
  adolescents, identity formation of, 186–187
  stereotypes of, television depiction of, 408
  students
    parental influences on, 428–429
    peer influences on, 428–429
    teacher's expectancies of, 429

MIS (Mullerian inhibiting substance), 246
Misconduct, peer pressure and, 467–468
Mixed-age peer interactions, 437–438
Modeling aggression, 294
Modeling influences
    on altruism, 322–324
    of peers, 466
Modeling therapies, for social-skills training,
    459–460
Modern evolutionary theory, vs. ethology,
    70–71
Monkeys, social isolation effects on,
    152–153
Moral affect, 327
Moral behavior
    of children, social models and, 348
    definition of, 327
    development of, 344–348
Moral character, consistency of, 344–345
Moral conduct
    consistency of, 344–345
    moral reasoning and, 343
    reinforcement as determinant of, 345
Moral development
    cognitive prerequisites for, 337–338
    Kohlberg's theory of, 333–344
    learning theory of, 344–348
    Piaget's theory of, 329–330
    psychoanalytic explanations of, 327–328
Moral dilemmas, 333–334
Moral emotions, 343
Moral internalization, temperament, discipline
    and, 351
Morality
    of care, 342
    conventional, 334–335
    definition of, 326
    developmentalist view of, 326–327
    heteronomous, 329–330
    of individual principles of conscience, 336
    of justice, 341–342
    maintaining, social order in, 335
    Oedipal, 327–328
    preconventional, 334, 335–336
    principled, 335–336
    social learning theory and, 344–348
Moral principles, 306
Moral reasoning
    cognitive development and, 328–329
    definition of, 327
    moral conduct and, 343
    prosocial, 316–317
Moral relativism, stage of, 330
Moral rules, 332
Moral self-concept training, 347–348
Moral socialization, 307
Moral values, 6
Moratorium, 184
Mother
    abusive, 391
    adolescent, 267
        infants of, 267–268

employment of, 387–390
    influence on father/infant relationship, 359
    stepmothers, 386
Mother-infant attachment. See Attachment
"Mother-only" monkeys, 439
Mother-to-child effect, 359–360
Motivational definition of altruism, 307
Motive to achieve success (M_s), 205–206
Motive to avoid failure (M_{af}), 205–206
Motor capabilities, 473
M_s (motive to achieve success), 205–206
Mullerian inhibiting substance (MIS), 246
Mutual trust, 194

National Television Violence Study, 403
Natural clues to danger, 128
Natural experiment
    definition of, 25–26
    strengths/limitations of, 27
Naturalistic observation, 18, 21
Natural selection, 69
Nature versus nurture issue
    definition of, 11–12
    as false dichotomy, 475–476
Need achievement theory, 205–207
Need for achievement (n Ach), 201–202
Negative identity, 185
Negative reinforcement, 297
Negative reinforcer, 297
Neglected children
    behavioral correlates of, 457–459
    definition of, 454–455
    as parents, 141
    reasons for, 455–459
Neo-Freudians, 40, 43
Neonates (newborns)
    cognitive capabilities of, 53
    developmental study and, 2
    emotional expressions of, 106
    imitative capabilities of, 55
    sensorimotor development and, 53–54
    self-concepts of, 165–166
Nominations technique, 453
Nonorganic failure to thrive, 156, 157
Nonrepresentative sample, 28–29
Nonshared environmental influences (NSE)
    definition of, 77
    measuring effects of, 80–81
Nonsocial activity, 442
Normative altruism, 308
Norm of social responsibility, 309
Norms, 467
NSE. See Nonshared environmental influences

Object permanence
    beginning of, 131
    in cognitive-developmental theory, 124
    development of, 54–56, 473
Observation, 18–19
Observational learning
    of aggression, 46, 279–280
    of altruism, 310–311

definition of, 45
    description of, 254–255, 279
    of gender-typing, 254
    of moral behavior, 348
    origins of, 47–48
    in social-learning theory, 45–47, 253
    of social skills, 459–460
    television and, 403–412
    verbal mediators and, 48
Observer influence, 18–19
Occupations, feminine, 254
Oedipal morality, 327–328
Oedipus complex, 39, 76, 252, 327
Open classrooms, 420
Operant learning, 45
Operant learning theory, 45
Operational schemes, 51
Operations, cognitive, 56
Oral phase, 39
Organismic model, 98
Organization, 51–52
Organizational effect, on memory, 237
Original sin, 11, 37
Own-sex schema, 256–257

Parallel play, 442
Parental influence hypothesis, 367
Parental-leave policies, 160
Parental socialization hypothesis, 226
Parent/child relationship
    during adolescence, 371–373
    mother-infant, 5
        attachment and, 122–123
        emotional bonding and, 118–119
Parenting. See also Child-rearing
    authoritarian, 365
    authoritative, 225, 365
    by custodial parent, 384
    dimensions, 363–364
    of employed mothers, 388
    ethnic variations in, 217, 369–371
    high-quality, importance of, 159–161
    importance of, 478–480
    influences
        on development, 86–87
        on identity formation, 186–188
    patterns, 364–367
    permissive, 365
    styles
        popularity of children and, 455
        self-esteem and, 177
    uninvolved, 366
Parents. See also Father; Mother; Parenting
    abusive, 391
    acceptance/responsiveness, 363–364
    adaptability of, 479–480
    of altruistic children, 324–326
    as caregivers, 450–451
    conflict, children's aggression and, 296
    custodial, parenting by, 384
    disciplinary practices, prosocial behavior
        development and, 325–326

educational involvement, cross-cultural studies of, 432
gender curriculum of, 253
hostile/out-of-control, dealing with, 298
influences
    on academic achievement, 428–429
    on gender stereotypes, 238–239
    on peer interaction, 448–450
    insensitive, risk factors for, 141
internal working models, attachment and, 150
involvement in schooling
    educational importance of, 200
    ethnic minorities and, 428
    peer influences and, 428–429
as managers, 295–296
marital relationship of, effect on caregiving sensitivity, 141–142
moral development of children and, 332–333
of morally mature children, 348–352
noncustodial, social/emotional support from, 384–385
permissiveness of aggression, 295
working, assessment of, 159–161
Parents Anonymous, 396
Parsimony, 10
Particularistic development, 13–14
Passive genotype/environment correlations, 82
Passive victims of aggression, 287
Peer
    acceptance, 452–453
        behavioral correlates of, 457–459
        categories of, 453–455
        direction of effects issue, 458–459
        physical correlates of, 455–457
    conformity, 467
    as critics/agents of persuasion, 466–467
    cultural influences, on misconduct, 468
    cultures, 10
    definition of, 437
    groups
        definition of, 444
        formation of, 446
        influences on achievement, 217–218
        intergroup conflict, 446–447
        normative function of, 467–468
        reducing intergroup hostility, 447
    influences, 436, 466–470
        on academic achievement, 428–429
        on self-esteem, 177–178
        vs. adult influences, 468–470
    interactions
        frequency of, 438–439
        mixed-age, 437–438
        moral growth and, 338–339
        parental influence on, 448–450
        same-age, 437
        significance of, 437–438
        transactive, 338–339
    popularity with, 453–455

as promoters of positive developmental outcomes, 439–440
reinforcement, 466
sociability development and, 440–441
    in middle childhood/adolescence, 444–448
        parental influences on, 448–451
    in preschool, 442–444
"Peer-only" monkeys, 439
Pendulum problem, 60, 62
Perceptual perspective-taking, 58
Performance goals, 214, 215
Permissive cultures, sexuality in, 263
Permissive nonintervention, 352
Permissive parenting
    definition of, 365
    outcome from, 478–479
Personal agency, 166
Personal development, uniqueness of, 3
Personal fable, 62–63
Personal growth, socialization and, 2–3
Personality
    components of, 38
    development
        active, 473–474
        continuity in, 474–475
        cultural/historical context of, 477
        discontinuity in, 474–475
        historical perspective, 6–7
        holistic nature of, 473
        idiosyncratic, 476–477
        multiple perspectives for, 477–478
        normative, 476–477
        parenting patterns and, 478–480
        plasticity, 475
        social forces in, 480
        stages of, 39–40
    environmental influences, 79–81
    genetic contributions to, 78–81
    masculinity/femininity dimensions of, 259
    traits, children's stereotyping of, 240–241
Personal values, 307
Person perception, social experience and, 196
Perspective-taking, conceptual vs. perceptual, 58
Persuasion, by peers, 466–467
Phallic stage, 39, 252
Phase of indiscriminate attachments, 121
Phase of multiple attachments, 122
Phenotype, 73
Physical aggression, film violence and, 25
Physical competence, 174
Physical correlates, of peer acceptance, 455–457
Physical perspective-taking, 316
Physical punishment, 352
Plasticity, of development, 475
Play activities, preschool, 442–444
Popular children, 453–454
Poverty, children in, 362
Power assertion, 348–349
Power-assertive discipline, 294–295

Preadapted characteristic, 125
Preconventional morality, 334, 335–336
Pregnancy, unwanted, insensitive caregiving and, 141
Premoral period, 329
Preoperational period, 192
Preoperational reasoning, deficiencies in, 57–59
Preoperational stage, 56–59
Preschool children
    activities
        parental monitoring of, 448–449
        structured, 450
    aggression of, 284–285
    racial categorization and racism in, 190
    schooling for, 418
    self-recognition and, 168–169
    sociability development and, 442–444
    television violence and, 405
Pretend play, symbolism and, 56–57
Pride
    in accomplishment, 109
    in achievement, 201, 203
Primary circular reactions, 53
Primary or basic emotions, 106–107
Principled morality, 335–336
Private self (I), 169
Private speech, 92
Proactive aggressors, 281
Proactive victims of aggression, 287
Professions, masculine, 227
Proprioceptive feedback, 165
Prosocial activists, types of, 324–325
Prosocial behavior
    definition of, 306–307
    development theories, 308–313
    educational television and, 410
    origins of, 313–314
Prosocial moral dilemmas, 343
Prosocial moral reasoning, 316–317
Prospective study, 325
Protest phase, in separation, 131
Provocative victims of aggression, 287
Psychoanalytic theory, 37–42
    of aggression, 274
    of altruism/prosocial behavior development, 309
    of attachment, 122
    definition of, 20
    evaluation of, 252–253
    of gender-typing, 252–253
    historical aspects, 8
    of moral development, 327–328
    overview of, 100
Psychobiosocial model, of gender-role development, 250, 252
Psychological androgyny, 259–262
Psychological comparisons phase, 191
Psychological constructs phase, 191
Psychological self-awareness, 168
Psychosexual development, stages, 76
Psychosexual theory, 37–40

Psychosocial theory, 41–42
Puberty timing, peer acceptance and, 456–457
Public self (me), 169
Punisher, 44
Punishment
    consistency of, 346
    in establishing moral prohibitions, 345–348
    intensity of, 346
    in resistance to temptation, 346
    timing of, 346
Punishment-and-obedience orientation, 334
Pygmalion effect, 422–423

Quasi-experiment
    definition of, 25–26
    strengths/limitations of, 27
Questionnaire
    as research tool, 8, 21
    structured, 16–17

Race
    achievement and, 216–218
    categorization, in young children, 190
    stereotypes, television depiction of, 408
    stereotype threat and, 219
Racism, in young children, 190
Random assignment, 24
Reactive aggressors, 281
Reactive attachment disorders, 155, 161
Recapitulation, law of, 7
Reciprocal altruism, 309n
Reciprocal determinism, 12, 49
Reciprocal interaction, 12, 49
Reciprocal relationship, emotional attachment as, 116–117
Reciprocity, 313
Reconstituted families, 362
Reinforcement
    and achievement, 224–225
    and gender-typing, 253
    and moral development, 345
    by peers, 466
    for social-skills training, 459–460
    verbal, of altruism, 321–322
Reinforcer, 44
Rejected-aggressive children, 458
Rejected children
    definition of, 454–455
        aggression of, 458
        behavioral correlates of, 457–459
        reasons for, 455–459
        withdrawal of, 458
    improving social skills of, 459–461
    reasons for, 455–459
Rejected-withdrawn children, 458
Relational aggression, 292
Relational logic, growth of, 59–60
Relational self-worth, 176
Relationships
    causal, assessment of, 25
    detecting

correlational design and, 21–23
    experimental design, 23–25
    direction of, 22
    marital. See Marital relationship
    parent/child. See Parent/child relationship
    reciprocal, emotional attachment as, 116–117
    strength of, 22
    thinking about, role taking and, 194
Reliability, 15–16
Remarriage, 362, 385–387
Repression, 38
Research study designs
    for child development, 26–30
    strengths/limitations of, 27
Resistant attachment, 137, 139, 161
Restrictive cultures
    sexuality and, 263
    sexuality in, 263
Retaliatory aggression, 286
Reversibility, 58–59
Risk taking behavior, gender differences in, 235
Robber's Cave, 445, 446–447
Role taking
    aggression and, 285
    altruism and, 316, 318
    and moral reasoning, 331, 337–338
    skills, 192
    social experience as contributor to, 195–196
    in social-skills training, 460
    theory, 192–194
    thinking about relationships and, 194
Rouge test, 166, 167
Rules, socially defined
    as moral absolutes, 329
    premoral period and, 329
Rule training, in combating gender stereotypes, 262

Same-sex modeling, 254
SAT (Scholastic Assessment Test), 183
Scaffolding, 92
Schemes
    constructing, 51–52
    definition of, 51
Schizophrenia, 81
Scholastic Assessment Test (SAT), 183
Scholastic influences, on identity formation, 188
School
    ability tracking and, 419–420
    classrooms
        goal restructuring, 214
        instruction, cross-cultural studies of, 431–432
        management of, 421
        open, 420
        organization of, 420
        transitional, 420
    class size and, 419

computer usage in, 413–415
    culturally compatible instruction in, 421–422
    developmental influence of, 416
    discipline in, 421
    effective, 417–418
        contributing factors for, 420–422
        misconceptions about, 419–420
        scholastic atmosphere of, 421
    "goodness of fit" with students, 421–422
    informal curriculum of, 416
    instructional techniques and, 426–427
    monetary support for, 419
    promotion of cognitive development and, 416–417
    secondary, transition to, 424–425
    student body
        meeting needs of, 427–431
    students
        effort, cross-cultural studies of, 432–433
        involvement, cross-cultural studies of, 432
        with special needs, 430–431
    study body
        composition of, 420–421
    teachers. See Teachers
    teacher's influence in, 422–427
    testing procedures, impact of, 423–424
Scientific method, 15
Scientific theory, 10
SE. See Shared environmental influences
Secondary circular reactions, 53
Secondary or complex emotions, 107
Secondary reinforcer, 123
Secure attachment
    changes in, 150–151
    definition of, 137
    history of, 150–151
    long-term correlates of, 147–148
    quality of caregiving and, 140
Secure base, 121–122, 130
Security, from friendships, 463
Seduction hypothesis, 264
Selective attrition, 28–29
Selective breeding experiments, 74
Self
    definition of, 164
    vs. nonself, 164, 165
Self-actualization goal, 357
Self-assertion, 180
Self-care children, 389–390
Self-concept
    in adolescence, 171–172
    altruism in, 319–320
    cultural influences on, 174
    development of, 165–172, 195
    early psychological, 168–169
    initiative and, 168
    looking-glass self and, 164
    in middle childhood, 171–172
Self-conscious emotions, 107

Self-control
  definition of, 178
  development of, 178–188, 195
  early, as predictor of later life outcomes, 183
  emergence, in early childhood, 179–181
  growth of, 164
  as valued asset, 182–183
Self-disclosure, 462
Self-esteem
  changes in, 176–177
  definition of, 172–173
  development of, 173–177, 195
  global, determinants of, 173–174, 176
  origins of, 173–177
  social contributors to, 177–178
Self-fulfilling prophecy
  definition of, 238–239
  Pygmalion effect and, 422–423
Self-fulfillment, 201
Self-interest, moral growth and, 342
Self-oriented distress, 317
Self-recognition
  contributors to, 167
  definition of, 166–168
  emotional consequences of, 167
  preschoolers and, 168–169
  social consequences of, 167
Self-regulation, emotional, 179–180
Self-reliance, 183
Self-reports, 16–18, 21
Self-sacrifice
  altruism and, 314
  moral growth and, 342
Self-worth, relational, 176
Sensitive period, 70, 118, 157
Sensorimotor stage, 53–56
Separation anxiety
  cognitive-developmental viewpoint of, 130–131
  "conditioned anxiety" hypothesis, 127–128
  definition of, 127
  easing pain of, 132
  ethological viewpoint of, 128–129
Separations, behavioral phases of, 131
Sequential design, 29, 31
Seriation, 59, 60
SES (socioeconomic status), 218
Sesame Street, 411–412
Sex. See also Gender
  of child, impact of divorce and, 382–383
  differences
    in achievement, 227–228
    in aggression, 289–291, 292
    in altruism, 314–315
    cultural myths of, 236–238
    as group averages, 236
    in identity formation, 184–185
    scholastic influences, 239
    in suicidal attempts, 178
  psychological differences in, 234–238
Sex instinct, maturation of, 68
Sex-role socialization, 231

Sexual abuse, of child, 394–395
Sexual behavior
  of adolescents, 265–266
  social values/customs and, 5
Sexuality, 263
Sexually transmitted disease (STD), 267
Sexual orientation, 264
Shame, in failure to achieve, 203
Shared environmental influences (SE)
  definition of, 77
  measuring effects of, 81
Shyness, culture and, 117
Sibling rivalry, 374–375, 376
Siblings
  as attachment objects, 377
  as contributors to social-cognitive understandings, 378
  as models/tutors, 377–378
  relationships
    over course of childhood, 375–377
    positive contributions of, 377–378
Single adults, 361
Single-parent family, 362
Situational compliance, 180–181
Slow-to-warm-up temperament, 115
Sociability
  cross-cultural study of, 452
  definition of, 440–441
  as heritable attribute, 448
  parental effects on
    direct, 448–450
    indirect, 450–451
  peer, in infancy/toddlerhood, 441–442
  peer, in middle childhood/adolescence, 444–448
  peer, in preschool period, 442–444
Social acceptance, 174
Social class
  differences in achievement, 218–222
  differences in aggression, 293–294
  differences, in child-rearing, 367–369
  gender typing and, 244–245
Social cognition
  definition of, 63–64, 164
  developmental milestones, 195
  developmental theories, 191–196
  knowing about others, 188–196
Social-cognitive interventions, for aggression, 302–303
Social-cognitive theory, 45
Social comparison, 177–178
Social-contract orientation, 335–336
Social-conventional rules, 332
Social deprivation
  early
    harmfulness of, 155
    recovering from, 155, 157
  in humans, 153–155
  of institutionalized children, 26, 153–155
Social development
  active, 473–474
  continuity in, 474–475

cultural/historical context of, 477
discontinuity in, 474–475
father's contributions to, 146–147
future research directions, 481
holistic nature of, 473
idiosyncratic, 476–477
multiple perspectives for, 477–478
normative, 476–477
parenting patterns and, 478–480
plasticity, 475
social forces in, 480
television viewing and, 401–402
Social/emotional support, from noncustodial parent, 384–385
Social experience, in morality development, 330
Social-experience hypothesis, 338–339
Social impact, of computers, 414–415
Social inequalities, computers and, 415
Social influences, on social-cognitive development, 195–196
Social information-processing theory
  of aggression, 281–284
  contributions/criticisms, 97–98
  of moral development, 346–348
  overview of, 101
  in social and personality development, 94–97
Social interactions
  among friends/acquaintances, 462–463
  in cognitive development, 91
Social isolation. See also Social deprivation
  of dogs, 151–152
  of monkeys, 152–153
Socialization
  culture and, 2, 4
  definition of, 2, 356–357
  extra-familial agents and, 6
  historical perspective, 6–7
  moral, 357
  sex differences in, 232
  societal benefits of, 2–3, 357
  television for, 412–413
Social judgment, aggression as, 274, 275
Social learning, collaborative, 92
Social-learning theory
  of aggression, 279–281
  of altruism/prosocial behavior development, 309–311
  contributions/criticisms of, 49–50
  of gender identity, 253–255
  sex differences in aggression and, 290
  television violence and, 403
Social models, on children's moral behavior, 348
Social order
  in maintaining morality, 335
  socialization and, 3, 357
Social origins, of early competencies, 91–93
Social perspective-taking
  definition of, 316
  stages of, 192–194

Social problem-solving skills, from friendships, 463–464
Social problem-solving training, 461
Social referencing, 110–111, 112
Social self, 164
Social-situational triggers, to child abuse, 392–393
Social skills
  definition of, 442
  improving, for rejected children, 459–461
  training, cognitive approaches for, 460–461
Social stereotypes
  academic performance and, 219
  television as source of, 408
Social stimulation hypothesis, 155, 161
Social support
  for divorcing families, 385
  from friends, 463
  for insensitive caregivers, 142
Sociocultural theory
  contributions/criticisms of, 93–94
  focus of, 64, 91–94
  of intellectual development, 91–94
Socioeconomic status (SES), 218
Sociometric techniques, 453
Sociomoral Reflection Measure-Short Form (SRM-SF), 334
Special-needs children, education of, 430–431
Specific attachments phase, 121
SRM-SF (Sociomoral Reflection Measure-Short Form), 334
Standards, use of, 203
STD (sexually transmitted disease), 267
Stepparents, 386
Stereotypes, gender-role, development of, 240–242
Stereotype threat, 219
Stranger anxiety
  cognitive-developmental viewpoint, 130–131
  combating, 128–129
  "conditioned anxiety" hypothesis, 127–128
  definition of, 127
  ethological viewpoint of, 128–129
"Strange Situation," 136–137, 138, 144, 161, 377
Stress, minimizing, during divorce, 385
Structured interviews, 16–17
Structured observation, 19, 21
Structured questionnaires, 16–17
Subcultural influences
  on achievement, 215–222
  on aggression, 291–294
  in gender typing, 244–245
Subjective interpretation, in clinical method, 18
Success
  expectancies of, 207
  value of, 206
Sudden infant death syndrome, 357
Suicide, adolescent, 178–179
Superego, 38

Superordinate goals, 447, 448
Survival goal, 357
Survival of the fittest, 72
Symbolic function, 56–57
Symbolic representations, 47, 54
Symbolic schemes, 51
Sympathetic empathic arousal, 317
Synchronized routines, 119–121

Tablua rasa (blank slate), 2, 11, 44, 72, 474
Teachers
  as appraisers/evaluators, 422–426
  evaluations of child's conduct and, 424–426
  expectancies of, 429
  expectancy effects of, 422–423
  influence of, 422–427
  responses, to children from lower socioeconomic background, 220, 429
  stereotyped beliefs of, 239
  teaching styles of, 426–427
Teenage pregnancy/childbearing, 267
Teen Outreach program, 268
Television
  commercial messages, children's reactions to, 408–409
  educational
    cognitive development and, 410–412
    criticisms of, 412
    prosocial behavior and, 410
  harmful effects, reduction of, 409–410
  literacy, 402–403
  relative deprivation and, 294
  for socialization of children, 412–413
  as social stereotype source, 408
  viewing
    age and, 401
    children's lifestyles and, 401–402
  violence
    aggression and, 406, 407–408
    childhood aggression and, 22–24
    correlational surveys, 404
    as desensitizing agent, 407
    effects of, 403–408
    field experiments, 404, 405–407
    laboratory experiments, 404–405
    The Mighty Morphin Power Rangers and, 406
Temperament
  of child, impact of divorce and, 382
  child rearing and, 115–116
  children's adjustment and, 115
  development and, 112–113
  difficult, 115
  discipline and, 350–351
  early profiles, later development and, 115
  easy, 115
  environmental influences on, 113–114
  hereditary influences on, 113–114
  personality development and, 105
  popularity and, 455
  slow-to-warm-up, 115
  stability of, 114–115

Temperament hypothesis, 143, 161
Temporal stability, 16
Temptation, learning to resist, 345–348
Ten Commandments, 336
Tertiary circular reactions, 53–54
Test anxiety, 423–424
Testicular feminization syndrome (TFS), 246–247, 250–251
Testosterone, 246–247
TFS (testicular feminization syndrome), 246–247, 250–251
Thantos, 38, 272–273
Theory. See also specific theories
  definition of, 10
  in scientific investigation, 10
Three-mountain problem, 58
Time-out technique, 301–302
Timidity, gender differences in, 235
Timing of puberty effect, 247
Toddlers
  peer sociability and, 441–442
  racial categorization and racism in, 190
Tools of intellectual adaptation, 91
Traditional nuclear families, 359
Trait inferences, 192
Traits, male vs. female, 233
Transactive interactions, 338–339
Transgressions, moral, 312, 332
Transitional classrooms, 420
Transitivity, 60
Trust versus mistrust, 41, 42
Twin design, 74, 75
Twins
  discordant, 81
  separated identical, 83–84
Twin studies, of sociability, 448

Unconscious motivation, 40
Unconscious motives, 38
Uninvolved parenting, 366
Universal development, 13–14
"Universal Parenting Machine," 3–5

Validity
  definition of, 15, 16
  ecological, 24–25
Value
  achievement, 206
  of success, 206
Variable
  confounding, 24
  dependent, 23, 26
  independent, 23, 26
Verbal ability, gender differences in, 234
Verbal mediators, observational learning and, 48
Verbal reinforcement, of altruism, 321–322
Videogames, concerns about, 415
Violence
  in films, physical aggression and, 25
  on television. See Television, violence

Visual/spatial abilities, gender differences in, 234

Weiner's attribution theory, 207–211
Western societies
  individualistic nature of, 200
  prosocial conduct and, 322–323
Withdrawal

permanent, from human relationships, 133
  of rejected children, 458
Women, workforce participation of, 361
Word processing, 414
Worldviews, developmental theories and, 98–99
World Wide Web (WWW), 415

X chromosome, 231
X-linked recessive traits, 247

Y chromosome, 231
Younger-peer therapy, 153

Zone of proximal development, 92